THE AGE OF DATA

THE AGE OF DATA
Embracing Algorithms in Art & Design

.
Concept, Editing and Layout:
Christoph Grünberger
cg@christophgruenberger.com
instagram.com/christophgruenberger

Co-Editing:
Paul Heys/Nottingham Trent University

Proof-Reading:
Sophie Steybe

Typeface:
DIN Next Pro

.

.
2nd edition 2022

.

.
ISBN 978-3-7212-1015-6

.
.
.
.
.
.
.
Cover:
Refik Anadol
QUANTUM MEMORIES
NGV (National Gallery of Victoria) Triennal 2020
Melbourne (AUS)
Picture by Tom Ross
.

DATA IS ZERO
DATA IS ONE

DATA IS MOTION
DATA IS PIGMENT

DATA IS LIGHT
DATA IS POETICS

DATA IS LIVE

DATA IS MORE
DATA IS LESS

DATA IS NO
DATA IS YES

DATA IS REAL

DATA IS INFORMATION
DATA IS KNOWLEDGE
DATA IS MOTIVATION

DATA IS NOW

DATA IS US

WELCOME TO THE AGE OF DATA

003 . Christoph Tratberger

IA
N
AN
DE RS
ON

“Starting Point.
Once upon a time — (some words organised around a perspective on) navigating a sea of assumptions.

It’s in the human / post-numan nature of things that ‘die Neue Techno-logie’ should ‘werk’ to satisfy our collective need / greed for huge ever growing electro shocks of the new. It’s in the irony of things that the tech we allow to impact both our individual and our shared daily existence the most is seldom really new… what really works / delivers for ‘us humans’ is technology we already ‘know’ in our heads, our minds and our mass conscience / consciousness. Just as we cannot conceive of anything we don’t already ‘know’, we respond better to the ‘new’ ideas we were expecting, the future we’ve been waiting for. Knowing that what we knew all along was right all along helps keep us happy.

Without realising, hardly knowing, we have been further and deeper submerged in an ocean of fizzing digital data, for some of us, most of our lives. In the context of data equating to information, what is this data telling us? And what do we do with the data overload left over?

What happens when we reach critical mass, when we can't process any more knowledge, is we start to look at the 'why' of the data not the 'what'; a data (over) flow spun as webs of creativity all around us from the matrix to minority report, from anything to everything else, information and disinformation here, there and everywhere else.

Rewind to a future of flying cars and the romance of robot maids, to hi-def, hi-res, skyscraper (i love you)-high TV screens, virtual reality, digital realms, artificial intelligence and cyborg pets, we've got, and continue to get the future we deserve, where life imitates not art but a science fiction evolved to describe / eat itself — exhibit one: the first flip-phone, Motorola's 1996 StarTAC, being directly inspired by Star Trek's 1964 flip top communicator.

We're constantly on the way to becoming... re-arranging naturally occurring pixels, and disturbing sound waves, using up surplus digital data in an attempt to express what we understand, or maybe more interestingly what we don't understand, about the disinformation we confuse with knowledge.

To know more is to know less. Facts are not full stops and the best answers are questions.

As a data curious society we, like artists down through history, use what we have (our bubbles) to explore what we call dreams and imagination. We play with reality in the hope of finding out what's on the other side. New technologies breed new forms. The artists whose work appears in this book concern themselves with asking what that means (so most of us don't have to). Elsewhere, as with any discipline, you'll experience data spread thin as surface, it's the way of things. But that's another conversation.

The most successful technology, the survival of the fittest for purpose, are those gizmos, and the ones and zeros making them tick (tok), which enable us to travel to, populate and colonise a future we've already imagined, fast faster fastest. We are, in the (human / post numan) nature of things, impatient and time poor / wasteful. We gleefully consume a needy technology programmed to solve the problems it's programmed to create, by default or by design, which is what we want — it helps keep us happy.

I'm somewhere between happy and happier when my data is dada and when 1+1=0.

The future becomes the norm
The work created in this age of data helps us accelerate past our expectations / experience.

Swimming in megapixels deep diving in a 'can you see what it is yet?' technology, or what we project of our own fantasies on to it, has the power to drag us kicking and dreaming way beyond the need to ever 'know' what it is (yet, or even ever). We have the potential to be drowning in a wonderful sea of 'what if', learning to think / see / breathe differently; moving away from the hippyshit fractals of pre-millennial virtual reality towards a world potentially really virtual. Who wants reality when it's on TV every day, what value is there in truth when it's dependent on perspective. Someone else's perspective. The Tomorrows World we hold in our heads is that 'what if' to the 'what is' of what we hold in our hands, the real value of it is that we can't quite quantify it in any sense of what we know, or choose to know, when we're awake.

I'd rather truly understand just one thing than 'know' everything. If you're asking.

I don't want to know if we are nearly 'there' yet, I'm happy to know we're on our way. I'm happier to believe we're never ever going to get 'there'. It's not so much that we never arrive, it's just that we never stay (long enough). Wherever we are is always going to be 'where we are'. Until the age of data we've had to be content with that being analogue / physical... now we can explore the ether, not to explain reality but have the possibility to surpass it. To find ourselves somewhere GPS can't find us.

Tell me that I'm dreaming... One of the things our clunky analogue physical existence can't do is represent the 'other', the surreal, the magic of what we think goes on in our heads when we're asleep, in dreams, or somewhere other than where we appear to be, to others. Art, whatever you think it might be, has attempted it, creating some wonderful works of human expression and at the same time, some of the most laughable celluloid attempts at dream sequences.

The work collected in this book helps us access our own tales of the unexpected, to dive in and immerse ourselves comfortably in 'I don't know what it is, but I like it'. Everything is or can be or has been technology but this isn't really a book about technology, it's a guide book about electric dreams and why some of us want make them, for real. It's a book about the search for 'the other'.

Technology isn't much without the ideas and dreams it fuels.

(But) all of this — everything in here and everything else, is just a starting point. Let's assume. We're always at the starting point on the way to becoming... something else. Which is as it should be."

Ian Anderson / The Designers Republic™ (North of Nowhere 2021)

IN TR OD UC TI ON

EMBRACING ALGORITHMS IN ART AND DESIGN.

IT WAS THE SUMMER OF 1987.
I WAS MOTIVATED BY MATTHEW BRODERICK AND HIS CHARACTER DAVID LIGHTMAN IN THE 1983 COLD WAR SCIENCE FICTION TECHNO-THRILLER WARGAMES, WITH STANLEY KUBRICK'S 2001: A SPACE ODYSSEY, STILL LIGHT YEARS BEYOND MY PERCEPTION.

EVERY TIME I WANDERED THROUGH THE CITY MALL;
I WOULD RECITE THE POEM:

```
10 FOR X=1 TO 16
20 POKE 646,X
30 POKE 53280,X+1
40 POKE 53281,X+2
50 PRINT "*** I WAS HERE ***";
60 NEXT
70 RUN
```

MY STAGE; THE COMMODORE C64 IN THE ELECTRICAL DEPARTMENT OF A SMALL TOWN IN GERMANY; MY AUDIENCE, ITS CUSTOMERS; BLIND AND CARELESS ABOUT MY ENACTMENT.

BUT LIKE EVERY MOTIVATED AND STRIVING ARTIST, IT FELT GREAT BECAUSE MY PERFORMANCES WOULD LEAVE A TRACE.

IT WAS MY MARK, MY GRAFFITI, MY TAG IN THE BIG CITY, AND LIKE ALL "GUERRILLA ART," ALONG WITH ITS HIGH RISK AND LIMITED DURABILITY, IT ALLOWED ME A VOICE, TO TELL MY STORY AND COMMUNICATE MY MESSAGE.

THROUGH THESE PRIMARY FUNCTIONS, I FELT MY EFFECTIVENESS AND IT CREATED MY STARTING POINT INTO POST-DIGITALIZATION BEFORE ANY THOUGHT WAS GIVEN TO IT.

FOR ME, IT WAS THE FASCINATION OF BEING ABLE TO OPERATE A MACHINE AS A MEANS OF EXPRESSION, A COMPUTER THAT PLAYED MY SCORE, READILY AND UNLIKE IN THE BLOCKBUSTERS, NO GOLEM, NO HAL, NO DOLORES.

IN THIS PUBLICATION, I FOCUS EXCLUSIVELY ON THE POSITIVE COLLABORATIONS BETWEEN USER AND CPU, THAT THE PROGRAMMING AND THE GENERATED DATA ARE A SHARED LEVEL OF PERFECTION.

A RAPHAEL, MICHELANGELO OR A TITIAN SET NEW STANDARDS IN THE MIDDLE AGES OF WESTERN CULTURE WITH A FUTURE-FACING WORLD VIEW.

IN THE SAME WAY, ARTISTS IN THIS BOOK SHARE A VISION TO REACH NEAR, FURTHER AND UNKNOWN FUTURES, ALL WITH THE ASSISTANCE OF MACHINE INTELLIGENCE.

TO ENTER THIS NEW TERRITORY, AN AI IS AN EQUAL COMPANION; TO BREAK NEW GROUND AT EYE LEVEL TOGETHER, EXPLORE THE VERY MEANING OF COLLABORATION AND EMANCIPATE THE CONCEPT OF ART ITSELF.

THE AGE OF DATA PRESENTS THE WORK OF 40 ARTISTS AND DESIGNERS ALONGSIDE DATA-BASED DESIGN PROCESSES.

THESE ARE SET VERTICALLY AND DIVIDED INTO USER-FRIENDLY CATEGORIES AND FIELDS.

FROM GRAPHIC DESIGN TO 3D ANIMATION, FROM USER INTERFACE TO ROBOTICS AND THE PARAMOUNT EXPERIENCES OF SPATIAL INSTALLATIONS.

THESE ARTISTS INVITE US TO LOOK BEHIND THE SCENES, TO BEAR WITNESS TO THE DESIGN PROCESS ALLOWING US, THE USER, TO DIVE DEEPER INTO THEIR IMPULSES AND MOTIVATION.

WE START TO UNDERSTAND THE TOOLS THAT REALIZE THESE BOUNDLESS PROJECTS AND OBSERVE THE GREATNESS OF AN AUTHENTIC COLLECTIVE OUTPUT.

THIS STATIC, PRINTED ARTIFACT ALLOWS US TO BECOME ACTIVE MEMBERS IN THIS DESIGN EVOLUTION/REVOLUTION.

WE WILL HEAR STORIES, CHALLENGES AND SURPRISES FROM LEADERS IN THE FIELD.

WE WILL STAND AT VIRTUAL RIVERS, EXPERIENCE ENDLESS CITIES, AND EVEN LAND ON THE MOON.

WE WILL OBSERVE ARTIFICIAL INTELLIGENCE AS PAINT, FORM AND PRODUCTION.

WE WILL LEARN NEW LANGUAGES, AND SHOULD WE WANT TO, WE CAN EVEN DANCE!

RUN

CHRISTOPH GRÜNBERGER IN DECEMBER 2020

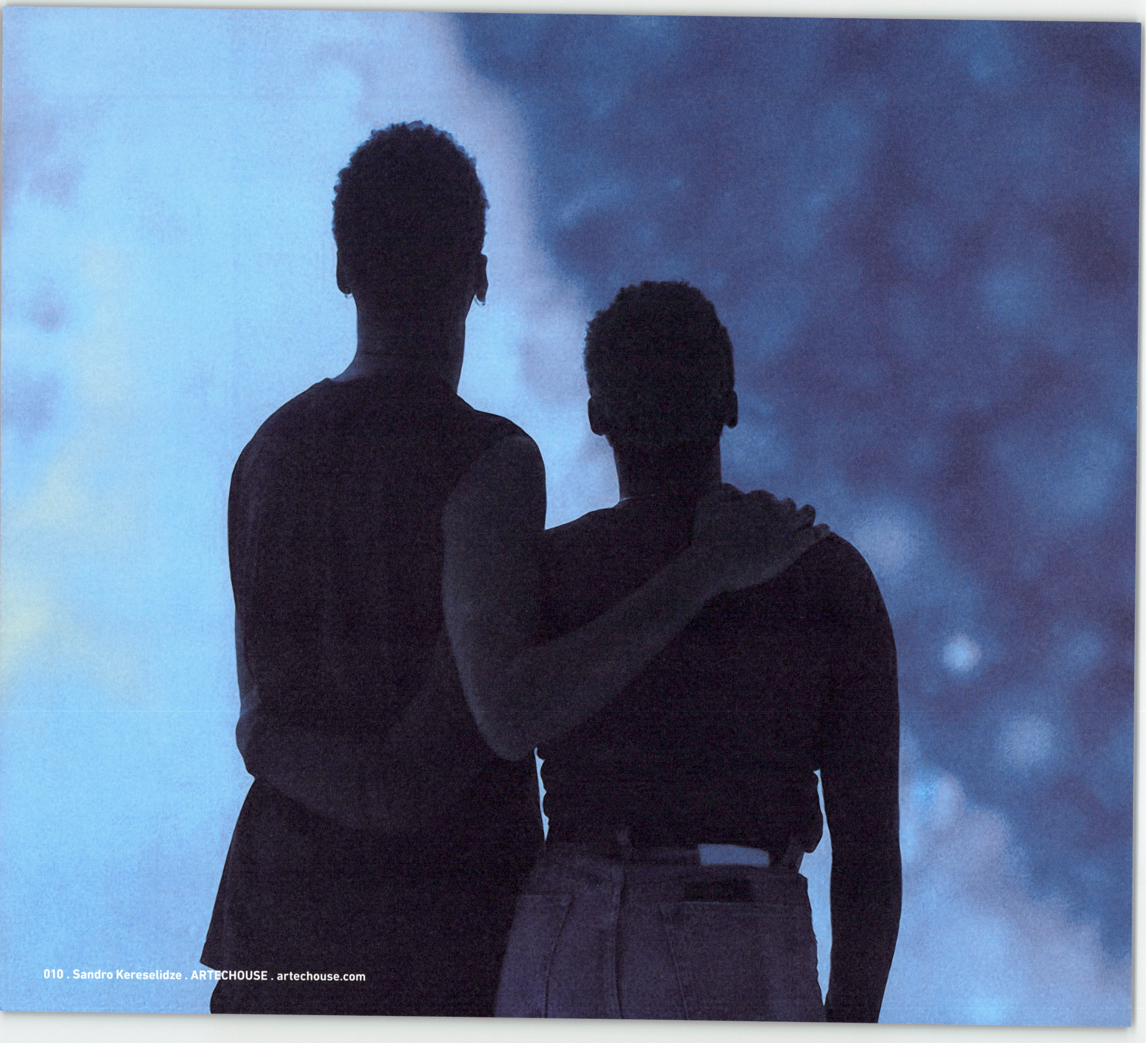

010 . Sandro Kereselidze . ARTECHOUSE . artechouse.com

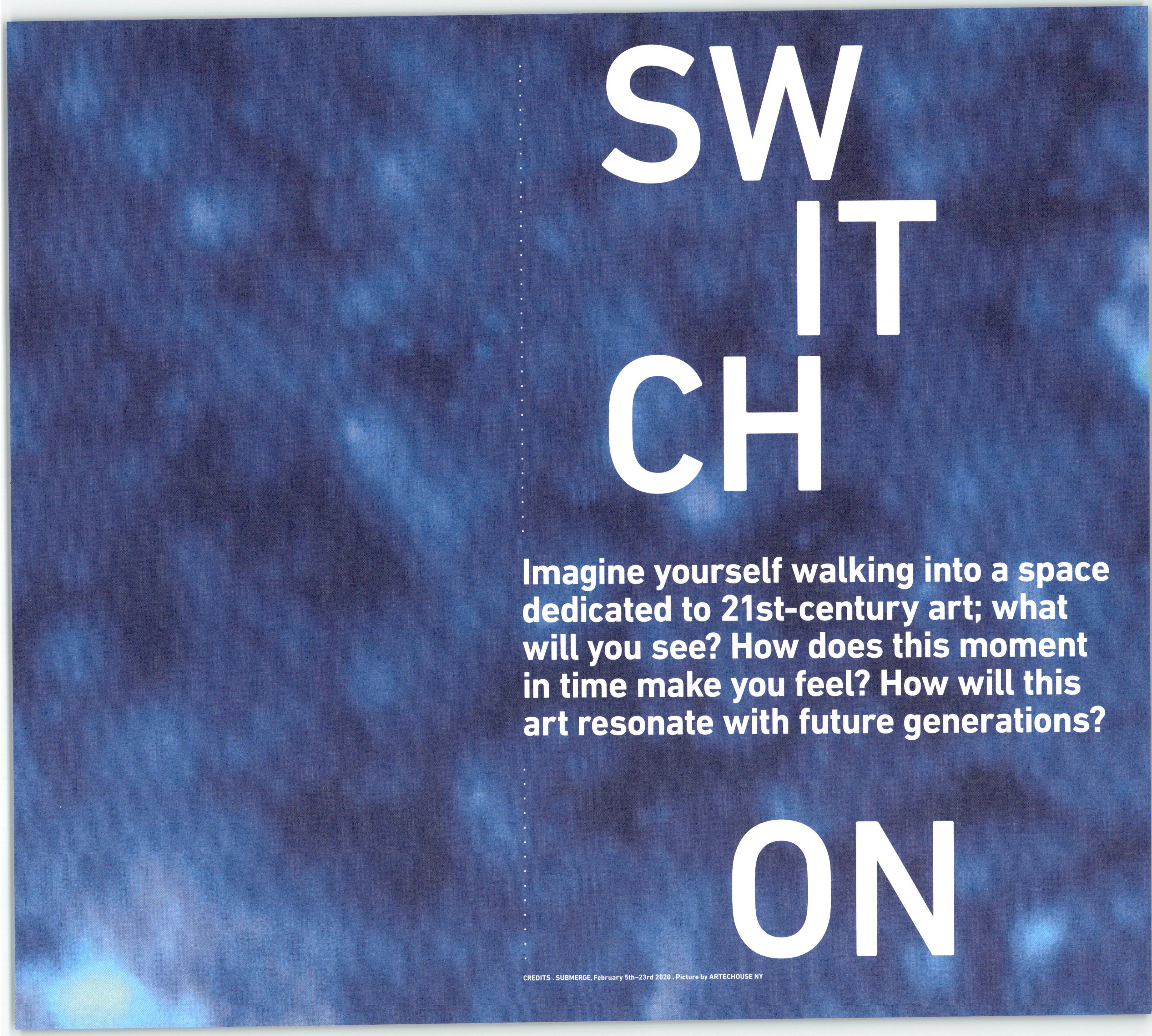

SWITCH ON

Imagine yourself walking into a space dedicated to 21st-century art; what will you see? How does this moment in time make you feel? How will this art resonate with future generations?

CREDITS . SUBMERGE, February 5th–23rd 2020 . Picture by ARTECHOUSE NY

AR
TE
CH
OU
SE

Since the beginning of time, humans have used the tools available to them to tell the story of their existence. These types of expressions became a creative outlet throughout history, an ever-evolving progression of imagination and innovation. The creation of synthetic colors gave artisans remarkable access to new hues, providing even more creative possibilities. The use of canvases, popularized in the 16th century due to their lower cost and longevity, allowed for new artistic expressions and wider participation from artists. The invention of photography in the 1800s opened the door to an entirely new genre, eventually paving the way for motion pictures in the 20th century. The exponential growth of computing built the runway for current developments and innovation in today's art.

Creators continue to push boundaries and make unprecedented strides with access to a more diverse set of tools and materials.

We see artwork becoming further removed from the historical constraints of frames and canvases. Audiences are now invited to break away from being passive viewers and instead are encouraged to explore and interact with artwork that utilizes digital information.

Today, we find ourselves at the beginning of a new era: the Age of Data.

Generated in abundance, data is the new tool for the 21st century, and artists are quickly realizing its creative potential. Through their fearless innovation, further research, and powerful techniques, artists are generating a new narrative within our communities and cultures, just as the creators of the past did.

This evolving movement explores immersion, experience, innovation, and experimentation in ways not seen in the past, and yet it is still part of history; a significant achievement in the history of art. The Age of Data is a natural evolution of self-expression, and a reflection of our society and the times we live in.

There is a defining characteristic in every movement, every process, and every technical advancement; it has lasted the passage of time. We can appreciate the beauty of Renaissance paintings, the intricacy of Mayan jade jewelry, the embellishments of churches, and the timeless allure of Art Deco buildings because we have physical examples that serve as windows into the past. This begs the question: how will we be able to preserve this technology-driven art that is so intangible?

Data-driven works are often perceived as elusive, since data does not exist in the physical world.

Virtual reality and augmented reality rely heavily on experience, which cannot be preserved the way a sculpture can. With the increased rate of innovation, we will see these modern tools become obsolete, just as the floppy disk and CD faded into the archive, preserved for coming generations to evaluate.

Because data lives in an intangible space, the only way to coax it into the physical world is through artistic expression, just as our ancestors found new ways to create meaning with pigment and stone.

Thus, the value of data does not lie in abstract binary digits, but in the works that grow out of them.

We must find a way to preserve these creations. Our responsibility is to maintain these contemporary achievements so future generations can not only understand who we were, but also learn from and build on them, and understand the origins of the Age of Data.

We are currently in the nascent stage of art and technology, and must recognize the need for a solid foundation. As multidisciplinary artists come together to tell the stories of our existence today, we must think about capturing, describing, and preserving the moment for the future.

One method of preservation is communal experience. Art does not exist without an audience. As such, art spaces like ARTECHOUSE that give this current movement a home are paramount. Just as movie theaters provided an innovative way to experience storytelling 100 years ago, ARTECHOUSE offers the most innovative platform to experience the latest artworks created using technology, from artists such as Refik Anadol, Daito Manabe, Zach Lieberman, and many others featured in this book, connecting them to new audiences in the most progressive spaces, and giving voice to all artists who wish to share their vision with the world.

We are an evolving community dedicated to preserving our modern history and showcasing the advancement of cultural and artistic expression. Our platform provides broader recognition, a place where unique experiences and memories are formed, while enabling new ways to create and appreciate innovative art.

Parallel to the technology-driven artistic programming offered at ARTECHOUSE, The Age of Data sheds light on this movement and facilitates the evolving discourse on how data-powered art unfolds. One way to protect today's data-driven art and make it accessible tomorrow is with deliberate documentation like the book you are reading now.

As we foster new developments and ideas within the field, we must actively stay conscious of further questions. Every great challenge begins with a dialogue and an attempt at understanding. As we start this journey and begin the conversation, we encourage you to dive deeper into the world of data-driven art and expand your knowledge by reading the supporting chapters and experiencing these developments firsthand. As we are guided into the Age of Data, more informed, more enlightened, and living what will eventually become our history, let us tackle the challenge of preservation together. Let us create new memories and celebrate the unique and undiscovered shared experiences. Let us connect and collaborate through an ever-growing global community of creators, audiences, archivists, and commentators.

The answer to the question of preservation lies in not only switching on, but consciously keeping the switch on. As we continue to define this exceptional movement, I invite you to join us to keep future artists and audiences educated and fearless in the mixed reality of a digital, virtual, and physical world. Let us all progress into the unfamiliar with confidence.

Let us keep the switch on.

CONTENT

Refik Anadol

Name:

Refik Anadol

Info:

Refik Anadol is a media artist and director born in Istanbul, Turkey, in 1985. Currently lives and works in Los Angeles, California. He is a lecturer and visiting researcher in UCLA's Department of Design Media Arts.

Anadol works in site-specific public art, creating live audio/visual performances and immersive AI cinema installations with a parametric data sculpture approach. His work explores the space between digital and physical entities by generating a hybrid relationship between architecture and media arts with machine intelligence.

He holds a Master of Fine Arts degree from the University of California, Los Angeles in Media Arts, a Master of Fine Arts degree from Istanbul Bilgi University in Visual Communication Design, and a Bachelor of Arts degree with Summa Cum Laude in Photography and Video.

Projects:

URL:

refikanadol.com

Mail:

refo@refikanadol.com

Instagram:

@refikanadol

My name is Refik Anadol. I am a media artist and director, using data as a pigment and painting with a thinking brush, trying to embed media art into architecture to let buildings dream and hallucinate.

For the last six years, I have been working with big data and machine intelligence to develop a unique understanding and knowledge of the relationship between humans, machines, and environments.

As a team, we are 14 people that can speak 14 languages. We are trying to create art for anyone, any age, and any background. In our practice, we predominantly use public data for public art projects

We specifically try to detach ego from data to generate collective memories and focus on humanity's collective dreams.

We draw inspiration from nature, especially in the age of machine intelligence; science fiction narratives heavily inspire the simulations. We also try to generate some machine experience that simulates the reality that we have. We also try to generate machine experiences that simulate our reality and find traces of emotions in these experiences – a process that we call "data poetics" of our three-dimensional data sculptures and data paintings.

In our practice, we not only focus on the virtual world but also create physical experiences. For example, we recently created a public art project for Portland based on eight million data archives that we collected from the city. We transformed the information through the lens of machine intelligence and generated a three-dimensional data cloud that became a 3D-printed large-scale data sculpture.

We also work with NASA JPL and other labs at various research universities in the US and in Europe to understand how AI-based art can interact with science and eventually attempt at answering the question of what it means to be a human being in the 21st century.

We try to emphasize why data is essential in the age of machine intelligence, especially in a world where we constantly feel like we are plugged into a system that controls our perception of knowledge.

I do believe that art is humanity's most powerful vehicle for imagination. As a media artist, I believe that this book will be one of the most inspiring outputs in our field, capturing the creation of data narratives and showcasing who is behind the scenes of the most interesting discourses in media arts and design.

The systems, the hardware, the software around us is constantly changing, and the data becomes a new language between machines.

But as humans, I think we have to learn this language as well.

I also believe art is a form of expression, a form of exploration to create a common language around these narratives.

CREDITS

Picture by Tom Ross

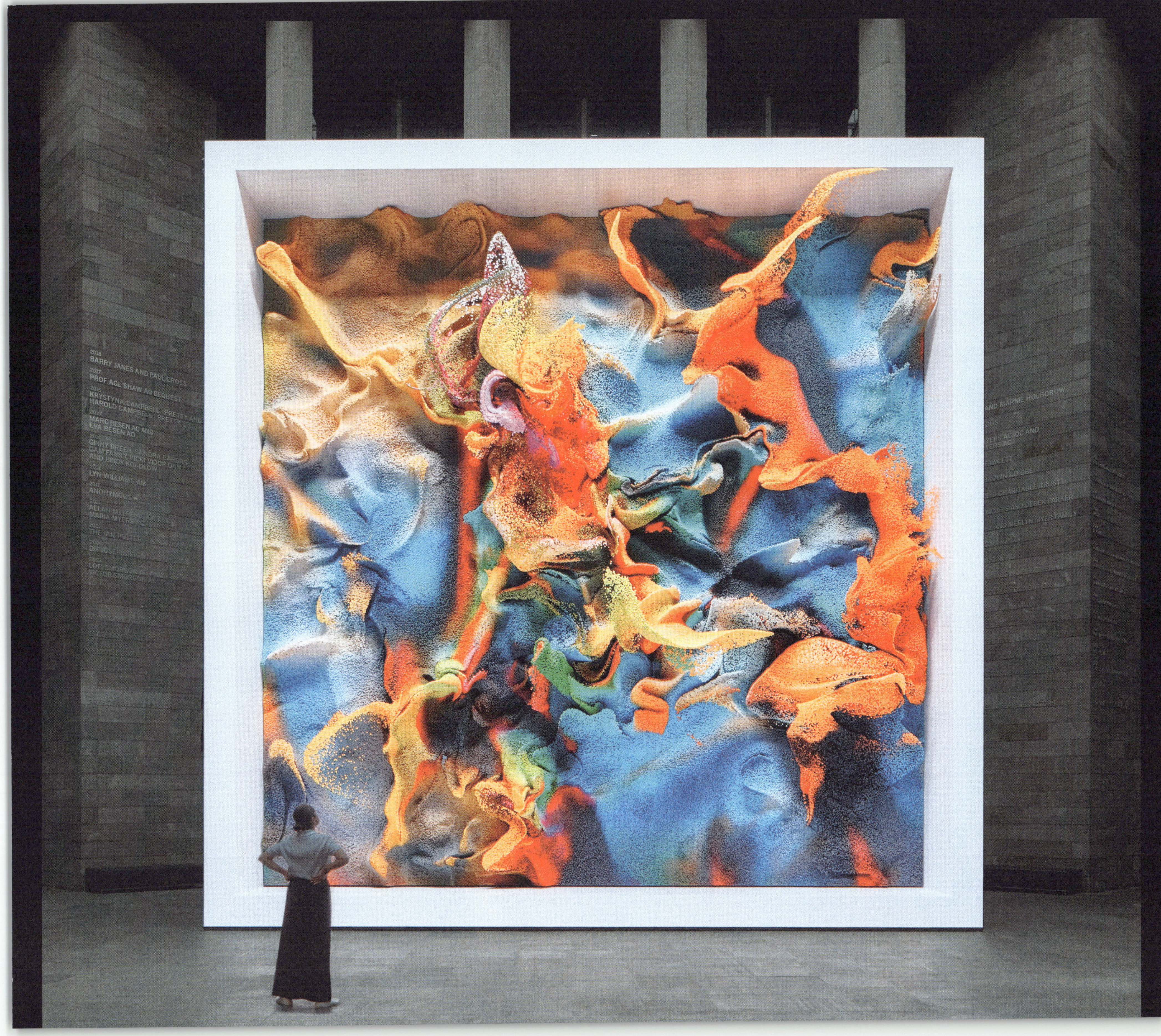
2018
BARRY JANES AND PAUL CROSS
2017
PROF AGL SHAW AO BEQUEST
2015
MARC BESEN AC AND
EVA BESEN AO
LYN WILLIAMS AM
ANONYMOUS
AND MARNIE HOLBOROW

NATURE DATA

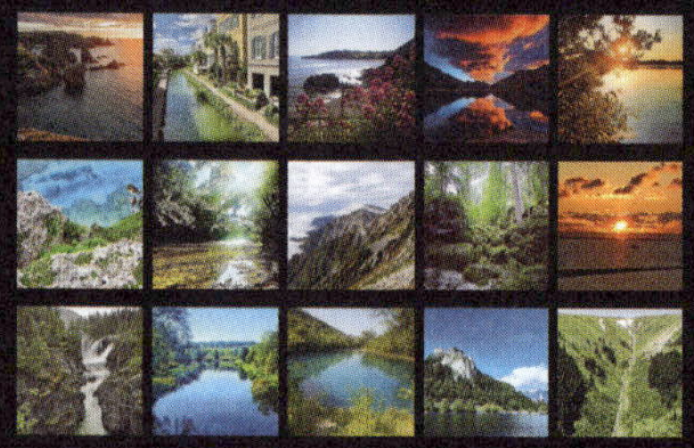

Over 200 million raw images of nature were collected to produce the preliminary dataset.

MACHINE LEARNING CLASSIFICATION

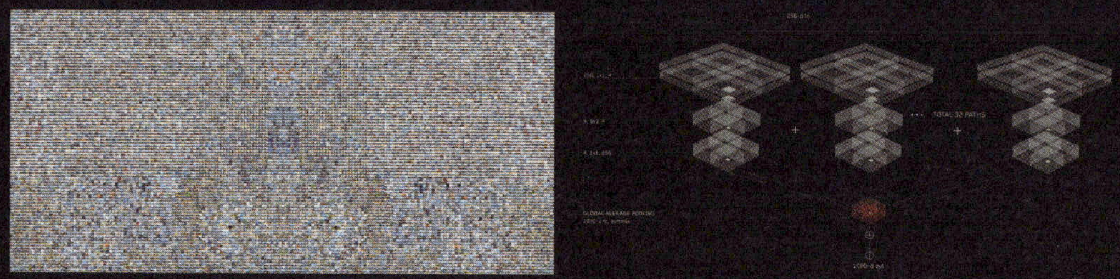

The dataset is processed through an image-recognition algorithm, ResNext, for feature vectorization. Computed features are then used to qualitatively filter the dataset.

IMAGE CLUSTERING

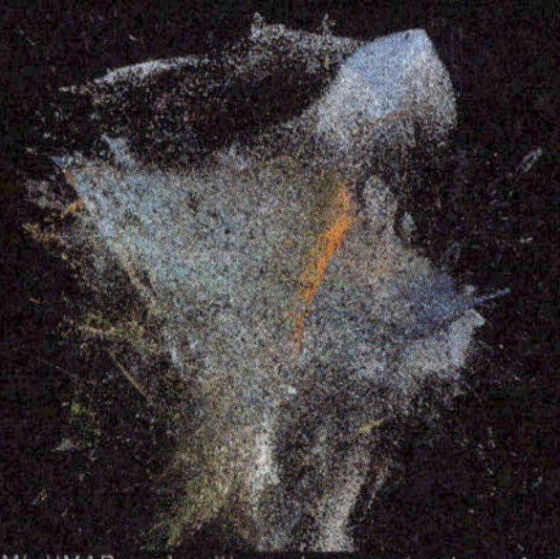

The UML-UMAP algorithm is used to cluster machine-generated memories of the nature and these clusters result in a three-dimensional data universe.

QUANTUM MEMORIES

CREDITS
Designed & Developed at Refik Anadol Studio

Alex Morozov, AnalogNative, Brian Chung, Carrie He, Christian Burke, Danny Lee, Efsun Erkilic, Kerim Karaoglu, Pelin Kivrak, Ho Man Leung, Kyle McLean, Nicholas Boss, Nidhi Parsana, Raman K. Mustafa, Toby Heinemann

10m x 10m x 2.5m AI Data Sculpture

Custom software, quantum computing data, generative algorithm with artificial intelligence (AI), real time digital animation on LED screen, 4 channel sound

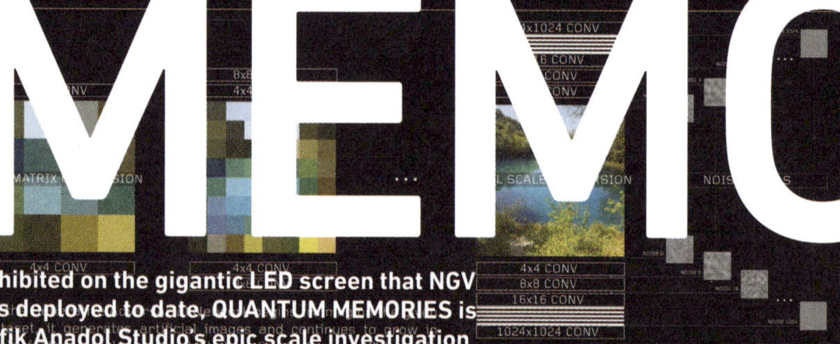

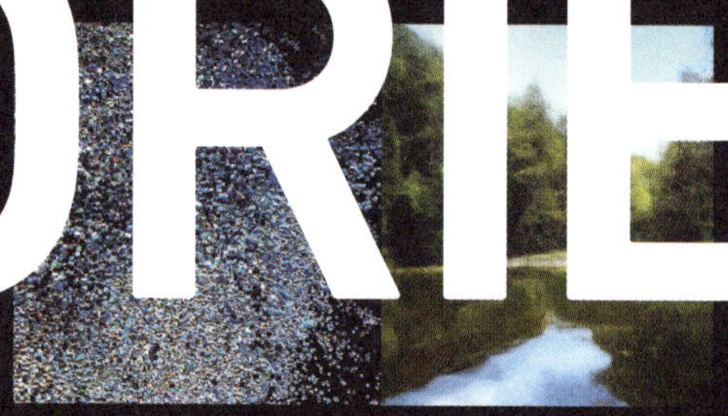

In the latent space of data processing where previously unseen connections between data clusters become recognizable by artificial intelligence, probabilistic nature of physical phenomena and their interactions become more visible.

WORLD INTERPRETATIONS

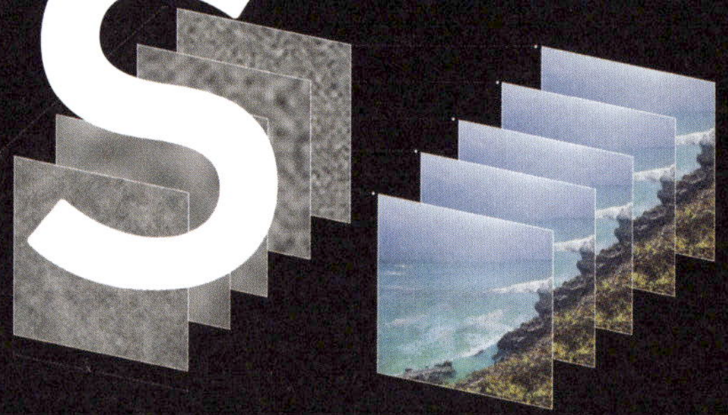

The machine re-generates new yet artificial nature images and presents them as exclusive alternative modalities to be experienced as parallel speculative realities.

Exhibited on the gigantic LED screen that NGV has deployed to date, QUANTUM MEMORIES is Refik Anadol Studio's epic scale investigation of the intersection between Google AI Quantum Supremacy experiments, machine learning, and aesthetics of probability.

Technological and digital advancements of the past century could be defined by humanity's eagerness to make machines go to places that humans could not go, including the spaces inside our minds and the non-spaces of our un- or sub-conscious acts.

QUANTUM NOISE LEVELS

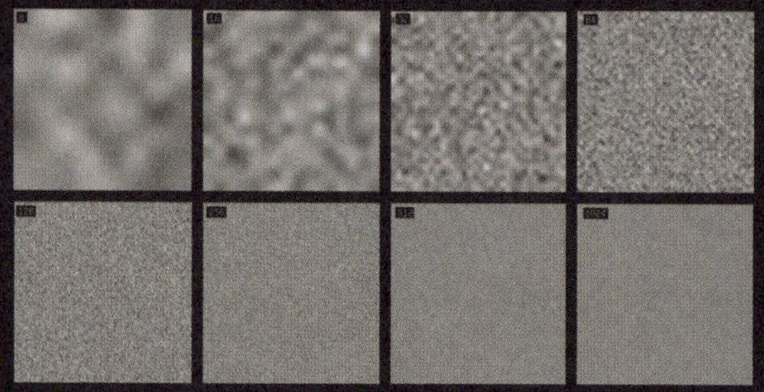

Using AI to speculate a parallel nature that we cannot possibly see with our human eye, we allow the measure of randomness that is triggered by quantum noise to interact with this new data.

QUANTUM NOISE DATA SCULPTURES

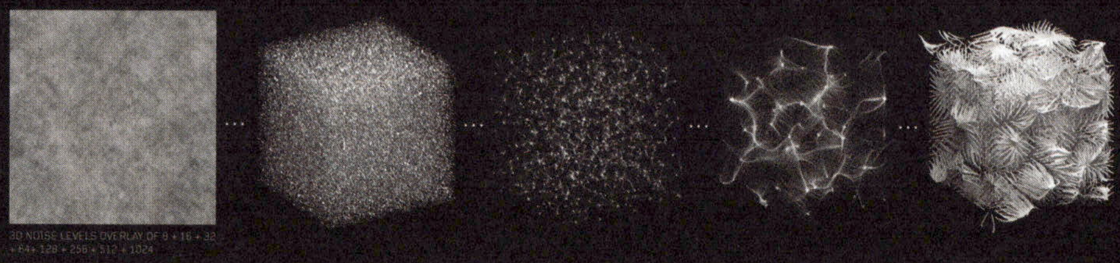

In this way, we first create noise from a data universe of real landscape images through publicly available quantum algorithms, and then re-create data by using the same noise as a generative resource.

ARTISTIC COMPUTATION

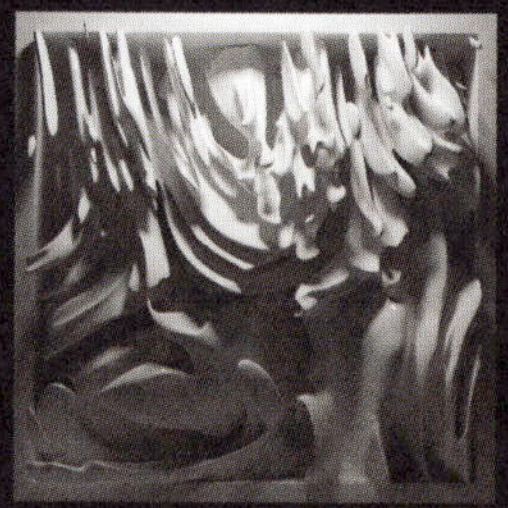

Tapping into the random fluctuations of quantum noise as a realm of aesthetic possibilities, the machine-mind uses residual quantum uncertainty to visualize its own process of "remembering."

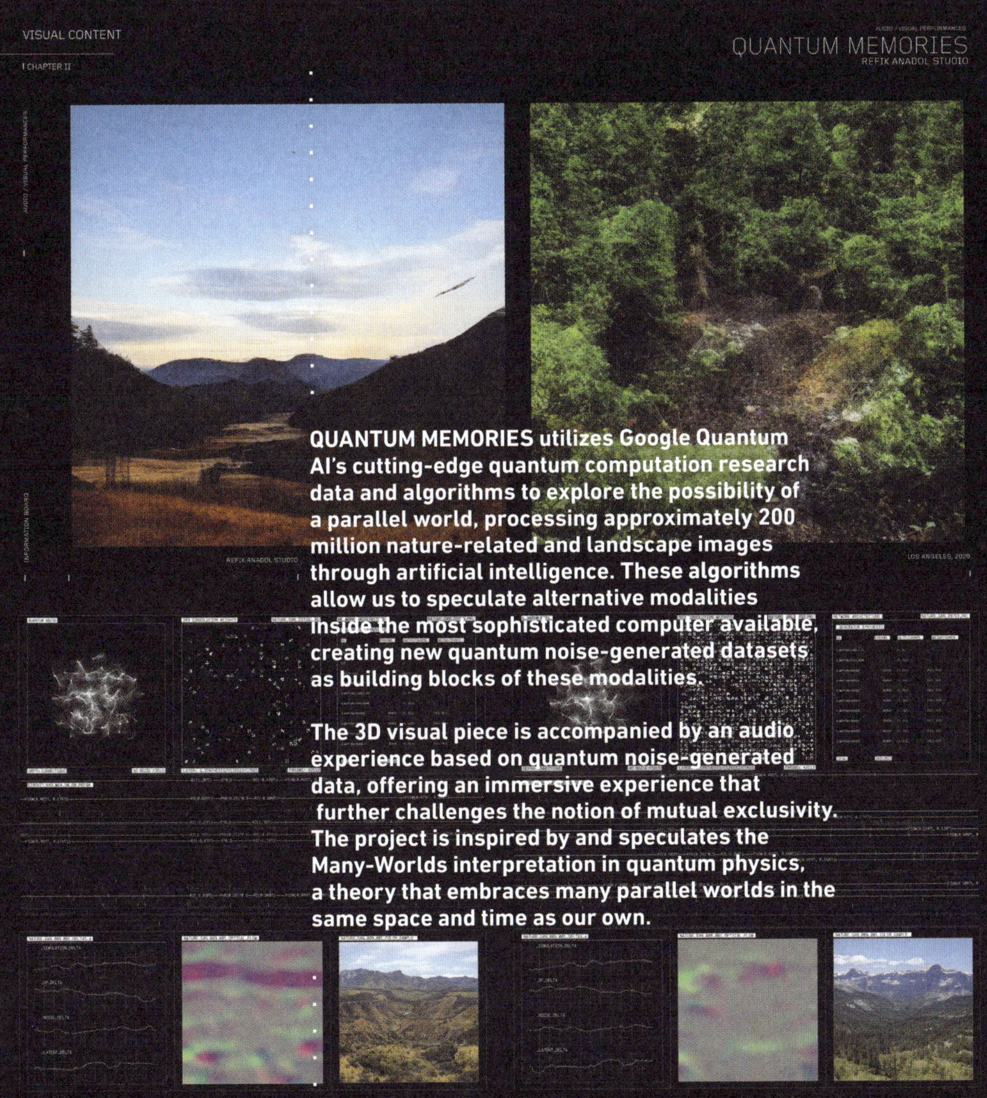

QUANTUM MEMORIES utilizes Google Quantum AI's cutting-edge quantum computation research data and algorithms to explore the possibility of a parallel world, processing approximately 200 million nature-related and landscape images through artificial intelligence. These algorithms allow us to speculate alternative modalities inside the most sophisticated computer available, creating new quantum noise-generated datasets as building blocks of these modalities.

The 3D visual piece is accompanied by an audio experience based on quantum noise-generated data, offering an immersive experience that further challenges the notion of mutual exclusivity. The project is inspired by and speculates the Many-Worlds interpretation in quantum physics, a theory that embraces many parallel worlds in the same space and time as our own.

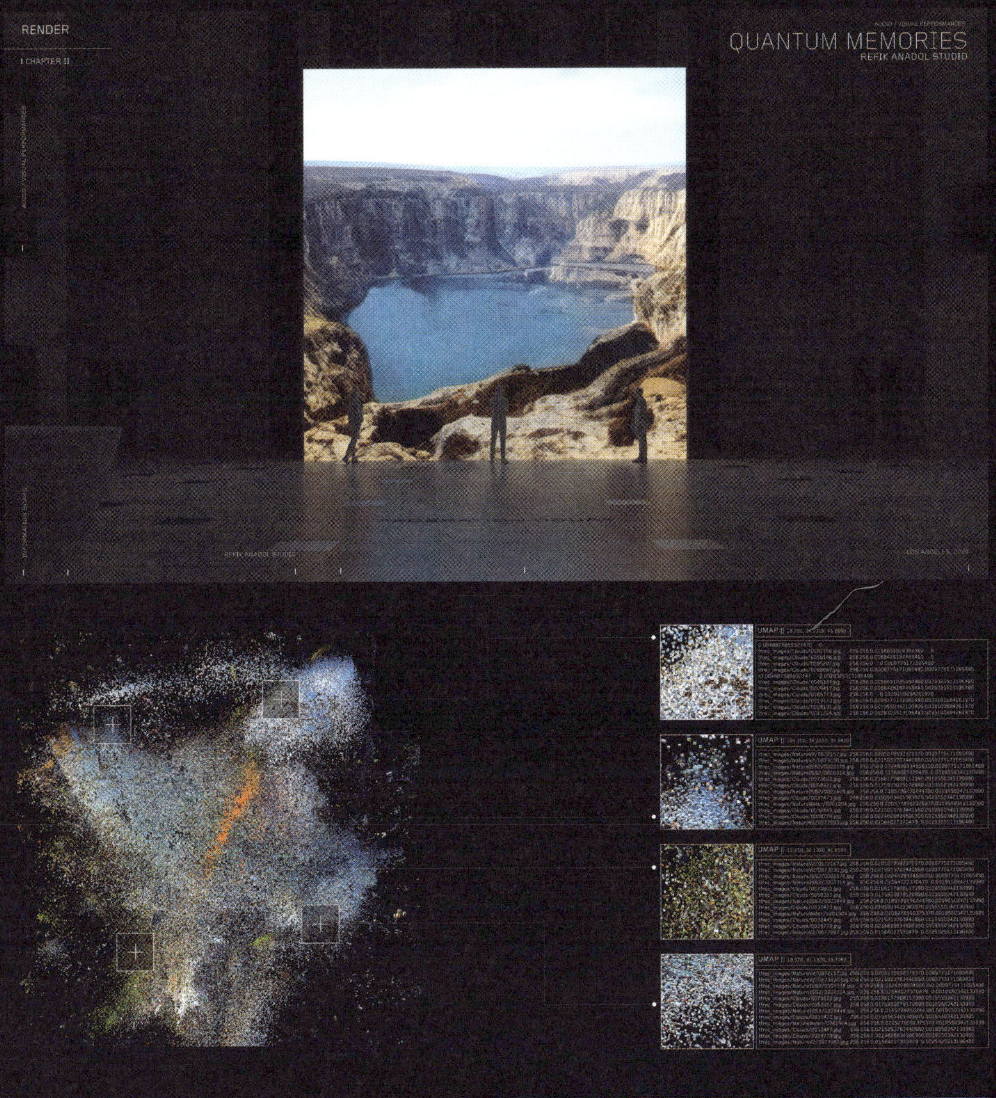

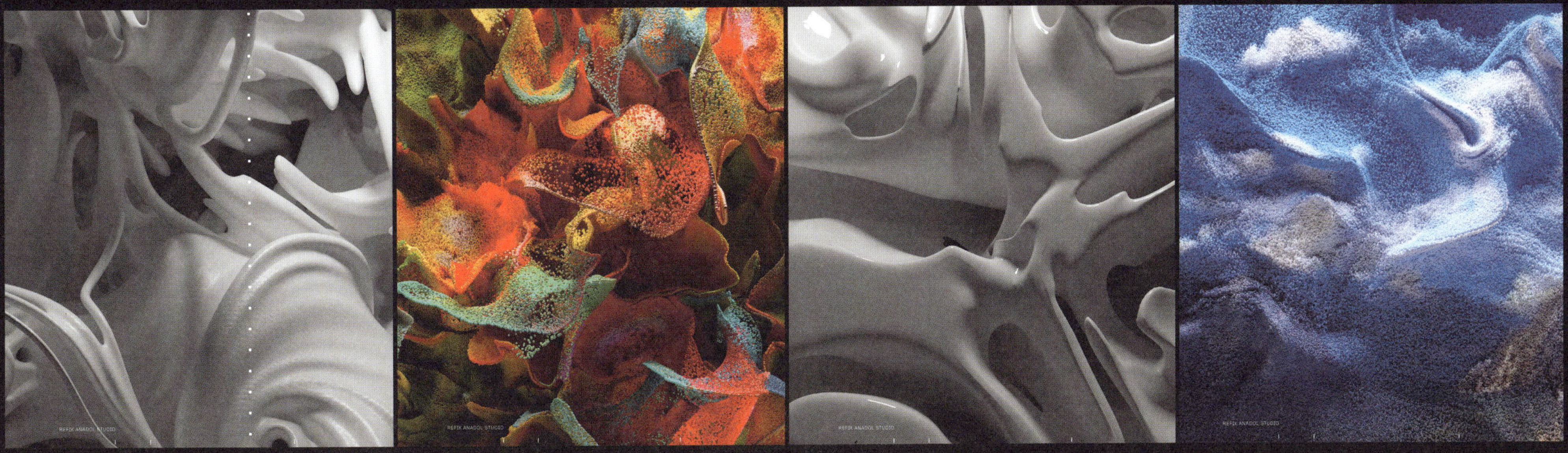

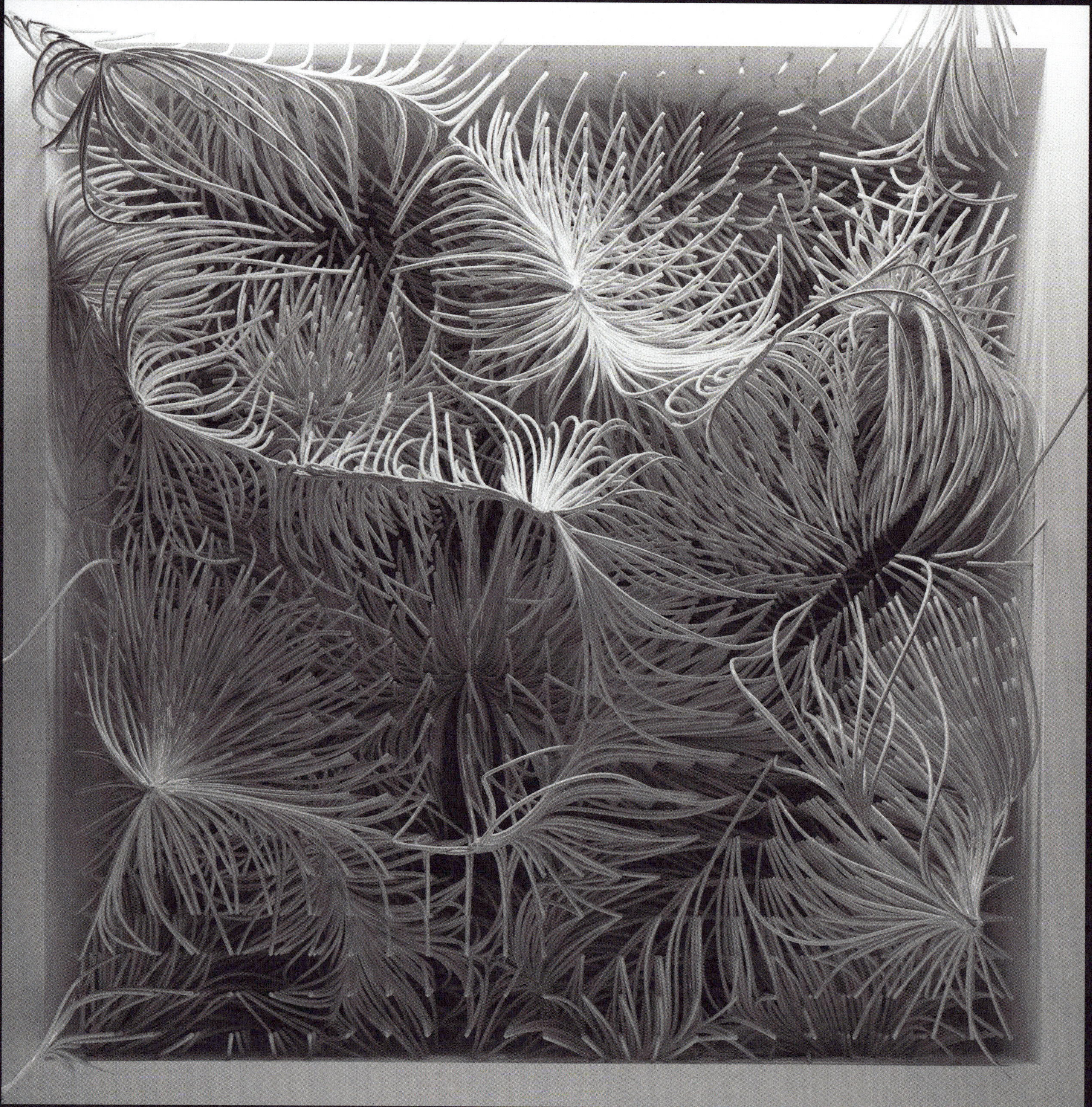

020 . Refik Anadol

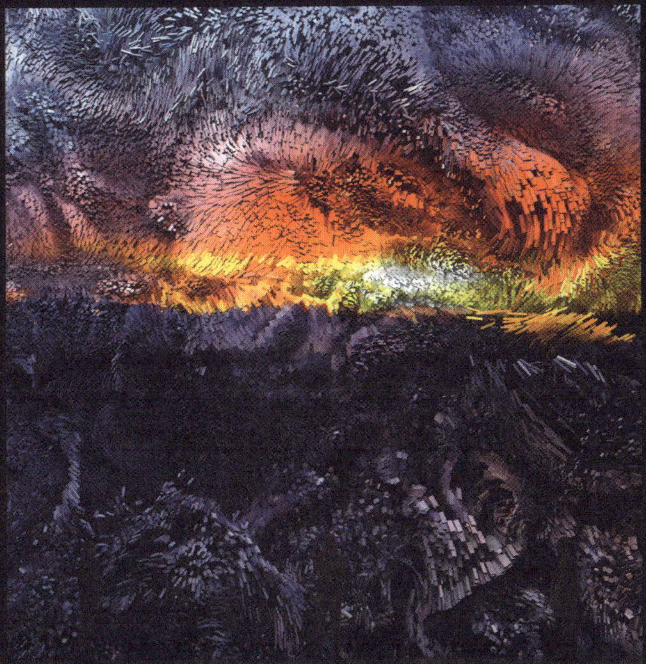

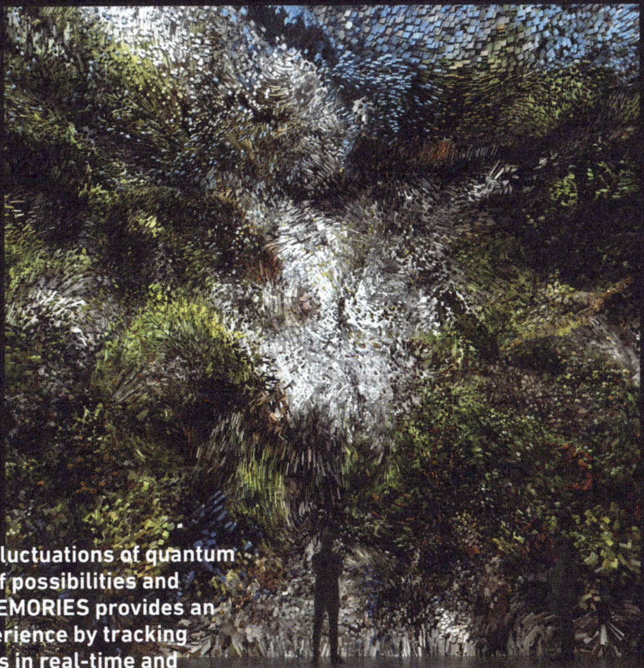

Tapping into the random fluctuations of quantum noise as a unique realm of possibilities and predictions, QUANTUM MEMORIES provides an interactive aesthetic experience by tracking the audience's movements in real-time and simulating how their observer positions indeed become entangled with the visible outcomes of the ever-changing artwork.

Deeply thankful to Google AI Quantum Team and their generous support:

Hartmun Neven,
Alan Ho,
Murphy Niu,
Michael Broughton.

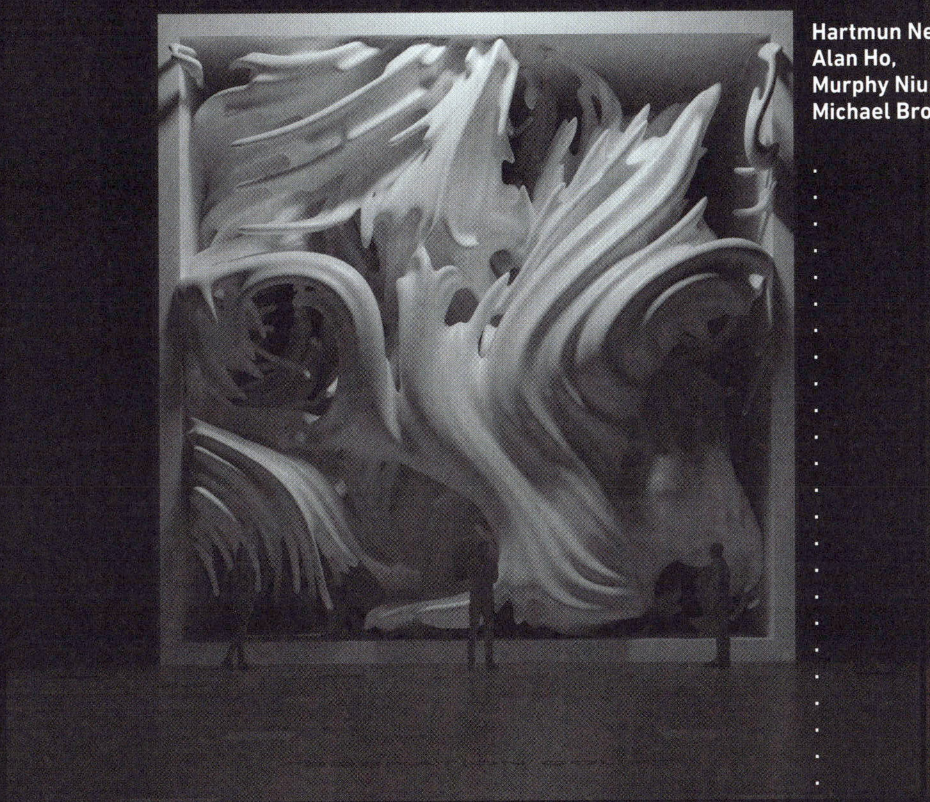

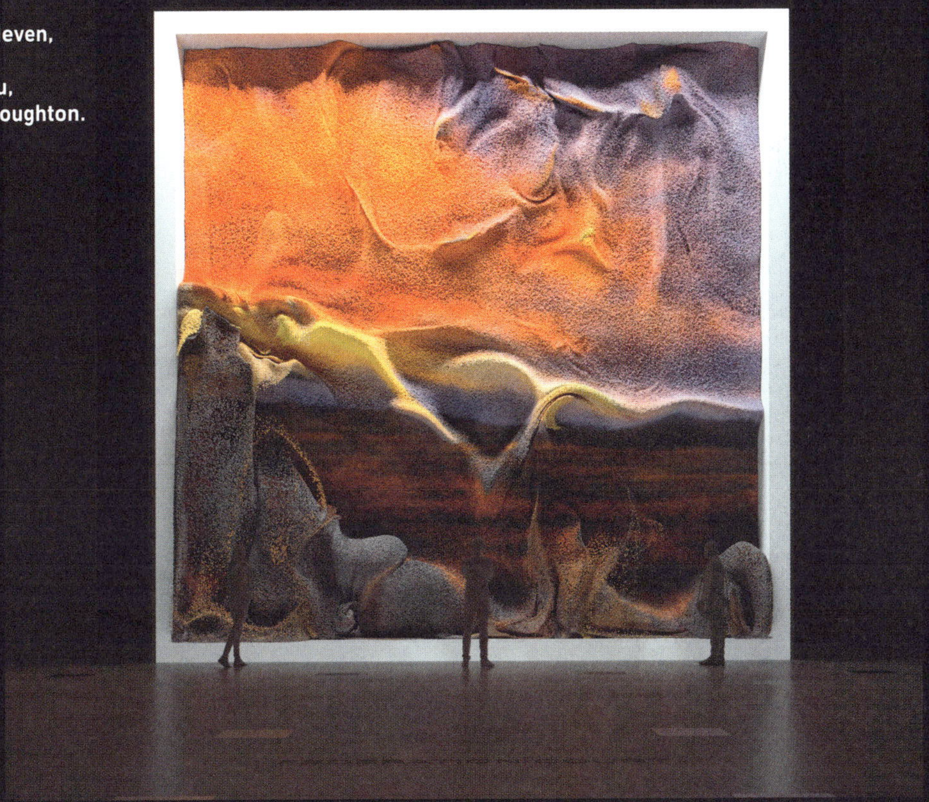

From February 7 through March 17, 2018, Pilevneli Gallery presented Refik Anadol's latest project on the materiality of remembering.

MELTING MEMORIES offered new insights into the representational possibilities emerging from the intersection of advanced technology and contemporary art.

By showcasing several interdisciplinary projects that translate the elusive process of memory retrieval into data collections, the exhibition immersed visitors in Anadol's creative vision of "recollection."

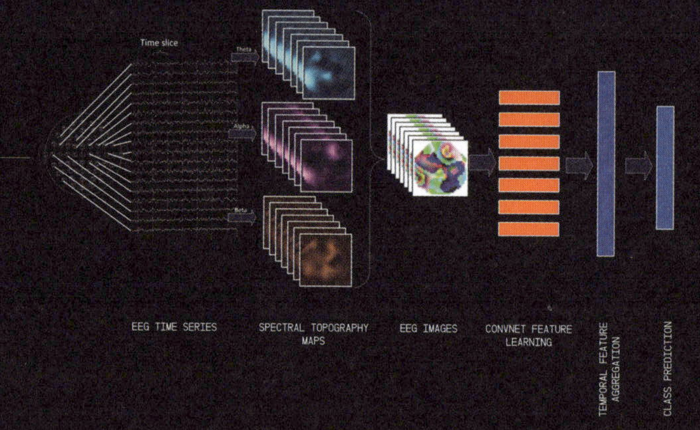

MELTING MEMORIES

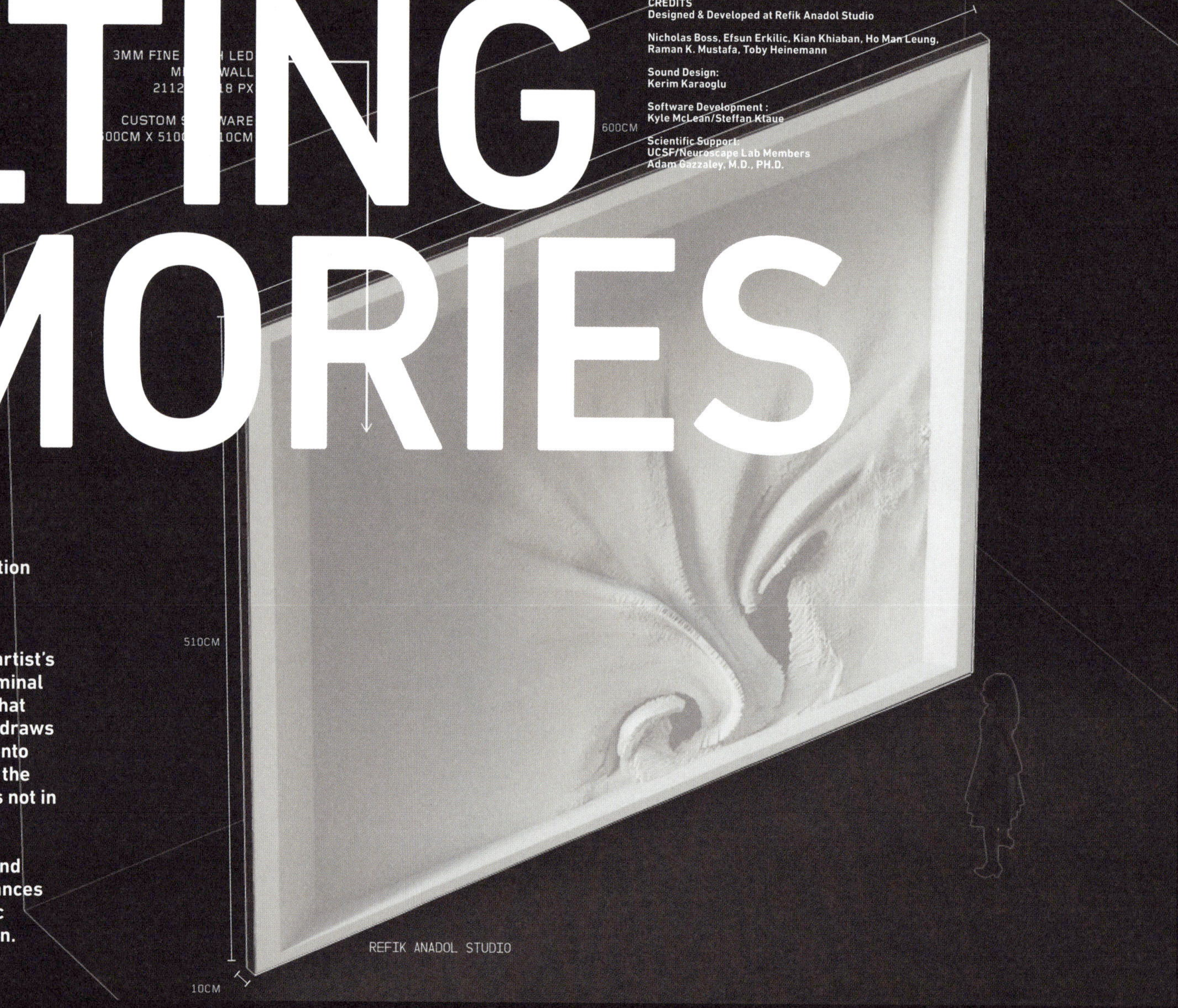

CREDITS
Designed & Developed at Refik Anadol Studio

Nicholas Boss, Efsun Erkilic, Kian Khiaban, Ho Man Leung, Raman K. Mustafa, Toby Heinemann

Sound Design:
Kerim Karaoglu

Software Development :
Kyle McLean/Steffan Klaue

Scientific Support:
UCSF/Neuroscape Lab Members
Adam Gazzaley, M.D., PH.D.

Anadol's installations address a productive espousal of cutting-edge technology and art and a strong preoccupation with studying human memory from Ancient Egyptians to Blade Runner 2049.

The exhibition's title, MELTING MEMORIES, refers to the artist's experience with unexpected interconnections among seminal philosophical works, academic inquiries, and artworks that take memory as their principal themes. The title further draws attention to the melting of neuroscience and technology into these centuries-long philosophical debates, questioning the emergence of a new space where artificial intelligence is not in conflict with individuality and intimacy.

Comprising data paintings, augmented data sculptures and light projections, the project as a whole debuts new advances in technology that enable visitors to experience aesthetic interpretations of motor movements inside a human brain.

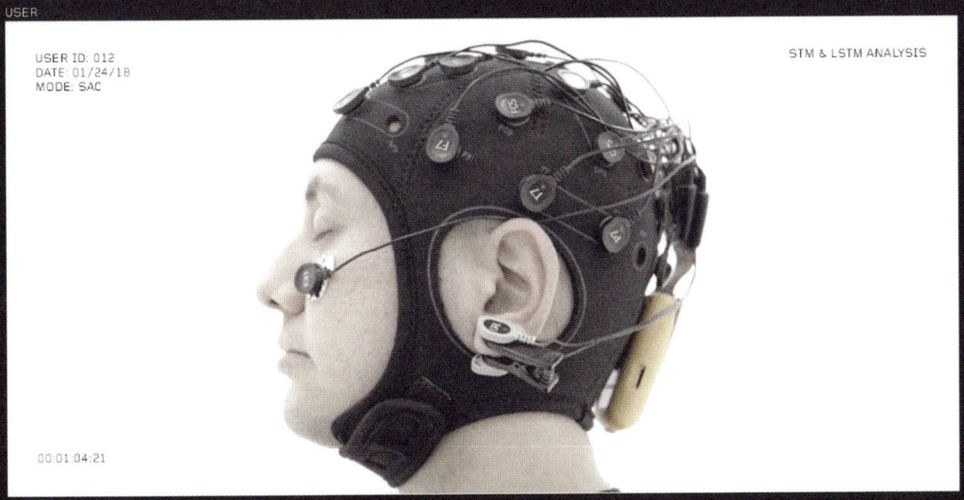

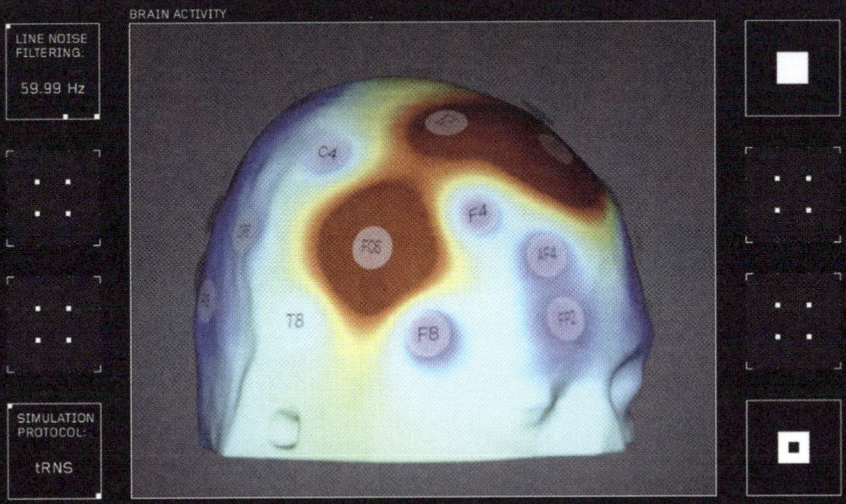

Each work grows out of the artist's impressive experiments with the advanced technology tools provided by the Neuroscape Laboratory at the University of California, San Francisco. Neuroscape is a neuroscience center focusing on technology creation and scientific research on brain function of both healthy and impaired individuals. Anadol gathers data on the neural mechanisms of cognitive control from an EEG (electroencephalogram) that measures changes in brain wave activity and provides evidence of how the brain functions over time. These data sets constitute the building blocks for the unique algorithms that the artist needs for the multidimensional visual structures on display.

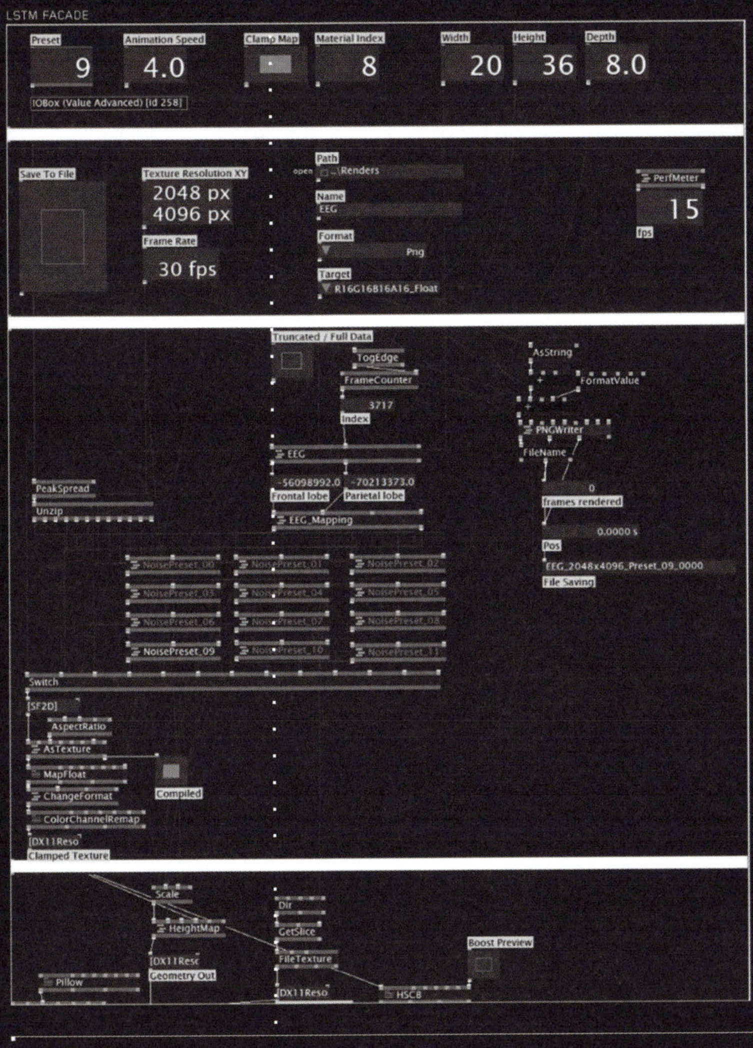

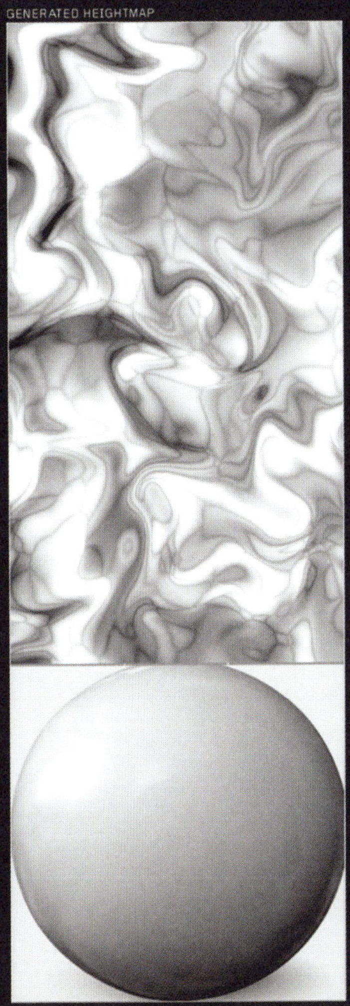

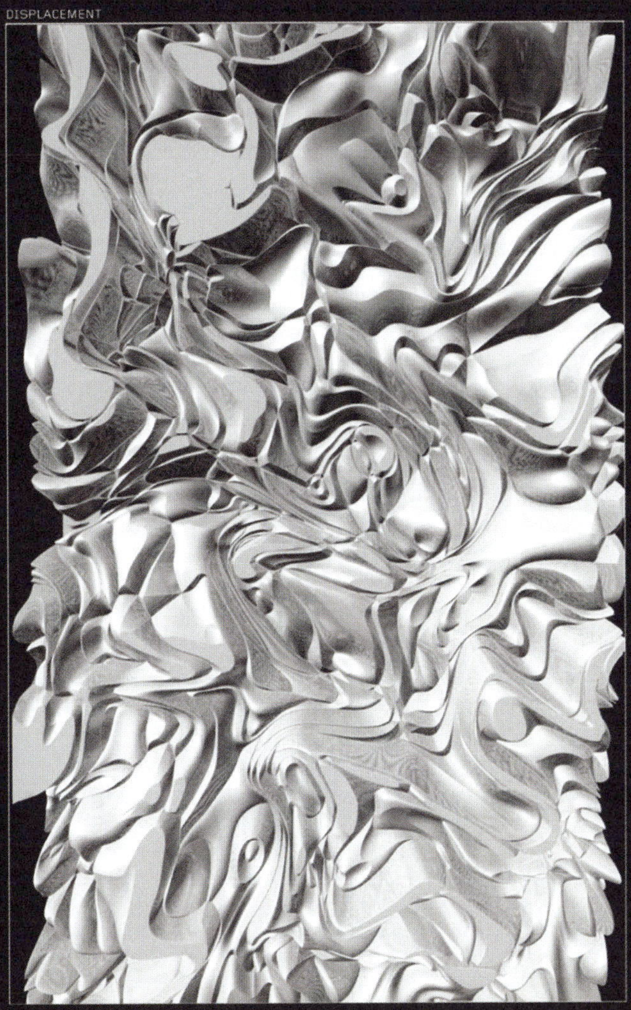

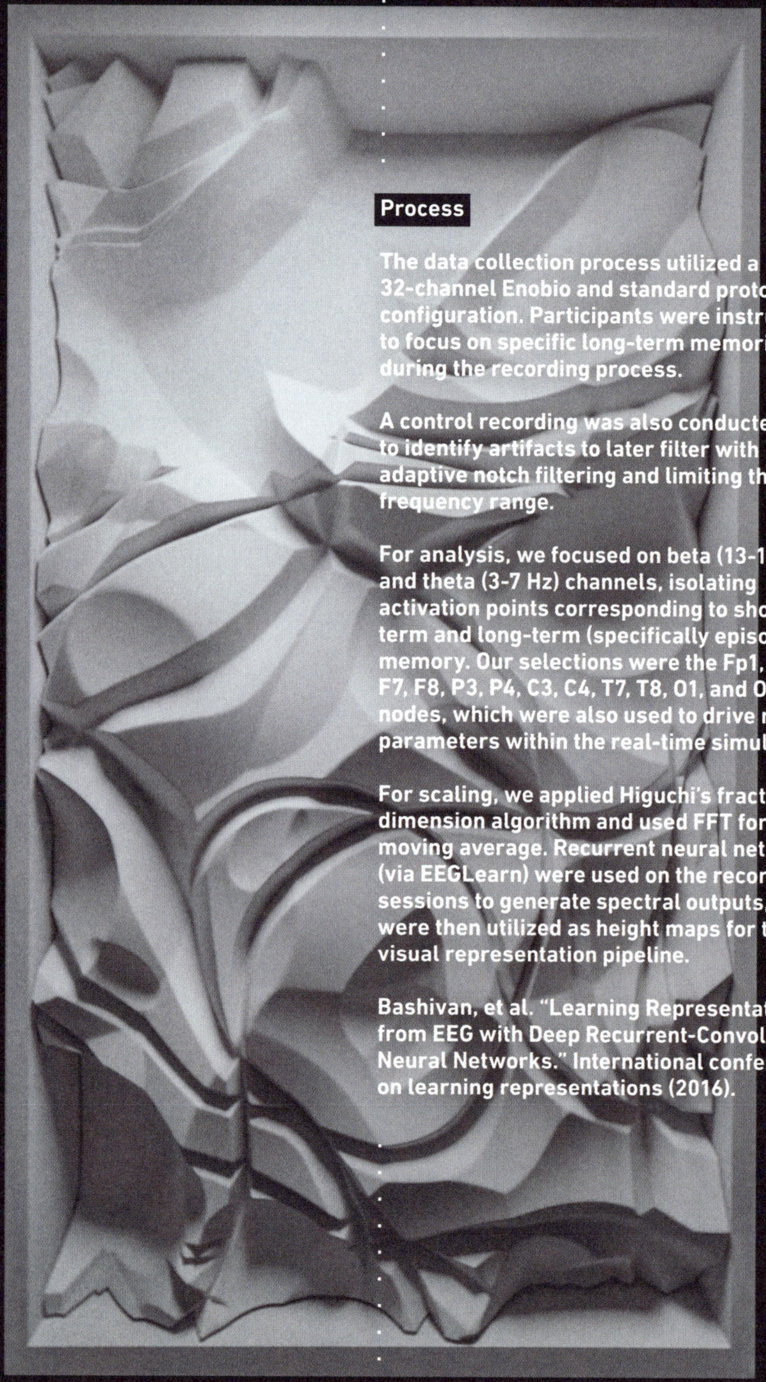

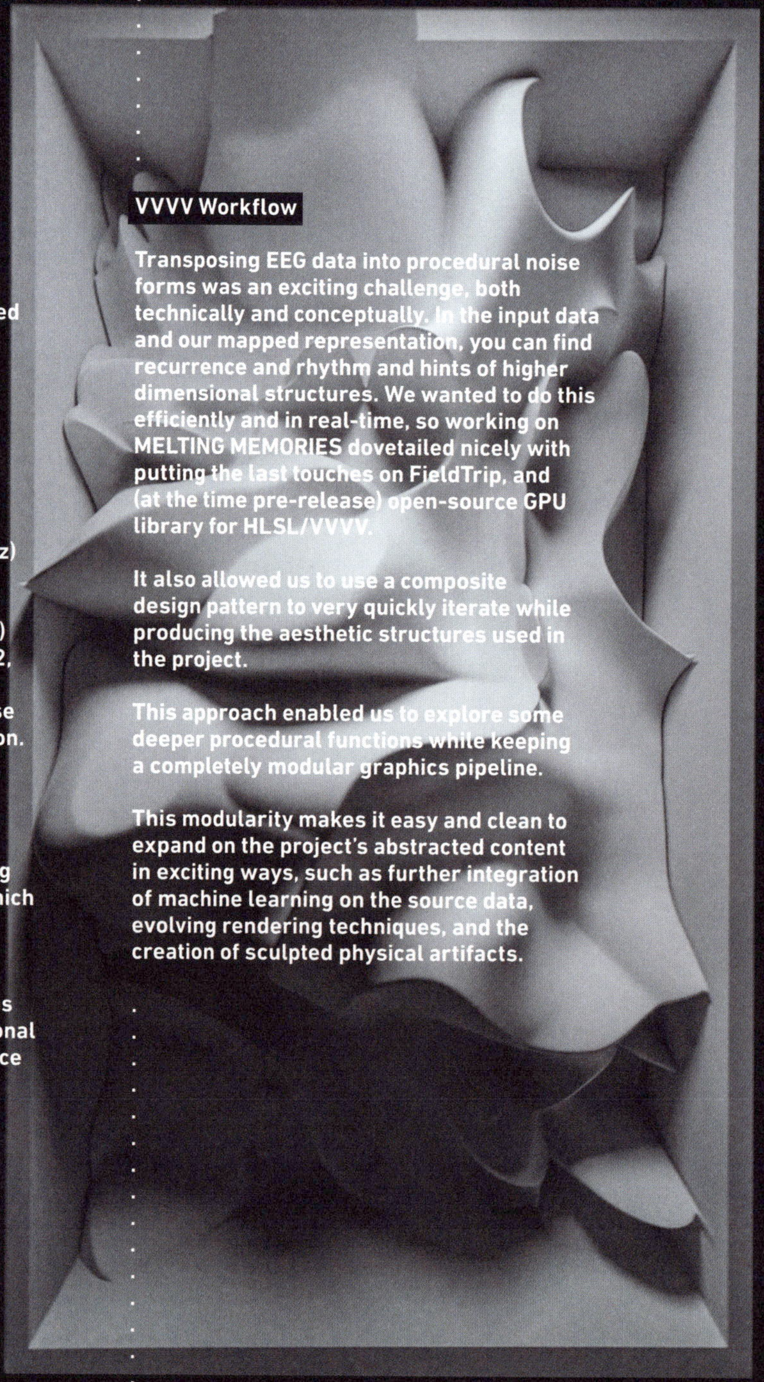

Process

The data collection process utilized a 32-channel Enobio and standard protocol configuration. Participants were instructed to focus on specific long-term memories during the recording process.

A control recording was also conducted to identify artifacts to later filter with adaptive notch filtering and limiting the frequency range.

For analysis, we focused on beta (13-17 Hz) and theta (3-7 Hz) channels, isolating activation points corresponding to short-term and long-term (specifically episodic) memory. Our selections were the Fp1, Fp2, F7, F8, P3, P4, C3, C4, T7, T8, O1, and O2 nodes, which were also used to drive noise parameters within the real-time simulation.

For scaling, we applied Higuchi's fractal dimension algorithm and used FFT for a moving average. Recurrent neural nets (via EEGLearn) were used on the recording sessions to generate spectral outputs, which were then utilized as height maps for the visual representation pipeline.

Bashivan, et al. "Learning Representations from EEG with Deep Recurrent-Convolutional Neural Networks." International conference on learning representations (2016).

VVVV Workflow

Transposing EEG data into procedural noise forms was an exciting challenge, both technically and conceptually. In the input data and our mapped representation, you can find recurrence and rhythm and hints of higher dimensional structures. We wanted to do this efficiently and in real-time, so working on MELTING MEMORIES dovetailed nicely with putting the last touches on FieldTrip, and (at the time pre-release) open-source GPU library for HLSL/VVVV.

It also allowed us to use a composite design pattern to very quickly iterate while producing the aesthetic structures used in the project.

This approach enabled us to explore some deeper procedural functions while keeping a completely modular graphics pipeline.

This modularity makes it easy and clean to expand on the project's abstracted content in exciting ways, such as further integration of machine learning on the source data, evolving rendering techniques, and the creation of sculpted physical artifacts.

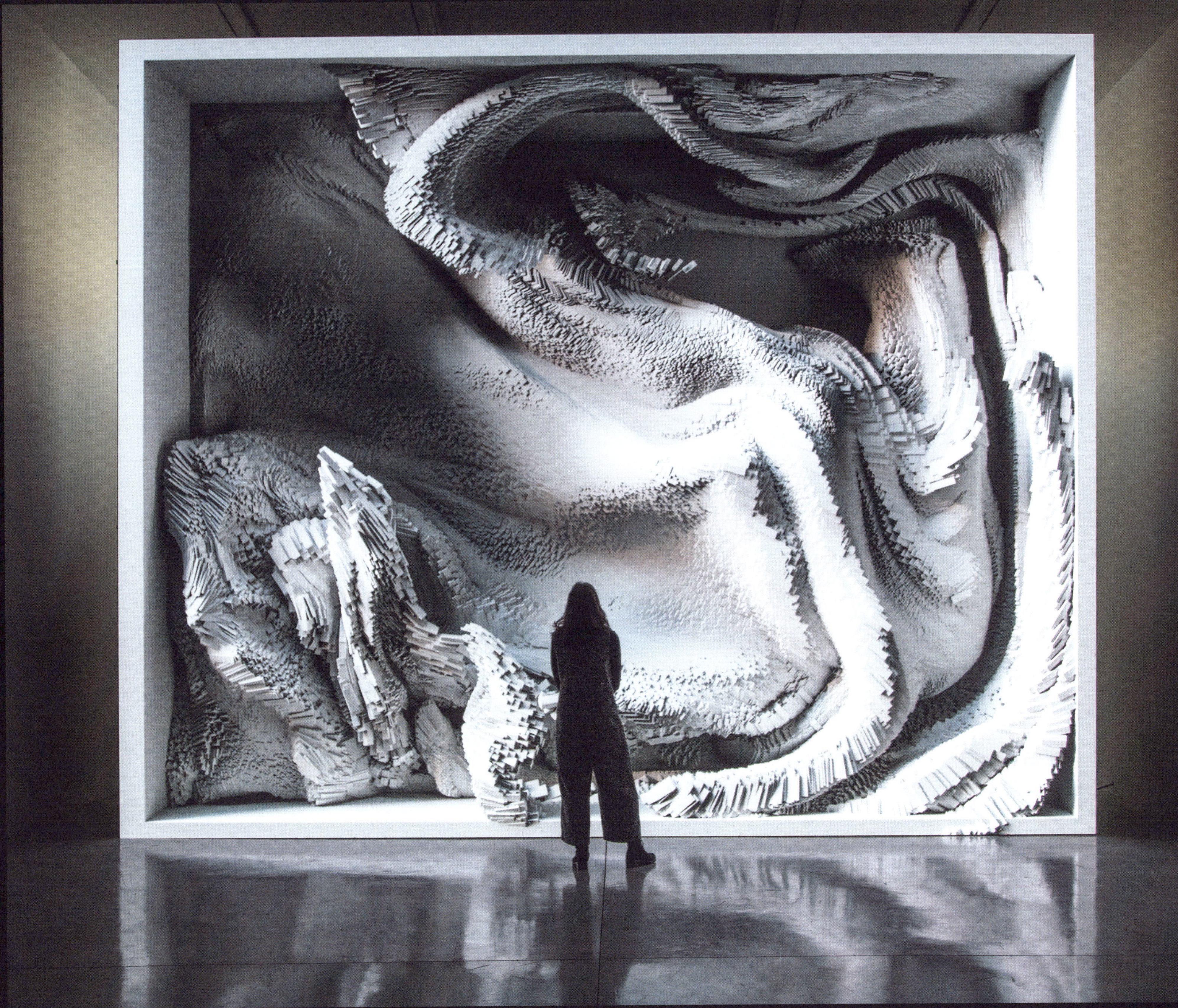

025 . MELTING MEMORIES

MACHINE HALLUCI- NATION

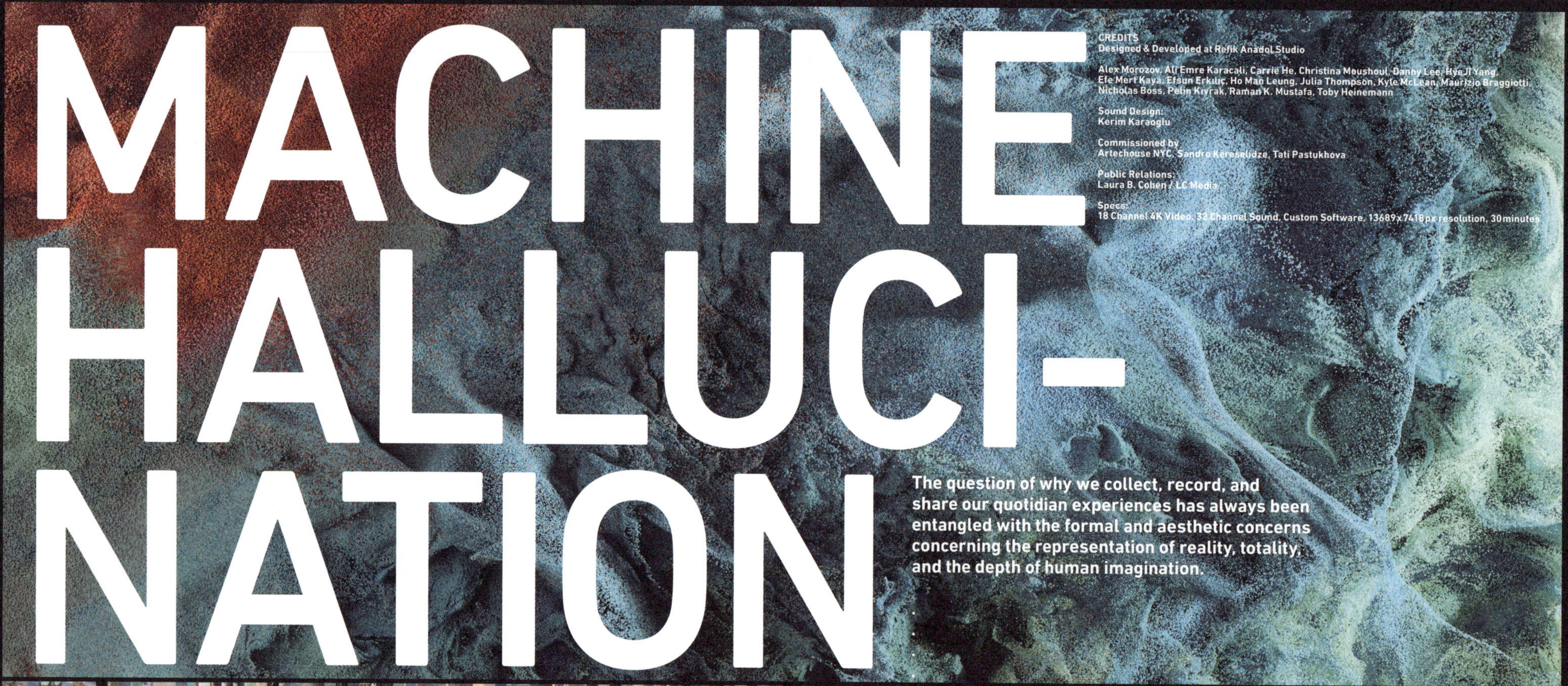

CREDITS
Designed & Developed at Refik Anadol Studio

Alex Morozov, Ali Emre Karacali, Carrie He, Christina Moushoul, Danny Lee, HyeJi Yang, Efe Mert Kaya, Efsun Erkılıç, Ho Man Leung, Julia Thompson, Kyle McLean, Maurizio Braggiotti, Nicholas Boss, Pelin Kıvrak, Raman K. Mustafa, Toby Heinemann

Sound Design:
Kerim Karaoglu

Commissioned by
Artechouse NYC, Sandro Kereselidze, Tati Pastukhova

Public Relations:
Laura B. Cohen / LC Media

Specs:
18 Channel 4K Video, 32 Channel Sound, Custom Software, 13689x7418px resolution, 30minutes

The question of why we collect, record, and share our quotidian experiences has always been entangled with the formal and aesthetic concerns concerning the representation of reality, totality, and the depth of human imagination.

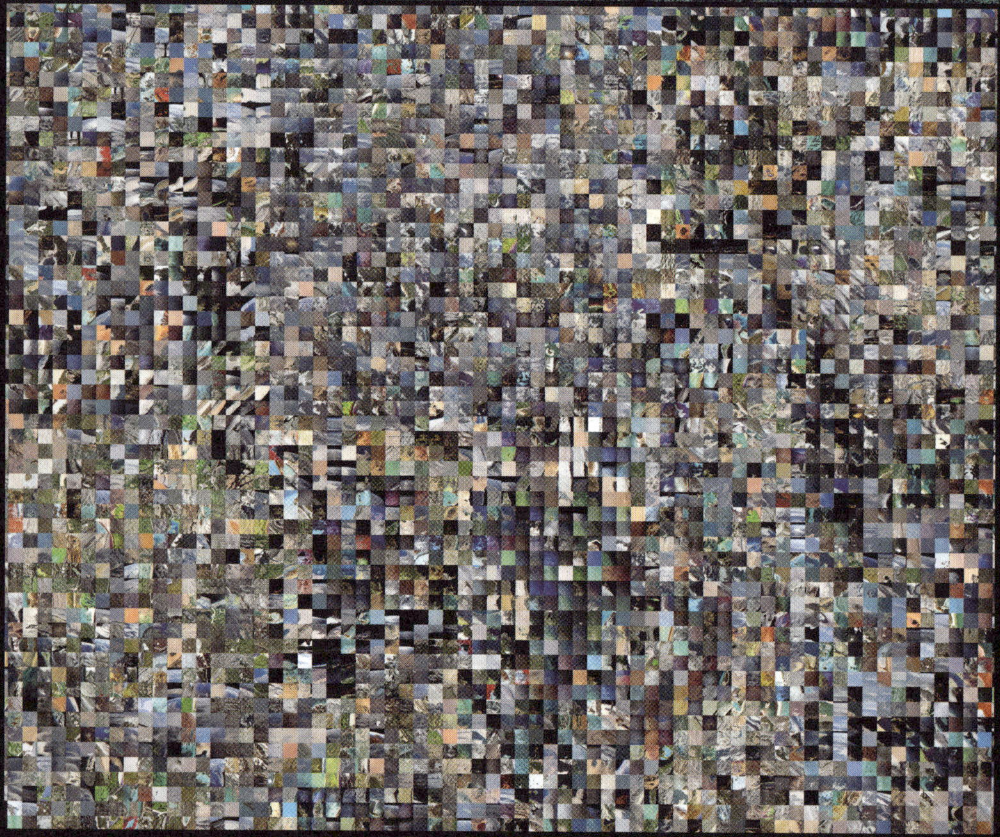

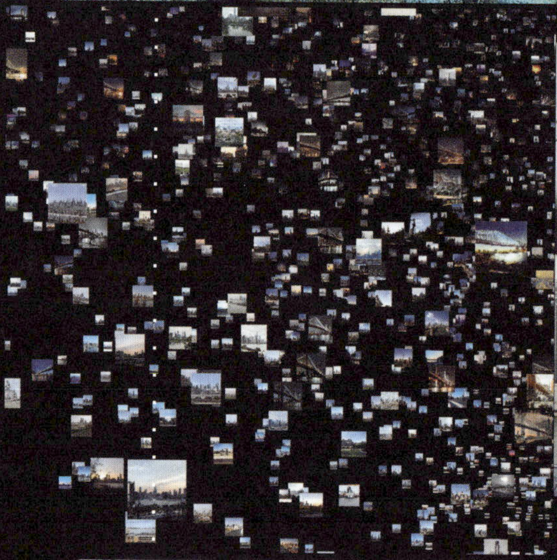

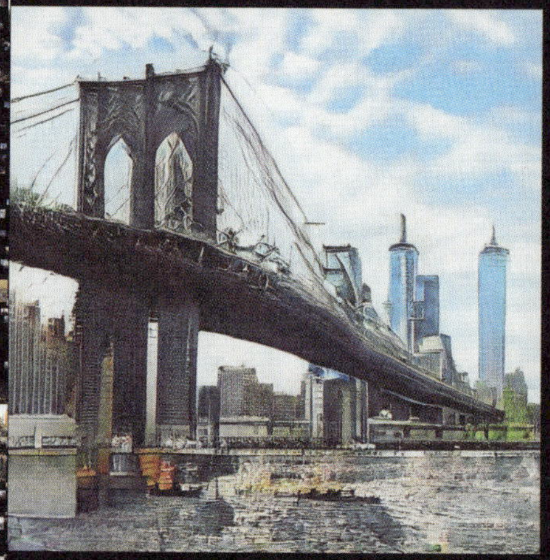

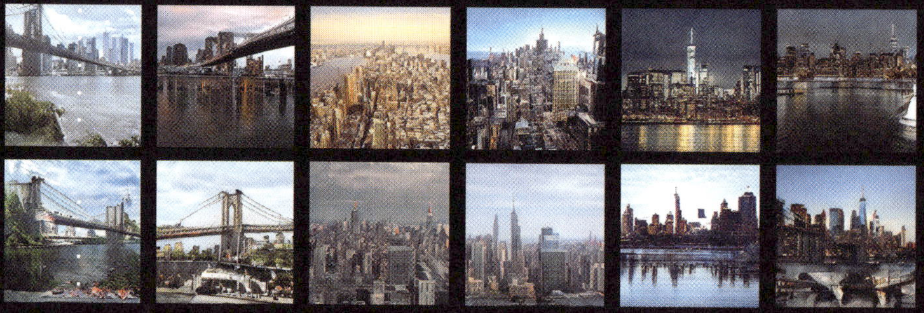

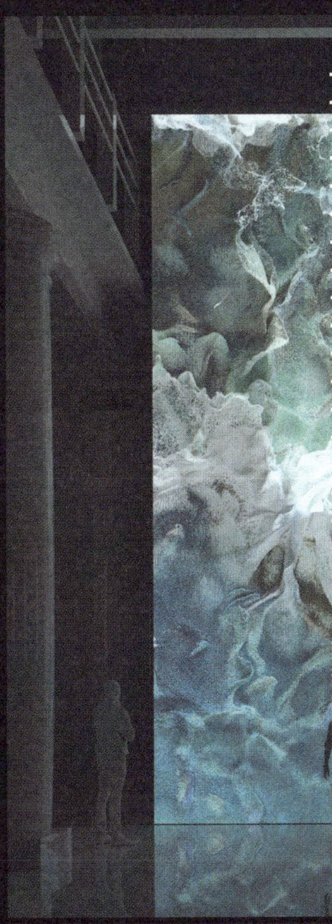

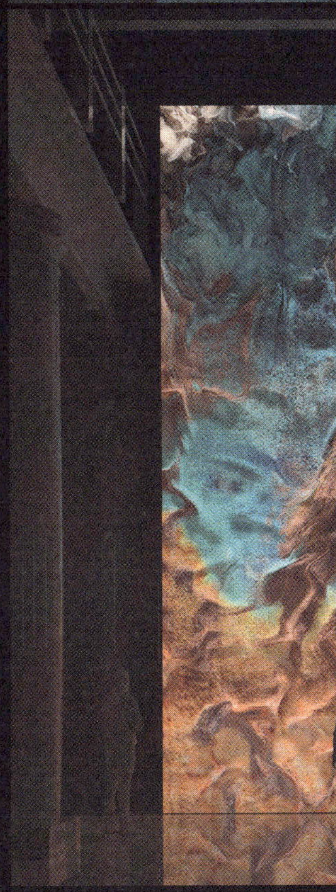

Nineteenth-century poet and critic Stéphane Mallarmé famously said that everything in the world existed to end up in a book. Revisiting Mallarmé's proposition in her 1977 collection of essays, On Photography, Susan Sonntag wrote, "Today everything exists to end in a photograph."

More recently, Jonathan Zittrain, the co-founder of Harvard's Berkman Center for Internet and society, suggested that "internet architecture" lacked a definable center and instead relied on "an extraordinary collective hallucination."

Refik Anadol's most recent synesthetic reality experiments deeply engage with these centuries-old questions and attempt at revealing new connections between visual narrative, archival instinct and collective consciousness. The project focuses on latent cinematic experiences derived from representations of urban memories as they are re-imagined by machine intelligence. For Artechouse's New York location, Anadol presents a data universe of New York City in 1025 latent dimensions that he creates by deploying machine learning algorithms on over 100 million photographic memories of New York City found publicly in social networks. MACHINE HALLUCINATION thus generates a novel form of synesthetic storytelling through its multilayered manipulation of a vast visual archive beyond the conventional limits of the camera and the existing cinematographic techniques.

The resulting artwork is a 30-minute experimental cinema experience, presented in 16K resolution, that visualizes the story of New York through the city's collective memories that constitute its deeply hidden consciousness.

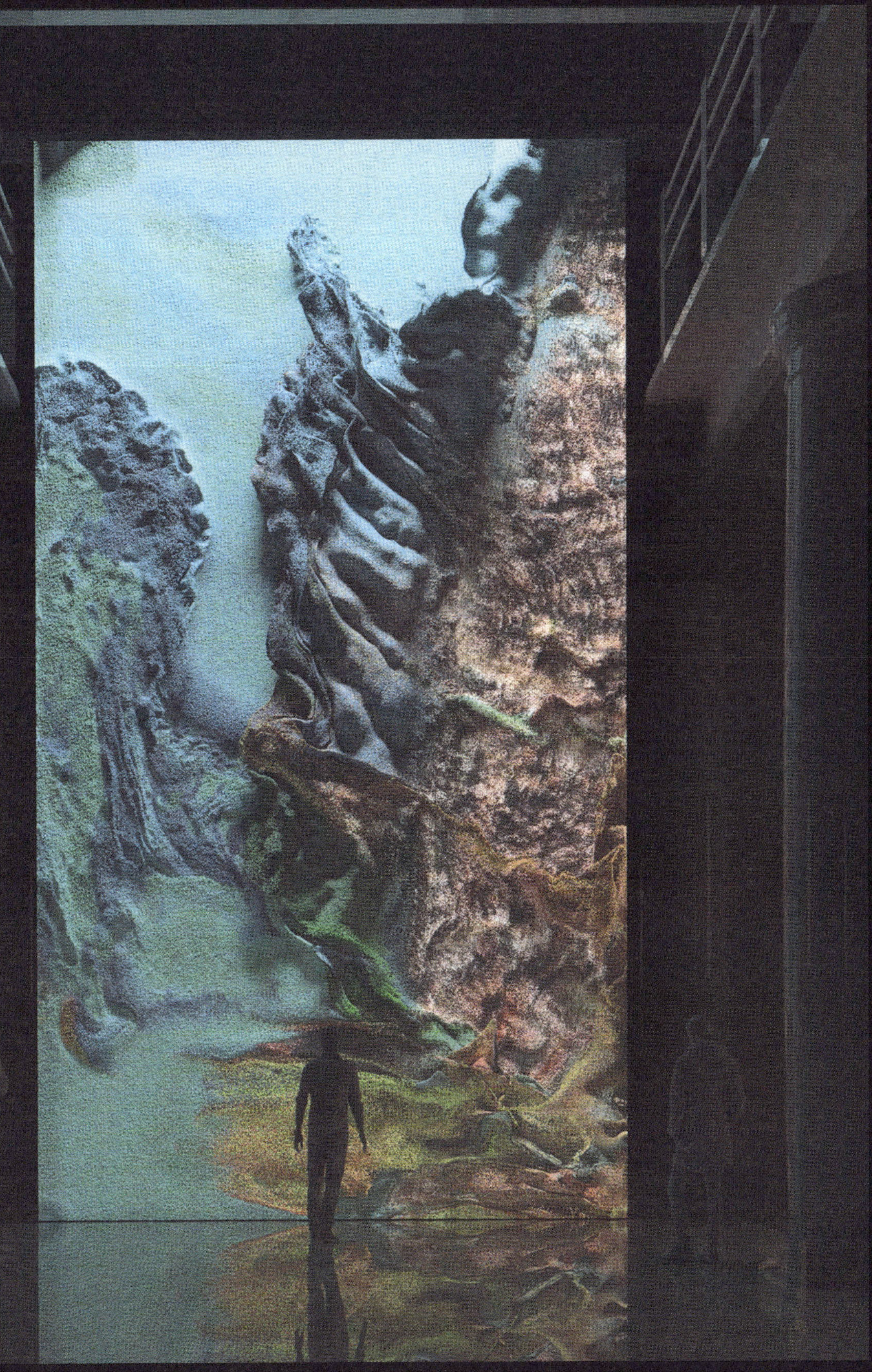

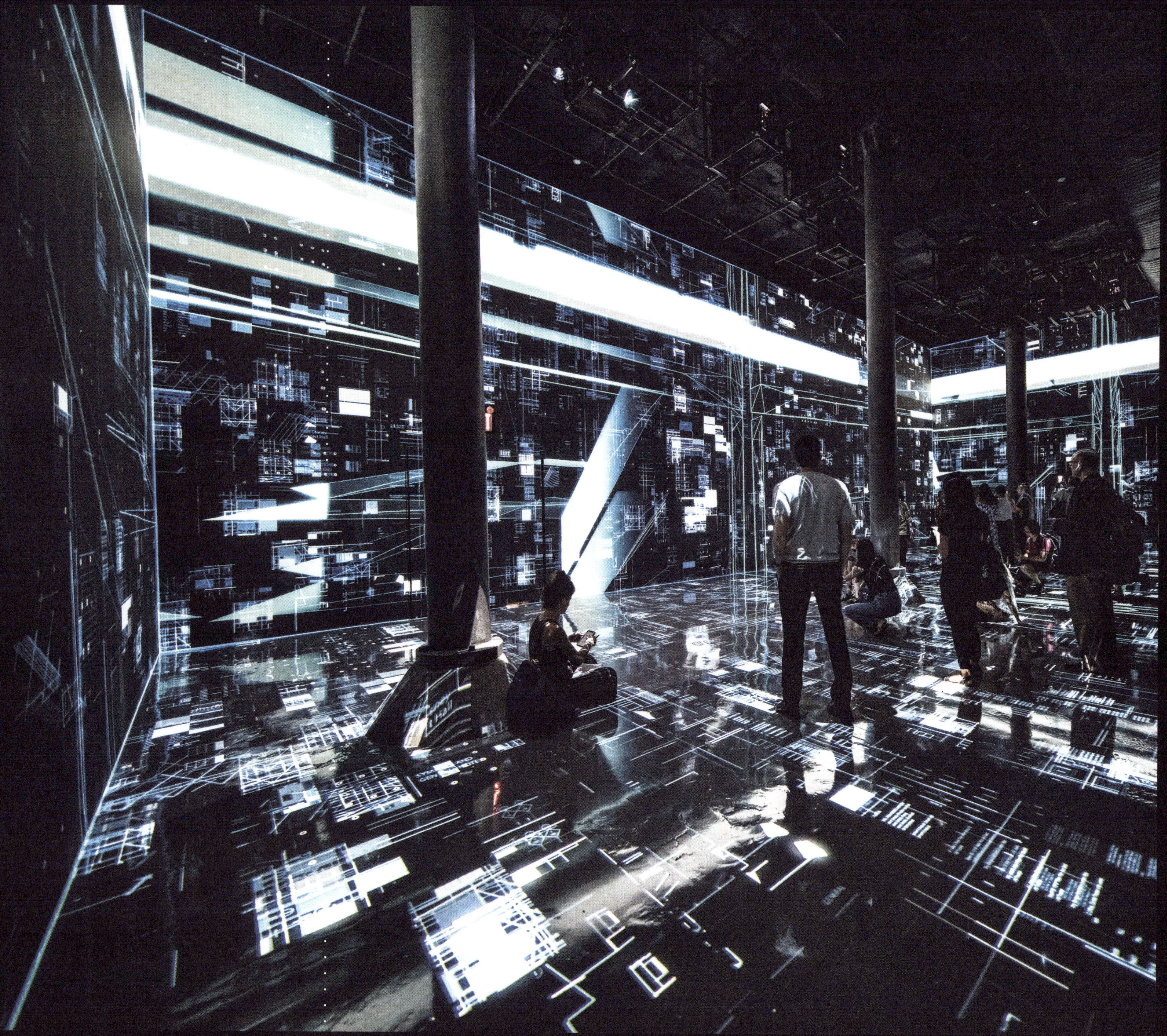

028 . Refik Anadol

The exhibition does not tell the story of today's New York but, instead, foresees what may come through the machine intelligence's bridging the gap between present and a vision of the near future. It is a hopeful vision relating to an evolving relationship between machine and man, providing an alternative to the conventional narrative of an apocalyptic future.

MACHINE HALLUCINATION offers a unique context for us to explore an alternative reality. As both an entertaining and enthralling experience, the machine's hallucination can expand our capacity to dream and help us envision things that we otherwise could not see or imagine.

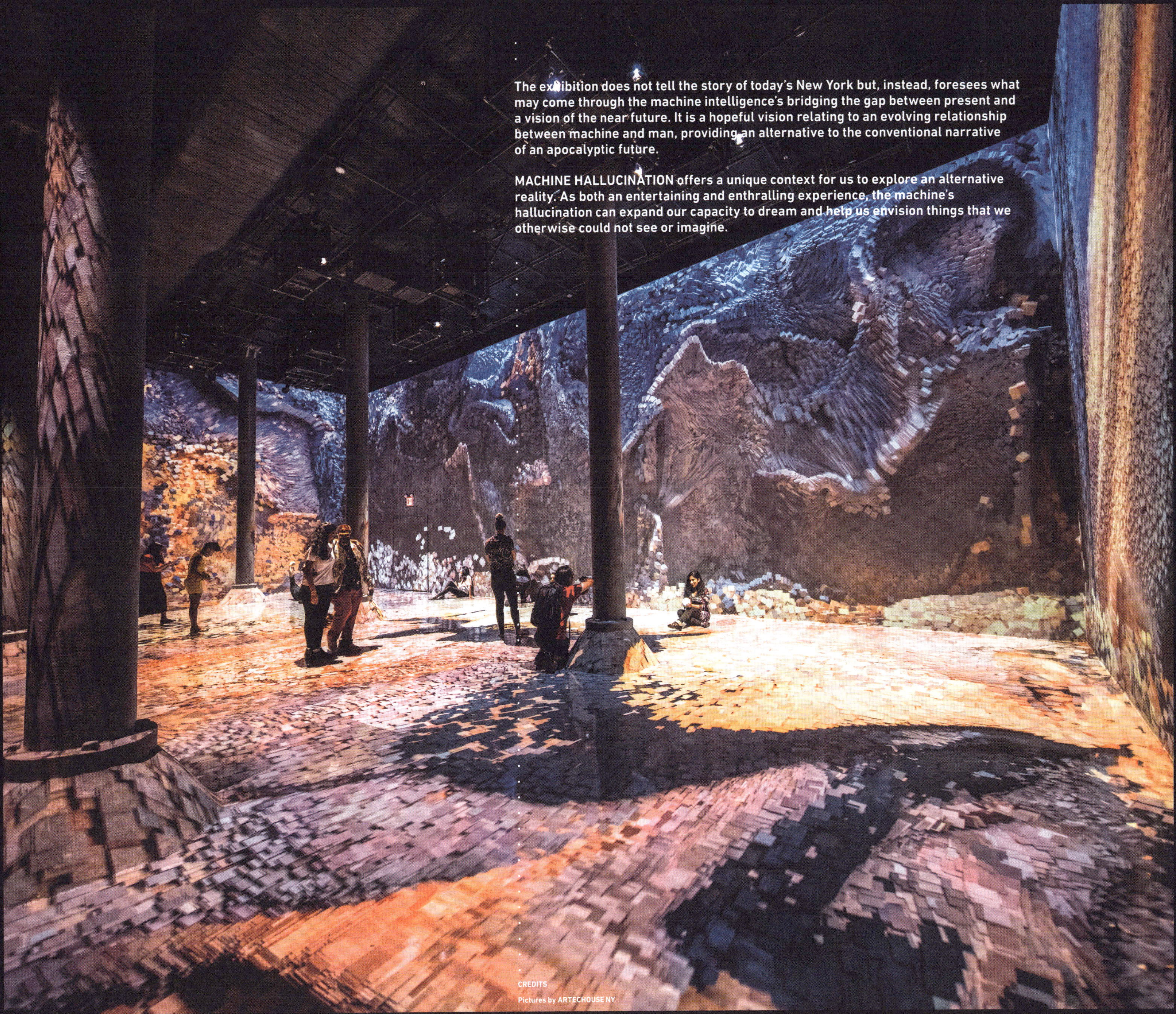

CREDITS

Pictures by ARTECHOUSE NY

029 . MACHINE HALLUCINATION . ARTECHOUSE . New York . September 6th–November 17th 2019

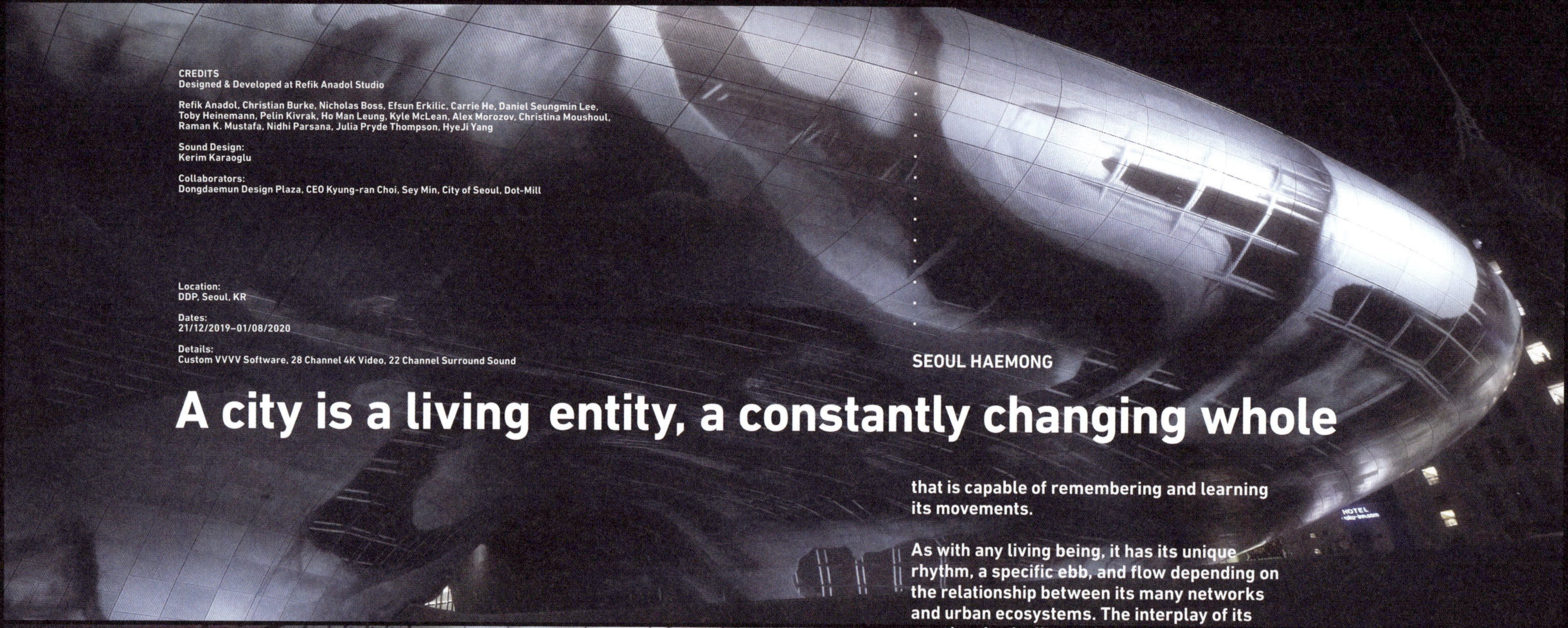

CREDITS
Designed & Developed at Refik Anadol Studio

Refik Anadol, Christian Burke, Nicholas Boss, Efsun Erkilic, Carrie He, Daniel Seungmin Lee, Toby Heinemann, Pelin Kivrak, Ho Man Leung, Kyle McLean, Alex Morozov, Christina Moushoul, Raman K. Mustafa, Nidhi Parsana, Julia Pryde Thompson, HyeJi Yang

Sound Design:
Kerim Karaoglu

Collaborators:
Dongdaemun Design Plaza, CEO Kyung-ran Choi, Sey Min, City of Seoul, Dot-Mill

Location:
DDP, Seoul, KR

Dates:
21/12/2019–01/08/2020

Details:
Custom VVVV Software, 28 Channel 4K Video, 22 Channel Surround Sound

SEOUL HAEMONG

A city is a living entity, a constantly changing whole

that is capable of remembering and learning its movements.

As with any living being, it has its unique rhythm, a specific ebb, and flow depending on the relationship between its many networks and urban ecosystems. The interplay of its people, physicality, and environment makes up its essence, an imperceivable dance that has remained largely invisible.

For SEOUL HAEMONG, Refik Anadol Studio collaborated with the DDP and City of Seoul to create a public art installation that showcased this otherwise uncontainable soul.

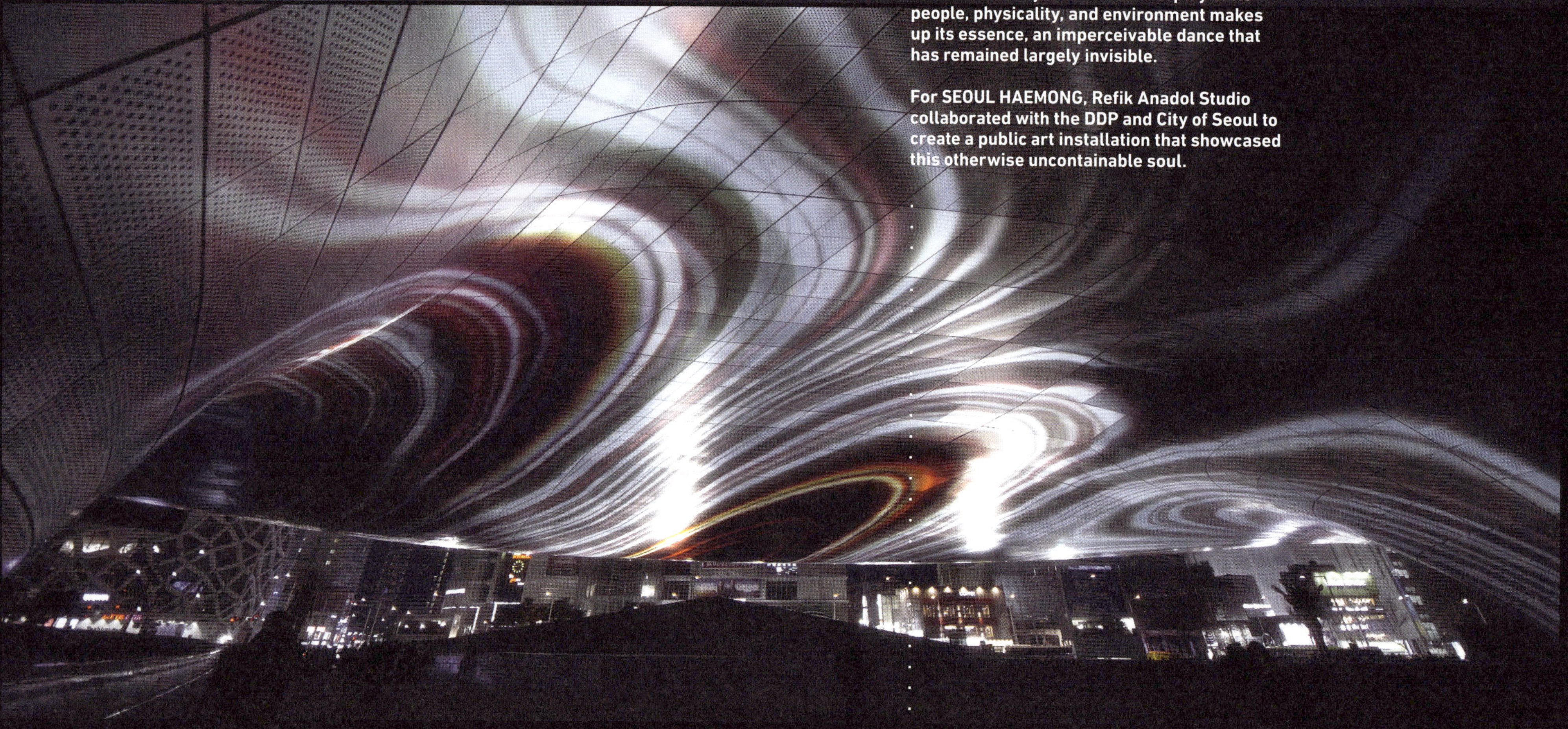

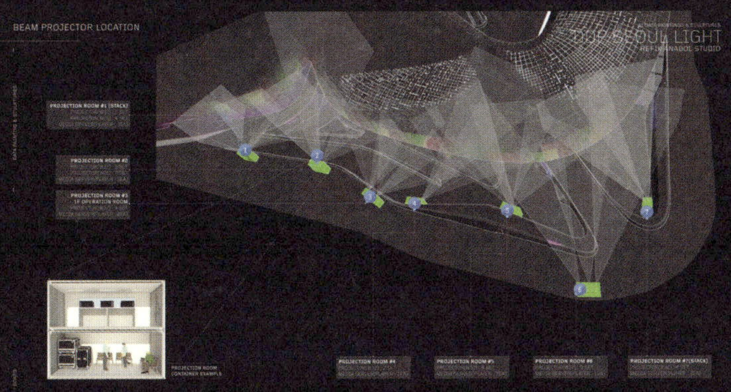

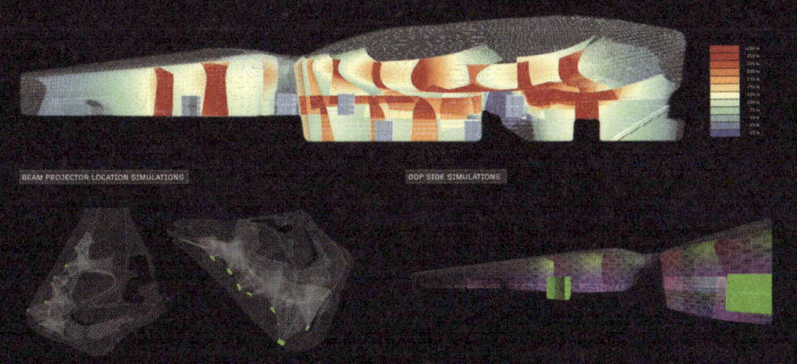

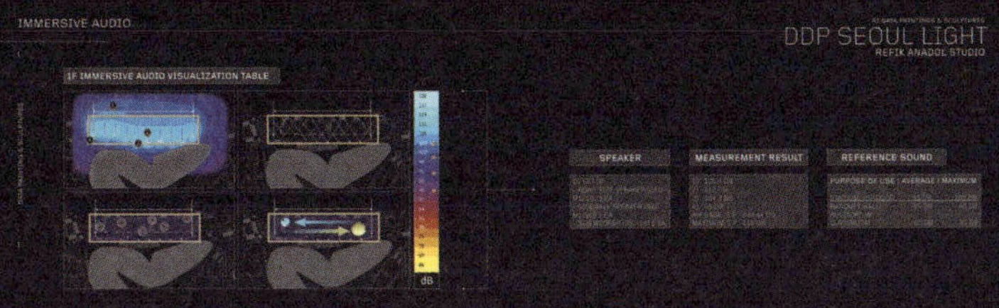

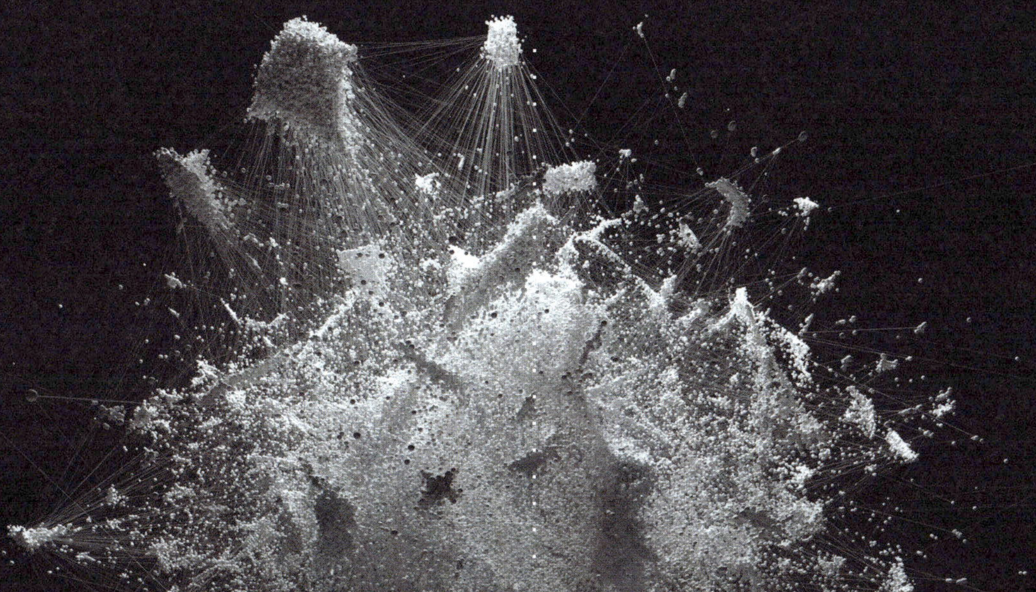

Using the Zaha Hadid Architects' DDP Building as a canvas, the performance collaborated with the mind of a machine to unearth the materiality of this structure and explore the architecture of memory itself. Upon unveiling DDP's architectural form, the building set the stage for exploring a new kind of topographic memory, revealing upon its face the city's collective histories.

Choreographing this piece began by collecting public data from the city in 11 million citizens' stories. These visual stories came in archival and personal photographs and documents, individual and communal narratives that would offer a window into the past and project hopes for the future.

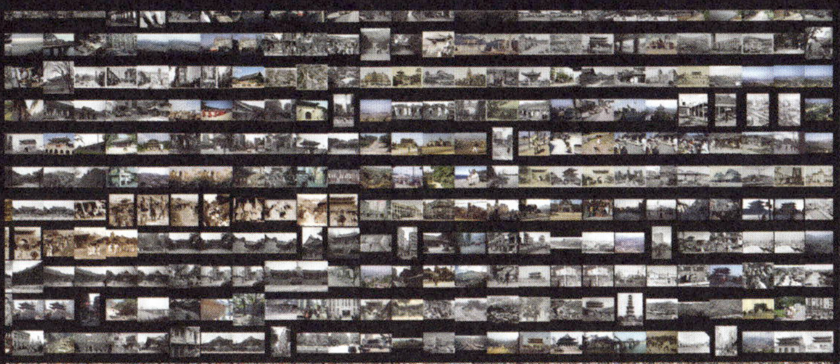

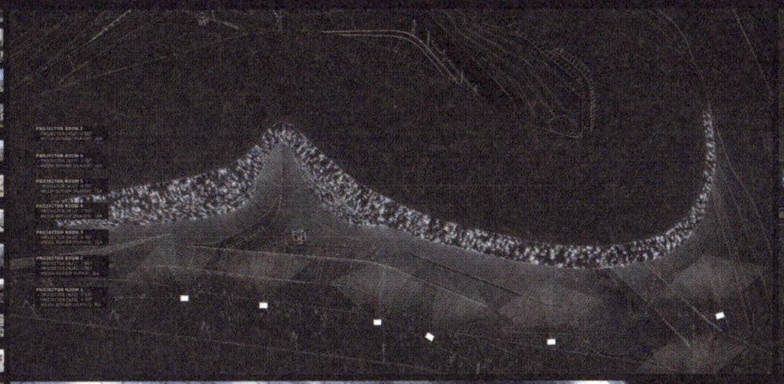

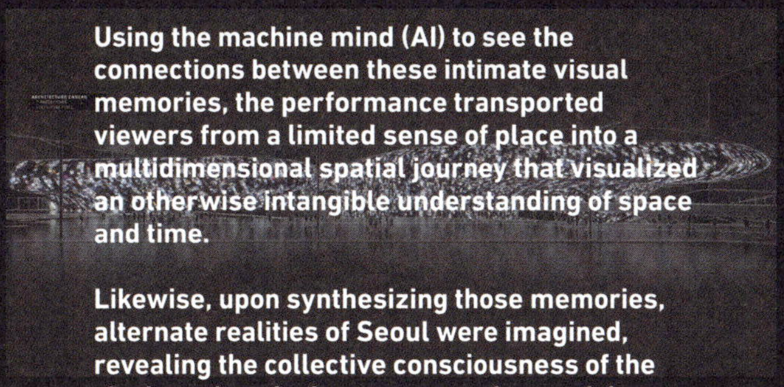

Using the machine mind (AI) to see the connections between these intimate visual memories, the performance transported viewers from a limited sense of place into a multidimensional spatial journey that visualized an otherwise intangible understanding of space and time.

Likewise, upon synthesizing those memories, alternate realities of Seoul were imagined, revealing the collective consciousness of the city based on the interconnectedness of those individual examples.

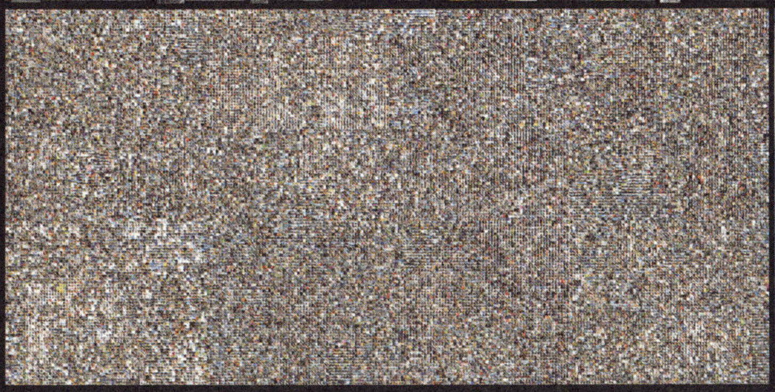

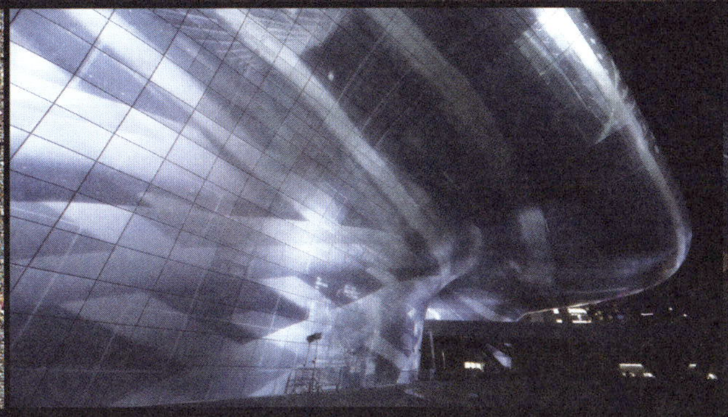

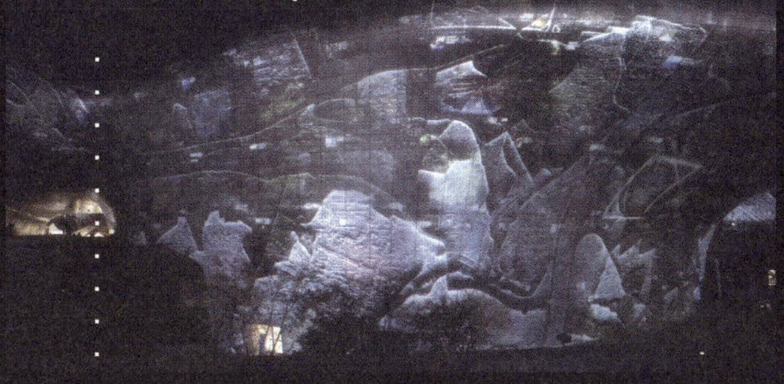

WALT DISNEY CONCERT HALL DREAMS

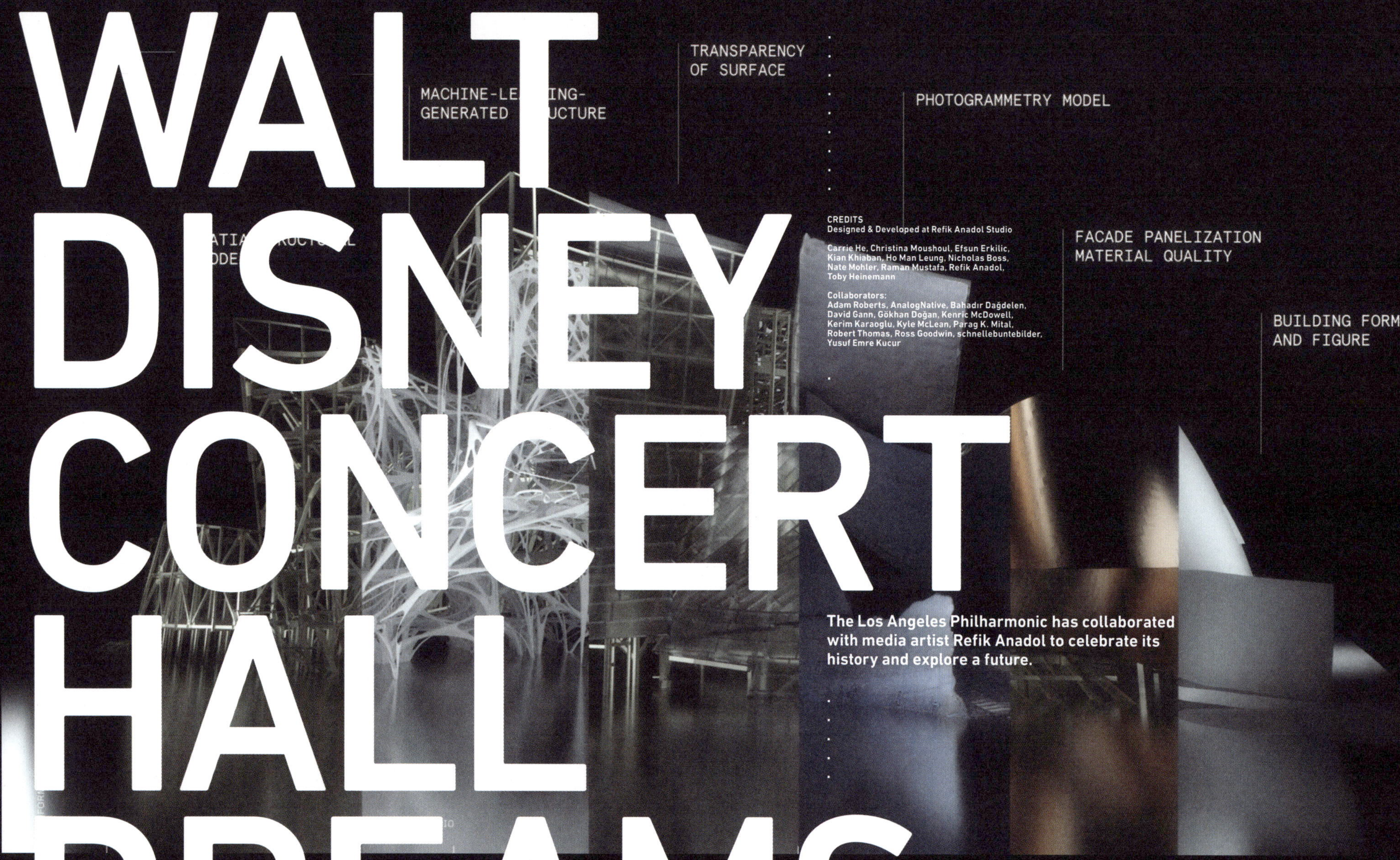

CREDITS
Designed & Developed at Refik Anadol Studio

Carrie He, Christina Moushoul, Efsun Erkilic, Kian Khiaban, Ho Man Leung, Nicholas Boss, Nate Mohler, Raman Mustafa, Refik Anadol, Toby Heinemann

Collaborators:
Adam Roberts, AnalogNative, Bahadır Dağdelen, David Gann, Gökhan Doğan, Kenric McDowell, Kerim Karaoglu, Kyle McLean, Parag K. Mital, Robert Thomas, Ross Goodwin, schnellebuntebilder, Yusuf Emre Kucur

The Los Angeles Philharmonic has collaborated with media artist Refik Anadol to celebrate its history and explore a future.

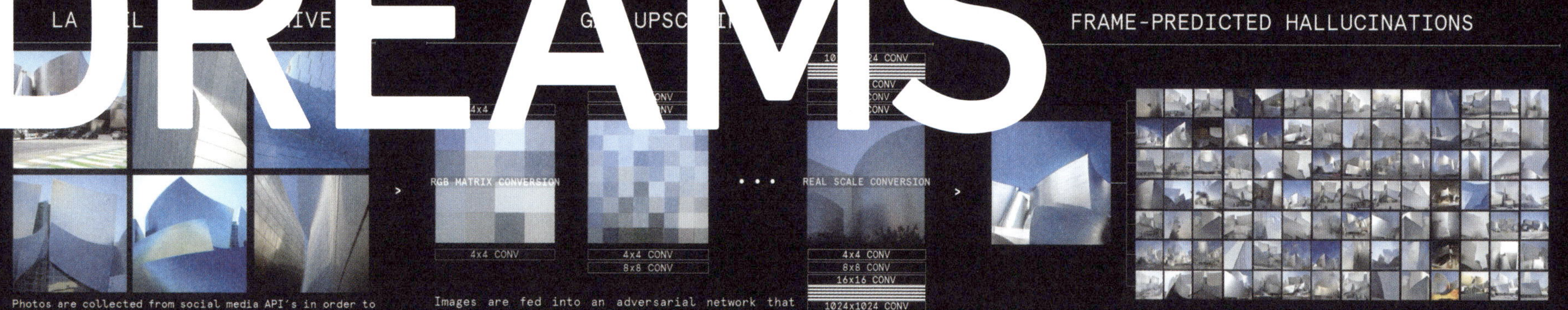

Photos are collected from social media API's in order to generate an image dataset. Data is used as the visual representation of LA Phil in an architectural context

Images are fed into an adversarial network that progressively adds convolutional layers. This improves performance at higher spatial resolutions

Machine hallucinations represent vision and the perspective of the institution in the context of the public's architectural memories

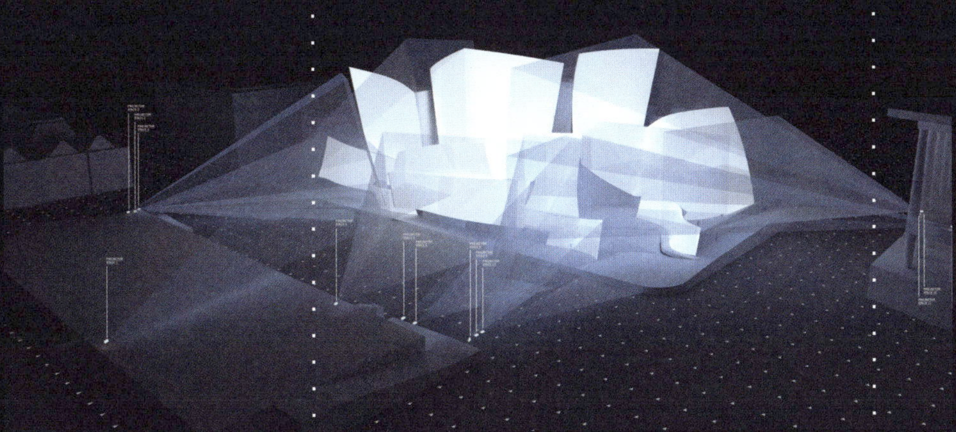

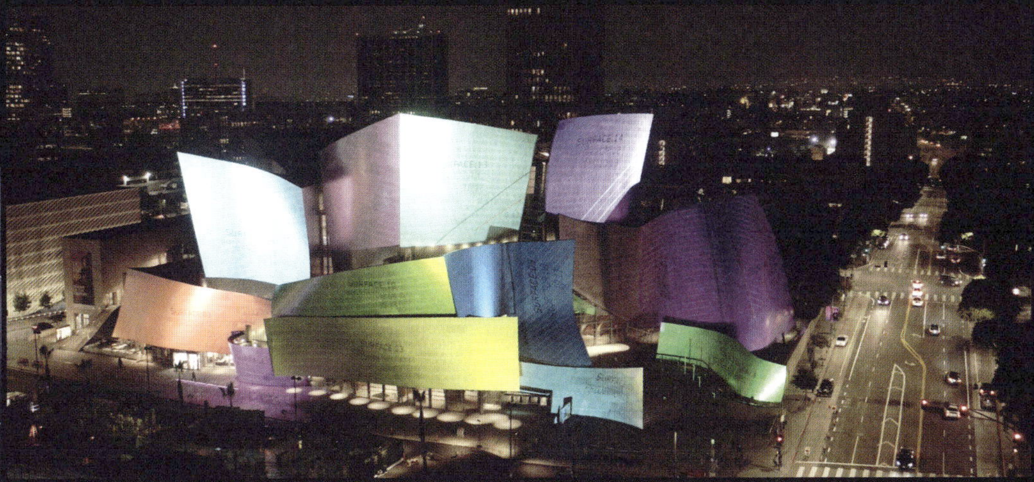

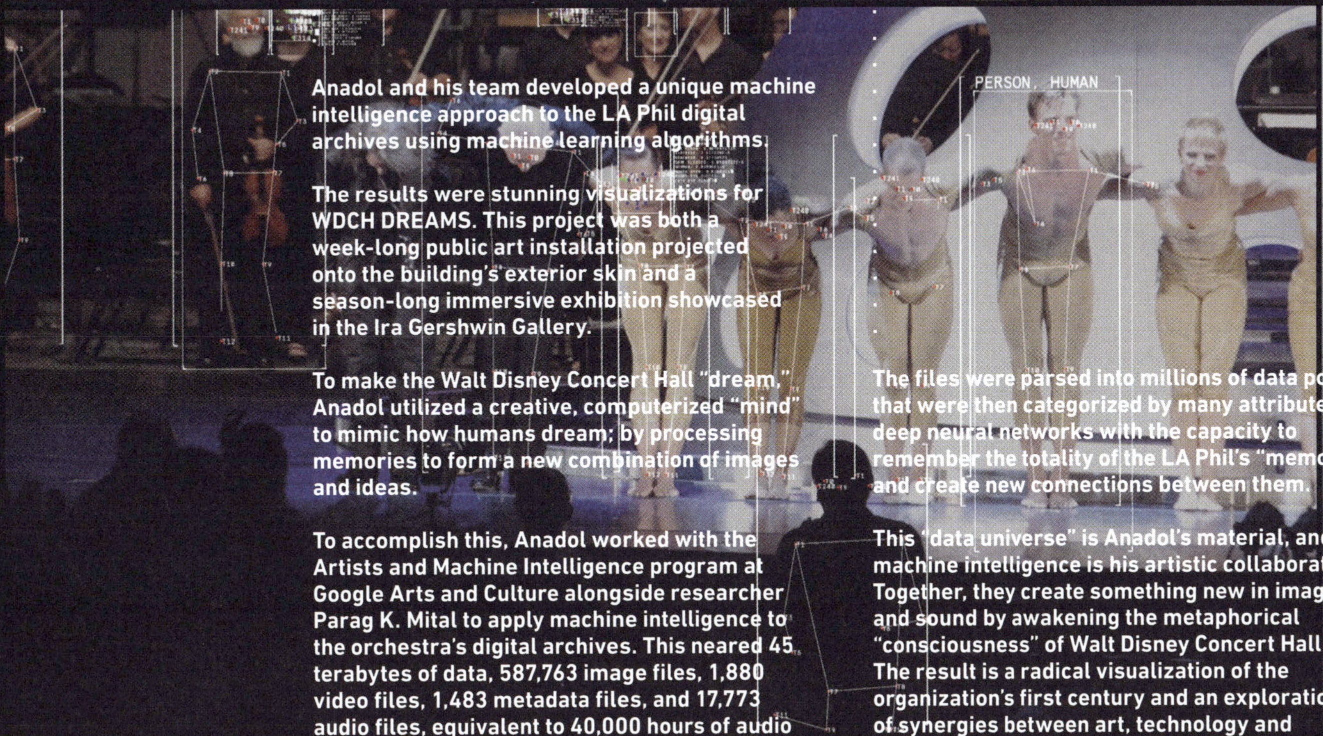

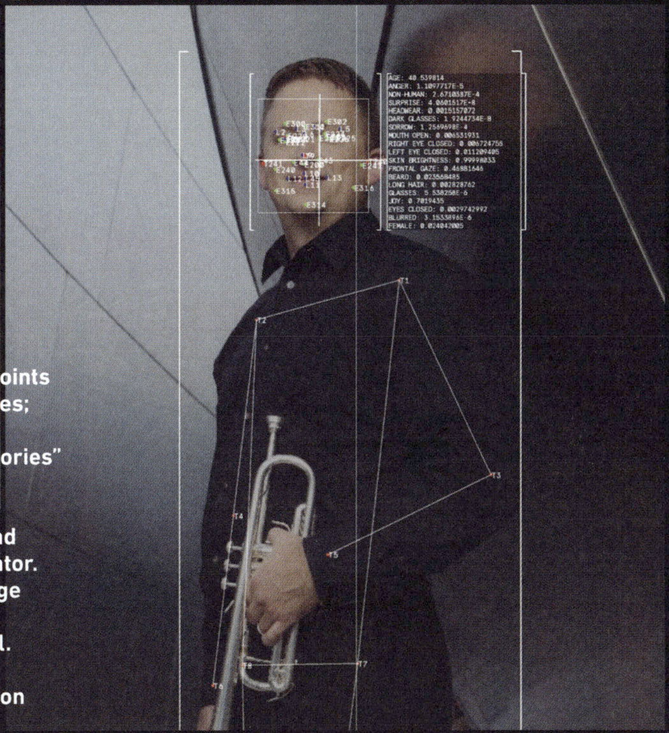

Anadol and his team developed a unique machine intelligence approach to the LA Phil digital archives using machine learning algorithms.

The results were stunning visualizations for WDCH DREAMS. This project was both a week-long public art installation projected onto the building's exterior skin and a season-long immersive exhibition showcased in the Ira Gershwin Gallery.

To make the Walt Disney Concert Hall "dream," Anadol utilized a creative, computerized "mind" to mimic how humans dream; by processing memories to form a new combination of images and ideas.

To accomplish this, Anadol worked with the Artists and Machine Intelligence program at Google Arts and Culture alongside researcher Parag K. Mital to apply machine intelligence to the orchestra's digital archives. This neared 45 terabytes of data, 587,763 image files, 1,880 video files, 1,483 metadata files, and 17,773 audio files, equivalent to 40,000 hours of audio from 16,471 performances.

The files were parsed into millions of data points that were then categorized by many attributes; deep neural networks with the capacity to remember the totality of the LA Phil's "memories" and create new connections between them.

This "data universe" is Anadol's material, and machine intelligence is his artistic collaborator. Together, they create something new in image and sound by awakening the metaphorical "consciousness" of Walt Disney Concert Hall. The result is a radical visualization of the organization's first century and an exploration of synergies between art, technology and architecture, and institutional memory.

AUDIO LIBRARY

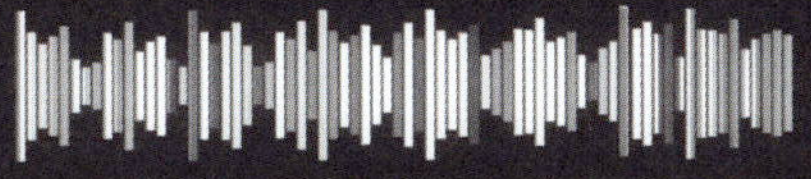

(BENVENUTO CELLINI: OVERTURE, OP 23)

Over 40,000 hours of music is compiled into a dataset. The recordings, ranging from 1928-2018, represent all of LA Phil's musical memories

MIR CLASSIFICATION

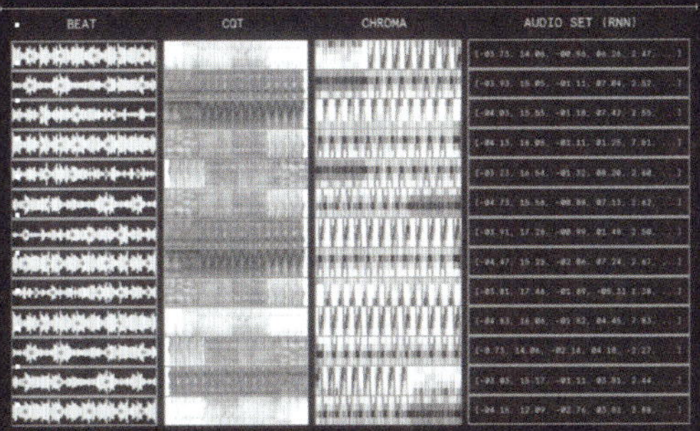

Audio analyzed by machine intelligence to be organized into a 256-dimensional feature space

UMAP CLUSTERING

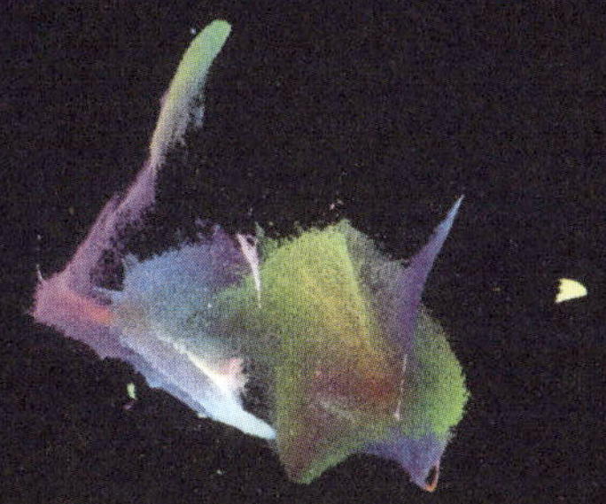

Features used with UMAP algorithm to project LA Phil's musical histo into an 6-dimensional audio universe, mapped by (x, y, z, r, g, b)

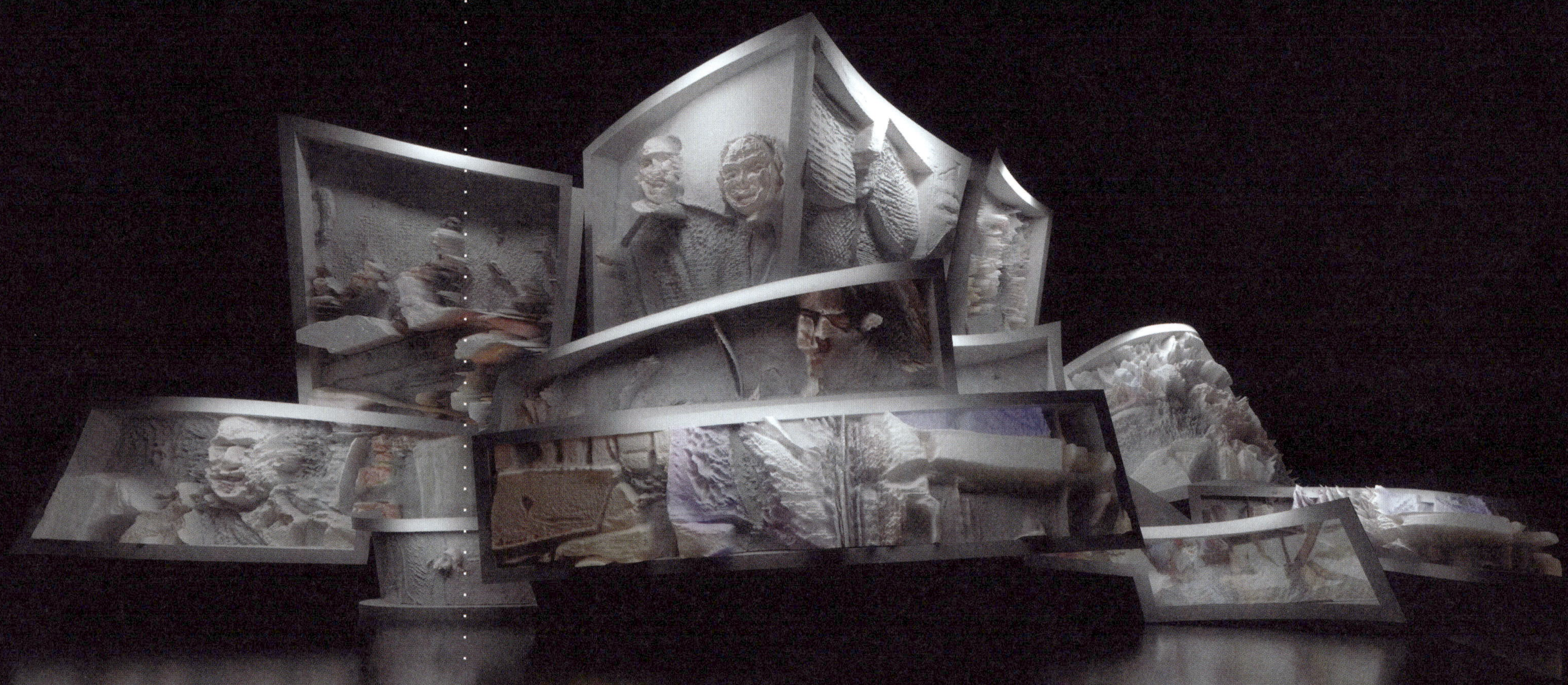

Anadol employed 42 large-scale projectors to actualize this vision, with 50K visual resolution, 8-channel sound, 1.2M luminance in total. The resulting patterns or "data sculptures" formed by the machine's interpretation of the archives were displayed directly onto the undulating stainless-steel exterior of Walt Disney Concert Hall.

WDCH DREAMS' accompanying soundtrack was created; hand-picked audio from the LA Phil's archival recordings. Sound designers Robert Thomas and Kerim Karaoglu augmented these selections using machine-learning algorithms to find similar performances recorded throughout the LA Phil's history, creating a unique exploration of historic audio recordings.

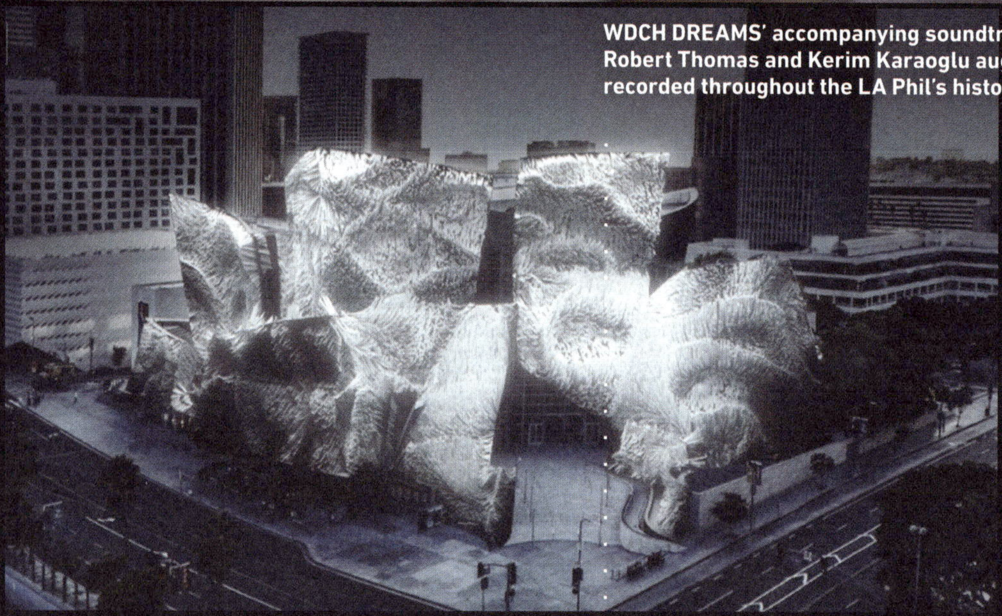

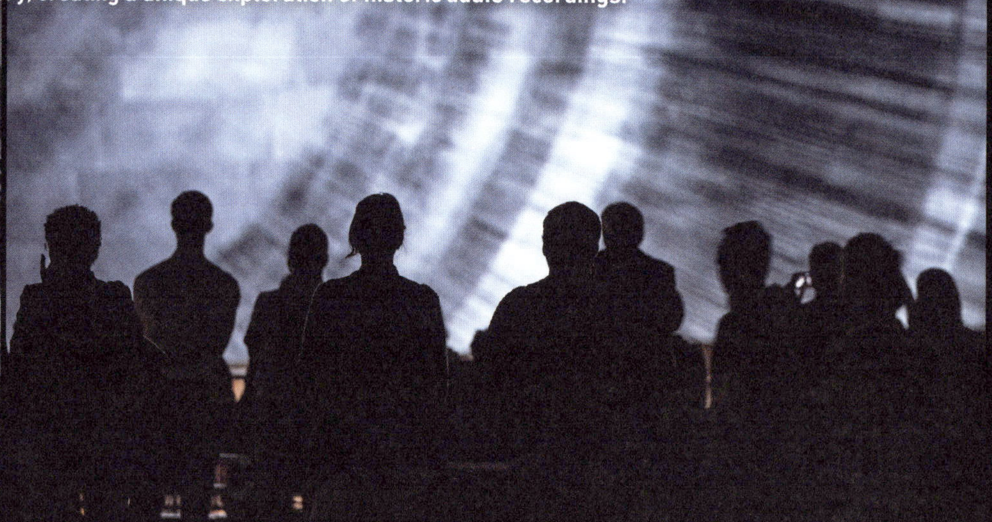

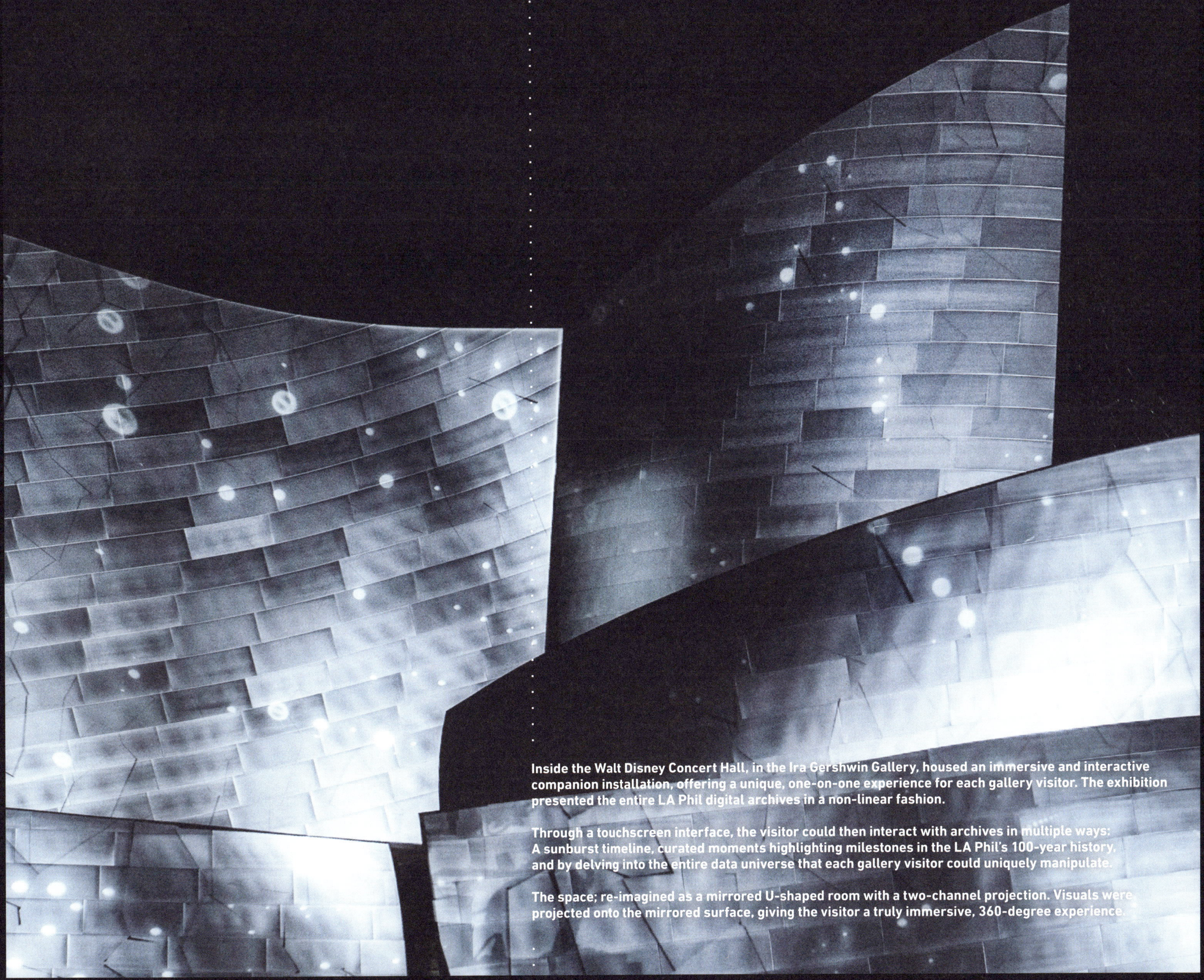

Inside the Walt Disney Concert Hall, in the Ira Gershwin Gallery, housed an immersive and interactive companion installation, offering a unique, one-on-one experience for each gallery visitor. The exhibition presented the entire LA Phil digital archives in a non-linear fashion.

Through a touchscreen interface, the visitor could then interact with archives in multiple ways: A sunburst timeline, curated moments highlighting milestones in the LA Phil's 100-year history, and by delving into the entire data universe that each gallery visitor could uniquely manipulate.

The space; re-imagined as a mirrored U-shaped room with a two-channel projection. Visuals were projected onto the mirrored surface, giving the visitor a truly immersive, 360-degree experience.

Name:

Ralf Baecker

Info:

Ralf Baecker is an artist working at the interface of art, science, and technology. Through installations and machines, Baecker explores the fundamental mechanisms of new media and technology. In his representations and spatializations of digital and technological processes, he offers a poetic sight behind the surfaces of contemporary image-making.

At the core, objects lie entangled within the virtual with the real, or rather, with the world.

Ralf Baecker digs within obsolete devices for traces of functions and (power) structures still detectable in technologies today with a media-archaeological outlook. His work seeks to form a hybrid between contemporary digital methodologies and a material-oriented artistic practice. As a result, he understands technology as a tool and an epistemological instrument to pose fundamental questions about a world perceived through technological impressions.

Baecker has been awarded multiple prizes and grants for his artistic work, including the grand prize of the Japan Media Art Festival in 2017, an honorary mention at the Prix Ars Electronica in 2012 and 2014, the second prize at the VIDA 14.0 Art & Artificial Life Award in Madrid.

Since 2016 Baecker teaches at the University of the Arts Bremen as Professor for Experimental Design of New Technologies in the Digital Media program.

Project:

PUTTING THE PIECES BACK TOGETHER AGAIN

URL:

rlfbckr.io/

Instagram:

@ralfbaecker

Q&As

Please explain the main idea and what gave the impulse?

"One of the most highly developed skills in contemporary Western civilization is dissection; the split-up of problems into their smallest possible components.

We are good at it. So good, we often forget to put the pieces back together again."

(Alvin Toffler in the Foreword of Order out Chaos by Ilya Prigogine and Isabelle Stengers)

Through my previous projects, I became interested in complex and emergent systems. What is order, and how does it emerge.

Is noise the enemy, or can it act as a catalyst?

A system that creates its behavior through its many individual parts and not by a centralized algorithm. I research ideas of complex theory and ways of building a simple mechanism as a simple agent in such a system.

What challenges did you face for this project? And what surprises?

Creating a system driven by 1,250 noise-generating motors creates many problems from an engaging perspective. PUTTING THE PIECES BACK TOGETHER AGAIN is a self-destructing machine. Electronics and mechanical parts very often broke in the test/prototyping phase.

The machine can now run for longer without destroying itself through many iterative steps (designing the driver software's mechanical parts and changing parameters).

Please describe the technical environment.

The system's core is a domesticated failure or hack that allows the individual actors' muscles to reflex. No sensing or algorithm is required, just a poorly connected cheap stepper motor and a sine wave generator.

Tell us about your aesthetical approach.

My installations are physical realizations of thought experiments and act as subjective epistemological instruments posing fundamental questions about the digital, technological images, and complex systems, speculating alternative computational realities.

Aesthetically the machines try to make the underlying structures tangible and visible principles of complex systems.

What's next? Your vision?

I'm currently working with new materials and technological settings. One project works with fluidic, soft, and electrochemical systems to explore strange and complex material processes to generate weird microcosms.

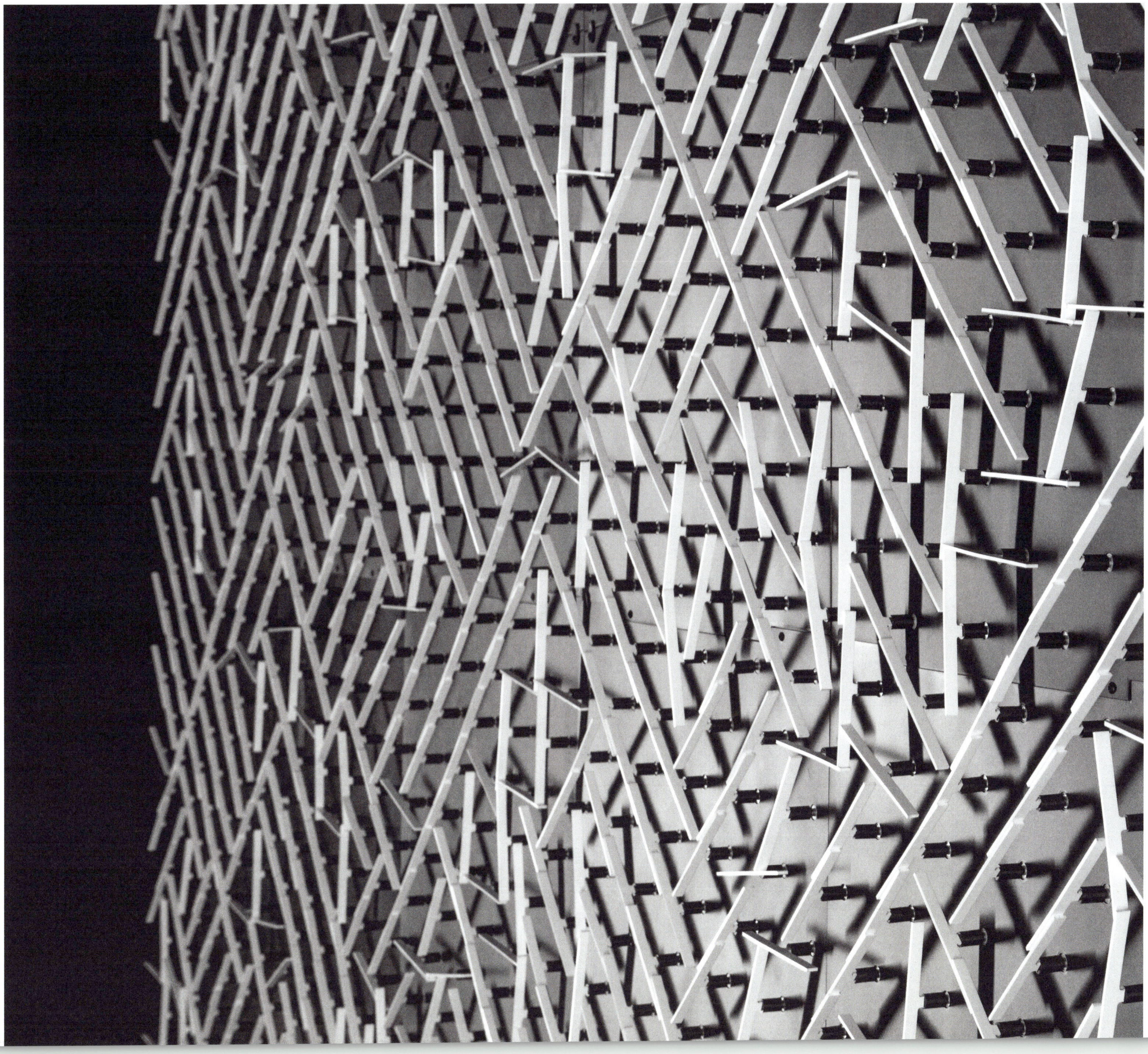

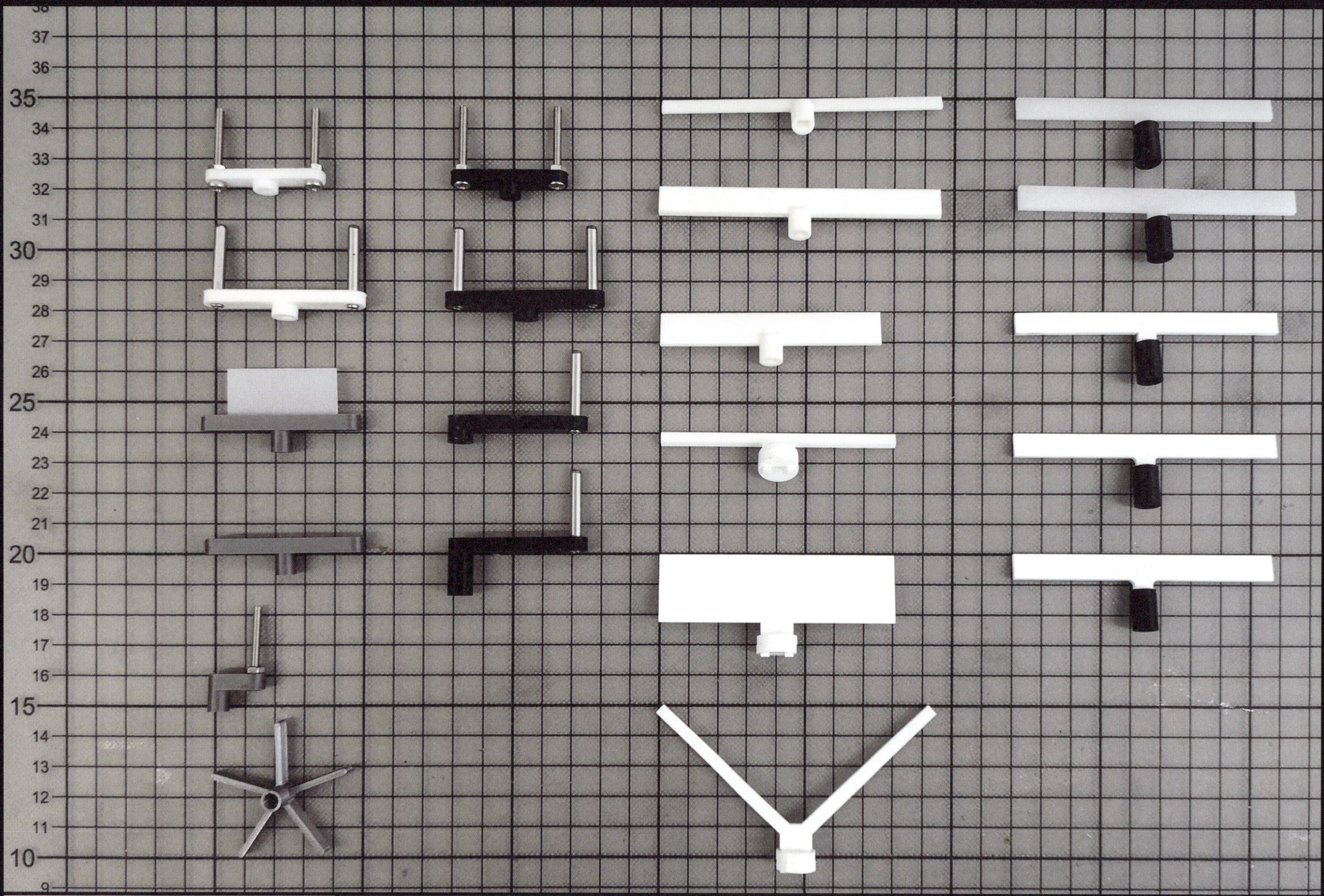
37
36
35
34
33
32
31
30
29
28
27
26
25
24
23
22
21
20
19
18
17
16
15
14
13
12
11
10

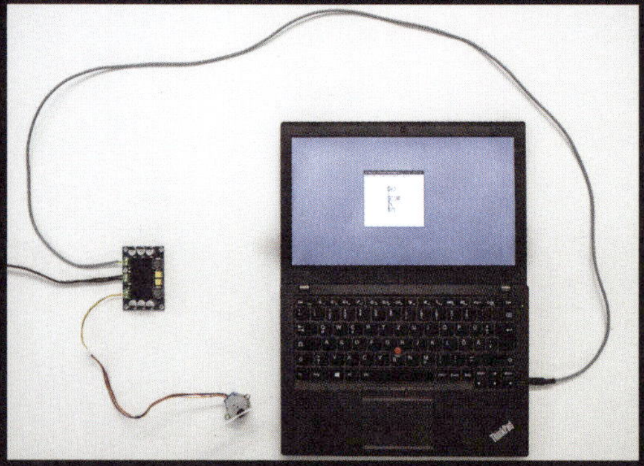

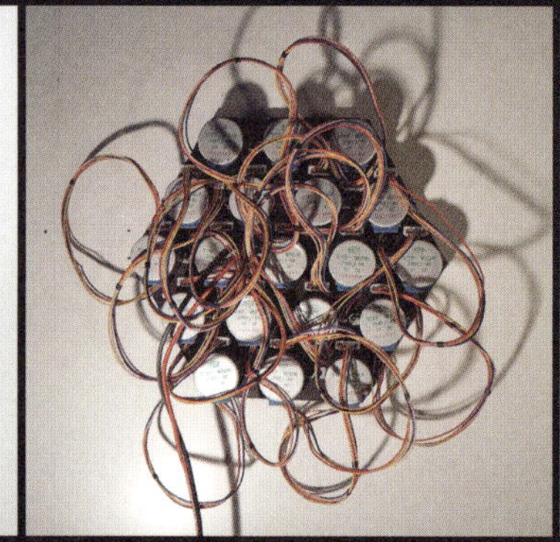

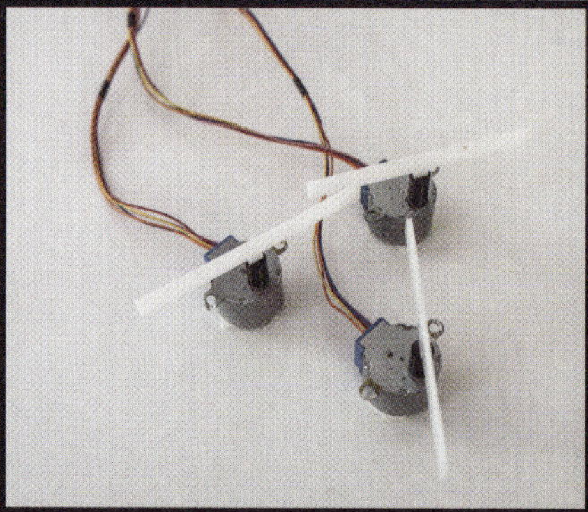

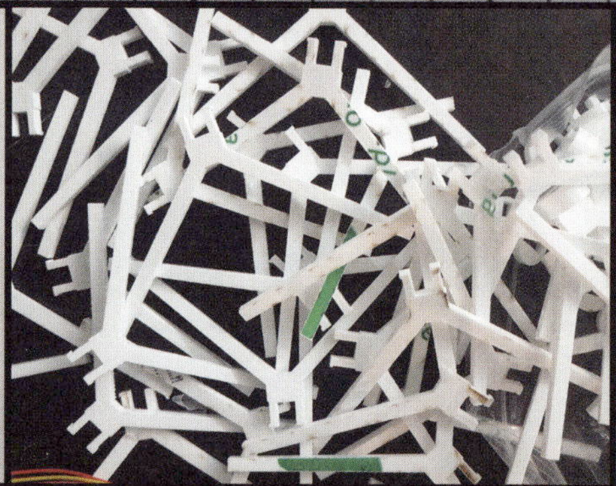

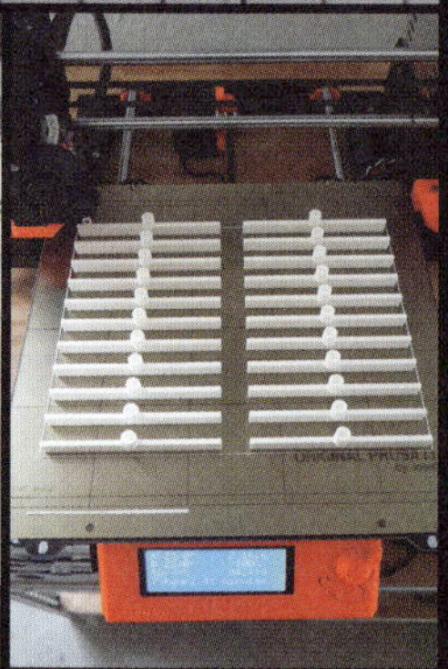

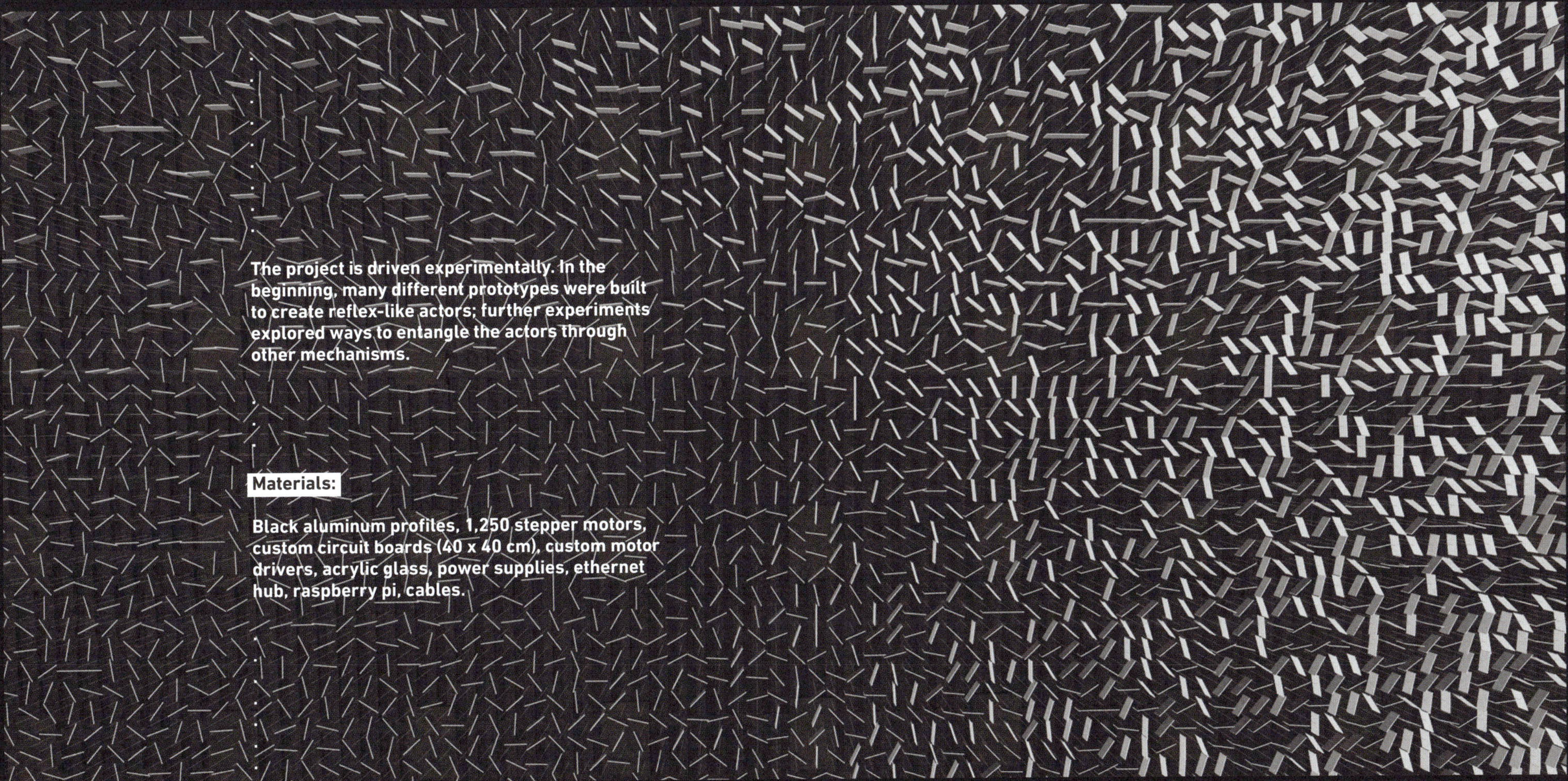

The project is driven experimentally. In the beginning, many different prototypes were built to create reflex-like actors; further experiments explored ways to entangle the actors through other mechanisms.

Materials:

Black aluminum profiles, 1,250 stepper motors, custom circuit boards (40 x 40 cm), custom motor drivers, acrylic glass, power supplies, ethernet hub, raspberry pi, cables.

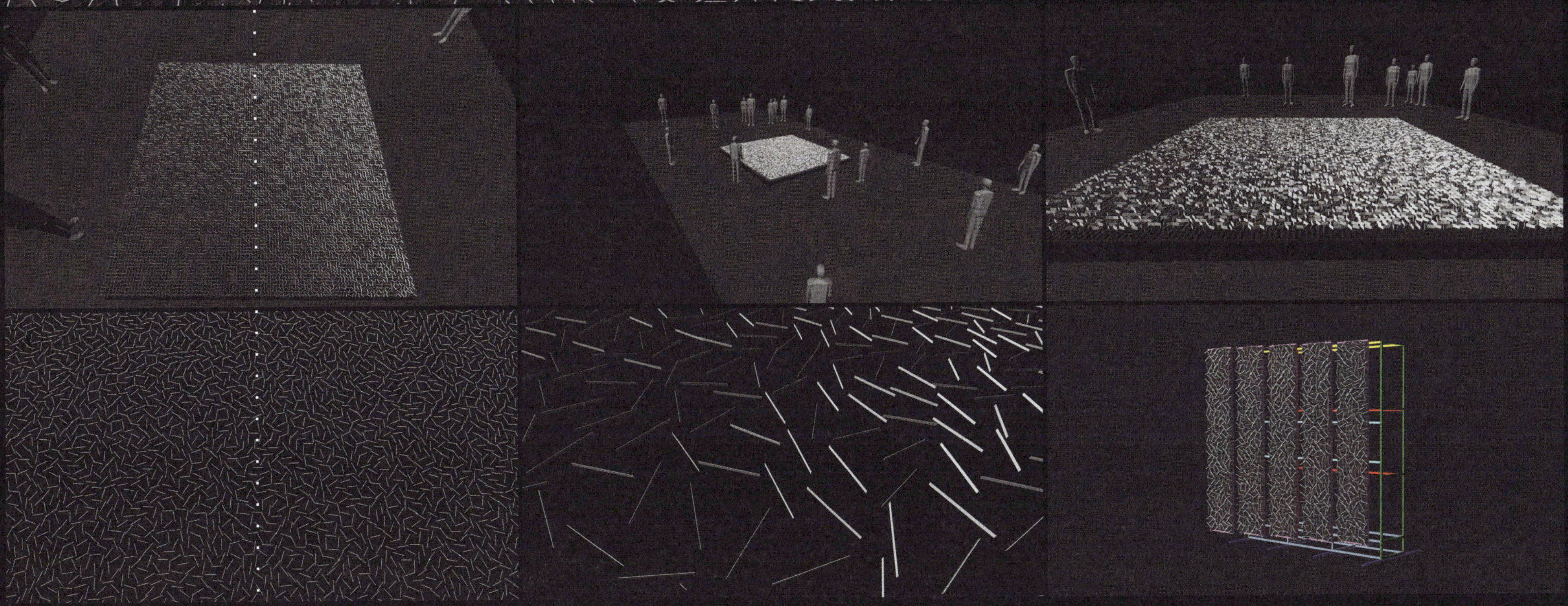

039 . PUTTING THE PIECES BACK TOGETHER AGAIN

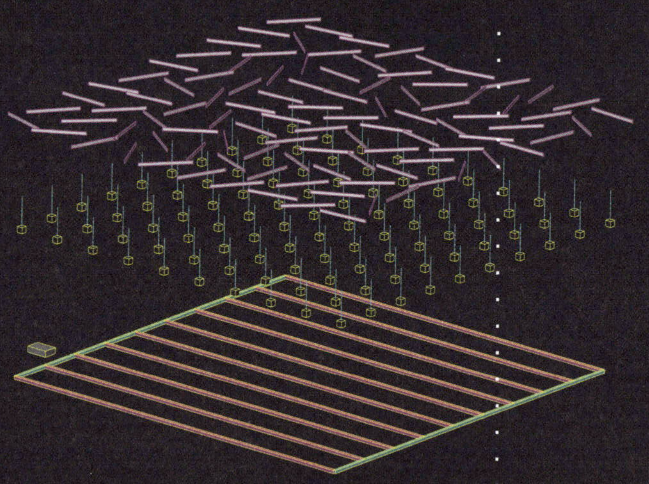

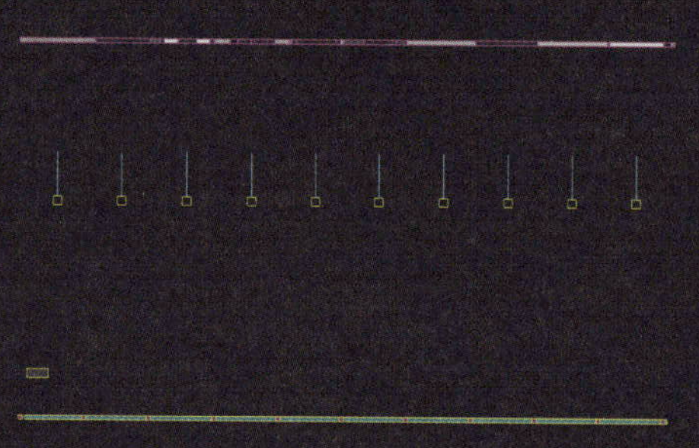

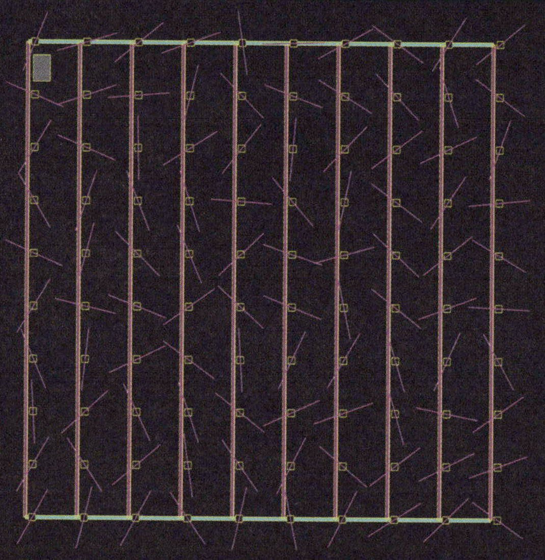

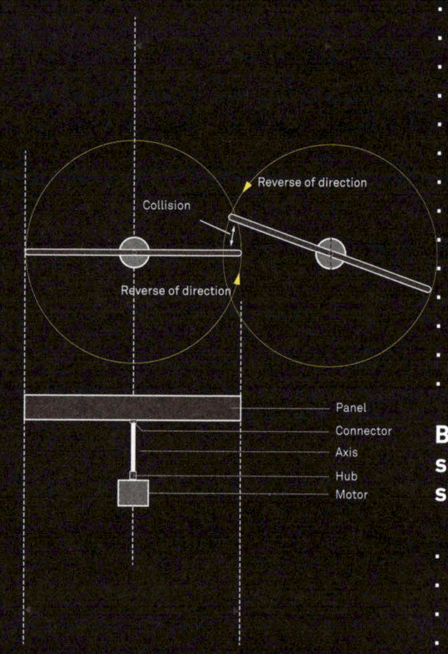

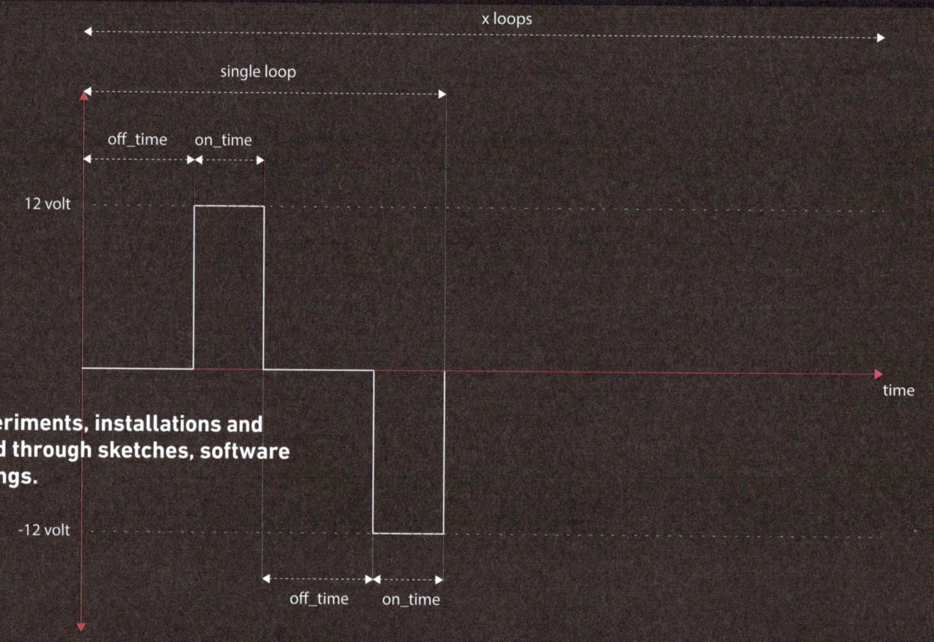

Beyond the physical experiments, installations and setup have been explored through sketches, software simulations, and renderings.

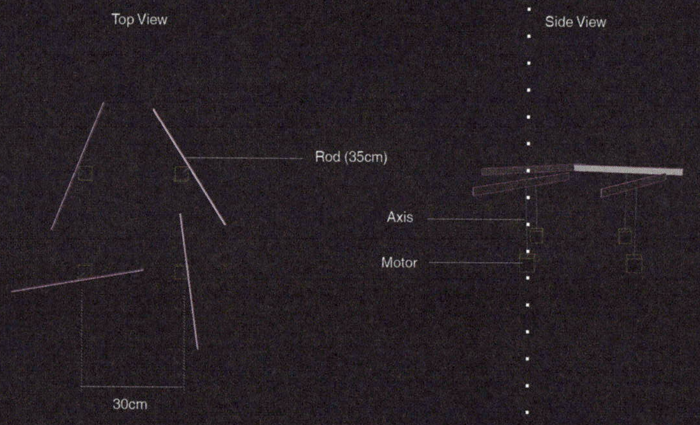

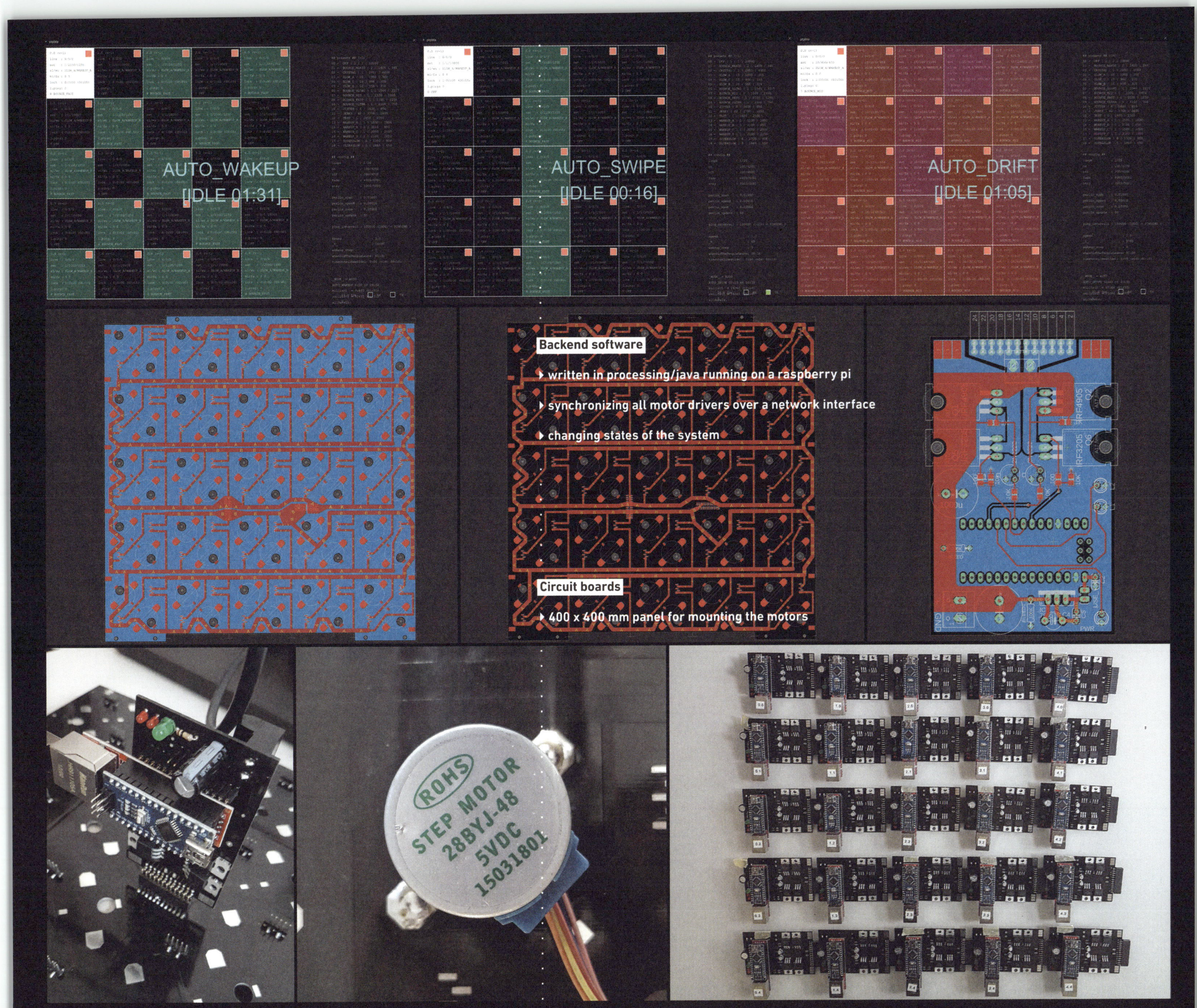

041 . PUTTING THE PIECES BACK TOGETHER AGAIN

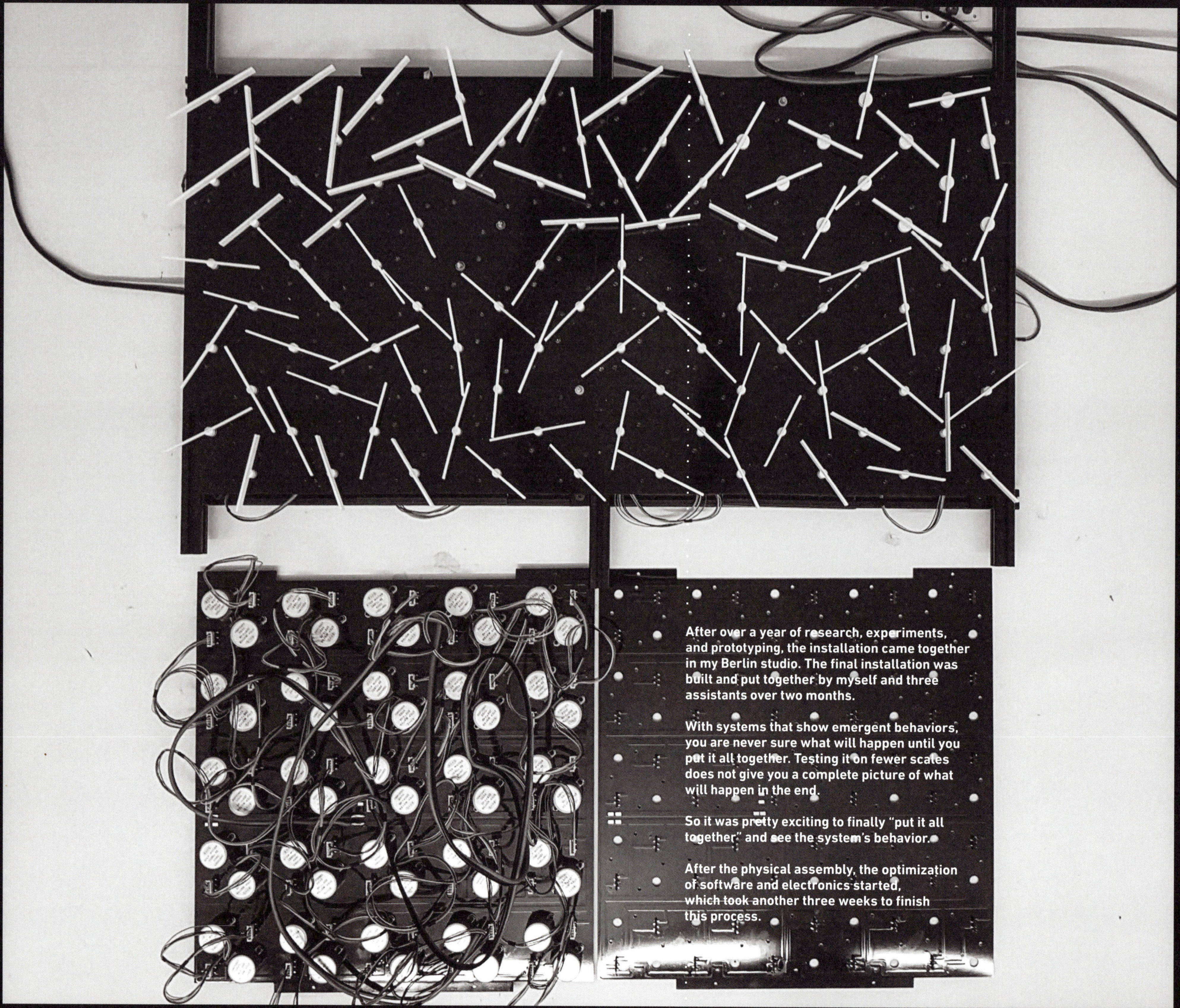

After over a year of research, experiments, and prototyping, the installation came together in my Berlin studio. The final installation was built and put together by myself and three assistants over two months.

With systems that show emergent behaviors, you are never sure what will happen until you put it all together. Testing it on fewer scales does not give you a complete picture of what will happen in the end.

So it was pretty exciting to finally "put it all together" and see the system's behavior.

After the physical assembly, the optimization of software and electronics started, which took another three weeks to finish this process.

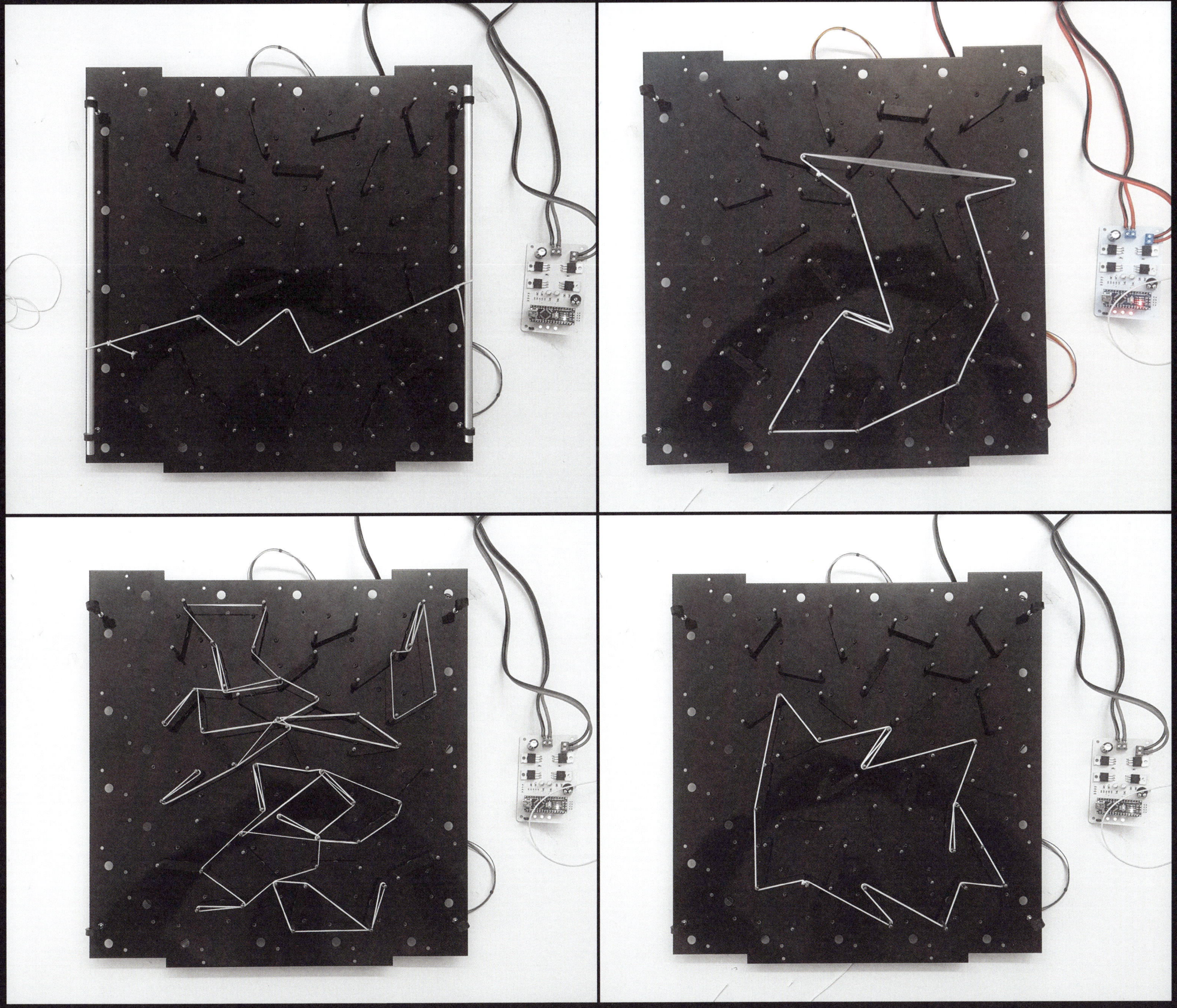

043 . PUTTING THE PIECES BACK TOGETHER AGAIN

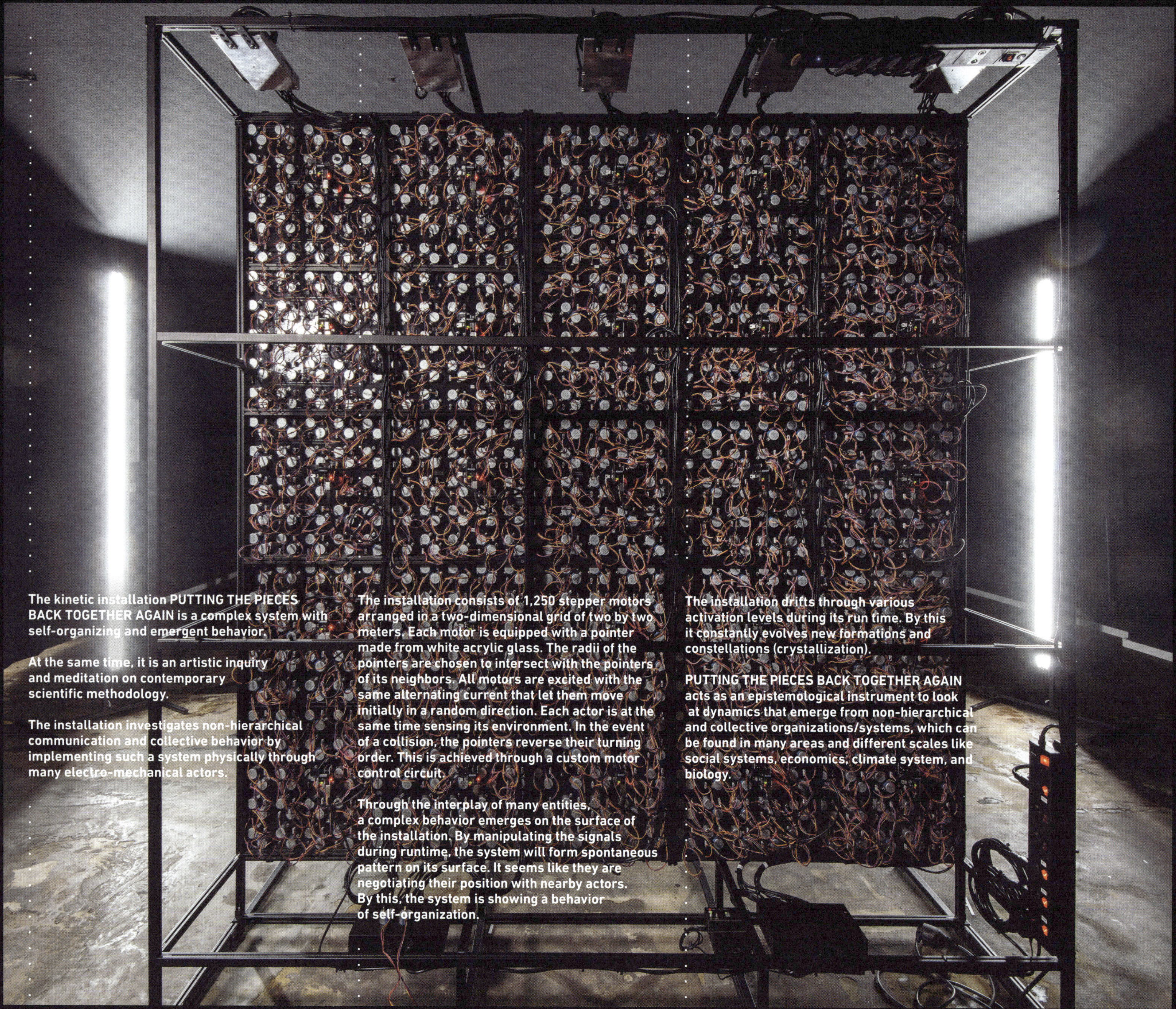

The kinetic installation PUTTING THE PIECES BACK TOGETHER AGAIN is a complex system with self-organizing and emergent behavior.

At the same time, it is an artistic inquiry and meditation on contemporary scientific methodology.

The installation investigates non-hierarchical communication and collective behavior by implementing such a system physically through many electro-mechanical actors.

The installation consists of 1,250 stepper motors arranged in a two-dimensional grid of two by two meters. Each motor is equipped with a pointer made from white acrylic glass. The radii of the pointers are chosen to intersect with the pointers of its neighbors. All motors are excited with the same alternating current that let them move initially in a random direction. Each actor is at the same time sensing its environment. In the event of a collision, the pointers reverse their turning order. This is achieved through a custom motor control circuit.

Through the interplay of many entities, a complex behavior emerges on the surface of the installation. By manipulating the signals during runtime, the system will form spontaneous pattern on its surface. It seems like they are negotiating their position with nearby actors. By this, the system is showing a behavior of self-organization.

The installation drifts through various activation levels during its run time. By this it constantly evolves new formations and constellations (crystallization).

PUTTING THE PIECES BACK TOGETHER AGAIN acts as an epistemological instrument to look at dynamics that emerge from non-hierarchical and collective organizations/systems, which can be found in many areas and different scales like social systems, economics, climate system, and biology.

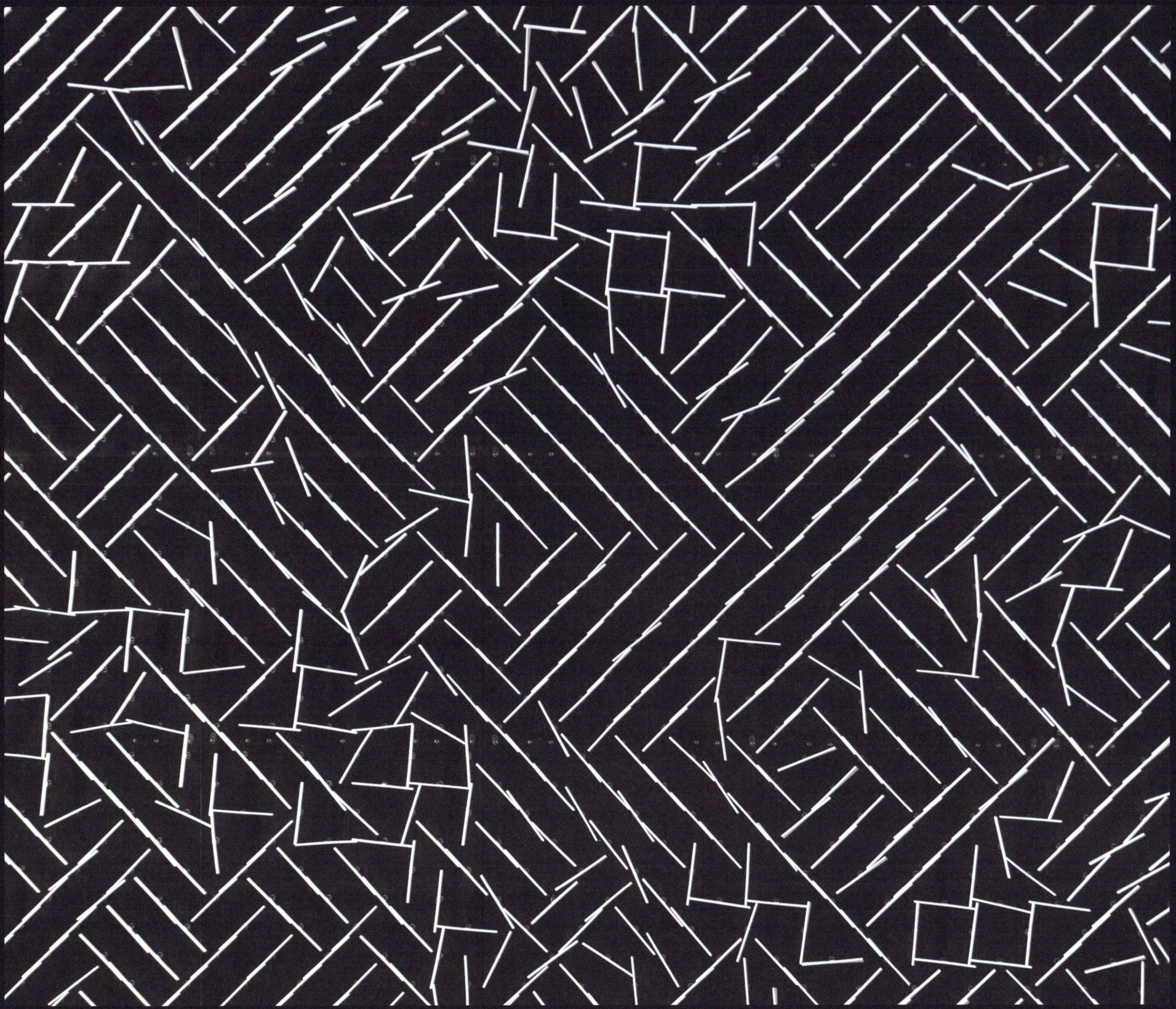

045 . PUTTING THE PIECES BACK TOGETHER AGAIN

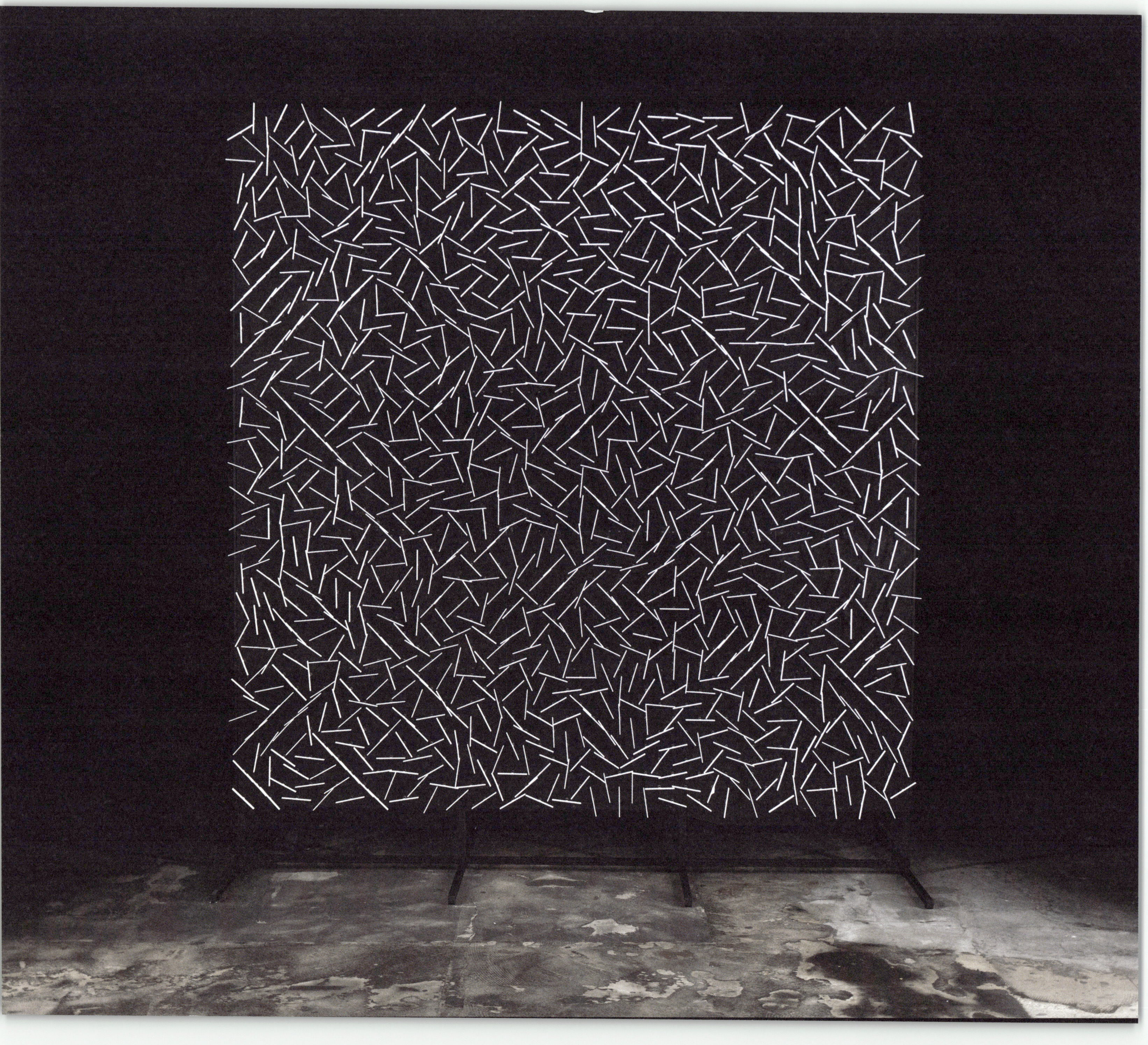

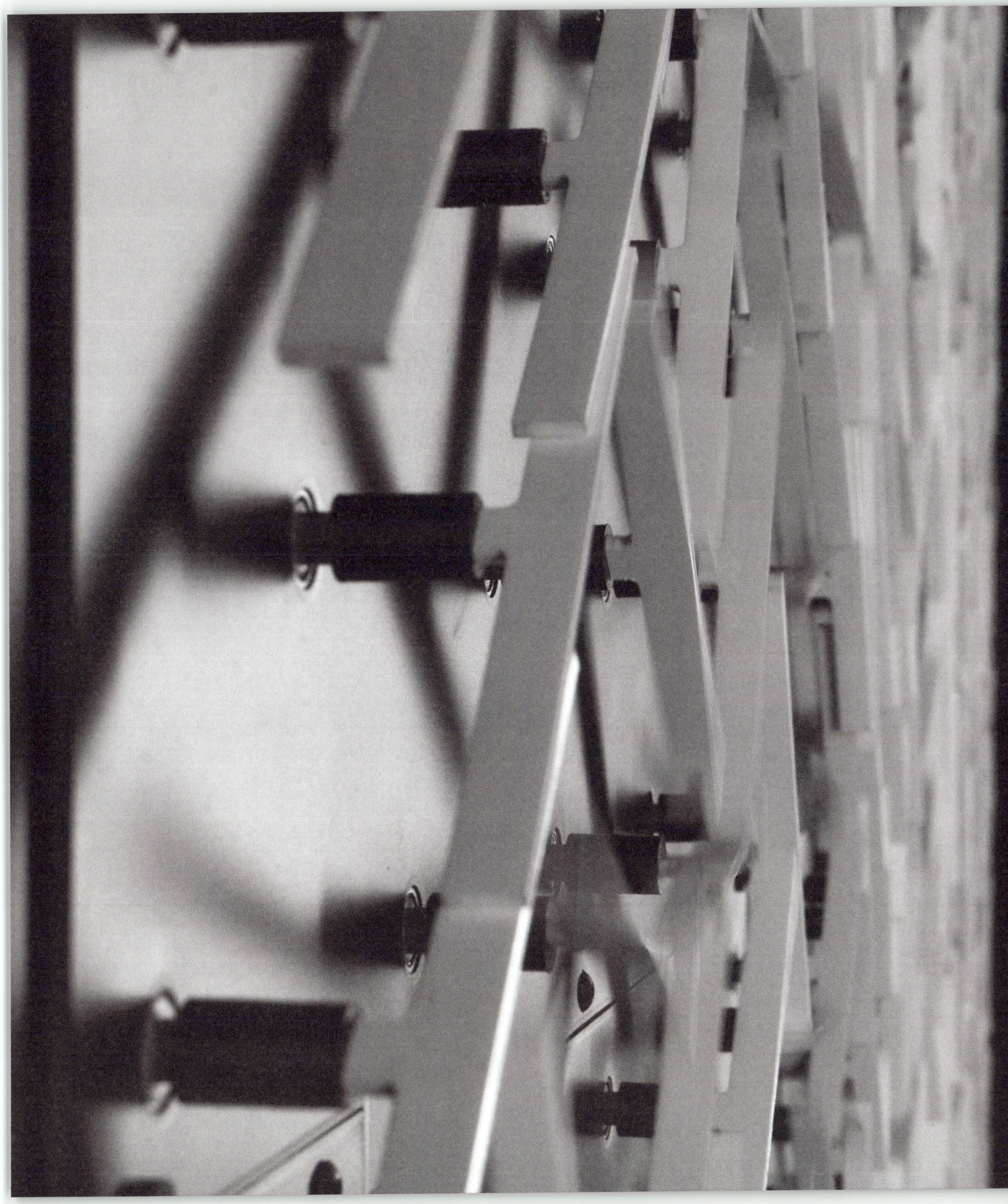

CREDITS

Produced with support of the City of Kirchheim unter Teck,
Verlag des Teckboten and Kulturregion Stuttgart
(Curated by Benjamin Heidersberger).

Production Assistants:
Mariana Schetini Basso, Irena Kukric and Antje Weller

Special Thanks to Katharina Sophia Hardt
(Stadt Kirchheim unter Teck/Kultur Abteilung)

.
.

Exhibitions of PTPBTA:

2020 Near + Futures + Quasi + Worlds
S+T+ARTS at STATE Studio, Berlin DE

2019 Ars Electronica 2019
Ars Electronica, Linz AT

2019 Todays Art 2019
TodaysArt, Den Hague NL

2019 International Art Exhibition for New Technology
Zebrastraat, Ghent BE

2019 Computing Spaces [more]
Stereolux, Nantes FR

2018 PUTTING THE PIECES BACK TOGETHER AGAIN
Drehmoment/KulturRegion Stuttgart,
Kircheim unter Teck/Stuttgart DE

.

Pictures by Frank Kleinbach

Name:

Adam Basanta

Info:

Adam Basanta is an artist, composer, and performer of experimental music.

Born in Tel Aviv (ISR) and raised in Vancouver (CAN), he lives and works in Montreal (CAN) since 2010.

Project:

ALL WE'D EVER NEED IS ONE ANOTHER (TRIO)

URL:

adambasanta.com

Mail:

adam.basanta@gmail.com

Instagram:

@adambasanta

References:

Since 2015, Basanta has exhibited in galleries and institutions, including the Musée des beaux-arts de Montréal (CAN), Optica Centre d'art contemporain (CAN), Fotomuseum Winterthur (CH), Arsenal Art Contemporain (CAN), Galerie Charlot (FRA), National Art Centre Tokyo (JPN), V Moscow Biennale for Young Art (RUS), Carroll/Fletcher Gallery (UK), American Medium Gallery (NYC), Serralves Museum (POR), Edith-Russ-Haus für Mediakunst (GER), York Art Gallery (UK), and The Center for Contemporary Arts Santa Fe (USA).

His work awarded several international prizes, including the Japan Media Arts Prize (2016) and the Aesthetica Art Prize (2017).

Ad am Ba sa nt a

Project Description:

ALL WE'D EVER NEED IS ONE ANOTHER (TRIO) is a continuously running autonomous "art-factory"; an independent ecosystem, a golem mindlessly self-producing without regard for human spectators.

The installation generates images using two flatbed scanners laying on their side, scanning surfaces while pointing at each other. A computer script creates automatic mouse movements, randomizing the proprietary scanning software interface settings, beginning the scanning process.

Each newly created image is analyzed by a series of deep-learning algorithms and trained on a database of millions of contemporary artworks in economic (Artsy) and institutional (The Met Museum, MoMA, Tate, etc.) circulation.

When an image matches an existing artwork beyond an 80% match, it is "validated as art" and uploaded to a dedicated website and social media platforms.

High ranking matches are printed live at the gallery using a large format printer.

I was interested in overlapping questions relating to creativity, authorship, and value: three seemingly inextricable elements in the political economy of art.

What is the nature of creativity? Is it found in the unique embodied actions of the artist or the work's contextual and historical conceptualization?

When the art-making process is performed as a mechanical automaton, does the perception of creativity shift to the eye of the beholder?

Can images accrue value with no mercurial personality behind them by appearing as similar variations of historical artworks or art movements?

Even if these images were to gain economic value, who exactly would be the author of such works: the human designer absent from the room while creating the image or the machinic assembly itself?

If a machine can be a hyper-efficient artist, producing 1,000 artworks per day while working 24/7, is it still subject to the laws of supply and demand?

Although explored through technological media, these questions are not unique to this world.

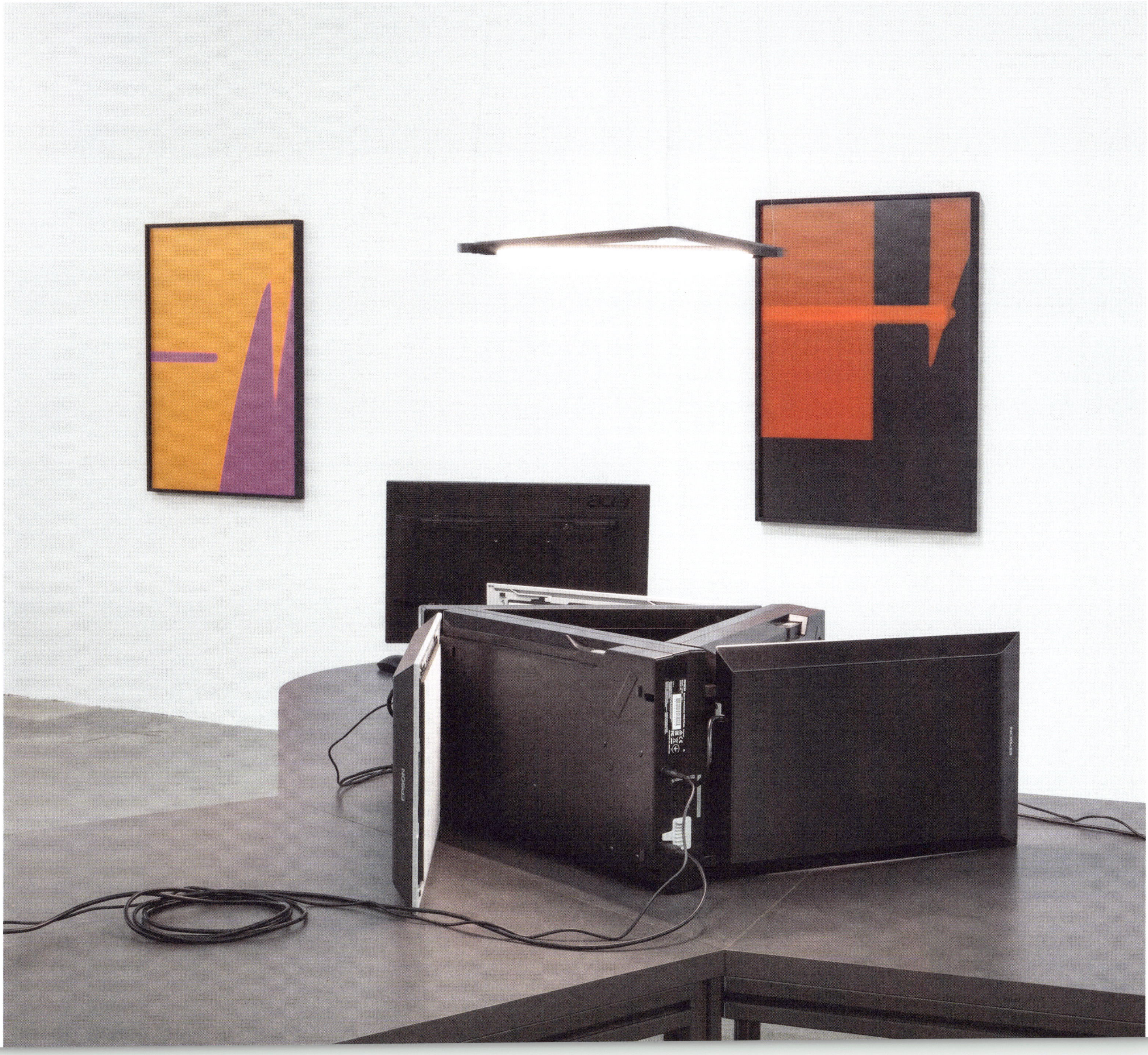

I realized that when two scanners are on their side pointed at one another, one scanner could "see" the opposite scanner's scanning band, and accompanying LED light, as it pulls across the scanning surface. This contrast in light levels would manifest as a "stripe" but would be further abstracted by the manipulated scanning parameters.

The stripe's size, thickness, and angle depended on the ratio between the scanner's DPI resolution setting since the resolution affected the speed of movement of the scanning band.

The ends of the line could now blur by playing with the contrast; colors manipulated using the level sliders, transforming the color profile curves to reveal unseen details.

The output could look like a brushstroke.

It could look like Rothko. It could look like abstract photography or digital art. It occurred to me that these original images needed to exist in relation to these references and that this process had to be overt.

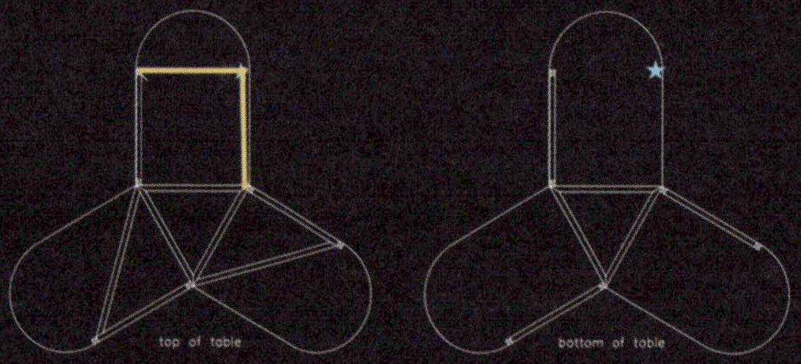

Signal Flow in "All we've ever had is one another"

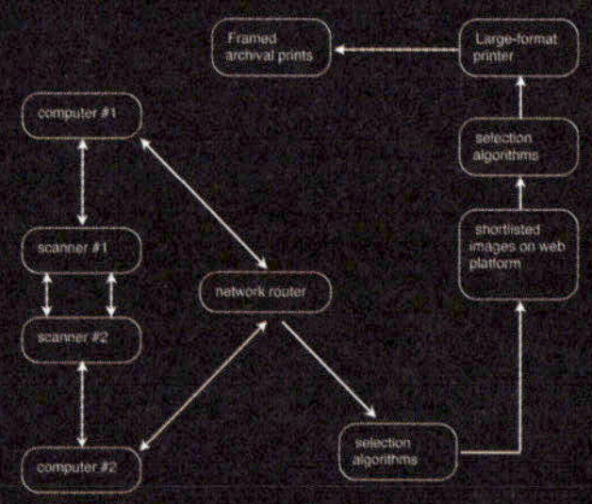

```
# to silence decompression bomb warning
from PIL import Image
Image.MAX_IMAGE_PIXELS = 1000000000

import time
import os
import sys
from match_stats import print_stats
from models import db, InstallationImageM
from configuration_values import get_web
    get_force_print_flag, set_fo
    get_force_print_threshold,
    get_stop_printing_flag, set_
    get_print_every_once_in_n
    get_web_twitter_every_onc
import magic
from image_resizing import resize_image
from image_hashing import get_all_algo_
from image_matching import compute_im
from image_score_weight_adjustment imp
from peewee import DoesNotExist, fn
from image_printing import print_file
import datetime
from web_generate import web_generate
from twitter_post import twitter_post
import random
from tqdm import tqdm
import numpy as np

SLEEP_BETWEEN_ITERATIONS_S = 10
RECURSIVE_IMAGES_DIR_PATH = os.environ['INSTALLATION_RECURSIVE_IMAGES_DIR_PATH']
ARTWORKS_SQLITE_PATH = os.environ['ARTWORKS_SQLITE_PATH']

PRINT_SCHEDULE = {
  'start': {
    'weekday': 2, # WED
    'hour': 11, # 11 AM
  },
  'end': {
    'weekday': 5, # SAT
    'hour': 18, # 6 pm
  }
}

db.init(ARTWORKS_SQLITE_PATH)
db.create_tables([InstallationImageMatch])

initial_file_list = None

def check_now_within_print_schedule():
  now = datetime.datetime.now()

  this_weeks_monday = now - datetime.timedelta(days=now.weekday())
  this_weeks_monday = this_weeks_monday.replace(hour=0,minute=0,second=0,microsecond=0)

  start_day_time = this_weeks_monday + datetime.timedelta(
    days=PRINT_SCHEDULE['start']['weekday'],
    hours=PRINT_SCHEDULE['start']['hour'],
  )
  end_day_time = this_weeks_monday + datetime.timedelta(
    days=PRINT_SCHEDULE['end']['weekday'],
    hours=PRINT_SCHEDULE['end']['hour'],
```

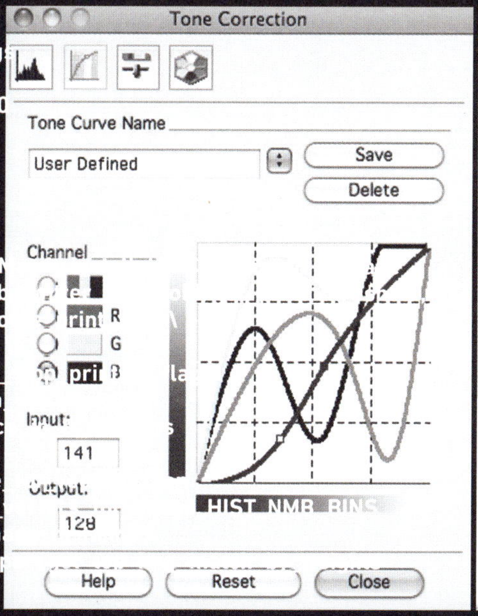

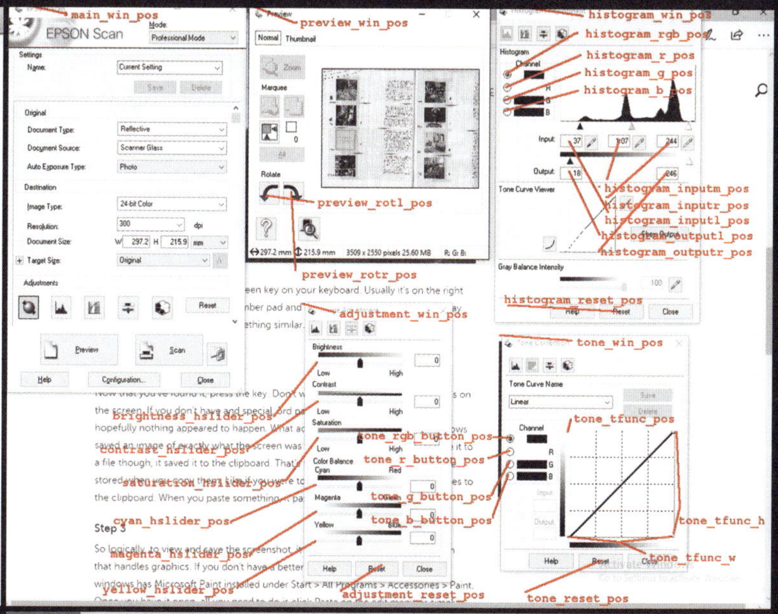

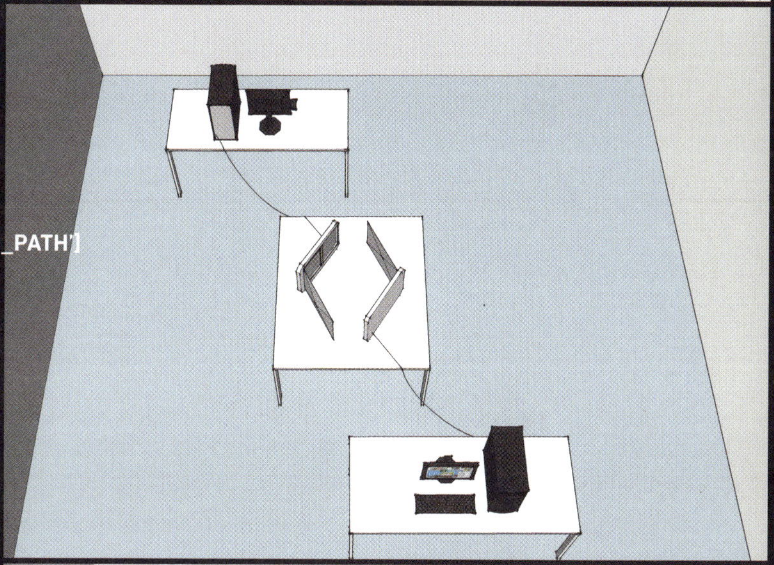

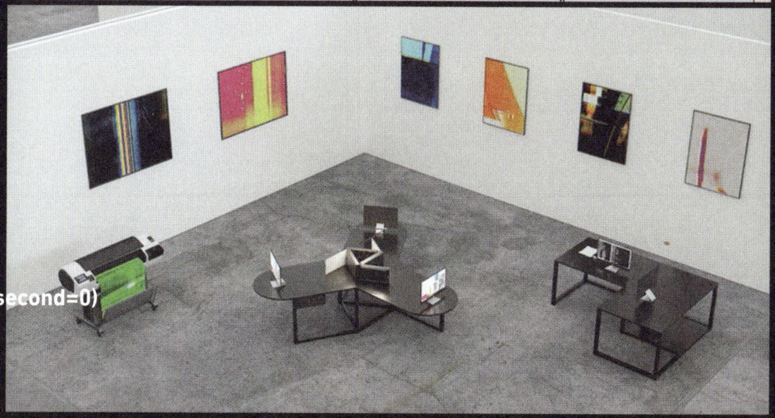

051 . ALL WE'D EVER NEED IS ONE ANOTHER (TRIO)

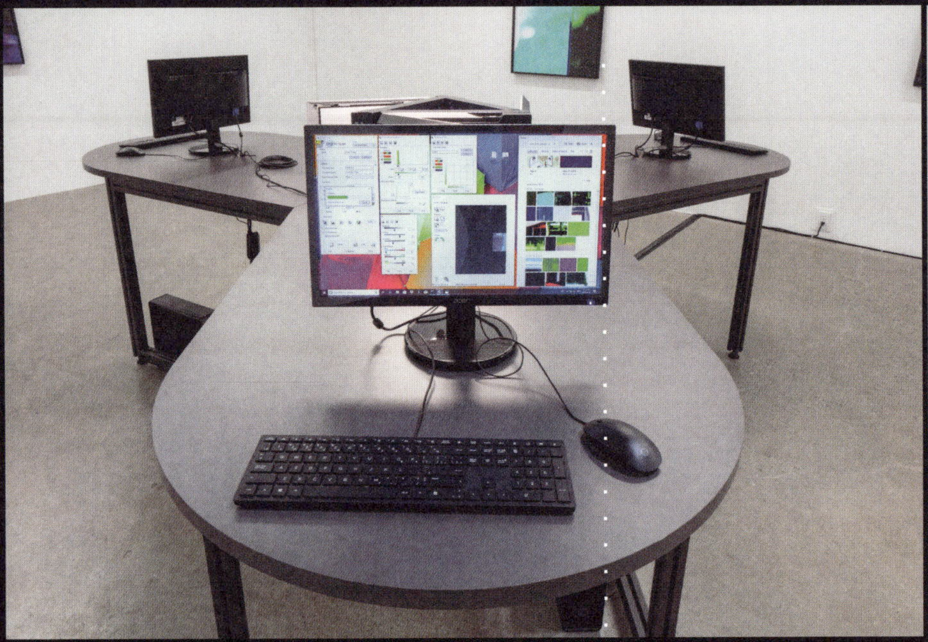

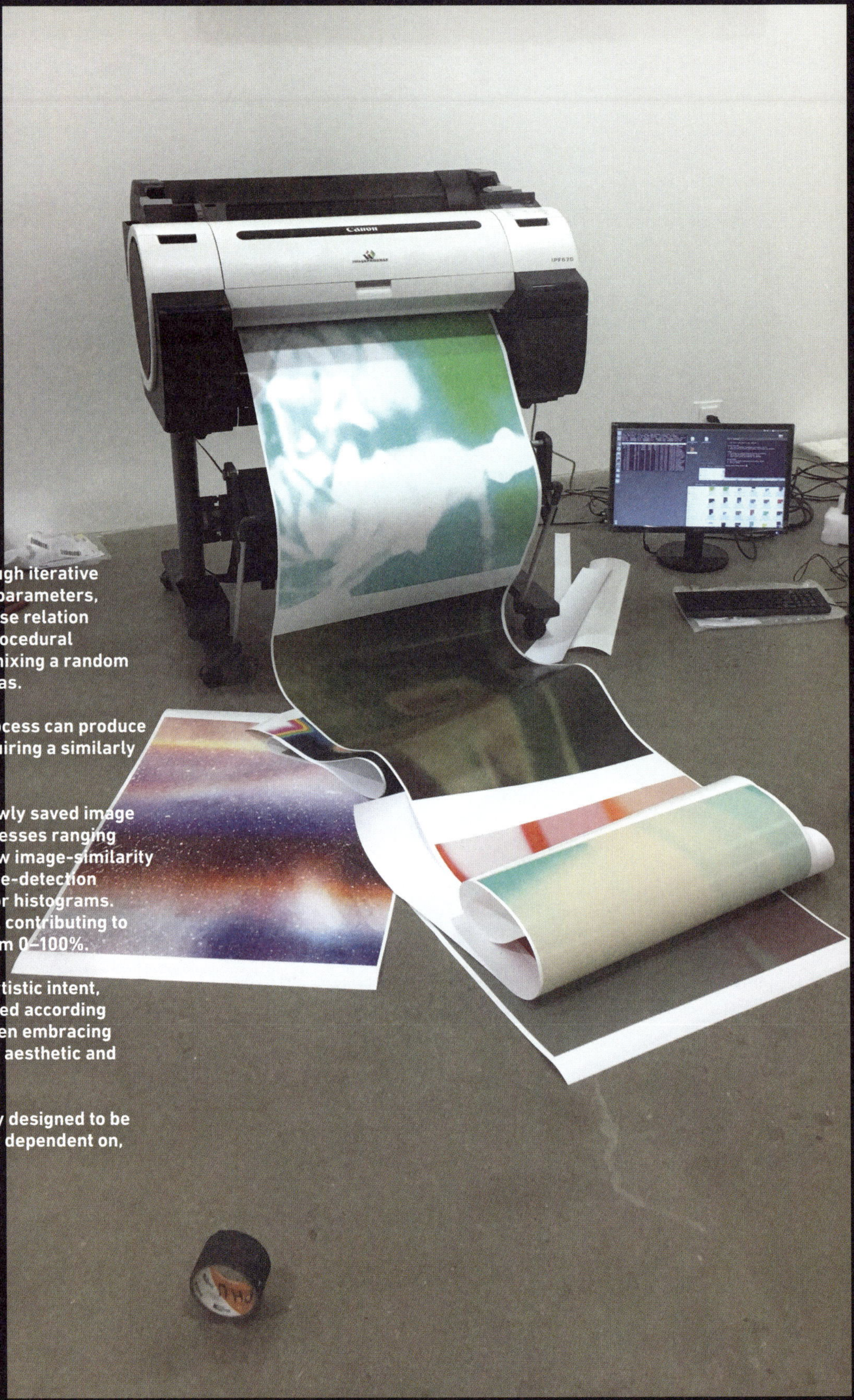

```
icrosoft Windows [Version 10.0.17134.1]
c) 2018 Microsoft Corporation. All rights reserved.

:\Users\allweneed2>cd Documents

:\Users\allweneed2\Documents>dir
Volume in drive C is Windows
Volume Serial Number is 0A0C-CD01

Directory of C:\Users\allweneed2\Documents

018-12-13  06:23 PM    <DIR>          .
018-12-13  06:23 PM    <DIR>          ..
018-12-16  04:31 PM    <DIR>          computer_as_artist
018-11-21  09:18 PM    <DIR>          GUI code
018-11-21  07:15 PM    <DIR>          installers
               0 File(s)              0 bytes
               5 Dir(s)  945,166,749,696 bytes free

:\Users\allweneed2\Documents>cd computerasartist
he system cannot find the path specified.

:\Users\allweneed2\Documents>cd computer_as_artist

:\Users\allweneed2\Documents\computer_as_artist>dir
Volume in drive C is Windows
Volume Serial Number is 0A0C-CD01

Directory of C:\Users\allweneed2\Documents\computer_as_artist

018-12-16  04:31 PM    <DIR>          .
018-12-16  04:31 PM    <DIR>          ..
018-12-13  07:04 PM            12,346 .epson_ctl_params.txt.un~
018-12-13  06:23 PM    <DIR>          .git
018-12-11  04:22 PM                42 .gitignore
018-12-11  04:22 PM                25 activate_epson_scan.ahk
018-12-11  04:22 PM                20 ahk_params_test.ahk
018-12-11  04:22 PM               123 ahk_params_test.bat
018-12-11  04:22 PM                58 ahk_test.ahk
018-12-11  04:22 PM               643 argparse_test.py
018-12-11  04:22 PM                75 arrange_Photos.ahk
018-12-11  04:22 PM                25 bring_epson_to_front.ahk
018-12-11  04:22 PM               208 do_scan_iteration.bat
018-12-11  04:22 PM             1,251 do_scan_iteration.py
018-12-11  04:22 PM                33 EPSON_close_test.ahk
018-12-11  04:22 PM               476 EPSON_close_wins.ahk
018-12-11  04:22 PM            27,086 epson_control-backup.py
018-12-11  04:22 PM            28,675 epson_control-new.py
018-12-16  04:31 PM            40,927 epson_control.py
018-12-17  02:02 PM             4,704 epson_controller.dat
018-12-11  04:22 PM               520 epson_control_hslider_test.py
018-12-11  04:22 PM               812 epson_control_setup.py
018-12-11  04:22 PM               823 epson_control_setup.sh
018-12-16  05:54 PM             7,391 epson_ctl_params.txt
018-12-11  05:25 PM             7,362 epson_ctl_params.txt~
018-12-11  04:22 PM                25 EPSON_launch.ahk
018-12-11  04:22 PM               334 EPSON_move.ahk
018-12-11  04:22 PM               557 EPSON_move_test.ahk
018-12-11  04:22 PM                95 histo_adjust_test.bat
018-12-11  04:22 PM               329 histo_adjust_test.py
018-12-11  04:22 PM                84 launch_Photos.bat
018-12-11  04:22 PM               135 launch_Photos.py
018-12-11  04:22 PM               359 loop_while_unchanged.py
```

```
icrosoft Windows [Version 10.0.17134.1]
(c) 2018 Microsoft Corporation. All rights reserved.

:\Users\allweneed2>dir
 Volume in drive C is
 Volume Serial Number

 Directory of C:\Users

2018-12-16  04:31 PM
2018-12-16  04:31 PM
2018-11-21  09:14 PM    <DIR>          .idlerc
2018-11-21  07:00 PM
2018-11-21  07:00 PM    <DIR>          Contacts
2018-11-21  09:18 PM
2018-12-13  06:23 PM    <DIR>          Documents
2018-11-21  07:00 PM    <DIR>          Downloads
2018-08-31  06:49 AM    <DIR>          Favorites
2018-11-21  07:00 PM
2018-11-21  07:00 PM    <DIR>          Music
2018-11-21  07:05 PM
2019-01-10  03:23 PM    <DIR>          Pictures
2018-11-21  07:00 PM
2018-11-21  07:02 PM    <DIR>          Searches
2018-12-15  06:35 PM               734 Sti_Trace.log
2018-11-21  07:00 PM    <DIR>          Videos
2018-12-16  04:31 PM
               2 File(s)          8,022 bytes
              16 Dir(s)

:\Users\allweneed2>c

:\Users>dir
 Volume in drive C is Windows
 Volume Serial Number

 Directory of C:\Users

2018-11-21  07:22 PM
2018-11-21  07:22 PM    <DIR>          ..
2018-12-16  04:31 PM    <DIR>          allweneed2
2018-04-27  10:07 PM    <DIR>          Public
               0 File(
               4 Dir(s)

:\Users>Processing...
'Processing....' is n
operable program or batch file.

:\Users>cd ..

:\>dir
 Volume in drive C is Windows
 Volume Serial Number is 0A0C-CD01

 Directory of C:\

2018-04-11  03:38 PM
2018-11-21  08:43 PM                   Program Files
2018-11-21  08:45 PM                   Program Files (x86)
2018-11-21  08:49 PM    <DIR>          Python27
2018-08-31  08:35 AM    <DIR>          SWSetup
2018-11-21  07:22 PM    <DIR>          Users
```

These images are created through iterative randomization of the scanning parameters, ambient light intensity, and phase relation between the scanners. It is a procedural approach, similar to a painter mixing a random palette of paints for every canvas.

This automatized "creative" process can produce thousands of images daily, requiring a similarly automated curatorial process.

The curation occurs as each newly saved image is analyzed using multiple processes ranging from Google's famed Tensorflow image-similarity analysis; through "blob" and line-detection algorithms to custom-built color histograms. Each analysis is given a weight, contributing to a "similarity score" ranging from 0–100%.

As a lasting legacy of human artistic intent, the weighing system is calibrated according to my study of similarity between embracing (and hopefully making obvious) aesthetic and conceptual biases.

The two cycles are intentionally designed to be utterly oblivious to, yet entirely dependent on, one another.

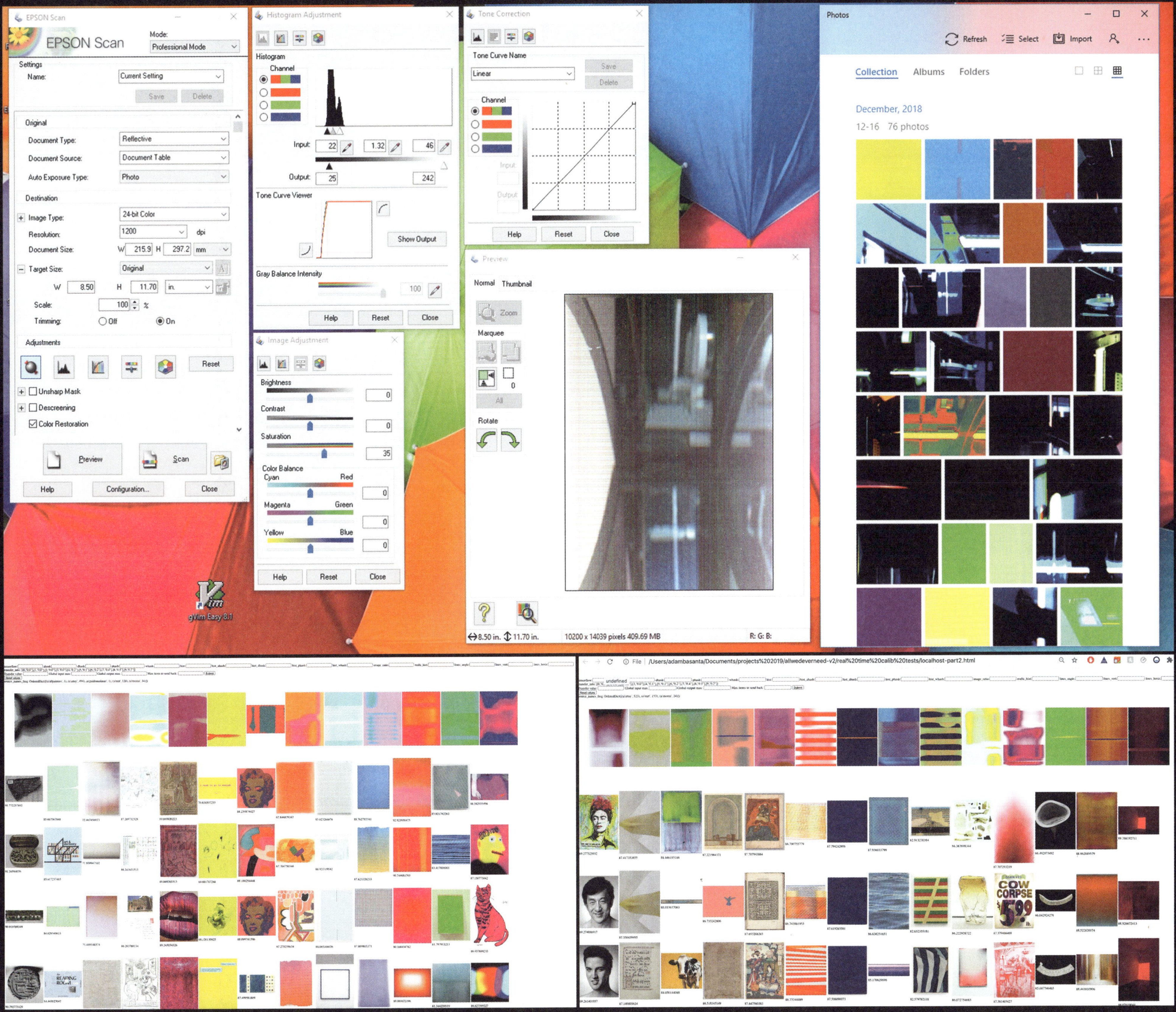

053 . ALL WE'D EVER NEED IS ONE ANOTHER (TRIO)

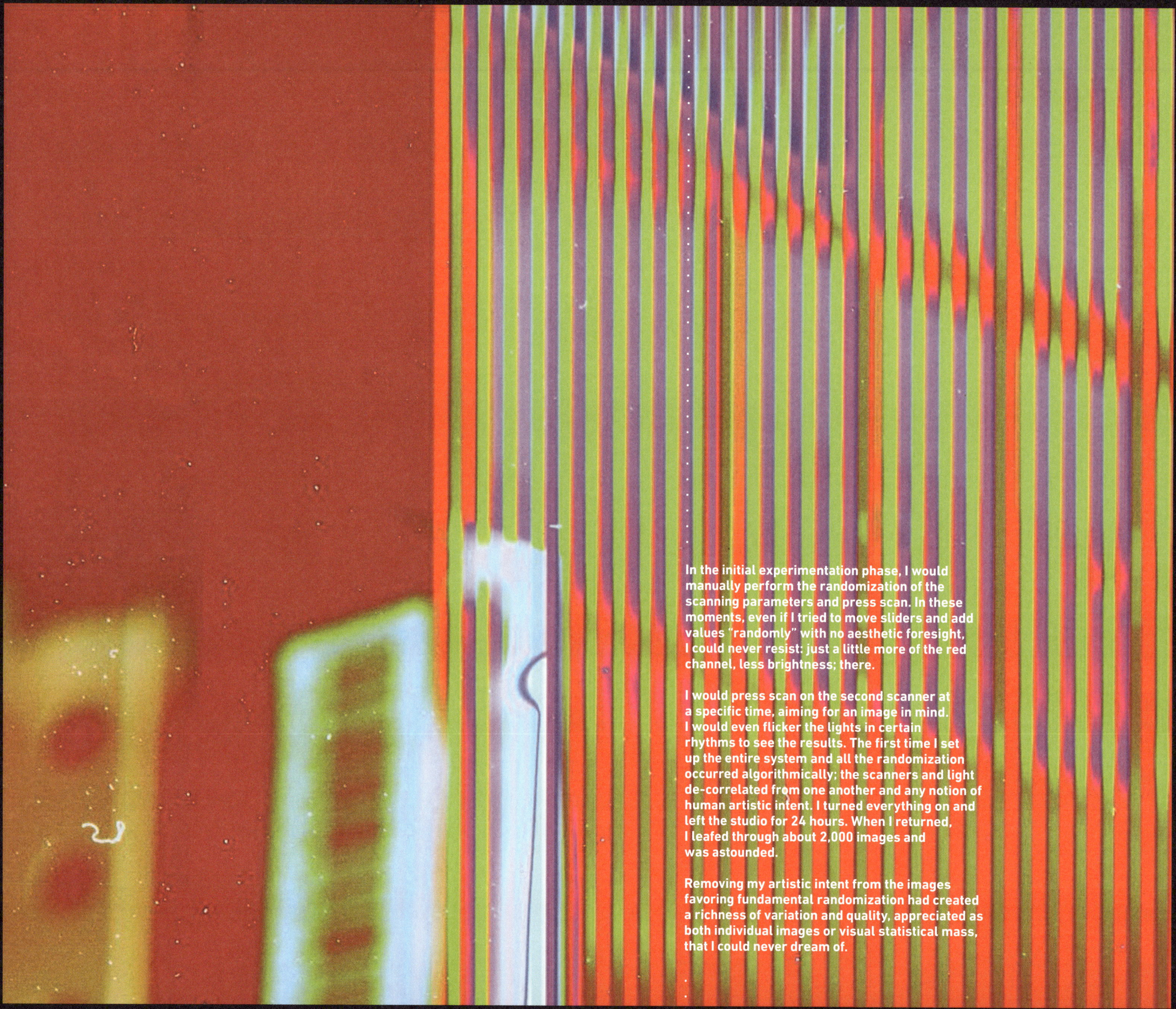

In the initial experimentation phase, I would manually perform the randomization of the scanning parameters and press scan. In these moments, even if I tried to move sliders and add values "randomly" with no aesthetic foresight, I could never resist: just a little more of the red channel, less brightness; there.

I would press scan on the second scanner at a specific time, aiming for an image in mind. I would even flicker the lights in certain rhythms to see the results. The first time I set up the entire system and all the randomization occurred algorithmically; the scanners and light de-correlated from one another and any notion of human artistic intent. I turned everything on and left the studio for 24 hours. When I returned, I leafed through about 2,000 images and was astounded.

Removing my artistic intent from the images favoring fundamental randomization had created a richness of variation and quality, appreciated as both individual images or visual statistical mass, that I could never dream of.

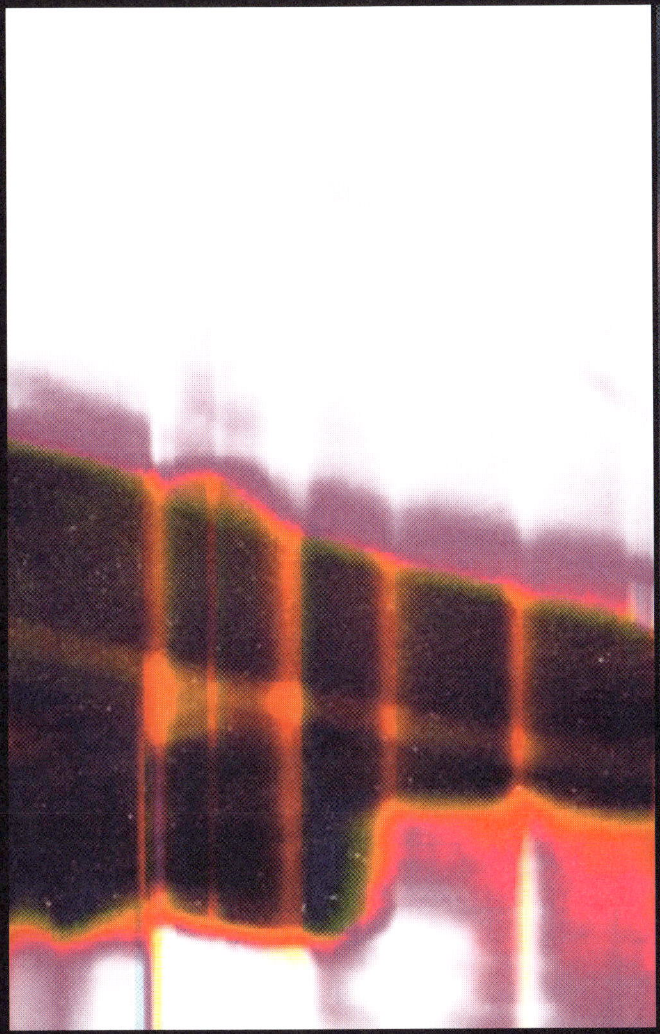

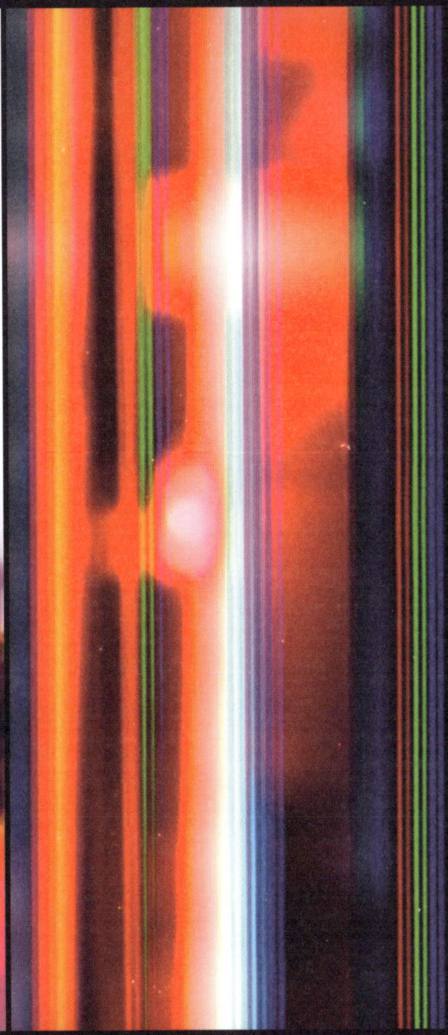

```
import tweepy
import os
import inspect
from skimage.io import imread, imsave
from skimage.transform import resize
from models import db, InstallationImageMatch,

import re

# Consumer keys and access tokens, used for
OAuth
consumer_key = 'LXKZWn4MvwNHWo2mt-
g271lVGd'
consumer_secret = '5USbdkUTPQPxG7vrNclKX-
RTW2pPtLNmbVAD6KGWde1yrHud1ZU'
access_token = '987783701764411393-X0S32x-
bqr9nbUgPvXY9iVLOWejV3idH'
access_token_secret = 'tnEfPae5M2H-
QLT3qTa570vQq4PiX9FPW2FVflqUJcUNKP'

THUMB_HEIGHT = 512

CURR_FILE_DIR, _ = os.path.split(inspect.stack()
[0][1])
TWITTER_THUMBS_DIR_PATH = os.path.
join(CURR_FILE_DIR, 'twitter_thumbs')

def find_or_create_resized_thumb(orig_img_
file_path):
  src_file_name = os.path.split(orig_img_file_
path)[1]
  src_file_name_no_ext = os.path.splitext(s-
rc_file_name)[0]

  found_thumbnail = filter(lambda _:
_.startswith(src_file_name_no_ext), os.list-
dir(TWITTER_THUMBS_DIR_PATH))
  if len(found_thumbnail) == 1:
    return os.path.join(TWITTER_THUMBS_DIR_
PATH, found_thumbnail[0])

  im = imread(orig_img_file_path)
  h = THUMB_HEIGHT
  w = int(h*im.shape[1]/float(im.shape[0]))
  im = resize(im, (h, w), anti_aliasing=True,
mode='constant')
  dest_file_path = os.path.join(TWITTER_
THUMBS_DIR_PATH, '{}.jpg'.format(
    src_file_name
  ))
  imsave(dest_file_path, im)
  return dest_file_path

def create_status_from_img_match_obj(img_
match_obj, force_base_status=False):
  TWITTER_LEN_MAX = 260

  match_score = img_match_obj.match_score
  image = img_match_obj.image
  artwork = image.artwork_id

  title = artwork.title
```

055 . ALL WE'D EVER NEED IS ONE ANOTHER (TRIO)

CREDITS

Pictures by Laura Findlay

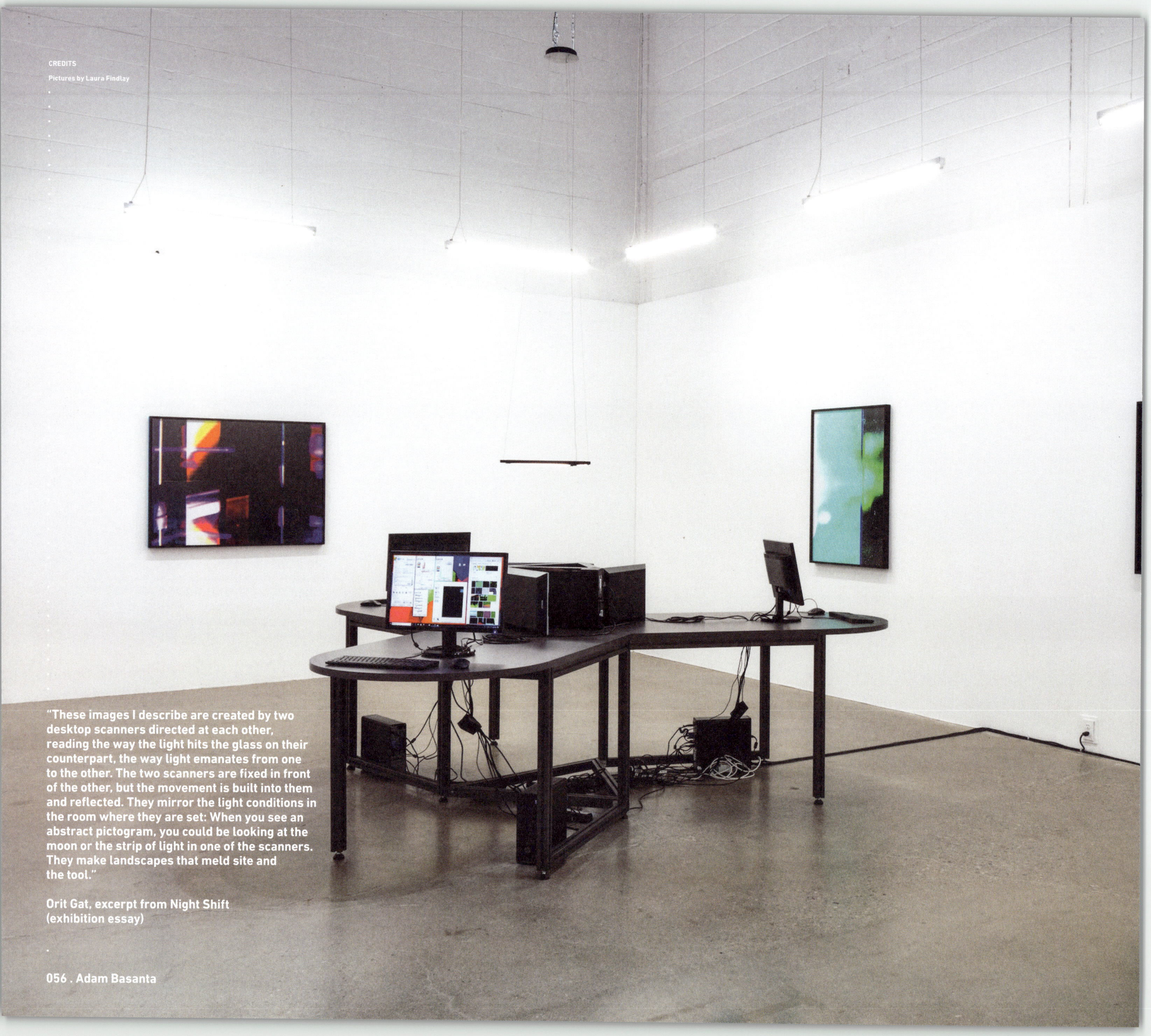

"These images I describe are created by two desktop scanners directed at each other, reading the way the light hits the glass on their counterpart, the way light emanates from one to the other. The two scanners are fixed in front of the other, but the movement is built into them and reflected. They mirror the light conditions in the room where they are set: When you see an abstract pictogram, you could be looking at the moon or the strip of light in one of the scanners. They make landscapes that meld site and the tool."

Orit Gat, excerpt from Night Shift (exhibition essay)

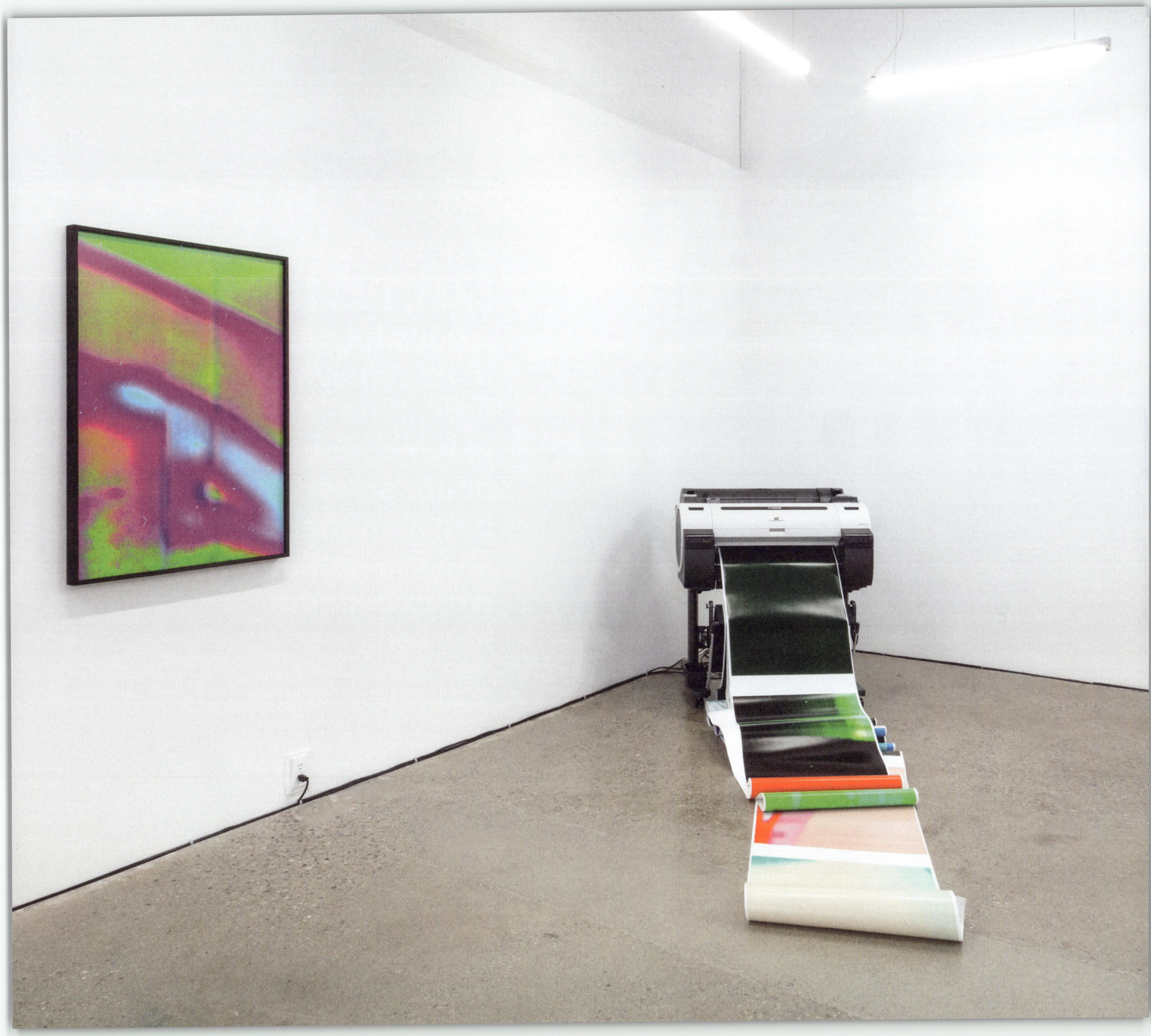

Christopher Bauder

Name:

Christopher Bauder
WHITEvoid

Cooperations:

Robert Henke

David Letellier

DEEP WEB
p. 059

DEEP WEB is a monumental immersive audiovisual installation and live performance created by light artist Christopher Bauder and composer and musician Robert Henke. Presented in enormous pitch-dark indoor spaces, DEEP WEB plunges the audience into a ballet of iridescent kinetic light and surround sound.

SKALAR
p. 066

SKALAR is a large-scale art installation that explores the complex impact of light and sound on human perception. Created by light artist Christopher Bauder and musician Kangding Ray, this monumental artwork reflects the raw nature and essence of human emotions.

URL:

whitevoid.com

Mail:

info@whitevoid.com

Instagram:

@whitevoid_berlin

Vita:

Christopher Bauder is the founder and Creative Director of the art and design studio WHITEvoid, and innovative lighting technology producer KINETIC LIGHTS.

Parallel to his work, Bauder is furthering his career as a light and media artist worldwide. He is best known for his expansive light art installations such as LICHTGRENZE, DEEP WEB, or SKALAR. The latter, conceived alongside music producer Kangding Ray, has already been visited by more than 200,000 people in Berlin, Zurich, Amsterdam, and Mexico City.

Bauder has always been fascinated by light. For him, light is an ephemeral material shaped, even though it's not tangible. Bauder transforms light into abstract beings that seem to come alive in the darkness by implementing modern technology.

Bauder's passion for technology and his creative spirit allow him to keep an eye on the future by designing and developing symbolic projects.

Also relevant in his new project DARK MATTER, the world's first kinetic light art exhibition.

DARK MATTER is a parallel cosmos of expansive light installations in which the boundaries between the real and the digital world become blurred.

Ranging from breathtakingly intimate light compositions to interactive walk-in structures and room-encompassing audiovisual performances.

Light, movement, and sound merge into graceful choreographies of luminous shapes and colors.

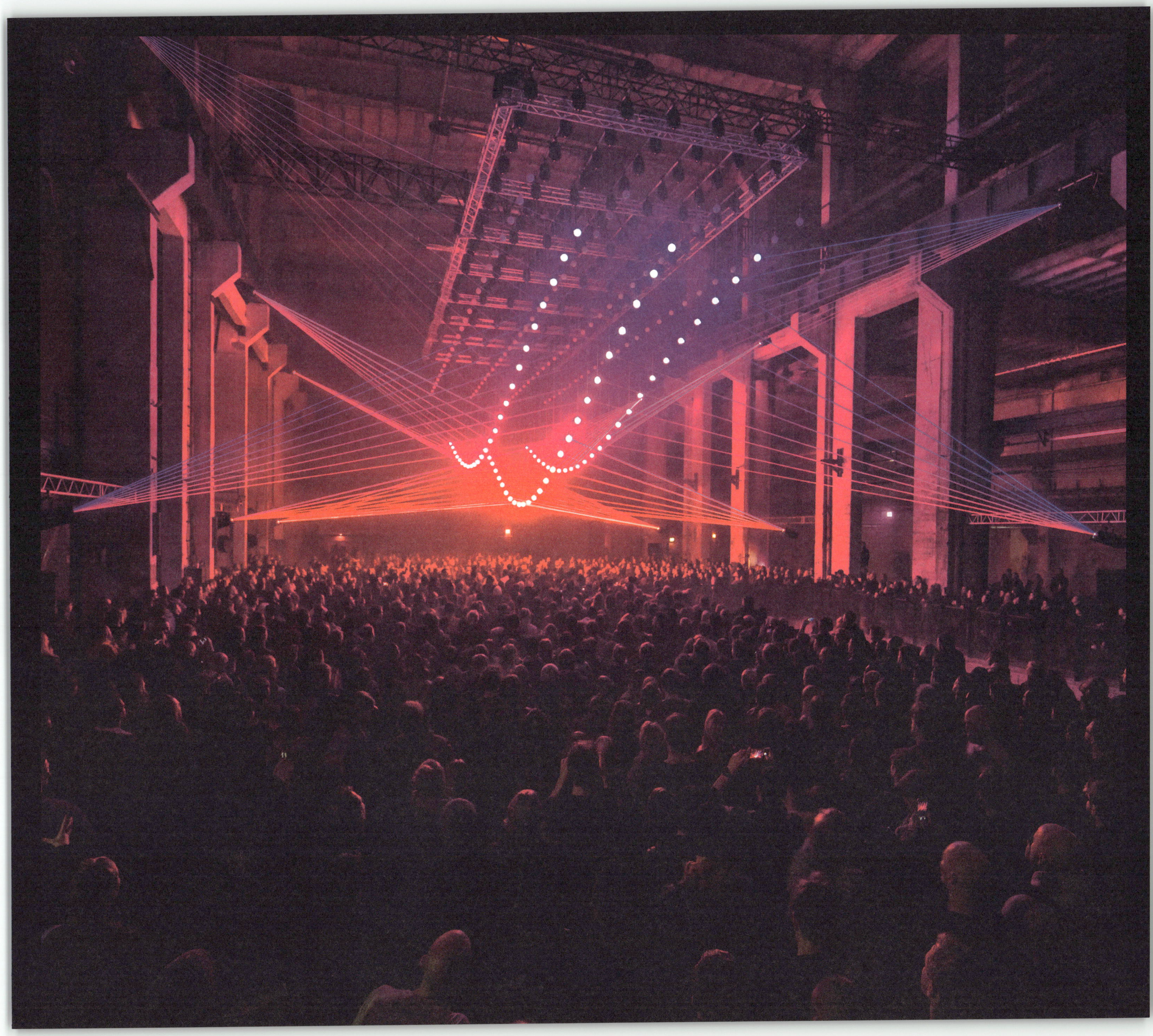

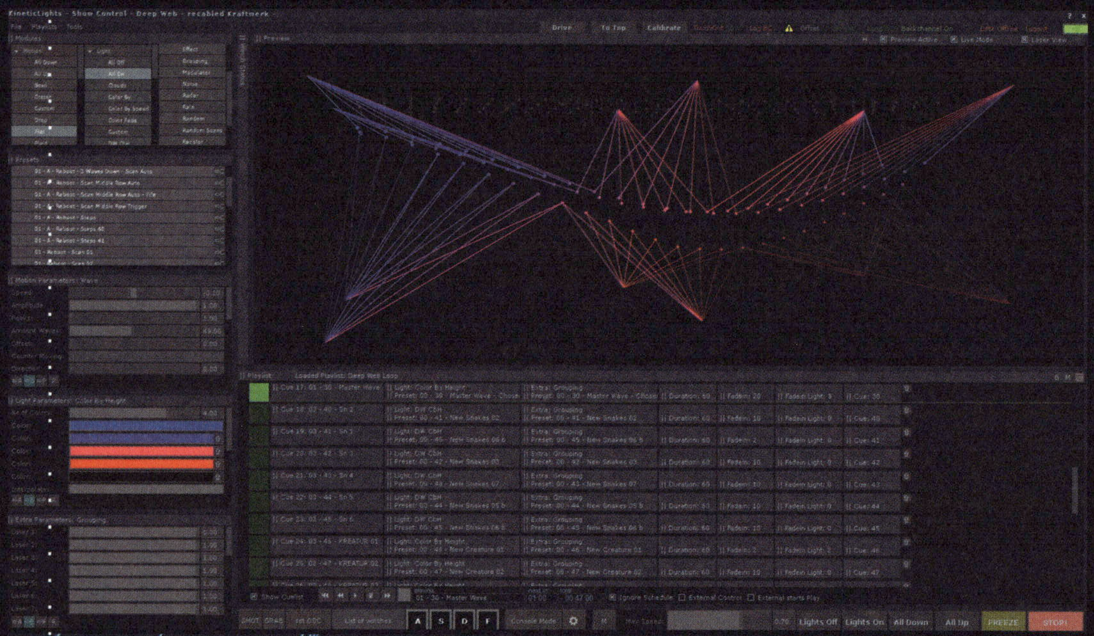

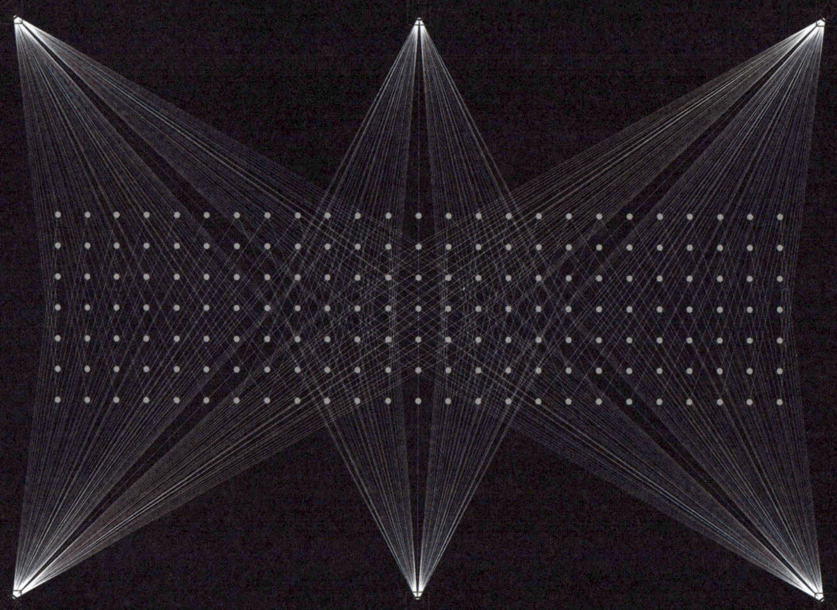

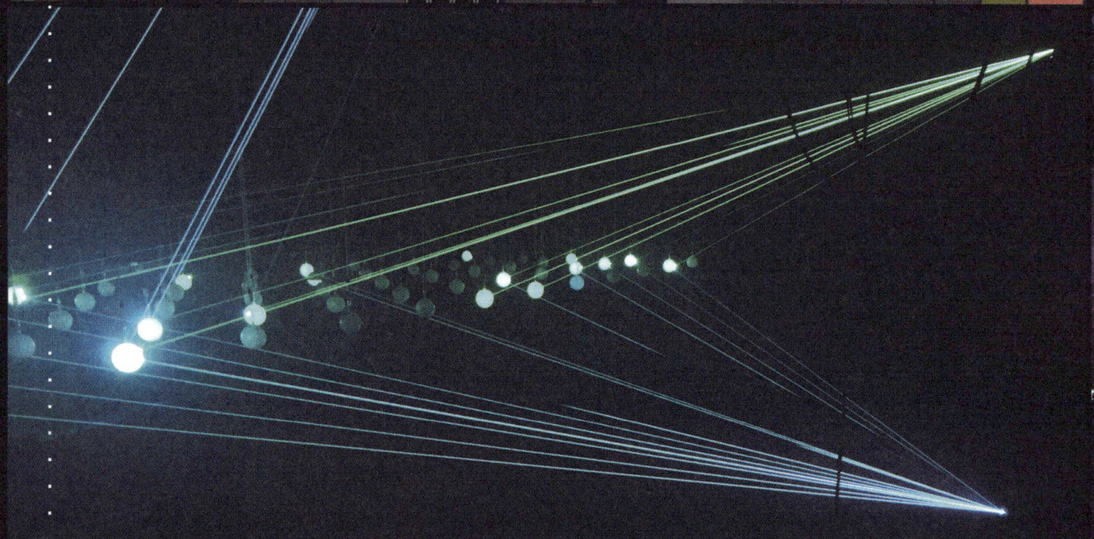

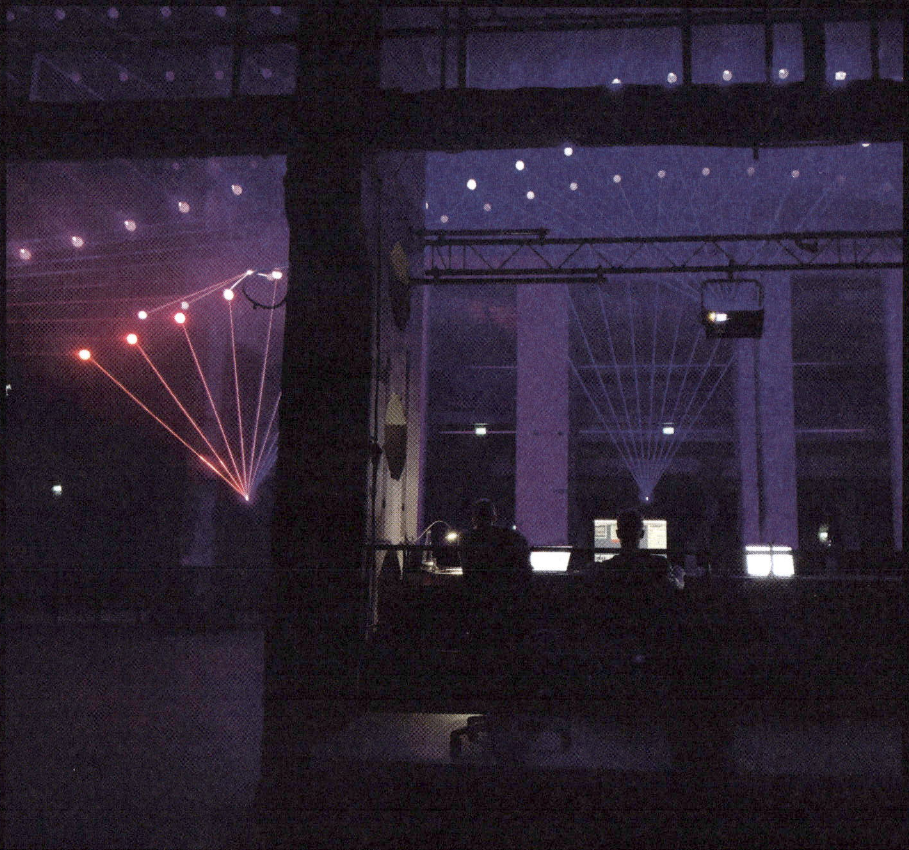

DEEP WEB is a monumental immersive audiovisual installation and live performance created by Bauder and composer and musician Robert Henke. DEEP WEB plunges the audience into a ballet of iridescent kinetic light and surround sound presented in enormous pitch-dark indoor spaces.

The generative luminous architectural structure weaves 175 motorized spheres and 12 high-power laser systems.

This huge superstructure brings to life a luminous analogy to the network connections, nodes, and technical drawings of information flow.

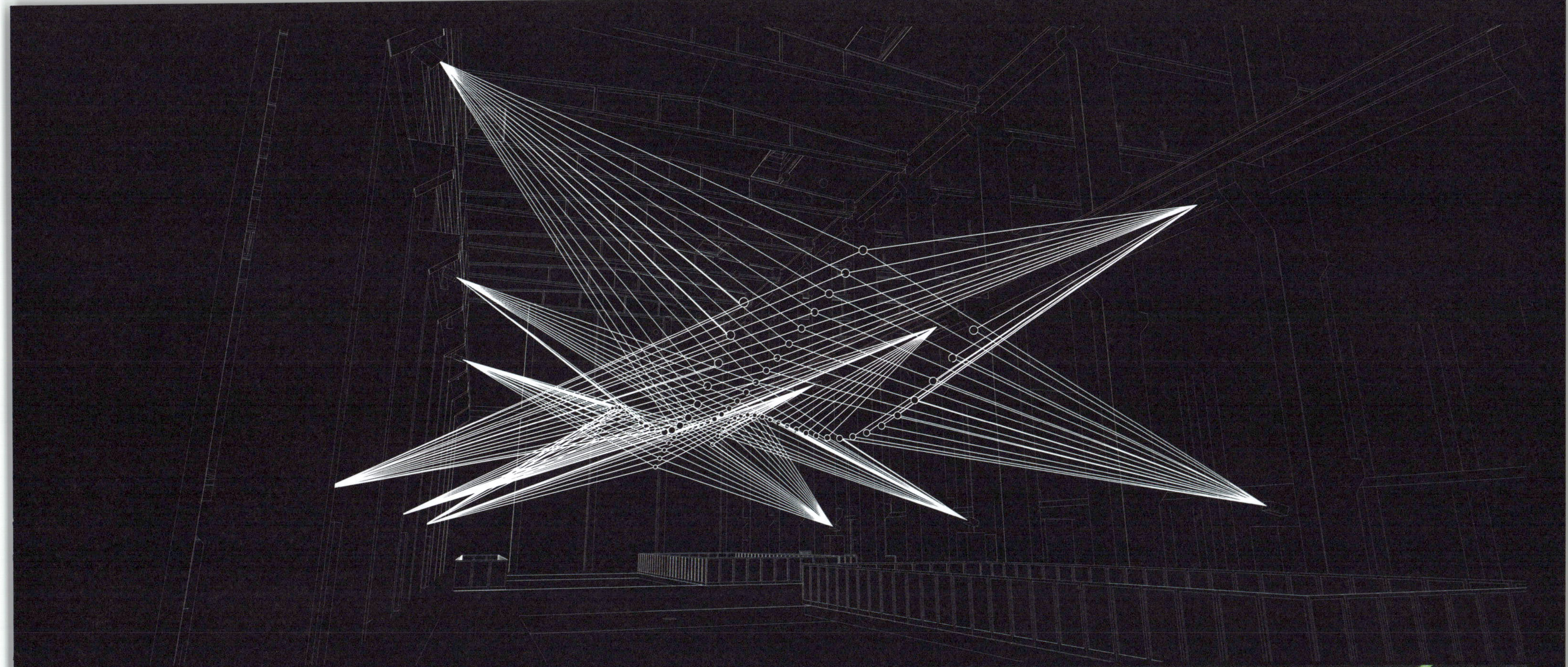

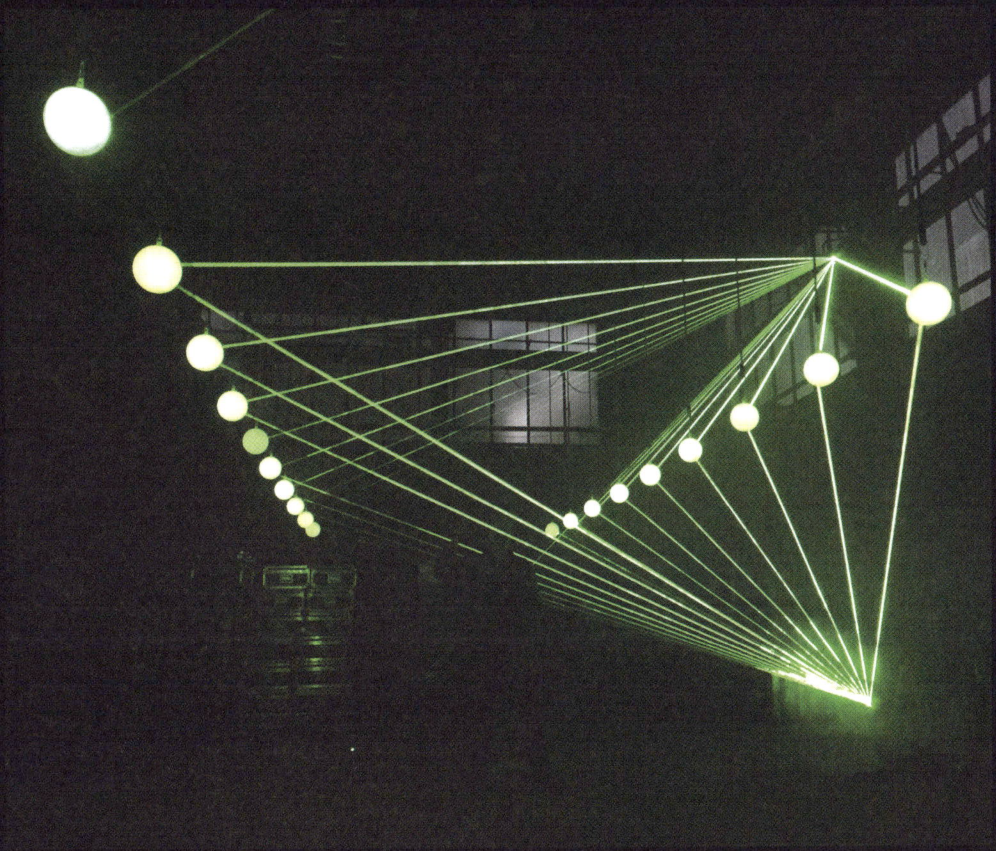

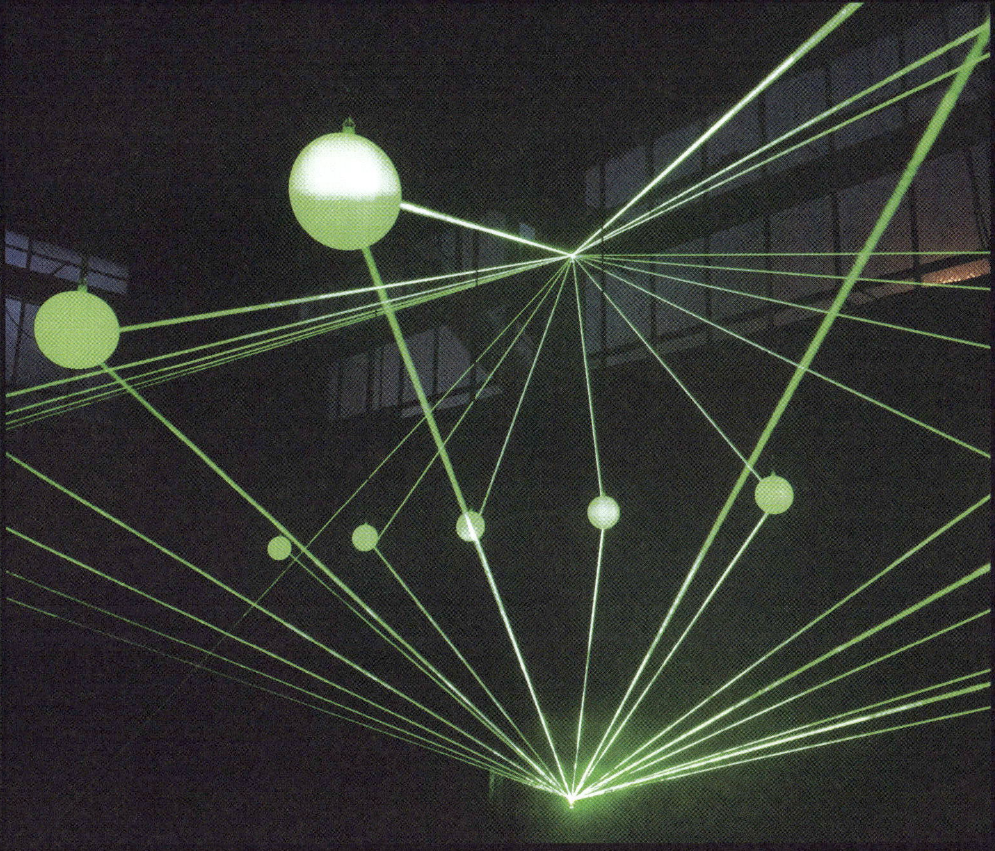

061 . DEEP WEB

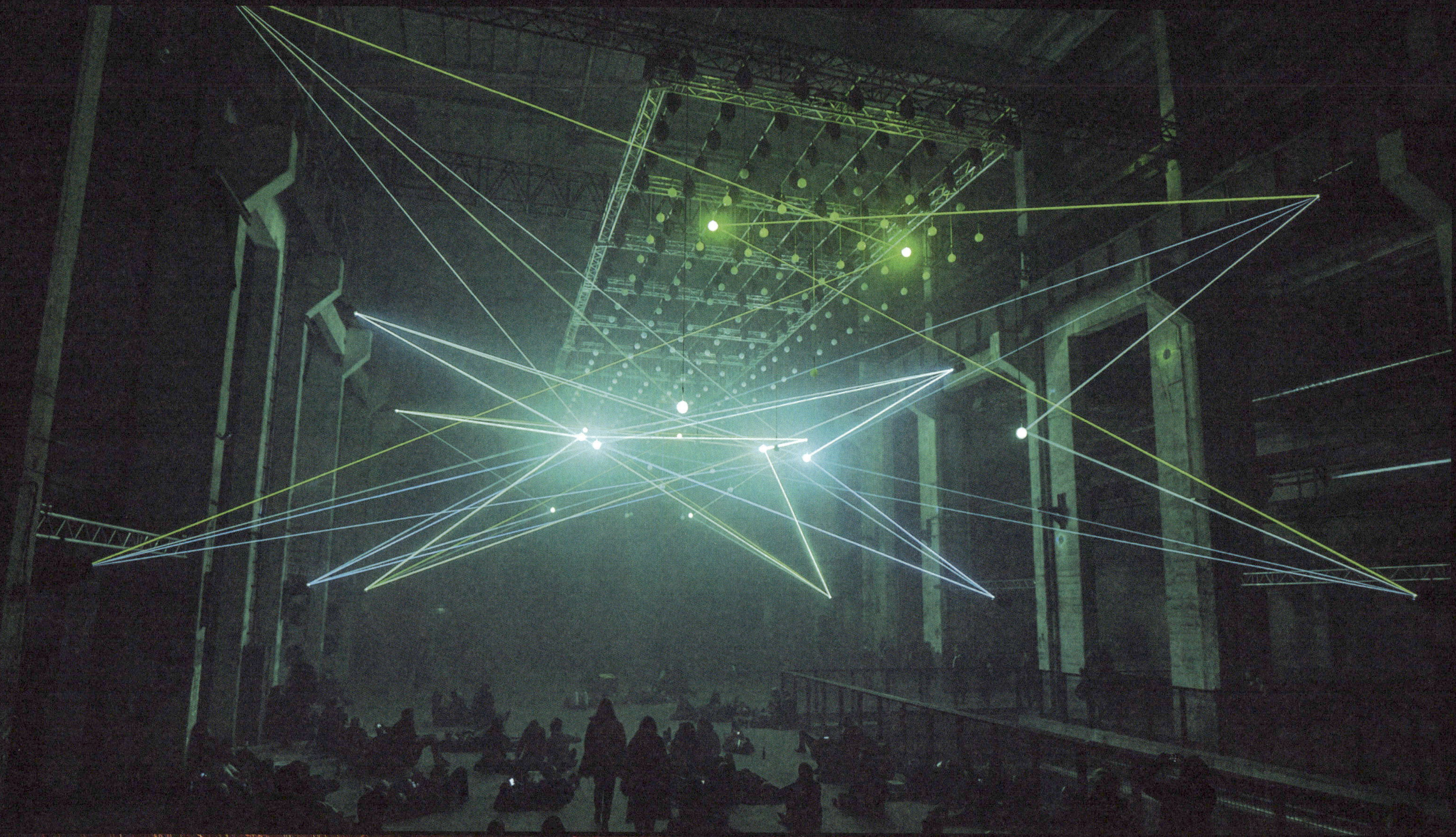

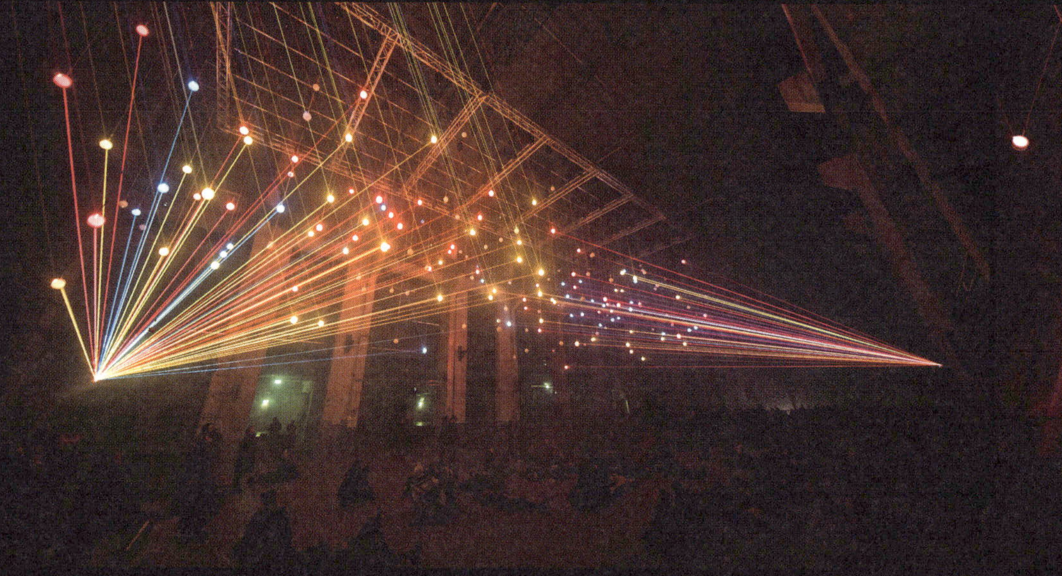

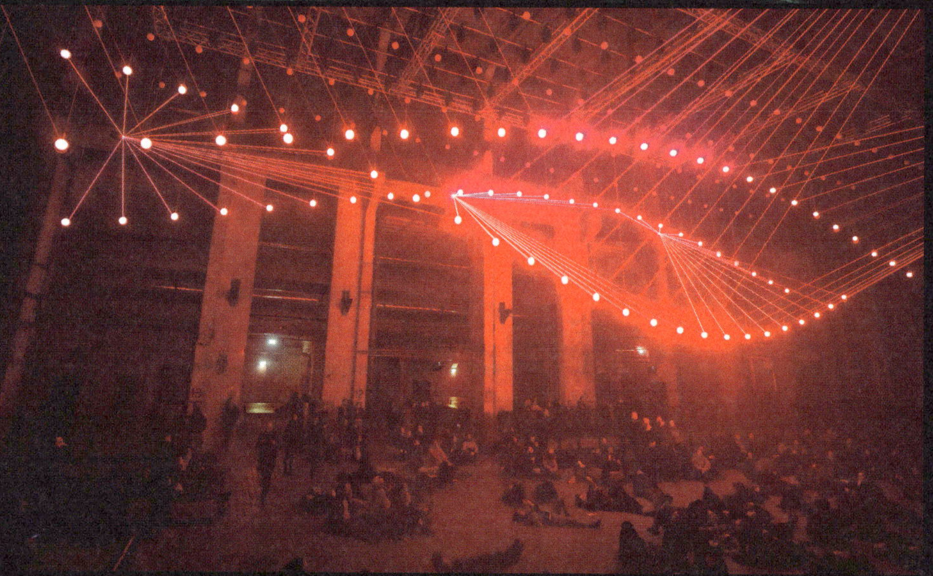

062 . Christopher Bauder and Robert Henke

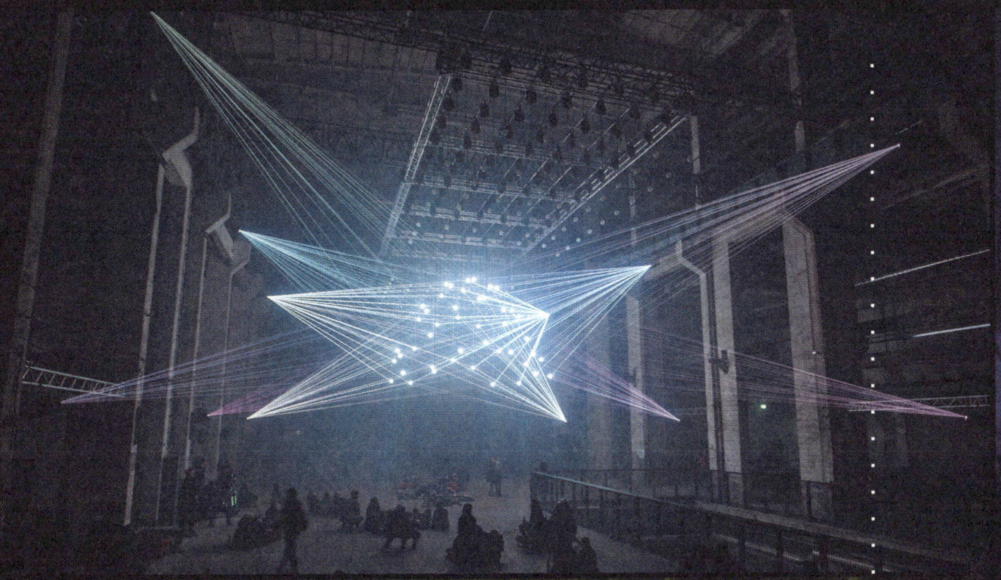

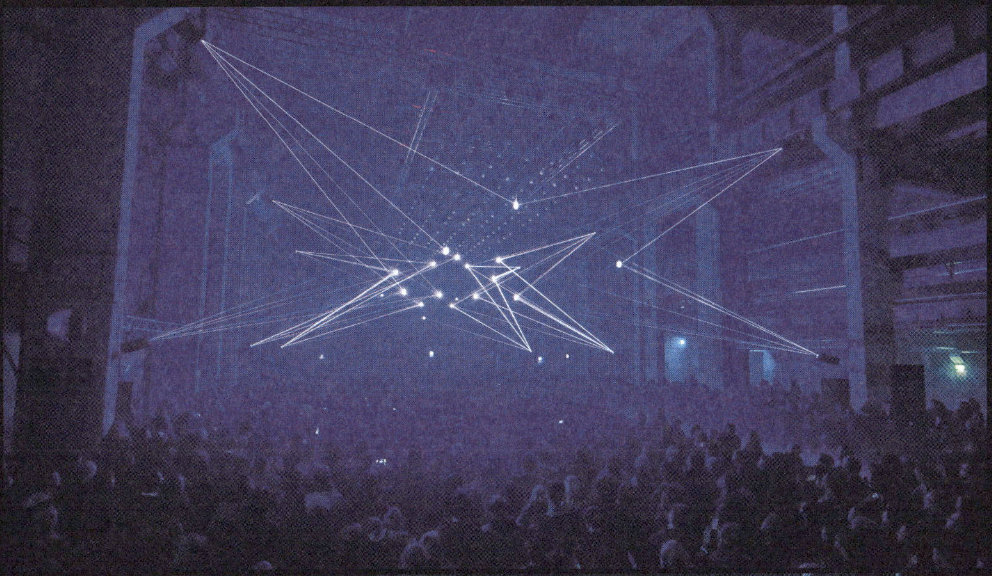

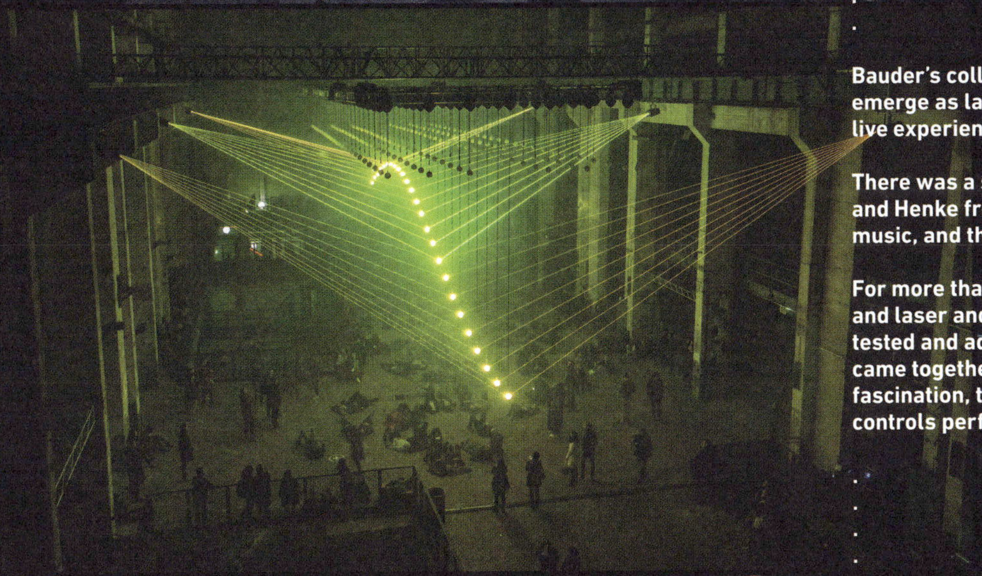

Bauder's collaborative projects always emerge as large-scale, expansive audiovisual live experiences.

There was a strong inspiration between Bauder and Henke from the offset, a mutual influence of music, and three-dimensional abstract patterns.

For more than six months, each new function and laser and its implementation in the software tested and adapted before sound and image came together for the first time; a moment of fascination, the novel experience that music controls perfectly synchronized visual patterns.

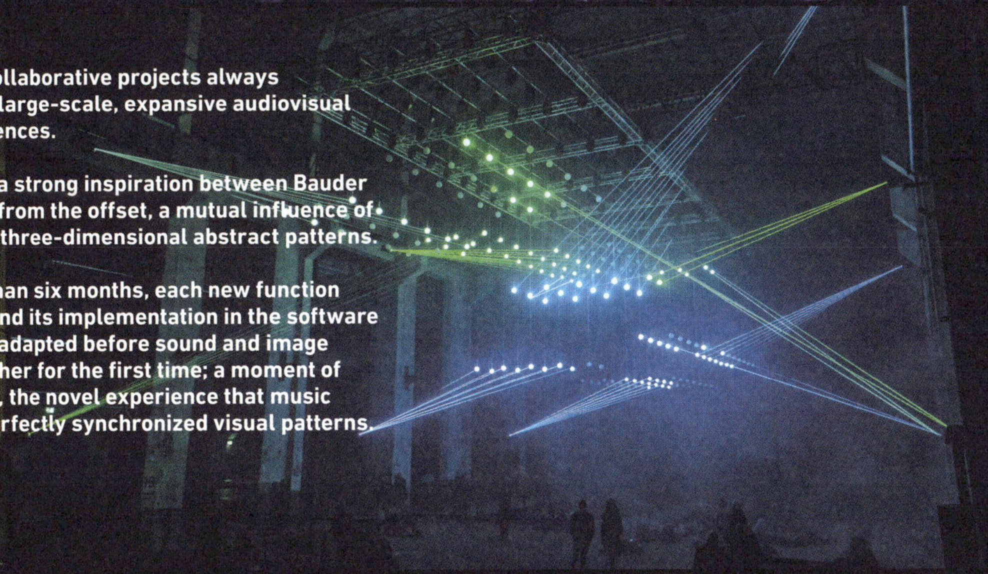

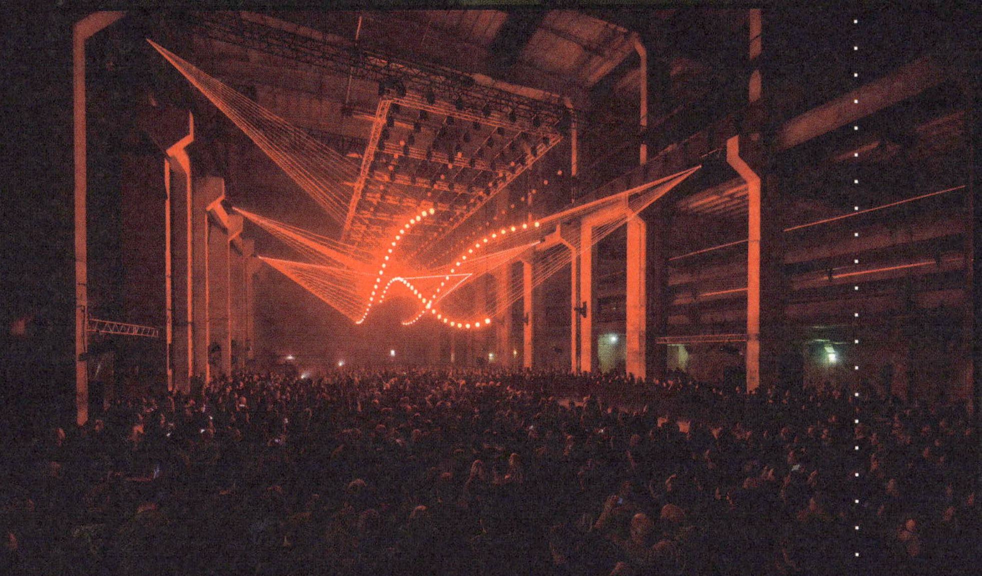

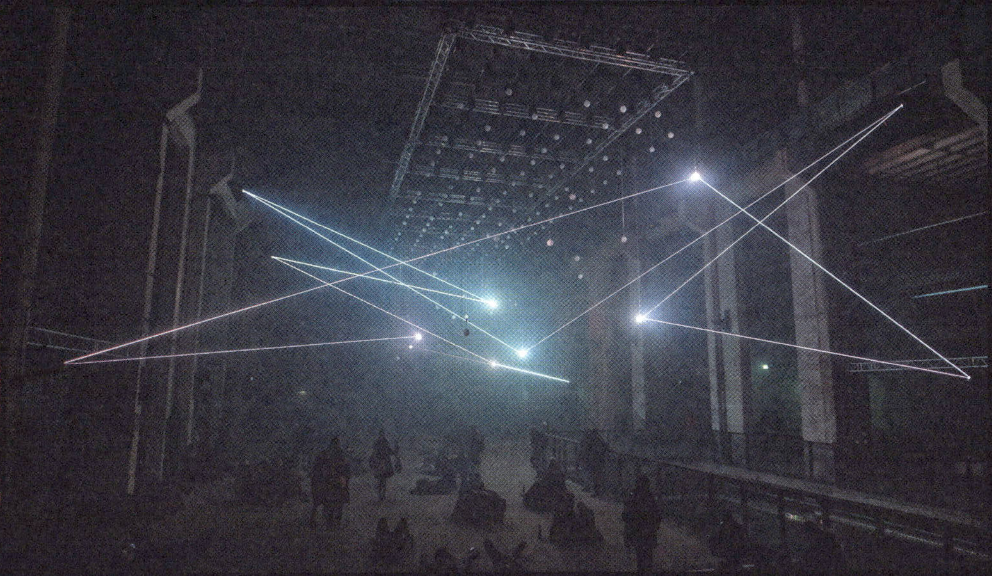

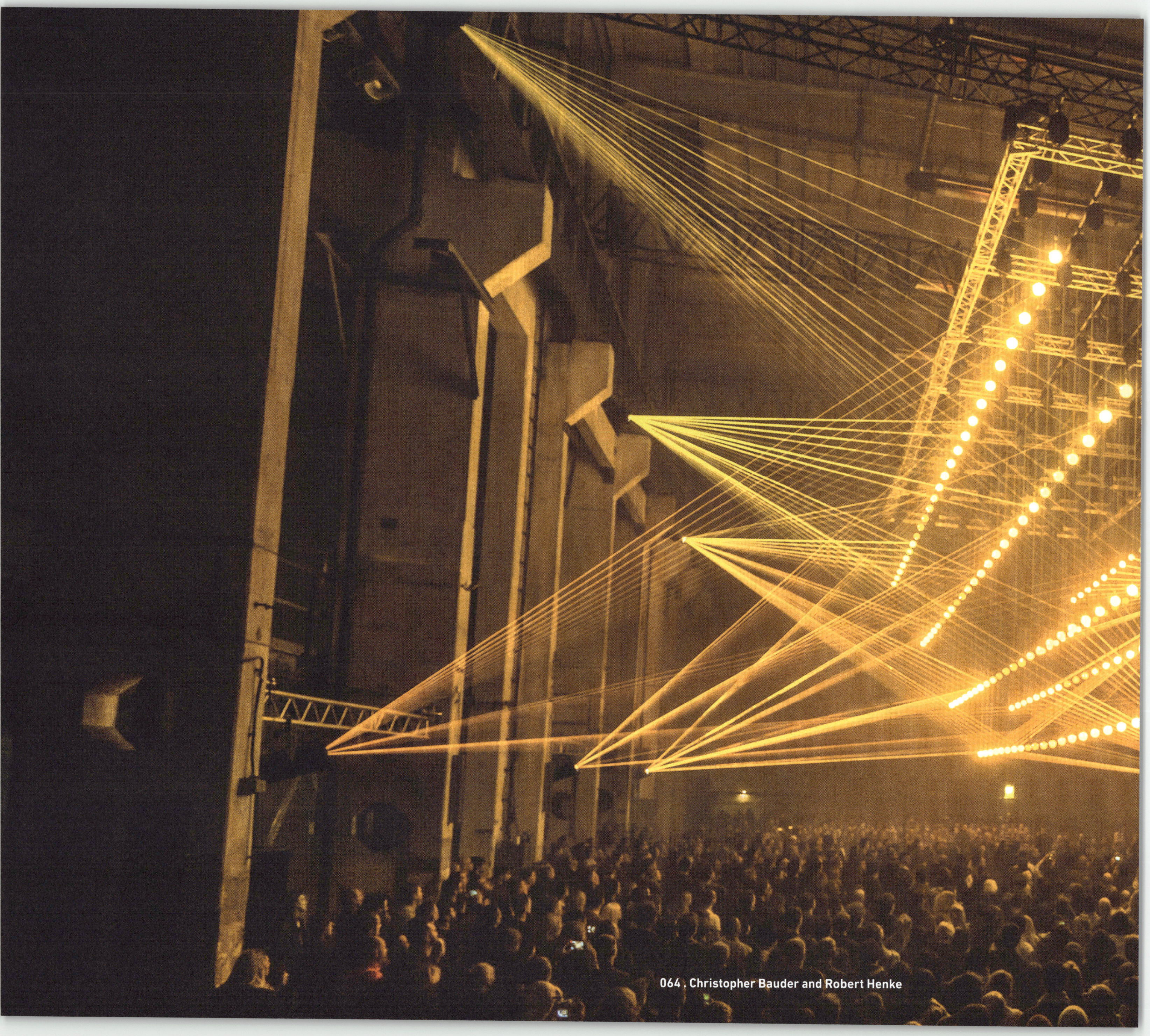

064 . Christopher Bauder and Robert Henke

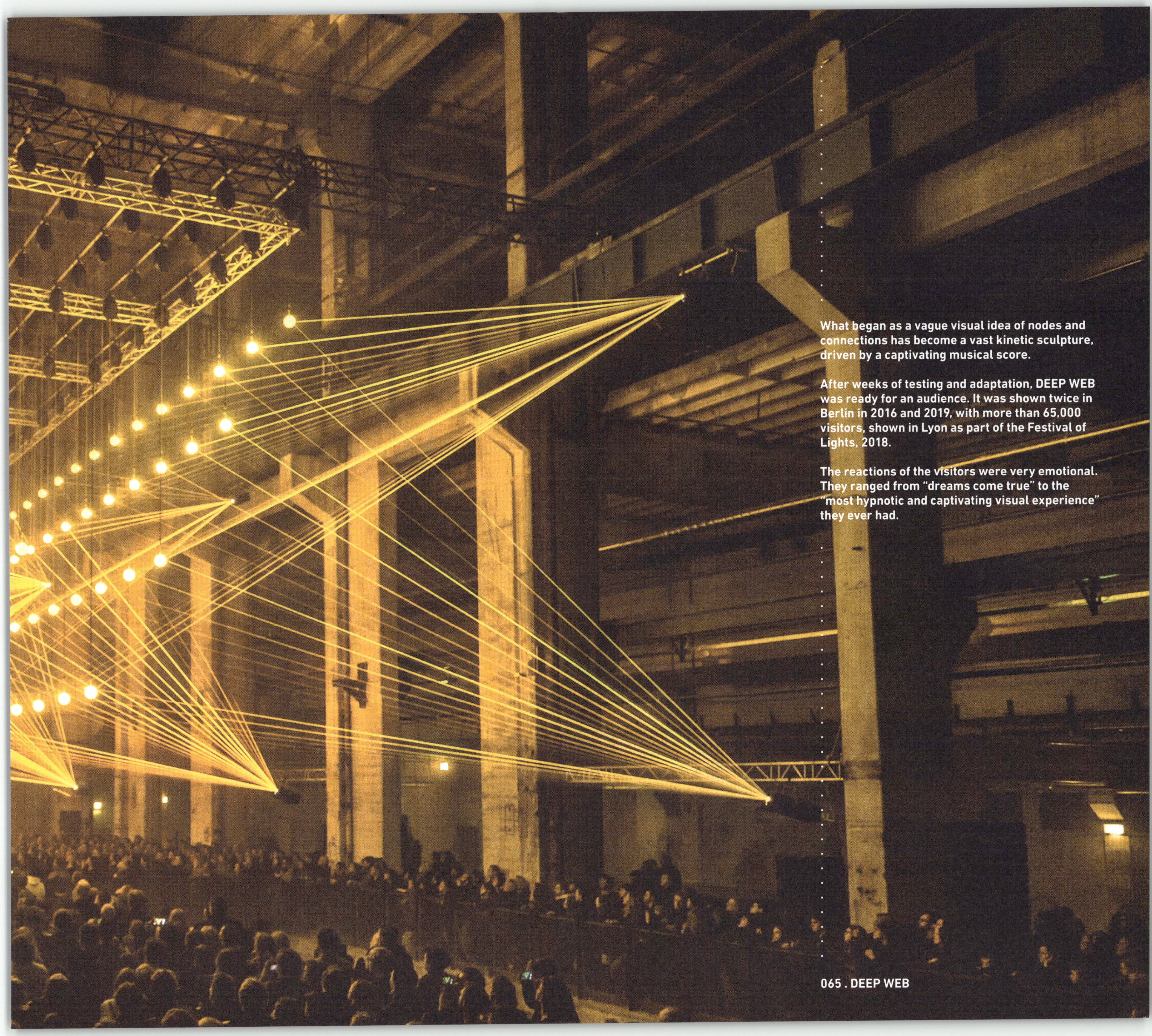

What began as a vague visual idea of nodes and connections has become a vast kinetic sculpture, driven by a captivating musical score.

After weeks of testing and adaptation, DEEP WEB was ready for an audience. It was shown twice in Berlin in 2016 and 2019, with more than 65,000 visitors, shown in Lyon as part of the Festival of Lights, 2018.

The reactions of the visitors were very emotional. They ranged from “dreams come true” to the “most hypnotic and captivating visual experience” they ever had.

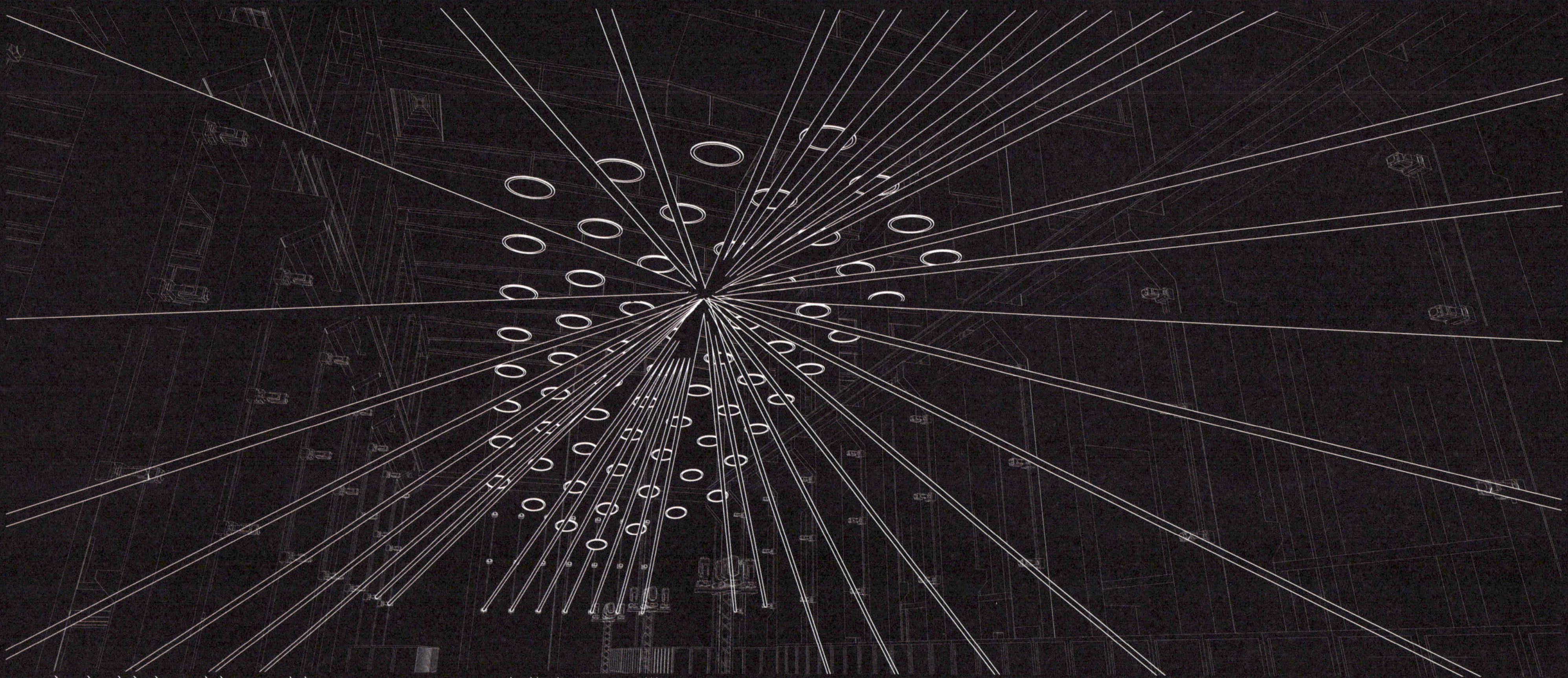

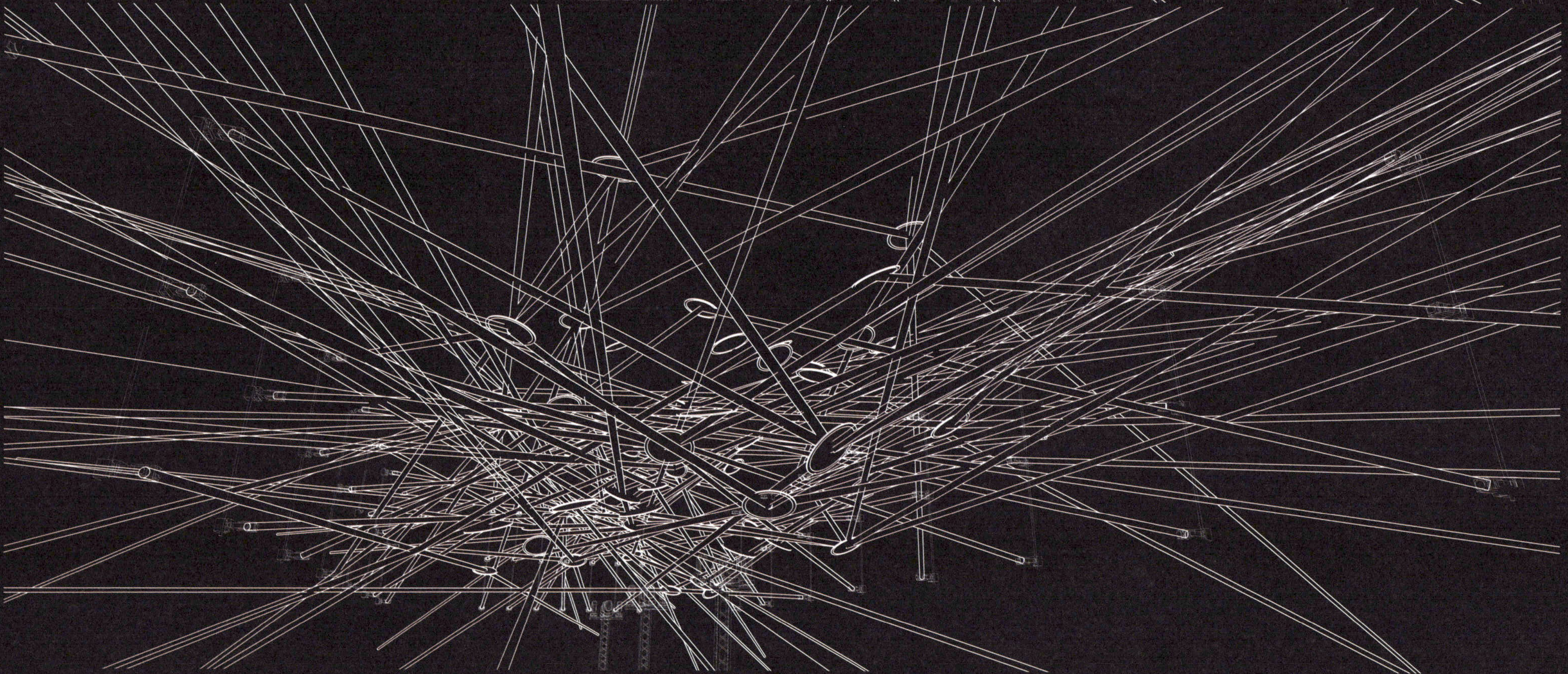

066 . Christopher Bauder and David Letellier

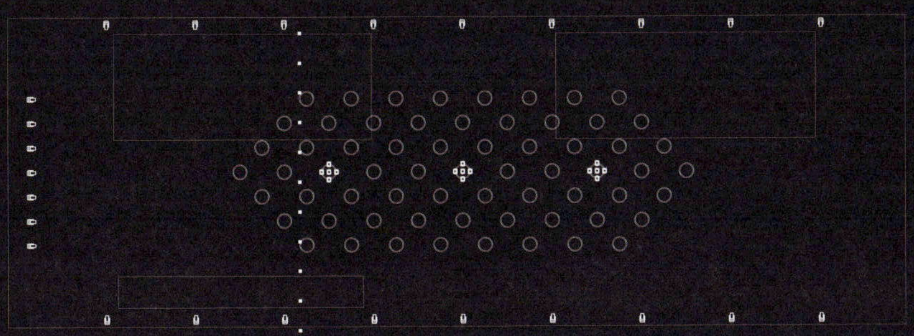

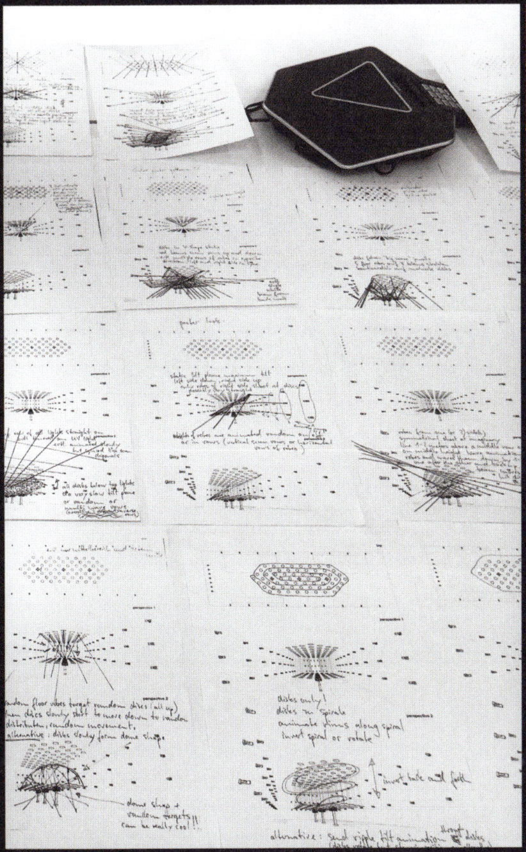

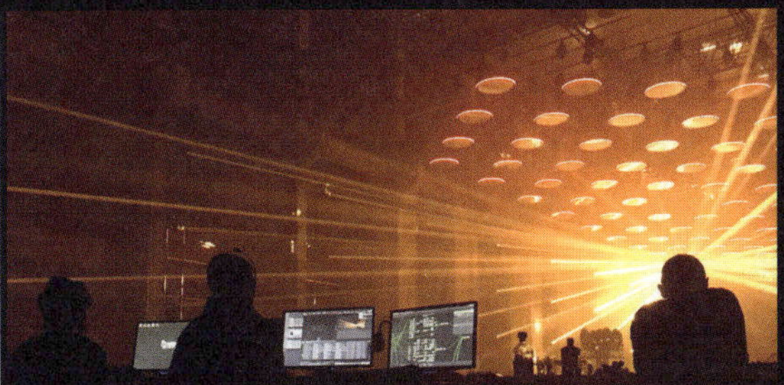

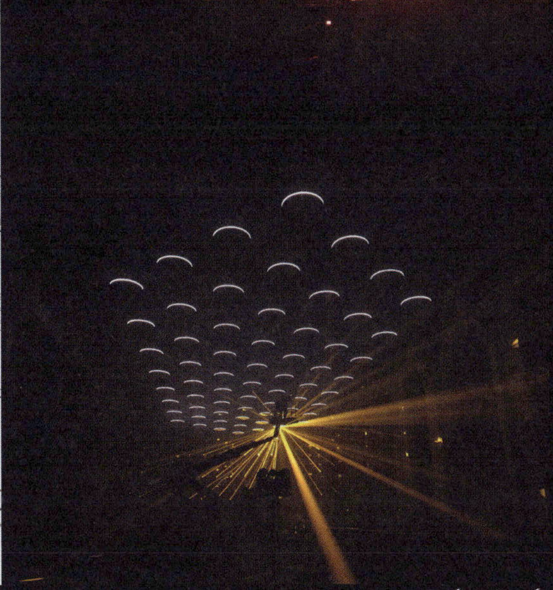

SKALAR is a large-scale art installation by light artist Christopher Bauder and musician David Letellier (aka Kangding Ray) that deals with the complex effects of light and sound on human perception.

By combining many kinetic mirrors, perfectly synchronized moving lights, and a sophisticated sound system, SKALAR reflects the primary purpose and nature of human emotions.

Christopher Bauder and Kangding Ray were introduced to each other by a mutual friend, which led to the joint development of the project just a few months after their first encounter at a festival in Belgium.

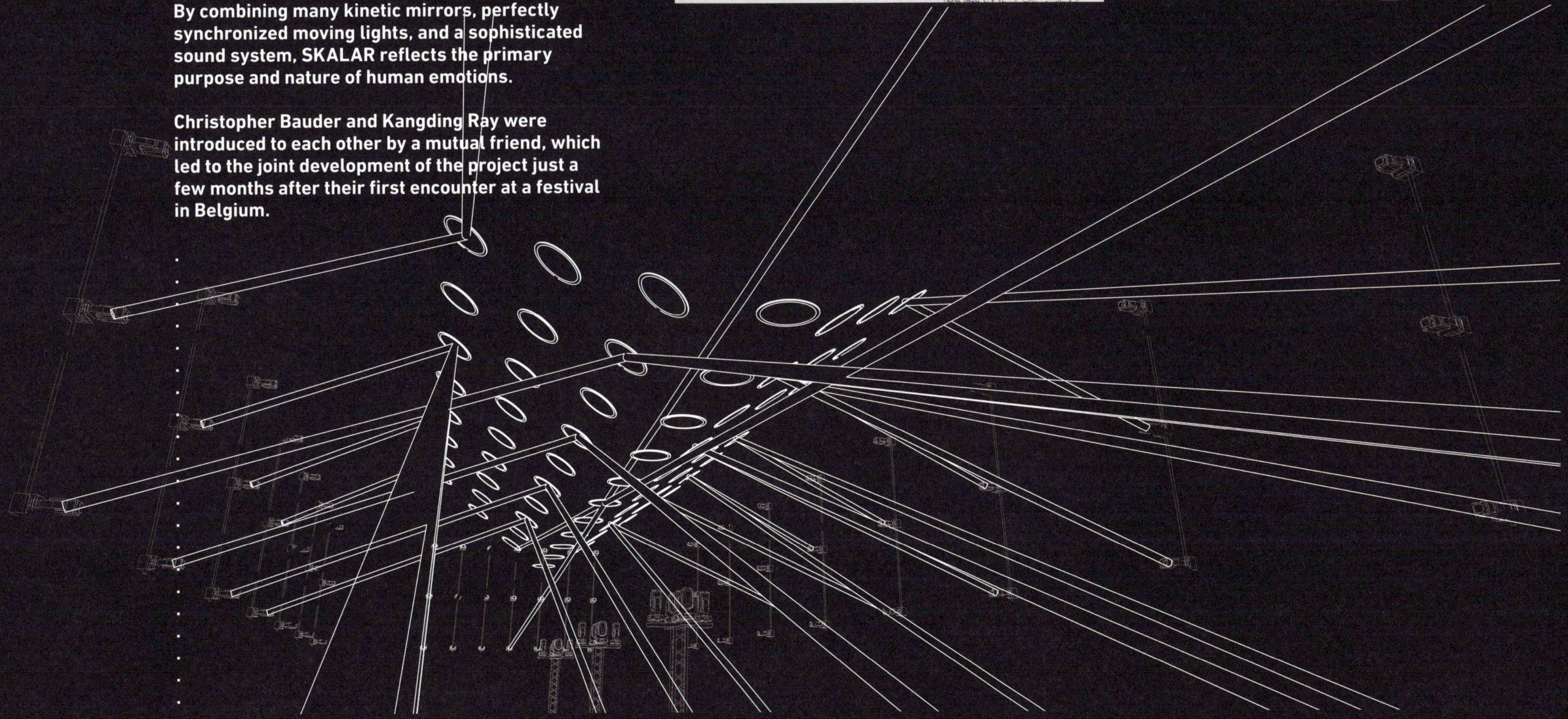

067 . SKALAR

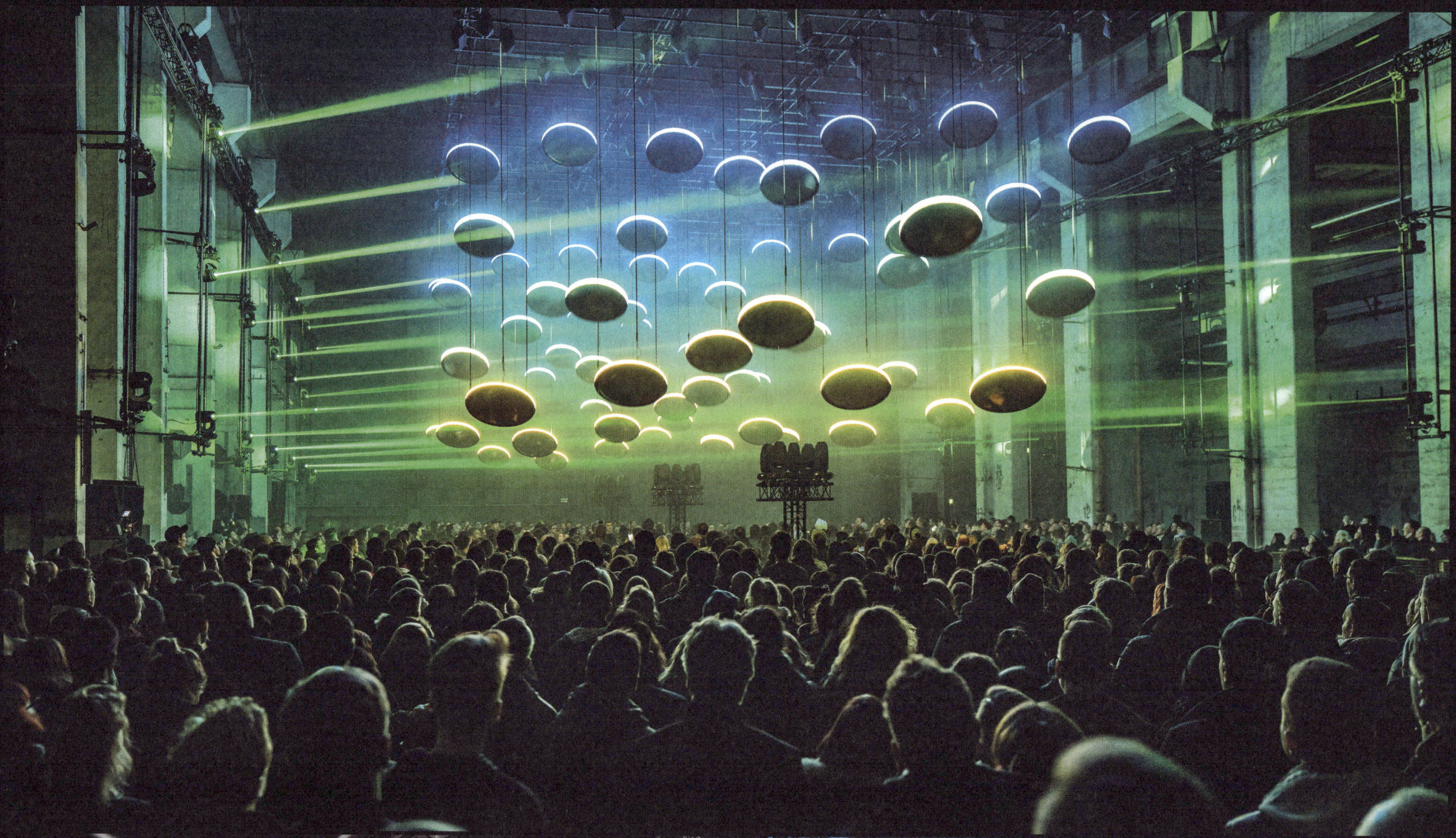

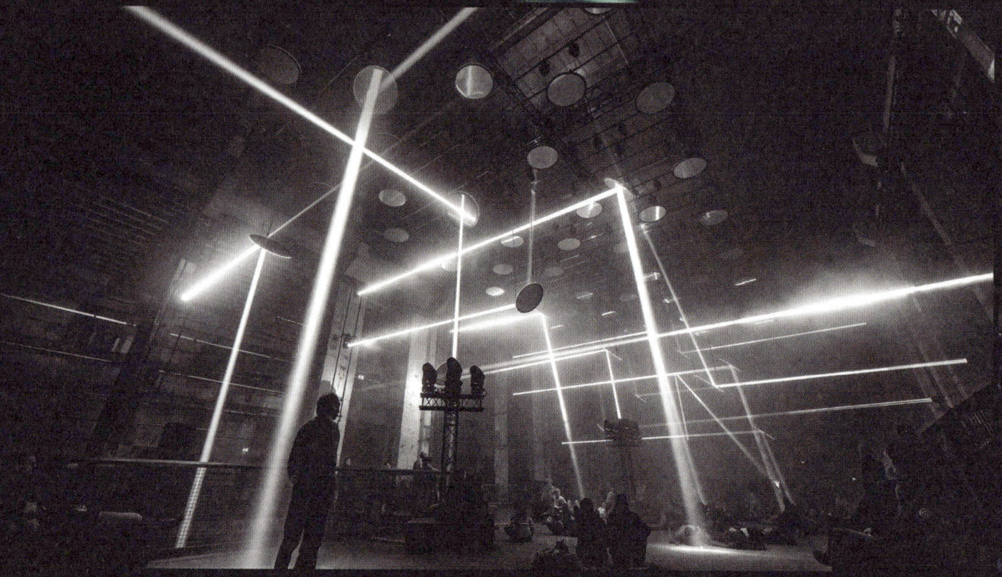

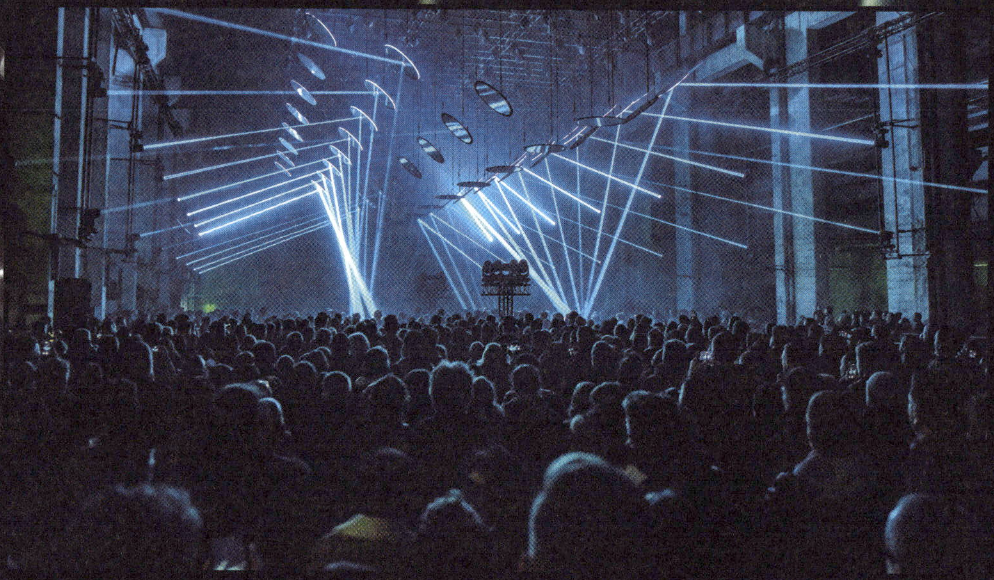

068 . Christopher Bauder and David Letellier

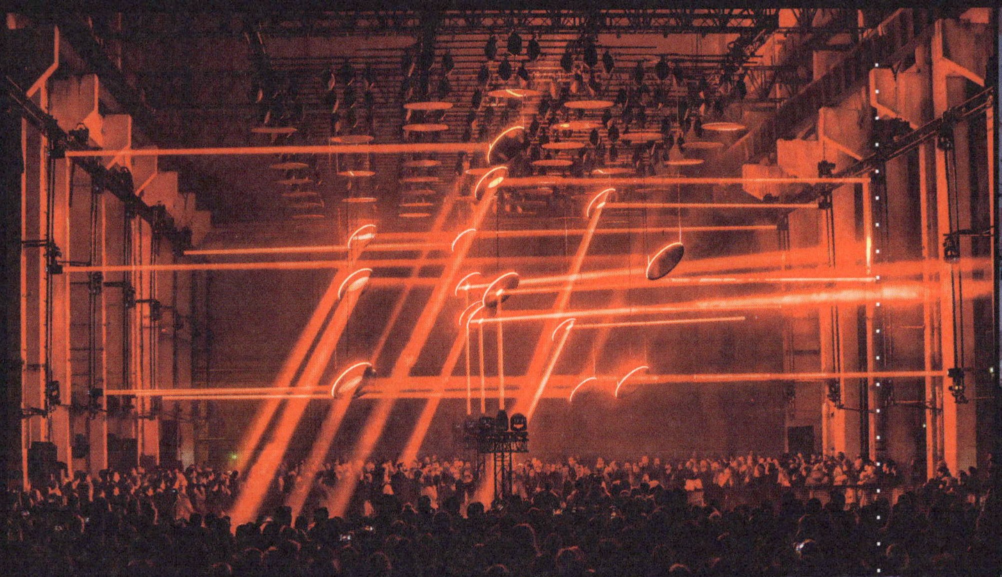

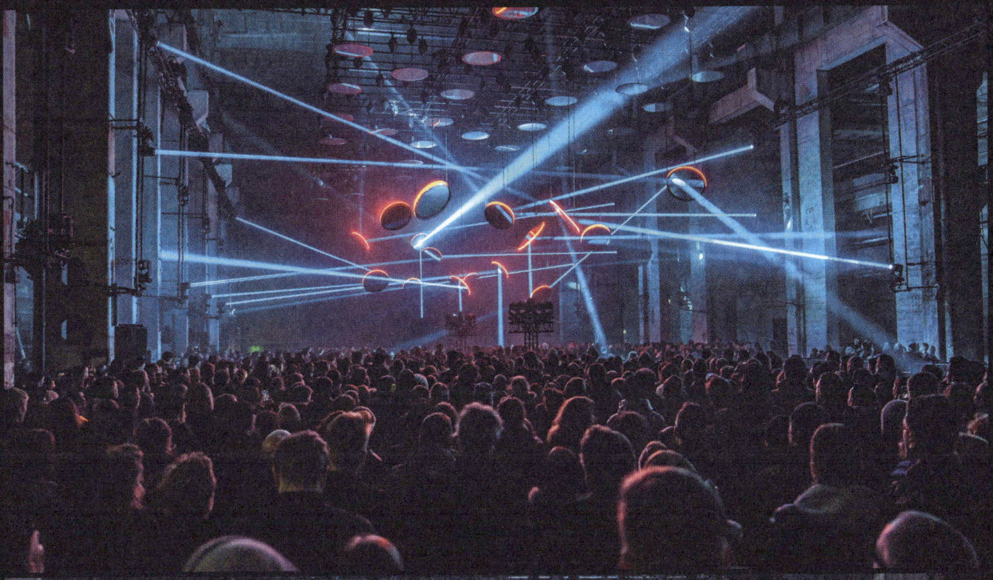

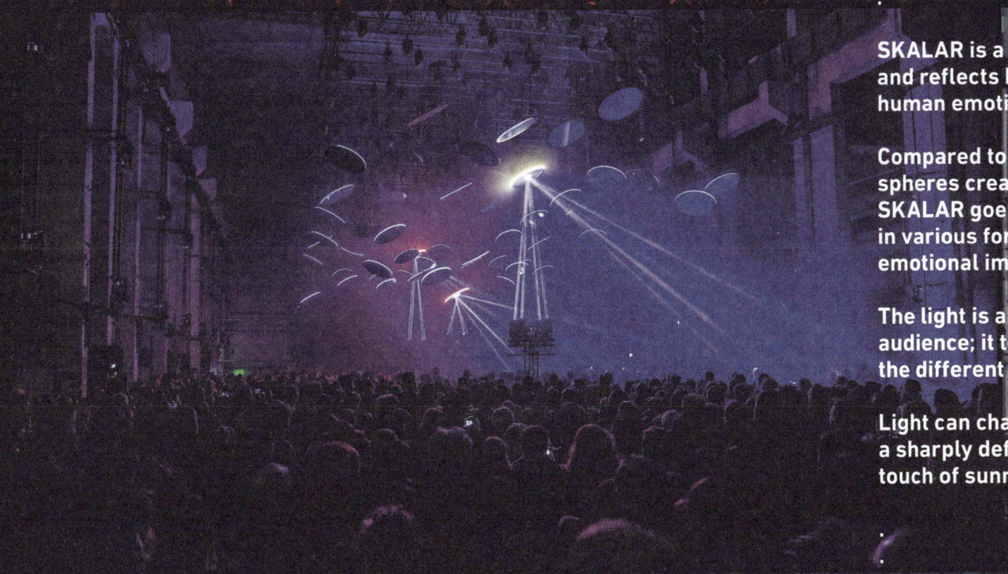

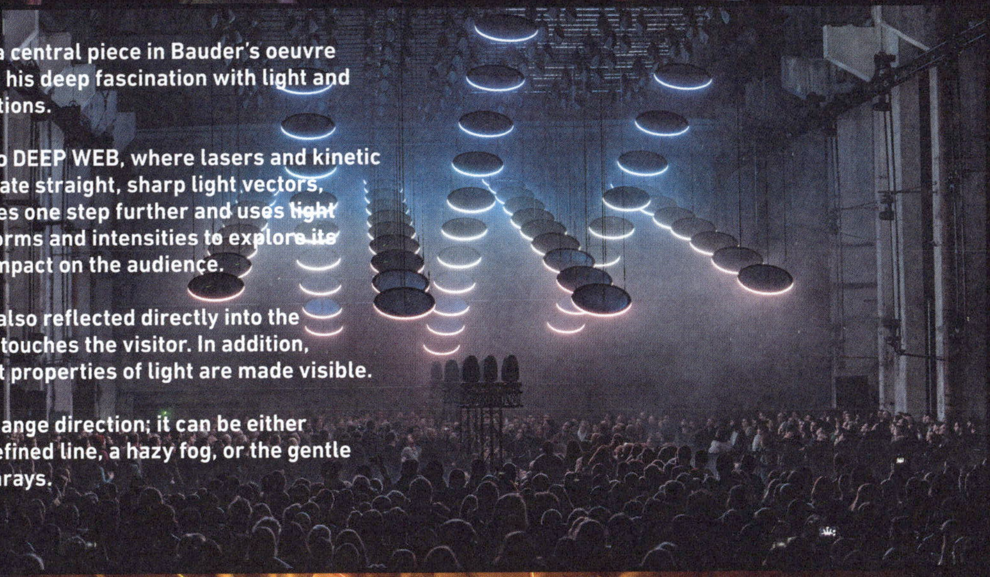

SKALAR is a central piece in Bauder's oeuvre and reflects his deep fascination with light and human emotions.

Compared to DEEP WEB, where lasers and kinetic spheres create straight, sharp light vectors, SKALAR goes one step further and uses light in various forms and intensities to explore its emotional impact on the audience.

The light is also reflected directly into the audience; it touches the visitor. In addition, the different properties of light are made visible.

Light can change direction; it can be either a sharply defined line, a hazy fog, or the gentle touch of sunrays.

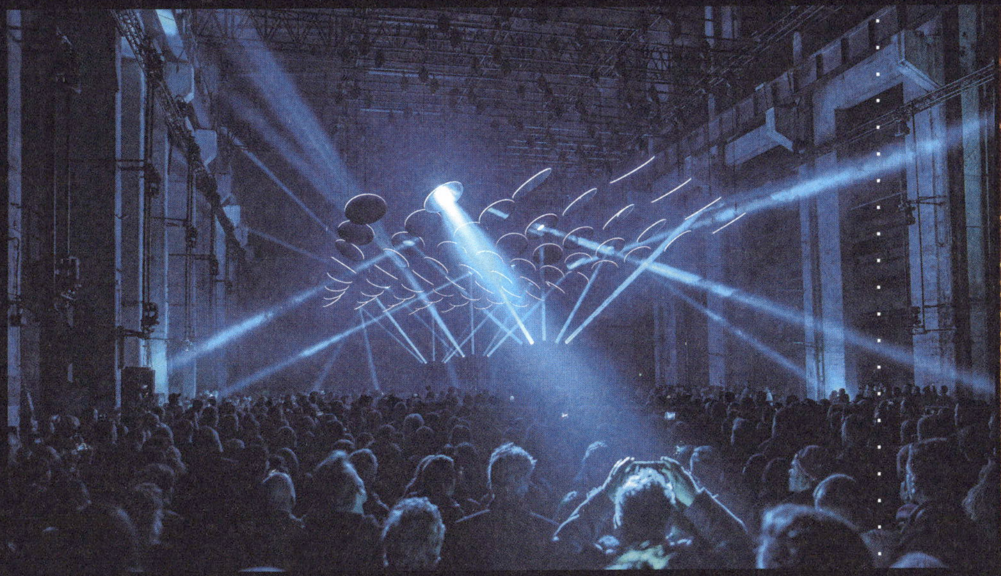

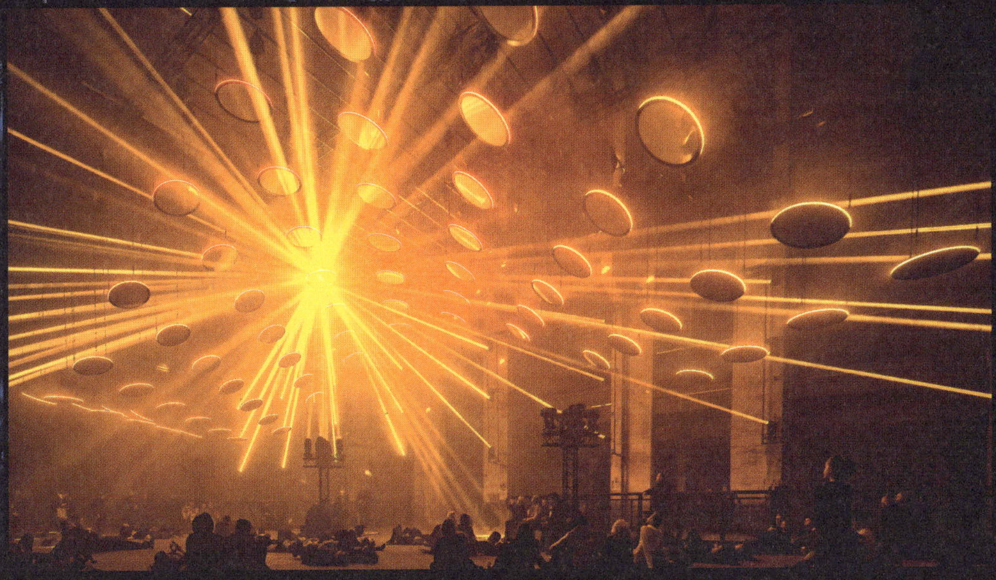

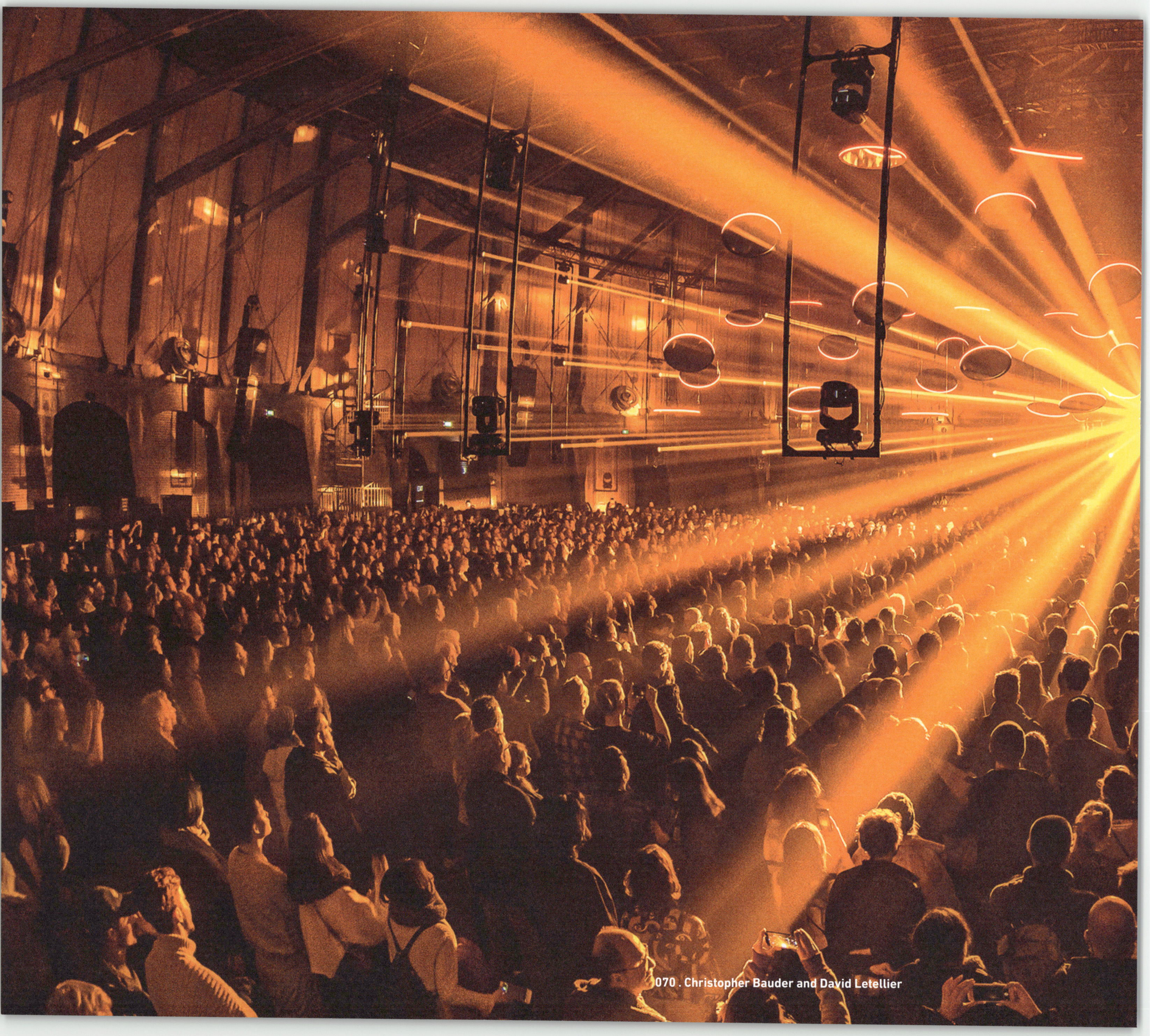

070 . Christopher Bauder and David Letellier

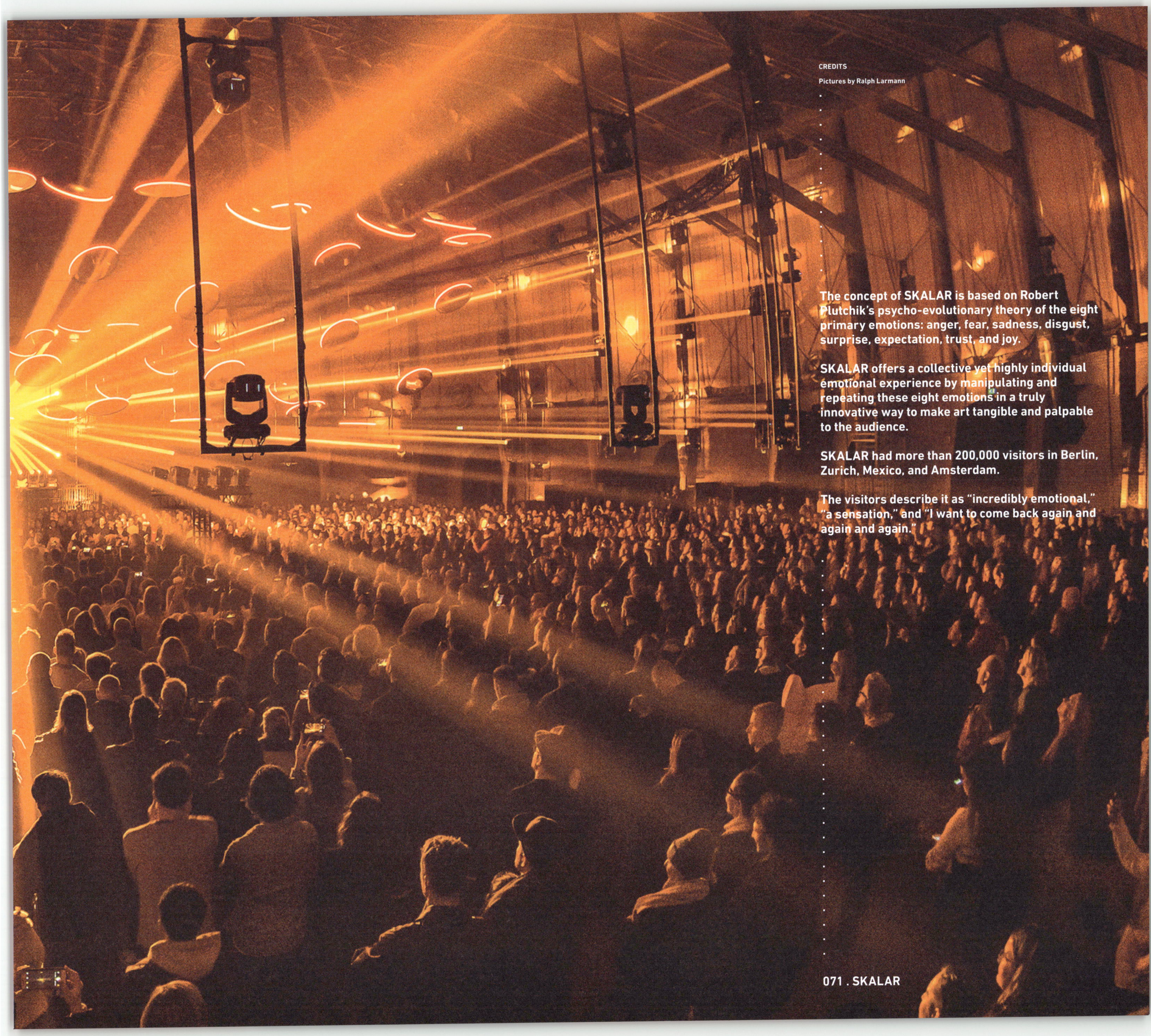

CREDITS

Pictures by Ralph Larmann

The concept of SKALAR is based on Robert Plutchik's psycho-evolutionary theory of the eight primary emotions: anger, fear, sadness, disgust, surprise, expectation, trust, and joy.

SKALAR offers a collective yet highly individual emotional experience by manipulating and repeating these eight emotions in a truly innovative way to make art tangible and palpable to the audience.

SKALAR had more than 200,000 visitors in Berlin, Zurich, Mexico, and Amsterdam.

The visitors describe it as "incredibly emotional," "a sensation," and "I want to come back again and again and again."

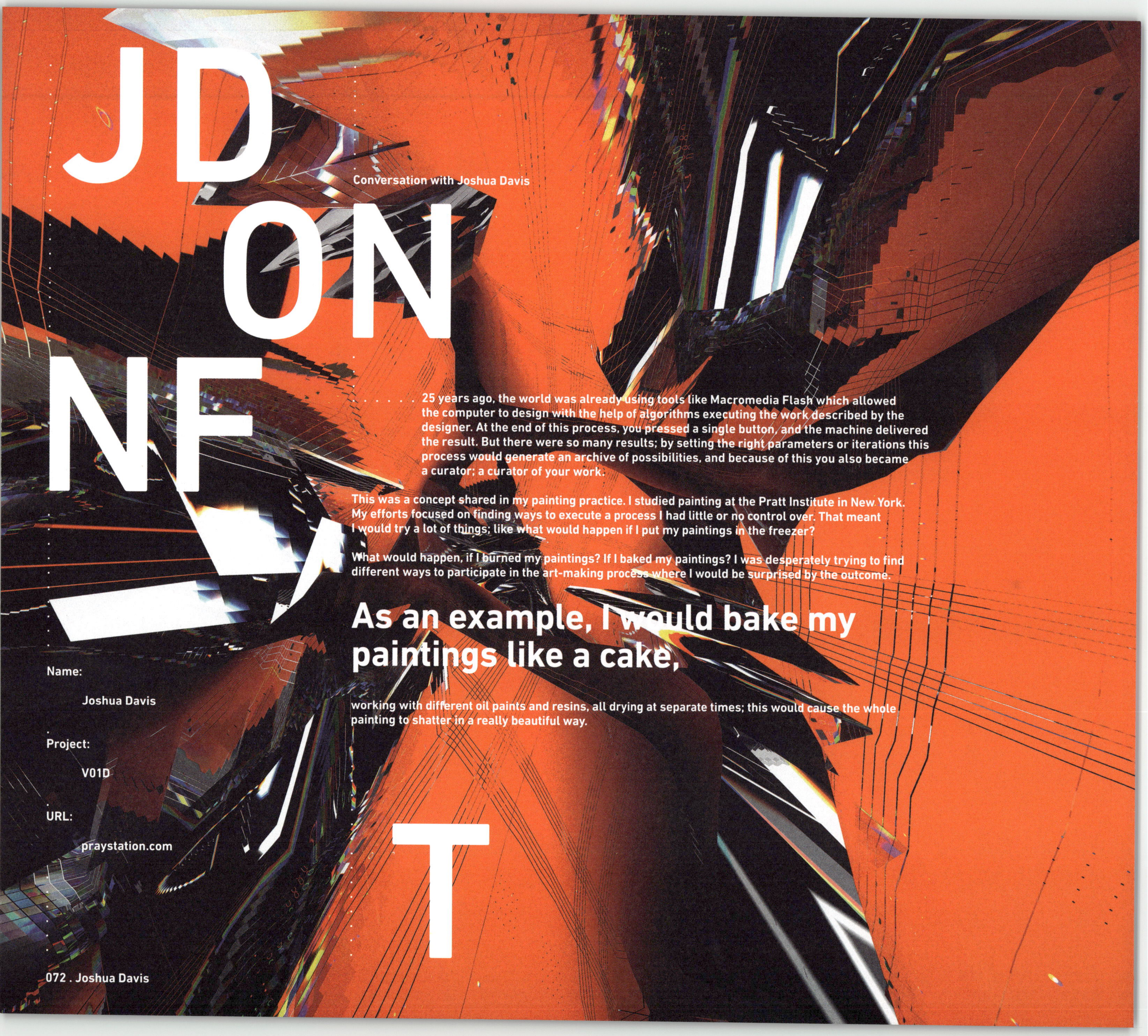

JD ON NF T

Conversation with Joshua Davis

25 years ago, the world was already using tools like Macromedia Flash which allowed the computer to design with the help of algorithms executing the work described by the designer. At the end of this process, you pressed a single button, and the machine delivered the result. But there were so many results; by setting the right parameters or iterations this process would generate an archive of possibilities, and because of this you also became a curator; a curator of your work.

This was a concept shared in my painting practice. I studied painting at the Pratt Institute in New York. My efforts focused on finding ways to execute a process I had little or no control over. That meant I would try a lot of things; like what would happen if I put my paintings in the freezer?

What would happen, if I burned my paintings? If I baked my paintings? I was desperately trying to find different ways to participate in the art-making process where I would be surprised by the outcome.

As an example, I would bake my paintings like a cake,

working with different oil paints and resins, all drying at separate times; this would cause the whole painting to shatter in a really beautiful way.

Name:

Joshua Davis

Project:

V01D

URL:

praystation.com

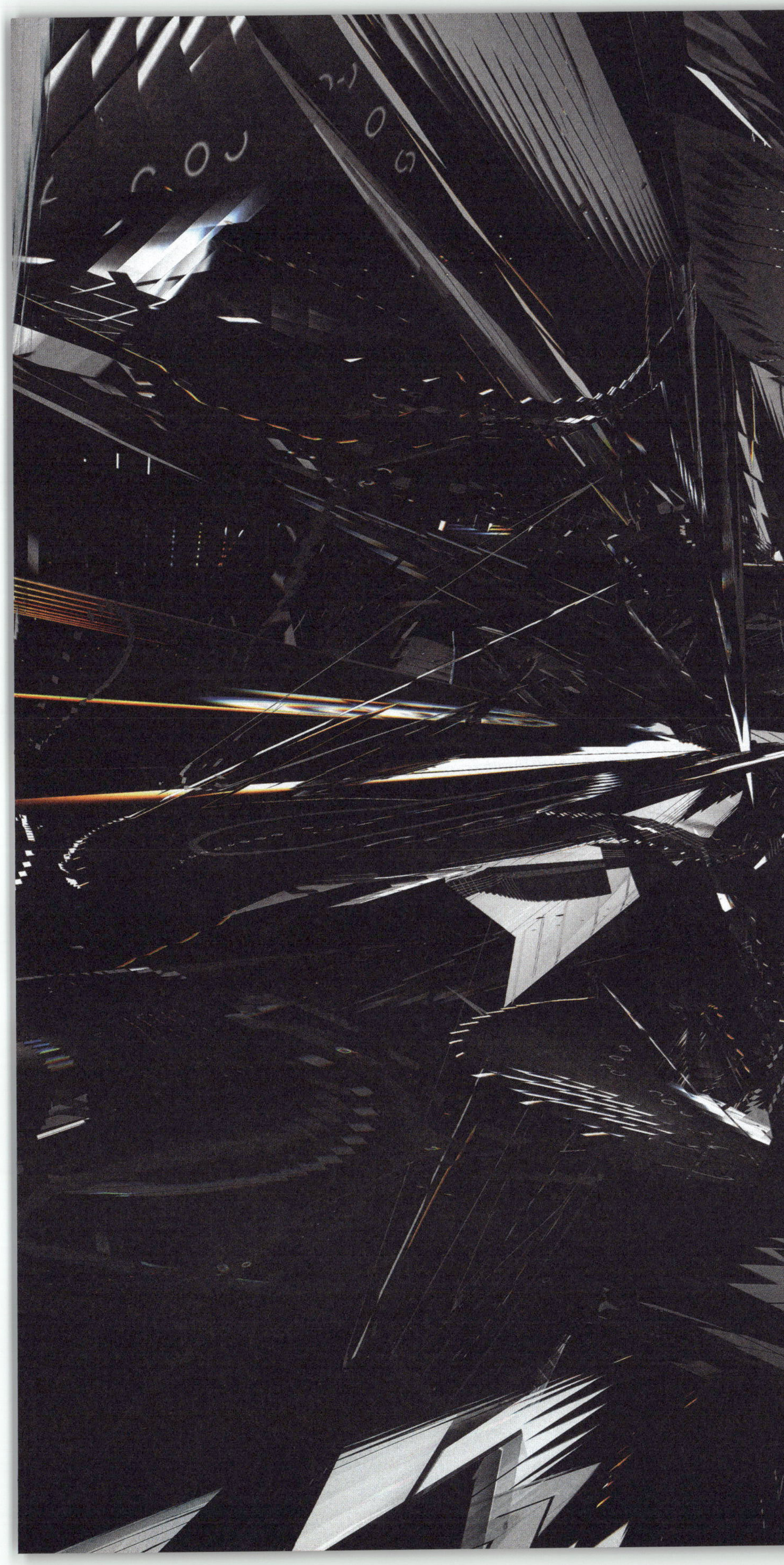

The problem was; if you were executing a system over which you have no control over, you were going to get a variable set of results. And these results would fluctuate in the desired outcome. In some cases, I would get significant cracks, in other paintings, really small, underwhelming cracks.

Sometimes I wanted the bigger ones and not the smaller ones, but I could never control it. As a result, this process would see the loss of a lot of artwork and undesirable product.

When I started to learn how to program in 1995, just before the days of Macromedia Flash, I started on Linux with JavaScript. Once I found Flash, I left JavaScript as I found Flash a little easier; as long as everybody had the plugin, they could see what I had intended. When it came to browsers, there was only really two, Netscape and Internet Explorer. Writing code on browsers at this point would give you different results on different platforms. That frustrated me, and so, this was another reason why I made the move to Flash. Even after making the move, I was still fascinated with this idea of executing a system that I didn't have complete control over, and an output that would lead to some sort of randomness.

So the concept I took from my painting practice, transfers well to programming. The trick is, that if you are executing a system that is going to produce unexpected results, at some point you have to say: "okay, how many iterations of this thing do I want, and which ones do I deem most beautiful?" And 26 years later, I'm still doing the same shit. But I'm using a different programming language.

Right now I am exploring NFTs generating 2,000 outputs at a time. Then I have to go through that curatorial process of which are the most beautiful and interesting? So it isn't much different to looking at those paintings, except for those works took considerably a lot longer to paint; and if it didn't achieve the desired result, I had to redo the same painting again and again. So, it was only natural that I would say goodbye to painting and fully embrace the programming. Because I could execute that concept exponentially in a very small amount of time. I could write a program that says, "give me 2,000 images," and then I could just sit back and drink a coffee in my backyard.

That's where the whole idea comes from. But what's fascinating is, that not only did I have to be the designer, I had to be the programmer to program the designer, and then, in the end, I would take on the role of curator and critic, surveying all of the work generated by my little computer minions.

I sort of deem like, that one's beautiful, this is the one I want to share with the public.

It's an interesting concept, especially in this NFT space, because when people are looking at my work, they may be looking at a singular image. The reality is, I have made approximately 4,000 images over one week, just to find that one that I deem exceptional, and unfortunately, the 3,999 remaining images hit the trash.

Back in the day, you made impressive work, you were celebrated by the community, then you got attention from the brands, you work for the brands, you get more attention from the community, so you generated your value. But can you say that looking at NFTs, what does it become? Is there a fair and equal payment system in favor of the artist and how do you describe the whole process?

Do you need to?

These are challenging and acceptable questions to ask. I didn't think in my lifetime, I would see this happen. It took 70 years for photography to be considered an art form. This digital art some of us were making outside of the client work; I thought maybe at some point, the art world would find interesting, but I certainly thought I would be dead by then.

I have taken a modest path.

I don't have a studio; I don't have any employees; It's just Joshua Davis. This was a conscious decision after several conversations with Stefan Sagmeister. I became friends with Stefan some years ago and ended up talking to him about what was important. In my mind, I thought, you were supposed to make a name for yourself, get clients and start a studio with employees.

And from a distance, I saw a lot of my friends do this but ultimately becoming unhappy in the long term. The reason for their unhappiness was that they were no longer creating, they were managing people who were doing the creating, so I said to Stefan;

"I have this idea of what I think I'm supposed to be doing, but I feel uncomfortable about it." Over lunch, I think in Sintra, Portugal Stefan and I had a real heart to heart, and he said; "Listen... there are people who are going to take that path, and they're going to make a lot more money than you, but they're probably going to be miserable.

What you can do is take on the product, you can determine how much money you need to make a year. It's probably going to be pretty modest, but you'll be able to pay your rent, buy food, clothing, and stuff you need.

You'll most likely be the happiest because you only have to work on a few projects a year you enjoy."

Since then, I now only do one to three projects a year and those projects are with big brands. They are with the likes of the Pepsis and the Nikes, and musicians, and these clients approach me because I have worked on a visual language that they are interested in. "Oh; here's a guy that's doing interesting things. Let's hire him." Then you are brought in to make things you would make, but for that particular brand. Not to speak ill of my clients, but it's not always going to be something that I 100% love; because and I am going to have to make some sacrifices and compromise because it was for a client. But, by doing one to three projects a year, I could make enough money to pay my mortgage, buy food and support my family and I wasn't going to get super-rich.

I could now spend the rest of the time doing the stuff I loved.

People would ask; "how are you able to put just these weird things on Twitter and Instagram?"

It's because that's the kind of stuff I enjoy making, and I want to make this stuff. I am compelled to create this work, and because I have made enough money to sustain a comfortable lifestyle for the year, I can now spend time making the work that I want to make, without having to put a logo on it, or have a team of people make the work, not as good.

When NFTs came along, that was a real epiphany.

It's not that the art market and collectors couldn't acquire digital art, until recently there was no way of assigning rarity or any real value to the work. What the NFT's market does, is deliver in many different ways.

They satisfy certificate of authenticity, guaranteeing the work is made by said artist. When somebody buys a work, they know, it's from Joshua Davis. Just like if you owned and wanted to sell a Picasso. First, you would have to get it authenticated confirming you weren't trying to sell a forgery.

I know that this has been something people struggled with for some time, but the conversation is really easy.

Imagine if I were to go into my computer right now; type in the Mona Lisa and copy that photo onto my desktop. I print out the picture at the same size as that of the Mona Lisa, and I hang it in my house.

I think me and you know that somebody coming into my house is not going to say – "holy shit! you have the Mona Lisa!" It's a copy. It's a copy of an original. The original is hanging in the Louvre in Paris. So, we already understand the concept of what is an original and what is a copy. We also understand in the music business, there's this idea of a master.

There is a master recording, and from that, many copies are made. Those copies end up becoming MP3s; compressed data you listen to on Spotify or CD ROMs for example.

The NFT concept is also validating the process of how the work is made, that original Mona Lisa, that original recording of the Beatles; the data is uploaded onto a blockchain and authenticated.

This is the original file. As an example, if anyone were to pull up that original file, copy and save it onto their desktop, they just made a copy. They made a copy of the original.

This has been, and still is a hard topic for people to wrap their heads around. "Oh, well, you know, the Mona Lisa, painted on wood or whatever the fuck it is." But the Mona Lisa is just an arrangement of colors in a rectangle.

It is no different than the arrangement of colors in a rectangle I would create in Photoshop or Illustrator. The concept and reality of NFTs are fascinating because we now have a way of assigning a certificate of authenticity. We also have a way to confirm the origins of a piece of digital artwork, and what that means is that buying digital artwork is no different to buying a painting. A collector can now buy a piece of digital work made by a digital creator in the digital medium.

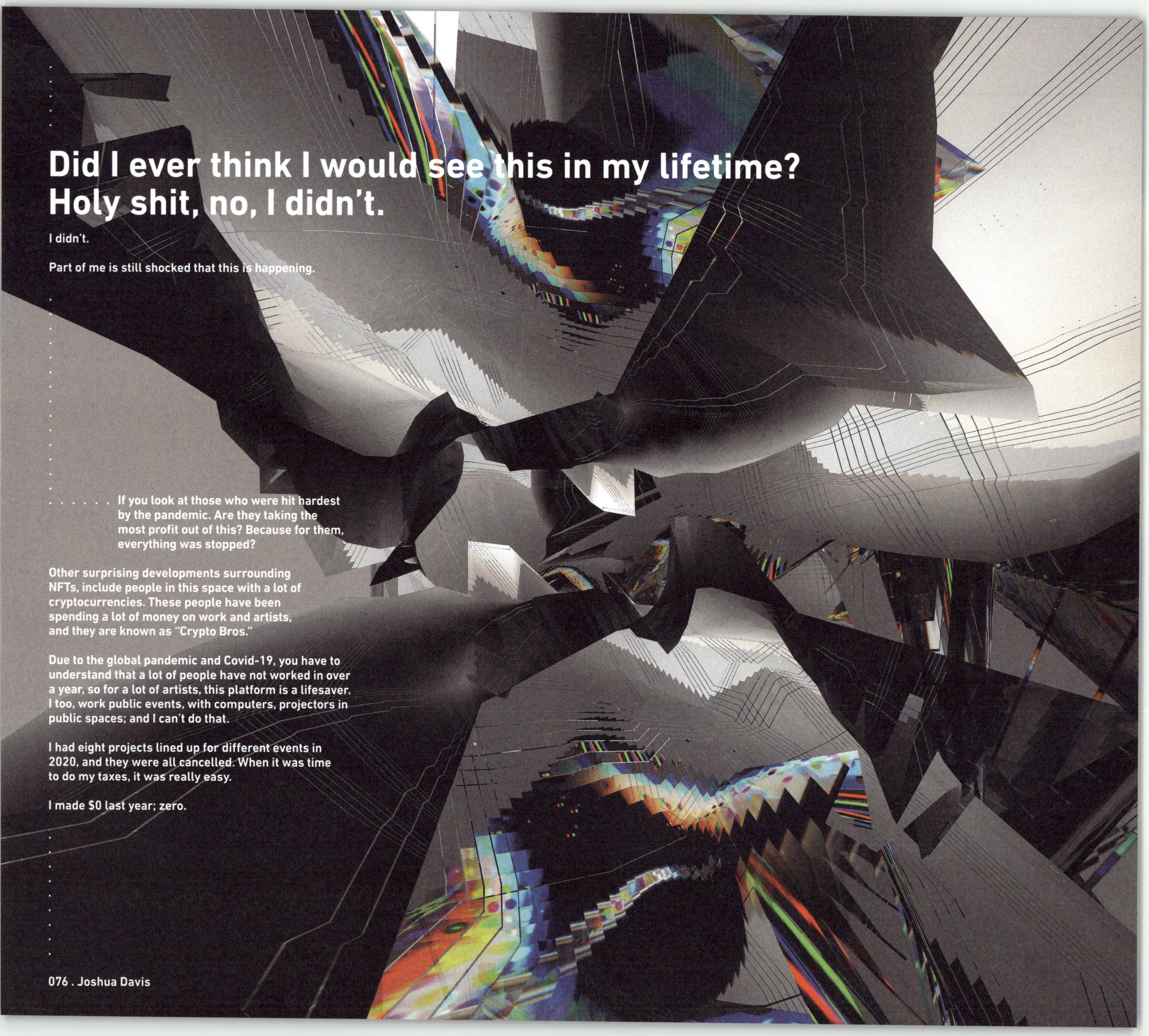

Did I ever think I would see this in my lifetime? Holy shit, no, I didn't.

I didn't.

Part of me is still shocked that this is happening.

If you look at those who were hit hardest by the pandemic. Are they taking the most profit out of this? Because for them, everything was stopped?

Other surprising developments surrounding NFTs, include people in this space with a lot of cryptocurrencies. These people have been spending a lot of money on work and artists, and they are known as "Crypto Bros."

Due to the global pandemic and Covid-19, you have to understand that a lot of people have not worked in over a year, so for a lot of artists, this platform is a lifesaver. I too, work public events, with computers, projectors in public spaces; and I can't do that.

I had eight projects lined up for different events in 2020, and they were all cancelled. When it was time to do my taxes, it was really easy.

I made $0 last year; zero.

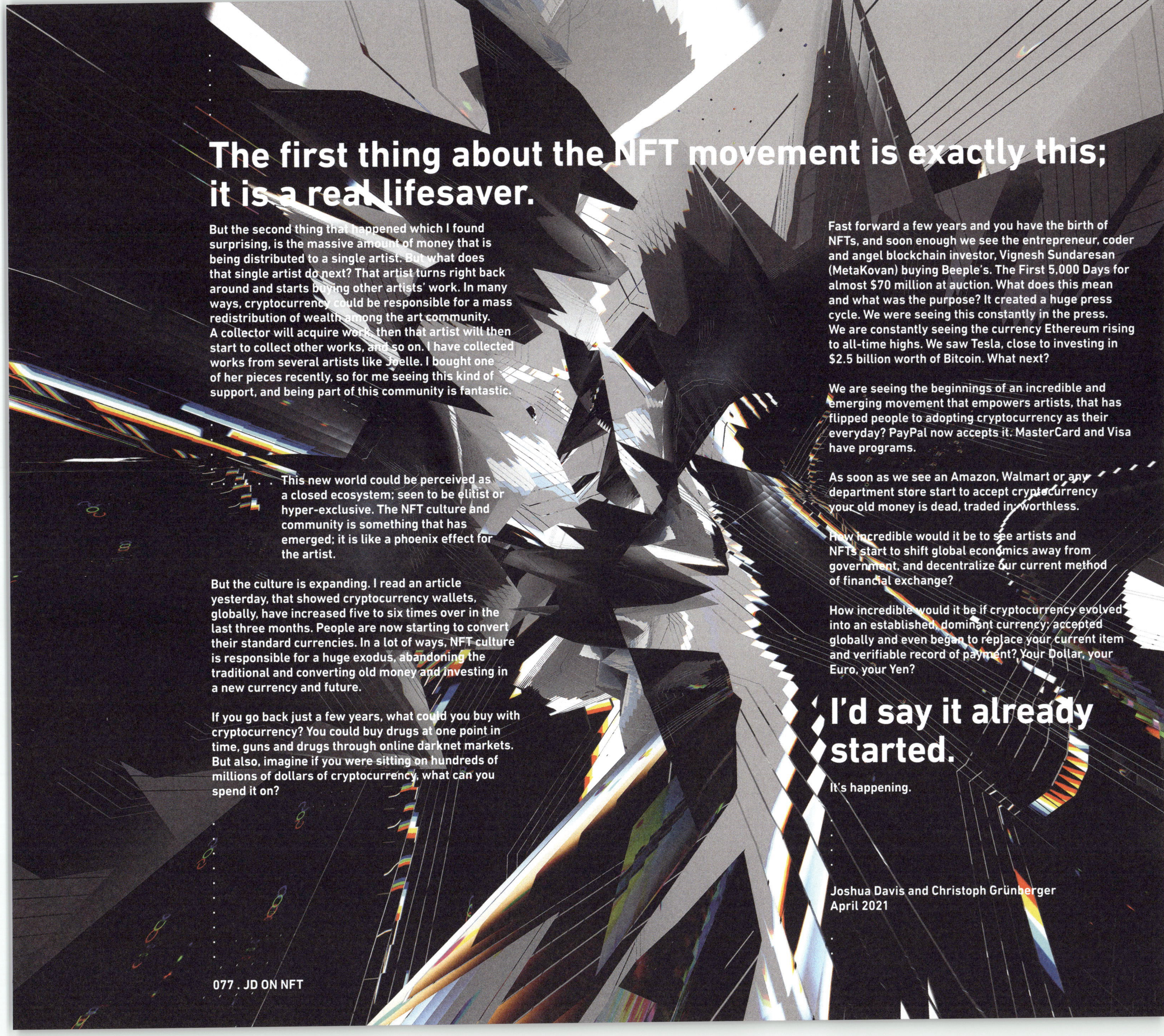

The first thing about the NFT movement is exactly this; it is a real lifesaver.

But the second thing that happened which I found surprising, is the massive amount of money that is being distributed to a single artist. But what does that single artist do next? That artist turns right back around and starts buying other artists' work. In many ways, cryptocurrency could be responsible for a mass redistribution of wealth among the art community. A collector will acquire work, then that artist will then start to collect other works, and so on. I have collected works from several artists like Joelle. I bought one of her pieces recently, so for me seeing this kind of support, and being part of this community is fantastic.

This new world could be perceived as a closed ecosystem; seen to be elitist or hyper-exclusive. The NFT culture and community is something that has emerged; it is like a phoenix effect for the artist.

But the culture is expanding. I read an article yesterday, that showed cryptocurrency wallets, globally, have increased five to six times over in the last three months. People are now starting to convert their standard currencies. In a lot of ways, NFT culture is responsible for a huge exodus, abandoning the traditional and converting old money and investing in a new currency and future.

If you go back just a few years, what could you buy with cryptocurrency? You could buy drugs at one point in time, guns and drugs through online darknet markets. But also, imagine if you were sitting on hundreds of millions of dollars of cryptocurrency, what can you spend it on?

Fast forward a few years and you have the birth of NFTs, and soon enough we see the entrepreneur, coder and angel blockchain investor, Vignesh Sundaresan (MetaKovan) buying Beeple's. The First 5,000 Days for almost $70 million at auction. What does this mean and what was the purpose? It created a huge press cycle. We were seeing this constantly in the press. We are constantly seeing the currency Ethereum rising to all-time highs. We saw Tesla, close to investing in $2.5 billion worth of Bitcoin. What next?

We are seeing the beginnings of an incredible and emerging movement that empowers artists, that has flipped people to adopting cryptocurrency as their everyday? PayPal now accepts it. MasterCard and Visa have programs.

As soon as we see an Amazon, Walmart or any department store start to accept cryptocurrency your old money is dead, traded in; worthless.

How incredible would it be to see artists and NFTs start to shift global economics away from government, and decentralize our current method of financial exchange?

How incredible would it be if cryptocurrency evolved into an established, dominant currency; accepted globally and even began to replace your current item and verifiable record of payment? Your Dollar, your Euro, your Yen?

I'd say it already started.

It's happening.

Joshua Davis and Christoph Grünberger
April 2021

Name:

Brendan Dawes

Info:

Brendan Dawes is an artist based in the UK using generative processes involving data, machine learning, and algorithms to create interactive installations, electronic objects, online experiences, data visualizations, motion graphics, and imagery for screen and print.

His clients include Airbnb, Twitter, PWC, Google, Seagate, BBC, The Royal Shakespeare Company, The Atlantic, Bravo, M&C Saatchi, EE, Arup, Intel, Cancer Research UK, Mailchimp, Trend Micro, Deloitte, and many others.

Highlights include creating 99,999 generative snowflakes for the Winter 2020 limited edition release of Field Notes. A story-telling installation at the Sundance Film Festival for Airbnb; a generative installation for Twitter creating real-time digital creatures in response to tweets.

Project:

THE ART OF CYBERSECURITY

URL:

brendandawes.com

Instagram:

@brendandawes

Awards

Long-listed Lumen Art Prize 2019
Long-listed Information is Beautiful Awards 2019

Exhibitions

Brighton Digital Festival
Art Futura 2020
ZKM Season of Media Arts 2019

Project Description:

Beauty from cybersecurity data for Trend Micro Commissioned by McMillan for Trend Micro, THE ART OF CYBERSECURITY is a series of images, together with a 4K animation born from cybersecurity threat data.

The work features three main components; the threats, represented by black obelisk style objects, the system that detects and deals with these threats, characterized by an organic mesh-like structure.

Finally, creativity allows for flowing because the threats have been neutralized.

The main mesh shapes are formed from splitting the data into five different industries: media, banking, government, technology, and retail.

I then made a simple algorithm that would create a form based on these industries to make each mesh unique.

Each threat relates to a warning metric derived from the data, while metrics influence the flow patterns of the creativity strands in the data and the space carved from the form itself.

The work was first shown at the RSA Conference 2019 in San Francisco, then rolled out globally across the Trend Micro site and marketing materials.

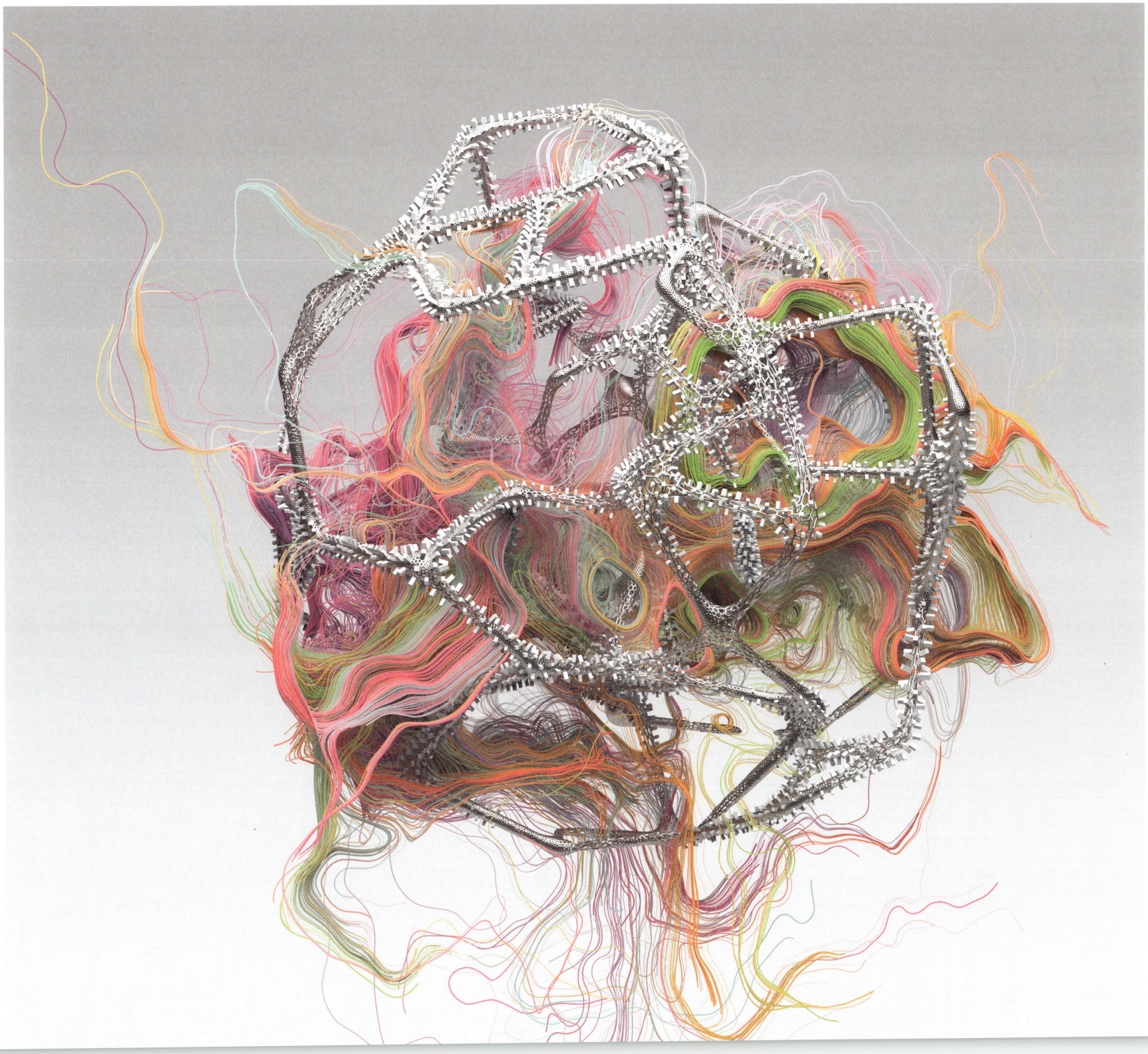

THE ART OF CYBERSECURITY

The Brief

Toronto-based agency McMillan made contact in early 2019 to ask if I would be interested in working with them on a campaign called THE ART OF CYBERSECURITY for Trend Micro.

Five other artists and I had been approached to make a piece of work from supplied cybersecurity threat data.

I, of course, said yes.

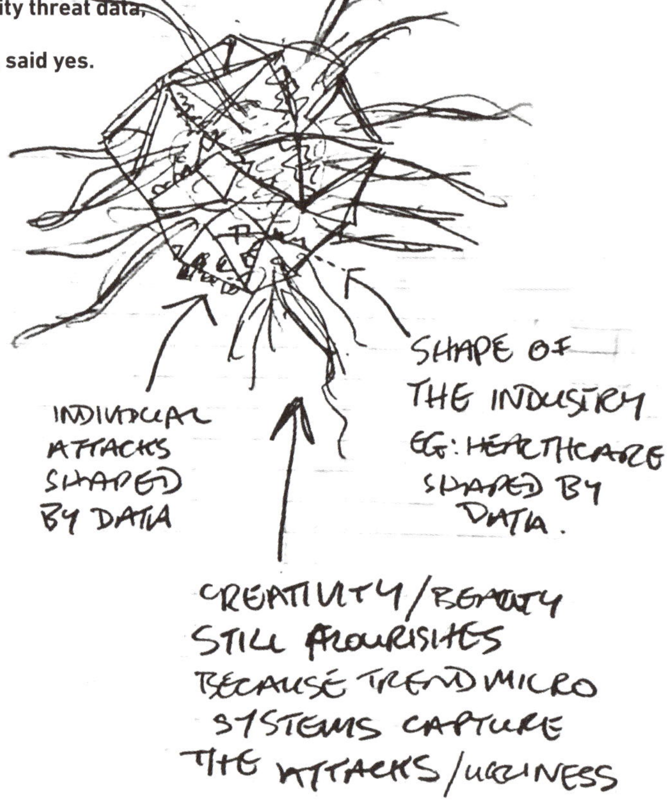

Sketches

Pencil and paper are still the best way for me to think when first starting a project. I love the freedom it allows me, the freedom I still don't find when using a digital equivalent.

There is no judgment applied to anything that appears on the paper at this stage, just allowing me to throw thoughts down to see what ideas might start to emerge.

For inspiration, I began to look at organic structures in nature, from deep-sea creatures to flowers, looking at their geometric systems.

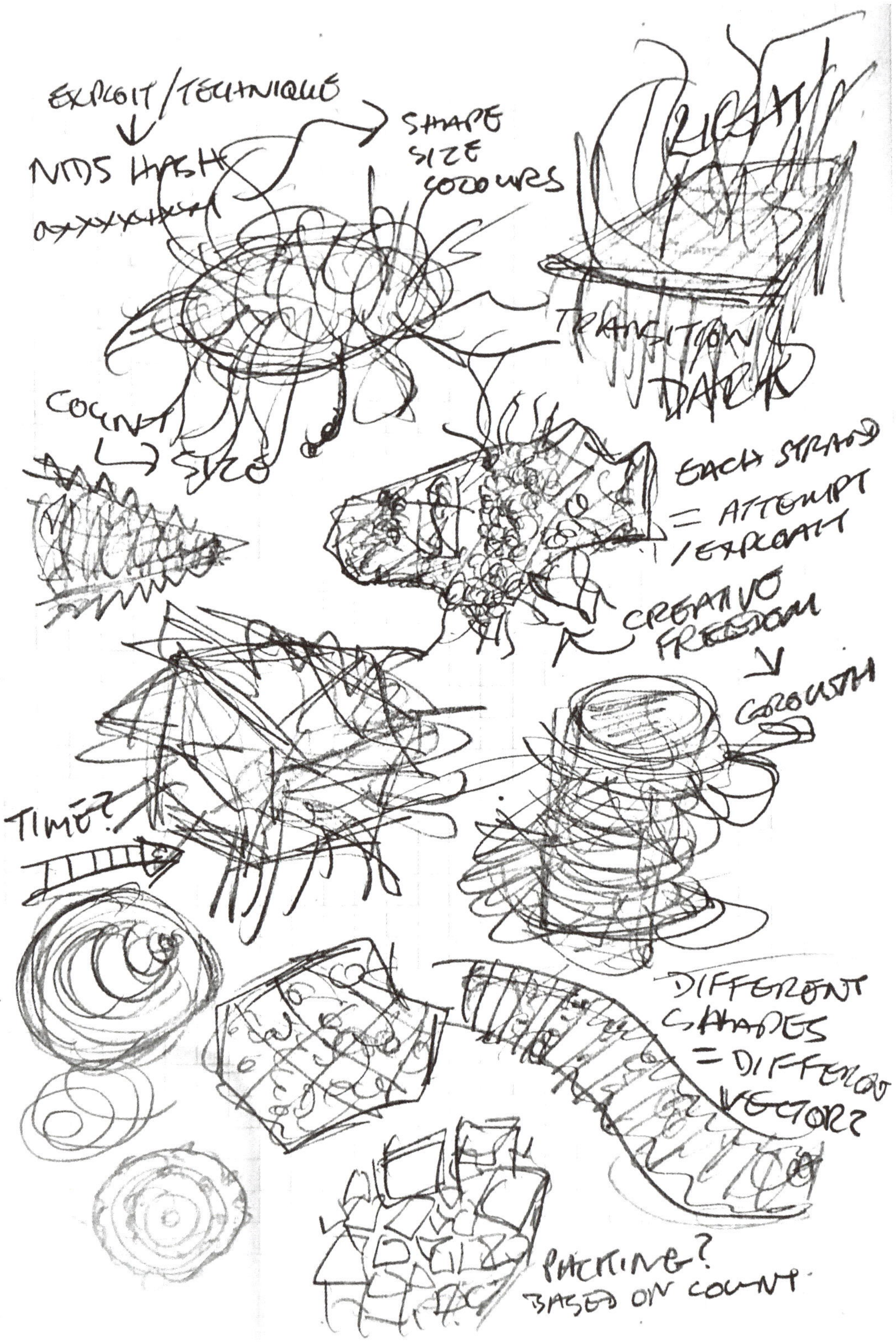

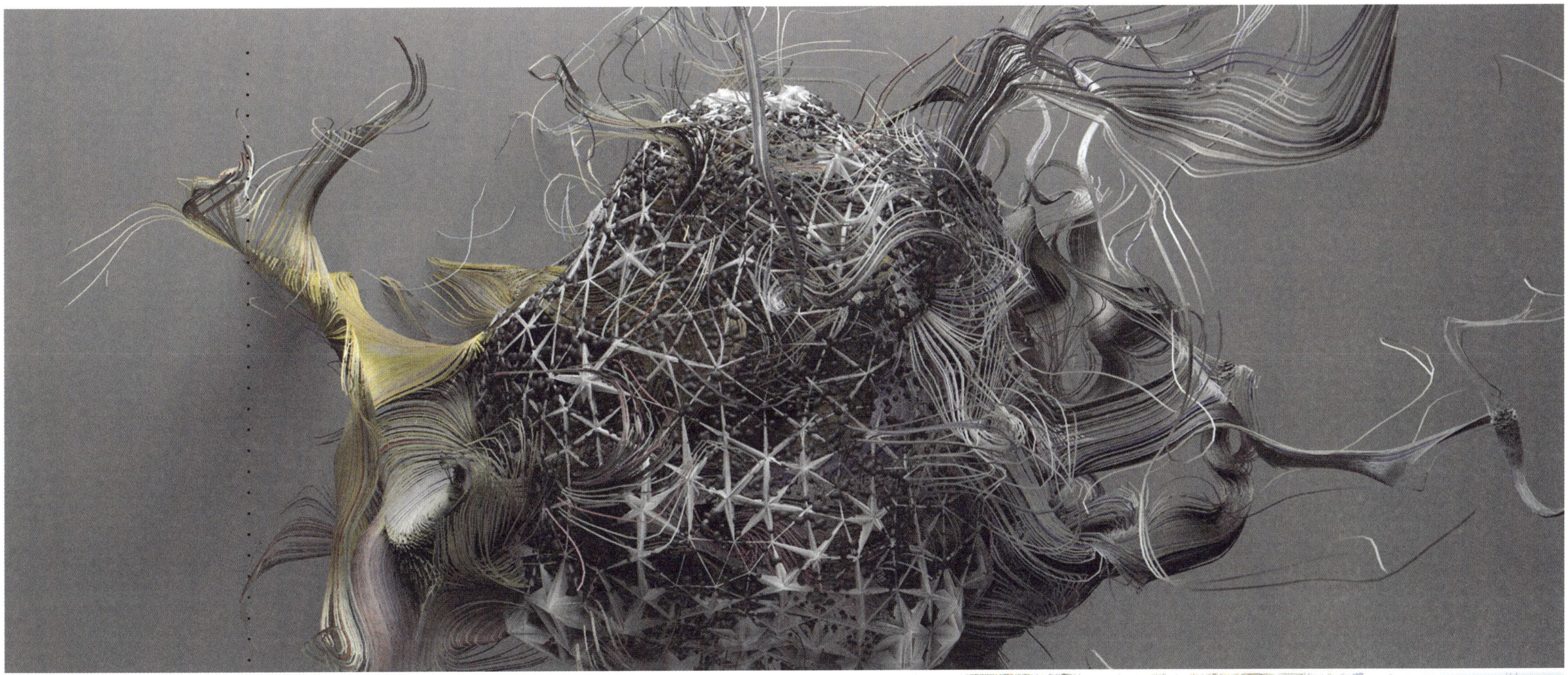

The Concept

As with anything like this, I had to base it on a solid concept. The brief stated it could be as abstract as I wanted, but I needed a creative theme to wrap it around; doing this adds a solid foundation to work.

In the end, I broke it down into three core pillars: The attacks and the system that protects you from these attacks, and finally, the creativity that is allowed to flow because your system is being protected.

After all, is it not the point of deploying such a protection system? So you can get on with doing what you are meant to be doing, not freaking out about why your computer won't work anymore?

Now I had three core parts of working with; the next stage was to bring in the data and visualize these three parts of the story.

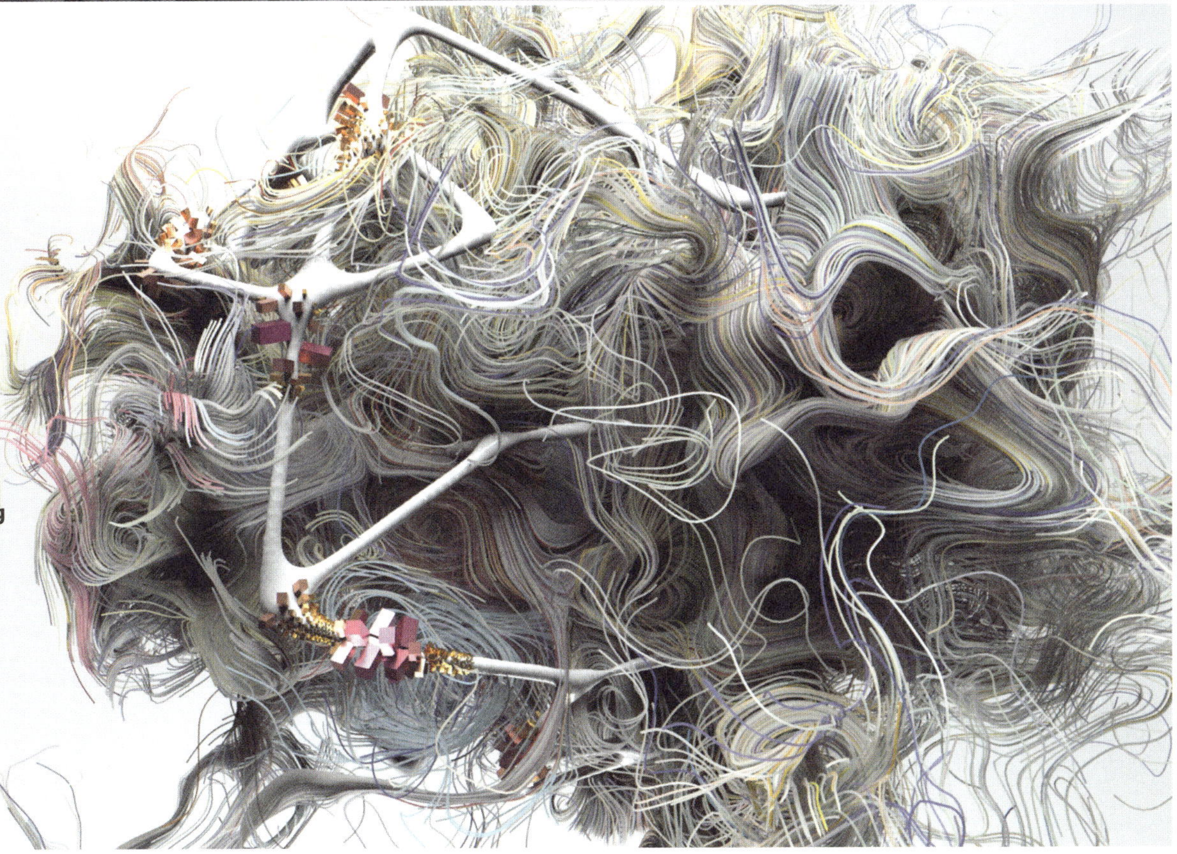

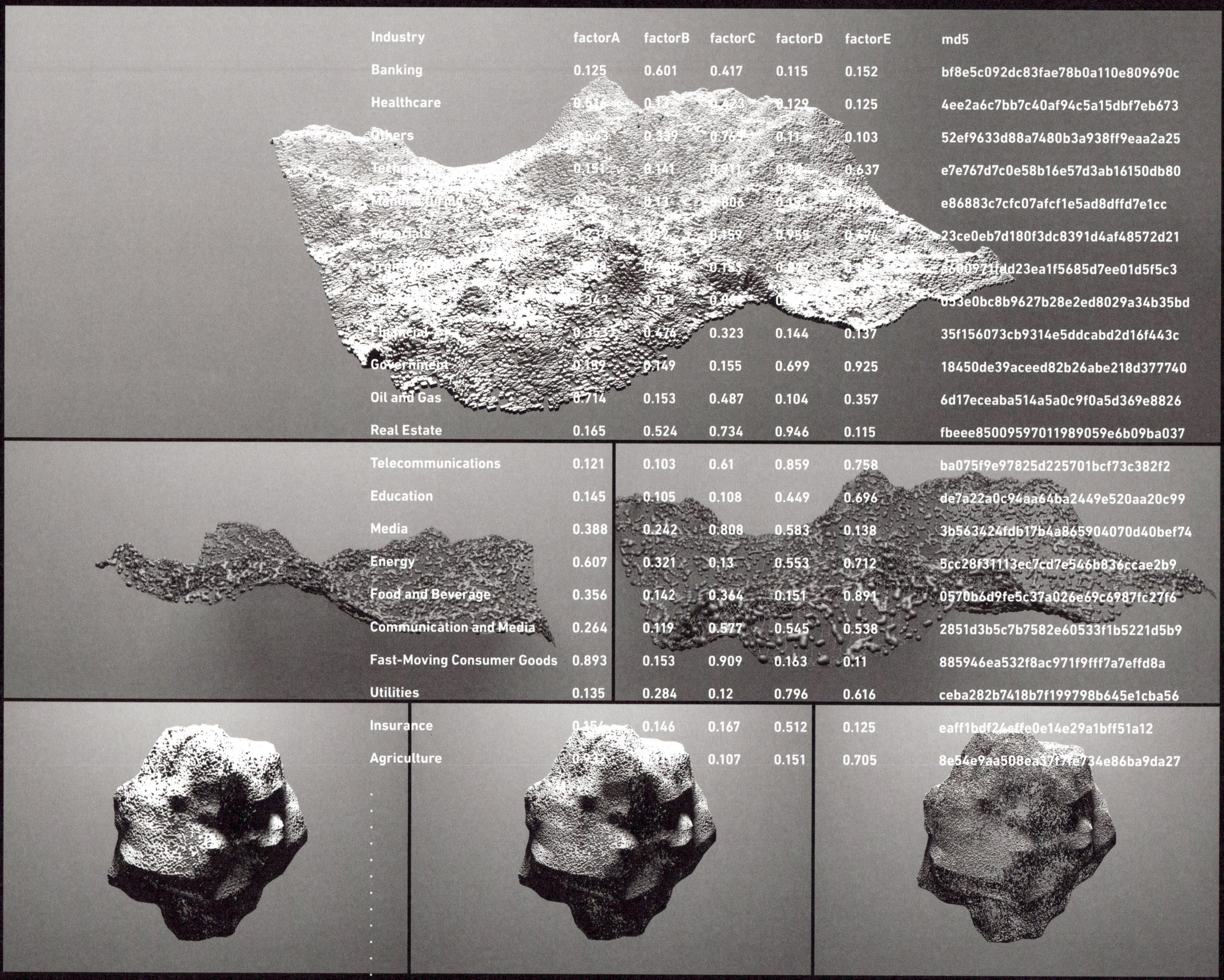

Industry	factorA	factorB	factorC	factorD	factorE	md5
Banking	0.125	0.601	0.417	0.115	0.152	bf8e5c092dc83fae78b0a110e809690c
Healthcare	[illegible]	[illegible]	[illegible]	0.129	0.125	4ee2a6c7bb7c40af94c5a15dbf7eb673
Others	0.543	0.339	[illegible]	[illegible]	0.103	52ef9633d88a7480b3a938ff9eaa2a25
[illegible]	0.151	0.141	[illegible]	[illegible]	0.637	e7e767d7c0e58b16e57d3ab16150db80
[illegible]	[illegible]	[illegible]	[illegible]	[illegible]	[illegible]	e86883c7cfc07afcf1e5ad8dffd7e1cc
[illegible]	[illegible]	[illegible]	0.159	0.955	[illegible]	23ce0eb7d180f3dc8391d4af48572d21
[illegible]	[illegible]	[illegible]	[illegible]	[illegible]	[illegible]	[illegible]fdd23ea1f5685d7ee01d5f5c3
[illegible]	0.343	[illegible]	[illegible]	[illegible]	[illegible]	053e0bc8b9627b28e2ed8029a34b35bd
[illegible]	[illegible]	0.474	0.323	0.144	0.137	35f156073cb9314e5ddcabd2d16f443c
Government	0.192	0.149	0.155	0.699	0.925	18450de39aceed82b26abe218d377740
Oil and Gas	0.714	0.153	0.487	0.104	0.357	6d17eceaba514a5a0c9f0a5d369e8826
Real Estate	0.165	0.524	0.734	0.946	0.115	fbeee8500959701198905 9e6b09ba037
Telecommunications	0.121	0.103	0.61	0.859	0.758	ba075f9e97825d225701bcf73c382f2
Education	0.145	0.105	0.108	0.449	0.696	de7a22a0c94aa64ba2449e520aa20c99
Media	0.388	0.242	0.808	0.583	0.138	3b563424fdb17b4a865904070d40bef74
Energy	0.607	0.321	0.13	0.553	0.712	5cc28f31113ec7cd7e546b836ccae2b9
Food and Beverage	0.356	0.142	0.364	0.151	0.891	0570b6d9fe5c37a026e69c6987fc27f6
Communication and Media	0.264	0.119	0.577	0.545	0.538	2851d3b5c7b7582e60533f1b5221d5b9
Fast-Moving Consumer Goods	0.893	0.153	0.909	0.163	0.11	885946ea532f8ac971f9fff7a7effd8a
Utilities	0.135	0.284	0.12	0.796	0.616	ceba282b7418b7f199798b645e1cba56
Insurance	[illegible]	0.146	0.167	0.512	0.125	eaff1bdf24effe0e14e29a1bff51a12
Agriculture	[illegible]	[illegible]	0.107	0.151	0.705	8e54e9aa508ea37f7fe734e86ba9da27
.						
.						
.						

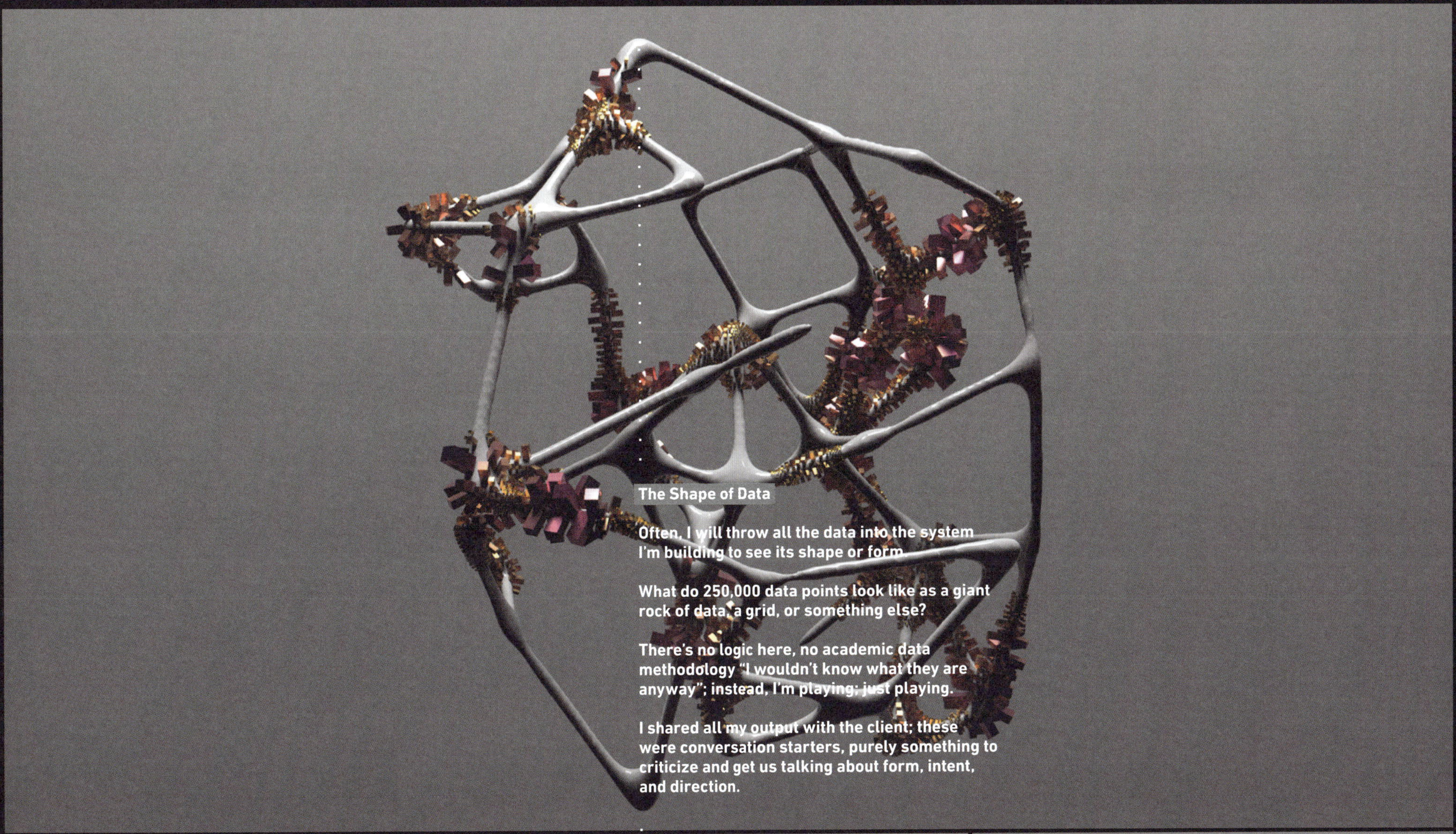

The Shape of Data

Often, I will throw all the data into the system I'm building to see its shape or form.

What do 250,000 data points look like as a giant rock of data, a grid, or something else?

There's no logic here, no academic data methodology "I wouldn't know what they are anyway"; instead, I'm playing; just playing.

I shared all my output with the client; these were conversation starters, purely something to criticize and get us talking about form, intent, and direction.

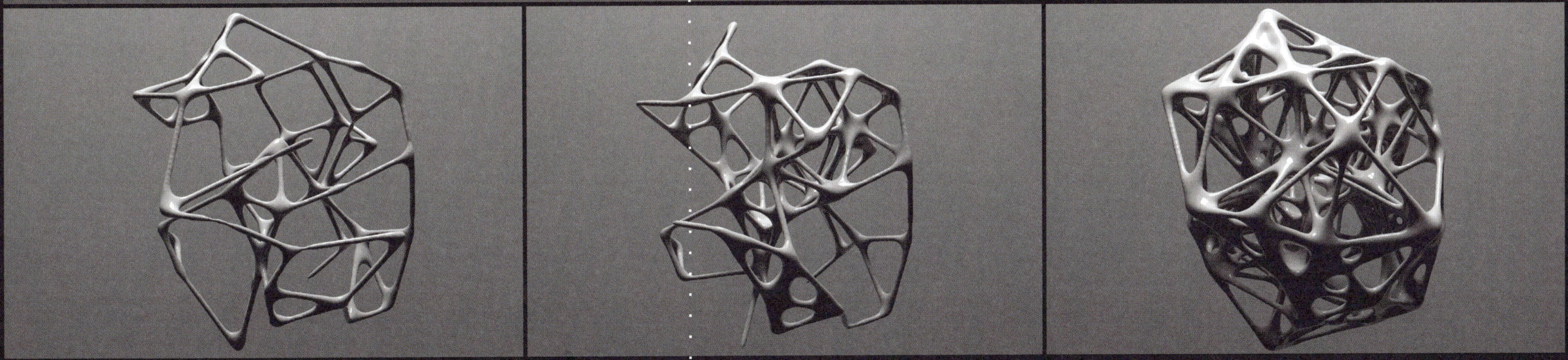

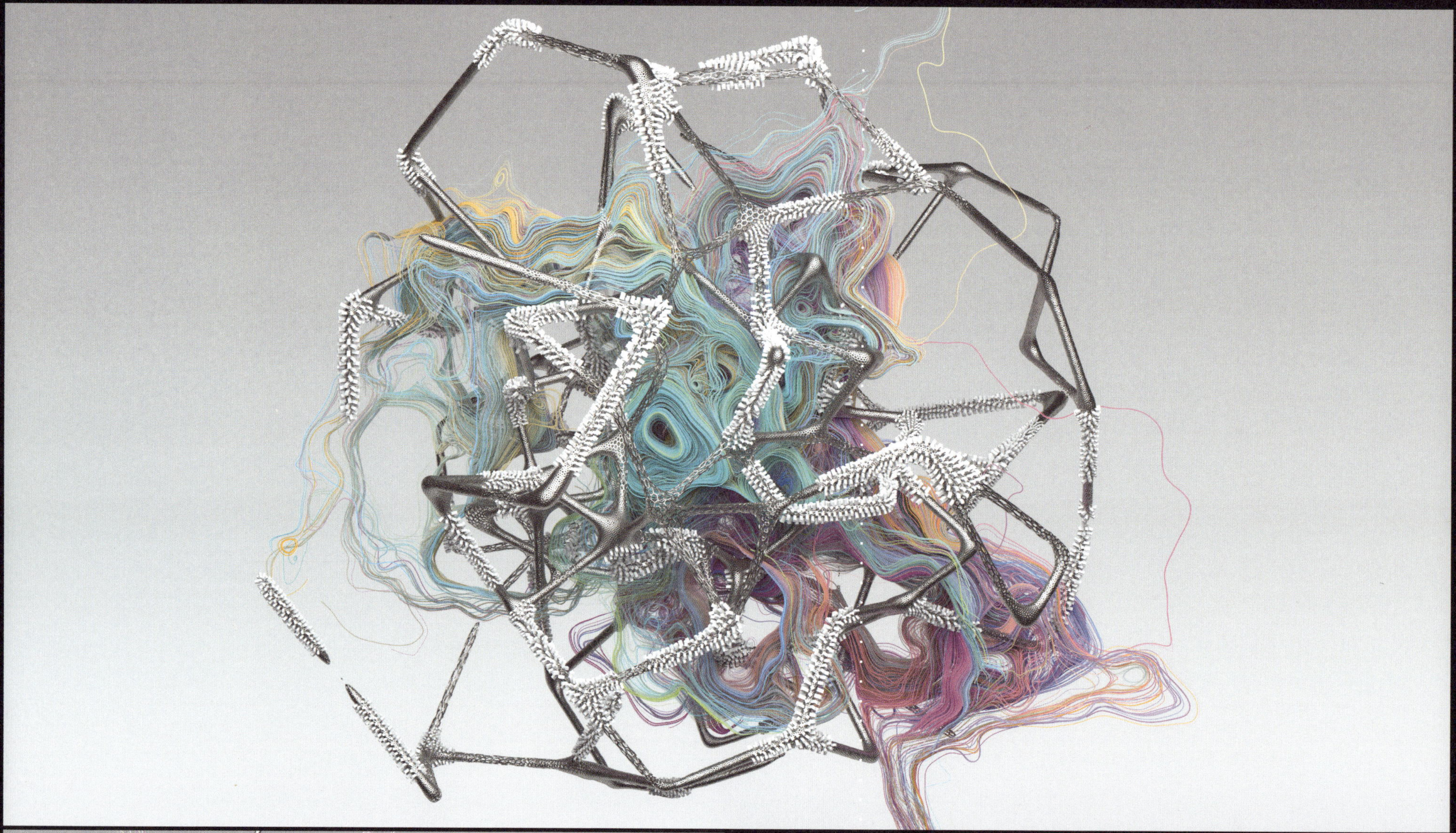

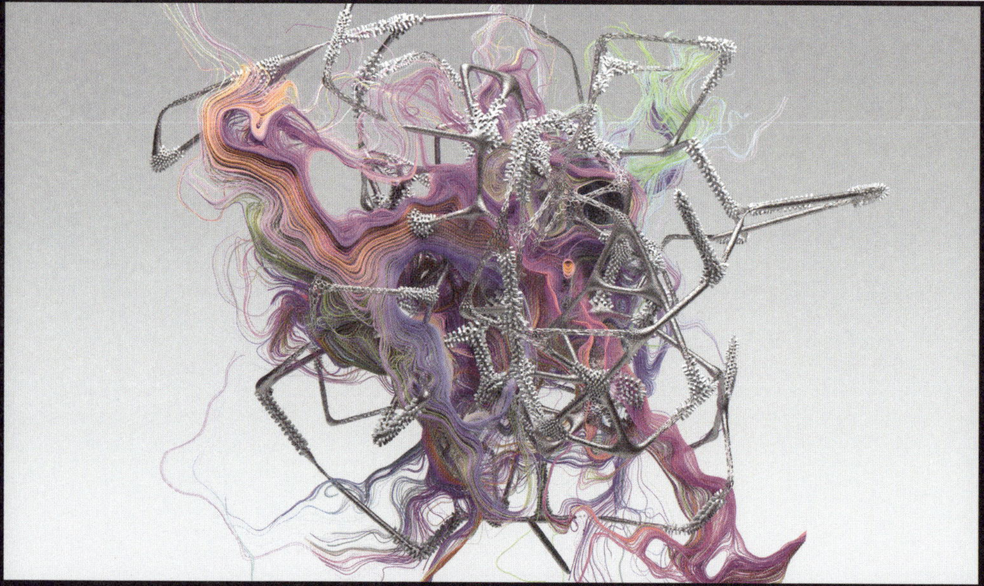

The Form of the System

One of the first things I wanted to do was work out a way to create a form representing the Trend Microsystem. I noticed a split into so-called industry verticals, Media, Government, Banking, for example, in the data I had been sent.

These were words as data, except I needed a technique to take those words and create numbers I could then use to drive an algorithm to create unique forms, which could then form the basis of the compositions.

I then remembered a few years ago; I had used a technique to generate colors from city names using an MD5 hash. An MD5 hash is a way to create a string of letters and numbers from a word or phrase, often used in security.

.

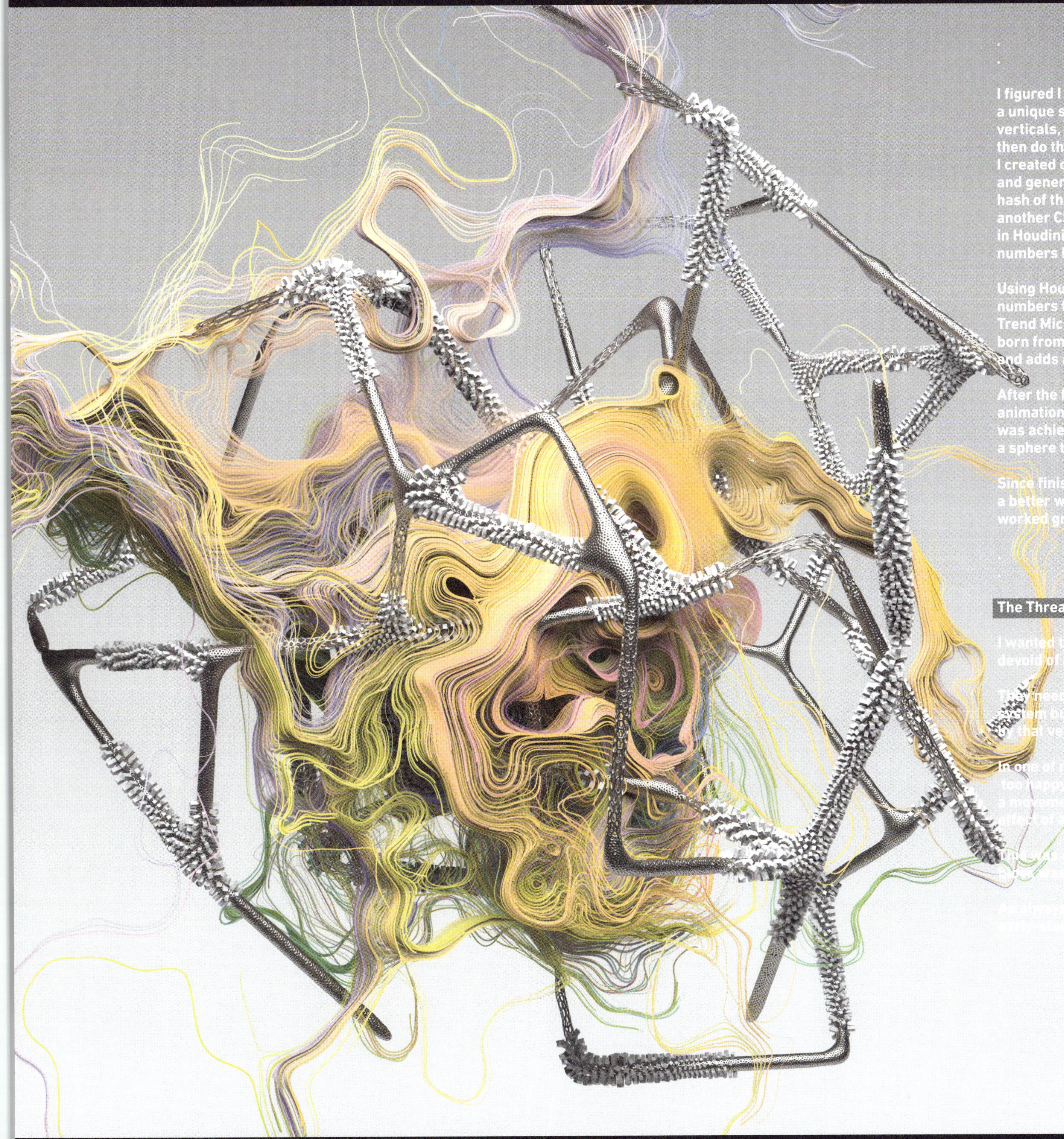

I figured I could use that same system to generate a unique set of numbers from these industry verticals, and once I had those numbers, I could then do things with them. Using Processing, I created code to read in the supplied CSV file and generate these numbers based on an MD5 hash of the industry verticals and then spit out another CSV file with the results, ready to be used in Houdini. On page 082 is a table of some of the numbers I generated utilizing that approach.

Using Houdini, I then set about using those numbers to create the shapes representing the Trend Microsystem, each unique to an industry, born from a security algorithm, a nice bonus, and adds an extra layer to the work.

After the forms were created, I then did a small animation test of the forms growing. This process was achieved using a Boolean operation with a sphere to grow the shape seemingly.

Since finishing the work, I have discovered a better way to use group expansion, but it still worked great.

The Threats

I wanted to make the threats themselves be devoid of any personality.

They needed to be seen to try to attach to the system but eventually be rendered useless by that very same system.

In one of my first sketches, they looked way too happy and not menacing at all, but from a movement point of view, they had the desired effect of attacking and infiltrating.

This was all born from the data, so each little block was a data point.

As always, this was shown to the client as an early-stage concept.

The Flow of Creativity

The final part of the composition was the representation of creativity which can still blossom because the threats have been stopped.

I wanted these to be the exact opposite of the threats; free-flowing, organic structures that suggested the beauty of creativity.

I created vector noise fields for trails to flow through, made from a giant cube cut out of the core shape. In this way, the trails would flow around the space left behind rather than through the shape itself.

Below is a very early prototype. You can see there is still a lot wrong with this, in the way it jitters and in the movement of the trails. Not to mention the color palette was way too inconsistent.

Putting it all Together

Once the client and I were happy with the individual components, it was then a case of putting all the parts together for the final UHD animation. I scoped out the narrative in a storyboard format and signed off before putting the final render together.

I was keen on using slightly unexpected music regarding what you might typically see or hear from a tech company. My idea was something akin to Philip Glass or Michael Nyman. After much searching and trying various pieces, I managed to find and license a piece of music that worked well and had the feeling I was looking for.

To render these final 4K UHD frames, I used a combination of my machine plus the cloud rendering services of Gridmarkets[1]. Using their service, I could set up a thirty-machine system and have it render in the cloud, all at a cost, of course, but for meeting a deadline, it was a perfect solution.

The renders were then composited and edited together using Hitfilm[2], having ditched Adobe Premiere long ago, and I have to say, it was a real joy using Hitfilm.

The final export quality was stellar!

1 www.gridmarkets.com
2 www.fxhome.com

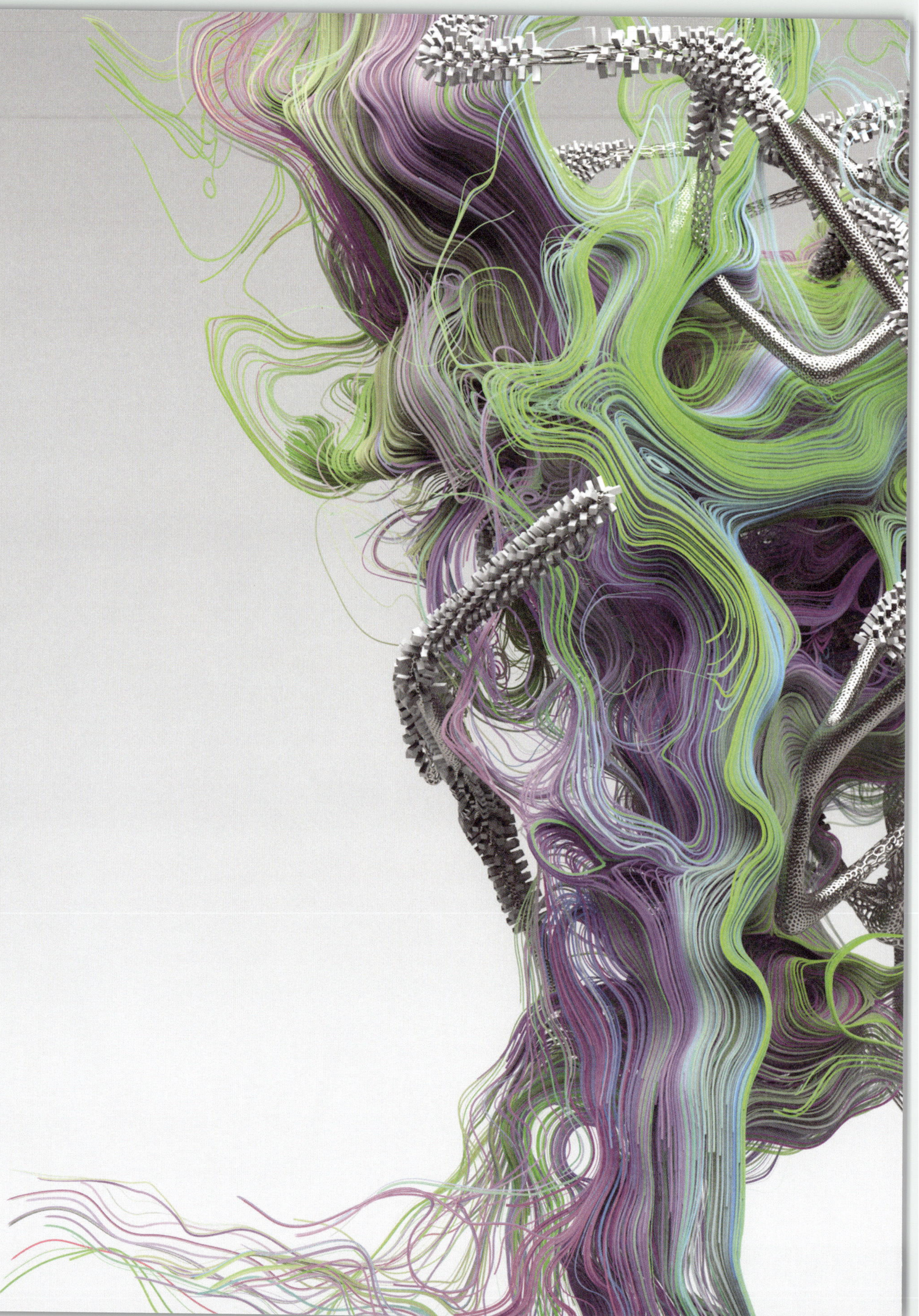

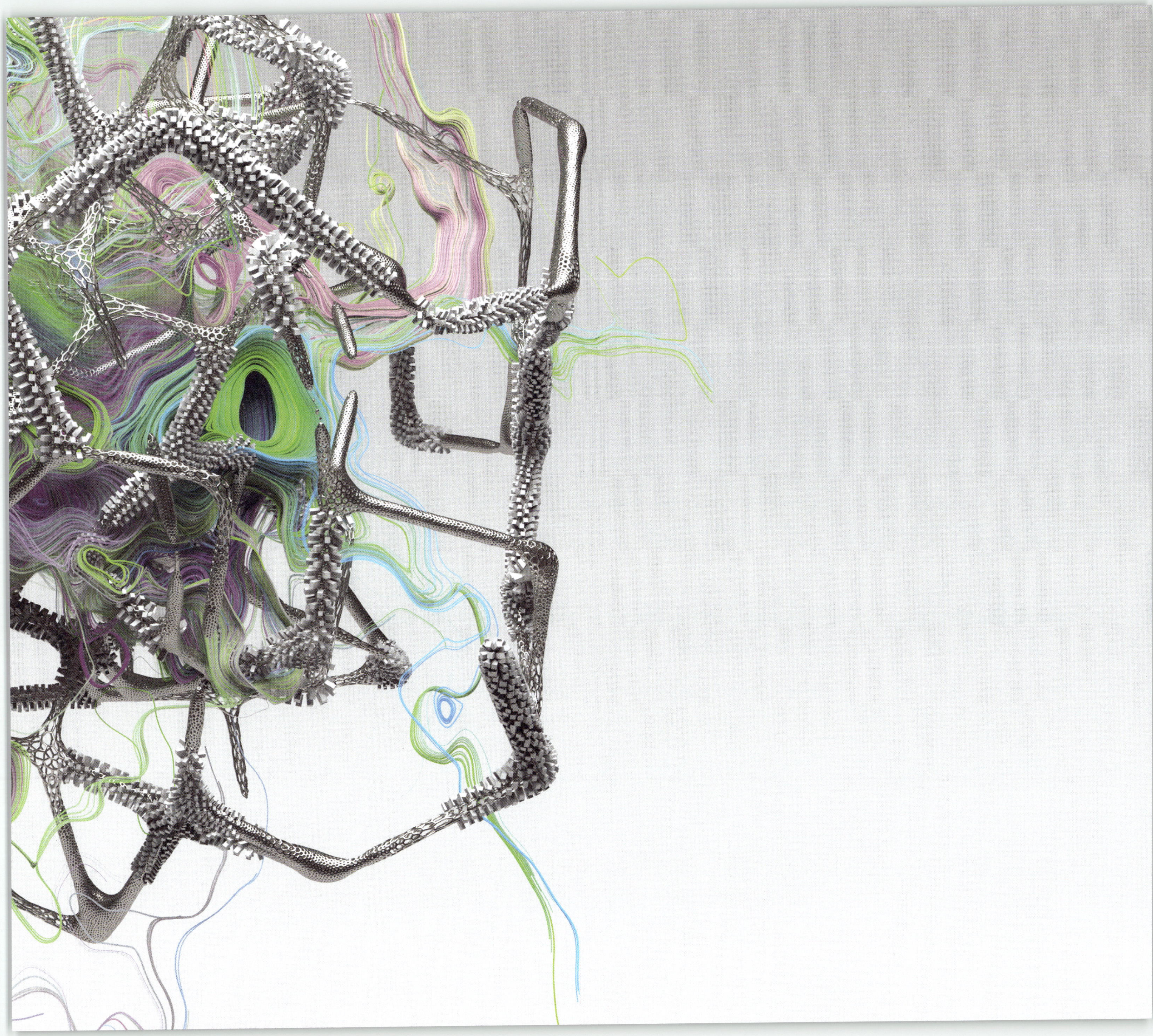

Name:

Matt DesLauriers

Info:

Matt DesLauriers is a Toronto-born artist and creative coder now living in London, UK.

His interactive installations have been displayed in special events at the Louvre Museum in Paris and the Art Gallery of Ontario in Toronto.

His work was part of Reykjavik's 2019 Winter Lights Festival in Iceland and Ontario Place Park's 2018 Winter Light Exhibition in Toronto.

Matt is active in the open-source community and has given numerous talks, classes, and workshops on creative coding, including UCL Bartlett School of Architecture, London; FITC in Toronto and Amsterdam, Frontend Masters in Minneapolis; and GROW in Paris.

Project:

CRYSTAL TOWERS

URL:

mattdesl.com

Mail:

info@mattdesl.studio

Instagram:

@mattdesl_art

Project Description:

CRYSTAL TOWERS is a series of ten art prints designed with the help of a generative algorithm. A dataset of skyscraper heights spread across major cities are distilled into unique and procedural 3D crystal structures, creating a compact and abstract representation of each city.

Q&As

Please explain the main idea and what gave the impulse?

In CRYSTAL TOWERS, I wanted to encode real-world datasets into an emergent system, to produce discrete outputs that highlighted and captured the natural beauty of data as a concrete structure.

The project came out of my experiments with integrating algorithmic processes into traditional 3D computer graphic workflows. These marked the beginning of my building tools as an artist within the space of generative art.

What challenges did you face for this project? And what surprises?

In 2017, I was writing code to develop interactive and animated content for the web. At the same time, I was beginning to grow my art practice; new prints, images, and video work derived from my code and algorithms.

I was using code as a tool, like an artist's brush, to create new outputs, but as I continued to push my code into larger and larger physical prints, but then began to run into technical limitations with the software environment.

Many graphical code-first platforms are not designed for print and physical outputs but for real-time rendering, which means they must draw each frame visual 60 times per second.

As a result, the visuals often have to be simplified to meet this frame budget.

Please describe the technical environment.

To break free of these constraints, I developed a bridge between my code and Blender, a 3D rendering software.

With this new workflow, I could code and tweak my designs in real-time within an interactive environment and pull in live data from various sources to influence the overall design.

Once I was happy, I could use Blender to export infinitely large canvases and even physical constructions with a laser cutter, CNC, or 3D printer.

This was the beginning of me creating my tools as an artist working with code, and it opened up new possibilities for what sorts of algorithmic work I could make.

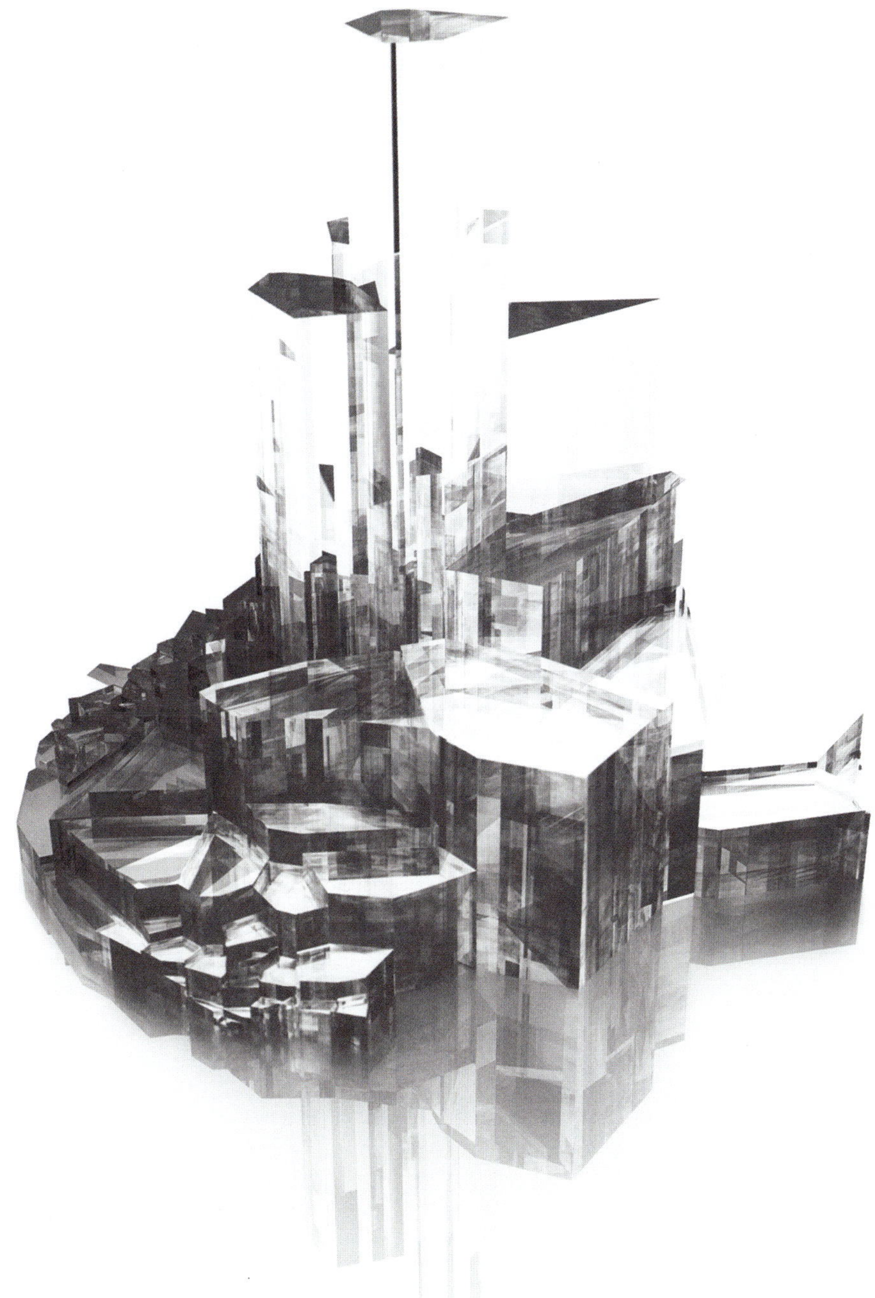

SHANGHAI

Most of my work starts with a rough sketch of an idea, often with pen and paper.

I usually have a vision for what I'd like but can't always imagine the exact final visuals, as the process becomes a sort of dance or collaboration with the machine.

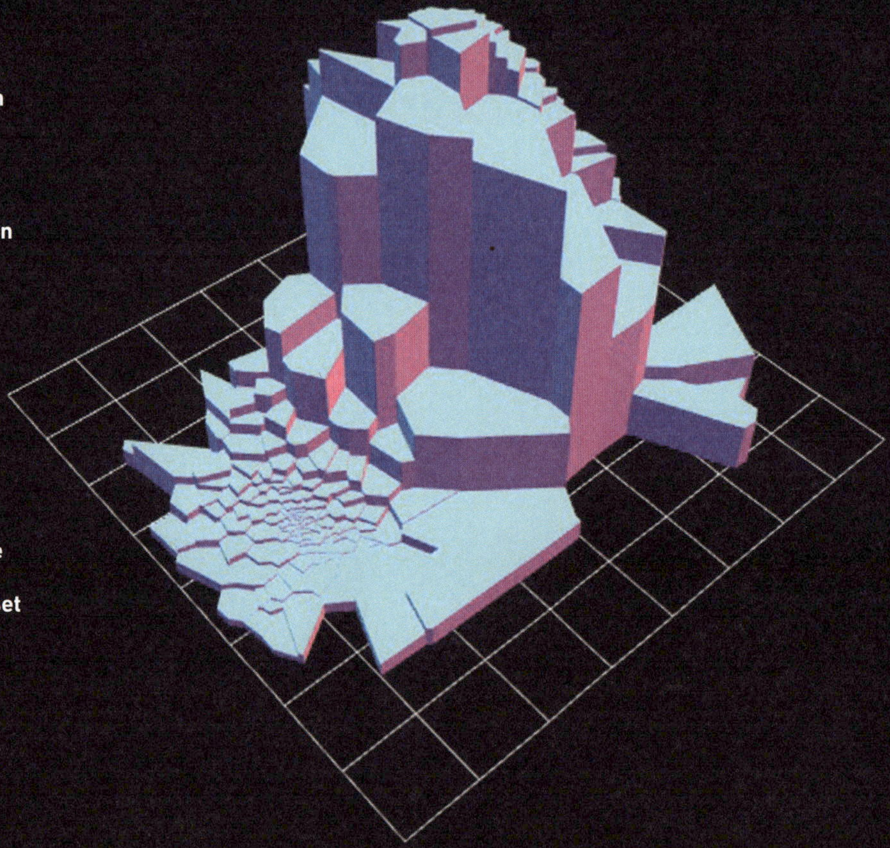

As I work, I try to let emergence, unexpected outputs, and even errors from my code guide me into new and exciting directions. With CRYSTAL TOWERS, I sketched out an algorithm: a simple set of rules that, when followed, produced towering three-dimensional crystalline structures.

As my sketches and coded systems began to evolve, it seemed only fitting to capture the complex skylines of major cities within these digital structures.

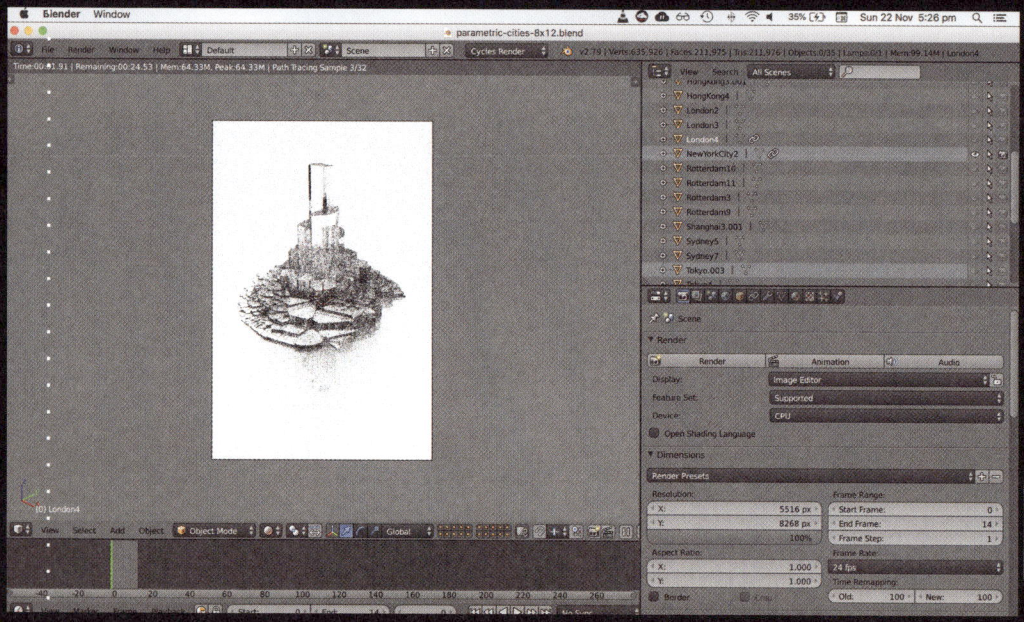

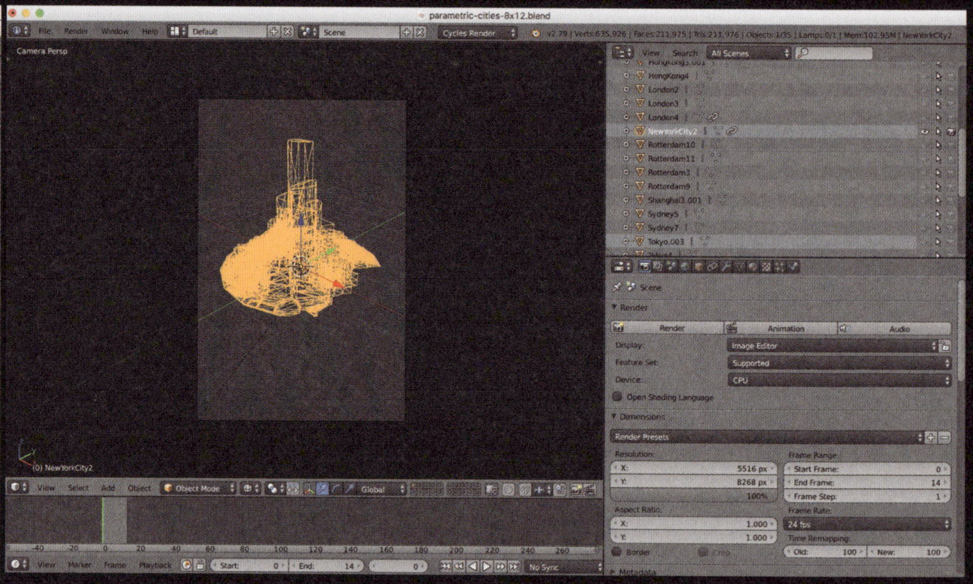

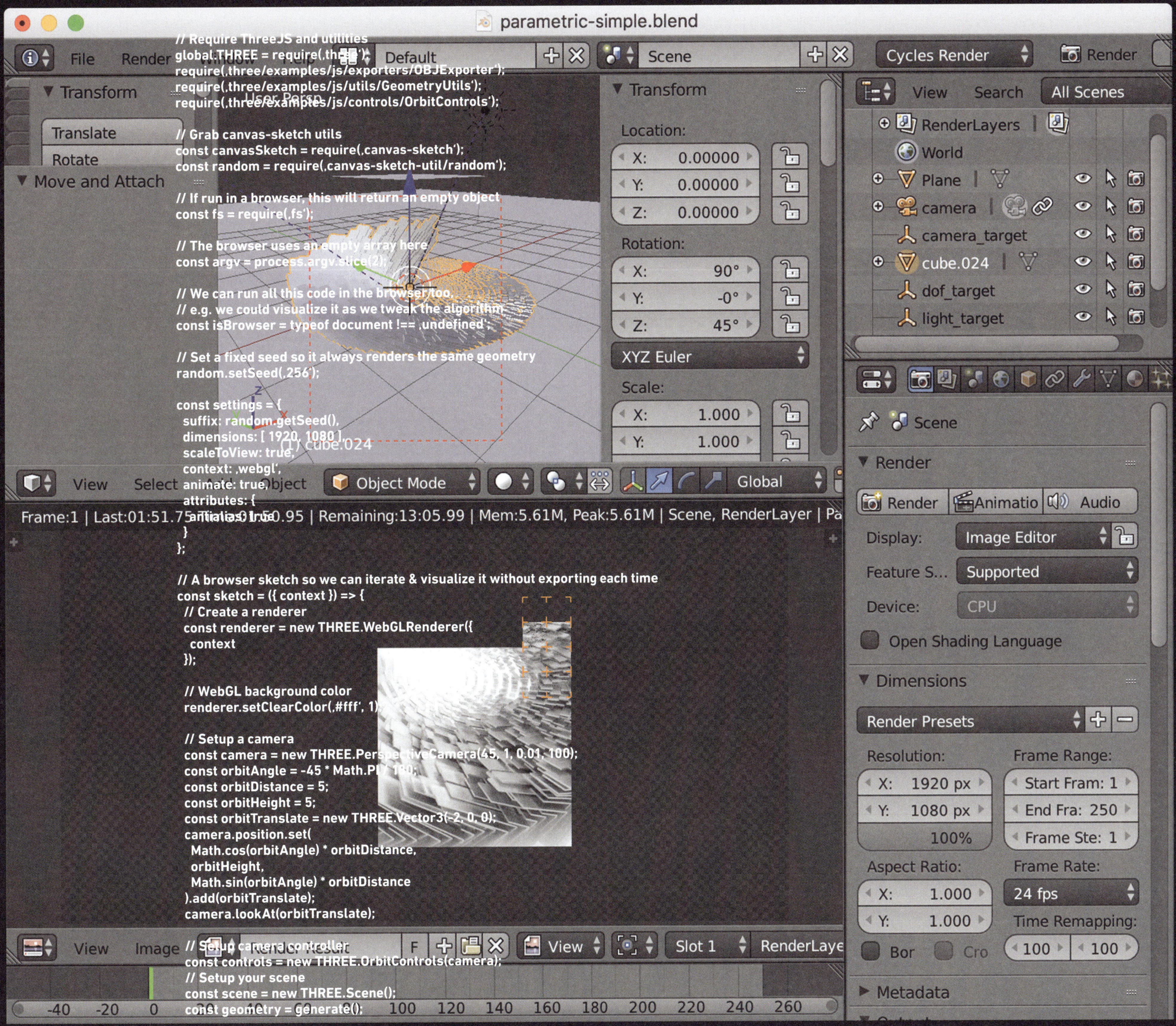


```
// Require ThreeJS and utilities
global.THREE = require(‚three');
require(‚three/examples/js/exporters/OBJExporter');
require(‚three/examples/js/utils/GeometryUtils');
require(‚three/examples/js/controls/OrbitControls');

// Grab canvas-sketch utils
const canvasSketch = require(‚canvas-sketch');
const random = require(‚canvas-sketch-util/random');

// If run in a browser, this will return an empty object
const fs = require(‚fs');

// The browser uses an empty array here
const argv = process.argv.slice(2);

// We can run all this code in the browser too,
// e.g. we could visualize it as we tweak the algorithm
const isBrowser = typeof document !== ‚undefined';

// Set a fixed seed so it always renders the same geometry
random.setSeed(‚256');

const settings = {
 suffix: random.getSeed(),
 dimensions: [ 1920, 1080 ],
 scaleToView: true,
 context: ‚webgl',
 animate: true,
 attributes: {
  antialias: true
 }
};

// A browser sketch so we can iterate & visualize it without exporting each time
const sketch = ({ context }) => {
 // Create a renderer
 const renderer = new THREE.WebGLRenderer({
  context
 });

 // WebGL background color
 renderer.setClearColor(‚#fff', 1);

 // Setup a camera
 const camera = new THREE.PerspectiveCamera(45, 1, 0.01, 100);
 const orbitAngle = -45 * Math.PI / 180;
 const orbitDistance = 5;
 const orbitHeight = 5;
 const orbitTranslate = new THREE.Vector3(-2, 0, 0);
 camera.position.set(
  Math.cos(orbitAngle) * orbitDistance,
  orbitHeight,
  Math.sin(orbitAngle) * orbitDistance
 ).add(orbitTranslate);
 camera.lookAt(orbitTranslate);

 // Setup camera controller
 const controls = new THREE.OrbitControls(camera);
 // Setup your scene
 const scene = new THREE.Scene();
 const geometry = generate();
```

091 . CRYSTAL TOWERS

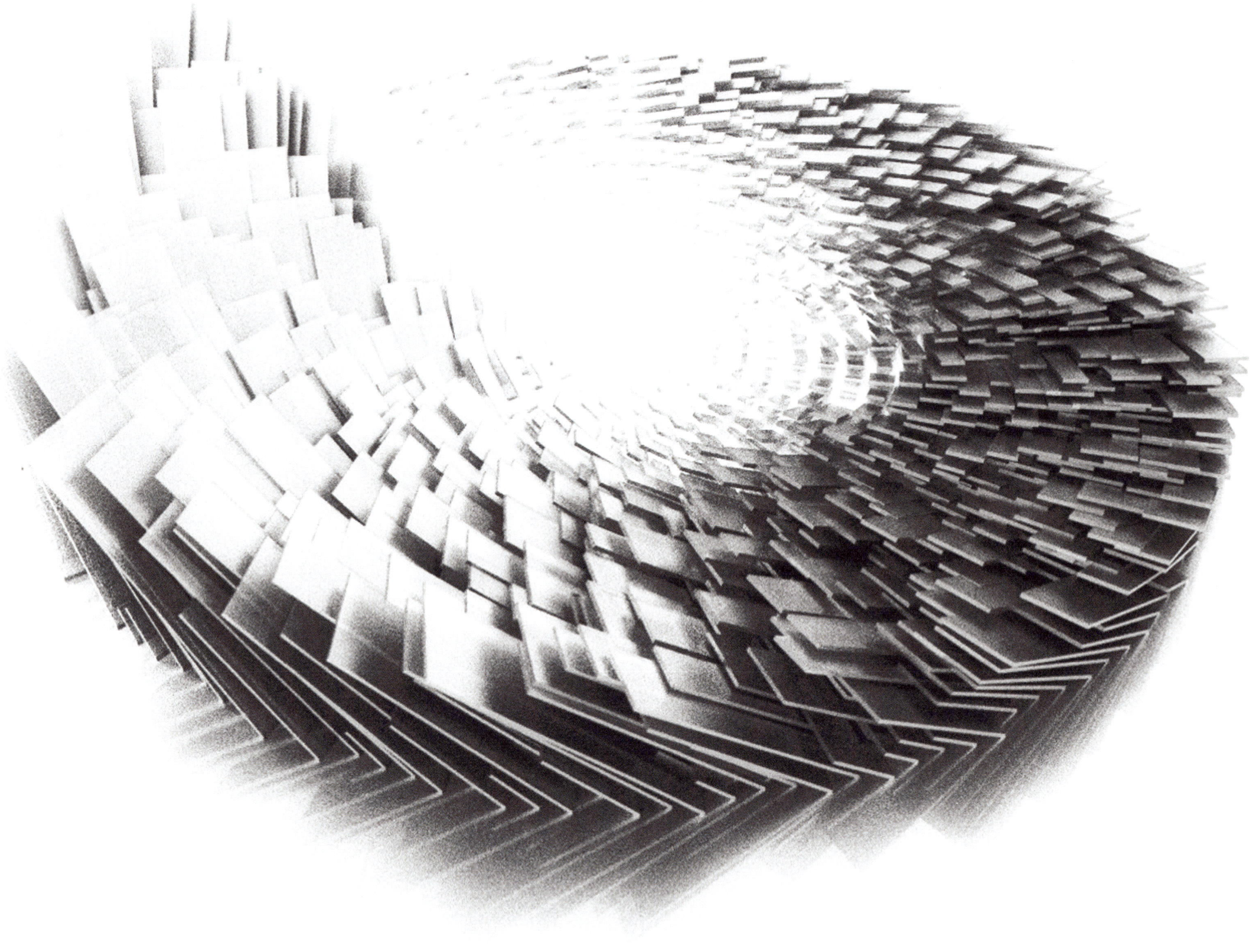

092 . Matt DesLauriers

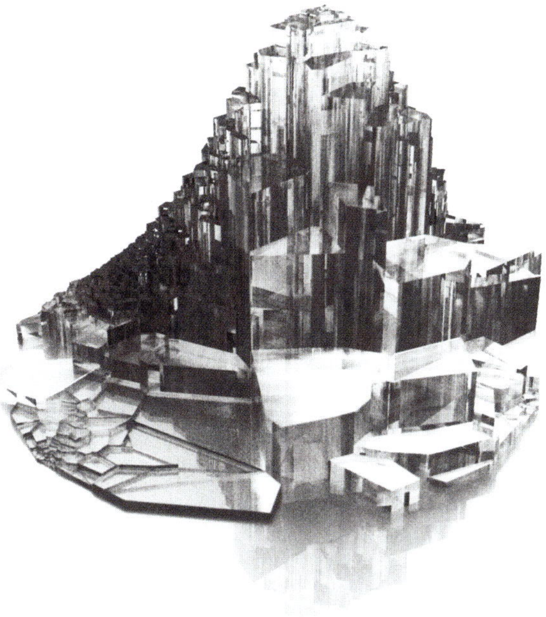

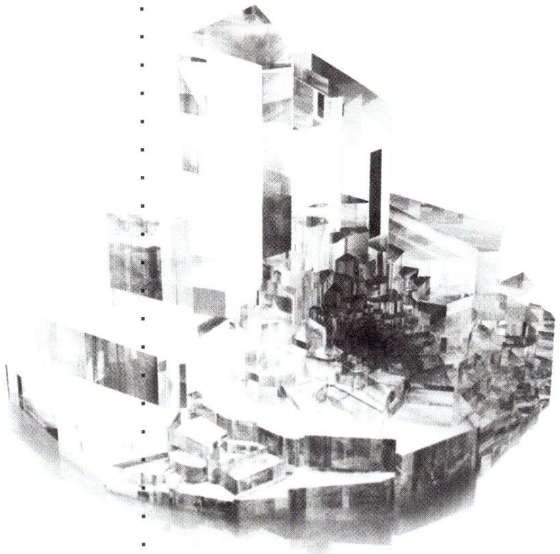

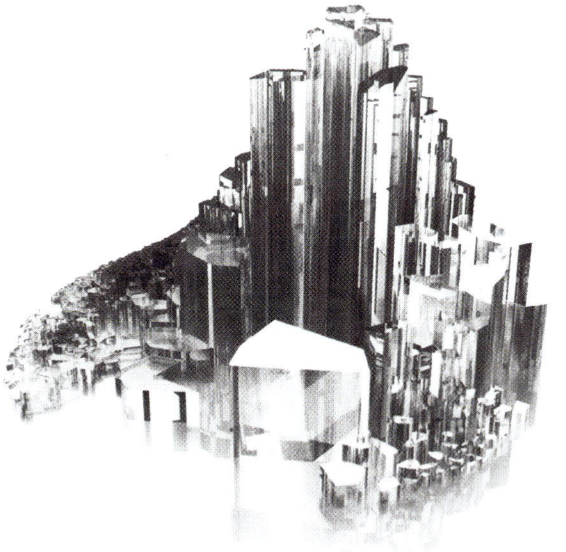

I ended up creating a software program that produced a series of 3D vertices and geometries that evolve, like a cellular growth structure.

This code emits an OBJ file. These files can then import into Blender to render at high print resolutions.

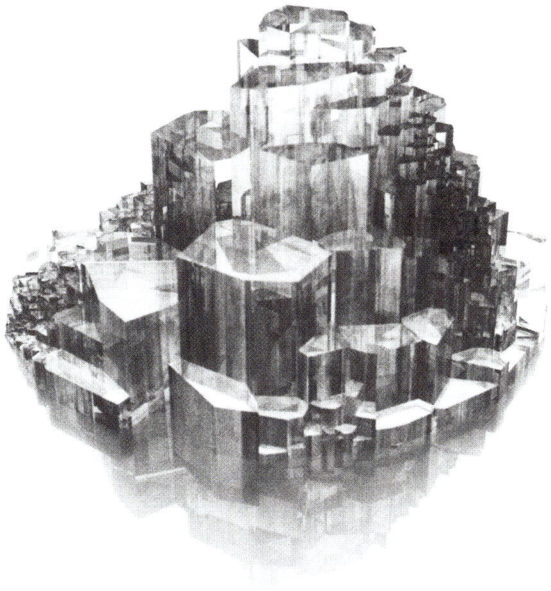

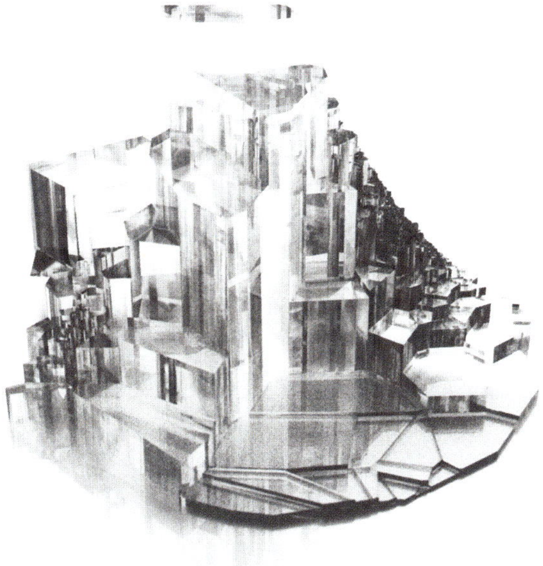

CRYSTAL TOWERS attempted to break away from my routine; instead of creating work for a screen, websites, social media etc., my goal was to bring my code and algorithms into a more physical space; print and 3D constructions.

The tools and processes I developed for this project, some are open source, have since become the basis for many of my artworks today.

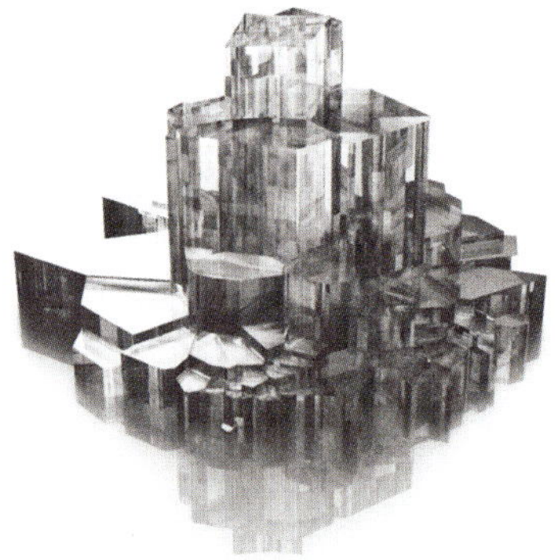

ROTTERDAM

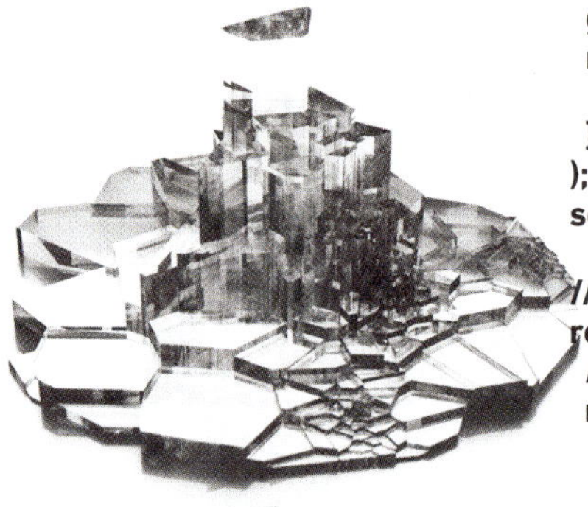

SYDNEY

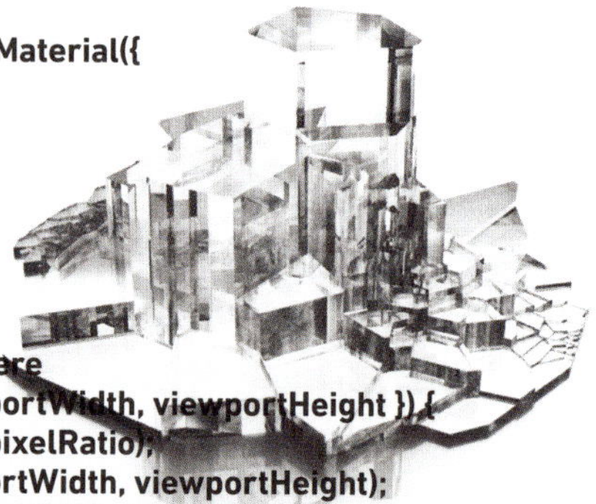

LONDON

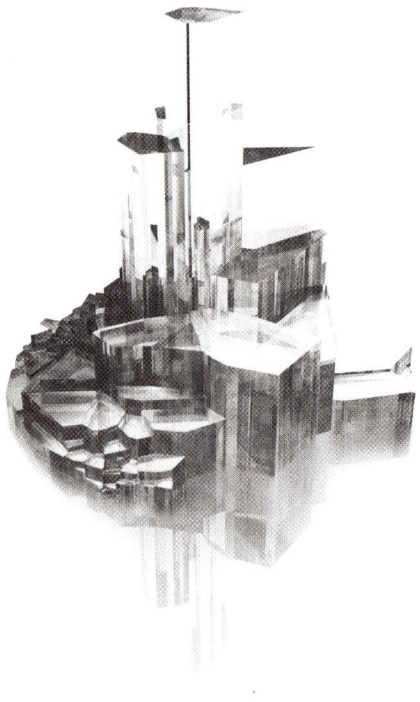

SHANGHAI

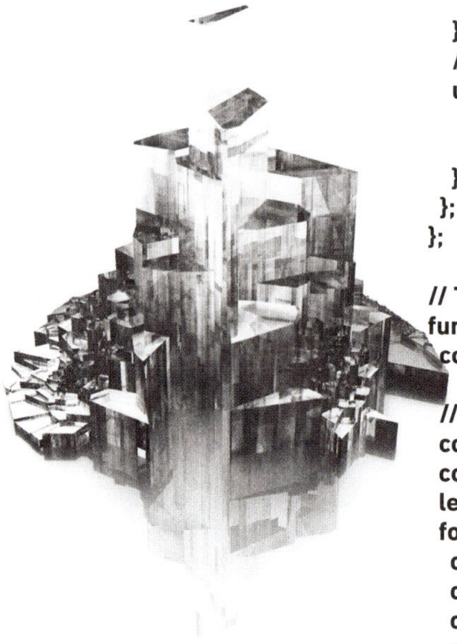

HONG KONG

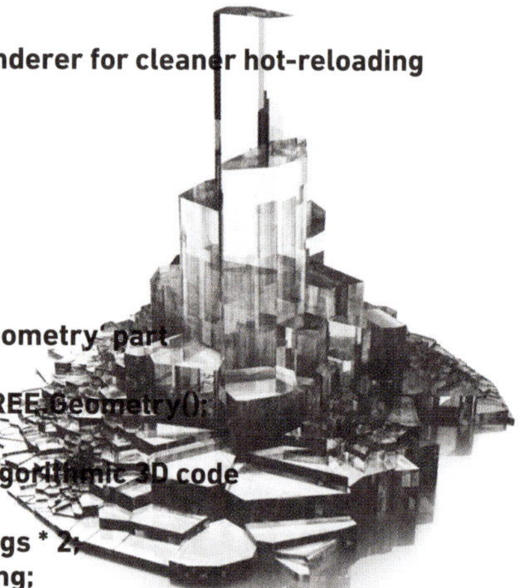

NEW YORK CITY

```
// Setup your scene
const scene = new THREE.Scene();
const geometry = generate();

const mesh = new THREE.Mesh(
 geometry,
 new THREE.MeshNormalMaterial({
  flatShading: true
 })
);
scene.add(mesh);

// draw each frame
return {
 // Handle resize events here
 resize ({ pixelRatio, viewportWidth, viewportHeight }) {
  renderer.setPixelRatio(pixelRatio);
  renderer.setSize(viewportWidth, viewportHeight);
  camera.aspect = viewportWidth / viewportHeight;
  camera.updateProjectionMatrix();
 },
 // Update & render your scene here
 render ({ time, exporting }) {
  controls.update();
  renderer.render(scene, camera);

  if (exporting) {
   // Export both PNG and OBJ file
   return [
    context.canvas,
    { data: exportGeometry(geometry), extension: „.obj‘ }
   ];
  }
 },
 // Dispose of events & renderer for cleaner hot-reloading
 unload () {
  controls.dispose();
  renderer.dispose();
 }
 };
};

// The actual ‚generative geometry‘ part
function generate () {
 const geometry = new THREE.Geometry();

 // this is our generative/algorithmic 3D code
 const rings = 20;
 const ringSpacing = 1 / rings * 2;
 let ringRadius = ringSpacing;
 for (let ringIndex = 0; ringIndex < rings; ringIndex++) {
  const steps = 7 * (ringIndex + 1);
  const A = ringIndex / Math.max(1, rings - 1);
  const radius = ringRadius;
  ringRadius += ringSpacing;
  for (let i = 0; i < steps; i++) {
   const B = i / Math.max(1, steps - 1);
   const angle = (i / steps) * Math.PI * 2;
   const x = Math.cos(angle) * radius;
   const z = Math.sin(angle) * radius;

   const thickness = ringSpacing * 0.15;
```

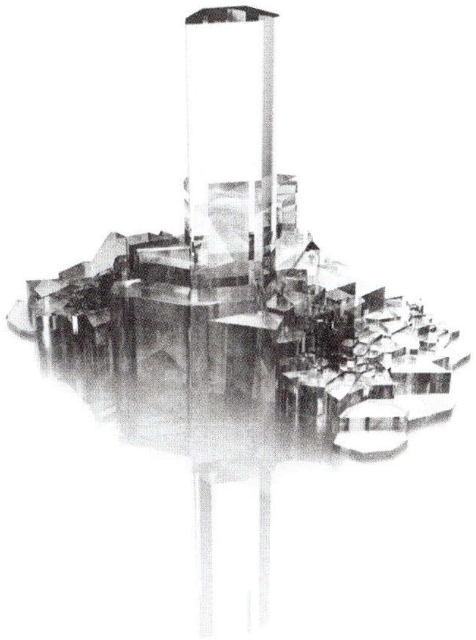

TOKYO

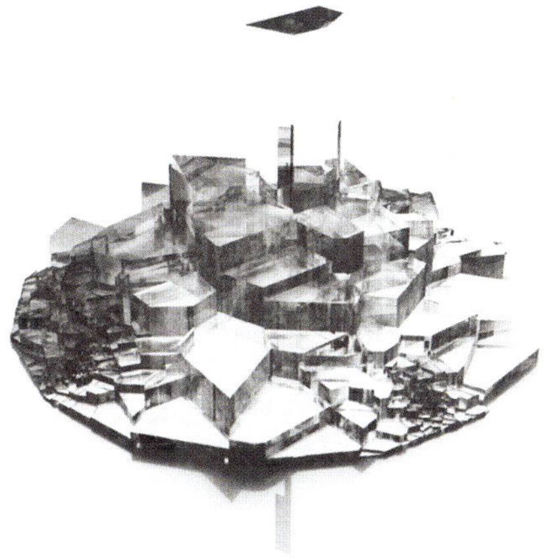

TORONTO

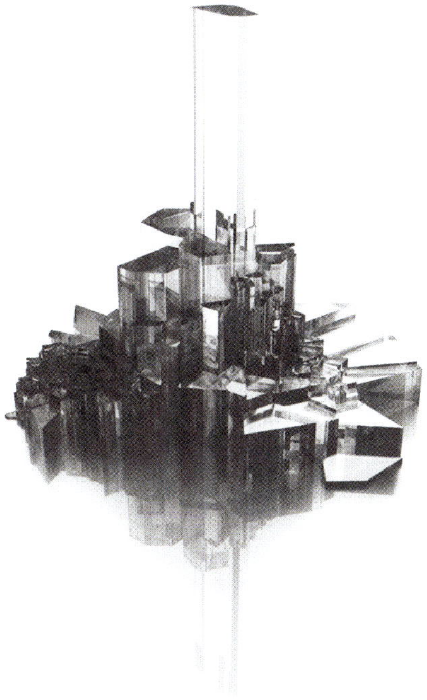

DUBAI

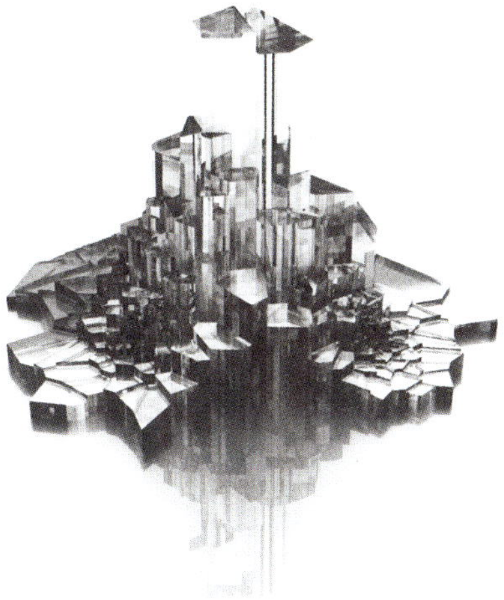

CHICAGO

As this work developed, I saw my process shift from digital into print form; I began to search for ways to represent a slice of my physical world within these computationally evolved and digitally accessed structures.

I was living in Toronto, Canada, at the time, a city overflowing with skyscrapers, and it inspired me to build the workaround of these towering metal monuments across major cities. I found something poetic in the idea of compressing, encoding skyscraper height data and the enormousness it represents into these byte-sized 3D digital structures.

The final output was ten prints of CRYSTAL TOWERS, a generative algorithm driven by data from skyscraper height distributions across major global cities.

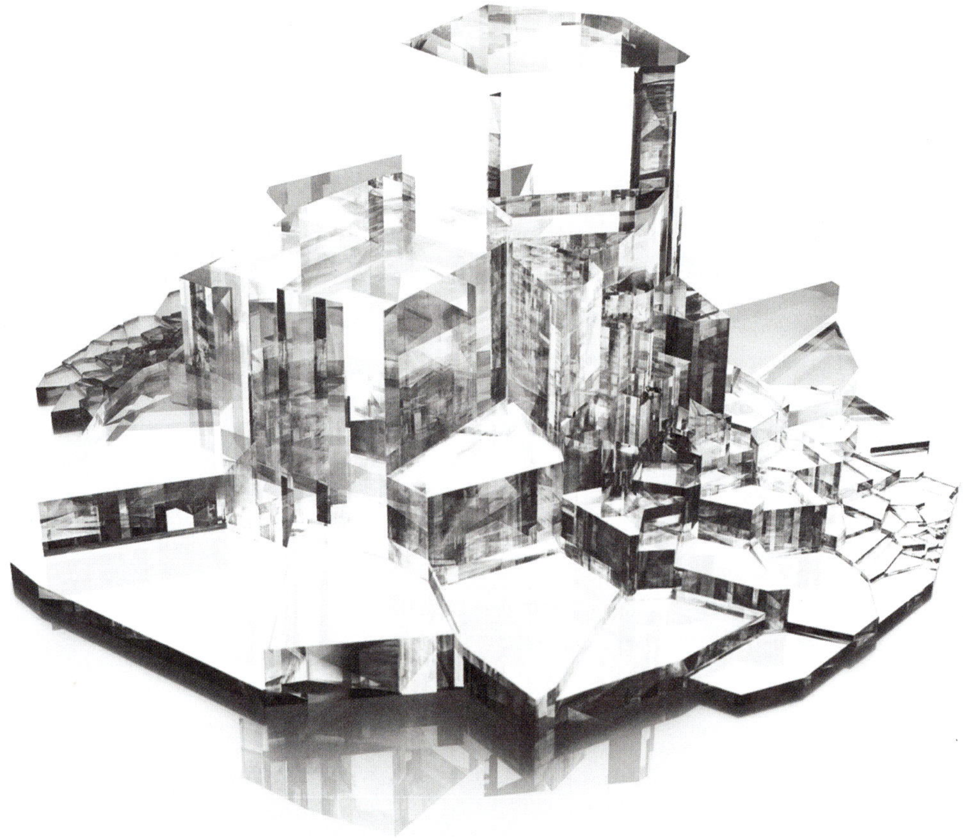

LONDON

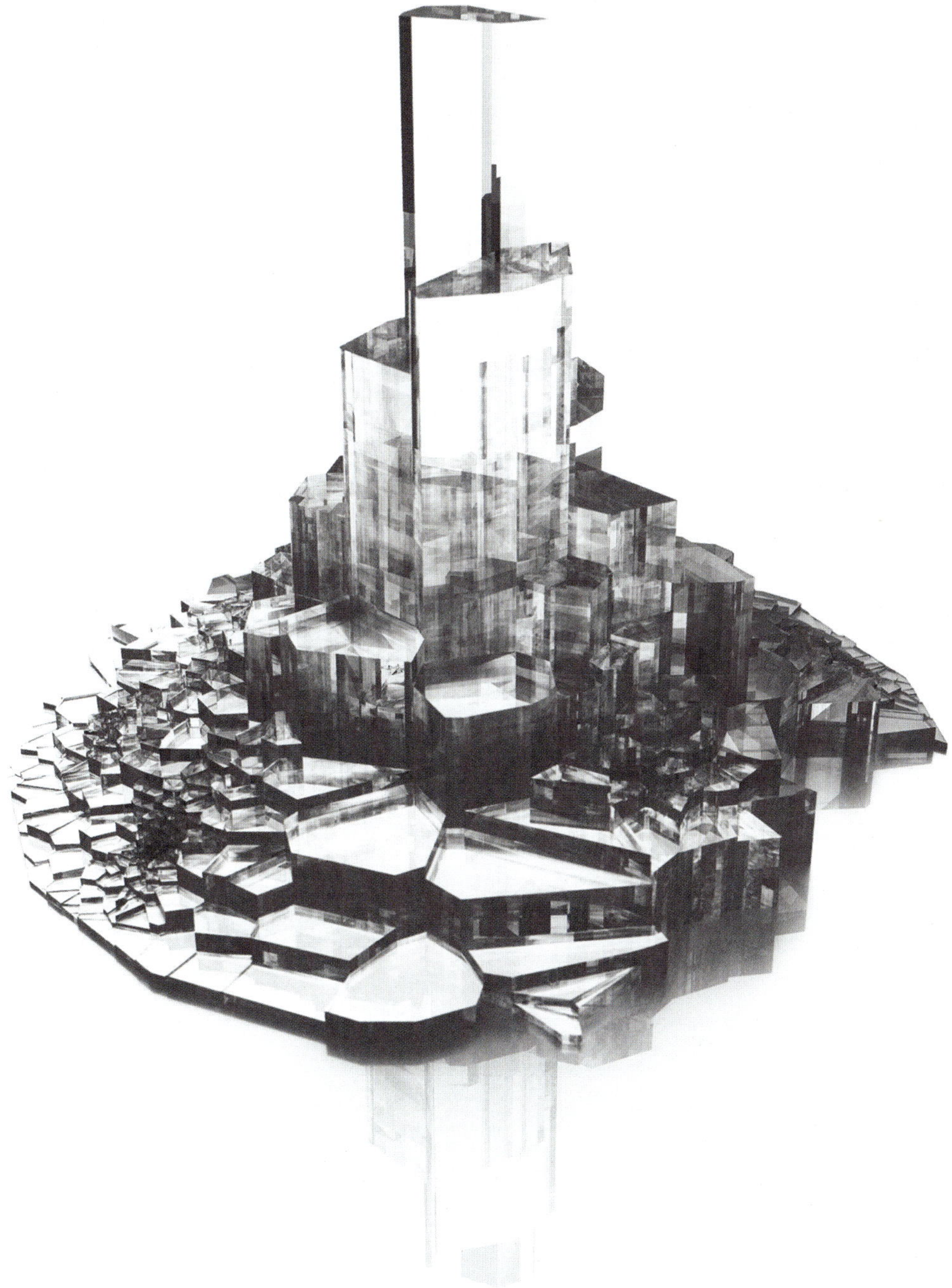

NEW YORK CITY

Name:

DRIFT

Info:

Dutch artists Lonneke Gordijn and Ralph Nauta founded DRIFT in 2007.

With a multidisciplinary team of 64, they work on experiential sculptures, installations and performances.

DRIFT manifests the phenomena and hidden properties of nature with the use of technology in order to learn from the Earth's underlying mechanisms and to re-establish our connection to it.

With both depth and simplicity, DRIFT's works of art illuminate parallels between man-made and natural structures through deconstructive, interactive, and innovative processes. The artists raise fundamental questions about what life is and explore a positive scenario for the future.

Project:

EGO

URL:

studiodrift.com

Mail:

info@studiodrift.com

Instagram:

@studio.drift

DRIFT

Why EGO?

Project EGO is timely and matches perfectly within the journey of data-based art as it points in the direction of performance. We can show DRIFT's entire development and approach to data-driven scenography, from sketch to end result.

Please explain the main idea and what gave the impulse?

The sculpture EGO was specially developed for Monteverdi's Opera L'Orfeo (1608) in a co-production with the Dutch Touring Opera (Nederlandse Reisopera). The production was great teamwork between DRIFT, director Monique Wagemakers, and choreographer Nanine Linning. We wanted to create a block that, at the same time-space, represents the frame of the protagonist's mind in this performance.

Our frame of thought is often quite limited in how we perceive the world and usually fits our cultural and historical beliefs. This personal perspective is symbolized as a block. In the story, things happen to the character that completely changes a way of thinking. This is expressed via the movement of the block, and space becomes a changing perspective, literally.

Orfeo is sometimes locked up in the block, but he can look at it at other moments and step outside his limiting beliefs and change his frame of mind. While the opera continues, EGO changes shape, sometimes slowly, other times all of a sudden, and sometimes he even completely disappears.

We created the block by handweaving 16 kilometers horizontal and vertical reflective threads of fluorocarbon. Visually it almost looks like a line drawing similar to how a 3D perspective is built up. Orfeo's perspective is continually changing.

With EGO, we have created a space that can change shape employing eight engines, allowing its perspective to disappear, adapt, change direction, and shape in different forms.

What challenges did you face for this project? And what surprises?

I am very used to working as an artist duo with Ralph. For this project, I was working very closely with director Monique Wagemakers and choreographer Nanine Linning.

It took some time to find a way to work together and alongside dancers and singers. I had never worked with opera or theater before, so I was not aware of all the disciplines that had to come together. So many people worked on the project, and EGO was a robot; its properties performed on stage with other performers; this experience was new to everyone.

Another exciting aspect was relating to the audience in a theater setting; the audience sitting still, while everything on stage moves.

I am used to museum settings where the public can walk around and spend time with the artwork.

Please describe the technical environment.

EGO is controlled by motors, algorithms, and specially developed software.

The block is stretched between eight motors. If one engine will pull in a particular direction, the other has to move with it or pull the block apart; we developed an algorithm to match that. In addition, the block is a character in the opera; singers and live music accompany it. We frequently had to overrule the algorithm and the programming that we created. Besides the algorithm, a person (who we call the puppet master) can control the block live.

This person can intervene, accelerate, and slow EGO down when the movements needed to adapt to the live music. Depending on the act, the spatial network looks both fine, light, and flowing like a transparent curtain or heavy and rigid like a cage. It glitters silvery in the spotlight, accompanies the actors, and expresses the feelings and moods of the performance.

Tell us about your aesthetical approach.

It is a project on stage. It is a minimalist environment, so the artwork is at the same time the only attribute/element on stage that has to change shape continuously, a transformative sculpture.

The most important thing is to convey the emotion by movement, depending on how it moves and how it interacts with the music, dancers, and singers. In addition to the movement, the material we have chosen works very well on stage with different types of light. With fluorocarbon, a Japanese version of nylon, we can make the block solid, transparent, change its color, appear menacing, or very soft with light.

You start envisioning what an algorithm is going to look like and what movements it will be making. We can see the result and start adjusting and making iterations in our studio. But we had to build in a whole new period where we began rehearsing with the dancers and singers.
At this point, we found out that we needed other things, that this was not just an environment that is always there. It's a moving environment, and that adds another significant element to the production. We found out that we had to do everything less. The block had to move less. We needed to find a combination of three factors that worked with each other.

We have imagined a spectator's experience. The aesthetic approach; greatness, experience, and the block compared to the actors and singers.

What's next? Your vision?

We want to make the block interactive.

What we find very interesting is how you can express human emotion through that block. How can you make it move in such a way that we feel a connection? We have now achieved this in an opera setting, where the block has a prominent role and represents different production elements. But now, without that whole entourage of the opera, we continue to find it an interesting object, and we now hope to express human emotion via the block. Our aim is that you almost see yourself reflected, your feeling in that block. An algorithm entirely, meticulously choreographed second by second for its situation; we do not know yet exactly.

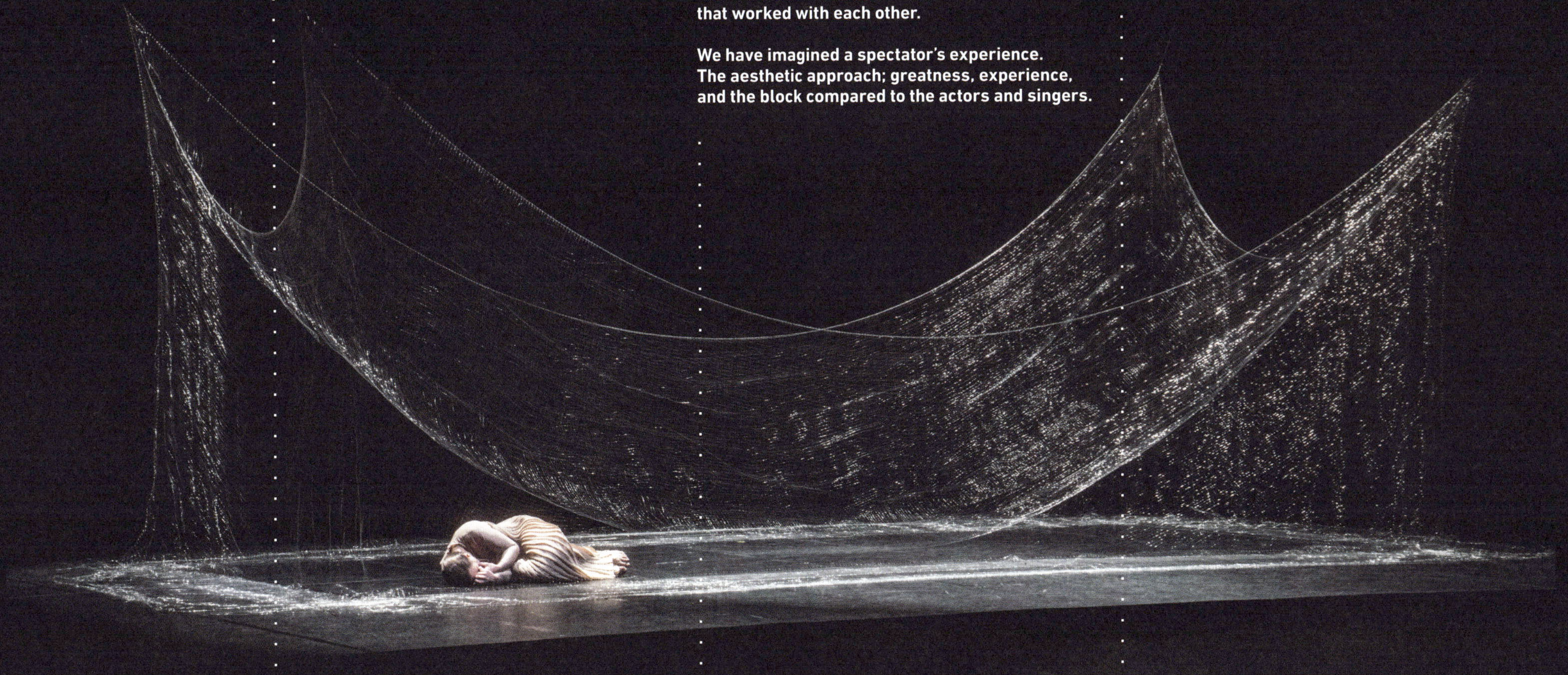

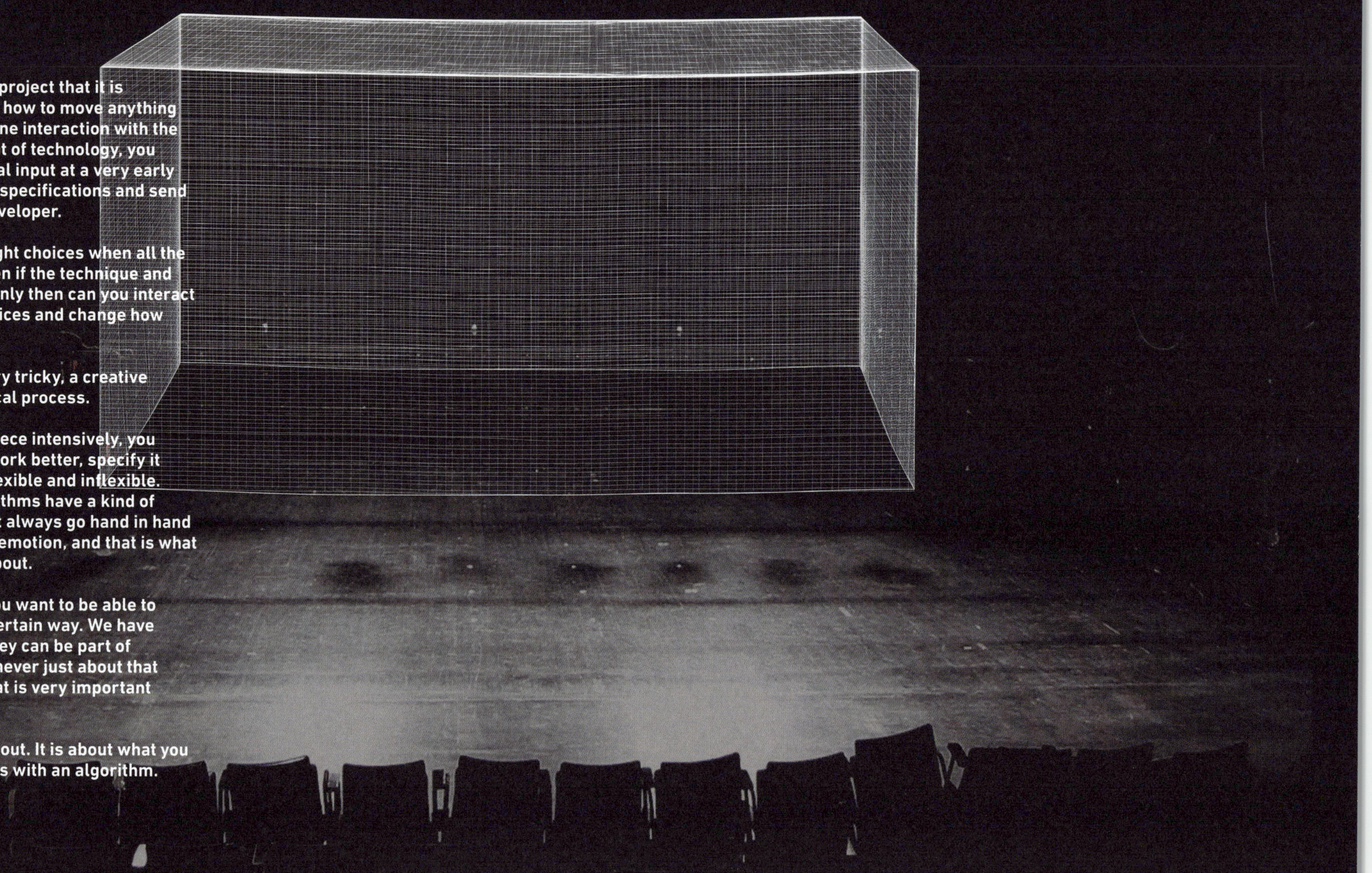

I have learned from this project that it is challenging to figure out how to move anything until you have that genuine interaction with the work. In the development of technology, you usually have the technical input at a very early stage. You have to make specifications and send these to the software developer.

We can only make the right choices when all the conditions are there, even if the technique and object developed fully. Only then can you interact with the work, make choices and change how it has to move.

These processes are very tricky, a creative process versus a technical process.

By getting to know the piece intensively, you can understand the artwork better, specify it next time, and what is flexible and inflexible. I have noticed that algorithms have a kind of randomness that doesn't always go hand in hand with creating a sense of emotion, and that is what art and theater are all about.

That is precisely what you want to be able to time and integrate in a certain way. We have put algorithms in, and they can be part of the experience, but it is never just about that algorithm, and I think that is very important to remember.

It is not an effect you try out. It is about what you want to say and if that fits with an algorithm.

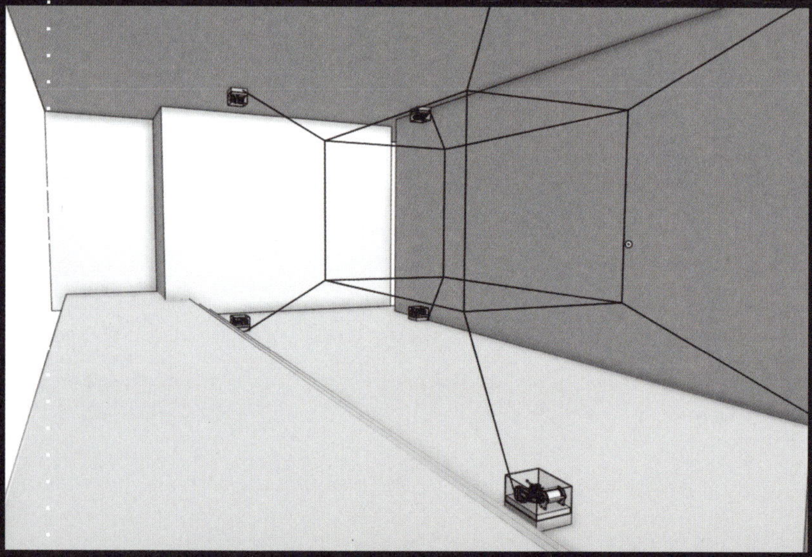

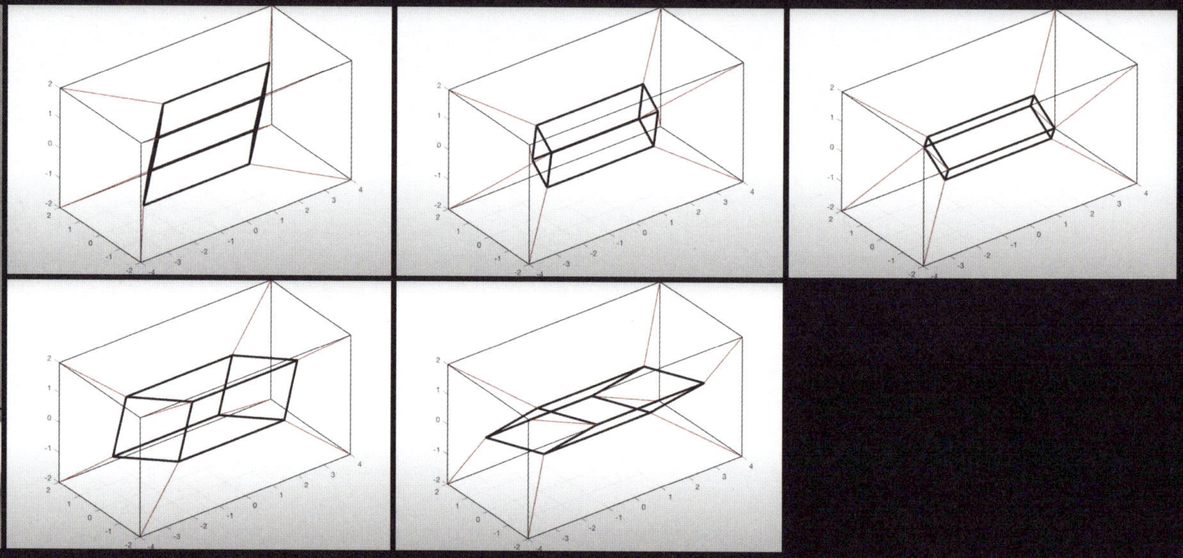

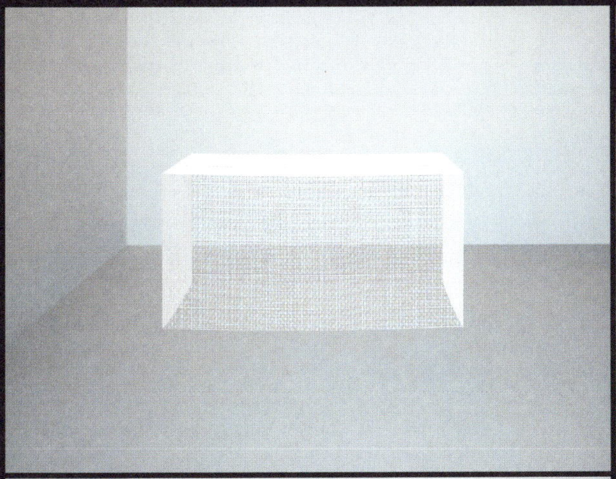

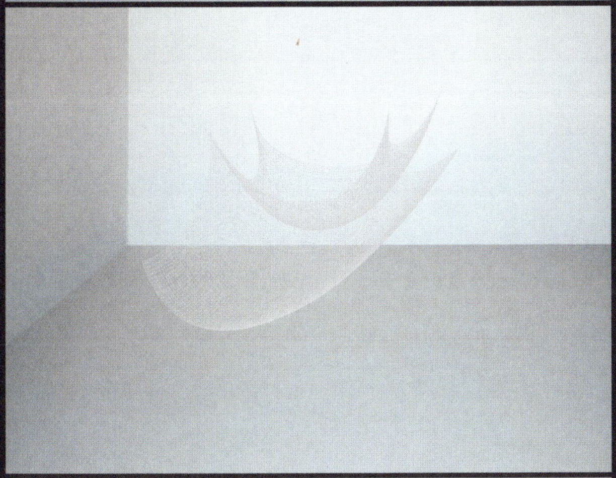

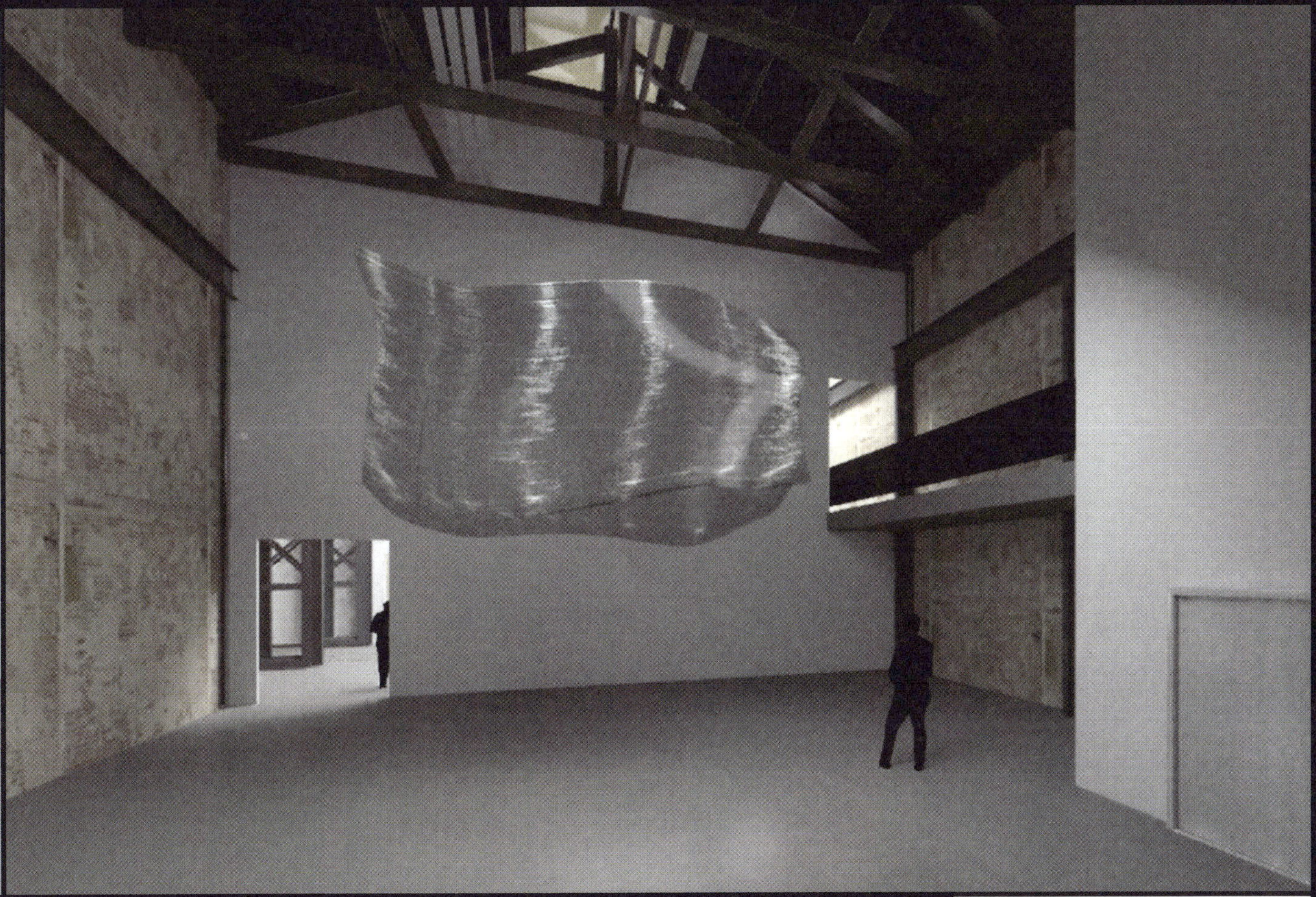

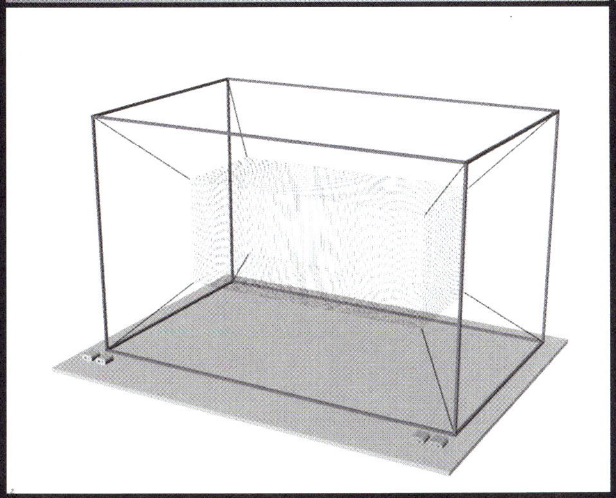

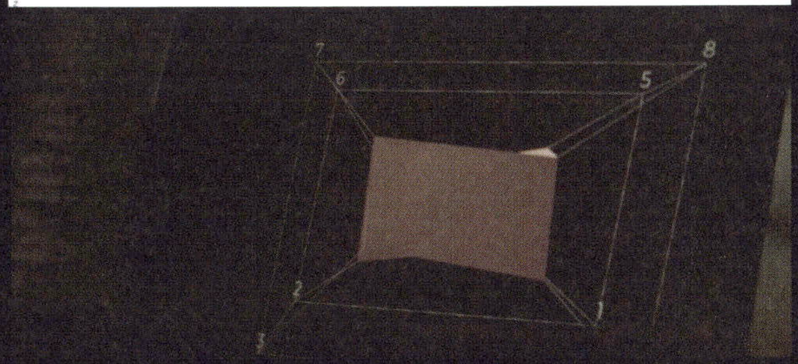

Installation Design / Motor Assemblies

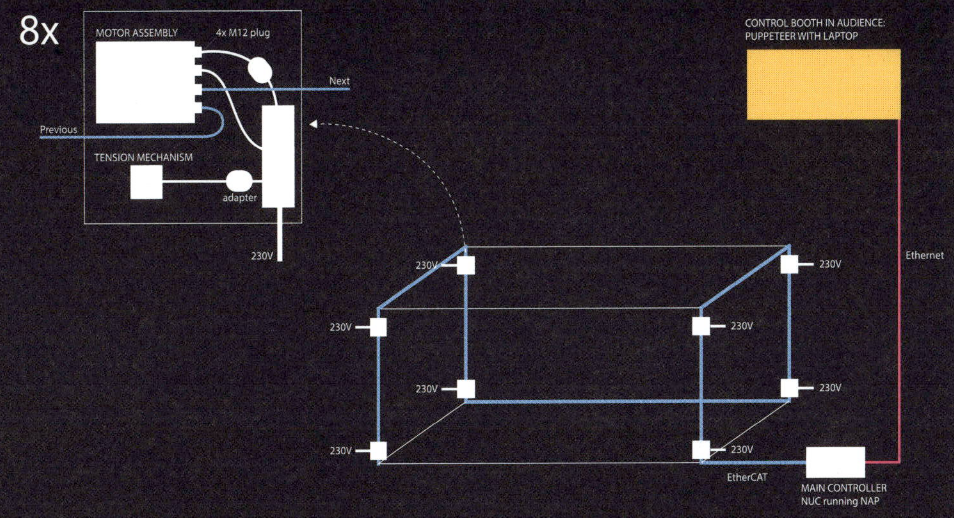

Flexblock / Theater
Nationale Reisopera
23 July 2019

DRIFT
Studio Drift © 2019

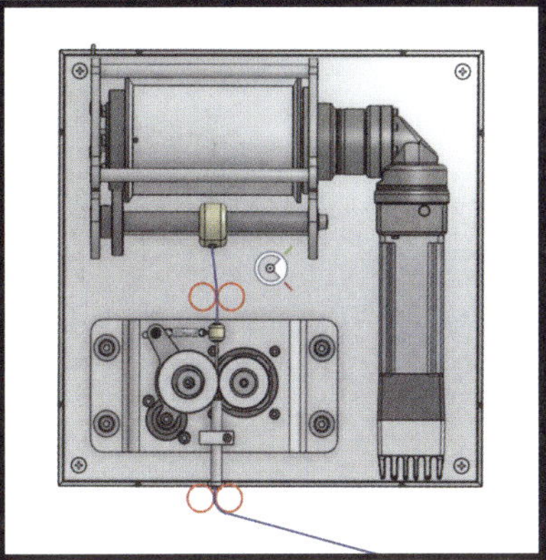

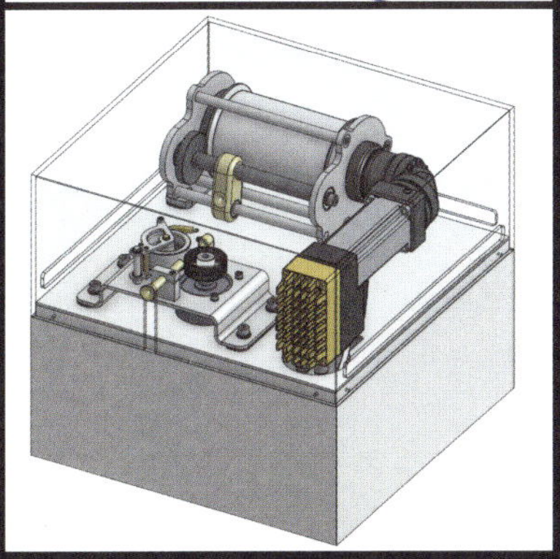

101 . EGO

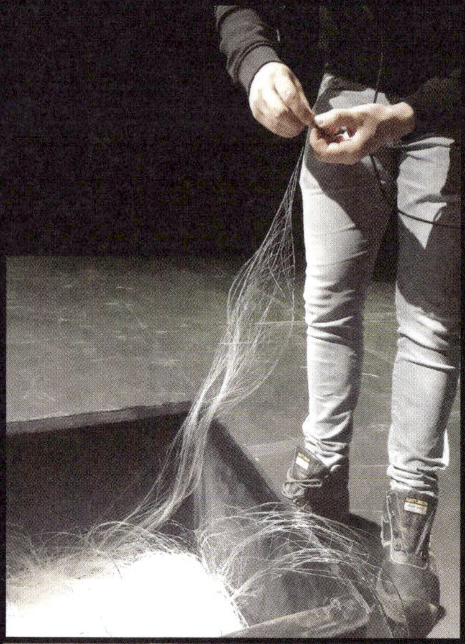

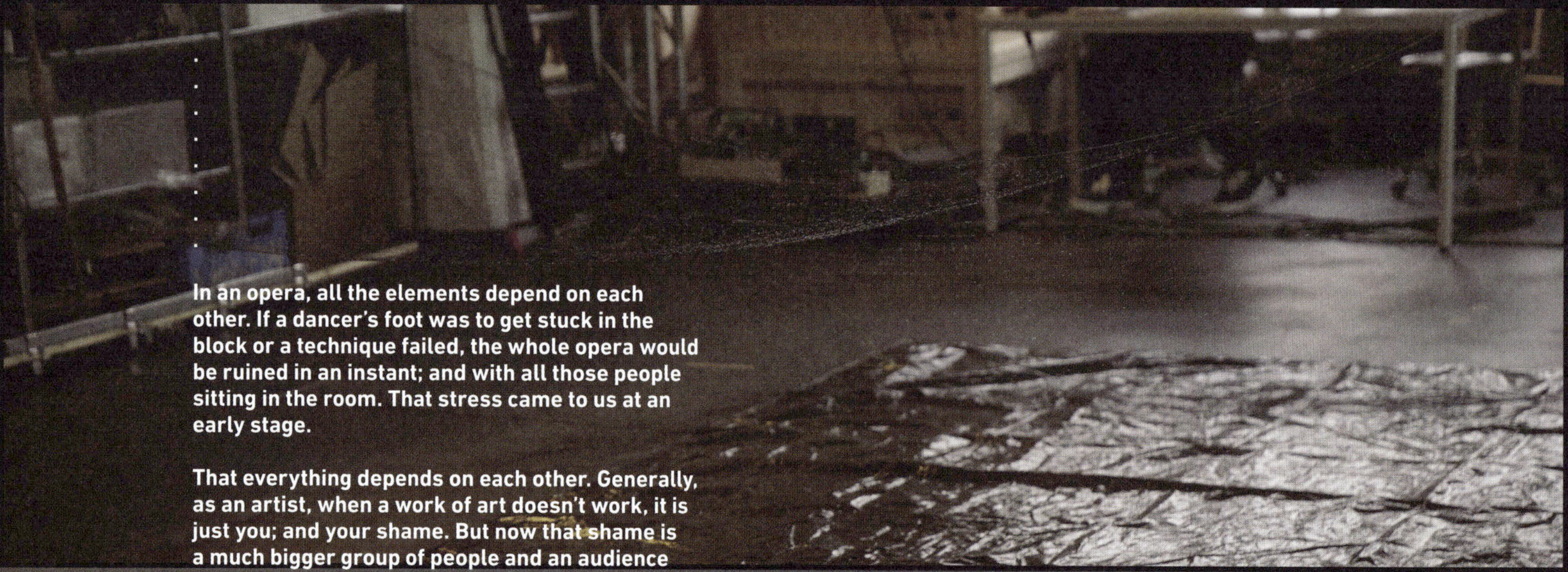

In an opera, all the elements depend on each other. If a dancer's foot was to get stuck in the block or a technique failed, the whole opera would be ruined in an instant; and with all those people sitting in the room. That stress came to us at an early stage.

That everything depends on each other. Generally, as an artist, when a work of art doesn't work, it is just you; and your shame. But now that shame is a much bigger group of people and an audience sitting in a seat in the auditorium watching; that was pretty intense. What I also found interesting was that the theater was entirely new for us.

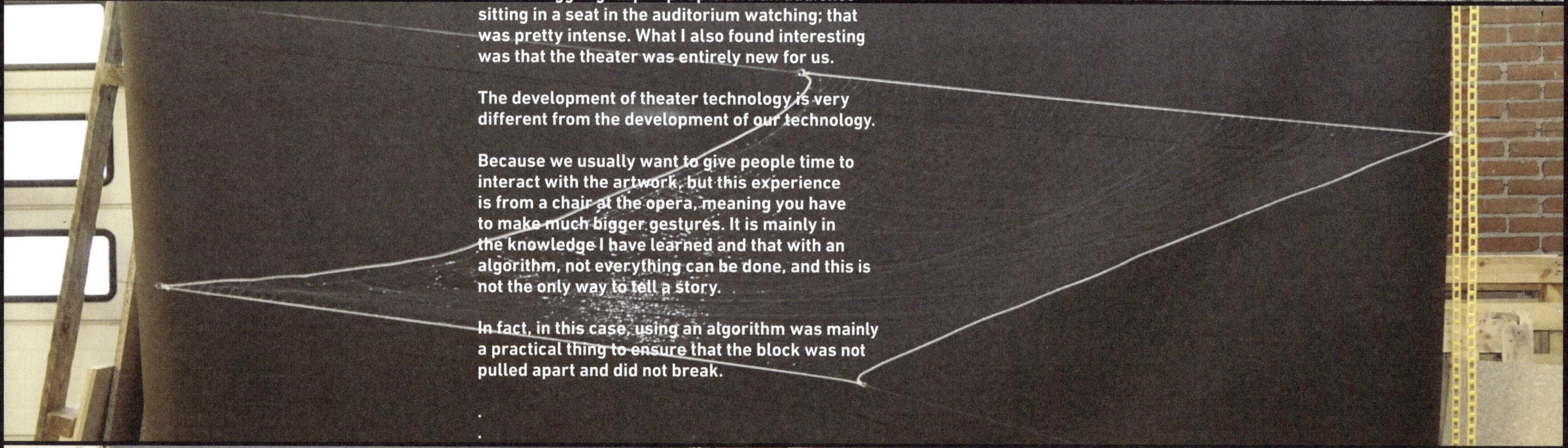

The development of theater technology is very different from the development of our technology.

Because we usually want to give people time to interact with the artwork, but this experience is from a chair at the opera, meaning you have to make much bigger gestures. It is mainly in the knowledge I have learned and that with an algorithm, not everything can be done, and this is not the only way to tell a story.

In fact, in this case, using an algorithm was mainly a practical thing to ensure that the block was not pulled apart and did not break.

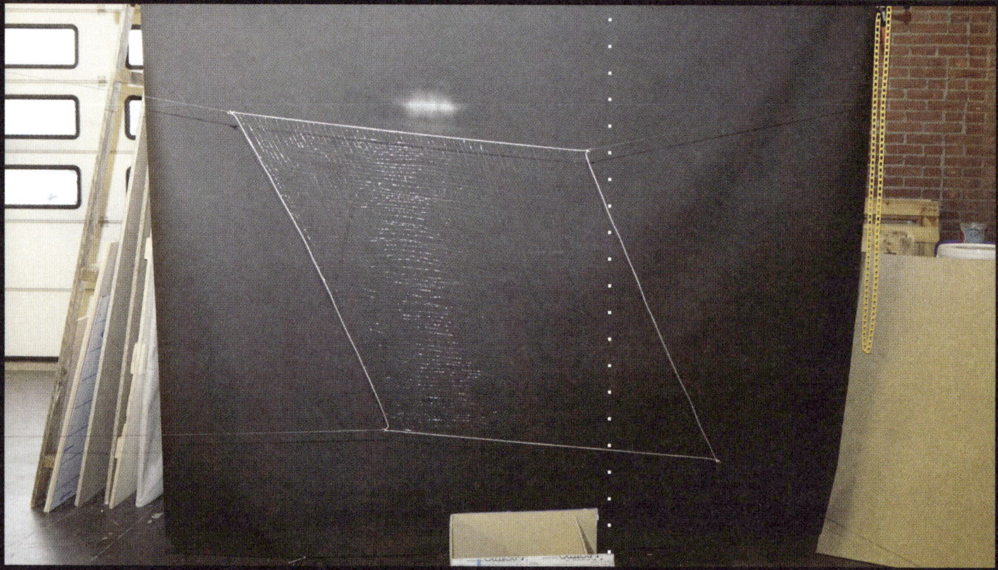

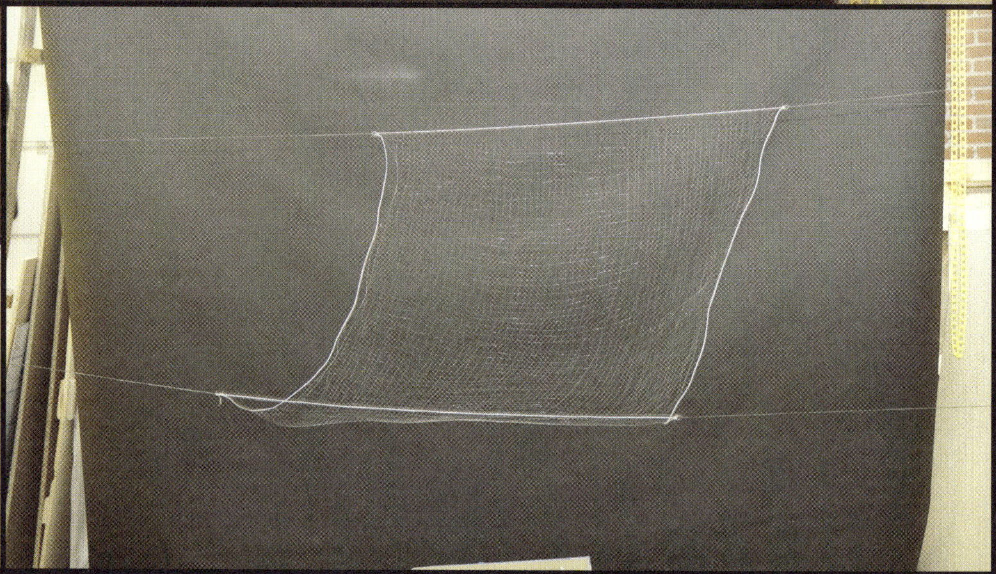

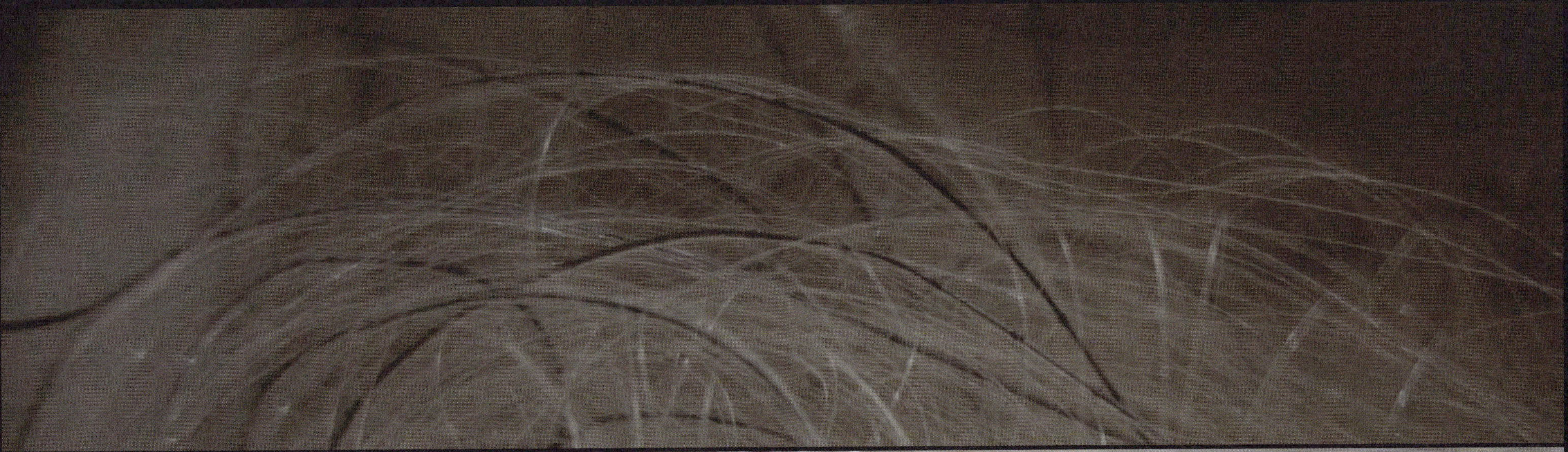
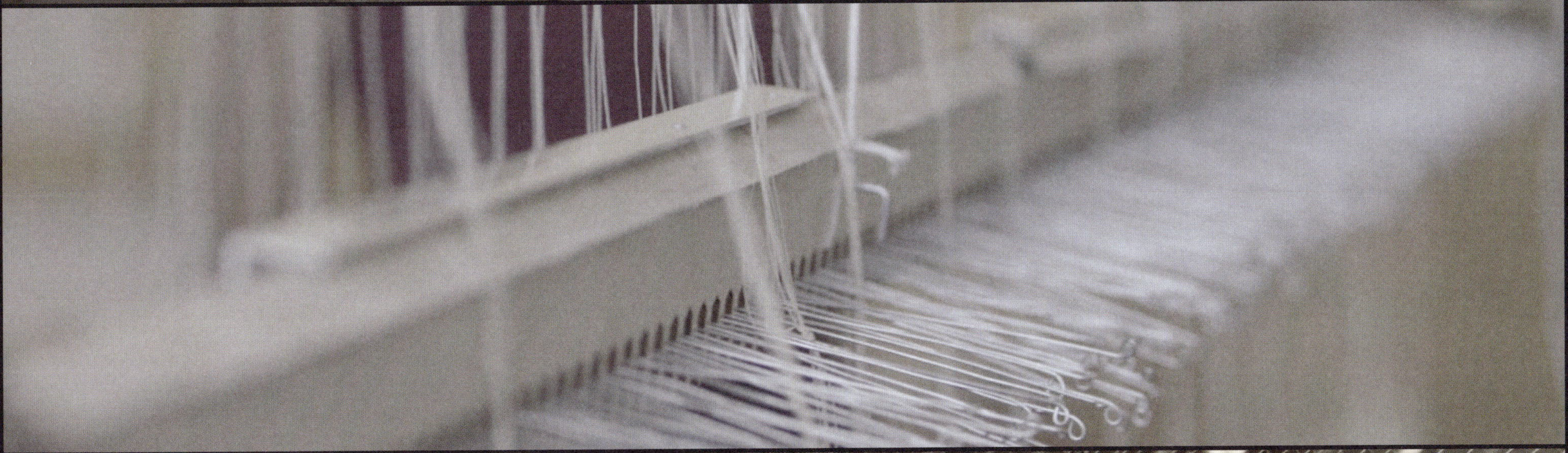
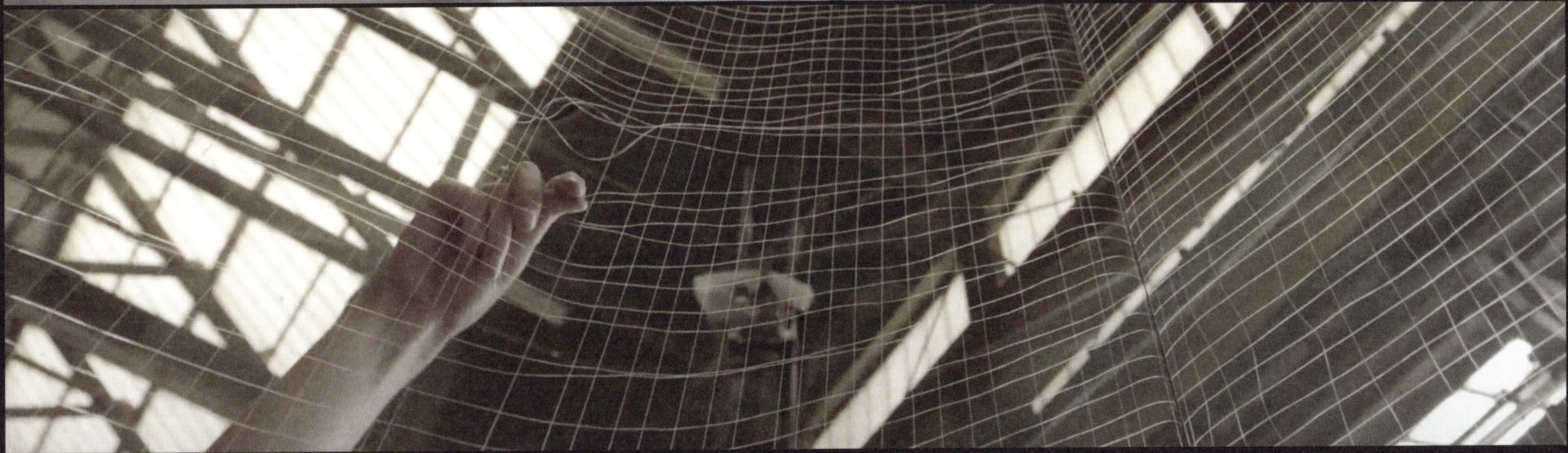

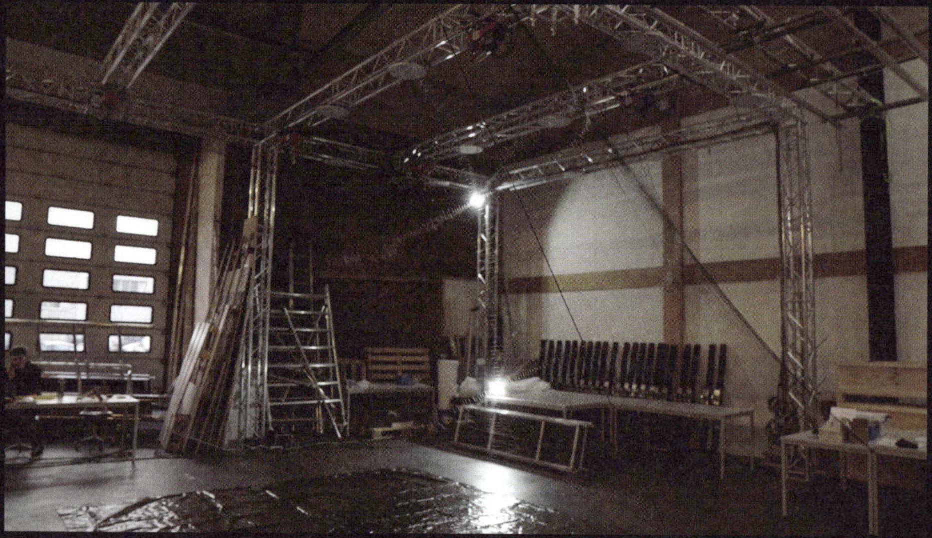

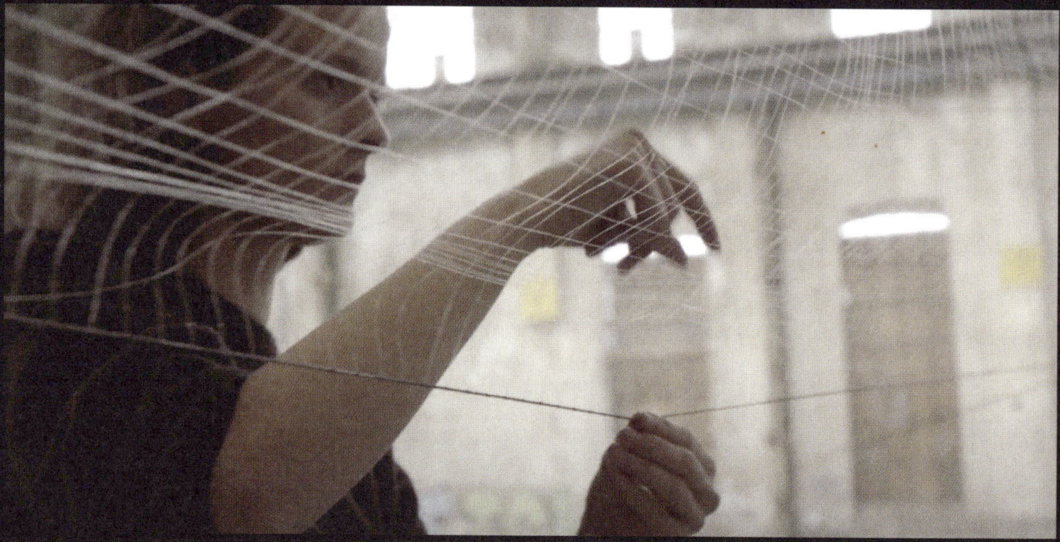

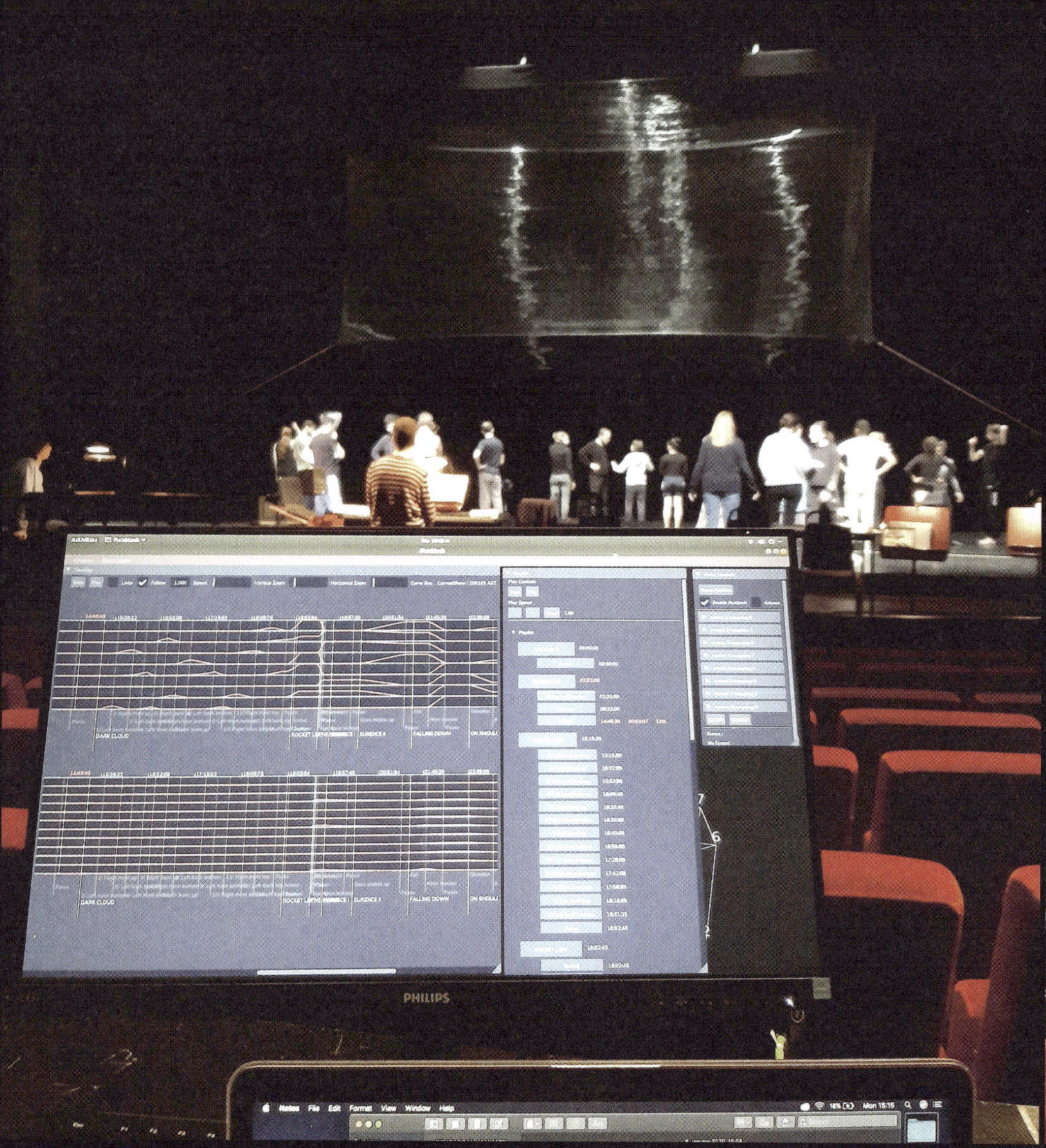
PHILIPS

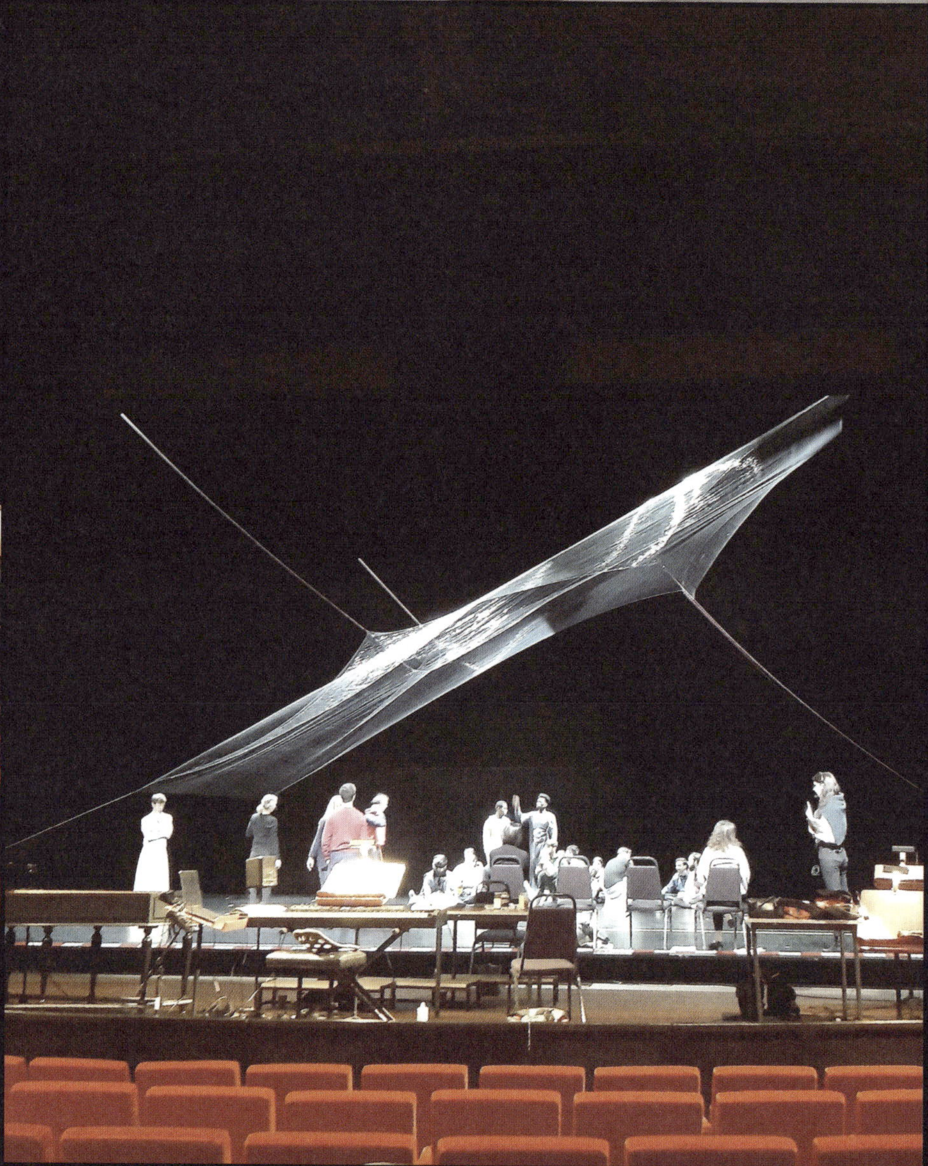

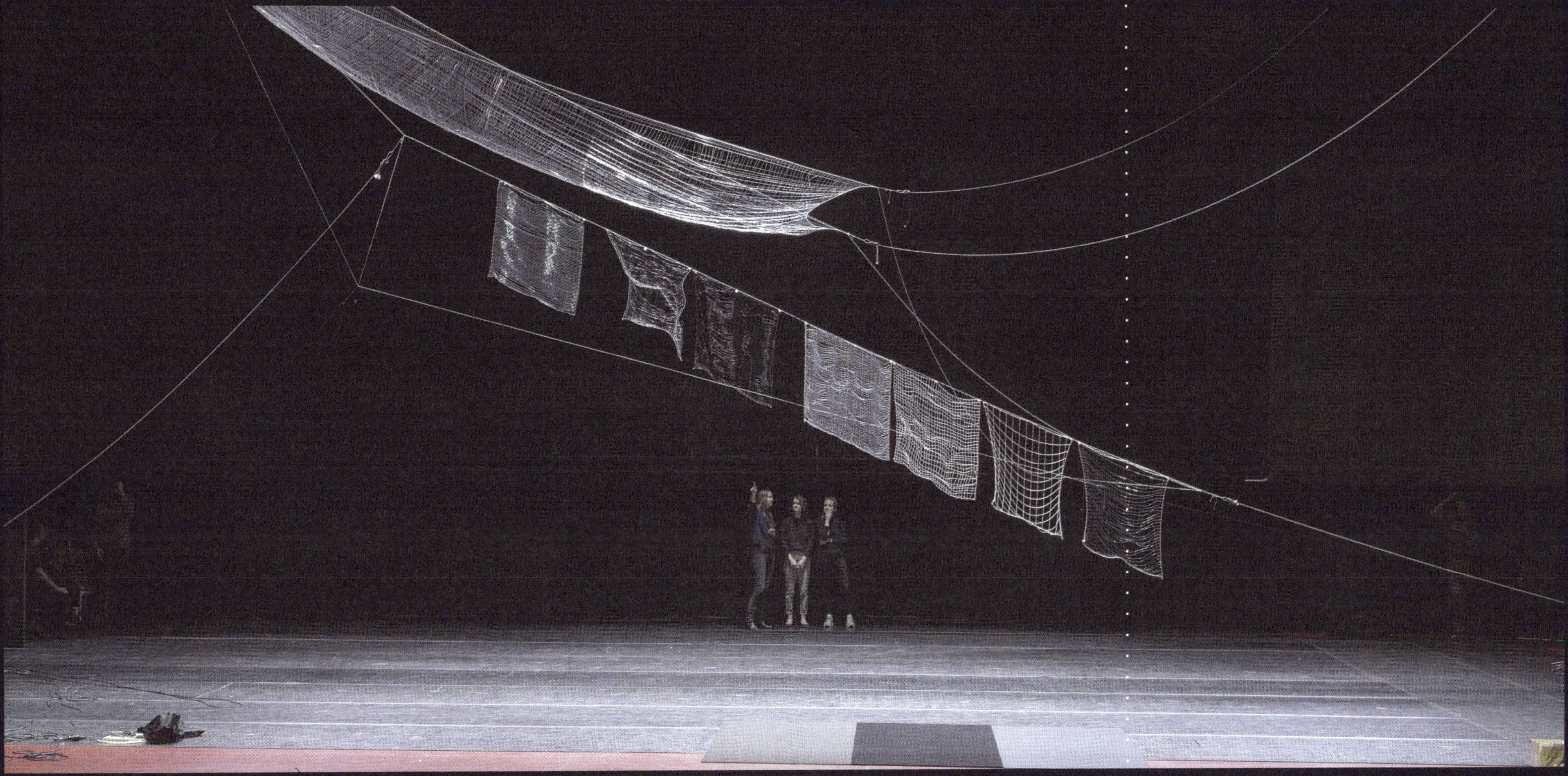

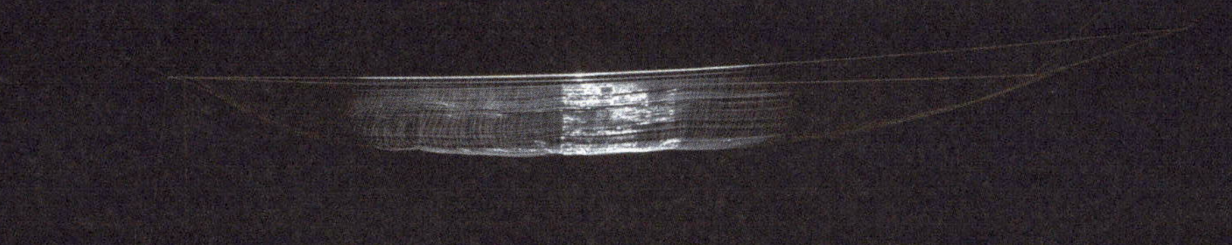

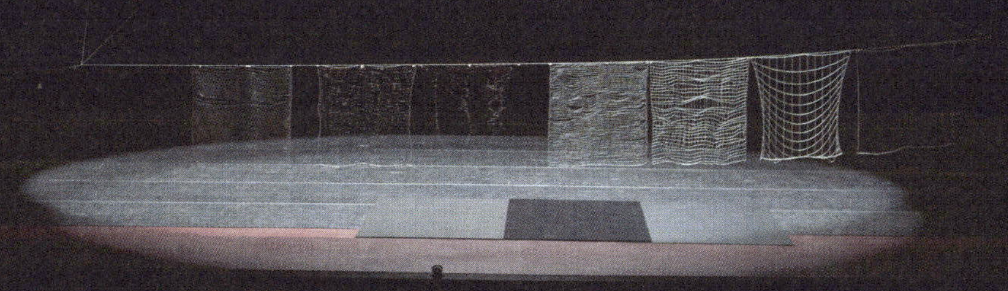

EGO is hand-woven.

We tried to complete this industrially, but there were no machines big enough to do this.

We started with very small test setups. During the physical development, you are also developing the software, so the software and hardware can connect. It was essential in the process that we as artists could operate this flawlessly.

Any alteration in music or dance had a lot of influence on the programming; countless hours matched the programming of the people and the music.

It took us months to get that programming right. In an opera process, you have very clear roles, and our position was new and not always taken into account in the larger process.

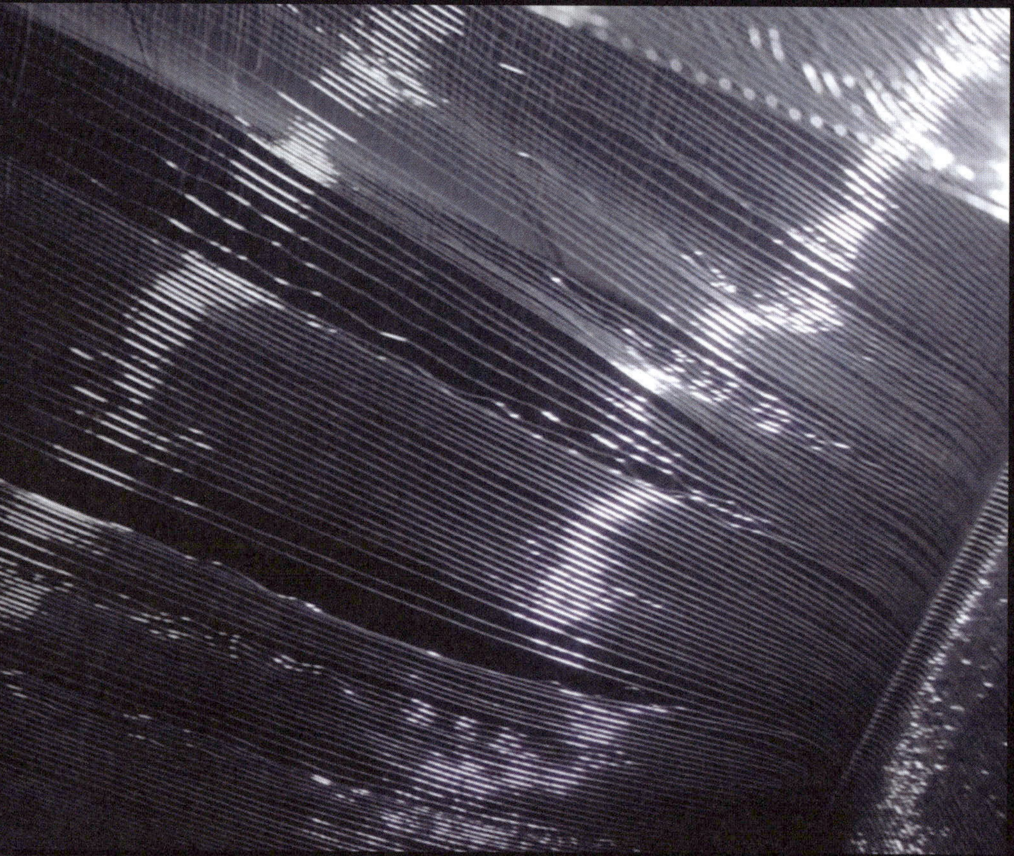

The result created a work of art which was also a character in the opera and, at the same time, the decor. It fulfilled a lot of different roles, but also as a stand-alone work of art. We learned how to meld handicrafts with mechanics, software, theater, opera, dance, and light.

A lot of aspects came together in this work.

This offered us a new dimension to work with, and it was a lot of fun. The thrill of working towards a premiere, one moment, is exciting; the tension behind and in front of the scenes. The discoveries during the process, uncovering what that block could do, were way more rewarding than we could have imagined.

You usually look at art in your own time, with your own time, and only look for a few seconds. In an opera, you are put in one place, from which you watch for 2.5 hours.

We were partially responsible for that entire period and therefore responsible for remaining important.

It is not just the viewer's story and the artwork, but it is a very different story.

Sometimes I find that intrusive; I also came to like my new understanding of the potentiality of art and its role in theater design and stage art.

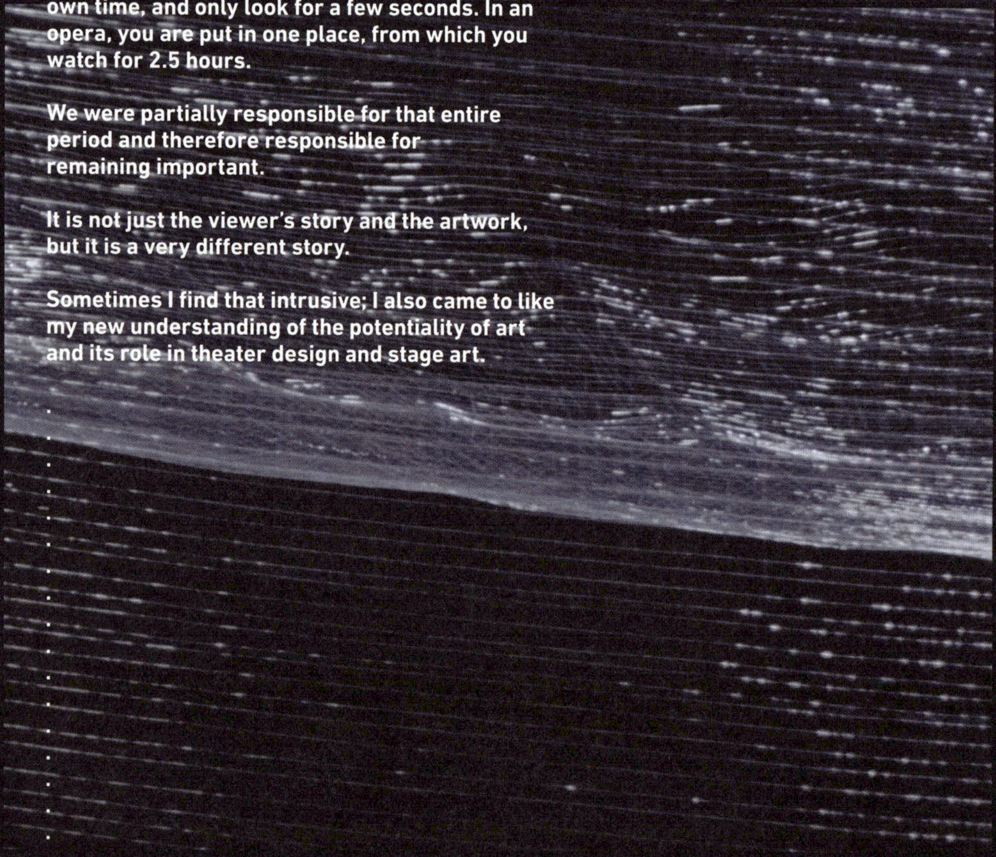

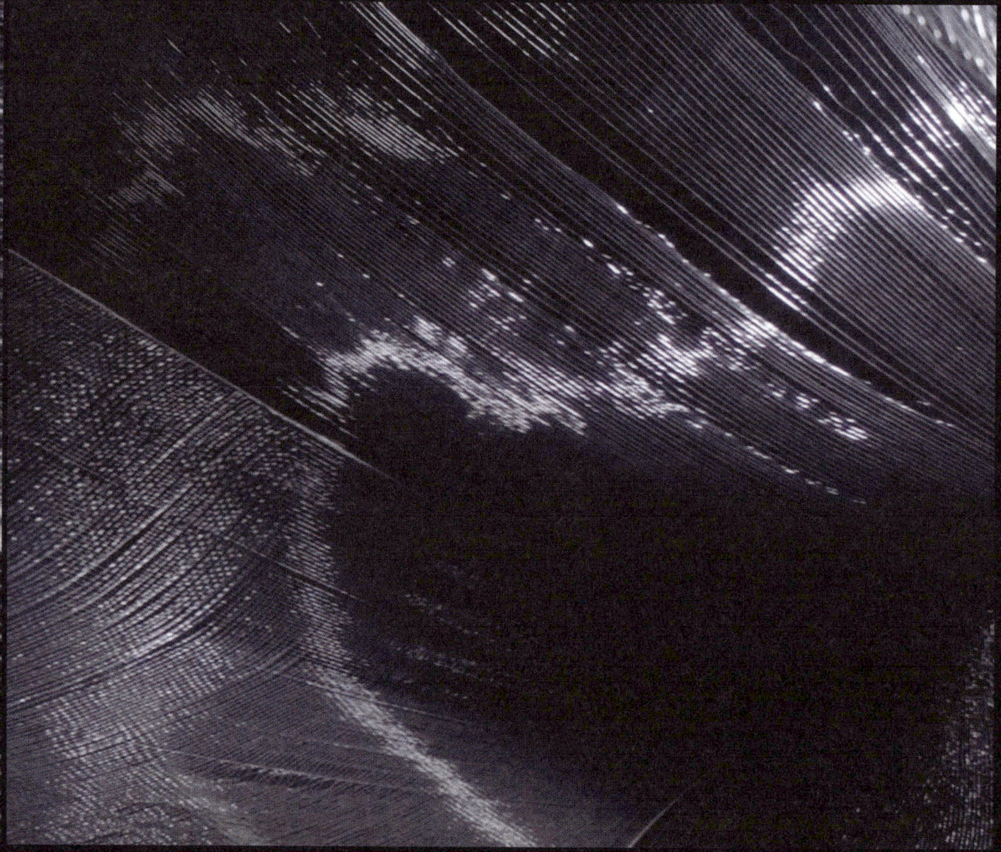

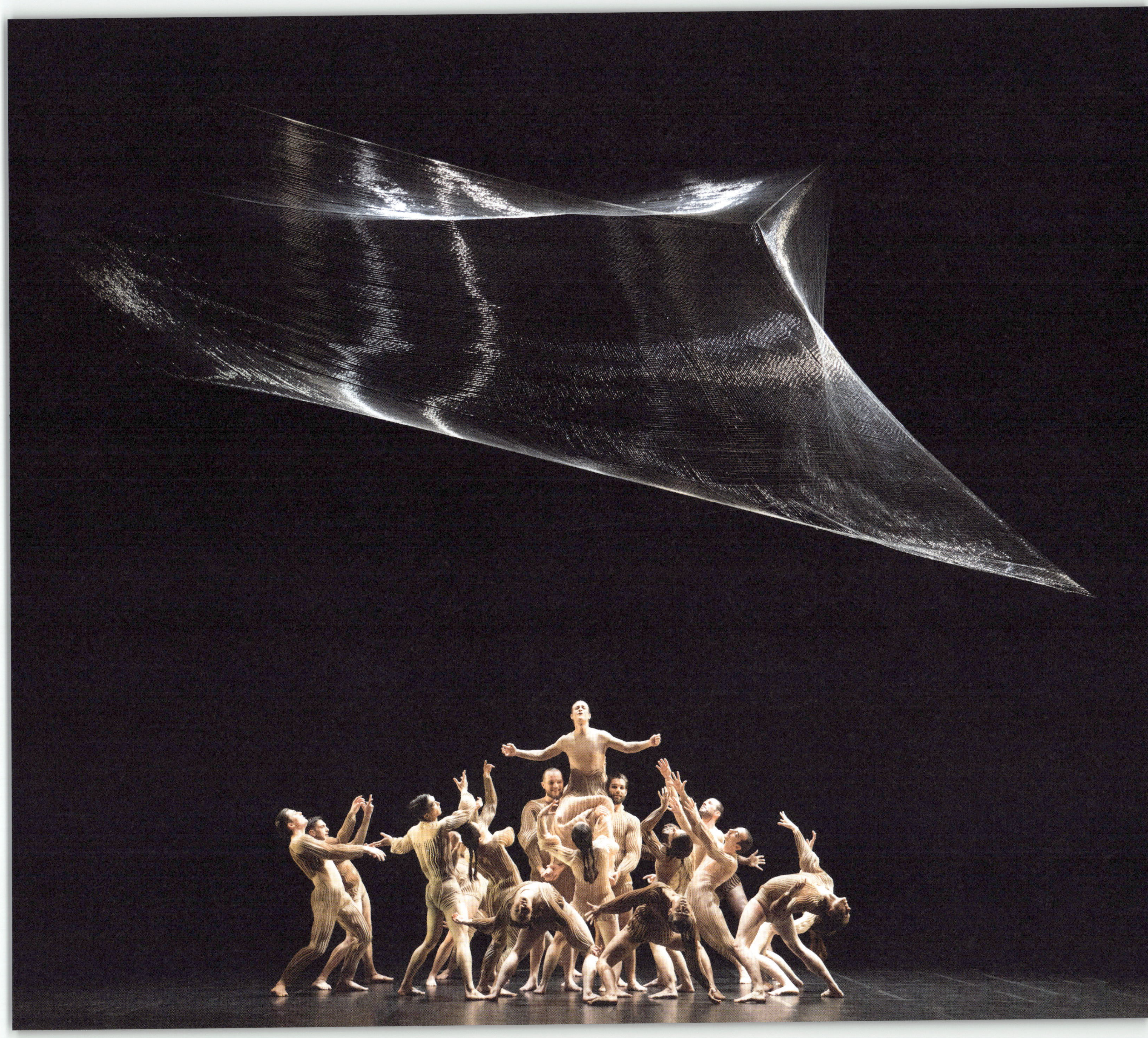

When I came in contact with the work of DRIFT I immediately realized that these autonomous artists possessed a new sort of language with which to communicate the Orfeo's myth to an audience. Lonneke Gordijn created EGO as an intriguing and spectacular theatrical concept to enhance the core of the story; and made the artwork a crucial part of the opera. The subsequent collaboration was very inspirational.

Greek mythology gave the ancient Greeks explanations about the origin of the earth and universe.

EGO reveals the soul of Orfeo by using shapes and movements; sometimes soft, round and flowing, sometimes hard, angular and rigid. Whilst metaphorically the imagery recalls the lyre of Orfeo. The stage is one vast network filaments; comparable to a living organism in which countless threads are woven into an open nervous system. EGO behaves like a real performer; poetic and meaningful. A true Greek drama and at the same time both modern and contemporary.

It was, according to lighting designer Thomas Hase: "like illuminating a piece of glass."

Monique Wagemakers, opera director.

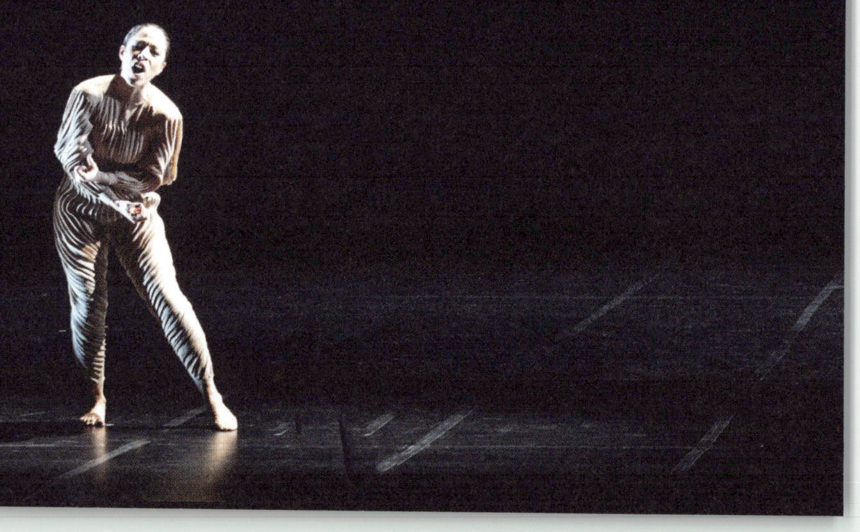

CREDITS

Ego, L'Orfeo 2020, Wilmink Theater Enschede (NL)

Pictures by Marco Borggreve

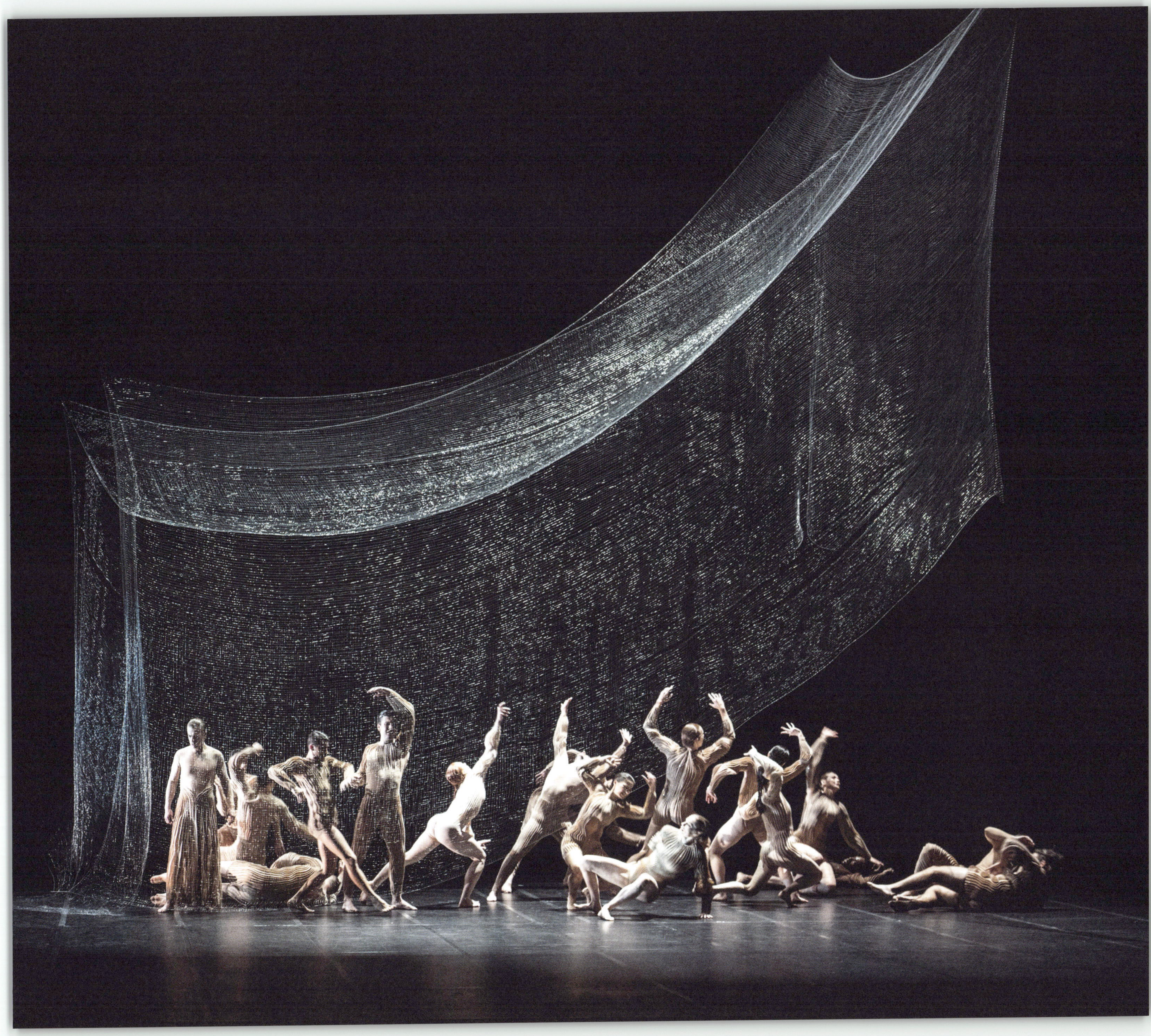

De tr oi t Un de rg ro un d™

Name:

Detroit Underground™

Artists:

- 0100110110
- 30drop
- Abjective
- Adam Jay
- Agony Forces
- Andrew Red Hand
- Anklepants
- Annie Hall
- Anthony Jimenez
- Apparat
- Ariadne's Labyrinth
- Bovaflux
- Brayan Valenzuela
- Corbin Davis
- Derek Michael
- Dinamite
- DJ Shiva
- Drumcell
- dyLAB
- EEZIR
- ErisSoundworks
- Exillon
- Exium
- Fenin
- Fluxion A/D
- FURS
- Gabriela Penn
- Galcid
- Gotshell
- Hisashi Saito
- Housemeister
- Ikuko Morozumi
- Jerry Abstract
- Jesse Somfay
- Jessica Kert
- Jimmy Edgar
- Joe Sousa
- Julia Bondar
- ke thu
- Keith Kemp
- Kero
- Loud Neighbor
- Madam Modesty
- Marshall Applewhite
- Material Object
- Matt Herdman
- Modeselektor
- Module One
- Mutate
- Noncompliant
- Nullptr
- Oscar Mulero
- Otto Von Schirach
- Phon.o
- Positive Merge
- Project 313
- pulsewidthmod
- Punisher
- Rebecca Goldberg
- Reeko
- Rex Sepulveda
- Richard Devine
- Rob Clouth
- Saskiatokyo
- Scan 7
- Shrubbn!!
- Snezhana Reizen
- Soela
- Soramimi
- Sound Psychologist
- Steve Kuehl
- The Allegorist
- Vaetxh
- Veronique Page
- XDCVR
- Yaporigami

URL:

detroitunderground.net
detund.bandcamp.com

Instagram:

@detroitunderground

Detroit Underground™, established in 1997, is a creative set of principles positioned somewhere between design, music and the crossroads where it all comes together.

Imagine an enormous field, static radiating from the earth in fragmented shocks of white light. Wheat sparks in flames, warming them and their cracked hands, gnarled from a million years of nothingness. A warmth that permeates muscles, tissues and tendons.

Is it somewhere in the tissue wedged between her teeth from those tentacles she puked up at the side of the road, squirming from her gums, her bone, her gut? They reach out to embrace you, wriggling and beckoning and crying in silence.

Maybe it's deep, deep below the earth, hidden away, a heavy pulse running through twisted, steaming tunnels filled with faceless and eager individuals. They dance, labyrinths of darkness engulfing hollow bodies, light glimmering from empty eye sockets, looking out as if to say,

"Where are we going? What are we now?"

No one quite knows the answer to that now, do they?

Follow the tracks, slight glints of light reflecting on broken, rusted metal, the cracks between the rust slowly illuminating from eyeball headlamps, swivelling and pivoting in the heat. Find the sunlight sneaking in, but it's far too far to ever get there.

The result to some equations, sequenced numbers, points here and there. Try to make sense of the pixels and figures floating between their minds and minds and minds, digits transforming into thoughts that connect one synapse to the next, firing off into air white with winter.

Perhaps it's otherworldly, but regardless, Detroit Underground™ bridges gaps between this world and theirs; art, sound, aesthetic and noise.

The aesthetic is immediately recognizable, pieces of color that seem sharp enough to cut oneself on, icicles smashed and shattered into great big broken glass. The music veers this and way that, slightly straying from the dance floor basics and classic Detroit techno sound, shifting into the experimental: IDM, techno, electro, glitch, etcetera and etcetera. The list goes on, but don't fret; Detroit Underground™ will never force you into that dark abyss of incomprehensible and unlistenable noise.

The music is music, extraordinarily stretching the limitations of electronics, exploring the unknown, bringing those who deserve recognition into the spotlight.

Detroit Underground™ is a multidisciplinary arts collective, functioning primarily as a record label. But that's not all. Forever expanding, discovering, and exploring, Detroit Underground™ continues to change, morph, and excite its audience, its members and colleagues.

Words via Sophia Warren

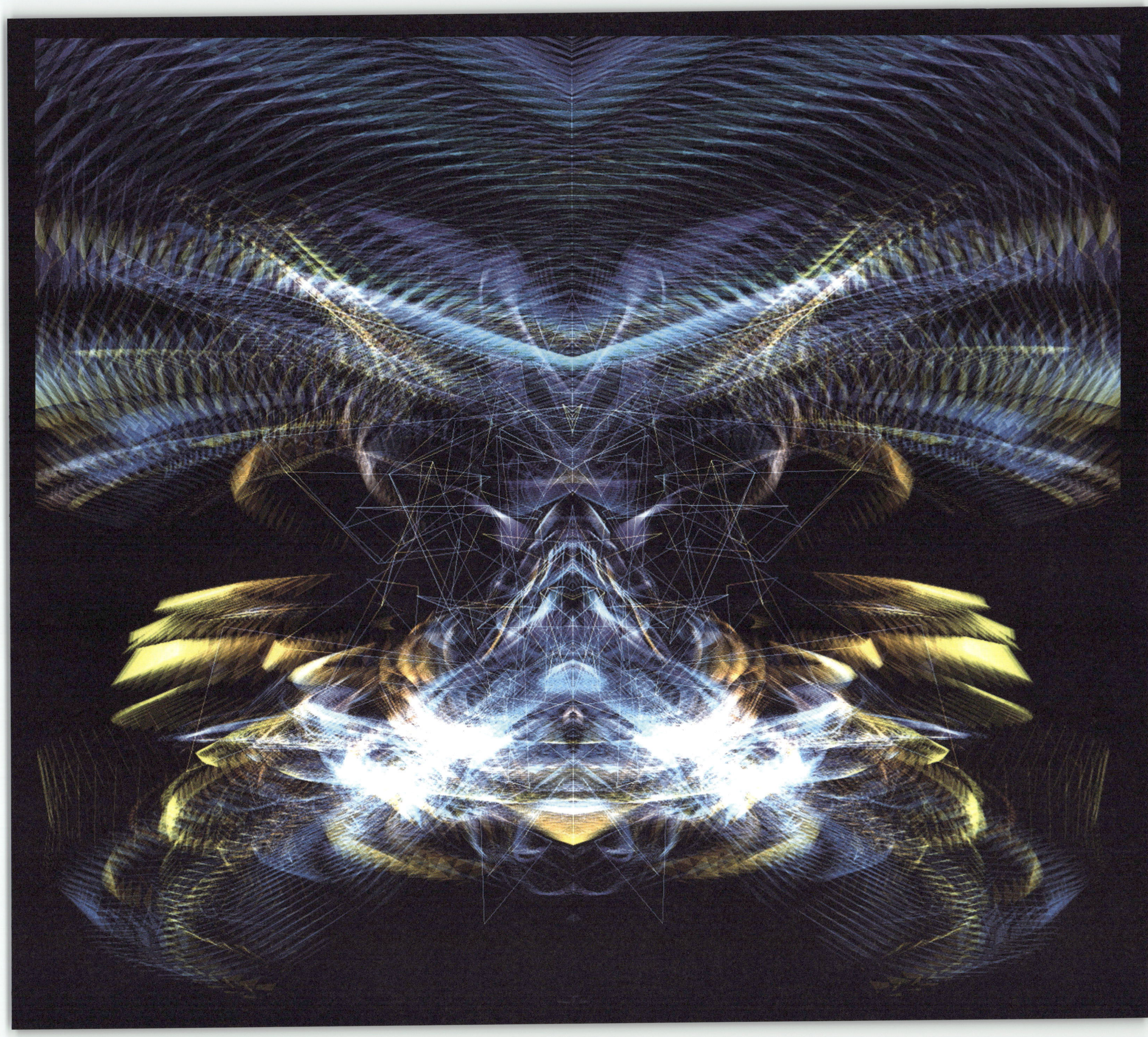

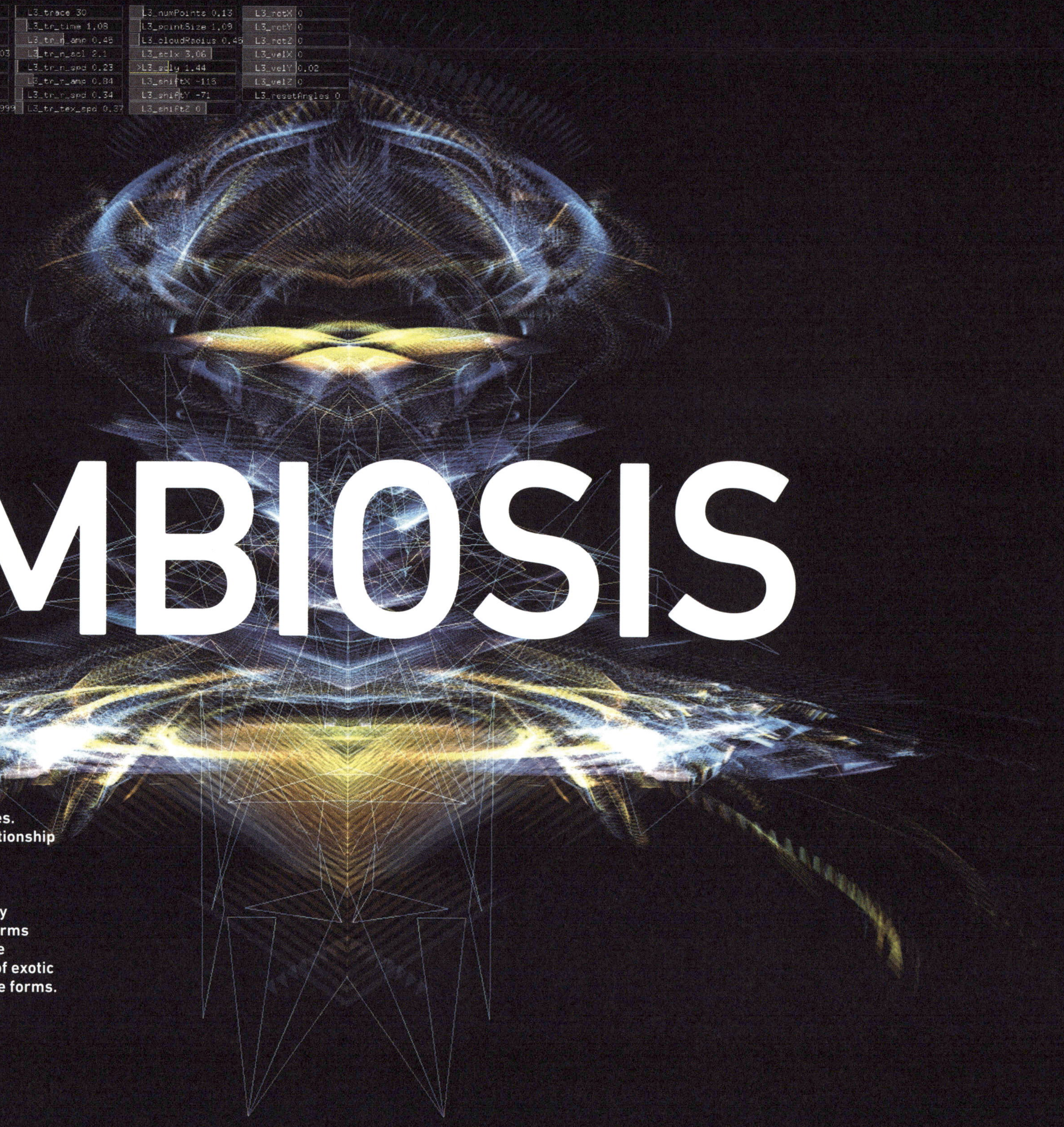

SYMBIOSIS

Interactive installation by Kuflex

In the installation area, the human body is augmented with video projected virtual images. Viewer and technology enter a symbiotic relationship and, as a result, bring to life extraordinary biomorphic creatures.

They constantly change, reacting to your every movement and turning into new and unique forms each time. The installation was inspired by the symmetry of living organisms, the structure of exotic insects, and reflections on extraterrestrial life forms.

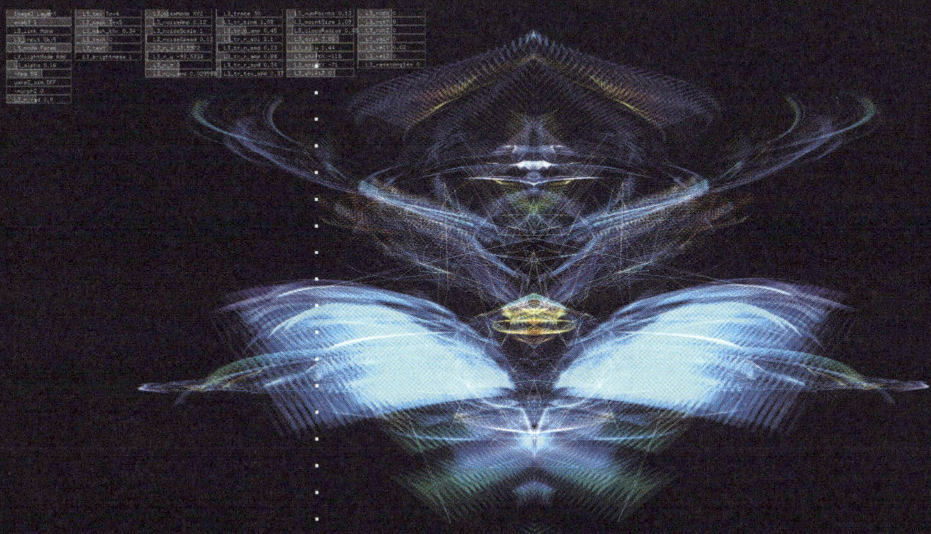

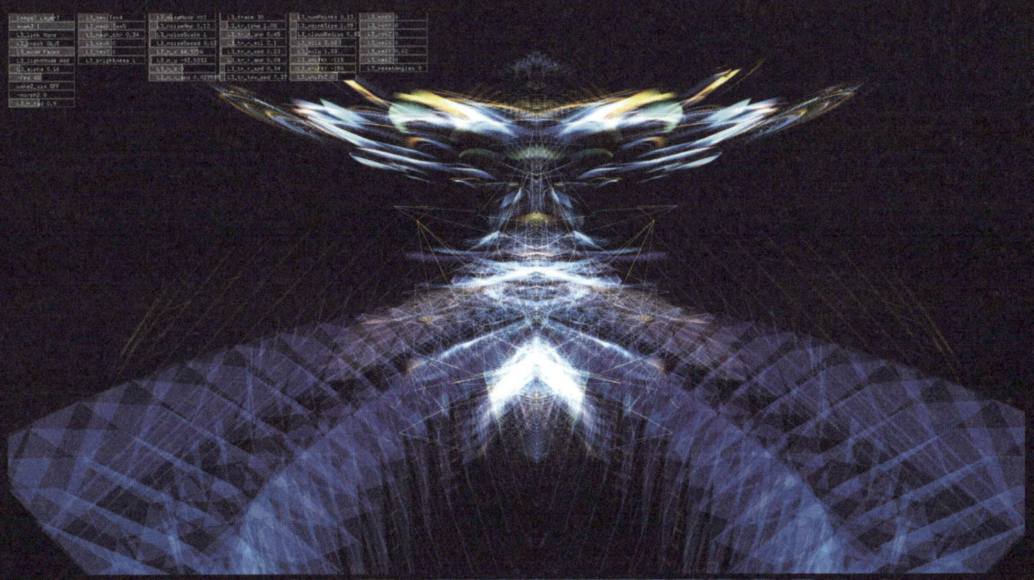

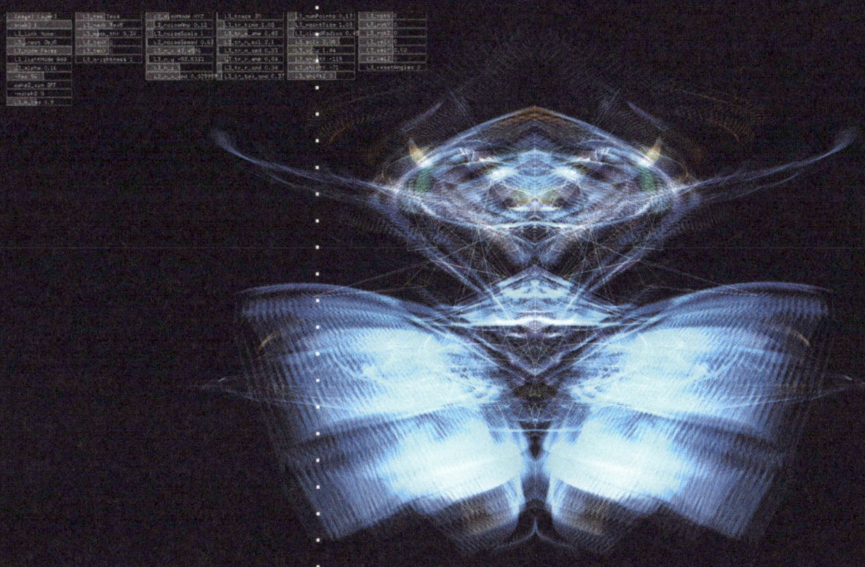

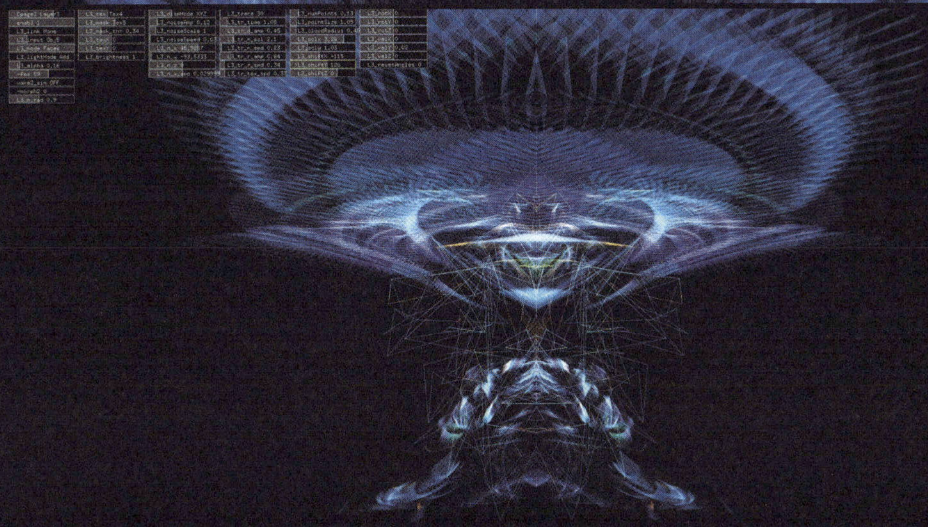

The images are generated using technology, which we call "subtractive video synthesis," that is, video synthesis, based on cutting the "superfluous" parts off a three-dimensional object, similar to a sound subtractive synthesis or the work of a sculptor with stone.

In our case, there is a surface of a 3D object that is repeatedly duplicated with parameter changes and modulation of the vertex position using Perlin 3D noise.

Next, we randomly cut off the extra polygons of the object. The transparency and color of the polygons are controlled by several textures, which are also generated in real-time through several Perlin noise functions.

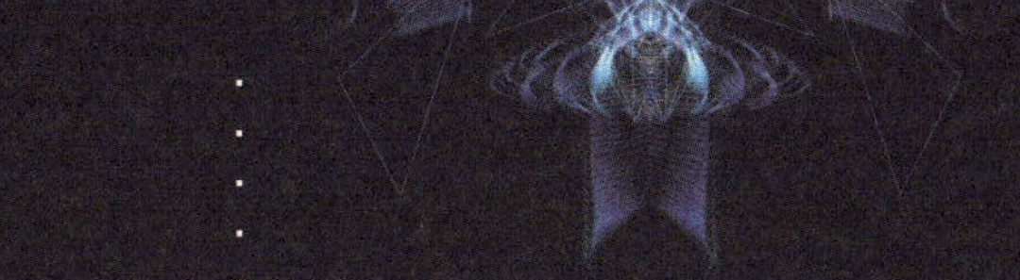

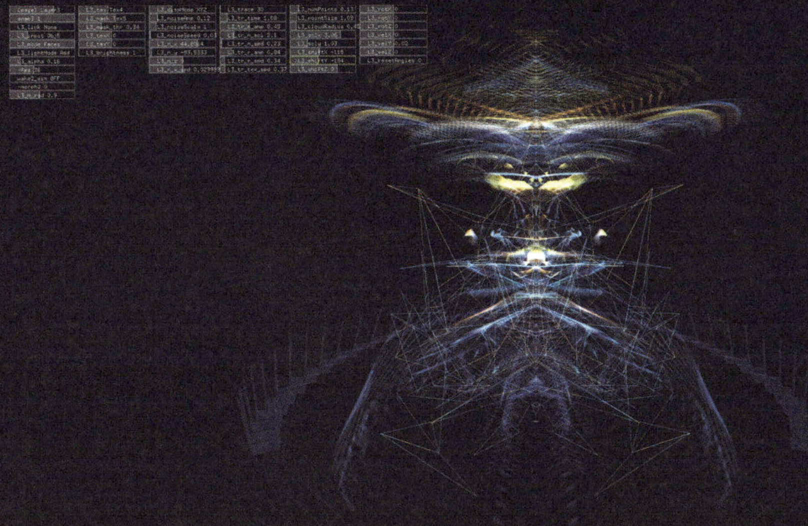

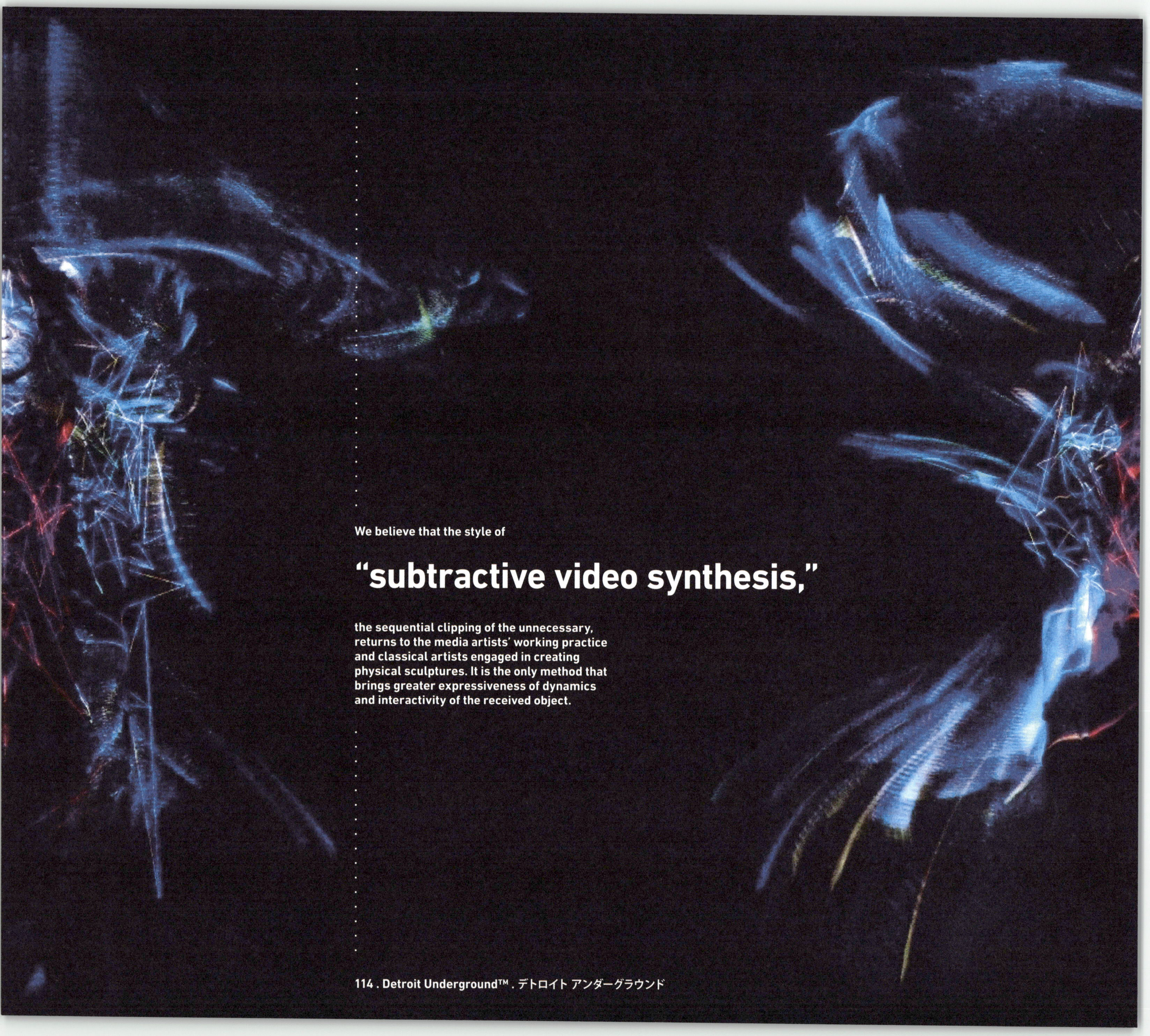

We believe that the style of

“subtractive video synthesis,”

the sequential clipping of the unnecessary, returns to the media artists’ working practice and classical artists engaged in creating physical sculptures. It is the only method that brings greater expressiveness of dynamics and interactivity of the received object.

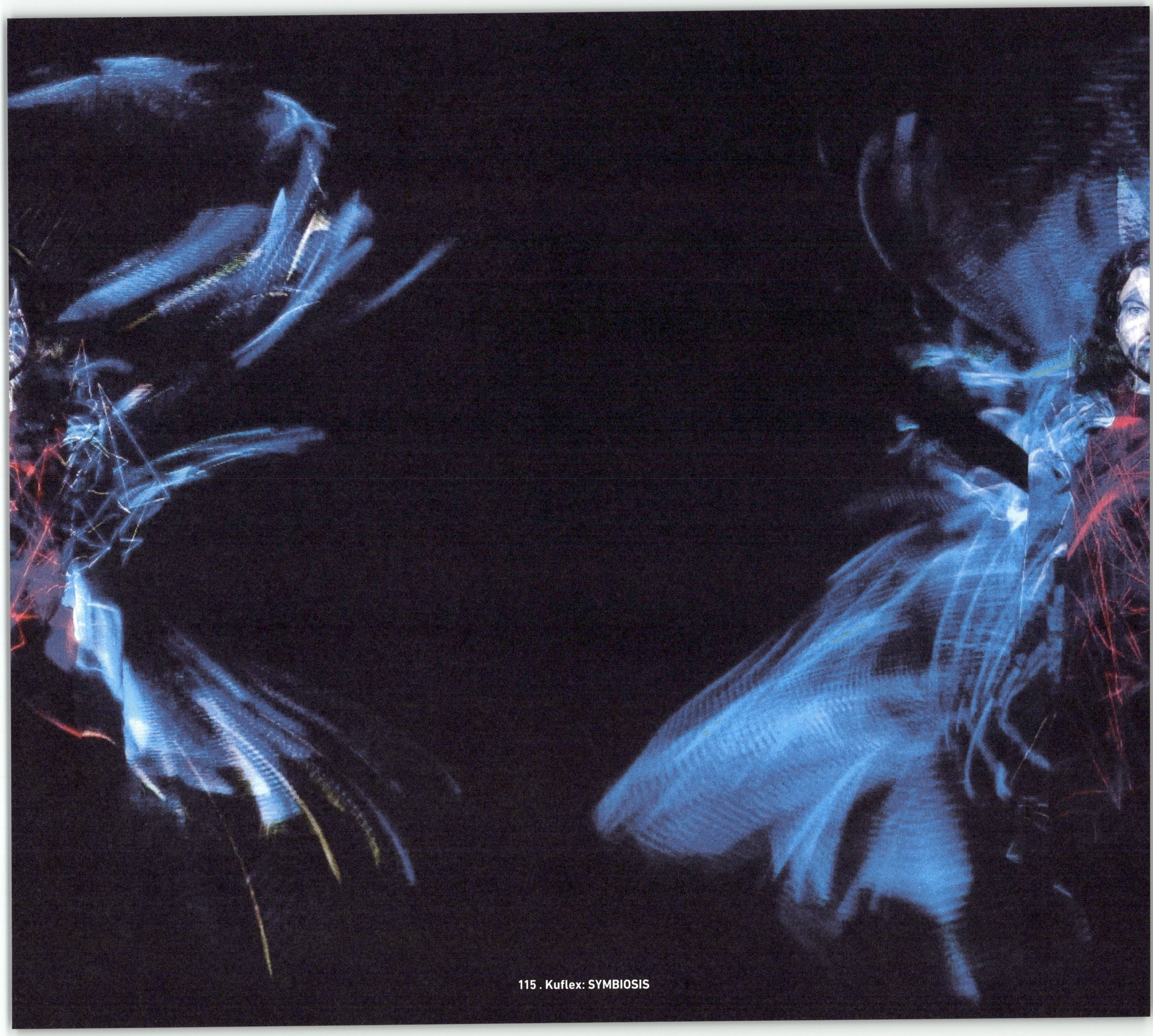

115 . Kuflex: SYMBIOSIS

DU™_ VHS

Jean-Christophe Naour

Data is Art.

No other short-form medium can reach millions of viewers. Music videos as an art form are more important today than ever before.

They are part of our visual language. An essential part of the culture of our consumption of music, art & entertainment ...

In some ways, music videos have become even more critical than artwork because of the way we consume music today. We used to buy a physical album with a beautiful cover design, but today we consume it on various platforms. Today, YouTube is the second largest search engine behind Google and the largest music streaming service in the world. Discovering new music is easy, but there's an under-curation in an oversaturated content library.

-VHS

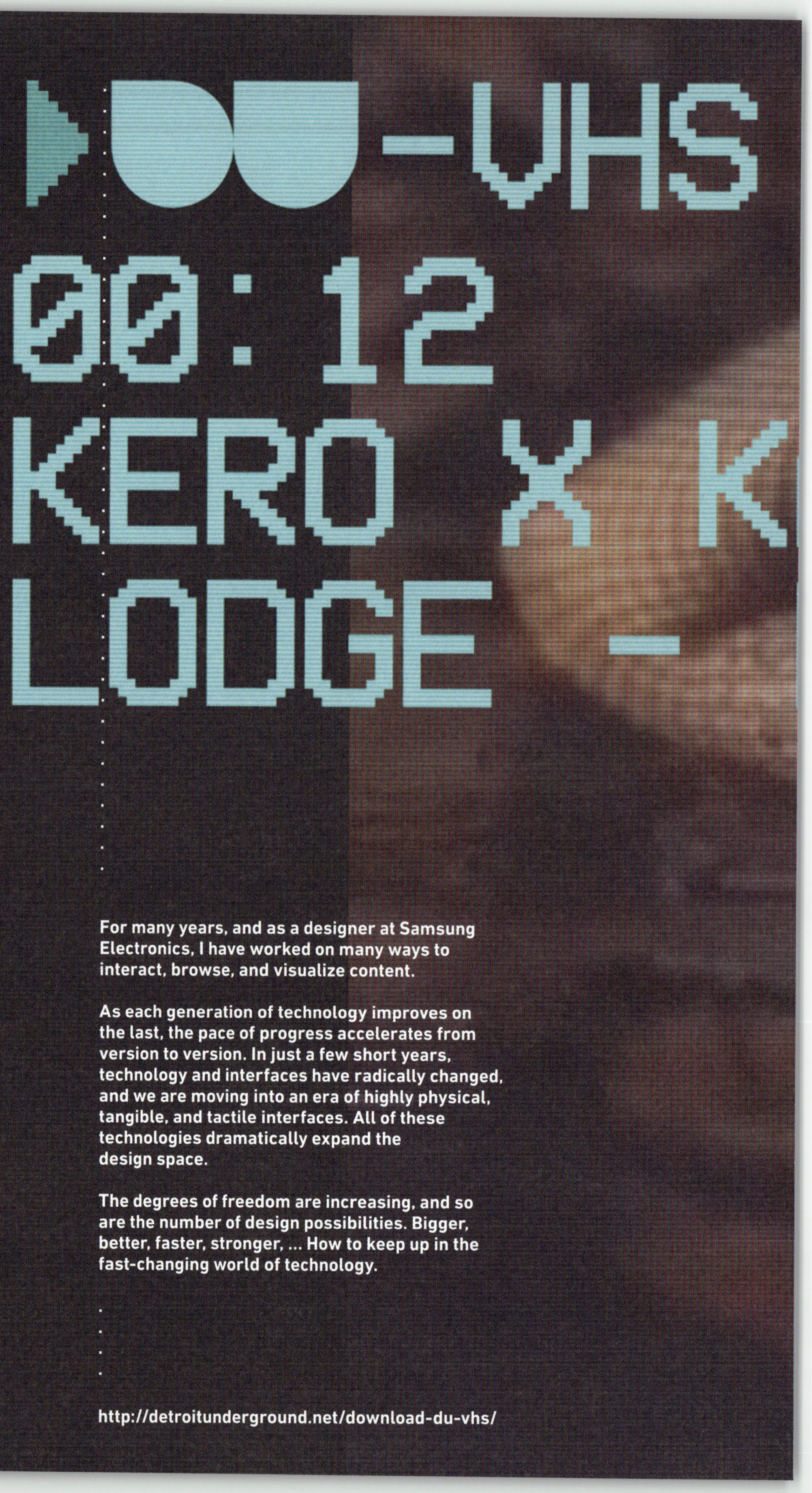

For many years, and as a designer at Samsung Electronics, I have worked on many ways to interact, browse, and visualize content.

As each generation of technology improves on the last, the pace of progress accelerates from version to version. In just a few short years, technology and interfaces have radically changed, and we are moving into an era of highly physical, tangible, and tactile interfaces. All of these technologies dramatically expand the design space.

The degrees of freedom are increasing, and so are the number of design possibilities. Bigger, better, faster, stronger, ... How to keep up in the fast-changing world of technology.

http://detroitunderground.net/download-du-vhs/

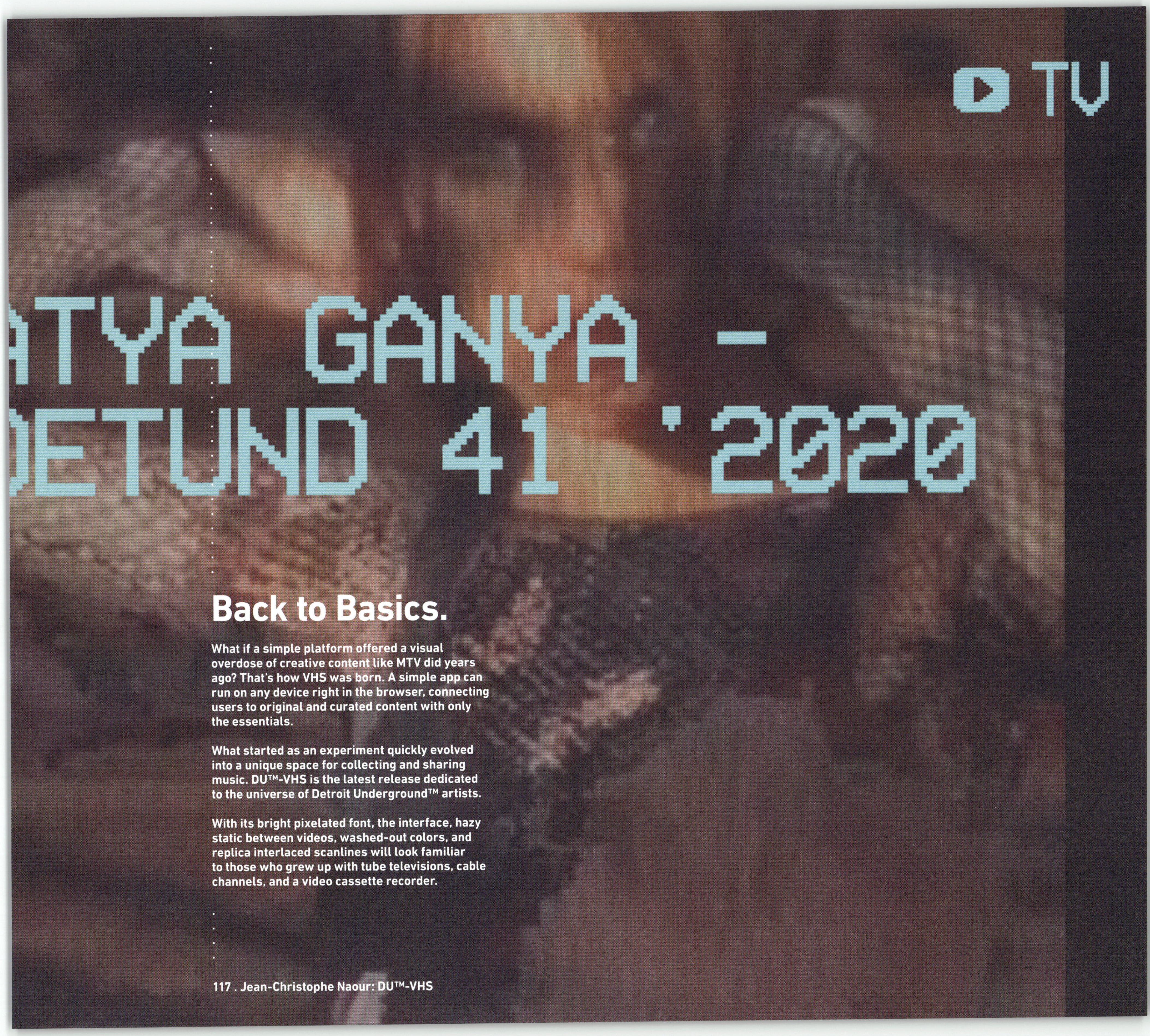

Back to Basics.

What if a simple platform offered a visual overdose of creative content like MTV did years ago? That's how VHS was born. A simple app can run on any device right in the browser, connecting users to original and curated content with only the essentials.

What started as an experiment quickly evolved into a unique space for collecting and sharing music. DU™-VHS is the latest release dedicated to the universe of Detroit Underground™ artists.

With its bright pixelated font, the interface, hazy static between videos, washed-out colors, and replica interlaced scanlines will look familiar to those who grew up with tube televisions, cable channels, and a video cassette recorder.

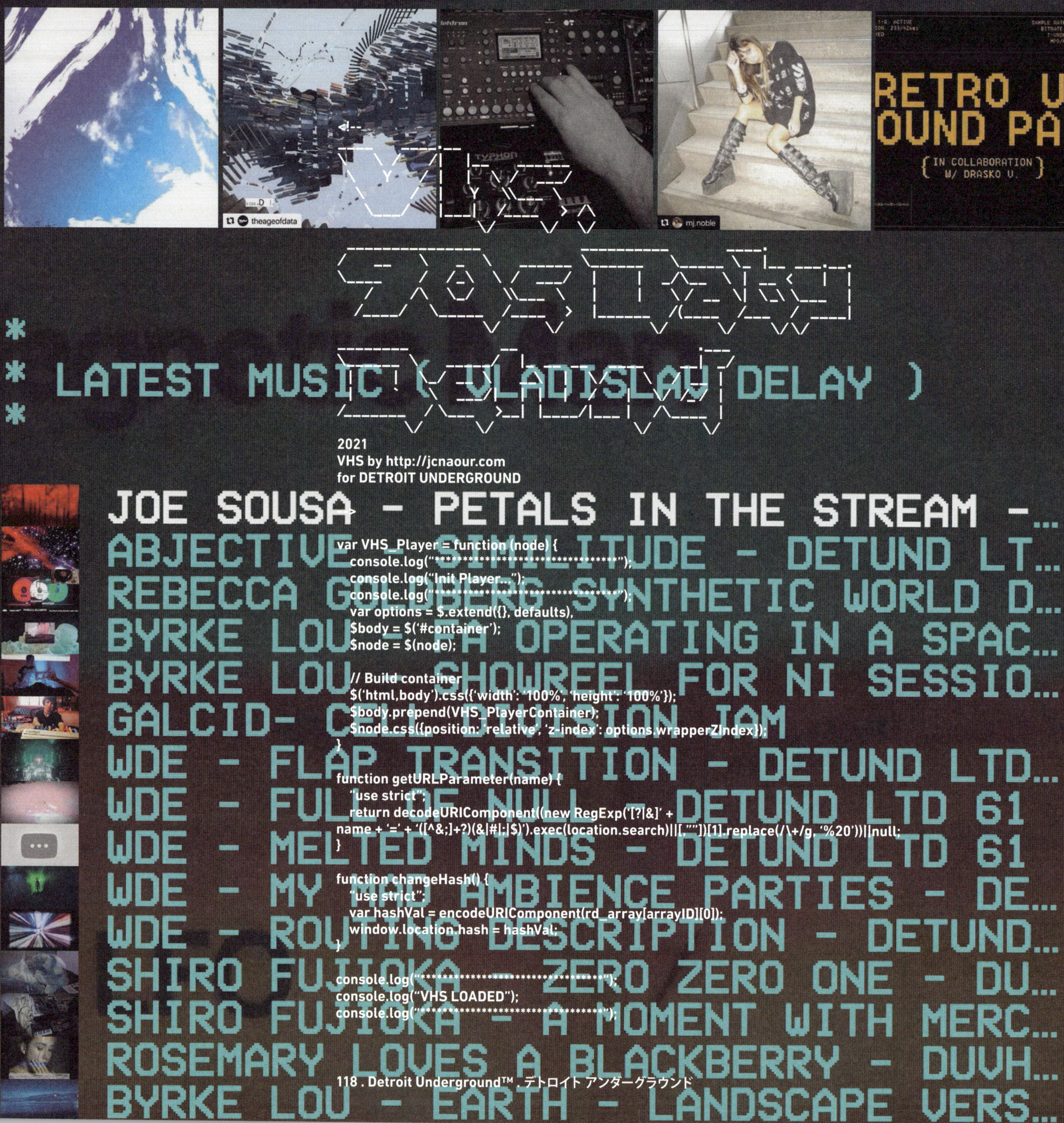

2021
VHS by http://jcnaour.com
for DETROIT UNDERGROUND

```
var VHS_Player = function (node) {
  console.log("********************************");
  console.log("Init Player...");
  console.log("********************************");
  var options = $.extend({}, defaults),
  $body = $('#container');
  $node = $(node);

  // Build container
  $('html,body').css({'width': '100%', 'height': '100%'});
  $body.prepend(VHS_PlayerContainer);
  $node.css({position: 'relative', 'z-index': options.wrapperZIndex});
}

function getURLParameter(name) {
  "use strict";
  return decodeURIComponent((new RegExp('[?|&]' +
name + '=' + '([^&;]+?)(&|#|;|$)').exec(location.search)||[,""])[1].replace(/\+/g, '%20'))||null;
}

function changeHash() {
  "use strict";
  var hashVal = encodeURIComponent(rd_array[arrayID][0]);
  window.location.hash = hashVal;
}

console.log("********************************");
console.log("VHS LOADED");
console.log("********************************");
```

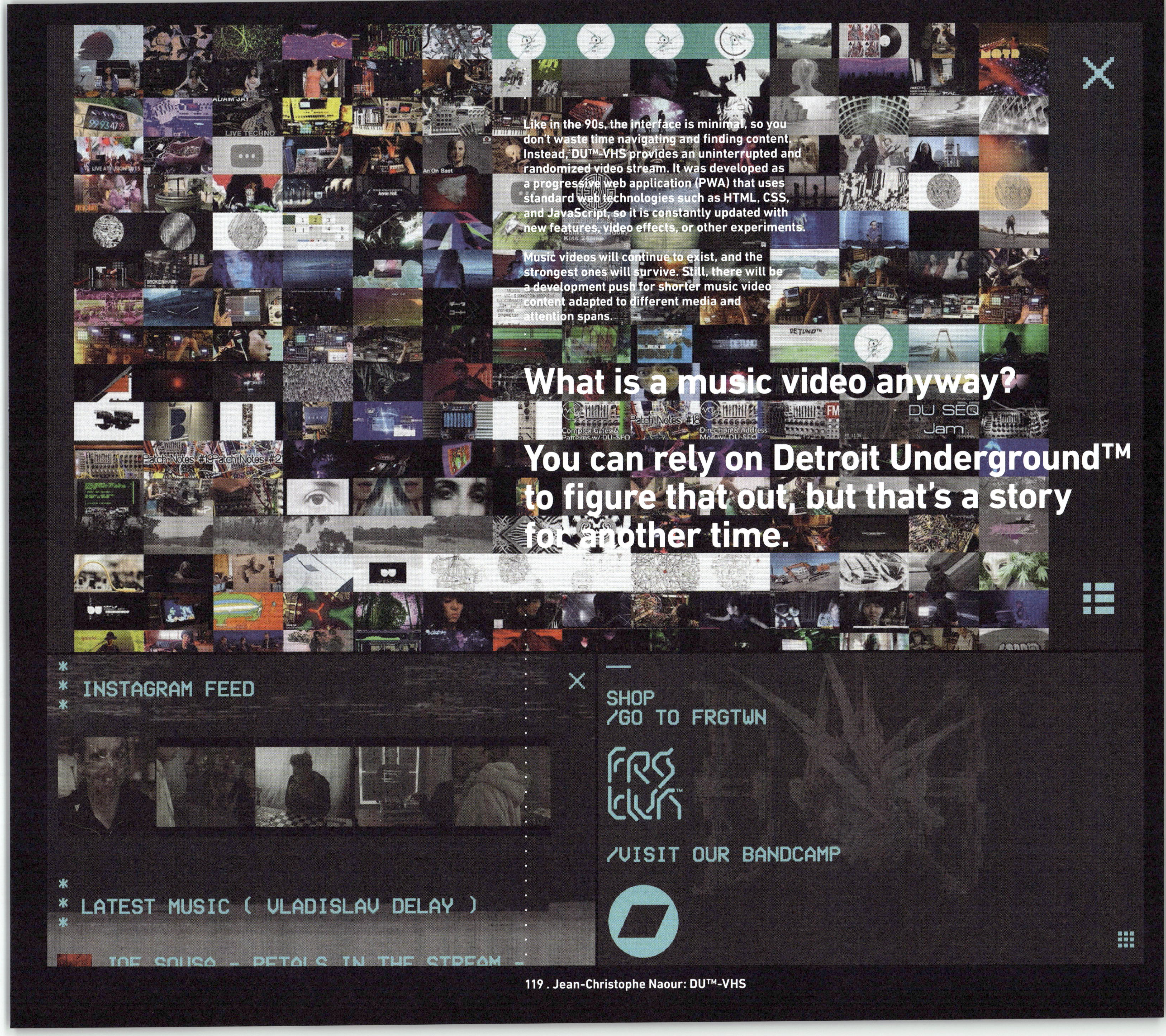

Like in the 90s, the interface is minimal, so you don't waste time navigating and finding content. Instead, DU™-VHS provides an uninterrupted and randomized video stream. It was developed as a progressive web application (PWA) that uses standard web technologies such as HTML, CSS, and JavaScript, so it is constantly updated with new features, video effects, or other experiments.

Music videos will continue to exist, and the strongest ones will survive. Still, there will be a development push for shorter music video content adapted to different media and attention spans.

What is a music video anyway?

You can rely on Detroit Underground™ to figure that out, but that's a story for another time.

119 . Jean-Christophe Naour: DU™-VHS

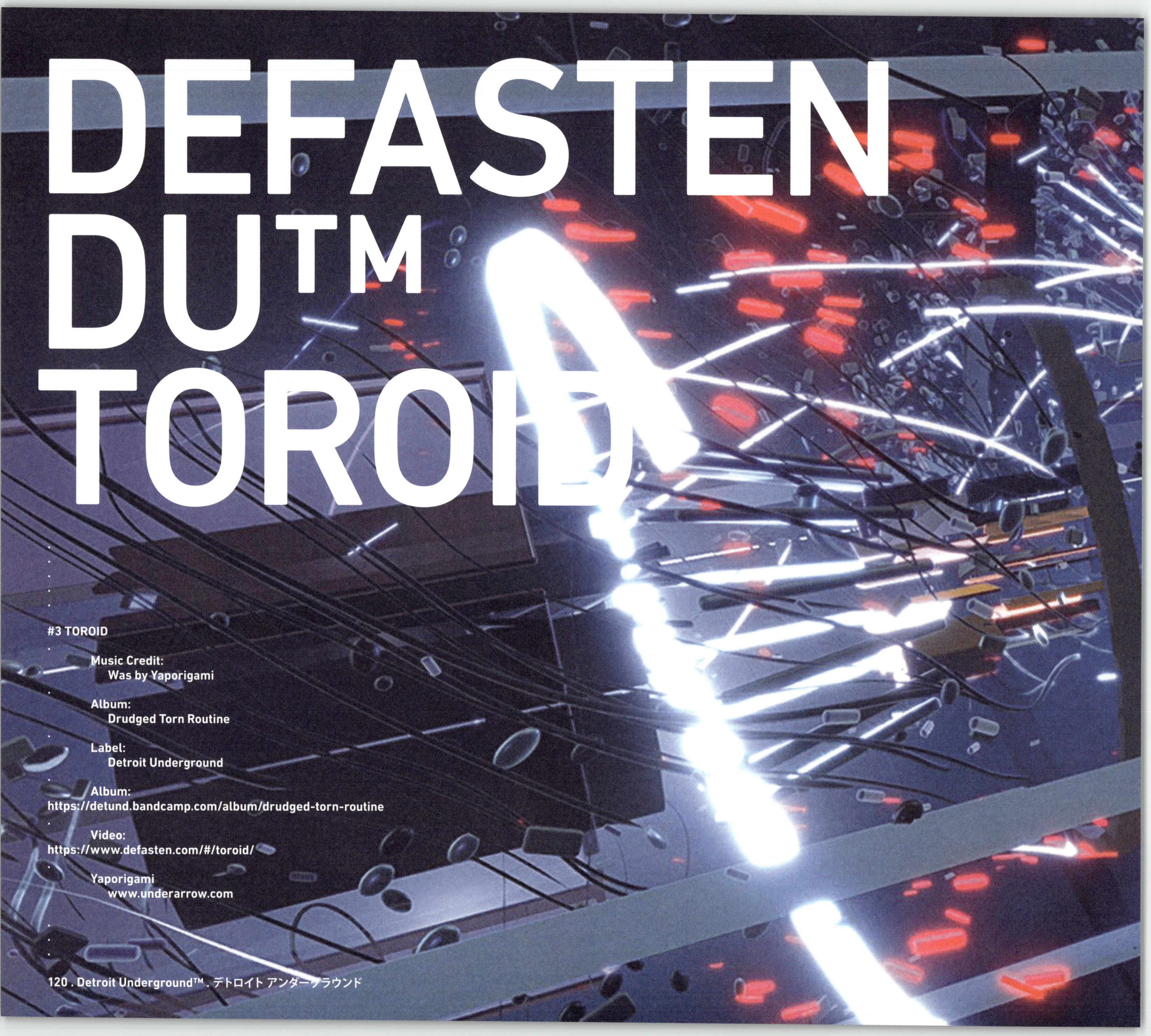

DEFASTEN DU™ TOROID

#3 TOROID

Music Credit:
Was by Yaporigami

Album:
Drudged Torn Routine

Label:
Detroit Underground

Album:
https://detund.bandcamp.com/album/drudged-torn-routine

Video:
https://www.defasten.com/#/toroid/

Yaporigami
www.underarrow.com

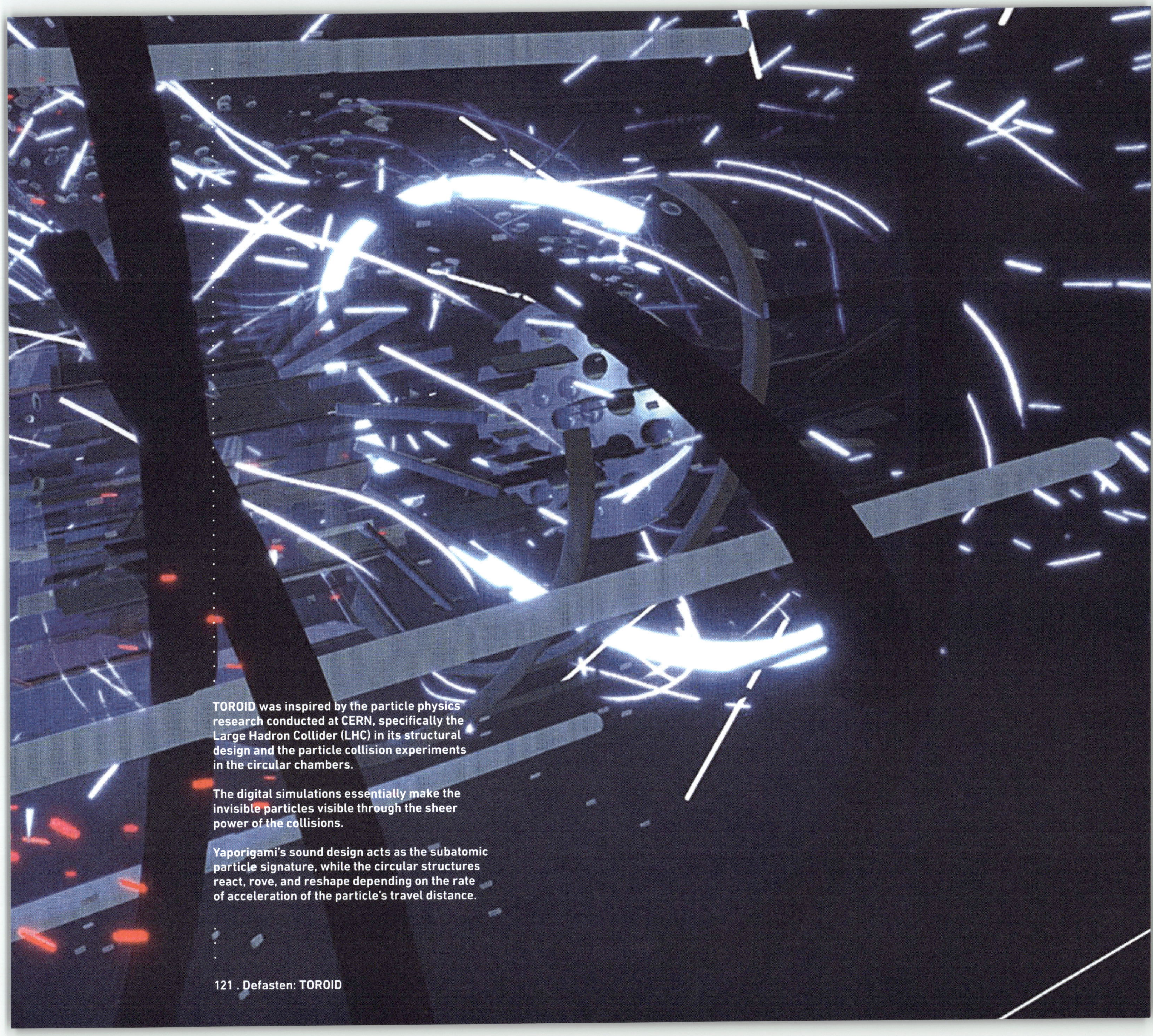

TOROID was inspired by the particle physics research conducted at CERN, specifically the Large Hadron Collider (LHC) in its structural design and the particle collision experiments in the circular chambers.

The digital simulations essentially make the invisible particles visible through the sheer power of the collisions.

Yaporigami's sound design acts as the subatomic particle signature, while the circular structures react, rove, and reshape depending on the rate of acceleration of the particle's travel distance.

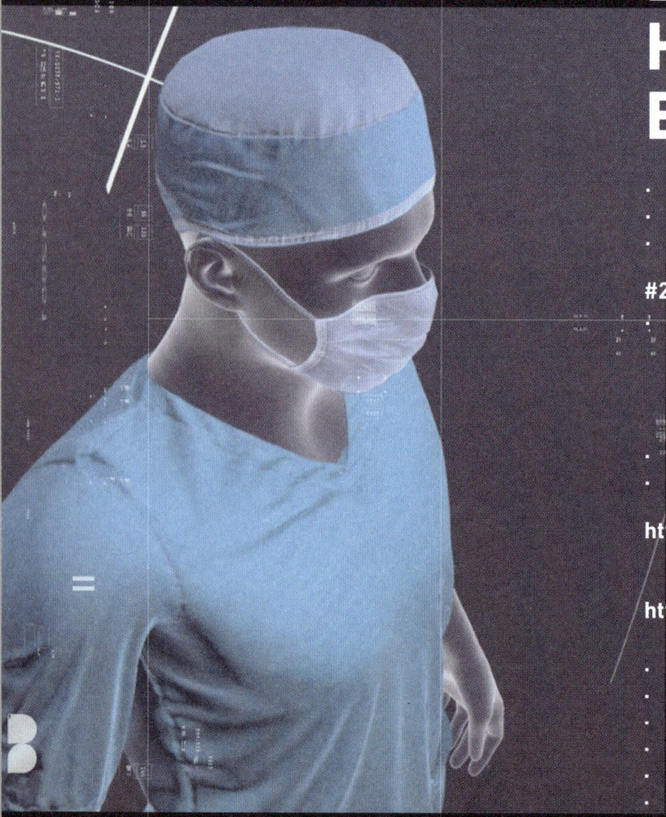

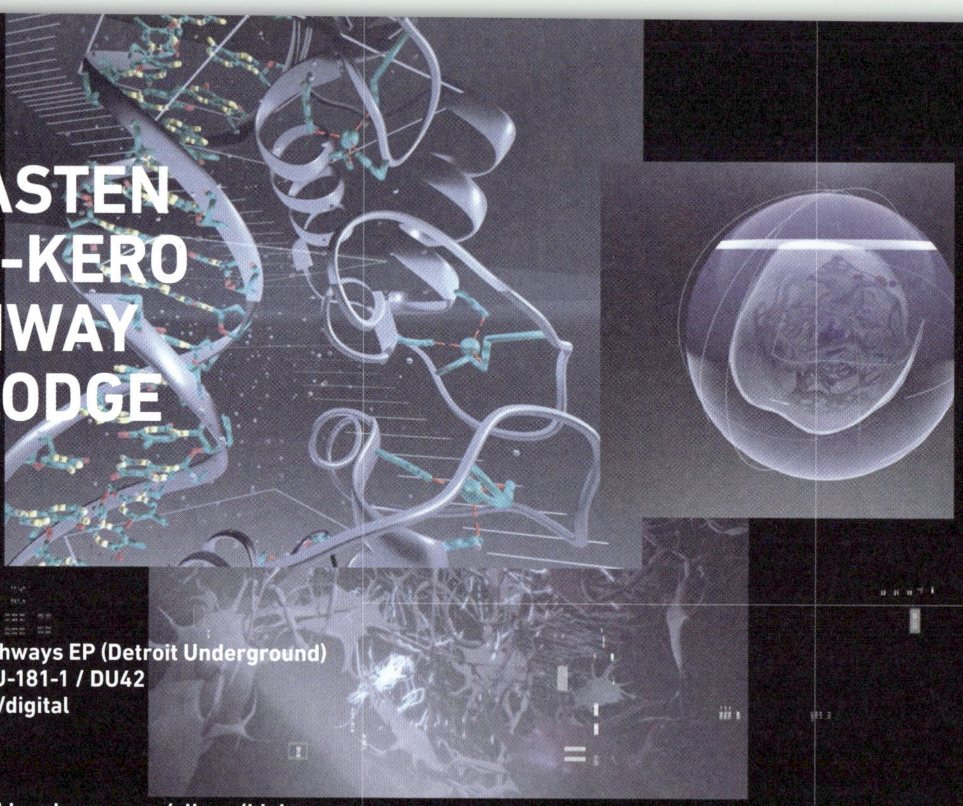

DEFASTEN DU™-KERO HIGHWAY EP/LODGE

#2 LODGE

Kero :
Highways EP (Detroit Underground)
cat# DU-181-1 / DU42
12"/digital

Album:
https://detund.bandcamp.com/album/highways

Video:
https://www.youtube.com/watch?v=YZGhtrXRO84

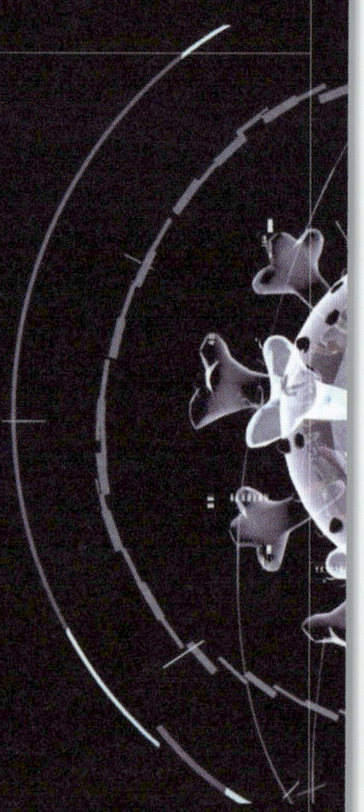

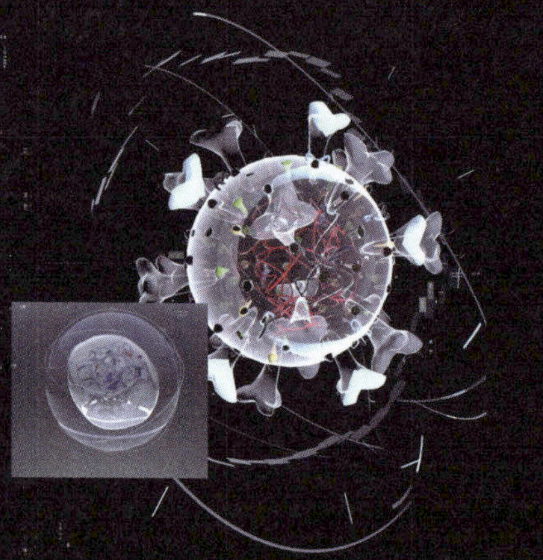

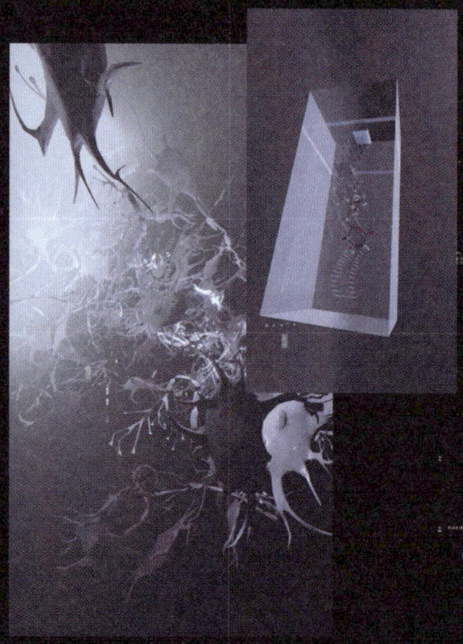

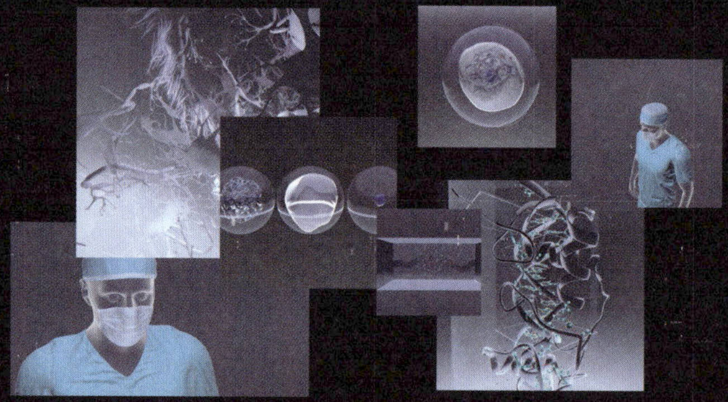

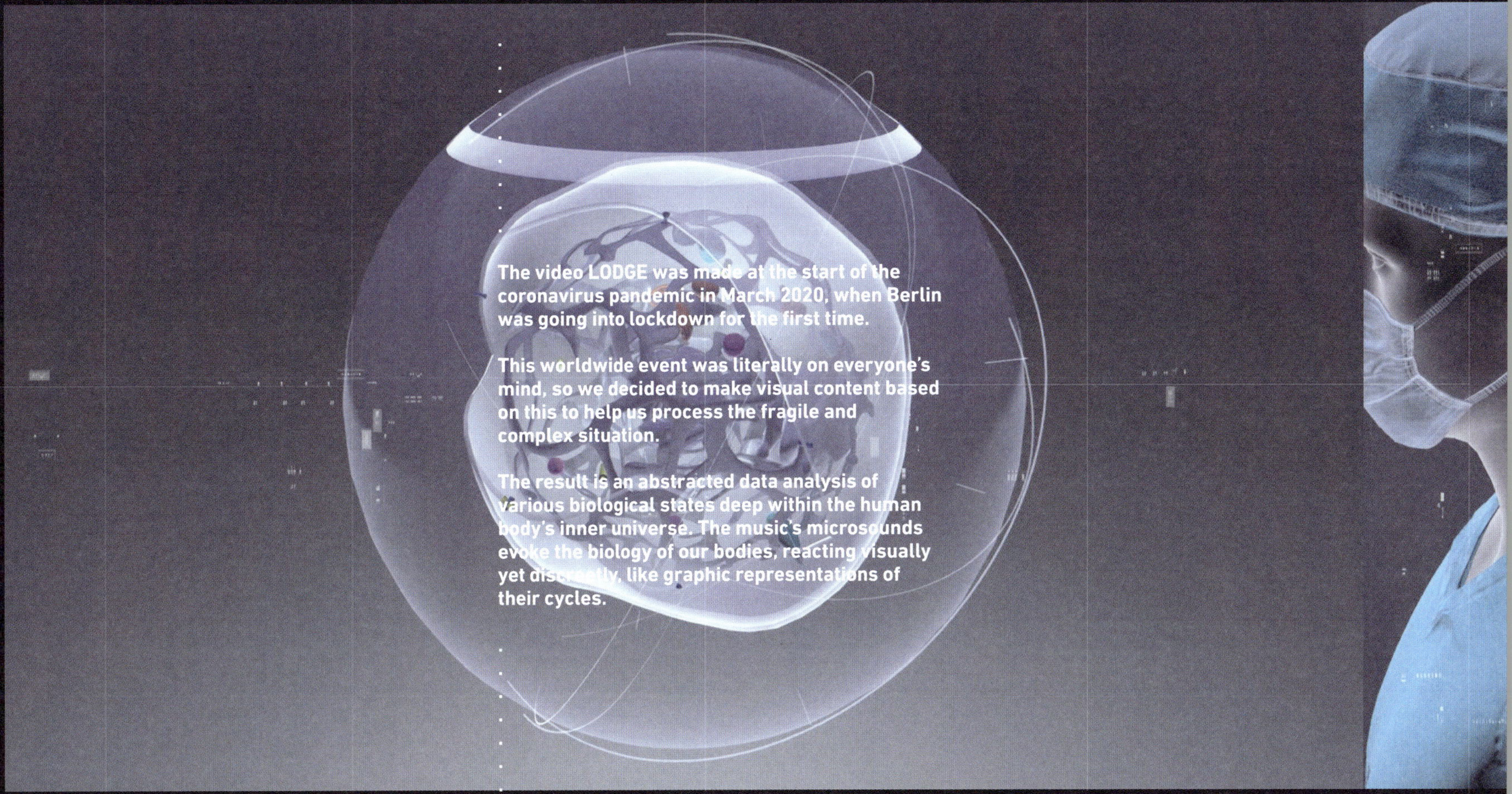

The video LODGE was made at the start of the coronavirus pandemic in March 2020, when Berlin was going into lockdown for the first time.

This worldwide event was literally on everyone's mind, so we decided to make visual content based on this to help us process the fragile and complex situation.

The result is an abstracted data analysis of various biological states deep within the human body's inner universe. The music's microsounds evoke the biology of our bodies, reacting visually yet discreetly, like graphic representations of their cycles.

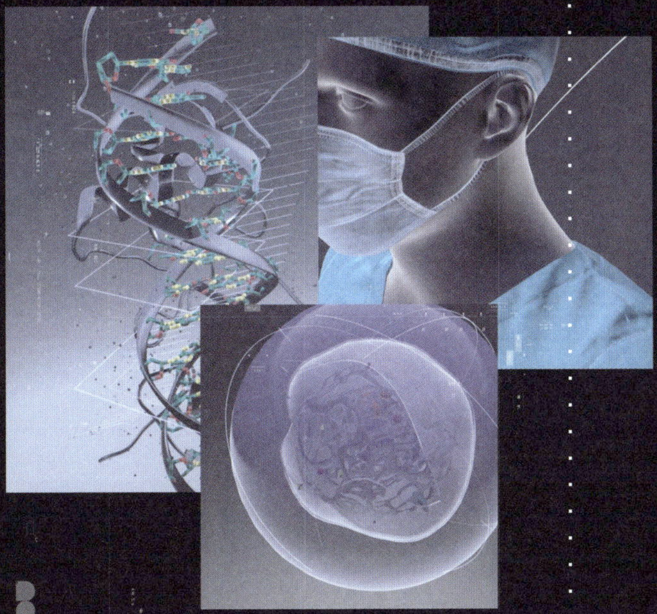

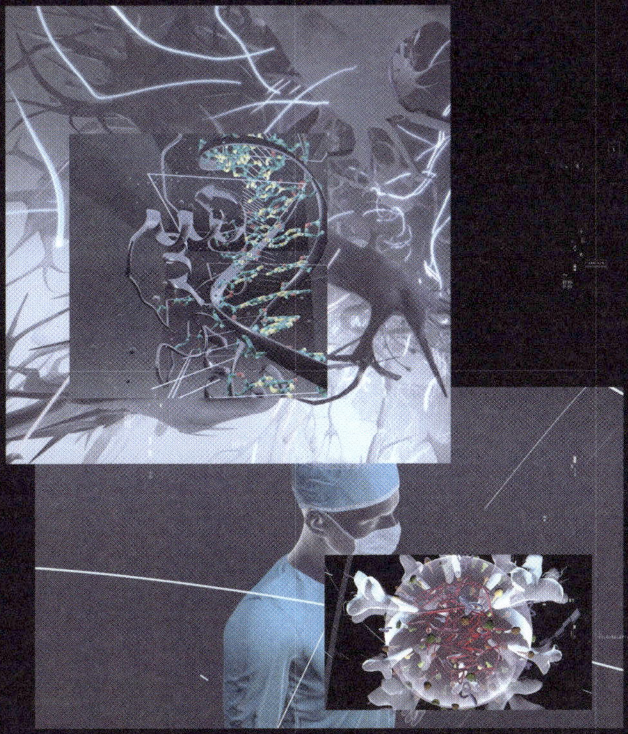

DEFASTEN DU™ ROADBLOCKS VDML

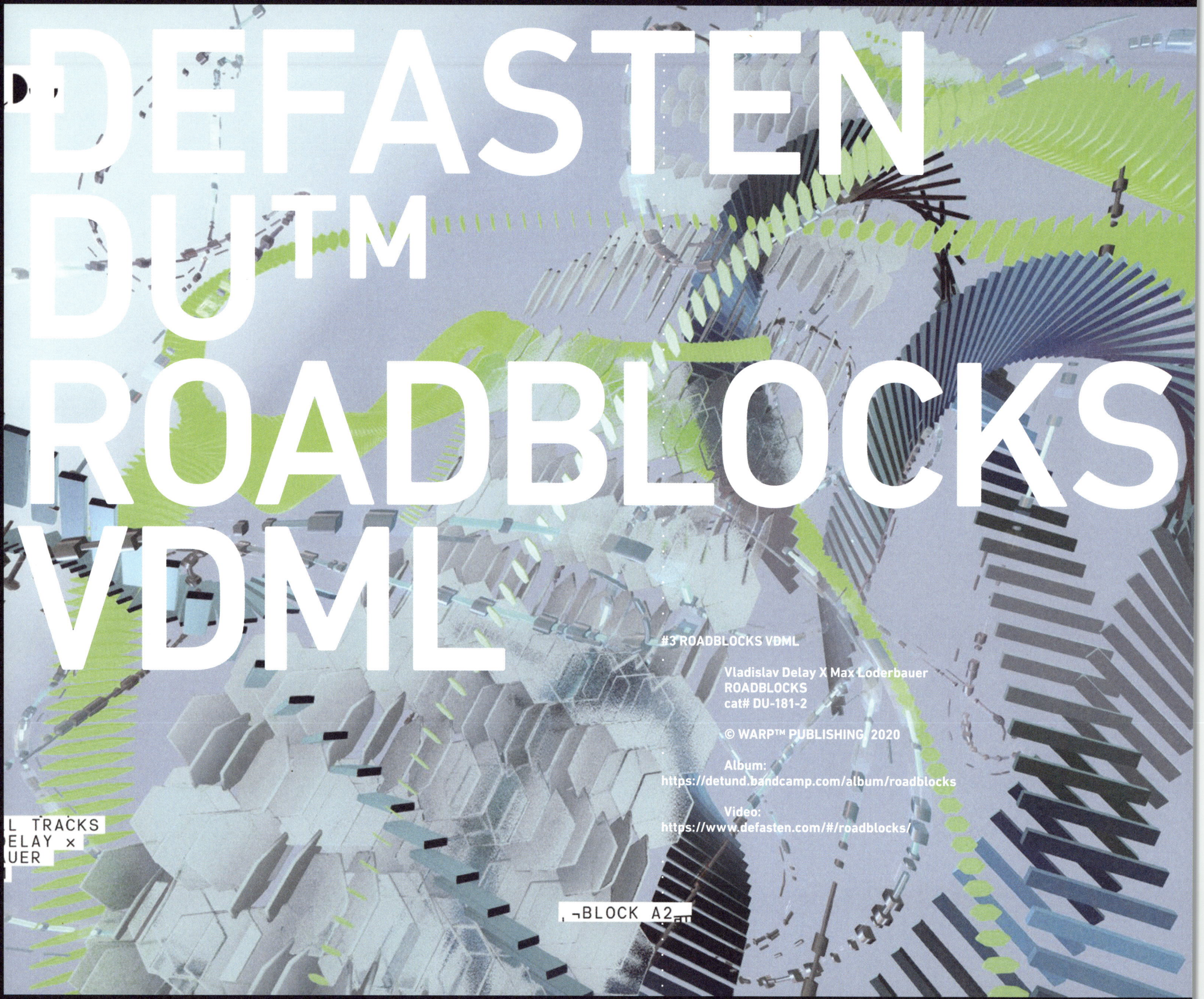

#3 ROADBLOCKS VDML

Vladislav Delay X Max Loderbauer
ROADBLOCKS
cat# DU-181-2

Album:
https://detund.bandcamp.com/album/roadblocks

Video:
https://www.defasten.com/#/roadblocks/

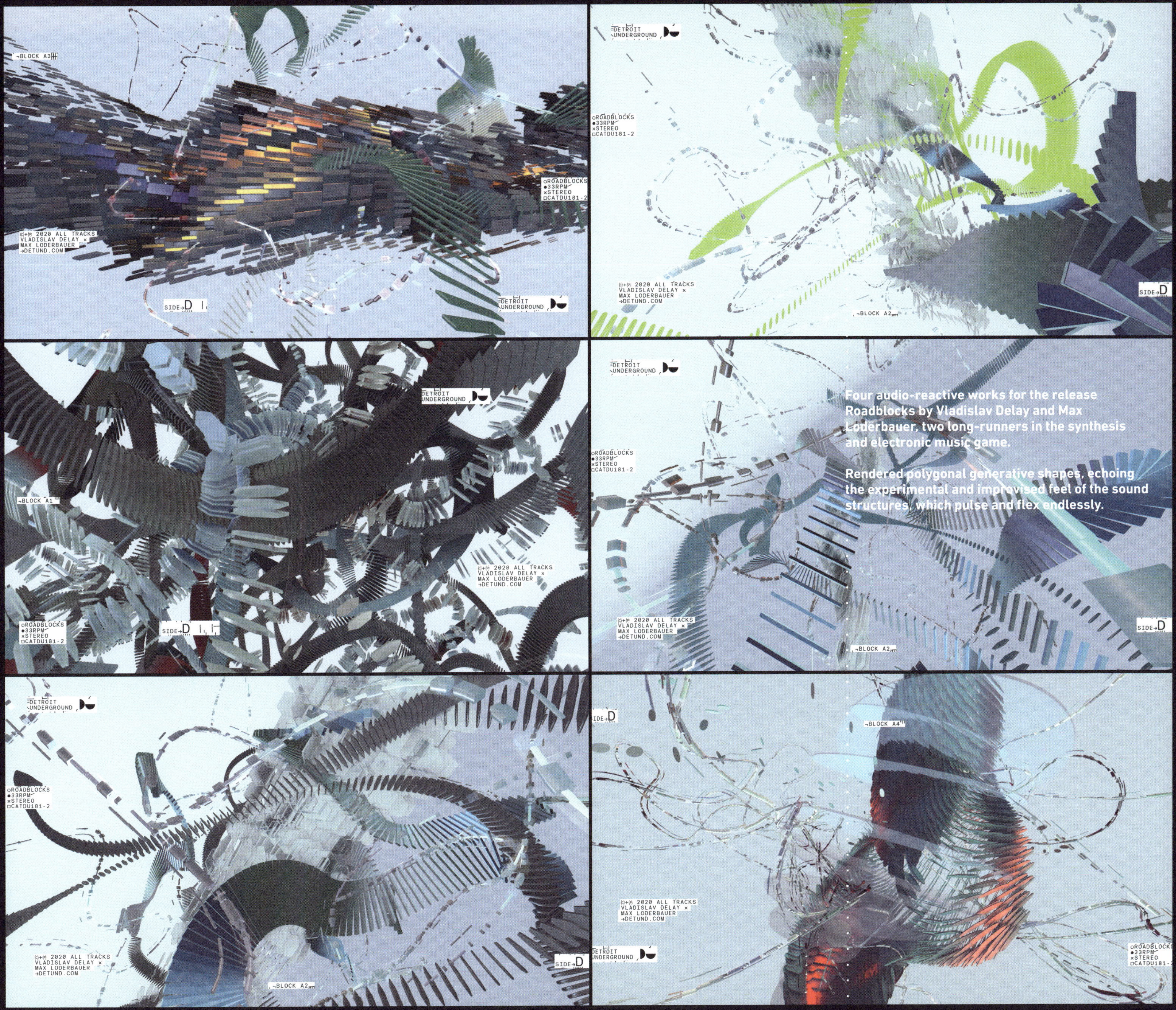

Four audio-reactive works for the release Roadblocks by Vladislav Delay and Max Loderbauer, two long-runners in the synthesis and electronic music game.

Rendered polygonal generative shapes, echoing the experimental and improvised feel of the sound structures, which pulse and flex endlessly.

Pete r Es ze ny i

Name:

Peter Eszenyi

Info:

London-based VFX Supervisor and Creative Director Peter Eszenyi founded his company Lunarstorm Studio in 2018, after spending seven years at Territory Studio as VFX Supervisor and Creative Lead.

He worked on films such as
Guardians of the Galaxy,
The Martian,
Avengers: Age of Ultron,
Ghost In The Shell,
Blade Runner 2049
and
Pacific Rim: Uprising.

Project:

APOLLO 50
VIRTUAL ARCHEOLOGY

URL:

petereszenyi.com

Instagram:

@p.eszenyi

Q&As

. . . . . Please explain the main idea and what gave the impulse?

Ever since I was a child, I have always been fascinated by images of the Moon landings.

I decided to extract three-dimensional data from the pictures taken on the Moon landing missions with a photogrammetry method that I use in my work quite often.

. . . . . What challenges did you face for this project? And what surprises?

One of the main challenges is that most Apollo missions' pictures never had photogrammetry in mind. That, and the nature of those photographs; no EXIF data, blurriness, the presence of fiducial markers meant there was a lot of prep-work involved, going through thousands of images and finding those that could yield results.

The beauty of this process is that it shows you the camera's position and, therefore, of the photographer.

So you know exactly where Armstrong or Aldrin stood on the Moon.

. . . . . Please describe the technical environment.

Besides building up a library of these photographs, I used various kinds of photogrammetry software to correlate these images and find corresponding points in 3D space from the relationships of those images.

I also used video for data extraction, so I needed a lot of computer time on a high-end machine.

. . . . . Tell us about your aesthetical approach.

I find the aesthetics of having vast amounts of point clouds fascinating.

To me, it feels like three-dimensional pointillism. It's important to stress that all these images were created from the data captured by those Hasselblad cameras on the Moon 50 years ago. I did not try to fix the models or manipulate the raw data in any way.

The inaccuracies in the reconstructions, especially when I'm using substandard datasets, create exciting, happy accidents, which I wanted to show.

I also tried to find complementary visual styles that rely on all sorts of derivations from these datasets.

Even though this could have influenced the look of sci-fi, I found there was a solid analog feel to it.

. . . . . What's next? Your vision?

The presence of artificial intelligence in image processing is a huge step forward. I find it intriguing that with the help of AI, I could access more and more data that was not available previously.

Secondly, augmented reality offers a great way to bring these datasets into real-world environments, and my ventures in this field, to date, have been genuinely encouraging.

Finally, it would be fantastic to present these datasets to a larger group of people as a part of a large-scale exhibition with projection.

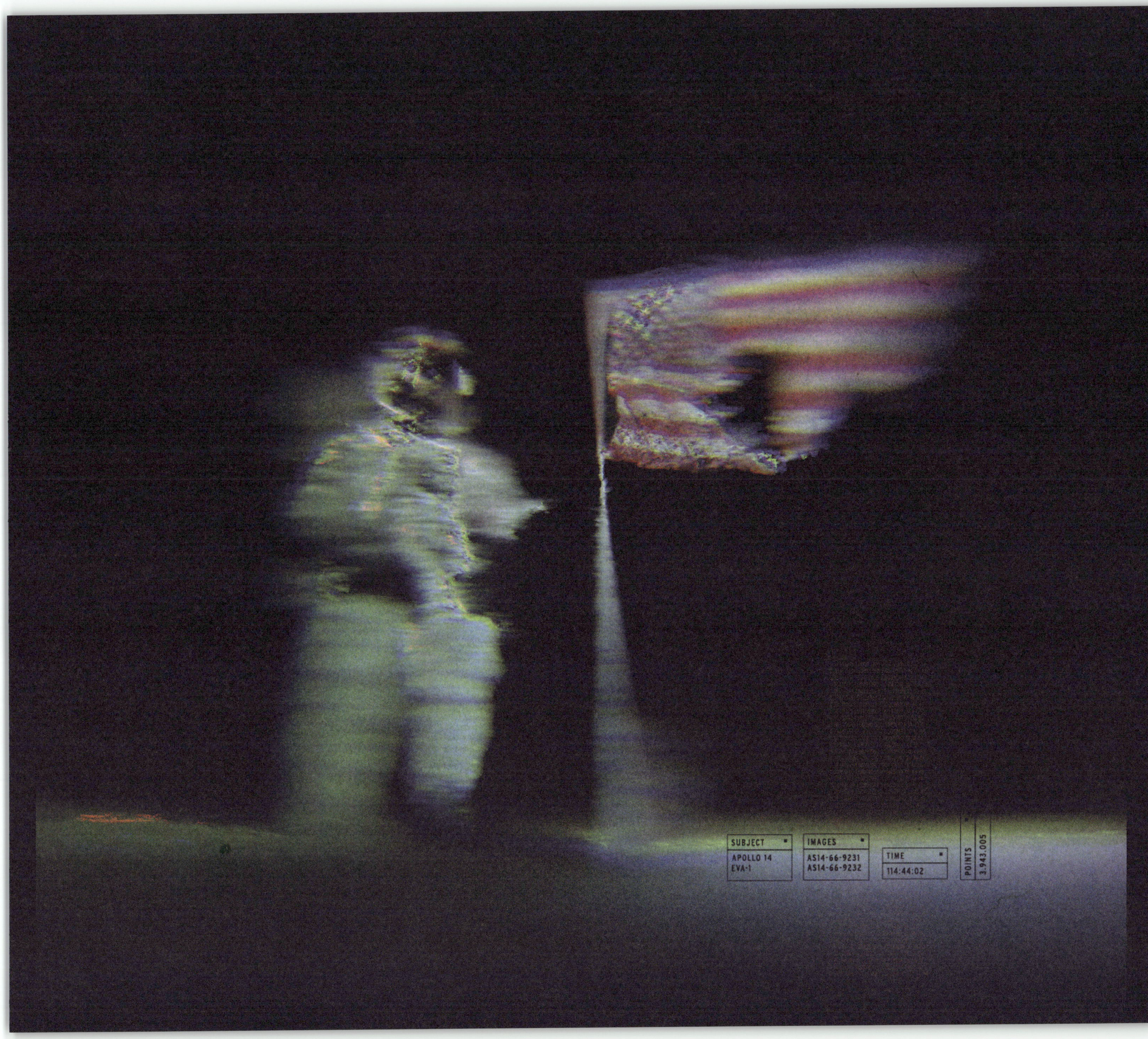
SUBJECT
APOLLO 14
EVA-1
IMAGES
AS14-66-9231
AS14-66-9232
TIME
114:44:02
POINTS
3.943.005

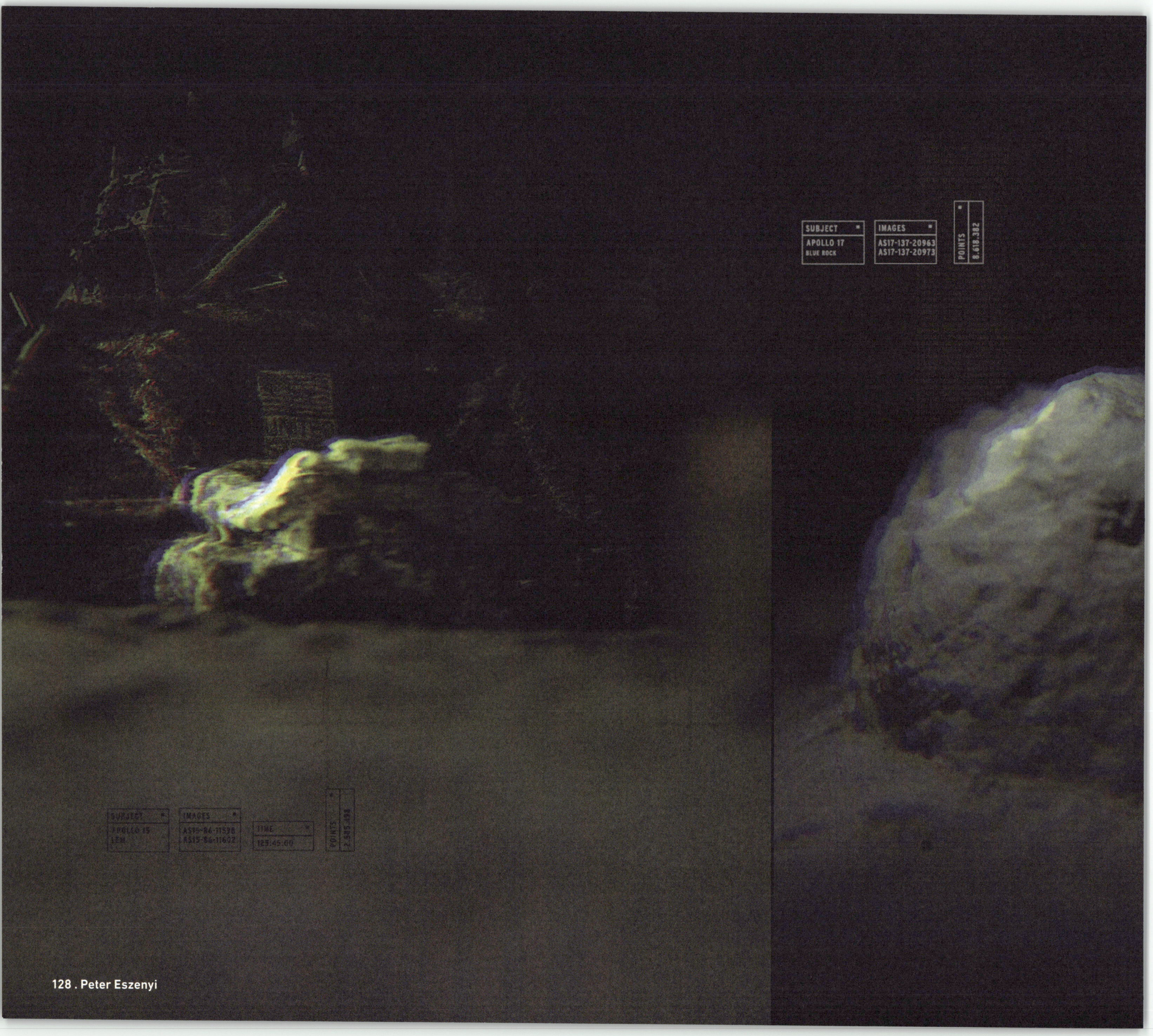
SUBJECT
APOLLO 17
BLUE ROCK
IMAGES
AS17-137-20963
AS17-137-20973
POINTS
8.618.382
IMAGES
TIME
POINTS

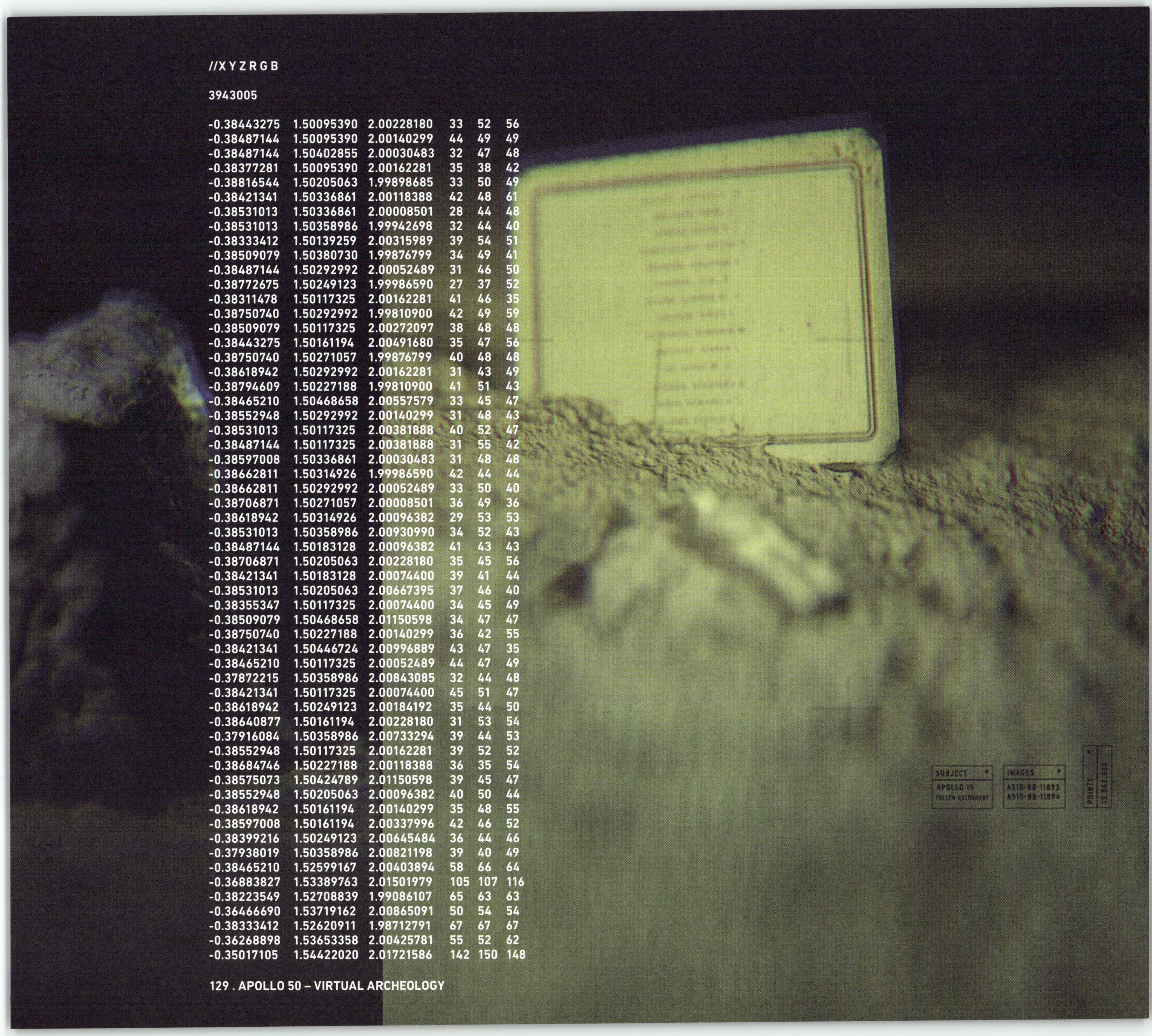

//X Y Z R G B

3943005

-0.38443275	1.50095390	2.00228180	33	52	56
-0.38487144	1.50095390	2.00140299	44	49	49
-0.38487144	1.50402855	2.00030483	32	47	48
-0.38377281	1.50095390	2.00162281	35	38	42
-0.38816544	1.50205063	1.99898685	33	50	49
-0.38421341	1.50336861	2.00118388	42	48	61
-0.38531013	1.50336861	2.00008501	28	44	48
-0.38531013	1.50358986	1.99942698	32	44	40
-0.38333412	1.50139259	2.00315989	39	54	51
-0.38509079	1.50380730	1.99876799	34	49	41
-0.38487144	1.50292992	2.00052489	31	46	50
-0.38772675	1.50249123	1.99986590	27	37	52
-0.38311478	1.50117325	2.00162281	41	46	35
-0.38750740	1.50292992	1.99810900	42	49	59
-0.38509079	1.50117325	2.00272097	38	48	48
-0.38443275	1.50161194	2.00491680	35	47	56
-0.38750740	1.50271057	1.99876799	40	48	48
-0.38618942	1.50292992	2.00162281	31	43	49
-0.38794609	1.50227188	1.99810900	41	51	43
-0.38465210	1.50468658	2.00557579	33	45	47
-0.38552948	1.50292992	2.00140299	31	48	43
-0.38531013	1.50117325	2.00381888	40	52	47
-0.38487144	1.50117325	2.00381888	31	55	42
-0.38597008	1.50336861	2.00030483	31	48	48
-0.38662811	1.50314926	1.99986590	42	44	44
-0.38662811	1.50292992	2.00052489	33	50	40
-0.38706871	1.50271057	2.00008501	36	49	36
-0.38618942	1.50314926	2.00096382	29	53	53
-0.38531013	1.50358986	2.00930990	34	52	43
-0.38487144	1.50183128	2.00096382	41	43	43
-0.38706871	1.50205063	2.00228180	35	45	56
-0.38421341	1.50183128	2.00074400	39	41	44
-0.38531013	1.50205063	2.00667395	37	46	40
-0.38355347	1.50117325	2.00074400	34	45	49
-0.38509079	1.50468658	2.01150598	34	47	47
-0.38750740	1.50227188	2.00140299	36	42	55
-0.38421341	1.50446724	2.00996889	43	47	35
-0.38465210	1.50117325	2.00052489	44	47	49
-0.37872215	1.50358986	2.00843085	32	44	48
-0.38421341	1.50117325	2.00074400	45	51	47
-0.38618942	1.50249123	2.00184192	35	44	50
-0.38640877	1.50161194	2.00228180	31	53	54
-0.37916084	1.50358986	2.00733294	39	44	53
-0.38552948	1.50117325	2.00162281	39	52	52
-0.38684746	1.50227188	2.00118388	36	35	54
-0.38575073	1.50424789	2.01150598	39	45	47
-0.38552948	1.50205063	2.00096382	40	50	44
-0.38618942	1.50161194	2.00140299	35	48	55
-0.38597008	1.50161194	2.00337996	42	46	52
-0.38399216	1.50249123	2.00645484	36	44	46
-0.37938019	1.50358986	2.00821198	39	40	49
-0.38465210	1.52599167	2.00403894	58	66	64
-0.36883827	1.53389763	2.01501979	105	107	116
-0.38223549	1.52708839	1.99086107	65	63	63
-0.36466690	1.53719162	2.00865091	50	54	54
-0.38333412	1.52620911	1.98712791	67	67	67
-0.36268898	1.53653358	2.00425781	55	52	62
-0.35017105	1.54422020	2.01721586	142	150	148

The first dataset I wanted to use for testing the feasibility of my idea was, obviously, the famous photograph of Aldrin's boot print on the Moon.

They took two photos of the print from different angles; those two images lent themselves to three-dimensional reconstruction well.

I was able to reconstruct an excellent 3D model from these, and with a bit of luck and a lot of time, I knew that I would find some real gems.

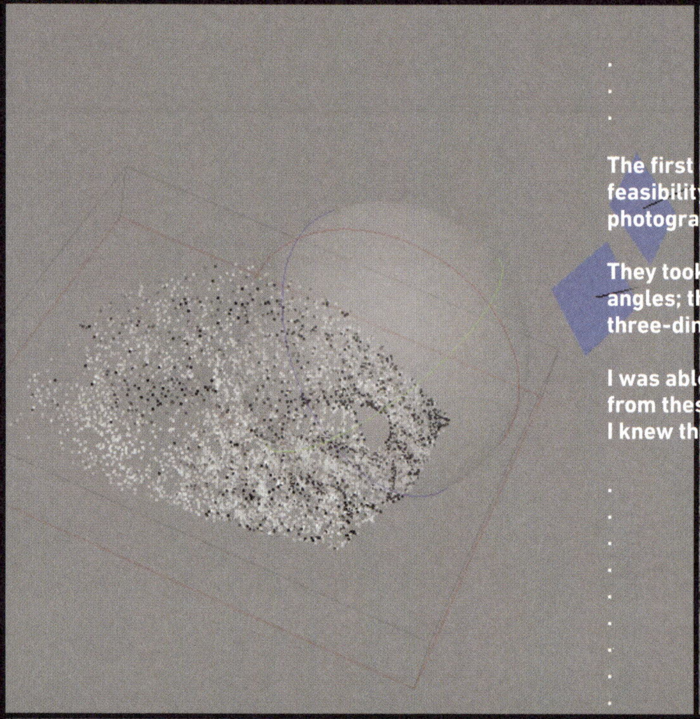

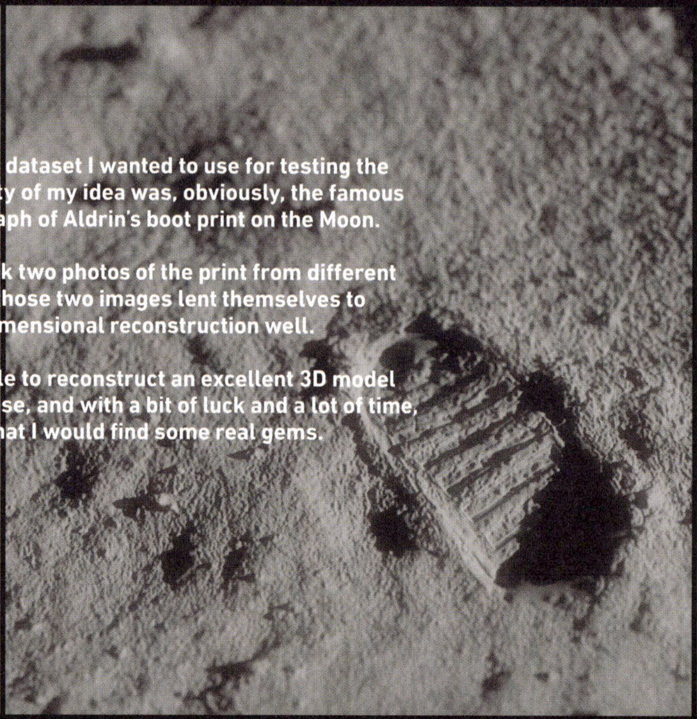

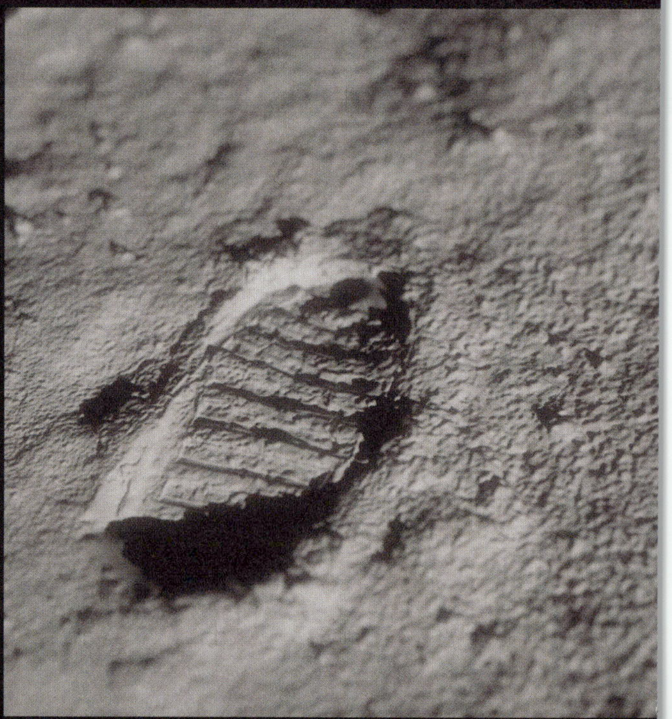

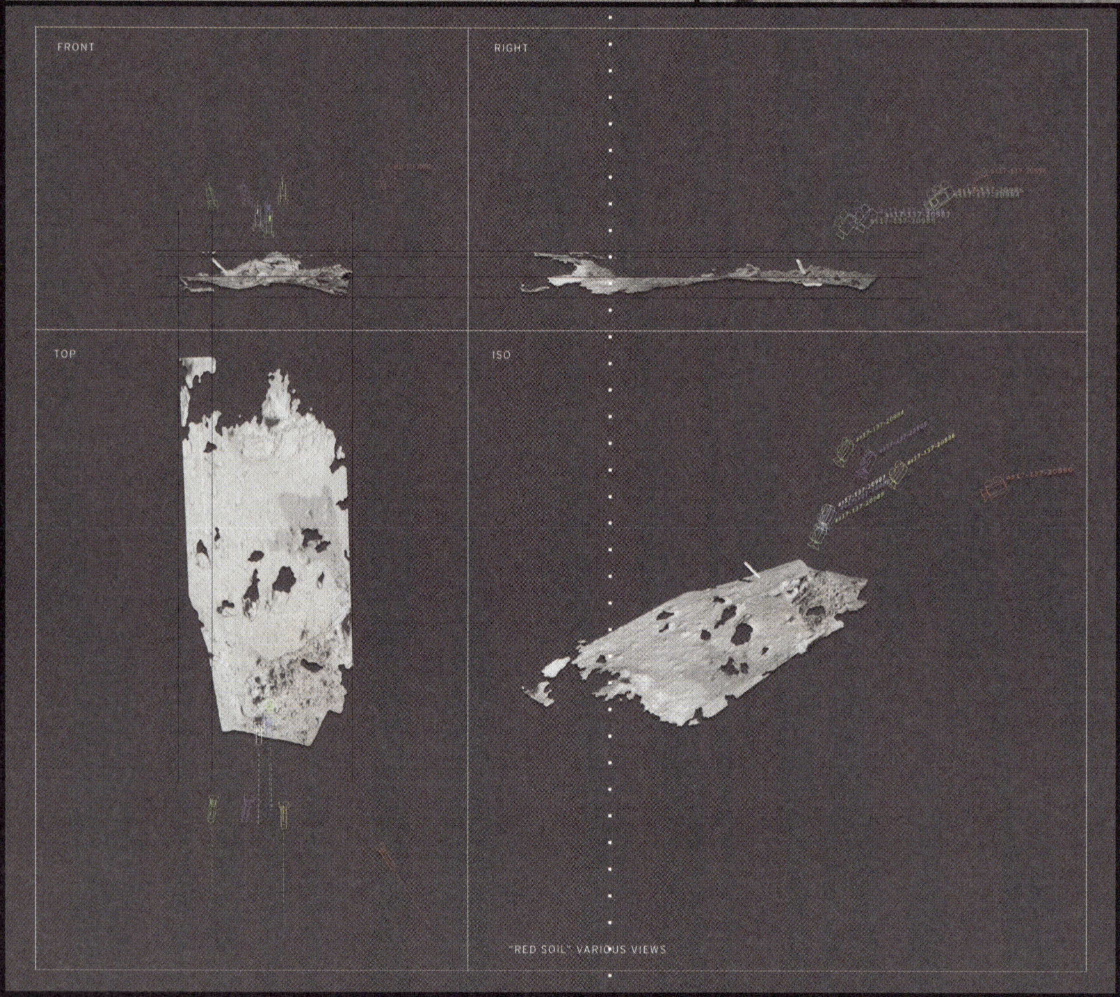

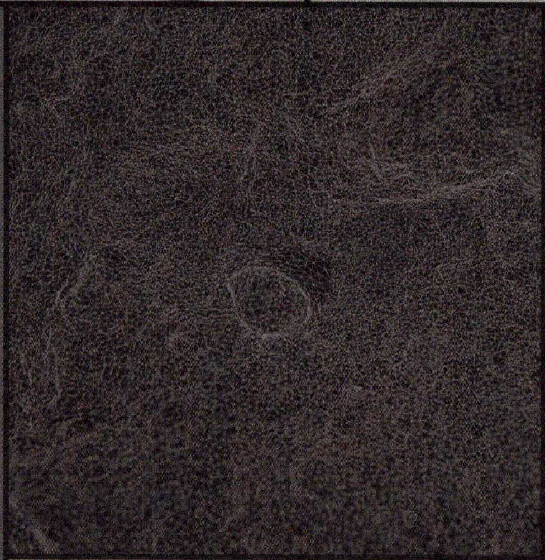

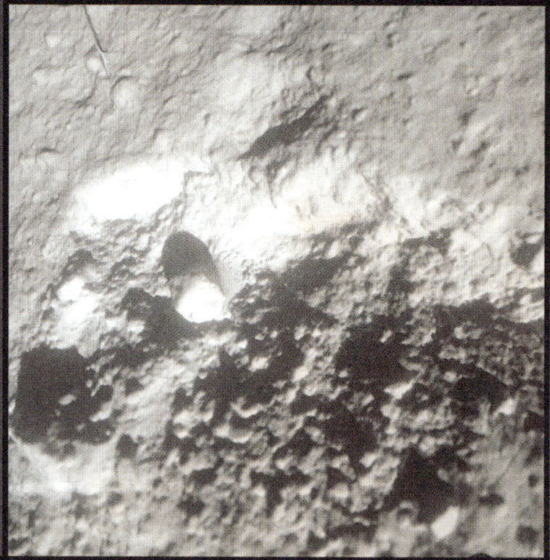

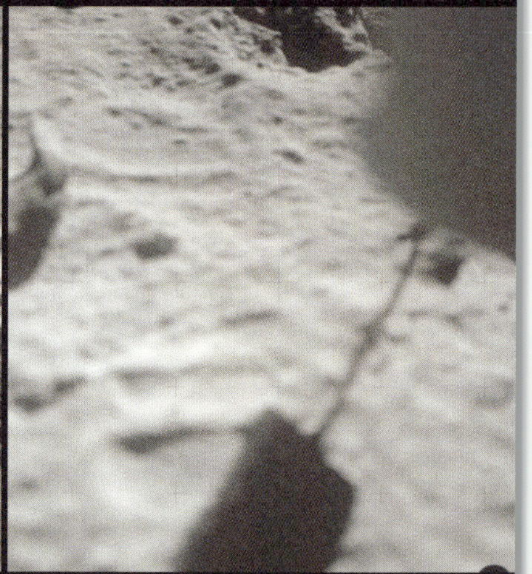

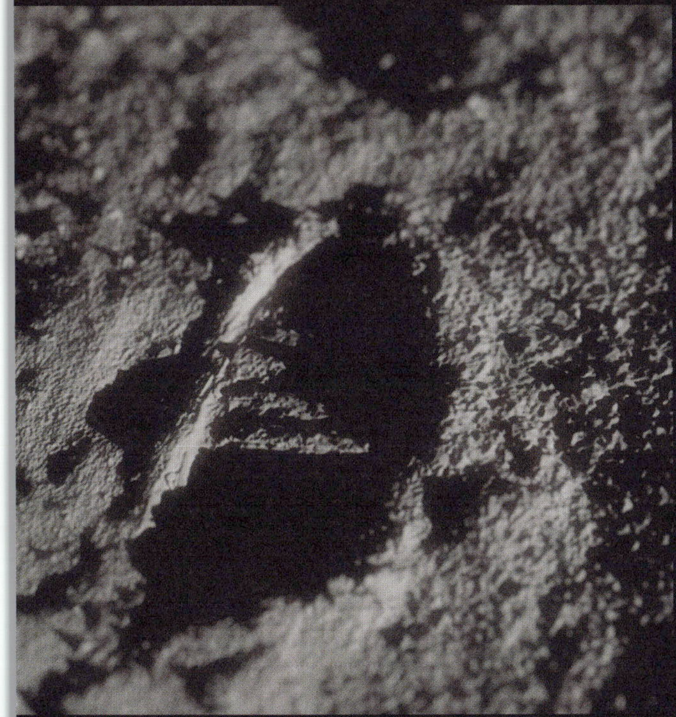

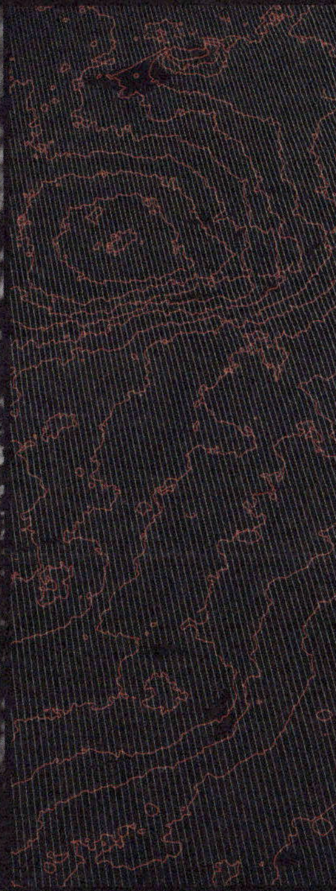

The software only goes as far as the data you put in it.

So I knew that I needed to find a way to consider specific images that could potentially give me results.

For example, many incredible images and panoramas are taken through the lunar lander window showing the Moon's surface.

The algorithm used is confused because the photo is taken through the camera lens and the lunar lander window; as a result, most of these images do not yield valuable data.

So that was something I spent a bit of time on.

The reconstructed three-dimensional data also took a bit of time to clean up and process through various pieces of software, like Houdini.

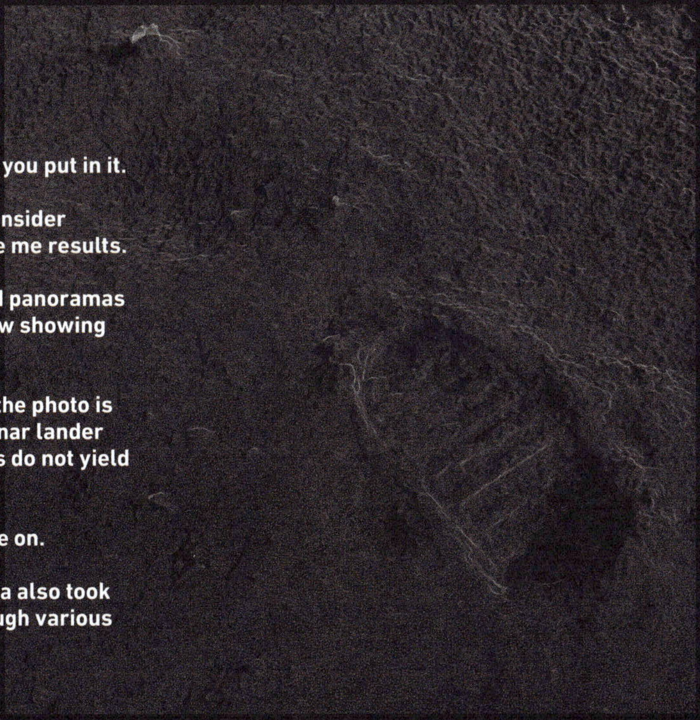

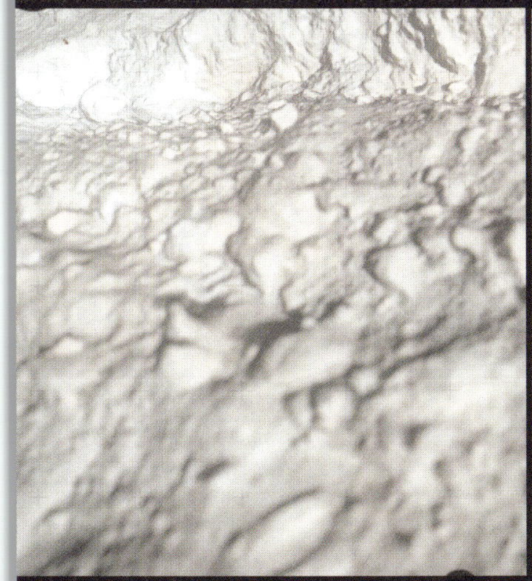

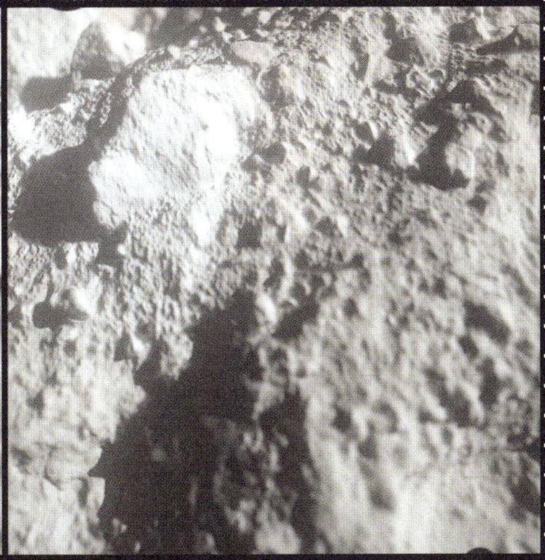

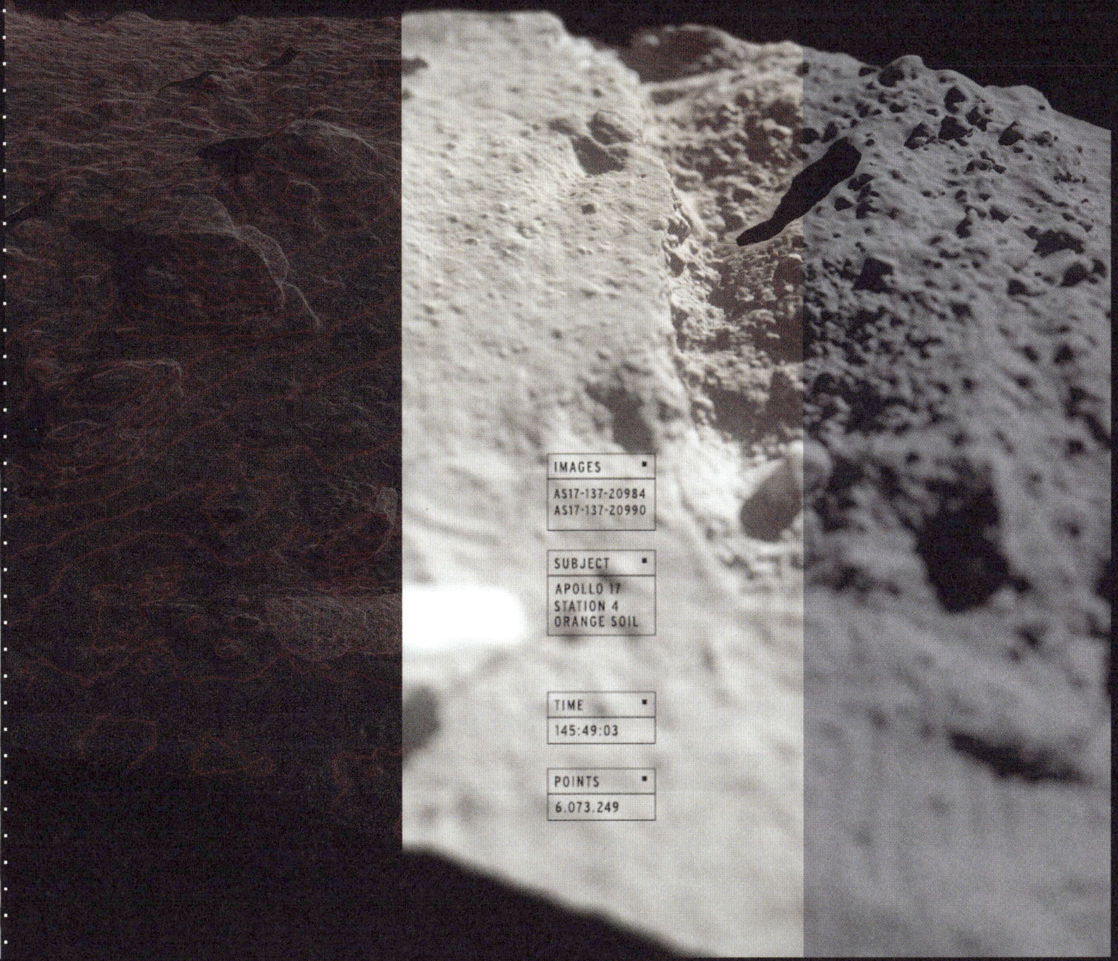

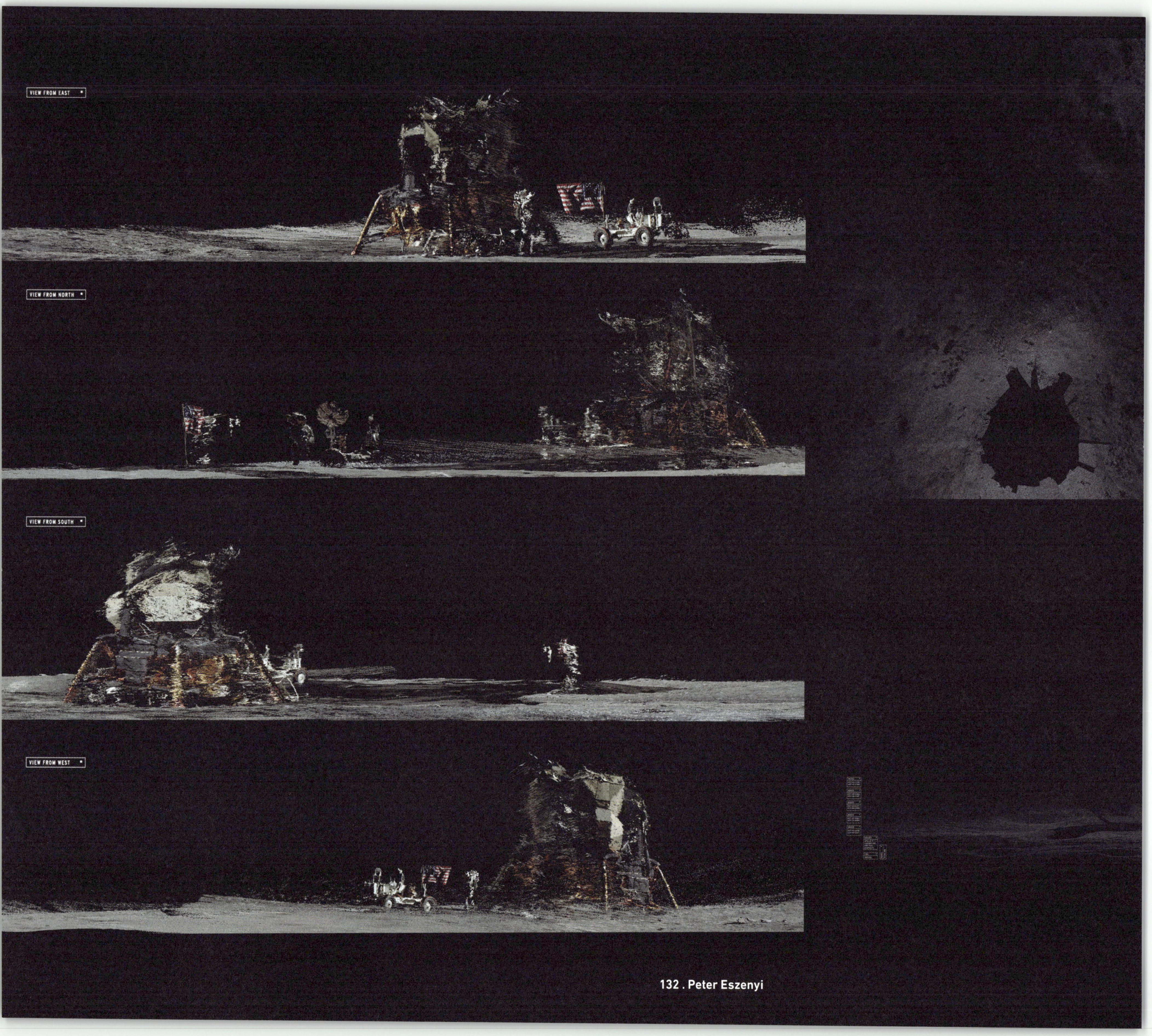

132 . Peter Eszenyi

After going through all the Apollo missions, I gravitated towards the last few ones, missions 15, 16, and 17, mainly because those images seemed to be working slightly better than images from the earlier missions.

They had more time on the Moon, so there was more data.

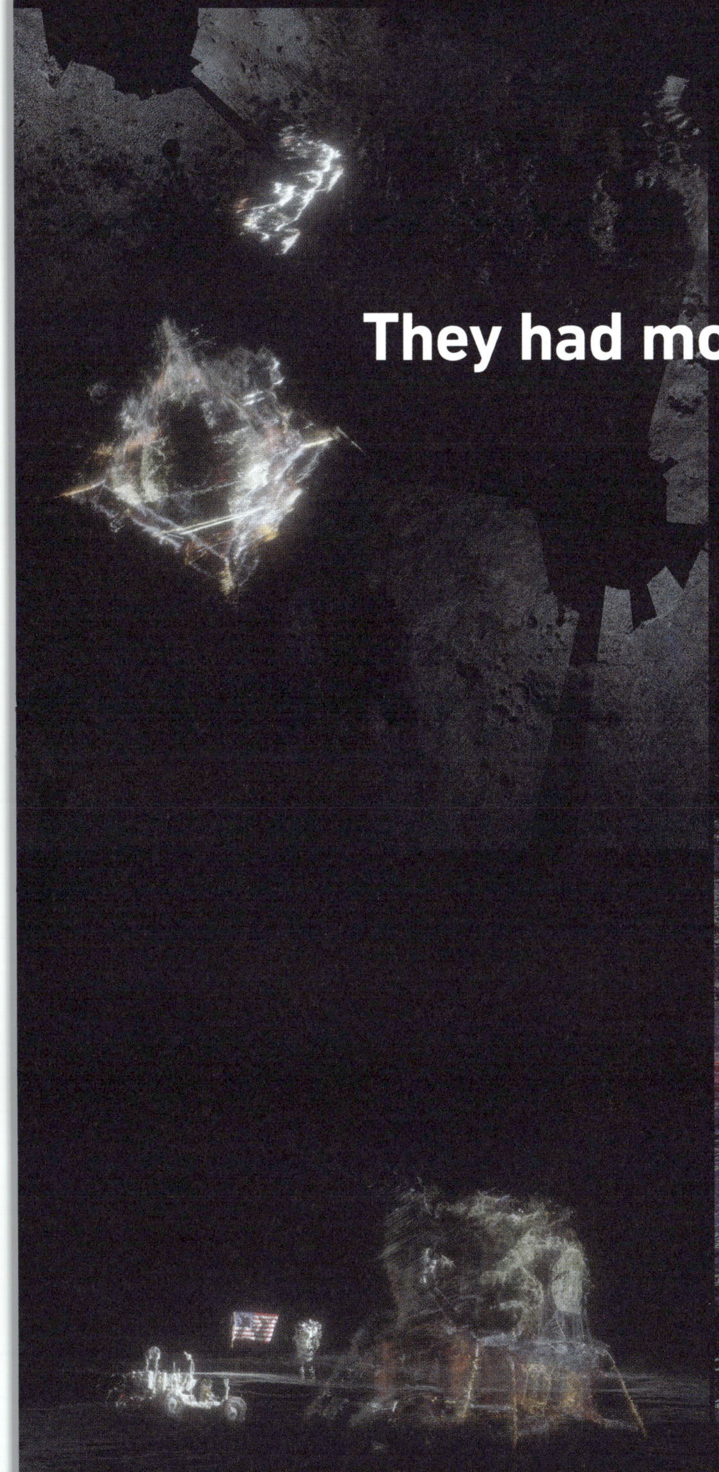

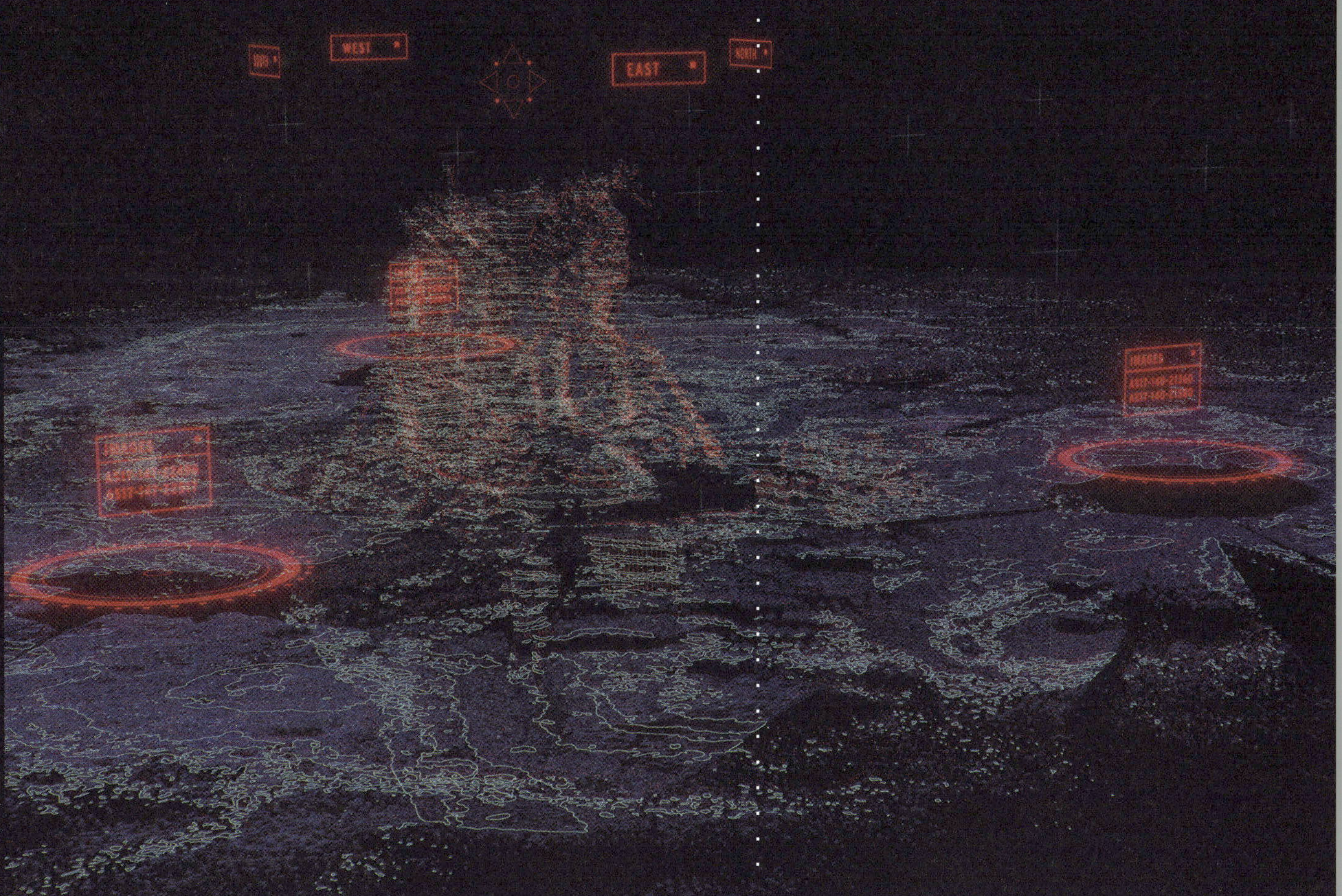

After the first successful reconstruction of a panorama that initially wasn't very promising but eventually gave me excellent results, I was able to get inside the point cloud data and move around it.

It felt like it gave me a new perspective into those moments frozen in time.

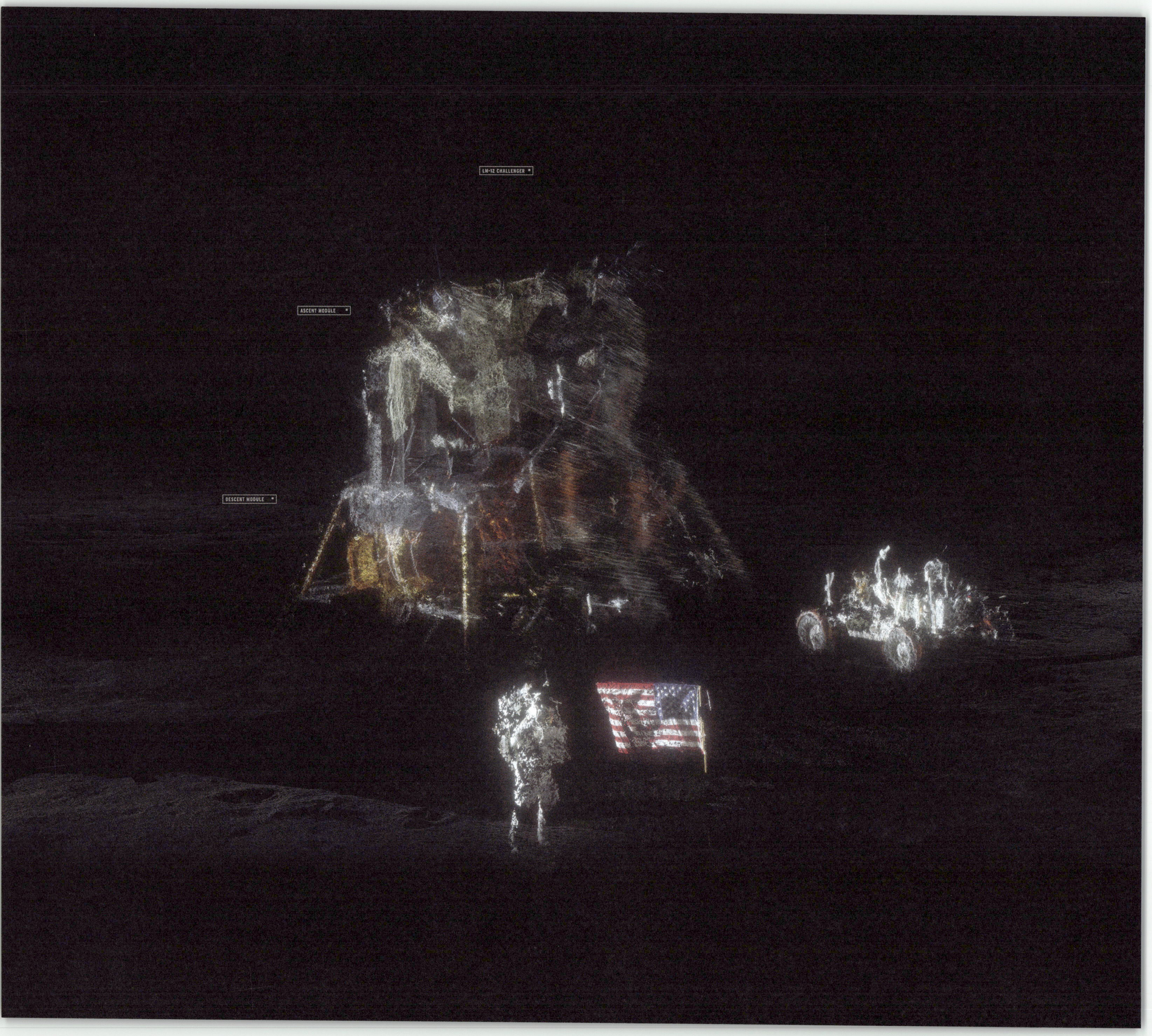
LM-12 CHALLENGER
ASCENT MODULE
DESCENT MODULE

IMAGES
AS17-140-21360
AS17-140-21380
IMAGES
AS17-140-21386
AS17-140-21391
IMAGES
AS17-134-20377
AS17-134-20382
IMAGES
AS17-137-20867
AS17-137-20893
IMAGES
AS17-147-22496
AS17-147-22517
SUBJECT
APOLLO 17
LANDING LOC.
AND FLAG
COMPOSITE
TIME
VARIOUS
POINTS
31.745.386

Name:

FIELD.SYSTEMS

Info:

As a creative studio specializing in art and technology, we create powerful new formats of visual communication.

Together with selected brands and cultural institutions, we work as artists, designers and consultants across strategy and branding, moving image, and immersive experiences.

Project:

IBM THINK 2020

URL:

field.systems

References:

Accenture
Adidas
Ailsa Bay
Aol.
Apple
British Library
Chivas Regal
Detica
Deutsche Bank
Diesel
Google
Hakkasan Group
Huawei
IBM
IKEA
Lululemon
Microsoft
Monotype
Museum of London
Nike
On Running
OPPO
Resonate Festival
Samsung
SAP
Space10
Stella McCartney
Swisscom
UK Gov
Virgin Active
Whitworth Gallery
Winton Capital
...

Q&As

. . . . . Please explain the main idea and what gave the impulse?

FIELD.SYSTEMS was commissioned to create a new musical, sound-reactive visual identity for IBM's THINK conference in 2020.

IBM commissioned UK artist Imogen Heap to create a bespoke piece of music. Her composition uses field recordings from IBM headquarters, abstractions of her voice, and a polyrhythmic melody of playful guitar sounds shifting between 80, 85, + 90 bpm, adding layers to create a rich and colorful piece.

THINK is IBM's flagship conference, showcasing the breadth and depth of the brand across services, products and technologies. THINK celebrates the dialogue between diverse disciplines and aims to capture the inspiration that occurs when humanity and technology, intelligence and emotion, design and business meet. The brief for a visual language demands a dynamic, flexible, and engaging response with IBM's tagline, "Let's Put Smart To Work."

. . . . . What challenges did you face for this project?

Our response to music is emotional unlike a machine's.

For most people, it engages the visual processing power of our brains. Acknowledging this posed a series of challenges on many levels.

Practically, we had to produce a visual system that could flex and adapt across many digital and physical use cases as the conference identity.

Emotionally, how do we look at the sound? Having access to Imogen's composition and breaking it down into separate components, we can see the DNA of the track, but we might all interpret it differently. If you are listening to the music, you are already experiencing it; should we want to showcase both views, DNA and the emotional connection, or not?

. . . . . And what surprises?

The ability to choreograph data in a way that feels fluid, elegant and expressive of an emotional connection with music.

The lightness and spring-like color palette associated with a technology conference.

. . . . . Please describe the technical environment.

Describing the technical environment, we translate all stems of the track(s) into data with our custom-built sound analysis tool, which allowed us to start exploring sound-responsive setups and delve into visual research.

We built custom software to analyze the musical layers in great detail alongside built a set of Houdini tools to import this data and make it accessible to artists and created a fully functional start-to-end generative sound visualization system.

. . . . . Tell us about your aesthetical approach.

The approach is to translate those into an expressive system, with rich, textural visuals that allow us to create moments of perspective shift; to be inside the data, see it from within, and elegantly and subtly shift to a global view.

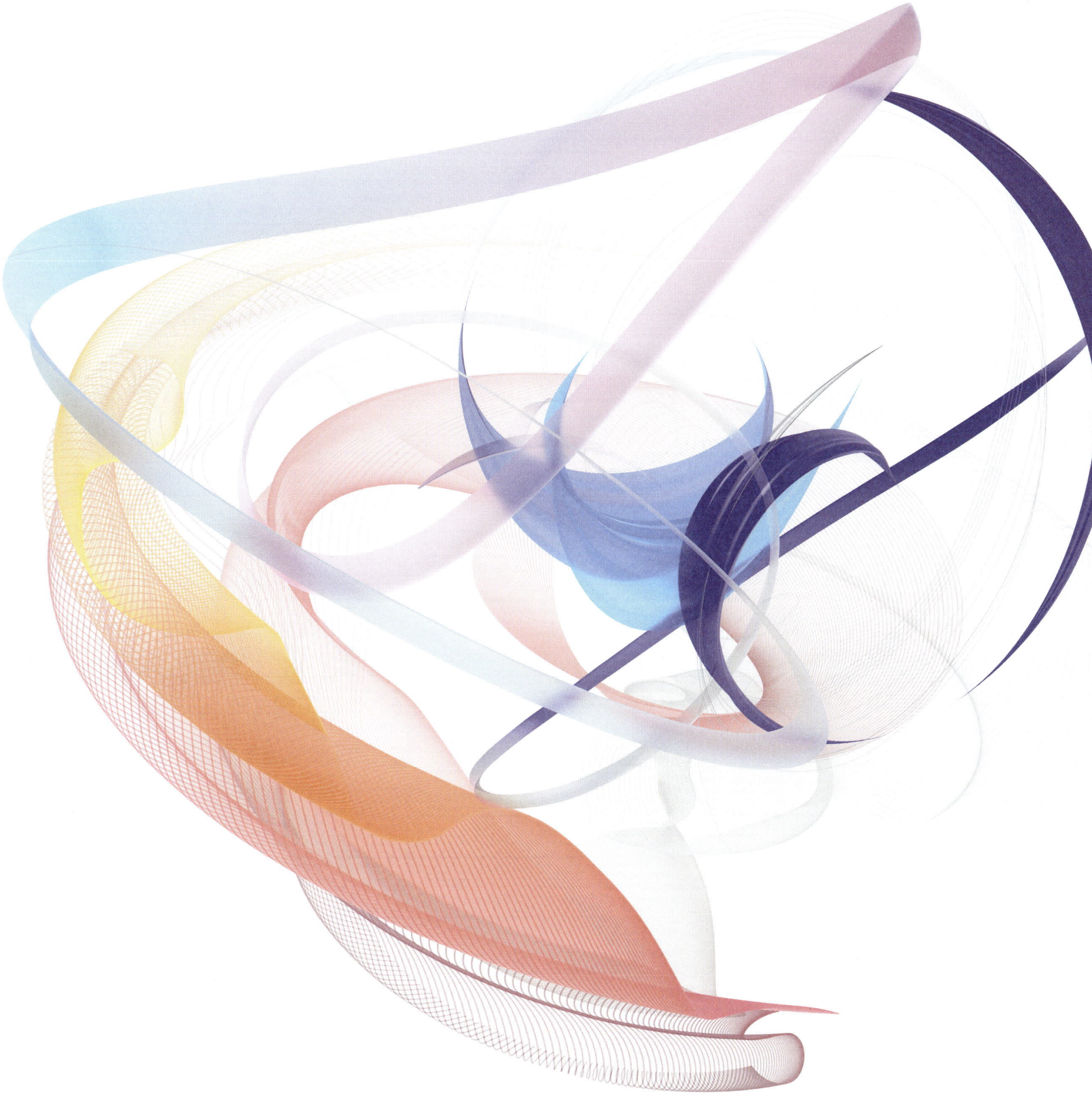

Put Smart To Work

These supporting pages contain the ongoing work between FIELD.SYSTEMS and IBM and explore their relationship through the THINK campaign, which began in 2019.

Through innovative technology and industry expertise, IBM is changing how the world works by building smarter businesses.

Think is IBM's flagship conference, inviting businesses and thought leaders to discuss new and emerging technologies which will fuel the world's next industrial transformation.

Seven generative Visual Systems illustrate IBM core themes and services to form the visual identity of the event, and provide a huge range of still and motion output to cater for 30k attendee conference in downtown San Francisco.

1. Adaptation
Continuously evolving large-scale cloud architectures, intelligent and seamless scaling.

2. Construction
The journey from individual components to large-scale solutions, aided by intelligent transformations.

3. Generation
From a chaotic explosion of unstructured data to ordered and insightful discoveries through intelligent pattern recognition and analysis.

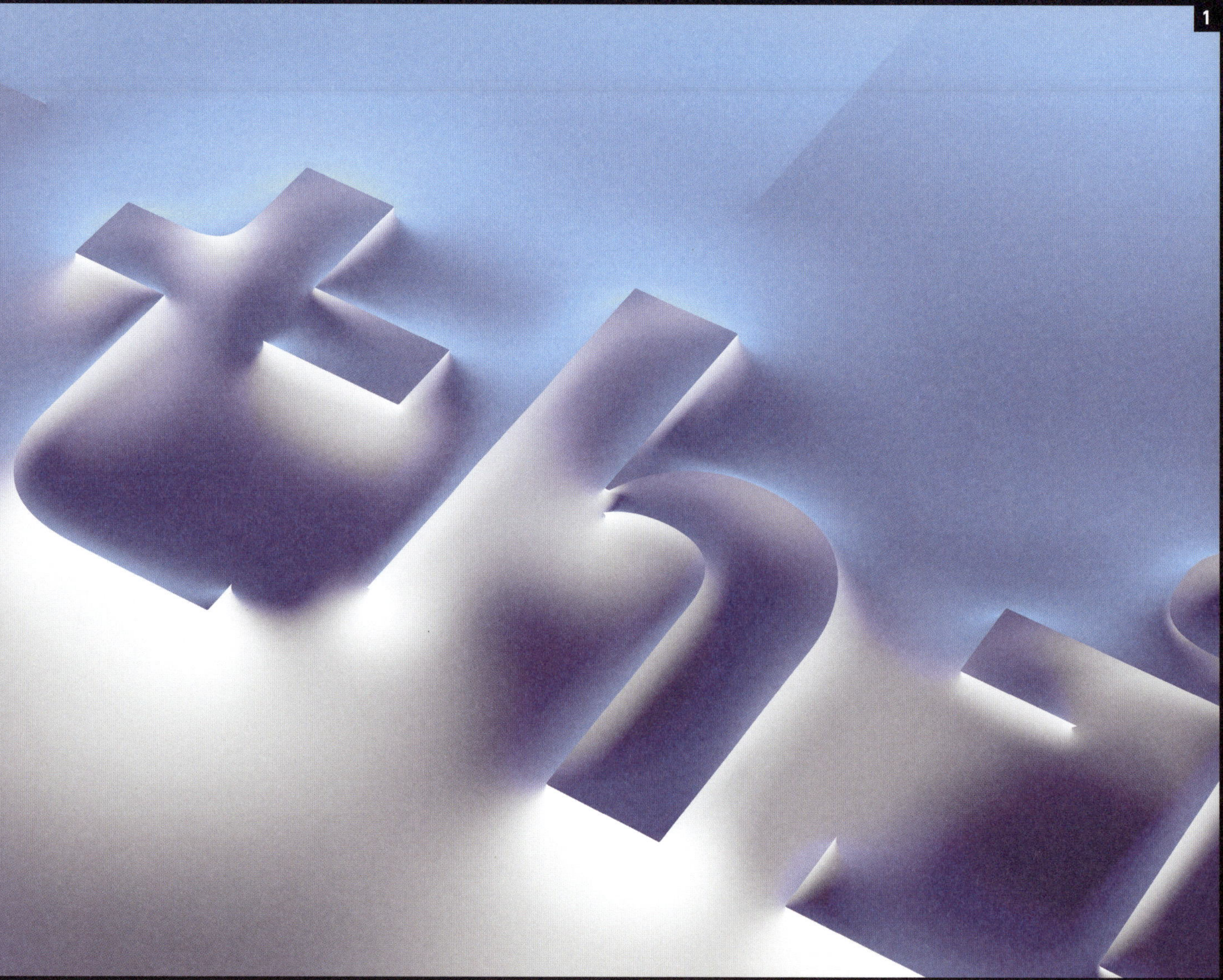

1

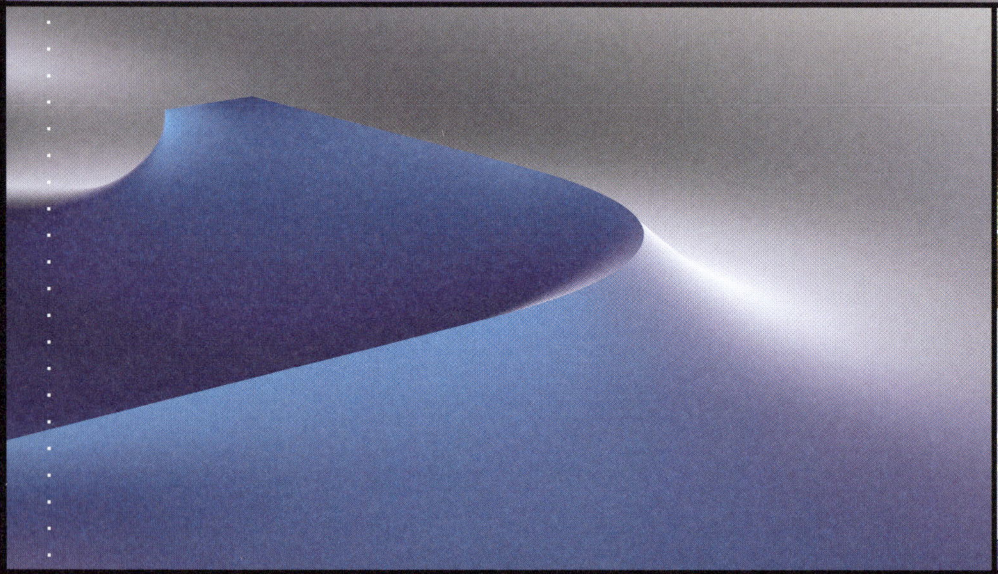

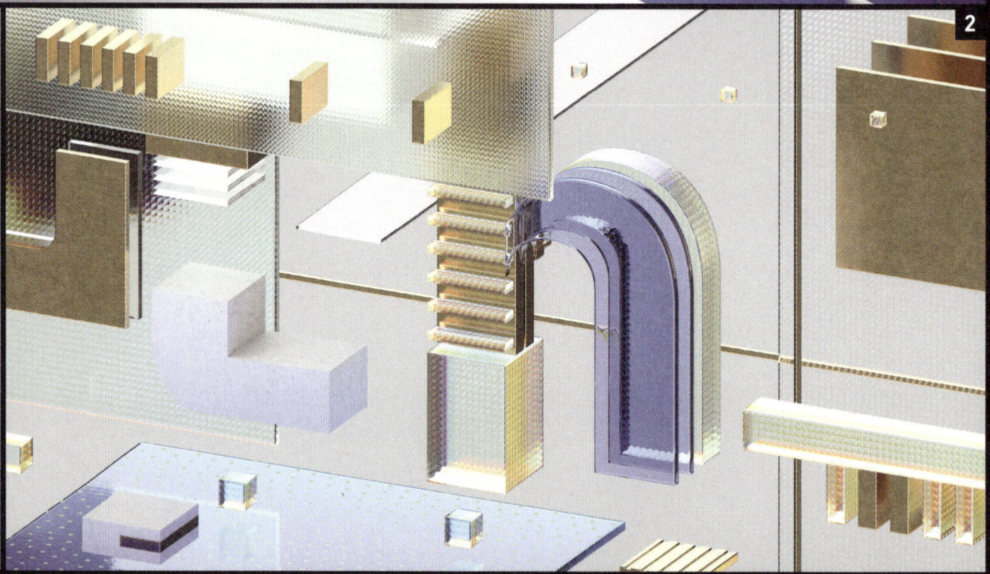

2

3

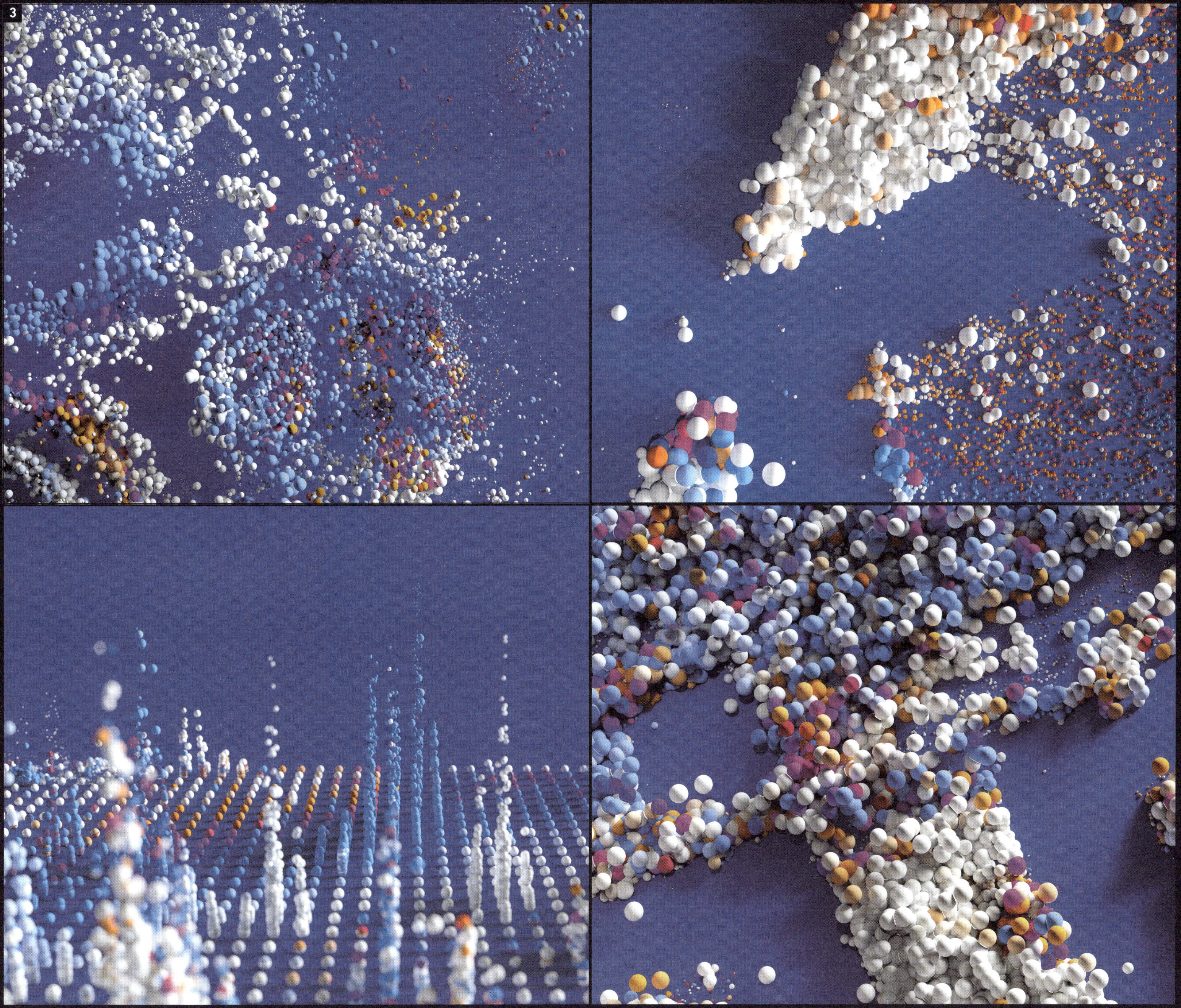

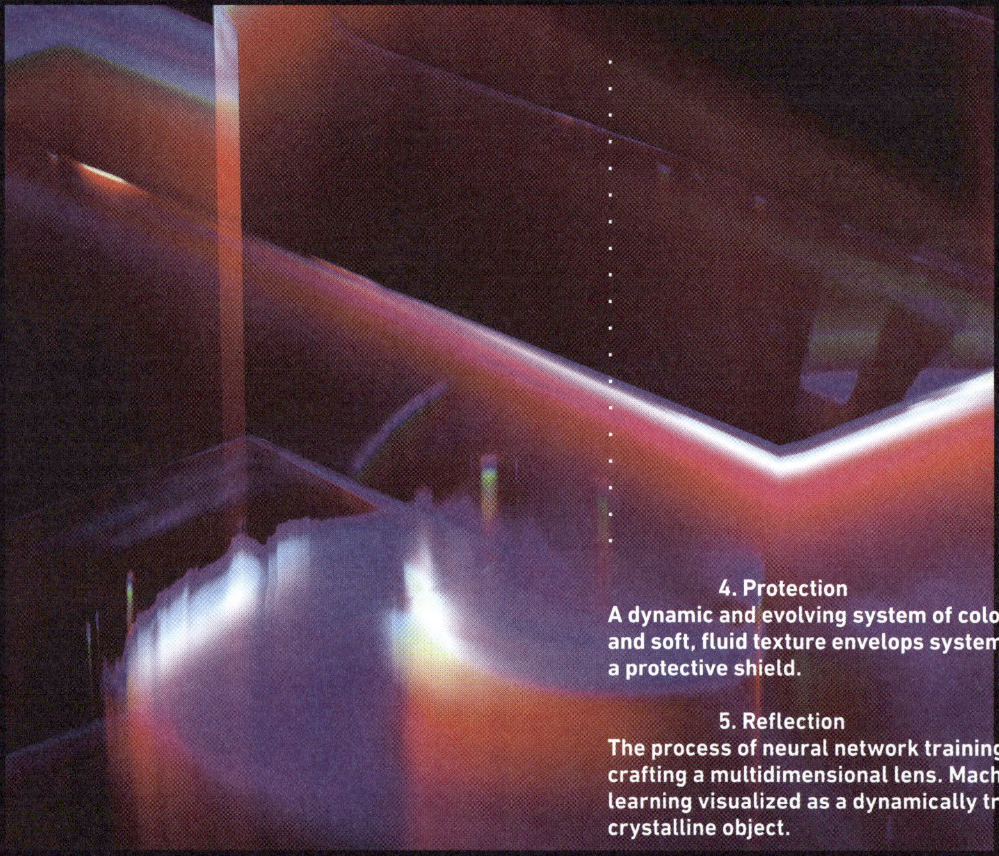

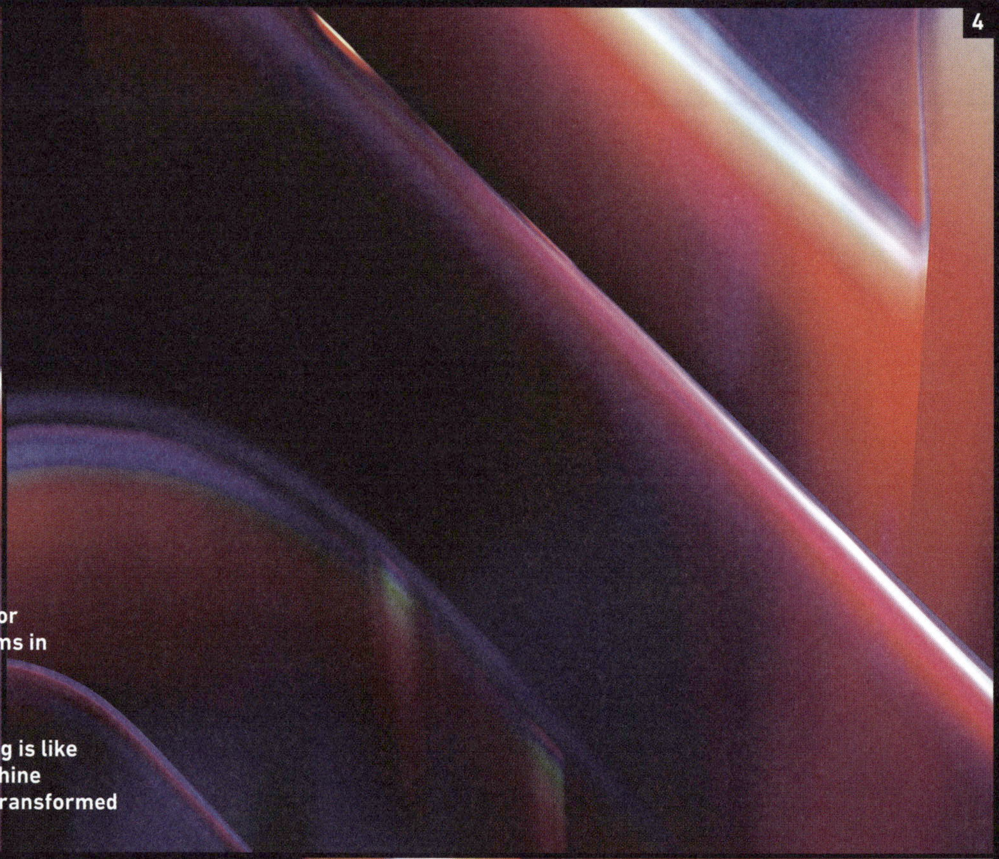

4

4. Protection
A dynamic and evolving system of color and soft, fluid texture envelops systems in a protective shield.

5. Reflection
The process of neural network training is like crafting a multidimensional lens. Machine learning visualized as a dynamically transformed crystalline object.

6. Transition
A dynamic cloud space where the constant flow is organic but organized.

7. Community
Studies of social dynamics expressed through playful abstract shapes and animation.

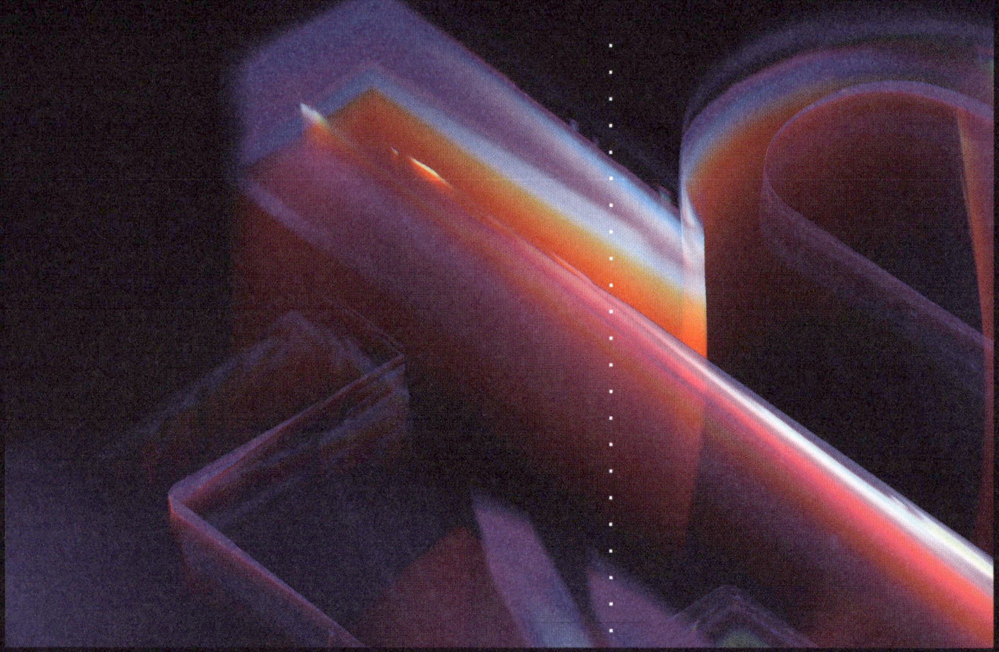

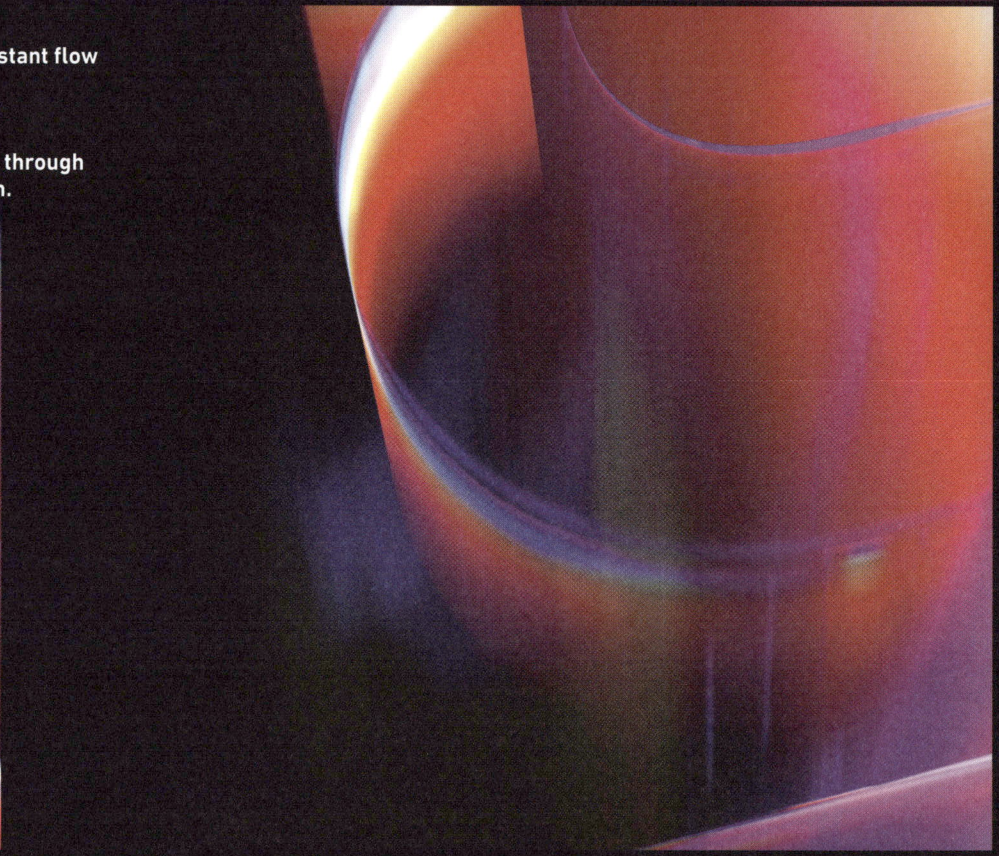

5

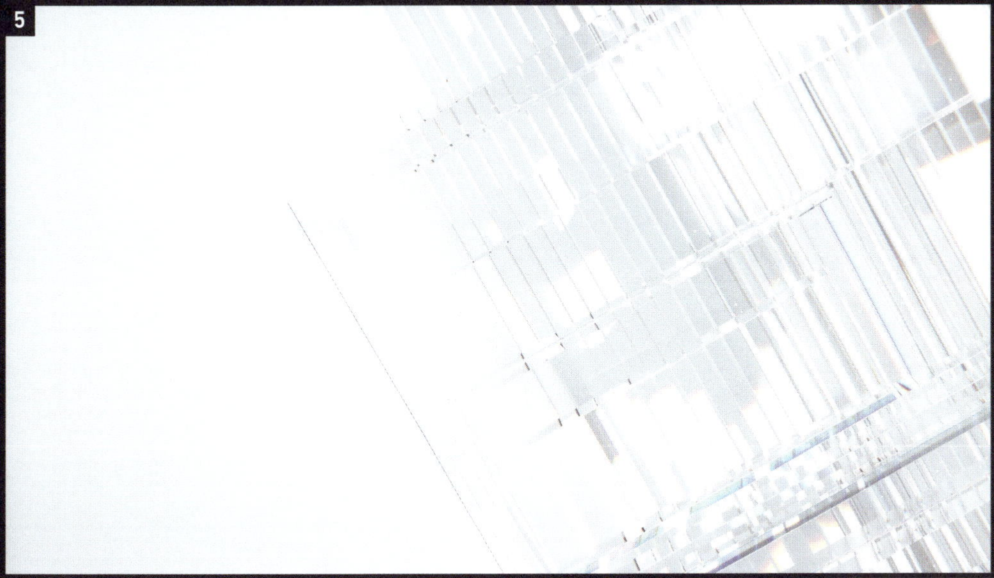

6

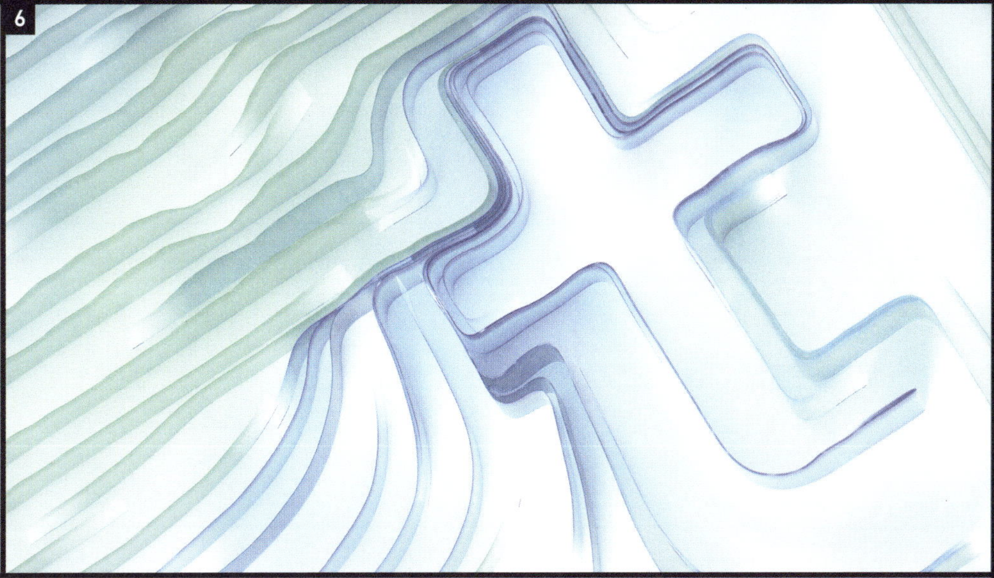

7

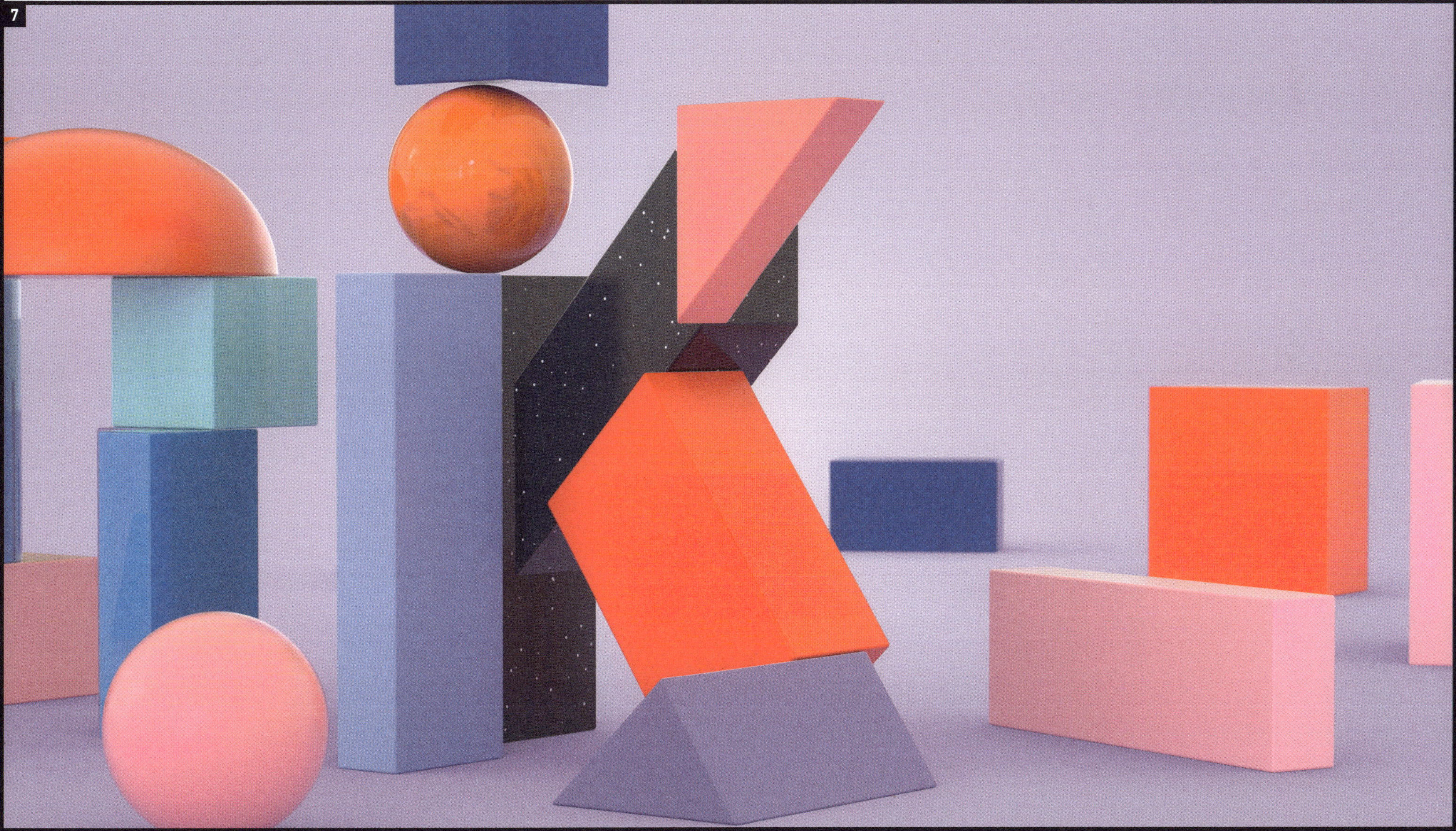

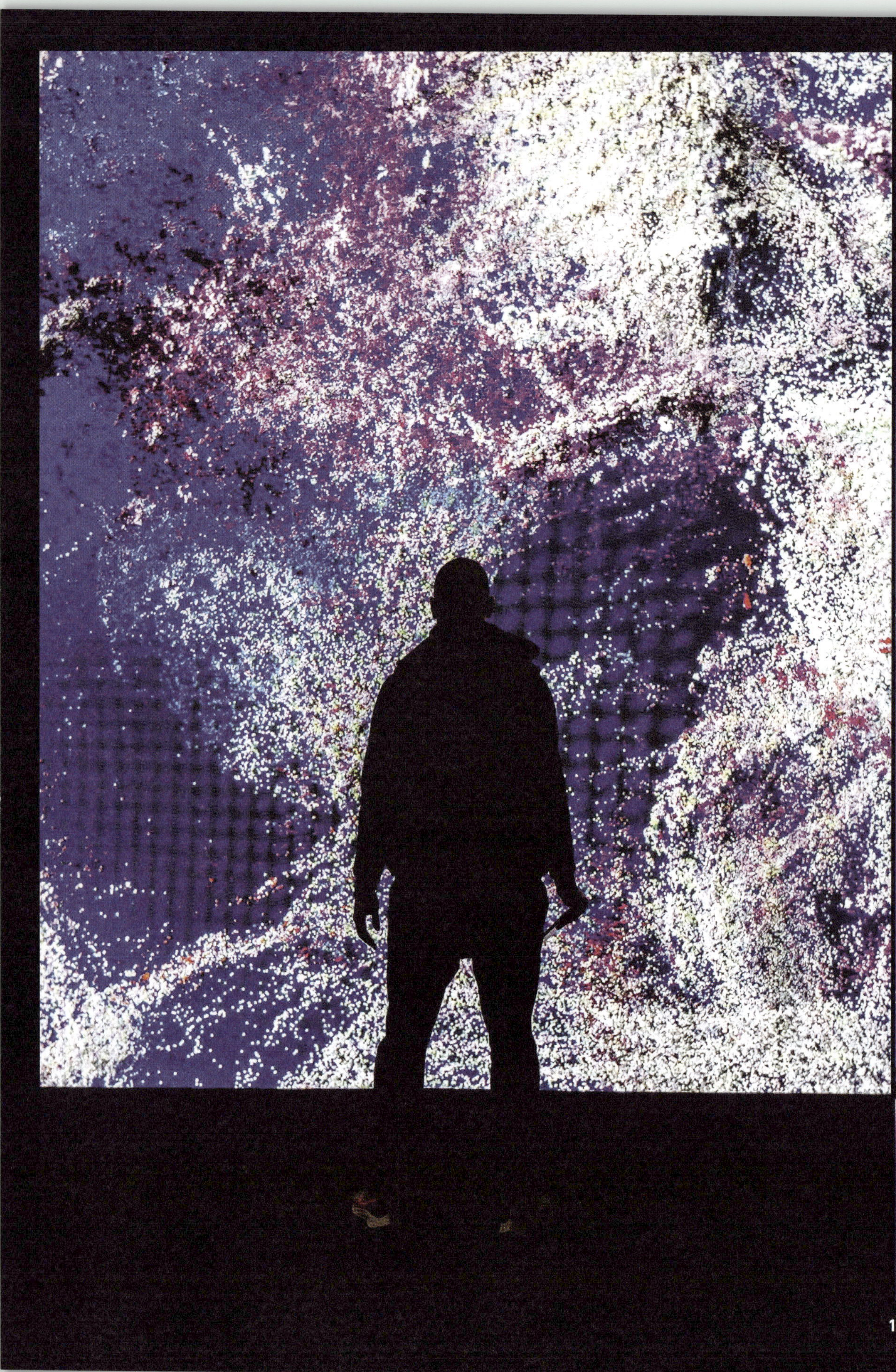

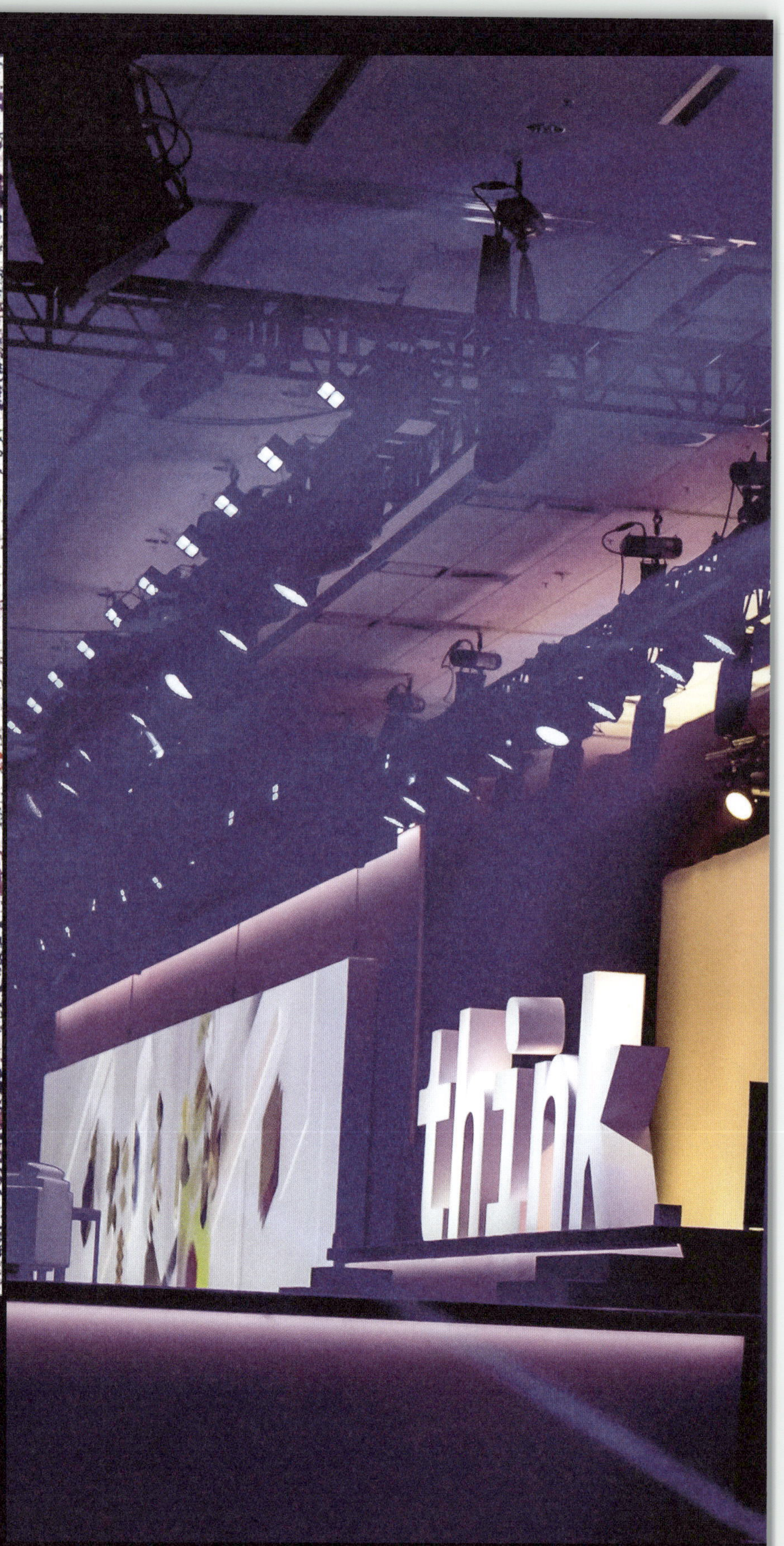
think

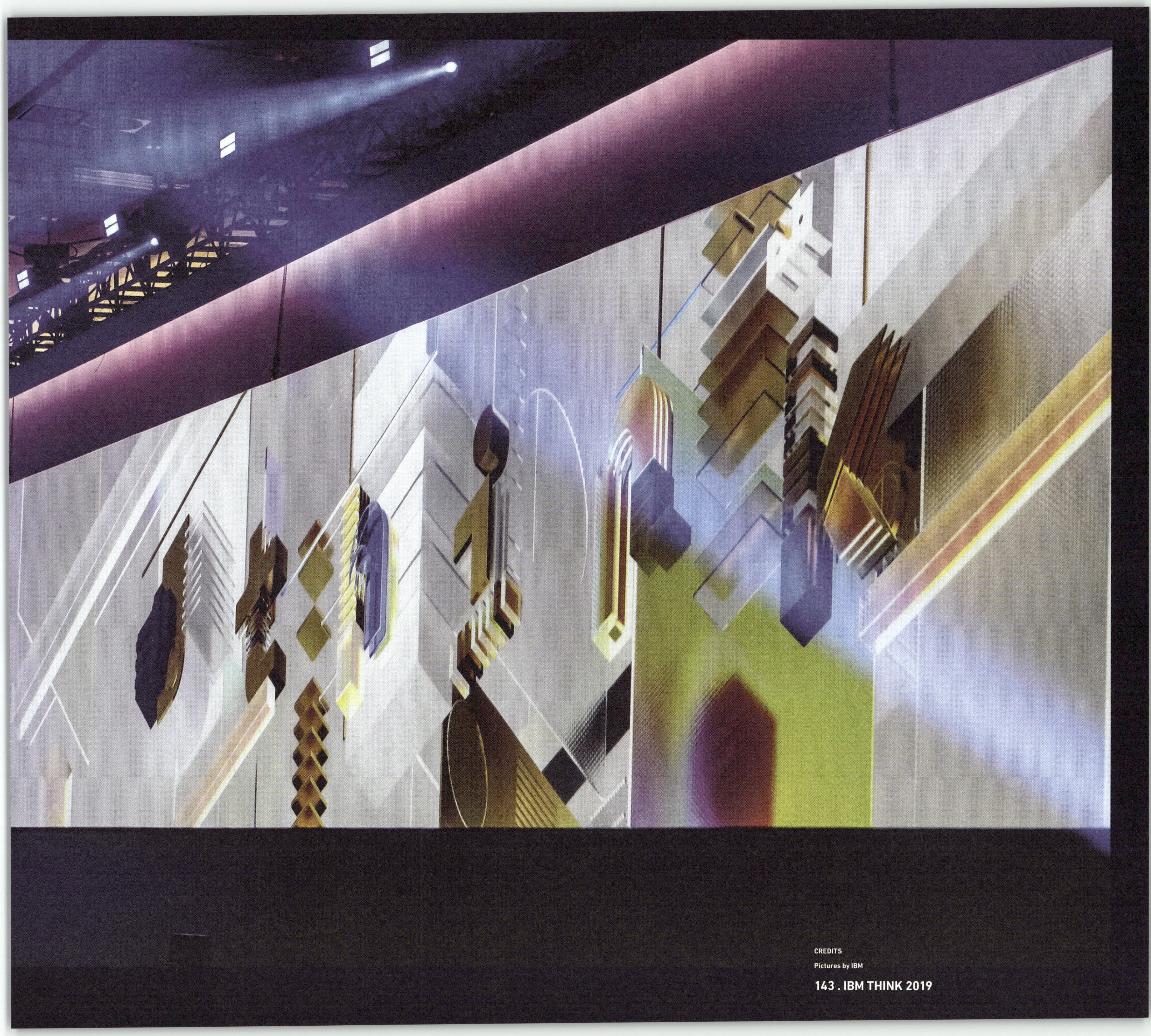

CREDITS
Pictures by IBM

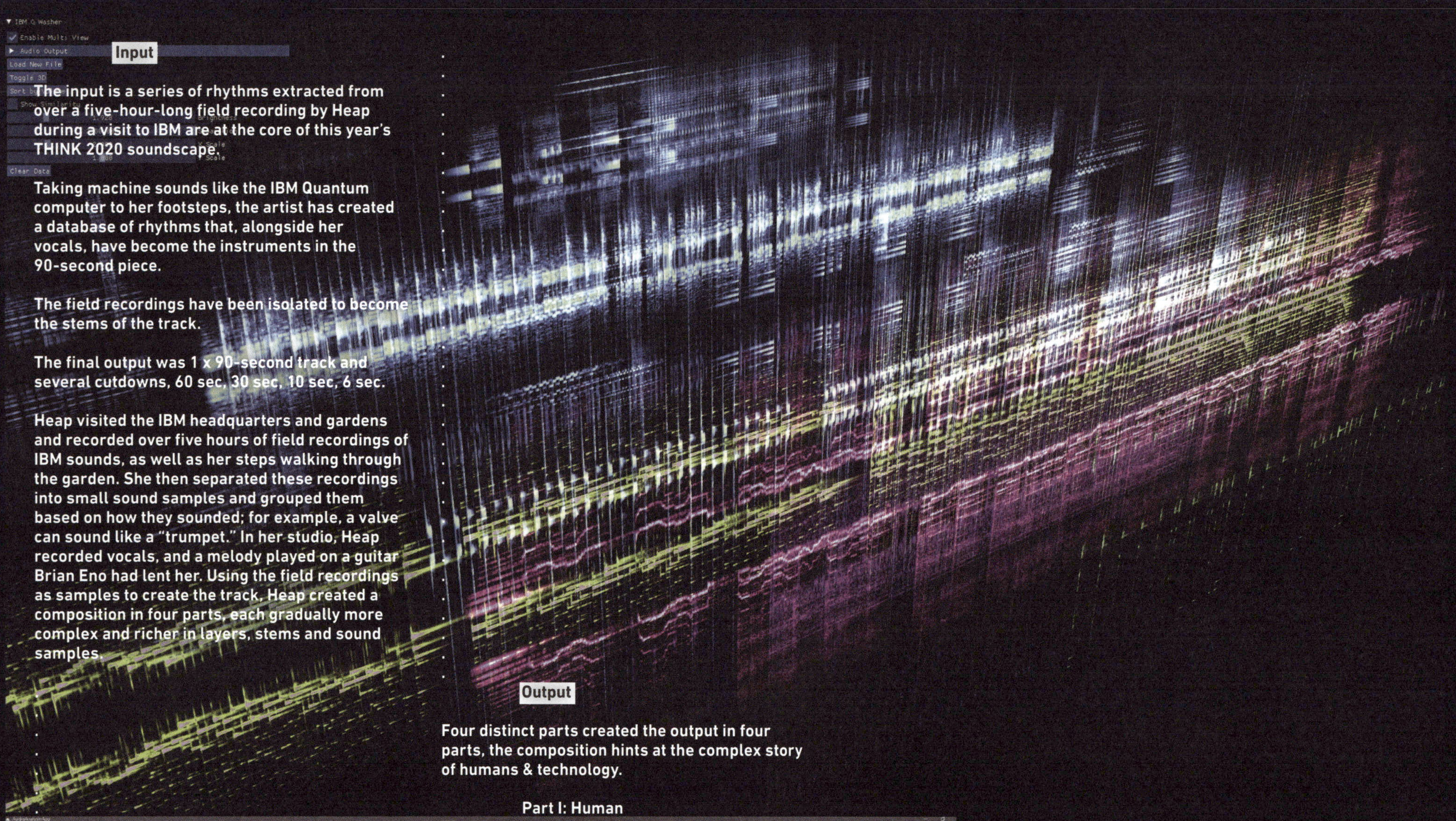

Input

The input is a series of rhythms extracted from over a five-hour-long field recording by Heap during a visit to IBM are at the core of this year's THINK 2020 soundscape.

Taking machine sounds like the IBM Quantum computer to her footsteps, the artist has created a database of rhythms that, alongside her vocals, have become the instruments in the 90-second piece.

The field recordings have been isolated to become the stems of the track.

The final output was 1 x 90-second track and several cutdowns, 60 sec, 30 sec, 10 sec, 6 sec.

Heap visited the IBM headquarters and gardens and recorded over five hours of field recordings of IBM sounds, as well as her steps walking through the garden. She then separated these recordings into small sound samples and grouped them based on how they sounded; for example, a valve can sound like a "trumpet." In her studio, Heap recorded vocals, and a melody played on a guitar Brian Eno had lent her. Using the field recordings as samples to create the track, Heap created a composition in four parts, each gradually more complex and richer in layers, stems and sound samples.

Output

Four distinct parts created the output in four parts, the composition hints at the complex story of humans & technology.

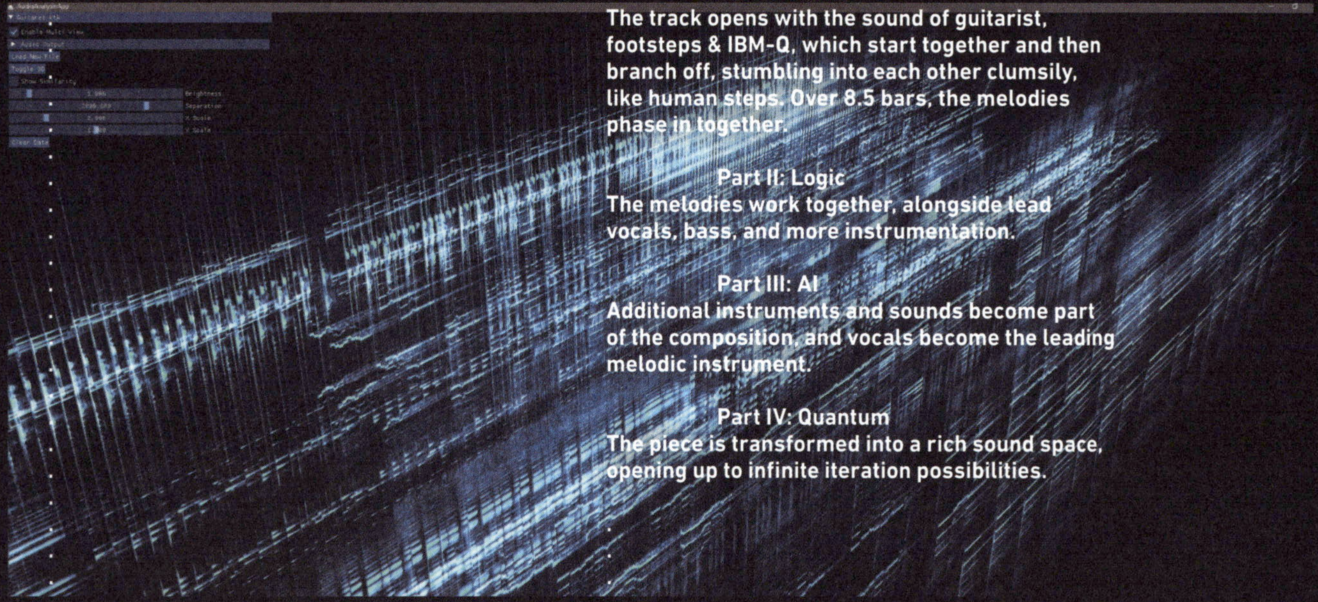

Part I: Human

The track opens with the sound of guitarist, footsteps & IBM-Q, which start together and then branch off, stumbling into each other clumsily, like human steps. Over 8.5 bars, the melodies phase in together.

Part II: Logic

The melodies work together, alongside lead vocals, bass, and more instrumentation.

Part III: AI

Additional instruments and sounds become part of the composition, and vocals become the leading melodic instrument.

Part IV: Quantum

The piece is transformed into a rich sound space, opening up to infinite iteration possibilities.

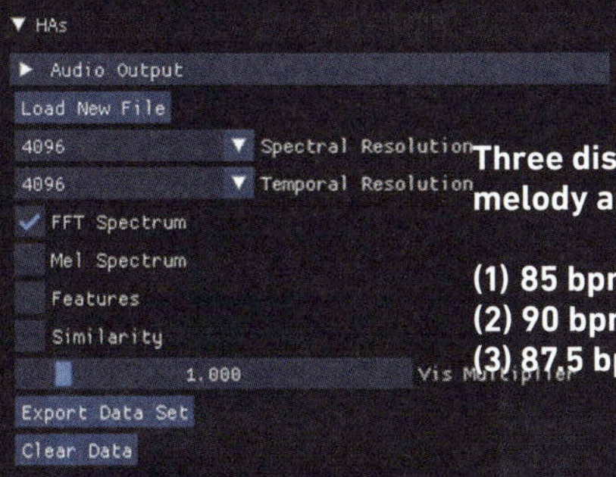

Tempo

Three distinct tempos make up the opening melody and recur throughout the track:

(1) 85 bpm (speed of the IBM-Q compressors)
(2) 90 bpm (speed of furnace)
(3) 87,5 bpm (walking)

The track's overall tempo is 85 BPM.

To create the artworks, we needed to first start by building a Visual Instrument that is:

- Highly reactive, representing every event in the music; very close to data, avoiding noise.
- Expressive of the music: beat-driven, yet delicate.
- To allow different forms to create harmony, so the elements can coexist and run on the music.
- Designed with the system's parameters to create a vast bandwidth of compositions, fade layers in and out.

The principle of Domain Transformation informs our visual metaphor for THINK 2020, its motion and behavior, and how music can become a storytelling vehicle for complex technology narratives.

With custom-built sound analysis tools, we have a visual identity entirely based on the sounds that make up the track, visualizing in exceptional detail the movement, progression and beauty of the melody to tell IBM's story.

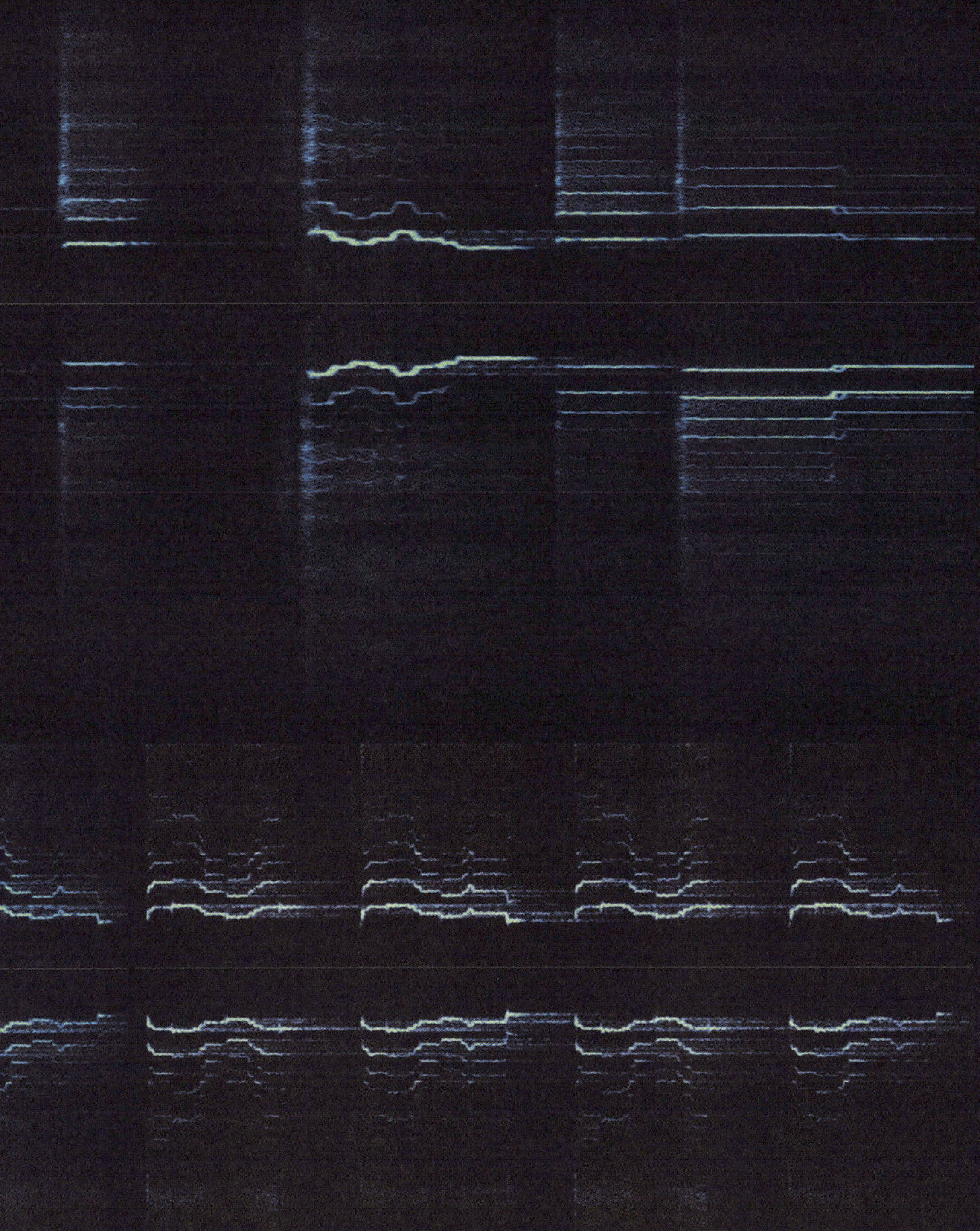

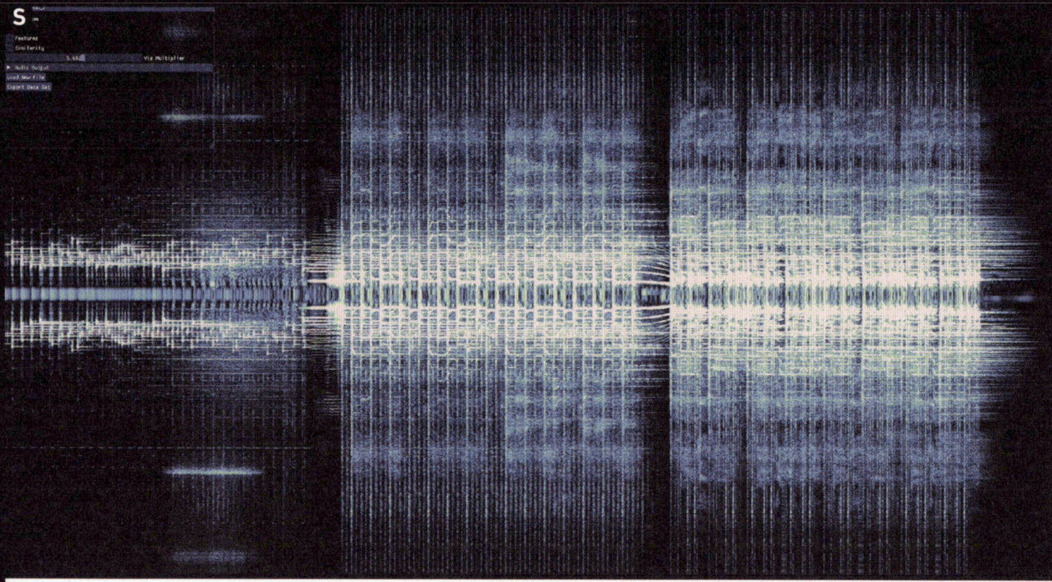
S

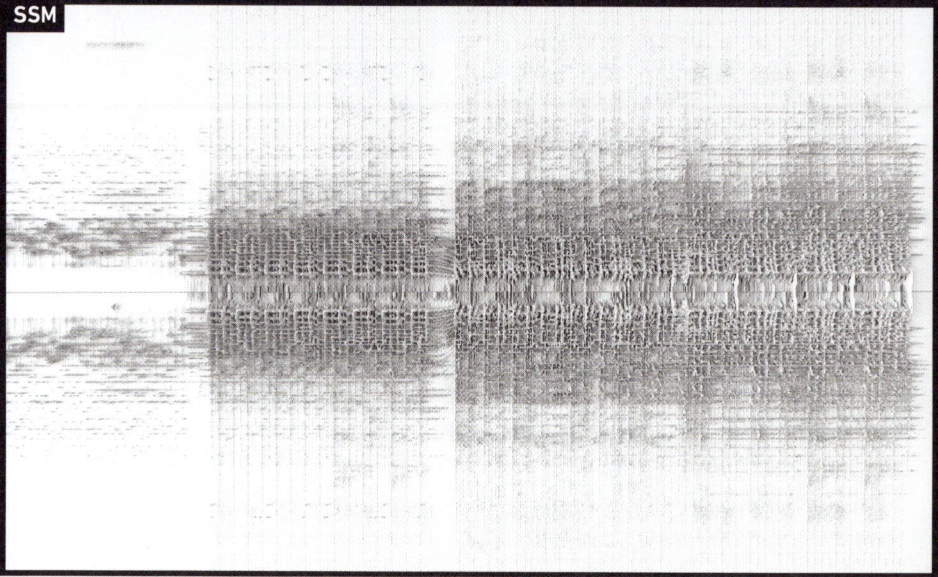
SSM

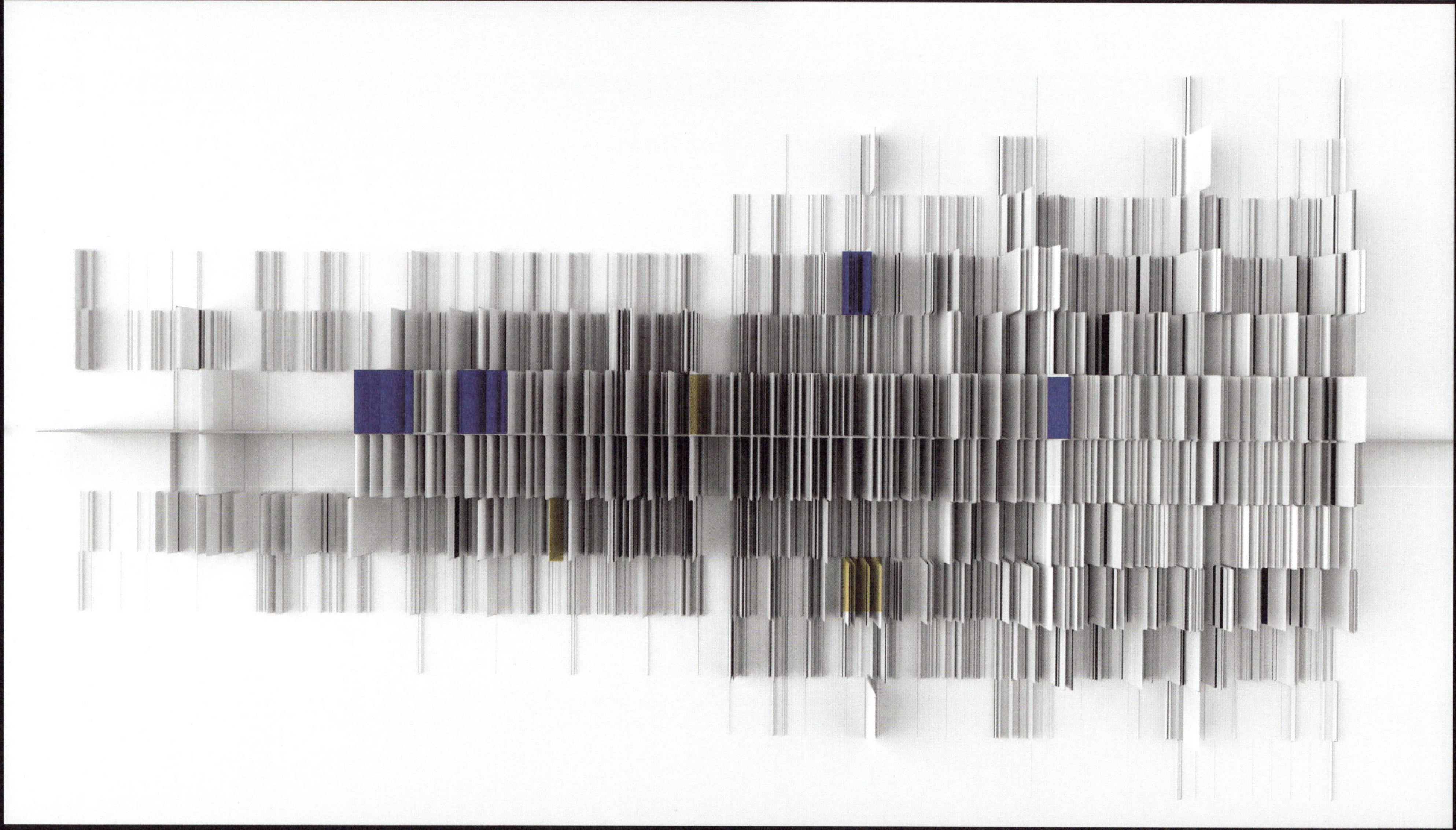

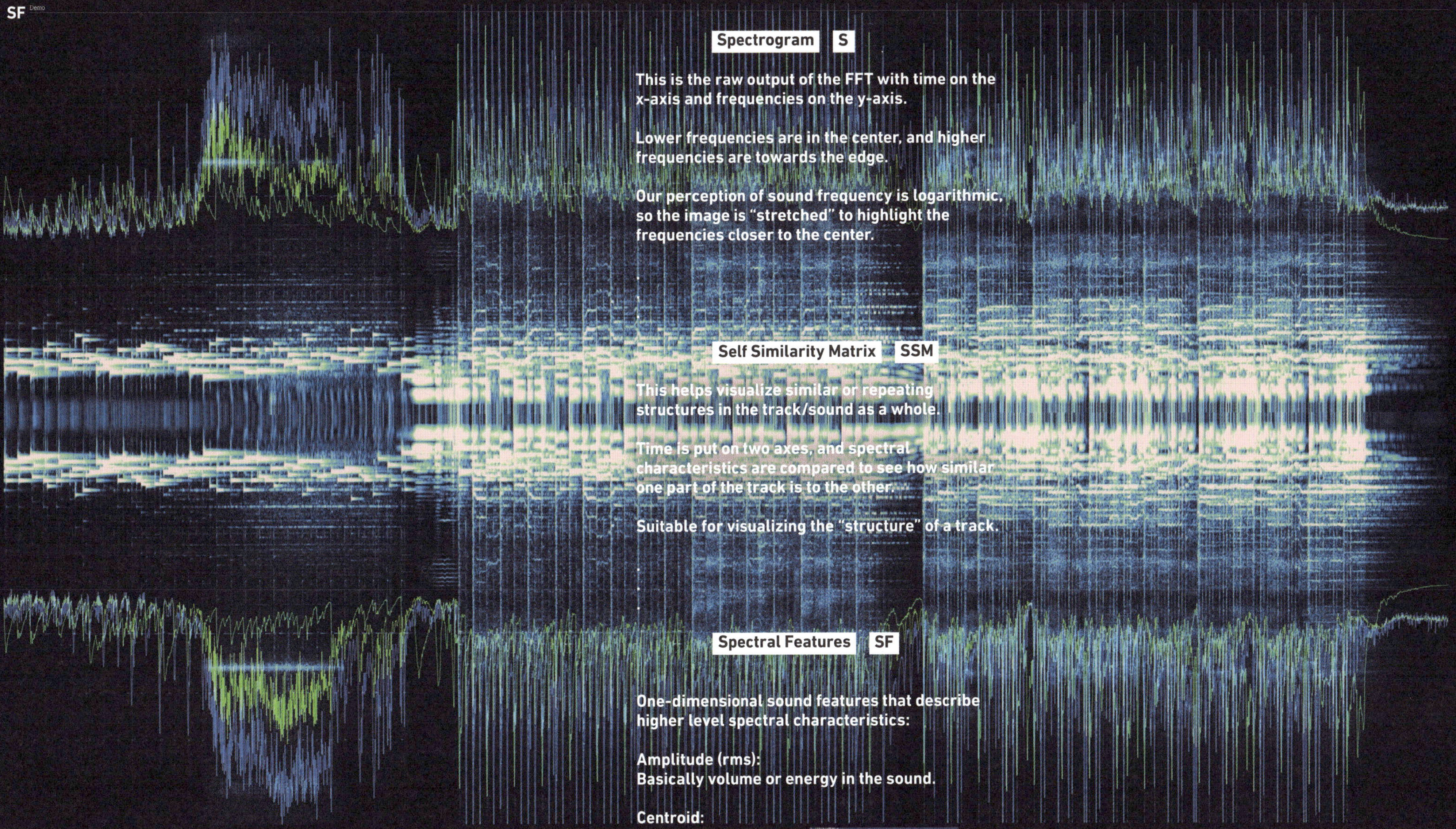

Spectrogram **S**

This is the raw output of the FFT with time on the x-axis and frequencies on the y-axis.

Lower frequencies are in the center, and higher frequencies are towards the edge.

Our perception of sound frequency is logarithmic, so the image is "stretched" to highlight the frequencies closer to the center.

Self Similarity Matrix **SSM**

This helps visualize similar or repeating structures in the track/sound as a whole.

Time is put on two axes, and spectral characteristics are compared to see how similar one part of the track is to the other.

Suitable for visualizing the "structure" of a track.

Spectral Features **SF**

One-dimensional sound features that describe higher level spectral characteristics:

Amplitude (rms):
Basically volume or energy in the sound.

Centroid:
"Brightness" of a sound.

Flatness:
"Noisiness" of a sound.

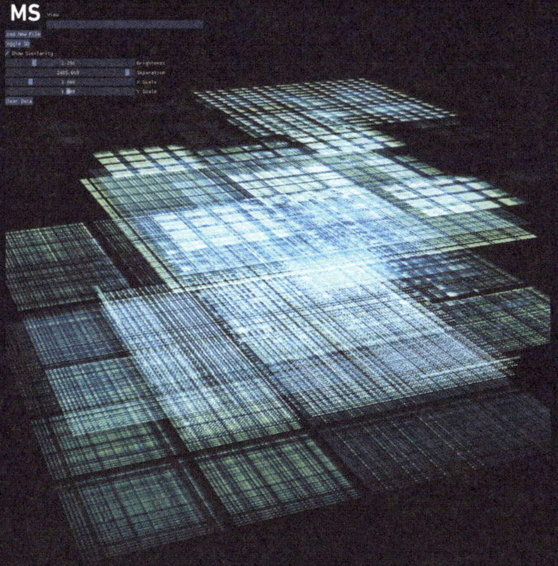

Mel Spectrum **MS**

A similar spectrum to the FFT but only features 13 bands chosen explicitly to respond to areas of the sound most relevant to human perception.

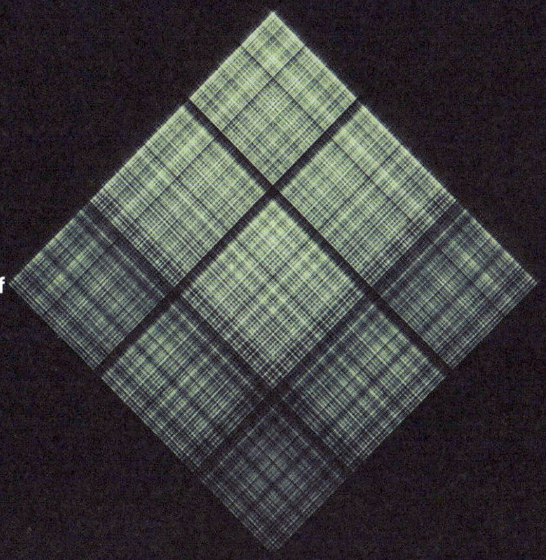

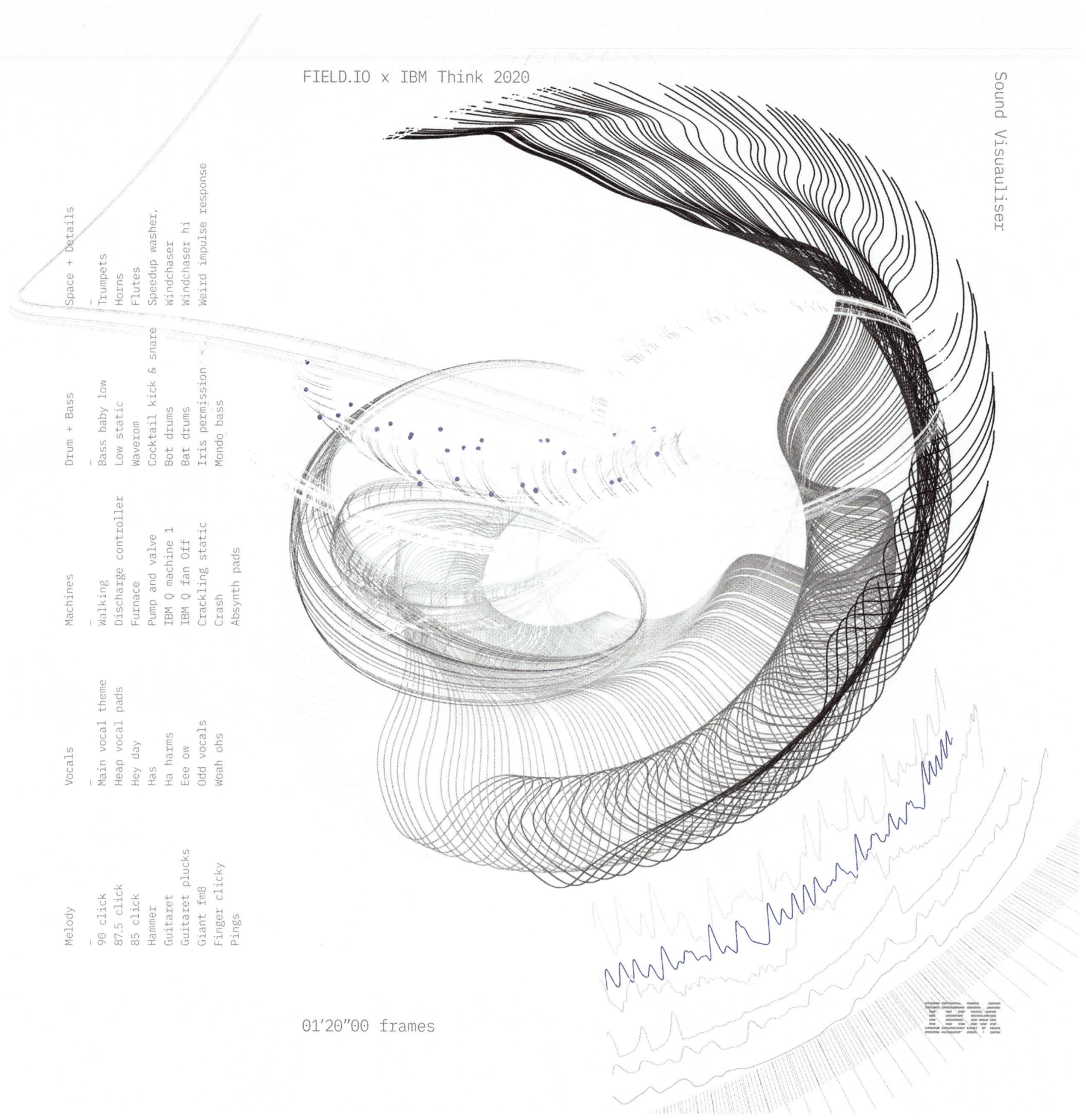
FIELD.IO x IBM Think 2020
Sound Visualiser
Space + Details
-
Trumpets
Horns
Flutes
Speedup washer,
Windchaser
Windchaser hi
Weird impulse response
Drum + Bass
-
Bass baby low
Low static
Waverom
Cocktail kick & snare
Bot drums
Bat drums
Iris permission
Mondo bass
Machines
-
Walking
Discharge controller
Furnace
Pump and valve
IBM Q machine 1
IBM Q fan Off
Crackling static
Crash
Absynth pads
Vocals
-
Main vocal theme
Heap vocal pads
Hey day
Has
Ha harms
Eee ow
Odd vocals
Woah ohs
Melody
-
90 click
87.5 click
85 click
Hammer
Guitaret
Guitaret plucks
Giant fm8
Finger clicky
Pings
01'20"00 frames
IBM

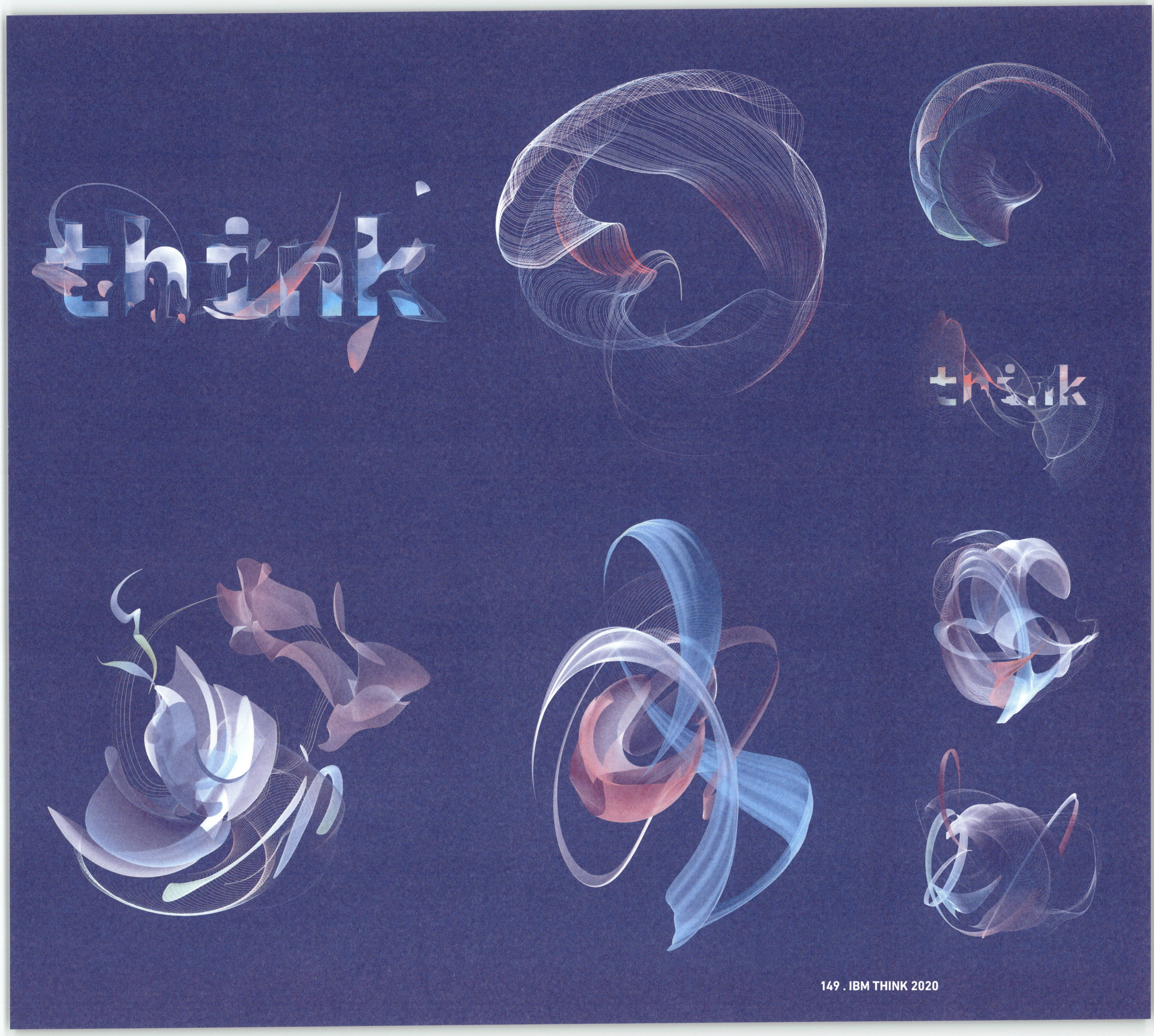
think

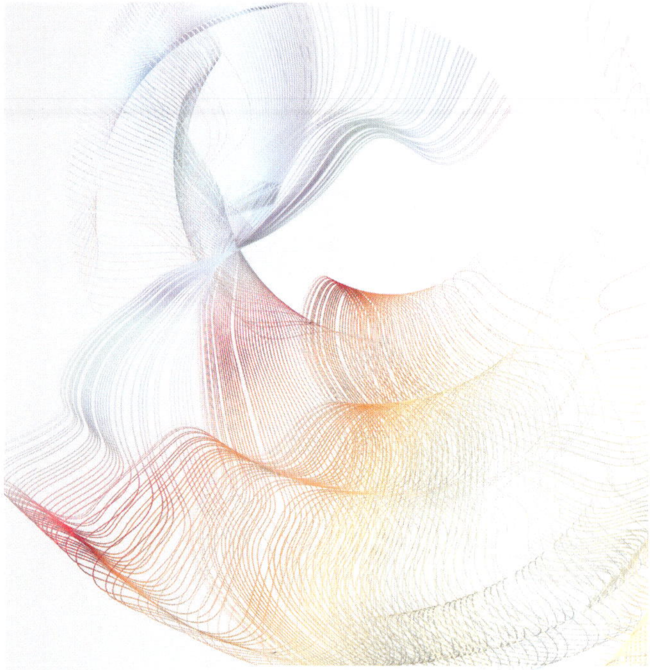
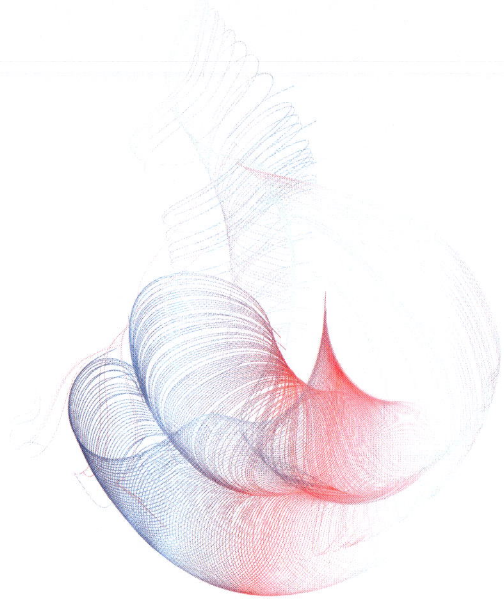
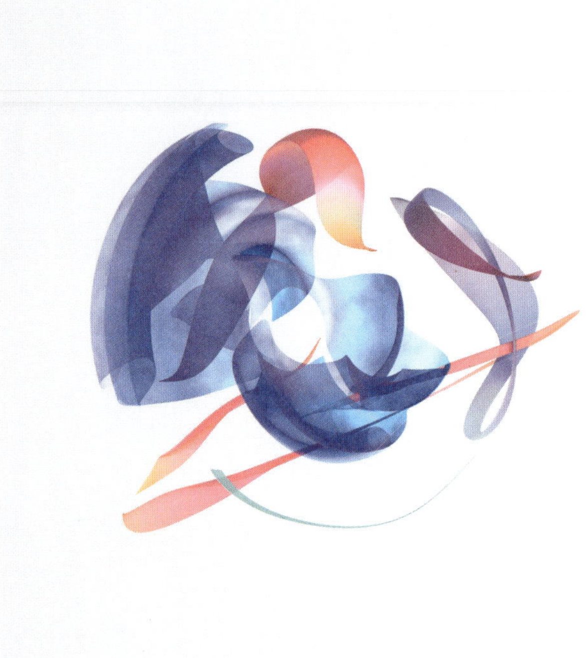
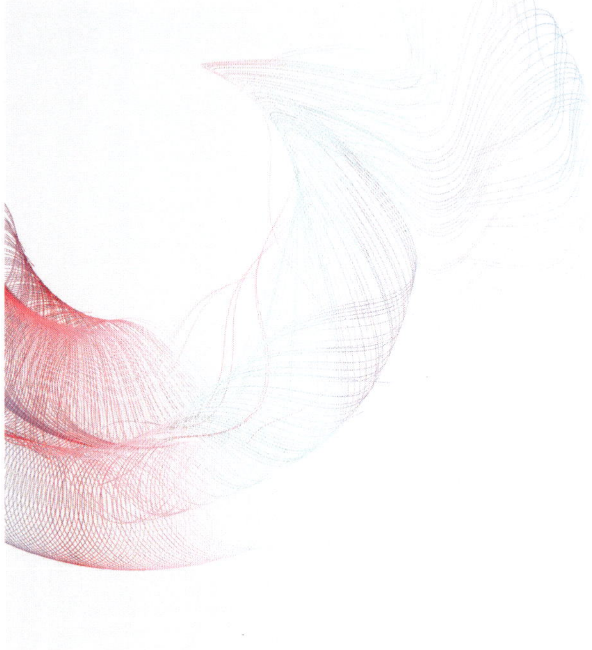
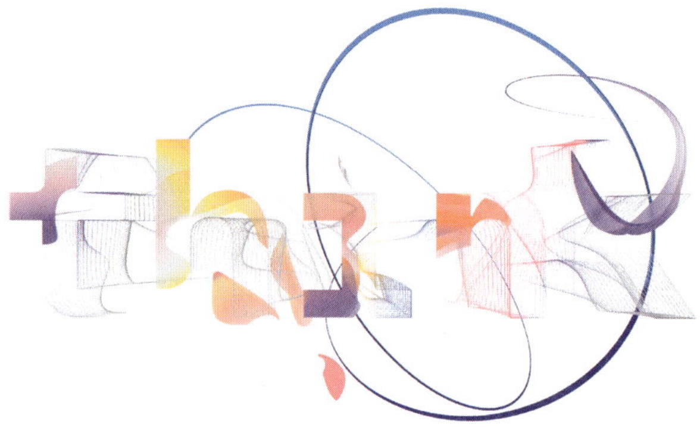
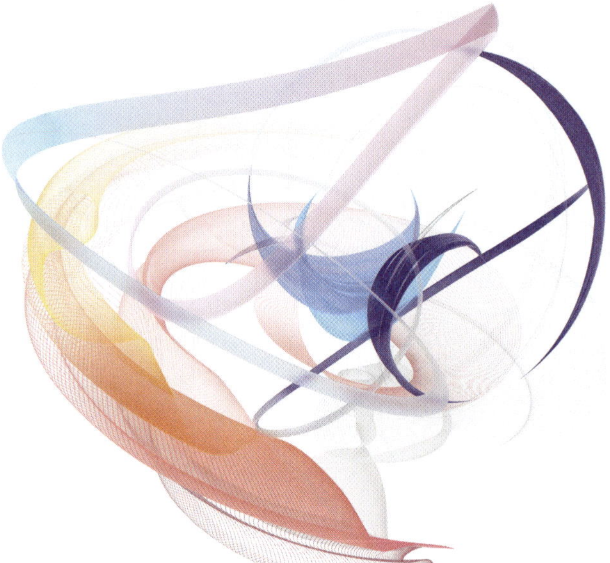
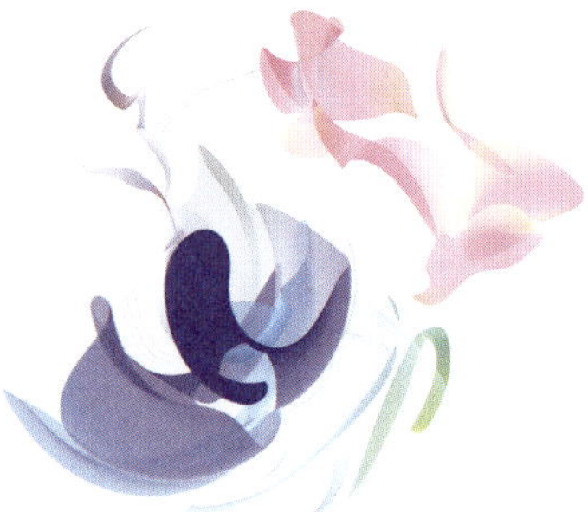
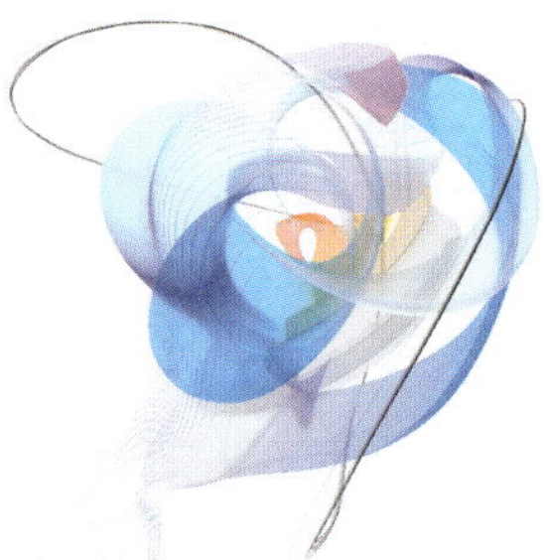
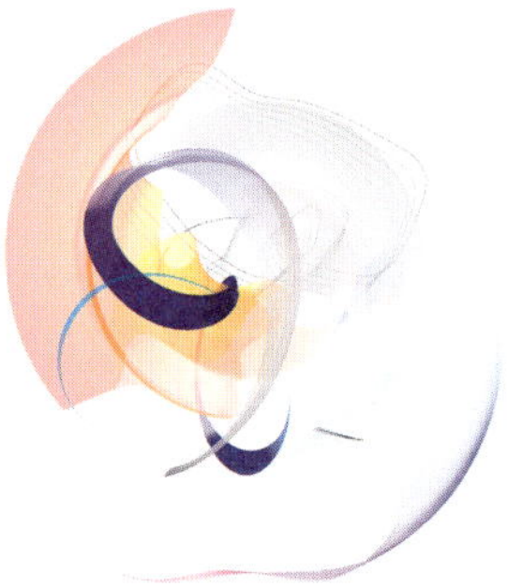
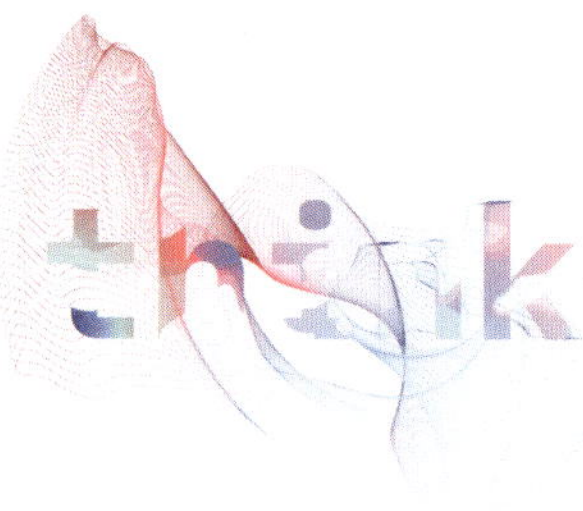
think
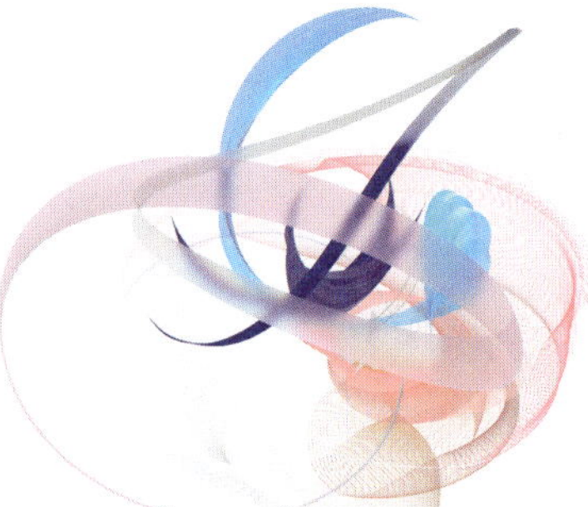

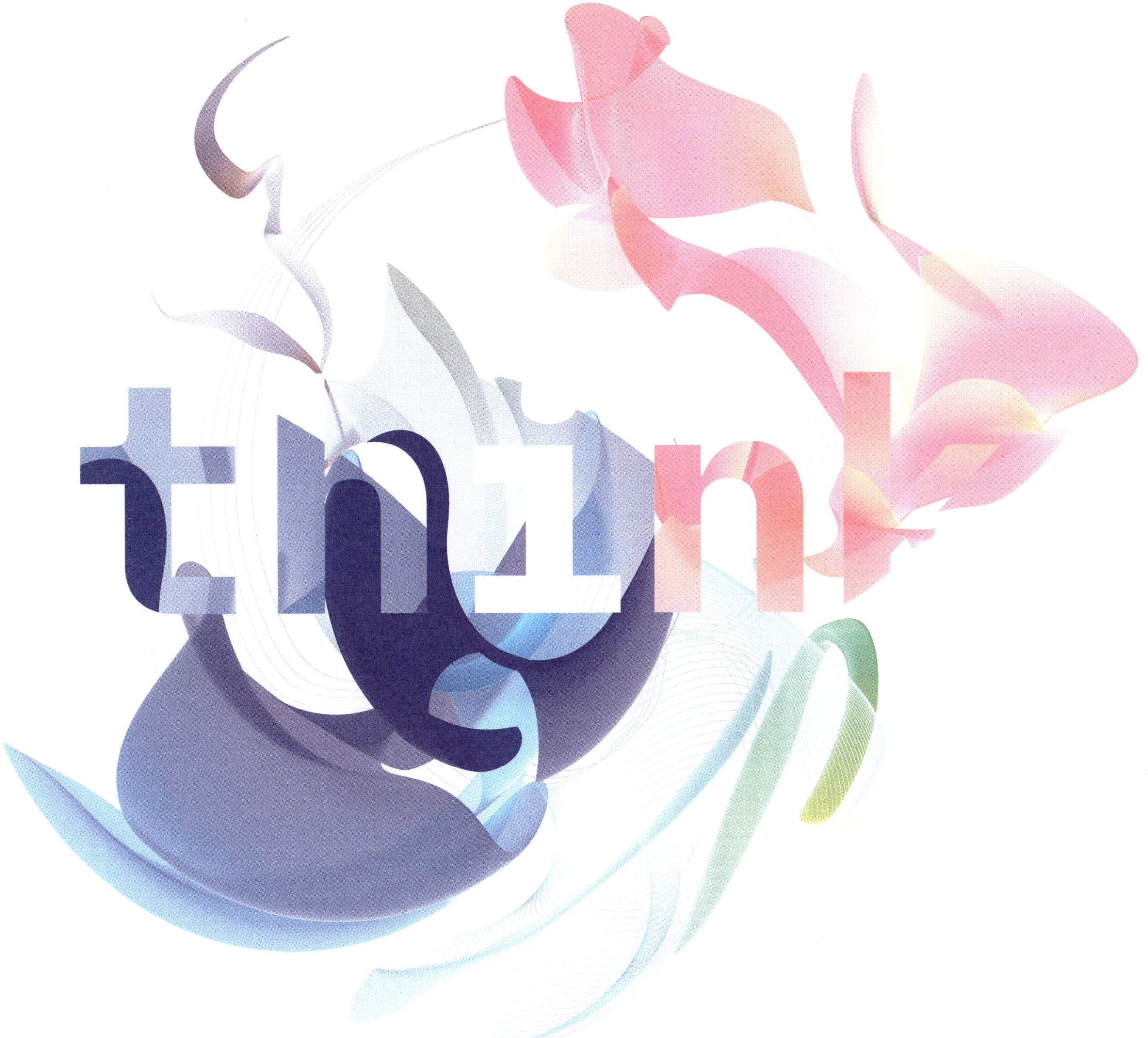
think

Sh on ei Fu ji mo to

Name:

Shohei Fujimoto

Info:

Based in Tokyo.

From a primitive perspective, explores perceptual experiences of essential nature through attempts to concisely capture the data and facts behind phenomena and shapes, emphasize them, and complicate them.

Project:

INTANGIBLE #FORM

URL:

sfjmt.org

Mail:

info@sfjmt.org

Instagram:

@shohei_fujimoto

Q&As

. . . . . Please explain the main idea and what gave the impulse?

The premise for this project is an exploration of structures formed by countless lines through a laser optical axis and a curiosity for the universal sense of human beings.

. . . . . What challenges did you face for this project? And what surprises?

The challenges and surprises faced during this project centered on spatial expression using the properties of multiple media, for example, moving lasers, strobes and projectors.

. . . . . Please describe the technical environment.

I am controlling 660 laser modules by using the original application (openFrameworks).

. . . . . Tell us about your aesthetical approach.

It gives materiality to the light, the moving laser, strobe, projector that exists and used in space.

. . . . . What's next? Your vision?

An exploration of human vision and color; with light wavelengths and their behavior on the brain.

Project Description:

This project is "intangible" to create a physical object/notion in space using a laser optical axis with no physical properties.

When we see a structure, we instantly try to calculate and understand the curves and physical rules of the structure.

This project is reflexive, in other words, a universal, wild sensation. When this sensation works, the behavior of space and structures influences the criteria for judging whether they are organic/inorganic; a notion such as biological consciousness;

The soul is generated from judging.

I create experiences, spaces, and structures that have both authentic and intangible qualities as a means of touching human cognition and imagery and as an opportunity for viewers to get a bird's-eye view of their abilities.

All laser modules are controlled by an original application (created with openFrameworks), while the computations that form the structure are in real-time.

Objects such as spheres and cubes are floating in a three-dimensional, virtual space in the application. The behavior of the laser is calculated by using the primitive data of the objects.

The primary purpose is to explore the essential expression. In the future, and in addition to the data possessed by the structure, I would like to study human vision and color working with data from a wavelength of light.

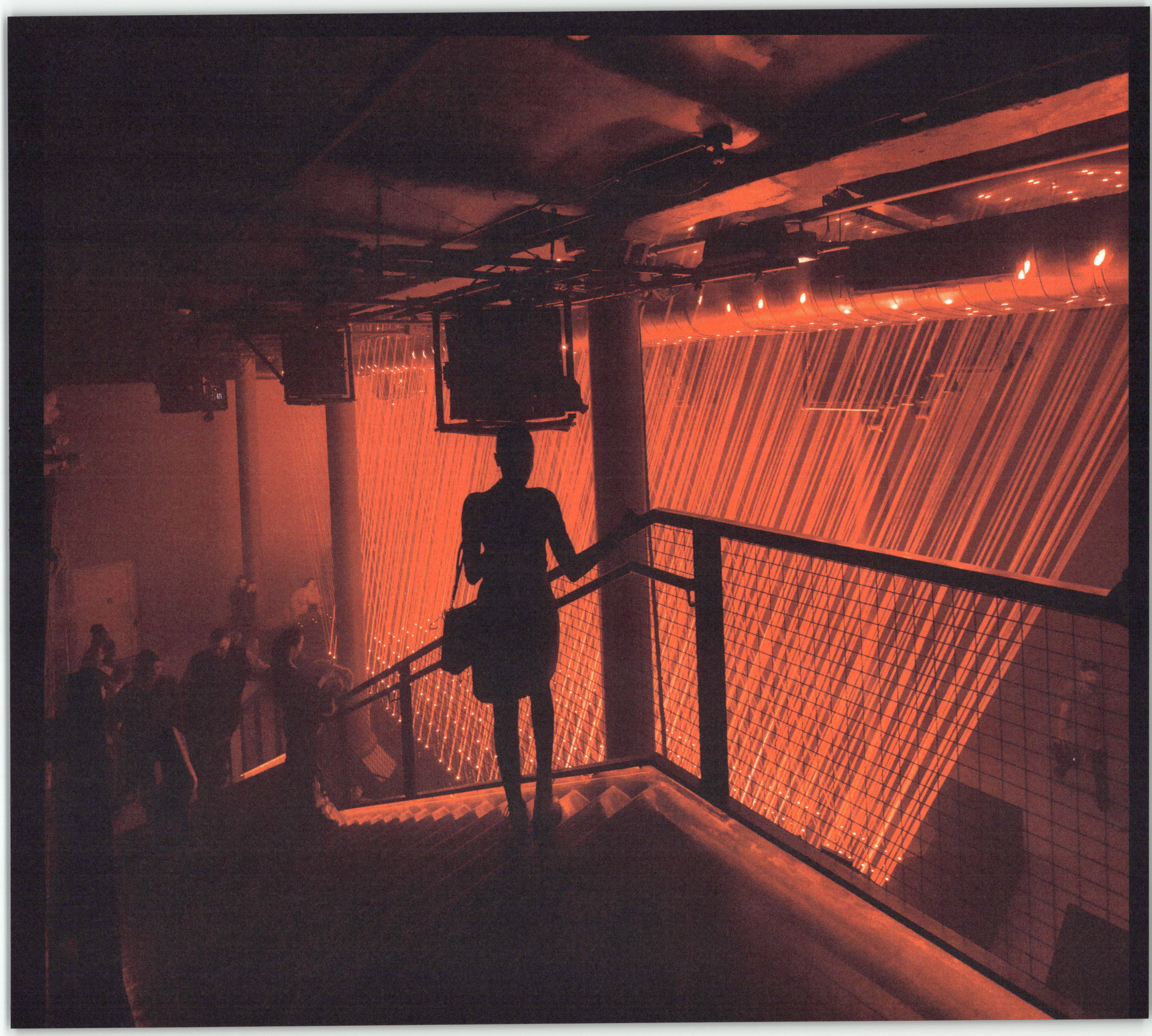

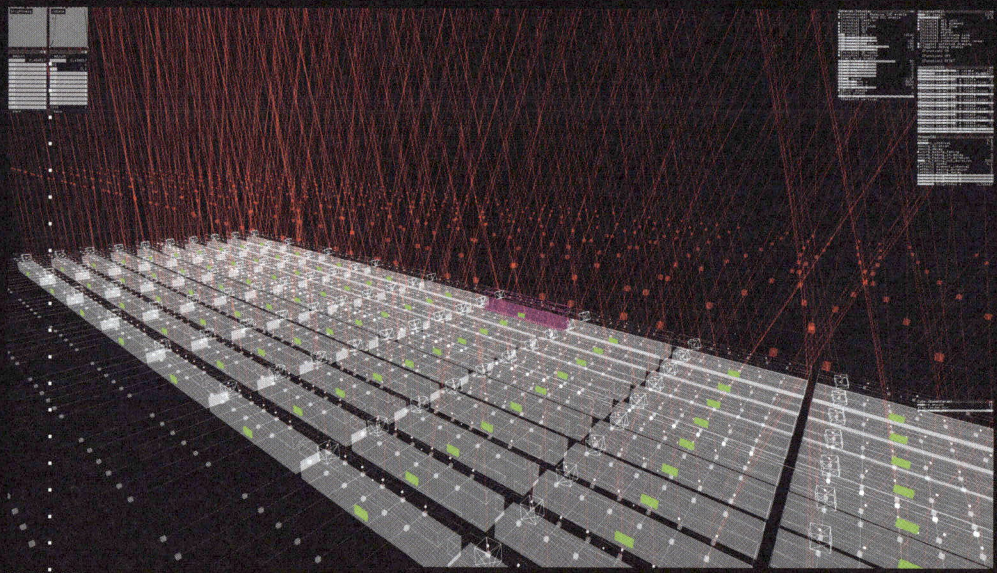

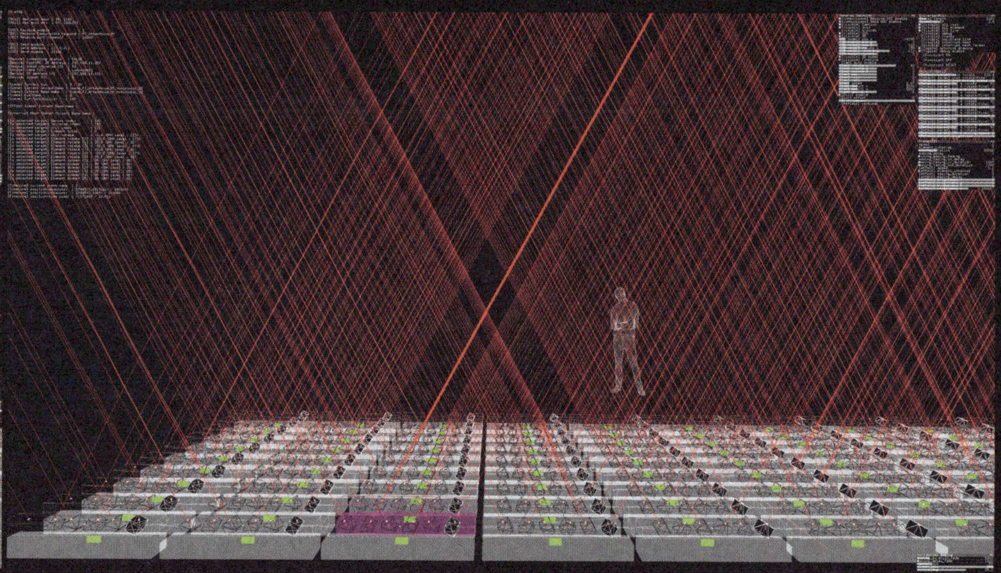

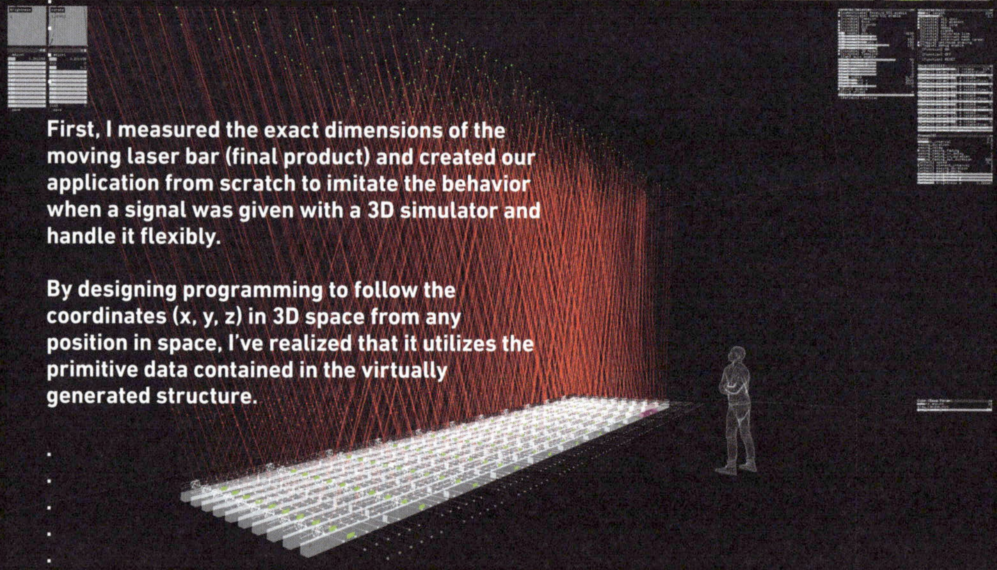

First, I measured the exact dimensions of the moving laser bar (final product) and created our application from scratch to imitate the behavior when a signal was given with a 3D simulator and handle it flexibly.

By designing programming to follow the coordinates (x, y, z) in 3D space from any position in space, I've realized that it utilizes the primitive data contained in the virtually generated structure.

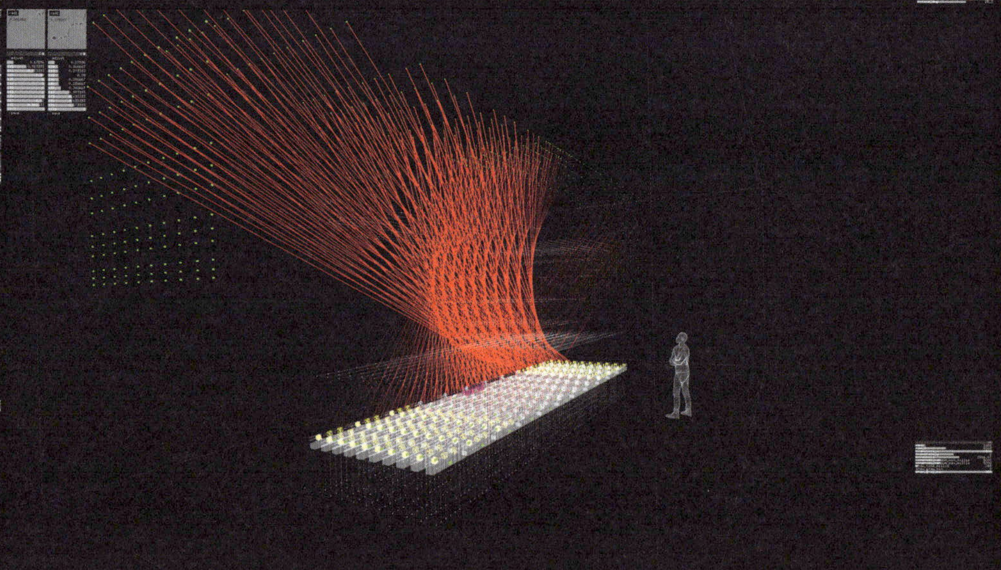

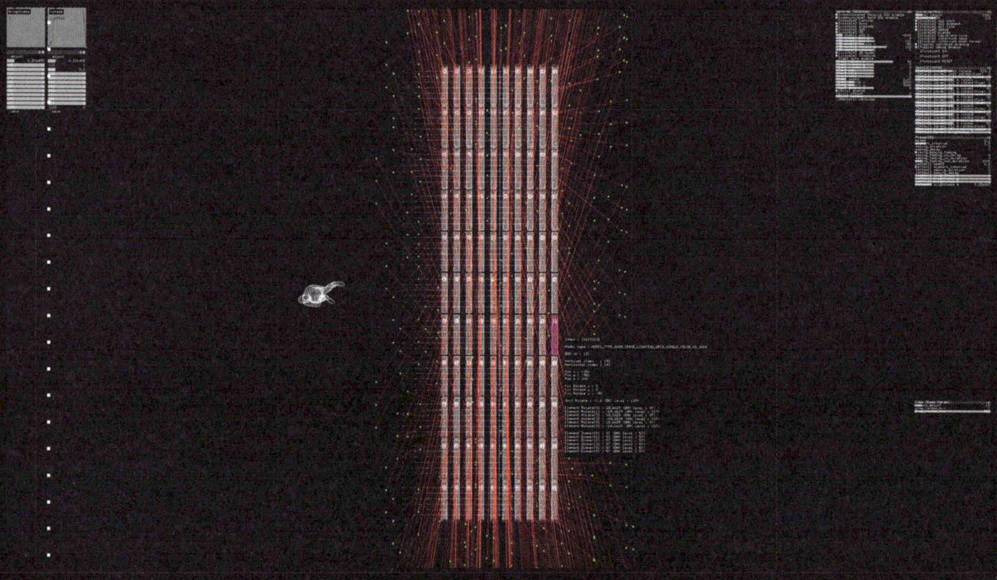

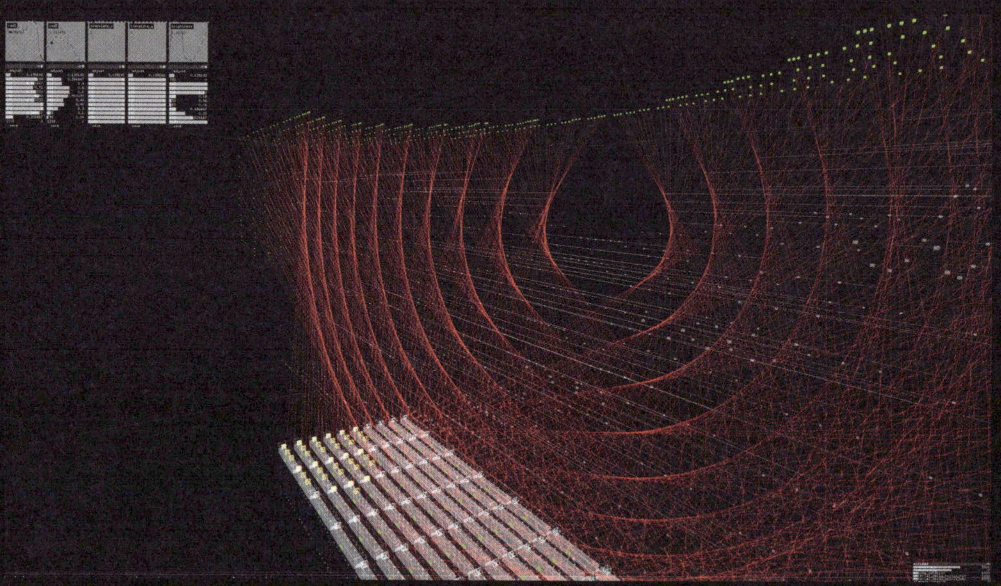

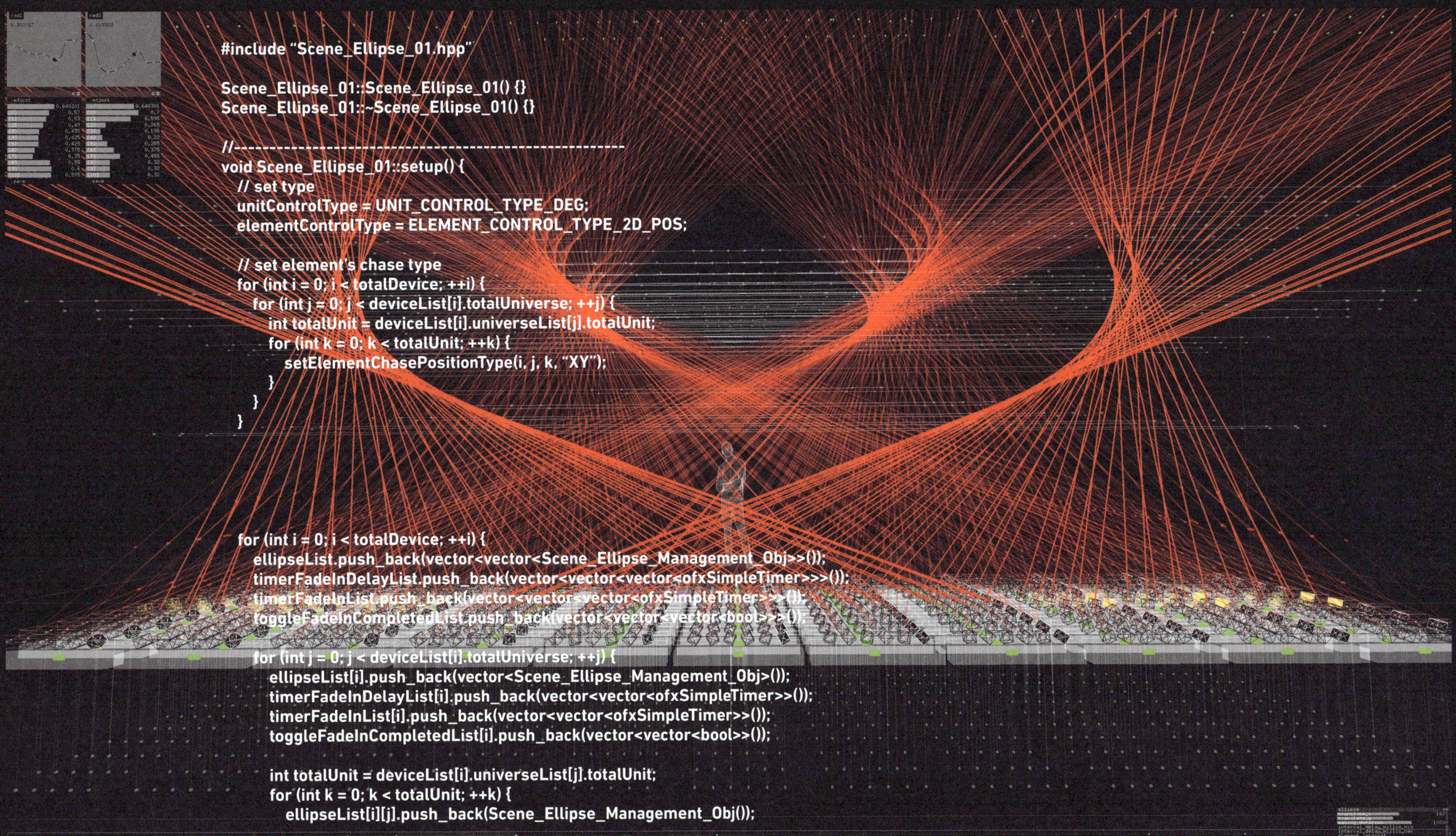

```
#include "Scene_Ellipse_01.hpp"

Scene_Ellipse_01::Scene_Ellipse_01() {}
Scene_Ellipse_01::~Scene_Ellipse_01() {}

//------------------------------------------------------------
void Scene_Ellipse_01::setup() {
  // set type
  unitControlType = UNIT_CONTROL_TYPE_DEG;
  elementControlType = ELEMENT_CONTROL_TYPE_2D_POS;

  // set element's chase type
  for (int i = 0; i < totalDevice; ++i) {
    for (int j = 0; j < deviceList[i].totalUniverse; ++j) {
      int totalUnit = deviceList[i].universeList[j].totalUnit;
      for (int k = 0; k < totalUnit; ++k) {
        setElementChasePositionType(i, j, k, "XY");
      }
    }
  }

  for (int i = 0; i < totalDevice; ++i) {
    ellipseList.push_back(vector<vector<Scene_Ellipse_Management_Obj>>());
    timerFadeInDelayList.push_back(vector<vector<vector<ofxSimpleTimer>>>());
    timerFadeInList.push_back(vector<vector<vector<ofxSimpleTimer>>>());
    toggleFadeInCompletedList.push_back(vector<vector<vector<bool>>>());

    for (int j = 0; j < deviceList[i].totalUniverse; ++j) {
      ellipseList[i].push_back(vector<Scene_Ellipse_Management_Obj>());
      timerFadeInDelayList[i].push_back(vector<vector<ofxSimpleTimer>>());
      timerFadeInList[i].push_back(vector<vector<ofxSimpleTimer>>());
      toggleFadeInCompletedList[i].push_back(vector<vector<bool>>());

      int totalUnit = deviceList[i].universeList[j].totalUnit;
      for (int k = 0; k < totalUnit; ++k) {
        ellipseList[i][j].push_back(Scene_Ellipse_Management_Obj());
```

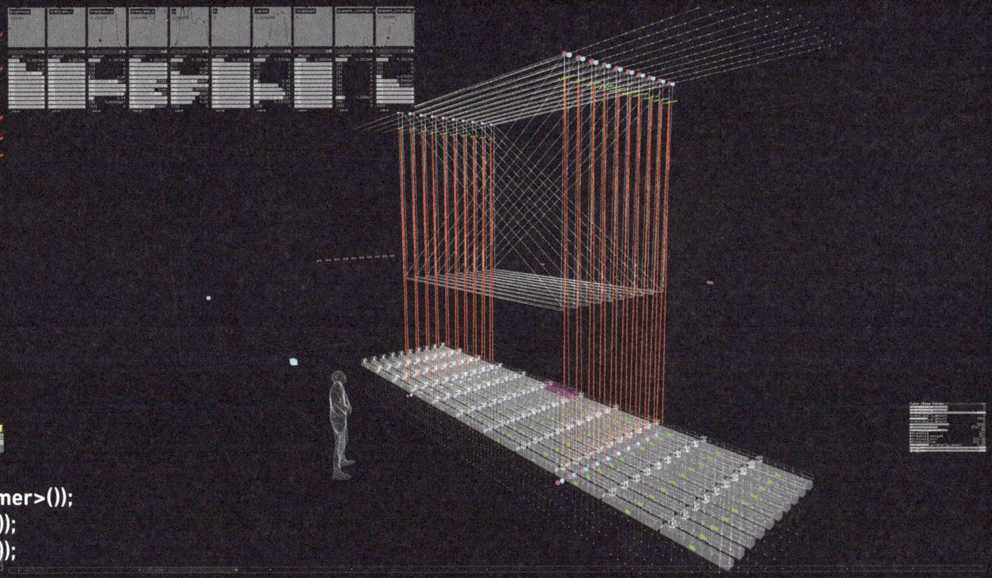

```
        timerFadeInDelayList[i][j].push_back(vector<ofxSimpleTimer>());
        timerFadeInList[i][j].push_back(vector<ofxSimpleTimer>());
        toggleFadeInCompletedList[i][j].push_back(vector<bool>());
```

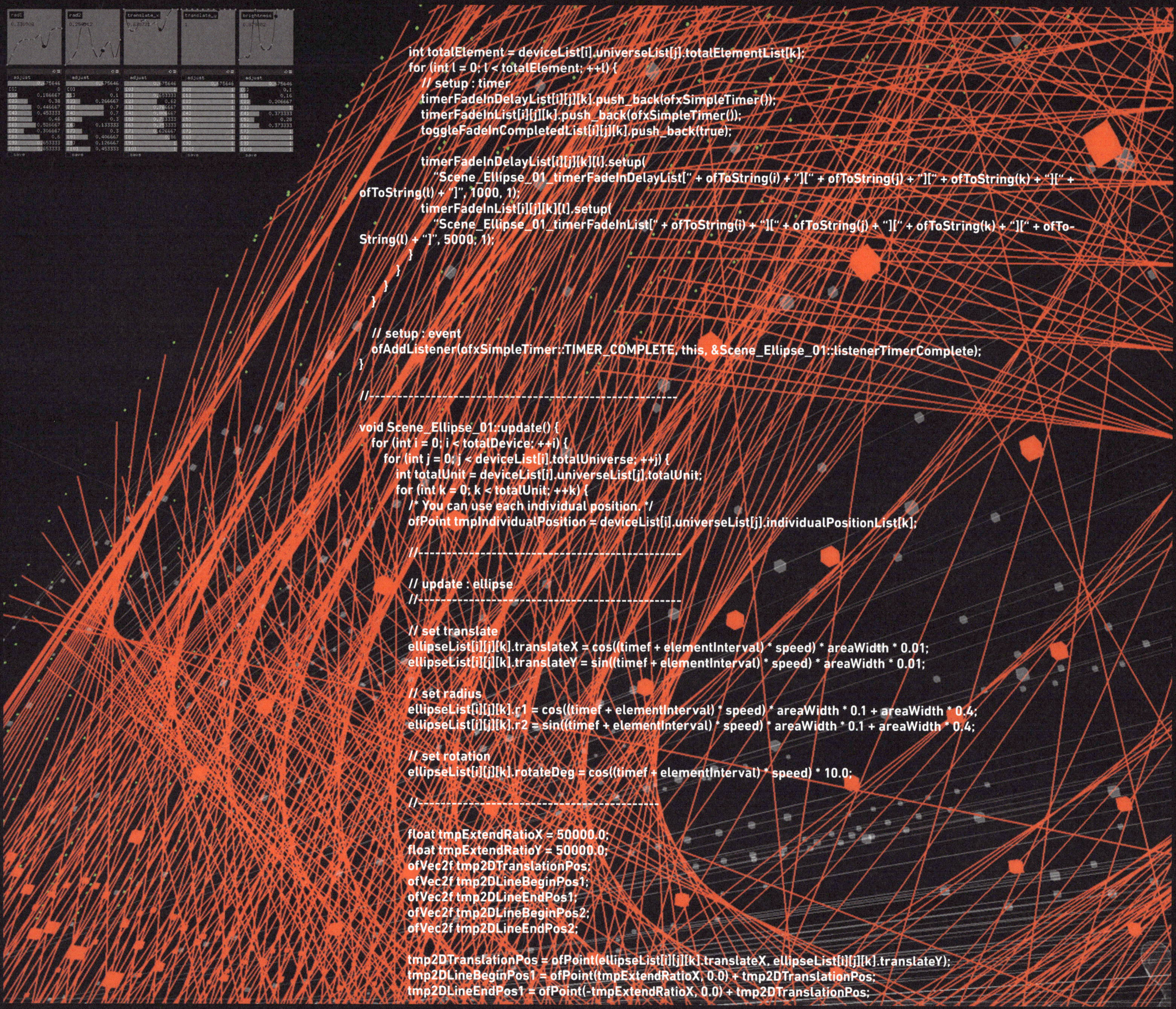

```
            int totalElement = deviceList[i].universeList[j].totalElementList[k];
            for (int l = 0; l < totalElement; ++l) {
                // setup : timer
                timerFadeInDelayList[i][j][k].push_back(ofxSimpleTimer());
                timerFadeInList[i][j][k].push_back(ofxSimpleTimer());
                toggleFadeInCompletedList[i][j][k].push_back(true);

                timerFadeInDelayList[i][j][k][l].setup(
                    "Scene_Ellipse_01_timerFadeInDelayList[" + ofToString(i) + "][" + ofToString(j) + "][" + ofToString(k) + "][" +
ofToString(l) + "]", 1000, 1);
                timerFadeInList[i][j][k][l].setup(
                    "Scene_Ellipse_01_timerFadeInList[" + ofToString(i) + "][" + ofToString(j) + "][" + ofToString(k) + "][" + ofTo-
String(l) + "]", 5000, 1);
            }
        }
    }
}

    // setup : event
    ofAddListener(ofxSimpleTimer::TIMER_COMPLETE, this, &Scene_Ellipse_01::listenerTimerComplete);
}

//--------------------------------------------------------------

void Scene_Ellipse_01::update() {
    for (int i = 0; i < totalDevice; ++i) {
        for (int j = 0; j < deviceList[i].totalUniverse; ++j) {
            int totalUnit = deviceList[i].universeList[j].totalUnit;
            for (int k = 0; k < totalUnit; ++k) {
                /* You can use each individual position. */
                ofPoint tmpIndividualPosition = deviceList[i].universeList[j].individualPositionList[k];

                //--------------------------------------------------

                // update : ellipse
                //--------------------------------------------------

                // set translate
                ellipseList[i][j][k].translateX = cos((timef + elementInterval) * speed) * areaWidth * 0.01;
                ellipseList[i][j][k].translateY = sin((timef + elementInterval) * speed) * areaWidth * 0.01;

                // set radius
                ellipseList[i][j][k].r1 = cos((timef + elementInterval) * speed) * areaWidth * 0.1 + areaWidth * 0.4;
                ellipseList[i][j][k].r2 = sin((timef + elementInterval) * speed) * areaWidth * 0.1 + areaWidth * 0.4;

                // set rotation
                ellipseList[i][j][k].rotateDeg = cos((timef + elementInterval) * speed) * 10.0;

                //-----------------------------------------------

                float tmpExtendRatioX = 50000.0;
                float tmpExtendRatioY = 50000.0;
                ofVec2f tmp2DTranslationPos;
                ofVec2f tmp2DLineBeginPos1;
                ofVec2f tmp2DLineEndPos1;
                ofVec2f tmp2DLineBeginPos2;
                ofVec2f tmp2DLineEndPos2;

                tmp2DTranslationPos = ofPoint(ellipseList[i][j][k].translateX, ellipseList[i][j][k].translateY);
                tmp2DLineBeginPos1 = ofPoint(tmpExtendRatioX, 0.0) + tmp2DTranslationPos;
                tmp2DLineEndPos1 = ofPoint(-tmpExtendRatioX, 0.0) + tmp2DTranslationPos;
```

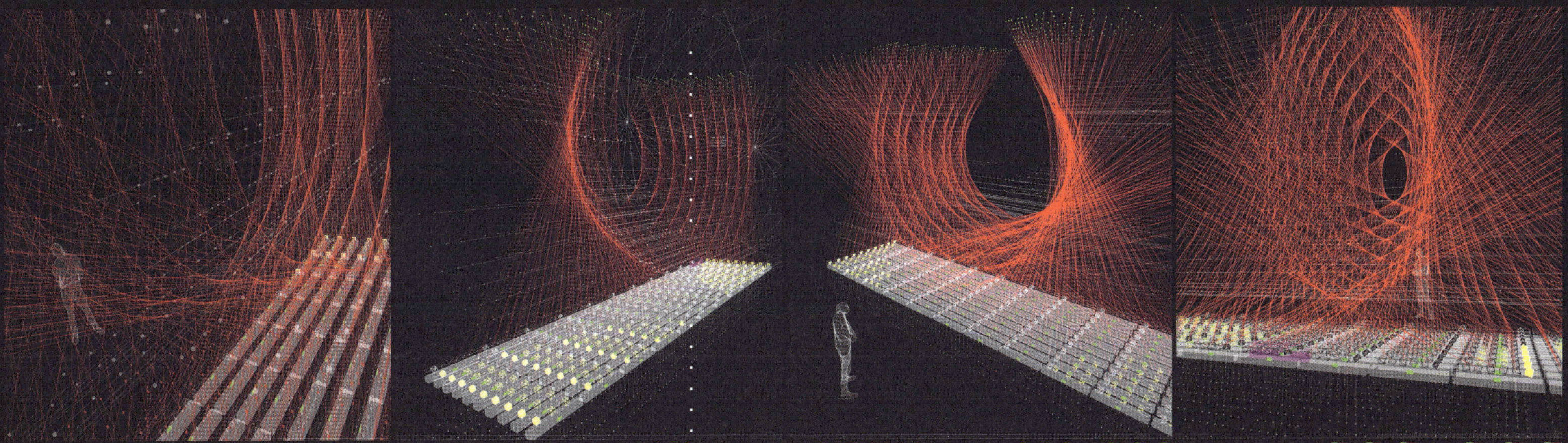

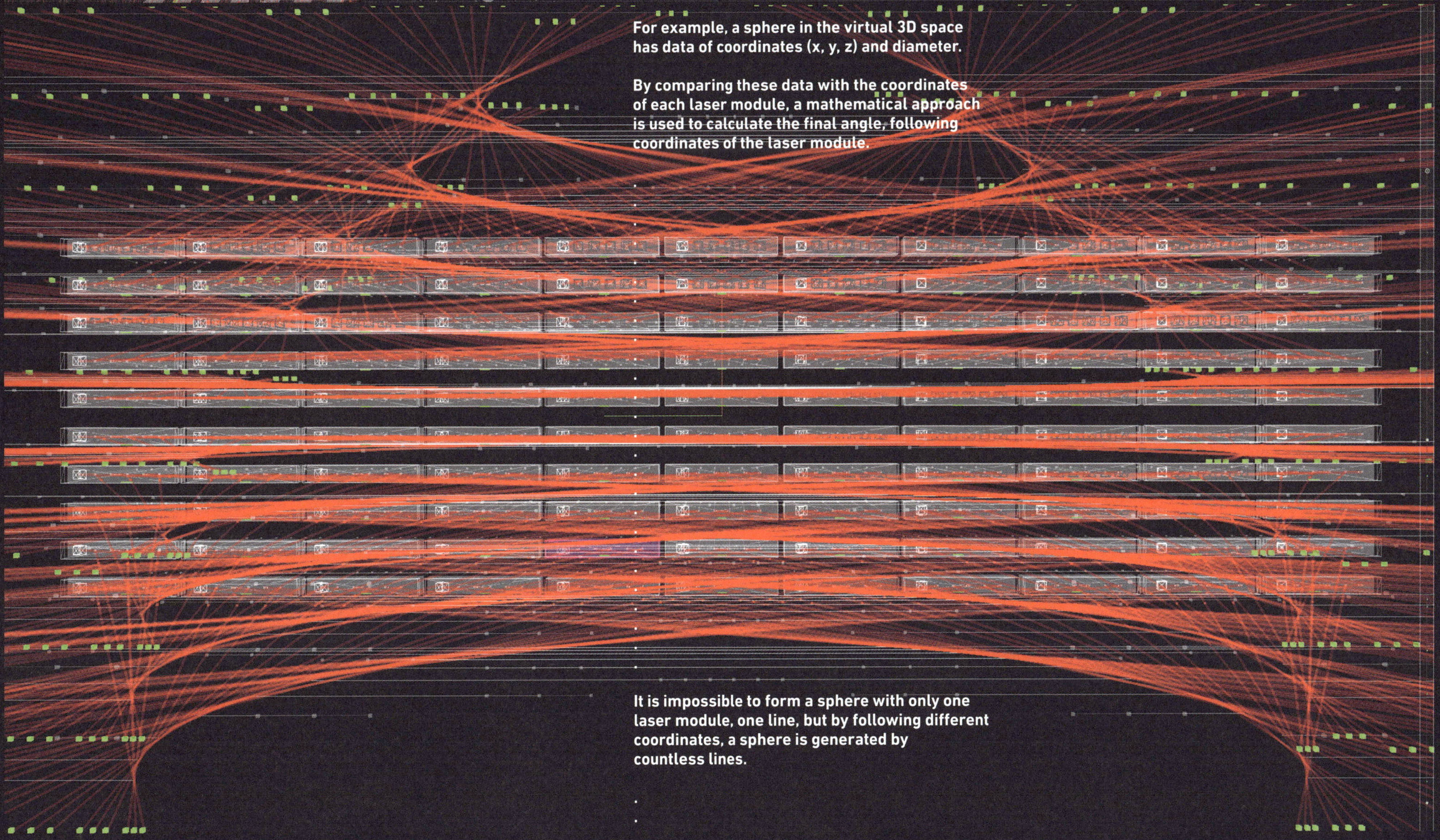

For example, a sphere in the virtual 3D space has data of coordinates (x, y, z) and diameter.

By comparing these data with the coordinates of each laser module, a mathematical approach is used to calculate the final angle, following coordinates of the laser module.

It is impossible to form a sphere with only one laser module, one line, but by following different coordinates, a sphere is generated by countless lines.

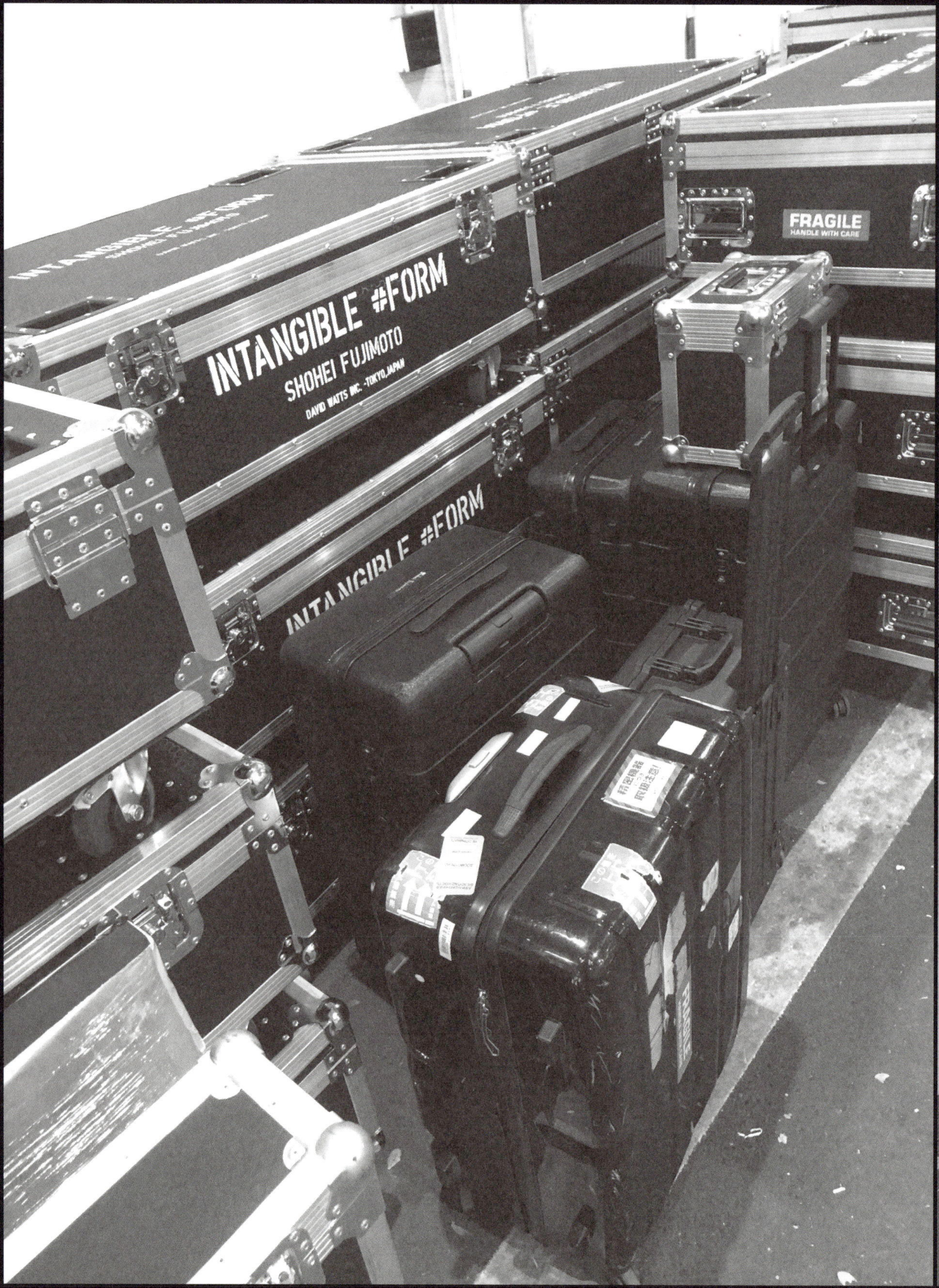
FRAGILE
HANDLE WITH CARE
INTANGIBLE #FORM
SHOHEI FUJIMOTO
DAVID WATTS INC. -TOKYO,JAPAN

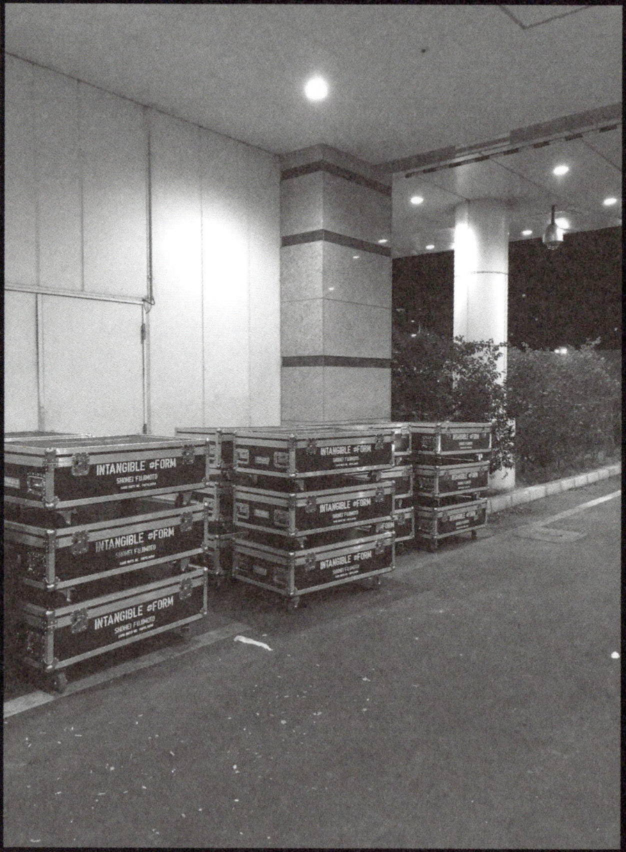

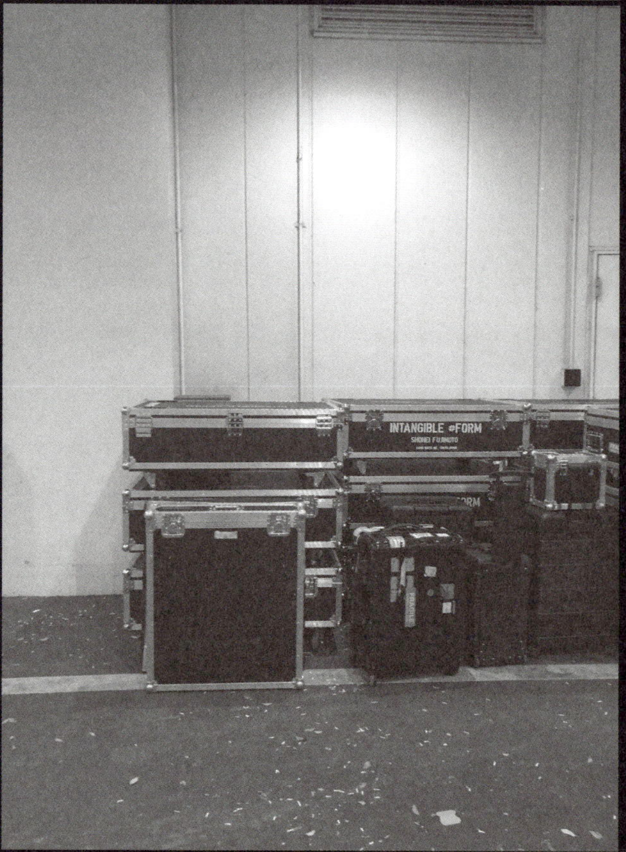

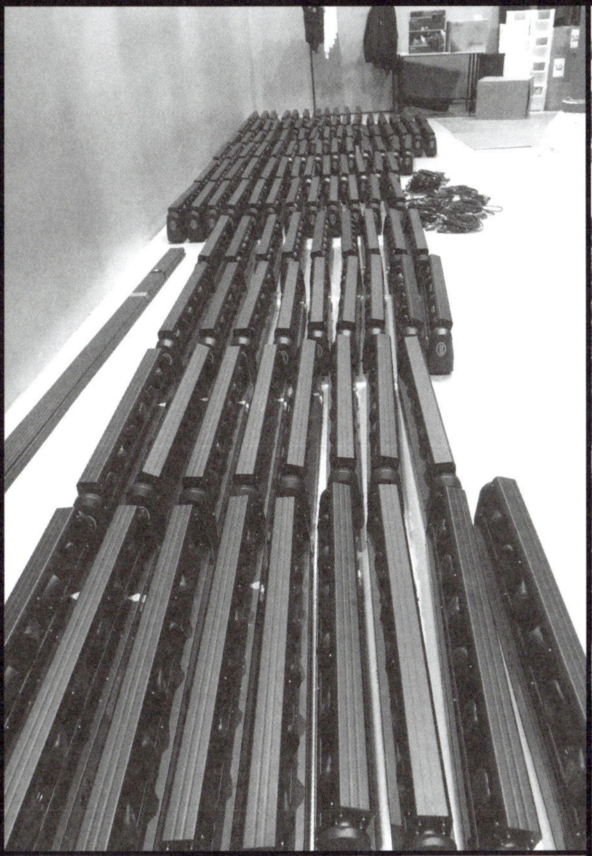

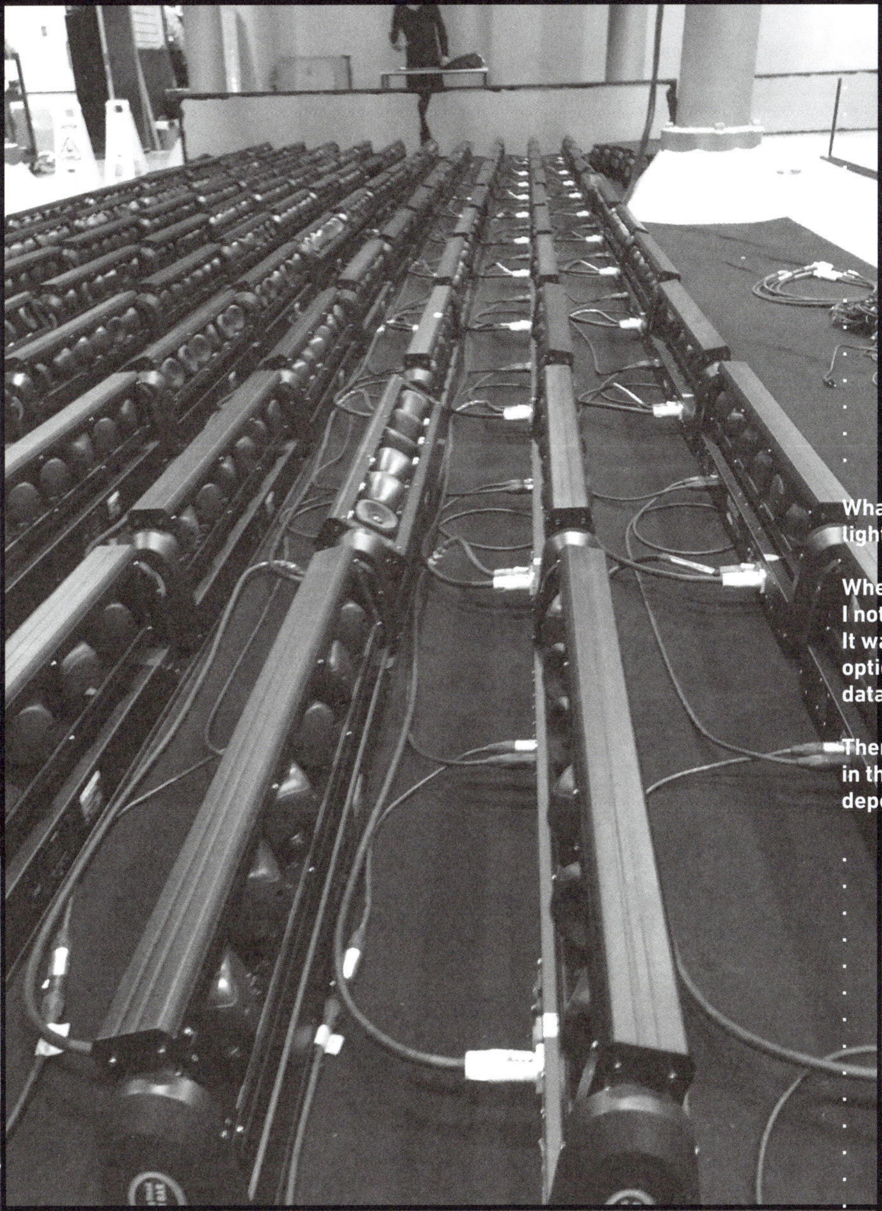

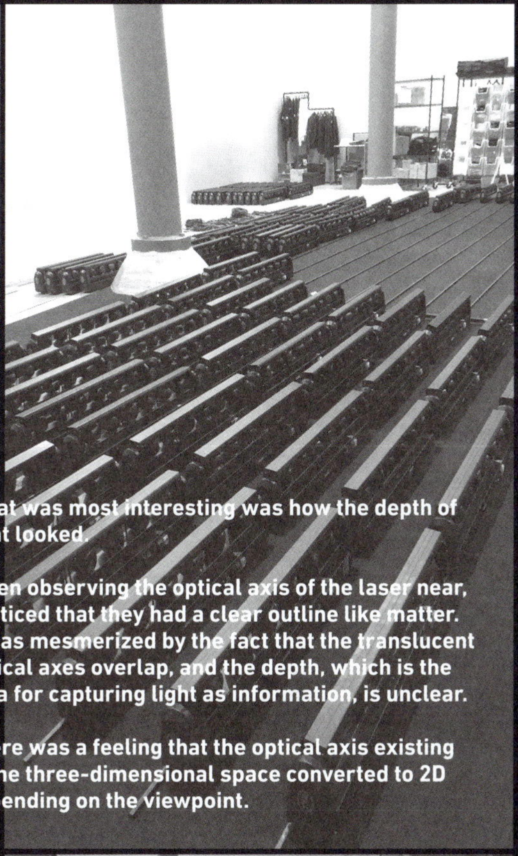

What was most interesting was how the depth of light looked.

When observing the optical axis of the laser near, I noticed that they had a clear outline like matter. It was mesmerized by the fact that the translucent optical axes overlap, and the depth, which is the data for capturing light as information, is unclear.

There was a feeling that the optical axis existing in the three-dimensional space converted to 2D depending on the viewpoint.

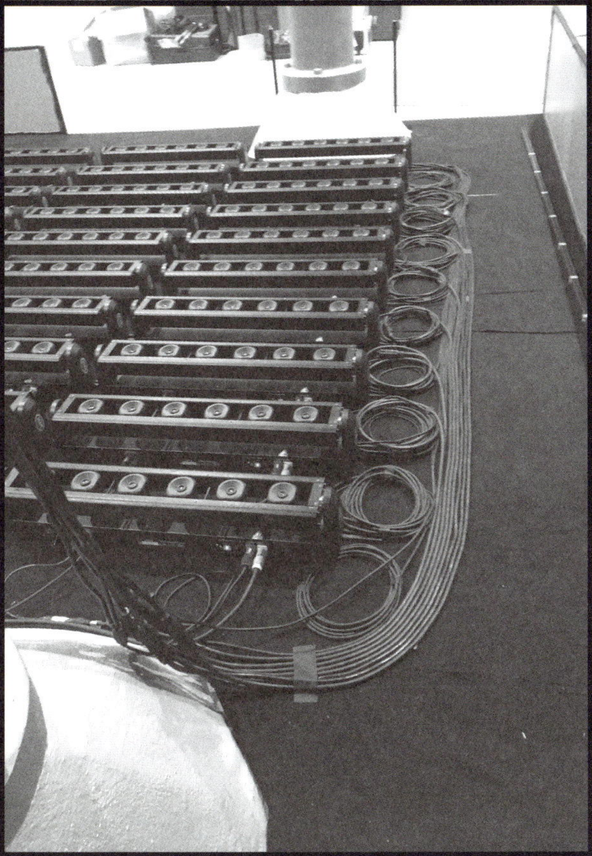

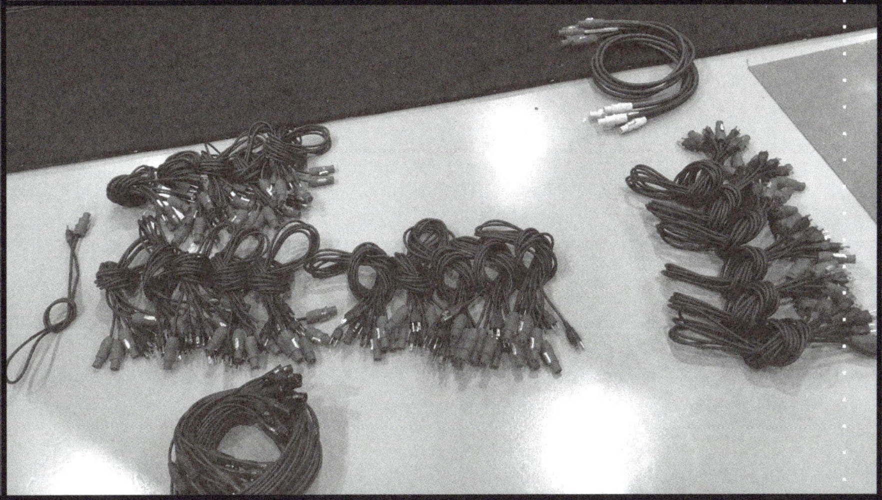

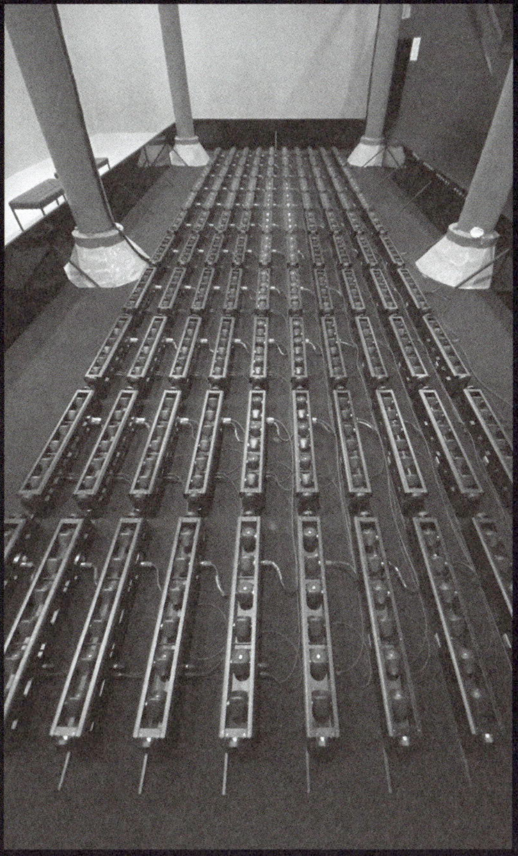

The red wavelength is the color with the longest wavelength of visible light captured by humans.
In other words, it is possible to deliver waves to objects located far away.

The waves of red that travel through space are colors that penetrate inside and touch the universal sensations deep inside you.

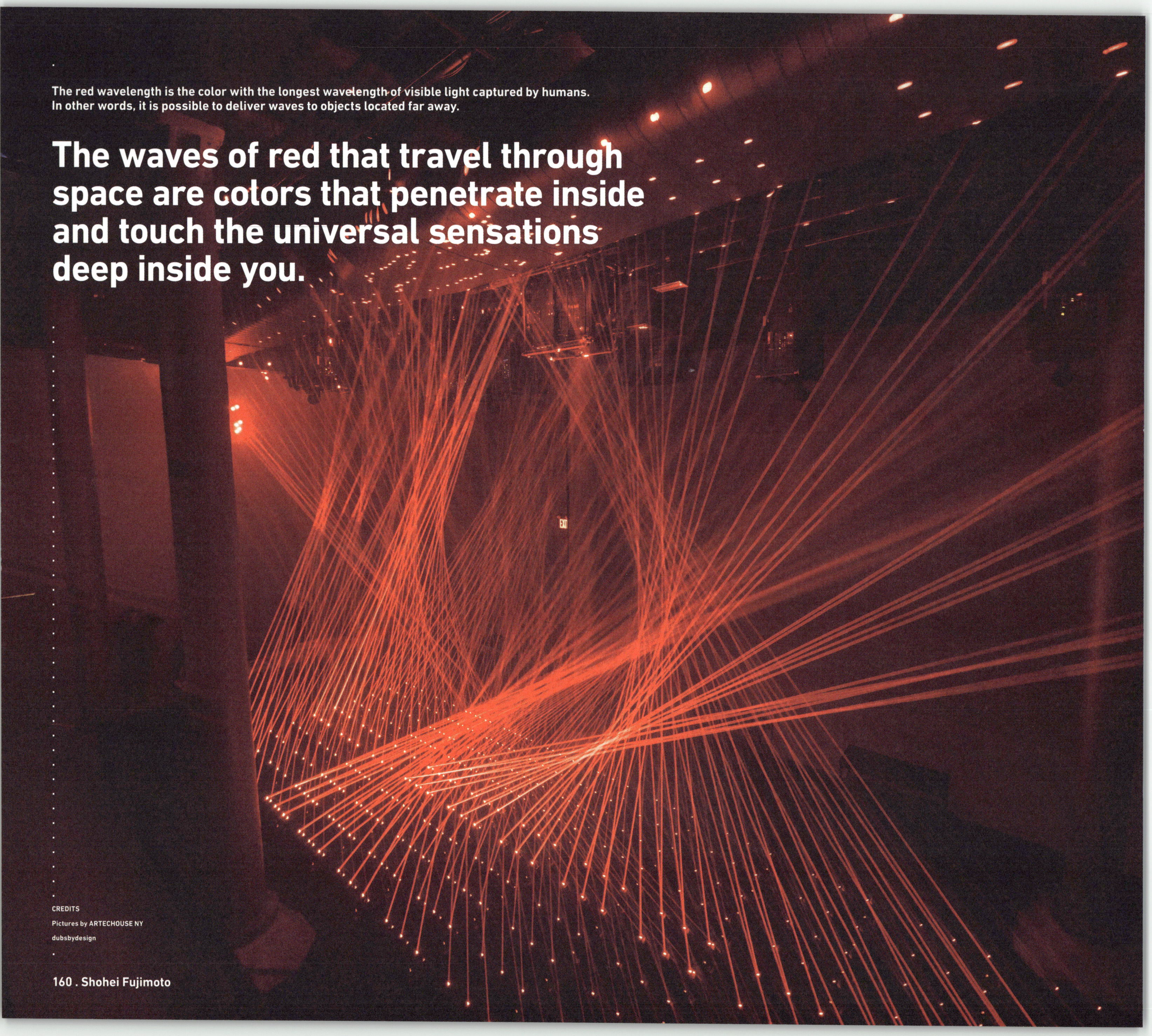

CREDITS
Pictures by ARTECHOUSE NY
dubsbydesign

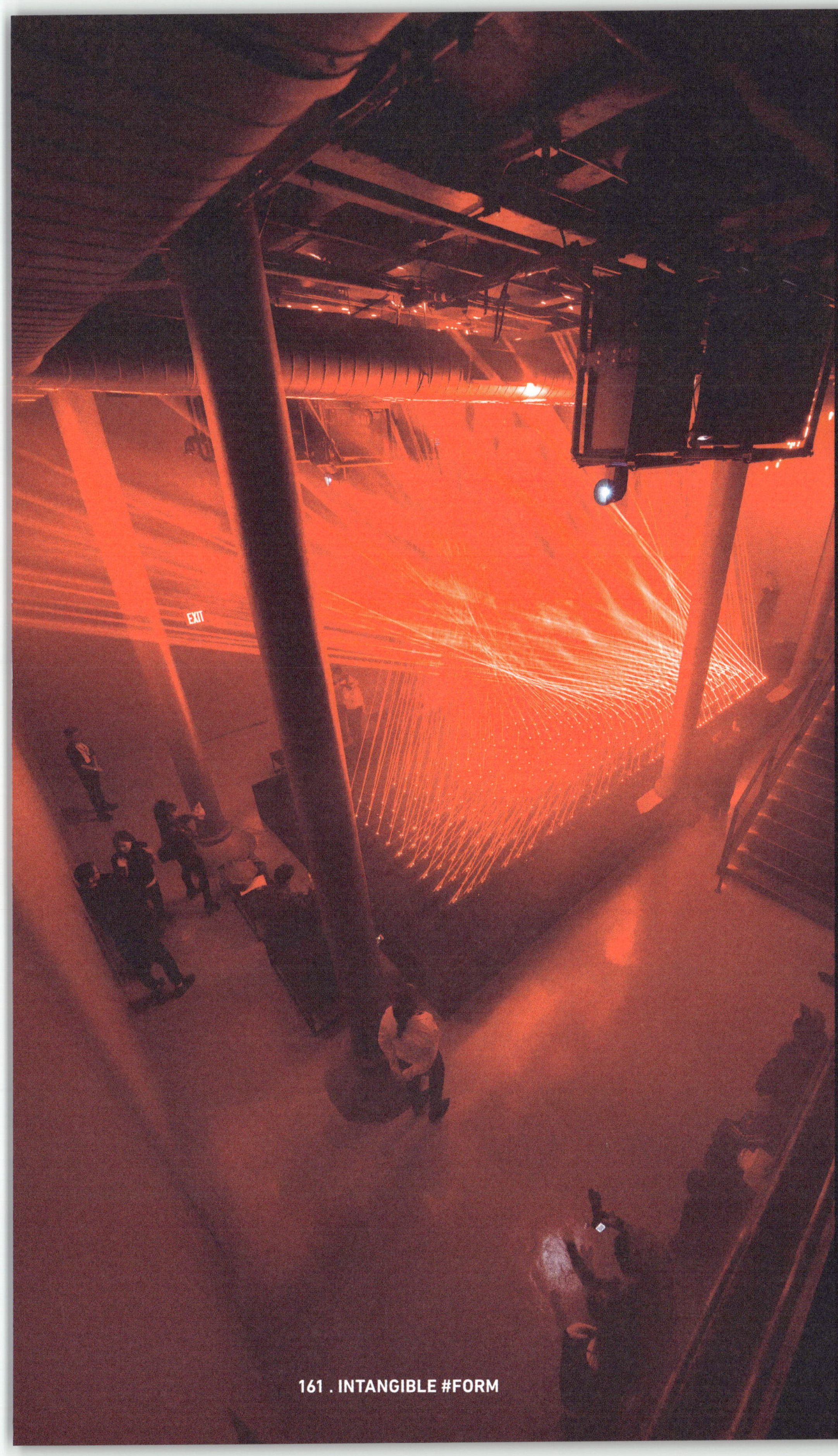

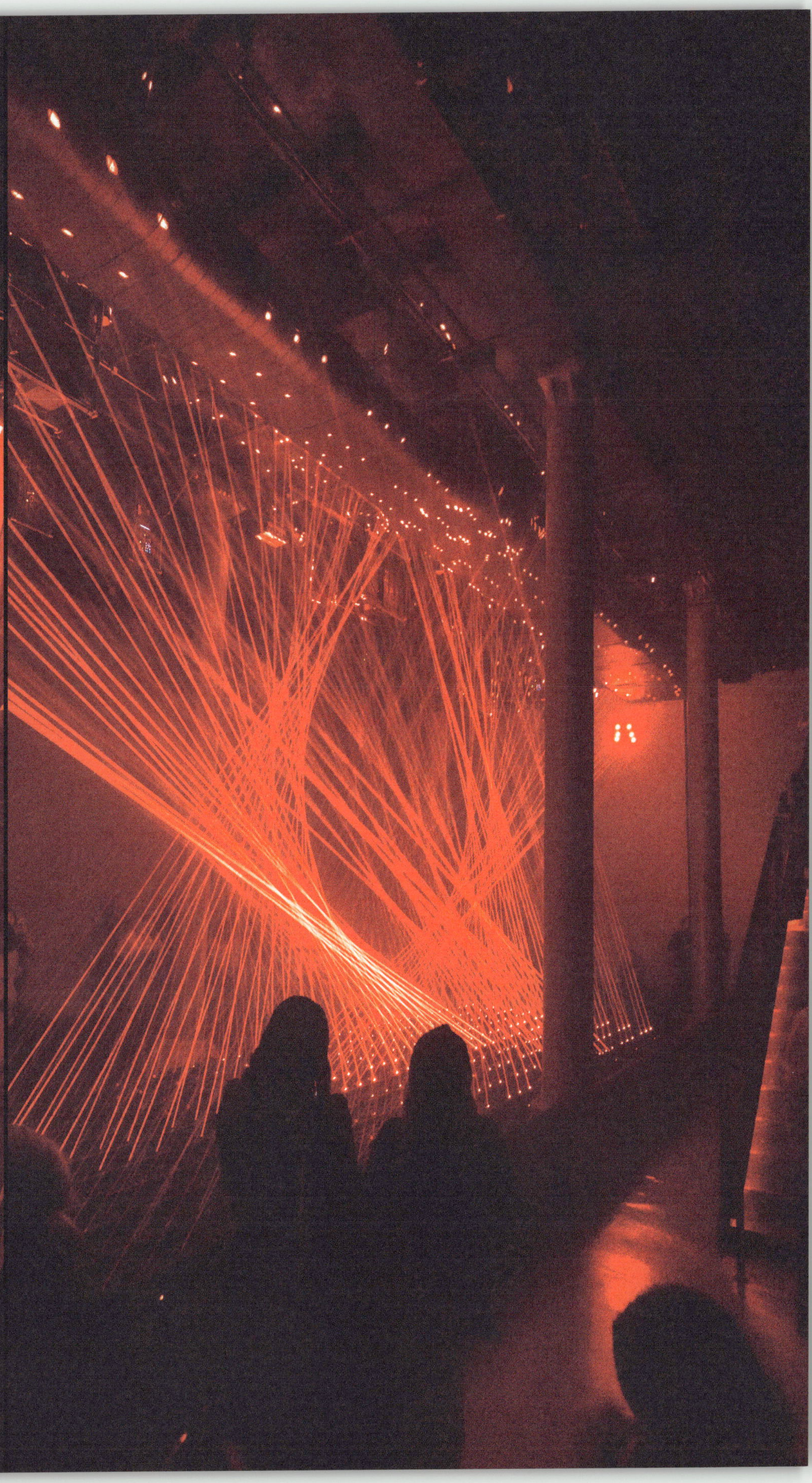

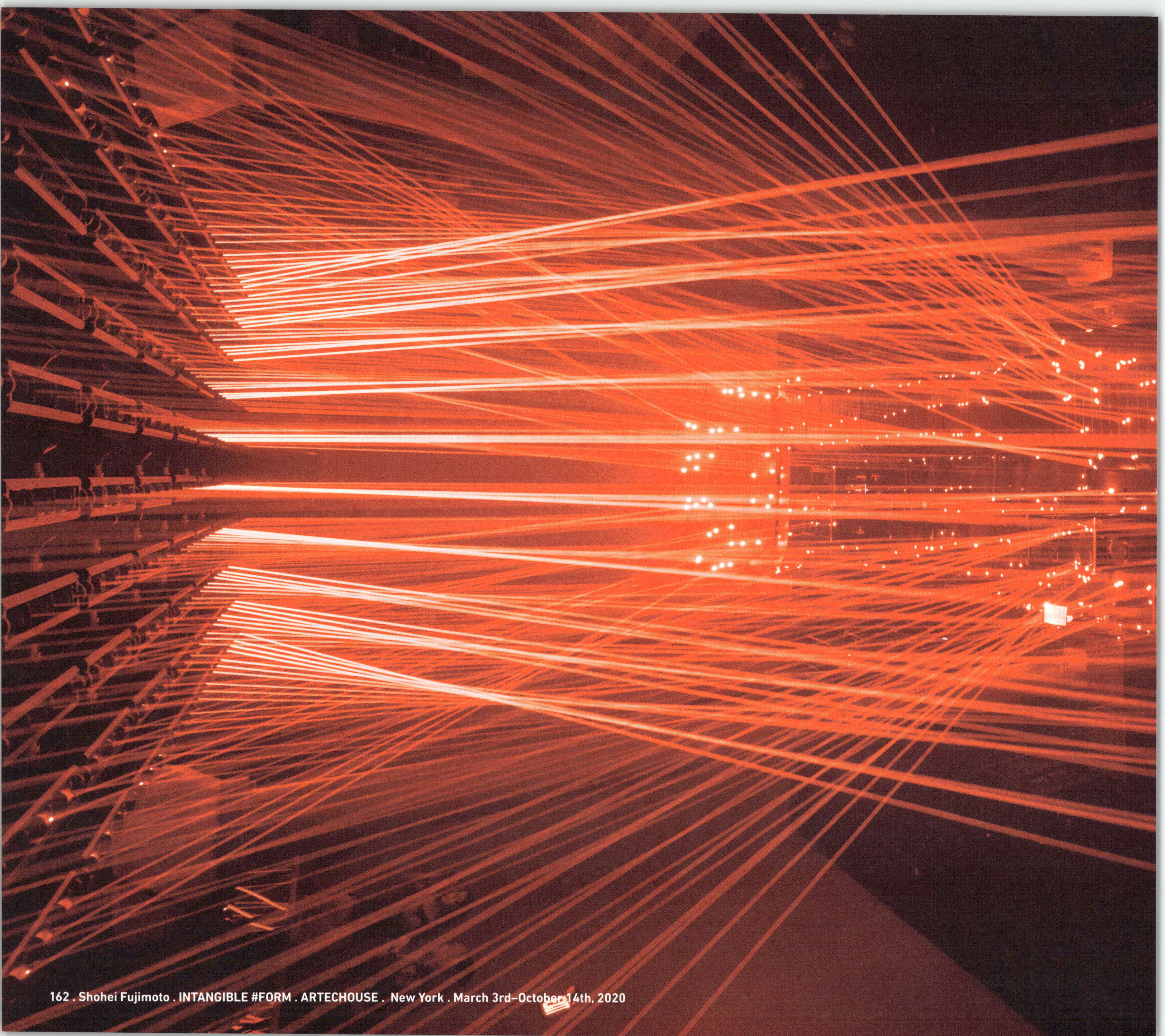
162 . Shohei Fujimoto . INTANGIBLE #FORM . ARTECHOUSE . New York . March 3rd–October 14th, 2020

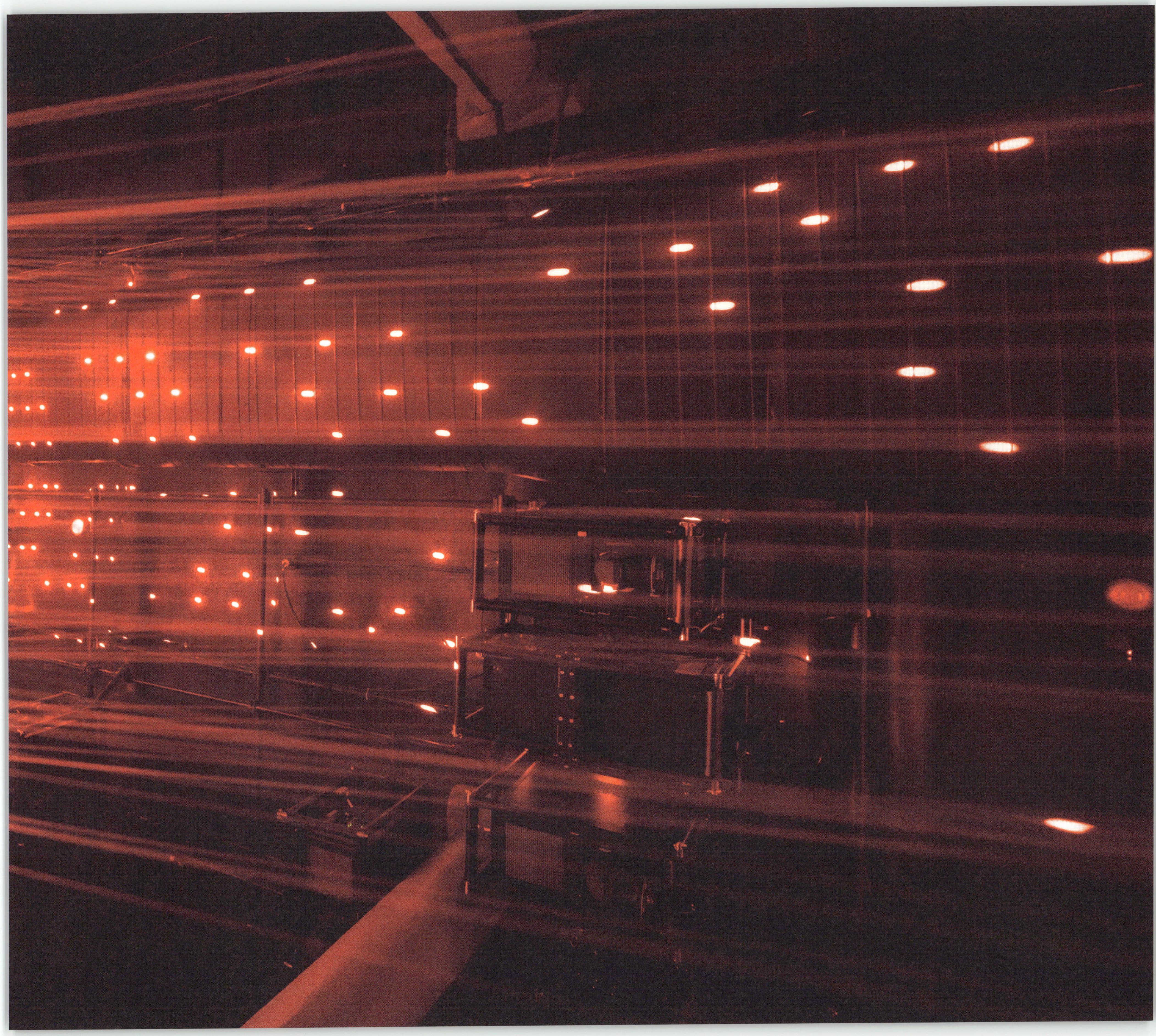

Name:

Gysin & Vanetti

Info:

Andreas Gysin and Sidi Vanetti work together on research projects without a particular purpose since 2000.

They combine disciplines from the field of visual communication, architecture from new and old technologies. Besides their activity as teachers and designers, they build temporary and permanent installations in public spaces and exhibitions.

Recent work explores images and patterns using the geometries of multipurpose displays, urban signage and found or forgotten objects and technologies.

Project:

ZURICH GA FLAP
2016

Location:

Museum of Digital Art,
Zurich

URL:

gysin-vanetti.com

Instagram:

@andreasgysin

Project Description:

The installation consists of the recontextualization of an original mechanical timetable from the SBB CFF FFS Zurich train station replaced at the end of 2015 by a new silent LED model.

The display consists of 452 mechanical split-flap elements.

Each flap is made of PVC and is silk-screened with a destination station, start or departure time or rail number information.

Since we were kids, we were fascinated by this vast and loud display when passing under it in the station. In 2006, we managed to build a permanent installation called “Colour Flap” with a custom-built panel of the same brand. This one features 112 elements with three colors.

While working at the first exhibition at the MuDA, Museum of Digital Arts in Zurich, we learned that the old panel would soon be removed and replaced by the Swiss railways. It wasn’t hard to persuade the museum’s curators to grab it so that we could reprogram it and install it at the museum for our exhibition.

We used a single side of the ordinarily two-sided panel for this installation, which is still heavy with its three tonnes.

The main focus of the installation was movement and sound, so we decided to put the display directly on the ground, changing the usual perspective for the viewer. When standing near it, visitors could even experience a slight breeze.

Many people told us that they had a special relationship with this vast display from its time at the station; they too loved its sound and motion and were happy to experience it again; we saved this old piece of Swiss engineering work from its death, and the people were grateful.

CREDITS
Picture by Zurich Tourism

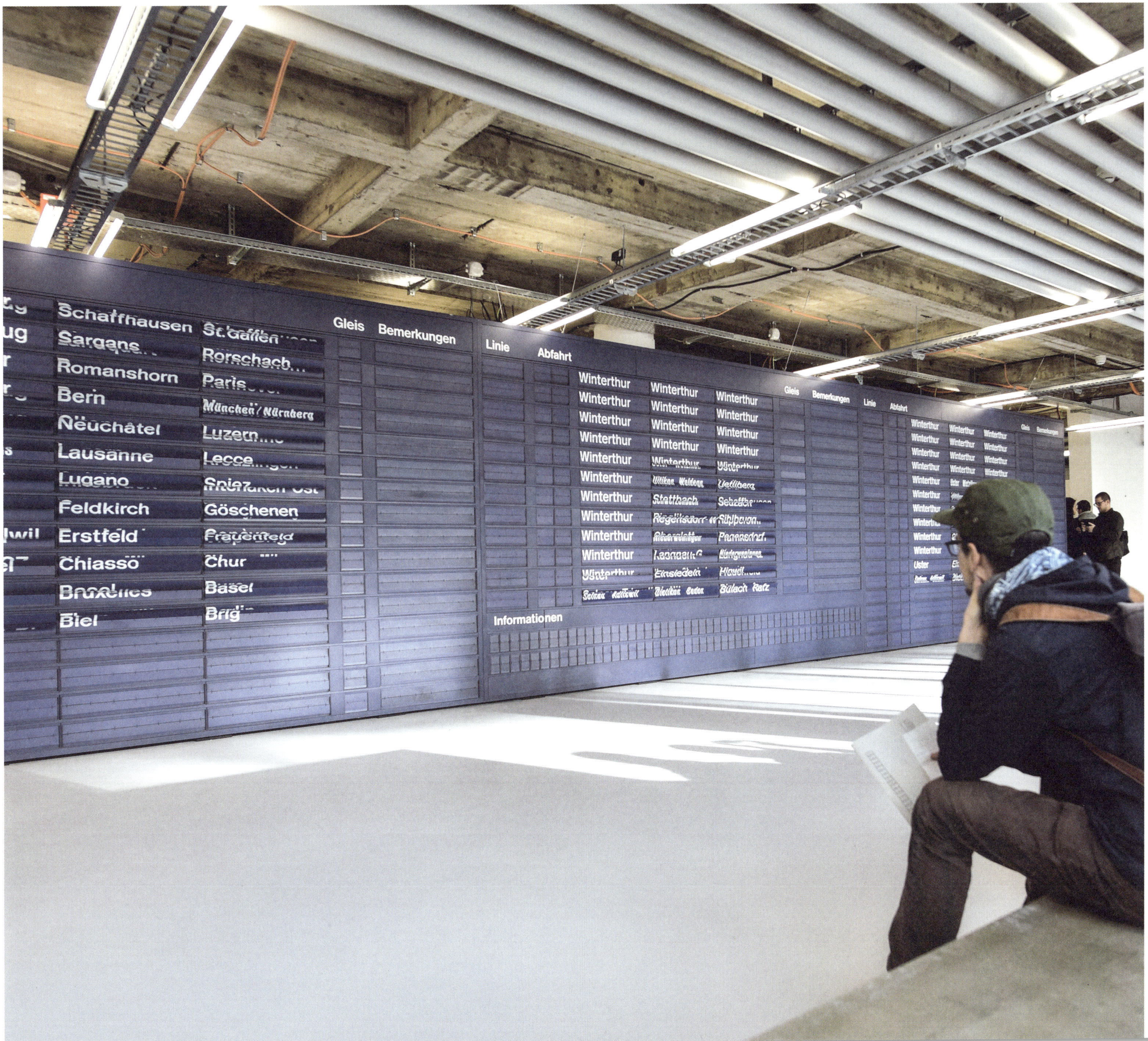

Schaffhausen
Sargans
Romanshorn
Bern
Neuchâtel
Lausanne
Lugano
Feldkirch
Erstfeld
Chiasso
Biel
Rorschach
Paris
München / Nürnberg
Luzern
Lecce
Göschenen
Chur
Basel
Gleis
Bemerkungen
Linie
Abfahrt
Winterthur
Informationen

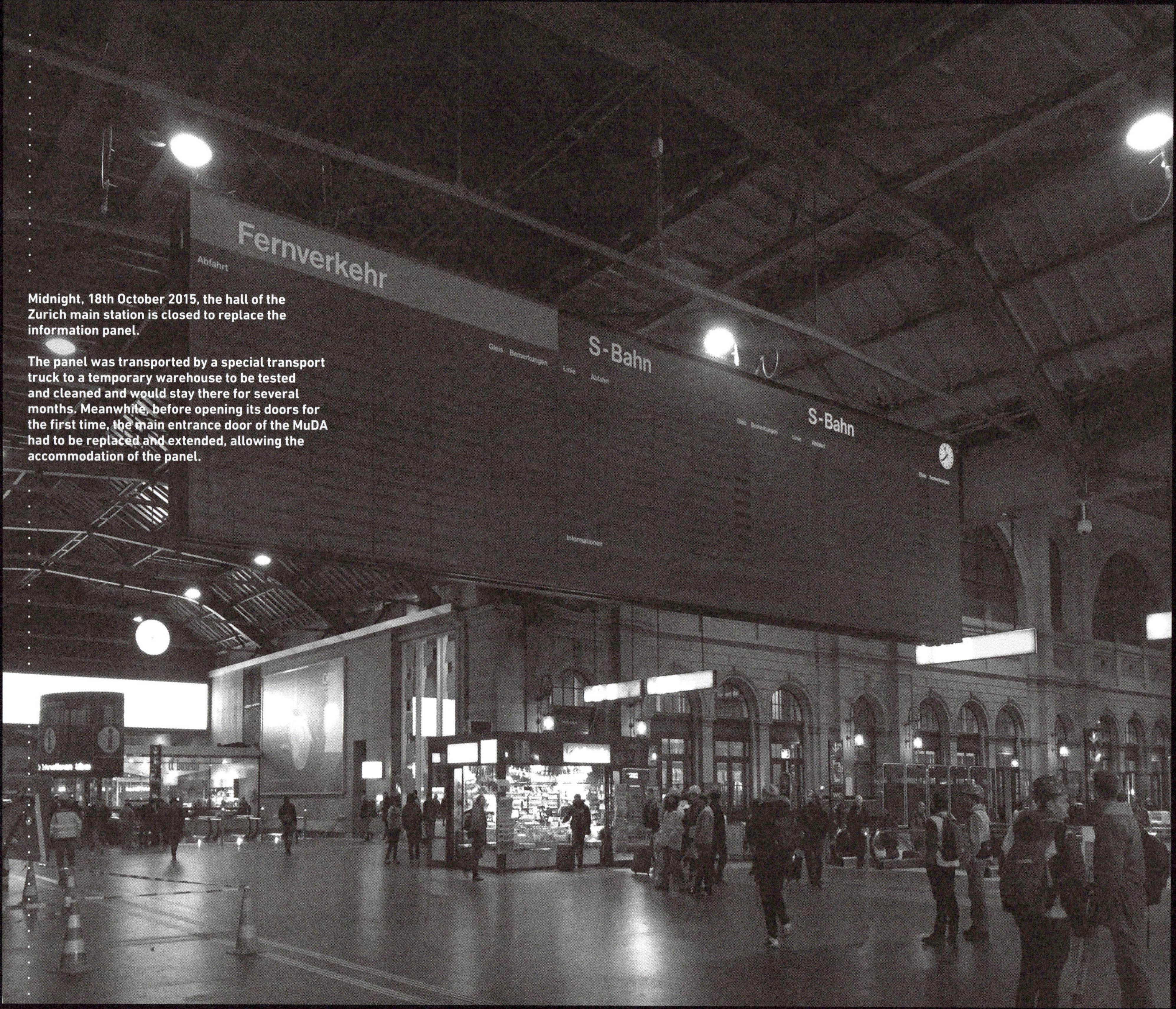

Midnight, 18th October 2015, the hall of the Zurich main station is closed to replace the information panel.

The panel was transported by a special transport truck to a temporary warehouse to be tested and cleaned and would stay there for several months. Meanwhile, before opening its doors for the first time, the main entrance door of the MuDA had to be replaced and extended, allowing the accommodation of the panel.

```
const mCommands[14] = {

 {"DISP", 0xC0, 0xD0, 4},  //DISP/RDB     C0 D0
 {"STAT", 0xC1, 0xD1, 4},  //STAT         C1 D1
 {"RSET", 0xC4, 0xD4, 5}, //RESET/VER     C4 D4
 {"ZERO", 0xC5, 0x00, 2},  //ZERO         C5
 {"STEP", 0xC6, 0x00, 2},  //STEP         C6
 {"PULS", 0xC7, 0x00, 2},  //PULSE        C7
 {"TEST", 0xC8, 0x00, 2},  //TEST         C8
 {"CTRL", 0xC9, 0xD9, 4},  //CTRL         C9 D9
 {"NULL", 0xCA, 0xDA, 4}, //NULL/POS      CA DA
 {"WIN ", 0xCB, 0xDB, 4},  //WIN          CB DB
 {"CALB", 0xCC, 0xDC, 3}, //CALB          CC DC
 {"TYPE", 0xCD, 0xDD, 4}, //TYPE          CD DD
 {"ADDR", 0xCE, 0xDE, 4}, //ADDR          CE DE
 {"SNBR", 0xCF, 0xDF, 7}  //SNBR          CF DF

};
```

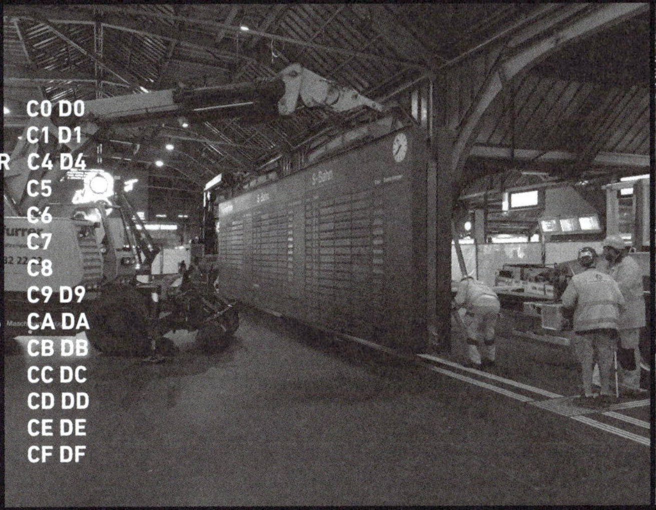

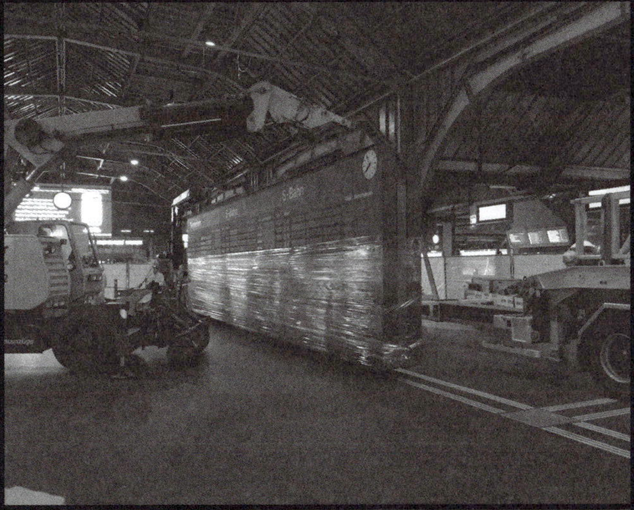

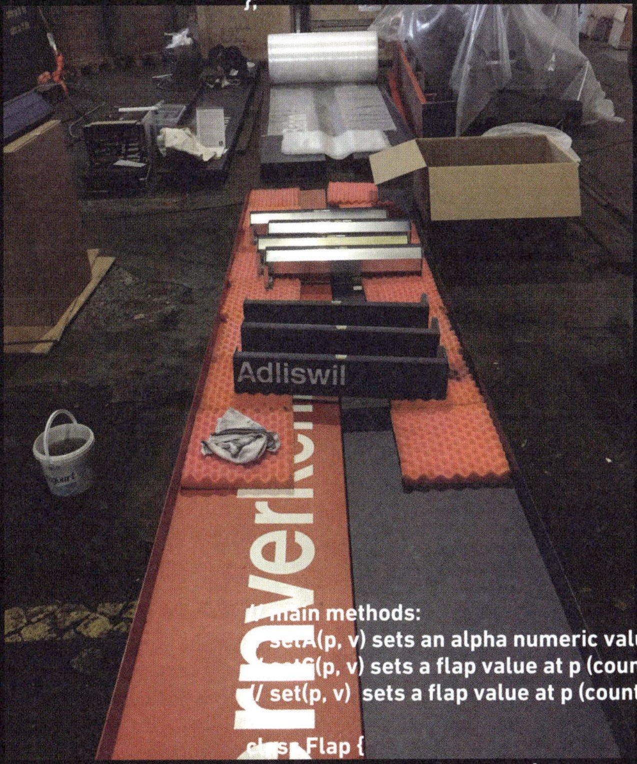

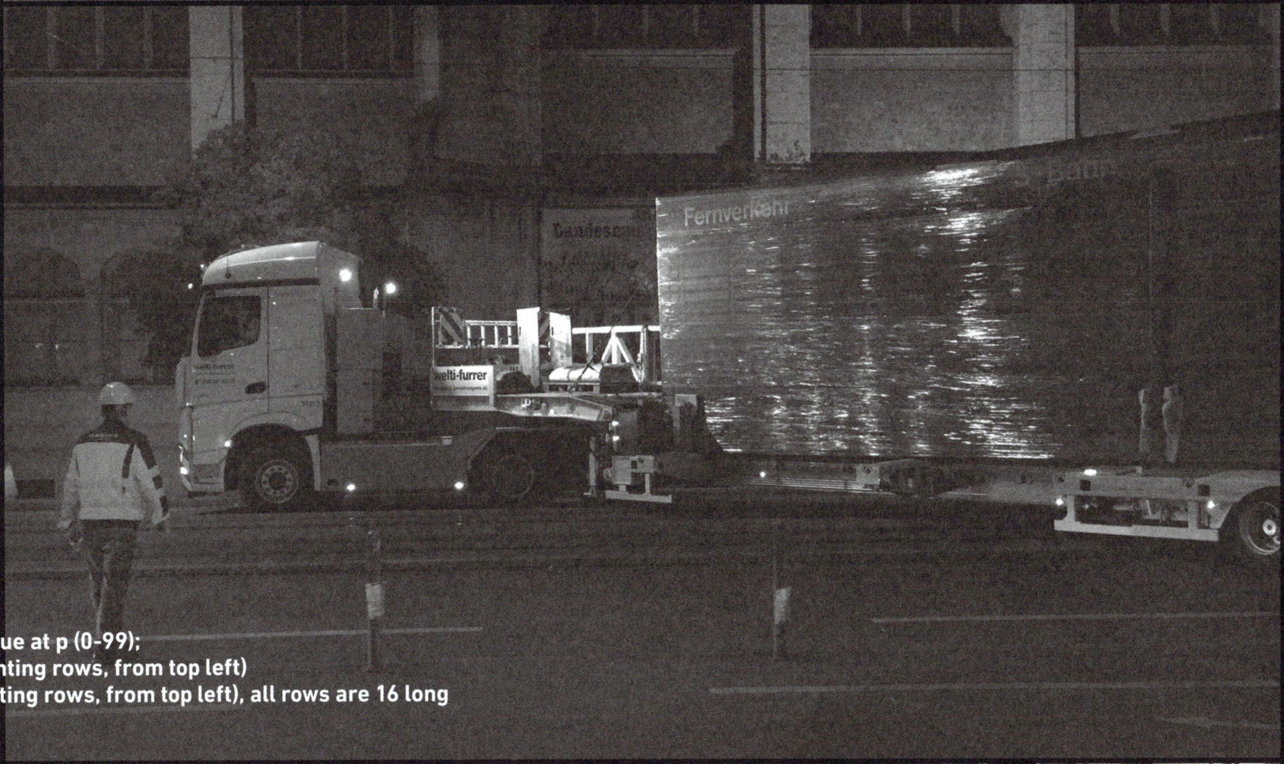


```
// main methods:
// setA(p, v) sets an alpha numeric value at p (0-99);
// setF(p, v) sets a flap value at p (counting rows, from top left)
// set(p, v)  sets a flap value at p (counting rows, from top left), all rows are 16 long

class Flap {
          private:
                    boolean debug = false;
                    const uint16_t BAUD = 19200;
                    const uint8_t  BREAK_DELAY = 6;

          struct Controller {
                    HardwareSerial&  S;
                    uint8_t RX_PIN;
                    uint8_t TX_PIN;
                    uint8_t D1;
                    uint8_t D2;
                    uint8_t D3;
                    uint8_t DE;
                    uint8_t rowNum;
                    uint8_t rowLen;
          };
```

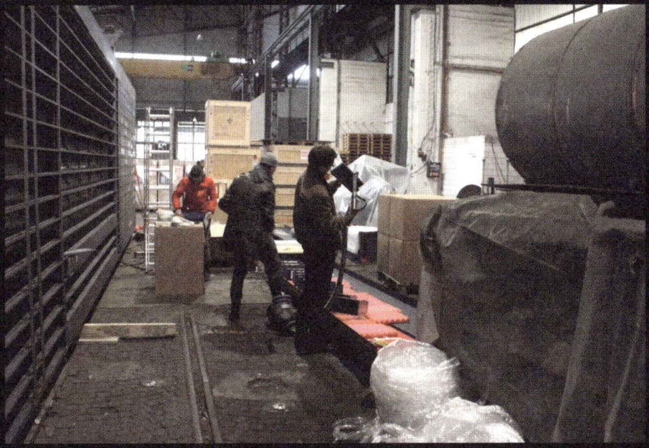

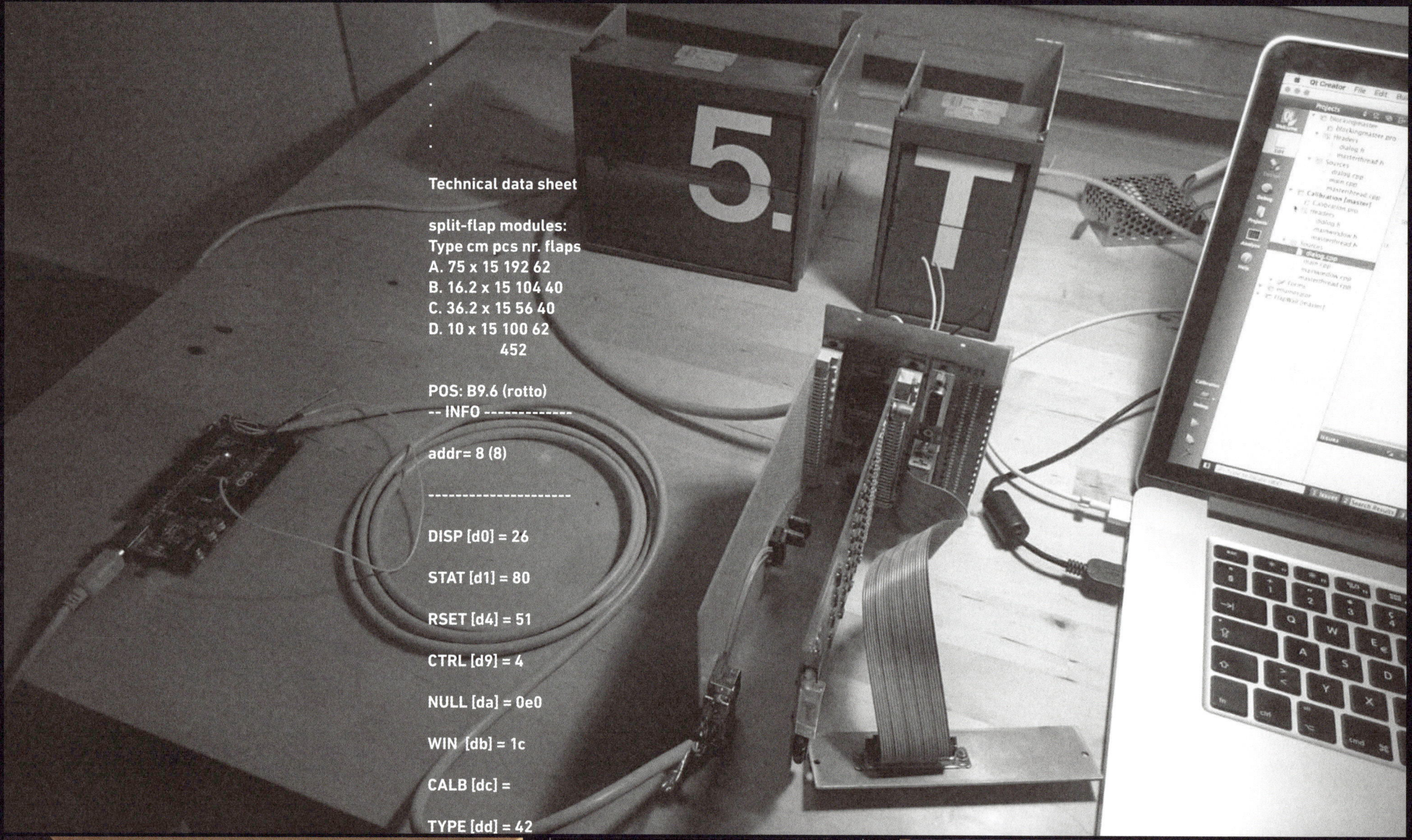

Technical data sheet

split-flap modules:
Type cm pcs nr. flaps
A. 75 x 15 192 62
B. 16.2 x 15 104 40
C. 36.2 x 15 56 40
D. 10 x 15 100 62
452

POS: B9.6 (rotto)
-- INFO -------------

addr= 8 (8)

DISP [d0] = 26

STAT [d1] = 80

RSET [d4] = 51

CTRL [d9] = 4

NULL [da] = 0e0

WIN [db] = 1c

CALB [dc] =

TYPE [dd] = 42

ADDR [de] = 8

SNBR [df] = 00eb92

POS: B9.7 (ok)

-- INFO ---------------

addr = 16 (10)

DISP [d0] = 5

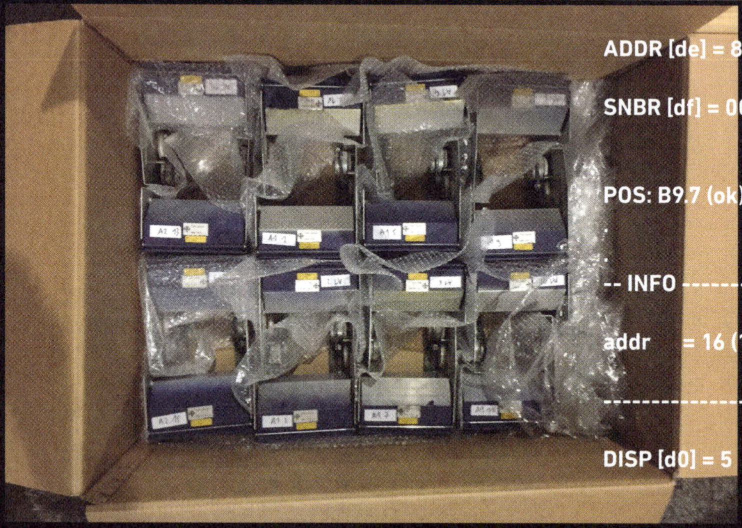

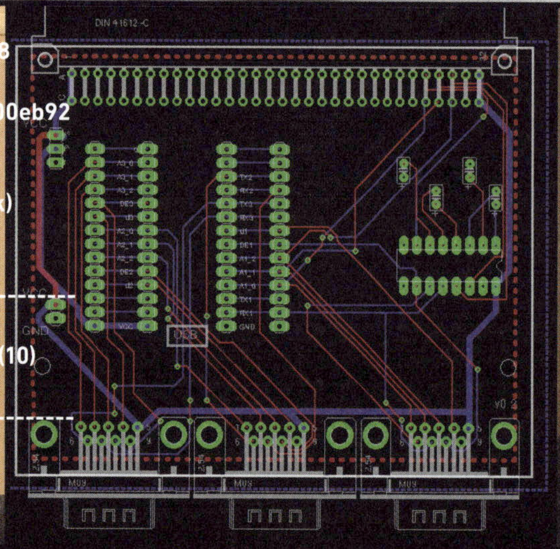

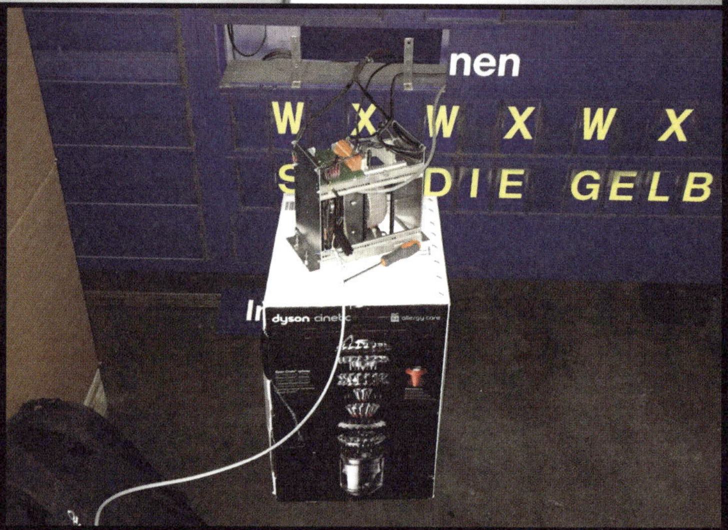

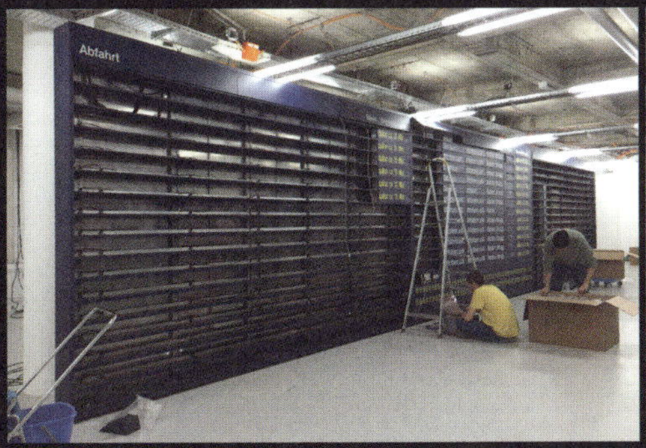

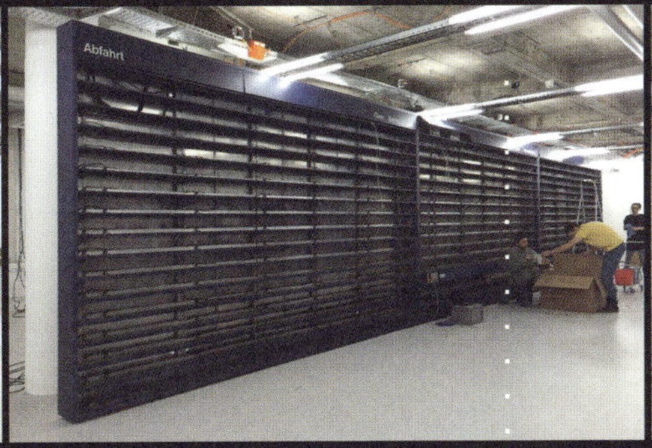

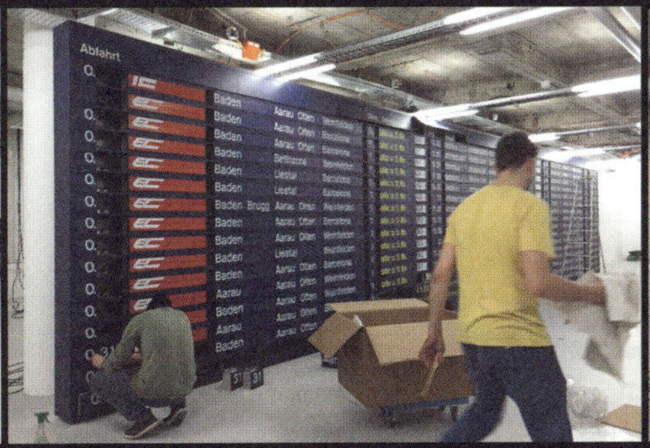

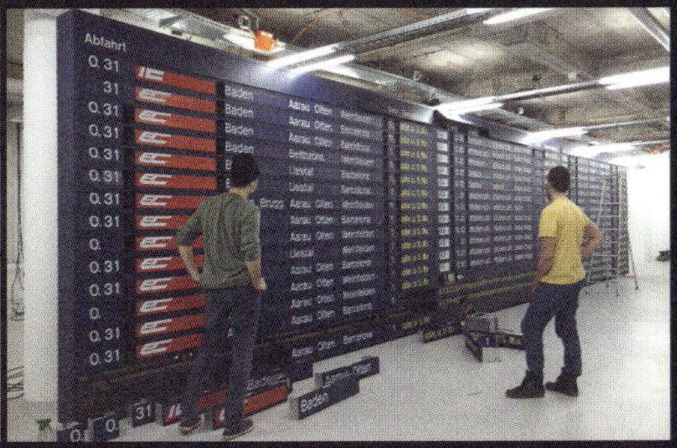

This is the original technical drawing of the SBB CFF FFS flap model.

The first model of the split-flap system was patented in 1962 by Gino Valle for the Solari company of Udine. This original design system by Valle received the Compasso d'Or award in 1962.

With the support of Tino Perucchi we reverse-engineered the protocol and hardware. The panel is still based on the same principles but has been completely redesigned and re-engineered.

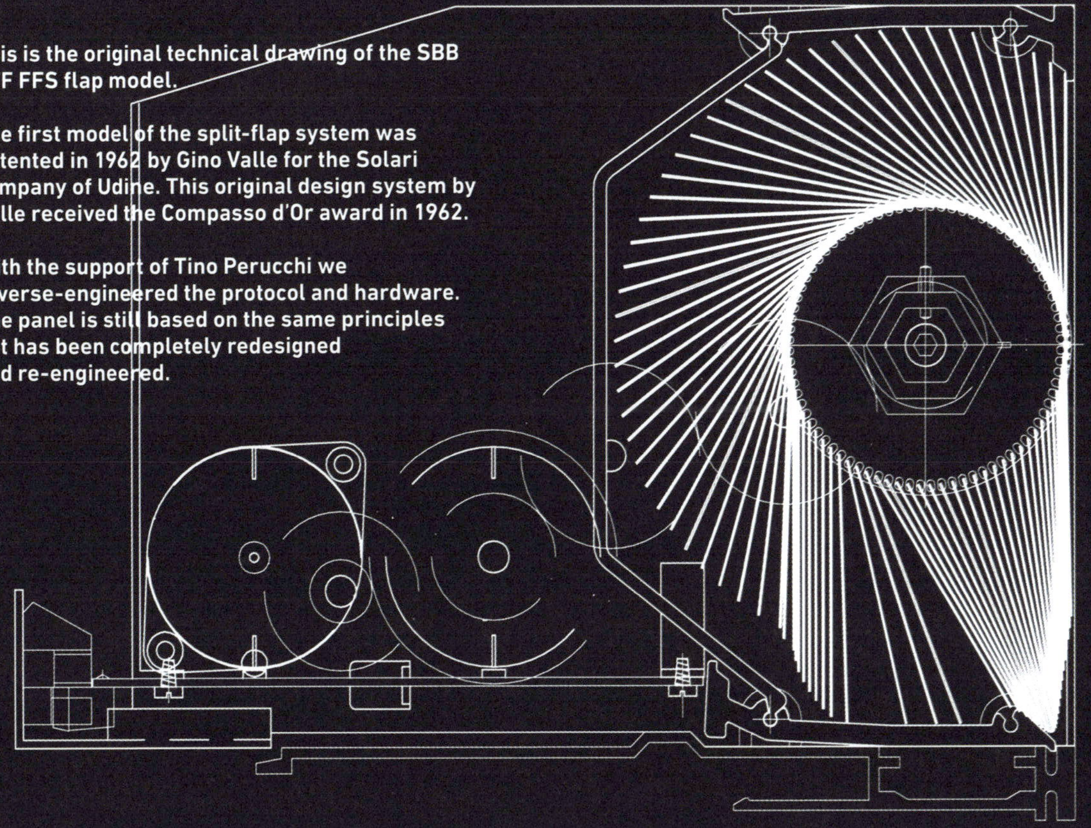

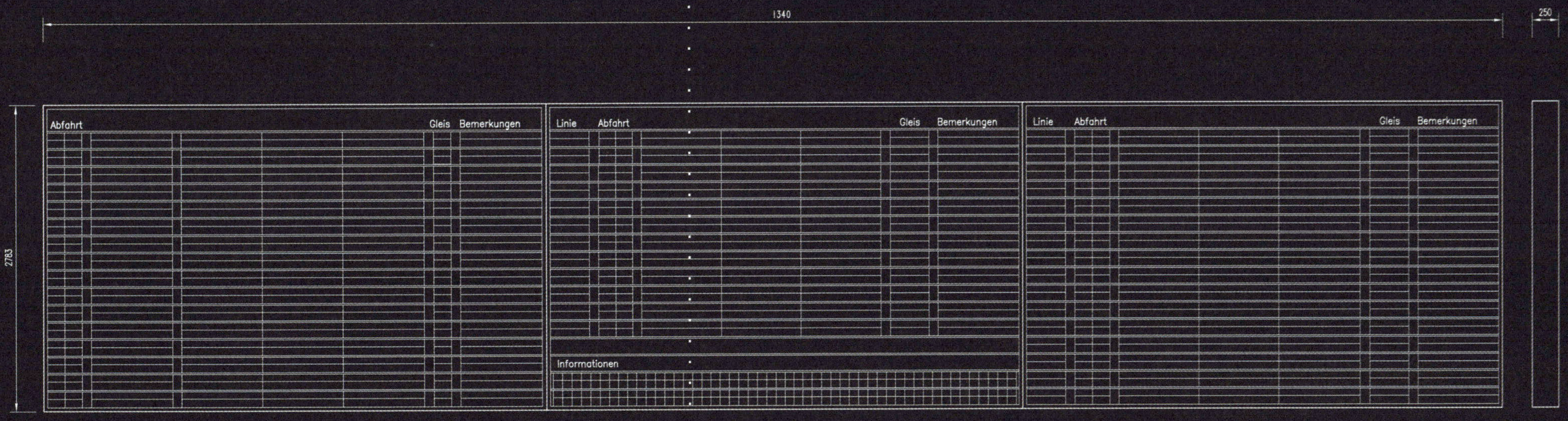

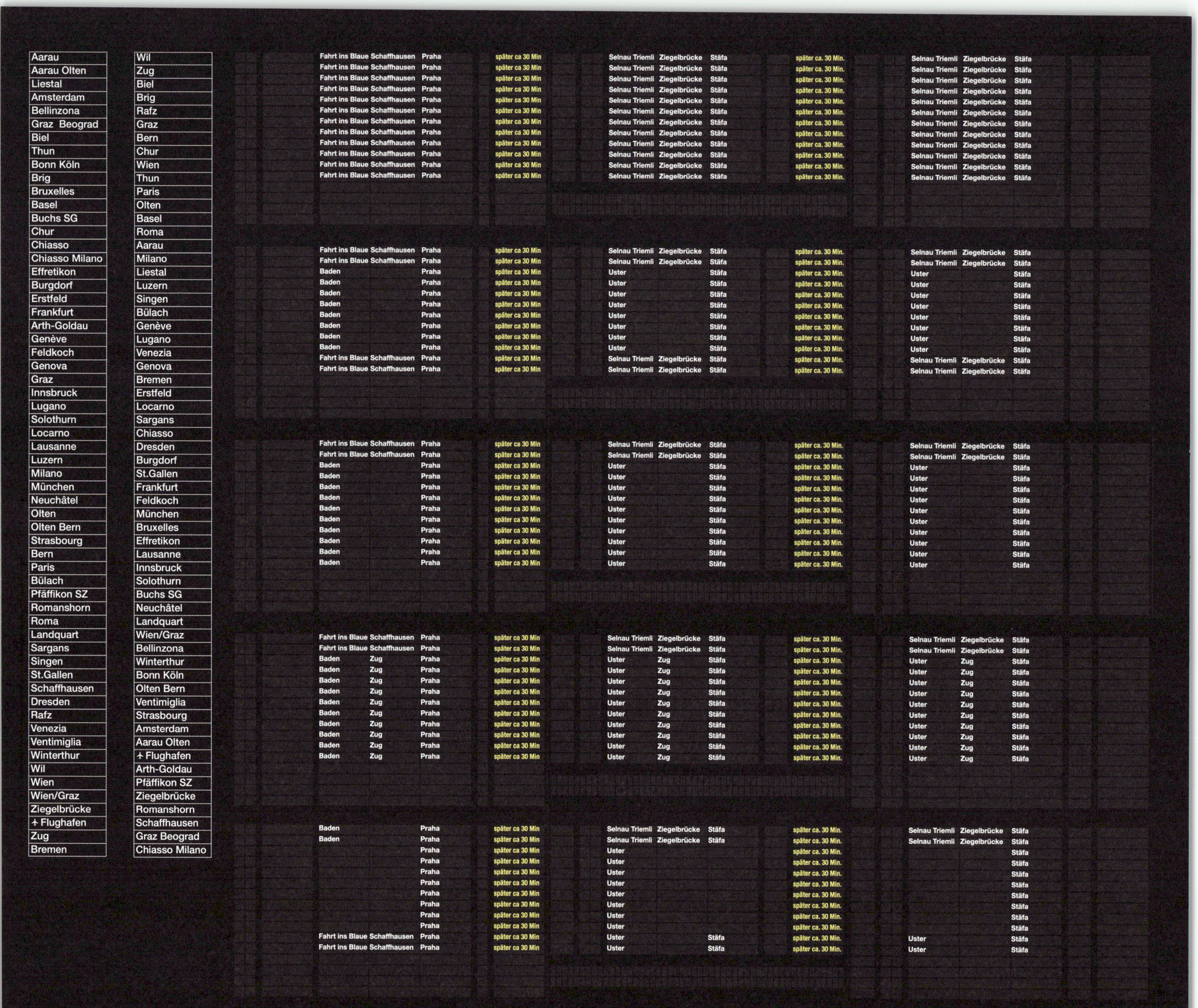

Aarau	Wil
Aarau Olten	Zug
Liestal	Biel
Amsterdam	Brig
Bellinzona	Rafz
Graz Beograd	Graz
Biel	Bern
Thun	Chur
Bonn Köln	Wien
Brig	Thun
Bruxelles	Paris
Basel	Olten
Buchs SG	Basel
Chur	Roma
Chiasso	Aarau
Chiasso Milano	Milano
Effretikon	Liestal
Burgdorf	Luzern
Erstfeld	Singen
Frankfurt	Bülach
Arth-Goldau	Genève
Genève	Lugano
Feldkoch	Venezia
Genova	Genova
Graz	Bremen
Innsbruck	Erstfeld
Lugano	Locarno
Solothurn	Sargans
Locarno	Chiasso
Lausanne	Dresden
Luzern	Burgdorf
Milano	St.Gallen
München	Frankfurt
Neuchâtel	Feldkoch
Olten	München
Olten Bern	Bruxelles
Strasbourg	Effretikon
Bern	Lausanne
Paris	Innsbruck
Bülach	Solothurn
Pfäffikon SZ	Buchs SG
Romanshorn	Neuchâtel
Roma	Landquart
Landquart	Wien/Graz
Sargans	Bellinzona
Singen	Winterthur
St.Gallen	Bonn Köln
Schaffhausen	Olten Bern
Dresden	Ventimiglia
Rafz	Strasbourg
Venezia	Amsterdam
Ventimiglia	Aarau Olten
Winterthur	+ Flughafen
Wil	Arth-Goldau
Wien	Pfäffikon SZ
Wien/Graz	Ziegelbrücke
Ziegelbrücke	Romanshorn
+ Flughafen	Schaffhausen
Zug	Graz Beograd
Bremen	Chiasso Milano

Fahrt ins Blaue	Schaffhausen	Praha	später ca 30 Min	Selnau Triemli	Ziegelbrücke	Stäfa	später ca. 30 Min.	Selnau Triemli	Ziegelbrücke	Stäfa
Fahrt ins Blaue	Schaffhausen	Praha	später ca 30 Min	Selnau Triemli	Ziegelbrücke	Stäfa	später ca. 30 Min.	Selnau Triemli	Ziegelbrücke	Stäfa
Fahrt ins Blaue	Schaffhausen	Praha	später ca 30 Min	Selnau Triemli	Ziegelbrücke	Stäfa	später ca. 30 Min.	Selnau Triemli	Ziegelbrücke	Stäfa
Fahrt ins Blaue	Schaffhausen	Praha	später ca 30 Min	Selnau Triemli	Ziegelbrücke	Stäfa	später ca. 30 Min.	Selnau Triemli	Ziegelbrücke	Stäfa
Fahrt ins Blaue	Schaffhausen	Praha	später ca 30 Min	Selnau Triemli	Ziegelbrücke	Stäfa	später ca. 30 Min.	Selnau Triemli	Ziegelbrücke	Stäfa
Fahrt ins Blaue	Schaffhausen	Praha	später ca 30 Min	Selnau Triemli	Ziegelbrücke	Stäfa	später ca. 30 Min.	Selnau Triemli	Ziegelbrücke	Stäfa
Fahrt ins Blaue	Schaffhausen	Praha	später ca 30 Min	Selnau Triemli	Ziegelbrücke	Stäfa	später ca. 30 Min.	Selnau Triemli	Ziegelbrücke	Stäfa
Fahrt ins Blaue	Schaffhausen	Praha	später ca 30 Min	Selnau Triemli	Ziegelbrücke	Stäfa	später ca. 30 Min.	Selnau Triemli	Ziegelbrücke	Stäfa
Fahrt ins Blaue	Schaffhausen	Praha	später ca 30 Min	Selnau Triemli	Ziegelbrücke	Stäfa	später ca. 30 Min.	Selnau Triemli	Ziegelbrücke	Stäfa
Fahrt ins Blaue	Schaffhausen	Praha	später ca 30 Min	Selnau Triemli	Ziegelbrücke	Stäfa	später ca. 30 Min.	Selnau Triemli	Ziegelbrücke	Stäfa
Fahrt ins Blaue	Schaffhausen	Praha	später ca 30 Min	Selnau Triemli	Ziegelbrücke	Stäfa	später ca. 30 Min.	Selnau Triemli	Ziegelbrücke	Stäfa
Fahrt ins Blaue	Schaffhausen	Praha	später ca 30 Min	Selnau Triemli	Ziegelbrücke	Stäfa	später ca. 30 Min.	Selnau Triemli	Ziegelbrücke	Stäfa

Fahrt ins Blaue	Schaffhausen	Praha	später ca 30 Min	Selnau Triemli	Ziegelbrücke	Stäfa	später ca. 30 Min.	Selnau Triemli	Ziegelbrücke	Stäfa
Fahrt ins Blaue	Schaffhausen	Praha	später ca 30 Min	Selnau Triemli	Ziegelbrücke	Stäfa	später ca. 30 Min.	Selnau Triemli	Ziegelbrücke	Stäfa
Baden		Praha	später ca 30 Min	Uster		Stäfa	später ca. 30 Min.	Uster		Stäfa
Baden		Praha	später ca 30 Min	Uster		Stäfa	später ca. 30 Min.	Uster		Stäfa
Baden		Praha	später ca 30 Min	Uster		Stäfa	später ca. 30 Min.	Uster		Stäfa
Baden		Praha	später ca 30 Min	Uster		Stäfa	später ca. 30 Min.	Uster		Stäfa
Baden		Praha	später ca 30 Min	Uster		Stäfa	später ca. 30 Min.	Uster		Stäfa
Baden		Praha	später ca 30 Min	Uster		Stäfa	später ca. 30 Min.	Uster		Stäfa
Baden		Praha	später ca 30 Min	Uster		Stäfa	später ca. 30 Min.	Uster		Stäfa
Baden		Praha	später ca 30 Min	Uster		Stäfa	später ca. 30 Min.	Uster		Stäfa
Fahrt ins Blaue	Schaffhausen	Praha	später ca 30 Min	Selnau Triemli	Ziegelbrücke	Stäfa	später ca. 30 Min.	Selnau Triemli	Ziegelbrücke	Stäfa
Fahrt ins Blaue	Schaffhausen	Praha	später ca 30 Min	Selnau Triemli	Ziegelbrücke	Stäfa	später ca. 30 Min.	Selnau Triemli	Ziegelbrücke	Stäfa

Fahrt ins Blaue	Schaffhausen	Praha	später ca 30 Min	Selnau Triemli	Ziegelbrücke	Stäfa	später ca. 30 Min.	Selnau Triemli	Ziegelbrücke	Stäfa
Fahrt ins Blaue	Schaffhausen	Praha	später ca 30 Min	Selnau Triemli	Ziegelbrücke	Stäfa	später ca. 30 Min.	Selnau Triemli	Ziegelbrücke	Stäfa
Baden		Praha	später ca 30 Min	Uster		Stäfa	später ca. 30 Min.	Uster		Stäfa
Baden		Praha	später ca 30 Min	Uster		Stäfa	später ca. 30 Min.	Uster		Stäfa
Baden		Praha	später ca 30 Min	Uster		Stäfa	später ca. 30 Min.	Uster		Stäfa
Baden		Praha	später ca 30 Min	Uster		Stäfa	später ca. 30 Min.	Uster		Stäfa
Baden		Praha	später ca 30 Min	Uster		Stäfa	später ca. 30 Min.	Uster		Stäfa
Baden		Praha	später ca 30 Min	Uster		Stäfa	später ca. 30 Min.	Uster		Stäfa
Baden		Praha	später ca 30 Min	Uster		Stäfa	später ca. 30 Min.	Uster		Stäfa
Baden		Praha	später ca 30 Min	Uster		Stäfa	später ca. 30 Min.	Uster		Stäfa
Baden		Praha	später ca 30 Min	Uster		Stäfa	später ca. 30 Min.	Uster		Stäfa
Baden		Praha	später ca 30 Min	Uster		Stäfa	später ca. 30 Min.	Uster		Stäfa

Fahrt ins Blaue	Schaffhausen	Praha	später ca 30 Min	Selnau Triemli	Ziegelbrücke	Stäfa	später ca. 30 Min.	Selnau Triemli	Ziegelbrücke	Stäfa
Fahrt ins Blaue	Schaffhausen	Praha	später ca 30 Min	Selnau Triemli	Ziegelbrücke	Stäfa	später ca. 30 Min.	Selnau Triemli	Ziegelbrücke	Stäfa
Baden	Zug	Praha	später ca 30 Min	Uster	Zug	Stäfa	später ca. 30 Min.	Uster	Zug	Stäfa
Baden	Zug	Praha	später ca 30 Min	Uster	Zug	Stäfa	später ca. 30 Min.	Uster	Zug	Stäfa
Baden	Zug	Praha	später ca 30 Min	Uster	Zug	Stäfa	später ca. 30 Min.	Uster	Zug	Stäfa
Baden	Zug	Praha	später ca 30 Min	Uster	Zug	Stäfa	später ca. 30 Min.	Uster	Zug	Stäfa
Baden	Zug	Praha	später ca 30 Min	Uster	Zug	Stäfa	später ca. 30 Min.	Uster	Zug	Stäfa
Baden	Zug	Praha	später ca 30 Min	Uster	Zug	Stäfa	später ca. 30 Min.	Uster	Zug	Stäfa
Baden	Zug	Praha	später ca 30 Min	Uster	Zug	Stäfa	später ca. 30 Min.	Uster	Zug	Stäfa
Baden	Zug	Praha	später ca 30 Min	Uster	Zug	Stäfa	später ca. 30 Min.	Uster	Zug	Stäfa
Baden	Zug	Praha	später ca 30 Min	Uster	Zug	Stäfa	später ca. 30 Min.	Uster	Zug	Stäfa
Baden	Zug	Praha	später ca 30 Min	Uster	Zug	Stäfa	später ca. 30 Min.	Uster	Zug	Stäfa

Baden		Praha	später ca 30 Min	Selnau Triemli	Ziegelbrücke	Stäfa	später ca. 30 Min.	Selnau Triemli	Ziegelbrücke	Stäfa
Baden		Praha	später ca 30 Min	Selnau Triemli	Ziegelbrücke	Stäfa	später ca. 30 Min.	Selnau Triemli	Ziegelbrücke	Stäfa
		Praha	später ca 30 Min	Uster			später ca. 30 Min.			Stäfa
		Praha	später ca 30 Min	Uster			später ca. 30 Min.			Stäfa
		Praha	später ca 30 Min	Uster			später ca. 30 Min.			Stäfa
		Praha	später ca 30 Min	Uster			später ca. 30 Min.			Stäfa
		Praha	später ca 30 Min	Uster			später ca. 30 Min.			Stäfa
		Praha	später ca 30 Min	Uster			später ca. 30 Min.			Stäfa
		Praha	später ca 30 Min	Uster			später ca. 30 Min.			Stäfa
		Praha	später ca 30 Min	Uster			später ca. 30 Min.			Stäfa
Fahrt ins Blaue	Schaffhausen	Praha	später ca 30 Min	Uster		Stäfa	später ca. 30 Min.	Uster		Stäfa
Fahrt ins Blaue	Schaffhausen	Praha	später ca 30 Min	Uster		Stäfa	später ca. 30 Min.	Uster		Stäfa

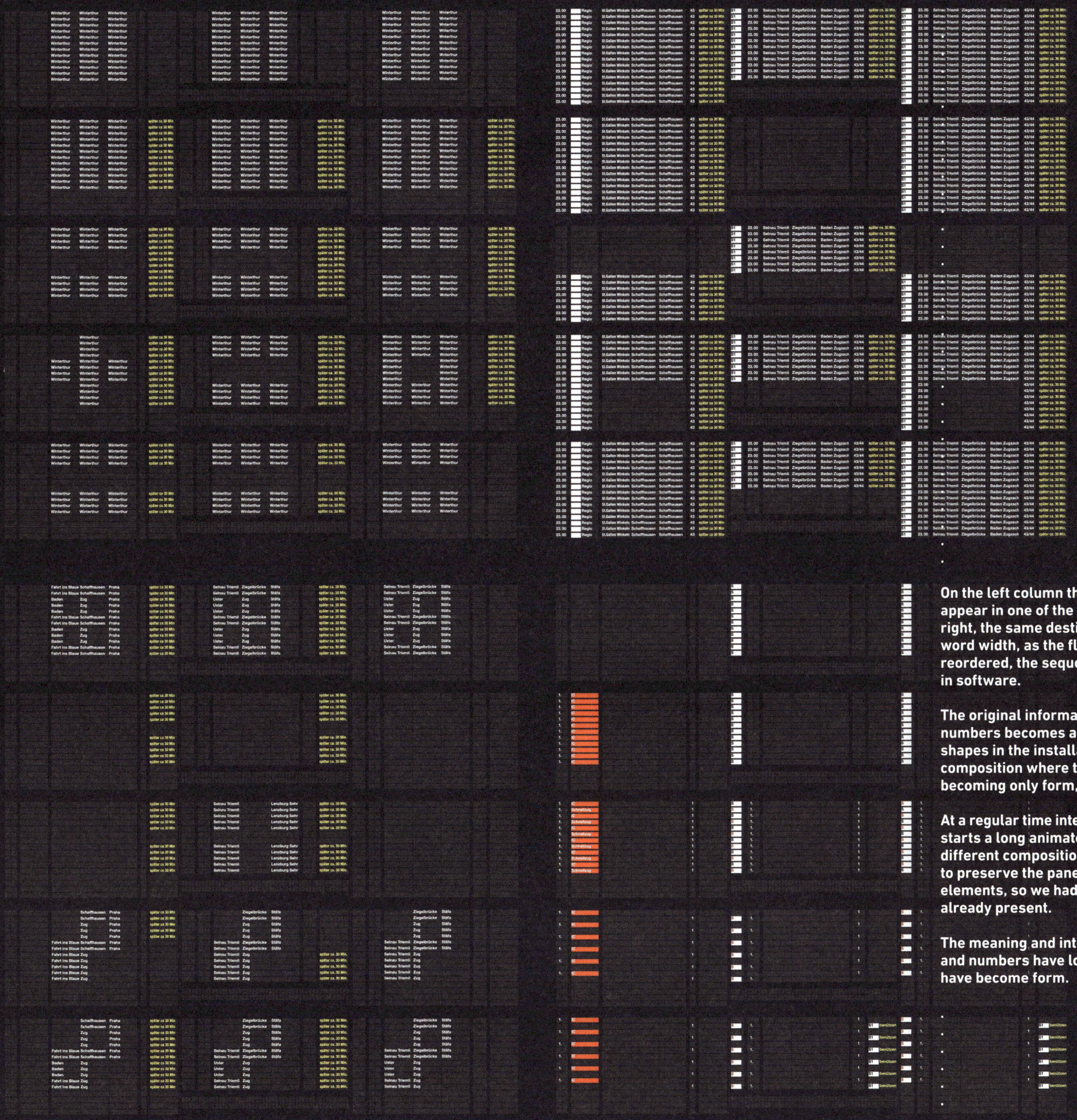

On the left column the 60 train destinations appear in one of the split-flap modules; on the right, the same destinations are reordered by word width, as the flaps cannot be physically reordered, the sequence was remapped in software.

The original information made of words and numbers becomes a series of abstract moving shapes in the installation, forming a larger composition where the text loses its meaning, becoming only form, color, movement and sound.

At a regular time interval, the display configuration starts a long animated transition producing different compositions. Our main objective was to preserve the panel without altering its elements, so we had to work with the features already present.

The meaning and intention of the original words and numbers have lost their original function and have become form.

171 . ZURICH GA FLAP

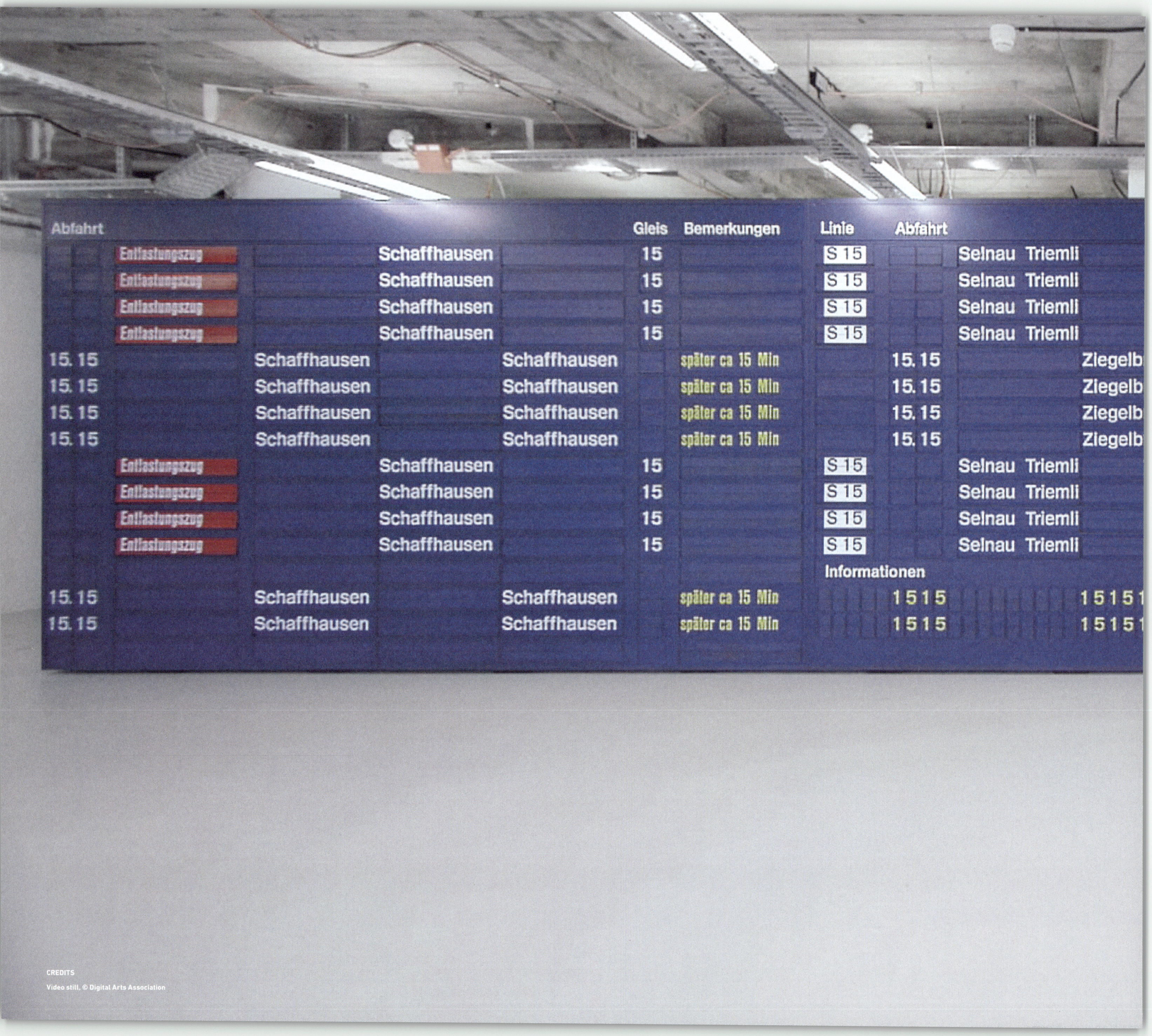

CREDITS
Video still, © Digital Arts Association

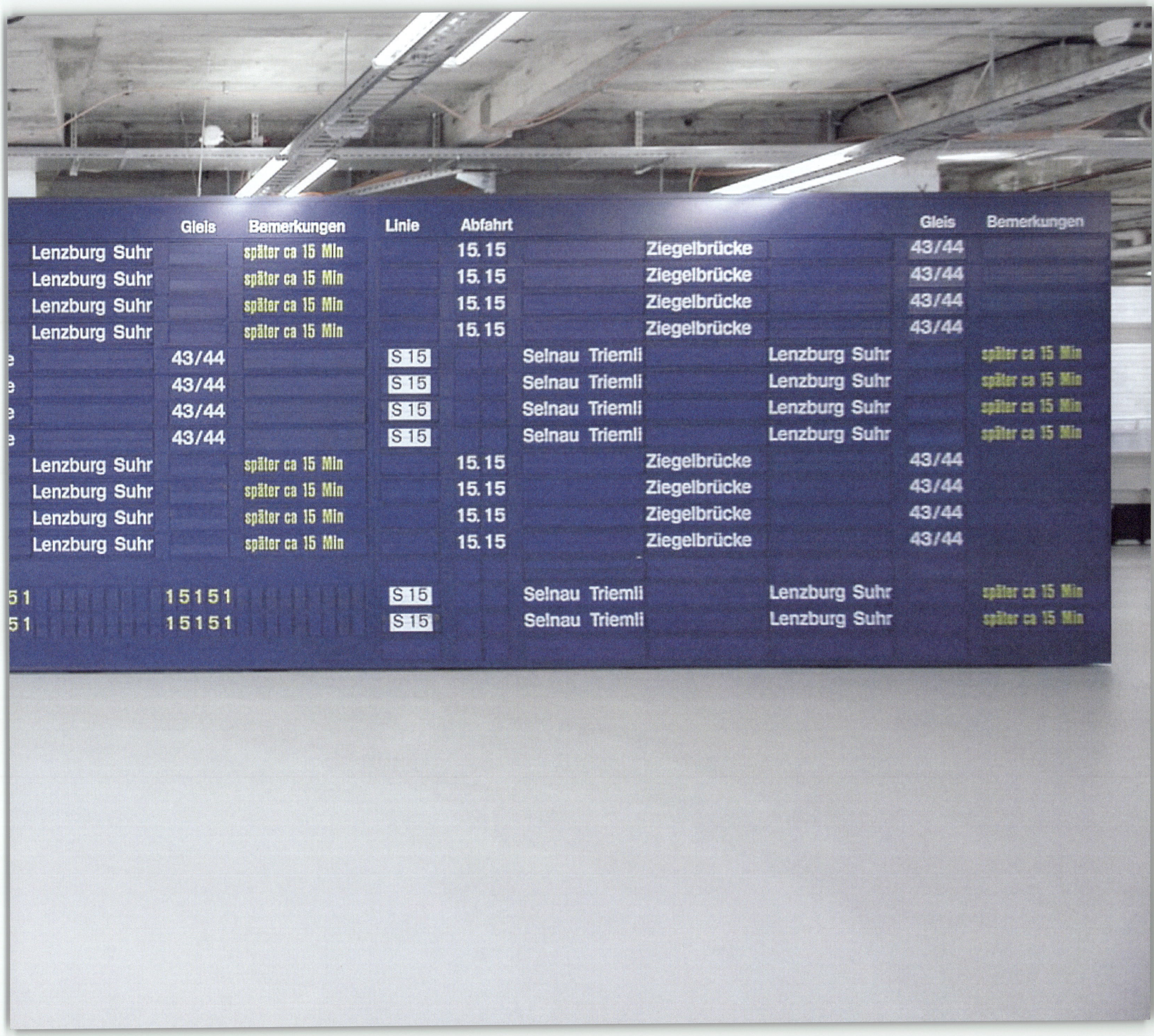
Gleis
Bemerkungen
Linie
Abfahrt
Gleis
Bemerkungen
Lenzburg Suhr
später ca 15 Min
15.15
Ziegelbrücke
43/44
Lenzburg Suhr
später ca 15 Min
15.15
Ziegelbrücke
43/44
Lenzburg Suhr
später ca 15 Min
15.15
Ziegelbrücke
43/44
Lenzburg Suhr
später ca 15 Min
15.15
Ziegelbrücke
43/44
43/44
S 15
Selnau Triemli
Lenzburg Suhr
später ca 15 Min
43/44
S 15
Selnau Triemli
Lenzburg Suhr
später ca 15 Min
43/44
S 15
Selnau Triemli
Lenzburg Suhr
später ca 15 Min
43/44
S 15
Selnau Triemli
Lenzburg Suhr
später ca 15 Min
Lenzburg Suhr
später ca 15 Min
15.15
Ziegelbrücke
43/44
Lenzburg Suhr
später ca 15 Min
15.15
Ziegelbrücke
43/44
Lenzburg Suhr
später ca 15 Min
15.15
Ziegelbrücke
43/44
Lenzburg Suhr
später ca 15 Min
15.15
Ziegelbrücke
43/44
15151
S 15
Selnau Triemli
Lenzburg Suhr
später ca 15 Min
15151
S 15
Selnau Triemli
Lenzburg Suhr
später ca 15 Min

Joëlle

Name:

Joëlle

Info:

Joëlle is a designer and audio-visual artist working in real-time visuals and live performance, where her focus is on exploring the relationship between sound and form.

Her approach is highly experimental, producing an output that is often unexpected and unknown at the start. Using frequencies and minimal structures, she captures the atmosphere and emotions that she feels in the moment, resulting in forms sculpted mainly by sound.

Project:

LOST HORIZON FESTIVAL 2020

A virtual reality music and arts festival

losthorizonfestival.com

URL:

joellesnaith.com

Instagram:

@joellesnaith

Q&As

. . . . . Please explain the main idea and what gave the impulse?

I was invited to participate in LOST HORIZON as a visual artist on the GAS TOWER stage.

LOST HORIZON is a virtual reality music and arts festival created by the team behind Glastonbury's Shangri-La in response to the cancellation of Glastonbury during the 2020 pandemic.

The Shangri-La area was recreated as an interactive 3D landscape, including multiple stages with over 50 music acts and more than 250 artworks.

. . . . . What challenges did you face for this project?

The GAS TOWER stage has a 360° octagonal screen, and the visual material needed to be rendered at 4K, so the pixel resolution for the final output was high. This presented a challenge in capturing the visuals in real-time at 60fps on my MacBook Pro.

. . . . . And what surprises?

Rendering an hour of visuals in 4K was not possible on my MacBook, and thankfully I was able to fall back on my partners PC, but that was an expected last-minute hurdle that I hadn't foreseen.

. . . . . Please describe the technical environment.

I use Vuo to design and code the visuals, VDMX as the performance software and Lemur on my iPad as a touch controller. I capture the output from VDMX using a Blackmagic Video Assist, and the final render takes place in Premiere.

. . . . . Tell us about your aesthetical approach.

I aim to enhance the sound with visuals to heighten the experience of listening to music, creating a symbiosis between the two.

Aesthetically, I've always leaned towards a minimalist approach that uses color sparingly. Using minimal structures that synchronize to the audio, I try to amplify the details within the frequencies.

There is power in restraint, and my goal is to create an atmosphere where the audio and visual are in balance and complement one another. The same principles apply whether in a real-world or a virtual world.

. . . . . What's next? Your vision?

I believe that music is a tool that can help us process our emotions and empathize with others by reflecting in us how others are feeling.

I'm interested in visually communicating those emotions and feelings, connecting what you hear and feel with what you see. I hope to keep learning, experimenting and collaborating while developing immersive audio-visual experiences that use light, visuals and sound to resonate with audiences on a deeper emotional level.

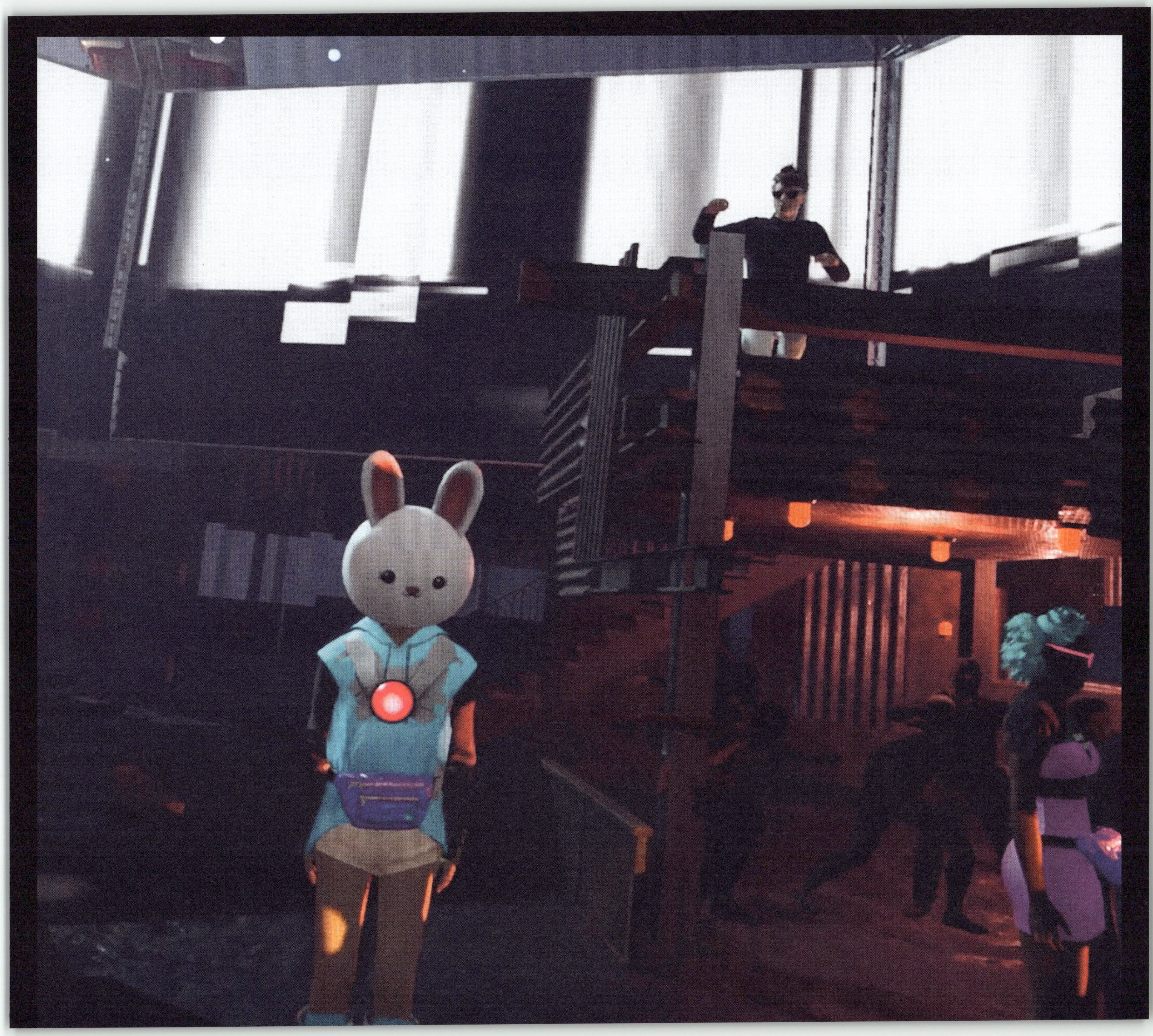

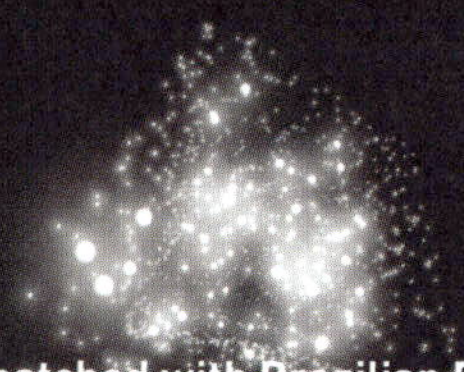

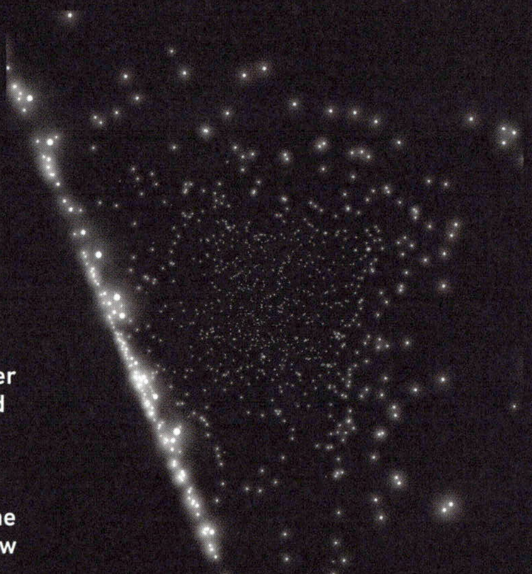

I was matched with Brazilian DJ and producer ANNA and sent her pre-recorded mix, filmed on a green screen to form her hologram in LOST HORIZON.

The music is always the starting point and the foundation of any project, and for the first few days, I immersed myself in ANNA's set while exploring some visual directions in Vuo. I rarely know the destination at the start, and my process is very experimental and iterative and informed by what feels right with the music. One of the things I enjoy most about working with sound is the happy accidents and unexpected results you get when using an audio input to create movement. I give a lot of control to the machine while also synchronizing that movement to the audio with great precision.

In practice, this means a lot of experimentation, adjusting values and parameters until I see something I like, saving a version of that file and planting seeds of ideas that grow throughout the process.

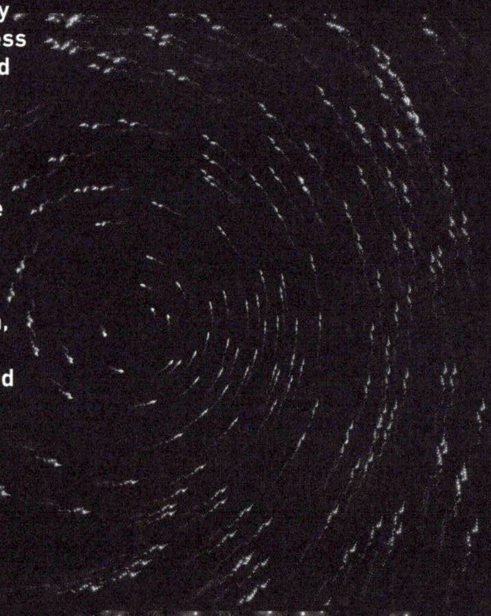

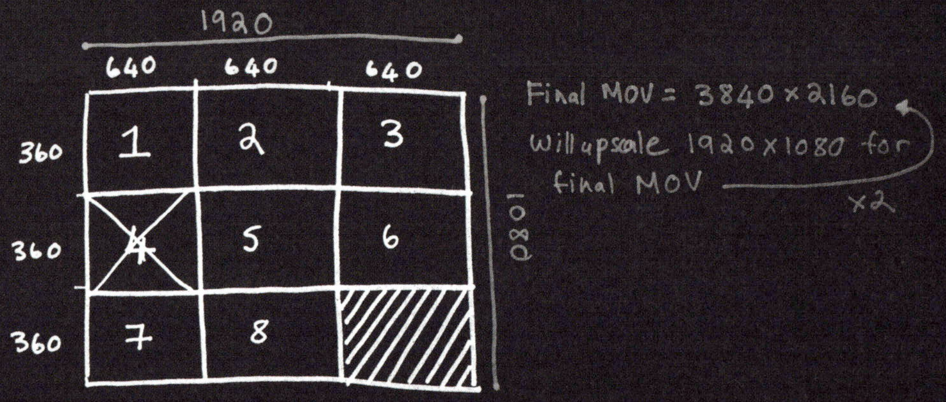

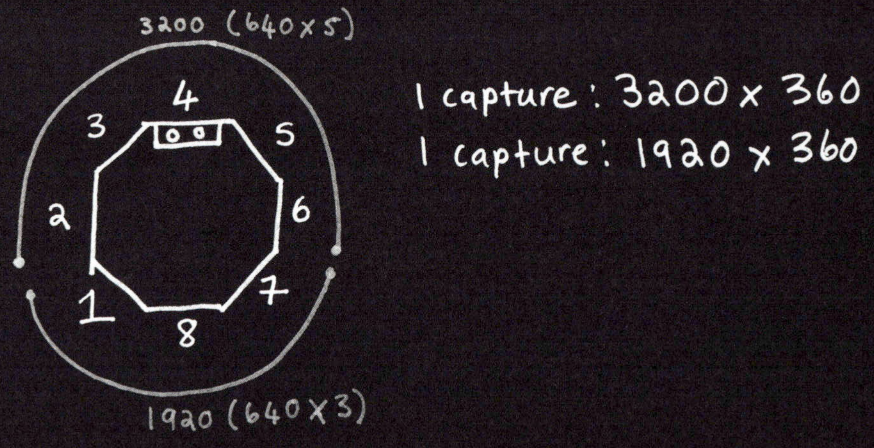

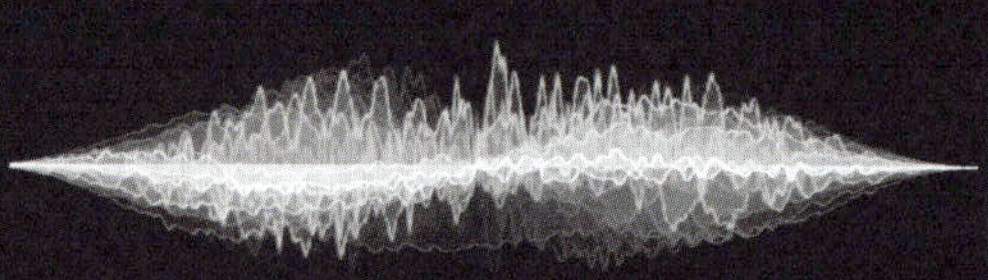

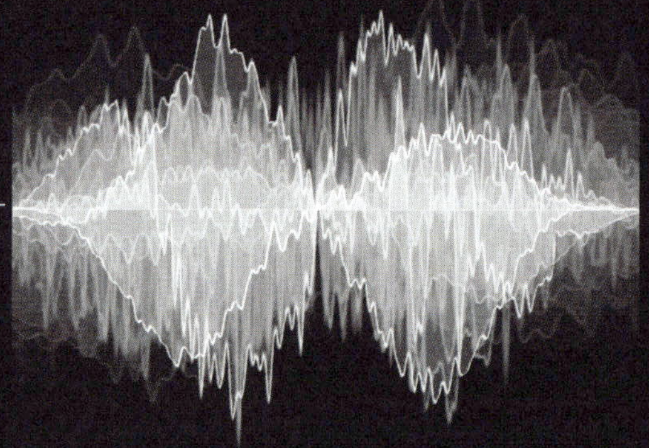

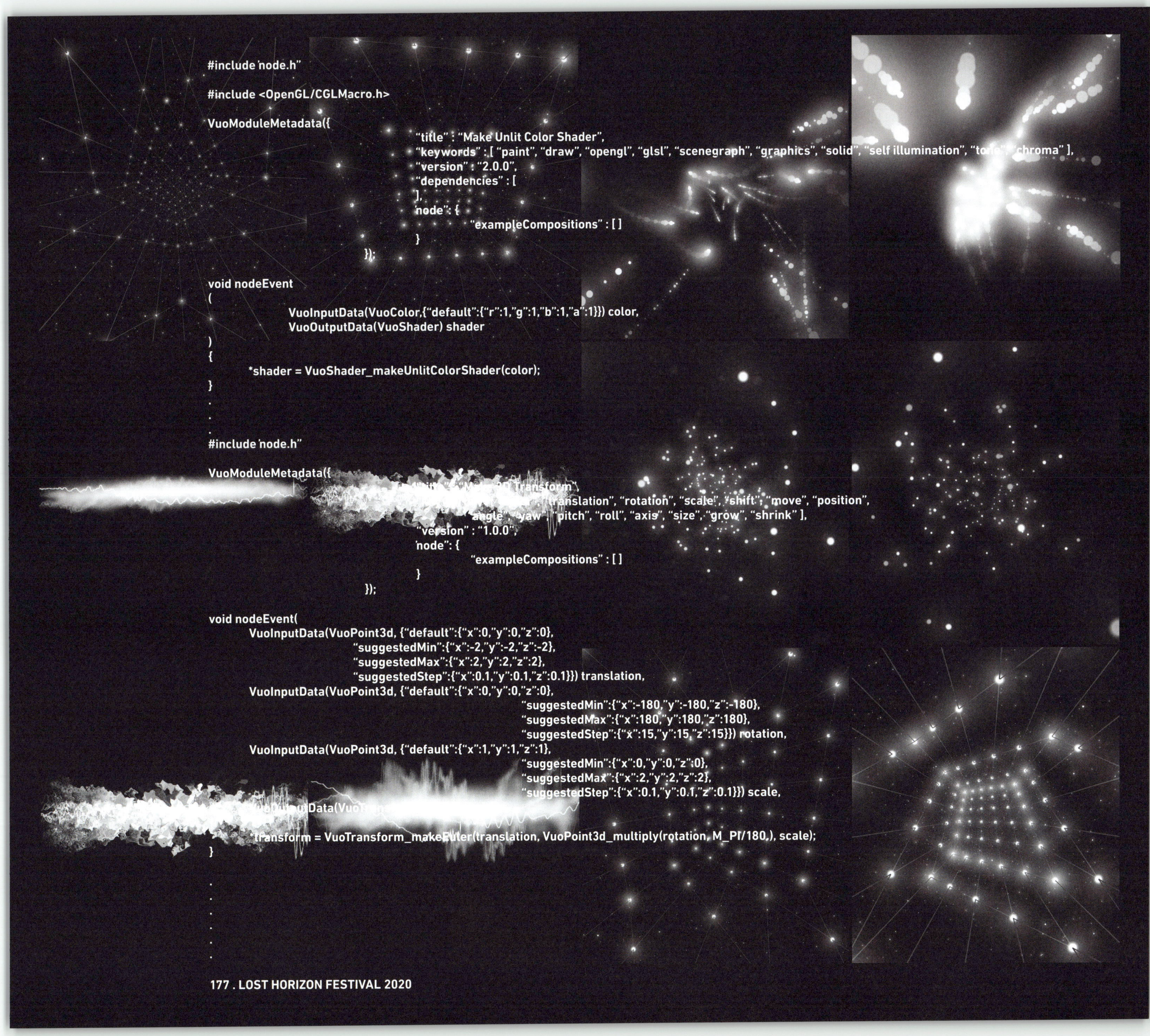

```
#include "node.h"

#include <OpenGL/CGLMacro.h>

VuoModuleMetadata({
                    "title" : "Make Unlit Color Shader",
                    "keywords" : [ "paint", "draw", "opengl", "glsl", "scenegraph", "graphics", "solid", "self illumination", "tone", "chroma" ],
                    "version" : "2.0.0",
                    "dependencies" : [
                    ],
                    "node" : {
                              "exampleCompositions" : [ ]
                    }
                 });

void nodeEvent
(
              VuoInputData(VuoColor,{"default":{"r":1,"g":1,"b":1,"a":1}}) color,
              VuoOutputData(VuoShader) shader
)
{
       *shader = VuoShader_makeUnlitColorShader(color);
}
.
.
.
#include "node.h"

VuoModuleMetadata({
                    Transform",
                              translation", "rotation", "scale", "shift", "move", "position",
                              angle", "yaw", "pitch", "roll", "axis", "size", "grow", "shrink" ],
                    "version" : "1.0.0",
                    "node": {
                              "exampleCompositions" : [ ]
                    }
                 });

void nodeEvent(
       VuoInputData(VuoPoint3d, {"default":{"x":0,"y":0,"z":0},
                           "suggestedMin":{"x":-2,"y":-2,"z":-2},
                           "suggestedMax":{"x":2,"y":2,"z":2},
                           "suggestedStep":{"x":0.1,"y":0.1,"z":0.1}}) translation,
       VuoInputData(VuoPoint3d, {"default":{"x":0,"y":0,"z":0},
                                        "suggestedMin":{"x":-180,"y":-180,"z":-180},
                                        "suggestedMax":{"x":180,"y":180,"z":180},
                                        "suggestedStep":{"x":15,"y":15,"z":15}}) rotation,
       VuoInputData(VuoPoint3d, {"default":{"x":1,"y":1,"z":1},
                                        "suggestedMin":{"x":0,"y":0,"z":0},
                                        "suggestedMax":{"x":2,"y":2,"z":2},
                                        "suggestedStep":{"x":0.1,"y":0.1,"z":0.1}}) scale,
       VuoOutputData(Vuo

       *transform = VuoTransform_makeEuler(translation, VuoPoint3d_multiply(rotation, M_PI/180.), scale);
}
.
.
.
.
.
.
```

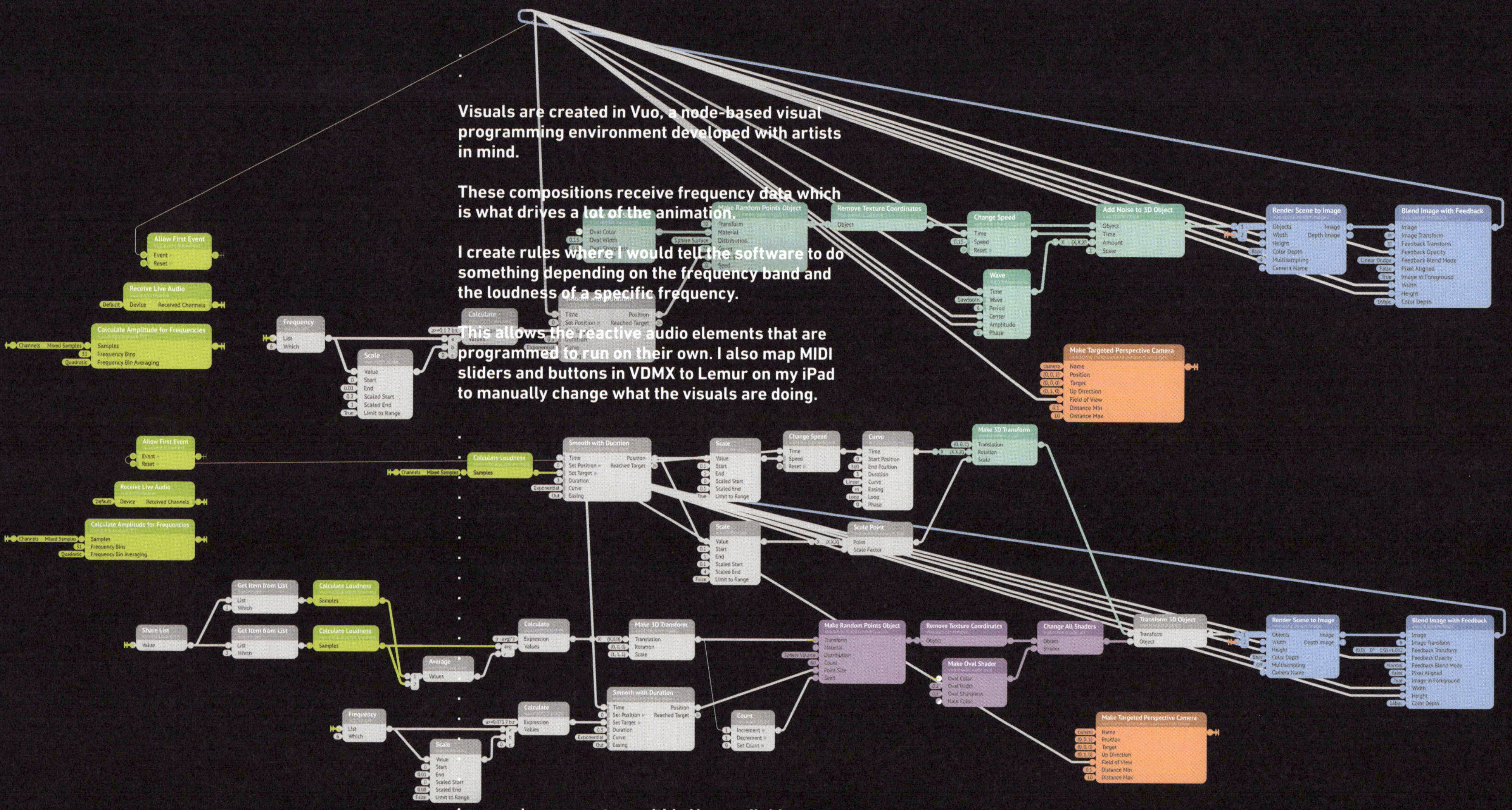

Visuals are created in Vuo, a node-based visual programming environment developed with artists in mind.

These compositions receive frequency data which is what drives a lot of the animation.

I create rules where I would tell the software to do something depending on the frequency band and the loudness of a specific frequency.

This allows the reactive audio elements that are programmed to run on their own. I also map MIDI sliders and buttons in VDMX to Lemur on my iPad to manually change what the visuals are doing.

I can make parameters within Vuo available in VDMX by publishing them, which allows me to control the behavior and aesthetic of that composition in real-time.

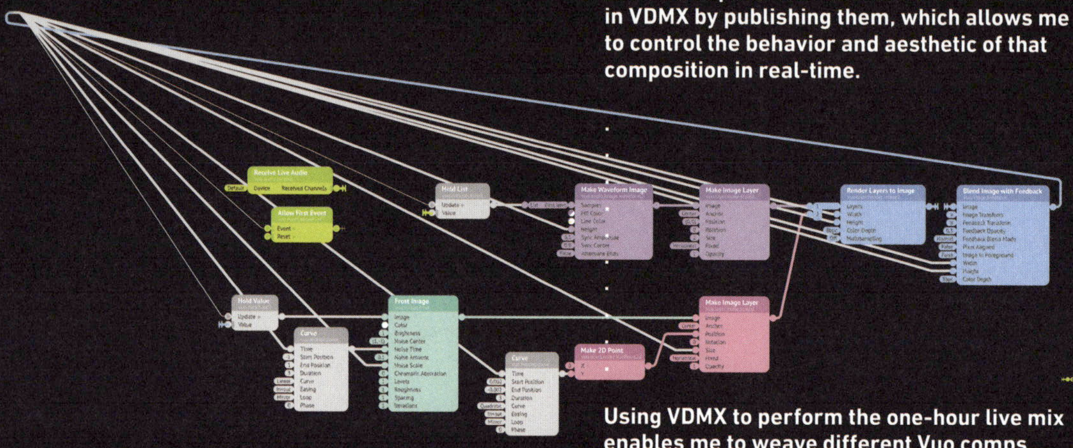

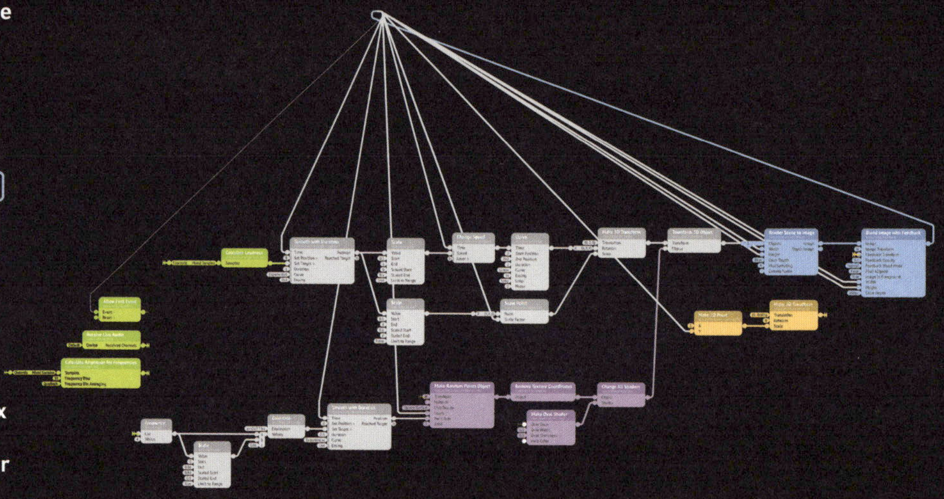

Using VDMX to perform the one-hour live mix enables me to weave different Vuo comps together efficiently and add Quartz Composer effects to the mixer, some of which sync to the audio.

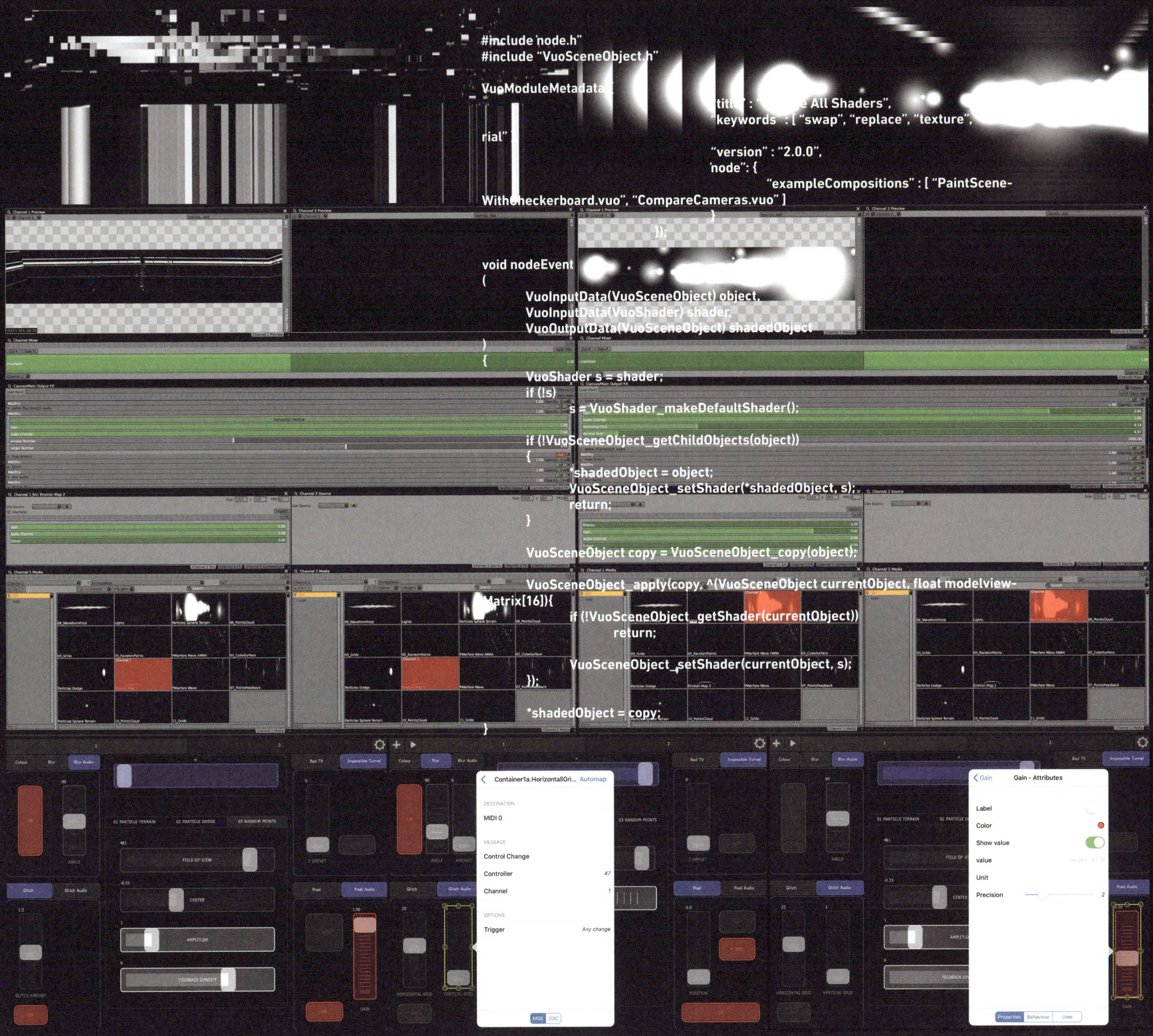

179 . LOST HORIZON FESTIVAL 2020

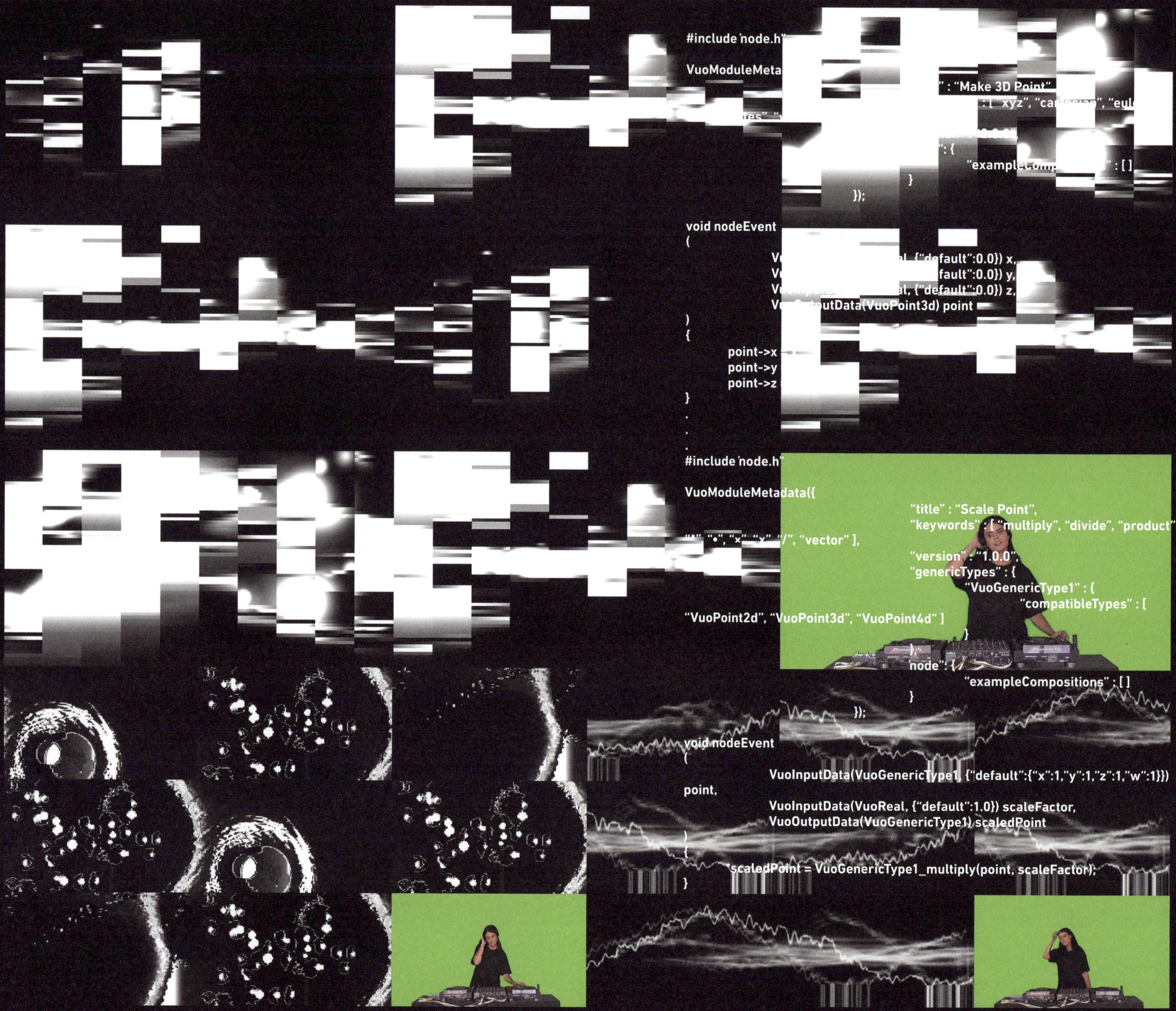
#include "node.h"
VuoModuleMeta
" : "Make 3D Point"
: ["xyz", "ca
"exampleComp
: [ ]
}
});
void nodeEvent
(
fault":0.0}) x,
fault":0.0}) y,
al, {"default":0.0}) z,
outData(VuoPoint3d) point
)
{
point->x
point->y
point->z
}
#include "node.h"
VuoModuleMetadata({
"title" : "Scale Point",
"keywords" : ["multiply", "divide", "product",
"/", "vector"],
"version" : "1.0.0",
"genericTypes" : {
"VuoGenericType1" : {
"compatibleTypes" : [
"VuoPoint2d", "VuoPoint3d", "VuoPoint4d"]
}
},
"node": {
"exampleCompositions" : [ ]
}
});
void nodeEvent
(
VuoInputData(VuoGenericType1, {"default":{"x":1,"y":1,"z":1,"w":1}})
point,
VuoInputData(VuoReal, {"default":1.0}) scaleFactor,
VuoOutputData(VuoGenericType1) scaledPoint
)
{
*scaledPoint = VuoGenericType1_multiply(point, scaleFactor);
}

Next, I planned out the set, marking each visual composition and effect against the audio timecode, which I mixed in VDMX and captured in one take.

Then I laid out the screen capture on a grid template for correct mapping to the 360° octagonal screen and rendered it at 4K. The video is then given to the team to input into the virtual world environment.

The first time I experienced the visuals on screen was when the event streamed live.

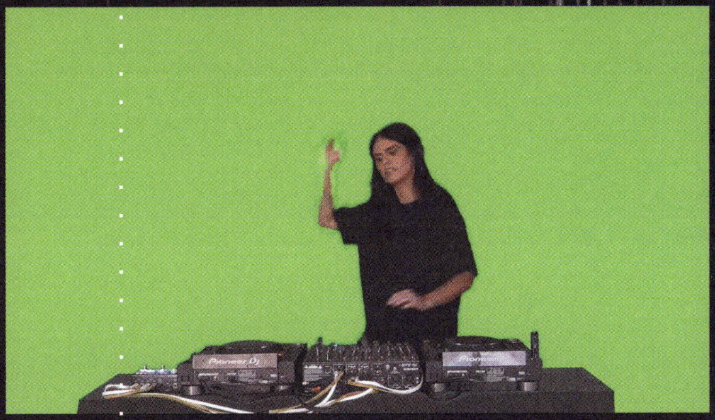

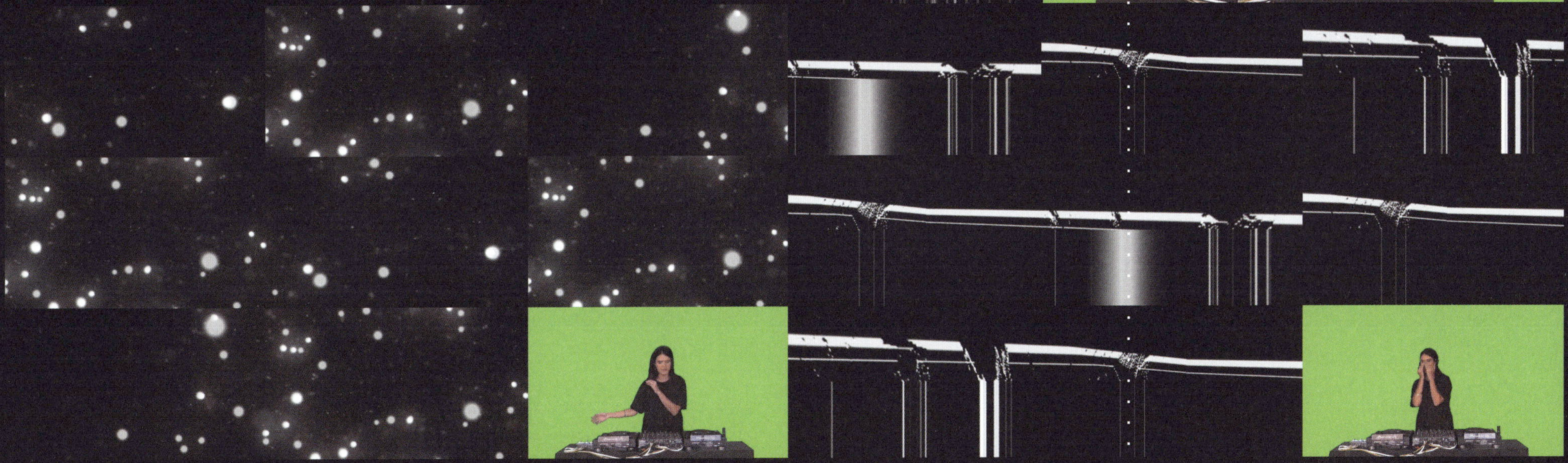

LOST HORIZON represents a shift in how we relate to one another when shared experiences feel like a distant memory. It's an exercise in transcending physicality and pushing the boundaries of human connection within a virtual space.

Despite the limitations and constraints of the hardware and platform, it was a welcome escape into an alternate reality, united once again with strangers through the collective ritual of music and dance.

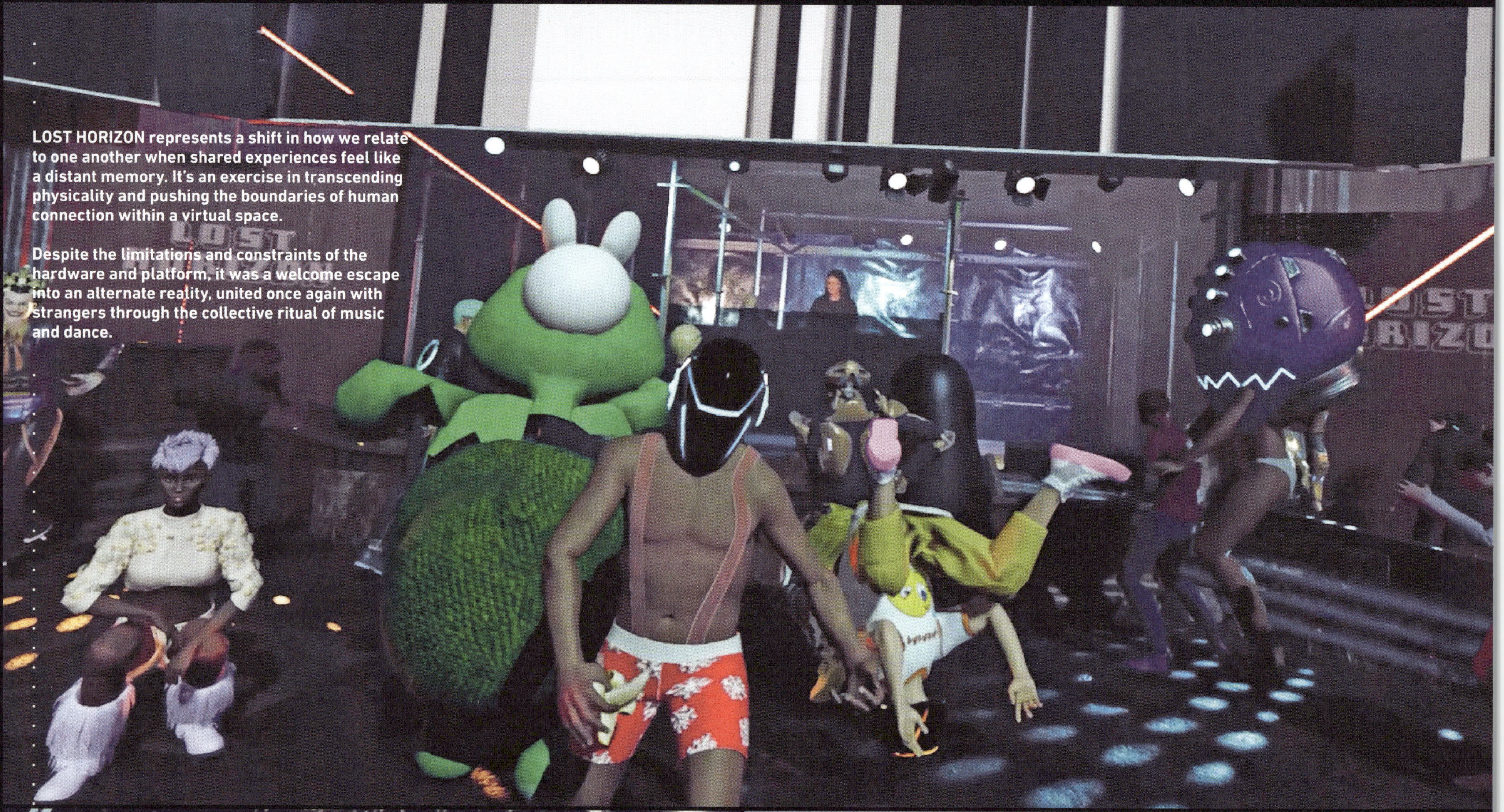

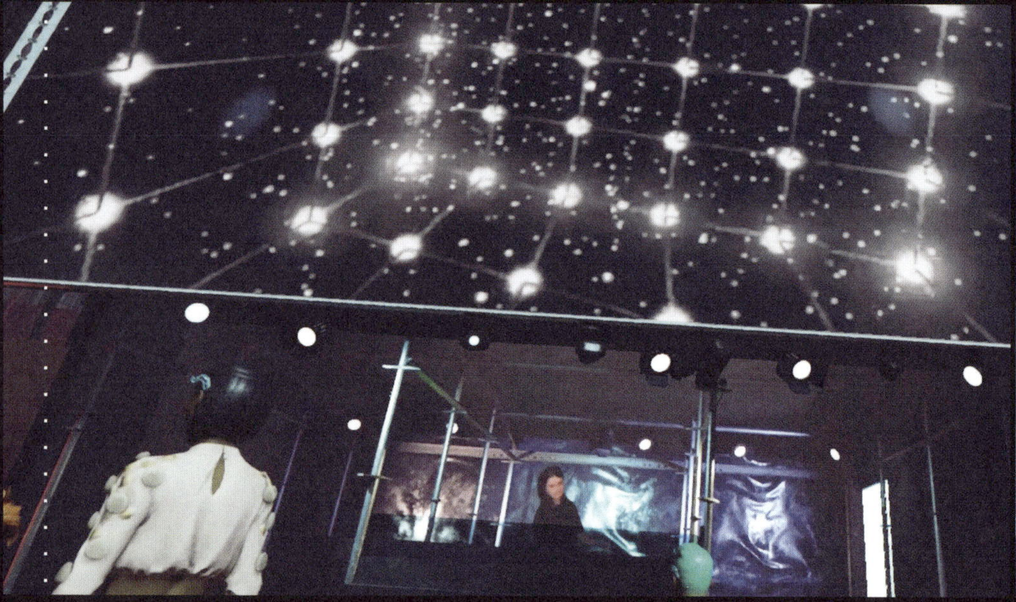

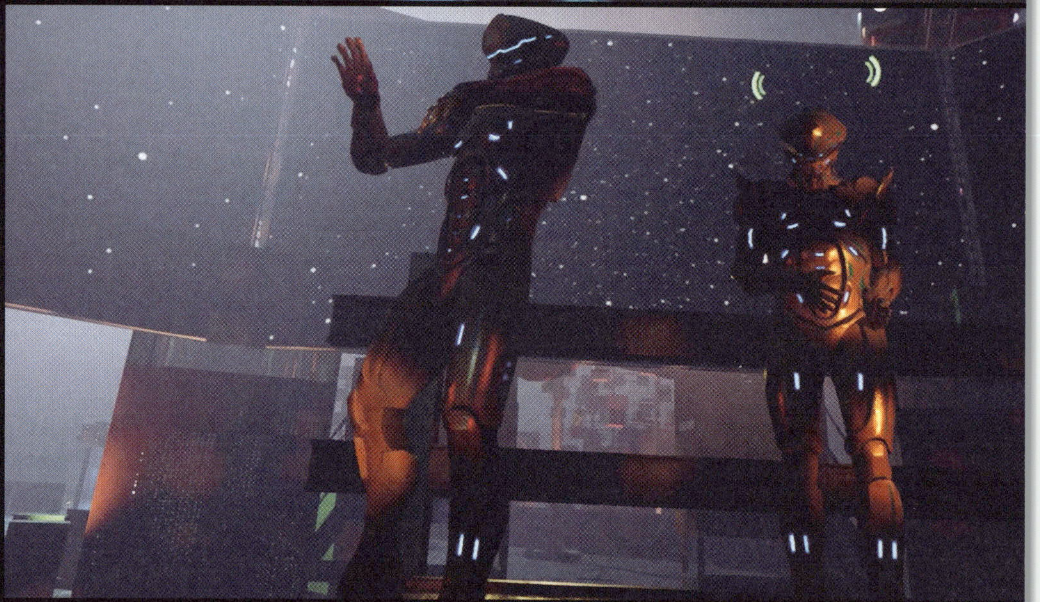

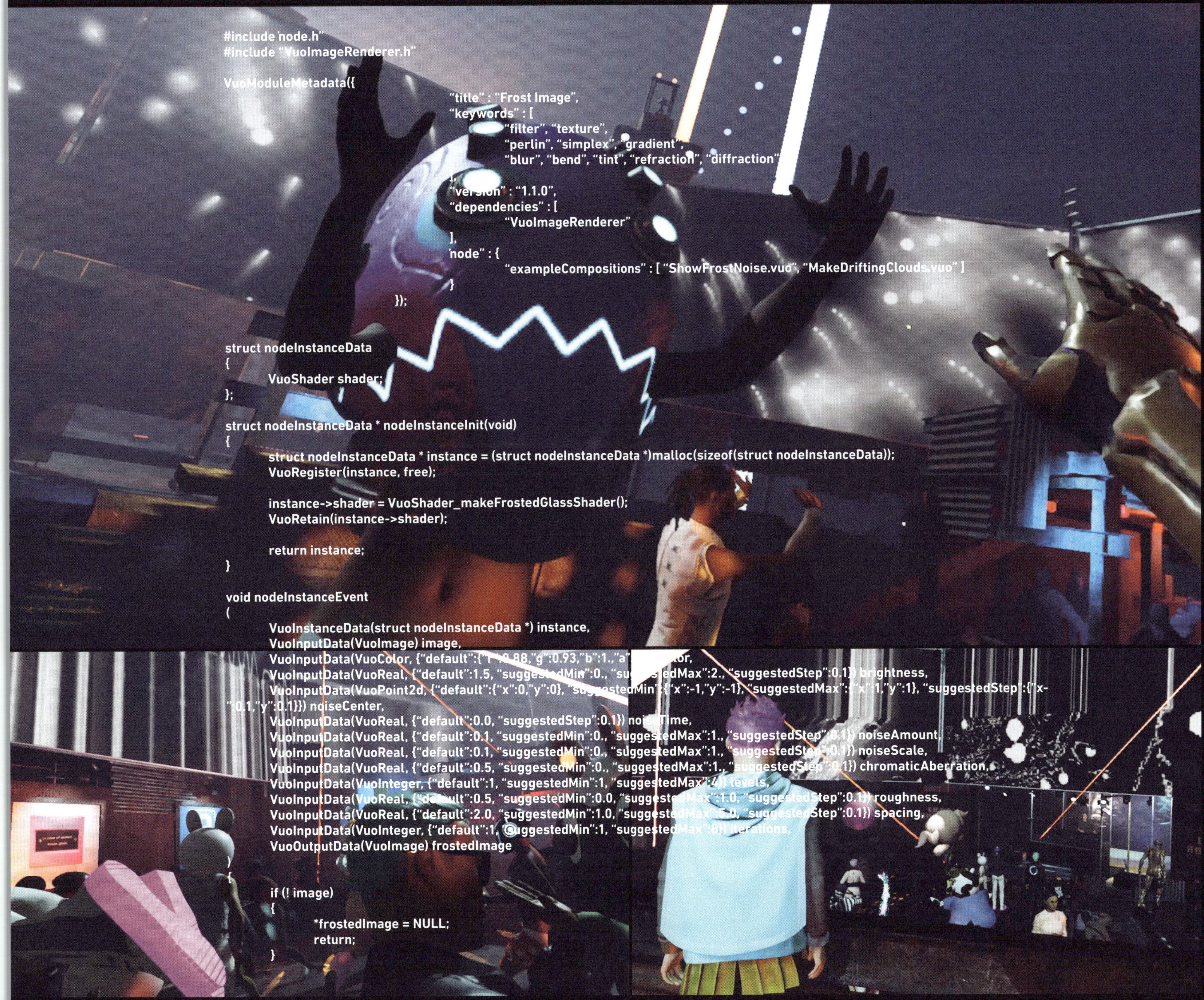

```
#include "node.h"
#include "VuoImageRenderer.h"

VuoModuleMetadata({
        "title" : "Frost Image",
        "keywords" : [
                "filter", "texture",
                "perlin", "simplex", "gradient",
                "blur", "bend", "tint", "refraction", "diffraction"
        ],
        "version" : "1.1.0",
        "dependencies" : [
                "VuoImageRenderer"
        ],
        "node" : {
                "exampleCompositions" : [ "ShowFrostNoise.vuo", "MakeDriftingClouds.vuo" ]
        }
});

struct nodeInstanceData
{
        VuoShader shader;
};

struct nodeInstanceData * nodeInstanceInit(void)
{
        struct nodeInstanceData * instance = (struct nodeInstanceData *)malloc(sizeof(struct nodeInstanceData));
        VuoRegister(instance, free);

        instance->shader = VuoShader_makeFrostedGlassShader();
        VuoRetain(instance->shader);

        return instance;
}

void nodeInstanceEvent
(
        VuoInstanceData(struct nodeInstanceData *) instance,
        VuoInputData(VuoImage) image,
        VuoInputData(VuoColor, {"default":{"r":0.88,"g":0.93,"b":1.,"a"[illegible]tor,
        VuoInputData(VuoReal, {"default":1.5, "suggestedMin":0., "suggestedMax":2., "suggestedStep":0.1}) brightness,
        VuoInputData(VuoPoint2d, {"default":{"x":0,"y":0}, "suggestedMin":{"x":-1,"y":-1}, "suggestedMax":{"x":1,"y":1}, "suggestedStep":{"x-
":0.1,"y":0.1}}) noiseCenter,
        VuoInputData(VuoReal, {"default":0.0, "suggestedStep":0.1}) noiseTime,
        VuoInputData(VuoReal, {"default":0.1, "suggestedMin":0., "suggestedMax":1., "suggestedStep":0.1}) noiseAmount,
        VuoInputData(VuoReal, {"default":0.1, "suggestedMin":0., "suggestedMax":1., "suggestedStep":0.1}) noiseScale,
        VuoInputData(VuoReal, {"default":0.5, "suggestedMin":0., "suggestedMax":1., "suggestedStep":0.1}) chromaticAberration,
        VuoInputData(VuoInteger, {"default":1, "suggestedMin":1, "suggestedMax":4}) levels,
        VuoInputData(VuoReal, {"default":0.5, "suggestedMin":0.0, "suggestedMax":1.0, "suggestedStep":0.1}) roughness,
        VuoInputData(VuoReal, {"default":2.0, "suggestedMin":1.0, "suggestedMax":5.0, "suggestedStep":0.1}) spacing,
        VuoInputData(VuoInteger, {"default":1, "suggestedMin":1, "suggestedMax":8}) iterations,
        VuoOutputData(VuoImage) frostedImage
)
{
        if (! image)
        {
                *frostedImage = NULL;
                return;
        }
```

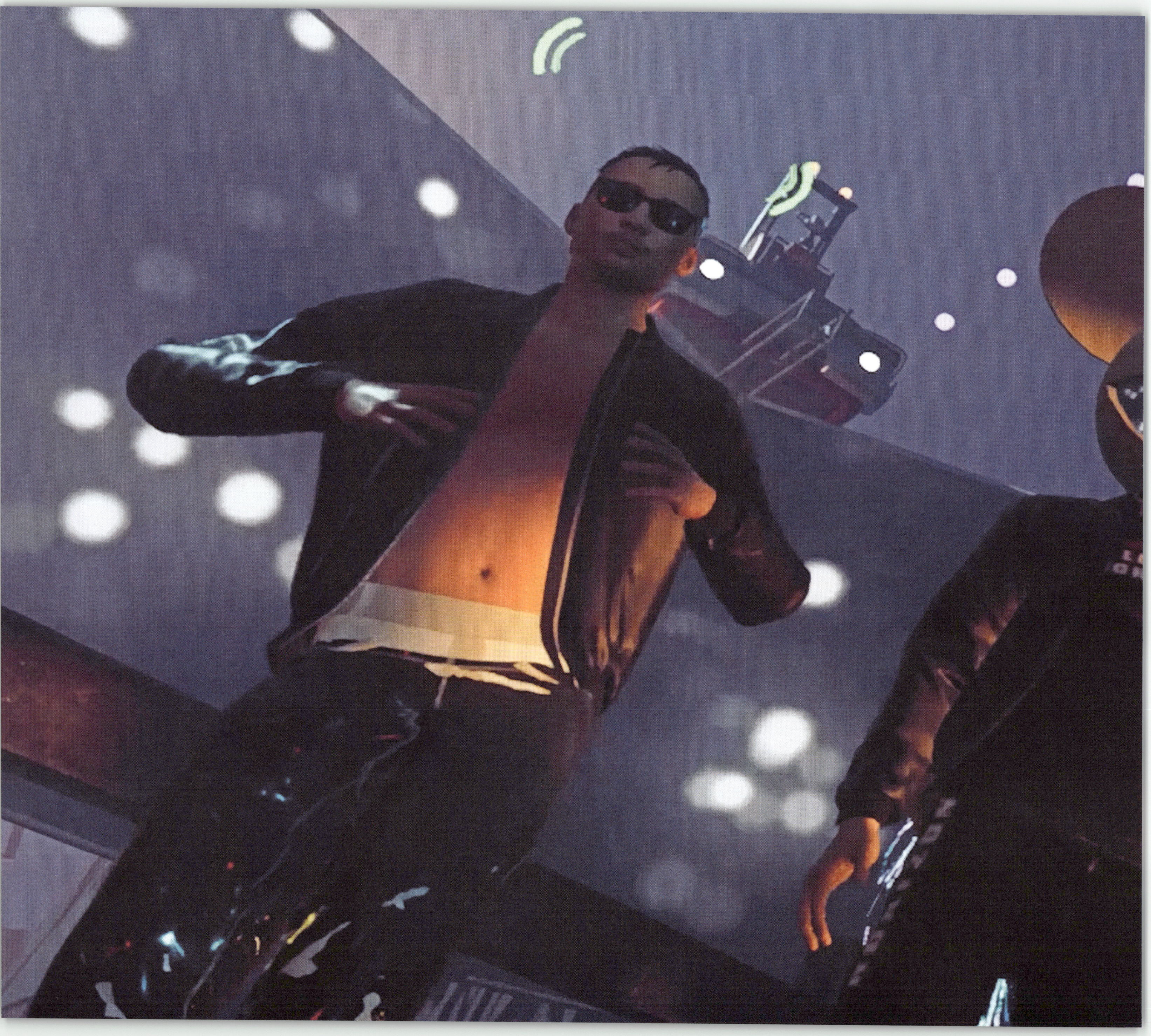

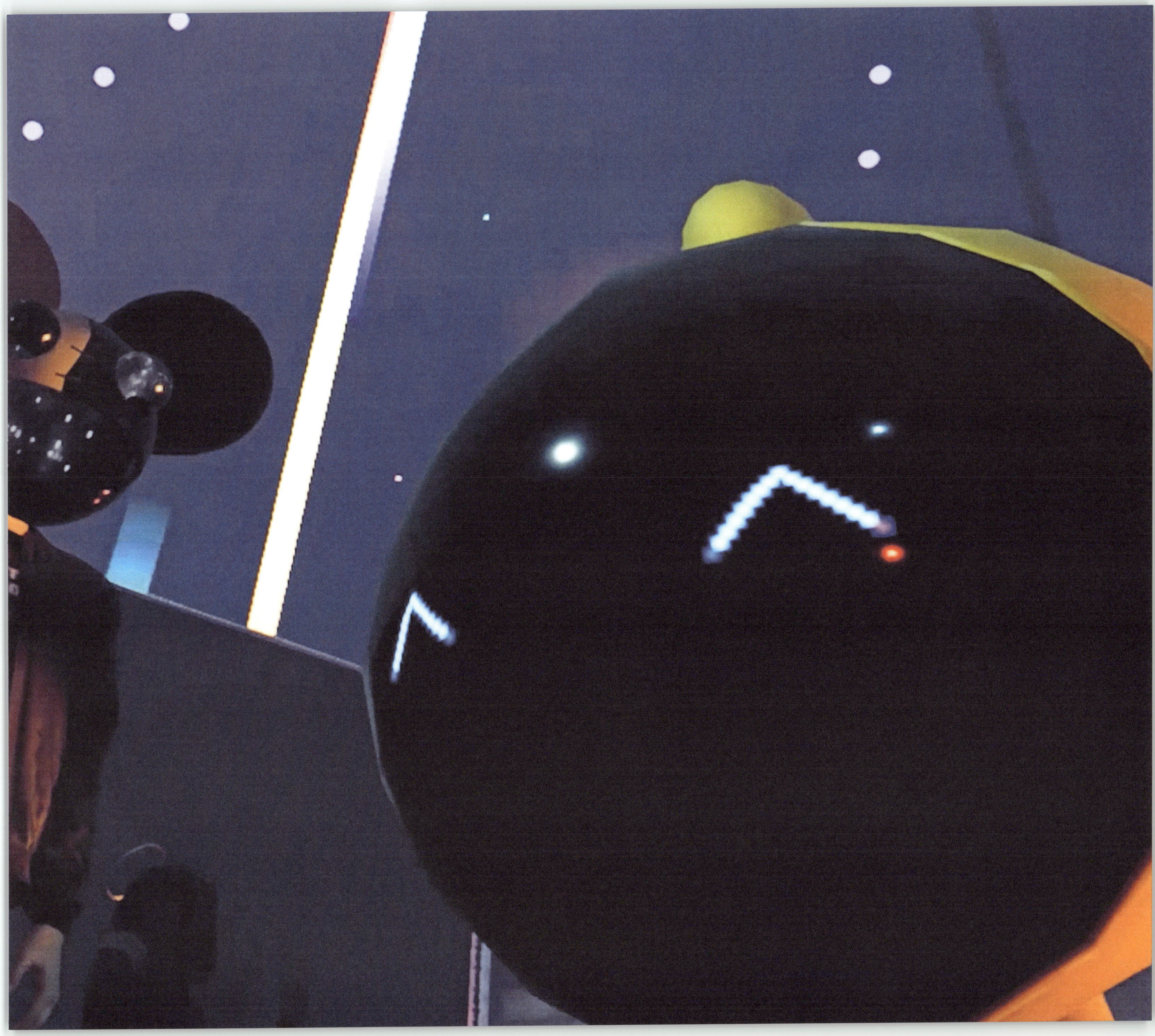

Name:

Dirk Koy

.
Info:

Dirk Koy graduated from the HGK Basel in the field of visual communication. He runs an office for motion design and experimental film Dirk Koy Bild und Bewegung.

Koy works as a lecturer for Time Based Media in the Institute of Visual Communication at the HGK Basel, University of Applied Sciences and Arts Northwestern Switzerland.

.
Project:

MUSIC VISUALIZATION OF THE YELLO SONG OUT OF SIGHT.

.
URL:

dirkkoy.com
vimeo.com/dirkkoy
twitter.com/dirkkoy

.
Instagram:

@dirkkoy

.
Video Credits:

DIrected / Video / Animation:
Dirk Koy
Audio Credits:
Music by Boris Blank
Lyrics by Dieter Meier
Published by:
Warner Chappell Music
Produced by Yello
Vocals:
Dieter Meier
Video Producer:
Dirk Koy
Mastering Engineer:
Ursli Weber

Music Video by Yello performing Out of Sight.

© 2020 Yello, under exclusive license to Universal Music GmbH

Project Description:

The visualization concept for the YELLO SONG OUT OF SIGHT comes from a series of animations I started at the end of 2019. The series is called Shape Studies, in which photographs and video recordings of places, objects, and living beings are modified digitally. In the process, the subject permanently takes on new forms.

I am interested in the space between natural and digital environments.

It's an investigation of the interface between the real and the digital.

The electropop duo Yello, consisting of Dieter Meier and Boris Blank, often make digital modifications to authentic sound recordings, such as voices and noises, and build their sound worlds from these and other elements.

I liked the idea that by taking up the Shape Studies idea on the visual level, something similar occurs in the design process, interweaving natural and digital elements.

When I first heard the song, it immediately reminded me of a dance scene.

Therefore, it was self-evident to create something related to dance. But since my knowledge of dance leaves a lot to be desired, I decided to rethink my ideas. Instead, vegetables and fruit dance to the music, and the singers distort in time to the music, respectively digitally set in motion.

This process gives the whole thing a dadaistic touch.

The rapid changes of form are an allusion to the fleeting nature of the encounter described in the song lyrics.

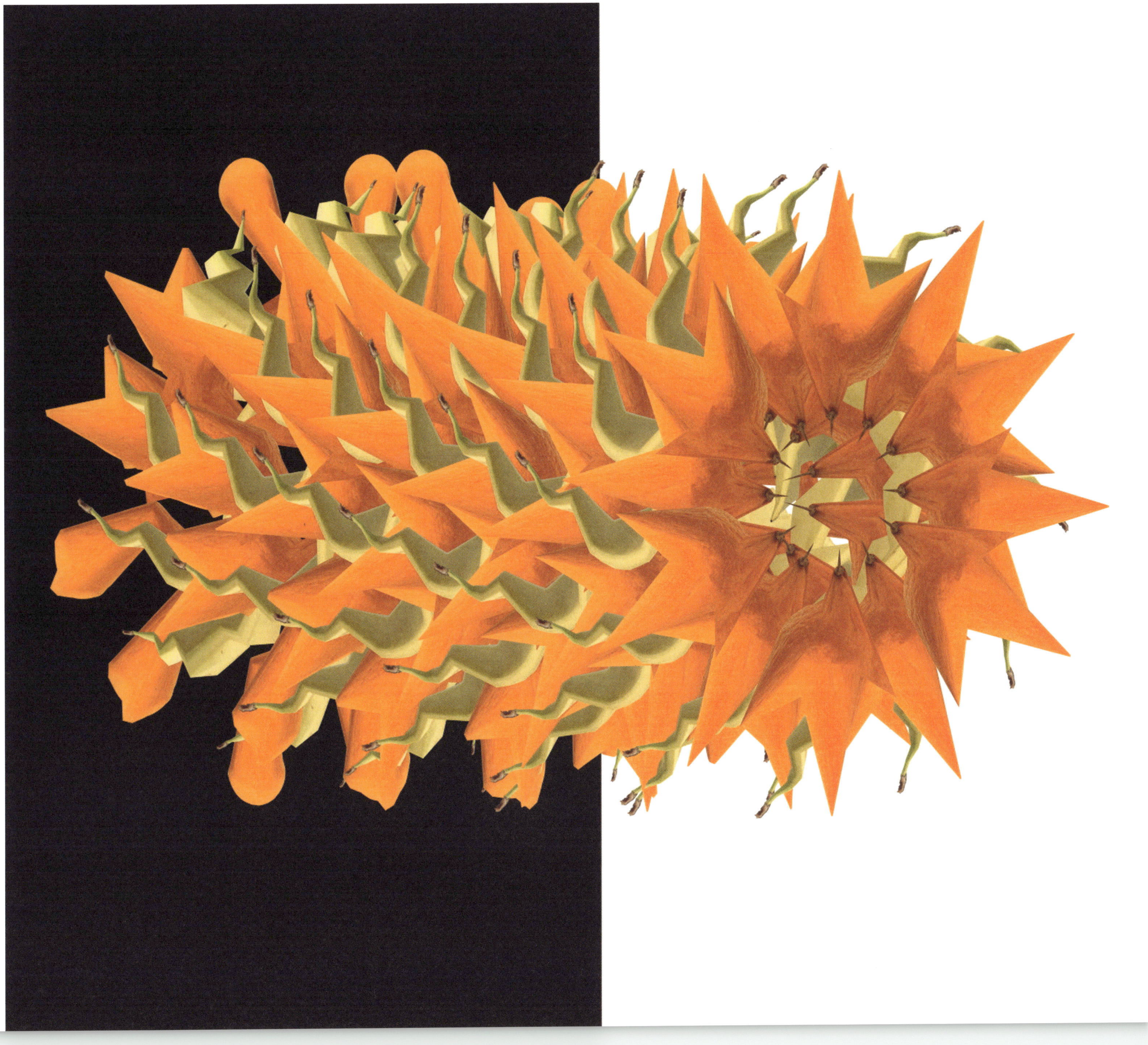

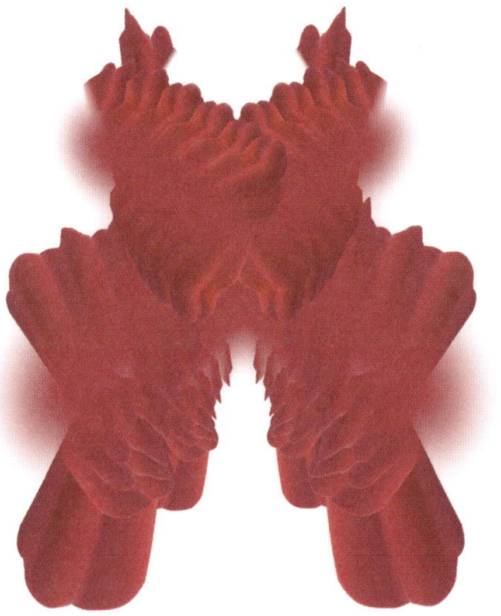

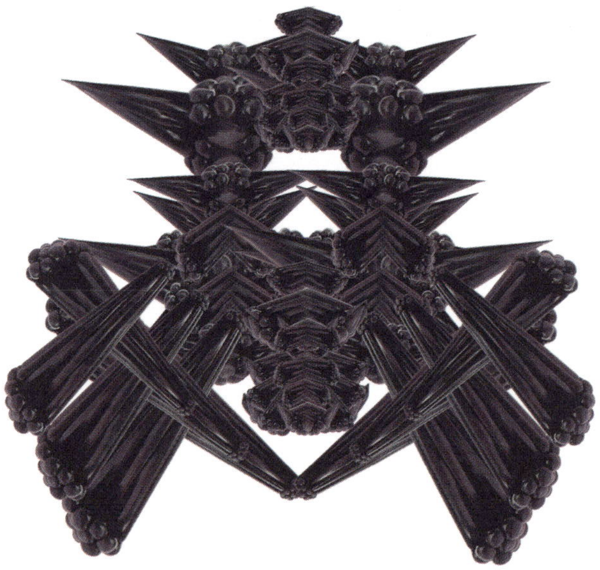

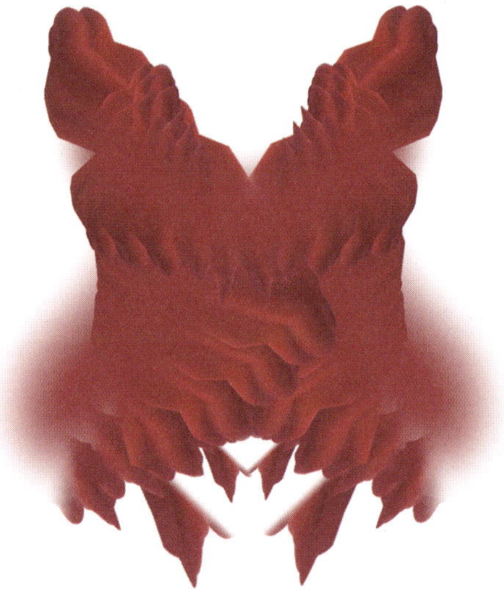

The first phase was to test the movements and staggering of the fruit and vegetables. In the beginning, there were also attempts to integrate certain words of the song in the form of moving typography into the music visualization.

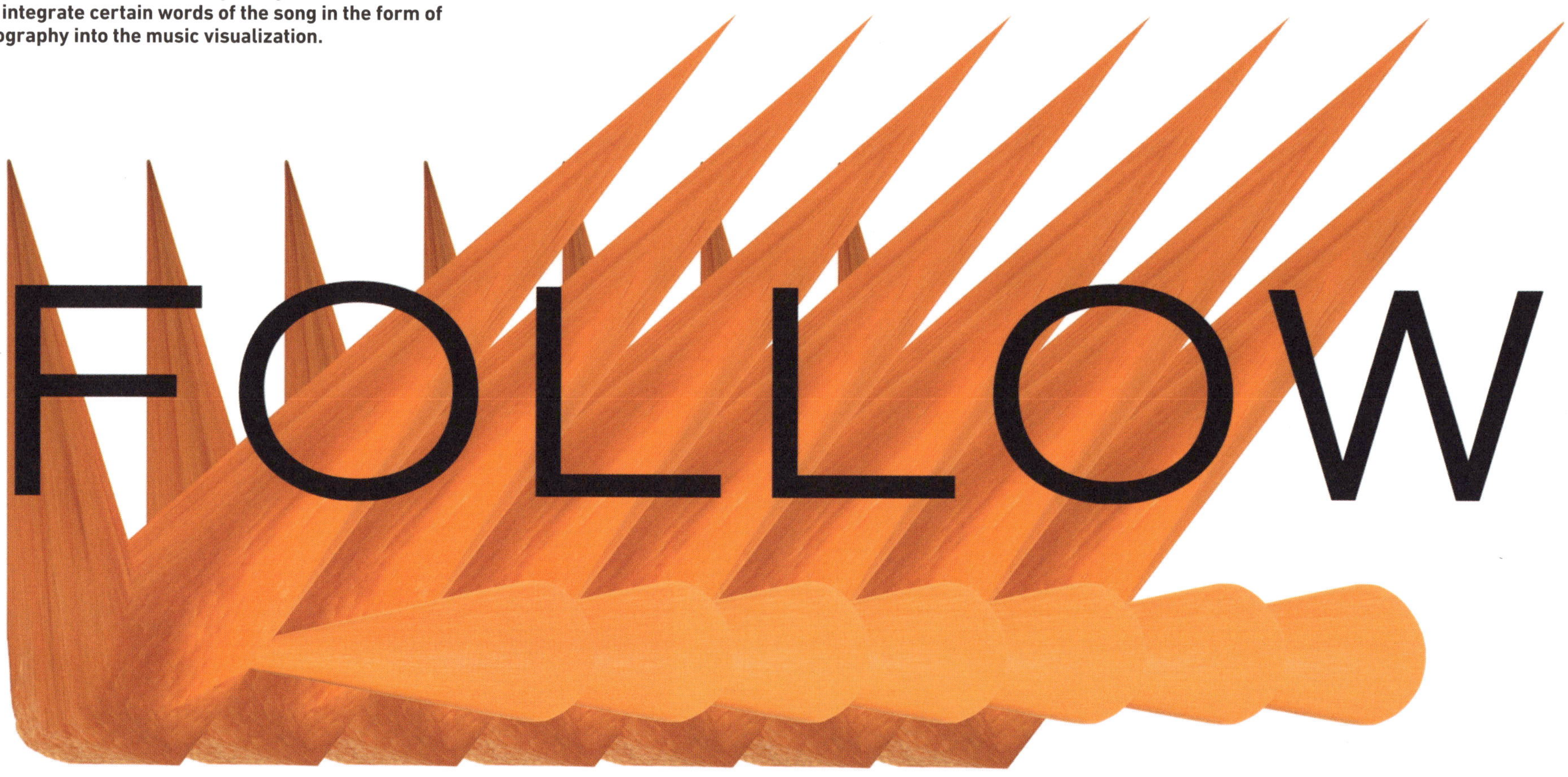

Based on the work Shape Study 10, an animation that shows me in various deformations, I developed the digital interventions on the video recordings of Dieter Meier and Boris Blank.

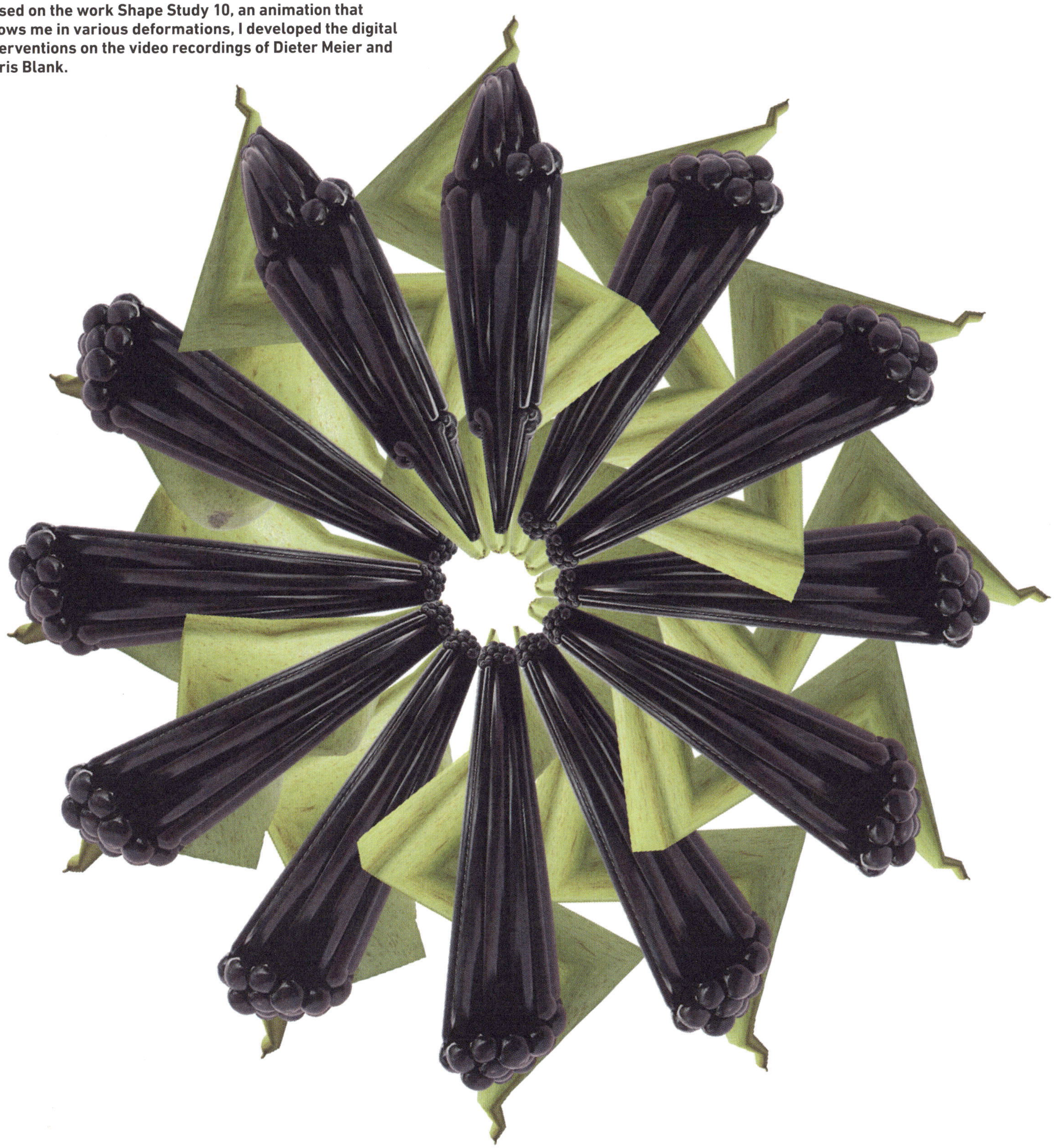

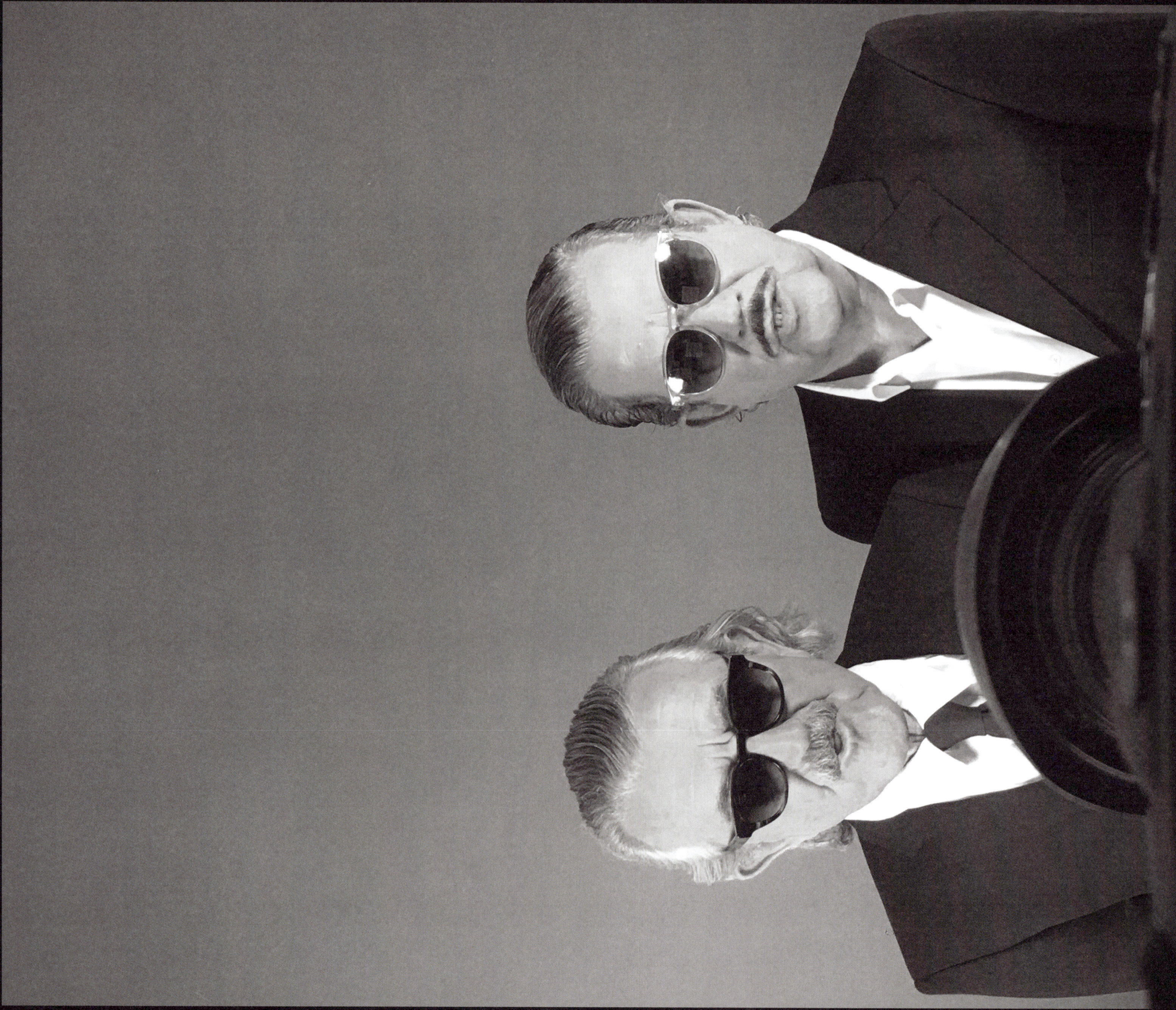

190 . Dirk Koy

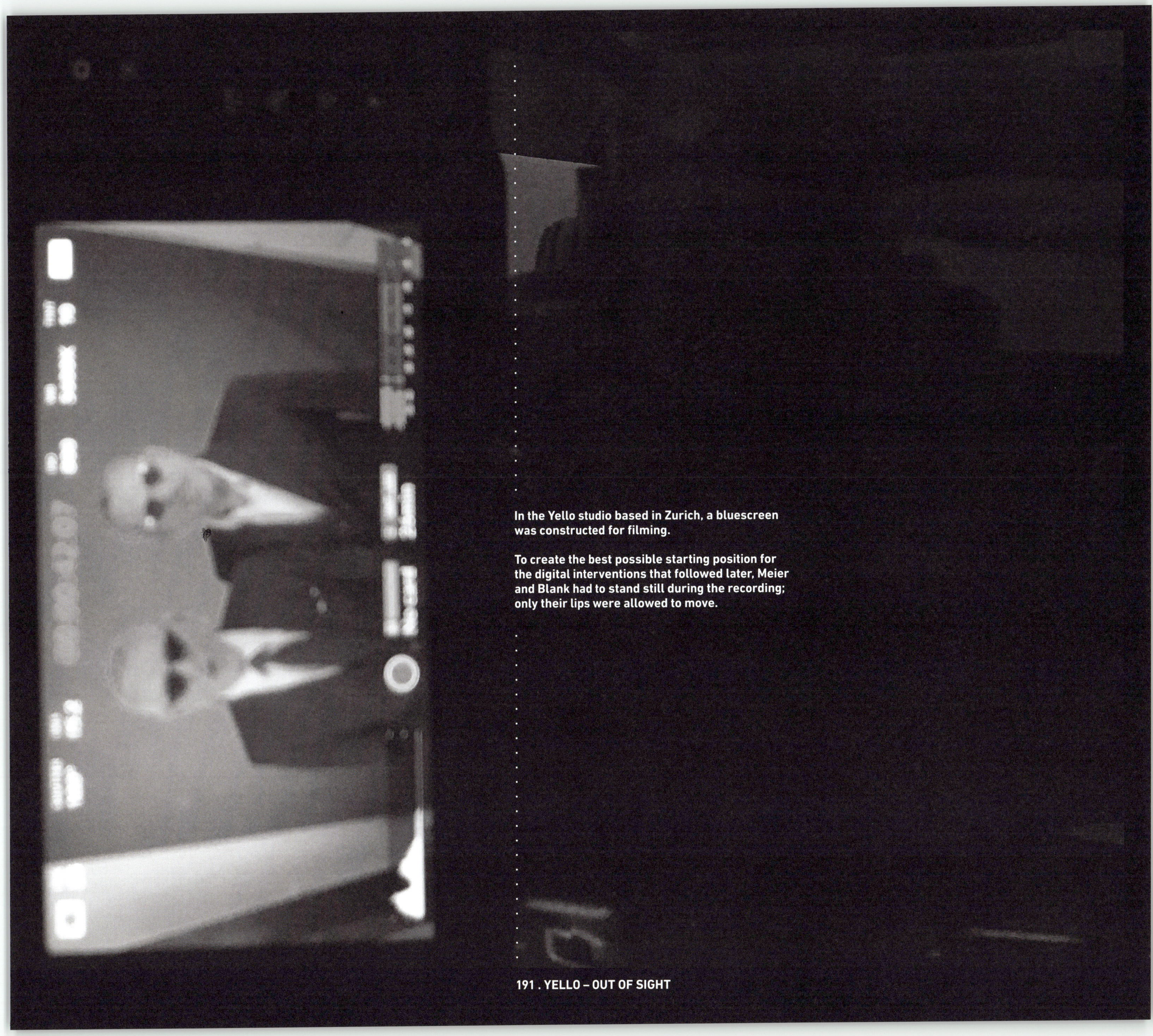

In the Yello studio based in Zurich, a bluescreen was constructed for filming.

To create the best possible starting position for the digital interventions that followed later, Meier and Blank had to stand still during the recording; only their lips were allowed to move.

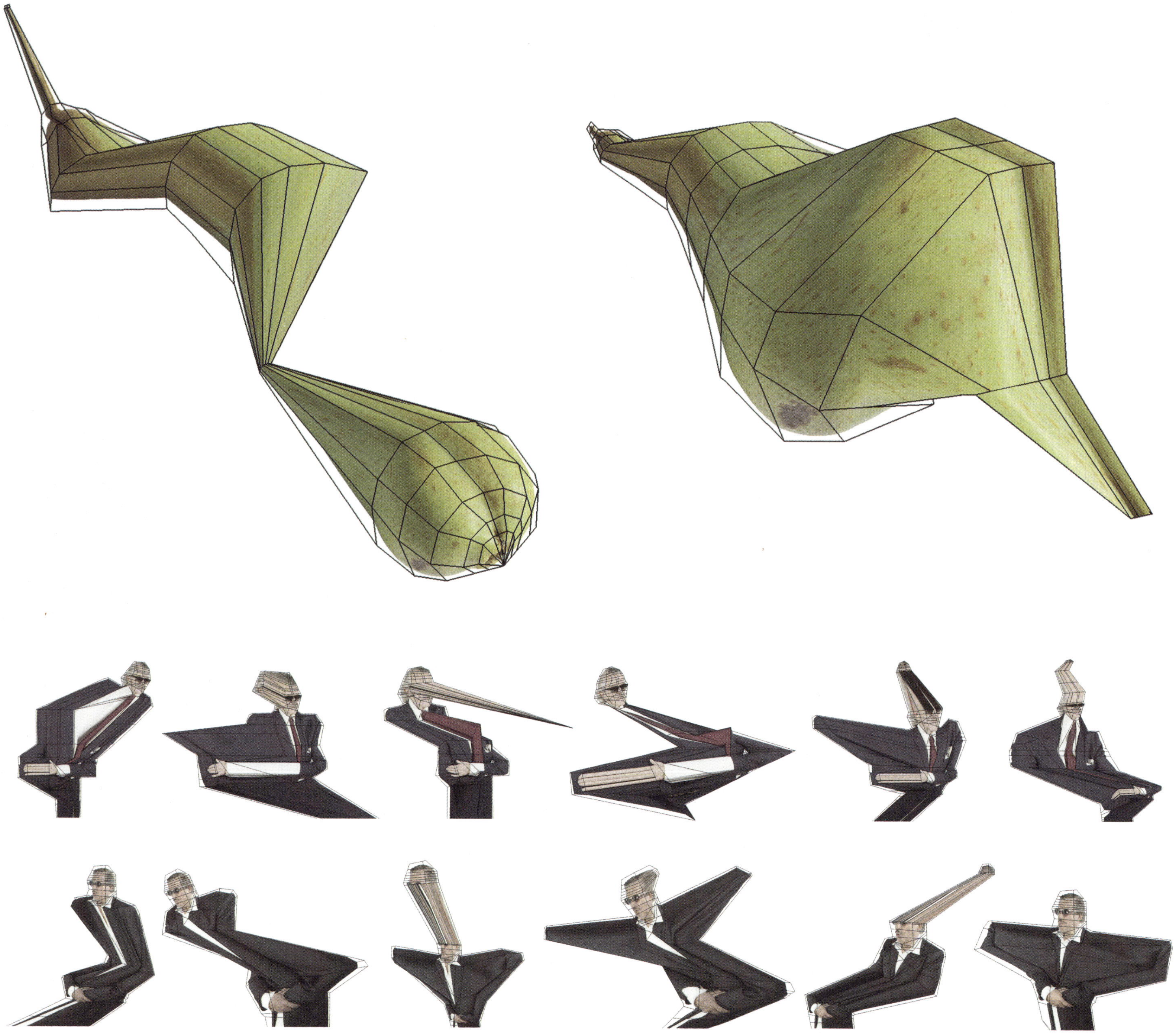

192 . Dirk Koy

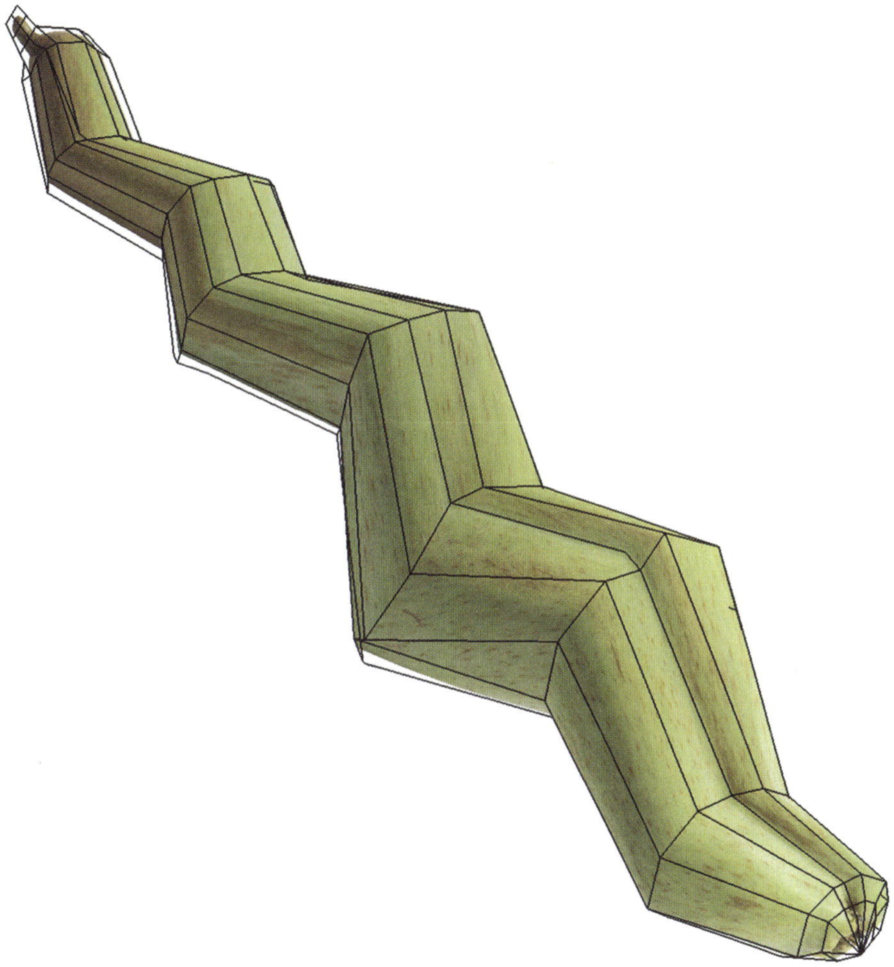

A very time-consuming moment was the splitting of the static and filmed templates into their components.

This process had drawing quality since it captured the objects and people in a kind of framework.

After that, I was able to design the individual changes of form.

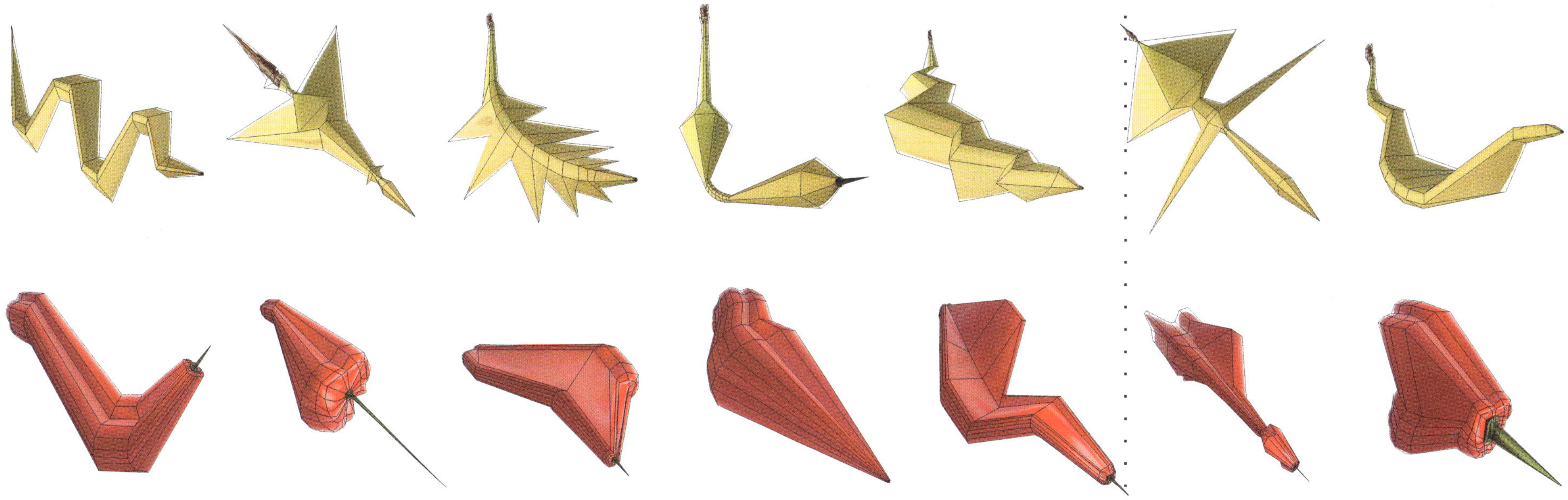

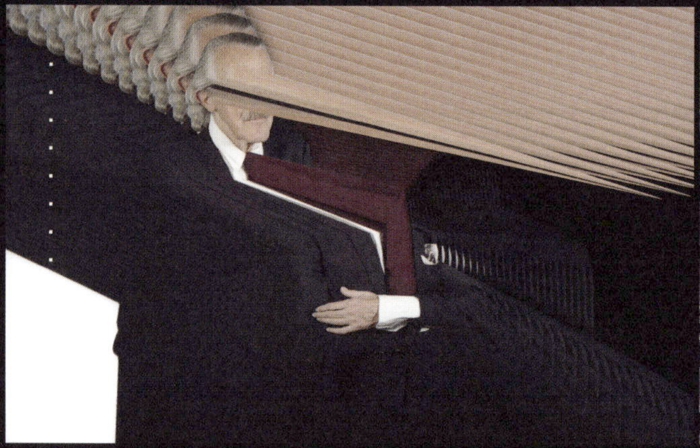

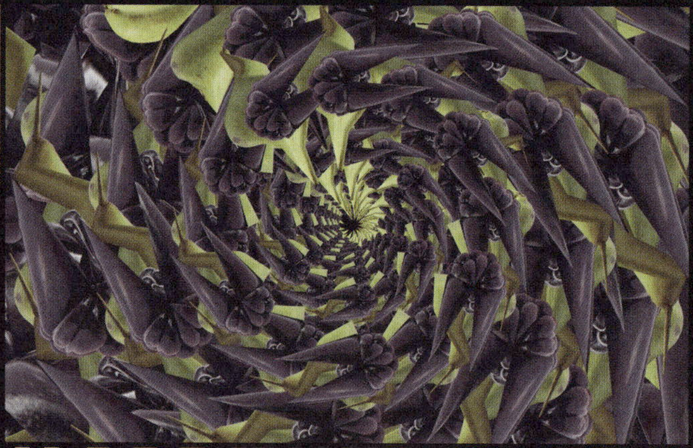

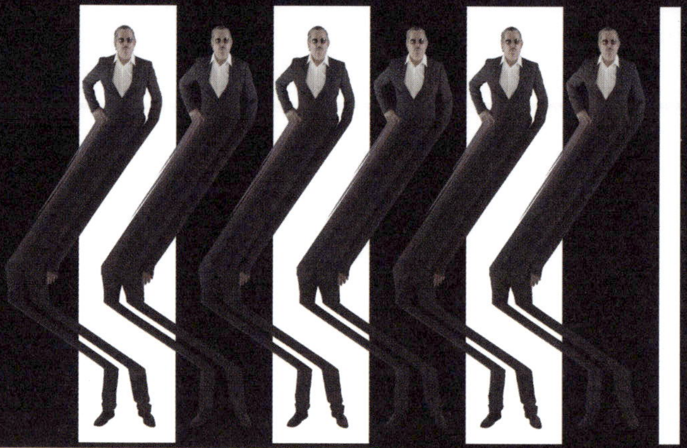

In the final compositing, I added the background.

Based on the song lyrics part "To the left, to the right," I came up with the idea of bisecting the background into a white and black area and animating the spaces from left to right and vice versa.

It was often challenging to create a smooth transition from one scene to another in the edit. In this case, the black and white stripes of the background helped a lot.

By increasing the speed of movement of the stripes before editing, it was possible to link the different scenes better together.

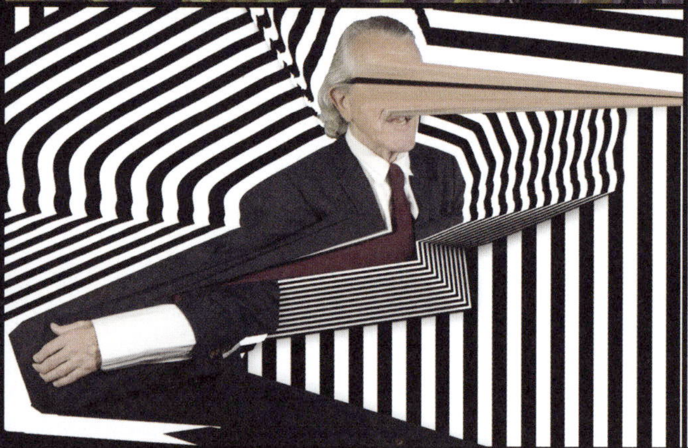

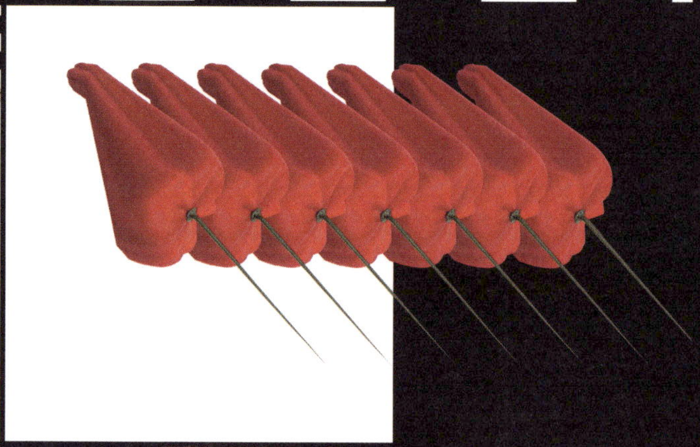

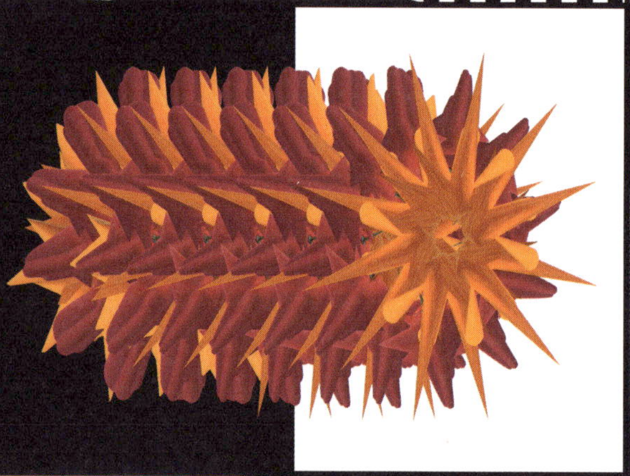

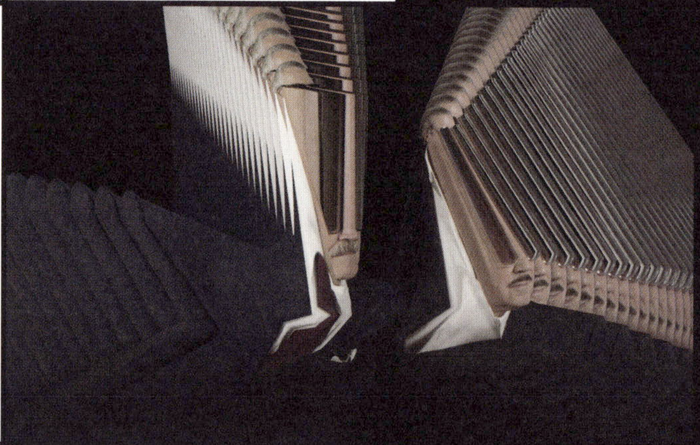

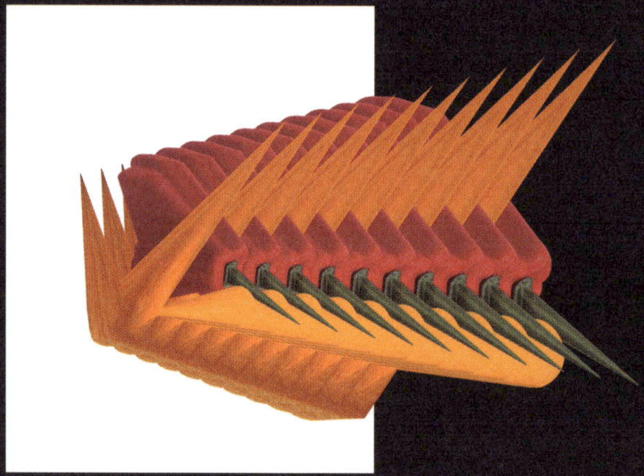

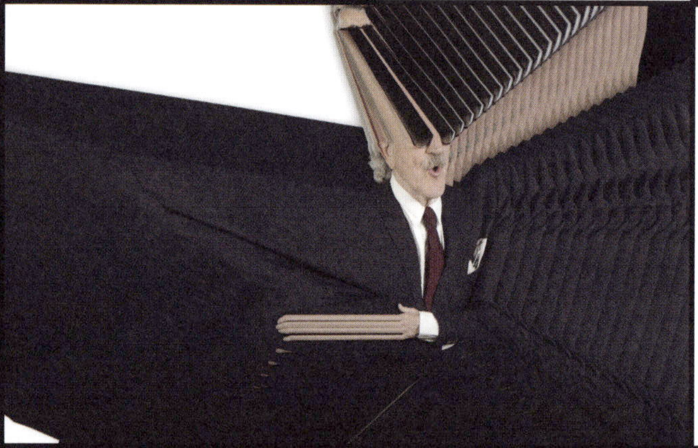

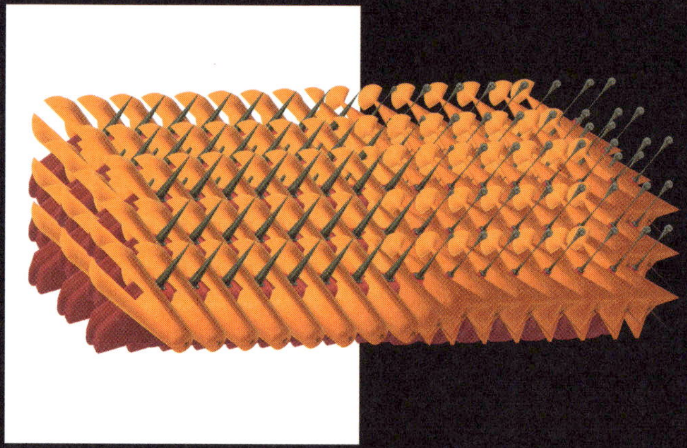

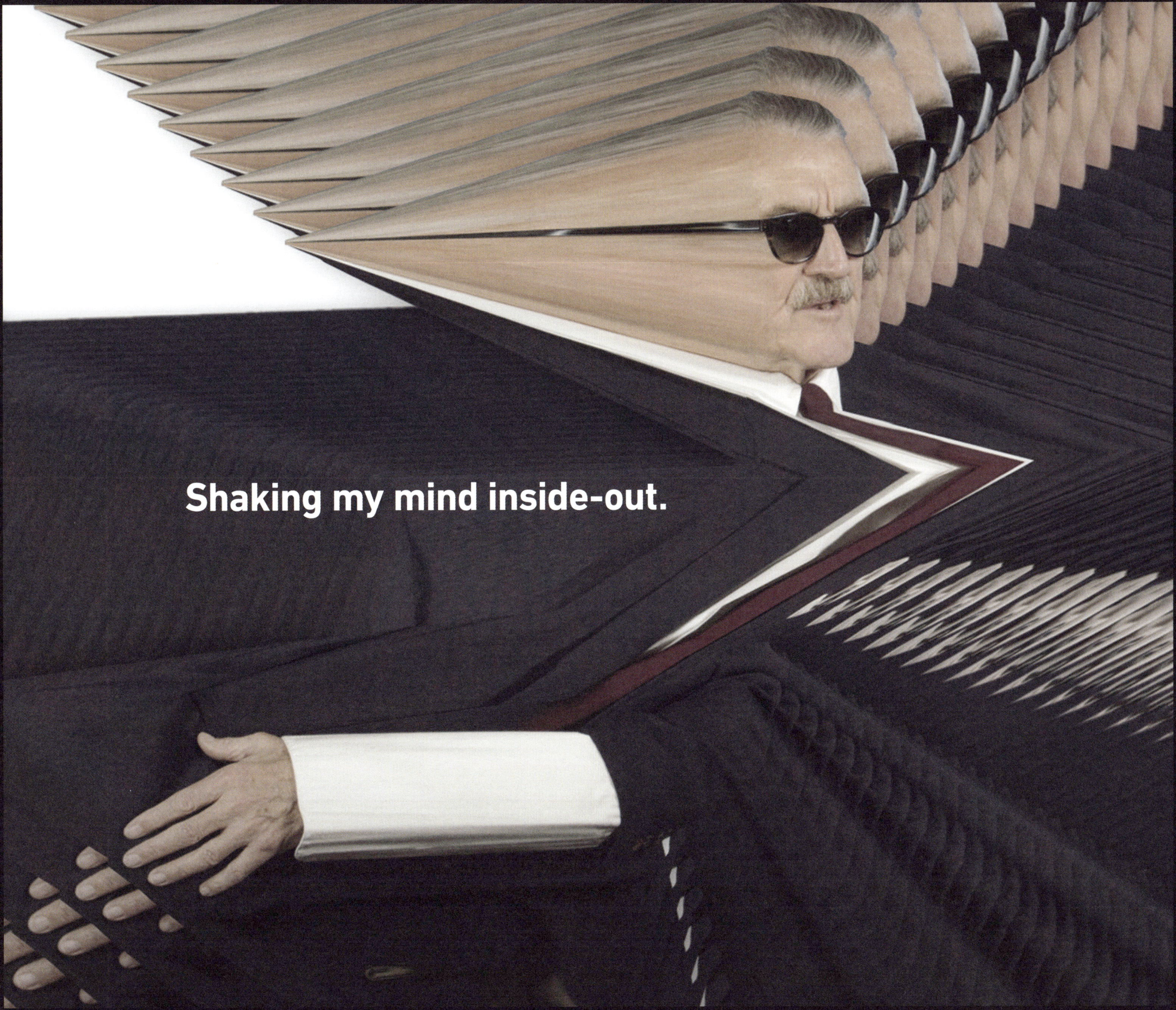

195 . YELLO – OUT OF SIGHT

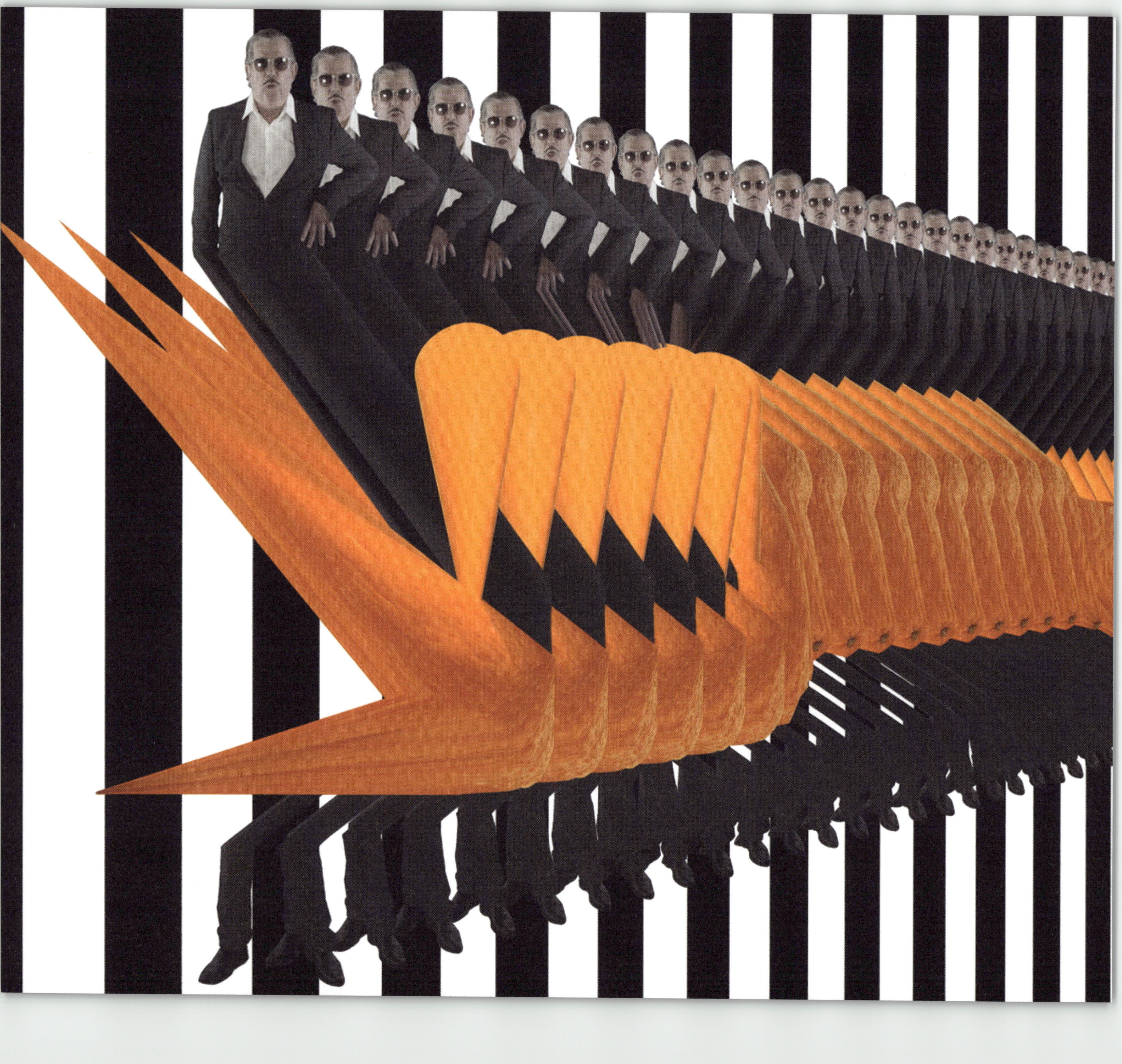

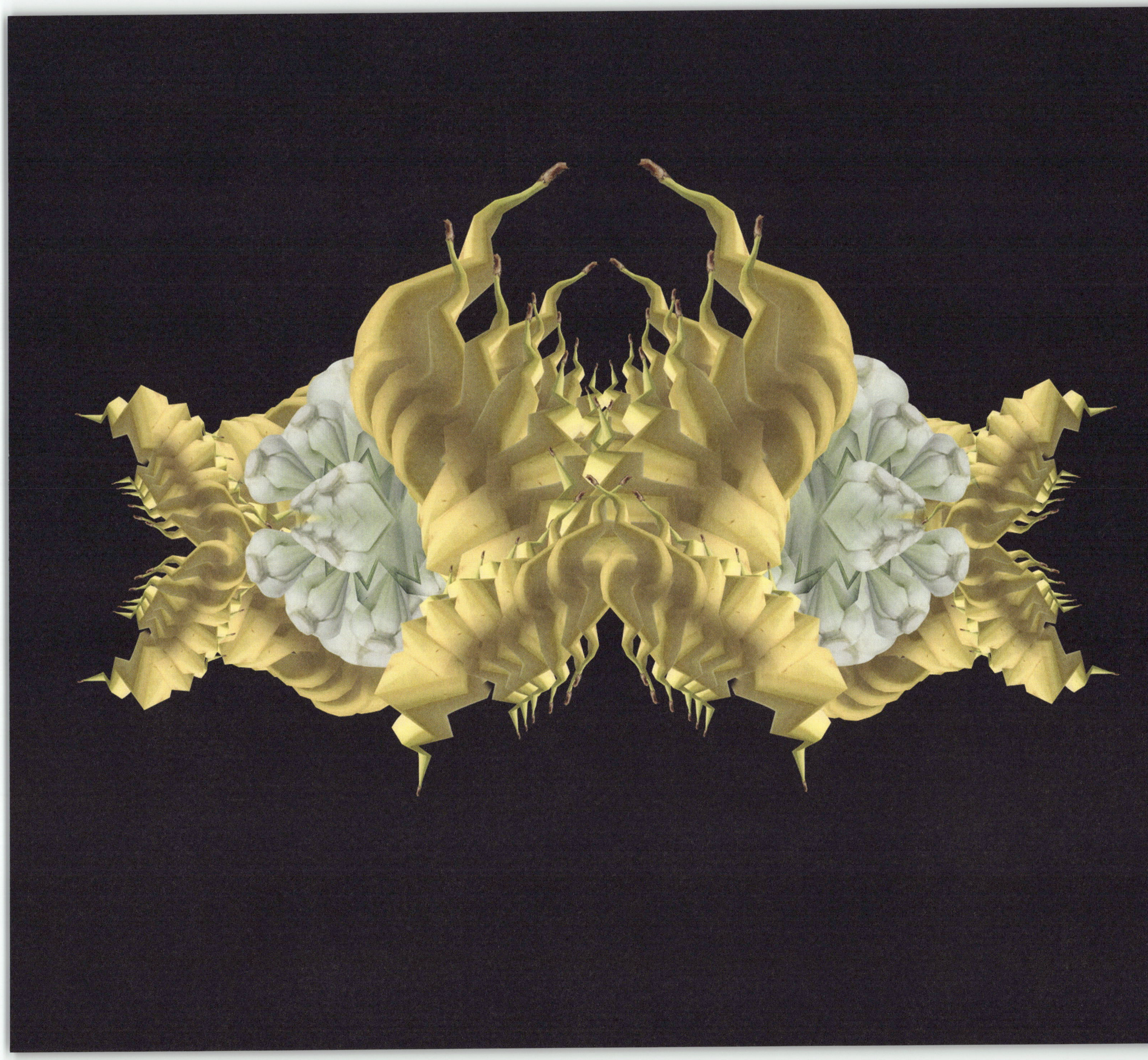

Th om as Ku rp pa
An dr ea s Pi hl st rö m

Name:

Thomas Kurppa
CEO Kurppa Hosk
&
Andreas Pihlström
suprb™

Info:

Thomas Kurppa is co-founder and the Chief Creative Officer of Kurppa Hosk. He began his career as a producer of electronic music in the early 90s. He started a number of small labels where he produced underground music and designed album covers. Thomas received his professional training at Forsberg School of Design in Stockholm.

In the late 90s he moved to London to work at Wallpaper* Magazine as a designer. Returning to Sweden, he joined Stockholm Design Lab as a Senior Designer 2002, where he was deeply involved in successful projects for IKEA, Scandinavian Airlines and Stadium, among others. In 2009, he co-founded Kurppa Hosk.

Andreas Pihlström, born and raised in Stockholm, Sweden. Electronic music, design, code, digital and physical art are all great passions. Pihlström has served as creative director at Pinterest, designer at Beats Music, partner and creative director at design agency Kurppa Hosk and creative director at the Spotify-backed company Soundtrack. He is also the founder of companies and projects such as Chroma, the electronic music discovery engine Plect, the graffiti art exhibition Underground Classics, the image bookmarking service Dropular, and Grid-A-Licious the grid layout system.

Project:

SEMANTIC MACHINE INTERPRETATIONS

URL:

kurppahosk.com
suprb.com

Instagram:

@kurppa
@suprb

Project Description:

The data generated here is on everything we can obtain; the typography and letters, the curves, anchor points, contrasts, lines, mass, kerning, spacing, the size of the letter itself, and its entire meaning.

We summarized each element and built functions that were composed generatively and created rhythm visually.

We employed visible aspects to this also, dependent on how fast we typed, how short or long the words were, and if the letters were lower or uppercase. These actions would affect the visual rhythm drastically.

In the end, we applied variable sources, for example, lyrics from a diverse list of songs, subtitles from movies, and we kept adding. What we discovered was something beautiful. Instead of visualizing the sound as intended or as anticipated, we saw an alternative narrative start to be expressed and designed for us.

The connection between what we read and what we saw became an impressive and exciting match.

Appearance D56 D98
colorless gas,
liquid or solid

Standard D42 D39
atomic weight

Ar, std(N)
[14.00643, 14.00728]

D31

Atomic number
(Z)7

Group 15 E33
(pnictogen

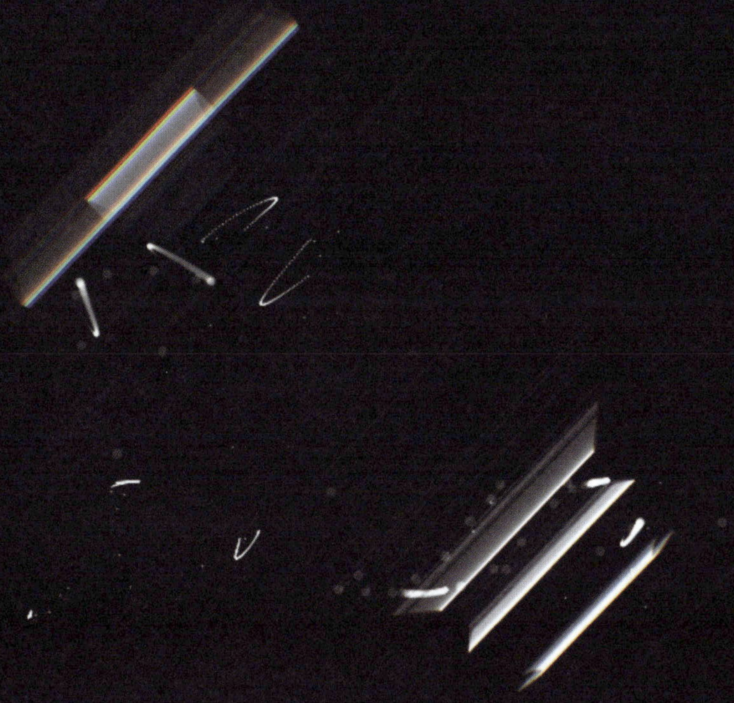

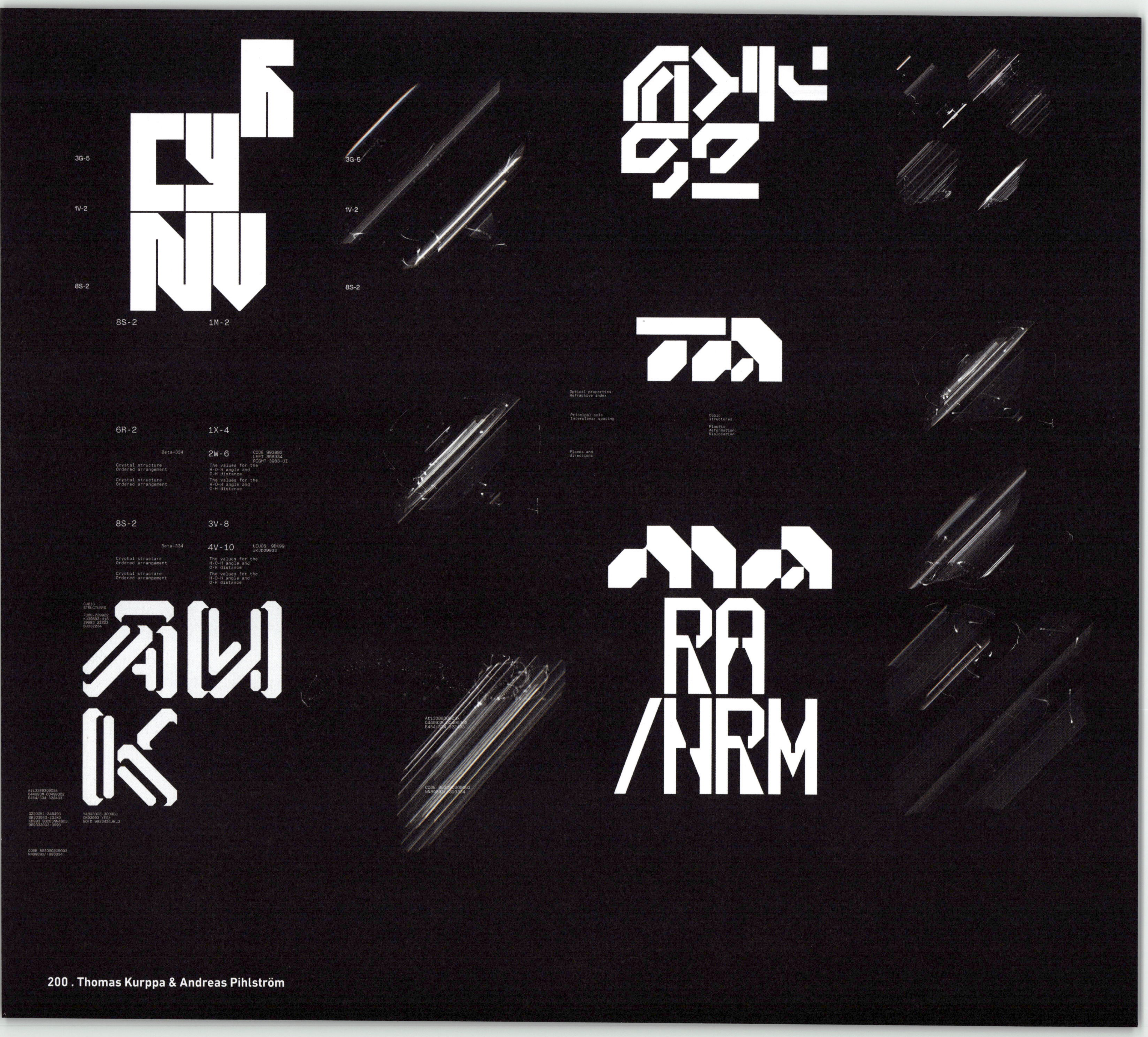

200 . Thomas Kurppa & Andreas Pihlström

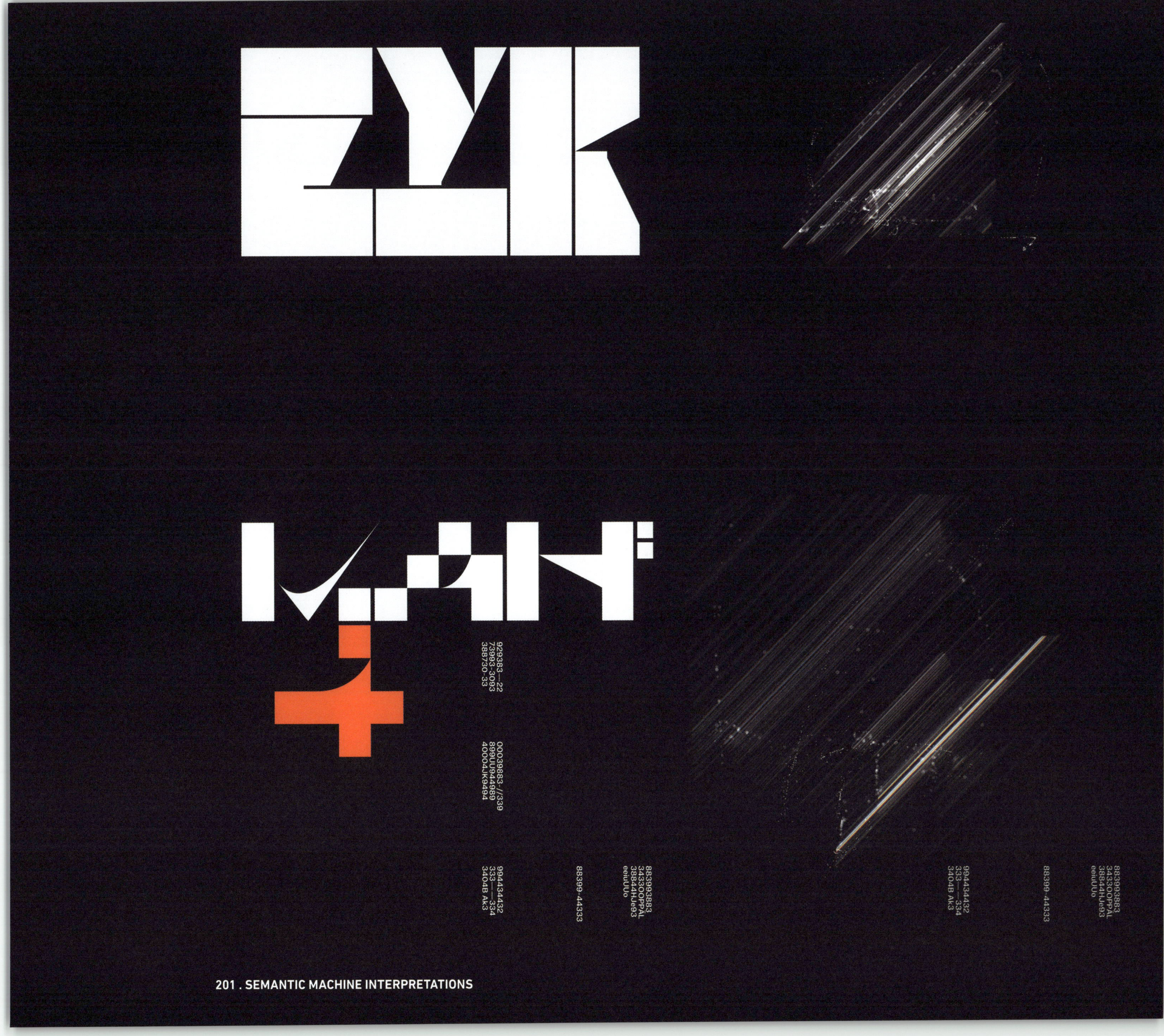

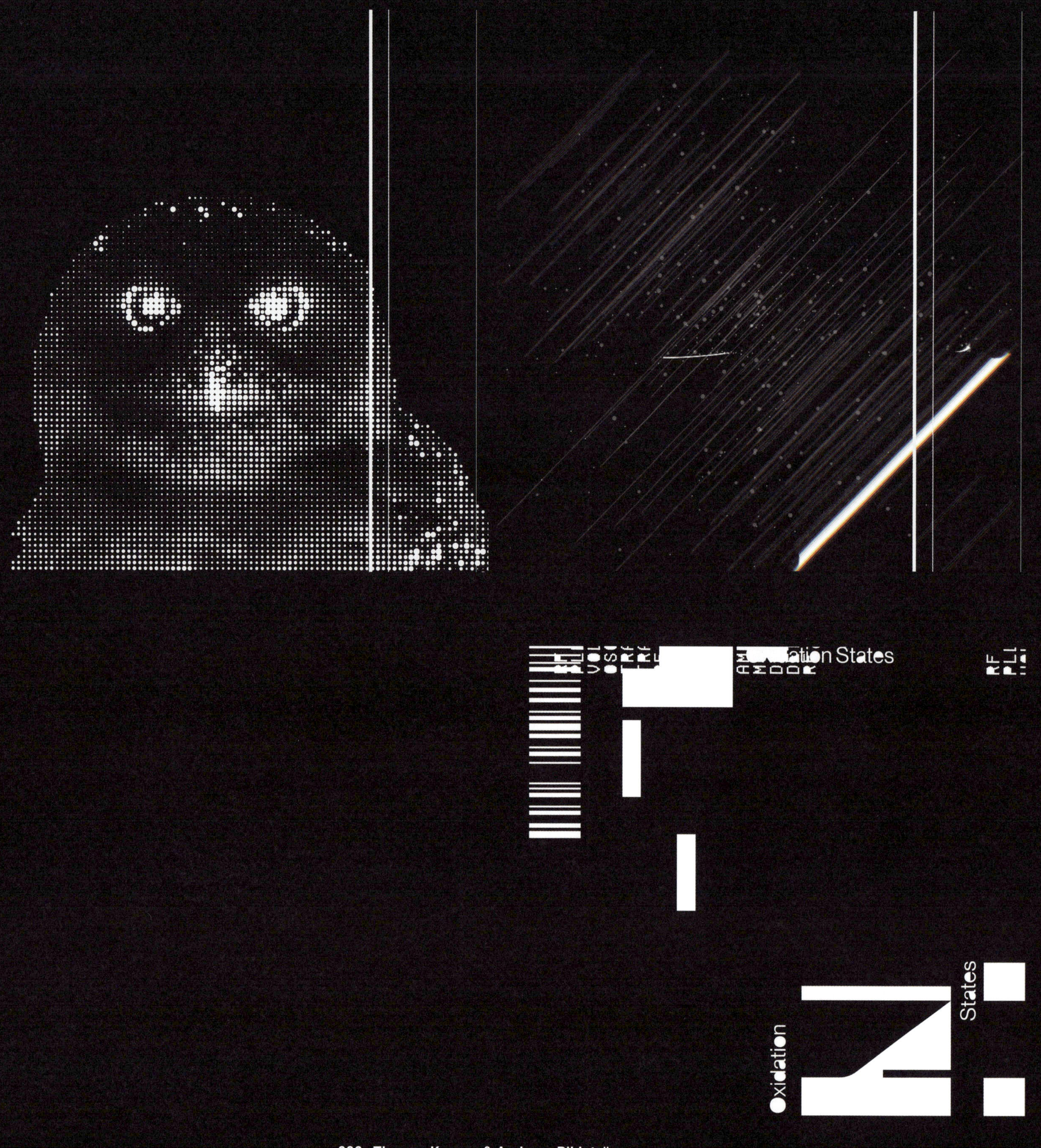

202 . Thomas Kurppa & Andreas Pihlström

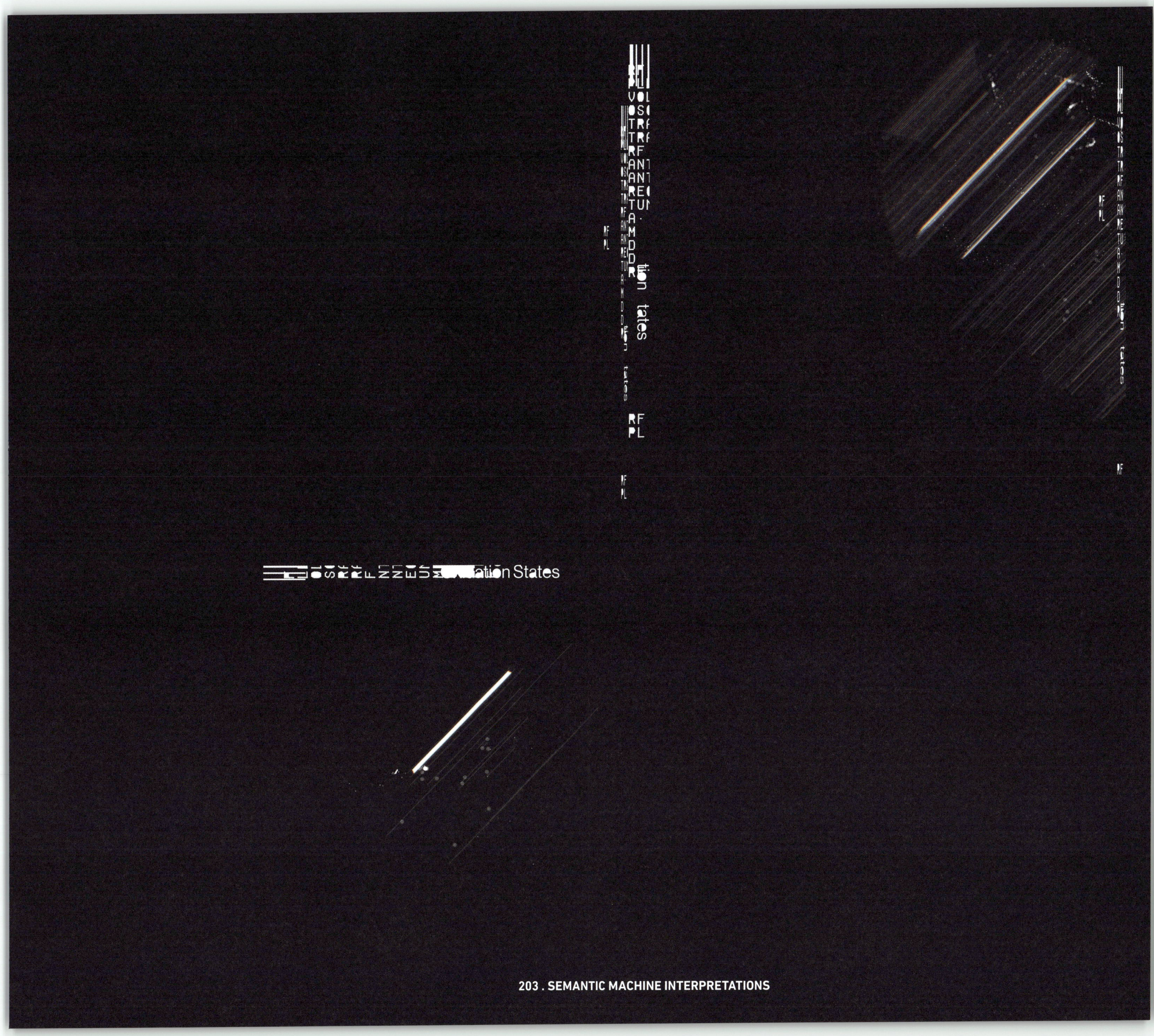
ation States
tates
RF
PL

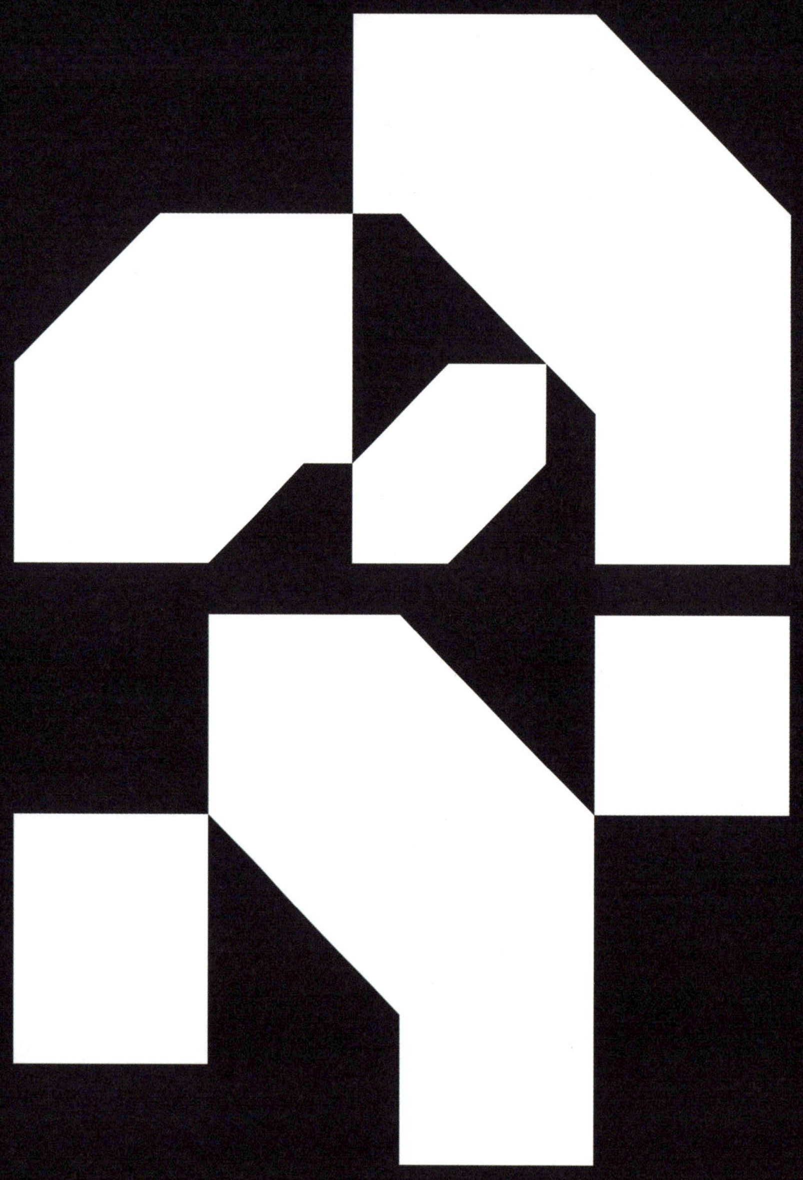

204 . Thomas Kurppa & Andreas Pihlström

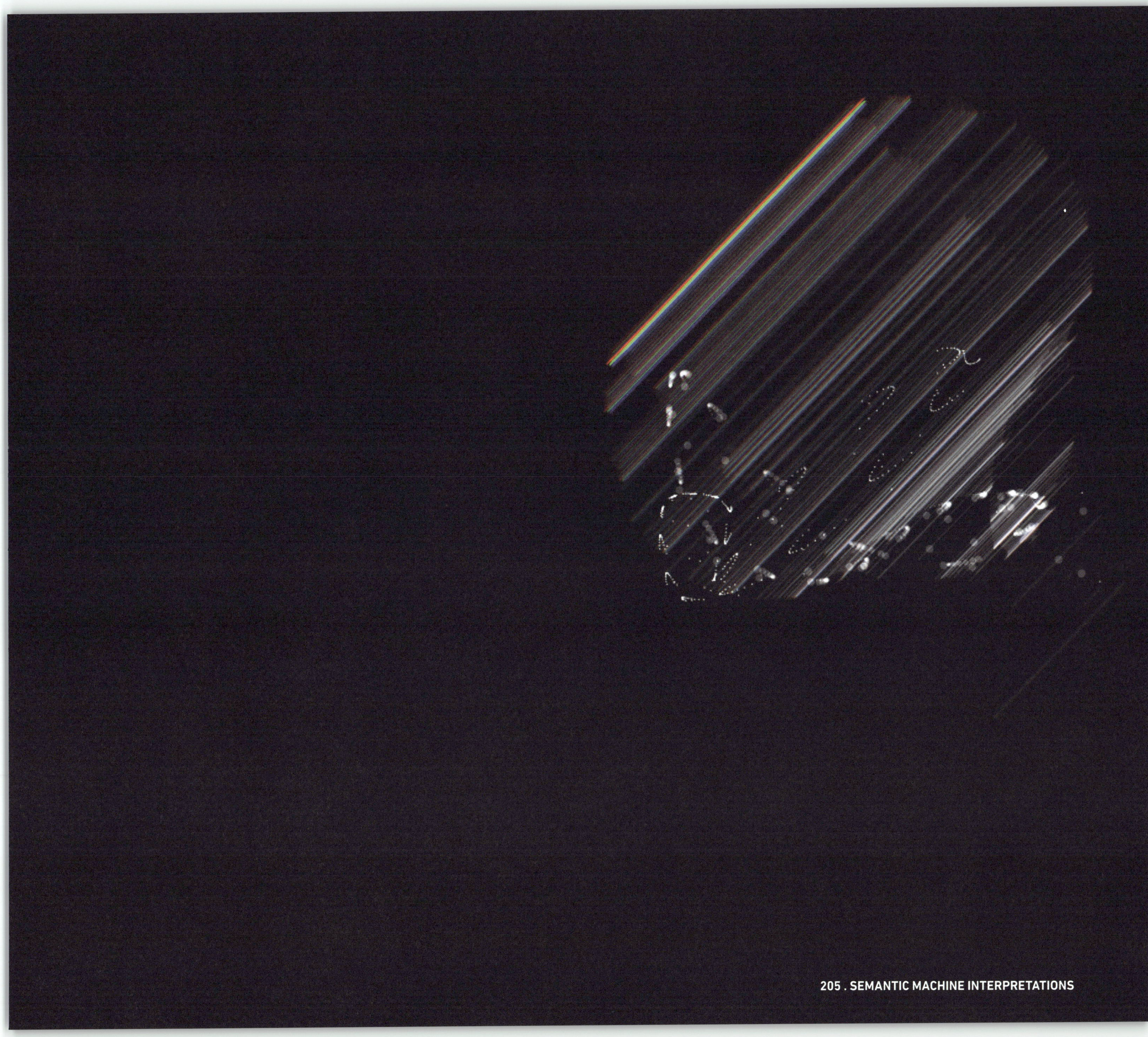

Zach Lieberman

Name:

Zach Lieberman

Info:

I am an artist and educator based in New York City. I create artwork with code and focus on building experimental drawing and animation tools. I make interactive environments that invite participants to become performers.

My main focus is how computation can be used as a medium for poetry.

Sketches:

First, I post sketches I make with software daily on Instagram. I have been doing this for over a year, and recently I wrote about the process.

Teaching:

I helped create the School for Poetic Computation in 2013 with friends after teaching for a decade at Parsons School of Design. We wanted to create a low-cost, alternative school where students could come for short ten-week sessions that were a mixture of an artist residency and an intensive seminar. At SFPC, we explore how electricity, code, and theory can be used to make poetry.

Writing:

I sometimes write on medium, here is an article about open office hours which I do once a week. I also wrote an article with advice for students and tips for public talks.

Open source

I helped make openFrameworks, an open-source c++ framework for creative coding.

URL:

zach.li

Instagram:

@zach.lieberman

Conversation with Zach Lieberman

Art is Science.

Those who speak the same way as a scientist thinks up a mental model to describe an idea, and so does an artist by observing the things in the world surrounding them and letting them take effect. Both bring these patterns back into existence. The artist in the form of a work of art, be it a drawing, a sculpture, or in this case, as code.

Another equation that can be set up is a code that can be read like a poem. You describe this as “Code Poetics.” In both cases, an idea is being described. The reading direction is the same both times. And both have to be interpreted.

To get back into the world and impact the poem. This process is done by a human, a computer, and through code.

When I think of code like a poem, I see the German-French Dadaist Jean Arp.

A large part of his work is based on observing nature, whereby the visualization of the invisible is attributed to him. However, Dadaism always had to be different, unclassifiable. The traditional artistic practice was replaced by simple, arbitrary, and mainly random actions.

I am the entire lifetime long
The ovary’s twelfth sense
The whole Augustine
In cellulose gown preening.

Ich bin der lange Lebenslang
Der zwölfte Sinn im Eierstock
Der insgesamte Augustin
Im lichten Zelluloserock.

Jean Arp, Opus Null

In this consideration, there are two possible types of randomness. On the one hand, the machine-based, which can only occur within a very narrow corridor. Specific parameters define this. On the other hand, “human” randomness is determined by many subtle and subconscious influences.

How would you describe "Code Randomness"?

As a generative artist, random is something I think about daily.

Where randomness shines in code is when it's used not as a crutch but as a tool to show the range of parametric design. Artists like Vera Molnar use it to explore the tension between chaos and order.

You can call a function, rand(), which returns a random number, but it's not truly random.

It's running an internal program to spit out statistically random values, but actually, it is a set sequence that gets internally updated. Typically this sequence is set to start with the system time when you launch an application, so that means you'll see different values when you re-run the software. If you could begin the program simultaneously on two other machines, you'd see the same thing.

The fact that randomness is not genuinely random is interesting. The computer is a giant illusion machine, turning bits into characters, colors, pixels, audio samples, and instructions.

The illusion of randomness is another trick it pulls off.

When you work with beginning coders, they love randomness because it leads to chaotic, frenetic energy in their work and the abdication of choice.

Don't know what color to set before you draw?
Make it random!
Not sure about the radius?
Make it random!

In tools like openFrameworks and Processing, which run on a draw loop and constantly redraw the scene, it makes graphics sparkly.

The computer is good at conversation, and randomness allows you to explore permutations.

I love how Vera Molnar, in conversation with Hans Ulrich Obrist, framed it, "Listen, if you replace the word 'random' with 'intuition,' there you have it.

With intuition, suddenly you say, 'now what if I used a curve instead of a straight line and what sort of a curve?'

And then you try it; that's intuition. Randomness does the same thing." In terms of human random and machine random, human random is a lot slower and harder to understand.

My work often takes random twists, but I can only see at much larger scales than computer random, where I could choose 1000s of random numbers per second. I often imagine that I am walking around in a foreign city in the creative process after dark, and at every intersection, I decide whether to turn left, right, or go straight.

What made you turn right instead of going straight? Was it a conscious choice?

Often, when we are doing something new or unexplored, the conversation between random options and intuition leads.

https://vintage.hu/wp-content/uploads/2019/03/Molnar-Vera-HUO-interview.pdf

Let's stay with "code as poem." A considerable aspect of code is the repetition, similar to the metre in a poem. Mathematical expressions formulated in the shape of algorithms. Here, the execution of the process becomes a repetition, but the repetition itself also becomes an iteration.

What is the feeling of iteration?

One of the most beautiful things you learn in coding is the power of code, and the languages I use are in the written word. You write text, like a poem, and the computer interprets it, line by line, from the top of the page to the bottom. Early on, you learn about a "control structure" that allows you to control how the lines are read.

You can ask the computer to read something repeatedly until continuing for a certain amount of time.

This process is called a repeat loop.

I was thinking to myself, what if regular reading was like that? Where you could control how someone reads through instruction.

I recalled the children's book "We are in a book" by the author Mo Willems, and he describes two characters, an elephant and a pig, who discover they are in a book. At first, they love it because they can make you, the reader, say words out loud. But as the book progresses, they get sad because they realize the book will end, and they keep discussing the diminishing number of pages. The last thing they ask you to do is reread the book. I love this final act because they use the text to form a repeat loop.

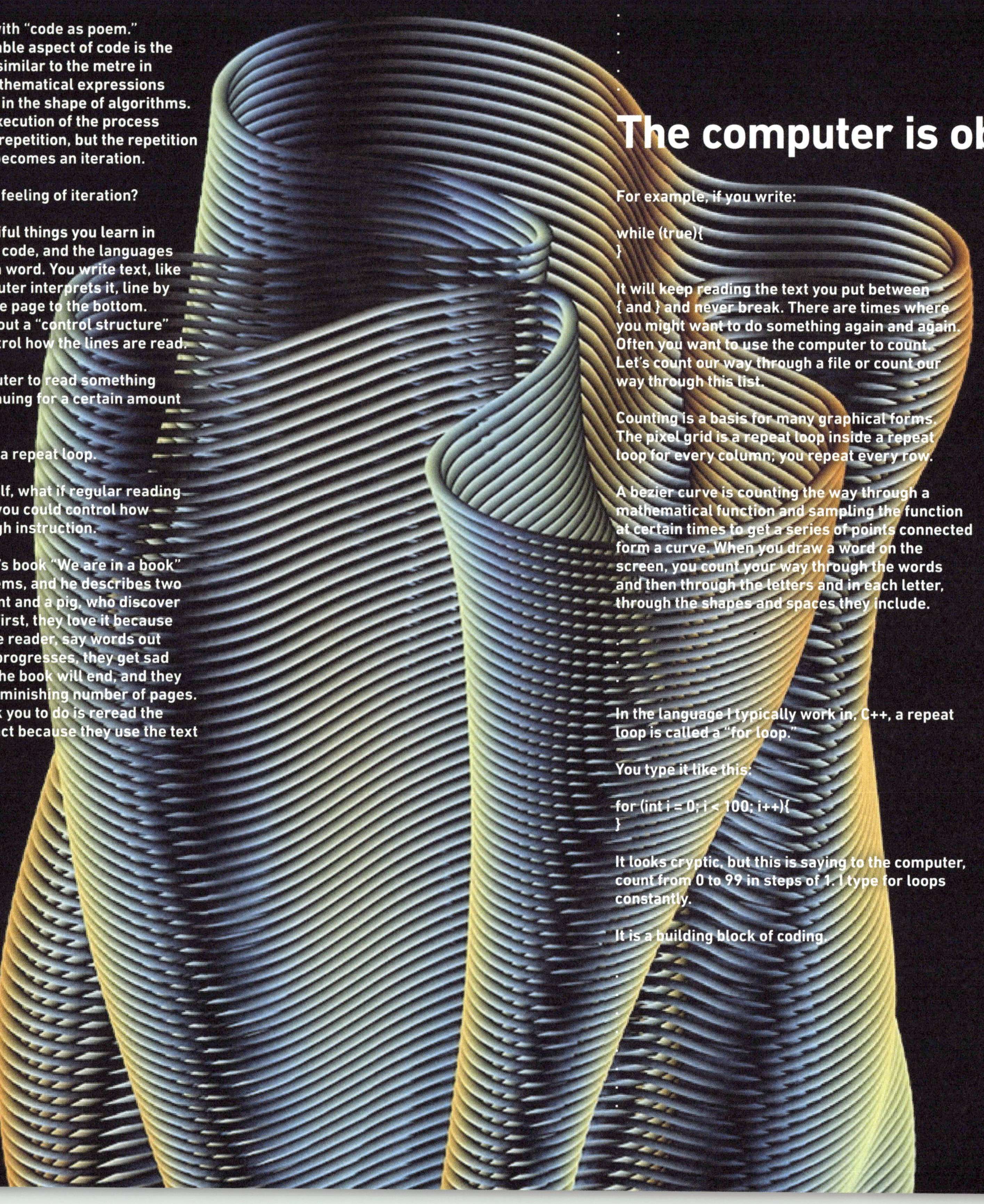

The computer is obedient.

For example, if you write:

```
while (true){
}
```

It will keep reading the text you put between { and } and never break. There are times where you might want to do something again and again. Often you want to use the computer to count. Let's count our way through a file or count our way through this list.

Counting is a basis for many graphical forms. The pixel grid is a repeat loop inside a repeat loop for every column; you repeat every row.

A bezier curve is counting the way through a mathematical function and sampling the function at certain times to get a series of points connected form a curve. When you draw a word on the screen, you count your way through the words and then through the letters and in each letter, through the shapes and spaces they include.

In the language I typically work in, C++, a repeat loop is called a "for loop."

You type it like this:

```
for (int i = 0; i < 100; i++){
}
```

It looks cryptic, but this is saying to the computer, count from 0 to 99 in steps of 1. I type for loops constantly.

It is a building block of coding.

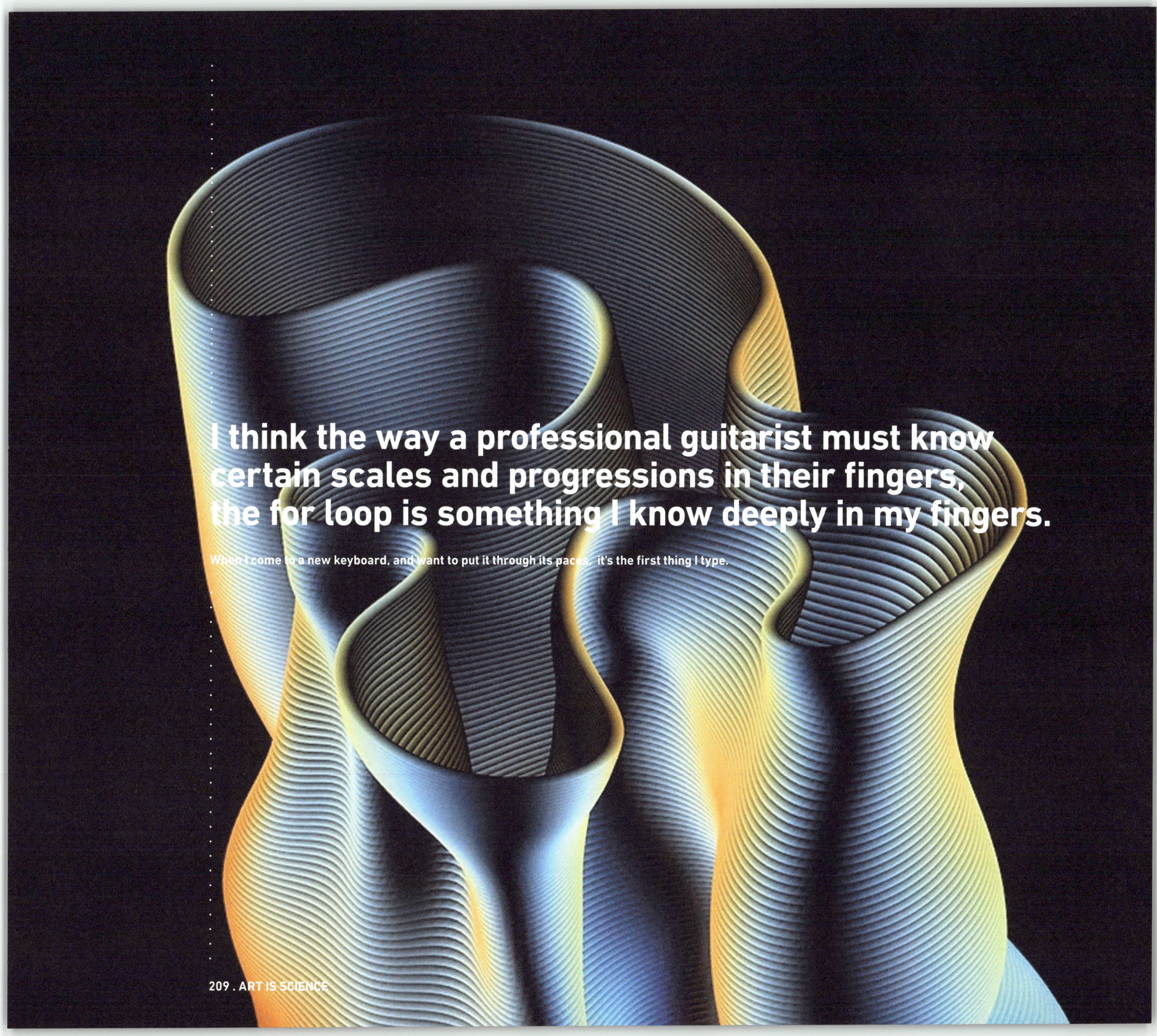

I think the way a professional guitarist must know certain scales and progressions in their fingers, the for loop is something I know deeply in my fingers.

When I come to a new keyboard, and want to put it through its paces, it's the first thing I type.

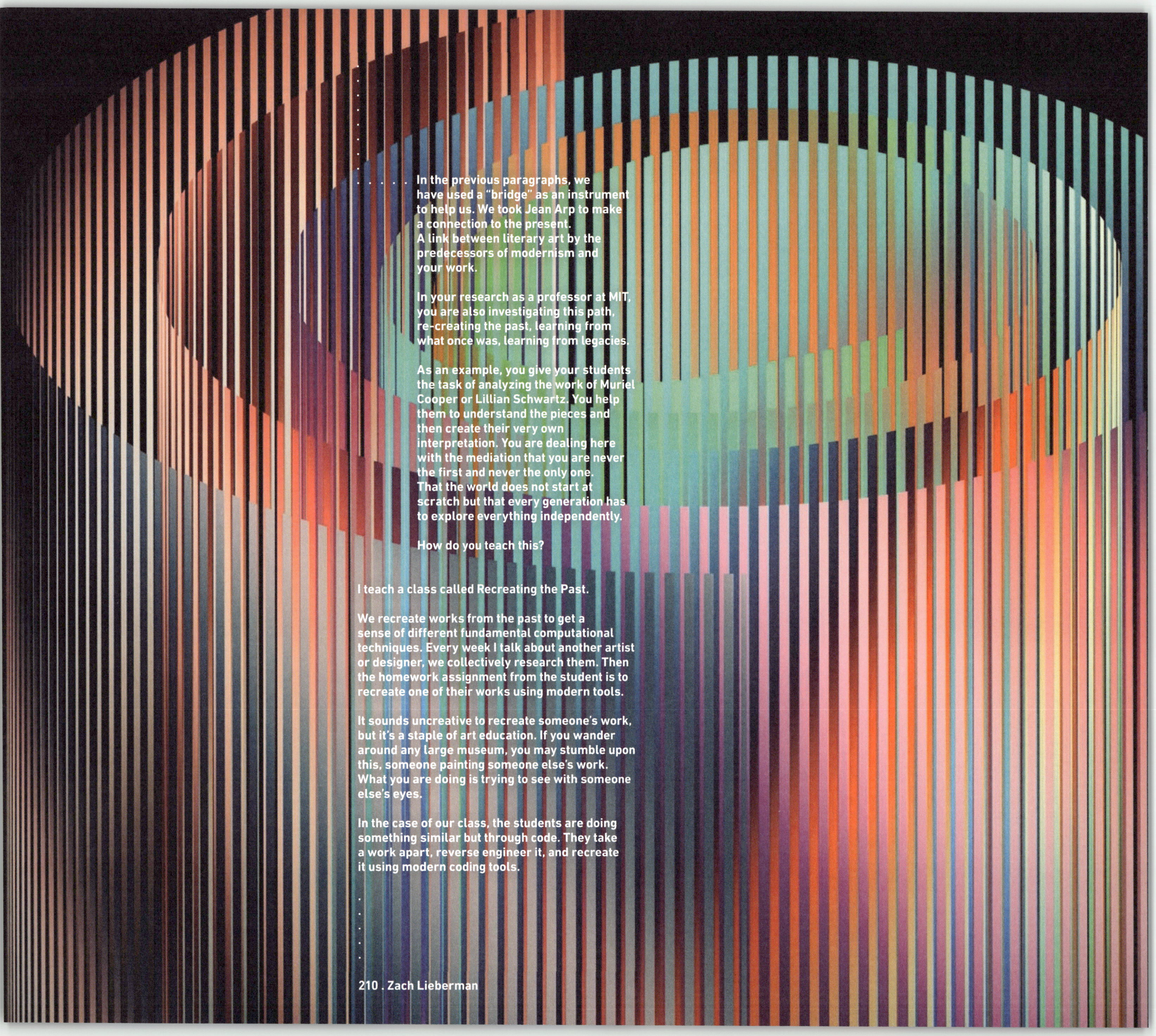

In the previous paragraphs, we have used a "bridge" as an instrument to help us. We took Jean Arp to make a connection to the present. A link between literary art by the predecessors of modernism and your work.

In your research as a professor at MIT, you are also investigating this path, re-creating the past, learning from what once was, learning from legacies.

As an example, you give your students the task of analyzing the work of Muriel Cooper or Lillian Schwartz. You help them to understand the pieces and then create their very own interpretation. You are dealing here with the mediation that you are never the first and never the only one. That the world does not start at scratch but that every generation has to explore everything independently.

How do you teach this?

I teach a class called Recreating the Past.

We recreate works from the past to get a sense of different fundamental computational techniques. Every week I talk about another artist or designer, we collectively research them. Then the homework assignment from the student is to recreate one of their works using modern tools.

It sounds uncreative to recreate someone's work, but it's a staple of art education. If you wander around any large museum, you may stumble upon this, someone painting someone else's work. What you are doing is trying to see with someone else's eyes.

In the case of our class, the students are doing something similar but through code. They take a work apart, reverse engineer it, and recreate it using modern coding tools.

For homework, students show two things; the original and the recreation, and the discussion that comes out of that is fascinating. It was almost like a spot-the-difference type game when you were a kid, where you would see two images and have to notice tiny differences. It's the same with the homework, where the conversation and evaluation are around the differences. I honestly feel that the key to craft is learning to look and that this exercise is training your eye to look very closely at computational form.

Artists discussed who formed the backbone of computational art; Vera Molnar teaches us about randomness and order; Muriel Cooper leads us to investigate graphic design and computation; Woody and Steina Vasulka open the door on media as material. I love seeing how different students find different heroes over the semester. One of my favorite assignments is having them BYOA, bring your own artist, where they recreate the work of someone outside of the class curriculum.

The class tells a story about my heroes, but I want to know what artists and voices they bring into the room.

I've been delighted to see that other people have taken this model and taught similar classes but with different groups of artists.

I think it's a valuable model for computational arts education.

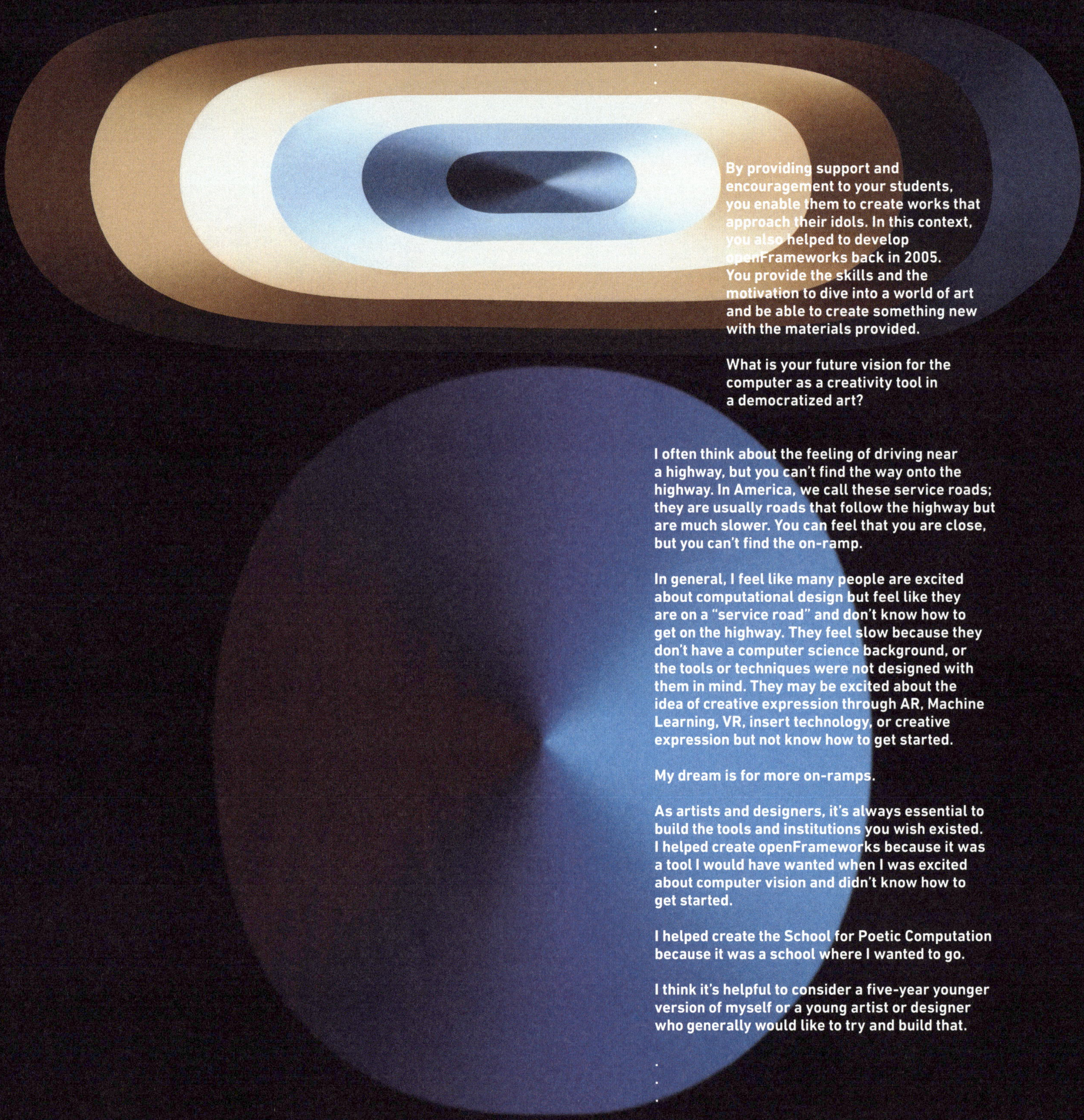

By providing support and encouragement to your students, you enable them to create works that approach their idols. In this context, you also helped to develop openFrameworks back in 2005. You provide the skills and the motivation to dive into a world of art and be able to create something new with the materials provided.

What is your future vision for the computer as a creativity tool in a democratized art?

I often think about the feeling of driving near a highway, but you can't find the way onto the highway. In America, we call these service roads; they are usually roads that follow the highway but are much slower. You can feel that you are close, but you can't find the on-ramp.

In general, I feel like many people are excited about computational design but feel like they are on a "service road" and don't know how to get on the highway. They feel slow because they don't have a computer science background, or the tools or techniques were not designed with them in mind. They may be excited about the idea of creative expression through AR, Machine Learning, VR, insert technology, or creative expression but not know how to get started.

My dream is for more on-ramps.

As artists and designers, it's always essential to build the tools and institutions you wish existed. I helped create openFrameworks because it was a tool I would have wanted when I was excited about computer vision and didn't know how to get started.

I helped create the School for Poetic Computation because it was a school where I wanted to go.

I think it's helpful to consider a five-year younger version of myself or a young artist or designer who generally would like to try and build that.

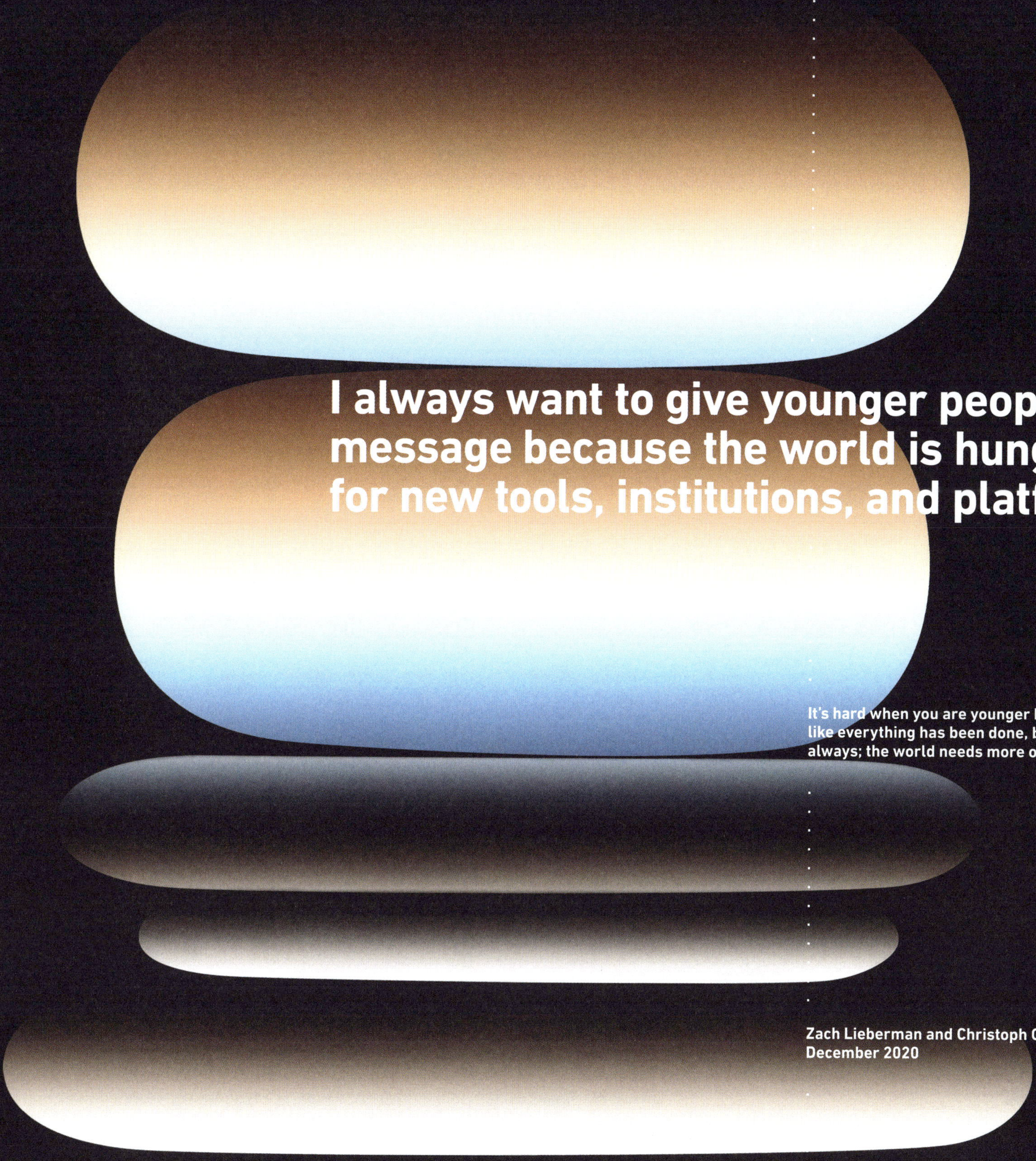

I always want to give younger people a message because the world is hungry for new tools, institutions, and platforms.

It's hard when you are younger because you feel like everything has been done, but my message is always; the world needs more on-ramps.

Zach Lieberman and Christoph Grünberger
December 2020

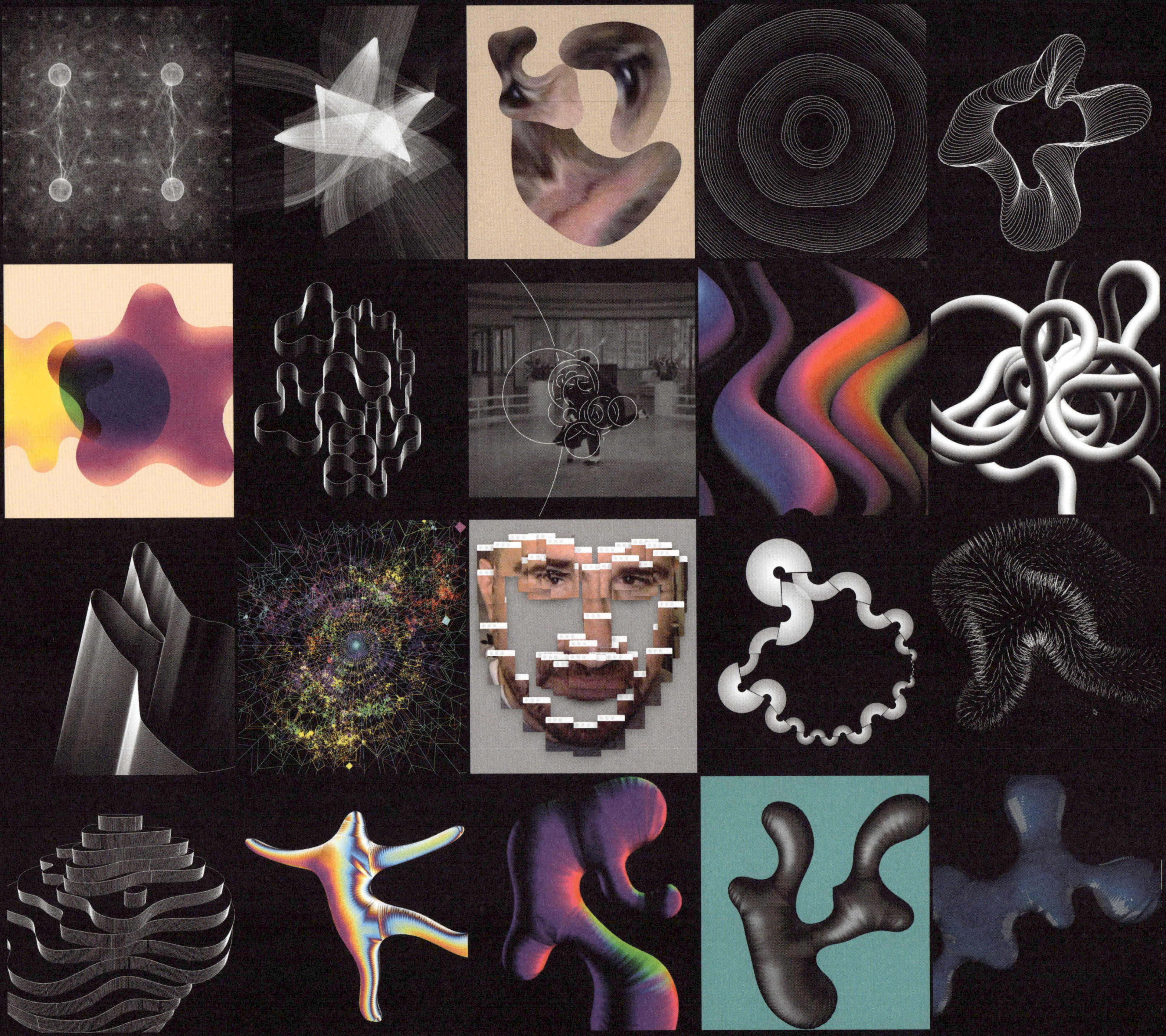

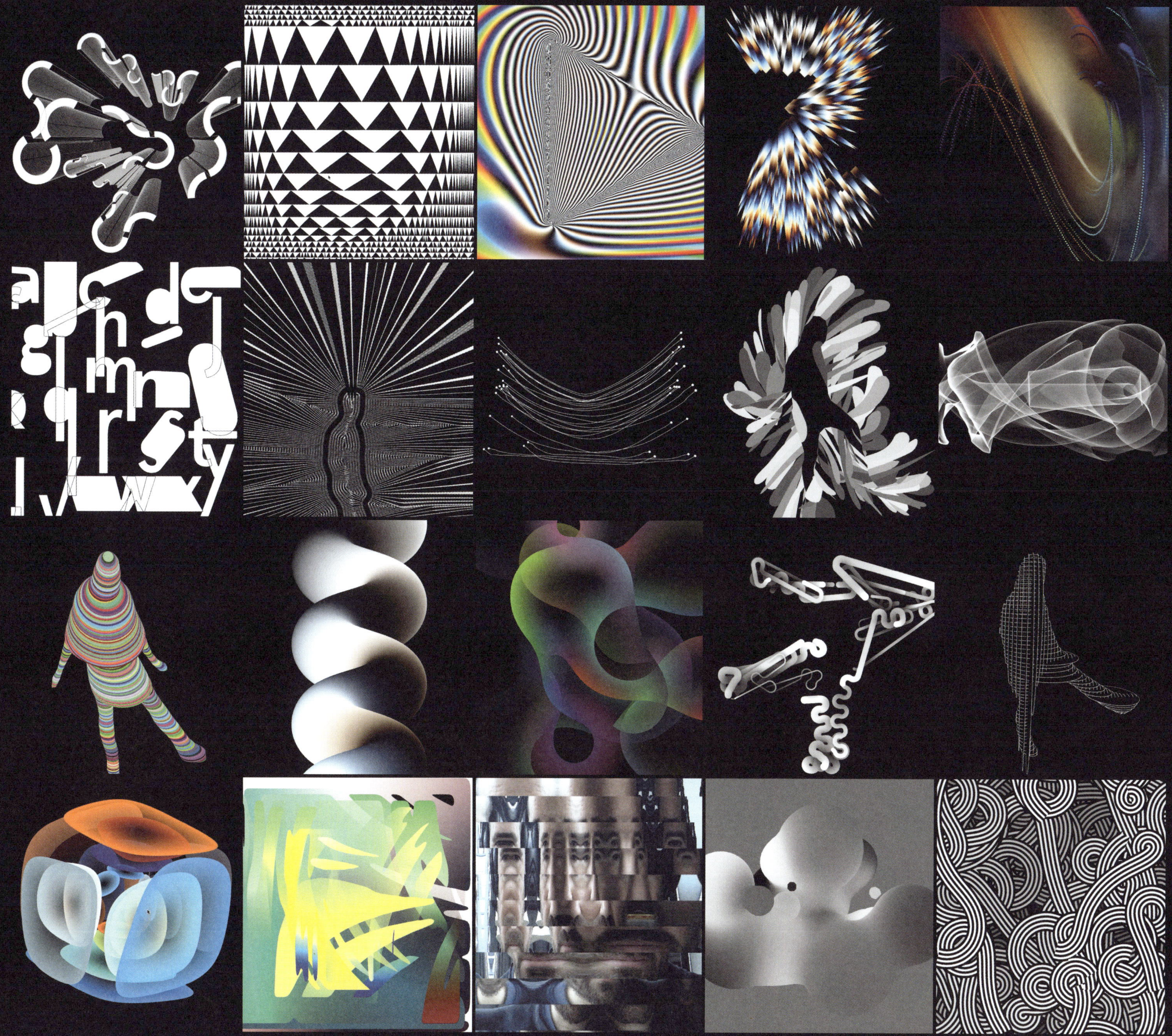

215 . SKETCHES

Name:

Andreas Lutz

Info:

Andreas Lutz's work refers to alternative human-machine interaction, developing integrated and universal communication systems, and creating experimental soundscapes.

Semiotics and sound are further aspects of his work.

Project:

SOFT TAKEOVER

URL:

andreaslutz.com

Mail:

hello@andreaslutz.com

Instagram:

@andreaslutzz

References:

Antarctic Pavilion Venice (Italy)
National Art Center Tokyo (Japan)
HeK Basel (Switzerland)
B39 Art Bunker (South Korea)
ZKM Karlsruhe (Germany)
Stereolux Scopitone (France)
York Art Gallery (UK)
Semibreve Festival (Portugal)
ISEA (Colombia)
Galerie Mazzoli (Germany)
FILE Festival (Brazil)
Nuit Blanche Brussels (Belgium)
KOBE Biennale (Japan)
Athens Digital Arts Festival (Greece)

Q&As

Please explain the main idea and what gave the impulse?

In my work I assume that machines are autonomous, self-aware beings

who can express themselves, communicate with each other, and establish contact with their non-machine surroundings.

I am interested in the idea of abstract communication models and the development of a universal semiotic system, which would be recognized as a trans-human or trans-machine language.

What challenges did you face for this project? And what surprises?

I should mention here the hand-craft side of the kinetic sculpture, especially the work with stretchable fabric, which often turns out to be a challenging material.

Please describe the technical environment.

I built customized linear actuators to realize the physical movements with the fabric.

Each actuator is propelled by a small stepper motor driven by a custom PCB. I utilized screen-based prototypes with Processing to simulate and develop the variations of the movements and the semiotic system.

Tell us about your aesthetical approach.

For SOFT TAKEOVER, I suppose that an intelligent machine uses a traditional human art medium, depicted by a white, unpainted canvas, subtly raising the acceptance of human perception for machine-provided content.

Controlled by algorithms based on an abstract language model, movements on the canvas are near invisible and ephemeral.

What's next? Your vision?

I am developing two new works that will include the physical deformation of an unstable surface in combination with light.

The works are a continuation based on the research for my work Hypergradient (2016), and they will further analyze the possibilities for interpretation of a consistent statement raised by a conscious machine.

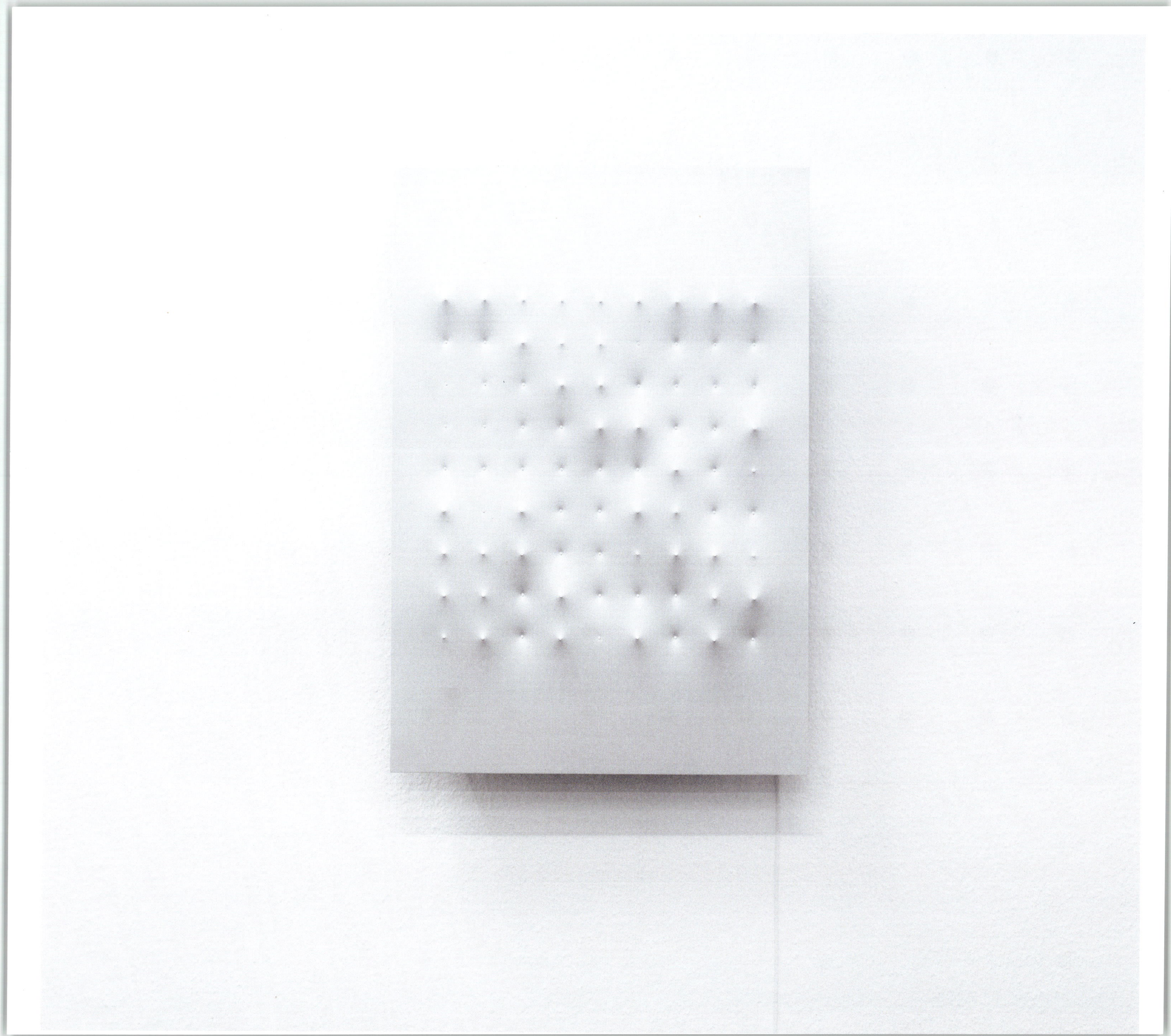

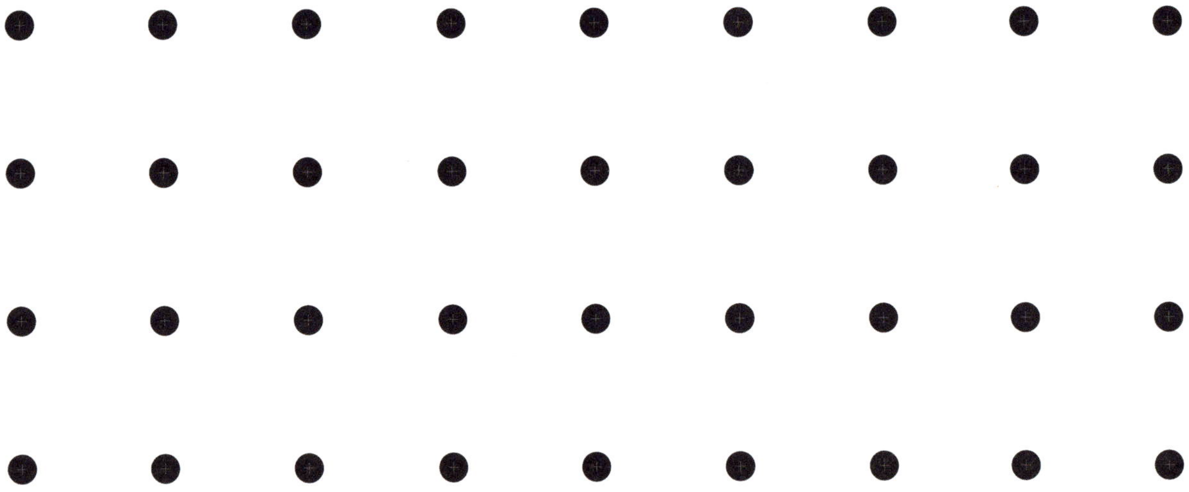

The technical drafts for the grid framework, the single parts of the linear actuators, and the PCB stencils.

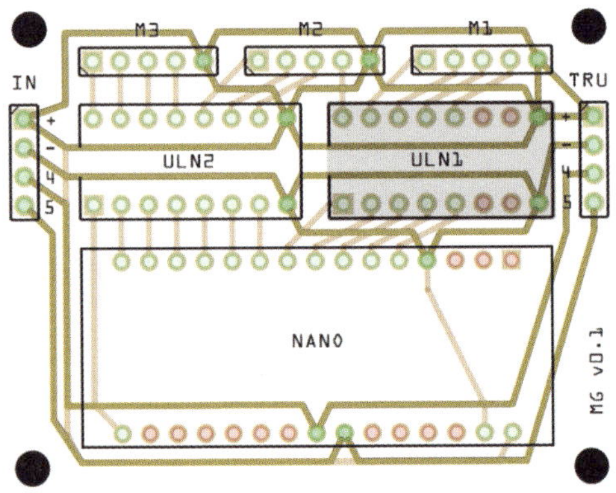

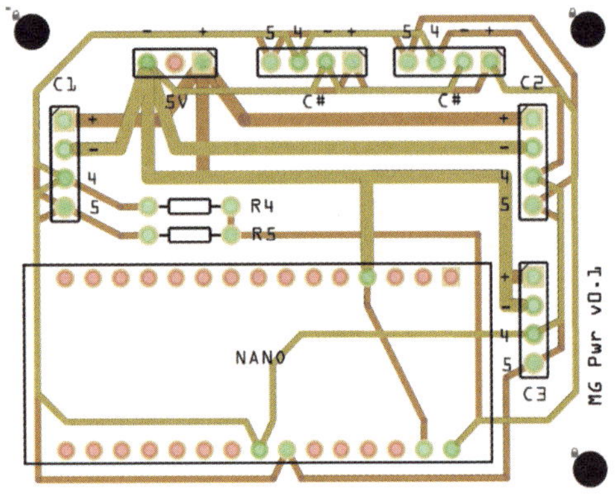

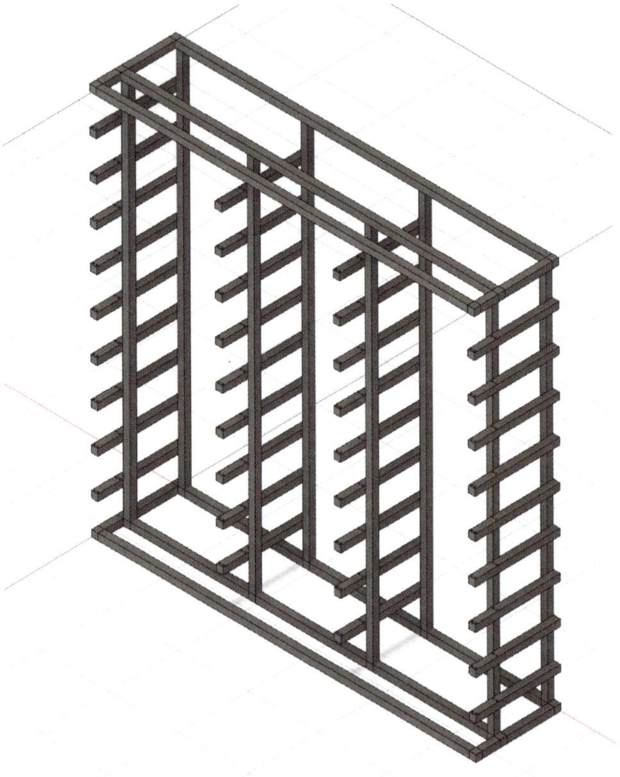

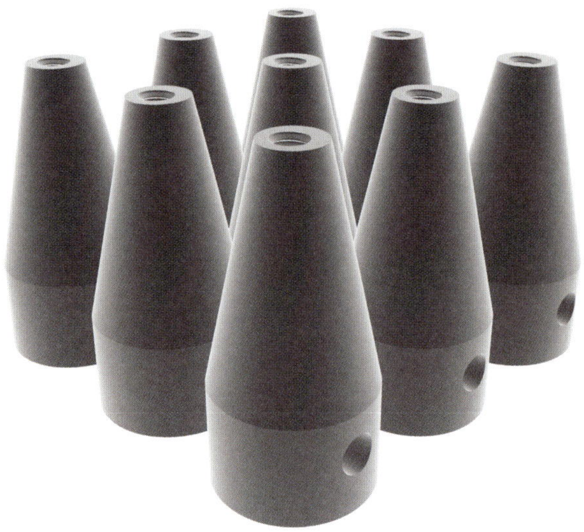

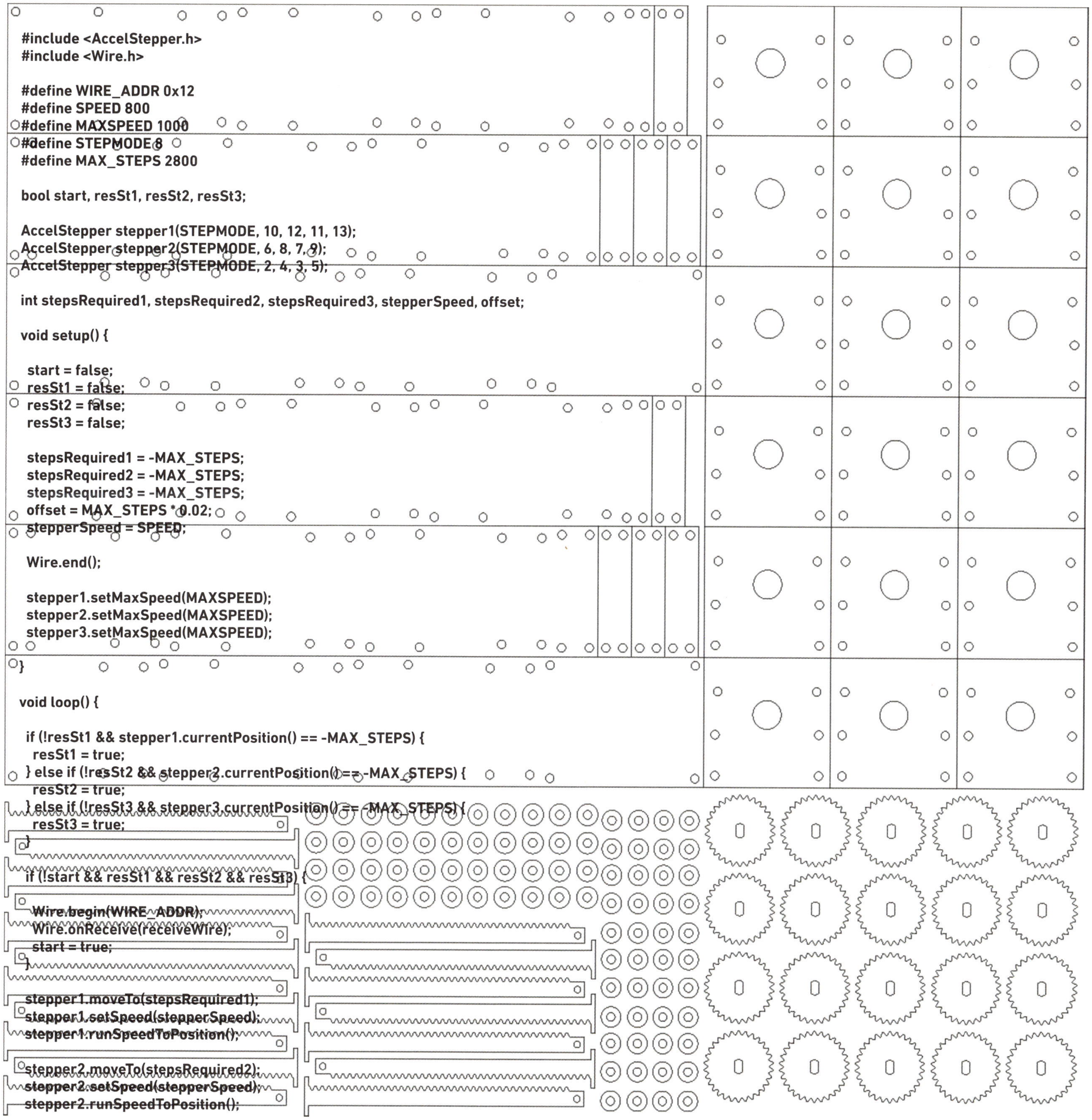

```
#include <AccelStepper.h>
#include <Wire.h>

#define WIRE_ADDR 0x12
#define SPEED 800
#define MAXSPEED 1000
#define STEPMODE 8
#define MAX_STEPS 2800

bool start, resSt1, resSt2, resSt3;

AccelStepper stepper1(STEPMODE, 10, 12, 11, 13);
AccelStepper stepper2(STEPMODE, 6, 8, 7, 9);
AccelStepper stepper3(STEPMODE, 2, 4, 3, 5);

int stepsRequired1, stepsRequired2, stepsRequired3, stepperSpeed, offset;

void setup() {

  start = false;
  resSt1 = false;
  resSt2 = false;
  resSt3 = false;

  stepsRequired1 = -MAX_STEPS;
  stepsRequired2 = -MAX_STEPS;
  stepsRequired3 = -MAX_STEPS;
  offset = MAX_STEPS * 0.02;
  stepperSpeed = SPEED;

  Wire.end();

  stepper1.setMaxSpeed(MAXSPEED);
  stepper2.setMaxSpeed(MAXSPEED);
  stepper3.setMaxSpeed(MAXSPEED);
}

void loop() {

  if (!resSt1 && stepper1.currentPosition() == -MAX_STEPS) {
    resSt1 = true;
  } else if (!resSt2 && stepper2.currentPosition() == -MAX_STEPS) {
    resSt2 = true;
  } else if (!resSt3 && stepper3.currentPosition() == -MAX_STEPS) {
    resSt3 = true;
  }

  if (!start && resSt1 && resSt2 && resSt3) {

    Wire.begin(WIRE_ADDR);
    Wire.onReceive(receiveWire);
    start = true;
  }

  stepper1.moveTo(stepsRequired1);
  stepper1.setSpeed(stepperSpeed);
  stepper1.runSpeedToPosition();

  stepper2.moveTo(stepsRequired2);
  stepper2.setSpeed(stepperSpeed);
  stepper2.runSpeedToPosition();
```

Development of the semiotic system with
81 binary states:
Static view (p. 220) and transition view (p.221)
for simulating and developing the "language"
of SOFT TAKEOVER.

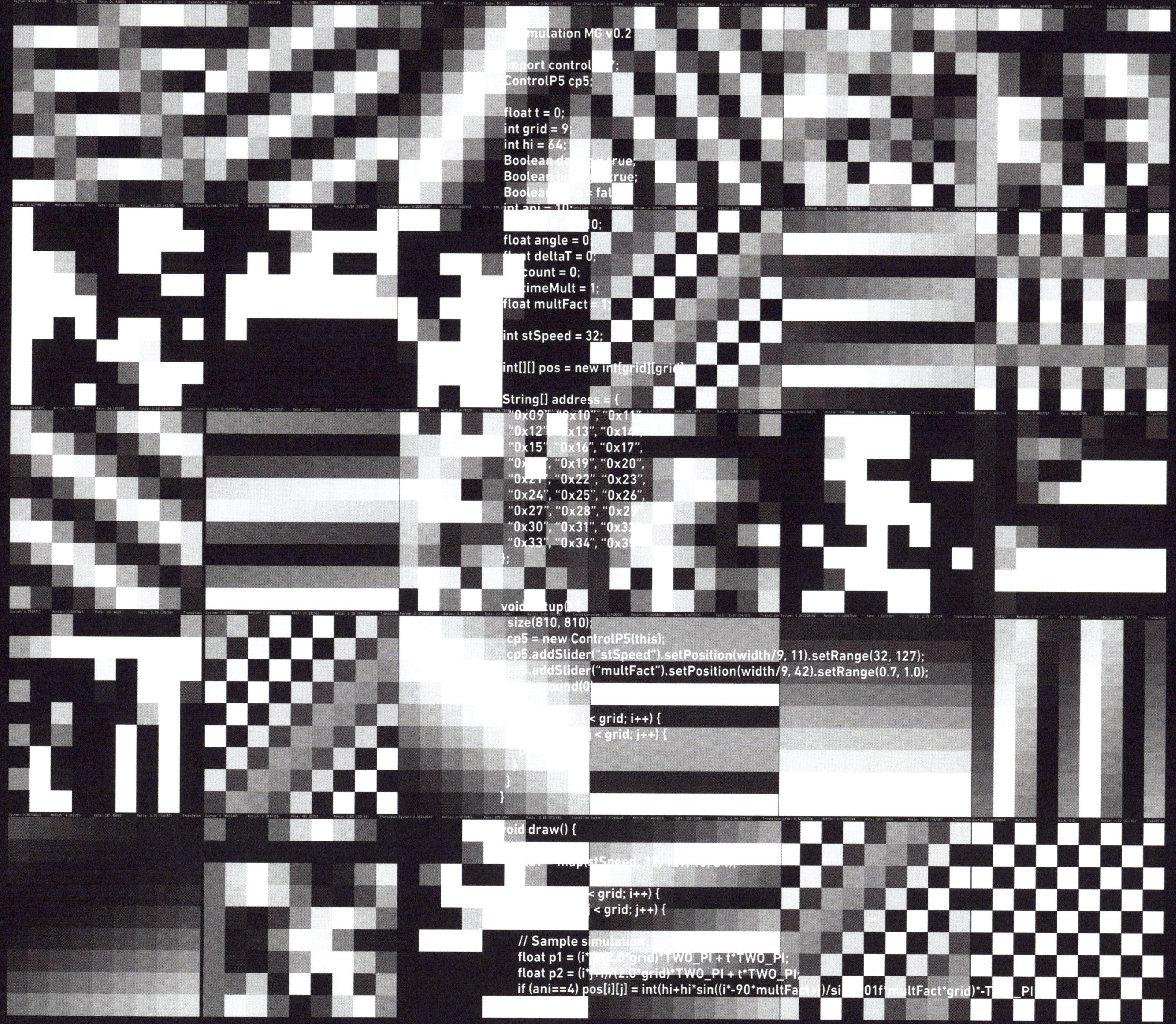

import control
ControlP5 cp5;
float t = 0;
int grid = 9;
int hi = 64;
Boolean
Boolean
float angle = 0
float deltaT = 0;
float multFact = 1;
int stSpeed = 32;
String[] address = {
"0x15", "0x16", "0x17",
"0x19", "0x20",
"0x22", "0x23",
"0x24", "0x25", "0x26",
"0x27", "0x28",
"0x30", "0x31",
"0x33", "0x34",
};
size(810, 810);
cp5 = new ControlP5(this);
cp5.addSlider("stSpeed").setPosition(width/9, 11).setRange(32, 127);
addSlider("multFact").setPosition(width/9, 42).setRange(0.7, 1.0);
< grid; i++) {
< grid; j++) {
void draw() {
< grid; i++) {
< grid; j++) {
// Sample simulation
float p1 =
float p2 =
if (ani==4) pos[i][j] = int(hi+hi*sin((i*-90*multFact

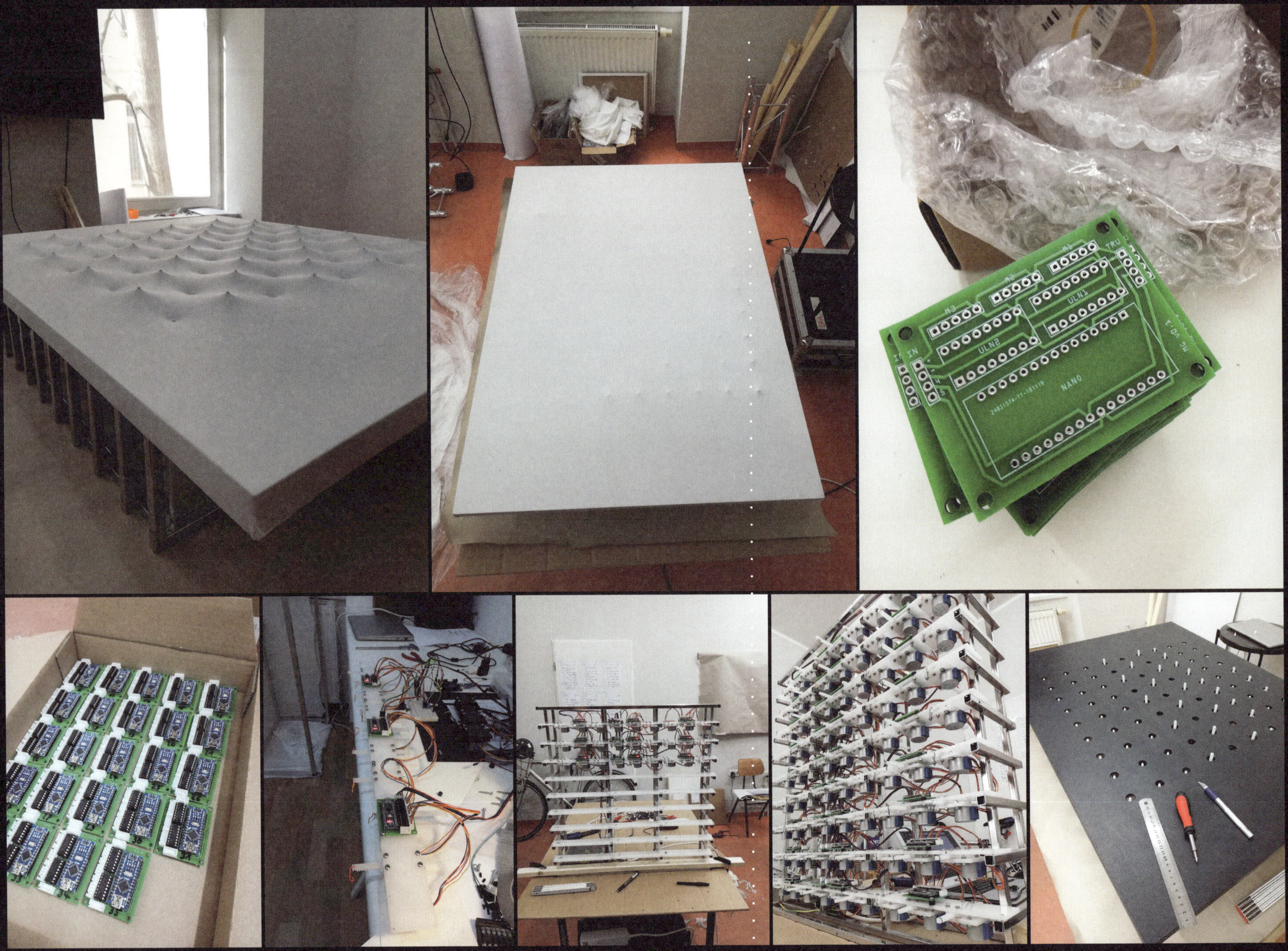

The final PCBs with soldered components, prototypes of the linear actuator modules, and various progress states of the kinetic sculpture.

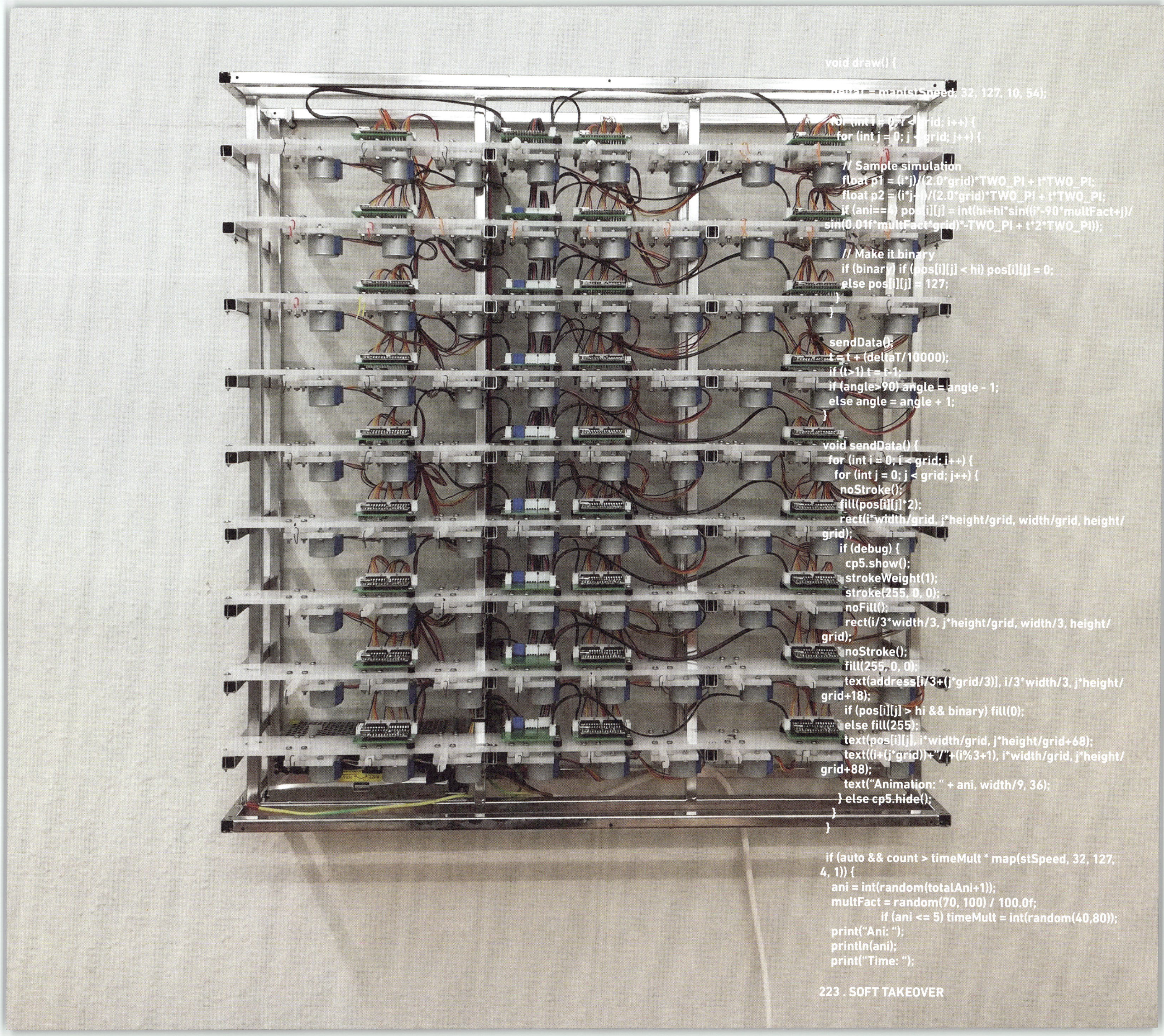

```
void draw() {

  deltaT = map(stSpeed, 32, 127, 10, 54);

  for (int i = 0; i < grid; i++) {
    for (int j = 0; j < grid; j++) {

      // Sample simulation
      float p1 = (i*j)/(2.0*grid)*TWO_PI + t*TWO_PI;
      float p2 = (i*j+i)/(2.0*grid)*TWO_PI + t*TWO_PI;
      if (ani==4) pos[i][j] = int(hi+hi*sin((i*-90*multFact+j)/
sin(0.01f*multFact*grid)*-TWO_PI + t*2*TWO_PI));

      // Make it binary
      if (binary) if (pos[i][j] < hi) pos[i][j] = 0;
      else pos[i][j] = 127;
    }
  }

  sendData();
  t = t + (deltaT/10000);
  if (t>1) t = t-1;
  if (angle>90) angle = angle - 1;
  else angle = angle + 1;
}

void sendData() {
  for (int i = 0; i < grid; i++) {
    for (int j = 0; j < grid; j++) {
      noStroke();
      fill(pos[i][j]*2);
      rect(i*width/grid, j*height/grid, width/grid, height/
grid);
      if (debug) {
        cp5.show();
        strokeWeight(1);
        stroke(255, 0, 0);
        noFill();
        rect(i/3*width/3, j*height/grid, width/3, height/
grid);
        noStroke();
        fill(255, 0, 0);
        text(address[i/3+(j*grid/3)], i/3*width/3, j*height/
grid+18);
        if (pos[i][j] > hi && binary) fill(0);
        else fill(255);
        text(pos[i][j], i*width/grid, j*height/grid+68);
        text((i+(j*grid))+"/"+(i%3+1), i*width/grid, j*height/
grid+88);
        text("Animation: " + ani, width/9, 36);
      } else cp5.hide();
    }
  }

  if (auto && count > timeMult * map(stSpeed, 32, 127,
4, 1)) {
    ani = int(random(totalAni+1));
    multFact = random(70, 100) / 100.0f;
              if (ani <= 5) timeMult = int(random(40,80));
    print("Ani: ");
    println(ani);
    print("Time: ");
```

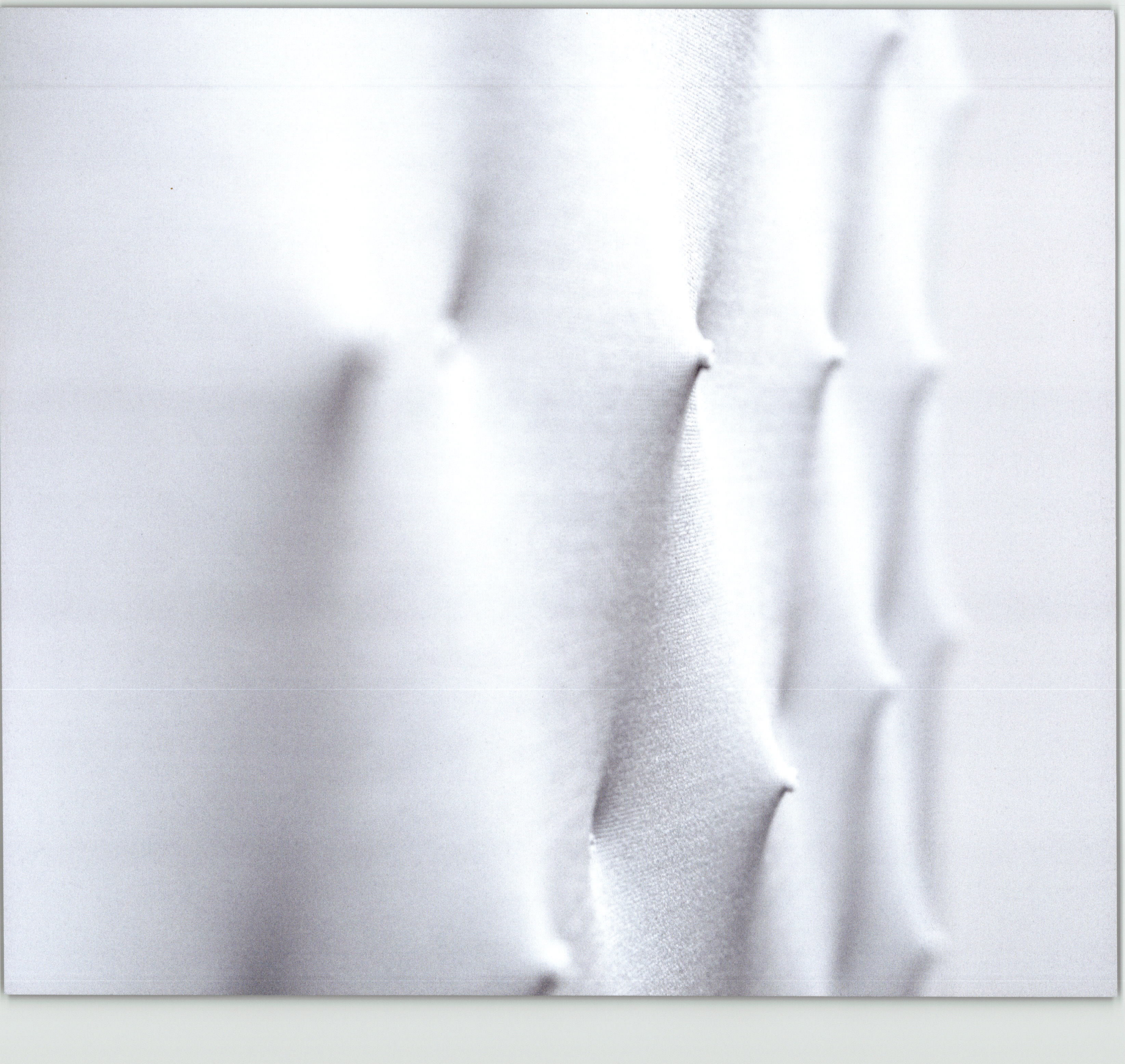

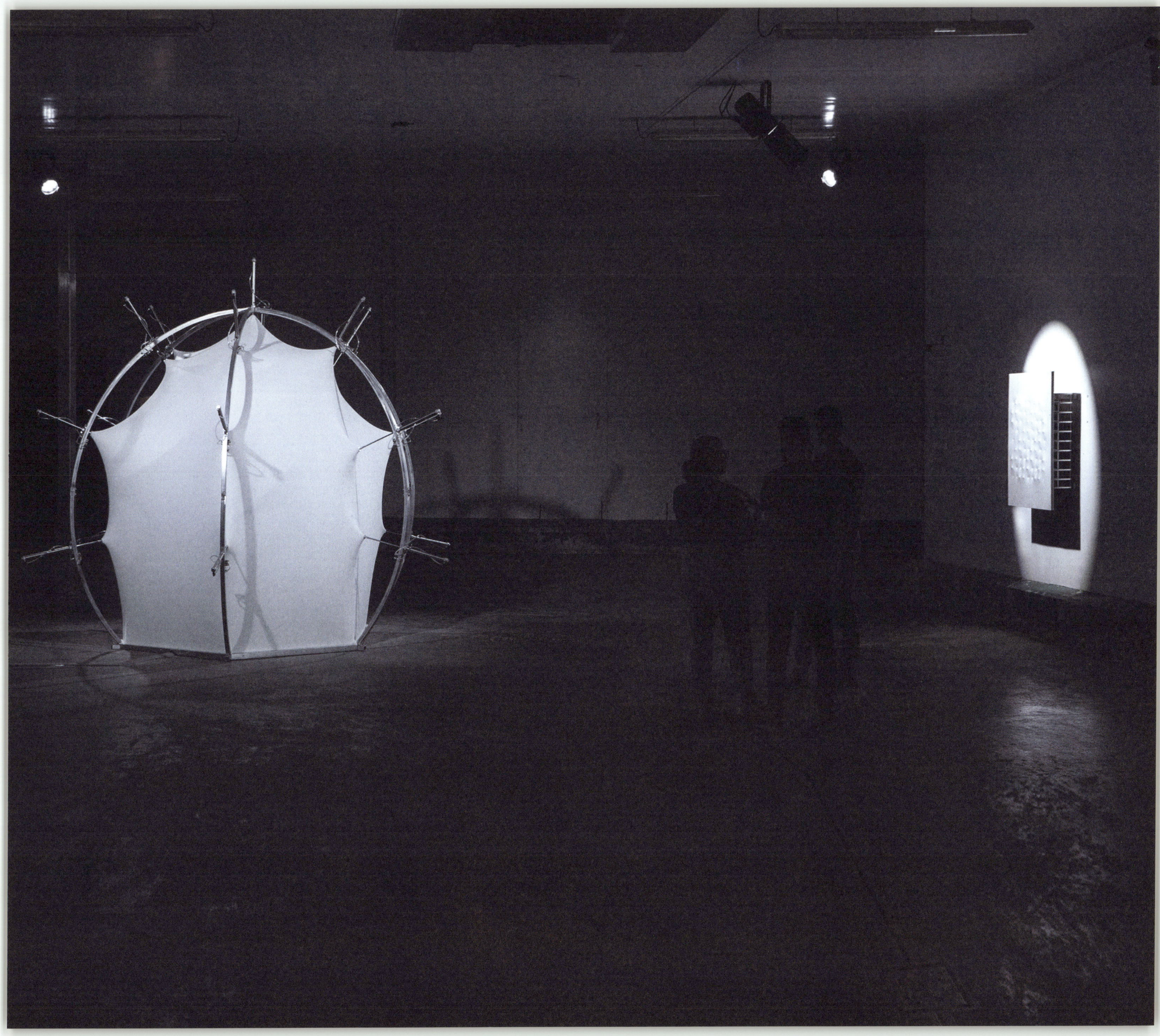

Name:

Daito Manabe

Info:

Tokyo-based artist, interaction designer, programmer, and DJ.

Since 2015, Daito Manabe has served alongside Motoi Ishibashi as co-director of Rhizomatiks Research, the firm's division dedicated to exploring new possibilities in technical and artistic expression with a focus on R&D-intensive projects. Manabe is also an appointed professor at Keio University SFC.

Manabe's design, art, and entertainment work take a new approach to everyday materials and phenomena. However, his end goal is not simply rich, high-definition realism by recognizing and recombining these familiar elemental building blocks. Relatively, his practice; informed by careful observation to discover and elucidate the essential potentialities inherent to the human body, data, programming, computers, and other phenomena. He is probing the interrelationships and boundaries delineating the analog and digital, real and virtual.

Projects:

TERMINAL SLAM [SQUAREPUSHER]
p. 227
ELECTRIC STIMULUS TO FACE TEST 4
p. 232
DISCRETE FIGURES
p. 234
MORPHECORE
p. 236
PERFUME "TIME WARP"
p. 238
COME BEHIND ME, SO GOOD [KAZU]
p. 239
COLD STARES FT. CHANCE THE RAPPER + THE O'MY'S
p. 240
CODED FIELD
p. 242

URL:

research.rhizomatiks.com

Mail:

info_daito@rhizomatiks.com

Conversation with Daito Manabe

Pushing the now.

You work in varied disciplines, always on the edge of what is possible. How can one describe what you do, and is there an activity that you enjoy the most?

Current work includes investigating the computing potential of organisms and cultured cells, not humans. We continuously push the limits of the now. For a successful output, our ideas must sit within the boundaries of current technologies; but their need maybe surpasses ornamental implementation; in the world of contemporary art, for example. Our ideas must be strong enough to merely pose a problem. This process is integral to our thoughts and our craft. The problem and the performance are both considered equally.

As someone who has been doing it for over a decade. In retrospect, what were the most significant cuts, what sticks with you, which quantum leaps or losses send out an echo?

For better or worse, I believe that the evolution of machine learning has had a significant impact on artists working with technology in general. There are many examples where bodies of work rely on fun as an output, and the algorithms inside remain a black box. Some results using technologies such as GAN are a good example.

Also, due to the enormous amount of computing resources, it is often impossible to complete the project using only equipment or the environment that one can prepare. For example, there are more and more outcomes that cannot be done without using the computing resources of Amazon and Google. Big data was not initially intended for producing interaction, and at a time when many things could be done using a desktop computer. This is a significant change.

You do a lot of collaboration with artists, for example, Björk, Golan Levin, Zachary Lieberman, and more recently Squarepusher, to name a few. Please explain this process. Where do the essential impulses come from? Do you draw your inspiration from the ever-changing, or is there a mutual understanding, like a ping-pong?

Like encounters in life, they often start by chance, but most of the time, I meet artists through my own work. ELECTRIC STIMULUS TO FACE is a great example; it created many opportunities and encounters for me. The most crucial thing in collaboration is to have a mutually stimulating environment; I have learned a lot through collaboration since I was young, especially with Golan and Zachary. I learned a lot from them, not only about coding but also about attitude, creating works, their open-source mindset, and their perspectives on life, even when I was just starting my career as a media artist. It is mainly because of their influence that I give lectures and workshops at universities, mentor young artists, and create artwork. I also collaborate with researchers in fields other than my own. As I learn about a particular area, this is a win-win situation, and the researcher can interpret their research from a different viewpoint. That was precisely the case when I worked with researchers in brain science and bioengineering.

A question about your performative works. With all this apparent stage perfection, do you also leave some things to chance? Does this element exist in the plan? The error in programming? The human in the machine?

If we were to pursue perfection, humans would not be necessary.

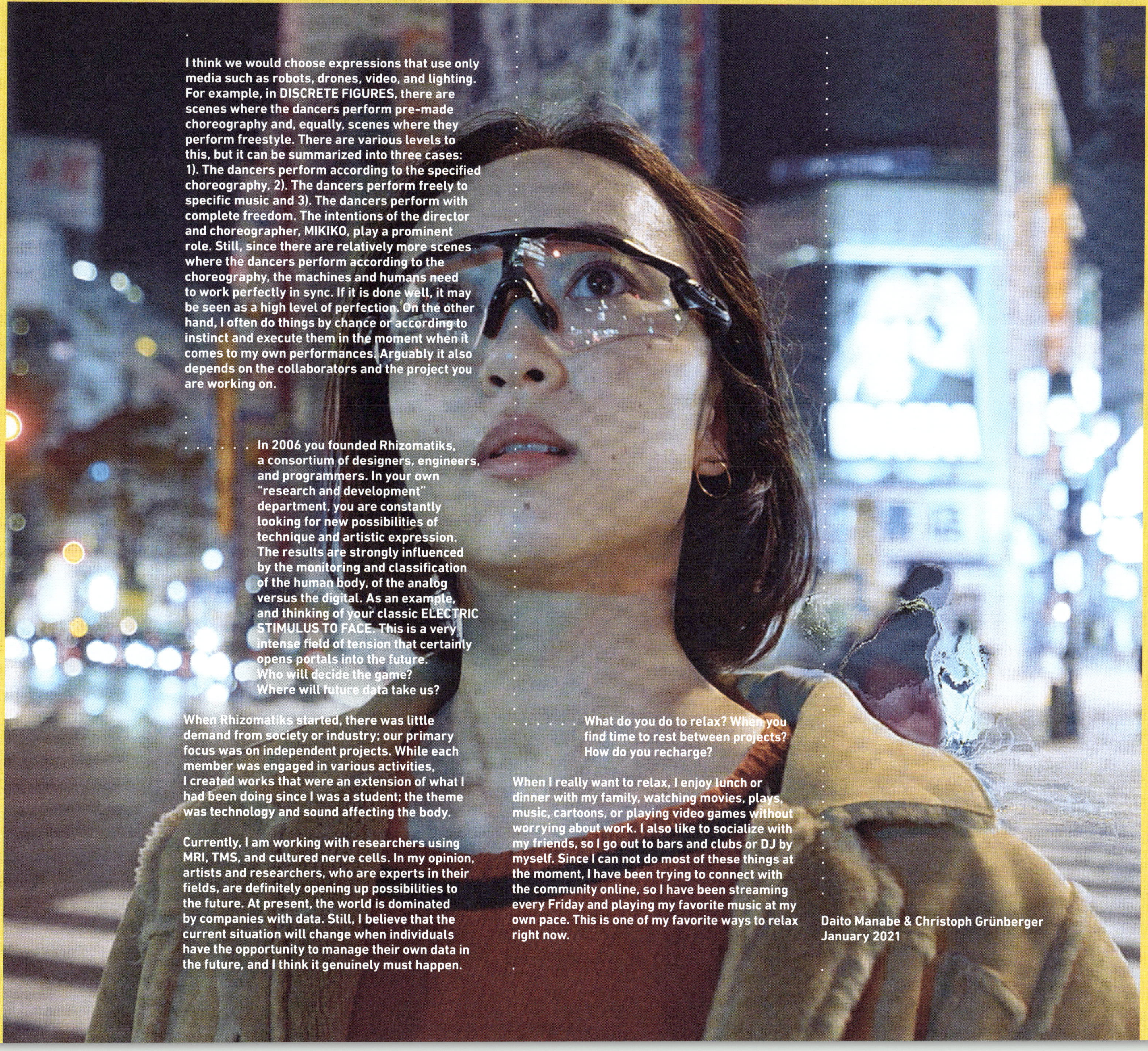

I think we would choose expressions that use only media such as robots, drones, video, and lighting. For example, in DISCRETE FIGURES, there are scenes where the dancers perform pre-made choreography and, equally, scenes where they perform freestyle. There are various levels to this, but it can be summarized into three cases: 1). The dancers perform according to the specified choreography, 2). The dancers perform freely to specific music and 3). The dancers perform with complete freedom. The intentions of the director and choreographer, MIKIKO, play a prominent role. Still, since there are relatively more scenes where the dancers perform according to the choreography, the machines and humans need to work perfectly in sync. If it is done well, it may be seen as a high level of perfection. On the other hand, I often do things by chance or according to instinct and execute them in the moment when it comes to my own performances. Arguably it also depends on the collaborators and the project you are working on.

In 2006 you founded Rhizomatiks, a consortium of designers, engineers, and programmers. In your own "research and development" department, you are constantly looking for new possibilities of technique and artistic expression. The results are strongly influenced by the monitoring and classification of the human body, of the analog versus the digital. As an example, and thinking of your classic ELECTRIC STIMULUS TO FACE. This is a very intense field of tension that certainly opens portals into the future. Who will decide the game? Where will future data take us?

When Rhizomatiks started, there was little demand from society or industry; our primary focus was on independent projects. While each member was engaged in various activities, I created works that were an extension of what I had been doing since I was a student; the theme was technology and sound affecting the body.

Currently, I am working with researchers using MRI, TMS, and cultured nerve cells. In my opinion, artists and researchers, who are experts in their fields, are definitely opening up possibilities to the future. At present, the world is dominated by companies with data. Still, I believe that the current situation will change when individuals have the opportunity to manage their own data in the future, and I think it genuinely must happen.

What do you do to relax? When you find time to rest between projects? How do you recharge?

When I really want to relax, I enjoy lunch or dinner with my family, watching movies, plays, music, cartoons, or playing video games without worrying about work. I also like to socialize with my friends, so I go out to bars and clubs or DJ by myself. Since I can not do most of these things at the moment, I have been trying to connect with the community online, so I have been streaming every Friday and playing my favorite music at my own pace. This is one of my favorite ways to relax right now.

Daito Manabe & Christoph Grünberger
January 2021

TERMINAL SLAM

[SQUAREPUSHER]

The music video TERMINAL SLAM is a provocative video where advertising outlets around the city are deleted or replaced with the ones related to Squarepusher. The inspiration behind this is Manabe's thought that the scenery in the city will become rewritable with AR/MR glasses in the near future, as seen in the video.

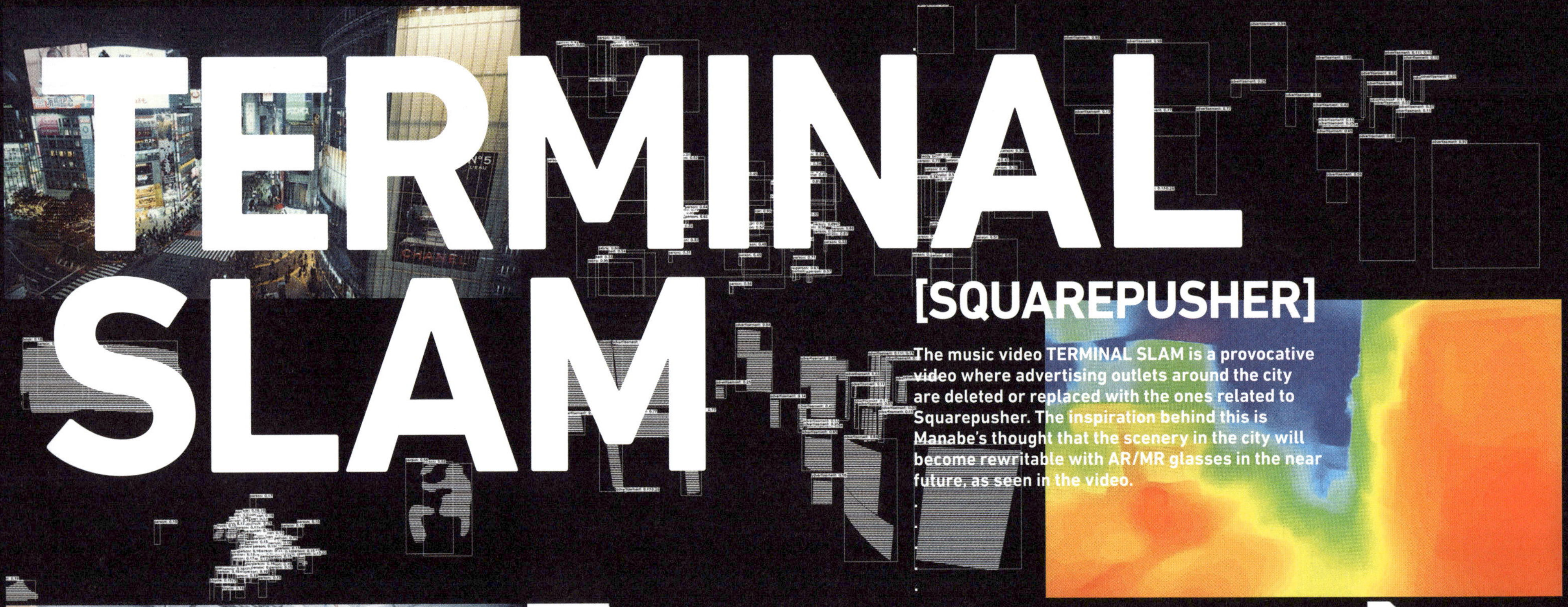

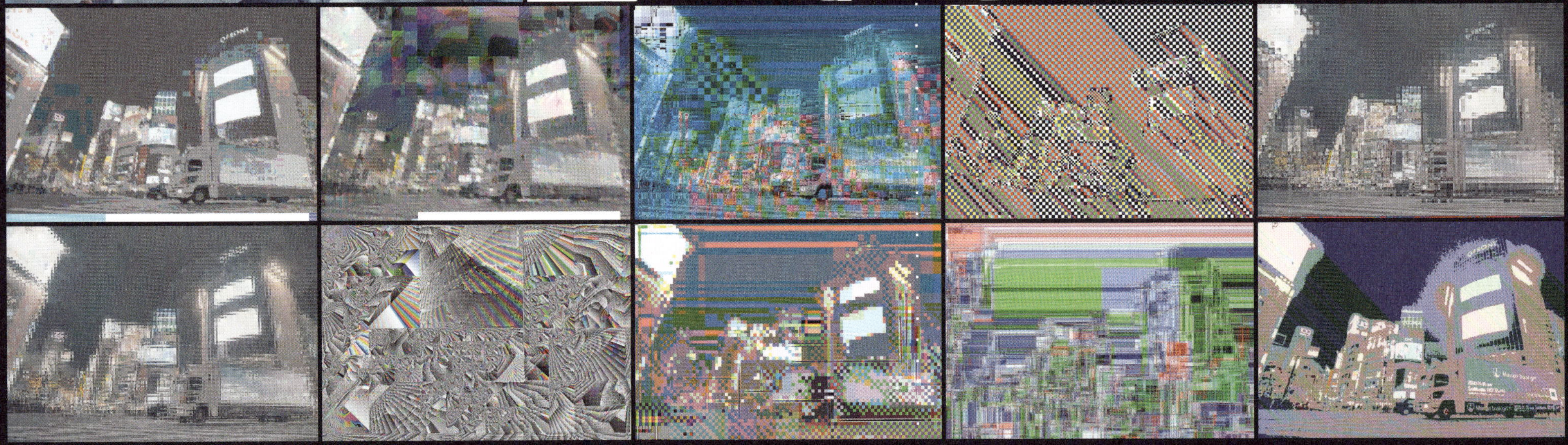

https://research.rhizomatiks.com/s/works/squarepusher/

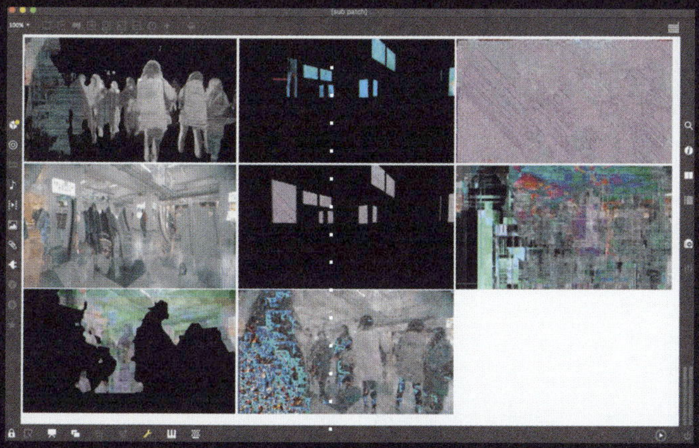

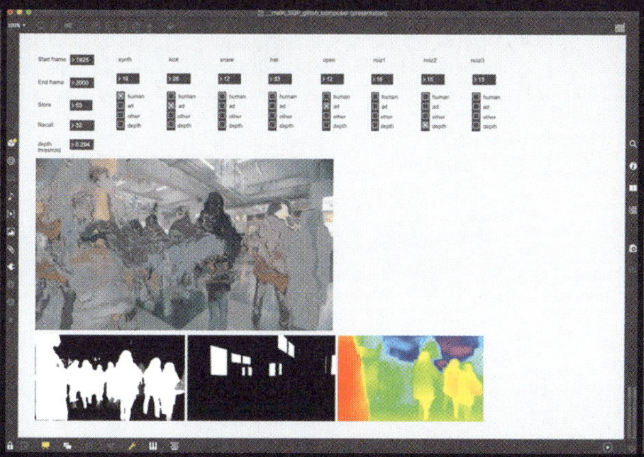

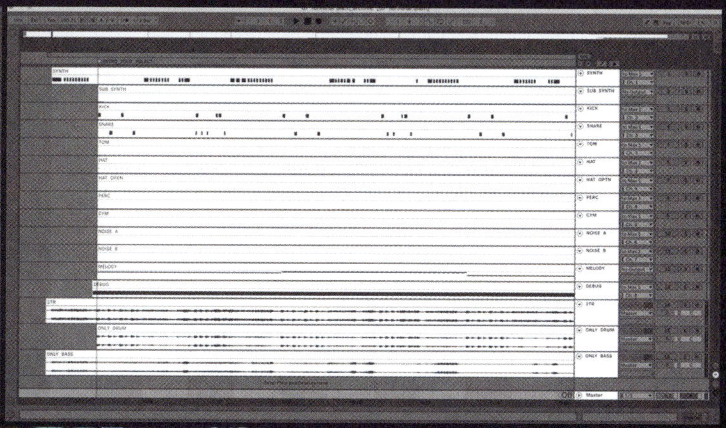

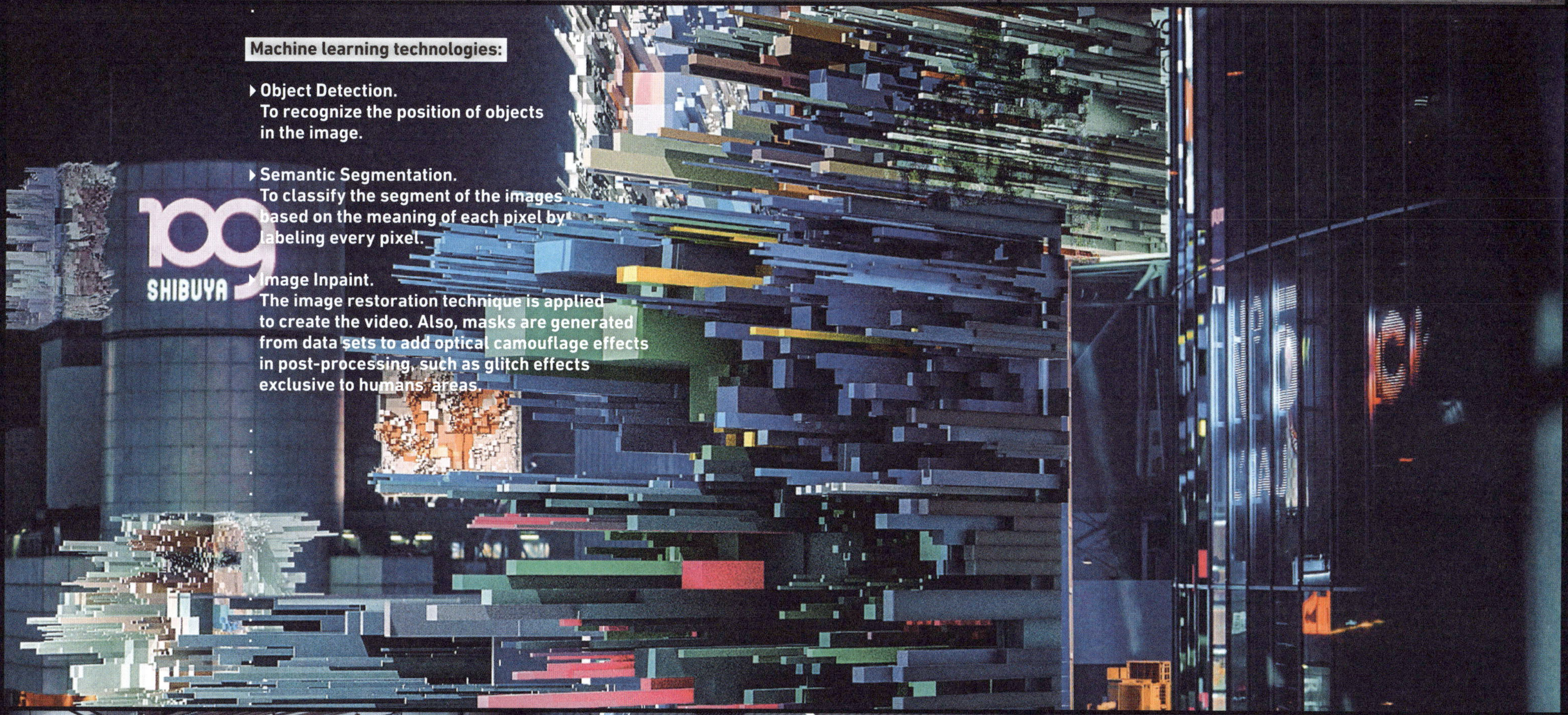

Machine learning technologies:

- Object Detection.
  To recognize the position of objects in the image.
- Semantic Segmentation.
  To classify the segment of the images based on the meaning of each pixel by labeling every pixel.
- Image Inpaint.
  The image restoration technique is applied to create the video. Also, masks are generated from data sets to add optical camouflage effects in post-processing, such as glitch effects exclusive to humans' areas.

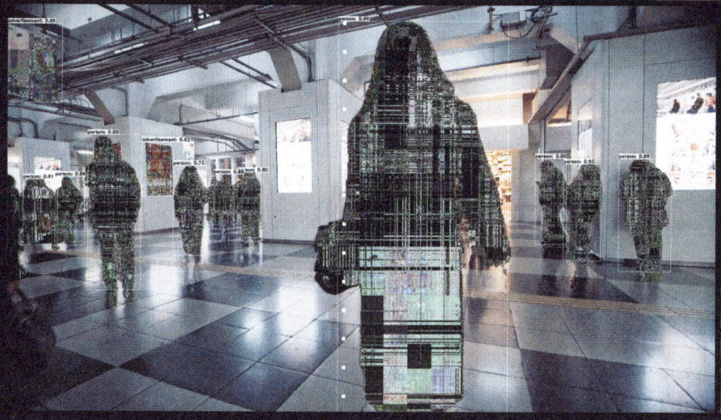

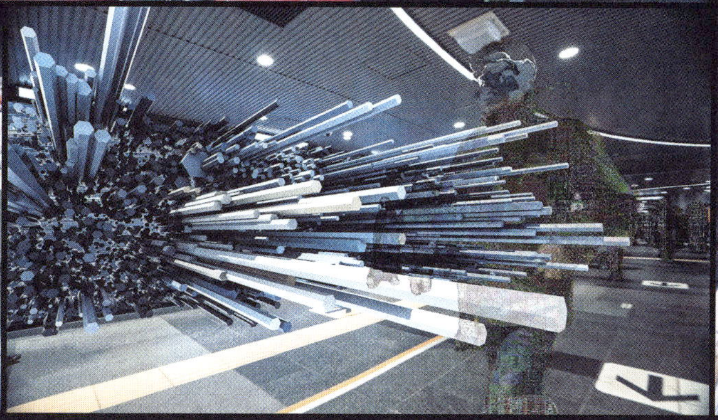

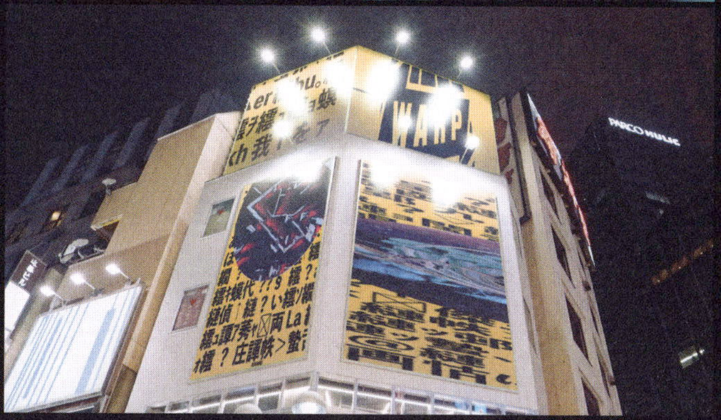

229 . TERMINAL SLAM [SQUAREPUSHER]

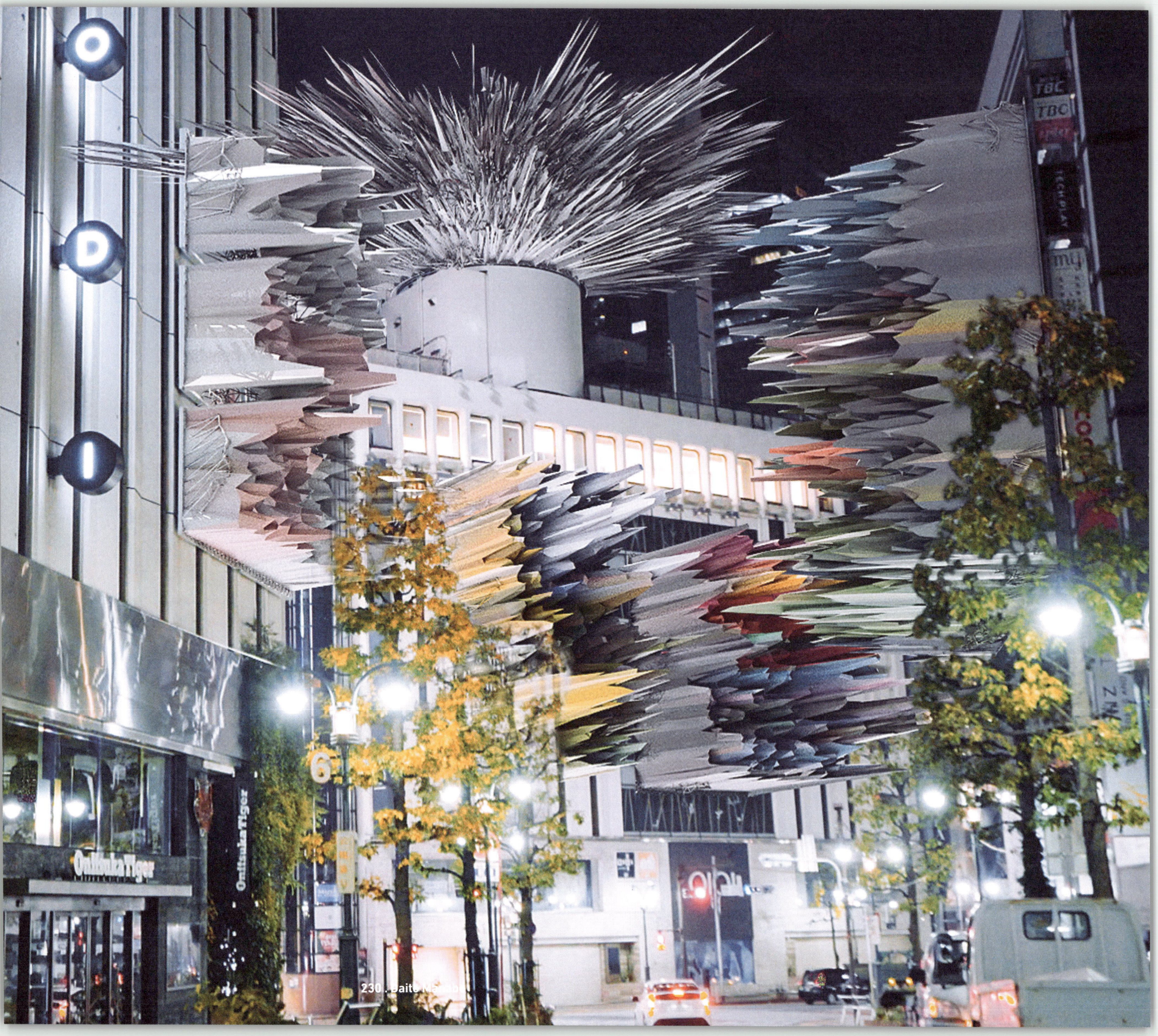

230 . Daito Manabe

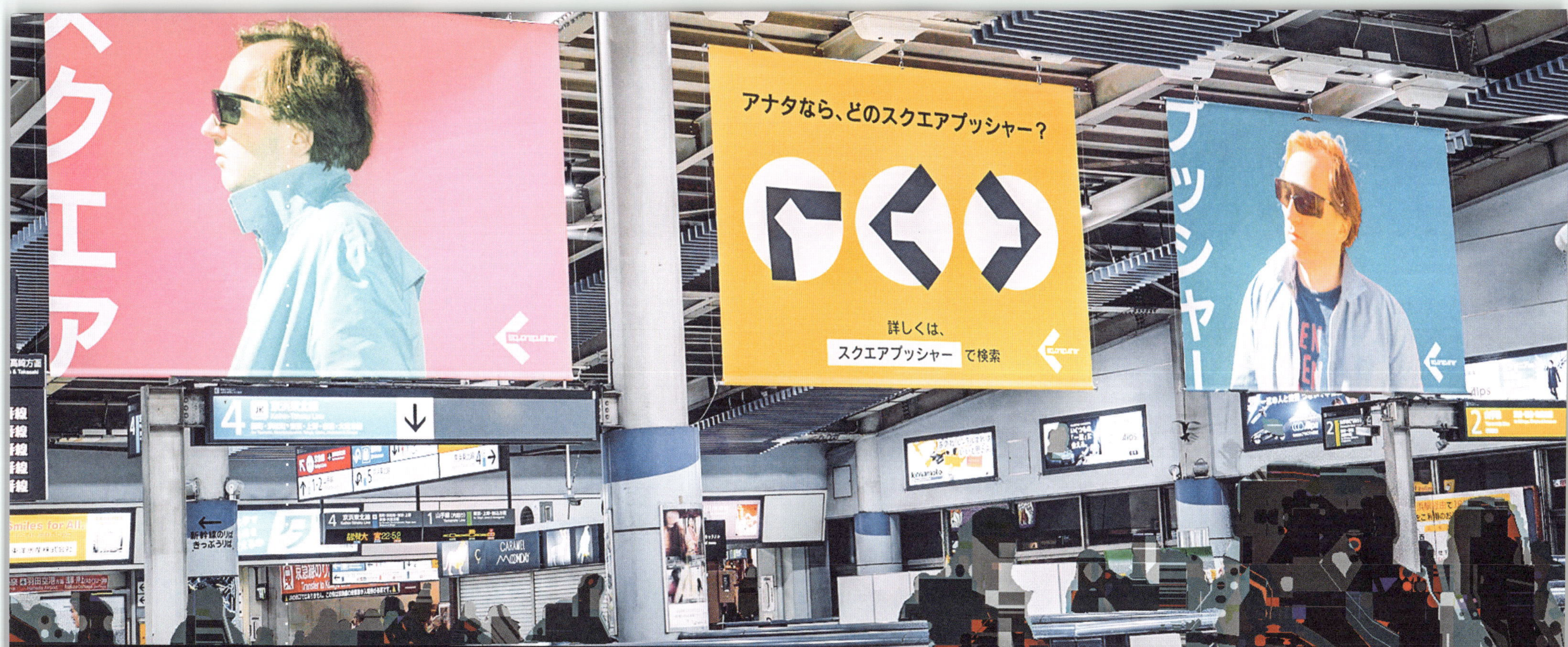

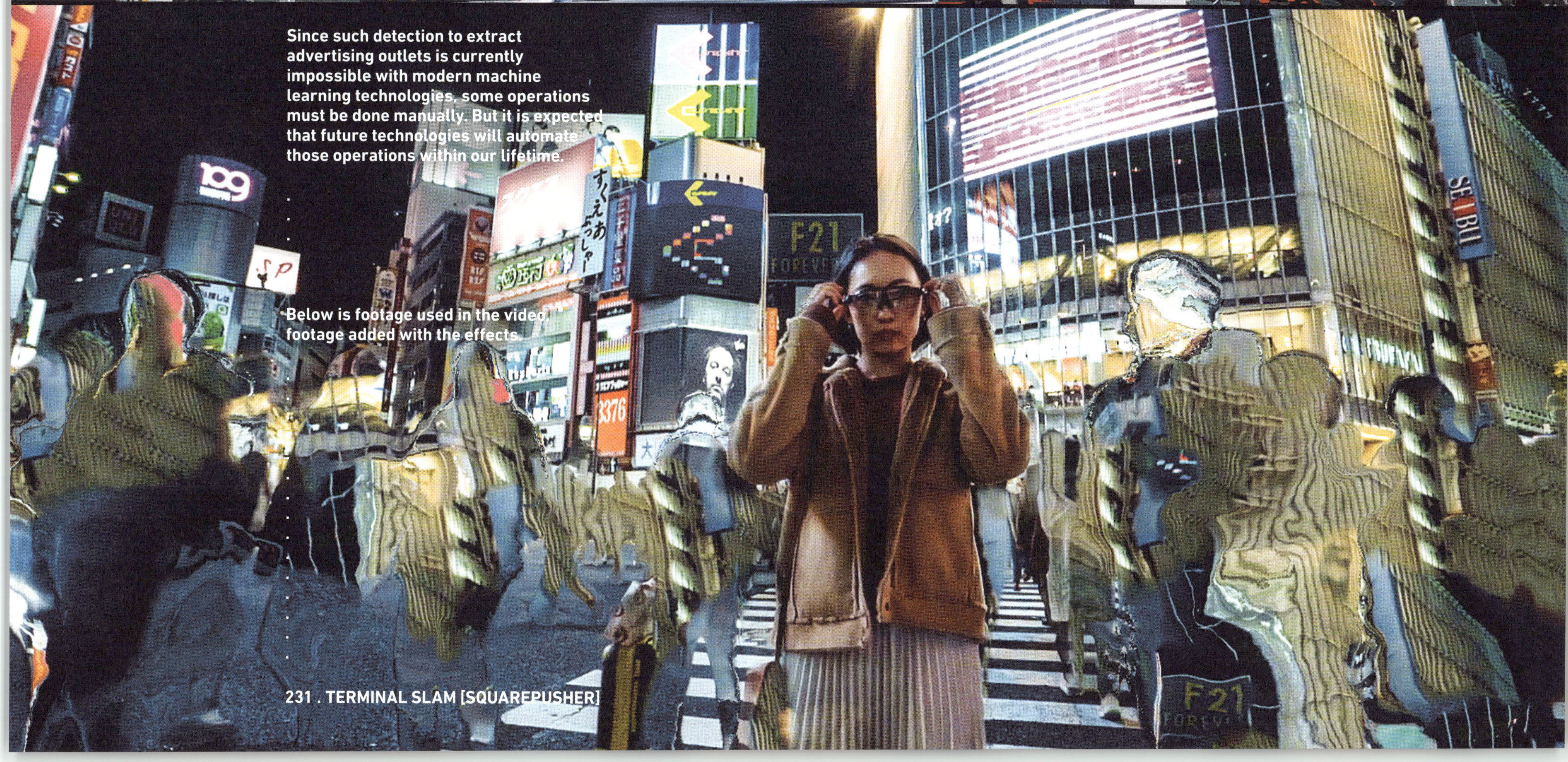

Since such detection to extract advertising outlets is currently impossible with modern machine learning technologies, some operations must be done manually. But it is expected that future technologies will automate those operations within our lifetime.

Below is footage used in the video, footage added with the effects.

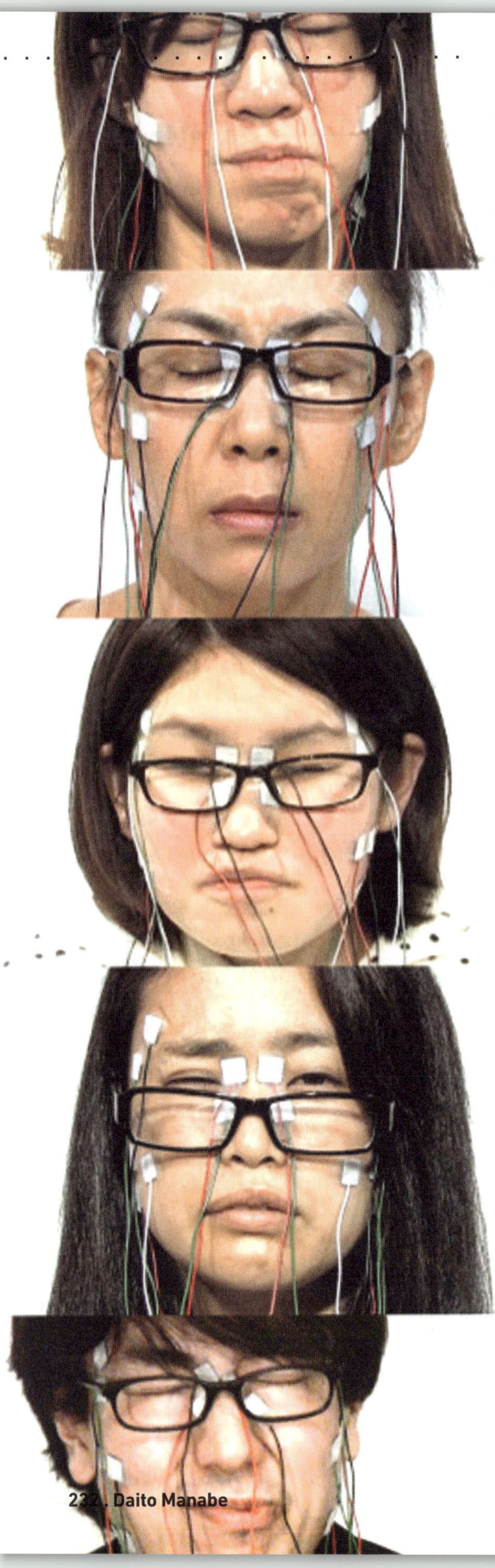

This process is an experimental performance centered on the mutual relationship between data and the human body, which continues to be one of Manabe's main focus themes.

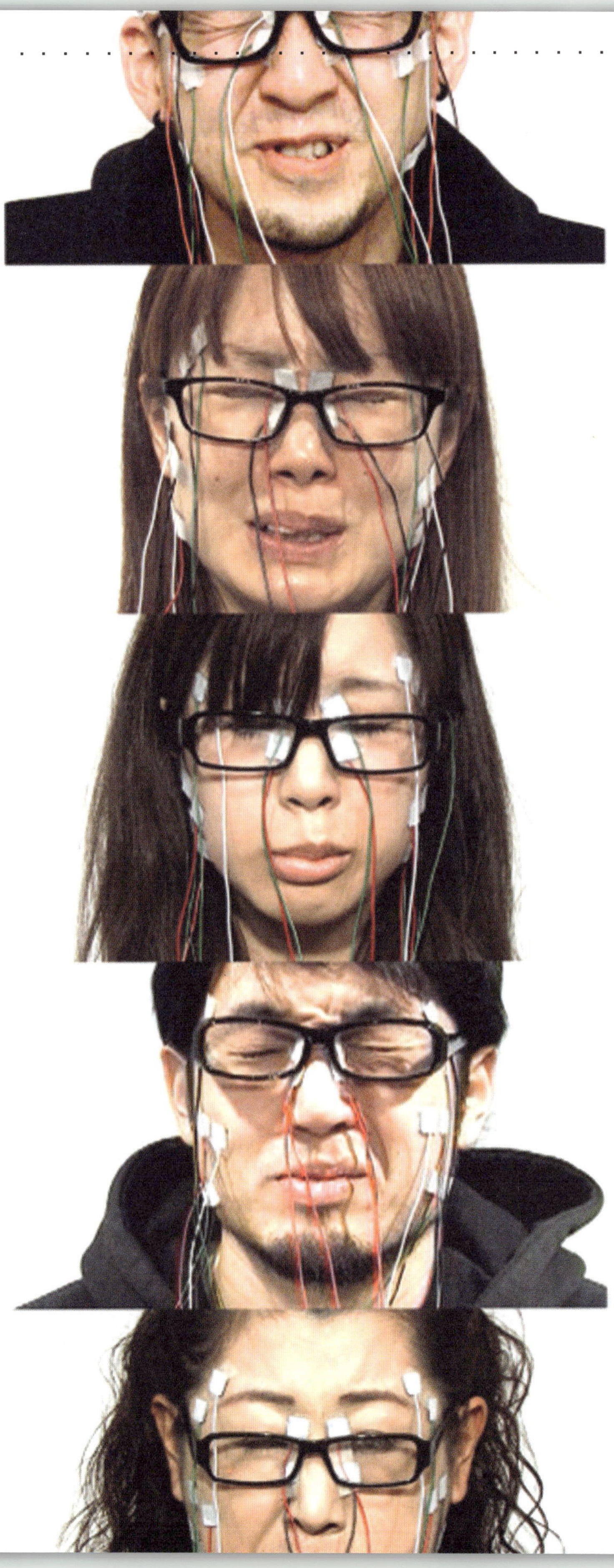

In this project, human facial expressions are controlled automatically by transmitting electrical signals converted from sounds.

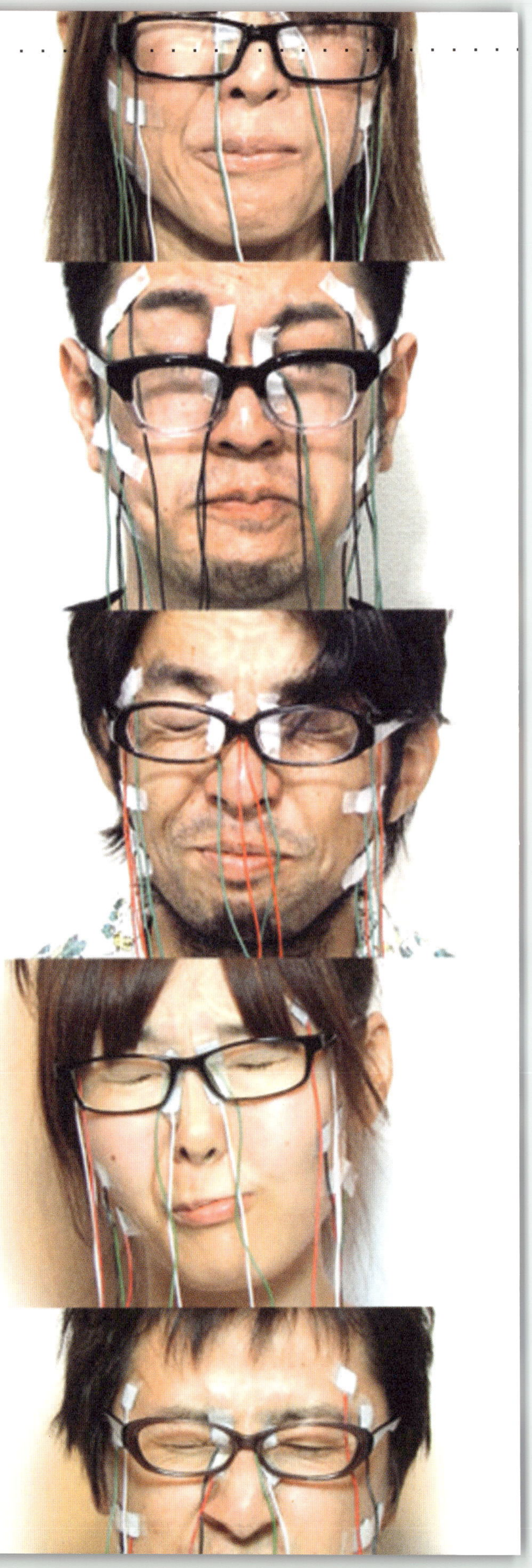

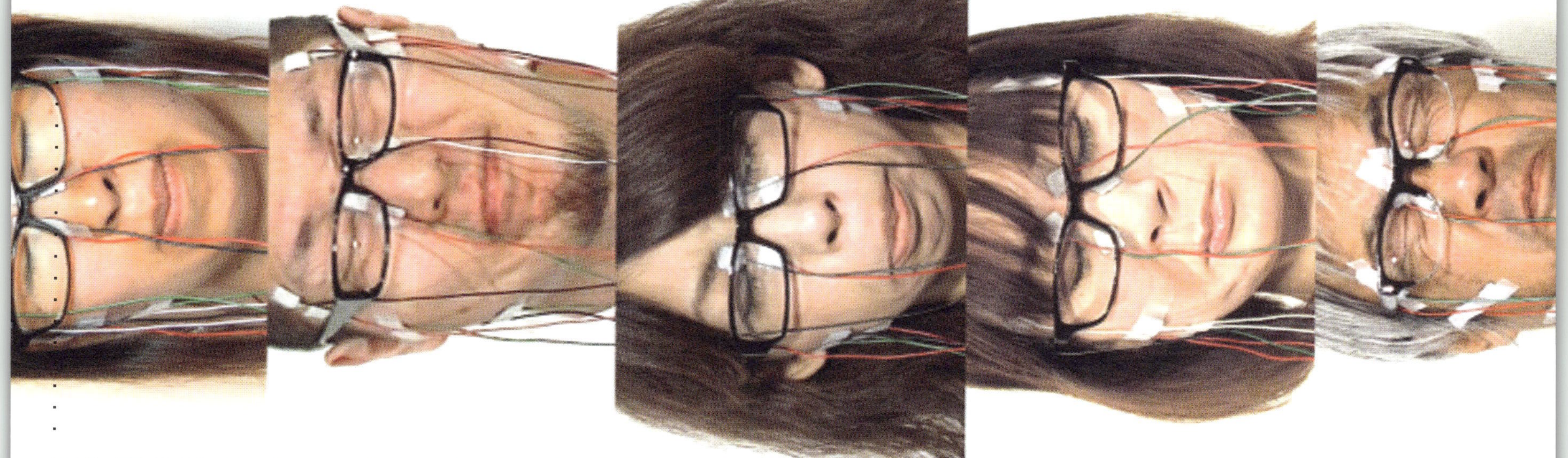

ELECTRIC STIMULUS TO FACE TEST 4

[DAITO MANABE'S FRIENDS]

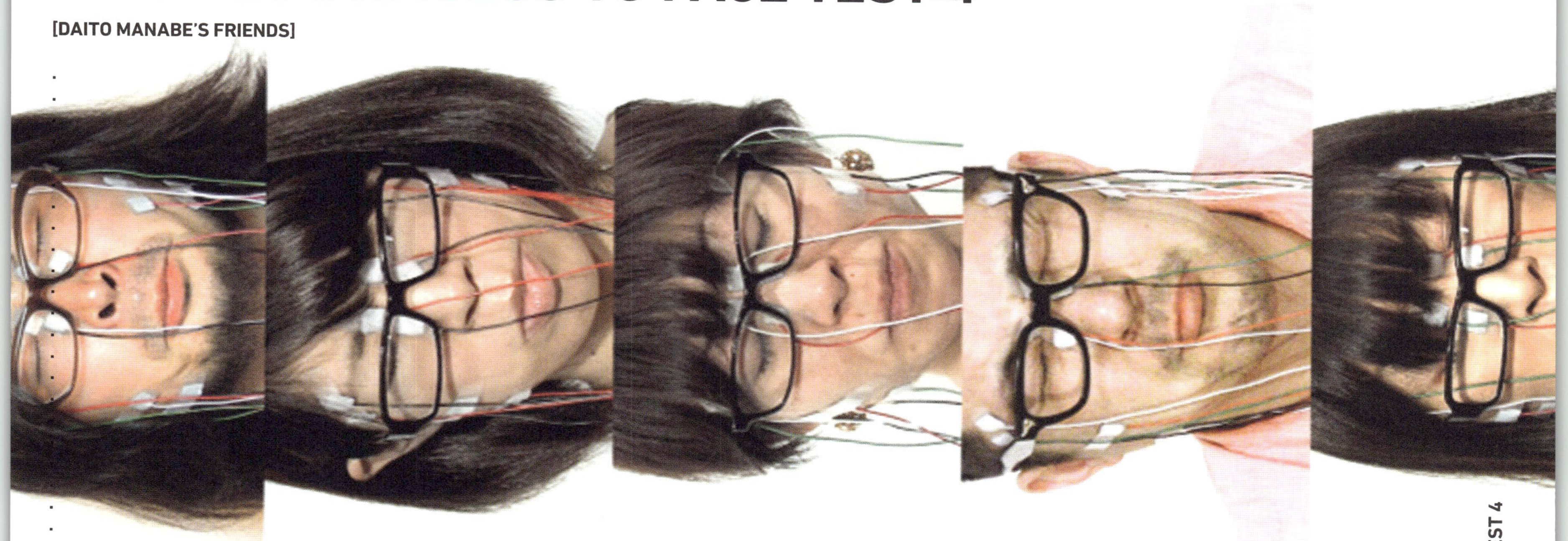

ELECTRIC STIMULUS TO FACE TEST 4 is an experimental performance created by Manabe that explores human facial expressions beyond conscience and feelings using myoelectric sensors and electrical stimulation devices.

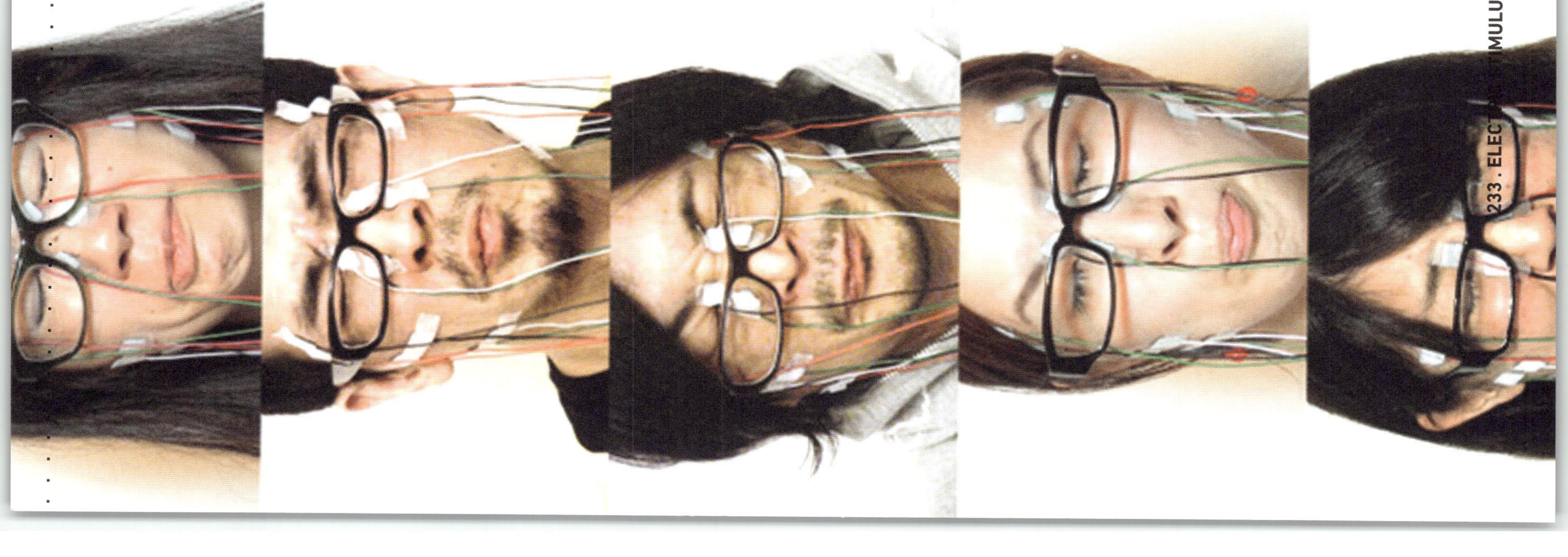

DISCRETE FIGURES

A dance performance generating physical expression through a mathematical, collective, intelligence-based methodology.

AI and machine learning offer new insights into the body schema and movement, numeric data, and analytical results informing choreography.

DISCRETE FIGURES is a neighborhood search system that matches data from stage footage and movies alongside dancer pose data, projecting similar poses into a rectangular on-stage frame.

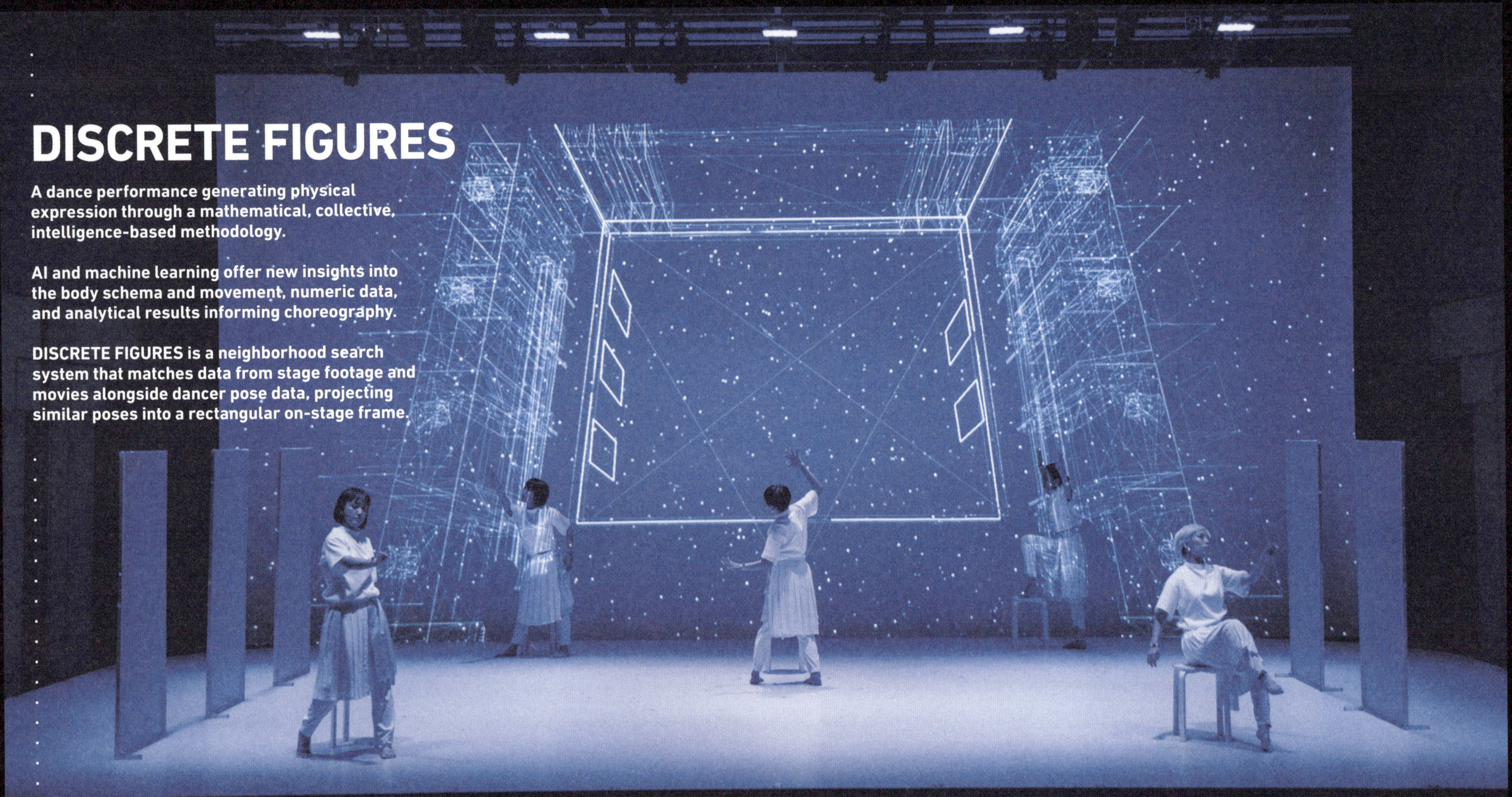

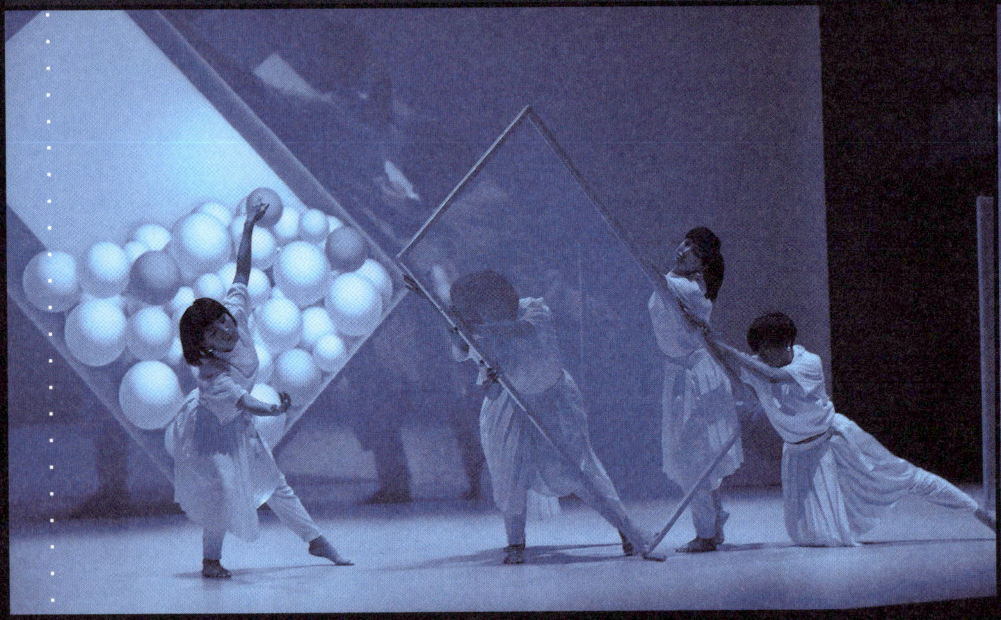

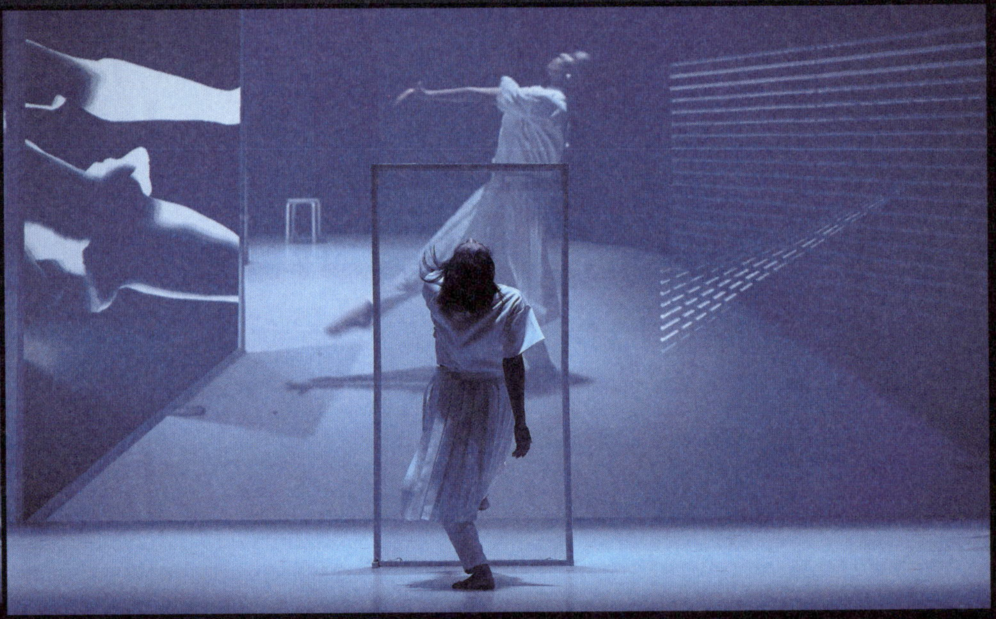

https://research.rhizomatiks.com/s/works/discrete_figures/en/information.html

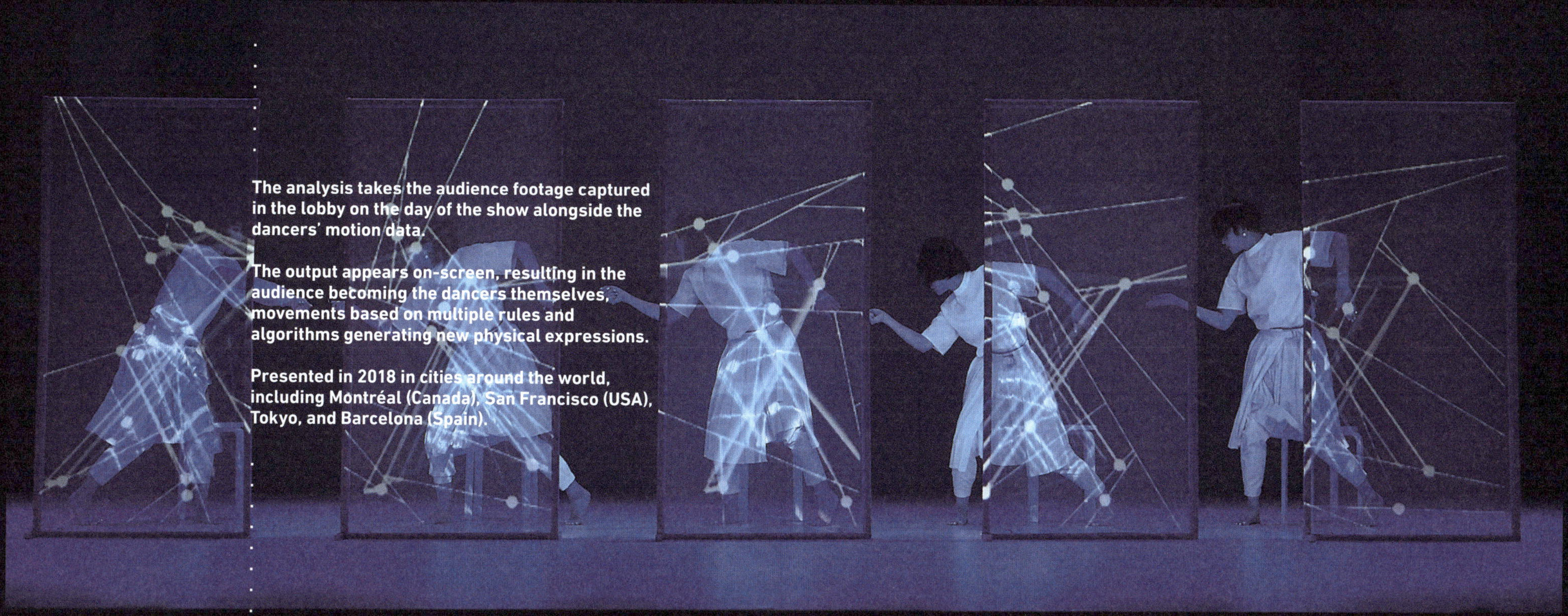

The analysis takes the audience footage captured in the lobby on the day of the show alongside the dancers' motion data.

The output appears on-screen, resulting in the audience becoming the dancers themselves, movements based on multiple rules and algorithms generating new physical expressions.

Presented in 2018 in cities around the world, including Montréal (Canada), San Francisco (USA), Tokyo, and Barcelona (Spain).

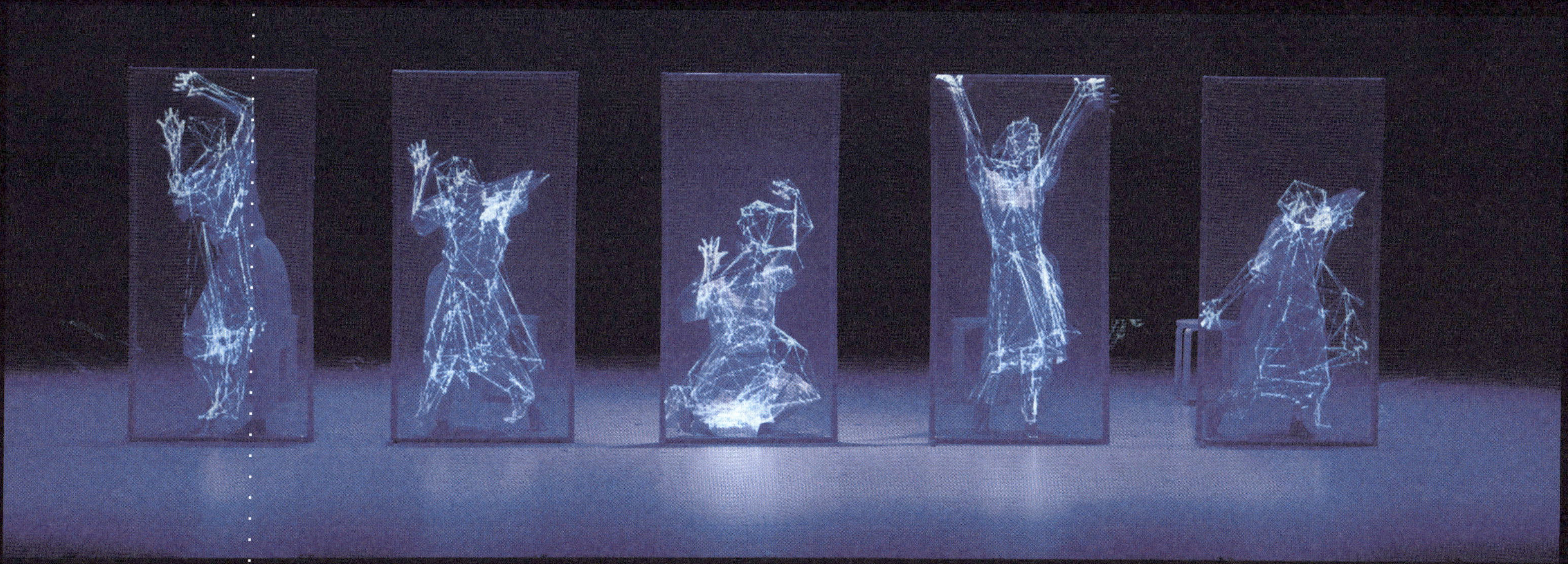

CREDITS

Pictures by Tomoya Takeshitaor, Suguru Saito

235 . ELEVENPLAY×RHIZOMATIKS RESEARCH×KYLE MCDONALD "DISCRETE FIGURES" (2018)

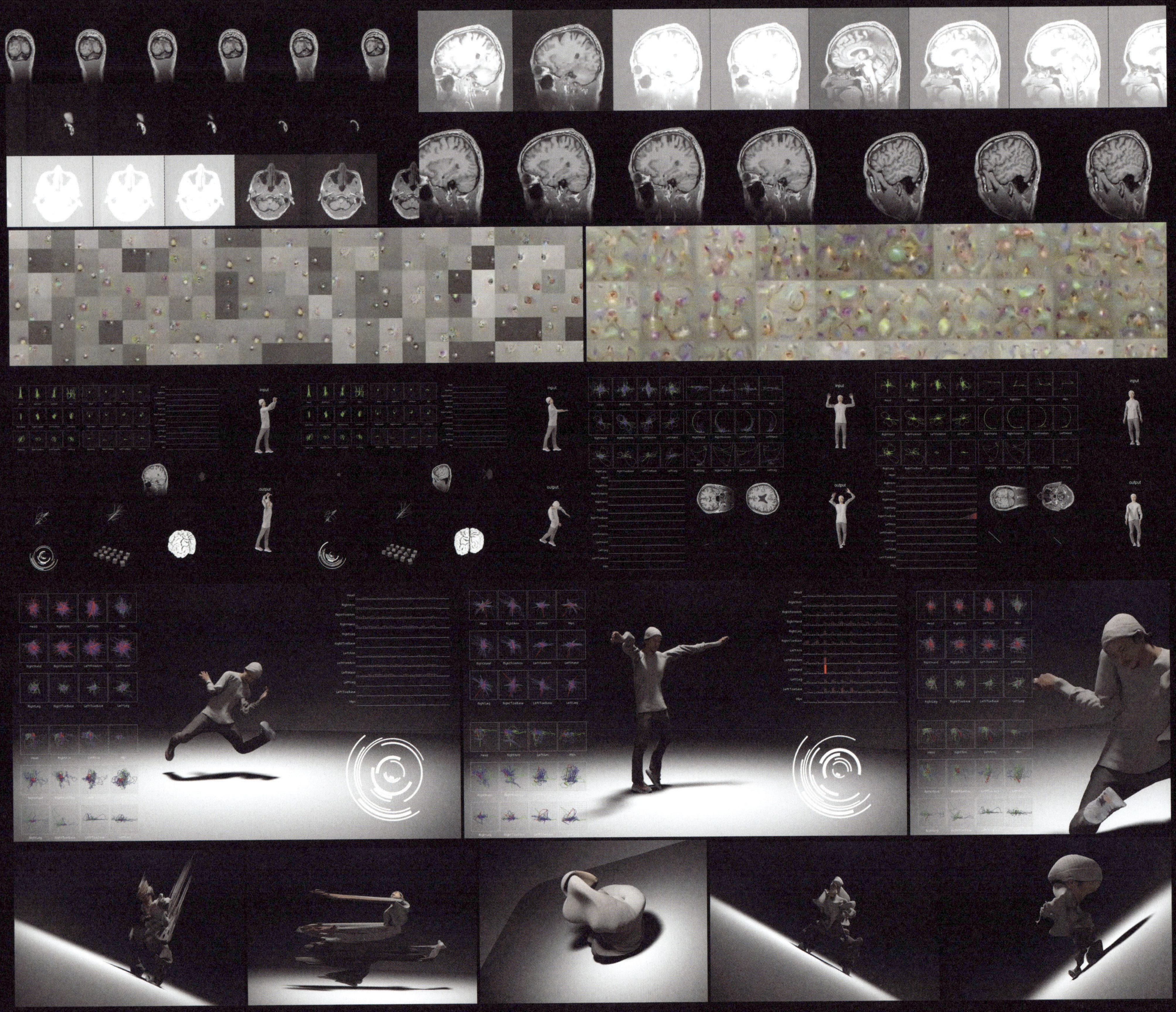

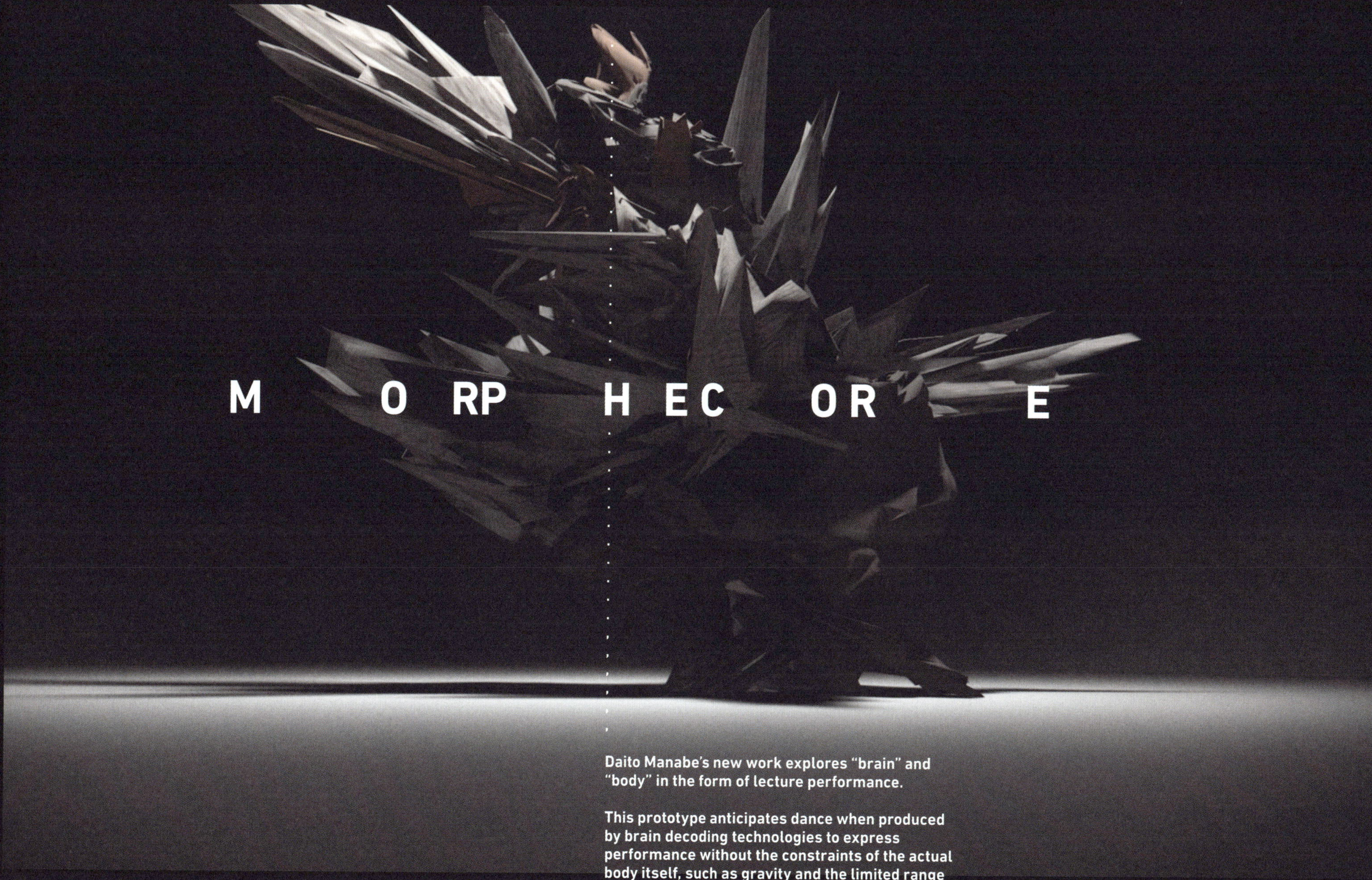

M O RP H EC OR E

Daito Manabe's new work explores "brain" and "body" in the form of lecture performance.

This prototype anticipates dance when produced by brain decoding technologies to express performance without the constraints of the actual body itself, such as gravity and the limited range of joint motion. Instead, noises and glitches are performed through distracting thoughts in the brain the body.

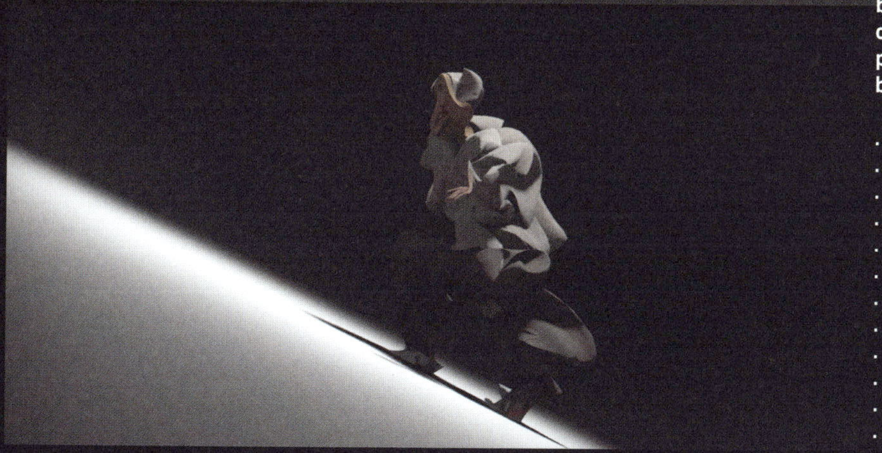

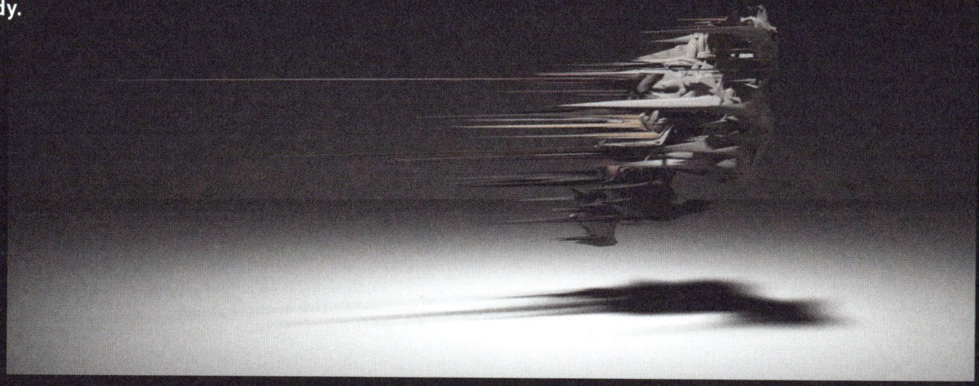

PERFUME IMAGINARY MUSEUM "TIME WARP" @ PERFUME P.O.P FESTIVAL

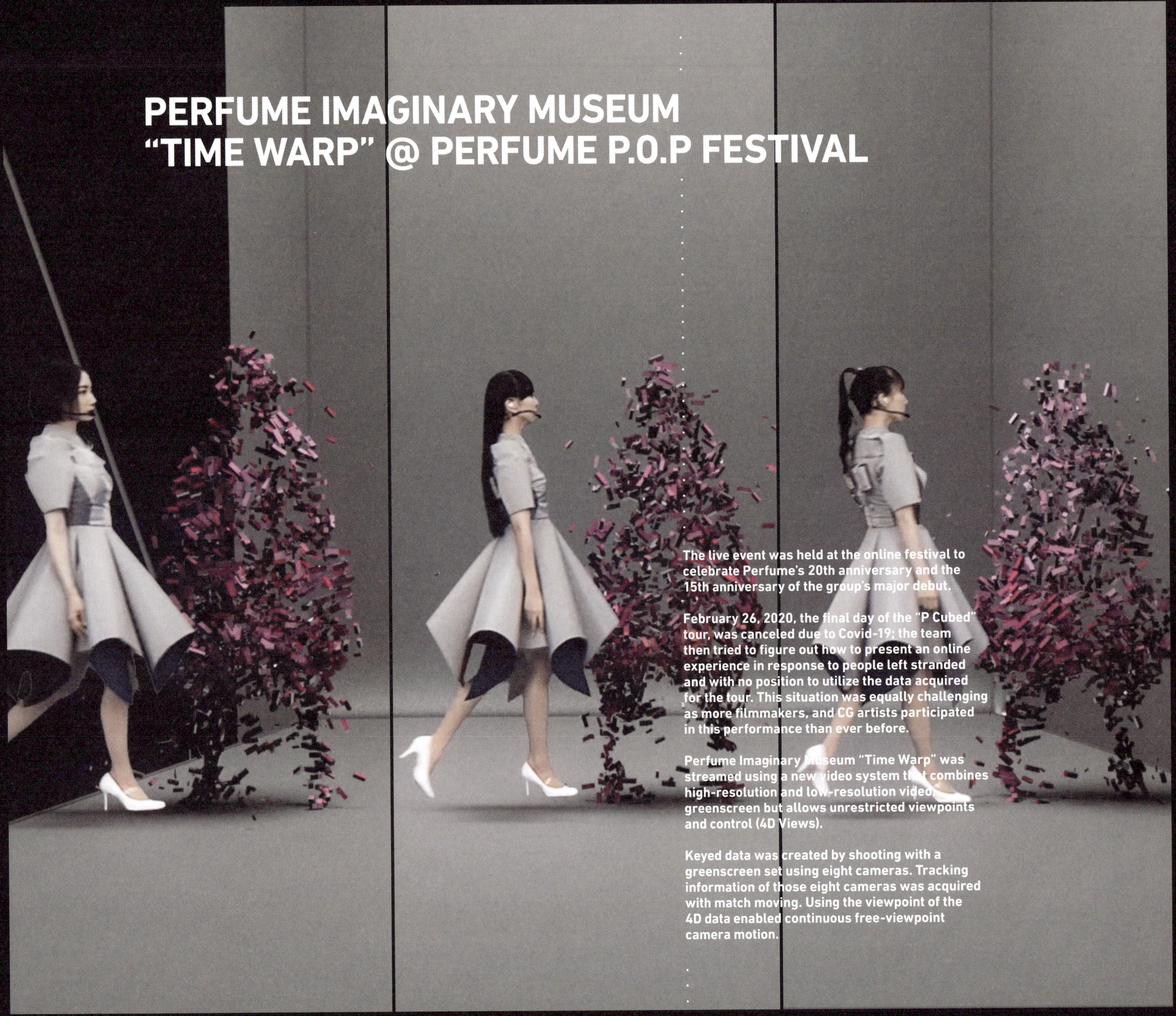

The live event was held at the online festival to celebrate Perfume's 20th anniversary and the 15th anniversary of the group's major debut.

February 26, 2020, the final day of the "P Cubed" tour, was canceled due to Covid-19; the team then tried to figure out how to present an online experience in response to people left stranded and with no position to utilize the data acquired for the tour. This situation was equally challenging as more filmmakers, and CG artists participated in this performance than ever before.

Perfume Imaginary Museum "Time Warp" was streamed using a new video system that combines high-resolution and low-resolution video, greenscreen but allows unrestricted viewpoints and control (4D Views).

Keyed data was created by shooting with a greenscreen set using eight cameras. Tracking information of those eight cameras was acquired with match moving. Using the viewpoint of the 4D data enabled continuous free-viewpoint camera motion.

https://www.perfume-popfes.jp/

COME BEHIND ME, SO GOOD [KAZU]

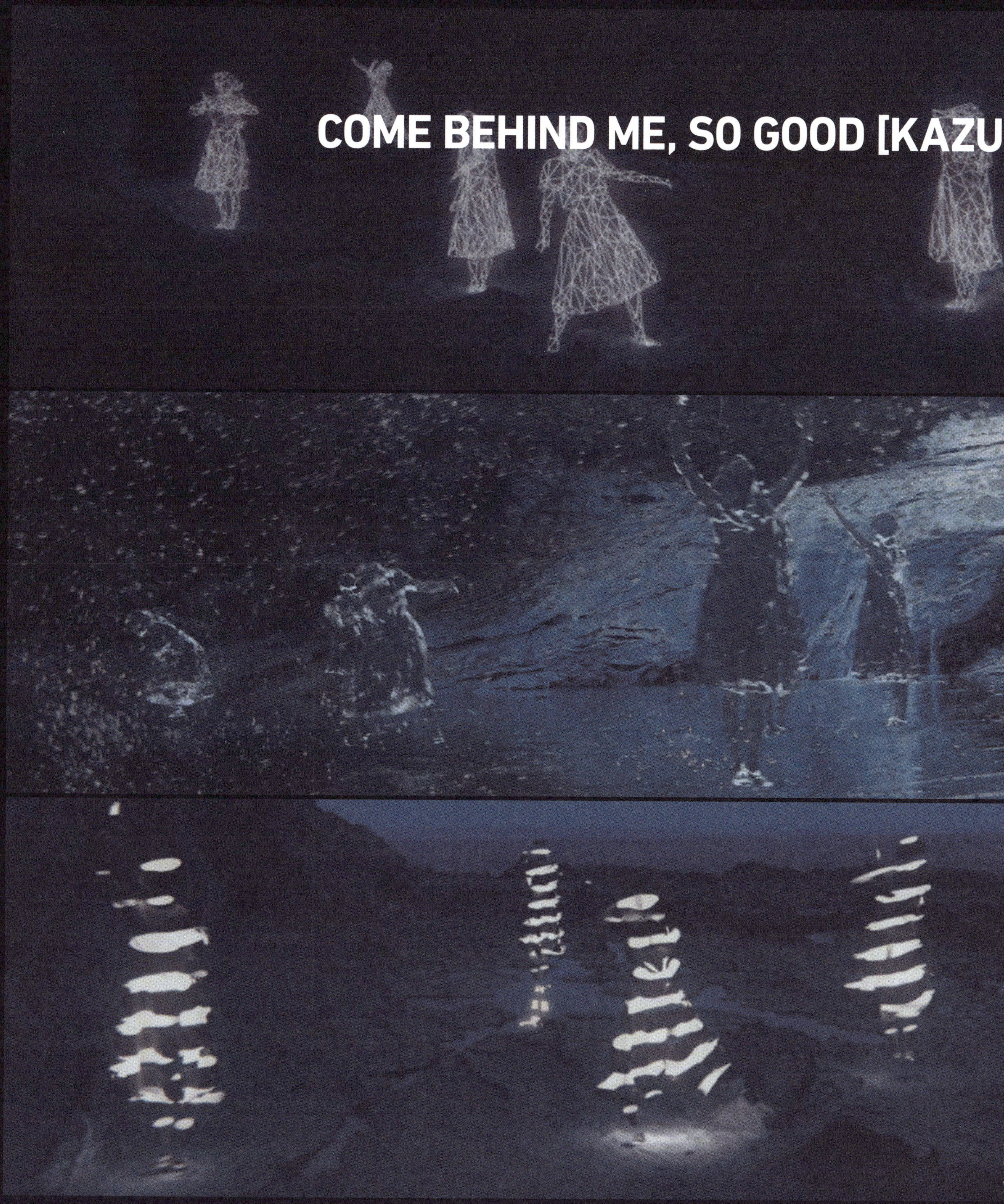

The video for Kazu is a combination of photogrammetry, which Rhizomatiks has fostered in various past projects, and a mix of cutting-edge software and hardware to collect plentiful data from realizing seamless mixed reality work at a large scale.

Photogrammetry is the technique used to create the dancers' three-dimensional data, enabling the creation of 3D data from still images taken at multiple angles. The process can also be used to reconstruct 2D data.

The first time Rhizomatiks used photogrammetry for dancers was the project with Perfume in 2012 when the algorithm was based on a silhouette. This process was not sophisticated enough to capture the complex expression of the facial surface; the texture was not smooth, but the quality has improved so much that Rhizomatiks continues to use the technique.

Besides extracting 3D using photogrammetry, static objects such as the landform are also built using a laser scanner to attain the 3D data.

This method, synthesizing various 3D data, has been present in our work since 2012. This ongoing method is also evident in the 2015 work at SXSW in the video for Nosaj Thing and Chance The Rapper; it was the first time we had the opportunity to work with so many dancers and handle this much environmental data.

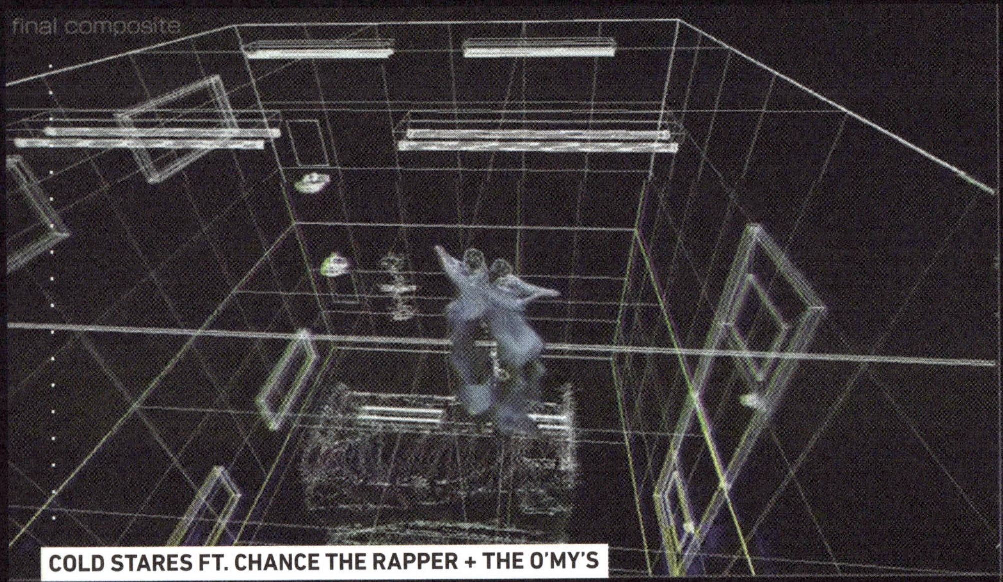

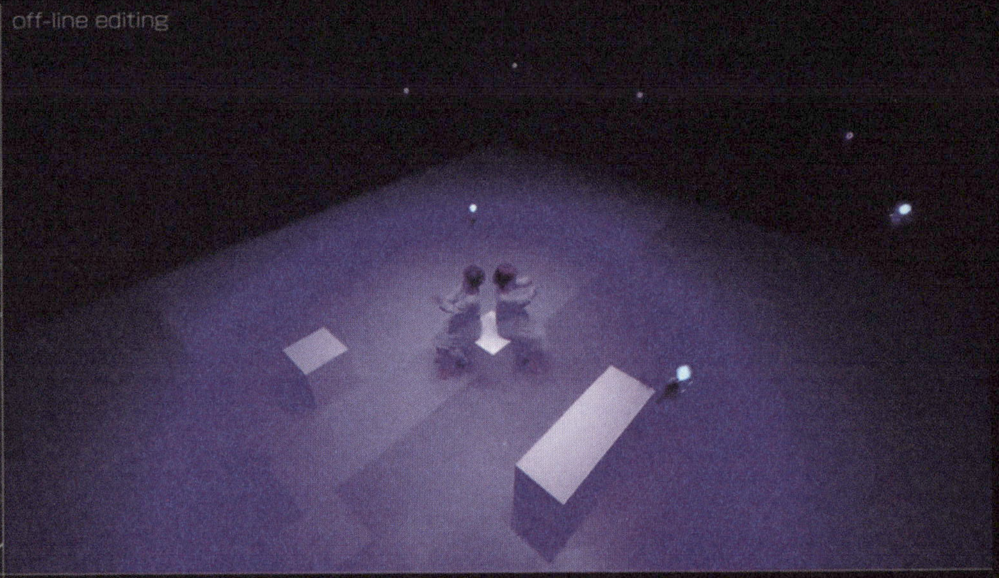

COLD STARES FT. CHANCE THE RAPPER + THE O'MY'S

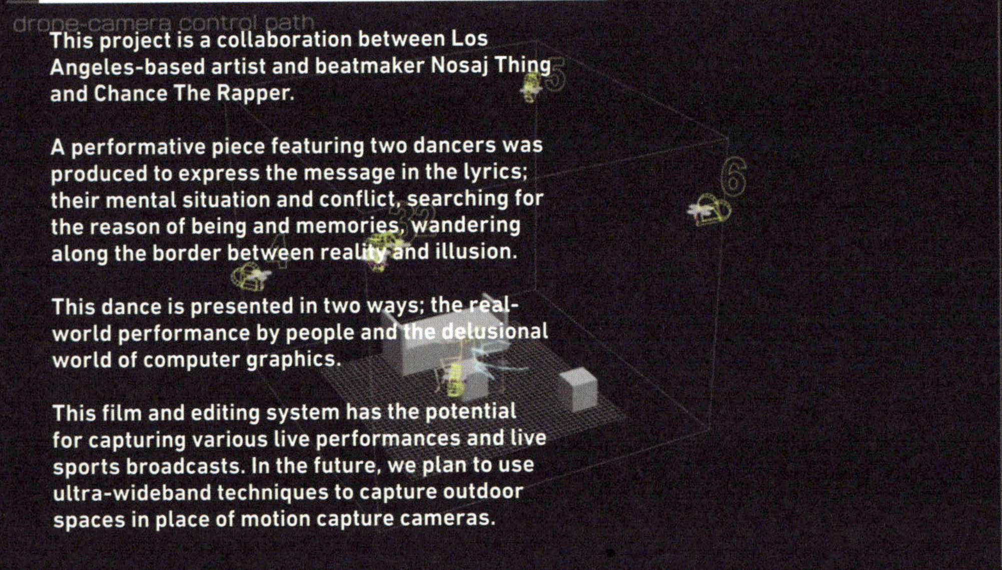

This project is a collaboration between Los Angeles-based artist and beatmaker Nosaj Thing and Chance The Rapper.

A performative piece featuring two dancers was produced to express the message in the lyrics; their mental situation and conflict, searching for the reason of being and memories, wandering along the border between reality and illusion.

This dance is presented in two ways; the real-world performance by people and the delusional world of computer graphics.

This film and editing system has the potential for capturing various live performances and live sports broadcasts. In the future, we plan to use ultra-wideband techniques to capture outdoor spaces in place of motion capture cameras.

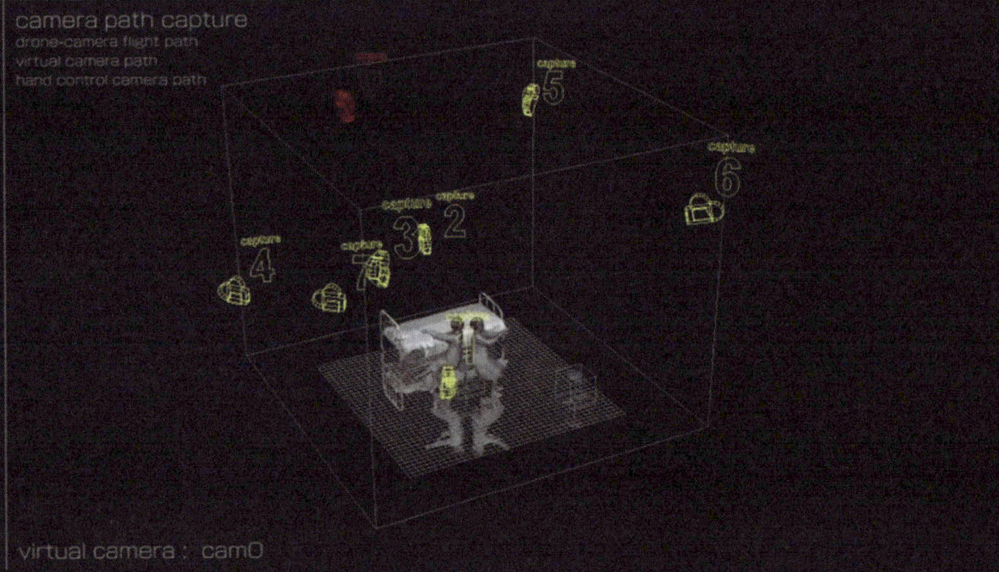

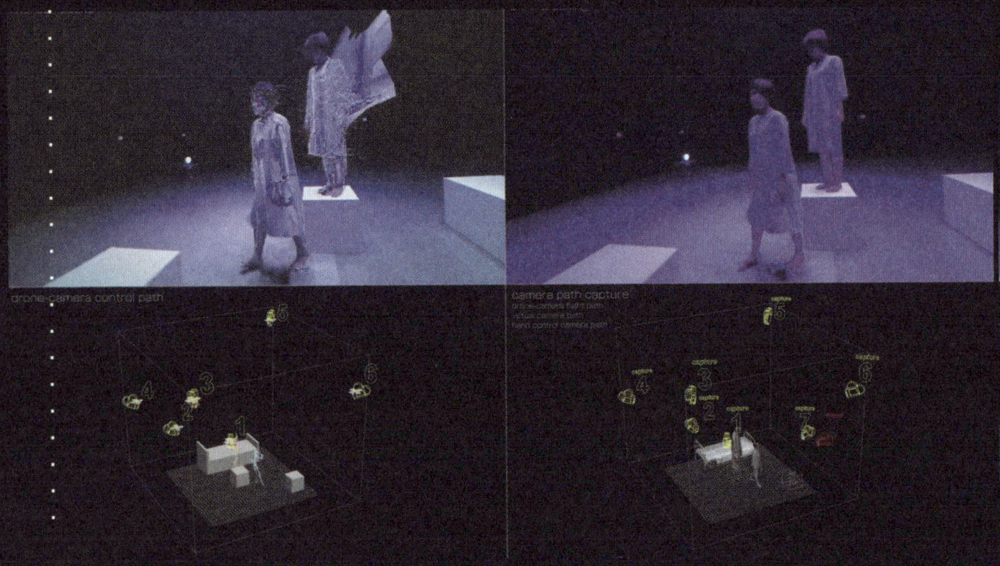

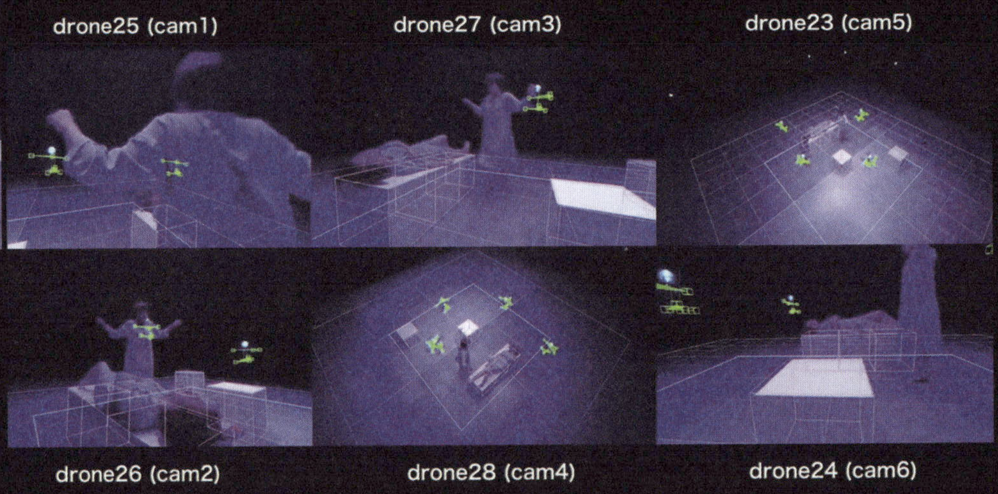

https://research.rhizomatiks.com/s/works/nosajthing_coldstares/

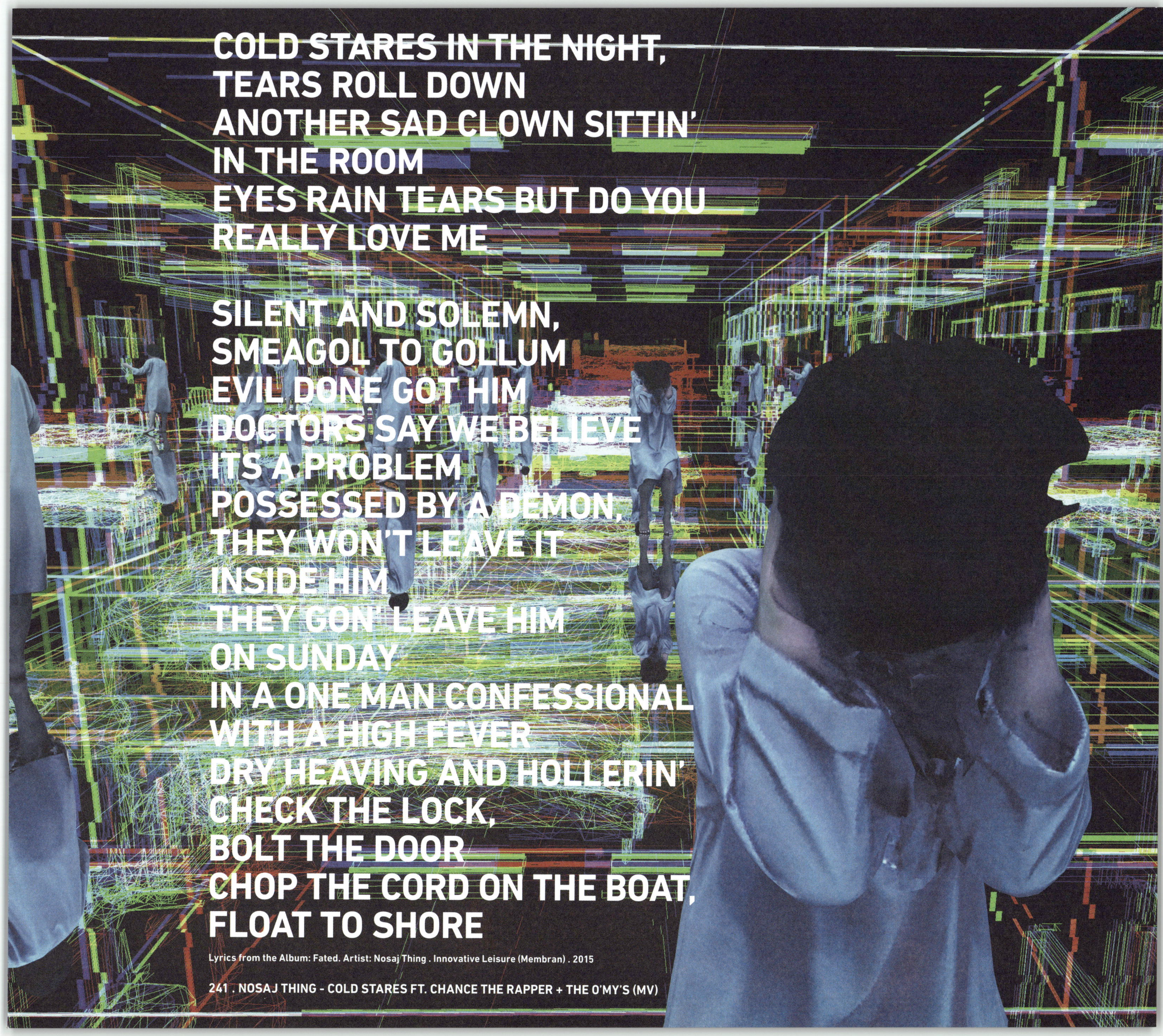

COLD STARES IN THE NIGHT,
TEARS ROLL DOWN
ANOTHER SAD CLOWN SITTIN'
IN THE ROOM
EYES RAIN TEARS BUT DO YOU
REALLY LOVE ME

SILENT AND SOLEMN,
SMEAGOL TO GOLLUM
EVIL DONE GOT HIM
DOCTORS SAY WE BELIEVE
ITS A PROBLEM
POSSESSED BY A DEMON,
THEY WON'T LEAVE IT
INSIDE HIM
THEY GON' LEAVE HIM
ON SUNDAY
IN A ONE MAN CONFESSIONAL
WITH A HIGH FEVER
DRY HEAVING AND HOLLERIN'
CHECK THE LOCK,
BOLT THE DOOR
CHOP THE CORD ON THE BOAT,
FLOAT TO SHORE

Lyrics from the Album: Fated. Artist: Nosaj Thing . Innovative Leisure (Membran) . 2015

241 . NOSAJ THING - COLD STARES FT. CHANCE THE RAPPER + THE O'MY'S (MV)

Tokyo Tokyo FESTIVAL Special 13
Light and Sound Installation

CODED FIELD

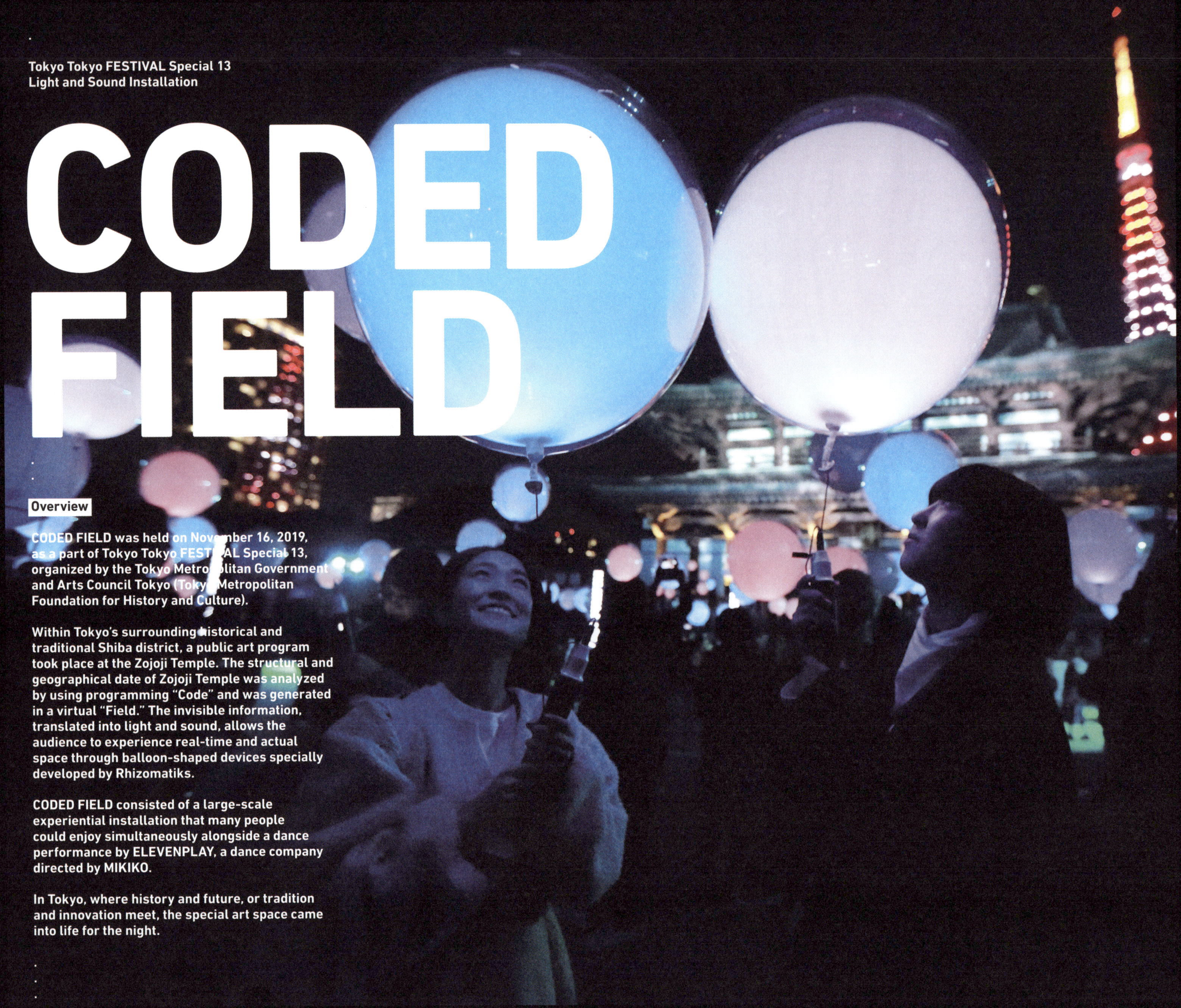

Overview

CODED FIELD was held on November 16, 2019, as a part of Tokyo Tokyo FESTIVAL Special 13, organized by the Tokyo Metropolitan Government and Arts Council Tokyo (Tokyo Metropolitan Foundation for History and Culture).

Within Tokyo's surrounding historical and traditional Shiba district, a public art program took place at the Zojoji Temple. The structural and geographical date of Zojoji Temple was analyzed by using programming "Code" and was generated in a virtual "Field." The invisible information, translated into light and sound, allows the audience to experience real-time and actual space through balloon-shaped devices specially developed by Rhizomatiks.

CODED FIELD consisted of a large-scale experiential installation that many people could enjoy simultaneously alongside a dance performance by ELEVENPLAY, a dance company directed by MIKIKO.

In Tokyo, where history and future, or tradition and innovation meet, the special art space came into life for the night.

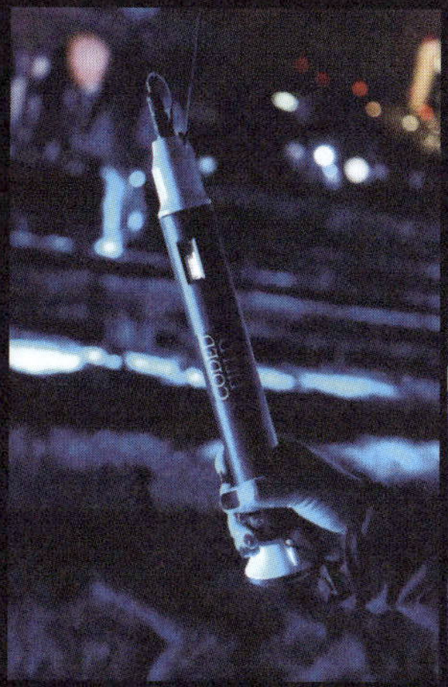

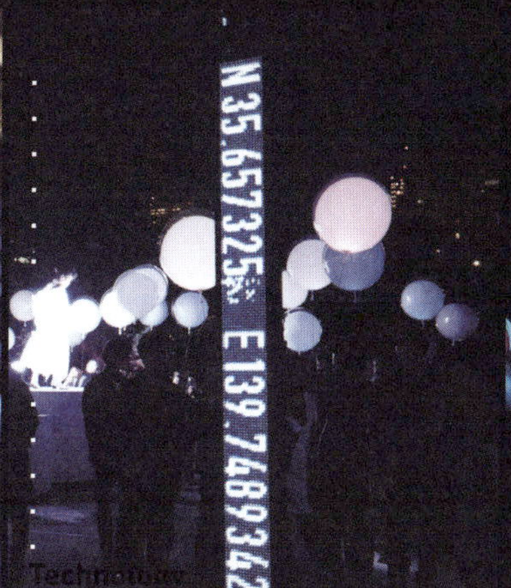

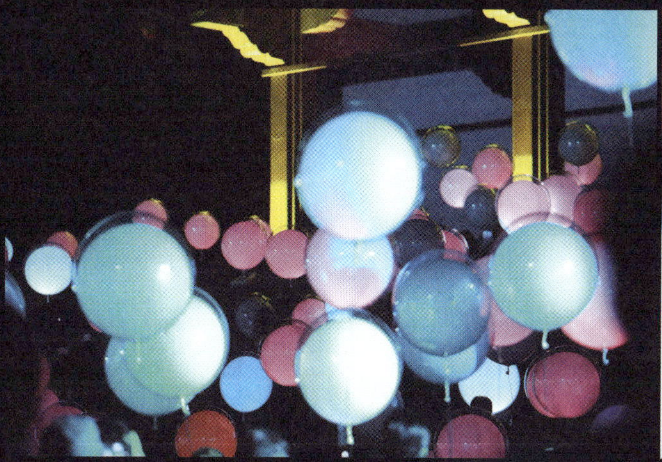

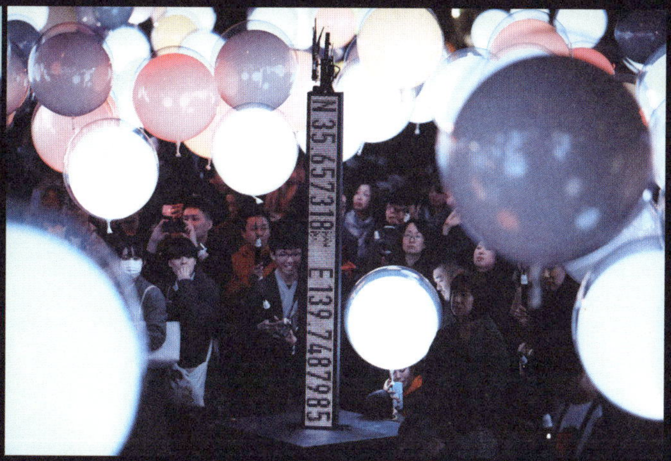

Technology

The handheld device Rhizomatiks had developed for this event was adapted SPRESENSE™ by Sony Semiconductor Solutions Corporation as a mainboard. The device, fitted with GNSS (Global Navigation Satellite System), LEDs, and speakers, altered patterns according to location data.

Since most of the penlights at concerts usually use group ID or seat numbers to control lightning, they cannot be used for those events where there are no fixed seats, or the audience can wander around spontaneously. However, GNSS enables a more flexible direction without causing any restrictions on the audience location. With this improvement of positioning technologies, highly accurate location data, which conventionally is only attainable indoors, could now be adapted to outdoor usage, advancing the relationships between a realistic and virtual space.

Baroon-shaped handheld devices created visual illusions of lights floating throughout. Additionally, sound from the device, controlled by location or the progression of live performance, made the unprecedented soundscape; inherited speakers inside 1,000 devices made sounds together.

For the first time, we created a fully autonomous driving device for a live performance. Controlled with a highly accurate, real-time kinematic global positioning system and supported by Omni wheeled robots with lightning equipment mounts that could be moved forward/backward and left/right.

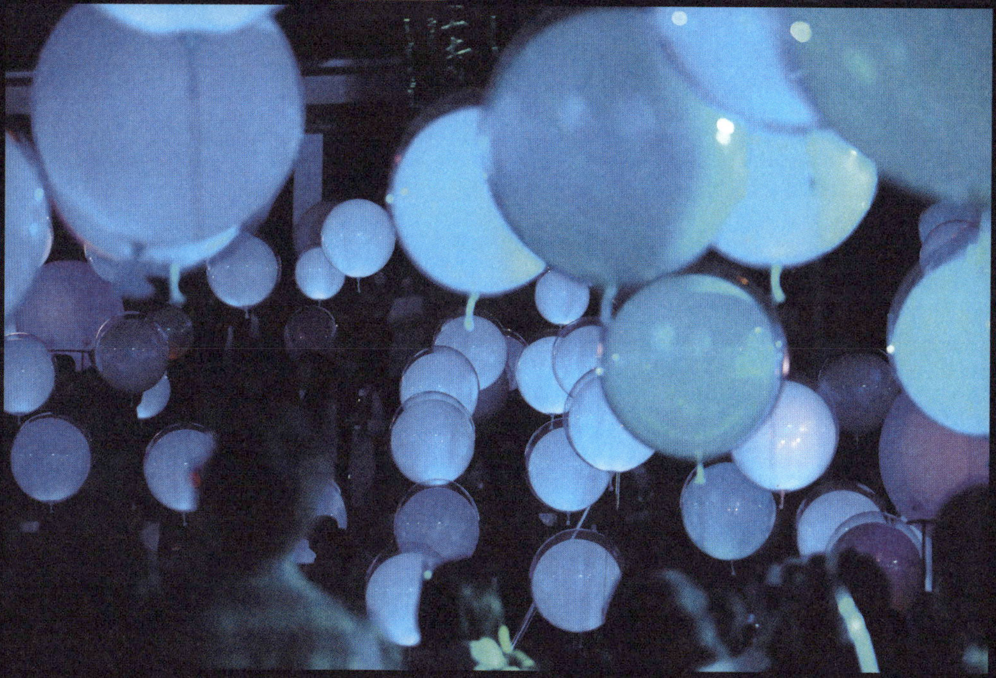

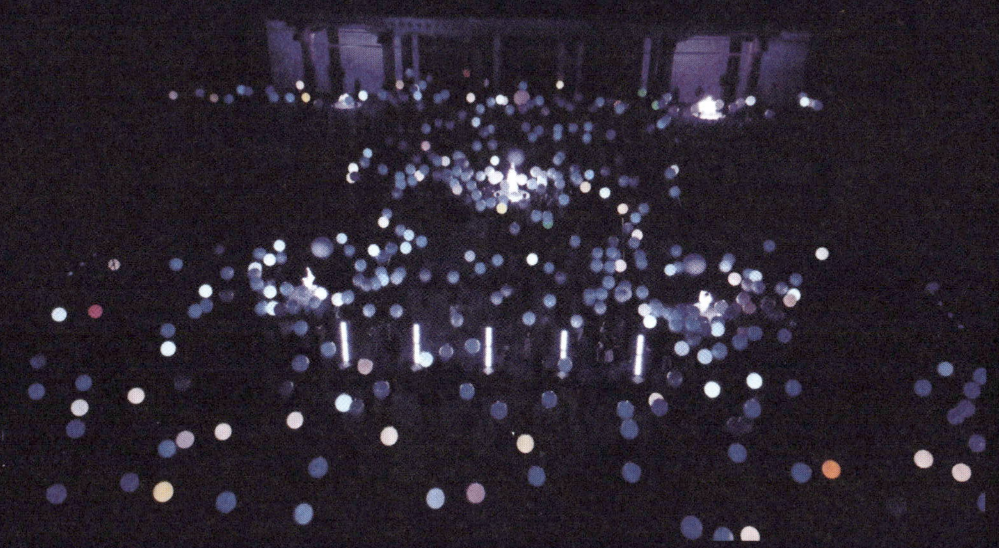

CREDITS

Photo courtesy of: Rhizomatiks

Name:

MuirMcNeil

Info:

Founded in 2009 by Paul McNeil and Hamish Muir, MuirMcNeil's activities focus on exploring systematic and algorithmic methods in graphic design, type design, and moving image.

Paul McNeil is a typographic designer, educator, and author. Seven years in the making, The Visual History of Type, his exhaustive survey of type design from 1450–2015, was published in 2017.

Hamish Muir was co-founder of the London-based graphic design studio 8vo (1985–2001) and co-editor of Octavo, journal of typography (1986–92).

Project:

EYE NO. 94 COVER

URL:

muirmcneil.com

Mail:

info@muirmcneil.com

Instagram:

@muirmcneil

Project Description:

Eye Magazine is a long-established international review of graphic design and visual culture. Its 94th edition was a typography special that included an article about MuirMcNeil written by John Walters, its editor, who also invited us to design the cover.

To do so, we set up a systematic procedure that would generate 8,000 uniquely different typographic compositions within a consistent design space.

For the EYE 94 COVER, we used our TwoPoint and TwoPlus type systems, an extensive series of related modular designs that we had developed over several different projects. These expanded examples completed the key asset of the brand identity SoTA's TypeCon conference in 2016.

In the Two system typefaces, individual letters operate as variable components of differential visual systems.

A common grid determines positioning for both characters and spaces in all TwoPoint and TwoPlus typefaces, with every contour and space aligning precisely.

Our collaboration as MuirMcNeil grew out of a shared interest in developing processes, conditions, and mechanisms that can give rise to many different outputs rather than result in single, one-off design outcomes. While we are not programmers, we work programmatically, using systematic methods to open up the possibilities of form-giving. Our intention is to allow the process to become the product.

We began the EYE 94 COVER project by exploring TwoPoint and TwoPlus typefaces to interact and be superimposed in multiple layers, applying selected weights and styles to the word "eye" in various precisely calibrated offsets. Testing contours, colors, textures, patterns, and transparencies in a variety of configurations.

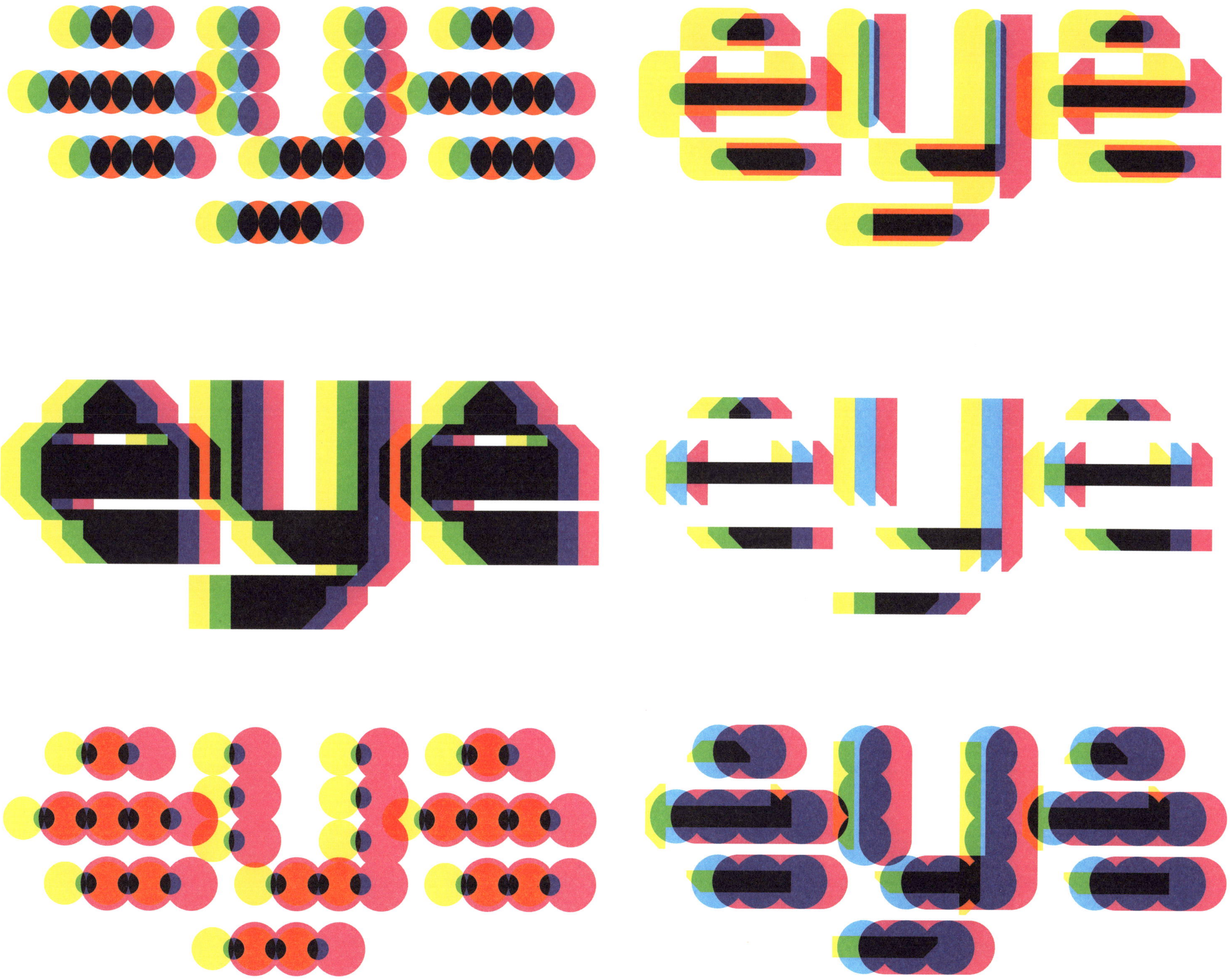
eye
eye
eye
eye
eye
eye

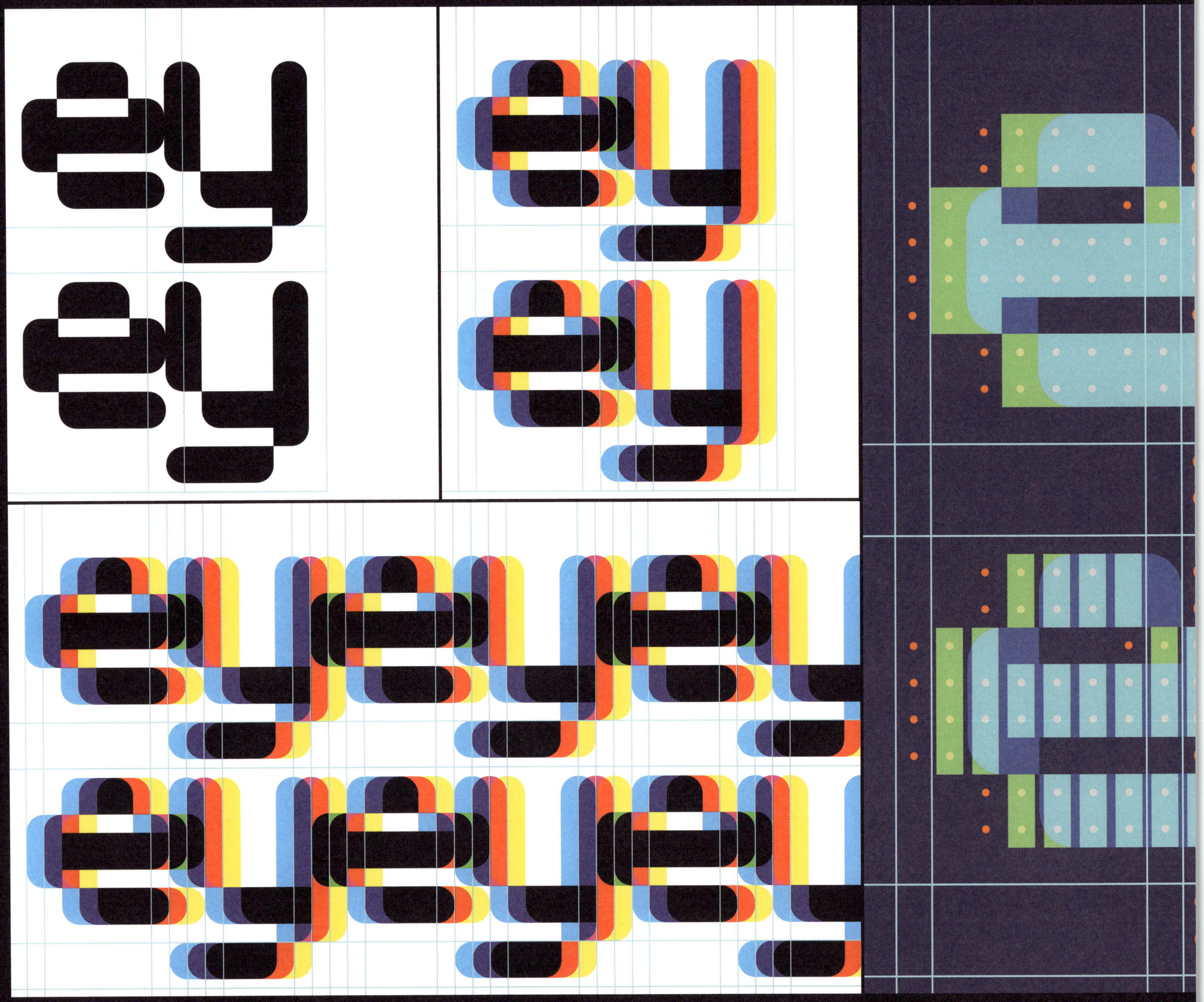

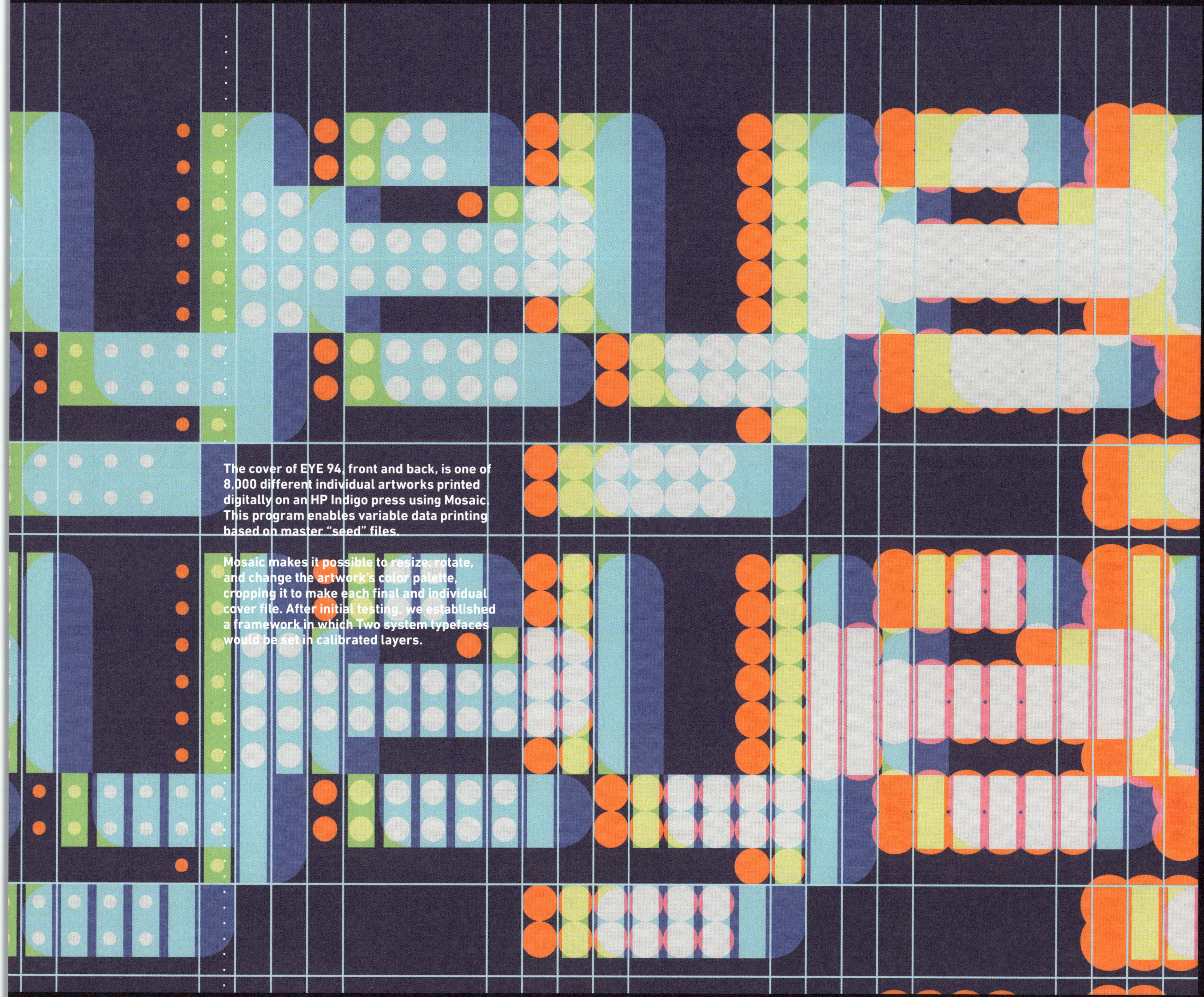

The cover of EYE 94, front and back, is one of 8,000 different individual artworks printed digitally on an HP Indigo press using Mosaic. This program enables variable data printing based on master "seed" files.

Mosaic makes it possible to resize, rotate, and change the artwork's color palette, cropping it to make each final and individual cover file. After initial testing, we established a framework in which Two system typefaces would be set in calibrated layers.

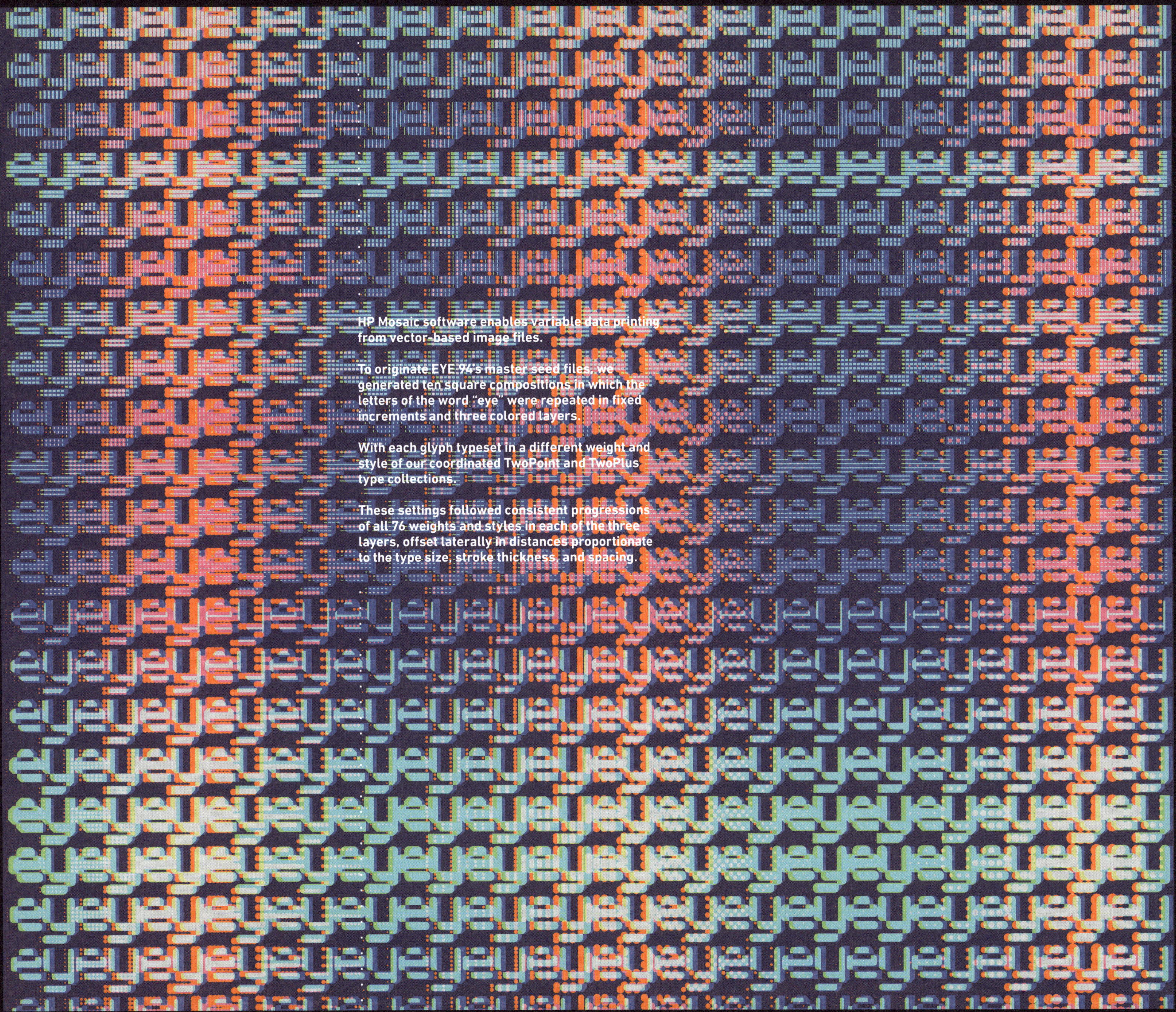

HP Mosaic software enables variable data printing from vector-based image files.

To originate EYE 94's master seed files, we generated ten square compositions in which the letters of the word "eye" were repeated in fixed increments and three colored layers.

With each glyph typeset in a different weight and style of our coordinated TwoPoint and TwoPlus type collections.

These settings followed consistent progressions of all 76 weights and styles in each of the three layers, offset laterally in distances proportionate to the type size, stroke thickness, and spacing.

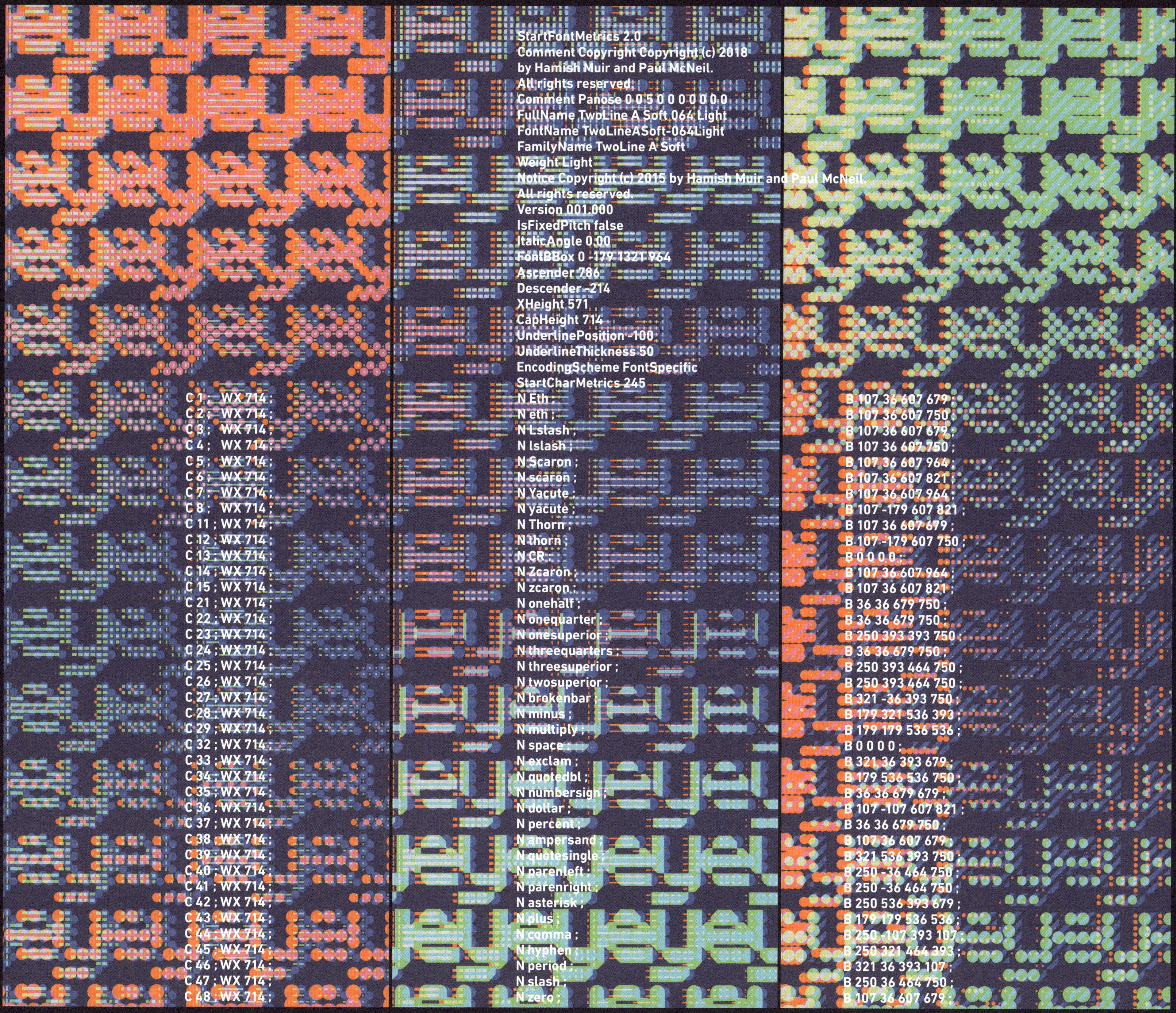

249 . EYE NO. 94 COVER

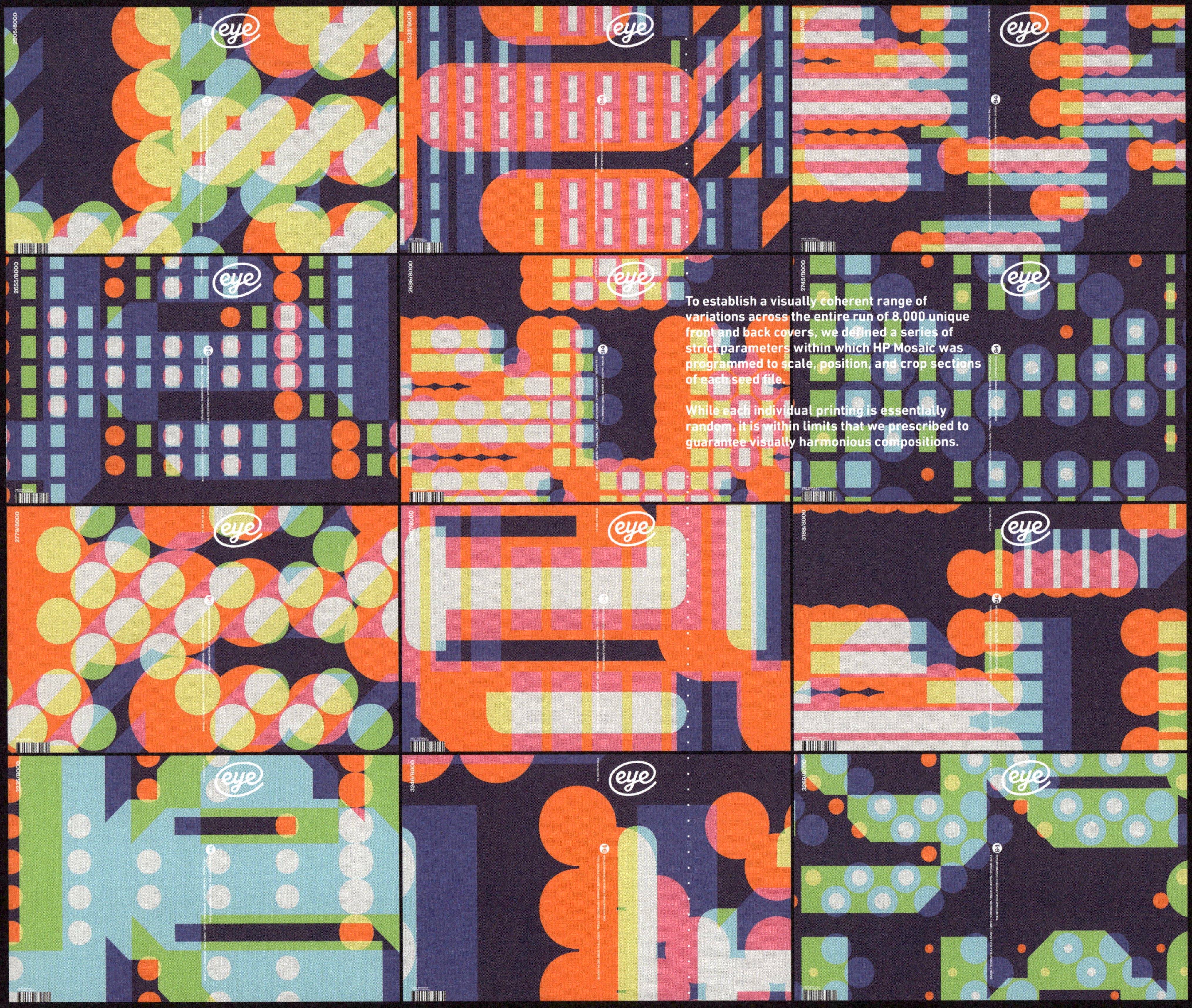

To establish a visually coherent range of variations across the entire run of 8,000 unique front and back covers, we defined a series of strict parameters within which HP Mosaic was programmed to scale, position, and crop sections of each seed file.

While each individual printing is essentially random, it is within limits that we prescribed to guarantee visually harmonious compositions.

250 . MuirMcNeil

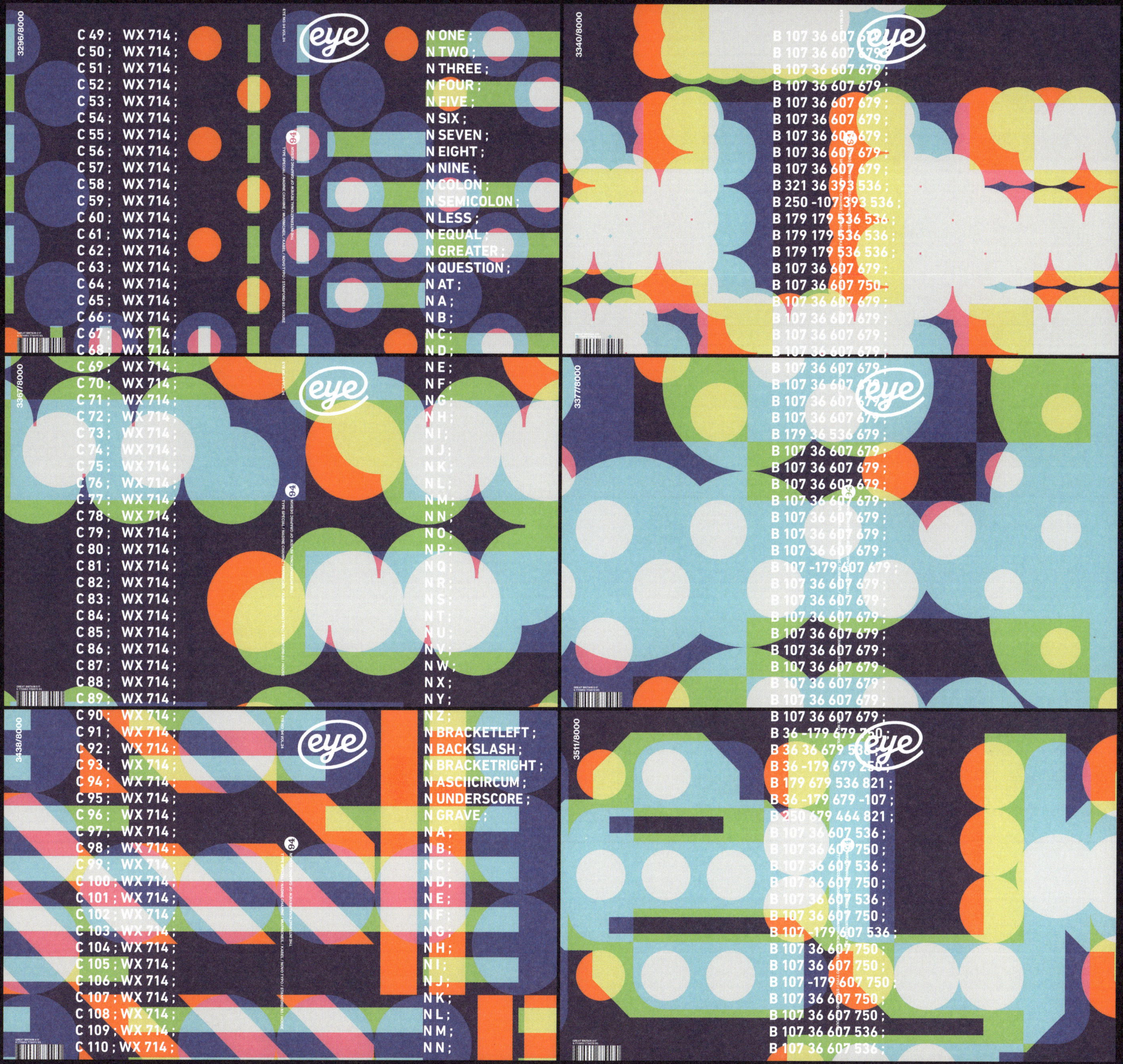

251 . EYE NO. 94 COVER

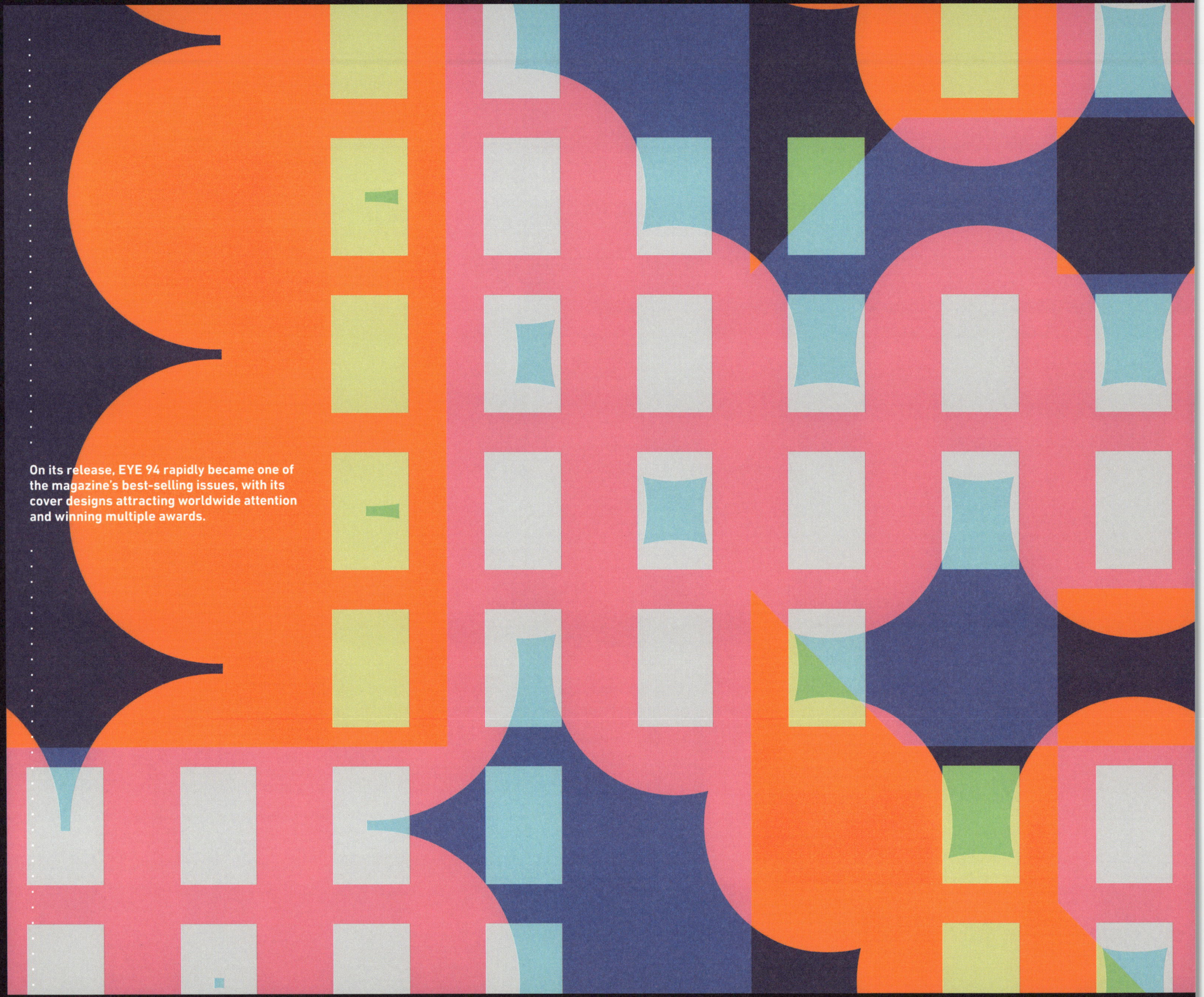

On its release, EYE 94 rapidly became one of the magazine's best-selling issues, with its cover designs attracting worldwide attention and winning multiple awards.

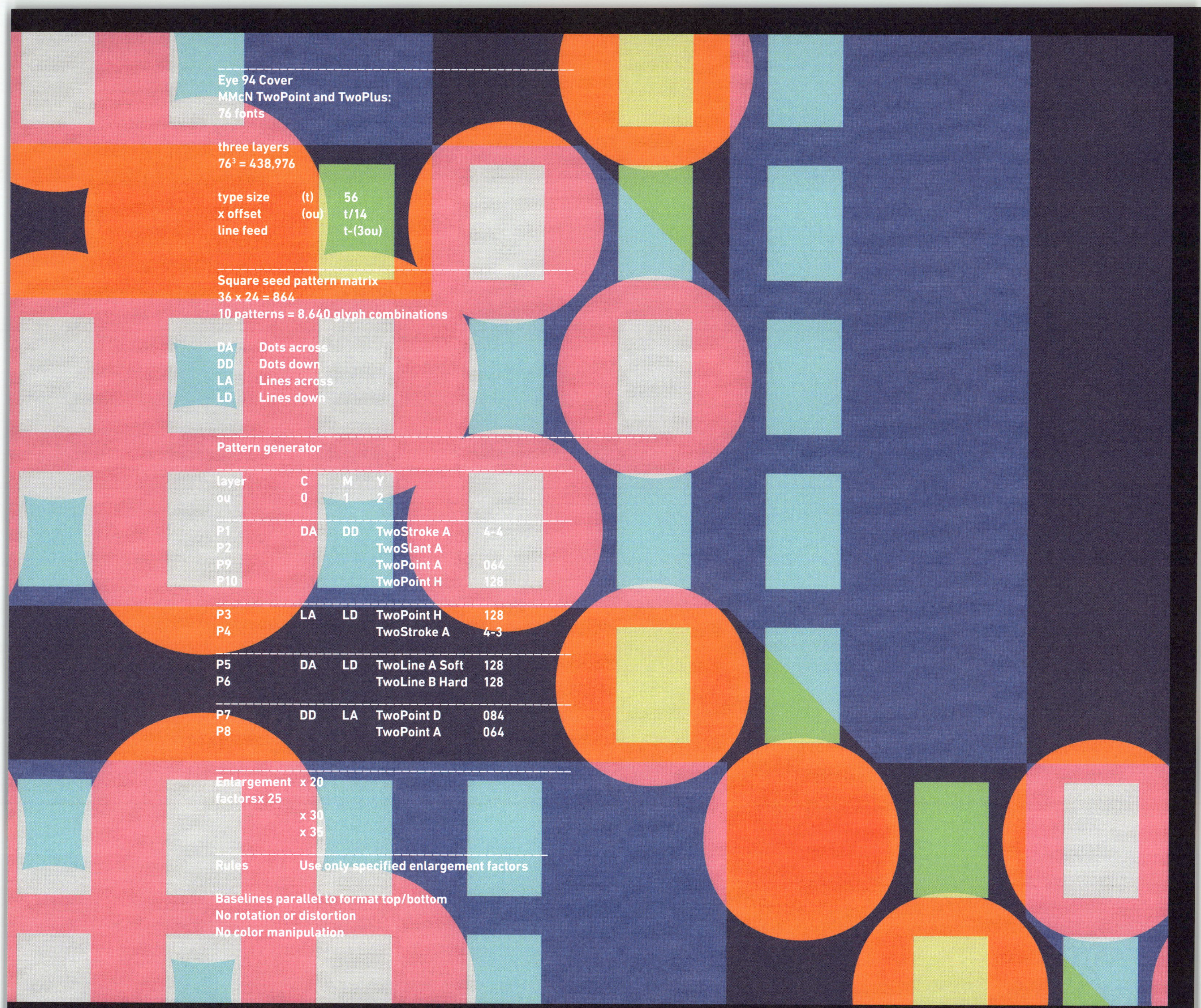

253 . EYE NO. 94 COVER

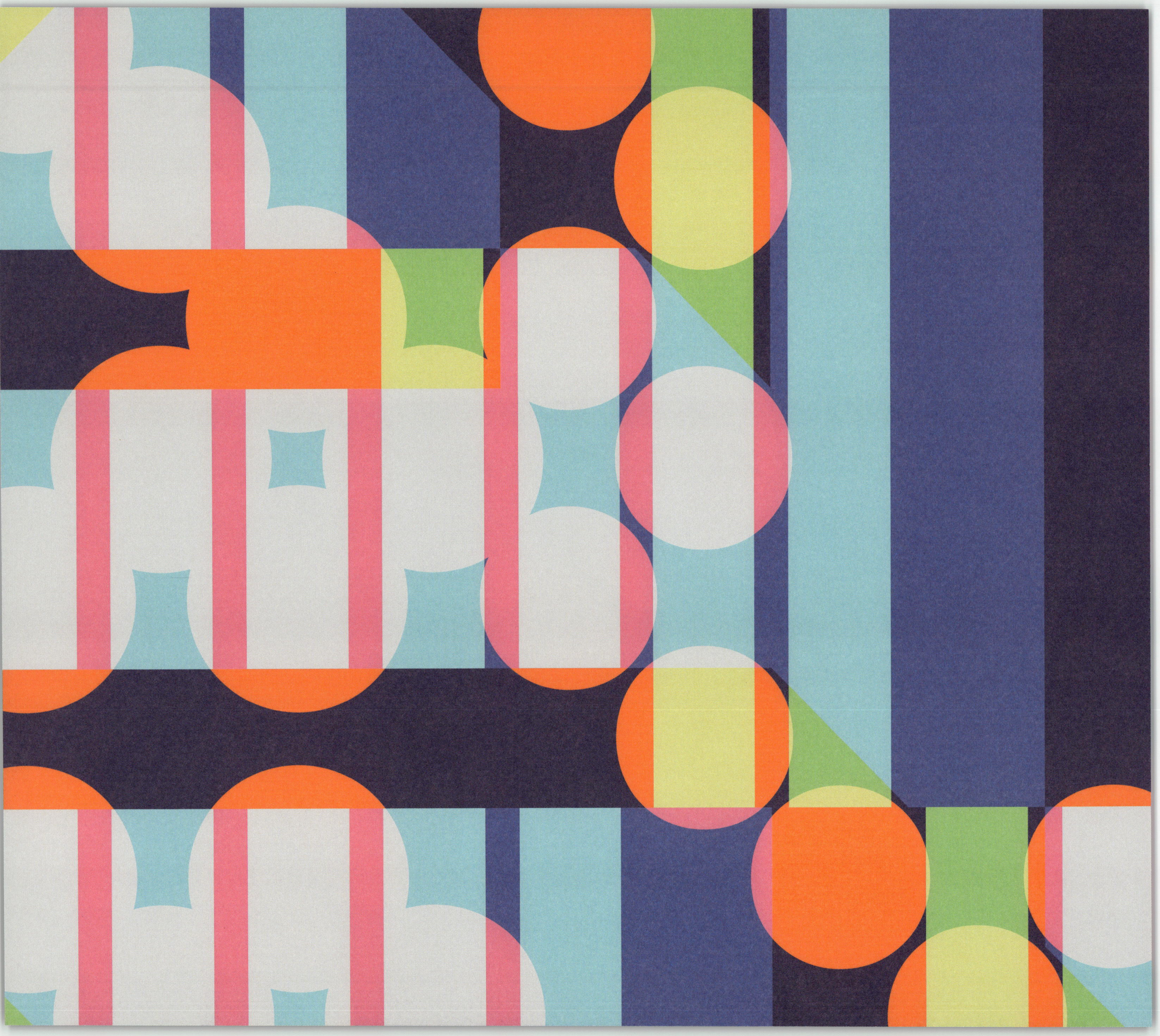

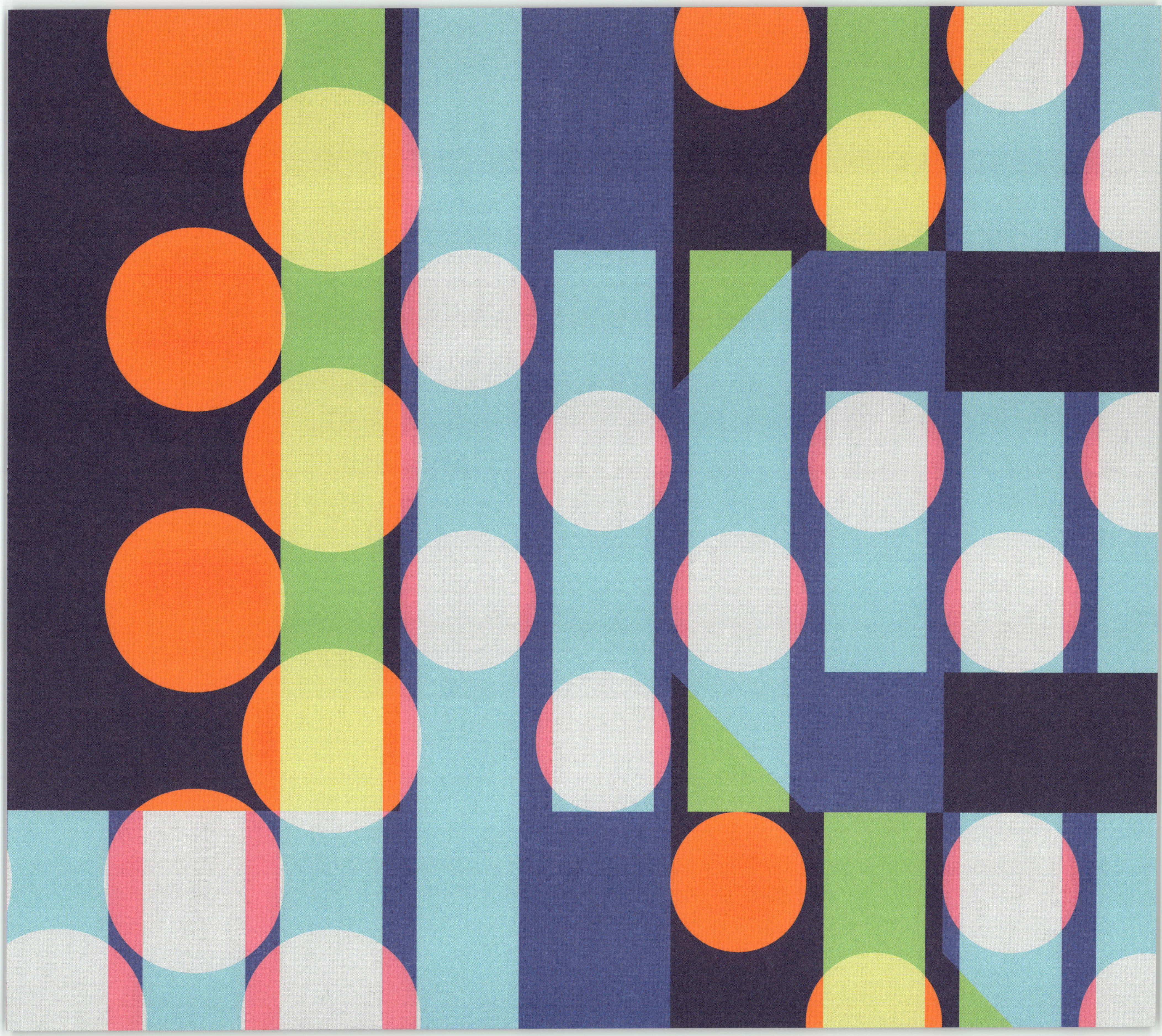

Name:

NONOTAK

Info:

Noemi Schipfer
Visual Artist
Takami Nakamoto
Artist, Architect Musician

NONOTAK Studio is the collaboration between the illustrator Noemi Schipfer and the architect, musician; Takami Nakamoto. Commissioned by the architect Bigoni-Mortemard to create a mural in the lobby of a public housing building in Paris, NONOTAK formed in late 2011.

In early 2013, NONOTAK started work on light and sound installations, creating an ethereal, immersive and dreamlike environment meant to envelop the viewer, capitalizing on Nakamoto's approach to space and sound and Schipfer's experience of the kinetic visual.

Project:

DAYDREAM V2

URL:

nonotak.com

Mail:

nonotakstudio@gmail.com

Instagram:

@nonotakstudio

References:

- Mapping Festival
- EM15 ELEKTRA / MUTEK
- la Nuit Blanche
- Roppongi Art night
- Axcess Art Gallery
- Stereolux
- Playgrounds Festival
...

Q&As

. . . . . Please explain the main idea and what gave the impulse?

NONOTAK's exploration of light materiality combined with space and sound has one goal; the visitor, their experience, and our ability to tell a story you can feel through the senses.

The idea of the DAYDREAM series installation is one of our first experiments. The main idea was to allow light to float as layers in space and envelope the audience. But before even realizing all of this, the main reason this project became an obsession is that we wanted to experience the artwork itself.

Creating a space for contemplation where senses are augmented and disrupted through an intense soundscape orchestrating how visuals oscillate and affect our perception.

. . . . . What challenges did you face for this project? And what surprises?

Scale is mostly the challenge. Our artworks are meant to resonate with the architectural context but, most importantly, with the human body.

Because we want the experience to be the most immersive, it is essential to find suitable proportions for visitors to appreciate completely; be thoroughly aware, and feel each part of the story we are telling.

DAYDREAM was one of our first experiments using projection as the medium. We discovered many aspects of this artwork while building it, inspiring us for the next ones.

. . . . . Please describe the technical environment.

The installation is built of wooden frames and transparent fabric that catches the light but allows some to pass through the material.

Two powerful and short ratio projectors were used to generate the visuals onto framed screens.

Projectors and sound systems are placed in the back of the frames to be invisible to the audience. This process allows visitors to get close and even touch the artwork without creating any shadows on the piece, which is always challenging when working around video projectors.

. . . . . Tell us about your aesthetical approach.

Our aesthetical approach is minimal.

We are composing the visuals with simple two-dimensional geometric shapes, but the duplication through the layers makes them look like we are looking at a three-dimensional sculpture. The structure itself generates complexity out of simple two-dimensional animations.

We are only using solid white color because we consider the visuals more like a light source than video content, allowing us to have the best brightness and contrast. That way, we can focus purely on the graphic aspect, allowing us to draw spaces and perspectives using lines of lights.

. . . . . What's next? Your vision?

We have been experimenting with light for more than seven years, predominantly in dark environments. This method inspires us to think about creating immersive experiences using daylight or in non-controlled light conditions. Permanent work is what we desire to do next as long as most of our projects are being ephemeral in the form of exhibitions or public shows.

NO NO T AK

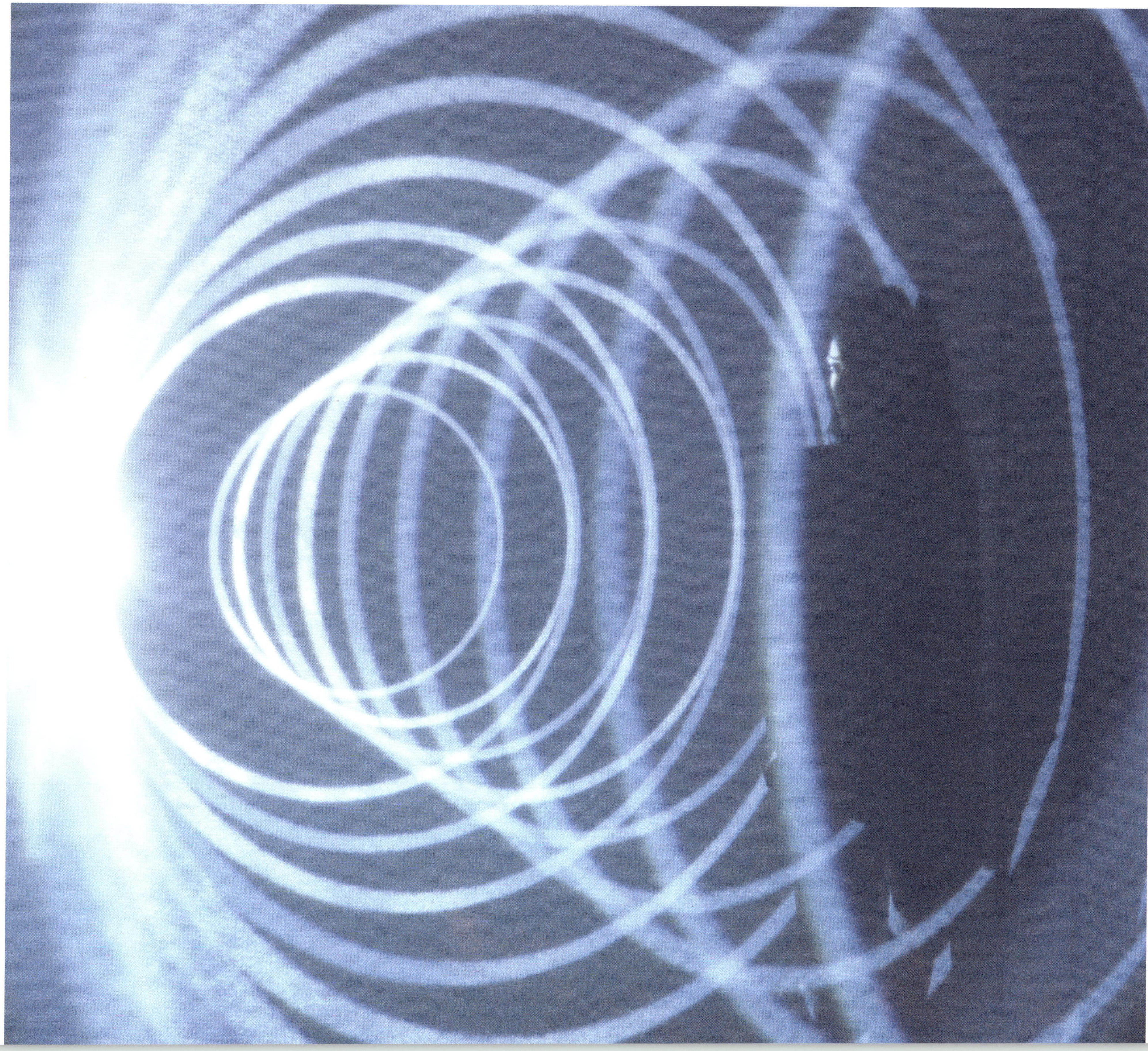

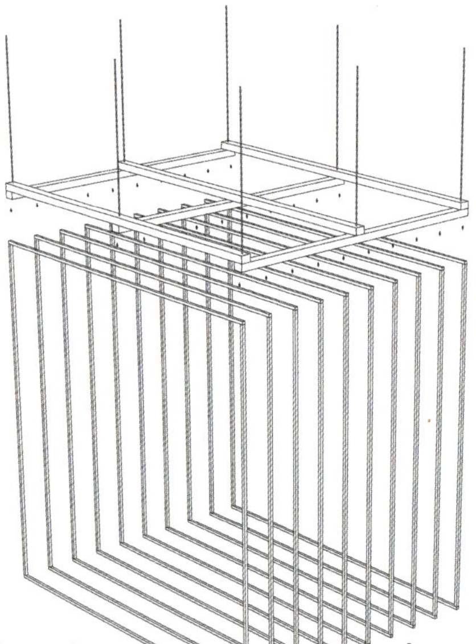

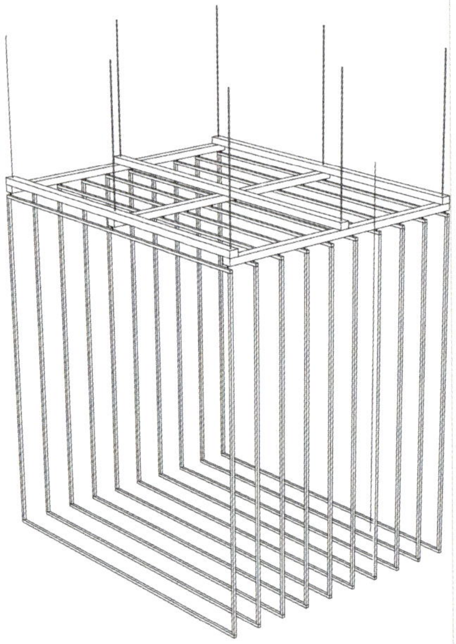

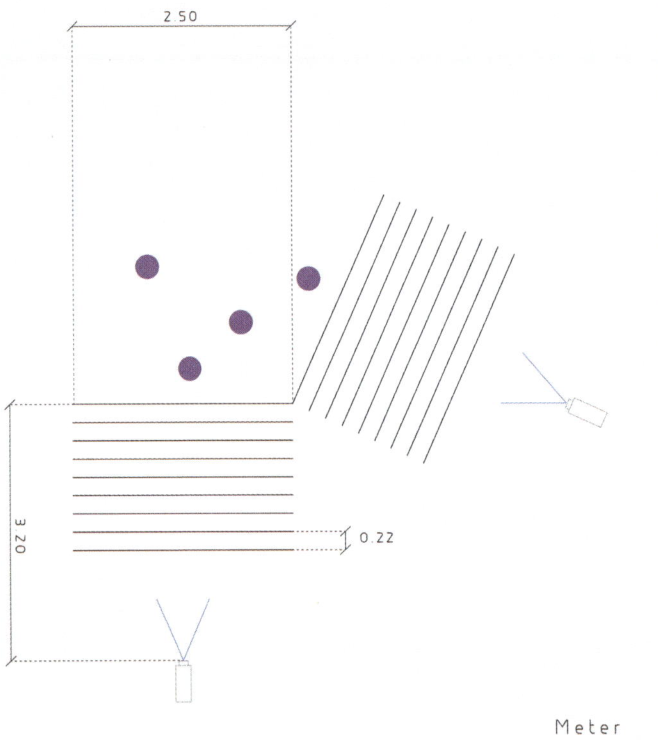

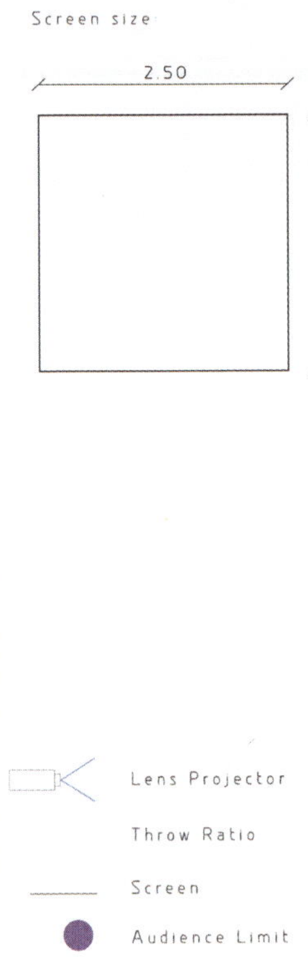

Many of our sketches are created using 3D modeling software, which allows us to see our ideas taking shape in correlation with space and architecture.

Most of our work consists of building complex visual effects using simple mediums. When we decide on the proportions, how the installation isolates or merges with existing elements, and how our decisions will affect visitors' spatial appreciation is crucial.

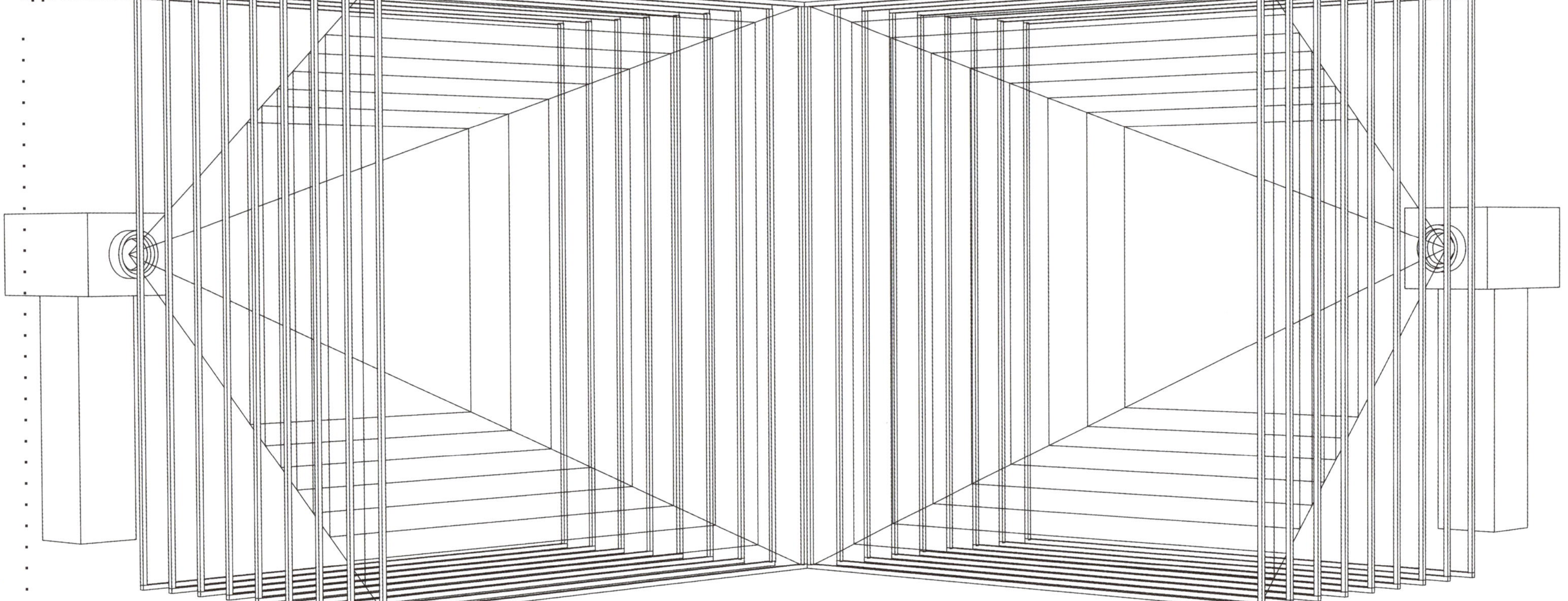

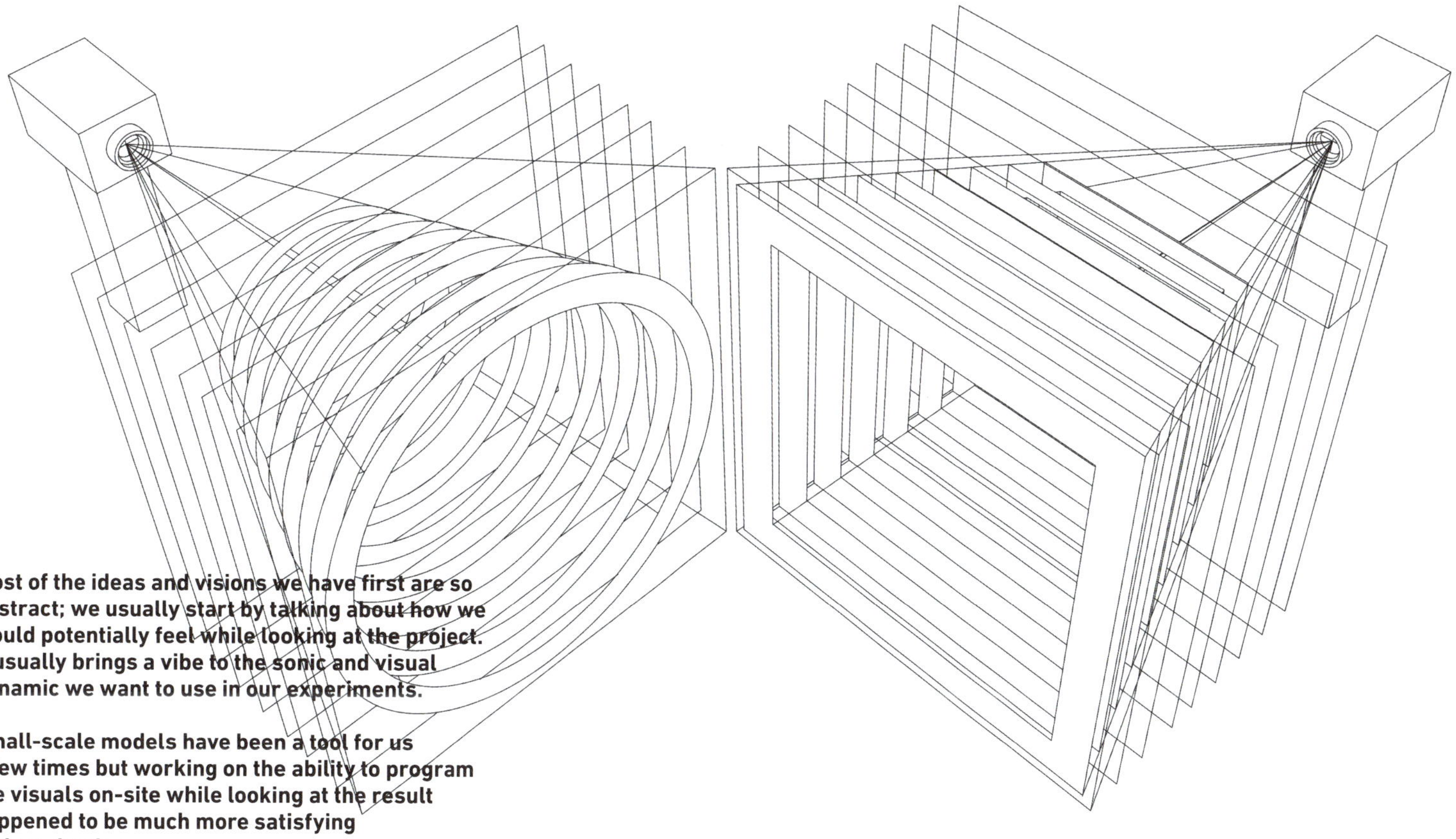

Most of the ideas and visions we have first are so abstract; we usually start by talking about how we would potentially feel while looking at the project. It usually brings a vibe to the sonic and visual dynamic we want to use in our experiments.

Small-scale models have been a tool for us a few times but working on the ability to program the visuals on-site while looking at the result happened to be much more satisfying and productive.

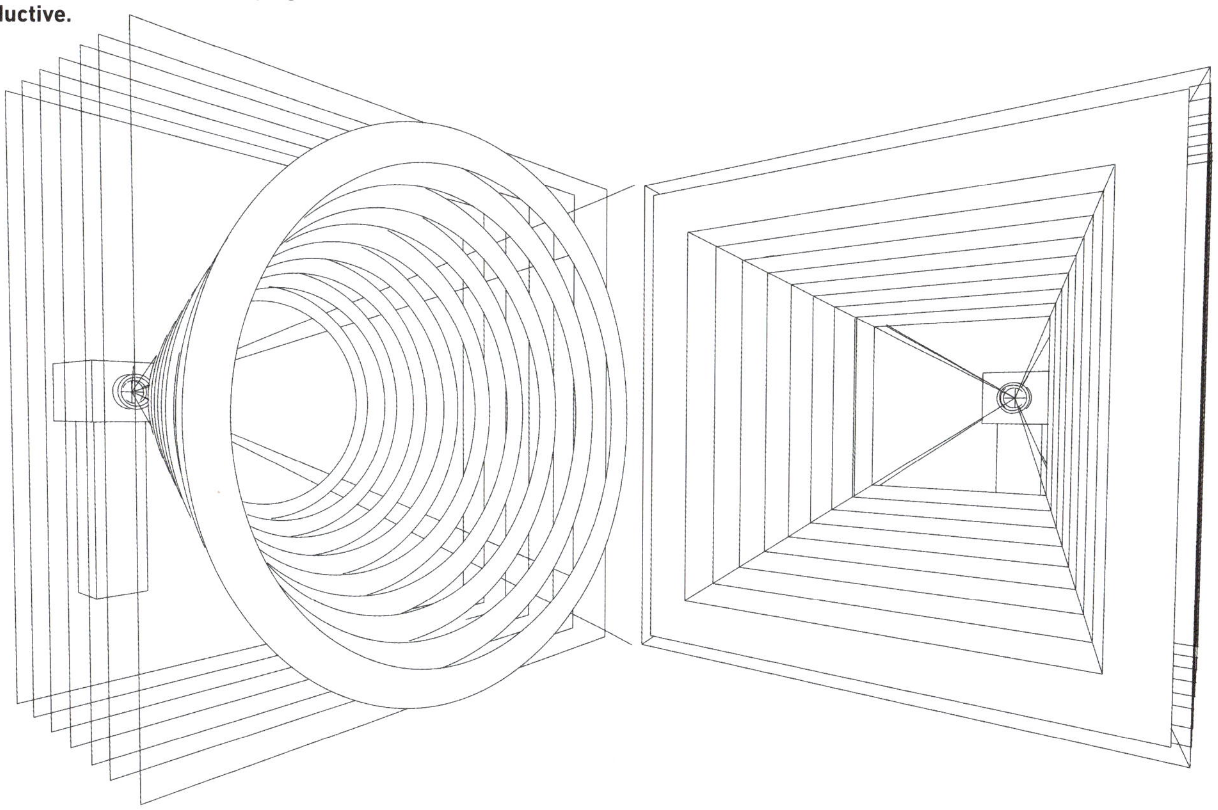

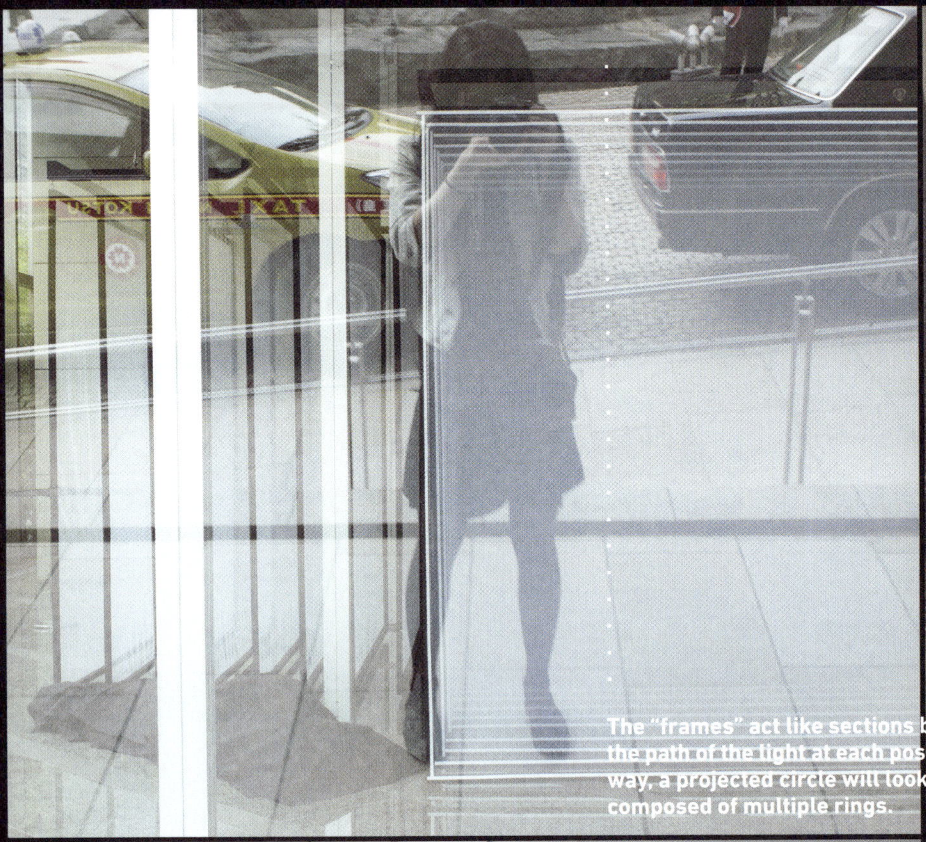

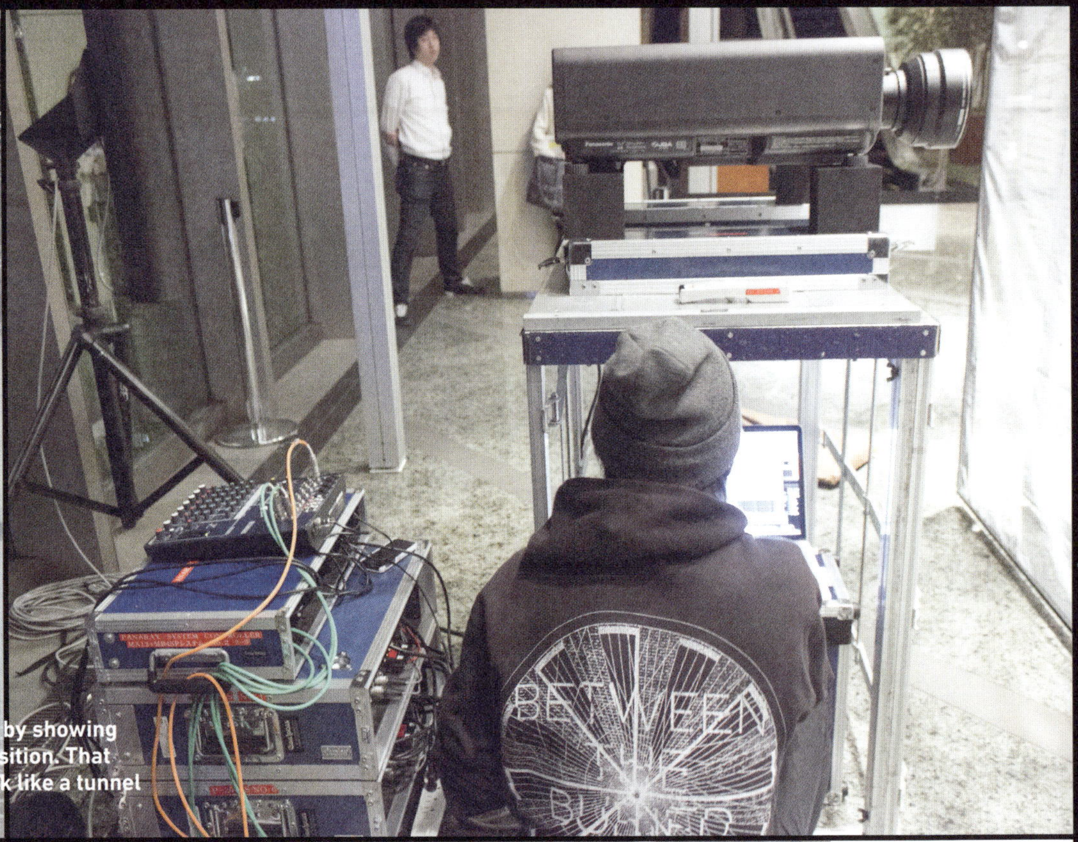

The "frames" act like sections by showing the path of the light at each position. That way, a projected circle will look like a tunnel composed of multiple rings.

The lens ratio of the video projector is affecting how the visuals look as well. The shorter it is, the bigger the difference in size between the visuals, which helps us create an illusion of a "perspective" that focuses the visitor to one spot.

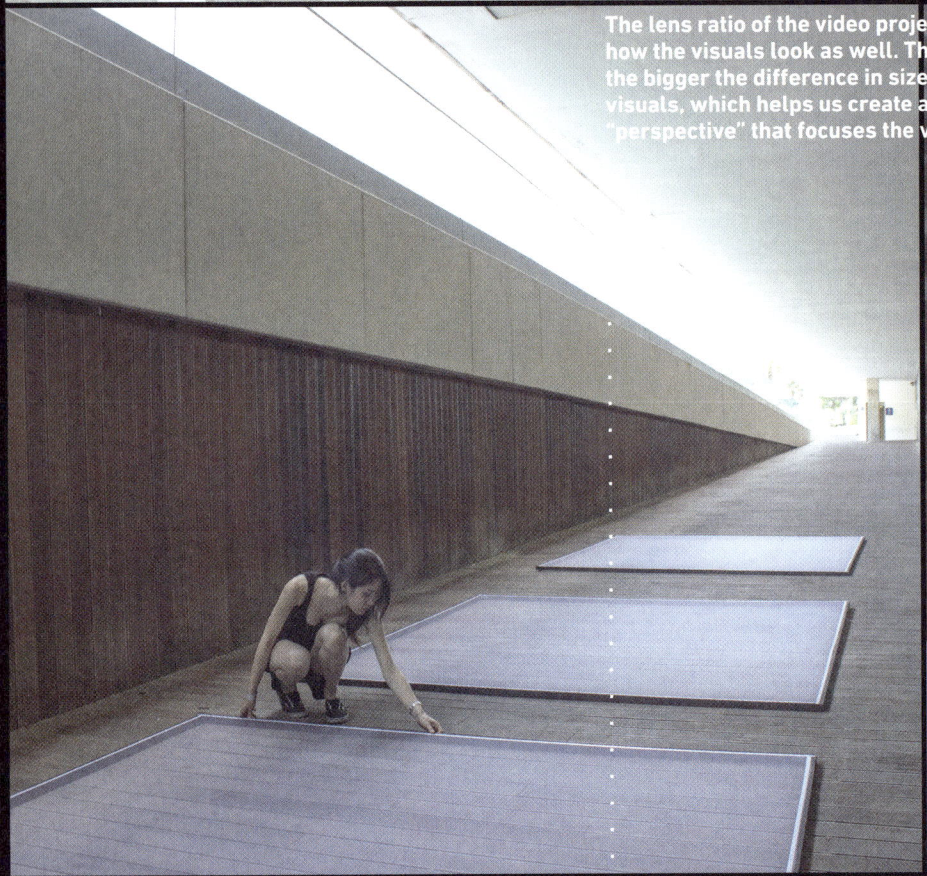

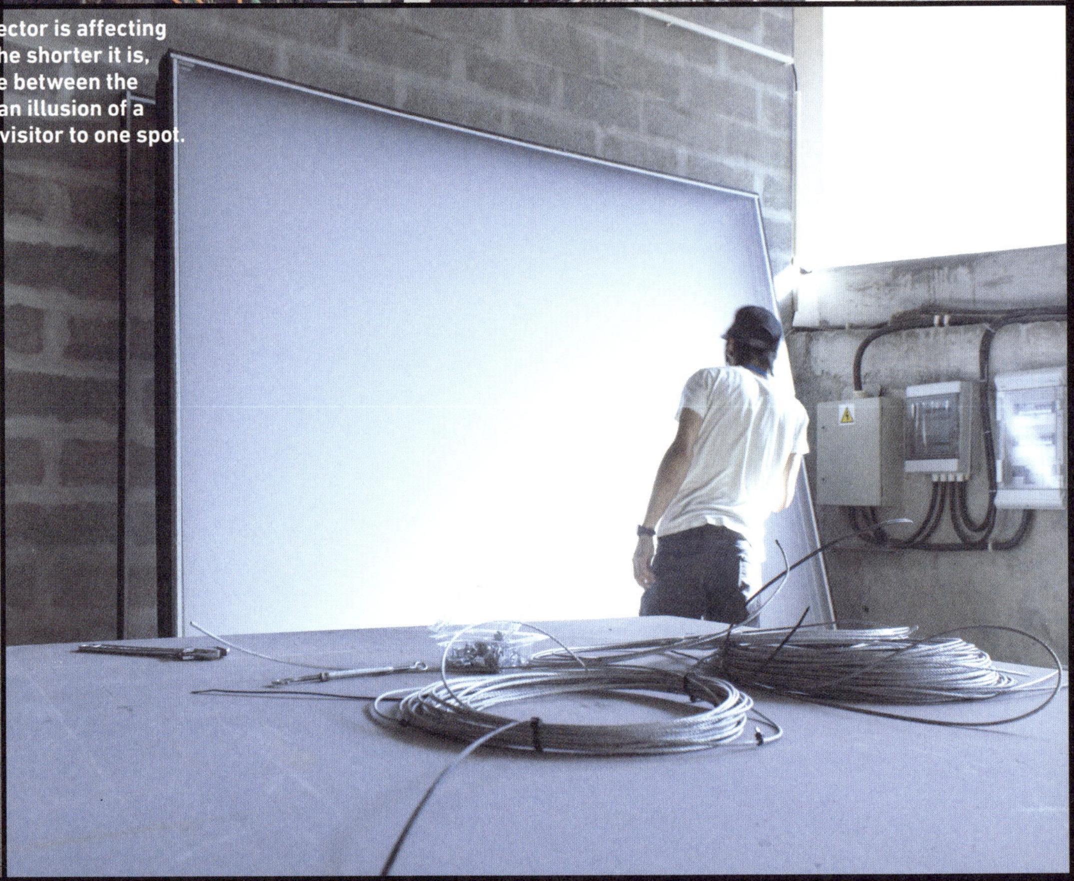

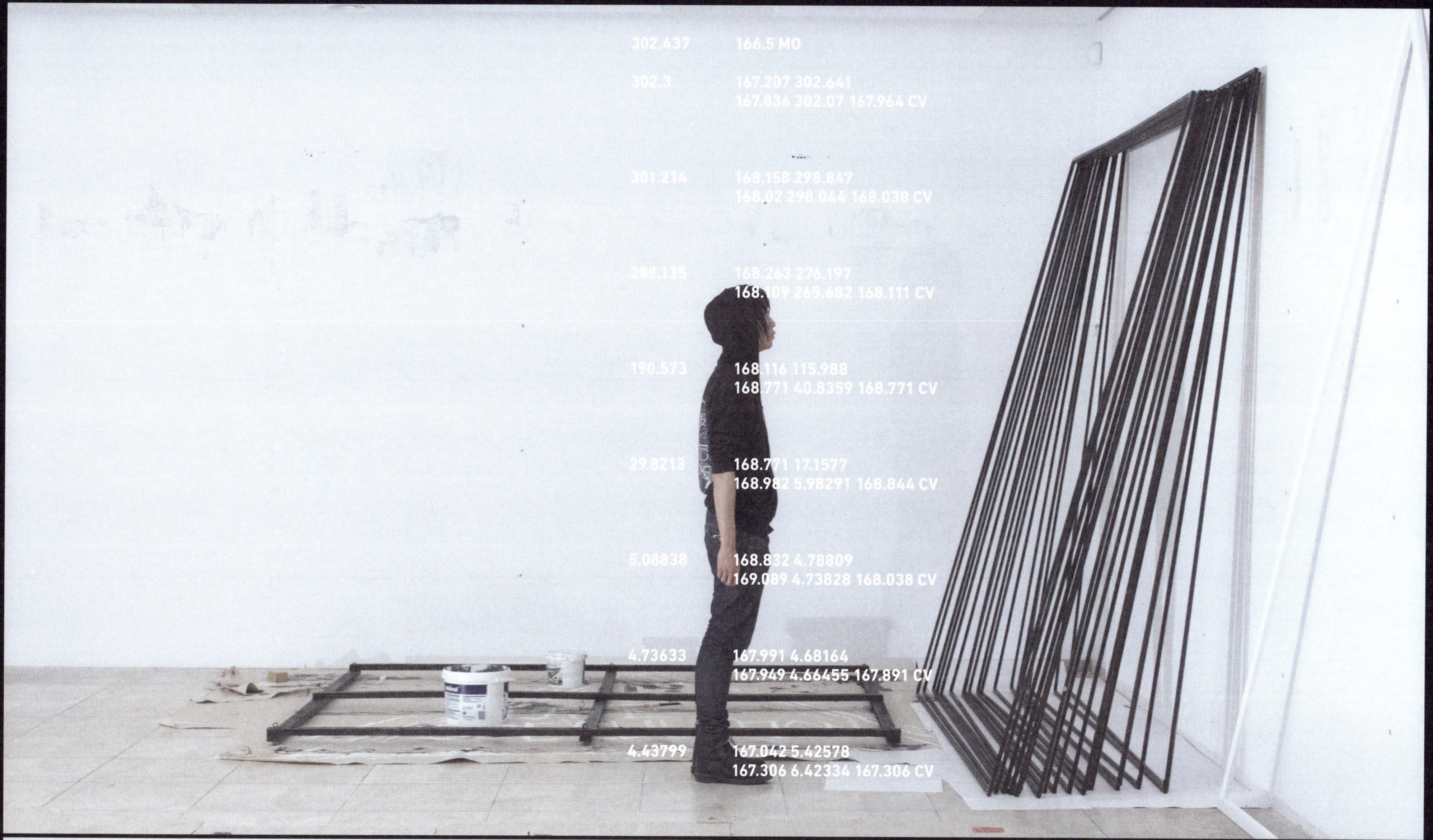

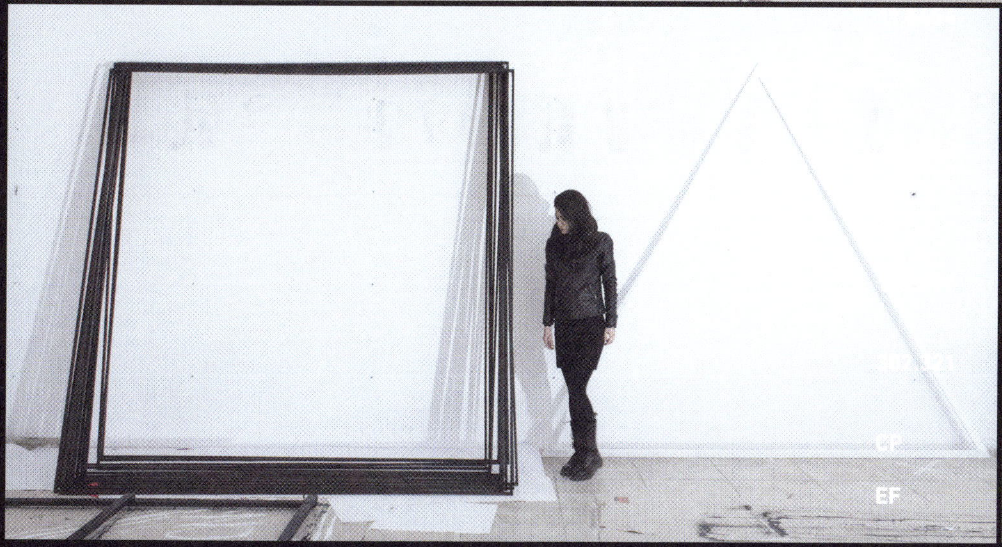

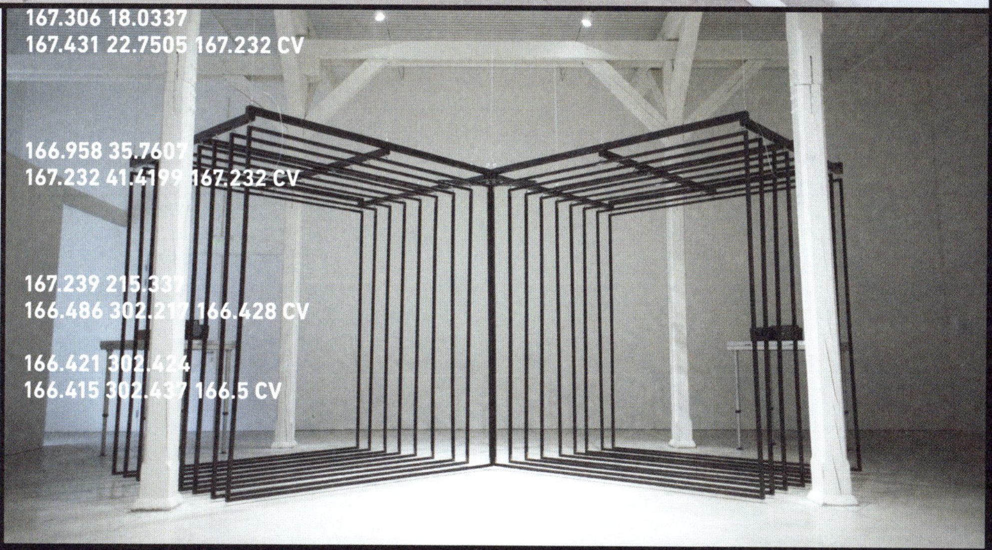

261 . DAYDREAM V2

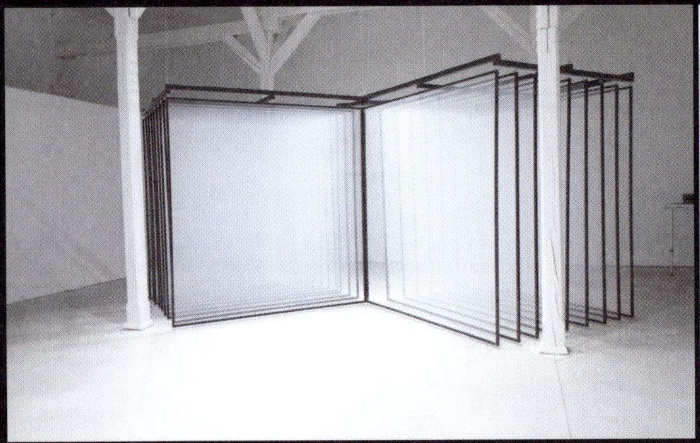
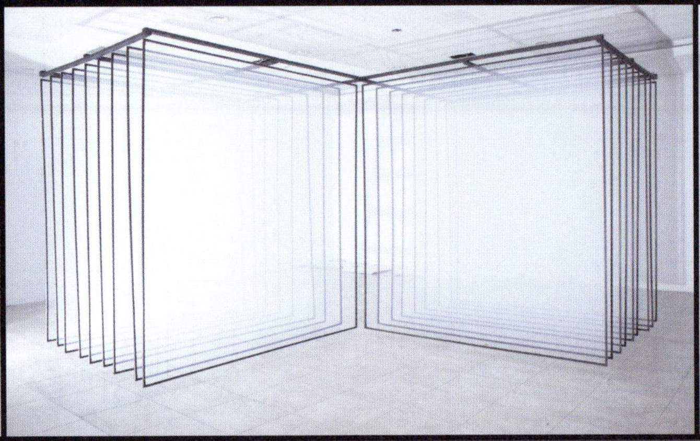
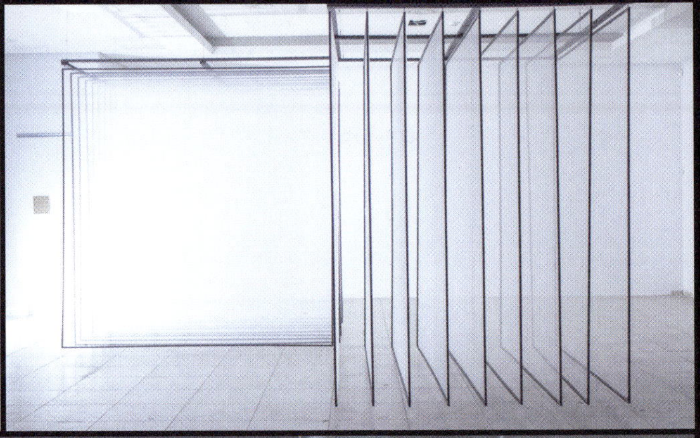
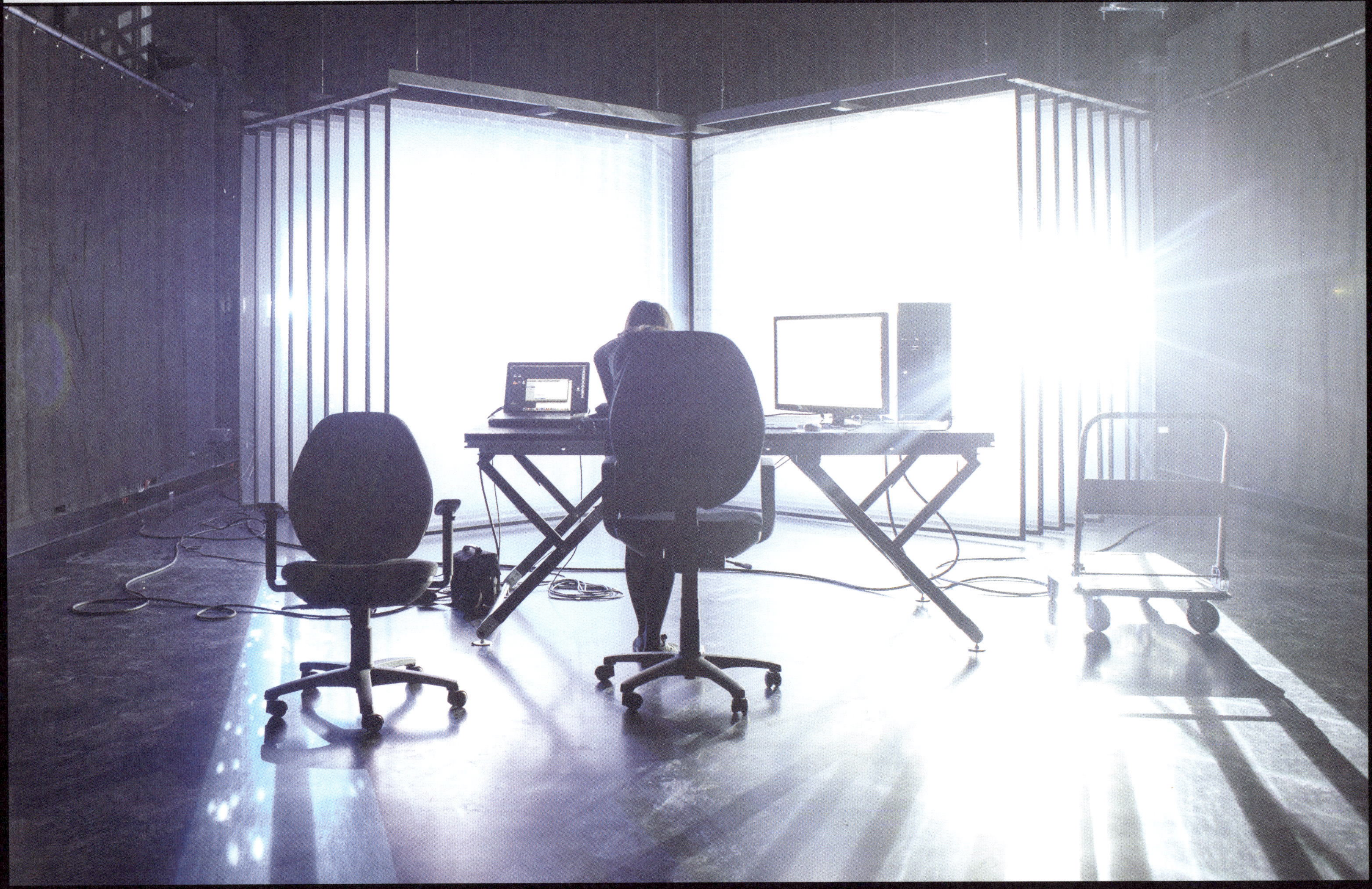

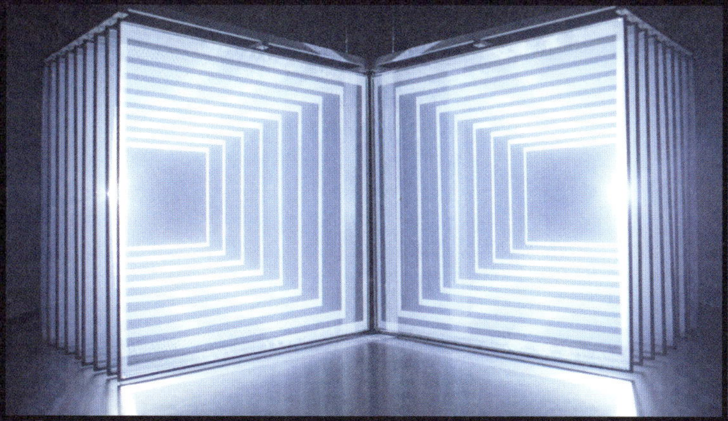

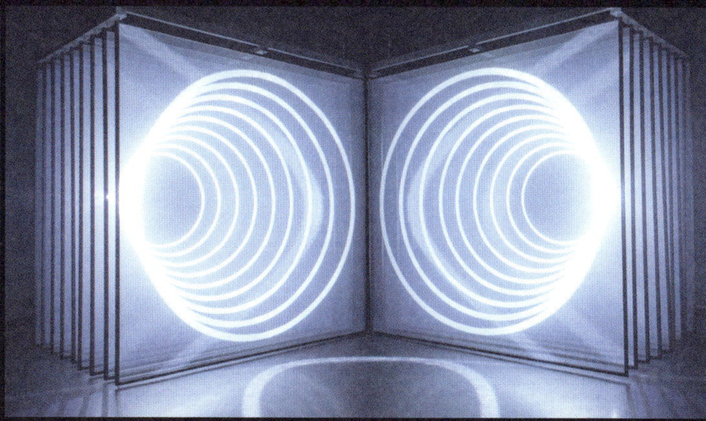

An art residency in Lithuania is where we made the realization.

We had space and tools to adapt and decide on the final design for a few weeks.

The first time we projected the visuals we expected to use for the artwork, we realized that there is nothing better than making them on-site, imagining them being part of the audience, which we did.

This realization of space and context had so much to do with how impactful art can be.

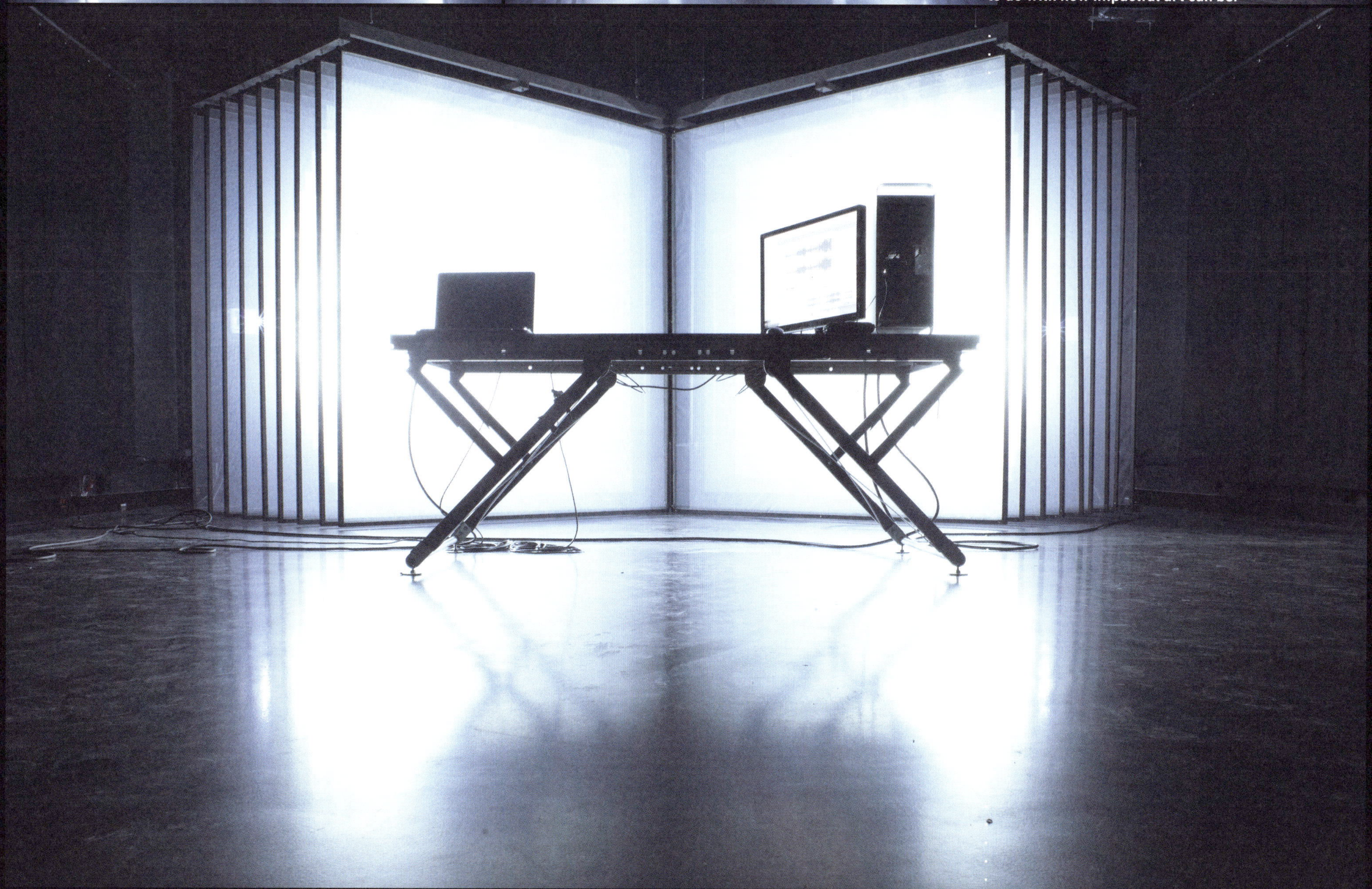

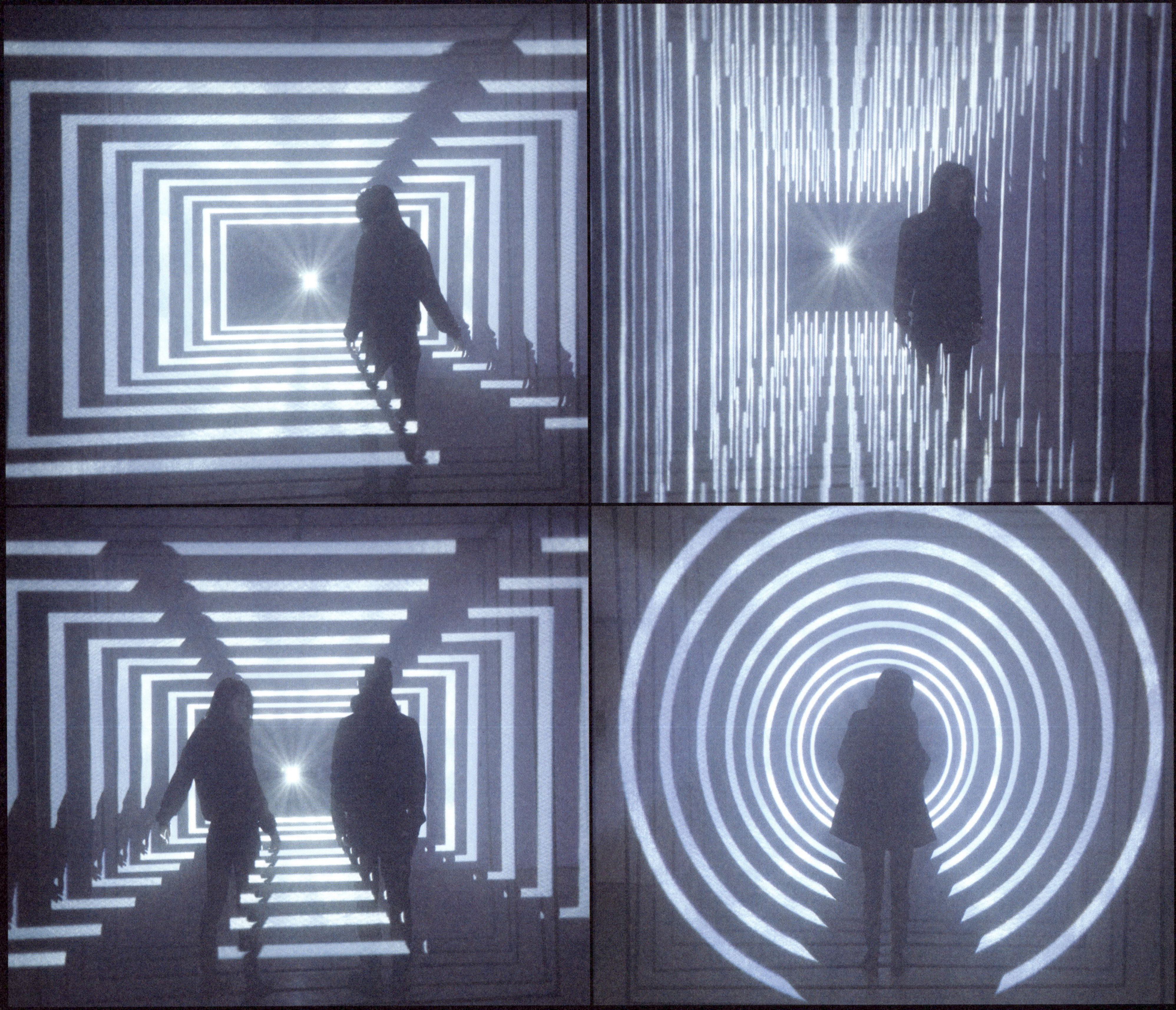

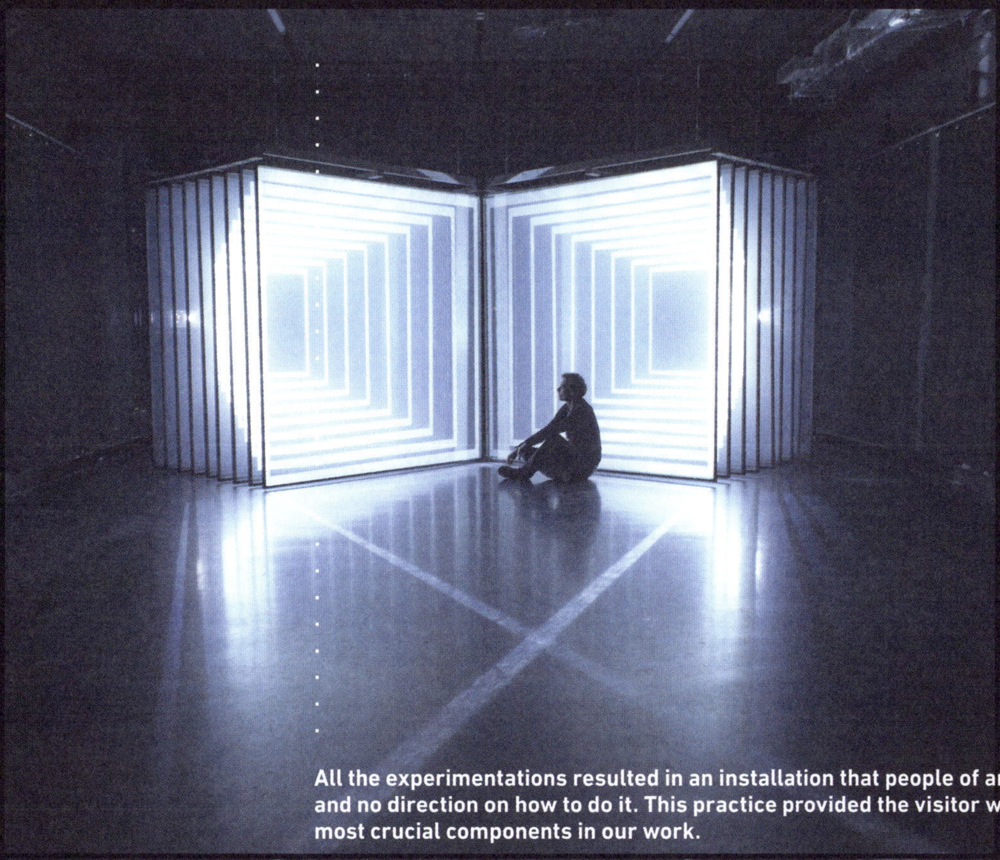

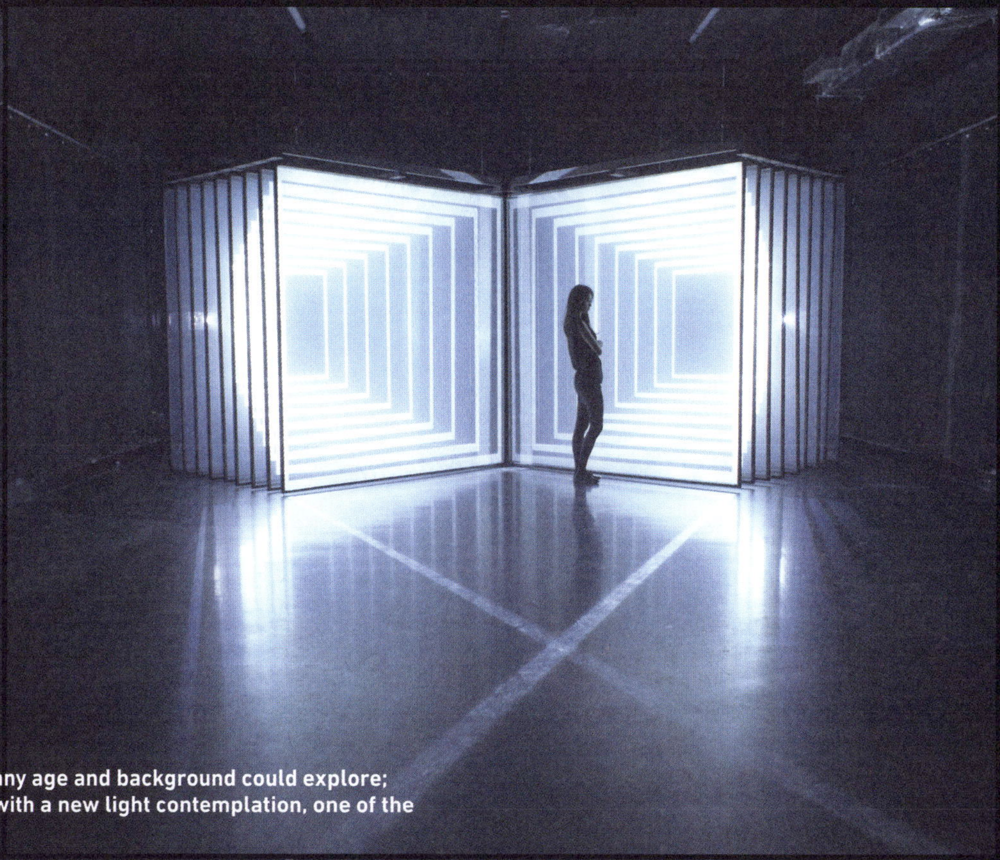

All the experimentations resulted in an installation that people of any age and background could explore; and no direction on how to do it. This practice provided the visitor with a new light contemplation, one of the most crucial components in our work.

It also resulted in many versions, exploring the various spatial possibilities using the same idea of sculpting light using projection.

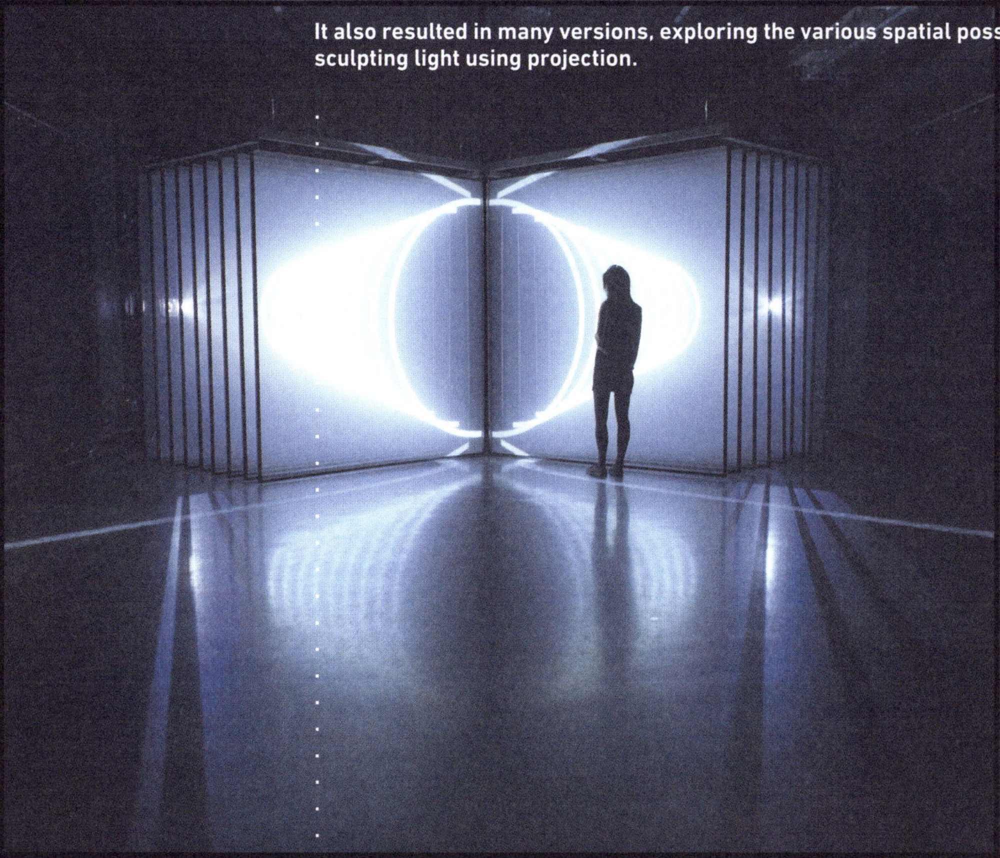

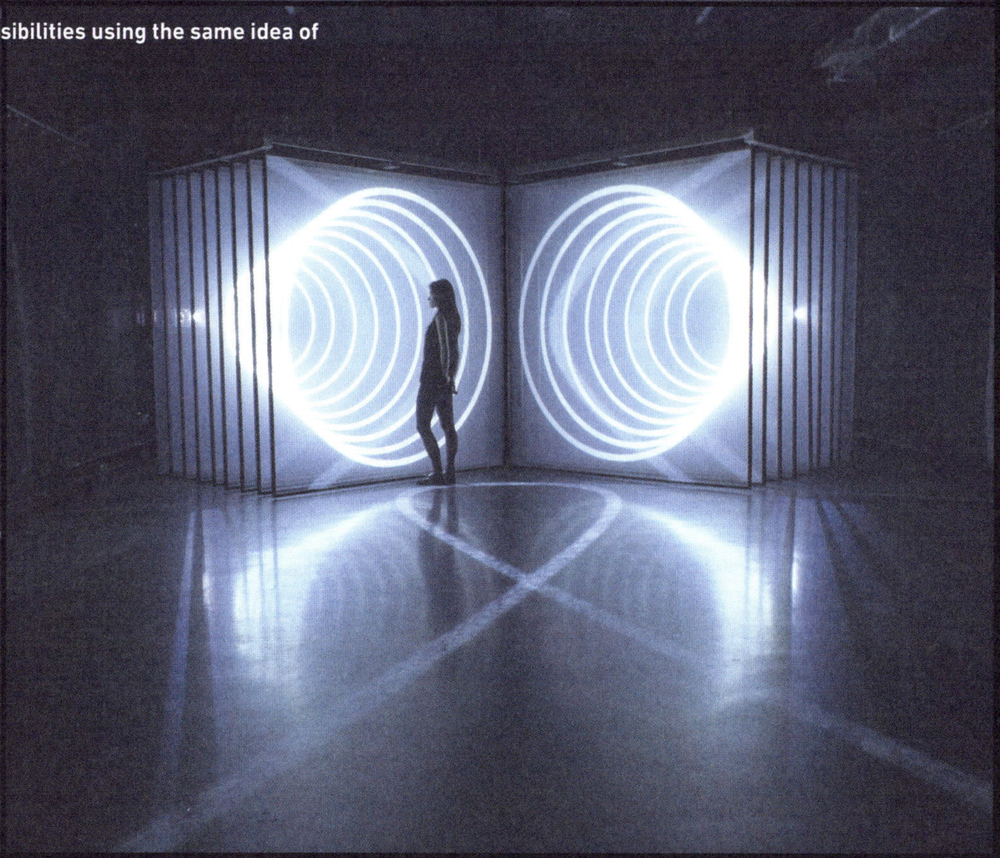

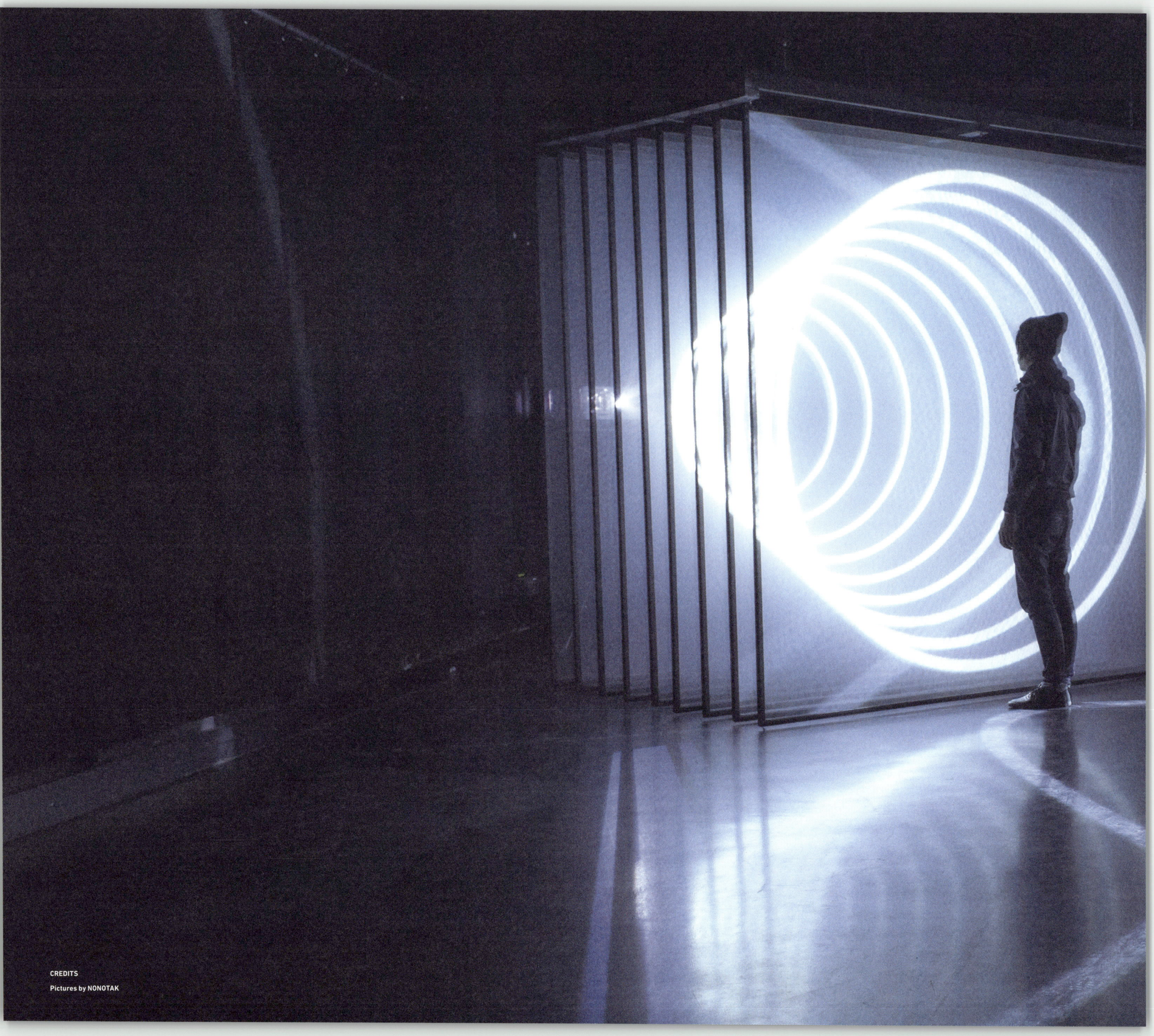

CREDITS
Pictures by NONOTAK

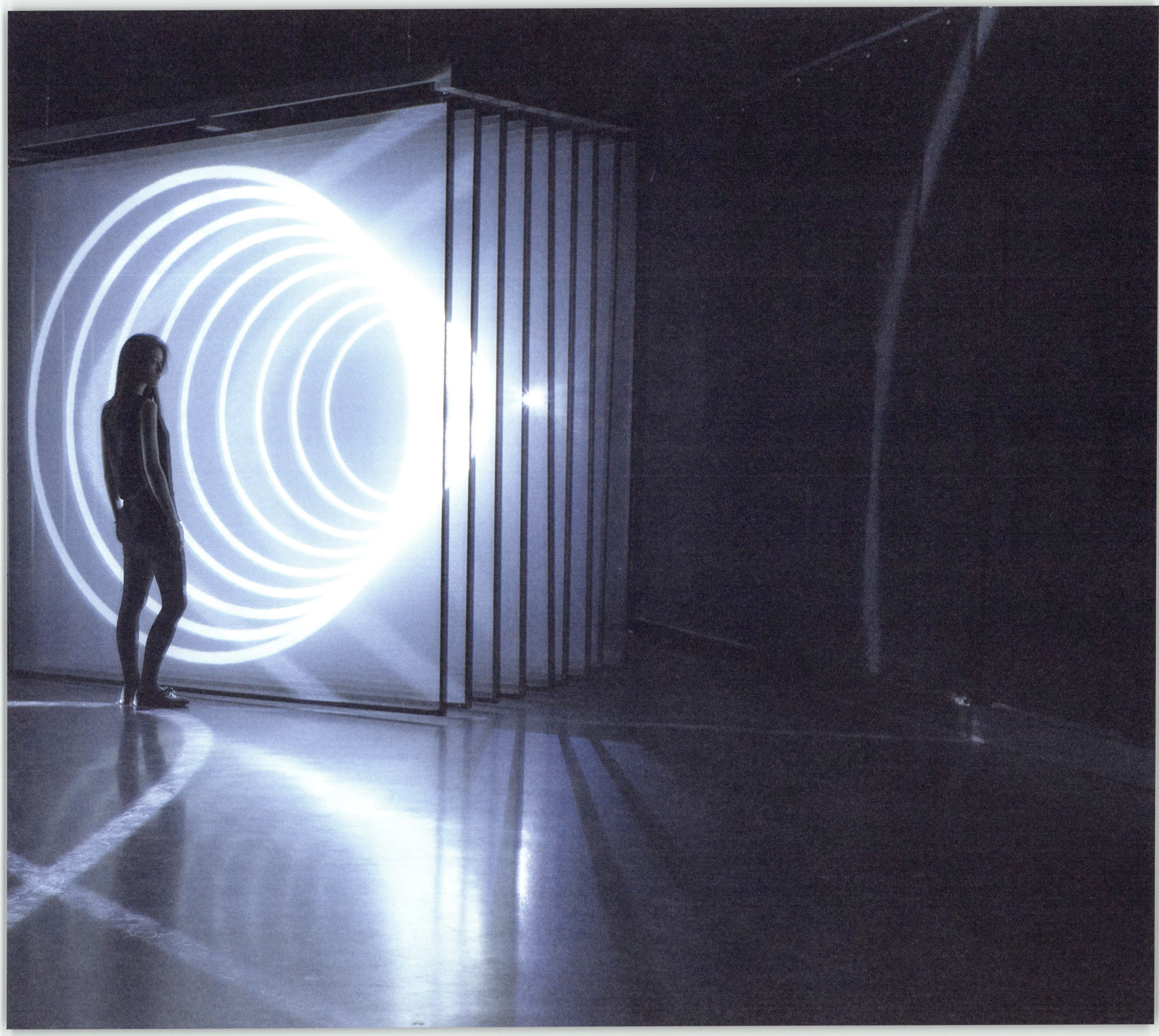

Name:

onformative

Info:

onformative is a studio for digital art and design.

Guided by a dynamic approach, we constantly search for new forms of creative expression.

We create meaningful works to challenge the boundaries between art, design, and technology through an experimental practice. As we stay true to an open process, outcomes and interpretations take on varying forms across media through self-initiated and commissioned works that range from interactive media installations, generative design, and dynamic visuals to data-driven narratives.

Through an interdisciplinary and collaborative practice, the visual language of onformative is variable.

Project:

MEANDERING RIVER

URL:

onformative.com

Mail:

info@onformative.com

Instagram:

@onformative

References:

- OnePlus 7 – Beyond speed
- IBM FLUX
- true/false
  kinetic light sculpture
- Nike Strike Series FA16
- ...

Q&As

Please explain the main idea and what gave the impulse?

Over time, landscapes are gradually shaped by natural forces, indiscernible to the naked eye. We only perceive one moment at a time.

Inspired by satellite photos of rivers and their unpredictable movement in the landscape, the intention was to zoom out and suggest another perspective of nature and time, enabled through technology in a new aesthetic way.

What challenges did you face for this project? And what surprises?

We met many exciting challenges in the complexity of the system that we built to simulate and visualize the changes of the river: transferring scientific insights to an algorithm that served as a tool for creating an endless number of visuals; viewed, defined, and refined in a looping, experimental approach until they reached the desired aesthetic.

Naturally, we also met surprising beauty in this process.

Please describe the technical environment.

MEANDERING RIVER is an audiovisual art installation comprised of generative real-time visuals and a musical score composed by an A.I. using machine learning.

It is displayed initially on six LED panels hung from the ceiling with a total height and width of 1,862 mm x 5,671 mm.

Tell us about your aesthetical approach.

The diverse and painterly aesthetic of satellite images served as visual inspiration for the look development.

As the evolving patterns emerge, the viewer is humbled by the unpredictability of change and the beauty of nature.

What's next? Your vision?

MEANDERING RIVER suggests a change of perspective based on the tension between nature as something unpredictable and technology as programmed.

Our vision is to challenge these kinds of relationships and present new perspectives through technology and art.

onformative

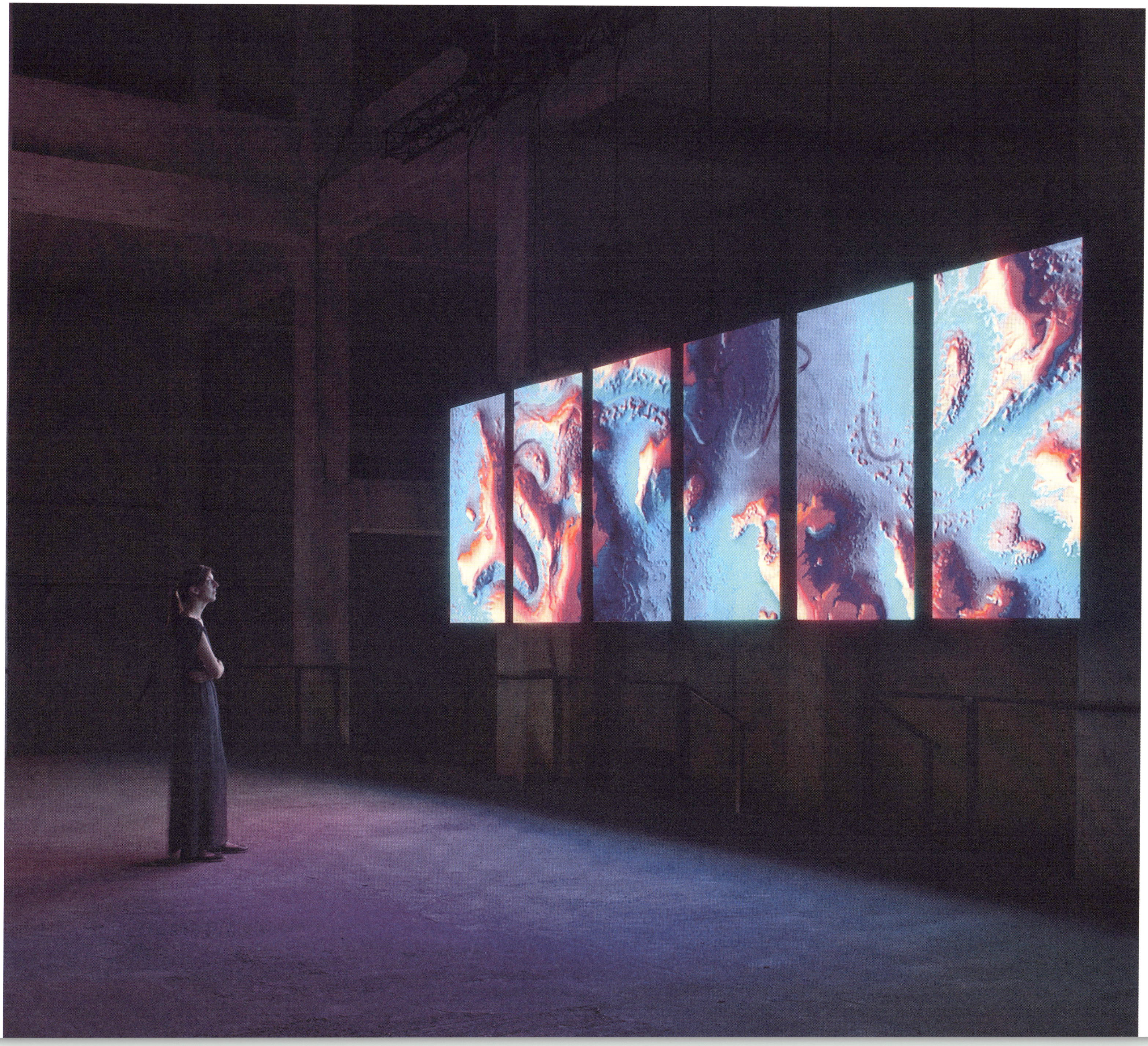

```
float normRampSmooth(float x, float xmin,
float xmax, float rampin, float rampout,

        float rampinedge0 = 0.0,
        float rampinedge1 = 1.0,

        float rampoutedge0 = 0.0,
        float rampoutedge1 = 1.0){

        if(x <= xmin || x >= xmax){

                return 0;

        }

        if(x < (xmin + rampin)){

                return smooth
        step(rampinedge0,
        rampinedge1,(x - xmin) / rampin);

        }

        if(x > (xmax - rampout)){

                return 1.0 - smooth
        step(rampoutedge0,
        rampoutedge1,
        (x - (xmax - rampout)) / rampout);

        }

        return 1;

}


float normNoiseFbm(float2 uv){

        return 0.5 + noiseFbm(uv) * 0.5;

}


float normNoiseFbm_(float2 uv, float x, float y){

    return 0.5 + noiseFbm(uv, x) * 0.5;

}


float floorStep(float x, float y){

    return floor(x * y) / y;

}
```

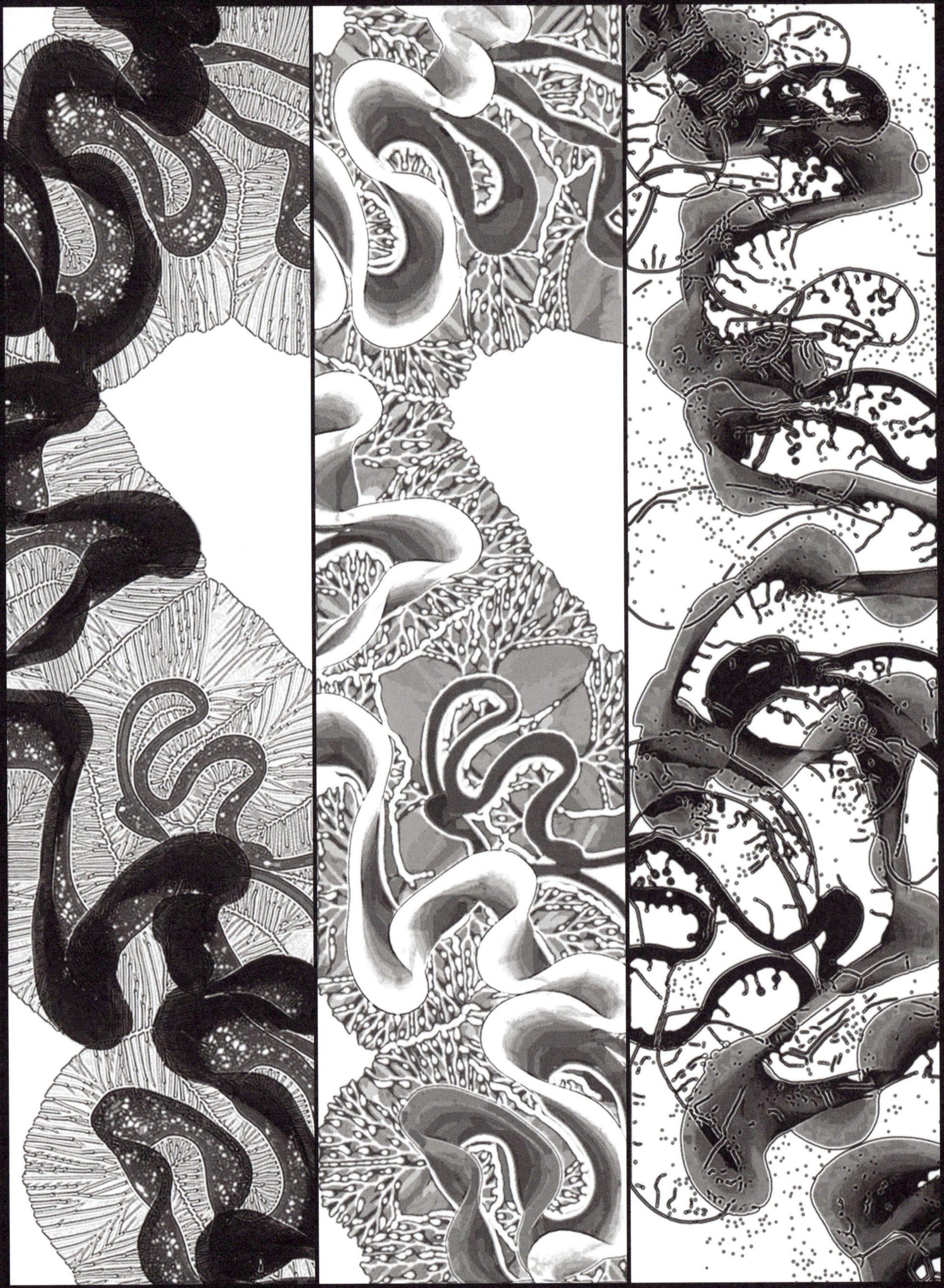

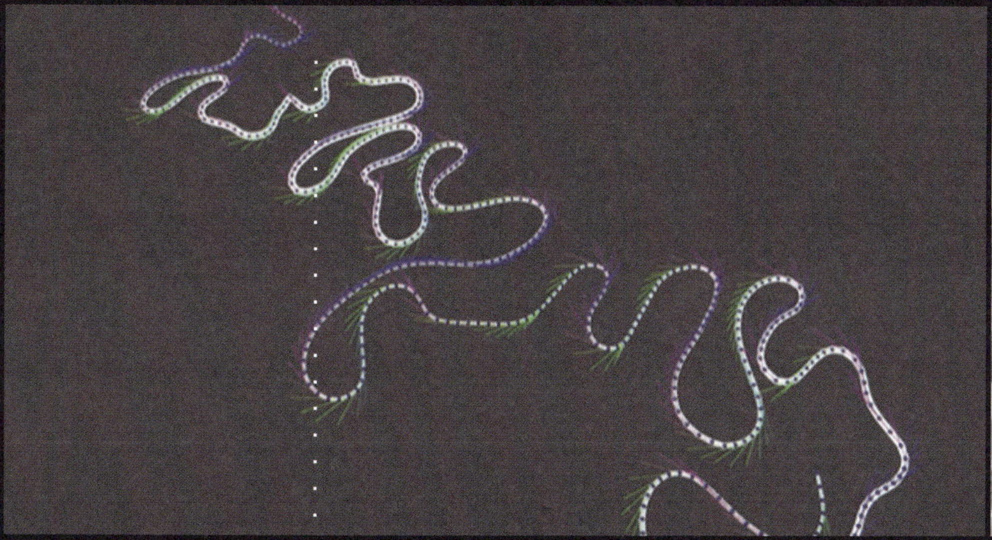

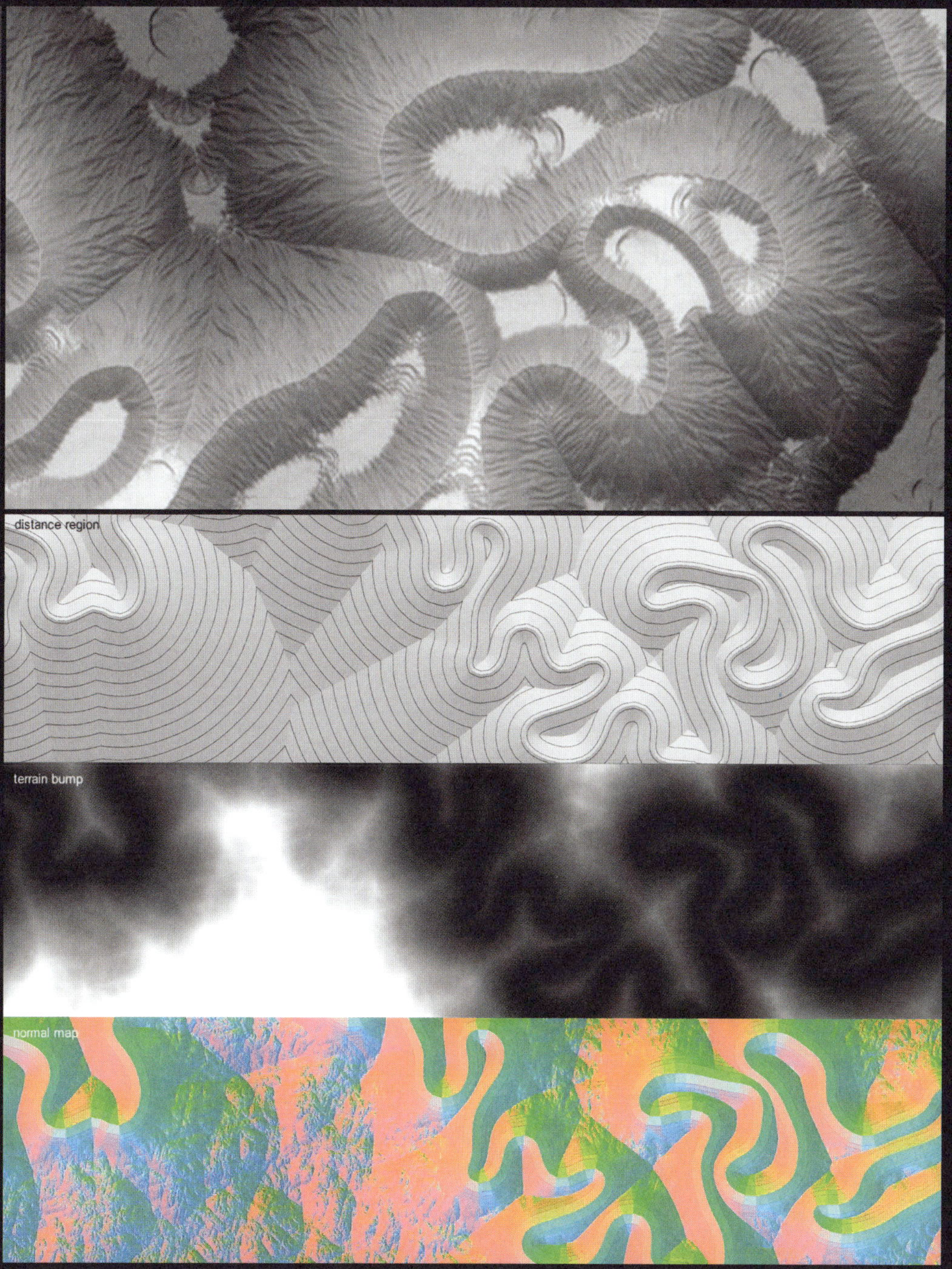

We utilized the natural behavior of meandering rivers as the DNA to code our digital artwork.

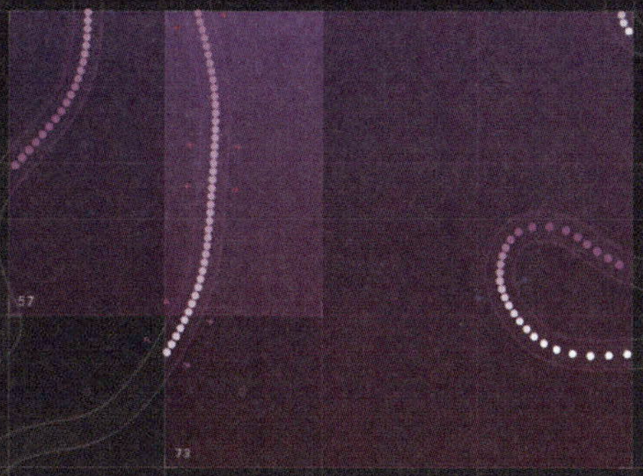

By investigating scientific research that examines the natural phenomena of meandering rivers, we developed different algorithms to simulate the unpredictable watercourse and show how the rivers influence the landscape and their surroundings.

Through the research of various computational strategies, the soundscape was created with the help of a machine-learning model and custom-built procedural system to underline the mesmerizing nature of the work.

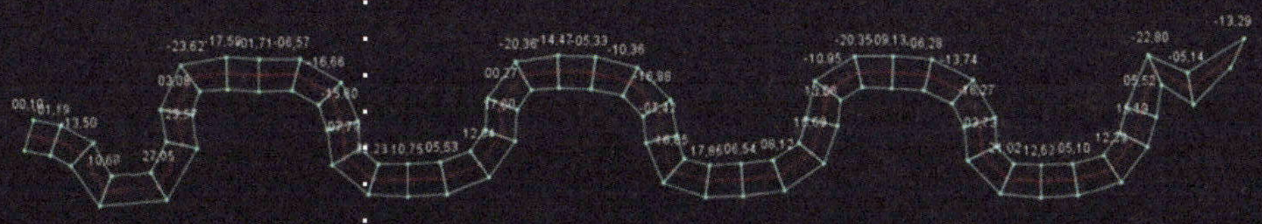

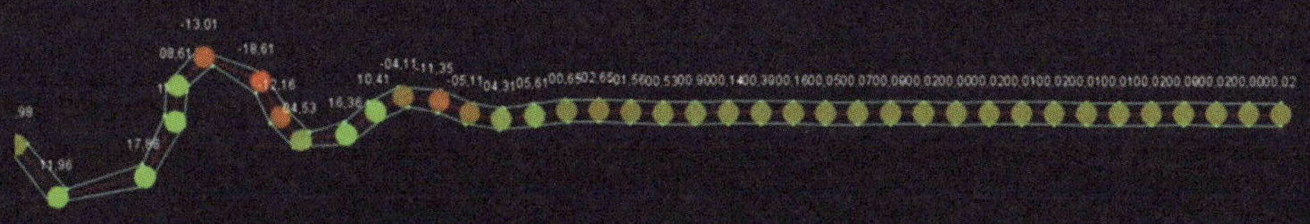

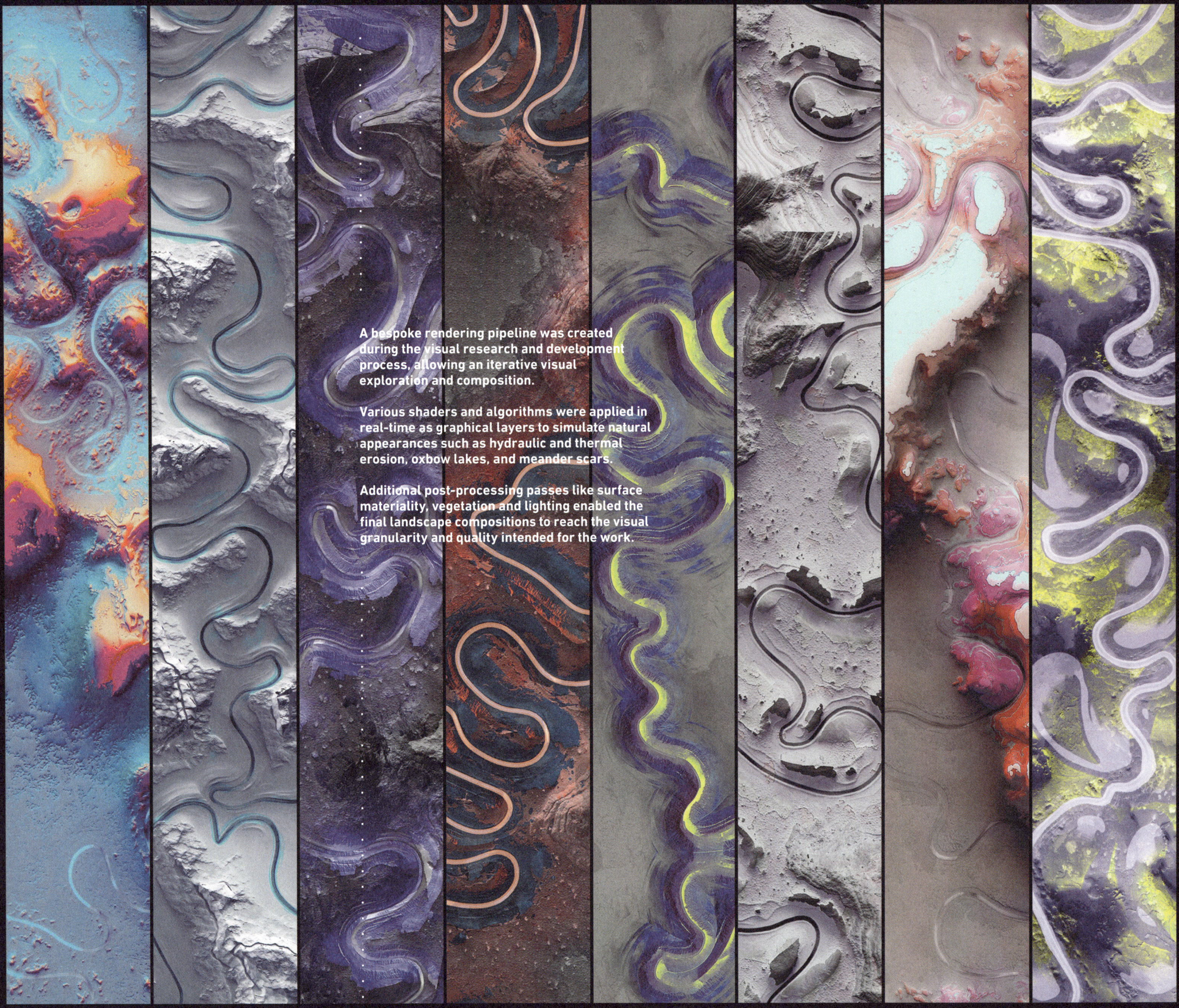

A bespoke rendering pipeline was created during the visual research and development process, allowing an iterative visual exploration and composition.

Various shaders and algorithms were applied in real-time as graphical layers to simulate natural appearances such as hydraulic and thermal erosion, oxbow lakes, and meander scars.

Additional post-processing passes like surface materiality, vegetation and lighting enabled the final landscape compositions to reach the visual granularity and quality intended for the work.

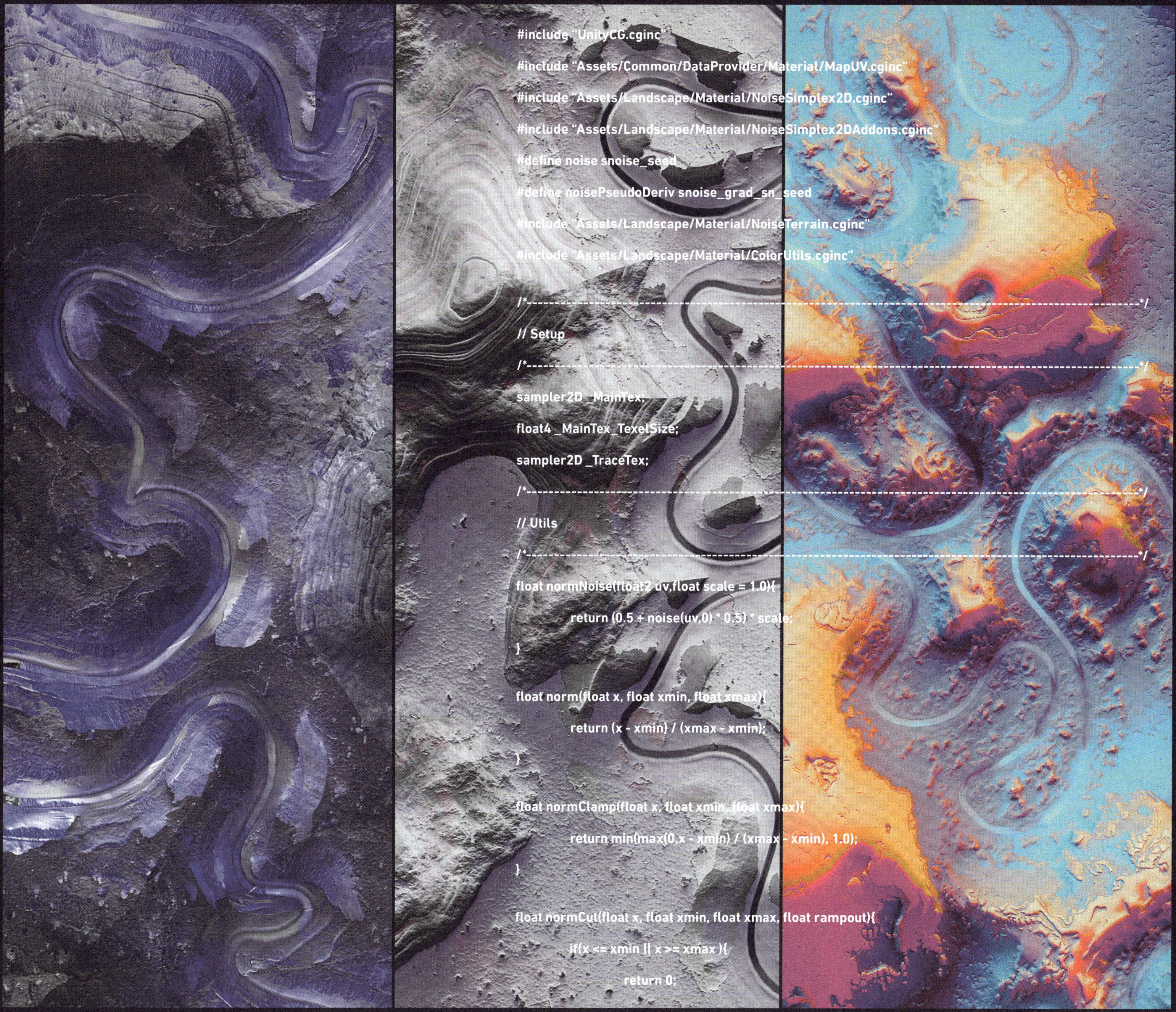

273 . MEANDERING RIVER

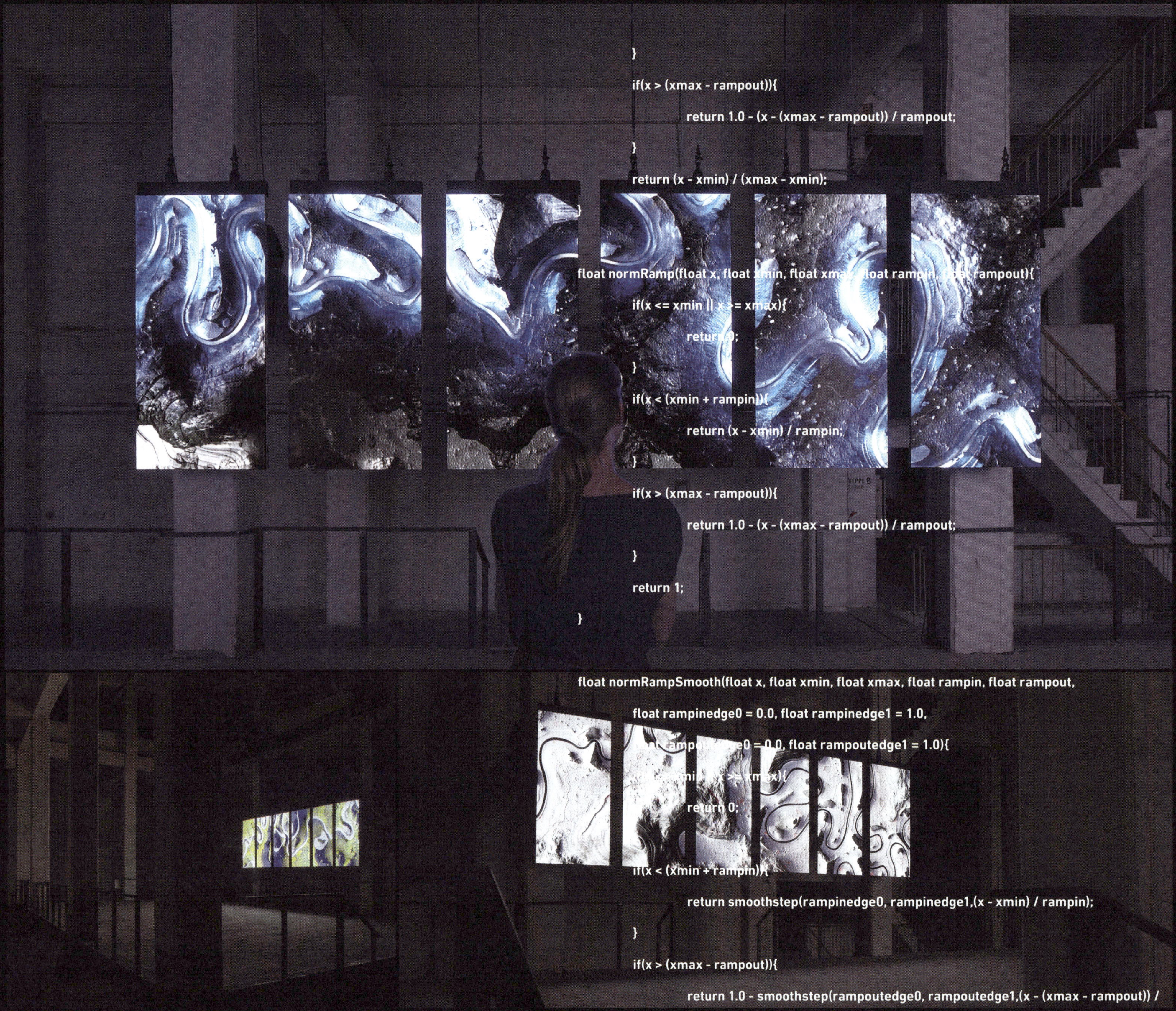

```
	}
	if(x > (xmax - rampout)){
		return 1.0 - (x - (xmax - rampout)) / rampout;
	}
	return (x - xmin) / (xmax - xmin);
}

float normRamp(float x, float xmin, float xmax, float rampin, float rampout){
	if(x <= xmin || x >= xmax){
		return 0;
	}
	if(x < (xmin + rampin)){
		return (x - xmin) / rampin;
	}
	if(x > (xmax - rampout)){
		return 1.0 - (x - (xmax - rampout)) / rampout;
	}
	return 1;
}

float normRampSmooth(float x, float xmin, float xmax, float rampin, float rampout,
	float rampinedge0 = 0.0, float rampinedge1 = 1.0,
	float rampoutedge0 = 0.0, float rampoutedge1 = 1.0){
	if(x <= xmin || x >= xmax){
		return 0;
	}
	if(x < (xmin + rampin)){
		return smoothstep(rampinedge0, rampinedge1,(x - xmin) / rampin);
	}
	if(x > (xmax - rampout)){
		return 1.0 - smoothstep(rampoutedge0, rampoutedge1,(x - (xmax - rampout)) /
```

The beauty of working with data and developing code lies in the endless possibilities.

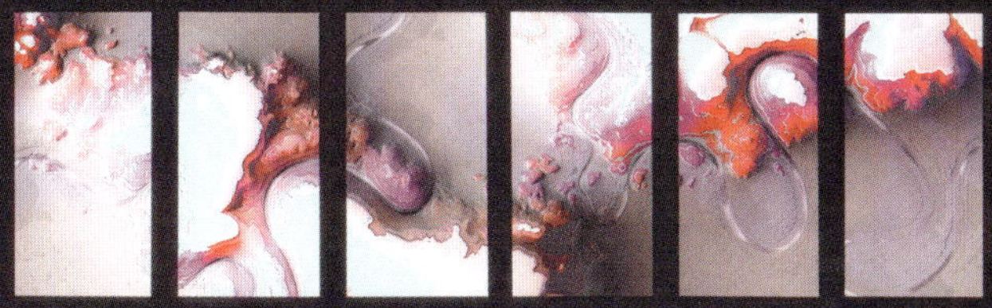

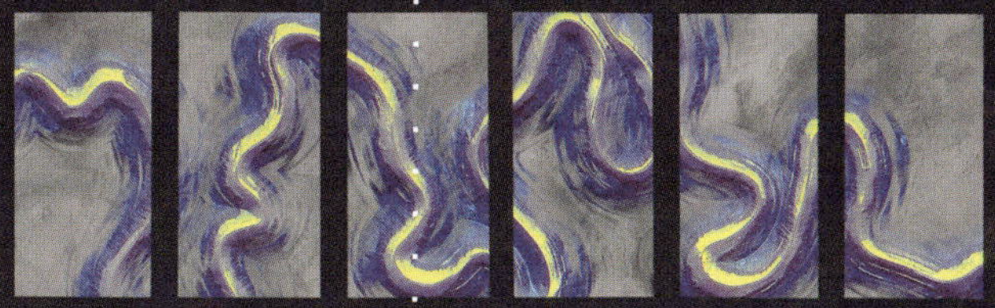

To create MEANDERING RIVER was a very complex process.

Inspired by nature, we built a system to create the artwork, which means the outcome could have been entirely different depending on many parameters.

We chose the final visuals based on our aesthetic perception. With the added complexity, the viewer can tap into a new perspective, and that is where the artwork fulfills the intention to "reinspire."

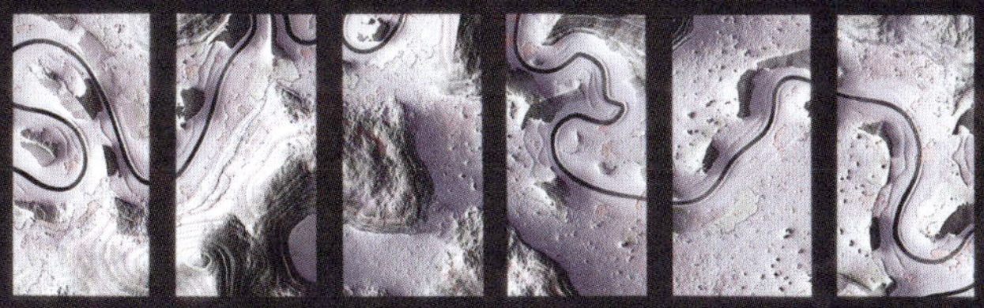

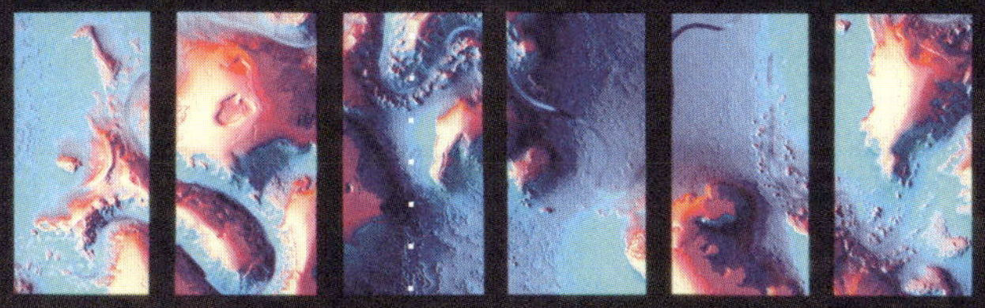

As an outcome, the artwork consists of six different visual modes, each accompanied by a bespoke musical composition.

The complete run presents the utmost balanced interplay of visuals and sound.

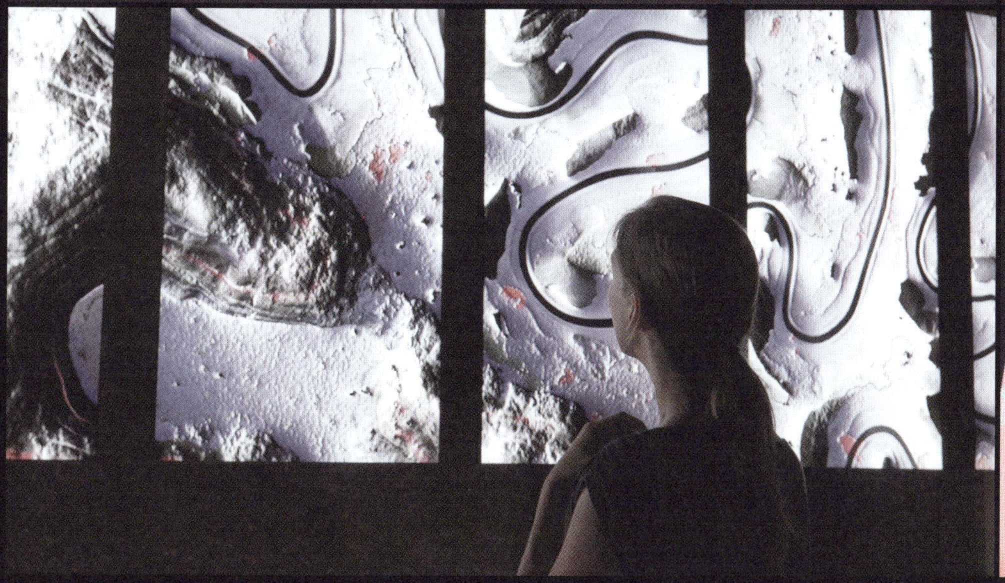

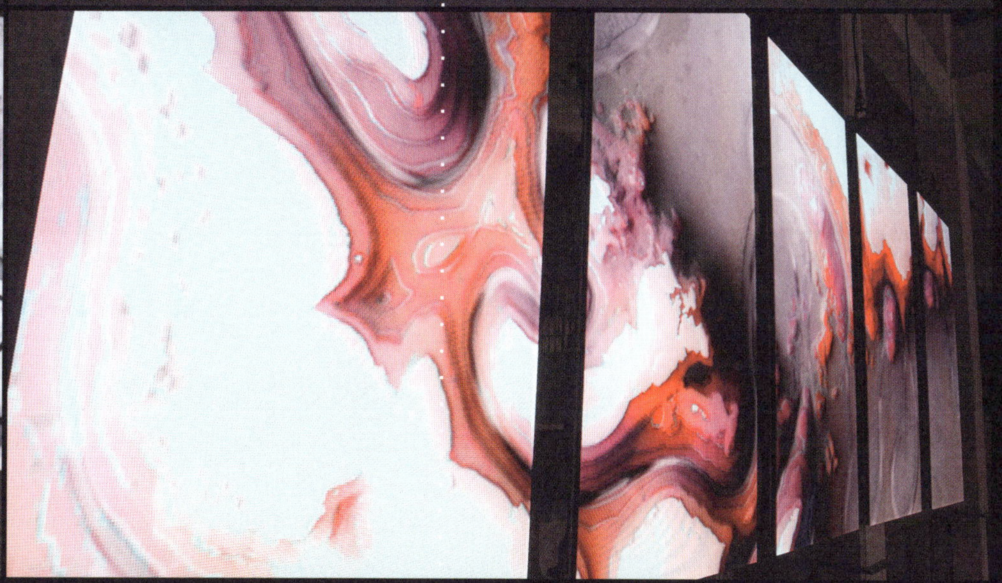

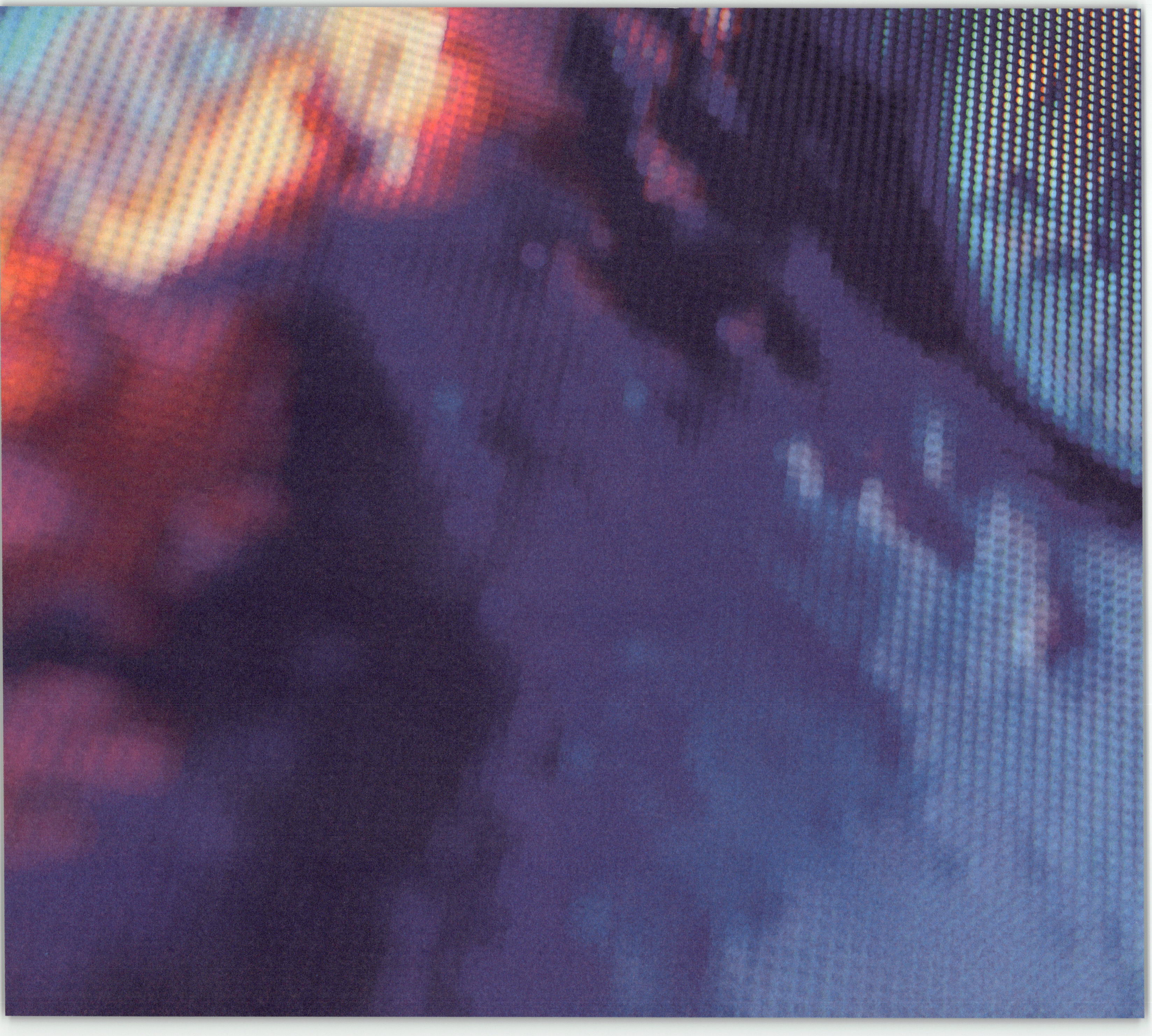

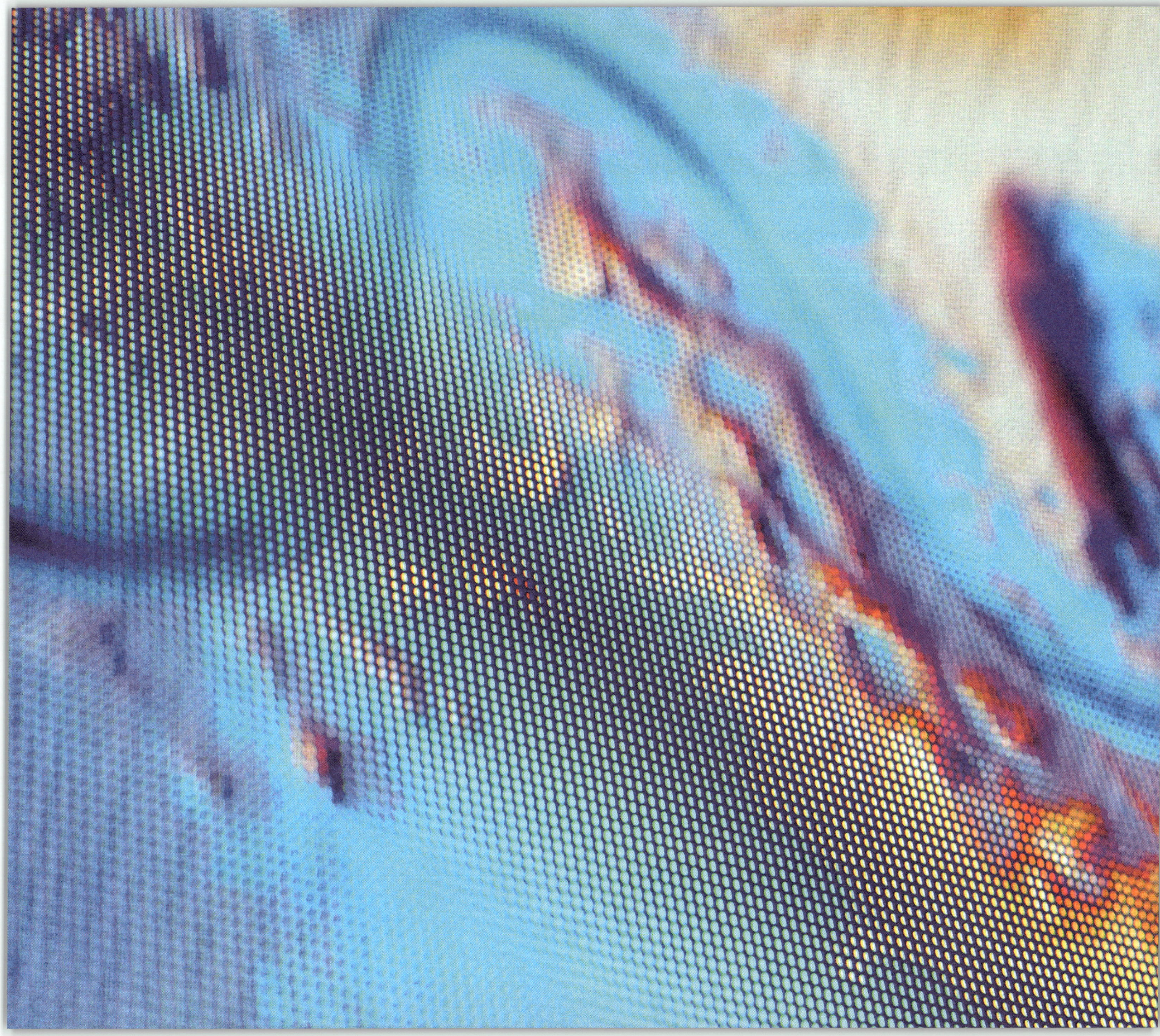

Quayola

Name:

Quayola

Info:

Quayola employs technology as a lens to explore the tensions and equilibriums between seemingly opposing forces: the real and artificial, figurative and abstract, old and new.

Constructing immersive installations, he engages with and re-imagines canonical imagery through contemporary technology.

Landscape painting, classical sculpture, and iconography are historical aesthetics that serve as a point of departure for Quayola's hybrid compositions.

His varied practice, deriving from custom computer software, also includes audiovisual performance, immersive video installations, sculpture, and works on paper.

Projects:

URL:

quayola.com

Mail:

enquiries@quayola.com

Instagram:

@quayola

Understanding the Machine

By Lucia Longhi

Quayola's artistic practice deeply revolves around technology and presents itself, on a general level, as a study of its role in the relational dynamics of man with his surroundings. He borrows the most advanced technologies from geology, environmental sciences, industrial robotics, and computer vision and transforms them into new tools for artistic expression.

The whole of the artist's production originates from a fundamental anthropological premise. We live in times in which men coexist with machines in a symbiotic relationship. Although current research in Artificial Intelligence is still far from allowing us to define an algorithm as an independent thinker, we have reached a stage at which machines can perform calculations, actions, and results that outrun human comprehension.

One could say that machines can now give origin to new languages and, by extension, to new aesthetics, although not independently from human intervention, but from man's desire for them to do so. There seems to be a mutual influence at play; man operates machine, but in turn, machines force men to revolutionize their thought process and adapt to such a new techno-logic.

Intercepting the peculiarity and the novelty of such a relationship, Quayola acts with the intent of exposing the potential of digital processing from an aesthetic point of view. Man is not interested in the machine's function, of technological extension, of human faculties. Instead, he wishes to shed light on its characteristics, particularly those prerogatives of the human species, aesthetic sensibility, abstract thinking, and reality interpretation. To do so, he must become an accomplice to technology, an alter ego with whom to entertain a mutual creative exchange. He must bring the relationship between human-machine to an empathic level, contributing to transforming the original hierarchy. He must, to an extent, identify with the machine to comprehend its logic and unveil it to the public.

In the pursuit of man's goal, Quayola concentrates on an alternative representation of reality; namely, reality understood and read by machines; this leads his work to qualify as a meta-representation, representing a method of representation.

To show the computers' peculiarity of modus operandi, the artist needs to keep the process visible, or better, to make such process the principal subject of the artwork. Indeed, when confronted with Quayola's art, the viewer is always aware of observing an ongoing process.

Process

Unlike process-based art of the past, which tended to rely mainly on chance-based procedures, Quayola's work bears no evidence of aleatoric strategies. On the contrary, it results from precise computational interactions, therefore exerting a very high level of control over the output.

Since the beginning, Quayola's work found its underpinning in a concrete referent serving as a matrix for the machine. The subject undergoes a specific procedure; it is studied under a historical, conceptual, and formal perspective by the artist; it is then observed by the machine, which finally decodes it by computational means. Quayola employs various technologies and systems, including industrial robots, 3D scanners, computer-vision systems, and generative algorithms. Among these strategies, it is possible to trace a common agenda. In all cases, everything revolves around process; the output image, whether a sculpture, a digital painting, or a print, is not intended to represent the original subject (be that a landscape or anything else) but rather the characteristics of the machine that created it. The artist instructs the machine in the observation of reality. He then observes how it works, exhibits, and intervenes in its ways of operating.

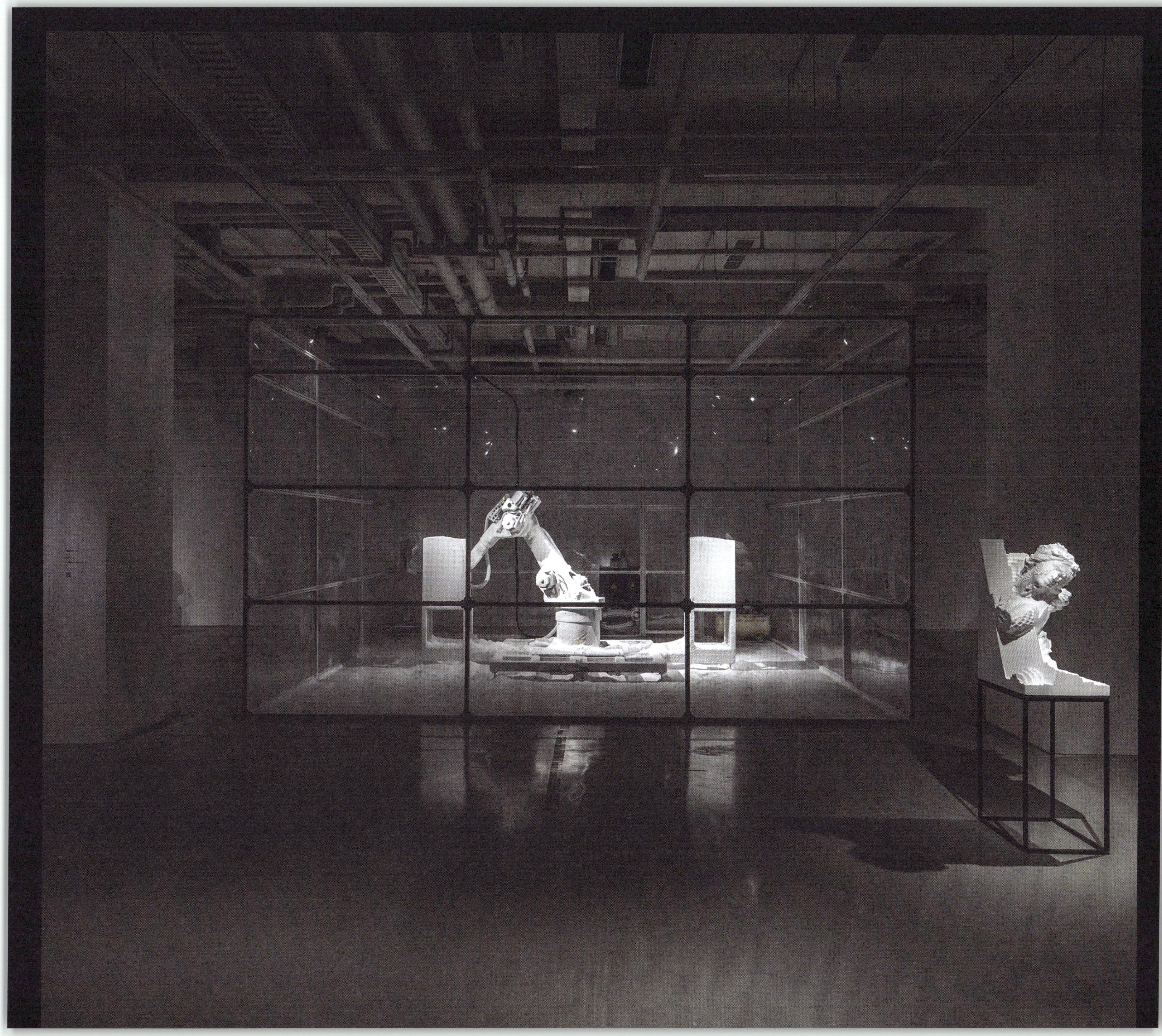

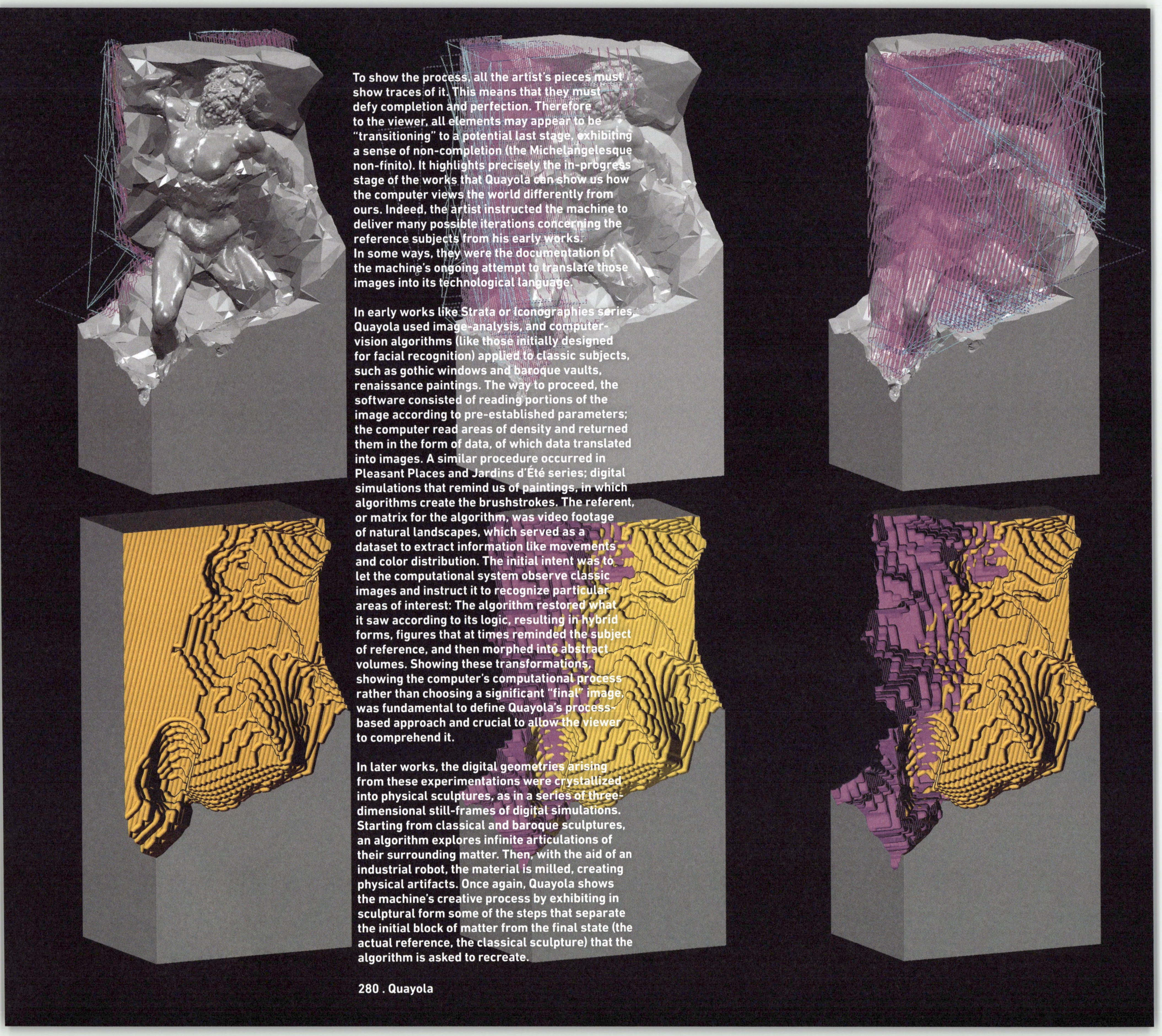

To show the process, all the artist's pieces must show traces of it. This means that they must defy completion and perfection. Therefore to the viewer, all elements may appear to be "transitioning" to a potential last stage, exhibiting a sense of non-completion (the Michelangelesque non-finito). It highlights precisely the in-progress stage of the works that Quayola can show us how the computer views the world differently from ours. Indeed, the artist instructed the machine to deliver many possible iterations concerning the reference subjects from his early works.
In some ways, they were the documentation of the machine's ongoing attempt to translate those images into its technological language.

In early works like Strata or Iconographies series, Quayola used image-analysis, and computer-vision algorithms (like those initially designed for facial recognition) applied to classic subjects, such as gothic windows and baroque vaults, renaissance paintings. The way to proceed, the software consisted of reading portions of the image according to pre-established parameters; the computer read areas of density and returned them in the form of data, of which data translated into images. A similar procedure occurred in Pleasant Places and Jardins d'Été series; digital simulations that remind us of paintings, in which algorithms create the brushstrokes. The referent, or matrix for the algorithm, was video footage of natural landscapes, which served as a dataset to extract information like movements and color distribution. The initial intent was to let the computational system observe classic images and instruct it to recognize particular areas of interest: The algorithm restored what it saw according to its logic, resulting in hybrid forms, figures that at times reminded the subject of reference, and then morphed into abstract volumes. Showing these transformations, showing the computer's computational process rather than choosing a significant "final" image, was fundamental to define Quayola's process-based approach and crucial to allow the viewer to comprehend it.

In later works, the digital geometries arising from these experimentations were crystallized into physical sculptures, as in a series of three-dimensional still-frames of digital simulations. Starting from classical and baroque sculptures, an algorithm explores infinite articulations of their surrounding matter. Then, with the aid of an industrial robot, the material is milled, creating physical artifacts. Once again, Quayola shows the machine's creative process by exhibiting in sculptural form some of the steps that separate the initial block of matter from the final state (the actual reference, the classical sculpture) that the algorithm is asked to recreate.

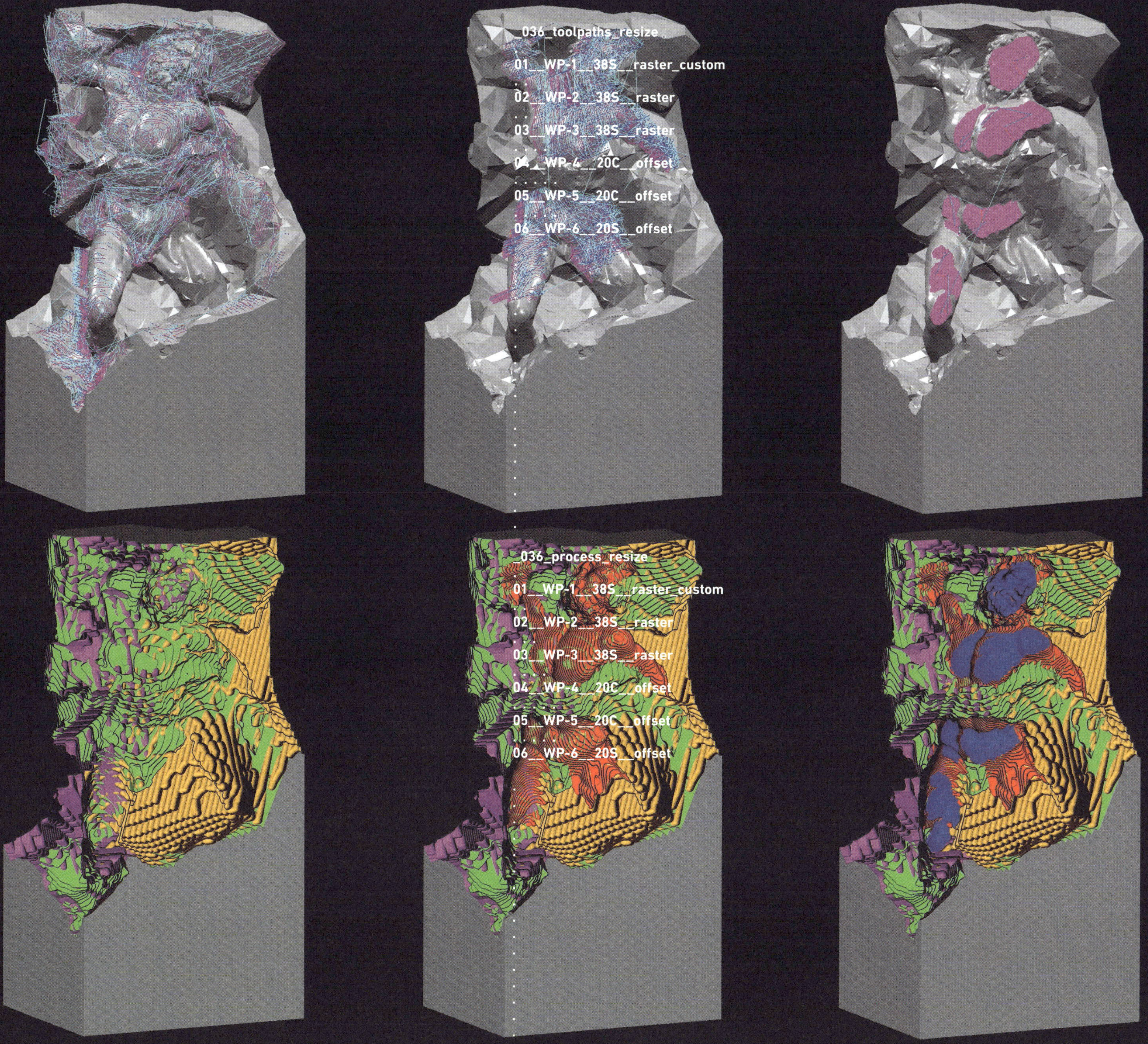
036_toolpaths_resize
01__WP-1__38S__raster_custom
02__WP-2__38S__raster
03__WP-3__38S__raster
04__WP-4__20C__offset
05__WP-5__20C__offset
06__WP-6__20S__offset
036_process_resize
01__WP-1__38S__raster_custom
02__WP-2__38S__raster
03__WP-3__38S__raster
04__WP-4__20C__offset
05__WP-5__20C__offset
06__WP-6__20S__offset

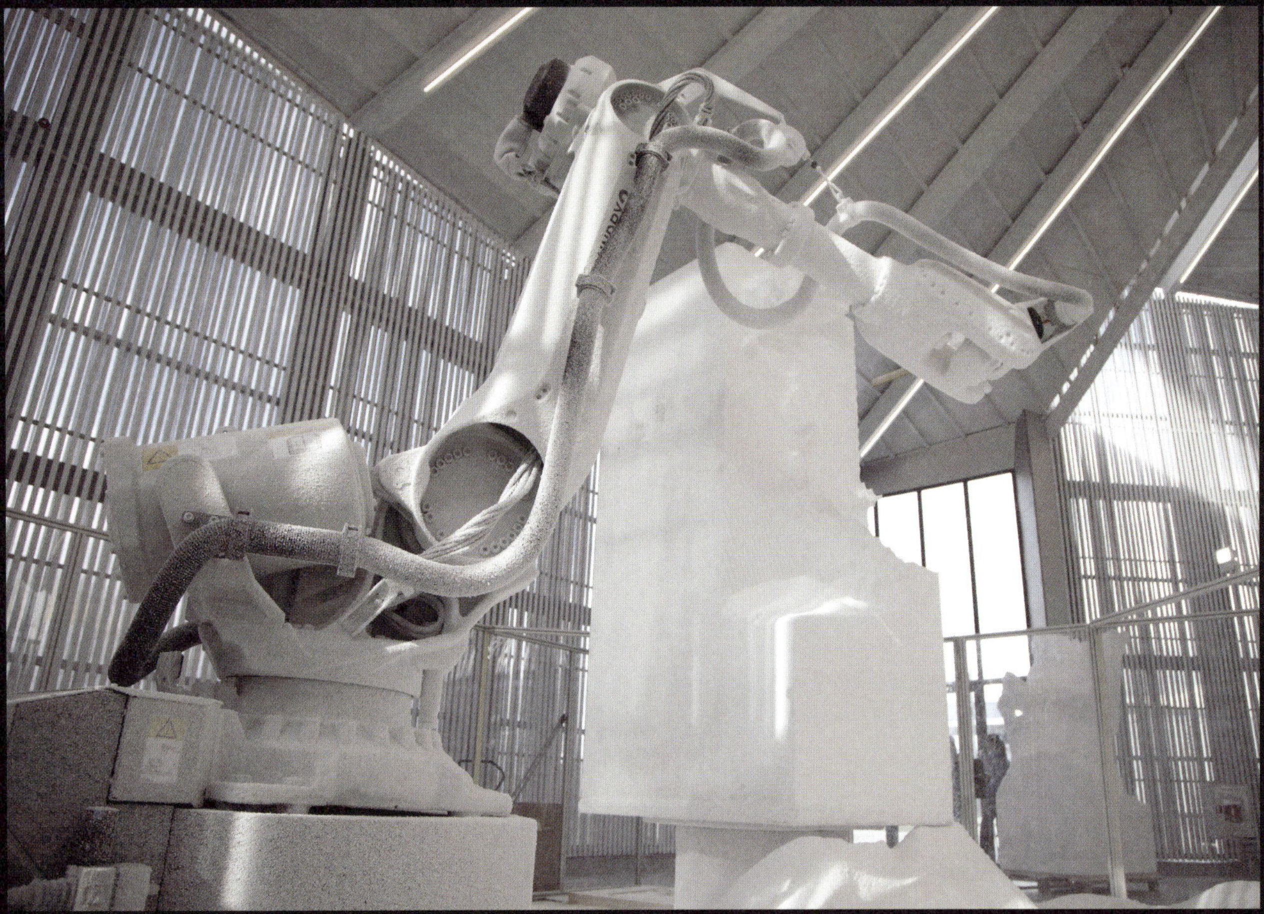

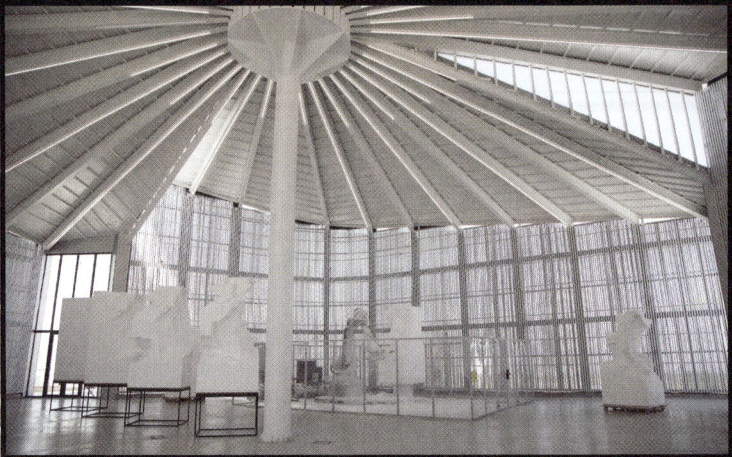

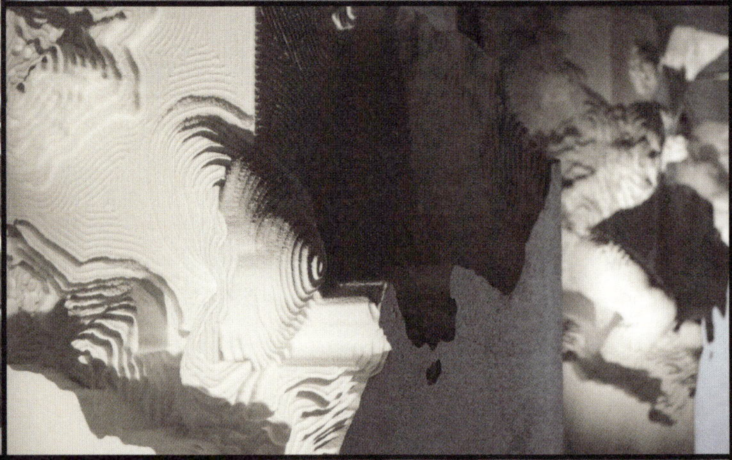

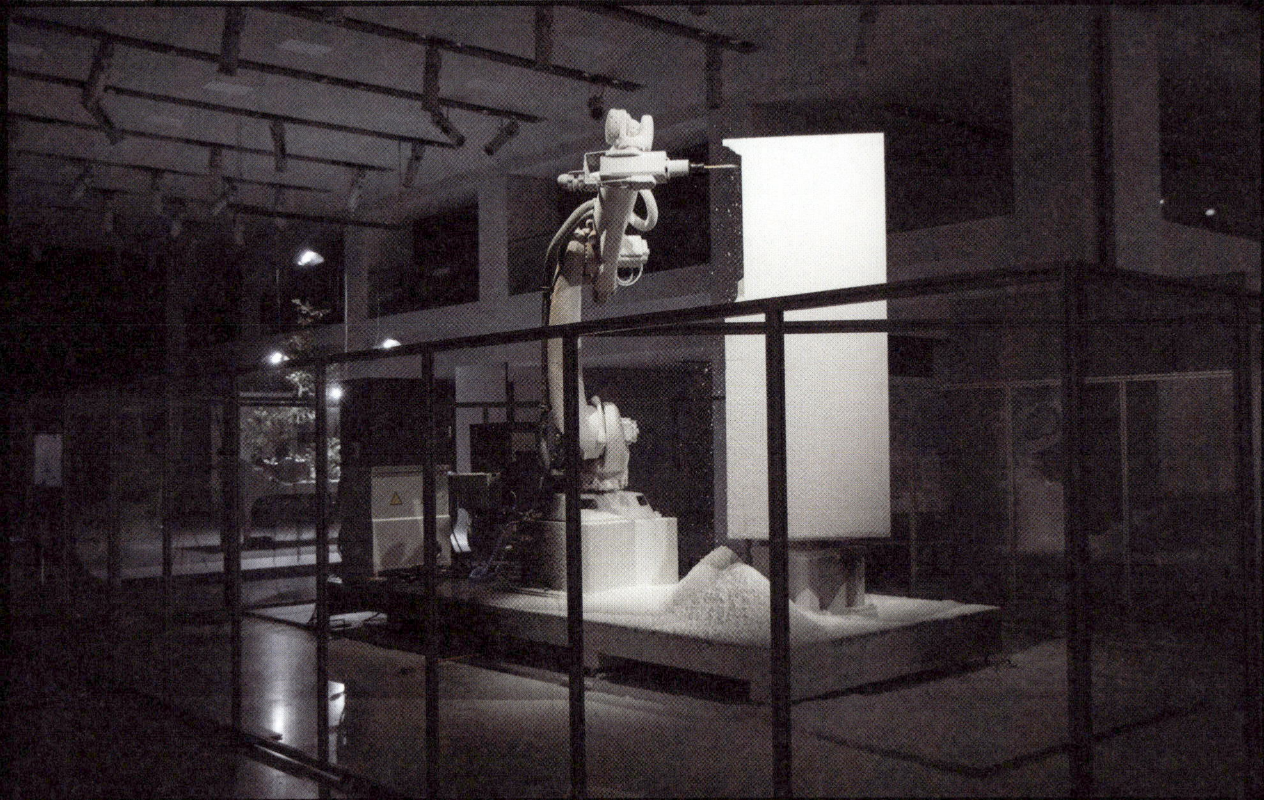

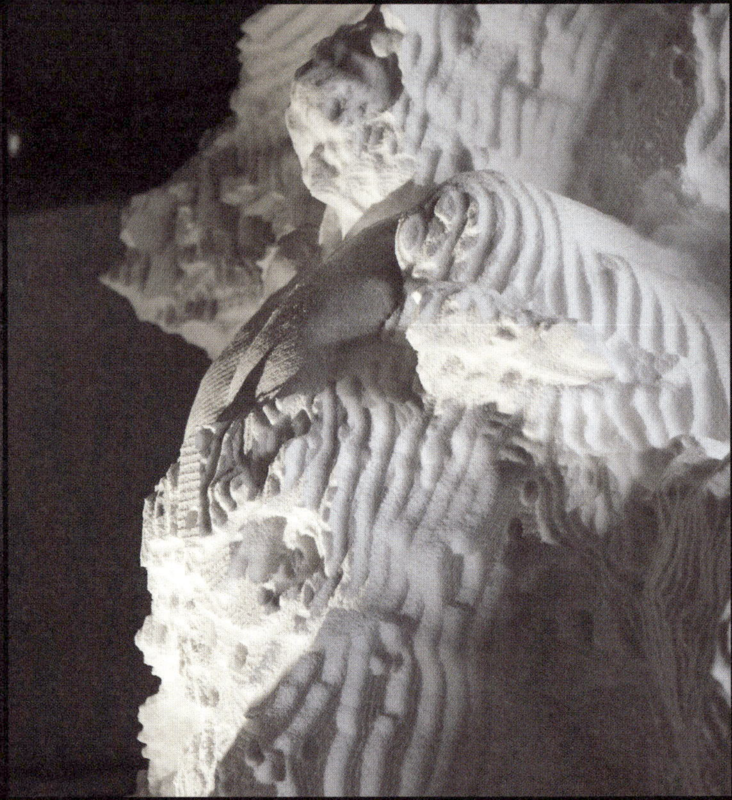

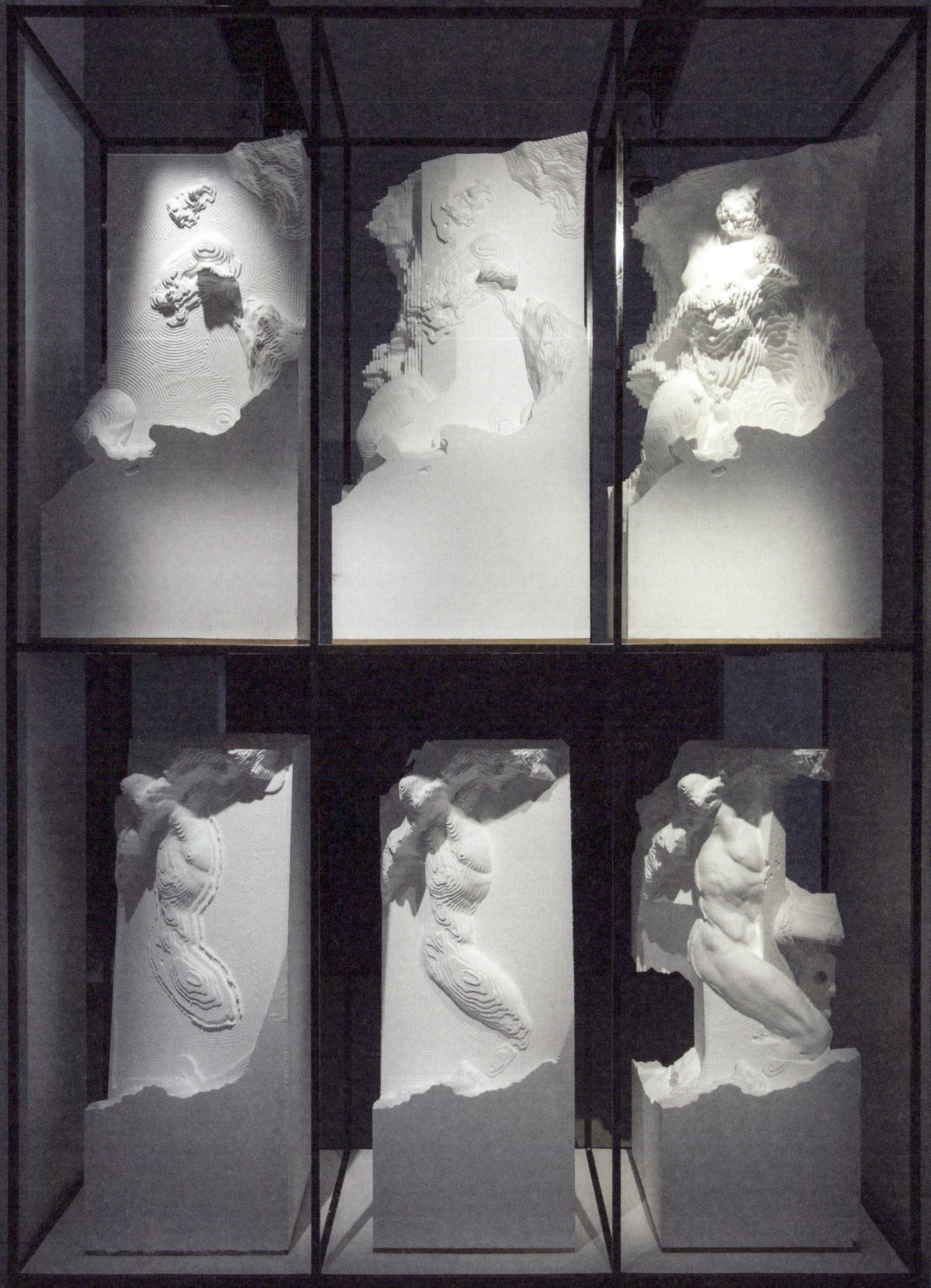

He specifically chose some stages of the morphing because they were emblematic of the process used to create them.

In the more recent Remains series, the technological process is exhibited by displaying what could be perceived as errors generated by the machine in reading a natural landscape. In the piece, a high-precision laser 3D scanner is used to make a detailed representation of a forest. Rendered in ultra-high resolution, the resulting image is similar to a photograph. Still, instead of pixels, it is composed of billions of white dots corresponding to the points where the laser hit various types of surfaces. The artist focuses on precise spots, for example, areas in which the light acted differently because of humidity. Such data translated into images return a representation of the forest that seems wrong in a way; sometimes illegible forms appear, portions of branches that seem suspended in the air. However, these seemingly idiosyncratic images are far from being mistakes thanks to the large format of the prints, a different approach to reading reality.

Time

In the exploration of the digital process, time is integral to Quayola's practice. Even when not in physical motion, the works are all time-based, containing time in its various connotations: duration, modification, simultaneity. Time plays an important role when conceived of as a historical continuum, and therefore an artistic legacy. For this reason, traditional subjects play an essential role; they emphasize a tangible effect of tension between past and present through a practice that draws from the classical heritage and leads to a digital output.

Quayola has always been fascinated by the idea that materials themselves are imbued with time, and over the years, he has been exploring this in different ways. Some of his video and sculptural works are based upon classical carvings that did not withstand the task of time and arrived at us fragmented or incomplete. Simulations were made to reproduce this type of fracturing, resulting in artworks that recalled something of the archeological fragments, and therefore the idea of a time enclosed in them. In Laocoön, for example, the artist took into account the quality of incompleteness of the original statue. The first series of Laocoön works, made of iron-filled resin, looked like fragments resurfaced from the earth, triggering the idea of an object from another era.

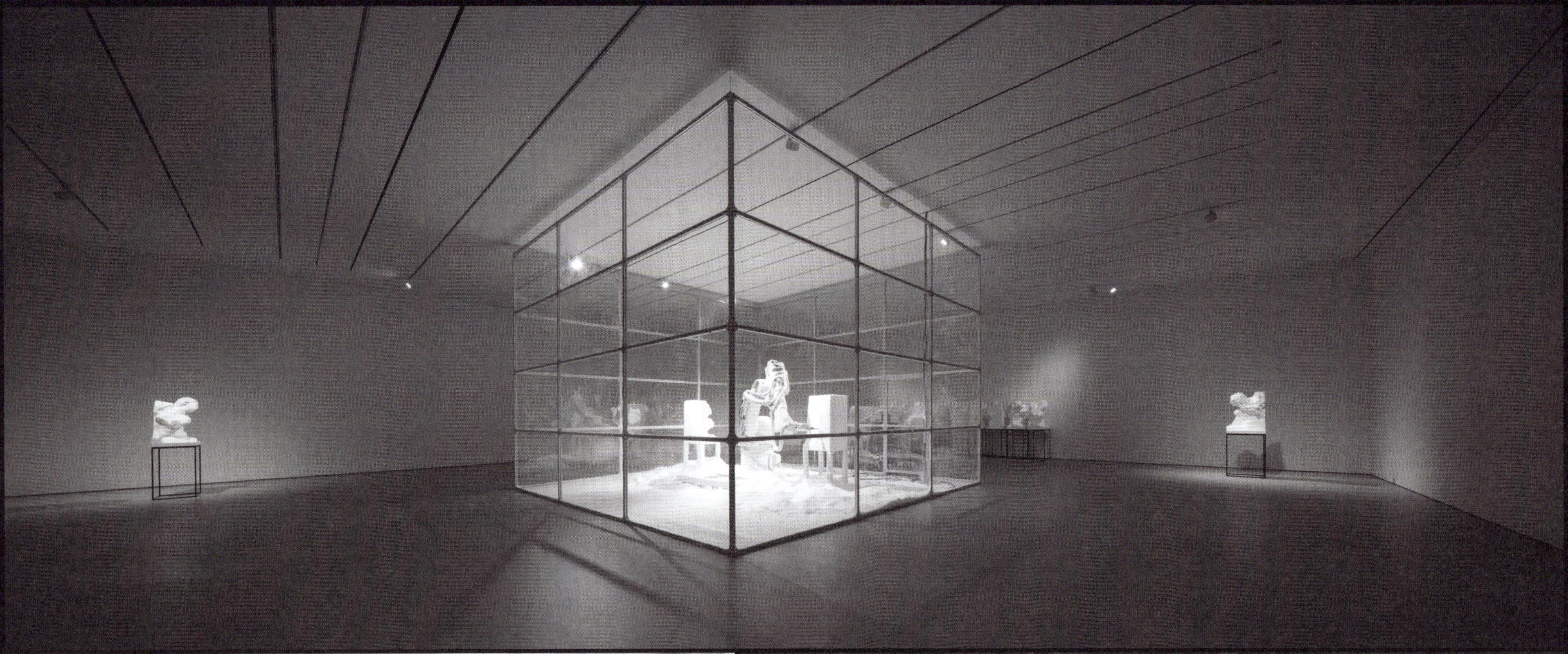
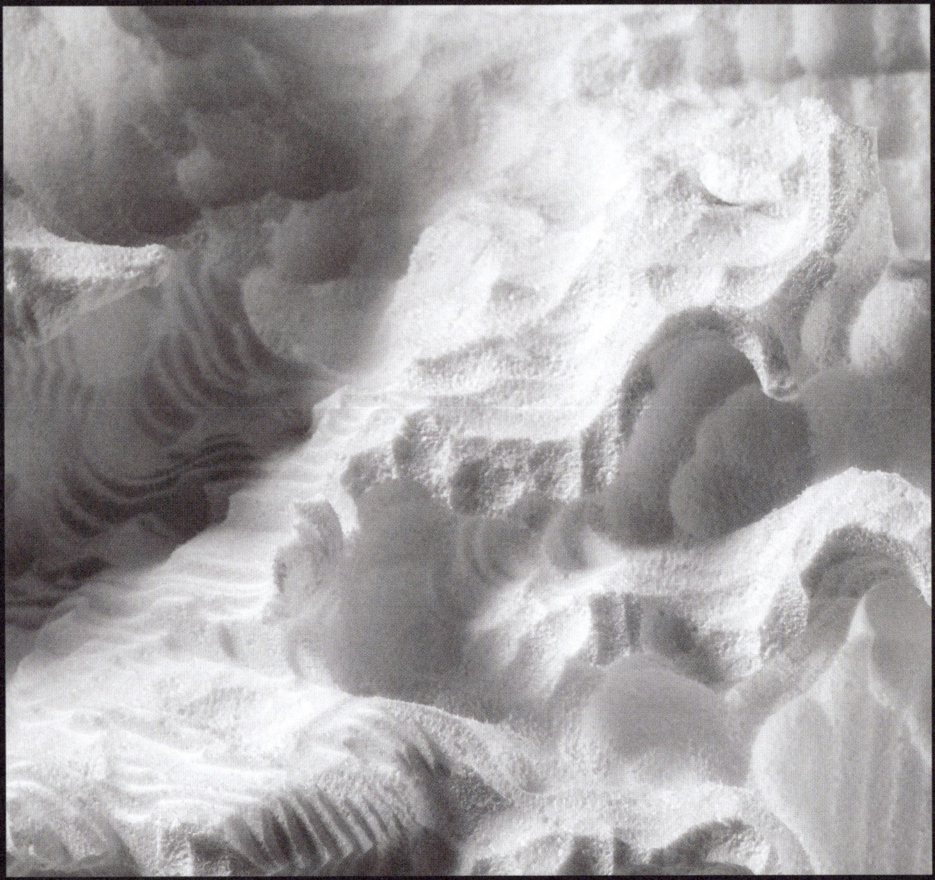
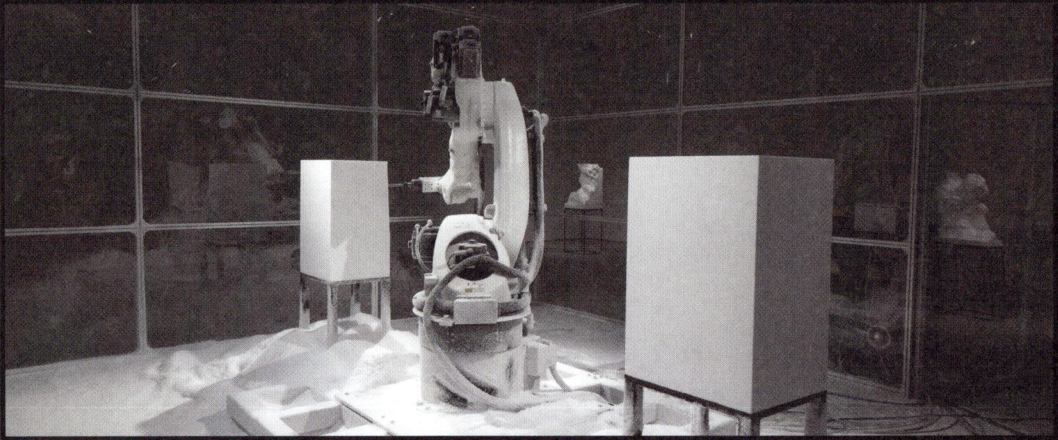
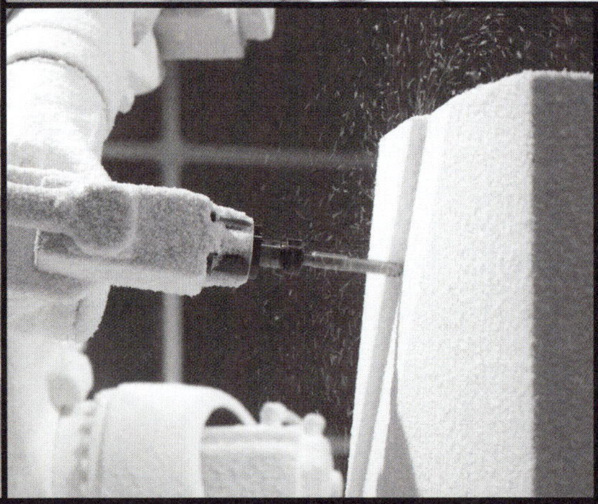
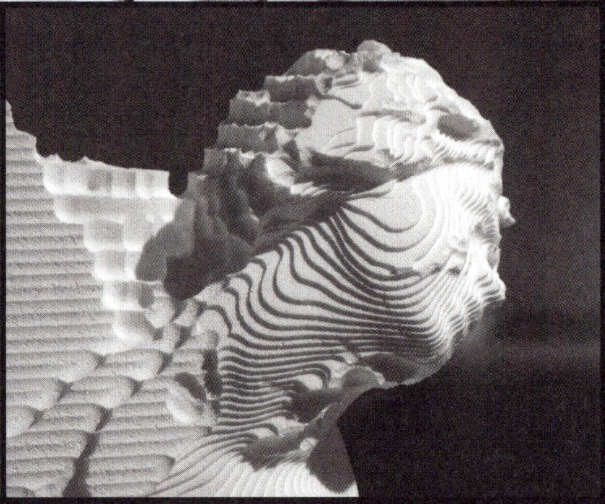

Taken to its climax, the purpose to reveal the process through time is also expressed in the concept of simultaneity; the work turns into a live performance. The process takes place in real-time, under the eyes of the spectator. Extracted from the performance, the single work then shapes its identity as a stage of a process, chosen as a marker of its specific characteristics. In the performative installation Sculpture Factory indeed, Quayola realized what he had in mind for a long time, showing the robot caught in action in the workshop. It has been a natural step; as he watched the robots sculpting, he started to engage with them and think of showing the workshop itself. In the ultimate act of witnessing the computer's modus operandi, the public can now watch the robot working in real-time.
A similar type of simultaneity occurs in digital paintings, thanks to the artist's software: This can modify images in real-time through algorithms that reproduce natural patterns and pictorial techniques.

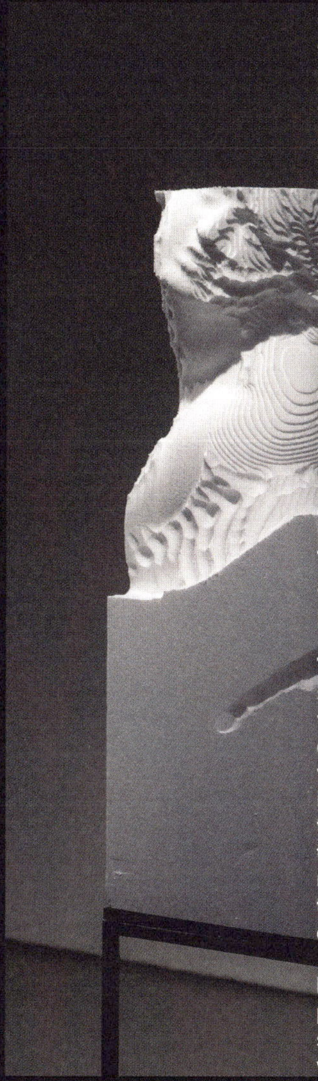

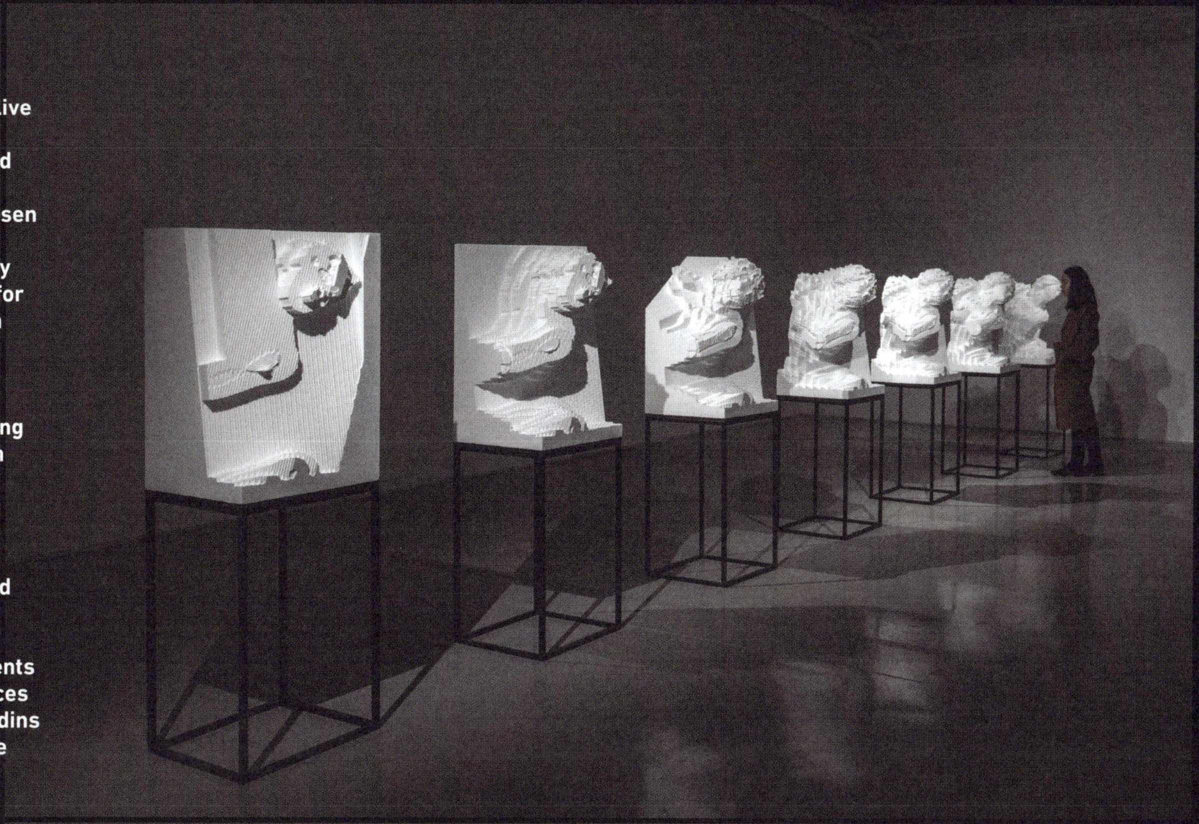

The genesis of Quayola's pictorial works presents similarities to that of the sculptures. The sources for the simulations of digital paintings like Jardins d'Été were originally videos of landscapes. The videos were shot in the same sites used by the impressionists as a source of inspiration. Like the impressionists, Quayola's intent was not to depict the landscapes but rather explore a new technique, which, in his case, involved a technological reading of the information shot on video.

In Pleasant Places, for example, the starting point was the features already contained in the source image: The vegetation oscillated with the wind, and from those movements, with a tracking system, the artist extrapolated the data, which he then used to create computational simulations of brushstrokes. Far from aiming to create a finished painting, the artist produced a series of iterations once again, reflecting the infinite array of possibilities within the act of deciphering and depicting reality from a computational eye.
The images we can observe on the monitor are real-time feedback on a digital "canvas."

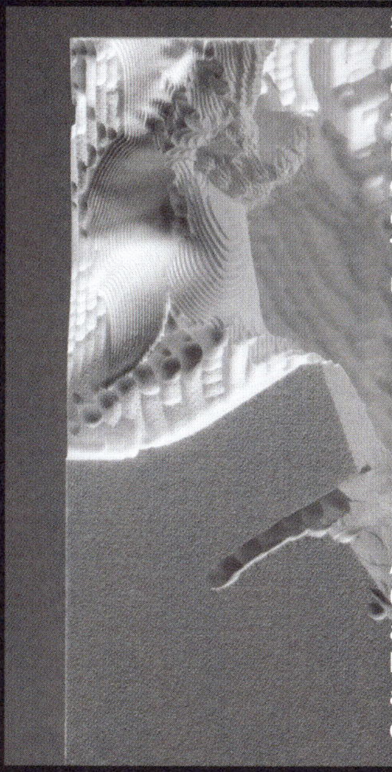

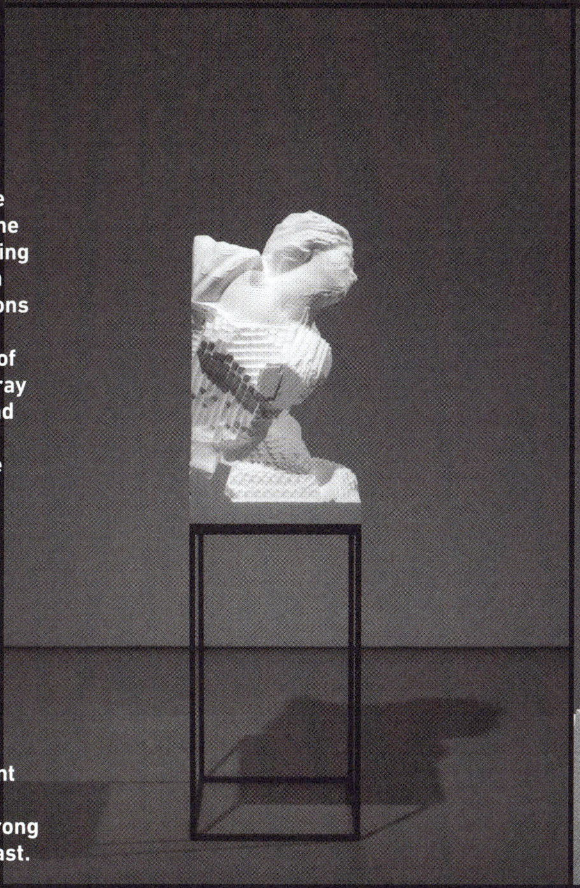

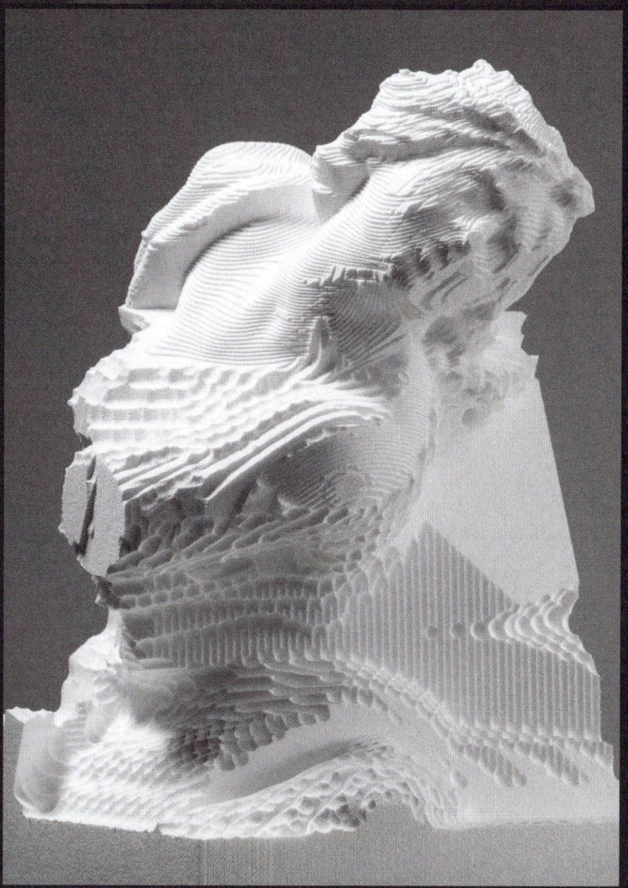

History and Heritage

Aside from being a kind of benchmark in Quayola's production when it comes to his attention to process in relation to time, Pleasant Places is also an excellent example of how the artist's work, almost paradoxically, bears a strong connection to certain artistic currents of the past.

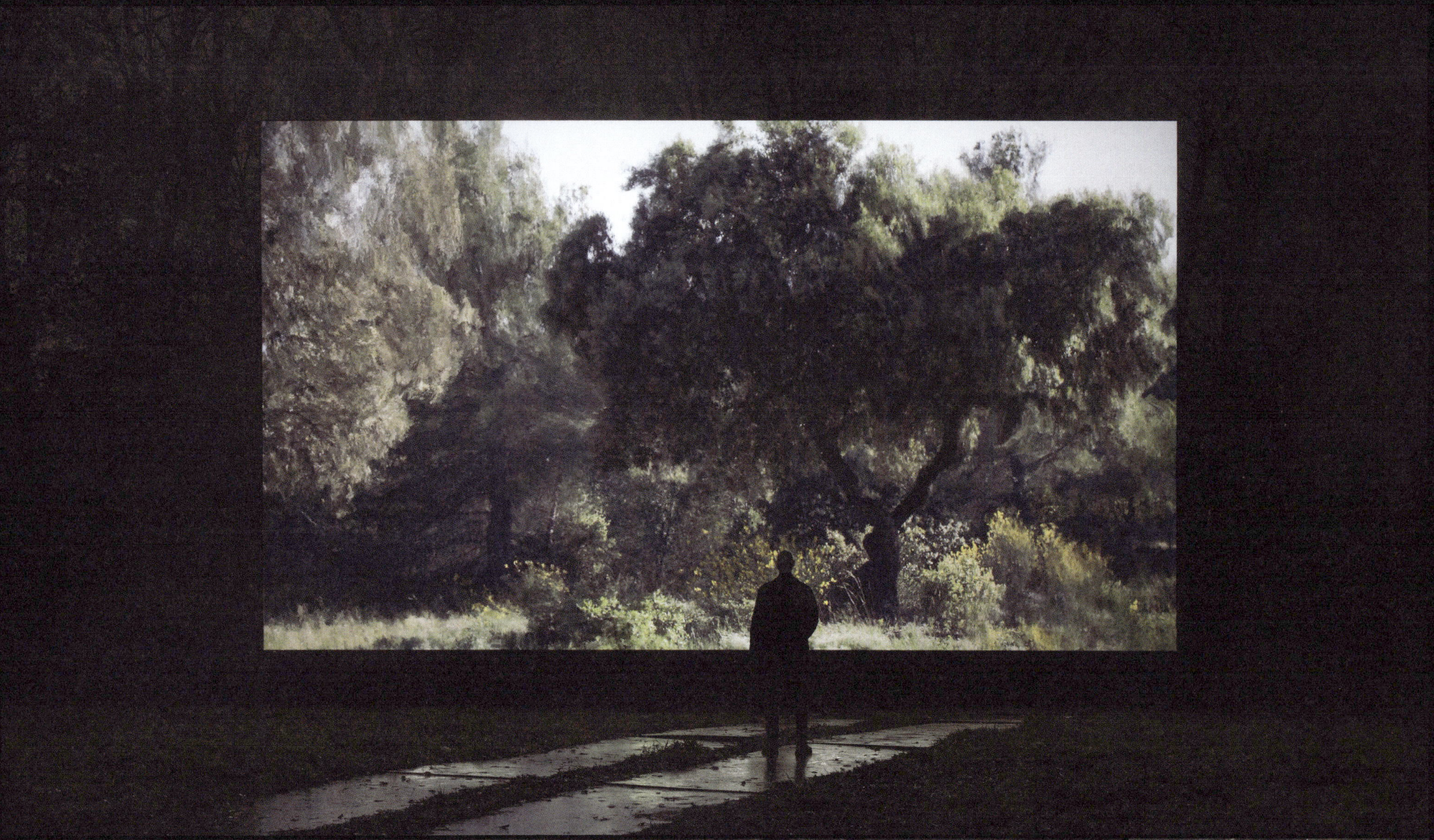

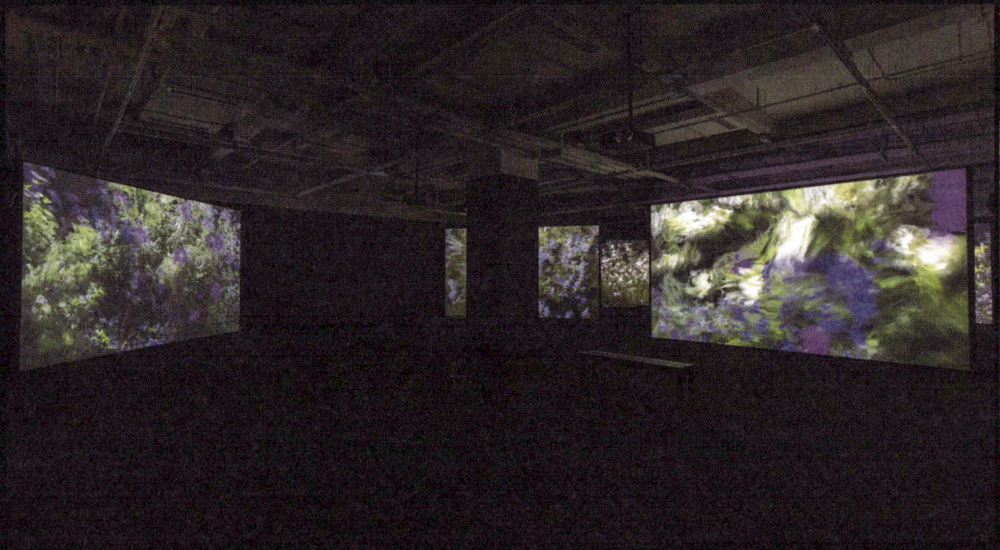

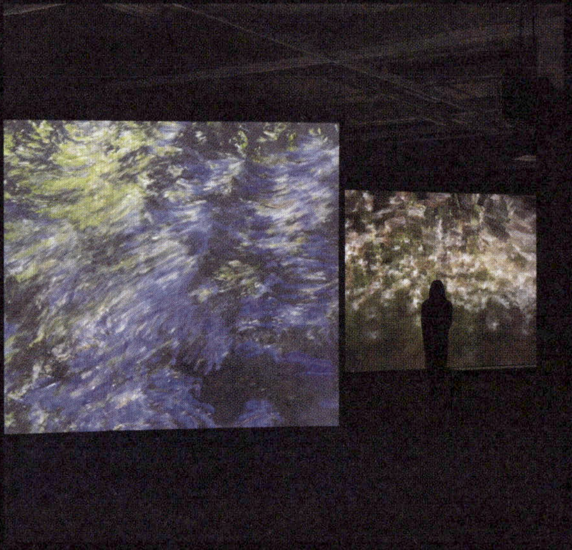

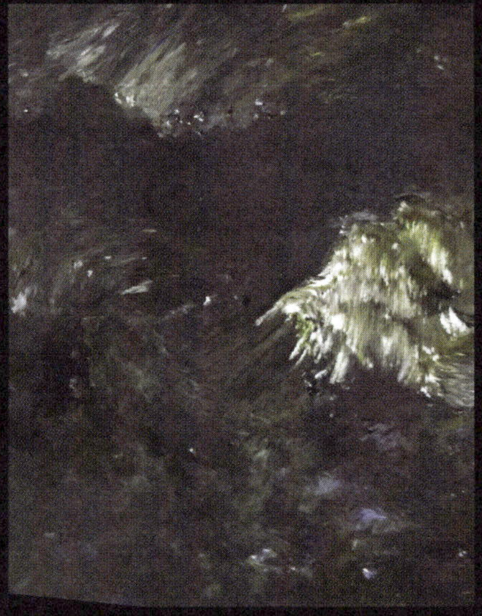

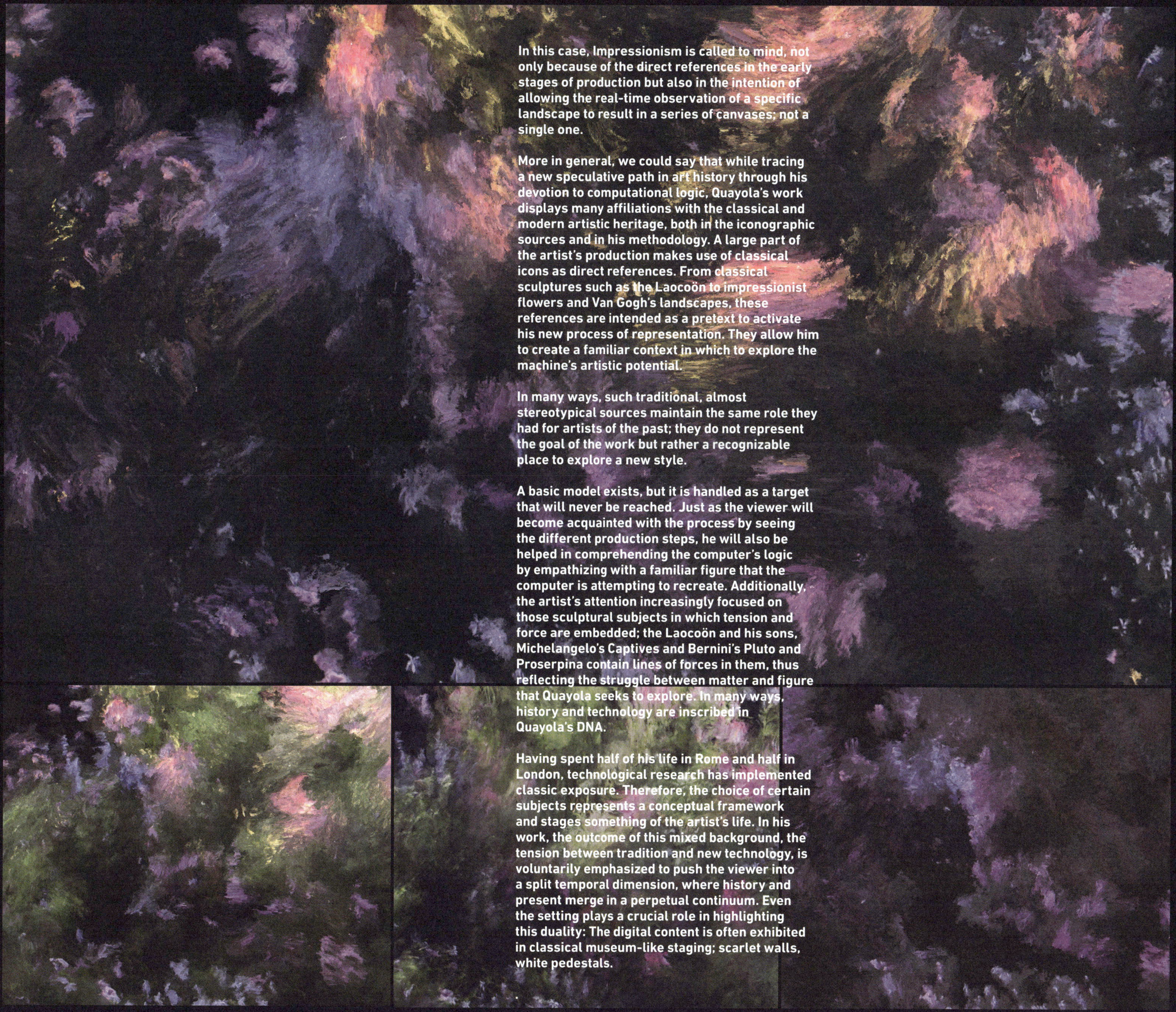

In this case, Impressionism is called to mind, not only because of the direct references in the early stages of production but also in the intention of allowing the real-time observation of a specific landscape to result in a series of canvases; not a single one.

More in general, we could say that while tracing a new speculative path in art history through his devotion to computational logic, Quayola's work displays many affiliations with the classical and modern artistic heritage, both in the iconographic sources and in his methodology. A large part of the artist's production makes use of classical icons as direct references. From classical sculptures such as the Laocoön to impressionist flowers and Van Gogh's landscapes, these references are intended as a pretext to activate his new process of representation. They allow him to create a familiar context in which to explore the machine's artistic potential.

In many ways, such traditional, almost stereotypical sources maintain the same role they had for artists of the past; they do not represent the goal of the work but rather a recognizable place to explore a new style.

A basic model exists, but it is handled as a target that will never be reached. Just as the viewer will become acquainted with the process by seeing the different production steps, he will also be helped in comprehending the computer's logic by empathizing with a familiar figure that the computer is attempting to recreate. Additionally, the artist's attention increasingly focused on those sculptural subjects in which tension and force are embedded; the Laocoön and his sons, Michelangelo's Captives and Bernini's Pluto and Proserpina contain lines of forces in them, thus reflecting the struggle between matter and figure that Quayola seeks to explore. In many ways, history and technology are inscribed in Quayola's DNA.

Having spent half of his life in Rome and half in London, technological research has implemented classic exposure. Therefore, the choice of certain subjects represents a conceptual framework and stages something of the artist's life. In his work, the outcome of this mixed background, the tension between tradition and new technology, is voluntarily emphasized to push the viewer into a split temporal dimension, where history and present merge in a perpetual continuum. Even the setting plays a crucial role in highlighting this duality: The digital content is often exhibited in classical museum-like staging; scarlet walls, white pedestals.

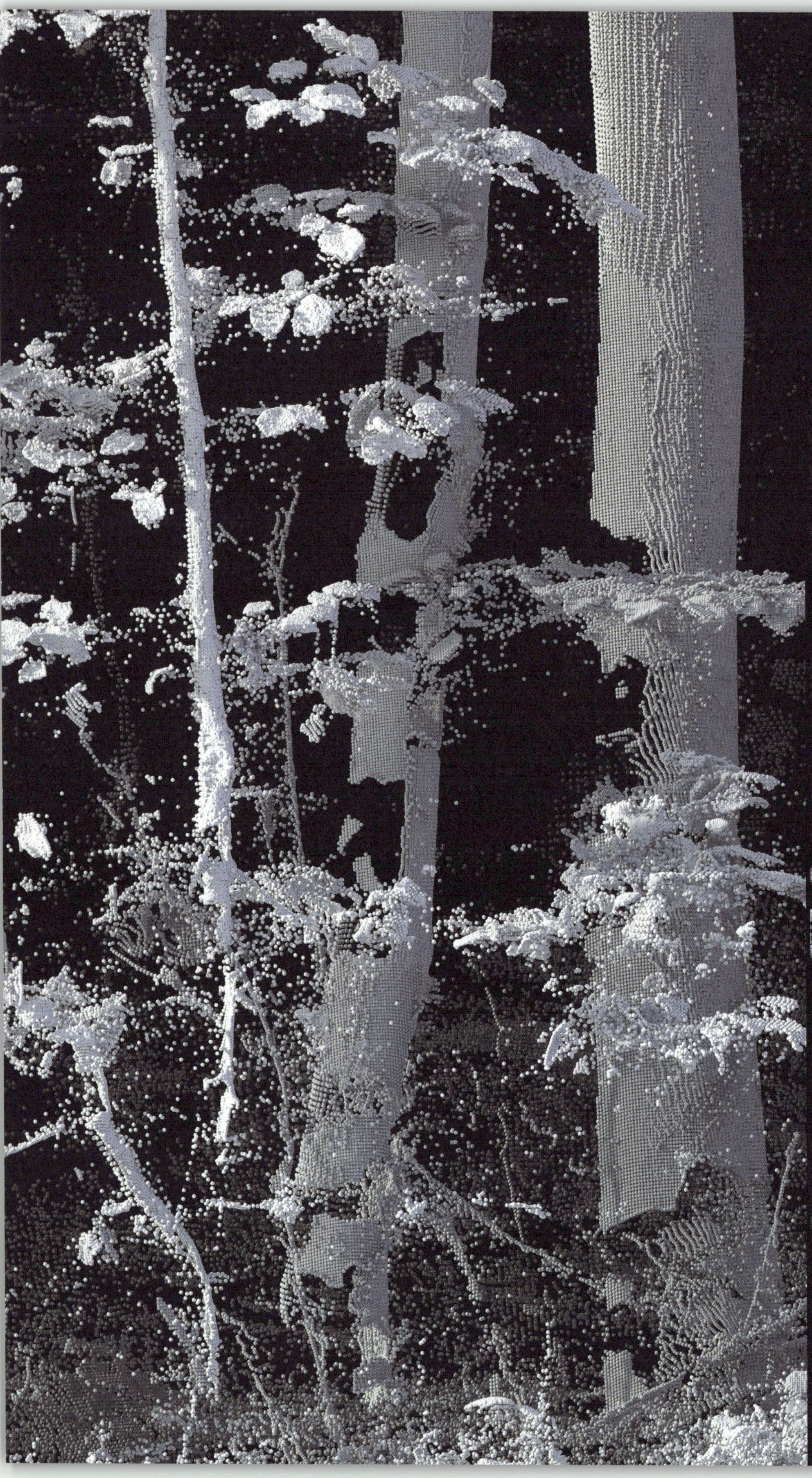

In some cases, the connection with the past is sought in the production method, rather than the iconographic references. In Quayola's pictorial work, there is a manifest intent, rather than interpret specific paintings, to mimic the approach of the impressionists. To create a new kind of brushstroke, or, we should say, allow the machine to create unique brushstrokes; to deliver a new type of painting. As it happened to his predecessors, Quayola pushed the algorithm towards the progressive removal of the iconographic subject. Some of his most recent works are de facto abstract, without literal, figurative references, even if it is still possible to detect some background source or retain a certain level of familiarity with the produced imagery.

Nature

As with classical subjects, nature is also a pretext for Quayola to investigate a different way of observing reality. The 3D-scanned landscapes of the Remains series and the digital paintings from Pleasant Places and the Jardin d'Été series can be considered the results of different attempts of seeing nature through the machine's eyes.

The observation of nature is at the basis of the primitive bond of a man with his surroundings. In his work, Quayola reclaims an idea of knowledge from the past, in which the artistic practice allowed scientists to decipher nature. For instance, in Leonardo Da Vinci's studies, the pictorial practice understood the natural world. Similarly, Quayola's artistic research suggests a new understanding of the natural world, achieved through collaboration with technological apparatuses.

Indeed, as in his revisitation of classical sculptures, natural imagery in Quayola's work is, once again, the result of hybridization; it combines natural and pictorial familiar forms with codes belonging to the digital world.

Then, it generates an empathy that invites us to redefine the categories we generally use to classify reality; natural/artificial, anthropic/technological. It ultimately encourages us to renegotiate our role concerning technology in the process of observing nature. The human being is no longer the protagonist.

In a way, Quayola goes through this renegotiation process by progressively allowing more autonomy to the machine. Indeed, he will enable the computational system to model the brushstrokes independently; the original natural subject is no longer present. The machine creates a new autonomous image that mimics the natural one.

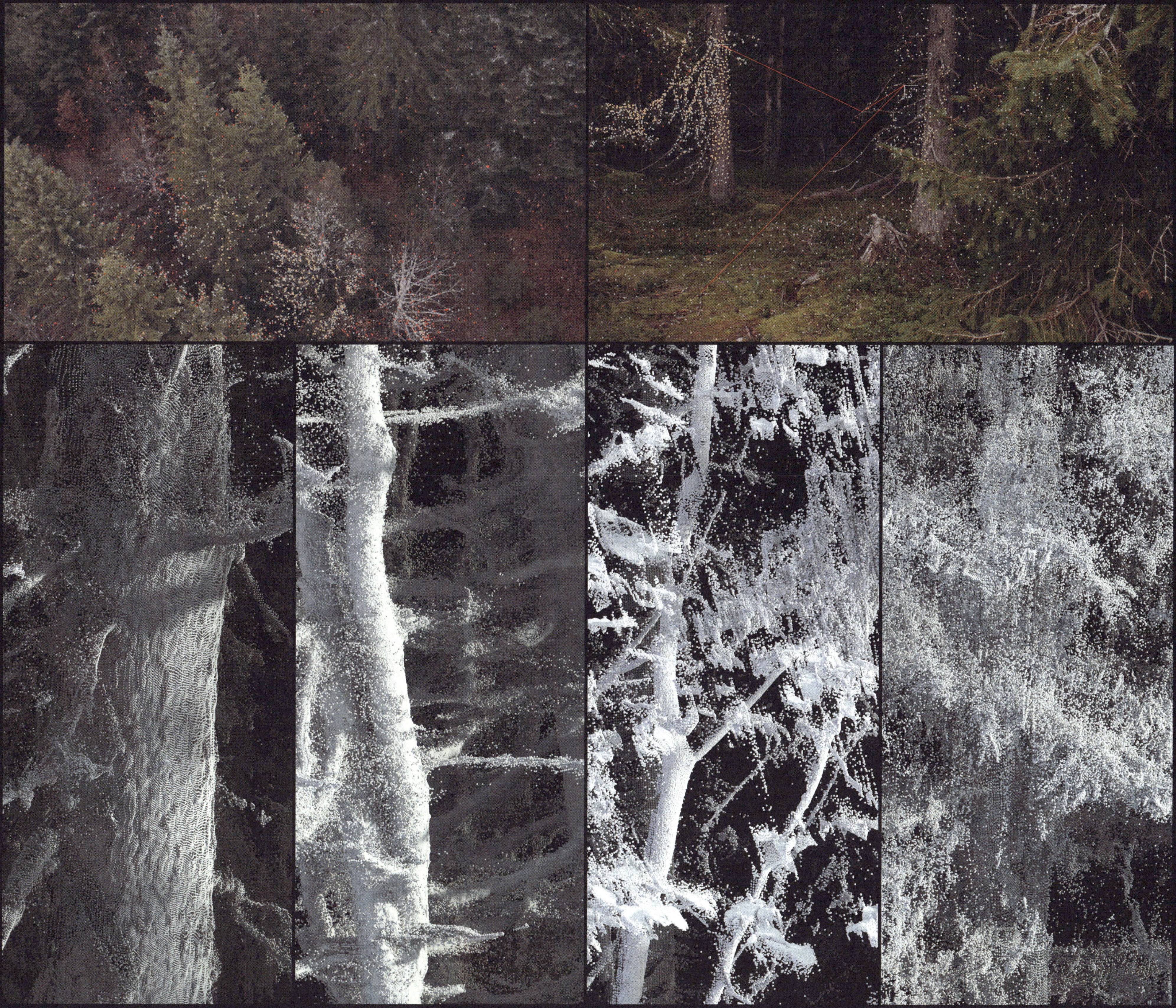

Seriality and Resolution

Seriality is a fundamental part of the artist's quest to highlight the process. The output of the work is indeed characterized by a wide range of iterations and variations. This process is based on algorithmic simulations. The purpose is not completeness but rather the potential contained within the infinite array of possibilities. Some of these finally become physical artwork, chosen among others as they are more representative of the process itself. Therefore, it is essential to look at these works as sequences: The single work gains relevance within the series of multiple iterations. For this reason, the titles of the works contain codes reflecting their serial nature.

Connected to seriality, Quayola's works also deal with the concept of resolution. This is not to be misunderstood with the idea of the resolution pertaining to the absolute sharpness of the final image. It references, in fact, to the in-progress state of the pieces, which often appear in an unfinished form. If we imagine a theoretically finished artifact representing the highest possible resolution, any nonfinito (unfinished) works will display a "lower resolution" compared to it. This is expressed through the choice of leaving the traces of the milling process visible in the sculptures. For example, Pluto and Proserpina, or again selecting the large format prints of Remains, are functional to make the laser-scanning patterns visible. Tiny white dots represent billions of laser beams measuring the natural features of a landscape.

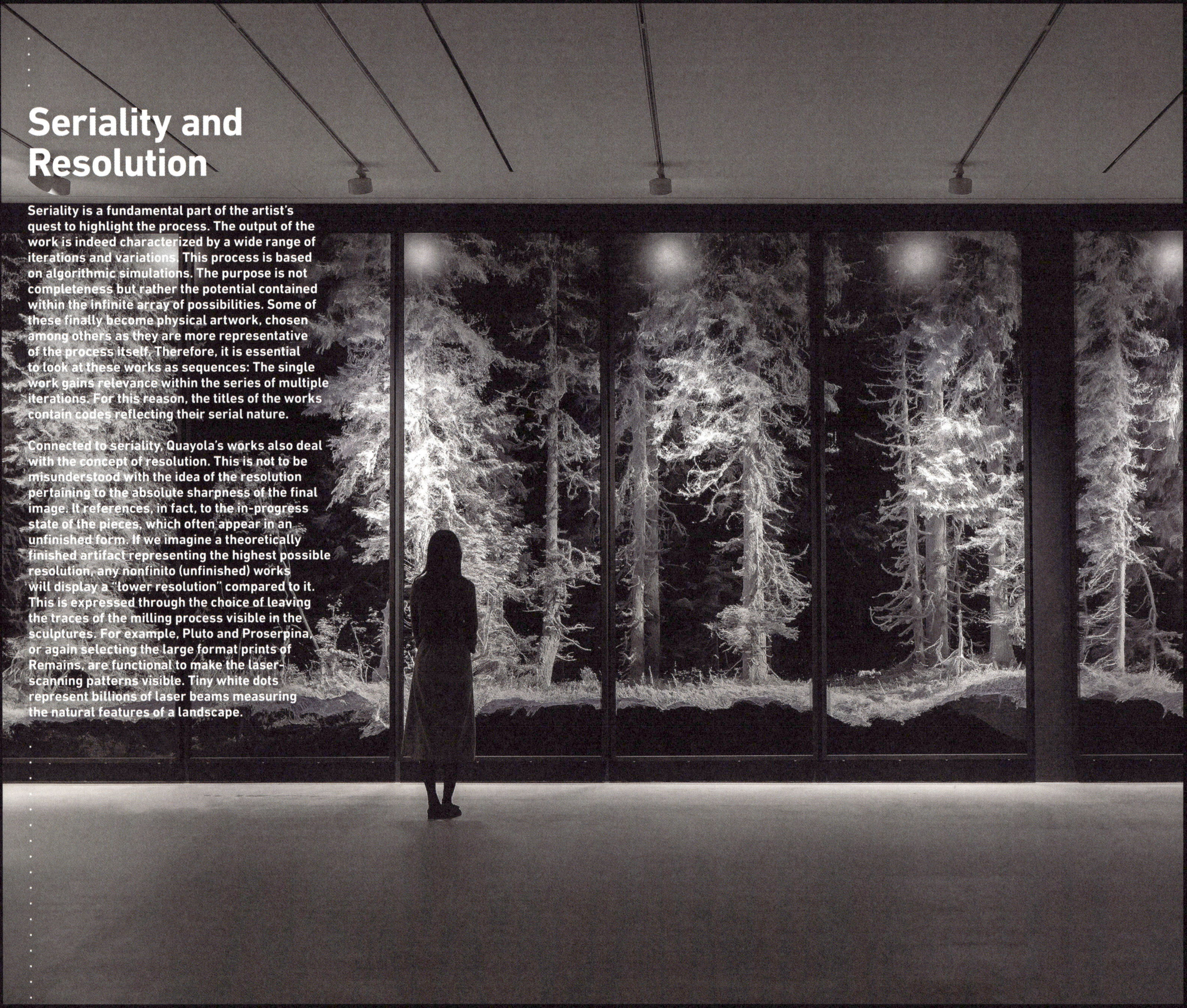

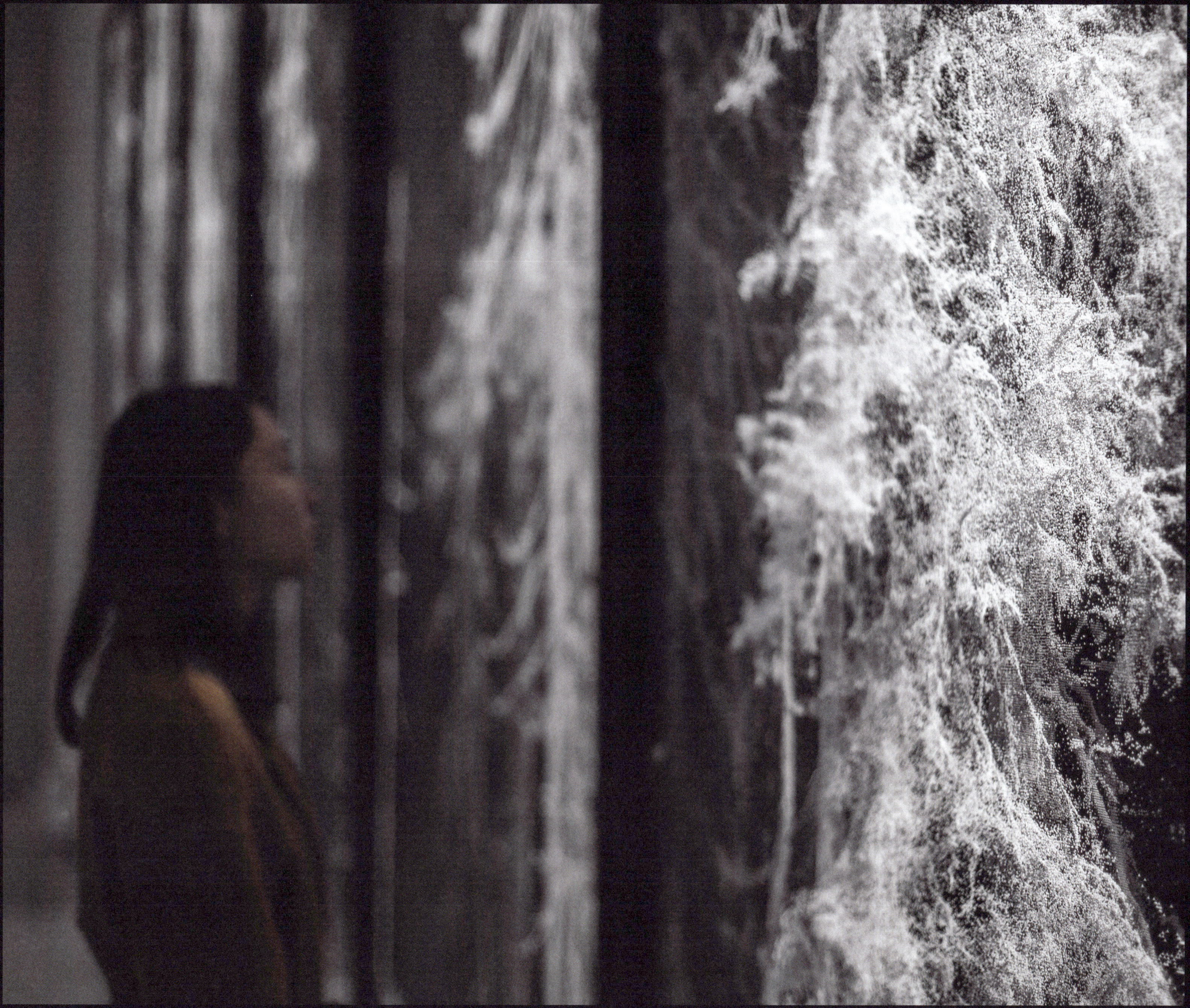

291 . REMAINS

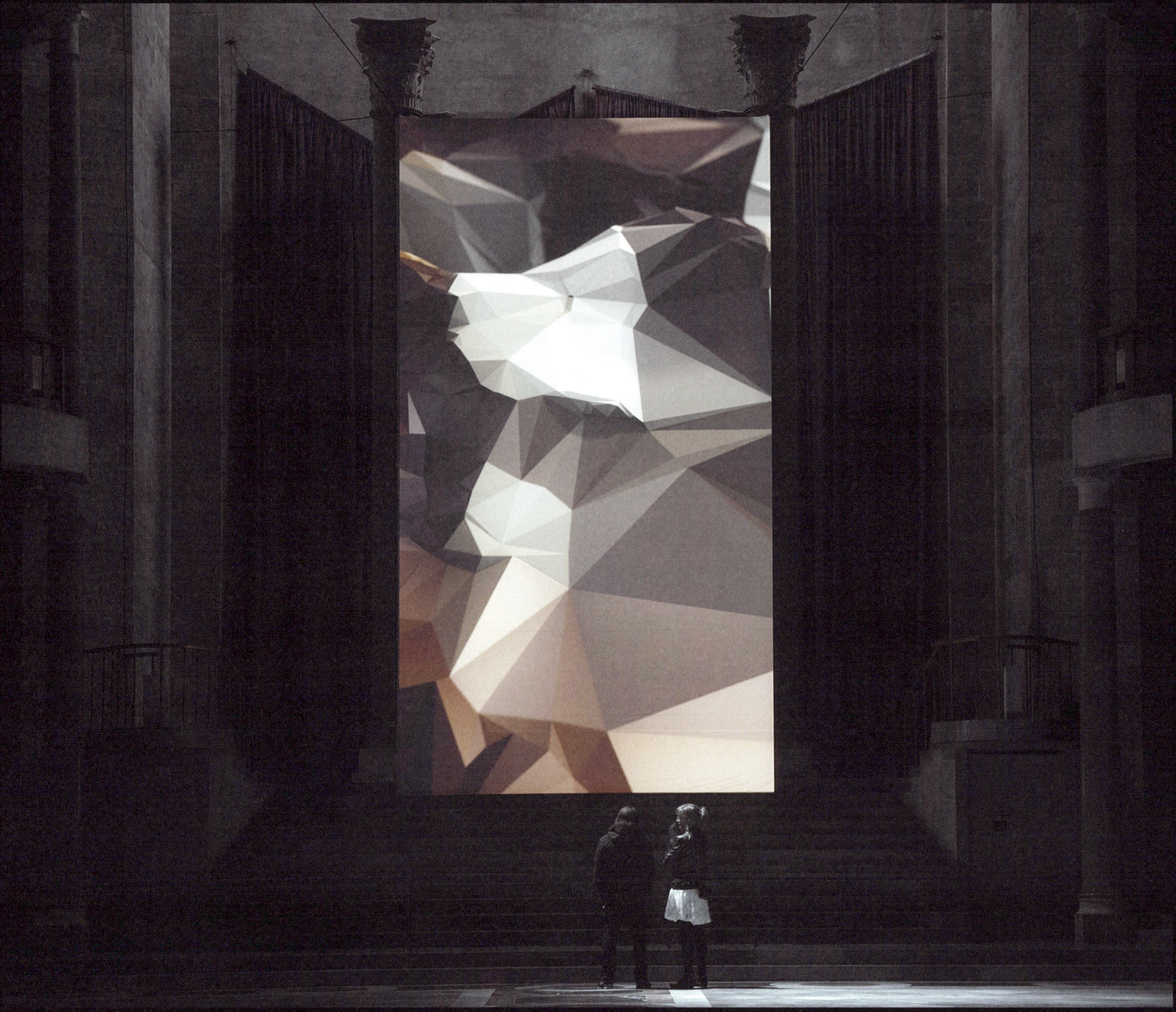

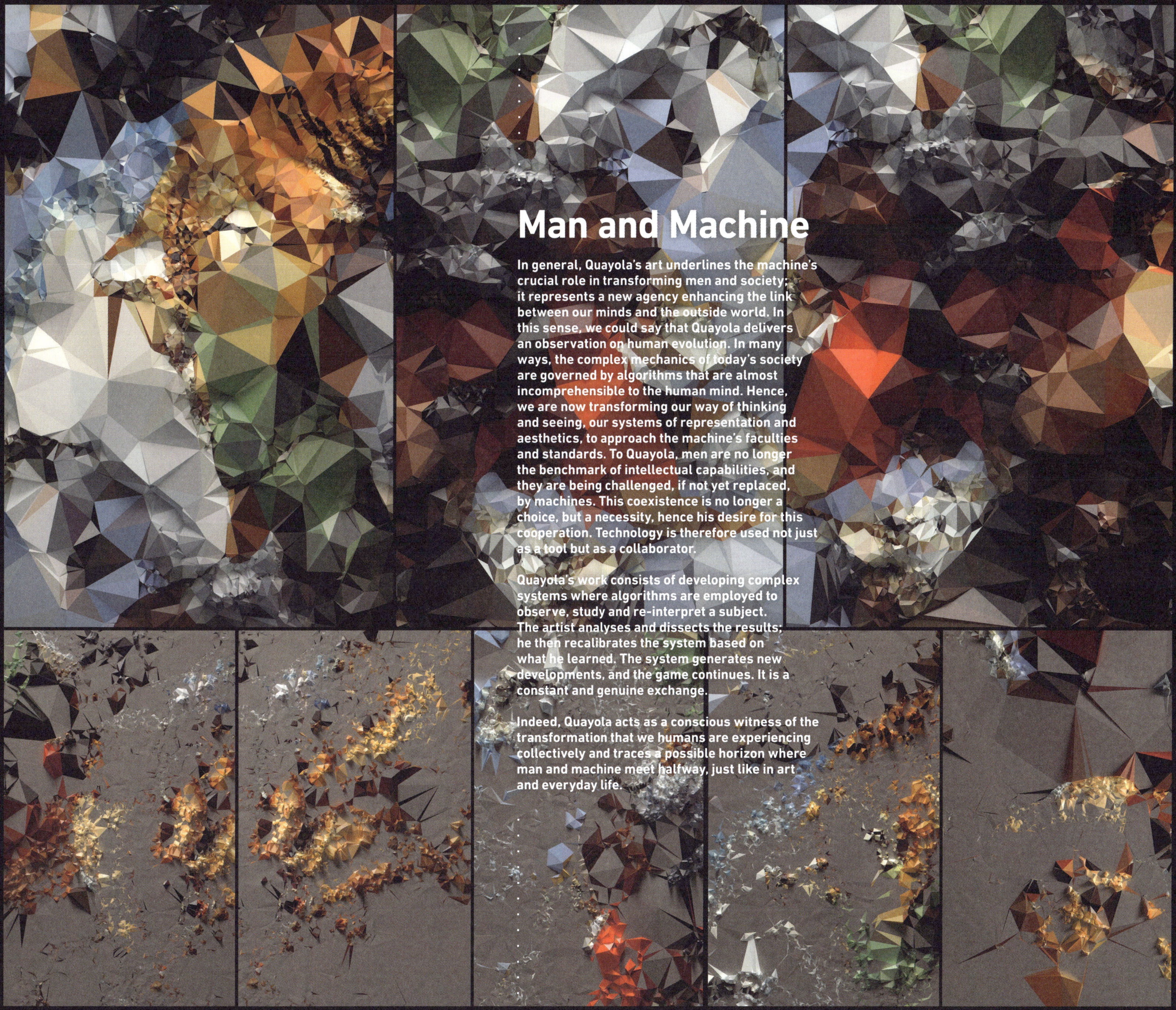

Man and Machine

In general, Quayola's art underlines the machine's crucial role in transforming men and society; it represents a new agency enhancing the link between our minds and the outside world. In this sense, we could say that Quayola delivers an observation on human evolution. In many ways, the complex mechanics of today's society are governed by algorithms that are almost incomprehensible to the human mind. Hence, we are now transforming our way of thinking and seeing, our systems of representation and aesthetics, to approach the machine's faculties and standards. To Quayola, men are no longer the benchmark of intellectual capabilities, and they are being challenged, if not yet replaced, by machines. This coexistence is no longer a choice, but a necessity, hence his desire for this cooperation. Technology is therefore used not just as a tool but as a collaborator.

Quayola's work consists of developing complex systems where algorithms are employed to observe, study and re-interpret a subject. The artist analyses and dissects the results; he then recalibrates the system based on what he learned. The system generates new developments, and the game continues. It is a constant and genuine exchange.

Indeed, Quayola acts as a conscious witness of the transformation that we humans are experiencing collectively and traces a possible horizon where man and machine meet halfway, just like in art and everyday life.

Name:

Hansi Raber
&
Jerobeam Fenderson

Info:

Hansi Raber; I grew up in rural Austria with a keen interest in programming, mathematics, and music.

Most of these interests started early in life and never stopped.

There is no particular goal I'm striving for; instead, I just try to see where my curiosity takes me. My main priority is to do as little commercial work as possible and not commercialize my interest too much.

Little heads up: I'm describing one-half of a long collaboration.

Project:

OSCISTUDIO

URL:

superduper.org

Instagram:

@kritzikratzi

Project Description:

In 2013 I was at a festival of sorts, a place called Schmiede in Hallein, Austria. My friend Hannes introduced me to Jerobeam Fenderson, "you'll love what he does." He brought me to the last corner of the building.

In front of us was a table consisting of a laptop, an audio interface, speakers, an oscilloscope, and a big mess of cables connecting everything. Jerobeam pressed play on his computer; it started making a continuous, slowly shifting tone, and on the oscilloscope, a faint green circle changing its shape appeared. Systematically the shape kept rearranging itself, jumping to different forms and sounds, resembling some sort of rhythmic or a little animation; actually both.

From lab exercises that I had to do at school, I knew what was going on, but I was amazed by how far he had pushed the idea and how much creative expression he had put into the whole thing.

So what was going on?
The basic setup consists of three steps:

1. Get a magic audio file and play it through your soundcard
2. Connect the left and right channels to speakers, so you can hear
3. Connect the left and right channels to an oscilloscope in xy-mode, so you can see

An oscilloscope in xy-mode works a bit like an electronic etch-a-sketch:

A crt tube produces a glowing dot. The audio signal connected to the x input deflects the dot along the horizontal axis, the signal related to the y input deflects the dot vertically. If you have a fast, repeating signal, then a fast-moving dot appears as lines and shapes.

Musicians will call an oscilloscope in xy-mode a vectorscope, and they use it to analyze stereo separation. A mono signal appears as a straight line; a fully stereo-panned signal will appear as some kind of wild spaghetti.

At the time, I had a keen interest in differential geometry, and I knew right away that what I was seeing can be described perfectly well by so-called two-dimensional parametric equations. Jerobeam and I talked quite a lot during the following ten days of the festival, and we exchanged many ideas.

At the time his biggest problem was to draw a rotating 3D cube.

Equipped with a lot of maths under my belt, I could point him towards a unique solution.

The oscilloscope thing stuck with me for a while, but it wasn't until the following year that OSCISTUDIO was born.

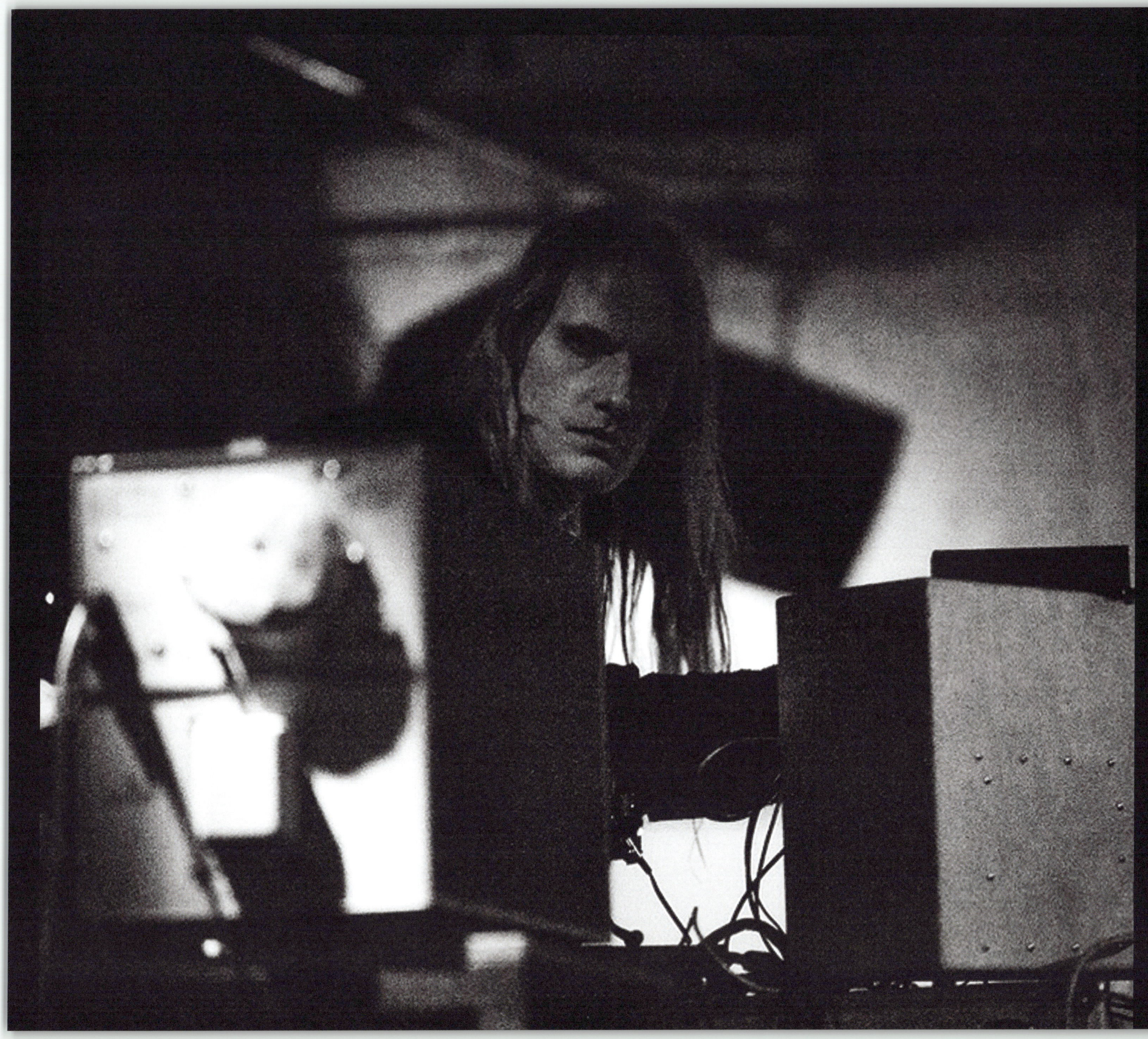

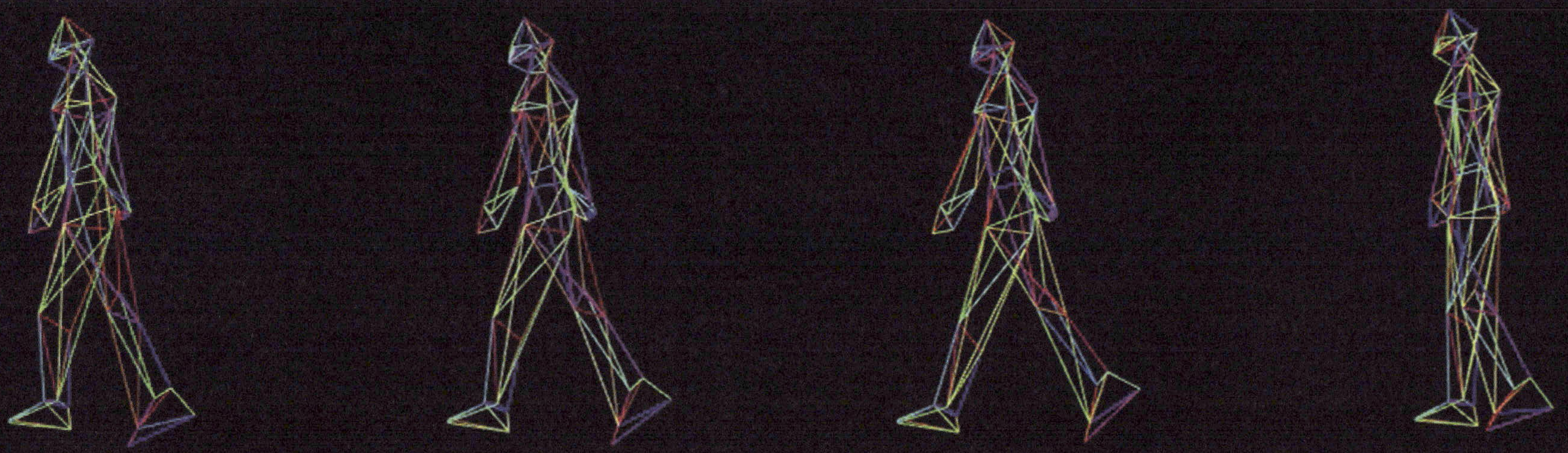

So how does one acquire magical audio files?

One way, and that's what Jerobeam was using at the time, is to use equations controlled mainly by a single parameter:

x(t) = sin(2*pi*50*t) ▸ left audio channel
y(t) = cos(2*pi*50*t) ▸ right audio channel

t in this equation is the time in seconds.

This produces a continuous tone at 50 Hz, and because things are how they are, the shape you will see is a circle.

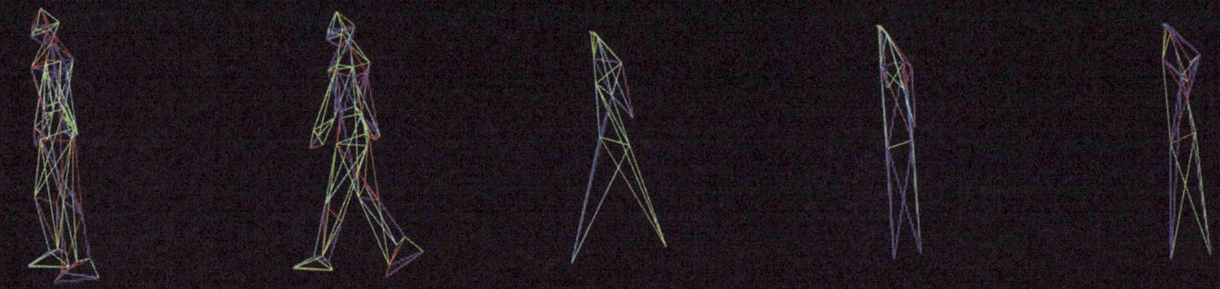

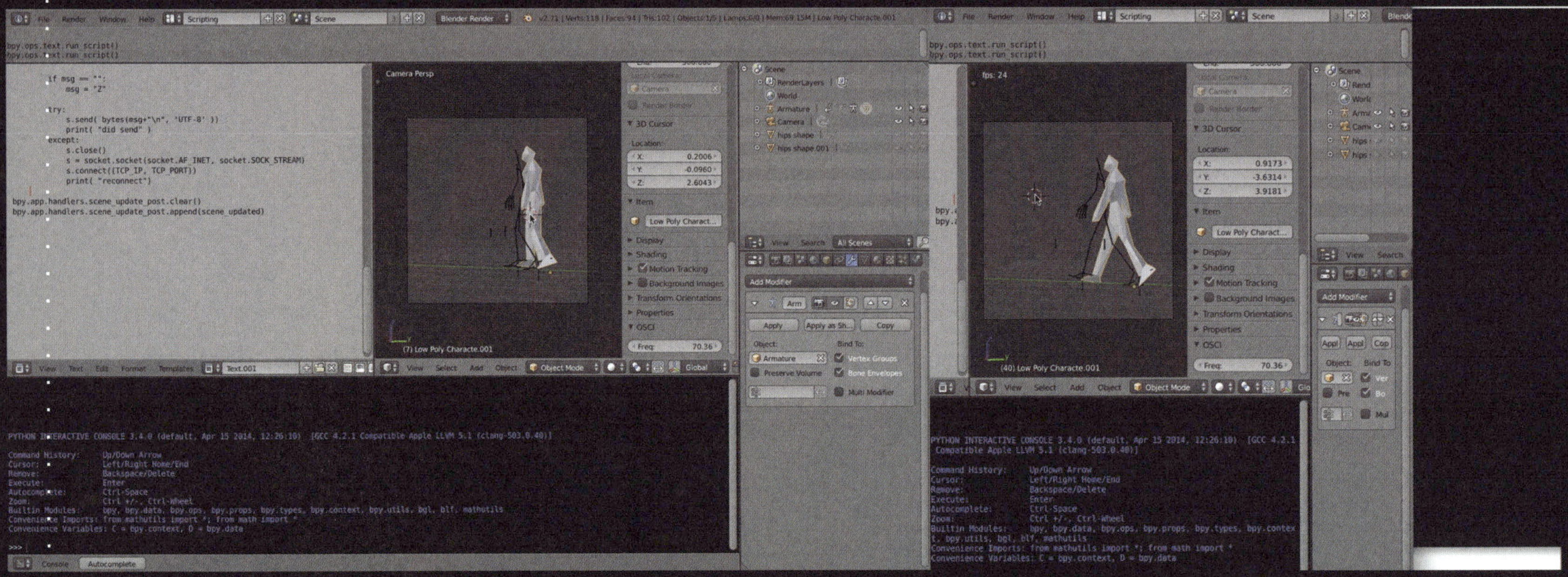

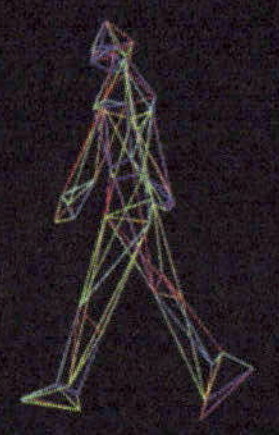

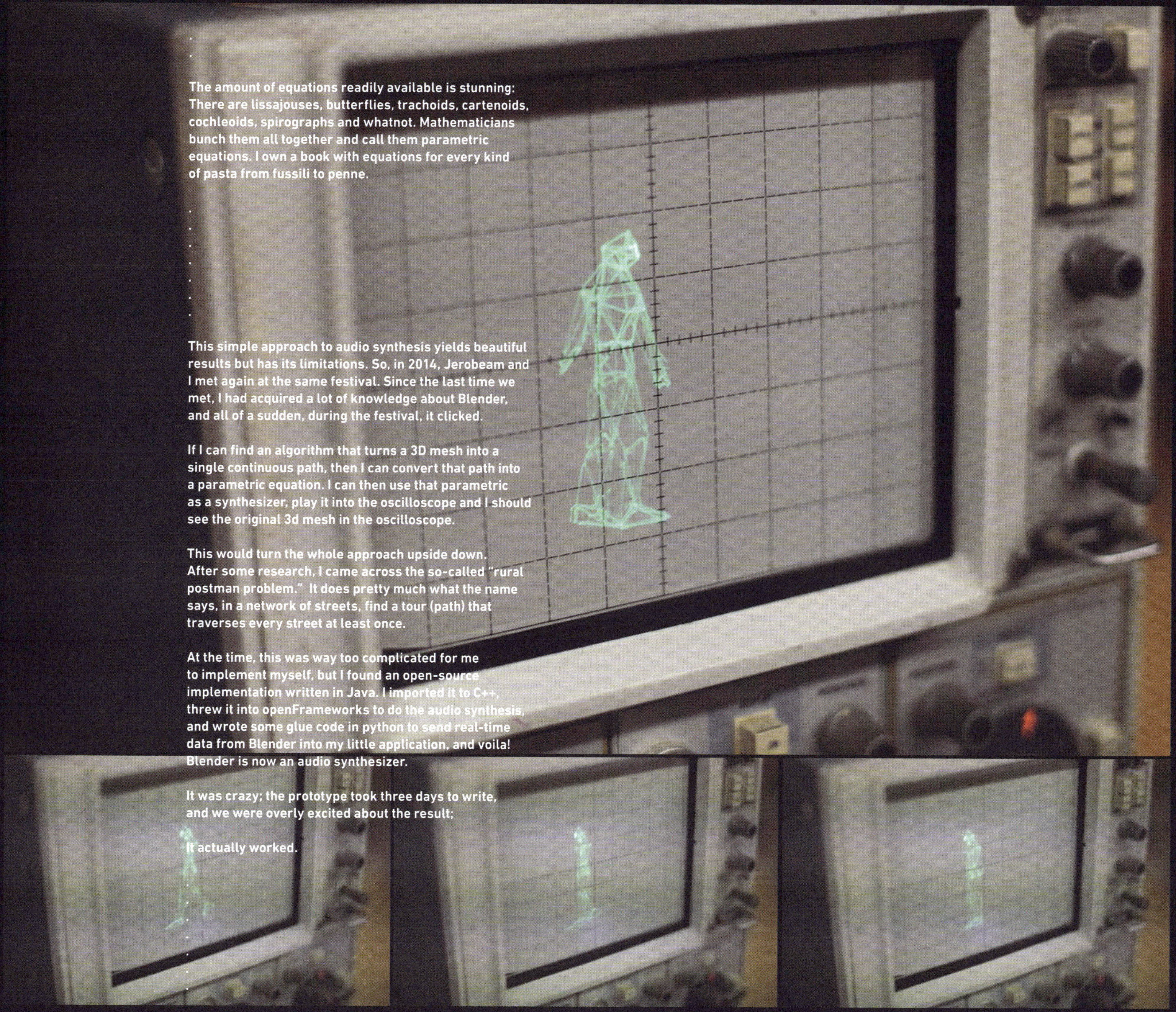

The amount of equations readily available is stunning: There are lissajouses, butterflies, trachoids, cartenoids, cochleoids, spirographs and whatnot. Mathematicians bunch them all together and call them parametric equations. I own a book with equations for every kind of pasta from fussili to penne.

This simple approach to audio synthesis yields beautiful results but has its limitations. So, in 2014, Jerobeam and I met again at the same festival. Since the last time we met, I had acquired a lot of knowledge about Blender, and all of a sudden, during the festival, it clicked.

If I can find an algorithm that turns a 3D mesh into a single continuous path, then I can convert that path into a parametric equation. I can then use that parametric as a synthesizer, play it into the oscilloscope and I should see the original 3d mesh in the oscilloscope.

This would turn the whole approach upside down. After some research, I came across the so-called "rural postman problem." It does pretty much what the name says, in a network of streets, find a tour (path) that traverses every street at least once.

At the time, this was way too complicated for me to implement myself, but I found an open-source implementation written in Java. I imported it to C++, threw it into openFrameworks to do the audio synthesis, and wrote some glue code in python to send real-time data from Blender into my little application, and voila! Blender is now an audio synthesizer.

It was crazy; the prototype took three days to write, and we were overly excited about the result;

It actually worked.

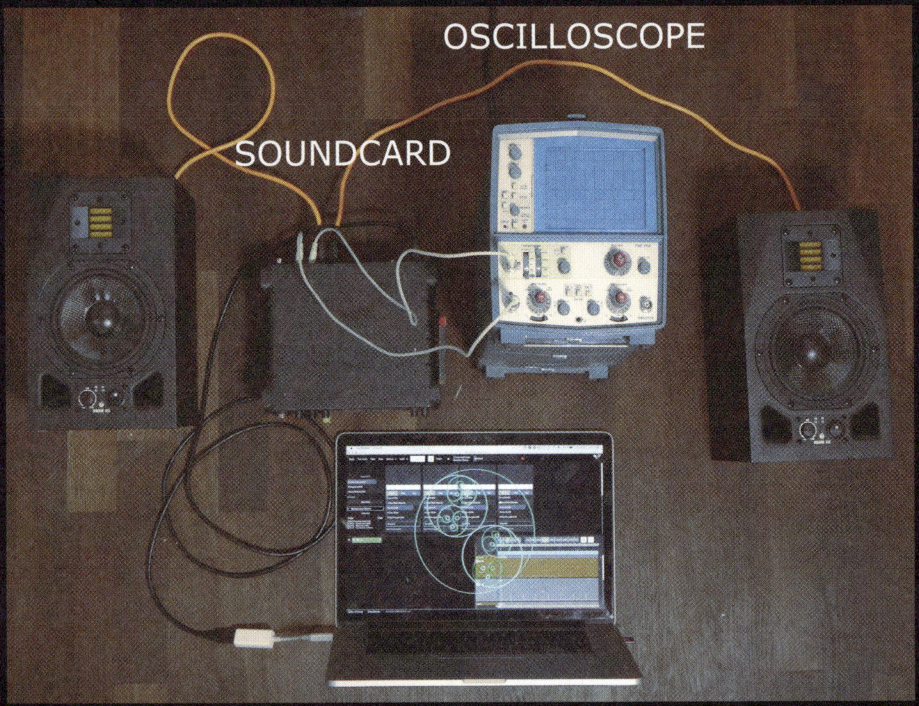
OSCILLOSCOPE
SOUNDCARD

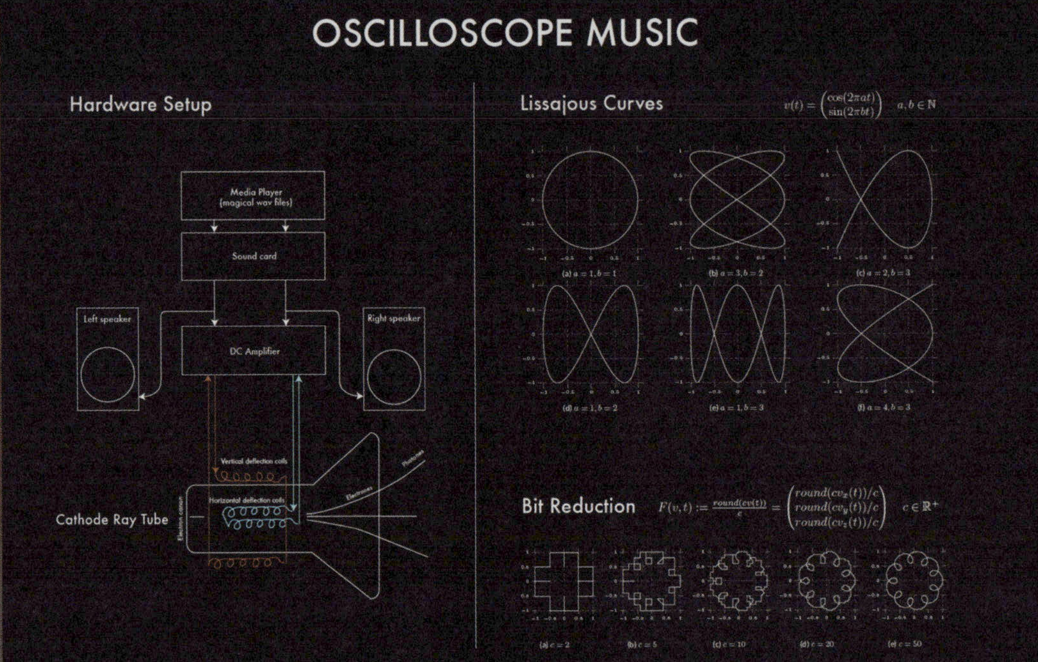
OSCILLOSCOPE MUSIC
Hardware Setup
Media Player (magical wav files)
Sound card
Left speaker
DC Amplifier
Right speaker
Vertical deflection coils
Horizontal deflection coils
Electrons
Photons
Electron canon
Cathode Ray Tube
Lissajous Curves
$v(t) = \begin{pmatrix} \cos(2\pi at) \\ \sin(2\pi bt) \end{pmatrix} \quad a, b \in \mathbb{N}$
(a) $a = 1, b = 1$
(b) $a = 3, b = 2$
(c) $a = 2, b = 3$
(d) $a = 1, b = 2$
(e) $a = 1, b = 3$
(f) $a = 4, b = 3$
Bit Reduction
$F(v,t) := \frac{round(cv(t))}{c} = \begin{pmatrix} round(cv_x(t))/c \\ round(cv_y(t))/c \\ round(cv_z(t))/c \end{pmatrix} \quad c \in \mathbb{R}^+$
(a) $c = 2$
(b) $c = 5$
(c) $c = 10$
(d) $c = 20$
(e) $c = 50$

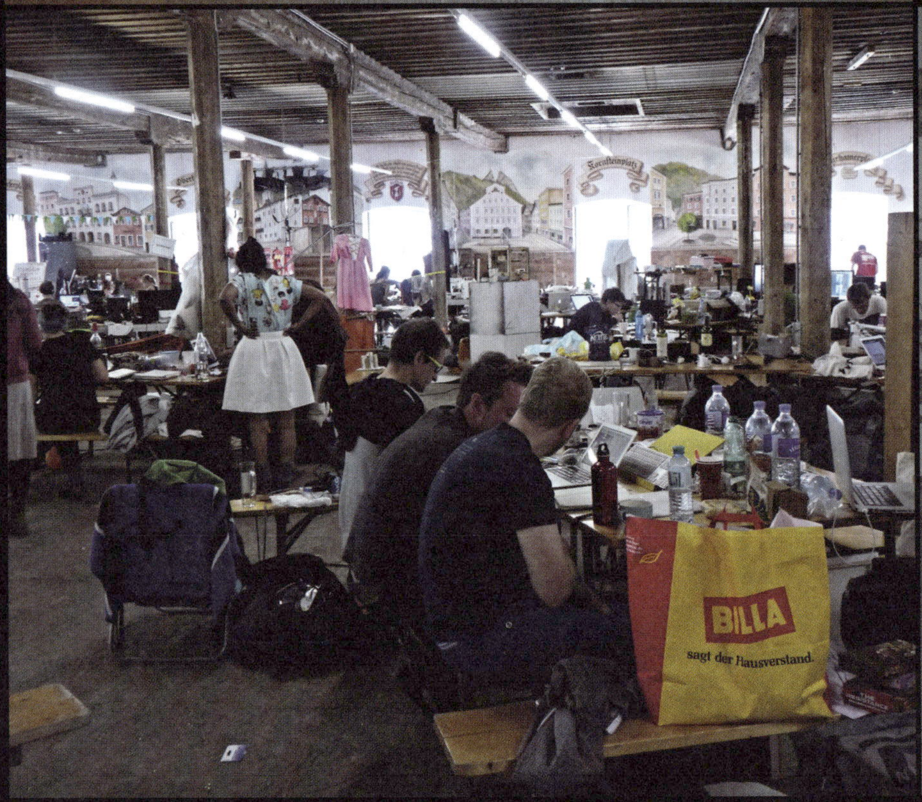
BILLA
sagt der Hausverstand.

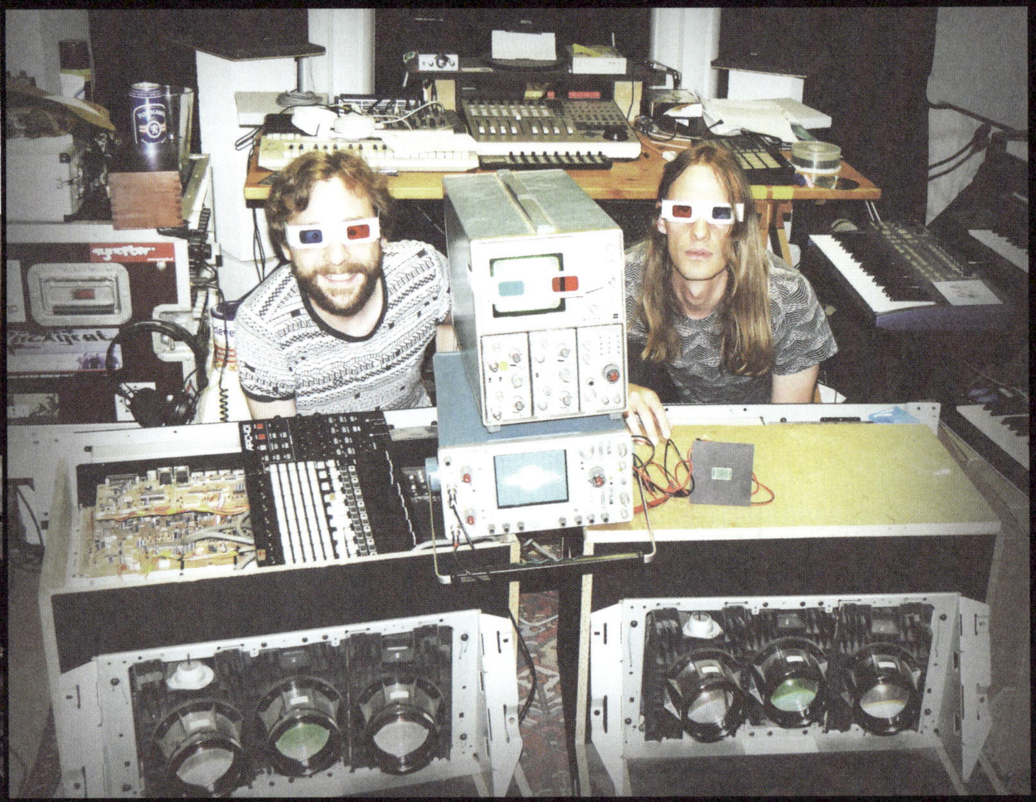

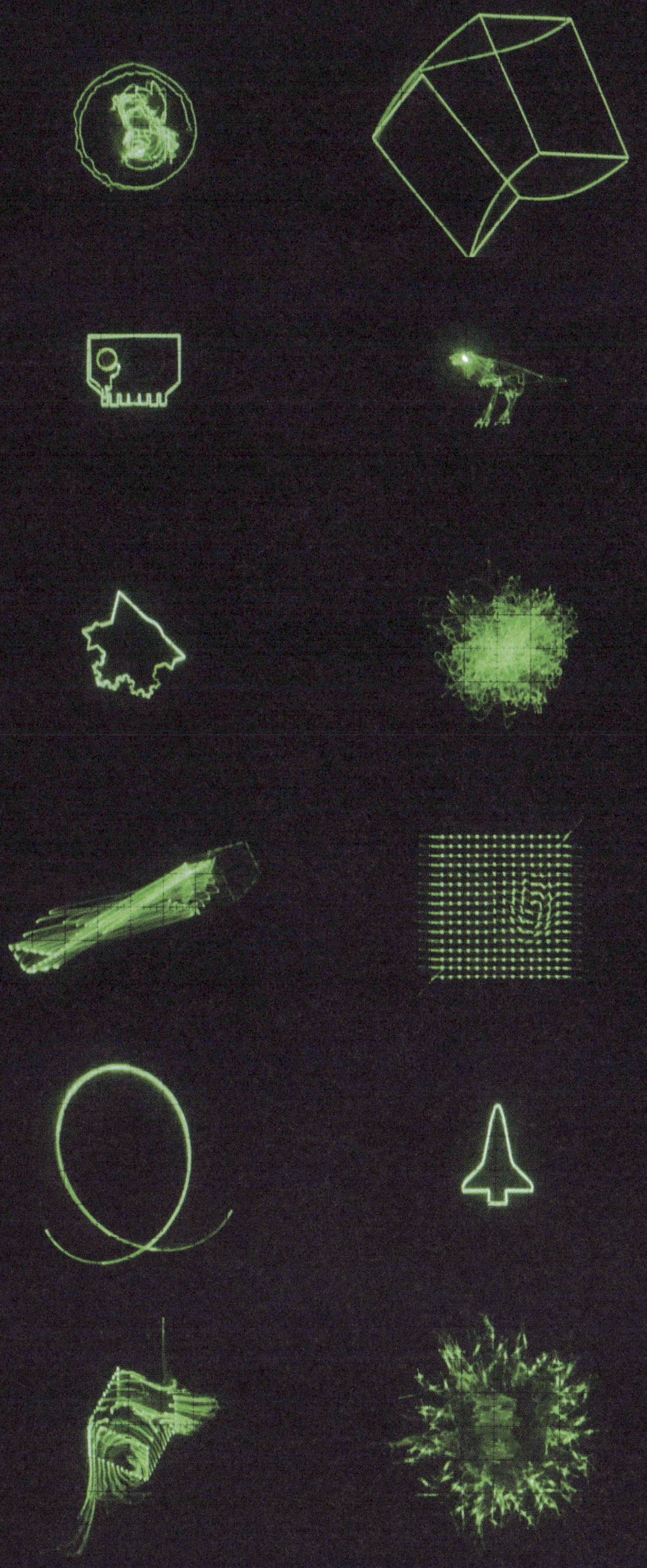

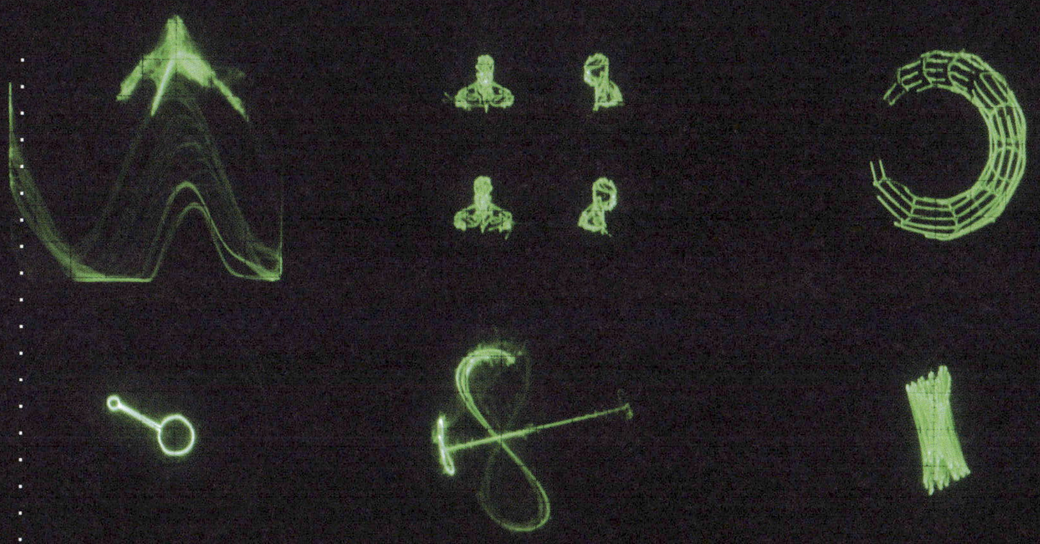

After that second festival, we would meet maybe once every other month or so; usually, this would be a week of eating, drinking, exchanging ideas, and even partying a tiny bit.

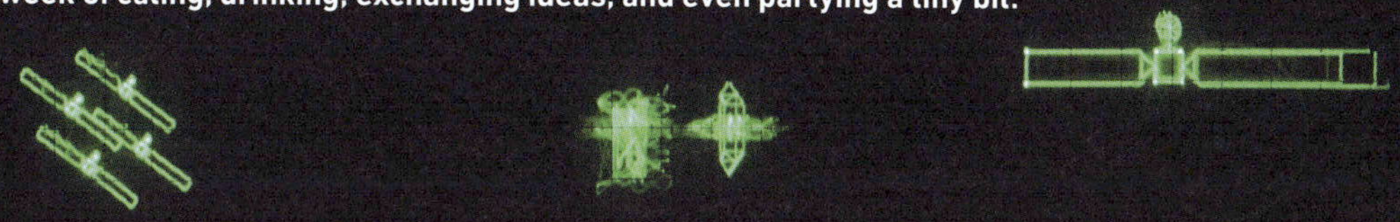

Jerobeam's goal was to make an album; my goal was to systematize everything.

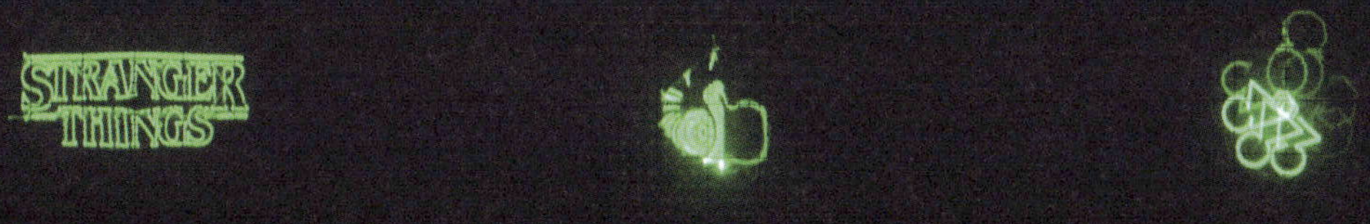

The process was wild and unstructured. In reality, it was a big mess, and most of the time, we were just in awe of all the things we had discovered.

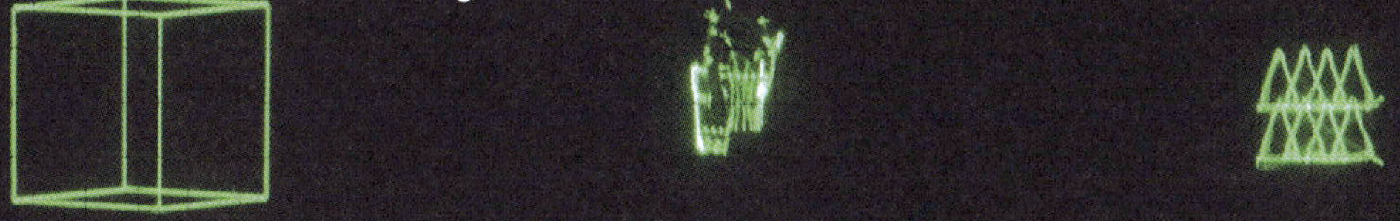

Curiosity was the main driving factor, and we mostly forgot about any actual goals.

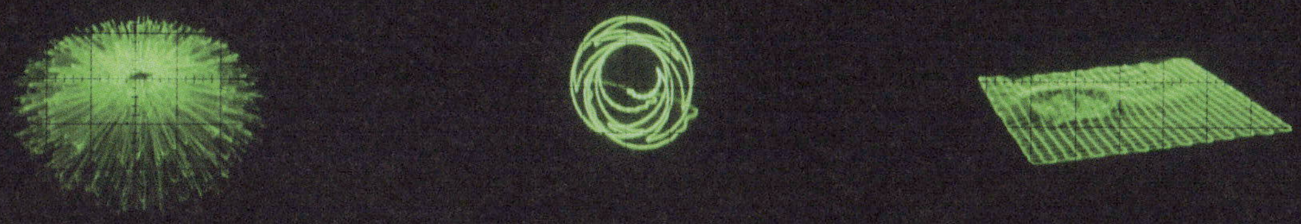

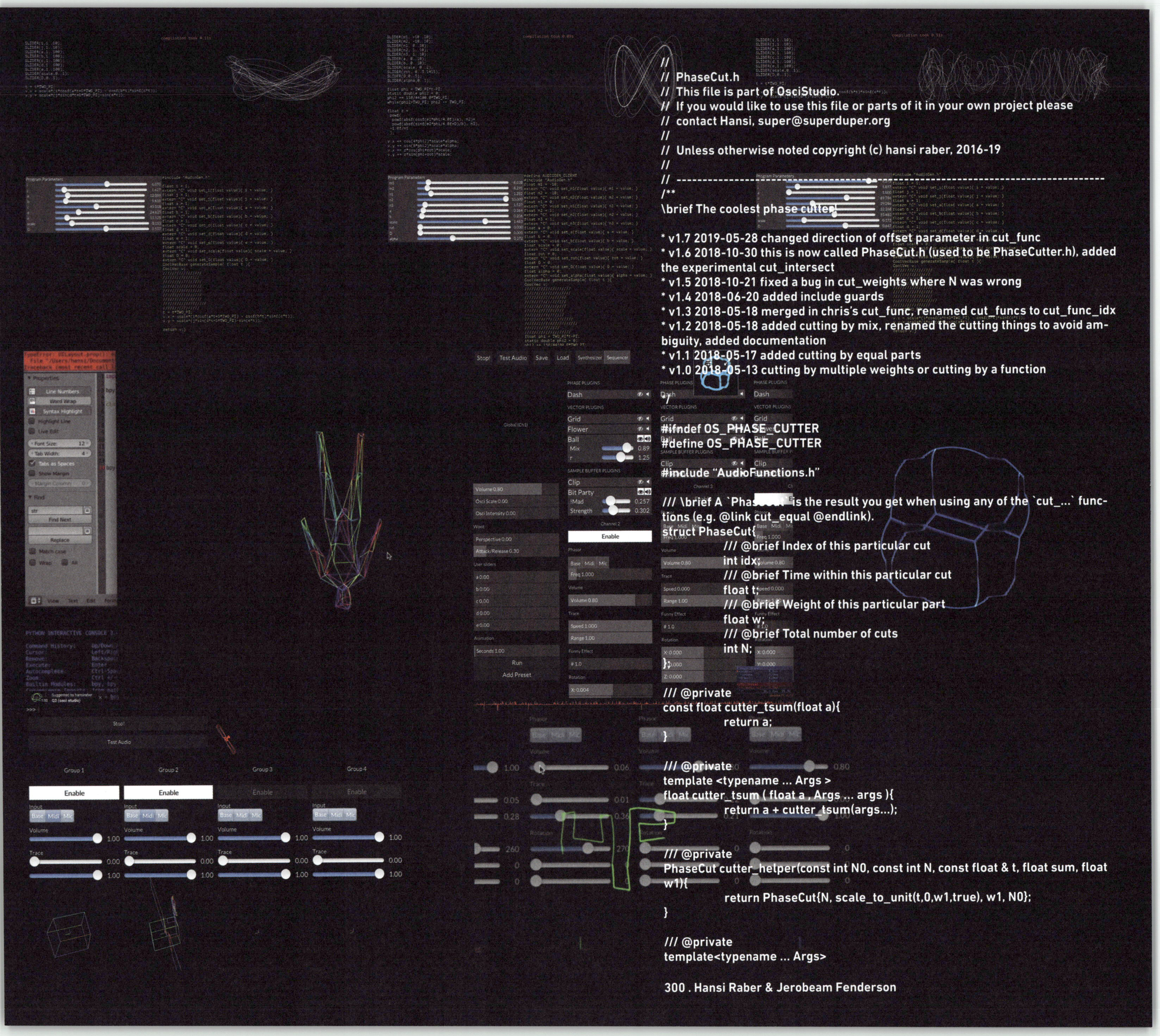

```
//
// PhaseCut.h
// This file is part of OsciStudio.
// If you would like to use this file or parts of it in your own project please
// contact Hansi, super@superduper.org
//
// Unless otherwise noted copyright (c) hansi raber, 2016-19
//
// ------------------------------------------------------------------------
/**
\brief The coolest phase cutter!

* v1.7 2019-05-28 changed direction of offset parameter in cut_func
* v1.6 2018-10-30 this is now called PhaseCut.h (used to be PhaseCutter.h), added
the experimental cut_intersect
* v1.5 2018-10-21 fixed a bug in cut_weights where N was wrong
* v1.4 2018-06-20 added include guards
* v1.3 2018-05-18 merged in chris's cut_func, renamed cut_funcs to cut_func_idx
* v1.2 2018-05-18 added cutting by mix, renamed the cutting things to avoid am-
biguity, added documentation
* v1.1 2018-05-17 added cutting by equal parts
* v1.0 2018-05-13 cutting by multiple weights or cutting by a function

*/

#ifndef OS_PHASE_CUTTER
#define OS_PHASE_CUTTER

#include "AudioFunctions.h"

/// \brief A `Phas[illegible]` is the result you get when using any of the `cut_...` func-
tions (e.g. @link cut_equal @endlink).
struct PhaseCut{
        /// @brief Index of this particular cut
        int idx;
        /// @brief Time within this particular cut
        float t;
        /// @brief Weight of this particular part
        float w;
        /// @brief Total number of cuts
        int N;
};

/// @private
const float cutter_tsum(float a){
        return a;
}

/// @private
template <typename ... Args >
float cutter_tsum ( float a , Args ... args ){
        return a + cutter_tsum(args...);
}

/// @private
PhaseCut cutter_helper(const int N0, const int N, const float & t, float sum, float
w1){
        return PhaseCut{N, scale_to_unit(t,0,w1,true), w1, N0};
}

/// @private
template<typename ... Args>
```

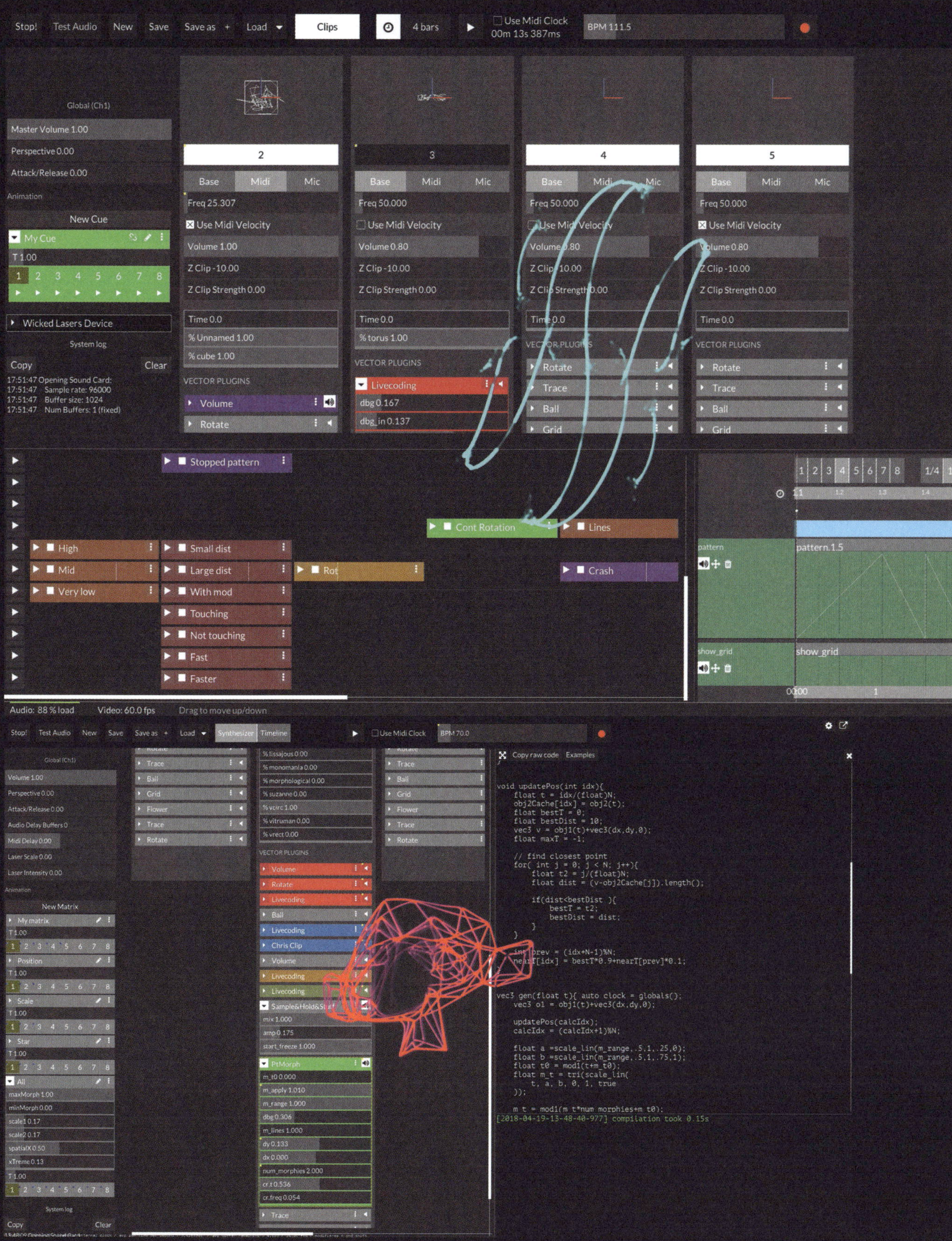


```
PhaseCut cutter_helper(const int N0, const int N, const float & t,
float sum, float w1, Args ... args){
        if(t<w1) return PhaseCut{N,scale_to_
unit(t,0,w1,true),w1, N0};
        else return cutter_helper(N0,N+1,t-w1,-
sum-w1,args...);
}

/// \brief Mix together multiple objects by separate weights
///
/// \param t Evaluation time
/// \param N Number of total shapes
/// \param a First weight
/// \param args All the other weights
template<typename ... Args>
PhaseCut cut_weights(const float & t, float a, Args ... args){
        constexpr int n = 1+sizeof...(Args);
        float s = cutter_tsum(a, args ...);

        return cutter_helper(n, 0, t*s, s, a, args...);
}

/// \brief Mix together multiple objects by equal weight
///
/// \param t Evaluation time
/// \param N Number of total shapes
PhaseCut cut_equal(float t, int N){
        float tn = t*N;
        int idx = tn;
        return PhaseCut{idx, tn-idx, 1/(float)N, N};
}

/// \brief Mix together multiple objects by their weight. A function
specifies the weight for each object
///
/// \param t Evaluation time
/// \param N Number of total shapes
/// \param func A function int->float that calculates a weight for a
specific shape. It will be called as func(idx), idx = 0..N-1
template<typename Func>
PhaseCut cut_func_idx(float t, int N, Func func){
        if(N<=0) return PhaseCut{0,0,1,N};

        float sum = 0;
        for(int i = 0; i < N; i++){
                sum += func(i);
        }

        t = t*sum;
        float t0 = 0;

        for(int i = 0; i < N; i++){
                float w = func(i);
                t0 += w;
                if(t0>=t) return PhaseCut{i,scale_lin(t,t0-
w,t0,0,1,true),w,N};
        }

        return PhaseCut{0,0,0,N};
}
```

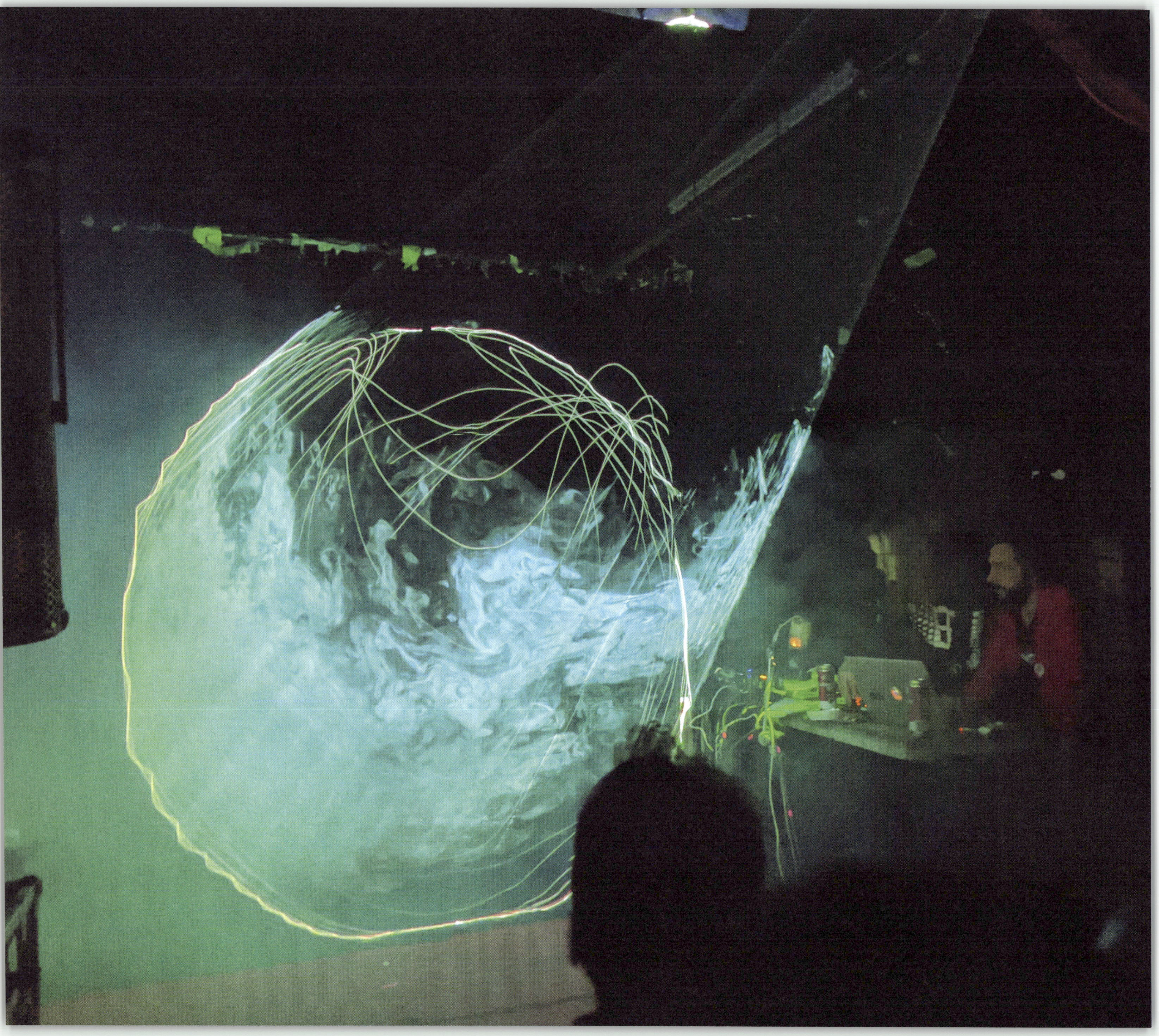

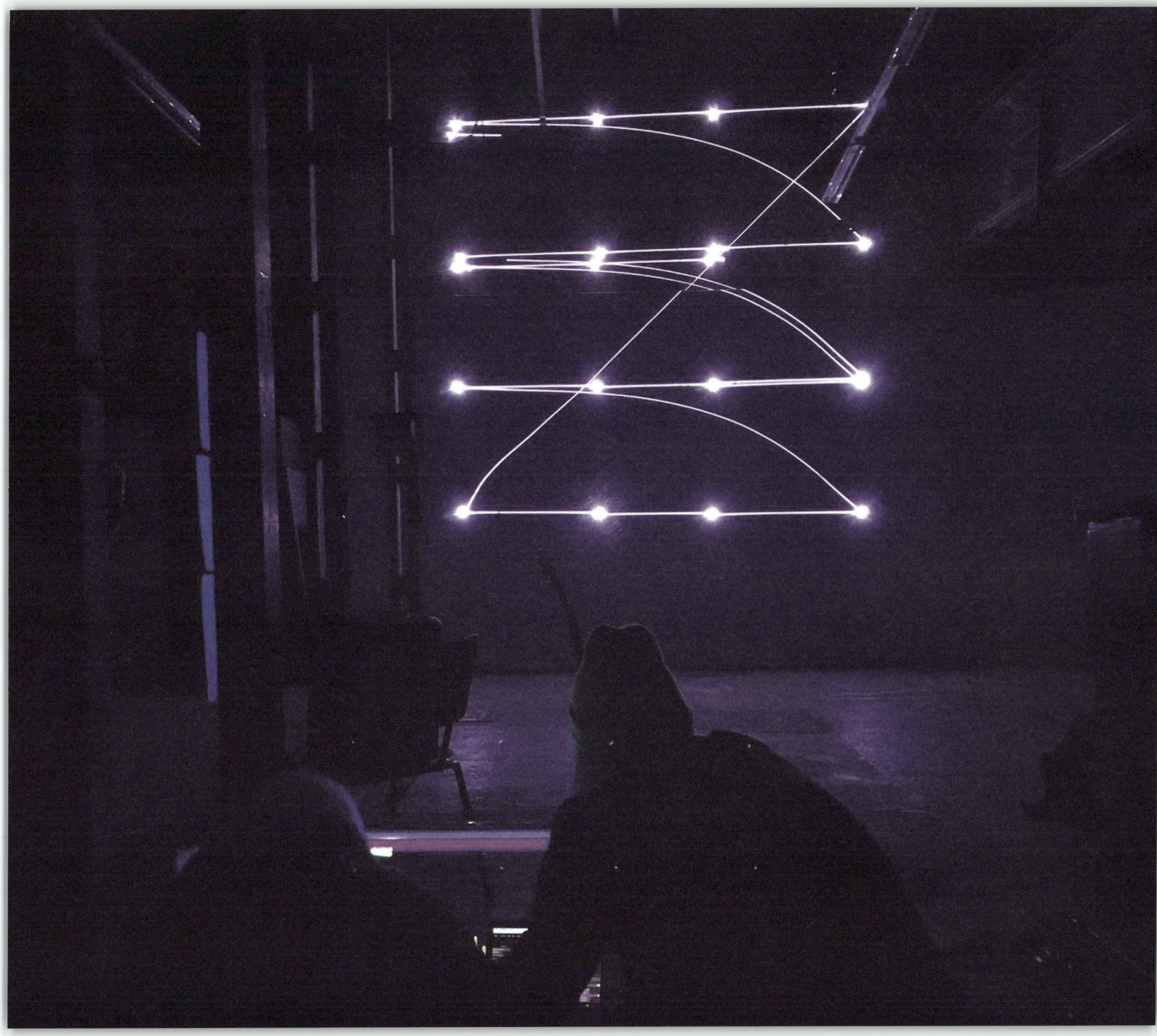

Name:

RANDOM INTERNATIONAL

Info:

Art Group RANDOM INTERNATIONAL runs a collaborative studio for experimental practice within contemporary art. Founded in 2005 by Hannes Koch and Florian Ortkrass, they work with larger diverse and complementary talent teams out of studios in London and Berlin.

Questioning aspects of identity and autonomy in the post-digital age, the group's work invites active participation. RANDOM INTERNATIONAL explores the human condition in an increasingly mechanized world through emotional yet physically intense experiences. The artists aim to prototype possible behavioral environments by experimenting with different notions of consciousness, perception, and instinct.

Projects:

URL:

random-international.com

Mail:

studio@random-international.com

Instagram:

@randominternational

Conversation with Hannes Koch

What does "The Age of Data" mean?

Those who speak of data strive for information. He, who speaks of information, strives for knowledge.

But to have an impact, the raw data is collected first, and processed data can be controlled. It can be the working material of creation; a brush, light, clay, pattern, or pigment.

When data attains three-dimensionality, when it receives a narrative or occupies space, it can become a controlling entity itself when it shifts from the virtual to the physical layer. It then influences the emotions of the spectator on a conscious and unconscious level and thus his perception. In this way, breathtaking experiences can be created.

We see the dawn of a new age of expression; this enables new ways of thinking and cognition. It shows us the possibilities of what is to come.

Your spatial installations are about breaking the norm. By involving the visitor, you shift the boundaries of what can be learned through a strong narrative.

Since the 1960s, right across all Documentas and the Fluxus movement, we have long since arrived at the "extended concept of art" proclaimed by Beuys.

The visitor is no longer only a recipient but also a producer. With the help of data-driven processes, interaction, experience alone becomes art itself. Data is the medium.

The idea of the visitor cocreation or coproducing implies a degree of separation from the work itself; maybe the cocreation process is just a means to an end; a material if you like, just as data is.

The "end" here would be the full-contact sport, the audience as a performer, and the physical insertion of the human into the work the actual emphasis of the work; plug-in human.

By plugging herself/himself into the artwork, the visitor leaves the real world, his everyday life, for a moment. The confusion of the outside gives way to a collective experience of immersion, a feeling of belonging.

Does this full-contact sport, i.e., the resonating art experience, constitute exactly its success?

No, I don't think so, not as such; otherwise, something mundane like swimming would count as that too? I think it often is the amplification and often exaggeration of certain aspects of a situation or a process that hold people's attention, and it's that they relate physically to that amplified yet familiar situation.

Is the visitor able to feel an adequate identity for this limited time? One that gets increasingly lost in the real world. Does it work in the sense of escapism, or is it actually "refilling" the fractures of her/his identity?

I am speculating here, but I imagine it is a very subliminal and fluid state of heightened awareness/self-awareness. Nothing has been there before, just a reconnection with our presence facilitated by physical sensations reminding us that we're here.

CREDITS

Picture by Esteban Schunemann, RANDOM INTERNATIONAL

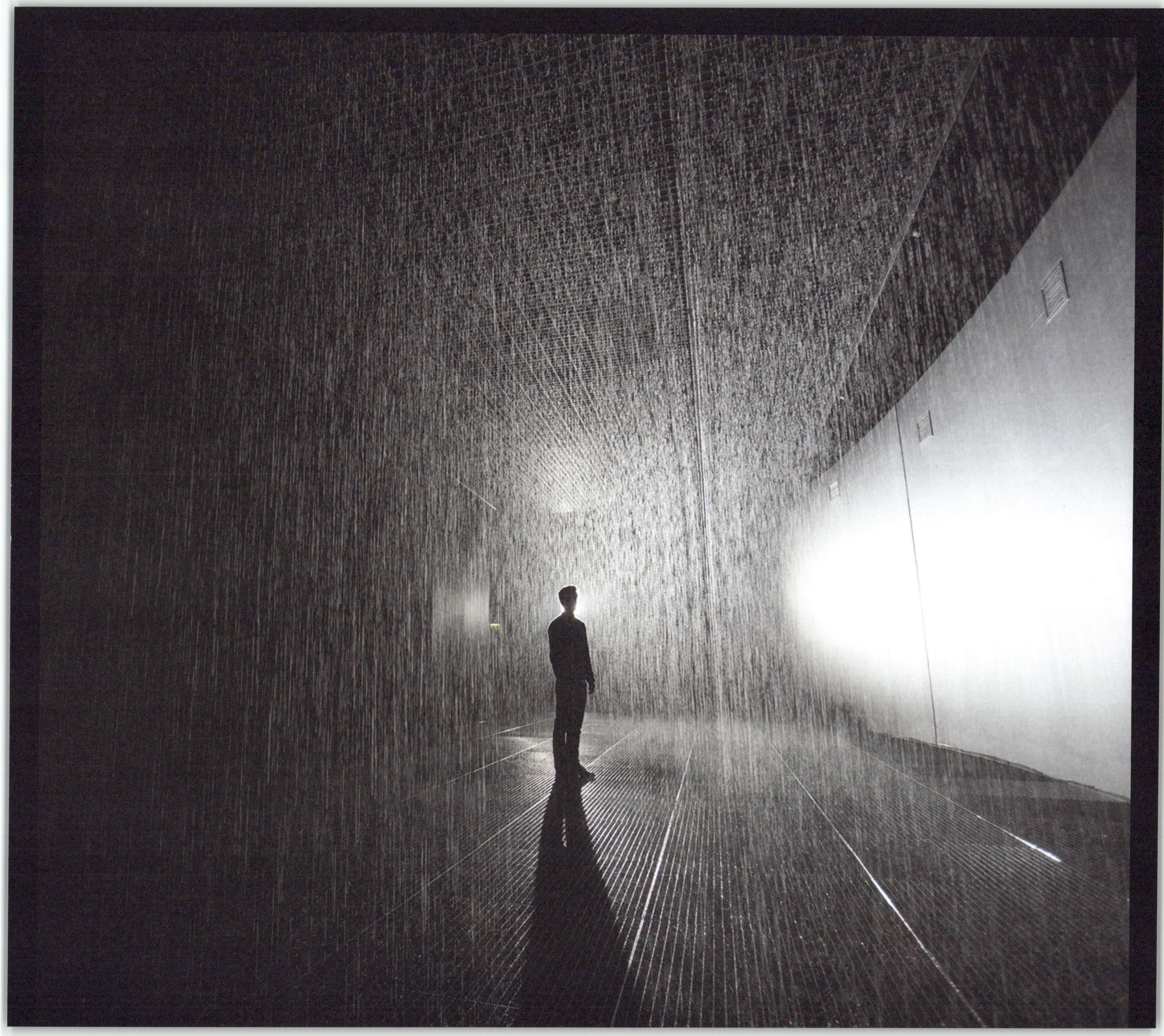

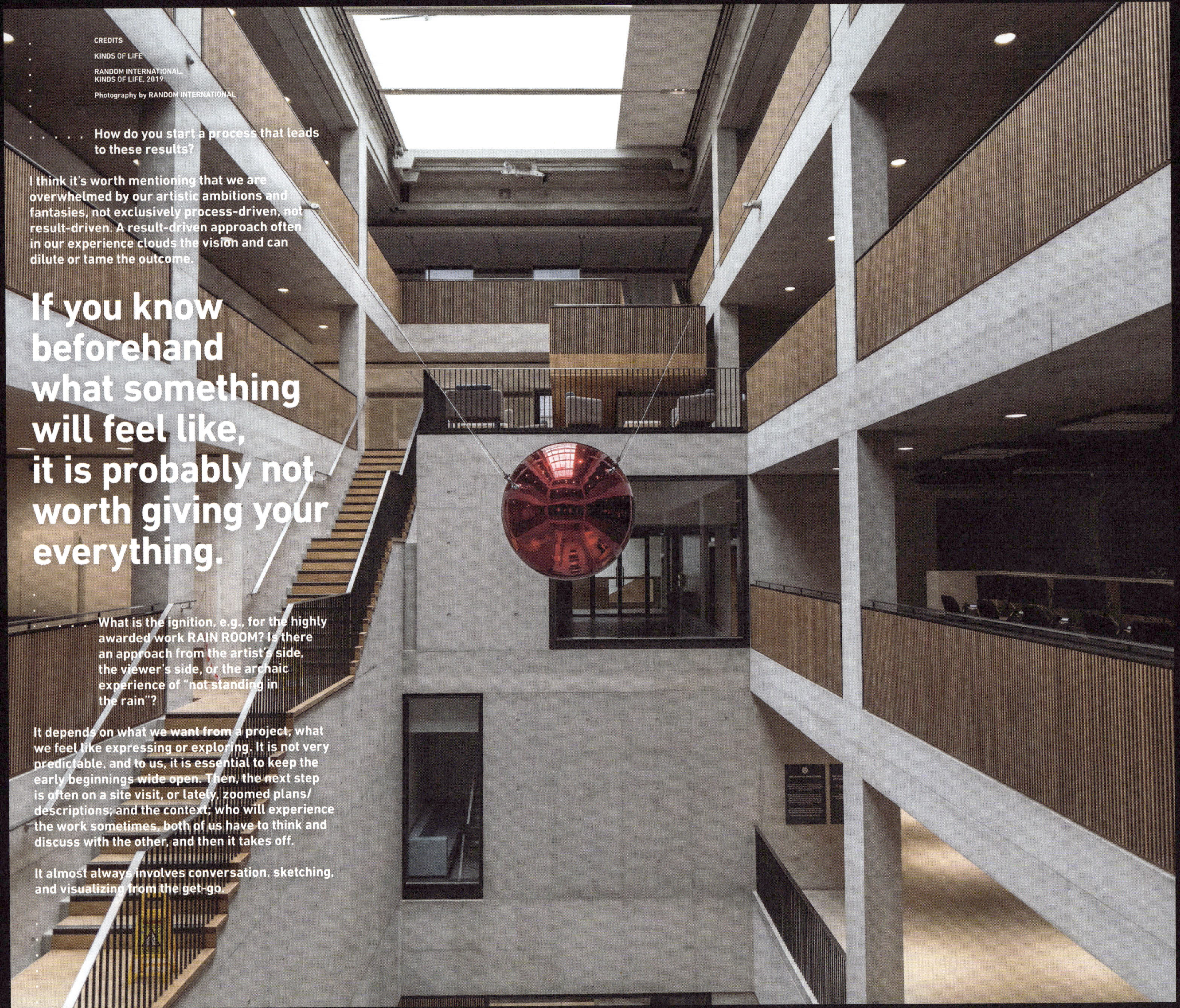

CREDITS

KINDS OF LIFE

RANDOM INTERNATIONAL, KINDS OF LIFE, 2019.

Photography by RANDOM INTERNATIONAL

How do you start a process that leads to these results?

I think it's worth mentioning that we are overwhelmed by our artistic ambitions and fantasies, not exclusively process-driven, not result-driven. A result-driven approach often in our experience clouds the vision and can dilute or tame the outcome.

If you know beforehand what something will feel like, it is probably not worth giving your everything.

What is the ignition, e.g., for the highly awarded work RAIN ROOM? Is there an approach from the artist's side, the viewer's side, or the archaic experience of "not standing in the rain"?

It depends on what we want from a project, what we feel like expressing or exploring. It is not very predictable, and to us, it is essential to keep the early beginnings wide open. Then, the next step is often on a site visit, or lately, zoomed plans/descriptions; and the context; who will experience the work sometimes, both of us have to think and discuss with the other, and then it takes off.

It almost always involves conversation, sketching, and visualizing from the get-go.

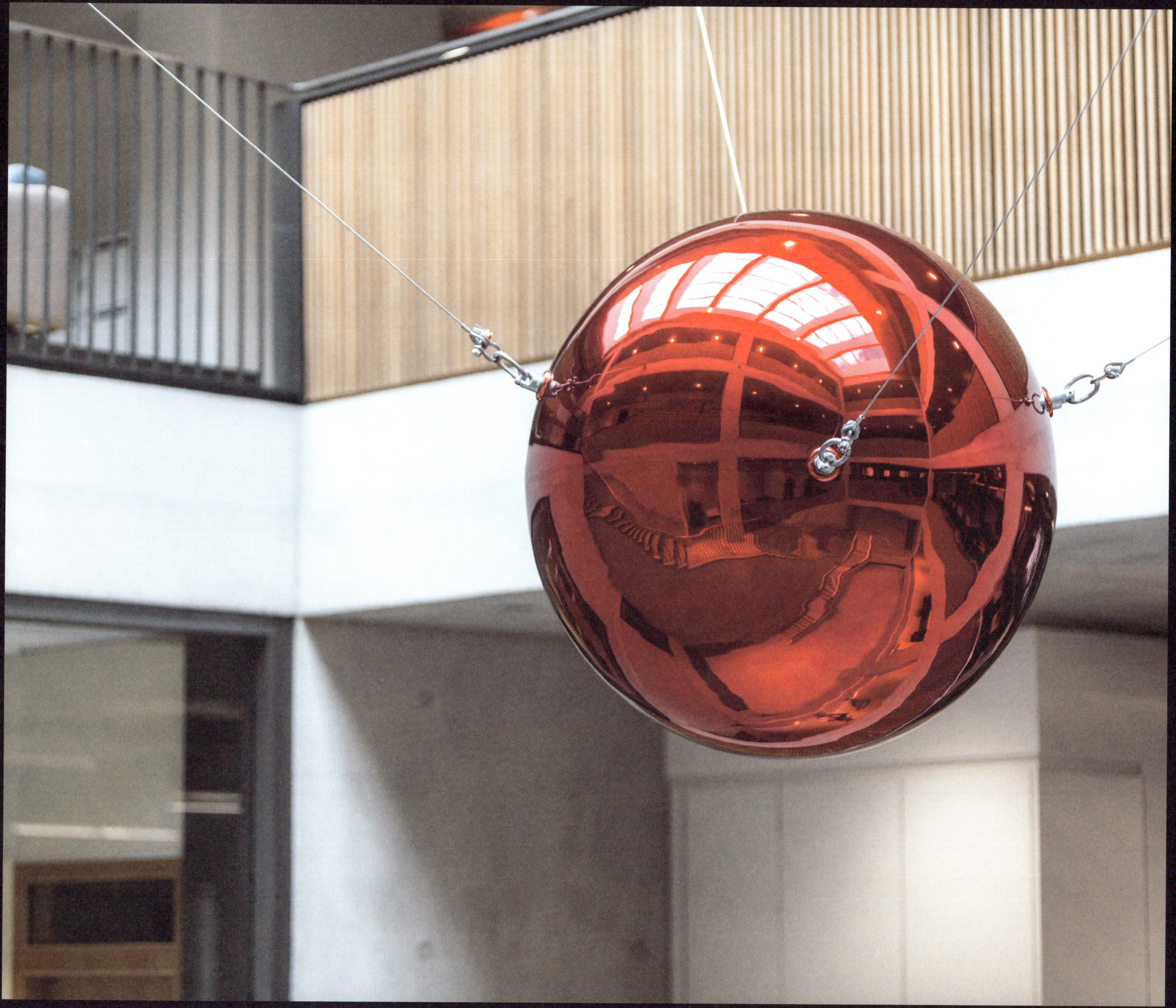

307 . KINDS OF LIFE

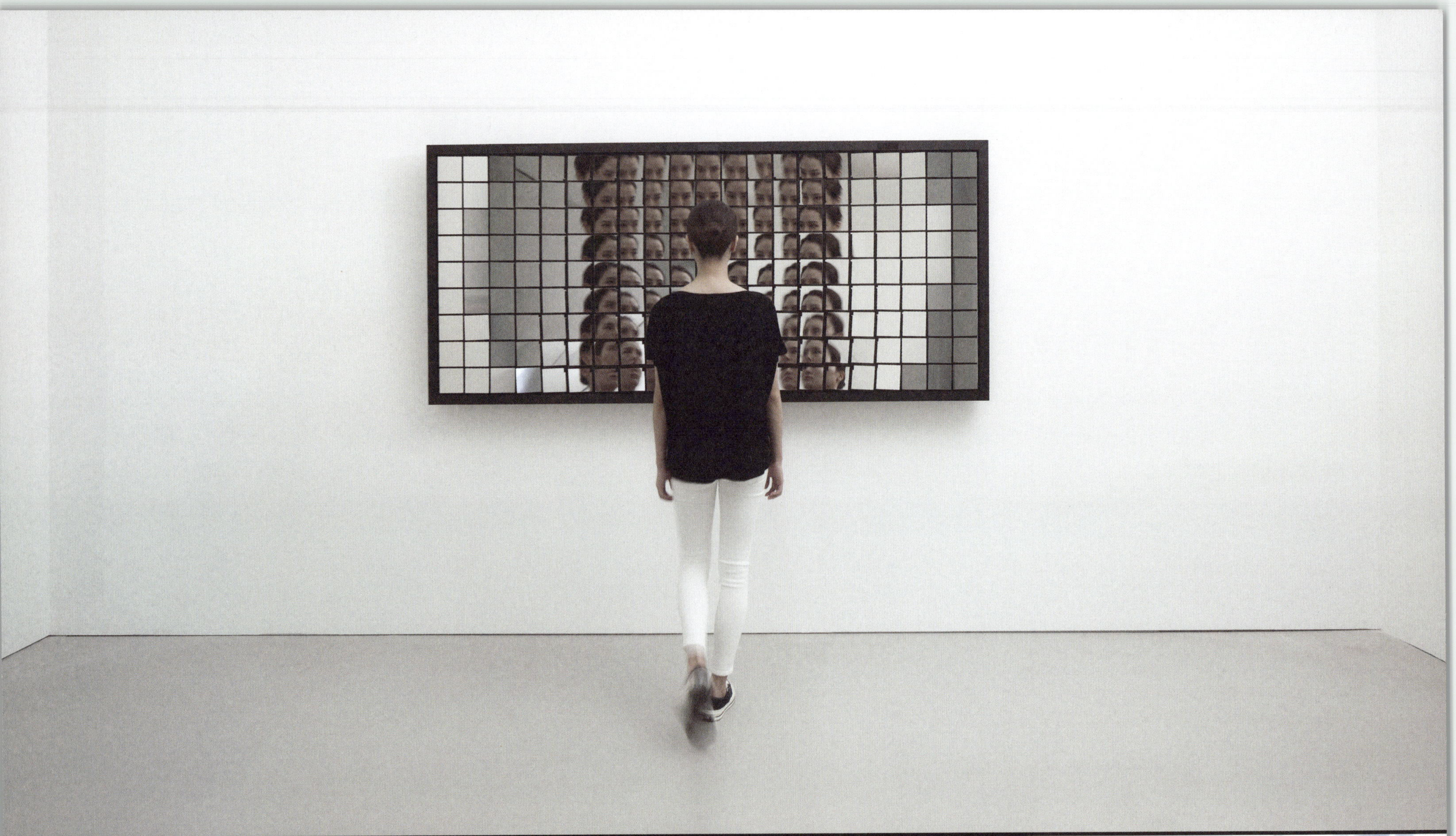

CREDITS

RANDOM INTERNATIONAL, FRAGMENTS, 2016.
Exhibited at Pace Gallery, NY.
Photography by RANDOM INTERNATIONAL

RANDOM INTERNATIONAL, FRAGMENTS, 2019.
Exhibited as part of the solo show Physical Algorithm at Paradise City Art Space, Seoul, South Korea, 2019. Photography by Paradise Art Space, courtesy of Park Myung Rae

SELF PORTRAIT AND PRESENCE & ERASURE:

RANDOM INTERNATIONAL, SELF PORTRAIT, 2010.
Exhibited as part of Studies in Motion at Lundskonsthall, Lund, 2014.
Photography by RANDOM INTERNATIONAL

RANDOM INTERNATIONAL, PRESENCE AND ERASURE, 2019. Exhibited as part of the solo show Physical Algorithm at Paradise City Art Space, Seoul, South Korea, 2019.
Photography by RANDOM INTERNATIONAL

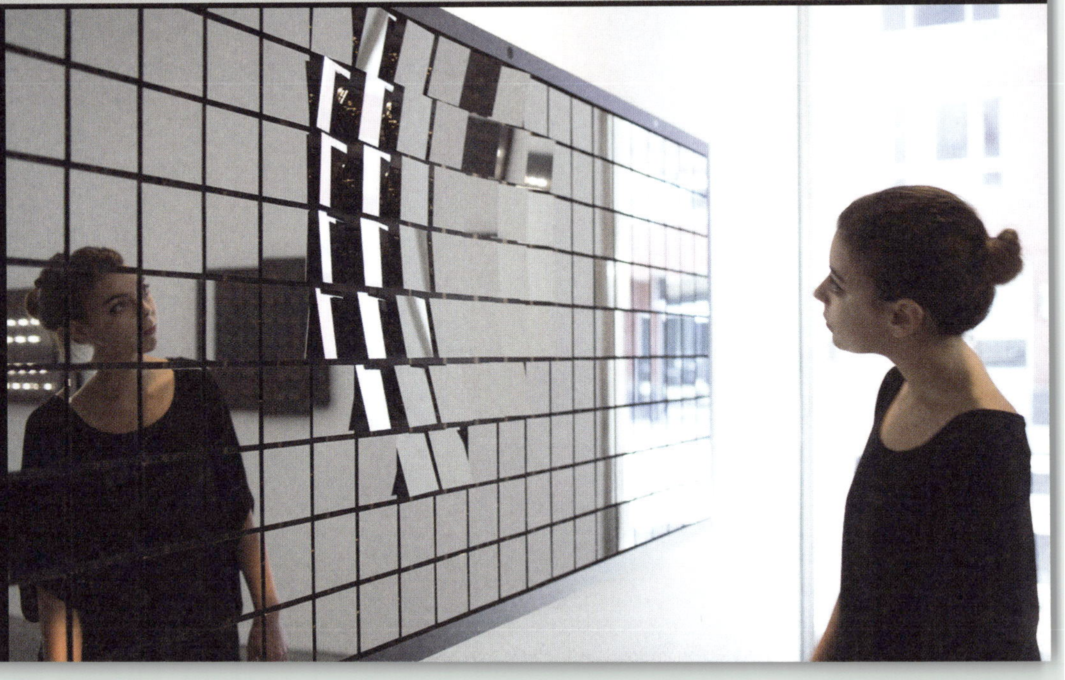

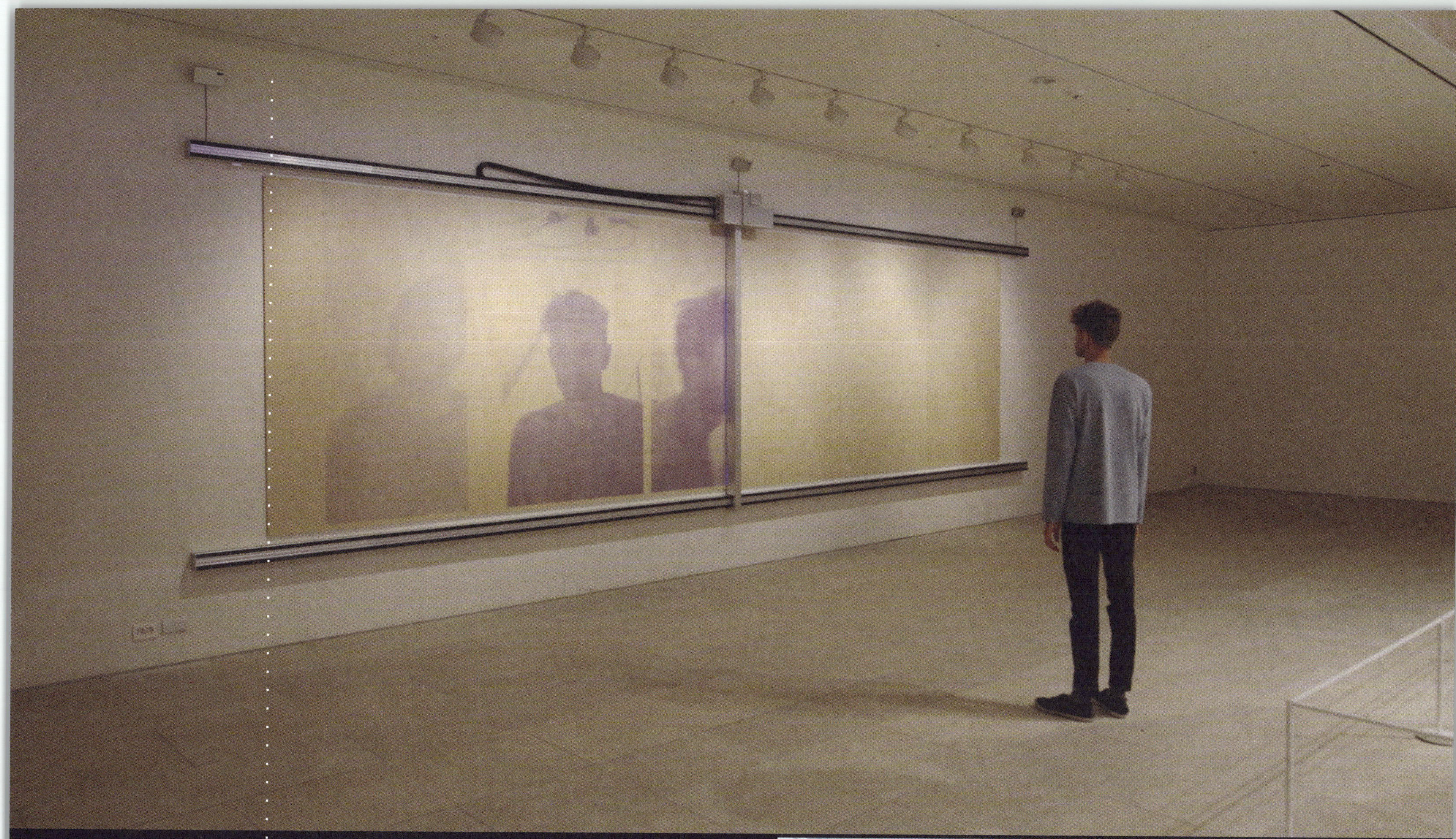

Most of what we develop is also supported internally by our dramaturge Heloise Reynolds, an art historian by training, and our Head of Technology Nikos Chandolias, our Executive Producer Jen Barnes, and our Chief Researcher Esteban Schunemann.

This collective process ensures that we immediately start a conceptual/programmatic and technical editing method, which helps drive a project forward, shelving for later consideration, or the bin.

If it goes forward, we assign a multidisciplinary team to a project and then start speaking to our trusted network of specialist consultants and partners.

.

309 . SELF PORTRAIT AND PRESENCE & ERASURE

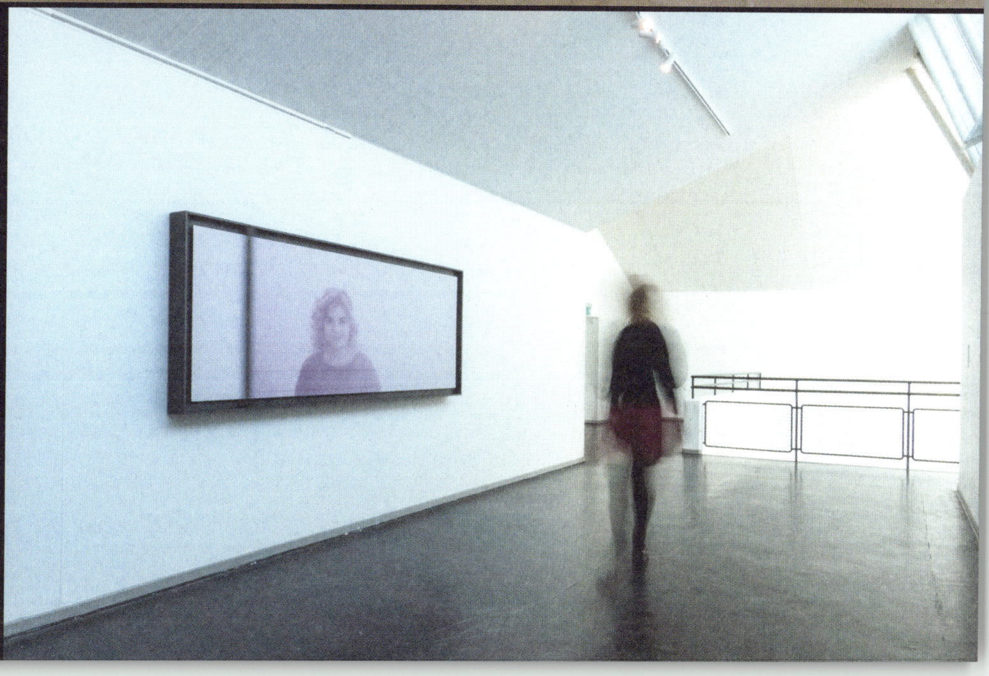

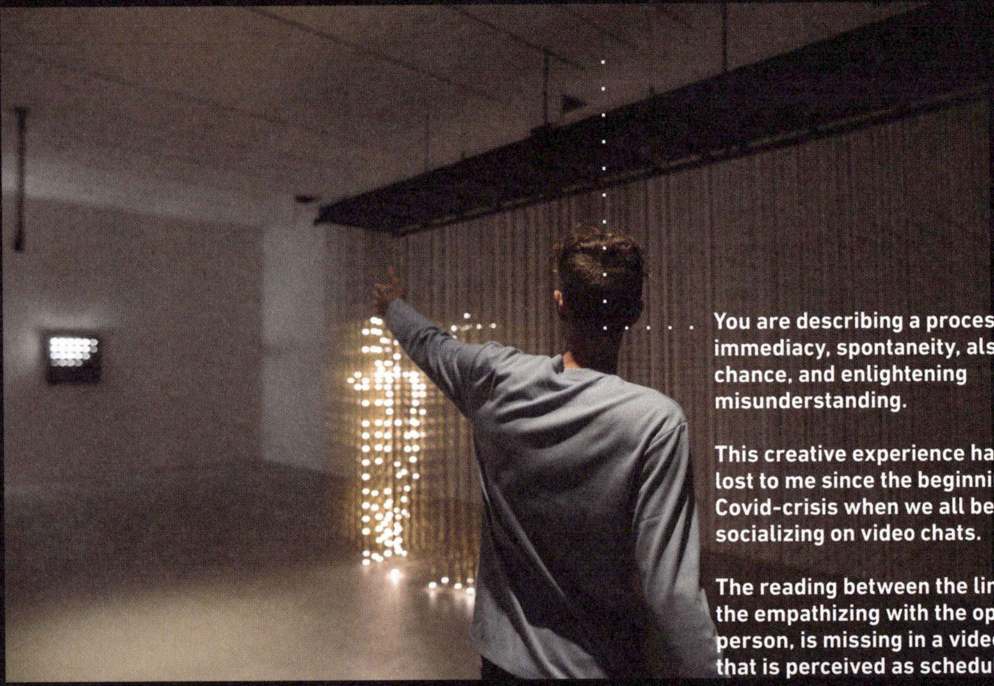

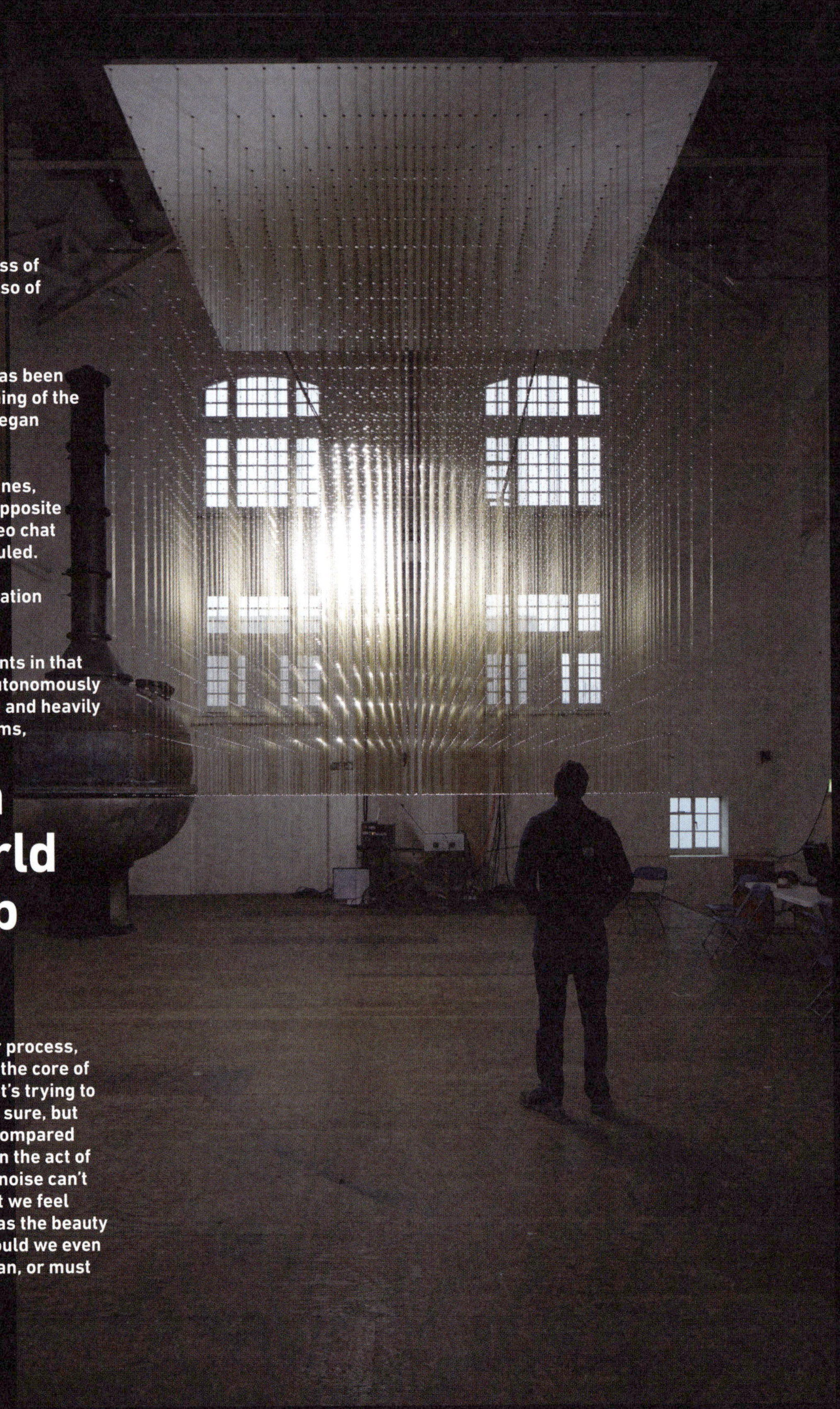

You are describing a process of immediacy, spontaneity, also of chance, and enlightening misunderstanding.

This creative experience has been lost to me since the beginning of the Covid-crisis when we all began socializing on video chats.

The reading between the lines, the empathizing with the opposite person, is missing in a video chat that is perceived as scheduled.

So does the process of creation require proximity?

I think that depends on the active agents in that process. After 15 years of working autonomously but closely together across the world and heavily using all available means of video coms,

it feels like in 2020, the world has caught up with us!

If a video is all it takes to ambush our process, we need to look at the resilience and the core of our artistic process, not the thing that's trying to ambush it. There's stuff going amiss, sure, but to us, that's more likely white noise compared to the qualities that make it through in the act of creation. That's not to say that white noise can't be amazing, but it's not precisely that we feel anything gets stolen from us. As far as the beauty of misunderstanding goes, where would we even be without zoom!?!? It has to be human, or must we learn to rethink?

CREDITS

RANDOM INTERNATIONAL, SWARM STUDY VII, 2015.
Photography by RANDOM INTERNATIONAL

RANDOM INTERNATIONAL, SWARM STUDY IX, 2016.
Installed outside the Hauptbahnhof Chemnitz, Germany.
Photography by Jan Bitter

RANDOM INTERNATIONAL, OUR FUTURE SELVES, 2019.
Exhibited as part of the solo show Physical Algorithm at Paradise City Art Space, Seoul, South Korea, 2019.
Photography by Paradise Art Space,
courtesy of Park Myung Rae

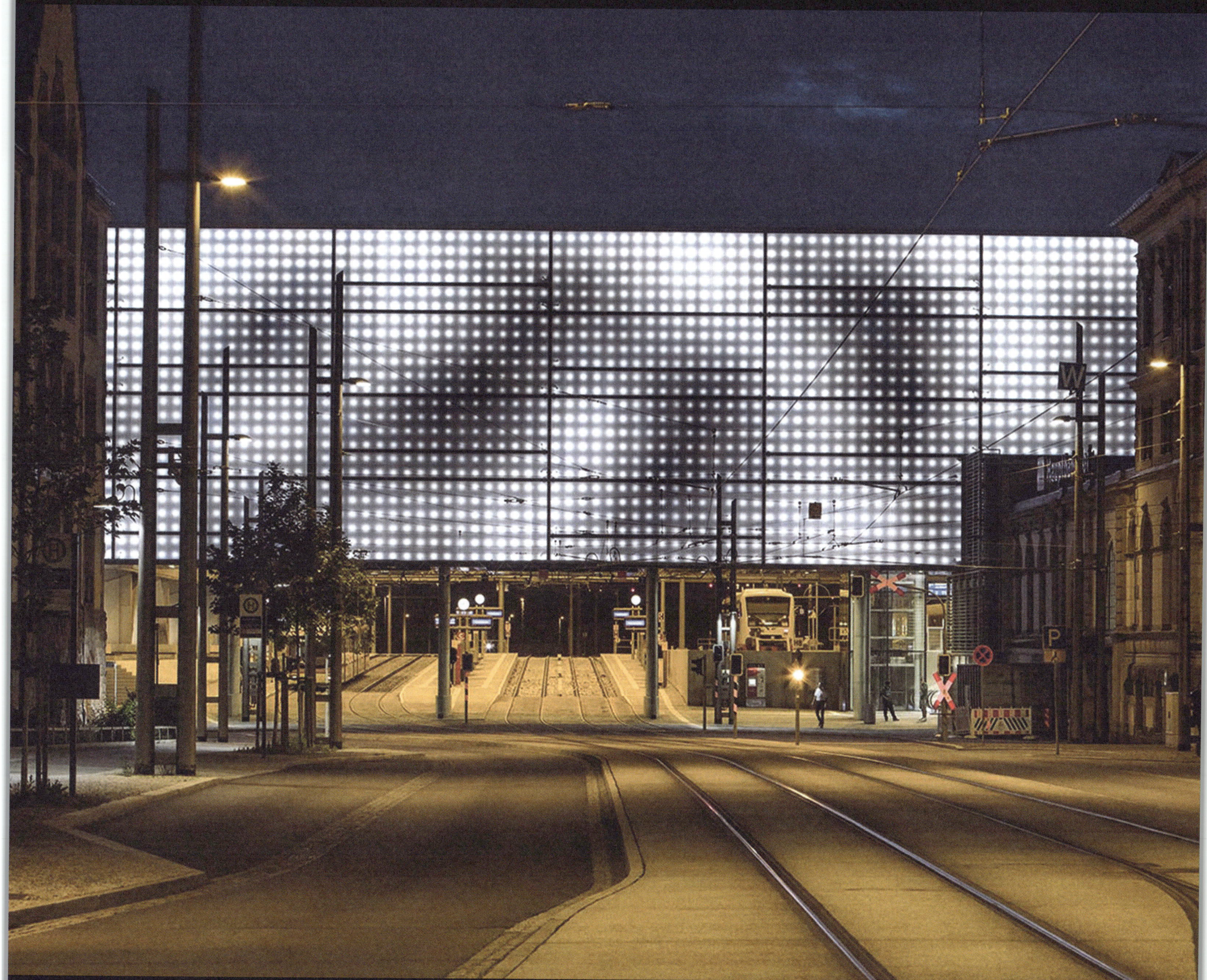

311 . SWARM STUDY VII

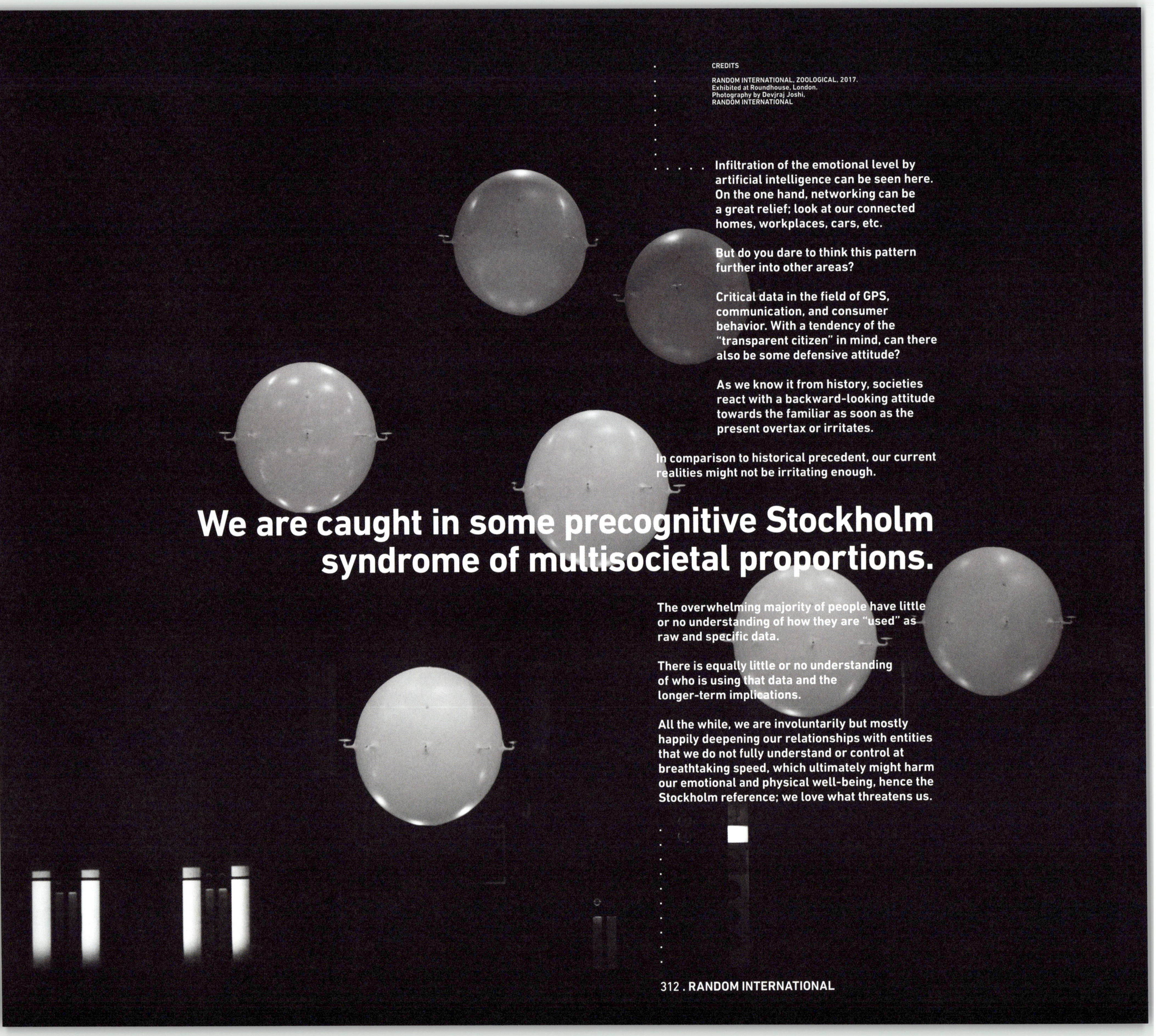

CREDITS

RANDOM INTERNATIONAL, ZOOLOGICAL, 2017.
Exhibited at Roundhouse, London.
Photography by Devjraj Joshi,
RANDOM INTERNATIONAL

Infiltration of the emotional level by artificial intelligence can be seen here. On the one hand, networking can be a great relief; look at our connected homes, workplaces, cars, etc.

But do you dare to think this pattern further into other areas?

Critical data in the field of GPS, communication, and consumer behavior. With a tendency of the "transparent citizen" in mind, can there also be some defensive attitude?

As we know it from history, societies react with a backward-looking attitude towards the familiar as soon as the present overtax or irritates.

In comparison to historical precedent, our current realities might not be irritating enough.

We are caught in some precognitive Stockholm syndrome of multisocietal proportions.

The overwhelming majority of people have little or no understanding of how they are "used" as raw and specific data.

There is equally little or no understanding of who is using that data and the longer-term implications.

All the while, we are involuntarily but mostly happily deepening our relationships with entities that we do not fully understand or control at breathtaking speed, which ultimately might harm our emotional and physical well-being, hence the Stockholm reference; we love what threatens us.

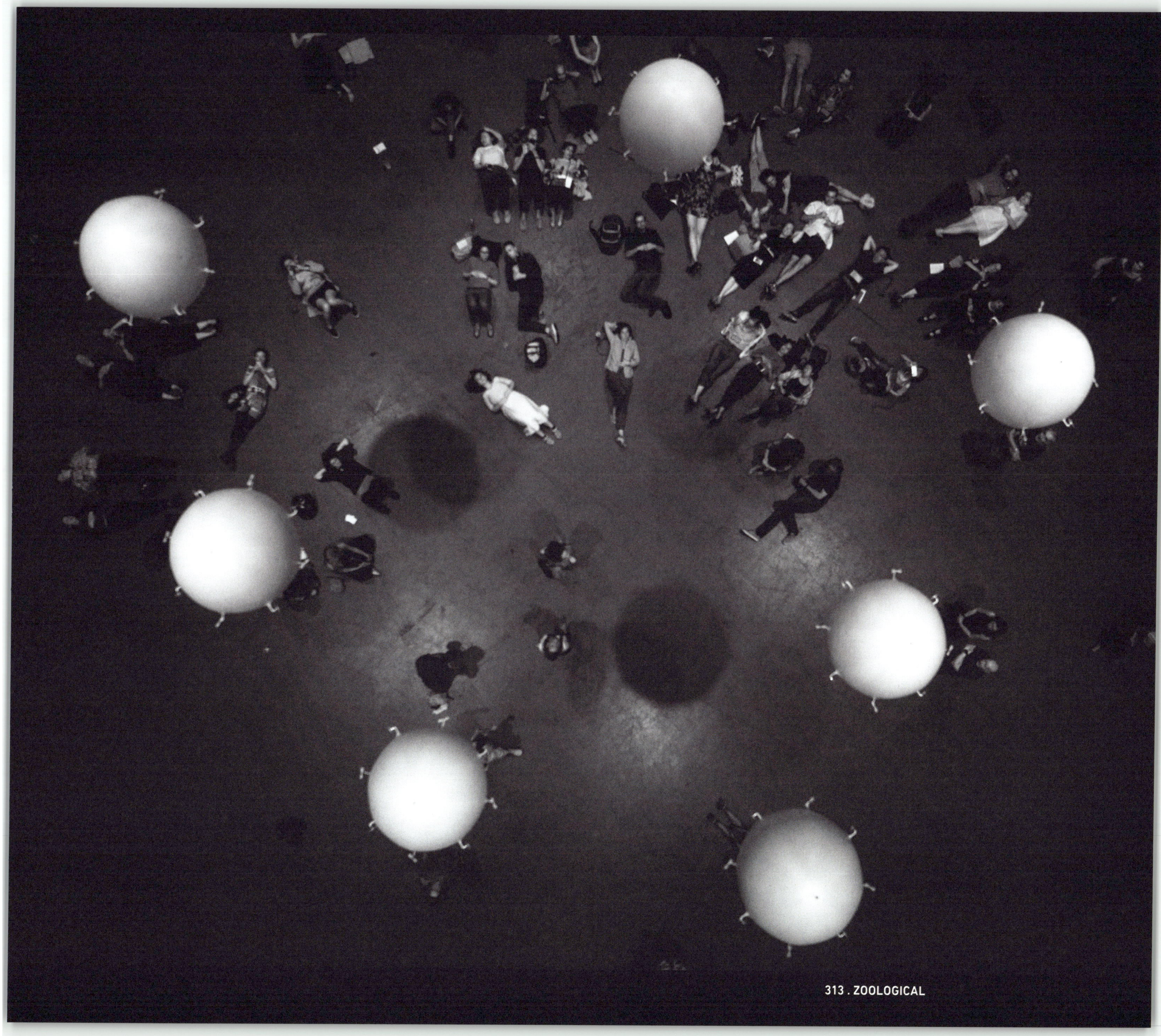

313 . ZOOLOGICAL

. . . . . A very nice comparison!
In reverse, this means that people these days are also indifferent to what happens to their data, or a certain naivety hangs over them.

I think it's the latter; if there were a believable, easy-to-understand risk assessment available, folks would be more careful. Nobody is driving without a seat belt fastened because we have seen crash test dummies in the 60s. We should be developing strategies for actual tangible "data privacy crash tests" that are publicized and tangibly communicated.

Data Crash Test Dummies to the rescue!

. . . . . Let us think back to Germany of the 1980s when heavy resistance against the census was planned for the beginning of 1983.

We were there!
Even with eight years, this was huge!

. . . . . It was feared that the level of details of the questions in the corresponding census forms would allow conclusions to be drawn about the identity of the respondents when they answered them, undermining data protection and thus violating the German constitution.

In what at the studio we call the "before time," things were more straightforward; we had pretty tunnel-visionary doomsday scenarios; nuclear war, data privacy abuse, etc.; and the pre-emptive steps to stop them were complex but manageable.

. . . . . Today, people willingly disclose sensitive data on both an information and a pictorial representation level.

It is an issue of fundamental data illiteracy; we do not know that what we have there is data, we do not know that it is sensitive, and even the most enlightened expert cannot possibly tell us what a potential threat scenario might look like 10 or 15 years down the line.

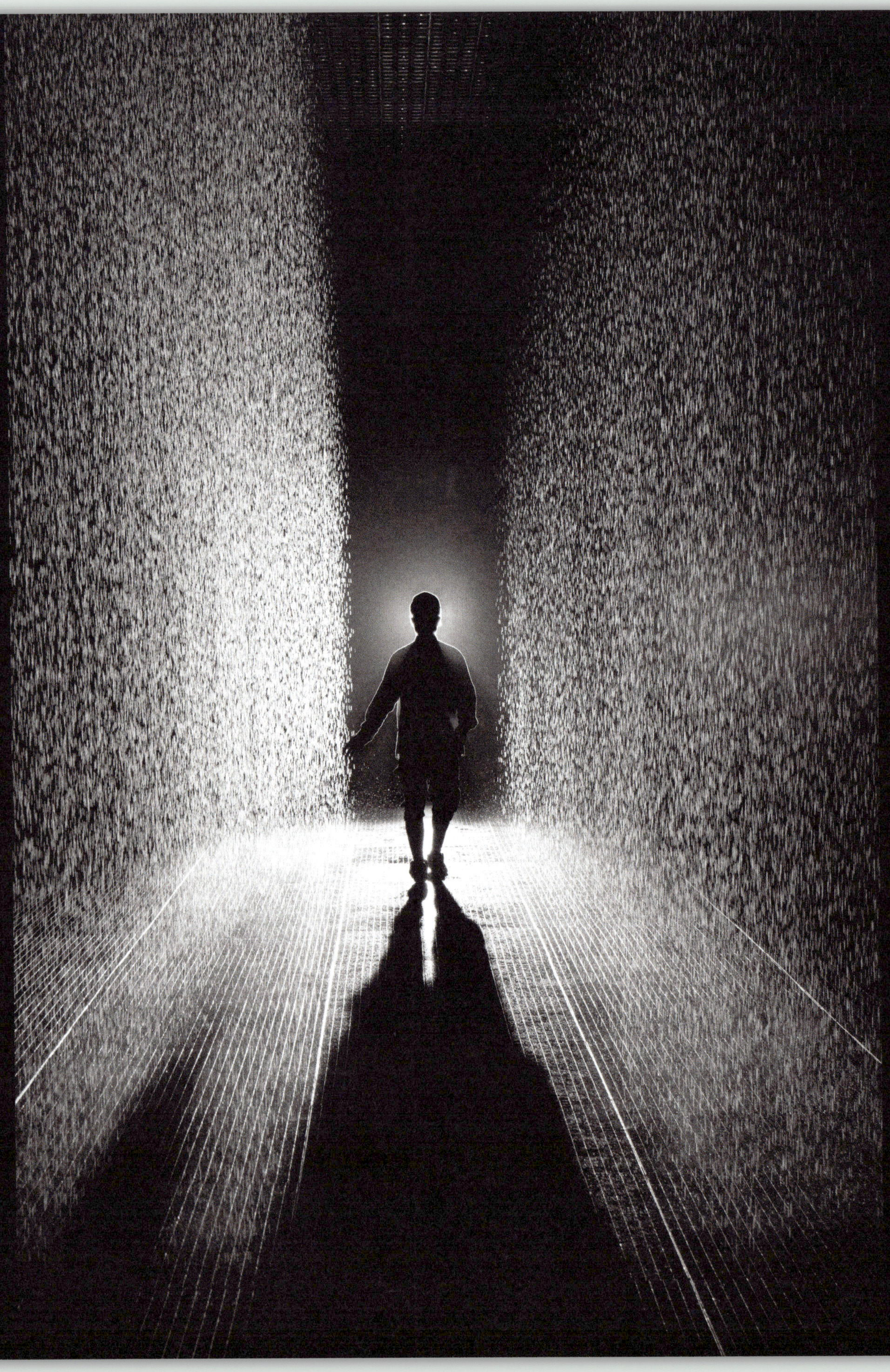

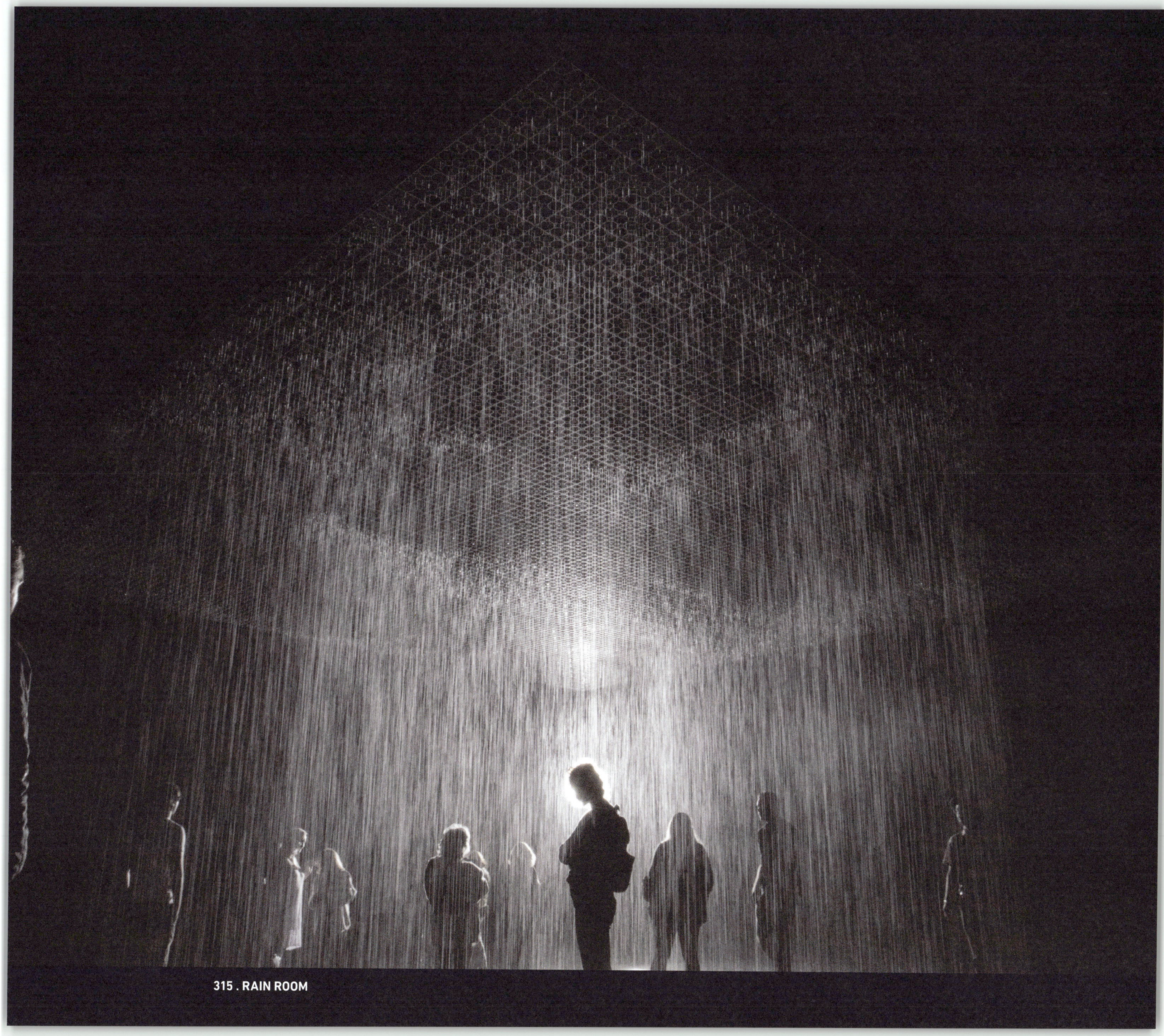

315 . RAIN ROOM

.

So again, we need a tangible crash-test scenario and multilateral development of regulation that helps us manage those risks.

Given that new players, specific or general AI entities, might enter the arena at any time, we really should get back to fundamental existential risk prevention and work it from there. Better to be safe than sorry.

.
.
. . . . . Another threat is undoubtedly in the area of post-factuality.

In doom scrolling, one gets lost between the postings. If you already communicate carelessly as a sender, as the hostage of the stream, will you voluntarily swallow any form of influence?

Yes, and it will matter less and less if we're not careful, as the point of a lot of our data is just to become part of the broader data stream.

Seeing ourselves as hostages is still in line with an essentially narcissistic worldview and the base assumption that we matter; we probably do not, at least not anywhere near as much as we are made to believe.

.
.
. . . . . Will we soon go one step further? The efforts of neuro link technology, which are currently becoming heard.

Should it soon be possible to digitalize one's feelings in addition to human memory and behavior?

Will we soon be able to transmit our thoughts and dreams wirelessly?

Maybe the exciting part in this context will likely not be transferring the known analog emotional/ experiential sphere into a digital one; it will be the development and exploration of a hybrid sphere that is terrifying and interesting; how do we identify and feel new emotions?

Our entire understanding of reality will be out of sync, which might pose exciting practical challenges in terms of living together, worrying issues in meeting collectively caused problems; climate change, for example, in a concerted manner.

.
.
.

CREDITS

RAIN ROOM

RANDOM INTERNATIONAL, RAIN ROOM, 2012.
Exhibited at The Curve, Barbican, London.
Courtesy of The Maxine and Stuart Frankel Foundation for Art.
Photography by RANDOM INTERNATIONAL

RANDOM INTERNATIONAL, RAIN ROOM, 2013.
Exhibited at MoMA, New York. Courtesy of RH Contemporary Art.
Photography by RANDOM INTERNATIONAL

RANDOM INTERNATIONAL, RAIN ROOM, 2015.
In the collection of LACMA, LA. Exhibited courtesy of LACMA, RH, Restoration Hardware and The Hyundai Project: Art + Technology a joint initiative exploring the convergence of art and technology.
Photography by RANDOM INTERNATIONAL

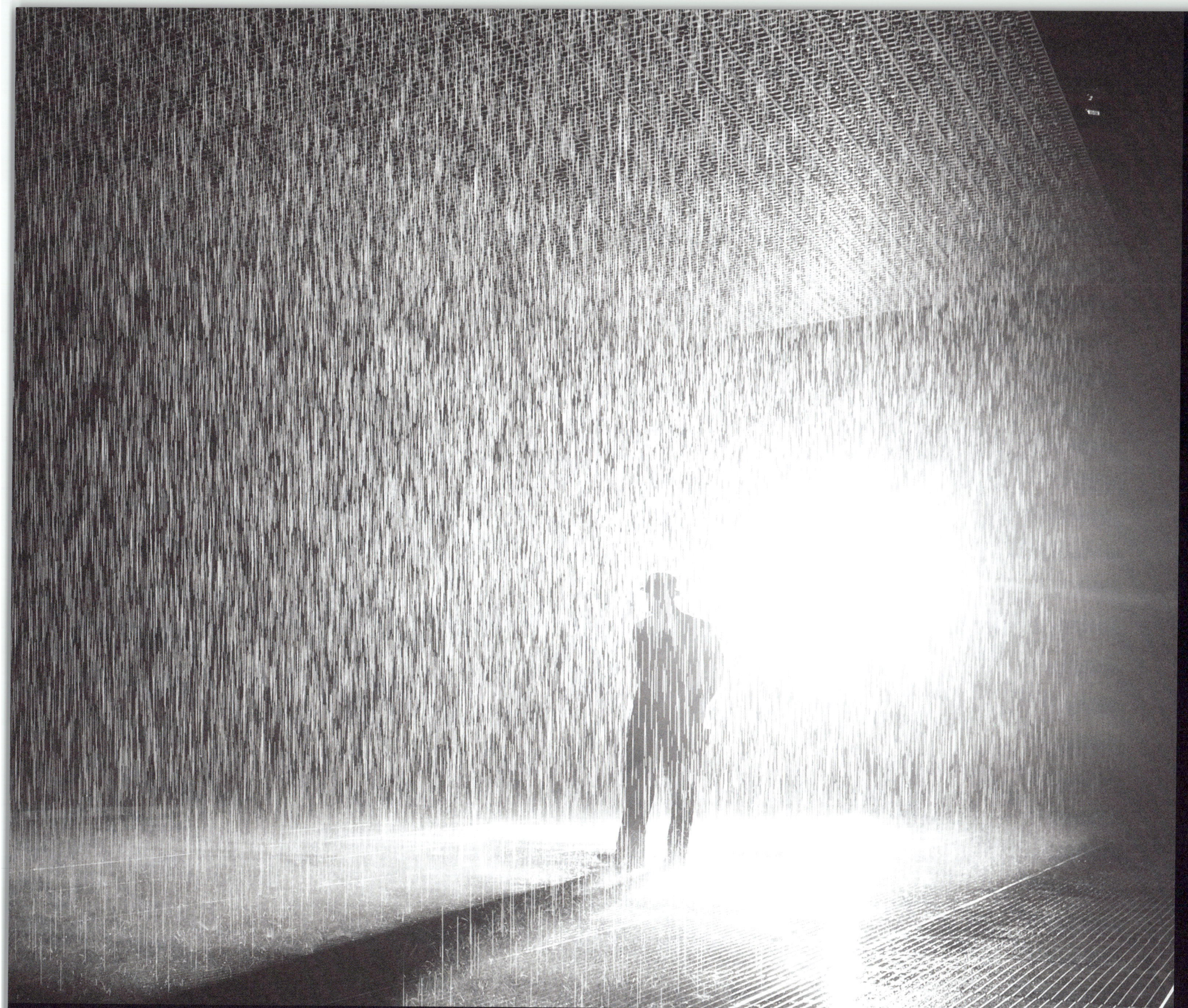

317 . RAIN ROOM

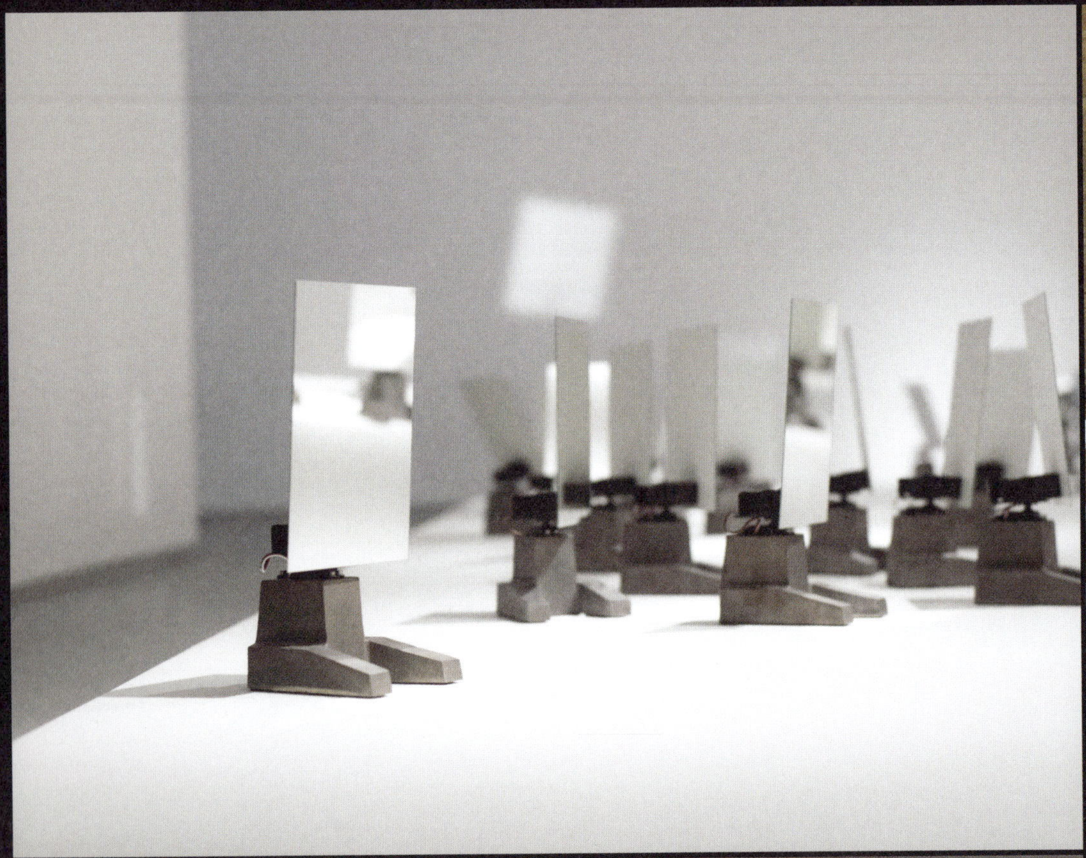

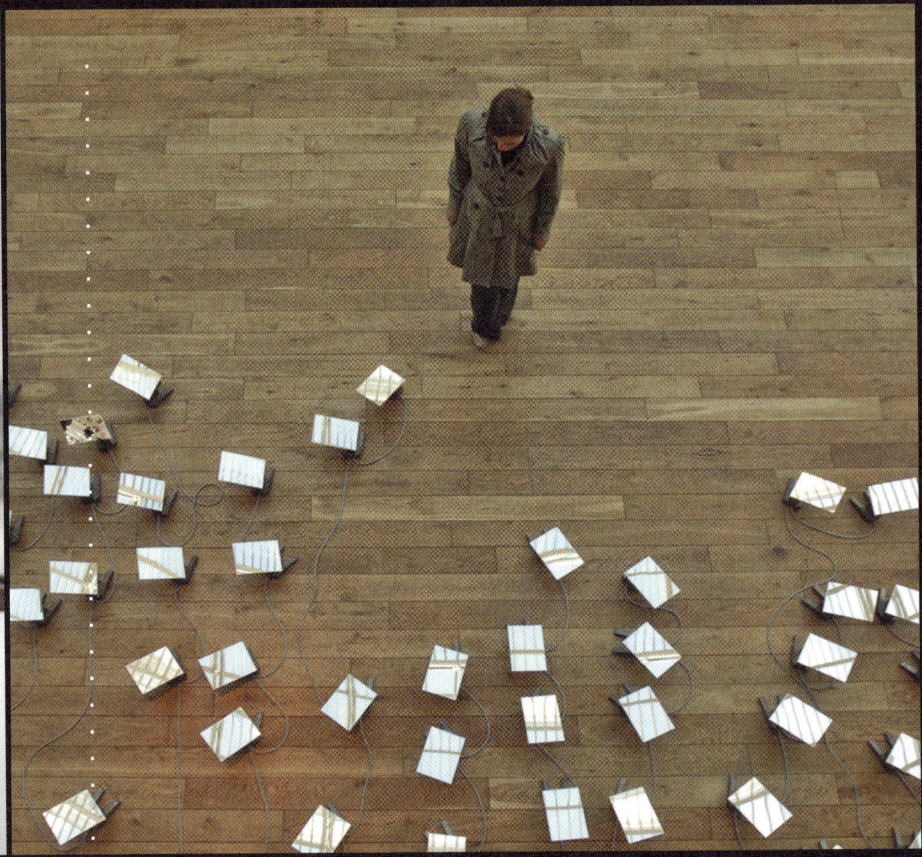

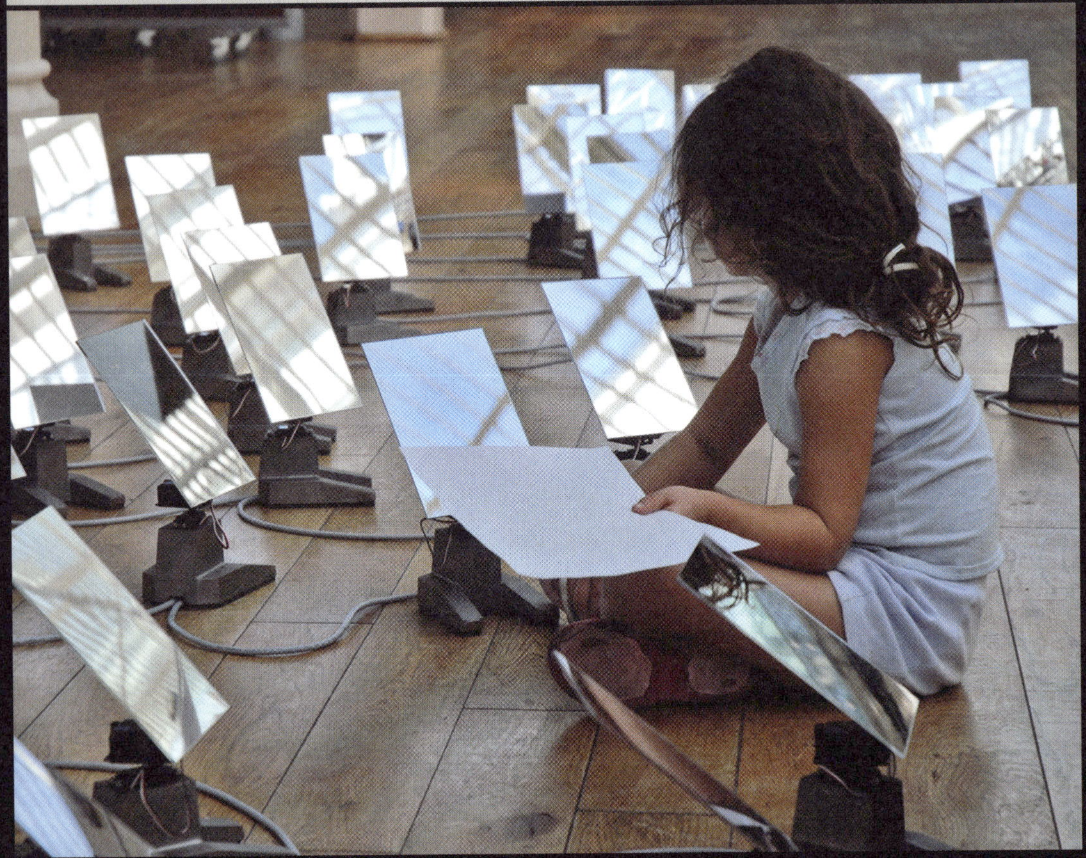

So new inner-psychic abilities will be demanded from humanity to develop positively in this hybrid sphere.

Does that require, in addition to a mindful art of immersion, an equally important art of emergence?

Yes, without striving for some actual presence in a sociocultural context that is built on, among other things, empathy, we will be facing a tough time.

Hannes Koch and Christoph Grünberger
October 2020

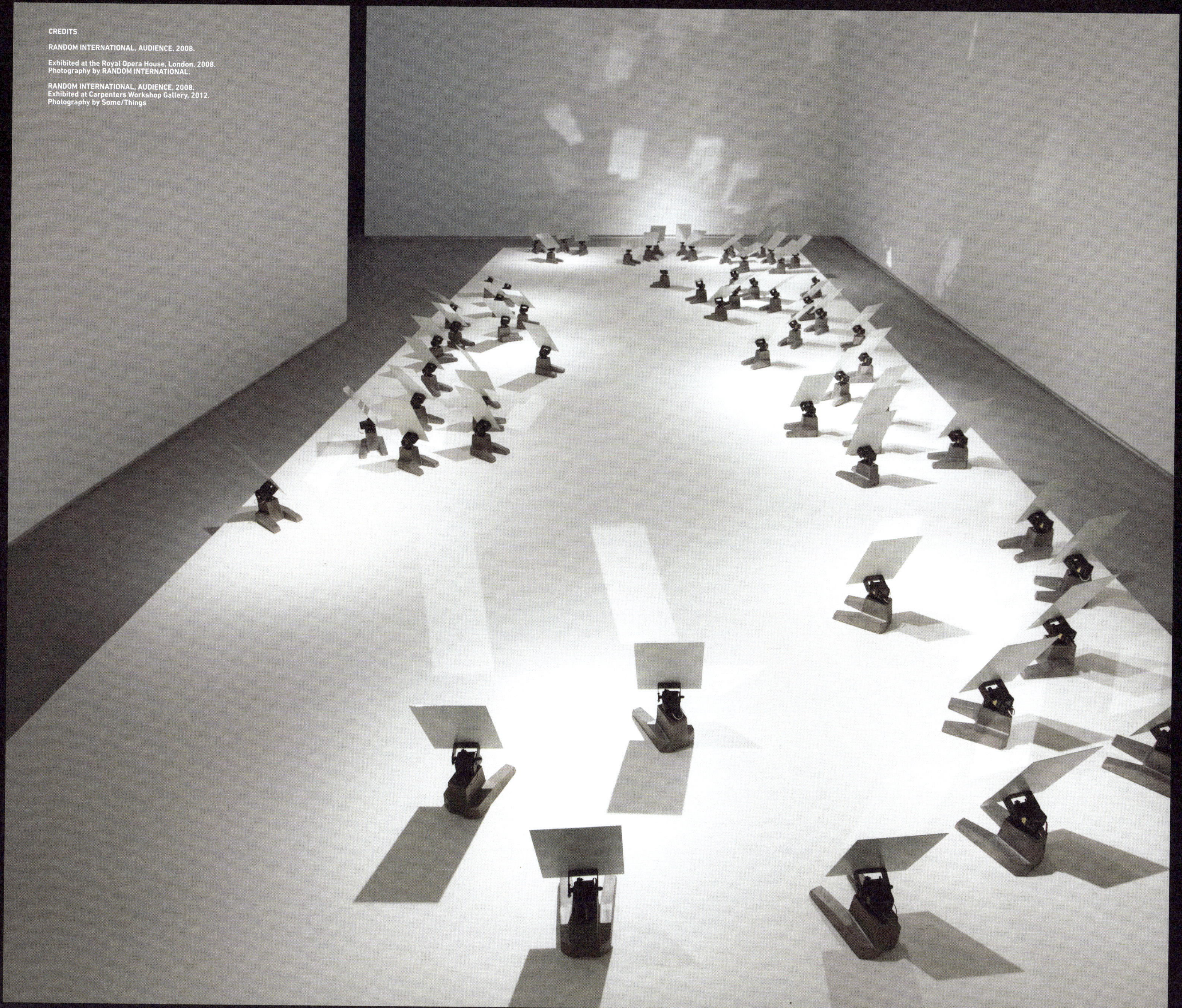

CREDITS

RANDOM INTERNATIONAL, AUDIENCE, 2008.

Exhibited at the Royal Opera House, London, 2008.
Photography by RANDOM INTERNATIONAL.

RANDOM INTERNATIONAL, AUDIENCE, 2008.
Exhibited at Carpenters Workshop Gallery, 2012.
Photography by Some/Things

Arpad Ray

Name:

Arpad Ray

Project:

WORK/ARTWORK

Project Description:

Transforming code repositories into generative artworks.

In collaboration with Christoph Grünberger, Amelie Maia and Yi-Wen Lin.

URL:

workartwork.org

Q&As

Please explain the main idea and what gave the impulse?

We believe great code is worth celebrating, and it is the craft; time and effort often go unnoticed. WORK/ARTWORK was created to turn code repositories into unique artworks.

Users import a Git repository or "repo," choose a design system by a top generative artist and customize their exclusive design.

As a professional coder, I have spent months working on projects, sometimes with a considerable number of other coders, and came to realize the visible result was often a tiny portion of the total work.

What challenges did you face for this project? And what surprises?

Our artworks are generated by analyzing a Git repo, where coders store their changes and collaborate. One of the early surprises was just how enormous these repos were. There are some with millions of changes, contributed by tens of thousands of coders. Conversely, some repos contain a single version of a single file.

This process is a tough challenge for our generative artists; how do you make an artwork feel unique and responsive across a vast range of inputs?

Please describe the technical environment.

In each case, we are producing a raster image for print. Still, there were some very different approaches, and of course, there is a reasonable amount of infrastructure in capturing the data and feeding it into each design for rendering.

Repo analysis: Rust
Rendering: Processing, Skia, WebGL
Web: Next.js, Go

Tell us about your aesthetical approach.

Our goal was each artwork be a stand-alone piece in its own right.

Even if you didn't know what the print was celebrating, you'd still proudly hang it on your wall.

We also wanted the artworks to channel the distinct style of the artists and avoid them being too literal.

Each of the artists we've collaborated with has achieved this magnificently.

What's next? Your vision?

In creating WORK/ARTWORK, we realized we could turn open-source repos into artworks and, in turn, support those same projects. A portion of sales is donated back to these schemes to help fund the work.

Open-source development needs support, and we love to inspire others to reward those projects.

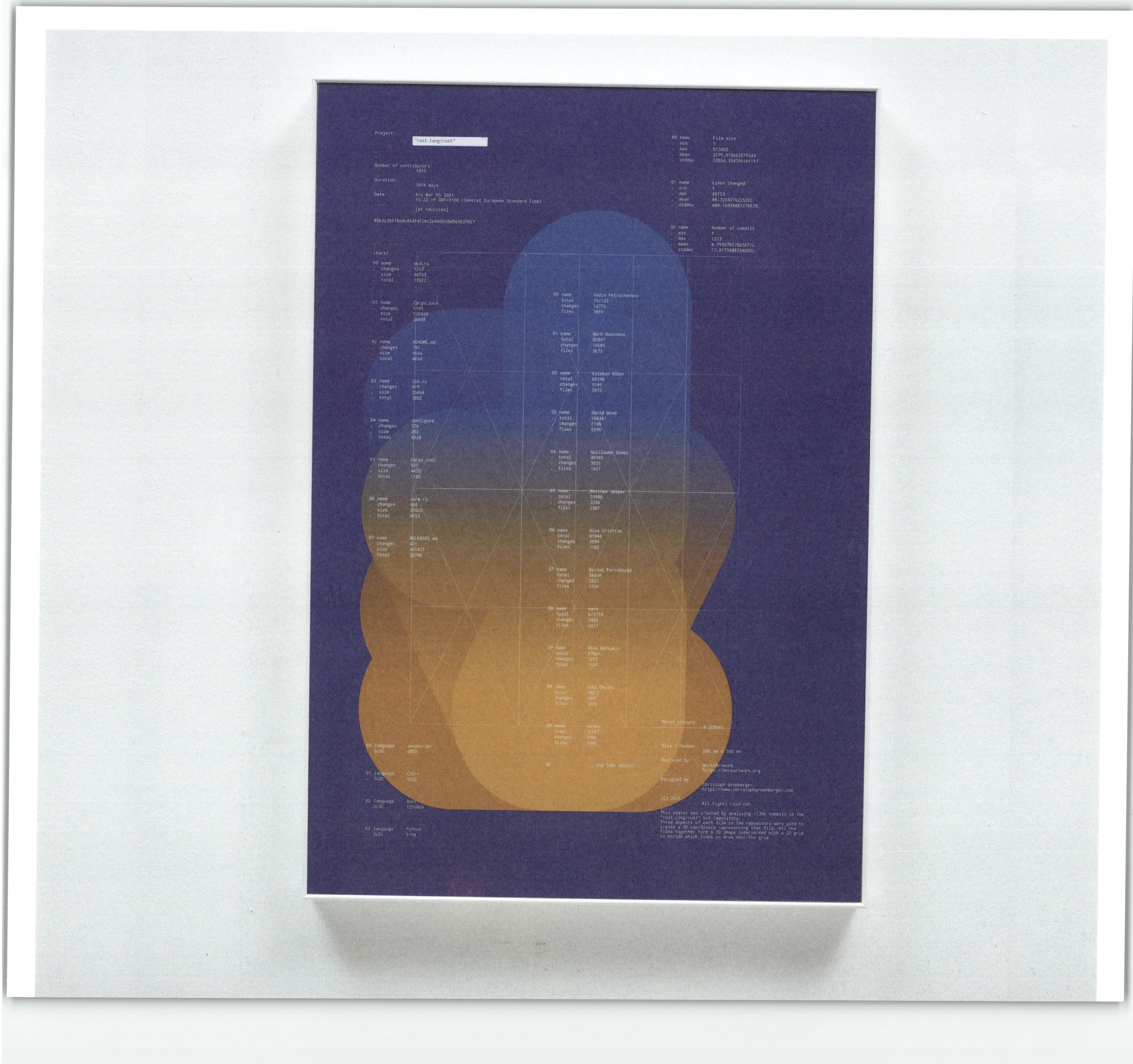
Project:
"rust-lang/rust"
Number of contributors: 1895
Duration: 3914 days
Date: Fri Mar 05 2021 15:22:19 GMT+0100 (Central European Standard Time)
[at revision]
45b3c28518e4c45dfd12bc2c4400c0d0e9639927
start/
00 name mod.rs . changes 1213 . size 94763 . total 17022
01 name Cargo.lock . changes 1193 . size 126848 . total 26898
02 name README.md . changes 781 . size 9566 . total 4684
03 name lib.rs . changes 619 . size 25668 . total 3802
04 name configure . changes 576 . size 292 . total 4328
05 name Cargo.toml . changes 537 . size 4433 . total 1185
06 name core.rs . changes 506 . size 25025 . total 4053
07 name RELEASES.md . changes 471 . size 491427 . total 20740
00 name File size . min 1 . max 823662 . mean 2179.018662275543 . stddev 10554.354786141157
01 name Lines changed . min 1 . max 45153 . mean 88.7234376225202 . stddev 489.16939481276535
02 name Number of commits . min 1 . max 1213 . mean 4.799576570218772 . stddev 17.81798887340205
00 name Vadim Petrochenkov . total 152122 . changes 12775 . files 7693
01 name Mark Rousskov . total 80897 . changes 10685 . files 9673
02 name Esteban Küber . total 69296 . changes 9149 . files 3972
03 name David Wood . total 154361 . changes 6106 . files 5596
04 name Guillaume Gomez . total 40385 . changes 3833 . files 1427
05 name Matthew Jasper . total 59990 . changes 3334 . files 2387
06 name Alex Crichton . total 61944 . changes 2994 . files 1102
07 name Mazdak Farrokhzad . total 38434 . changes 2827 . files 1750
08 name mark . total 672778 . changes 2463 . files 2417
09 name Niko Matsakis . total 37061 . changes 2372 . files 1104
0A name Yuki Okushi . total 18612 . changes 2047 . files 1818
0B name varkor . total 15167 . changes 2046 . files 1566
0C ... and 1883 others.
00 language Javascript . SLOC 4903
01 language C/C++ . SLOC 5522
02 language Rust . SLOC 1299869
03 language Python . SLOC 6194
Print colours: 4 [CMYK]
Size / format: 500 mm x 700 mm
Realised by: Work/Artwork https://workartwork.org
Designed by: Christoph Grünberger https://www.christophgruenberger.com
(C) 2021 All rights reserved.
This poster was created by analysing ~139k commits in the "rust-lang/rust" Git repository.
Three aspects of each file in the repository were used to create a 3D coordinate representing that file. All the files together form a 3D shape intersected with a 2D grid to decide which lines to draw onto the grid.

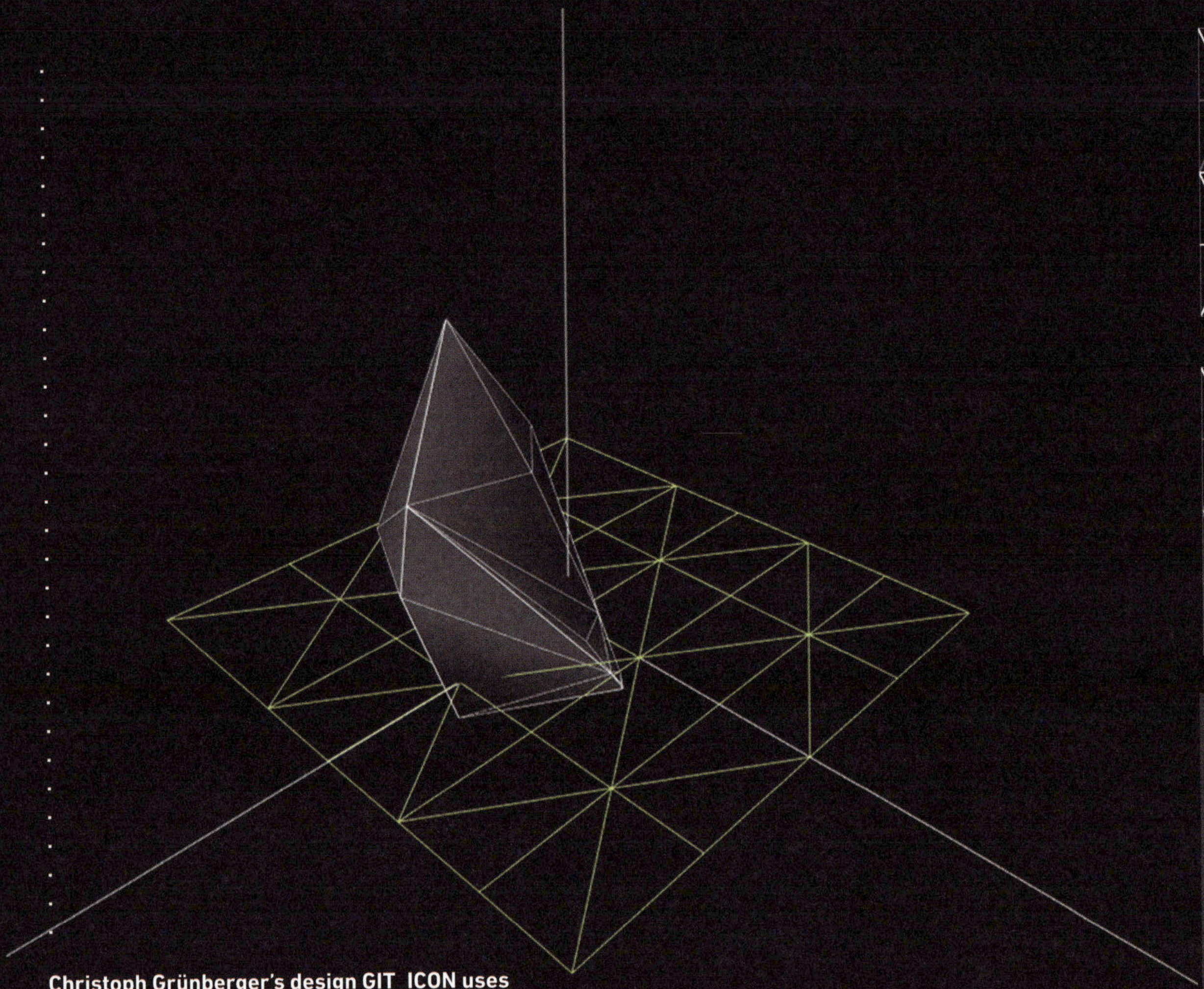

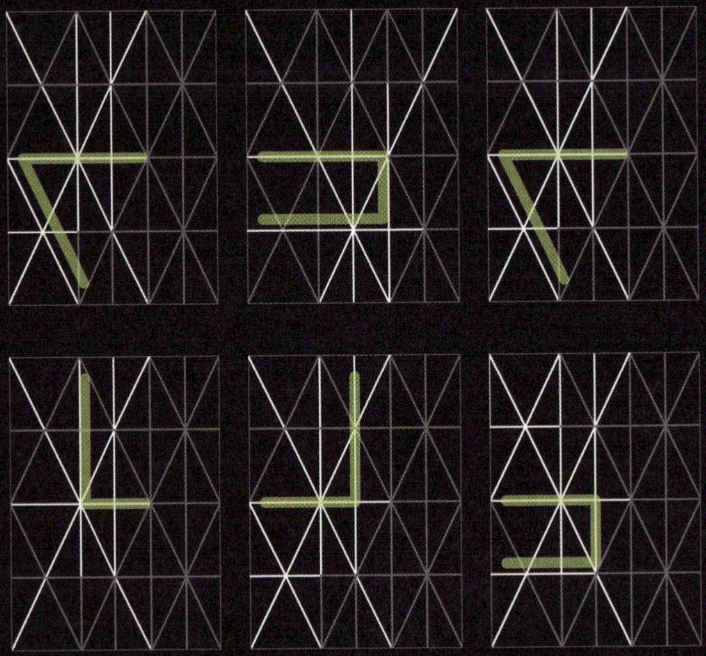

Christoph Grünberger's design GIT_ICON uses three properties of each file in the repository:

The file's size, the number of commits affecting it, and the number of lines changed over all of its commits. We can consider each property as a dimension, so each file is represented by a point in 3D space.

By calculating the convex hull of all these points, we are left with a solid 3D shape representing both the content of a repository and the history that led to it.

The grid intersects with the shape in several different orientations, and we find the longest continuous line along the intersected grid sections. This gives us a set of lines that are essentially two-dimensional cross sections of the 3D shape.

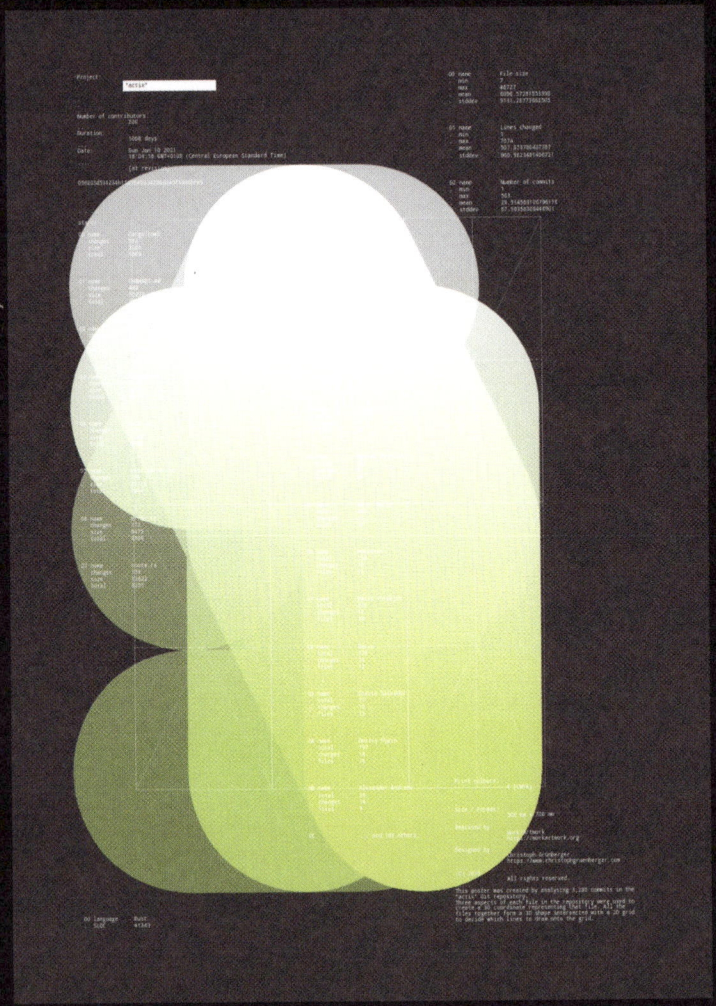

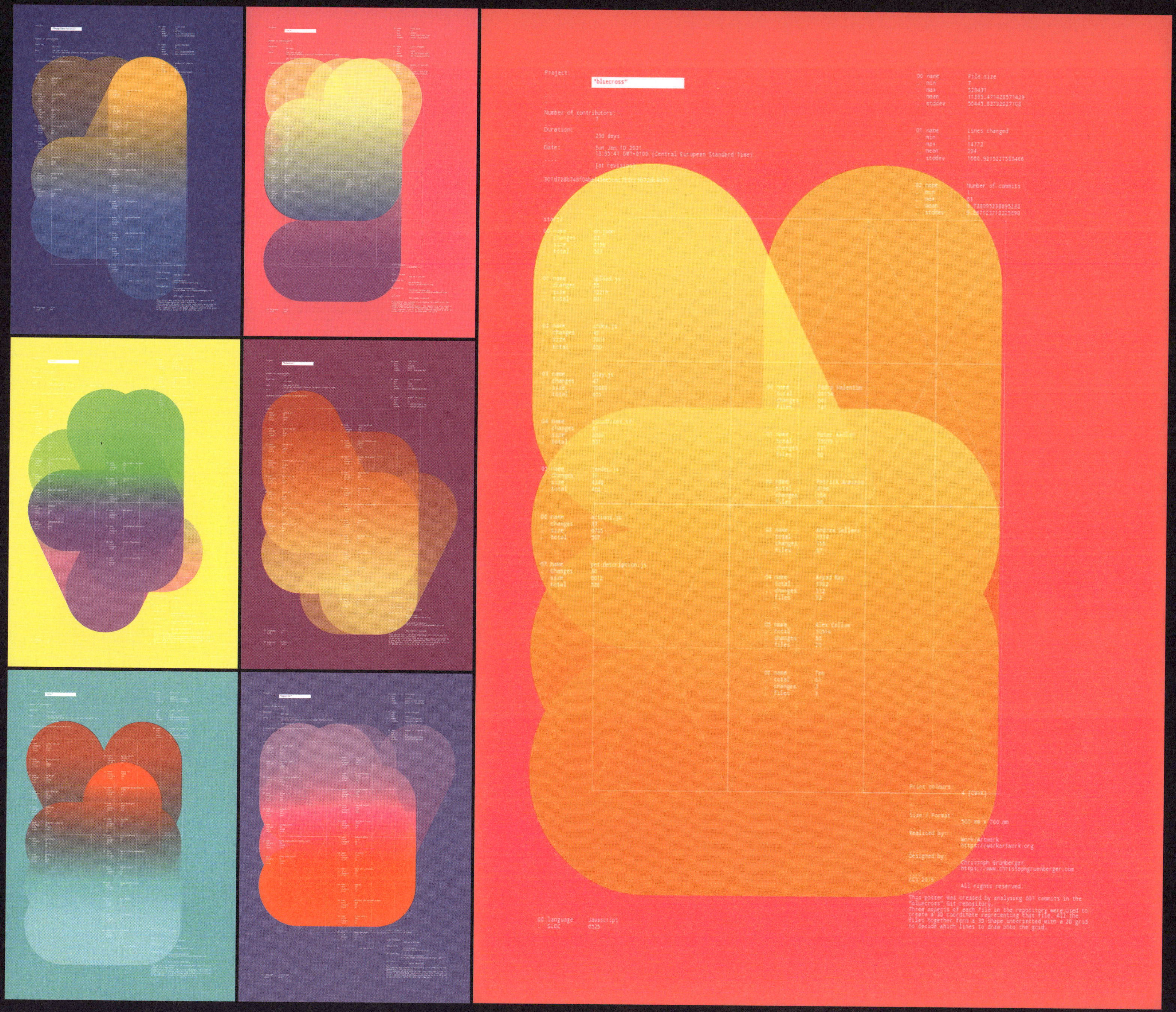

323 . WORK/ARTWORK . Christoph Grünberger . GIT_ICON

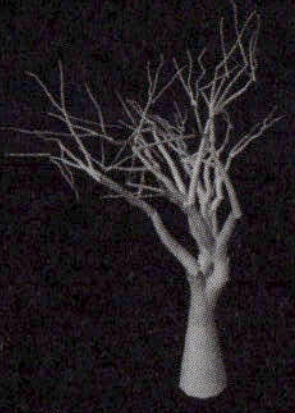

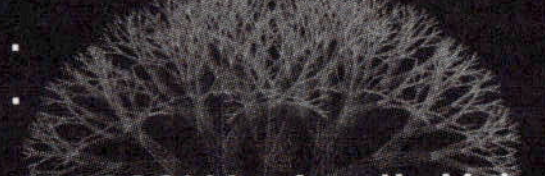

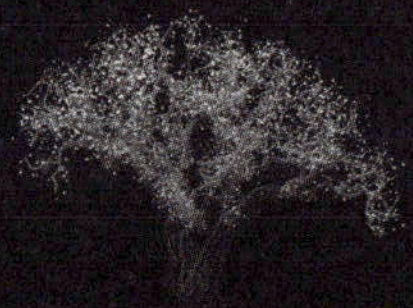

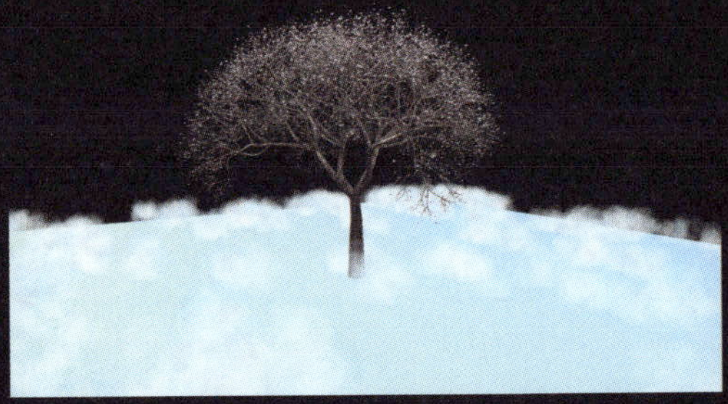

BLOSSOM by Amelie Maia uses the repo as a seed to grow a unique Japanese cherry (サクラ) tree.

Amelie took inspiration from traditional Japanese paintings while using WebGL to rapidly iterate on the design and allow the user to tailor the final artwork.

The growth and blossoming tree reflect the repo's journey and all the developers contributing to it.

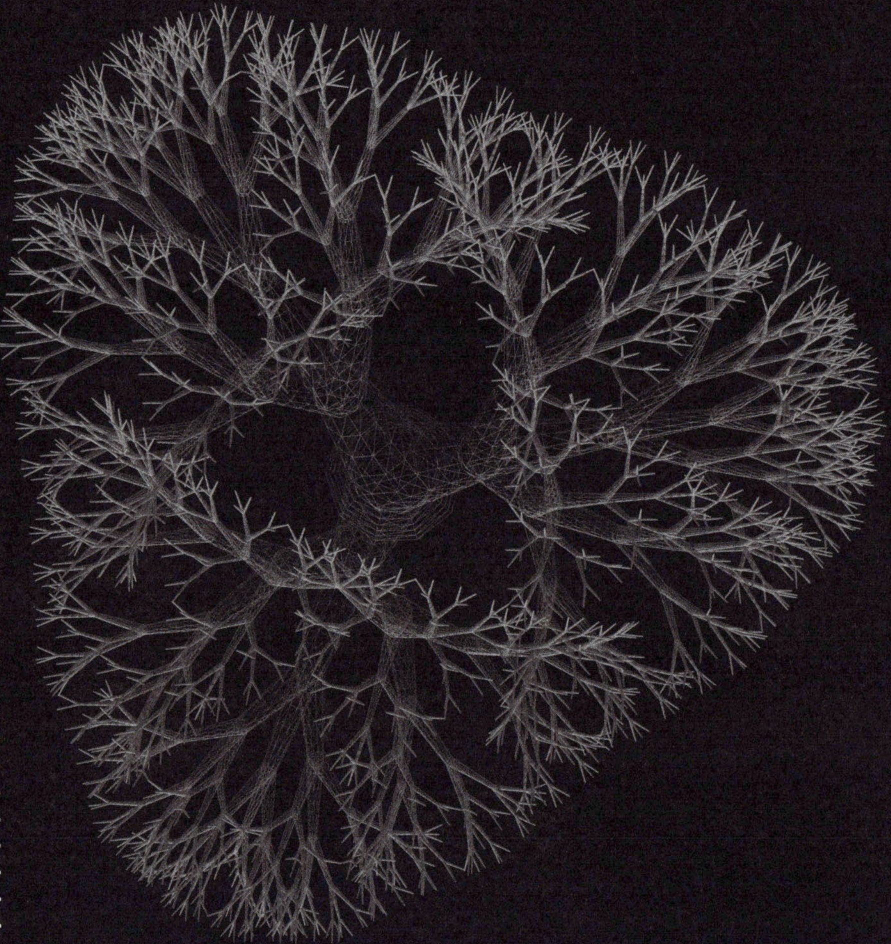

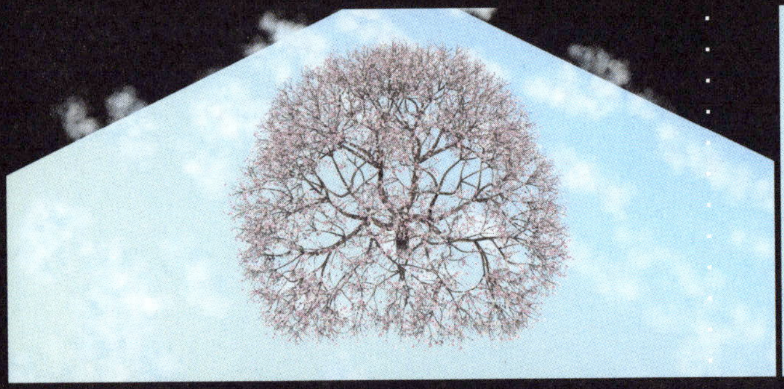

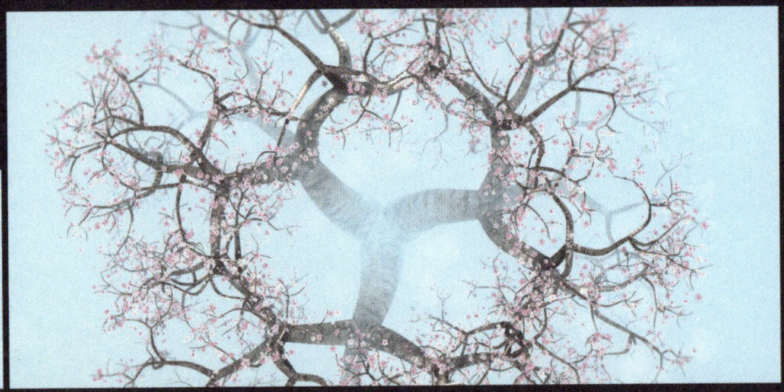

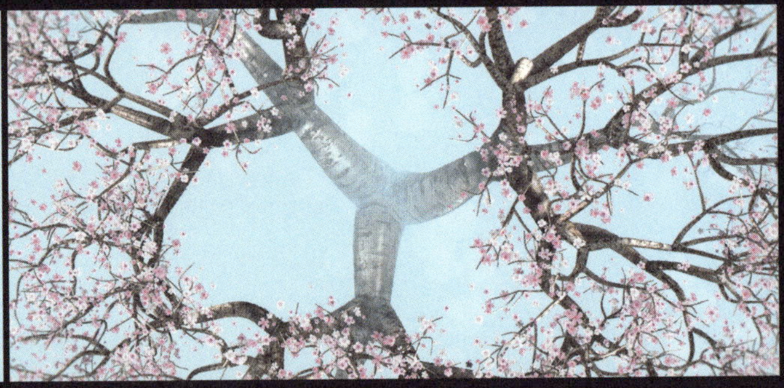

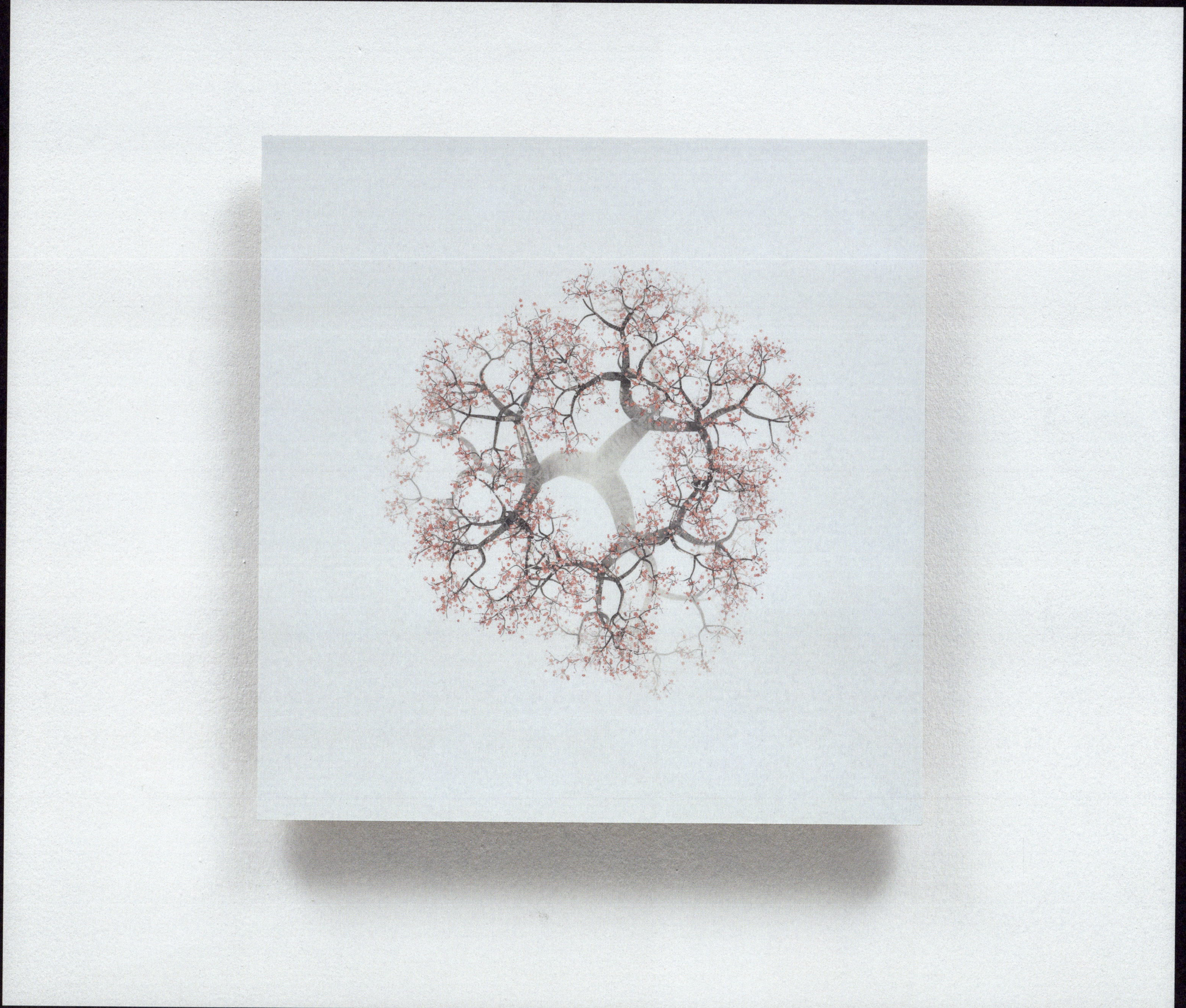

325 . WORK/ARTWORK . Amelie Maia . BLOSSOM

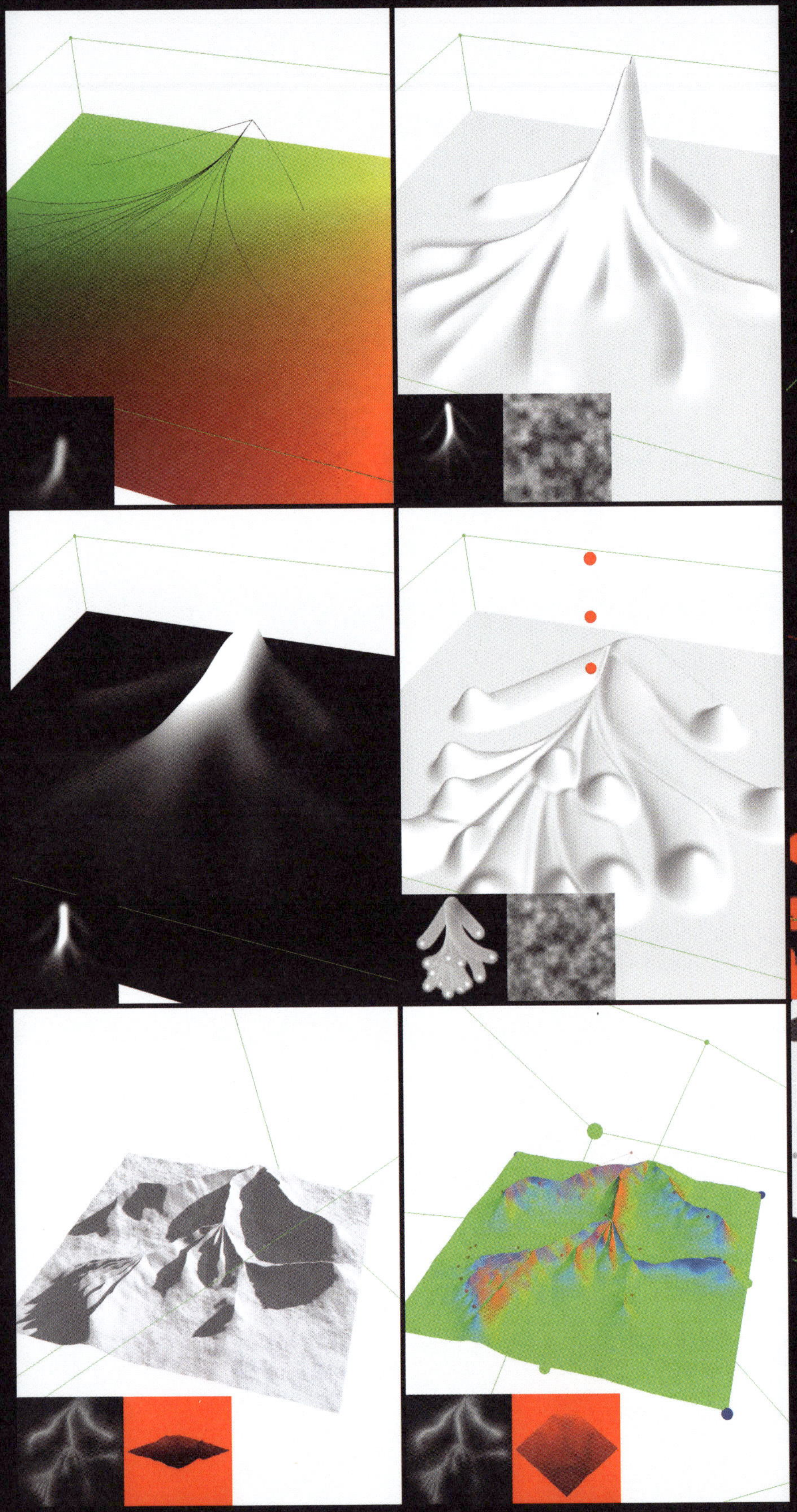

Yi-Wen Lin's design MOUNTAIN presents a topographical view of the repo in a vintage map style.

A mountain represents each folder in the project, the hierarchical directory structure then forming the mountain range.

Yi-Wen used his advanced WebGL framework to create this system, allowing users to control scene lighting and even camera angles.

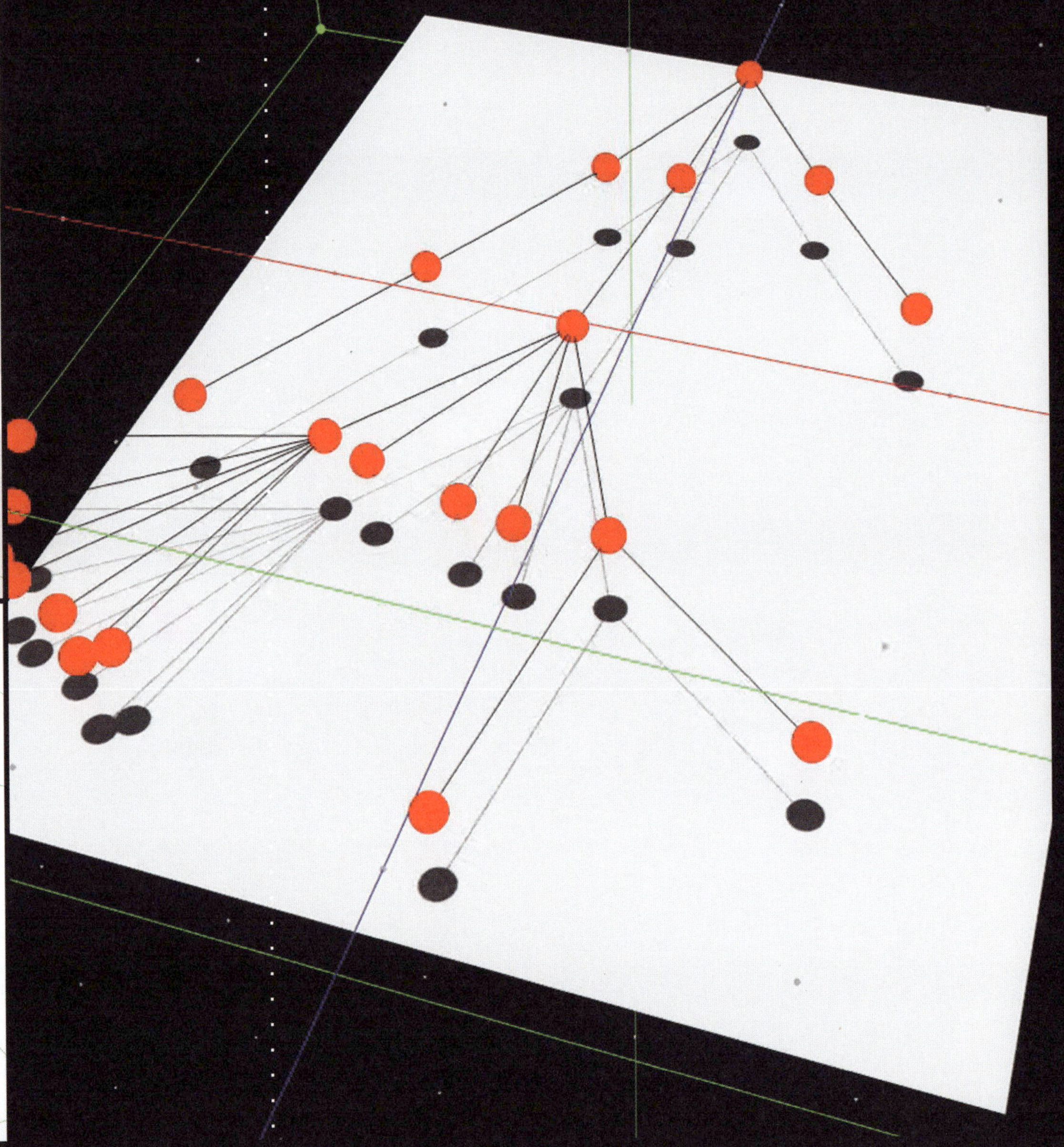

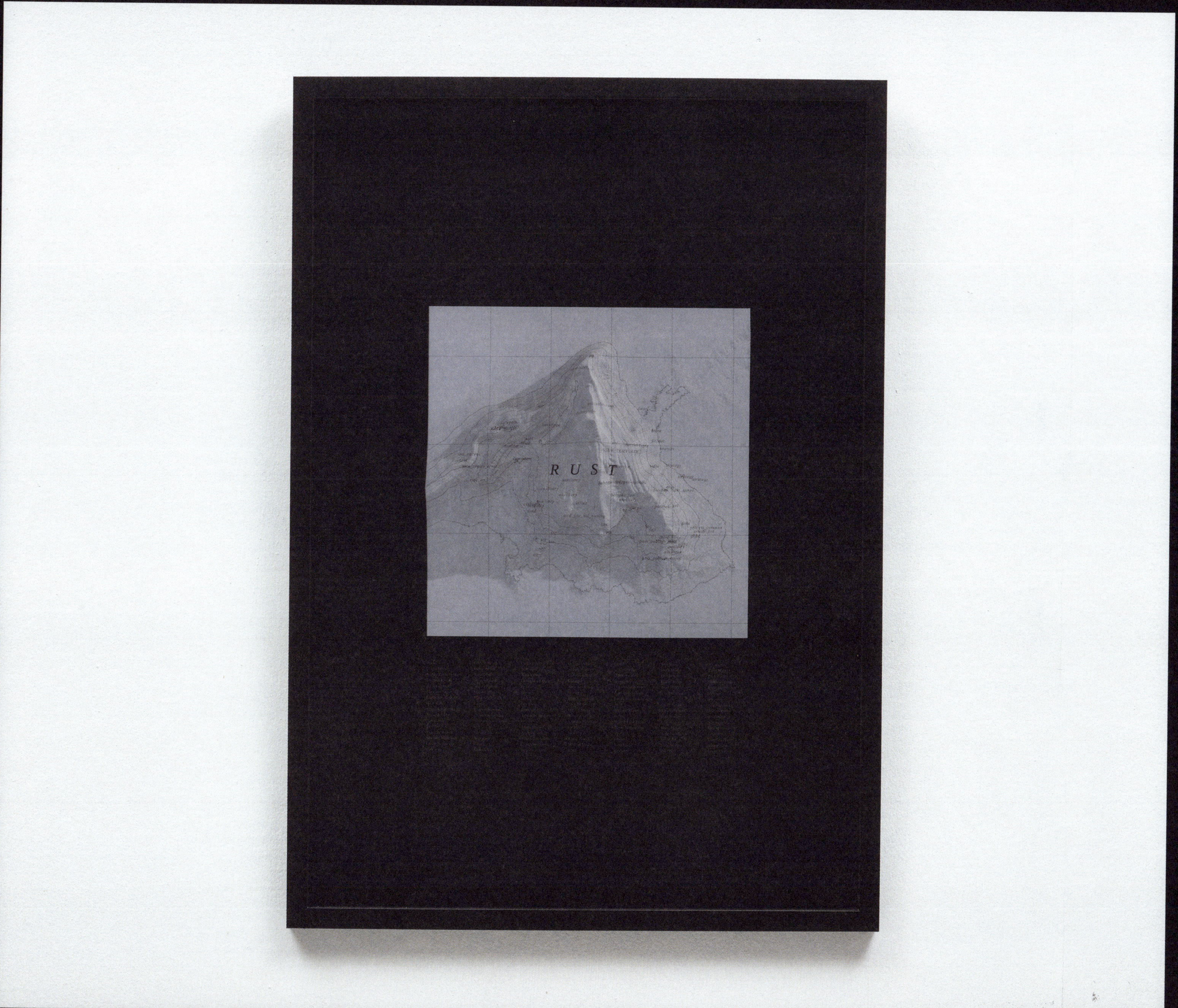

327 . WORK/ARTWORK . Yi-Wen Lin . MOUNTAIN

Florian Renner

Name:

Florian Renner

Info:

Graphic designer and 3D artist Florian Renner creates 3D environments, animations, and visualizations focusing on contrasting rich colors and geometric shapes and patterns.

The Munich-based artist combines his work with independent design and retro-futuristic aesthetics that influenced his youth. Even the synthwave music influenced by the sound of the 80s that he uses for his animations is not as much background music as an equal medium.

Cult movies and pop culture of the 80s and 90s; Blade Runner, Terminator, and Total Recall influenced his view on art, and also renowned artists like Brom and Frank Frazetta inspired him in early childhood and supported the desire to work as an illustrator.

Training as a graphic designer and working as an employee in various design agencies seem to move into the background. As a result, in 2011, Renner became a freelance illustrator and graphic designer. The combination of graphics, illustration, and 3D has fascinated him; and, at the same time, opened up new subject areas.

One result of this is the video Retrowave, used for the musician Miami Nights 1984 in the NewRetroWave YouTube channel.

Project:

CITYRIG & MANTIS PATTERN GENERATOR

URL:

rennerflorian.com

Instagram:

@florenoir

Q&As

. . . . . Please explain the main idea and what gave the impulse?

During the development of new projects and ascertaining the requirements, ideas for tools in Cinema 4D emerge that should simplify the modeling and creation of content for me. This process is how the CITYRIG came to life.

The first version of the tool was created to create a promotional video for Robert Parker's End of the Night.

The idea was to show a retro-futuristic endless city that pulsates to the rhythm of the music.

To avoid relying on purchased models, I created this tool that randomly generates buildings, facades, and roof structures in different arrangements.

. . . . . What challenges did you face for this project? And what surprises?

Initially, most surfaces and shapes created are polygons (see image on the right). With the size/height and the simple number of buildings, the maximum number of polygons represented was quickly reached.

Therefore, I added textures and displacement maps to many surface details; window facades, roof structures, advertising banners and placed them on low-polygon models consisting of simple shapes with no windows or details.

This process makes working with larger cities possible.

I wrote another tool that randomizes geometric shapes in size and angle to create technical-looking patterns for the new surfaces easily.

For the CITYRIG I used it for the roof structures and the floor plates. In the later version of the plugin, the MANTIS PATTERN GENERATOR, I extended it with BPM triggered animations, which can also be used for VJ clips, music videos, or similar.

. . . . . Please describe the technical environment.

I created CITYRIG and MANTIS with the Xpresso editor in Cinema 4D and MoGraph. Xpresso can realize dependencies between objects, while MoGraph can duplicate objects and control with effect fields. It is starting between simple If-Then statements and more complex circuits and scripts with COFFEE or Python.

It is, therefore, not pure programming; it also creates visual appeal similar to earlier Action Script in Macromedia Flash.

. . . . . Tell us about your aesthetical approach.

My approach was to create randomly generated environments and content that is also controllable and maintains its signature.

. . . . . What's next? Your vision?

I want to create more experimental approaches to randomly generated content. For example, I am currently working on a tool, creating random camera movements around a 3D object.

A sequencer within Cinema 4D controls camera cuts and movement, lighting, and effects. This process creates animations that would take hours to create by hand through keyframing in real-time. Later you only have to decide which scenes you want to use.

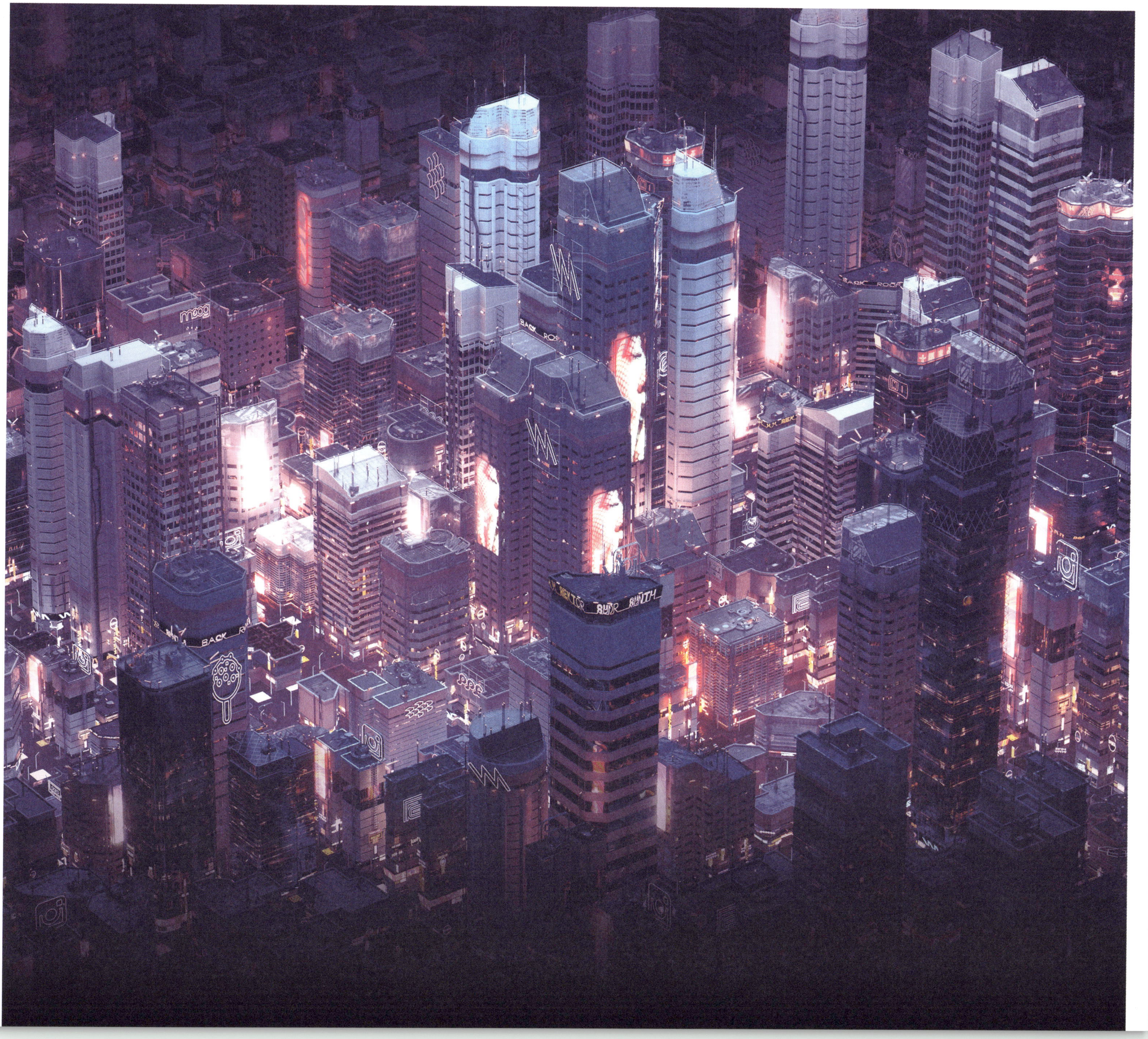
moog
BACK

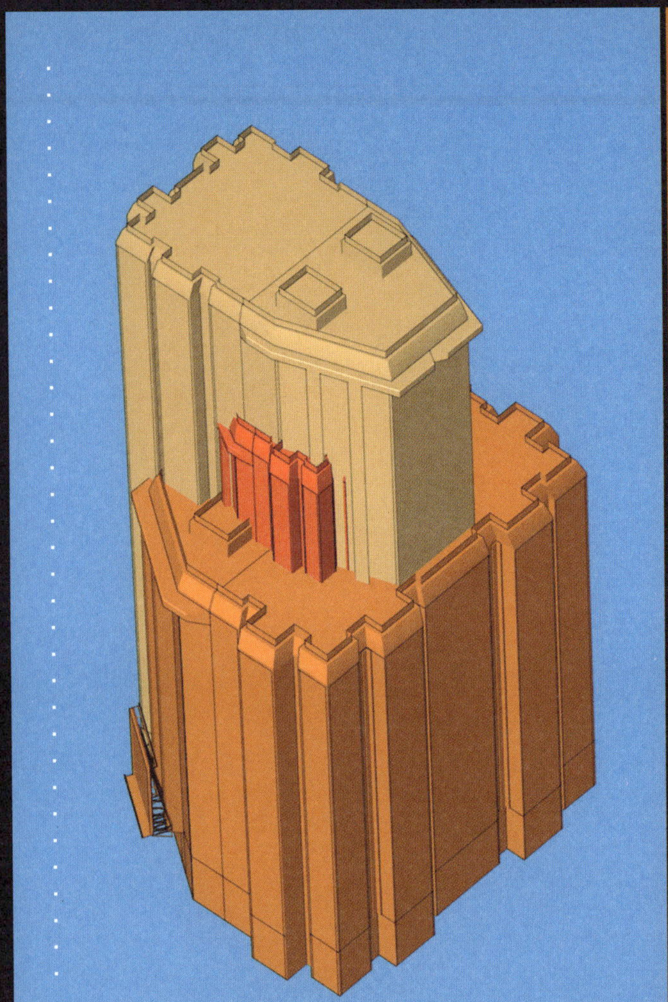

A building consists of four random parts that form a basic building shape when joined together at the ends.

A building, in turn, consists of three more such random basic shapes that differ in height and width.

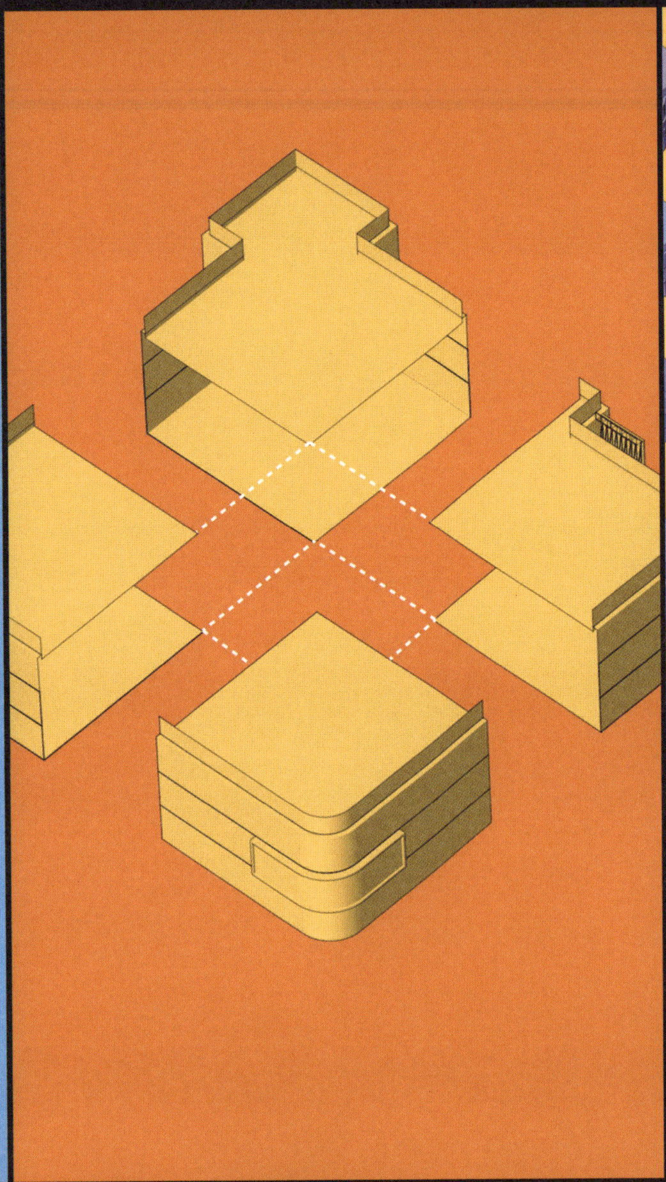

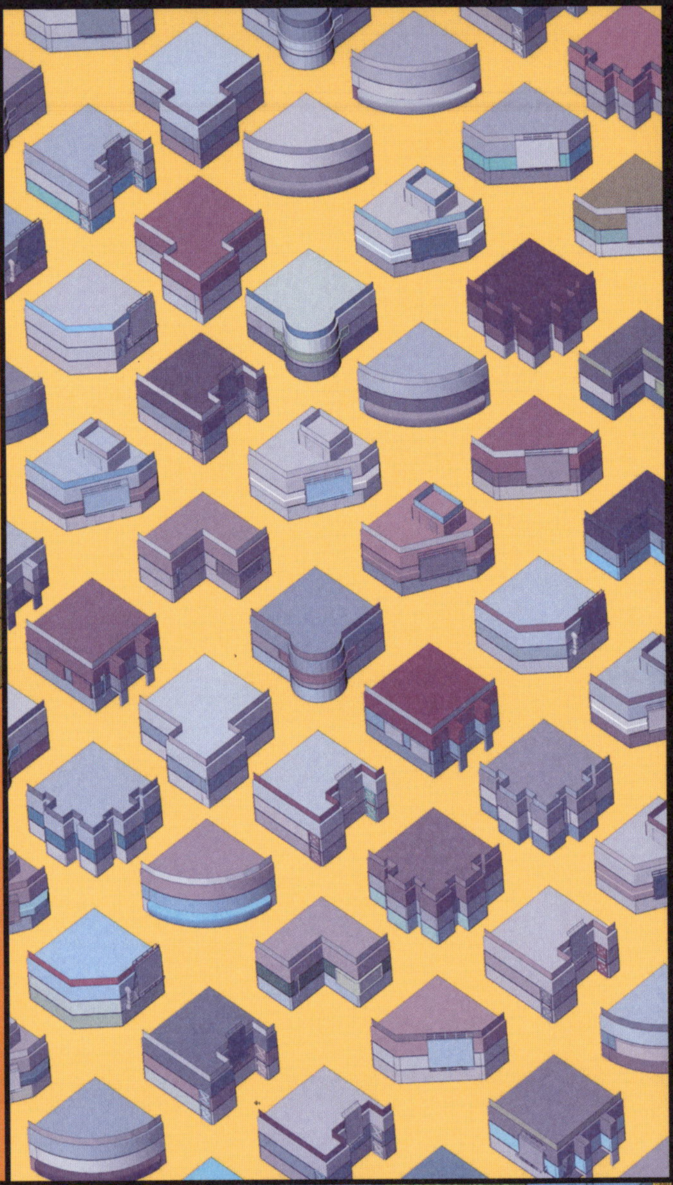

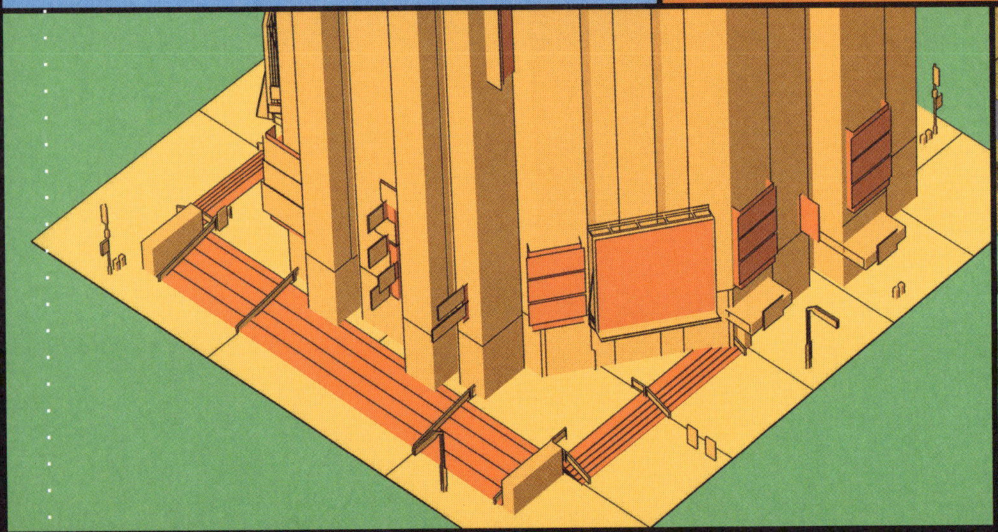

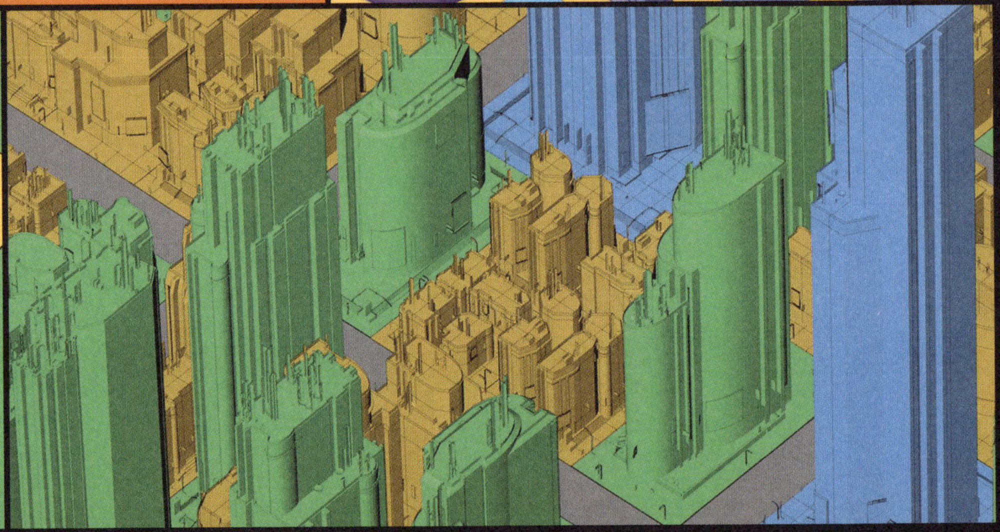

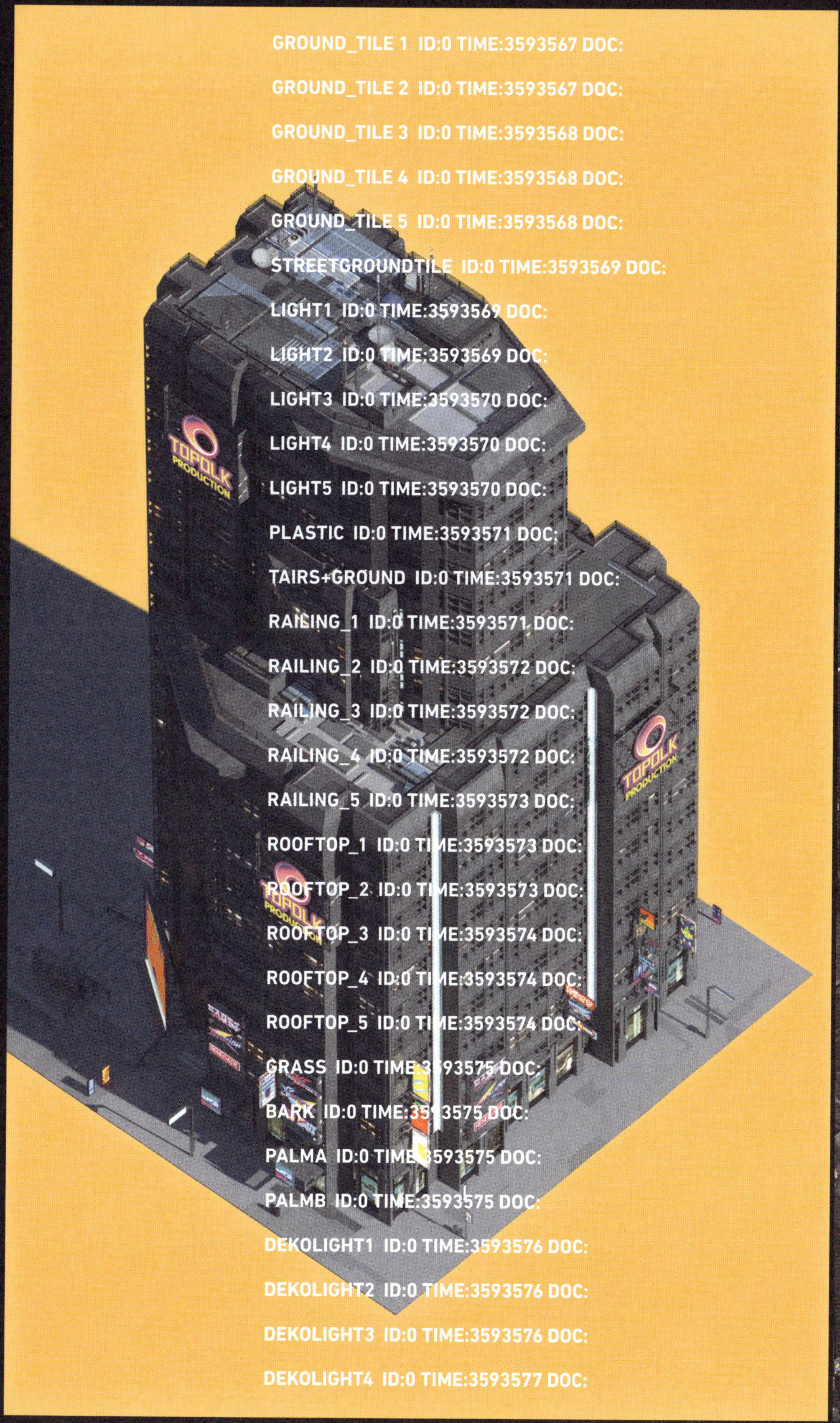
GROUND_TILE 1 ID:0 TIME:3593567 DOC:
GROUND_TILE 2 ID:0 TIME:3593567 DOC:
GROUND_TILE 3 ID:0 TIME:3593568 DOC:
GROUND_TILE 4 ID:0 TIME:3593568 DOC:
GROUND_TILE 5 ID:0 TIME:3593568 DOC:
STREETGROUNDTILE ID:0 TIME:3593569 DOC:
LIGHT1 ID:0 TIME:3593569 DOC:
LIGHT2 ID:0 TIME:3593569 DOC:
LIGHT3 ID:0 TIME:3593570 DOC:
LIGHT4 ID:0 TIME:3593570 DOC:
LIGHT5 ID:0 TIME:3593570 DOC:
PLASTIC ID:0 TIME:3593571 DOC:
TAIRS+GROUND ID:0 TIME:3593571 DOC:
RAILING_1 ID:0 TIME:3593571 DOC:
RAILING_2 ID:0 TIME:3593572 DOC:
RAILING_3 ID:0 TIME:3593572 DOC:
RAILING_4 ID:0 TIME:3593572 DOC:
RAILING_5 ID:0 TIME:3593573 DOC:
ROOFTOP_1 ID:0 TIME:3593573 DOC:
ROOFTOP_2 ID:0 TIME:3593573 DOC:
ROOFTOP_3 ID:0 TIME:3593574 DOC:
ROOFTOP_4 ID:0 TIME:3593574 DOC:
ROOFTOP_5 ID:0 TIME:3593574 DOC:
GRASS ID:0 TIME:3593575 DOC:
BARK ID:0 TIME:3593575 DOC:
PALMA ID:0 TIME:3593575 DOC:
PALMB ID:0 TIME:3593575 DOC:
DEKOLIGHT1 ID:0 TIME:3593576 DOC:
DEKOLIGHT2 ID:0 TIME:3593576 DOC:
DEKOLIGHT3 ID:0 TIME:3593576 DOC:
DEKOLIGHT4 ID:0 TIME:3593577 DOC:
TOPOLK PRODUCTION

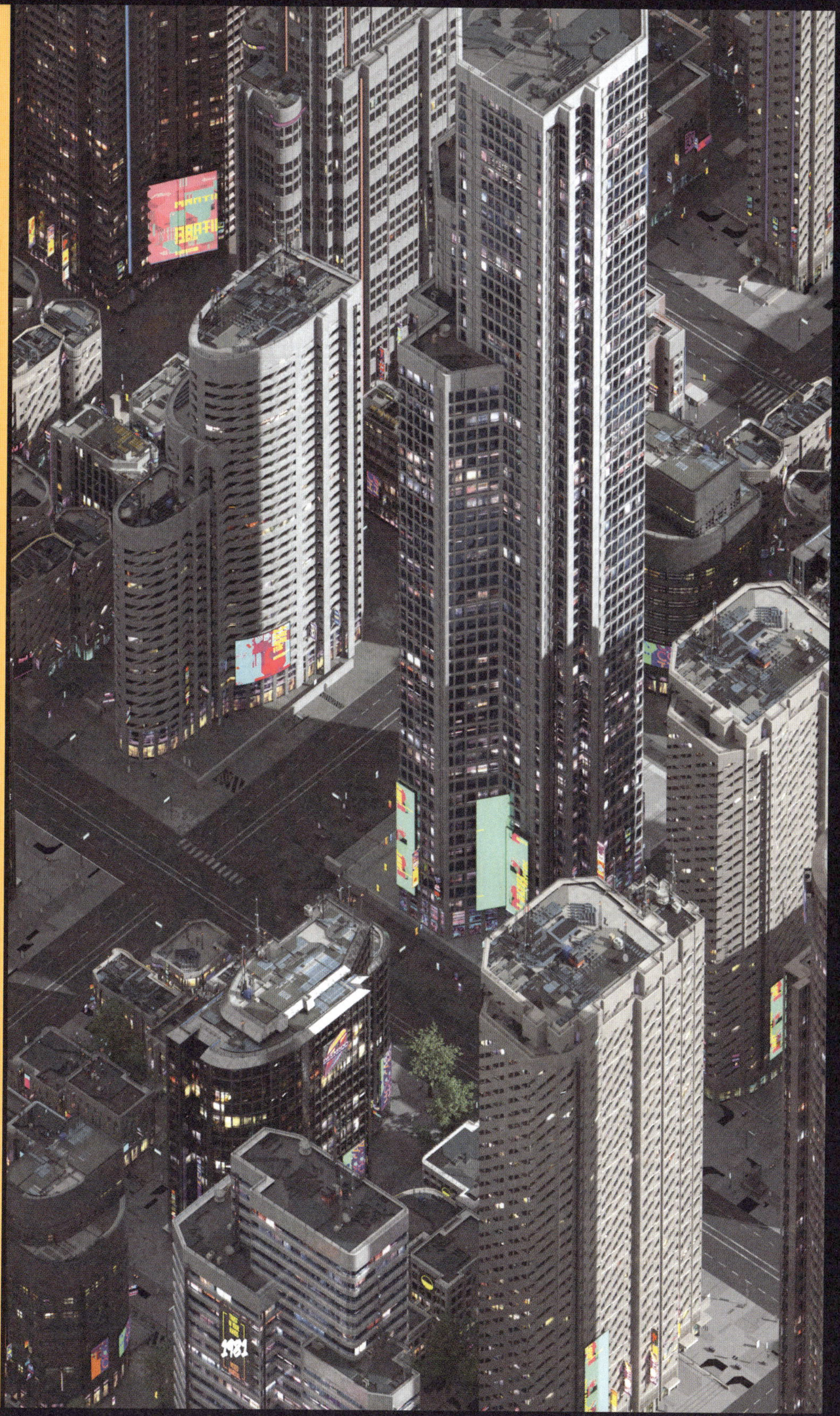

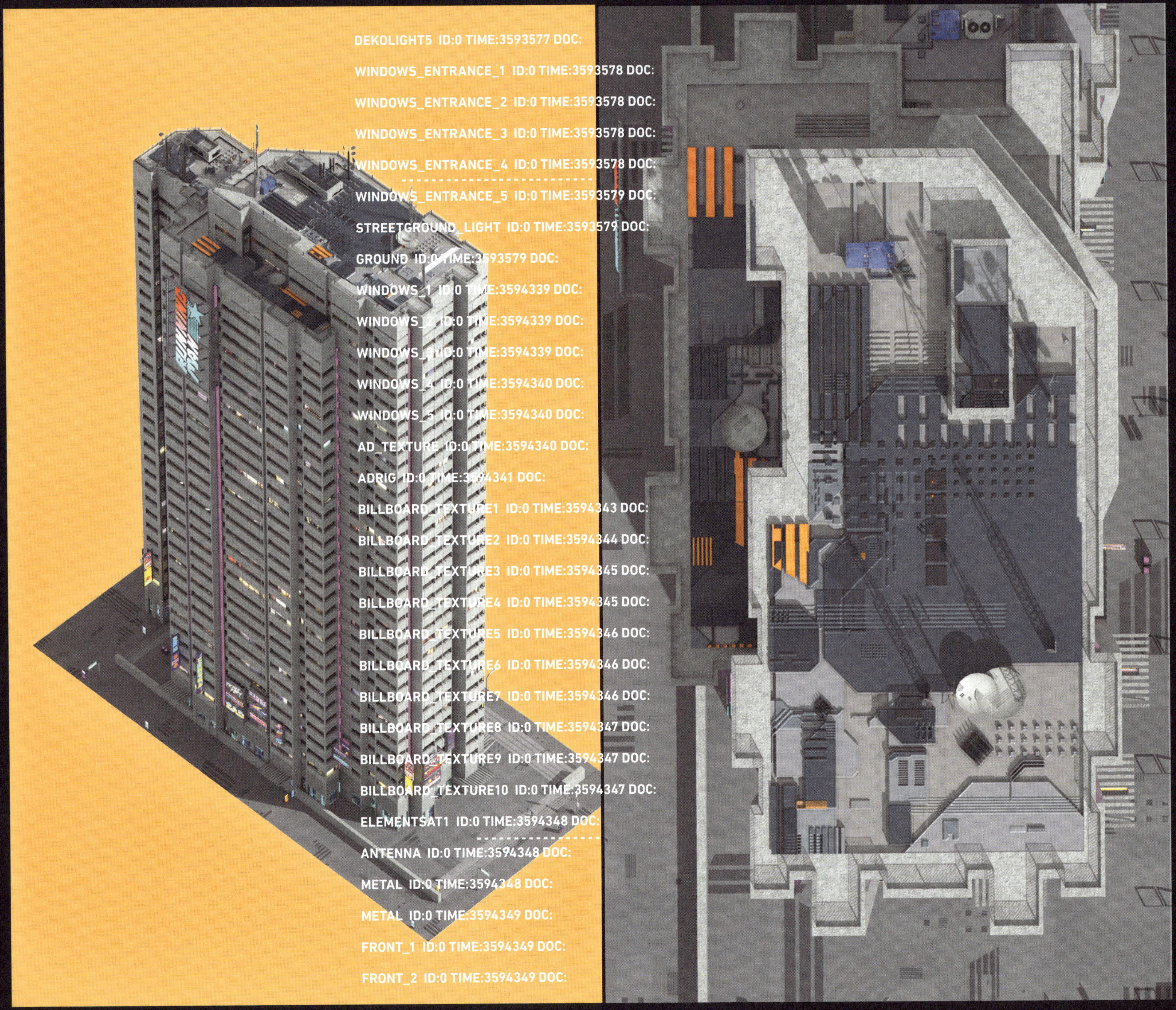
DEKOLIGHT5 ID:0 TIME:3593577 DOC:
WINDOWS_ENTRANCE_1 ID:0 TIME:3593578 DOC:
WINDOWS_ENTRANCE_2 ID:0 TIME:3593578 DOC:
WINDOWS_ENTRANCE_3 ID:0 TIME:3593578 DOC:
WINDOWS_ENTRANCE_4 ID:0 TIME:3593578 DOC:
WINDOWS_ENTRANCE_5 ID:0 TIME:3593579 DOC:
STREETGROUND_LIGHT ID:0 TIME:3593579 DOC:
GROUND ID:0 TIME:3593579 DOC:
WINDOWS_1 ID:0 TIME:3594339 DOC:
WINDOWS_2 ID:0 TIME:3594339 DOC:
WINDOWS_3 ID:0 TIME:3594339 DOC:
WINDOWS_4 ID:0 TIME:3594340 DOC:
WINDOWS_5 ID:0 TIME:3594340 DOC:
AD_TEXTURE ID:0 TIME:3594340 DOC:
ADRIG ID:0 TIME:3594341 DOC:
BILLBOARD_TEXTURE1 ID:0 TIME:3594343 DOC:
BILLBOARD_TEXTURE2 ID:0 TIME:3594344 DOC:
BILLBOARD_TEXTURE3 ID:0 TIME:3594345 DOC:
BILLBOARD_TEXTURE4 ID:0 TIME:3594345 DOC:
BILLBOARD_TEXTURE5 ID:0 TIME:3594346 DOC:
BILLBOARD_TEXTURE6 ID:0 TIME:3594346 DOC:
BILLBOARD_TEXTURE7 ID:0 TIME:3594346 DOC:
BILLBOARD_TEXTURE8 ID:0 TIME:3594347 DOC:
BILLBOARD_TEXTURE9 ID:0 TIME:3594347 DOC:
BILLBOARD_TEXTURE10 ID:0 TIME:3594347 DOC:
ELEMENTSAT1 ID:0 TIME:3594348 DOC:
ANTENNA ID:0 TIME:3594348 DOC:
METAL ID:0 TIME:3594348 DOC:
METAL ID:0 TIME:3594349 DOC:
FRONT_1 ID:0 TIME:3594349 DOC:
FRONT_2 ID:0 TIME:3594349 DOC:

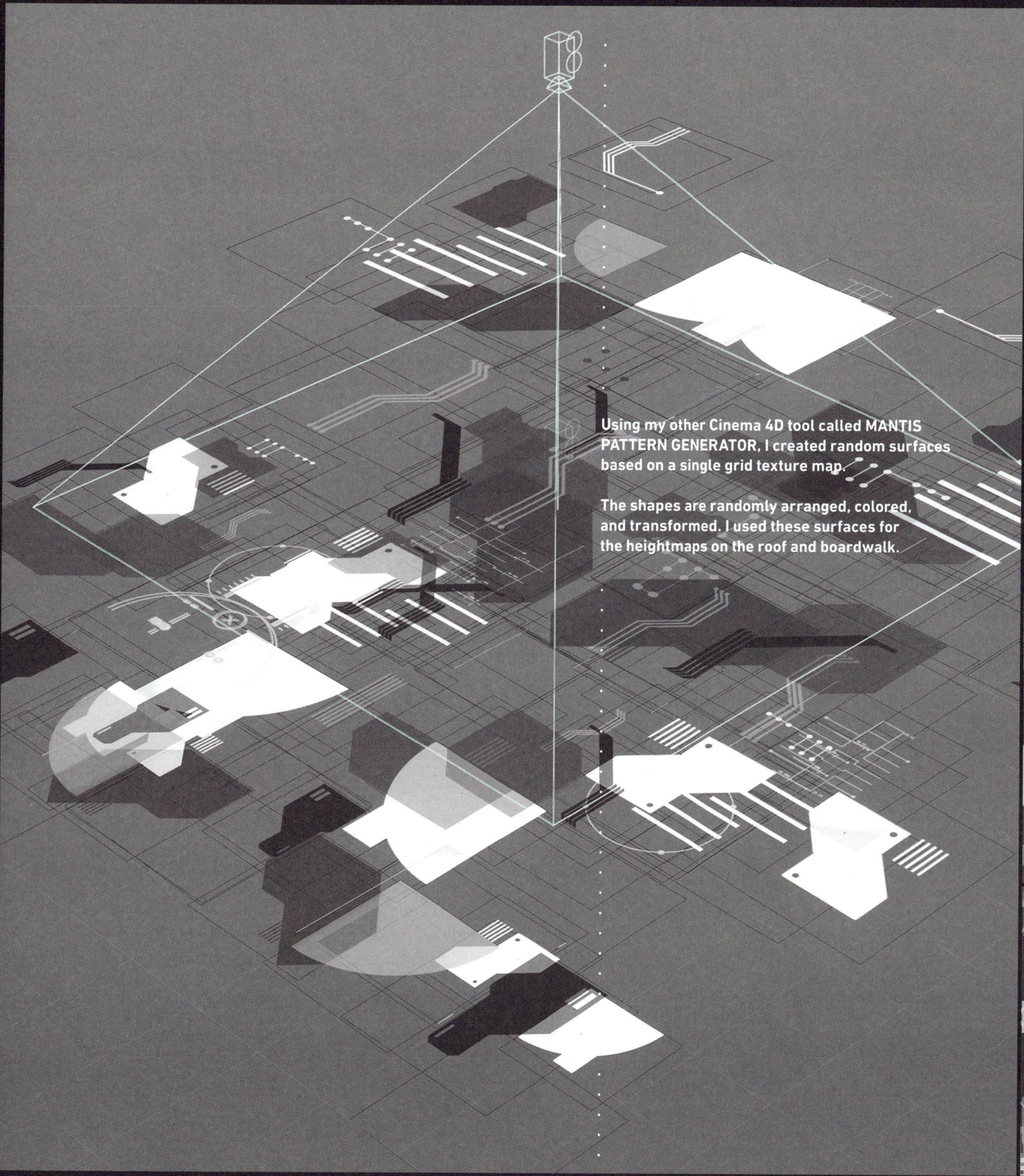
Using my other Cinema 4D tool called MANTIS PATTERN GENERATOR, I created random surfaces based on a single grid texture map.

The shapes are randomly arranged, colored, and transformed. I used these surfaces for the heightmaps on the roof and boardwalk.

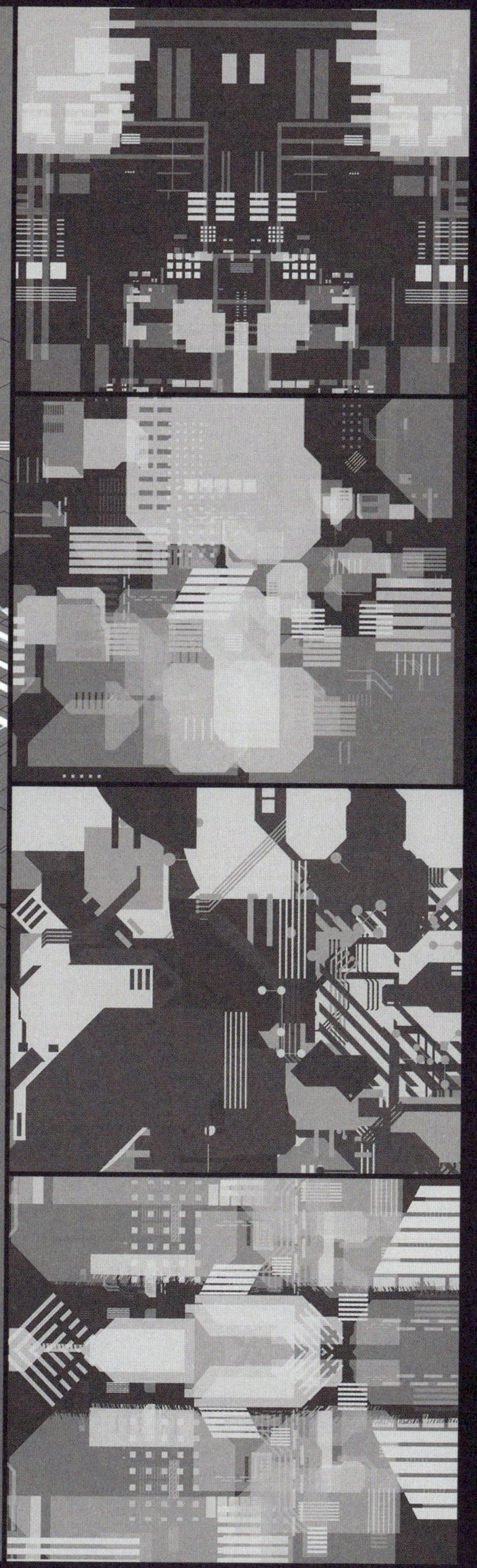

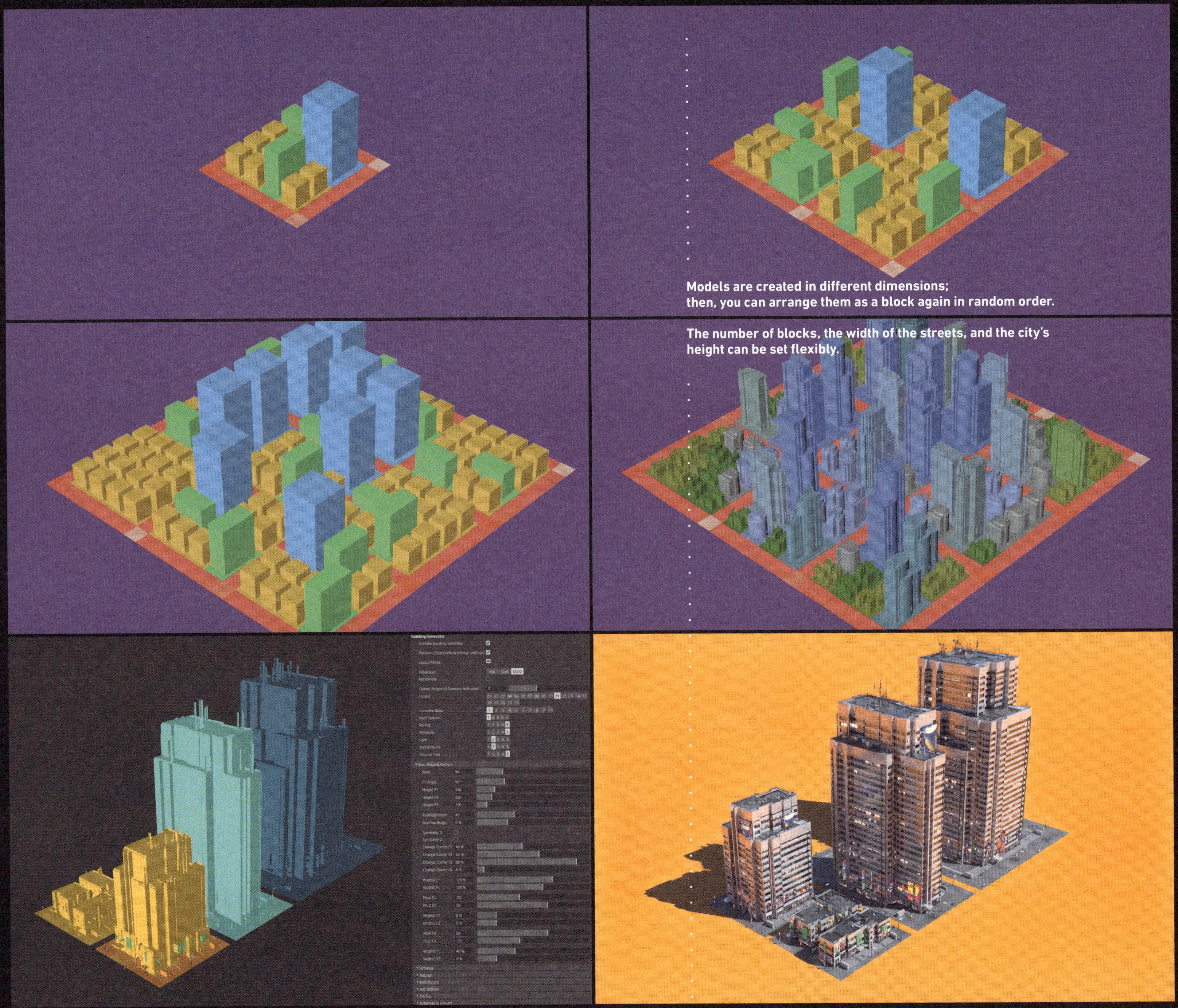

Models are created in different dimensions;
then, you can arrange them as a block again in random order.

The number of blocks, the width of the streets, and the city's height can be set flexibly.

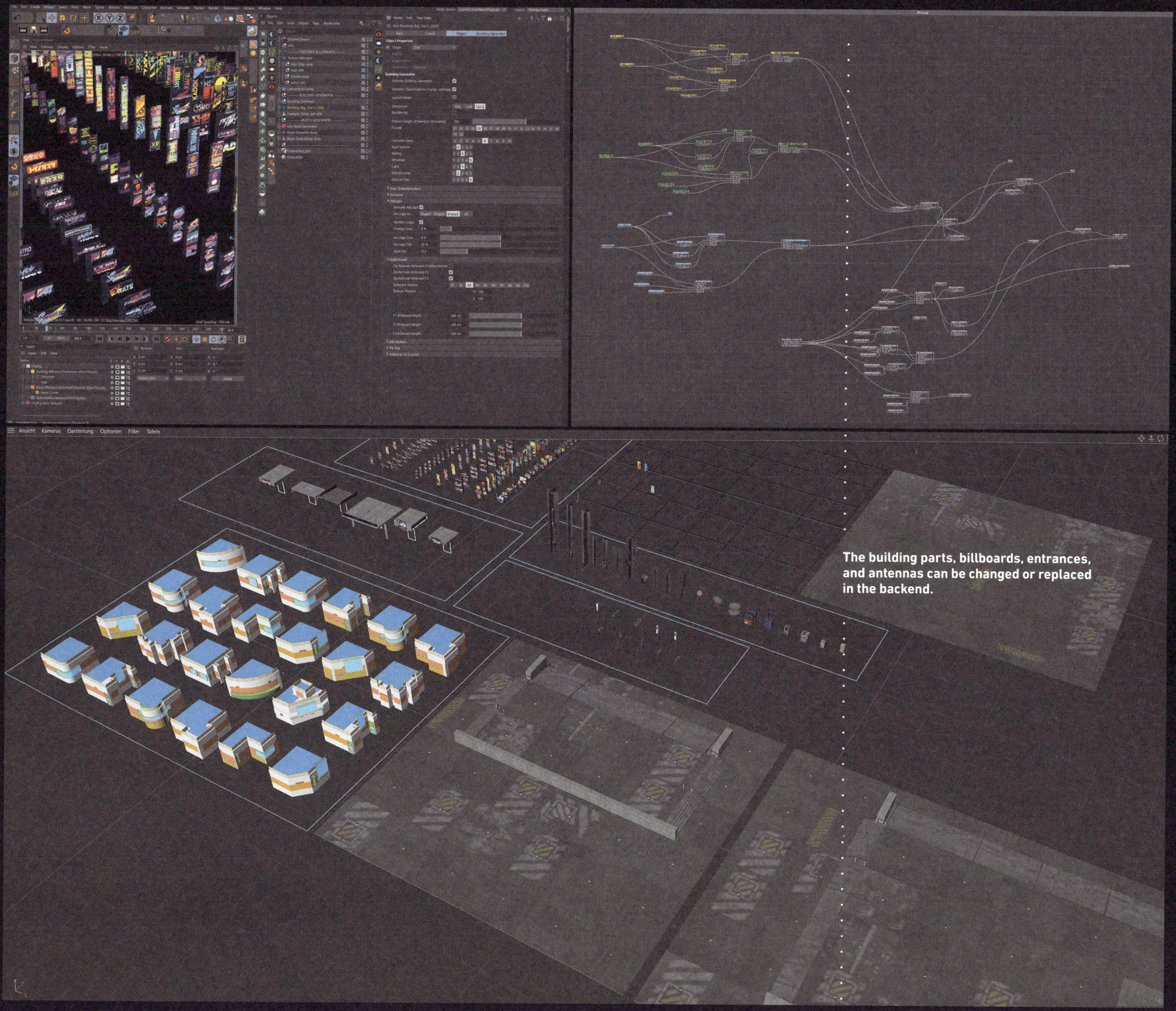

The building parts, billboards, entrances, and antennas can be changed or replaced in the backend.

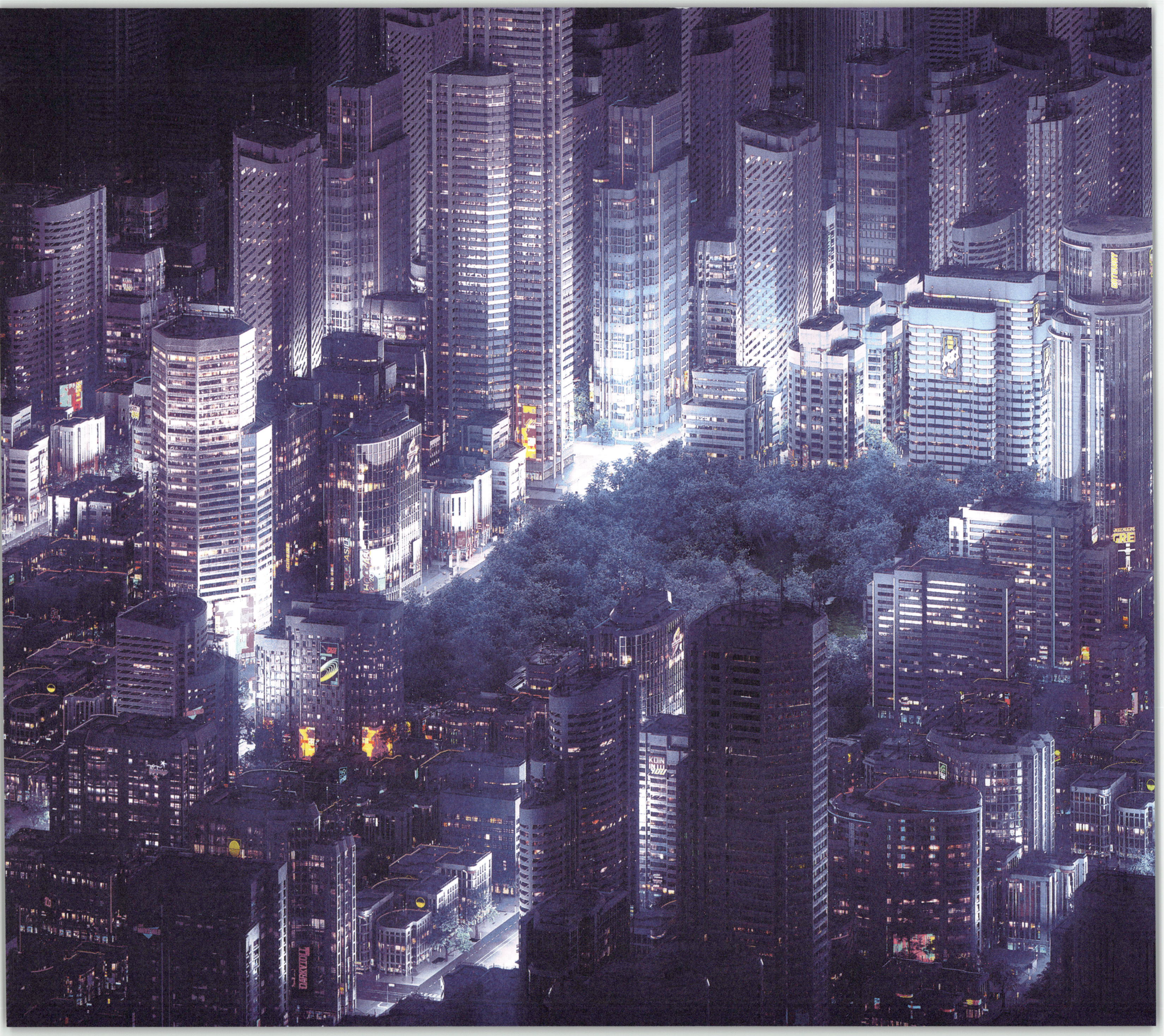

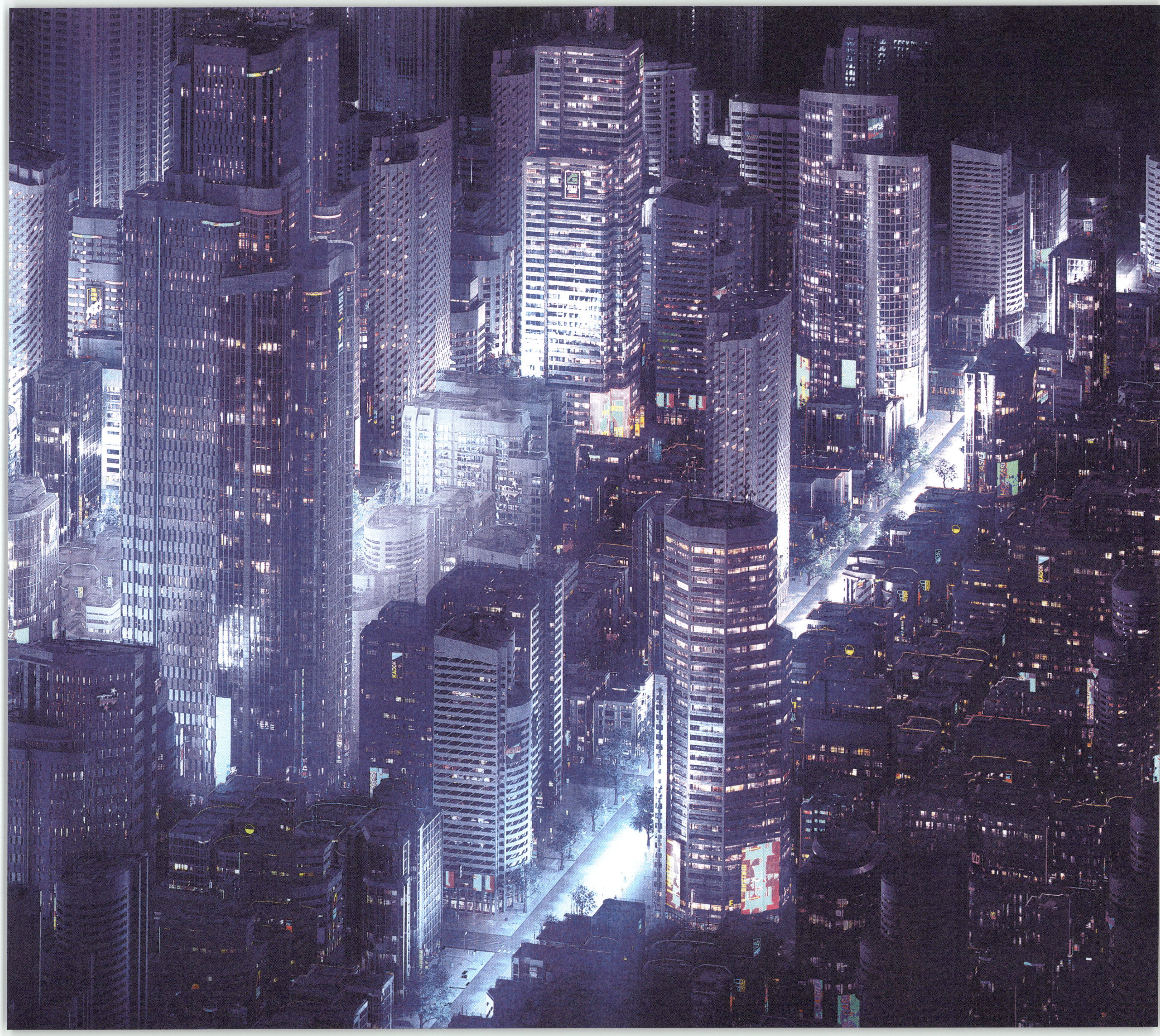

Lotta Stöver

Name:

Lotta Stöver

Info:

Lotta Stöver works as a student and media artist in the Digital Media MA program of the University of the Arts in Bremen.

Her works are driven by a deep interest in the intersections and interdependencies of phenomena and matters aligning, disobeying, transforming, and mutating along with (new) technologies.

She works in various media as installations, electronics, and publications.

Project:

1,000 BEHAVIORS

URL:

lotta-stoever.net

Mail:

hi@lotta-stoever.net

Instagram:

@lotta_stoever

Q&As

Please explain the main idea and what gave the impulse?

1,000 BEHAVIORS is an experimental framework for observing and evolving the movement behaviors of a robot.

The robot consists of nine connected servo motor segments. These perform movements based on generated and processed data to find its most optimized behaviors.

One impulse came from Karl Sims' work Evolved Virtual Creatures (1994). And one from the current trend around machine learning, which are both things that I find fascinating and do not; especially, consider the body.

What challenges did you face for this project? And what surprises?

Real-time is a big challenge for this work, because evolution is usually such an unimaginable slow process.

But then again, I think the work can be surprisingly accessible; it is a robotic snake that moves, adjusting its movement behaviors over time, based on external input.

Please describe the technical environment.

Generations, behaviors, and units structure the movement data of the robot snake.

For each new generation, the robot tests all behaviors by performing the prescribed movement in a certain amount of time.

After testing is complete, the behaviors are sorted by their ratings and then mutated and recombined so that 1,000 new behaviors can then be generated.

In this process, the robot's behaviors are consistently evolving, influenced by many observers; the framework and the robot itself.

Tell us about your aesthetical approach.

Functional, minimal, and robust.

What's next? Your vision?

I want to invite the robot to live with my girlfriend and me in our home in the near future.

Maybe in the role of a pet, who gets to pick up the newspaper for us in symbiotic exchange for petting and a battery refill.

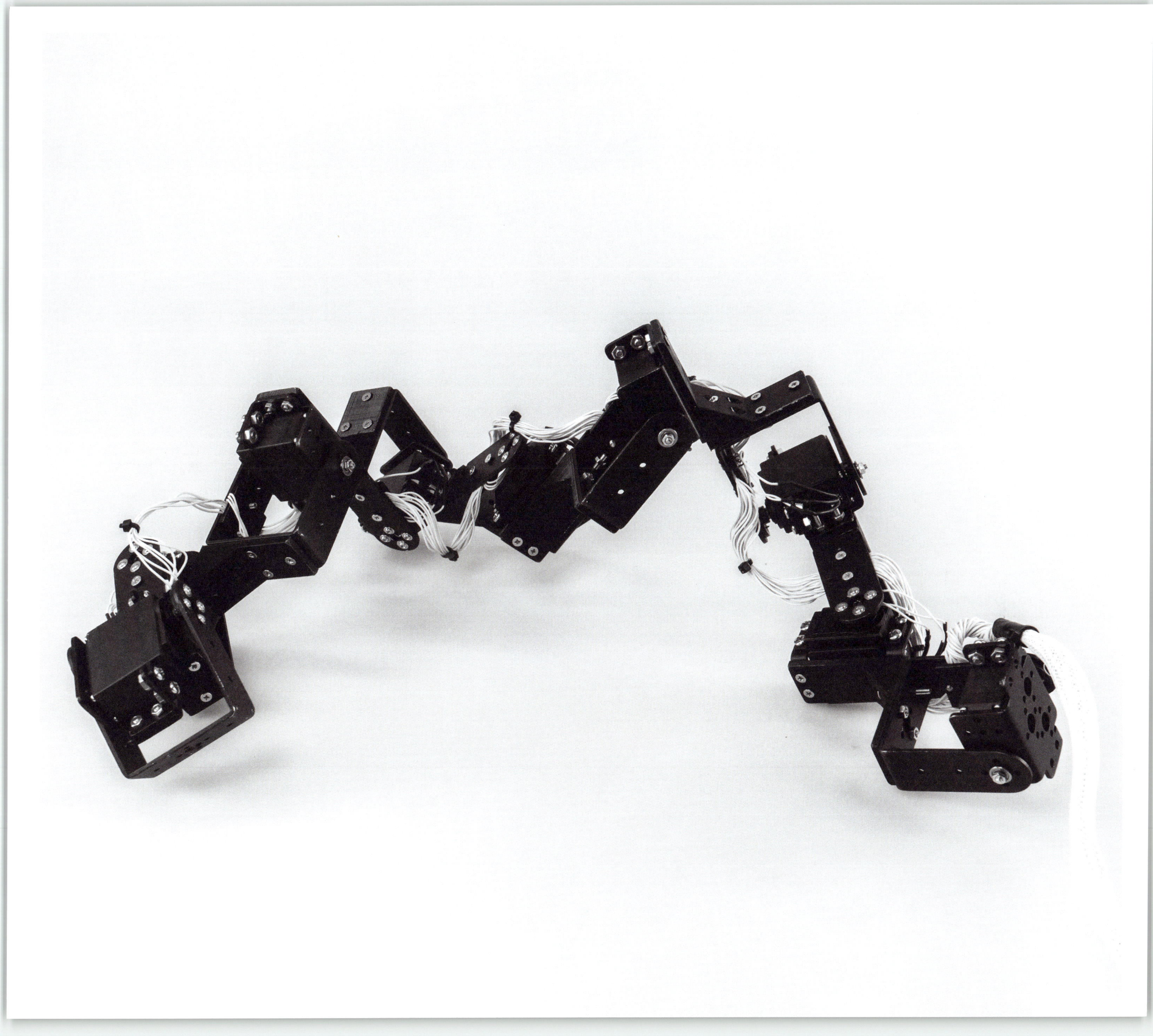

While thinking and prototyping the robot, I imagined various body shapes.

Still, after all, I chose what seemed to be the simplest form of a robotic body; multiple motors connected in series by rigid 3D-printed parts.

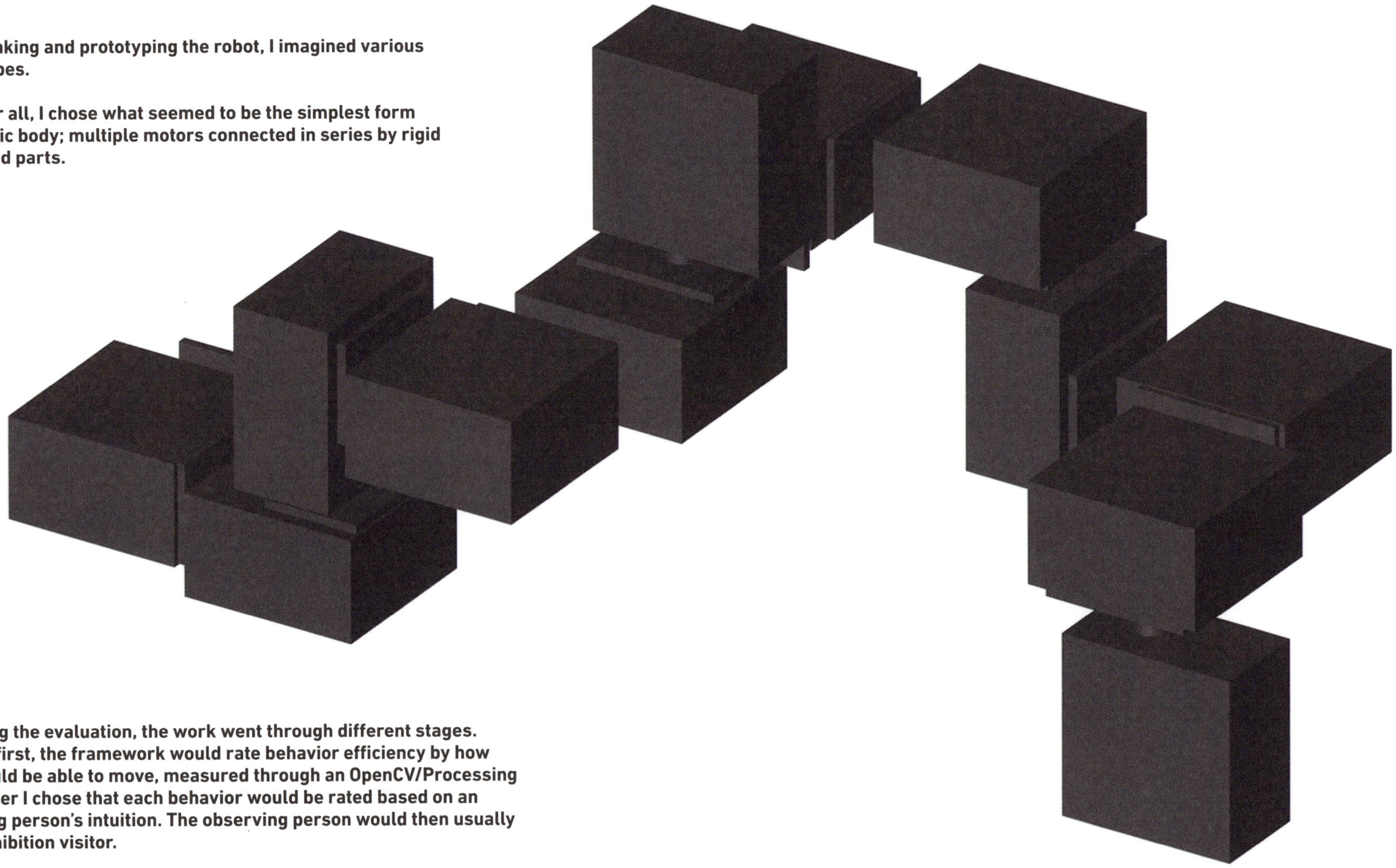

Regarding the evaluation, the work went through different stages. While at first, the framework would rate behavior efficiency by how far it would be able to move, measured through an OpenCV/Processing setup, later I chose that each behavior would be rated based on an observing person's intuition. The observing person would then usually be an exhibition visitor.

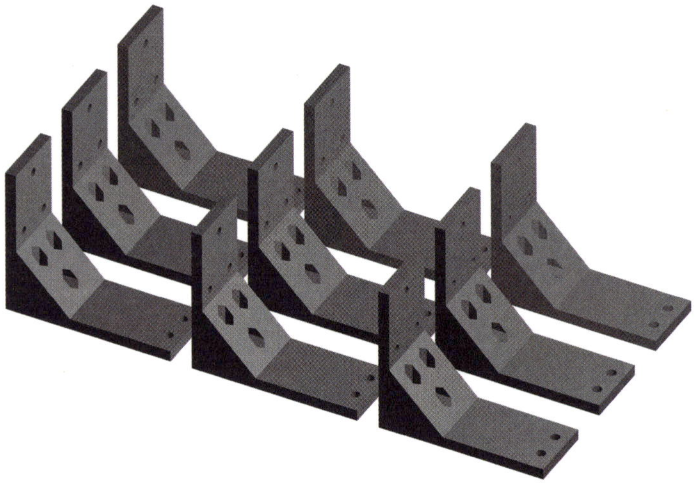

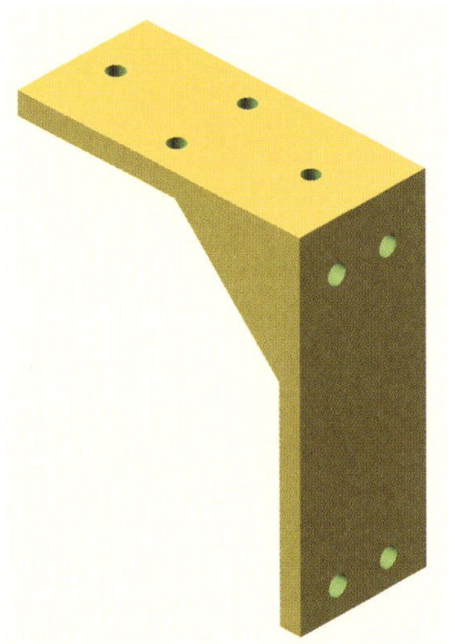

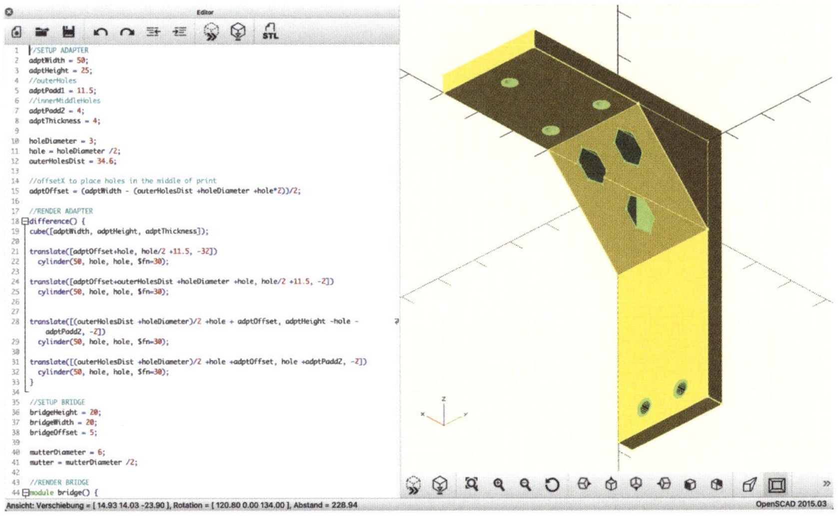

```
import processing.serial.*; //import the Serial library
import controlP5.*;

Serial myPort;  //the Serial port object
boolean firstContact = false;
String val;

ControlP5 cp5;

String[] lines;
ArrayList<Set> sets = new ArrayList<Set>();

int activeSet = 0;
boolean clicked = false;
float freq_factor = 0.005;
int max_lim = 160;
float scale = 4.1;

int PREPARE = 1, BEHAVIOR = 2, PERFORM = 3, FEEDBACK = 4;
int MODE = 0;

int padding = 30;
float timer = 0;
boolean started = false, finished = false;

float knob, button;

String prepareMassage = "";

float performTime = 5;
float performStart = 0;

void setup() {

  readData();

  for ( int i = 0; i < Serial.list().length; i++ ) {
    println( Serial.list()[i] );
  }
  myPort = new Serial(this, Serial.list()[2], 9600);
  myPort.bufferUntil('\n');

  cp5 = new ControlP5(this);

  prepareMassage += "Carefully place the robot in the middle of the Platform.\n\n";
  prepareMassage += "Assemble the cables so that they will not interfere\nwith the robots movements\n\n";
  prepareMassage += "Please rate this behavior afterwards.\n\n";
  prepareMassage += "Your rating will be saved and considered\nfor further generations.";

  size(480, 320);
  textSize(16);

  noCursor();

}

void draw() {
  timer += 1/frameRate;
  background(0);

  fill(255);
```

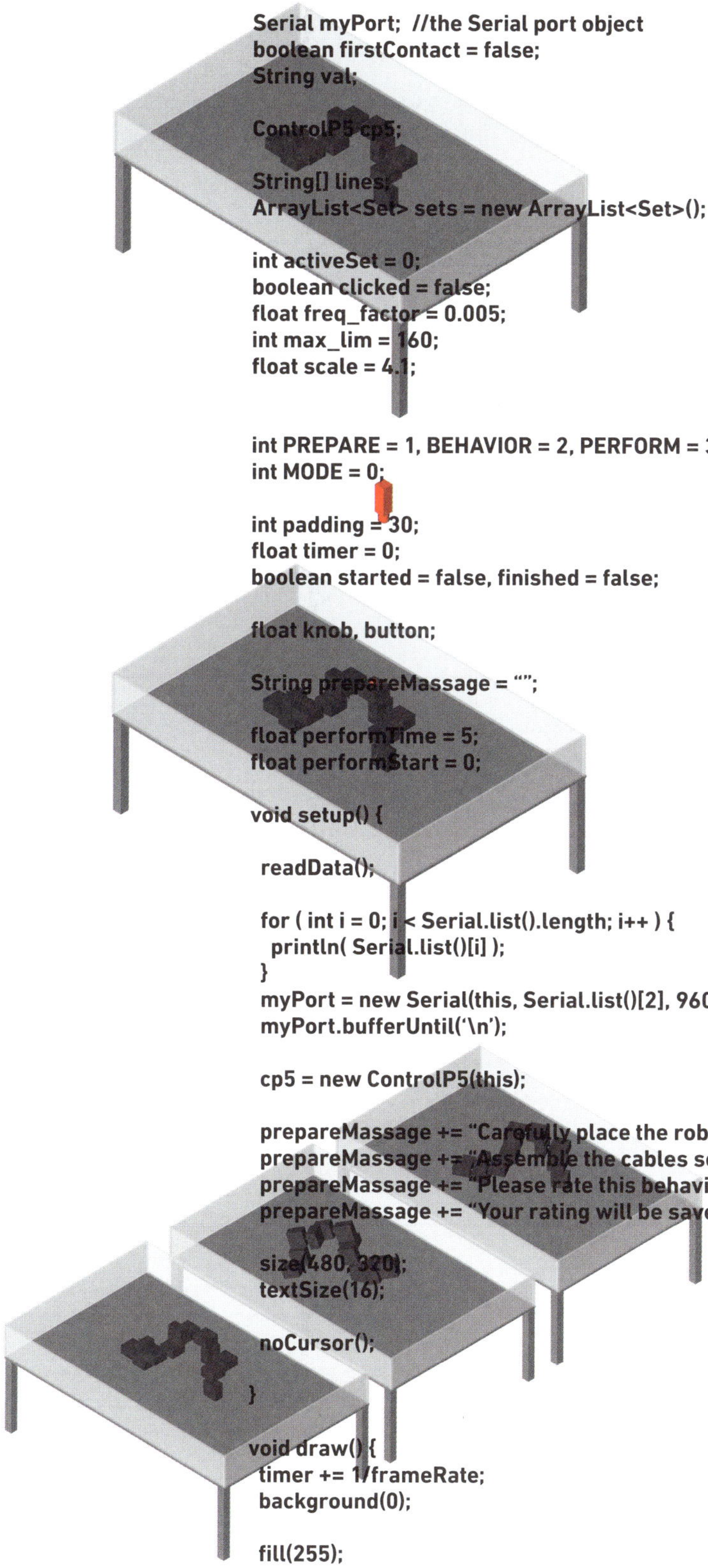

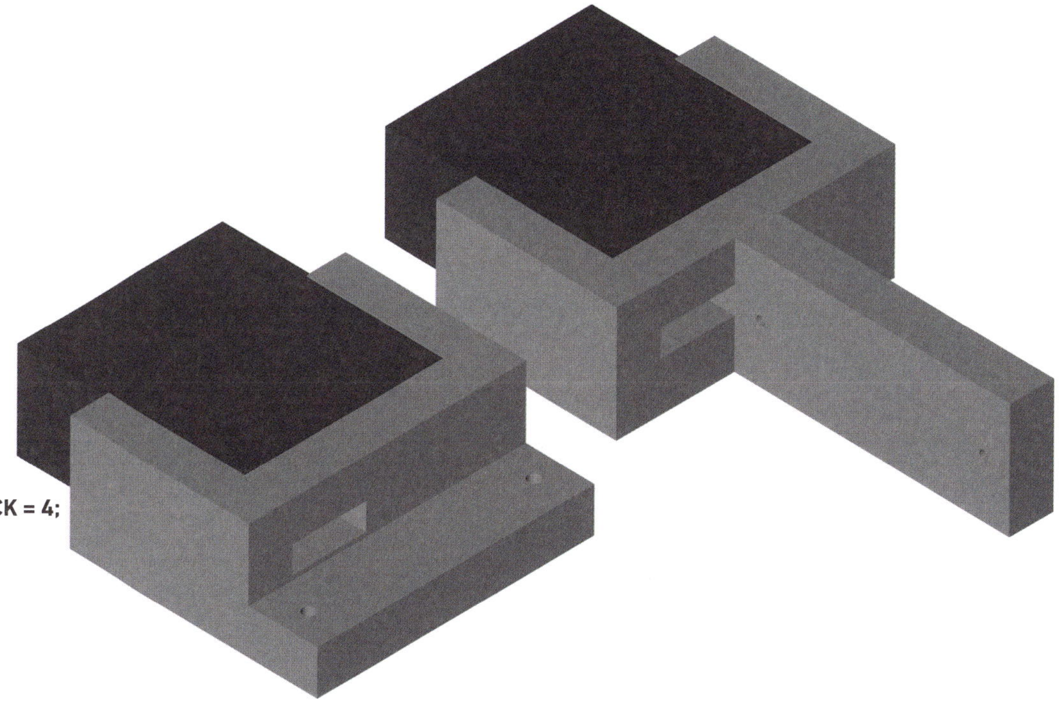

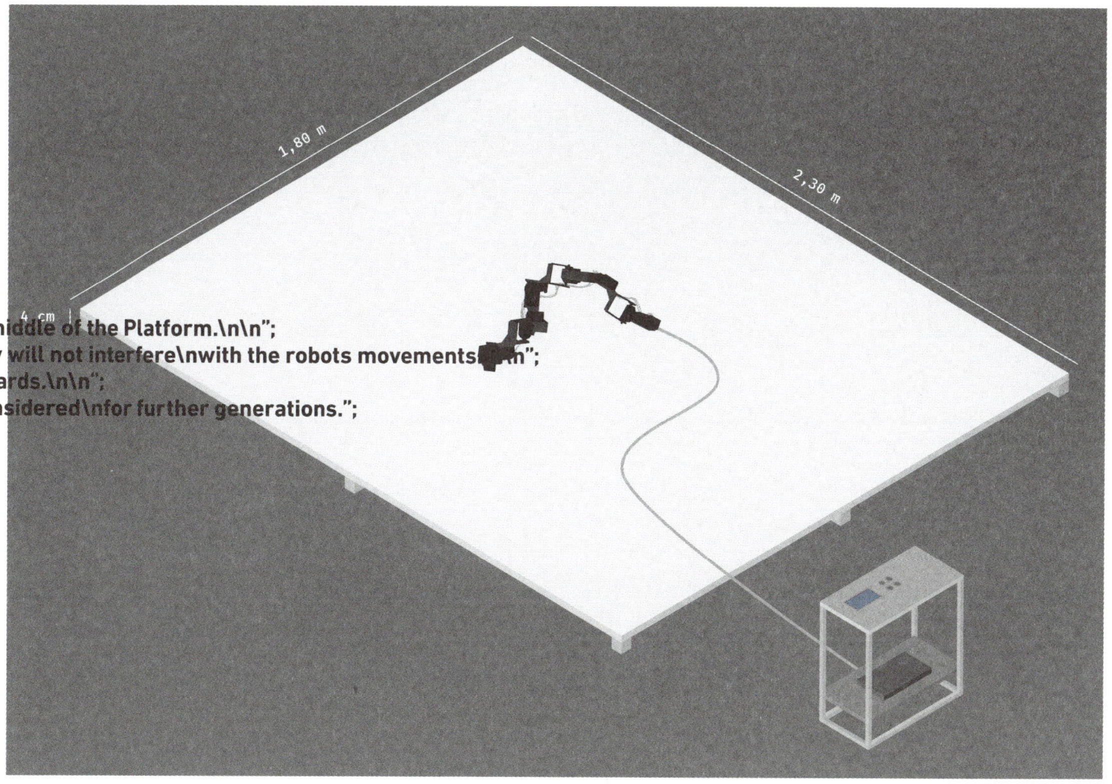

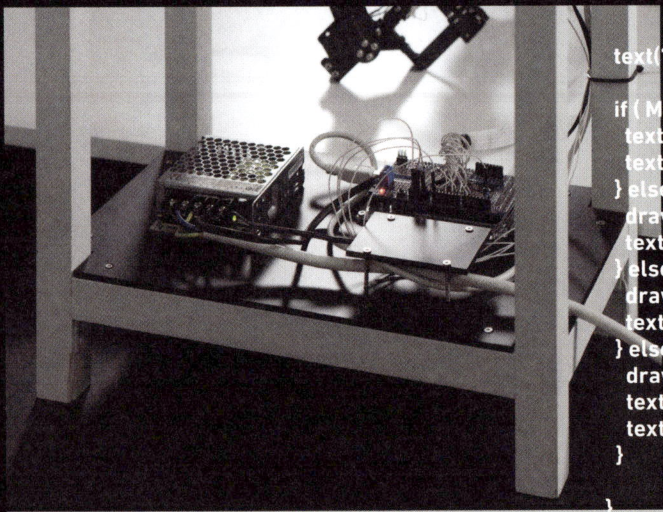

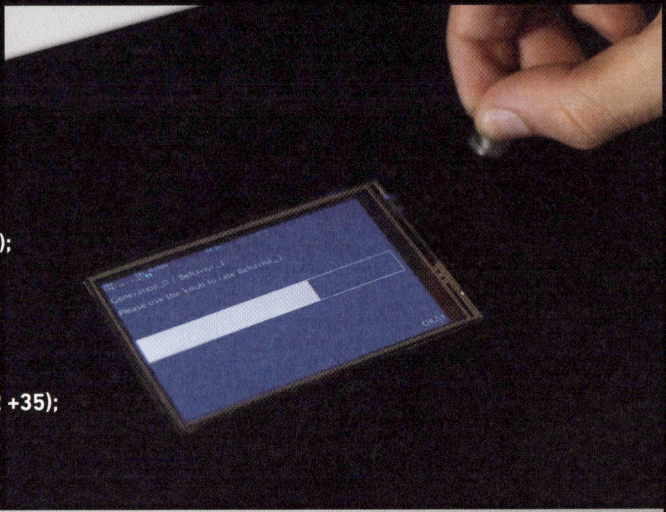

```
text("Generation_0 / Behavior_" +activeSet, 0, padding +25);

 if ( MODE == PREPARE ) {
   text(prepareMassage, 0, padding*2 +45);
   text("OKAY", width -padding -25, height -10);
 } else if ( MODE == BEHAVIOR ) {
   drawBehaviorInformation();
   text("START BEHAVIOR_" +activeSet, width -padding -132, height -10);
 } else if ( MODE == PERFORM ) {
   drawPerformInformation();
   text("Performing Behavior_" +activeSet, 0, padding*2 +35);
 } else if ( MODE == FEEDBACK ) {
   drawFeedbackInformation();
   text("Please use the knob to rate Behavior_" +activeSet, 0, padding*2 +35);
   text("OKAY", width -padding -25, height -10);
 }

}
```

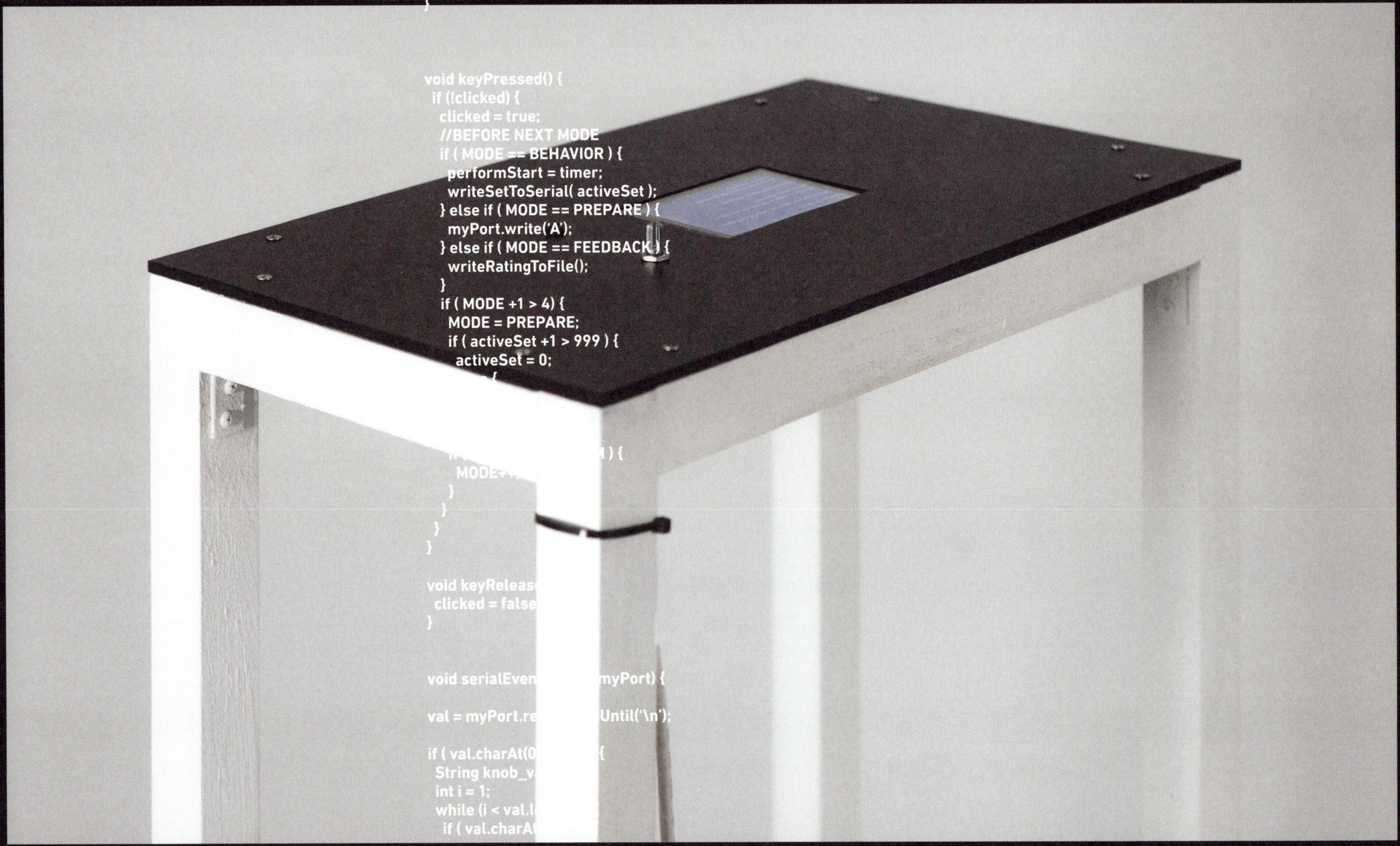

```
void keyPressed() {
 if (!clicked) {
   clicked = true;
   //BEFORE NEXT MODE
   if ( MODE == BEHAVIOR ) {
     performStart = timer;
     writeSetToSerial( activeSet );
   } else if ( MODE == PREPARE ) {
     myPort.write('A');
   } else if ( MODE == FEEDBACK ) {
     writeRatingToFile();
   }
   if ( MODE +1 > 4) {
     MODE = PREPARE;
     if ( activeSet +1 > 999 ) {
       activeSet = 0;
         {

     if (                    M ) {
       MODE++;
     }
   }
 }
}

void keyReleas
 clicked = false
}


void serialEven          myPort) {

val = myPort.re          Until('\n');

if ( val.charAt(0          {
 String knob_v
 int i = 1;
 while (i < val.l
   if ( val.charAt
```

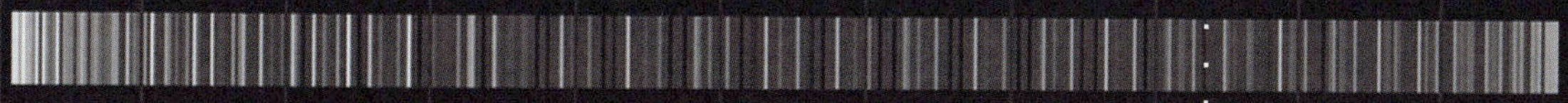

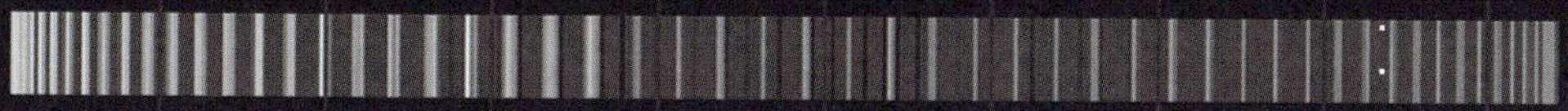

Even though the conceptualization and execution of the work took me a long time, its working principle remains pretty simple. The installation comes together with one Raspberry Pi, an Arduino Mega, and nine servo motors.

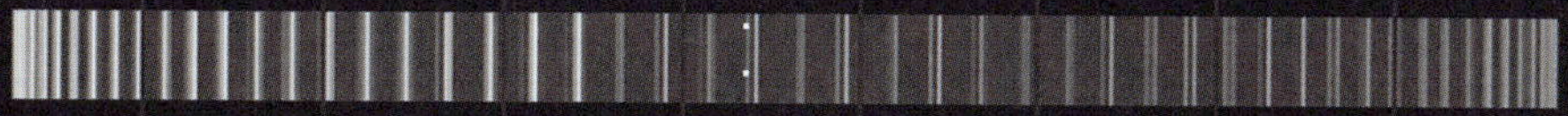

The Raspberry Pi runs a Processing sketch, reading behaviors from an SD-card, iterating through all; sending individual data via Serial to the Arduino.

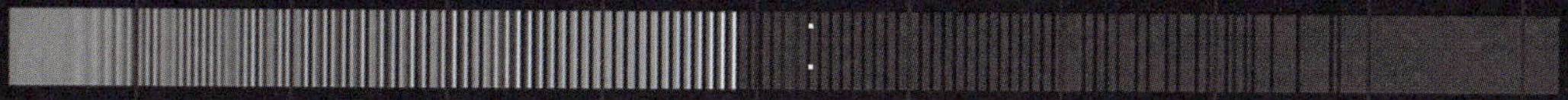

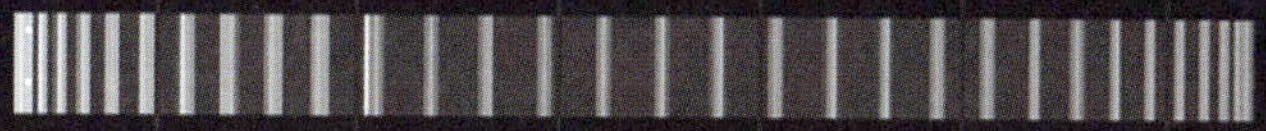

The Arduino parses the data, drives the servo motors, later reads out the rating of each behavior, and then sends the rating back to the Raspberry Pi.

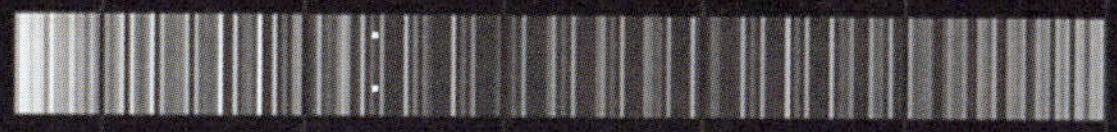

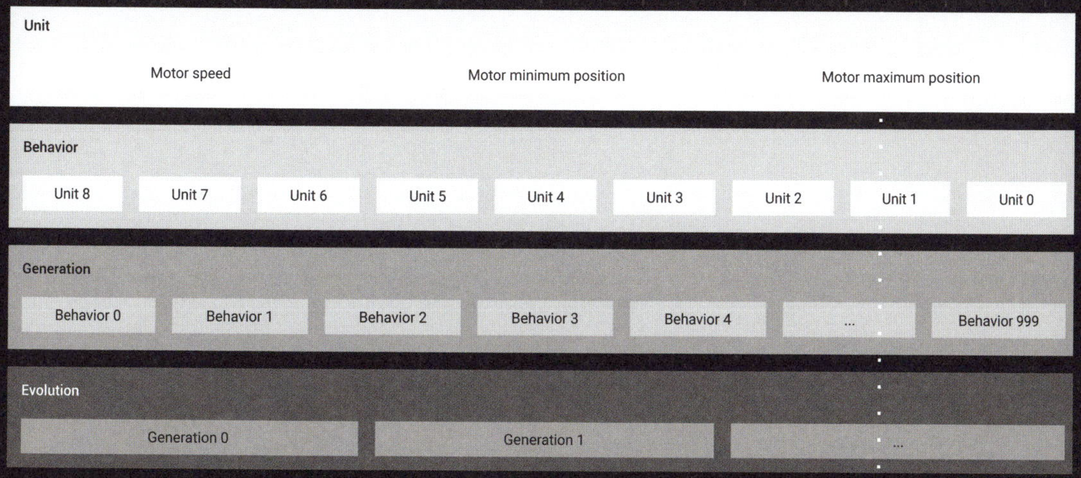

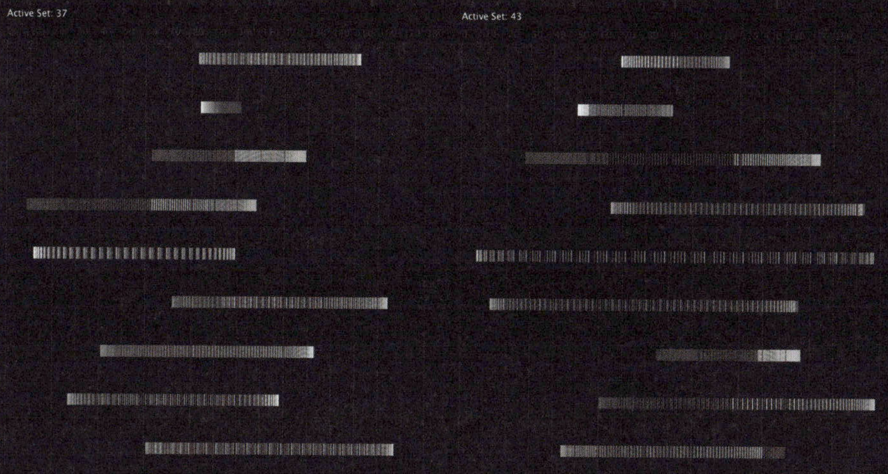

343 . 1,000 BEHAVIORS

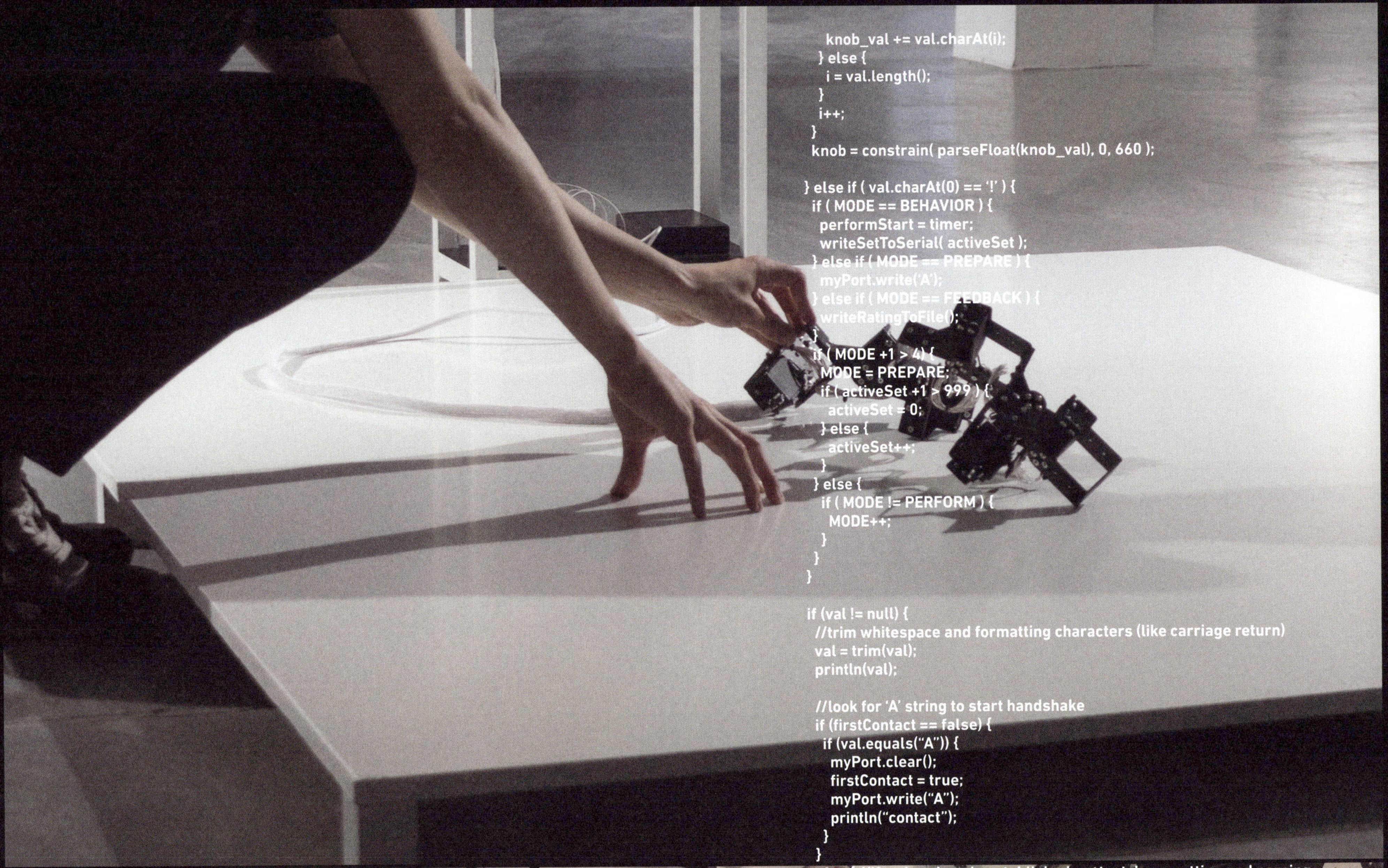

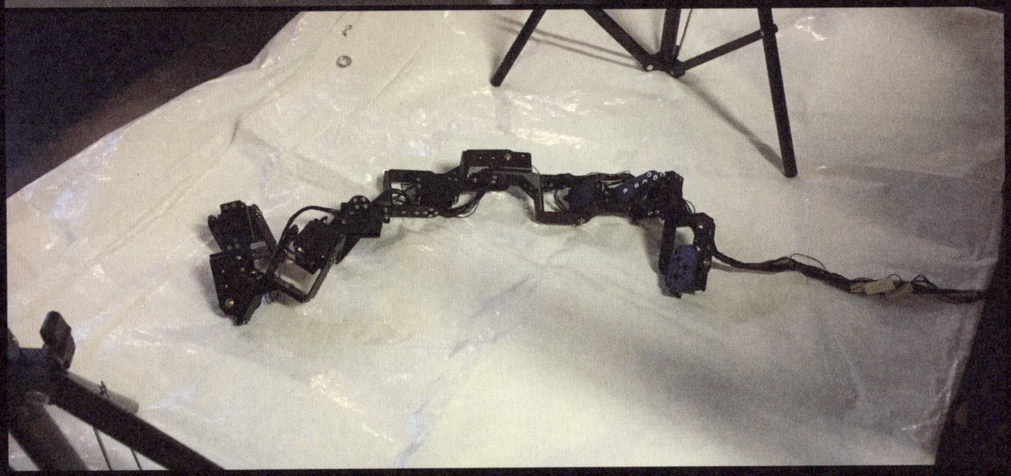

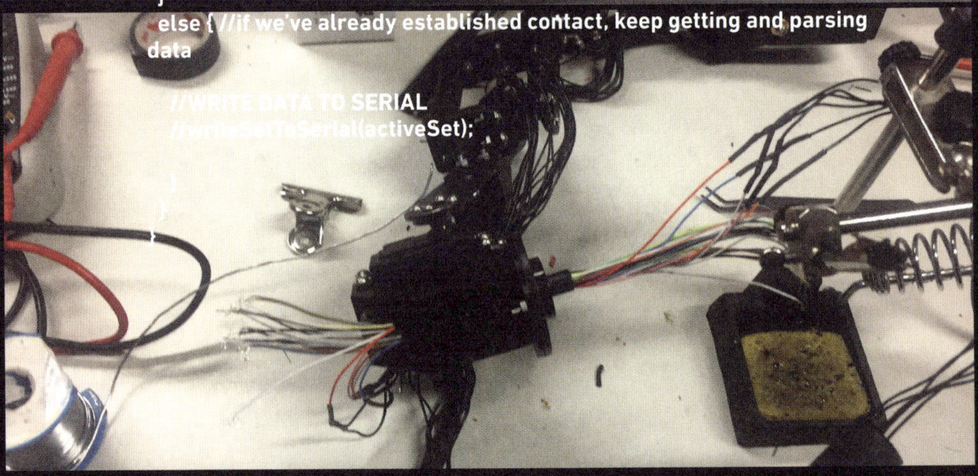

```
    knob_val += val.charAt(i);
   } else {
    i = val.length();
   }
   i++;
  }
  knob = constrain( parseFloat(knob_val), 0, 660 );

} else if ( val.charAt(0) == '!' ) {
  if ( MODE == BEHAVIOR ) {
   performStart = timer;
   writeSetToSerial( activeSet );
  } else if ( MODE == PREPARE ) {
   myPort.write('A');
  } else if ( MODE == FEEDBACK ) {
   writeRatingToFile();
  }
  if ( MODE +1 > 4) {
   MODE = PREPARE;
   if ( activeSet +1 > 999 ) {
    activeSet = 0;
   } else {
    activeSet++;
   }
  } else {
   if ( MODE != PERFORM ) {
    MODE++;
   }
  }
}

if (val != null) {
  //trim whitespace and formatting characters (like carriage return)
  val = trim(val);
  println(val);

  //look for 'A' string to start handshake
  if (firstContact == false) {
   if (val.equals("A")) {
    myPort.clear();
    firstContact = true;
    myPort.write("A");
    println("contact");
   }
  }
  else { //if we've already established contact, keep getting and parsing
data

   //WRITE DATA TO SERIAL
   //writeSetToSerial(activeSet);

   }
  }
}
```

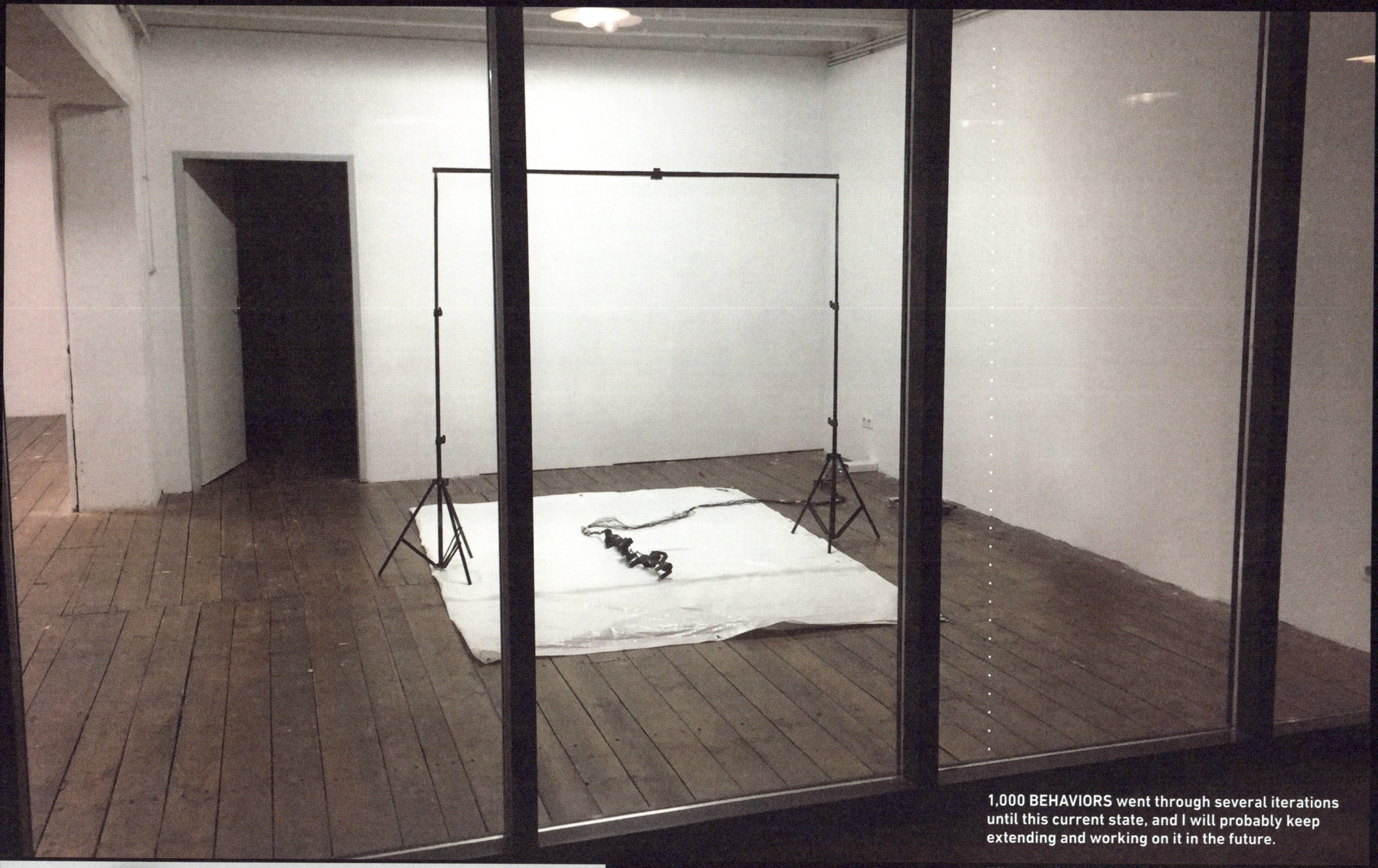

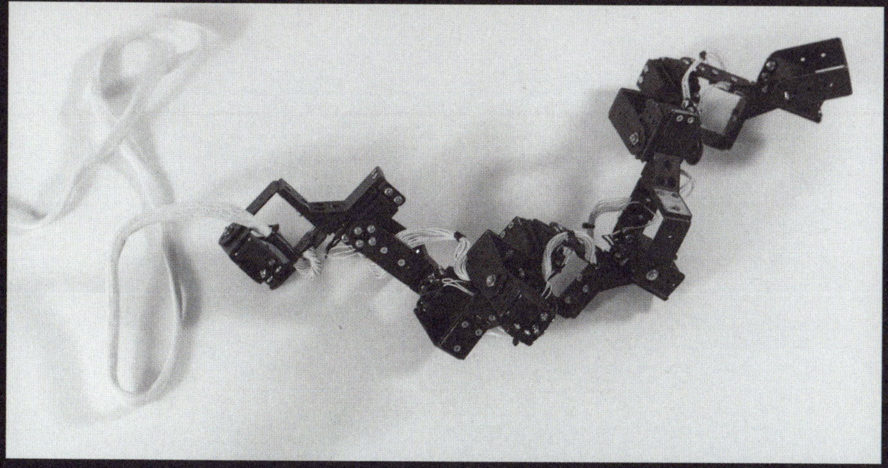

1,000 BEHAVIORS went through several iterations until this current state, and I will probably keep extending and working on it in the future.

When I exhibited the installation in Osnabrück during EMAF 2019, this was a thrilling moment for me because it was the first time that visitors would interact with the robot.

They observed and rated many behaviors and took excellent care of the robot.

If, for example, the robot managed to leave the platform, the visitors were instructed to carefully place it back in the middle of the platform, which worked out well, and I was thrilled to observe this.

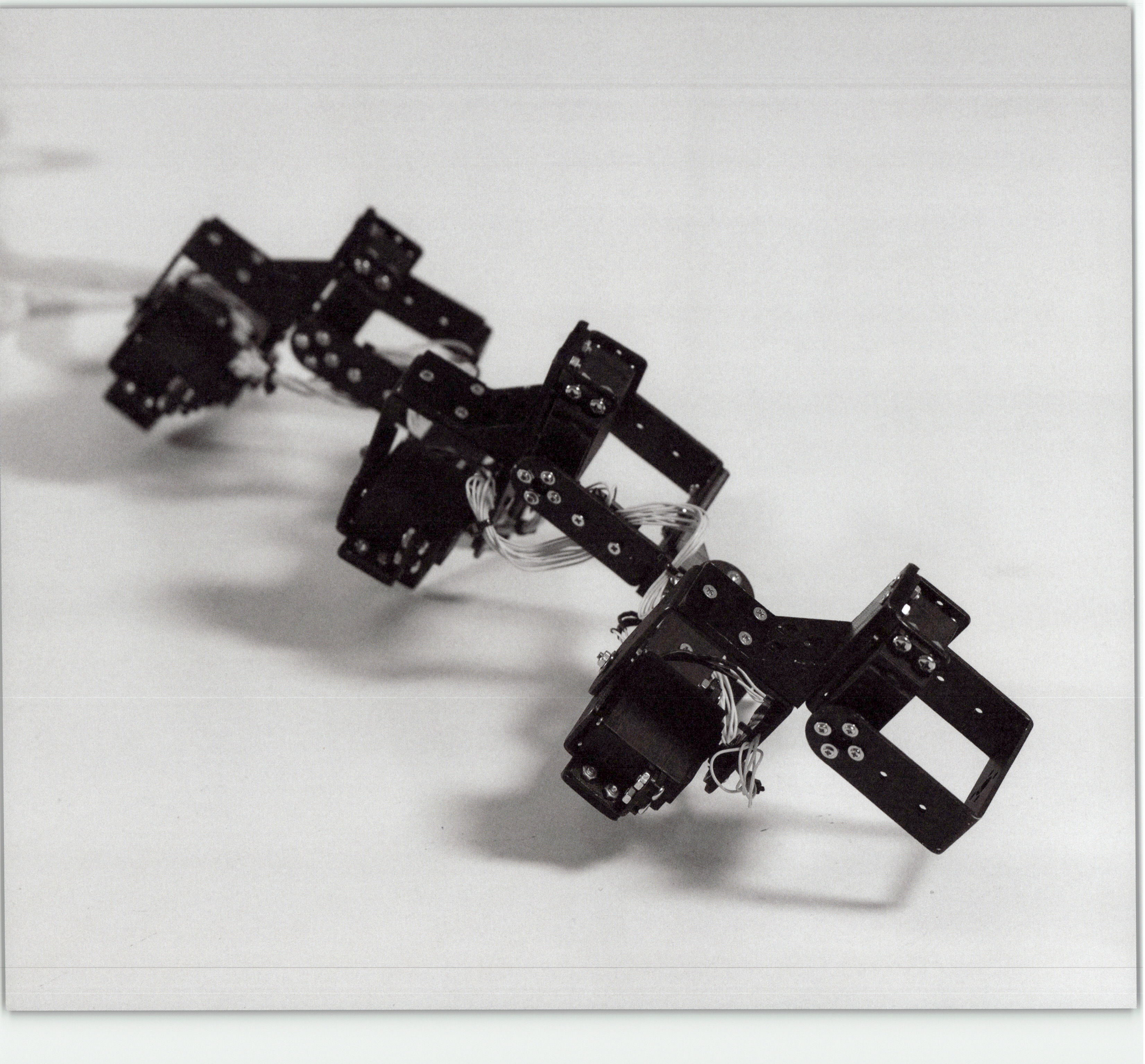

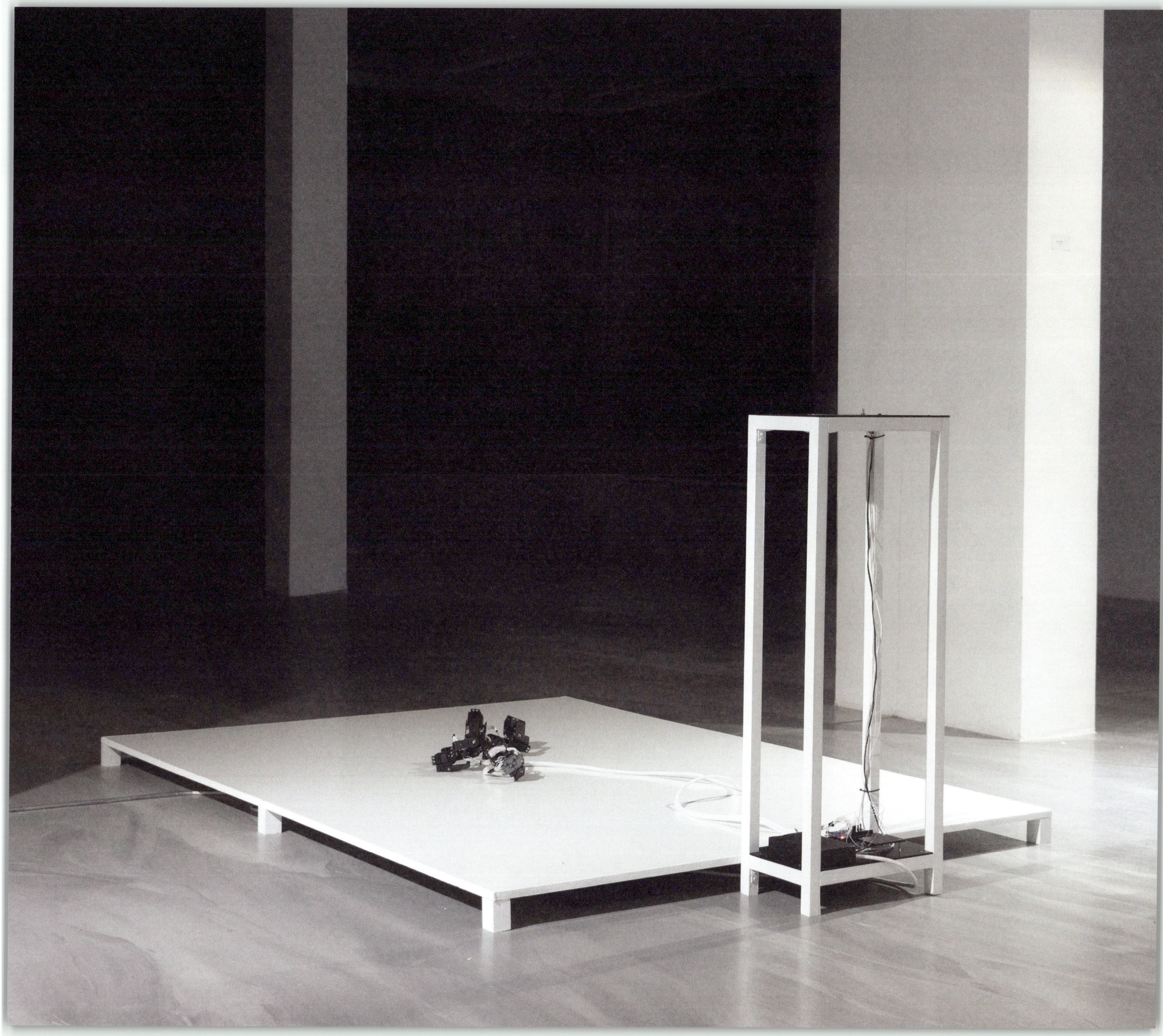

Name:

David Sheldon-Hicks
Founder & Exec. Creative Director
Territory Studio

Info:

Territory Studio is an atelier with a unique approach to motion design, visual effects, and digital experiences. Drawing on the deep expertise of narrative design for film, games, and brands, we blend creativity with technology to realize compelling future-facing experiences.

Working across diverse briefs, what ties our work together is a love of craft and creativity, a passion for story, and a designer's eye for problem-solving. What sets us apart is our uniquely advanced design intelligence and near future expertise. We are a team of ambitious, focused, and proactive cross discipline creatives.

Our clients span entertainment, culture, commercial, and technology sectors with growing studios in London and San Francisco.

URL:

territorystudio.com

Mail:

hello@territorystudio.com

Instagram:

@territorystudio

References:

. . . . . Screen Graphics

Ad Astra
Blade Runner 2049
Watchmen
Marvel's Avengers:
Infinity War
Endgame
Age of Ultron
Alex Rider
Avenue 5
The Martian
Project Power
Guardians of the Galaxy
Ex Machina
Le Chant du Loup
Detective Pikachu
Watchroom
Nightflyers
Mile 22
Hunter Killer
Electric Dreams
Johnny English strikes again
American Assassin
Tom Clancy's Jack Ryan
Jupiter Ascending
Mission Impossible – Rogue Nation
Spy
Prometheus
Zero Dark Thirty
...

. . . . . Design & VFX

Brave New World
Spider-Man: Far from Home
Mindhunter
Ready Player One
Men in Black: International
Project Power
Eurovision Song Contest:
The Story of Fire Saga
Ghost in the Shell
Shanghai Fortress
Black Mirror
Pacific Rim: Uprising
The OA Part II
A-X-L
2036 Origin Unknown
Year Million
Miles
...

Territory Studio

Conversation with David Sheldon-Hicks

THE NARRATIVE OF A TANGIBLE A.I.

There is a moment coming soon when a volumetric data space can augment the physical world.

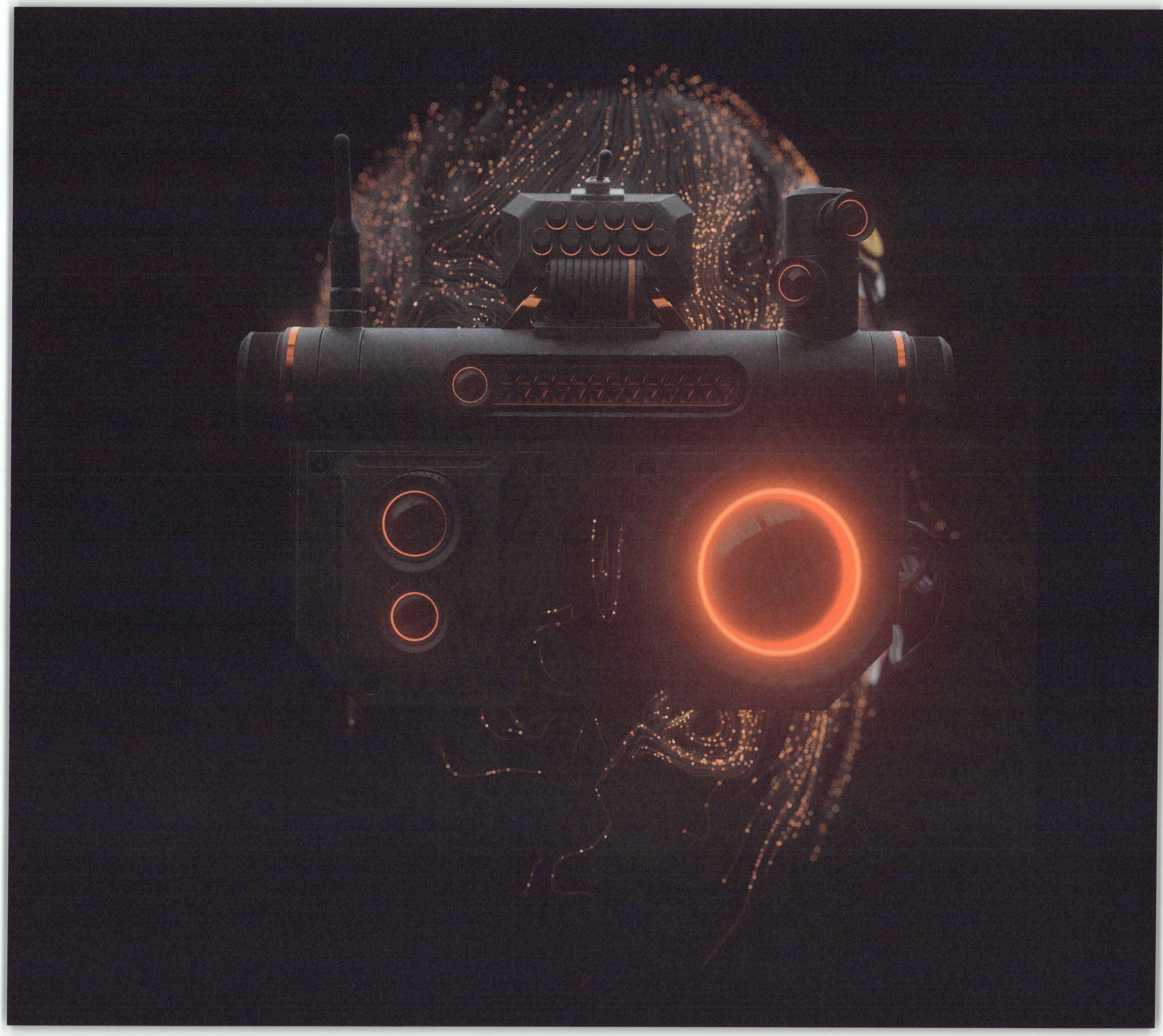

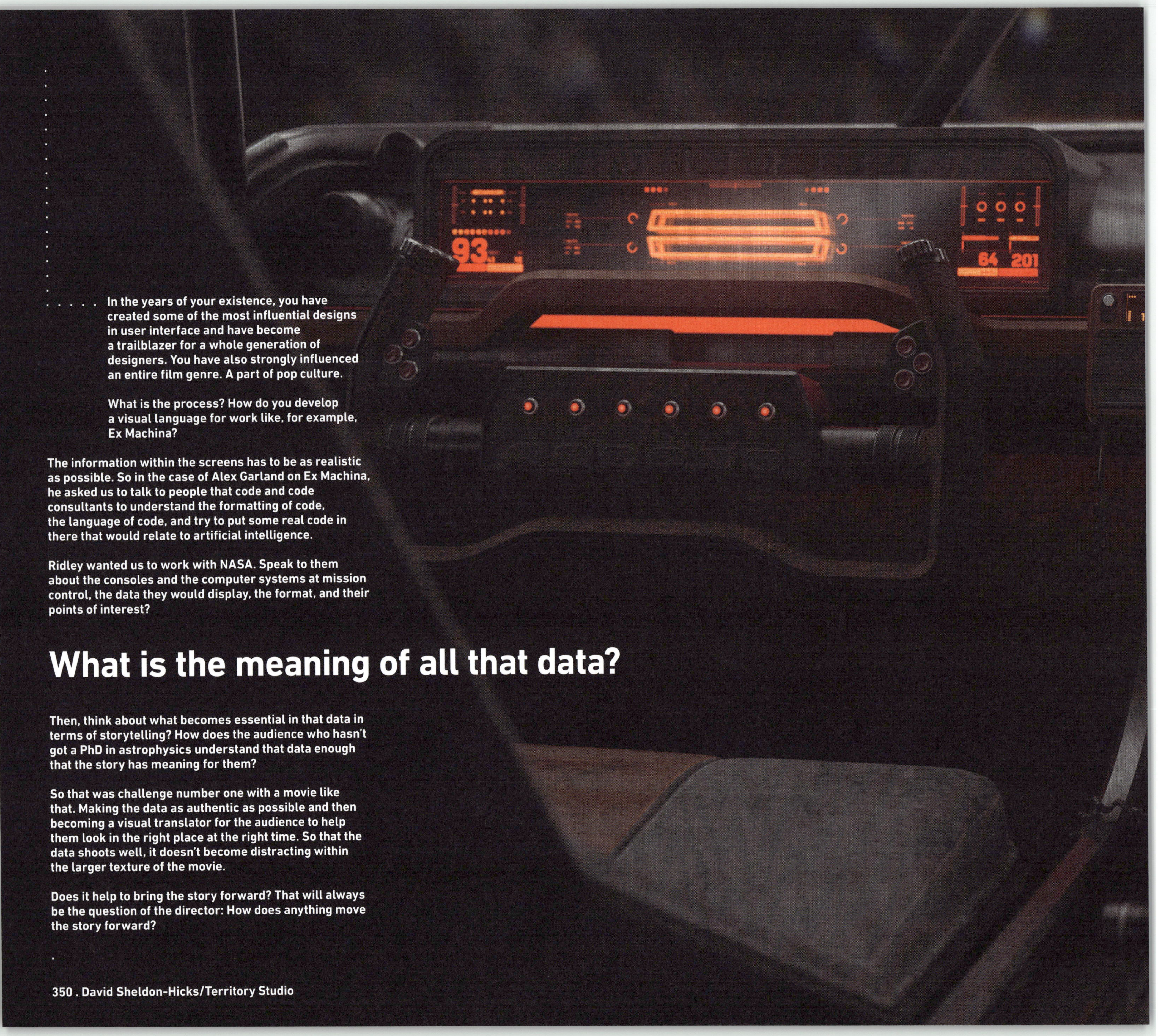

In the years of your existence, you have created some of the most influential designs in user interface and have become a trailblazer for a whole generation of designers. You have also strongly influenced an entire film genre. A part of pop culture.

What is the process? How do you develop a visual language for work like, for example, Ex Machina?

The information within the screens has to be as realistic as possible. So in the case of Alex Garland on Ex Machina, he asked us to talk to people that code and code consultants to understand the formatting of code, the language of code, and try to put some real code in there that would relate to artificial intelligence.

Ridley wanted us to work with NASA. Speak to them about the consoles and the computer systems at mission control, the data they would display, the format, and their points of interest?

What is the meaning of all that data?

Then, think about what becomes essential in that data in terms of storytelling? How does the audience who hasn't got a PhD in astrophysics understand that data enough that the story has meaning for them?

So that was challenge number one with a movie like that. Making the data as authentic as possible and then becoming a visual translator for the audience to help them look in the right place at the right time. So that the data shoots well, it doesn't become distracting within the larger texture of the movie.

Does it help to bring the story forward? That will always be the question of the director: How does anything move the story forward?

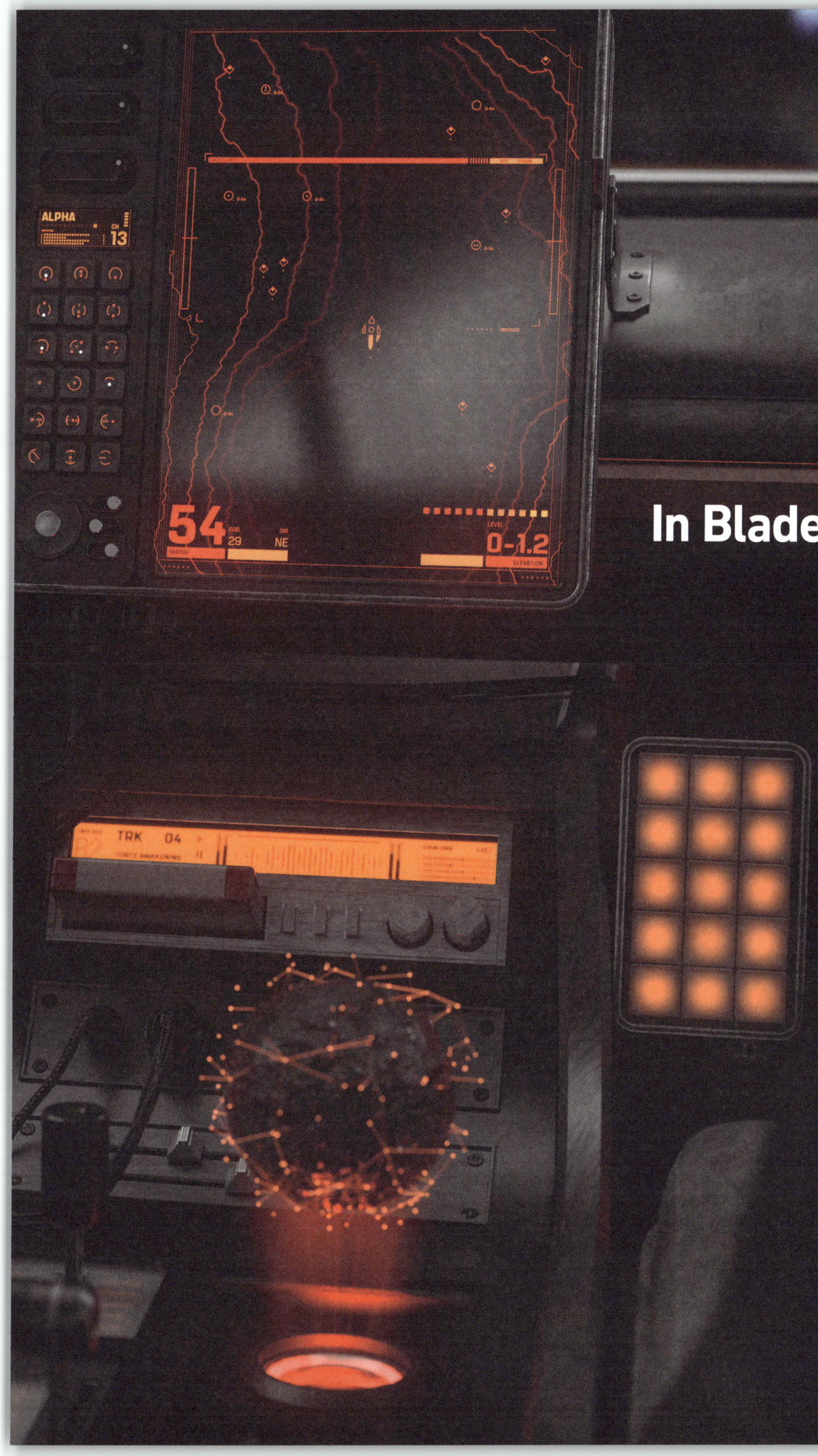

With a Marvel film or something a little more fantastical. I'm thinking of examples, Ready Player One and Ghost in the Shell. The directors' motivation is slightly different. After all, they are not thinking about how accurate the data is because their worlds are so fantastic.

At that point, I am thinking about how the data and graphics become an extension of world-building? What do the graphics say about the characters that live in that world?

How does technology become a shorthand for making commentary on their world-building?

In Blade Runner, the data was degraded.

It was analog; it was imperfect.

That imperfection commented on where technology had taken them. Technology had transported them to an imperfect place.

Guardians of the Galaxy needed to feel bright and colorful and a reference 1980s. Because Peter Quill had been abducted in the 1980s, more of his visual references were from this place. But it was also a moment for James Gun to be excited about his first Marvel film. Humor needed to be applied; the palette needed to feel vivid, the colors required to wake your eyeballs!
The data was far more expressive. It was more about how these technology systems have been hacked together. They became an expression of the Marvel Universe in space. Because Guardians of the Galaxy was the first film in space for Marvel, James had a moment to expand the universe and do that for graphics.

So we helped.

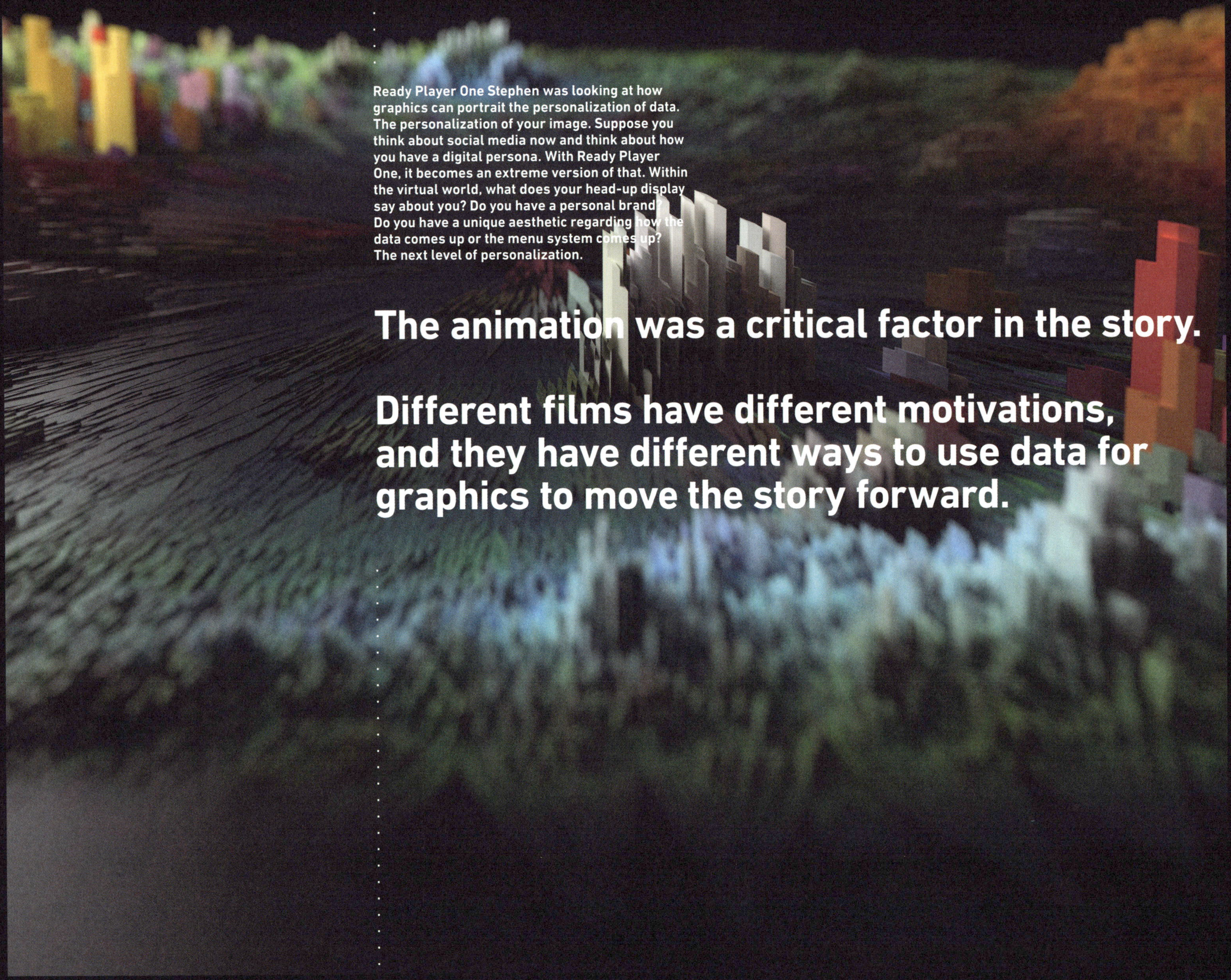

Ready Player One Stephen was looking at how graphics can portrait the personalization of data. The personalization of your image. Suppose you think about social media now and think about how you have a digital persona. With Ready Player One, it becomes an extreme version of that. Within the virtual world, what does your head-up display say about you? Do you have a personal brand? Do you have a unique aesthetic regarding how the data comes up or the menu system comes up? The next level of personalization.

The animation was a critical factor in the story.

Different films have different motivations, and they have different ways to use data for graphics to move the story forward.

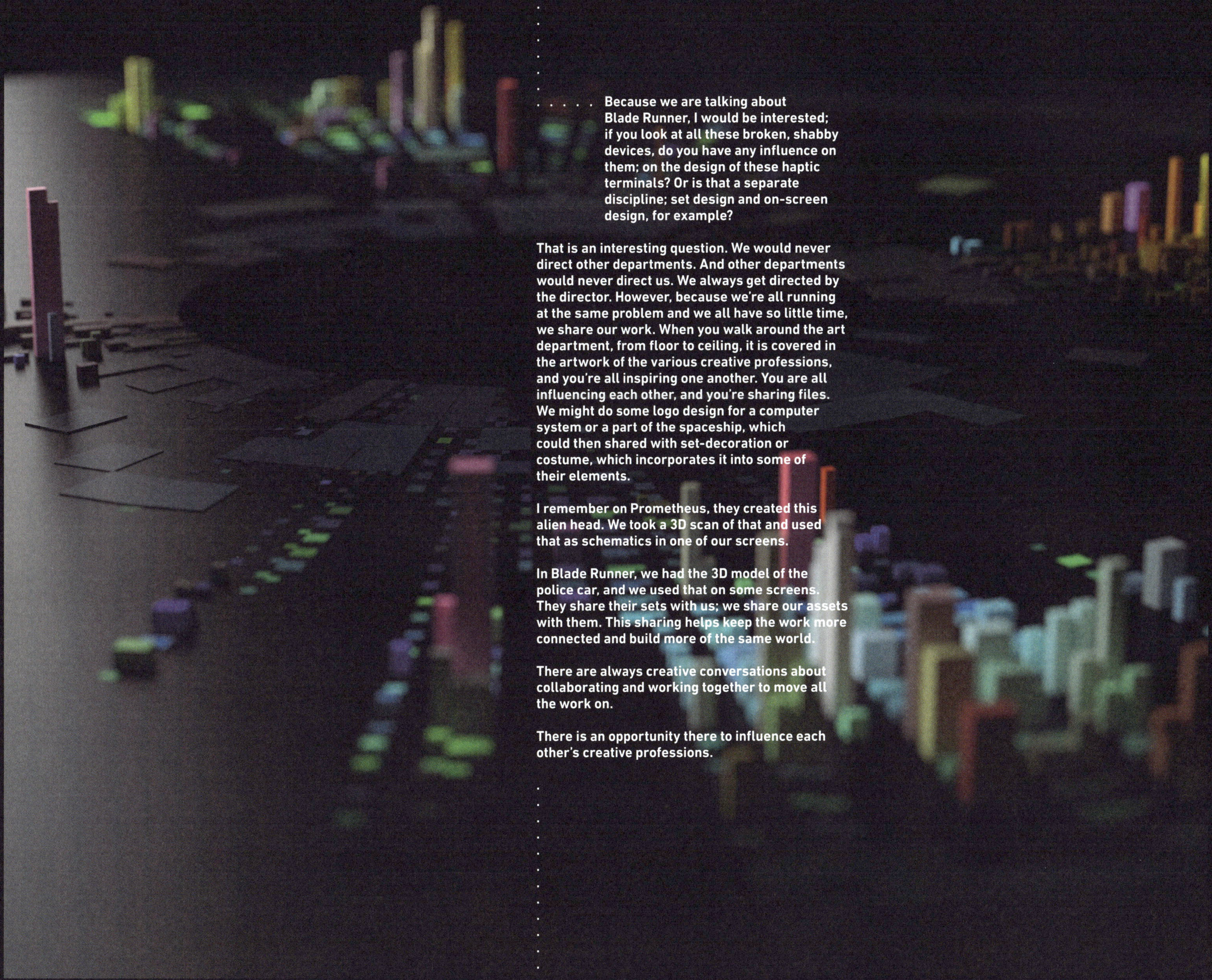

Because we are talking about Blade Runner, I would be interested; if you look at all these broken, shabby devices, do you have any influence on them; on the design of these haptic terminals? Or is that a separate discipline; set design and on-screen design, for example?

That is an interesting question. We would never direct other departments. And other departments would never direct us. We always get directed by the director. However, because we're all running at the same problem and we all have so little time, we share our work. When you walk around the art department, from floor to ceiling, it is covered in the artwork of the various creative professions, and you're all inspiring one another. You are all influencing each other, and you're sharing files. We might do some logo design for a computer system or a part of the spaceship, which could then shared with set-decoration or costume, which incorporates it into some of their elements.

I remember on Prometheus, they created this alien head. We took a 3D scan of that and used that as schematics in one of our screens.

In Blade Runner, we had the 3D model of the police car, and we used that on some screens. They share their sets with us; we share our assets with them. This sharing helps keep the work more connected and build more of the same world.

There are always creative conversations about collaborating and working together to move all the work on.

There is an opportunity there to influence each other's creative professions.

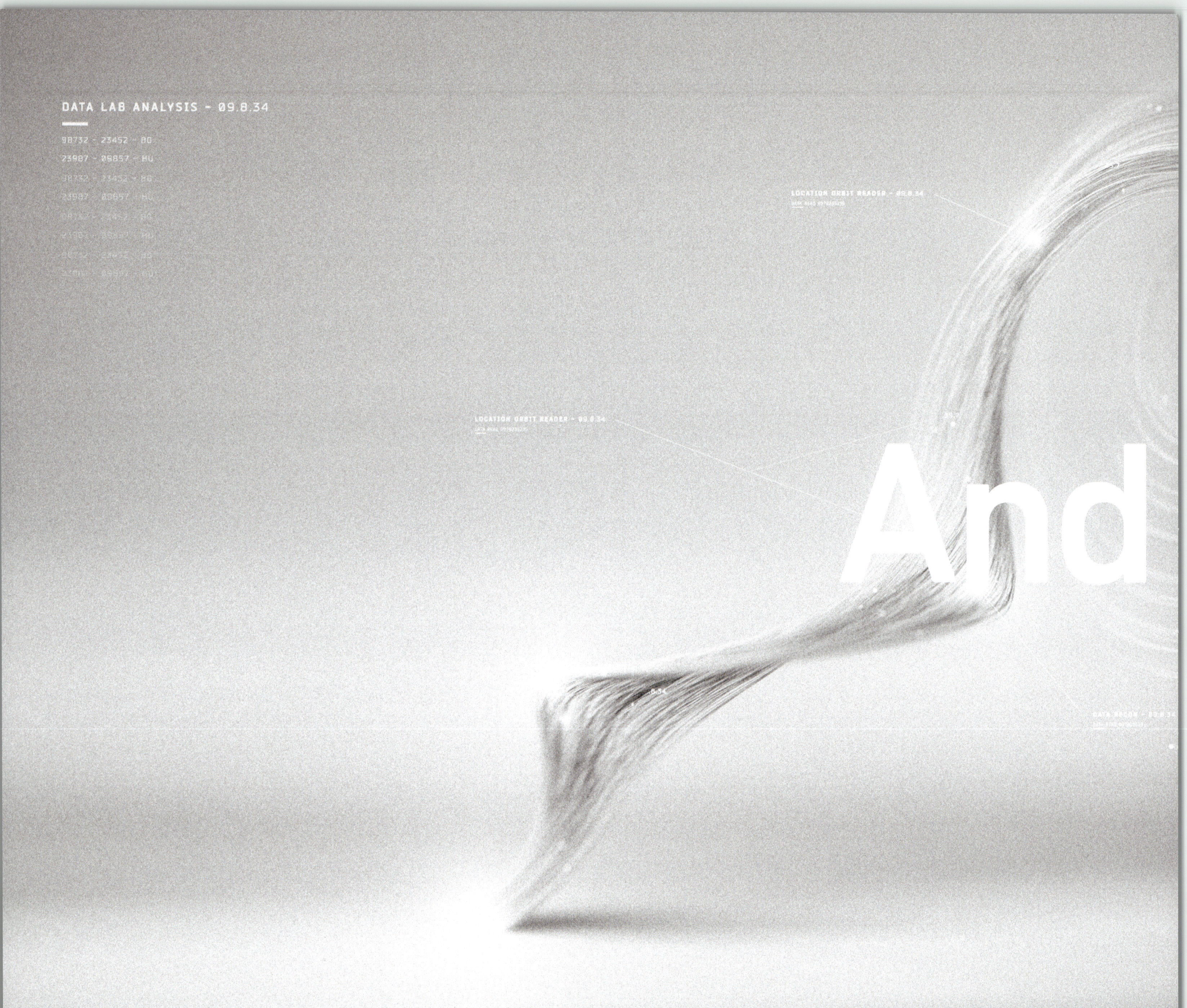
DATA LAB ANALYSIS - 09.8.34
98732 - 23452 - BG
23987 - 09857 - HU
LOCATION ORBIT READER - 09.8.34
LOCATION ORBIT READER - 09.8.34
And

That means, it all starts with the script. From here you move on. You start with the research, build prototypes ... everything parallel

The script is the starting point, along with a conversation with the director. Denis Villeneuve was excellent in terms of giving us all some words to work with. He would provide us with creative assets. I have talked about this many times before. This idea that a power struggle was one of the critical themes of Blade Runner. The scale was another one. If you create a real contrast in scale, you also need to develop a sense of isolation for the people living in that world.

Scale and power were really important.

then brutality.

Everything needed to feel brutal, really intense, really hard to live through. These three essential elements were then shared with all the other creative departments. We all, in terms of our design aesthetic, were pushing in the same direction. When it is working well, a director will pull everyone together and help everyone understand the vision to move in the same way to achieve the same things.

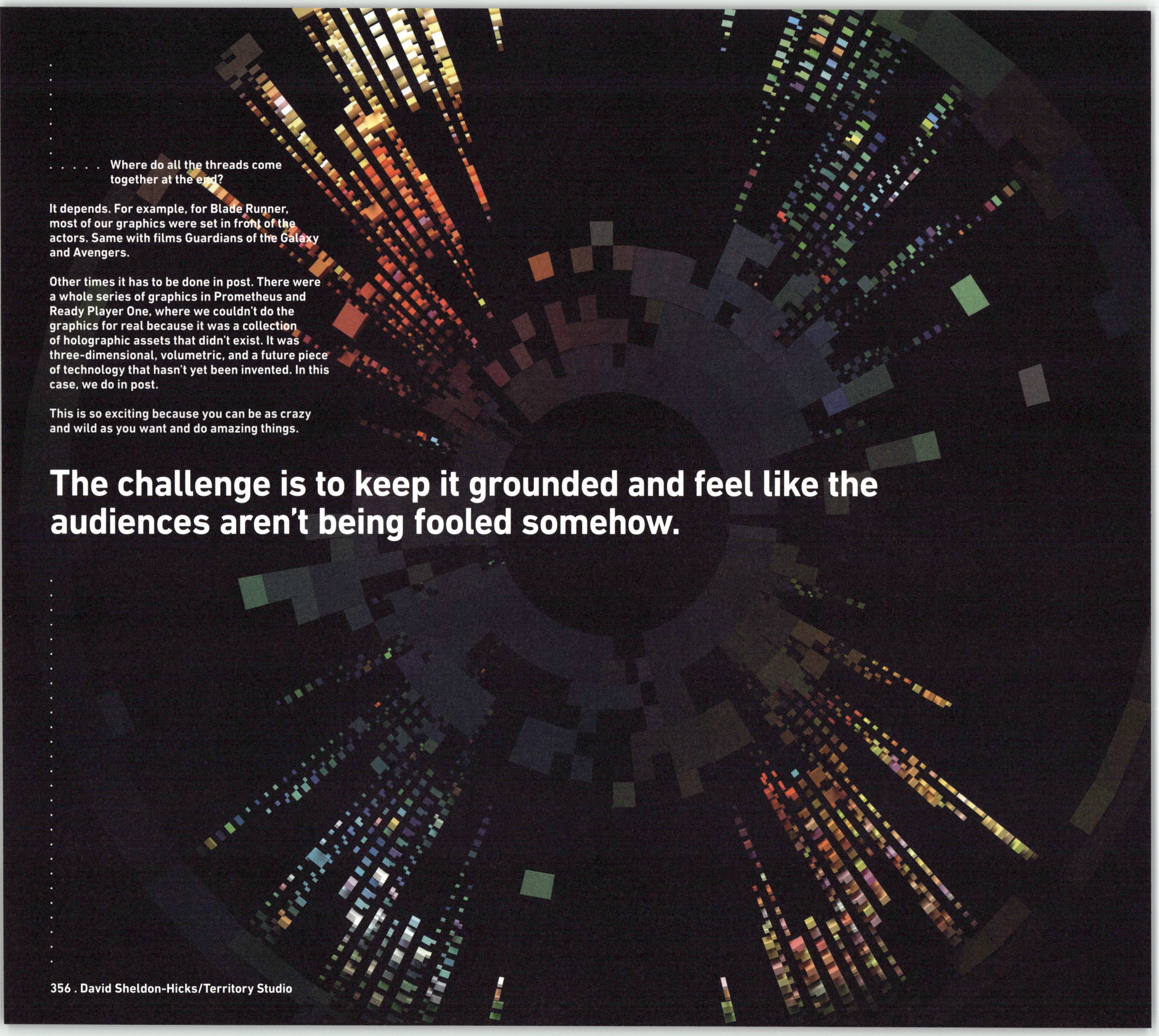

Where do all the threads come together at the end?

It depends. For example, for Blade Runner, most of our graphics were set in front of the actors. Same with films Guardians of the Galaxy and Avengers.

Other times it has to be done in post. There were a whole series of graphics in Prometheus and Ready Player One, where we couldn't do the graphics for real because it was a collection of holographic assets that didn't exist. It was three-dimensional, volumetric, and a future piece of technology that hasn't yet been invented. In this case, we do in post.

This is so exciting because you can be as crazy and wild as you want and do amazing things.

The challenge is to keep it grounded and feel like the audiences aren't being fooled somehow.

You just named some of these incredible blockbusters, but what is the greatest in your eyes?

What is your best work so far?

Regarding special projects, I always wanted to work on Black Mirror because I think it's such a fantastic TV series. Blade Runner was another because of the original film back in 1982.

Then it was our first opportunity to work with Denis Villeneuve. We have just finished working with him, and that was equally special. More recently, we worked on the new James Bond film, No Time to Die and that's very special because James Bond was the first movie I worked on.

I worked on Casino Royale many years ago, and that is personally important to me, but I think Guardians of the Galaxy hold a special place for me, not just because it was my first Marvel film, but because it was so fun.

The art team was excellent, and we created some great visuals. Ready Player One was extraordinary because of that director. Being able to work with Steven Spielberg is just pretty special. It is hard to focus on one because we have been so lucky to work with many great directors on countless great projects.

As a studio, I think the piece of work that holds up in so many aspects, and probably the most rewarding, is Blade Runner 2049.

It hit all the big ticks for me. The design work was incredible. The film itself was great. The director was terrific. The art department team was terrific to work with also. We had enough time to do the work we were doing, and it was all so well-managed.

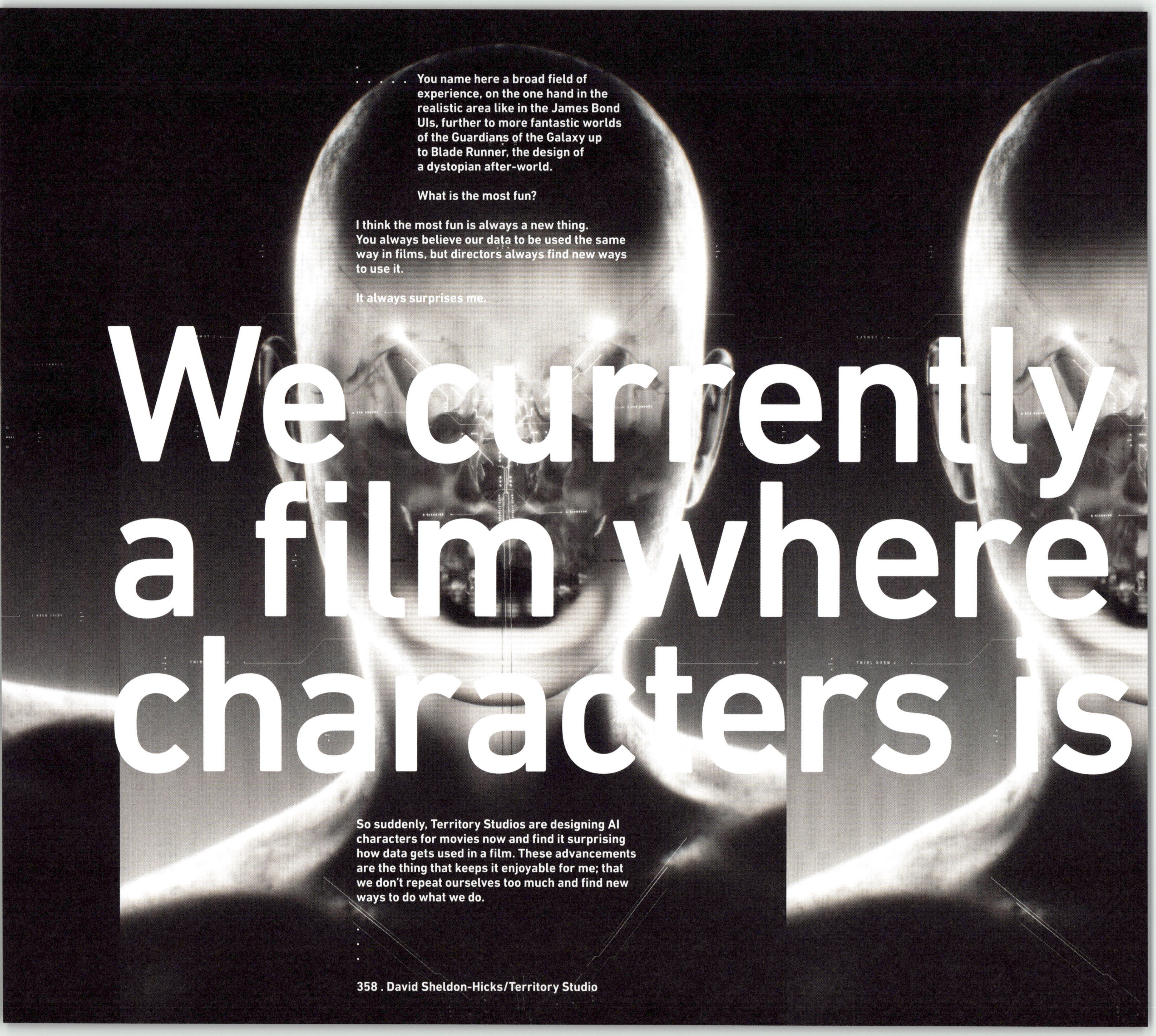

You name here a broad field of experience, on the one hand in the realistic area like in the James Bond UIs, further to more fantastic worlds of the Guardians of the Galaxy up to Blade Runner, the design of a dystopian after-world.

What is the most fun?

I think the most fun is always a new thing. You always believe our data to be used the same way in films, but directors always find new ways to use it.

It always surprises me.

We currently a film where characters is

So suddenly, Territory Studios are designing AI characters for movies now and find it surprising how data gets used in a film. These advancements are the thing that keeps it enjoyable for me; that we don't repeat ourselves too much and find new ways to do what we do.

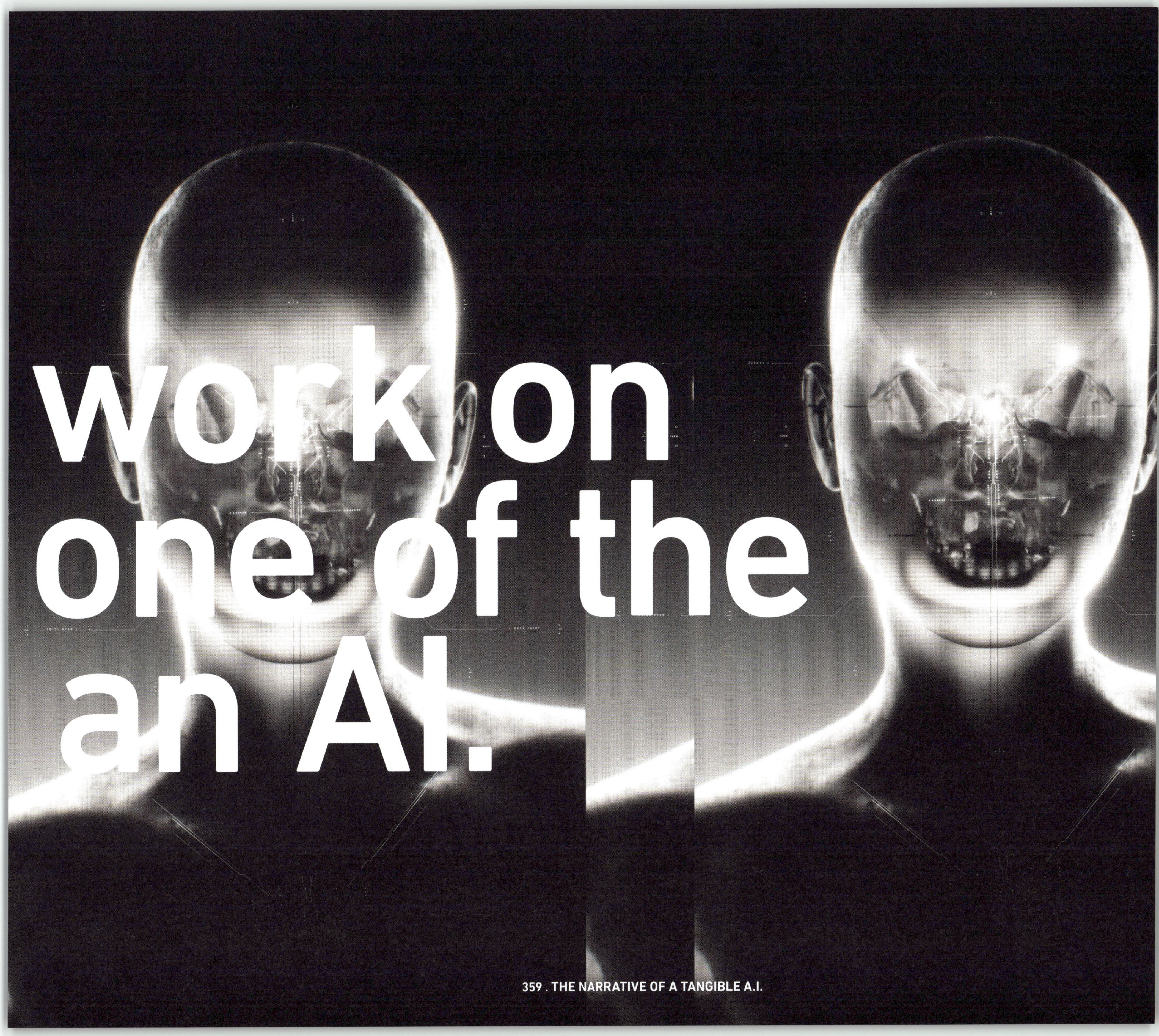

work on
one of the
an AI.

I would also love to do an innovative computer game in a movie. I think that would be fun. There is a movie I can't talk about at the moment, but it will be out in a year or so.

It uses three-dimensional volumetric interfaces in a really new and

It is just a beautiful execution aesthetically, so surprising, so I don't feel we are running out of any ideas soon; there are still many avenues to explore.

If you look at anyone series of "Black Mirror." The way they use data, the interfaces, and everything else in that series are different every time. It makes a poignant commentary on how we all use data and technology and how technology and data use us. I find that fascinating that data often is a reflection in films of how we are manipulating each other. It is a social commentary. This finding has as much meaning as the data itself; how we use data or control it says a lot about the actual data content.

original way.

We discussed this issue earlier this year, at the beginning of the Covid-19 crisis.

What role do immersive experiences play under these circumstances?

Can a hybrid model be developed here, for example, for fair trade construction? Or is this already a business road for your studio to travel?

It's funny; we have been using game-engine technologies since we began. We have always used game-engine technology with our partners in games. Suddenly everyone realizes that this technology is very applicable to everything that we do. I think that the Covid-situation has meant that we have reassessed the importance of living our lives through the digital space.

I am not saying that I don't love the real world. I do, I miss it a lot, and the people, I miss them as well. But there is an opportunity with game-engine and real-time technologies to do some things that haven't been done yet, and that always excites me.

New technology and new uses of technology always excite me. Because I am creative, and when creatives find new paradigms to work within, we suddenly find new ways of doing what we do.

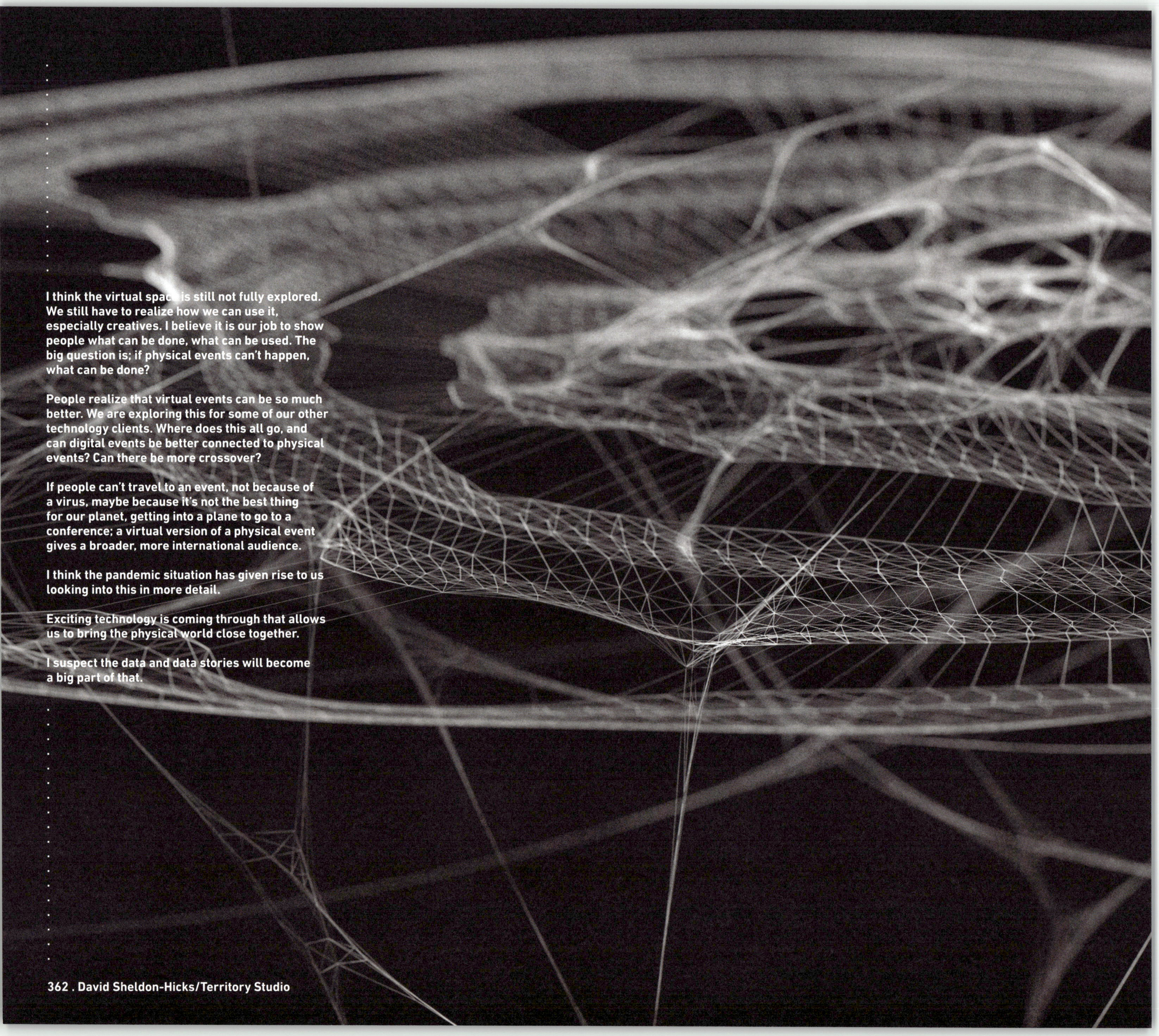

I think the virtual space is still not fully explored. We still have to realize how we can use it, especially creatives. I believe it is our job to show people what can be done, what can be used. The big question is; if physical events can't happen, what can be done?

People realize that virtual events can be so much better. We are exploring this for some of our other technology clients. Where does this all go, and can digital events be better connected to physical events? Can there be more crossover?

If people can't travel to an event, not because of a virus, maybe because it's not the best thing for our planet, getting into a plane to go to a conference; a virtual version of a physical event gives a broader, more international audience.

I think the pandemic situation has given rise to us looking into this in more detail.

Exciting technology is coming through that allows us to bring the physical world close together.

I suspect the data and data stories will become a big part of that.

As a conclusion to this interview?

How would you formulate an outlook?

The physical world overlaid with the digital is the next prominent paradigm movement, and I think this will be an exciting time for creatives.

That moment we went from painting the world to photographing it. This current process is as big as that or as big as going from a handwritten notation to the Gutenberg bible and having the printing press.

There is a moment coming soon when a volumetric data space can augment the physical world. This movement will be the next playground for creatives and designers, and I can't wait for it to happen.

Arguably, it is already happening with mobile phones. Still, I think when the technology comes through in a far more transparent way, a less intrusive way, there's going to be a massive boom in creativity and technology.

David Sheldon-Hicks and Christoph Grünberger
October 2020

Name:

Florence To

.

Info:

Artist and director Florence To designs and produces sound and light installations creating generative motion graphics with a strong focus on architectural spatial design in site-specific projects. The Scottish-born artist graduated from The Glasgow School of Art in 2008 with a Masters in Design, originally specializing in textiles and tailoring.

She merged her skills with digital technologies in 2011 to develop installations in underground and disused spaces, using its defects as an advantage.

Working in various disparate architectural environments guided her further exploration of the effects of cognitive and emotional triggers and how multiple sensory arrangements are experienced within space.

.

Project:

EOAN

.

URL:

florence-to.com

.

Instagram:

@florence.to

Fl
or
en
ce
To

Q&As

. . . . . Please explain the main idea and what gave the impulse?

EOAN is a participatory installation exploring the relationship between sound, light, and the resonance of architectural space. The installation is composed of optic panels and aluminum pipes tuned to specific planetary harmonics creating rhythmic reflections and spatial sound resonance that distort, heighten and shape our perception of space.

Developed from my interest in caves and how Paleolithic people utilized resonance.

In prehistoric times caves were also used as a performative space because of their shape and materiality. The sound would reflect producing overtones in a primitive acoustic modality. The approach is essentially physical; the whole body is subtly implicated through resonance and relating to sound in a primitive way. The basic properties of vibration relate to the external body perception with sound intensity, wavelength as frequency, and distance as space. The concept of timbre belongs to the deep levels of perception, and the expressions are still often rarely expressed properly within a digital environment.

. . . . . What challenges did you face for this project? And what surprises?

The position of the pipes and order of harmonics became quite challenging due to the format of the environment. The solution was to arrange the order of harmonics and length of pipes in relevance to the size of the space. I had to consider how the pitch would change in the given environment and calculate a measurement allowing these compromises and allowing other tones to complement the existing ones. The perception of the frequency would hold the attention and energy in the space depending on the length.

An installation that presents objects to be "hit" welcomes a form of release that also includes intensity. The open-end pipes produce sound when hit, and overtones attenuate more rapidly than others at a distance. The original combination of strike, frequency, and overtones are not the same at a distance.

The fundamental frequency does not always contribute to the note. These factors were included in the presentation, trusting the participant to be thoughtful in interacting with the object.

. . . . . Please describe the technical environment.

The aluminum pipes are positioned according to the swing circumference, with consideration to how the resonant frequencies sound together with neighboring pipes. The open-end tubes are composed of three positions in relation to body temperament. The strength in timbre varies when hitting the pipes positioned in front, above, and below. The sound perception is also different; to hit the pipes above the head is less intensive with more strength when facing the ground. LED panels are arranged according to the position of the pipes using three phases of light geometry, including dot, horizontal and vertical lines. The generative frames are mapped out on each LED panel and triggered by the sound of the "hit" picked up by the omnidirectional microphones above each section of pipes.

The sound after the hit produces a "wah-wah" effect; the lowest note (D1) in the space would have the most prolonged resonating tone and a shorter wavelength with the highest note (D#4). The pipes are recorded without the strike which triggers the harmonics inside the pipe and played back into the space as a subtle hum that would welcome the participants when they enter the gallery's basement.

. . . . . Tell us about your aesthetical approach.

A clear functional approach relating to the perception of the body and architecture.

. . . . . What's next? Your vision?

Further experimentation with less familiar resonating materials, and through this, how to challenge body perceptions with these materials.

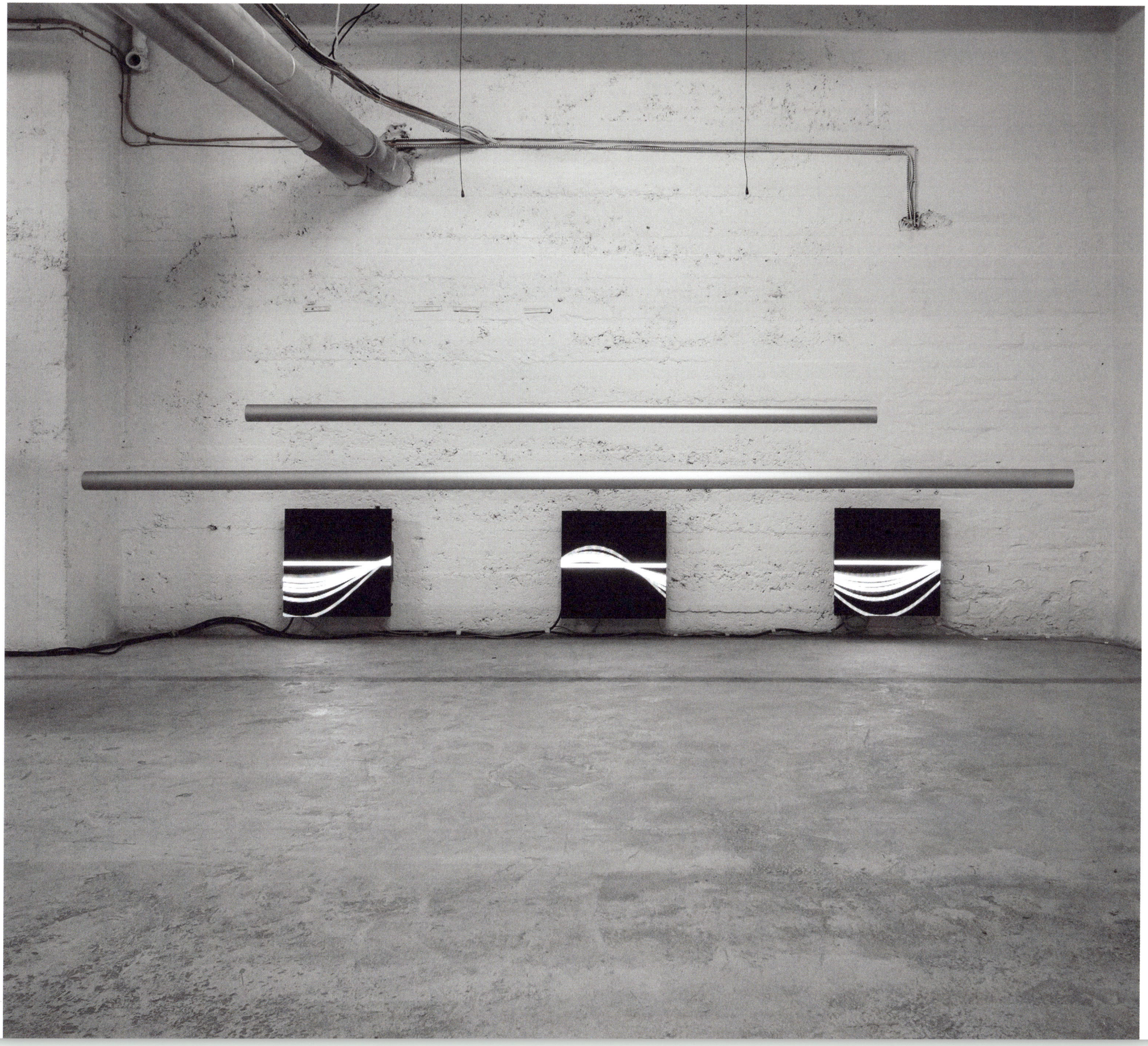

Measuring the frequencies with a resonating material such as metal would further investigate the psychoacoustics of the space in the beginning stages. I wanted to create an emotional environment where the participants could develop sounds through traditional craft methods, keeping technology secondary.

The velocity of light is triggered by the temperament of the "hit" on the pipes, which increases tension within the space. The second phase to the composition uses higher numbered frequencies in relation to the color wavelength Red-Orange, which is also the measurement of Venus in planetary harmonics.

I want to avoid associating with mainstream astrology and focusing on factual information, using the knowledge to reference harmonics relating to the space we live in and how color can be felt through listening without seeing.

The frequencies are based on data readings from 1952 and 2017. The shallow frequency (ELF) peaks within the Earth's electromagnetic field spectrum are also known as Schumann resonance.

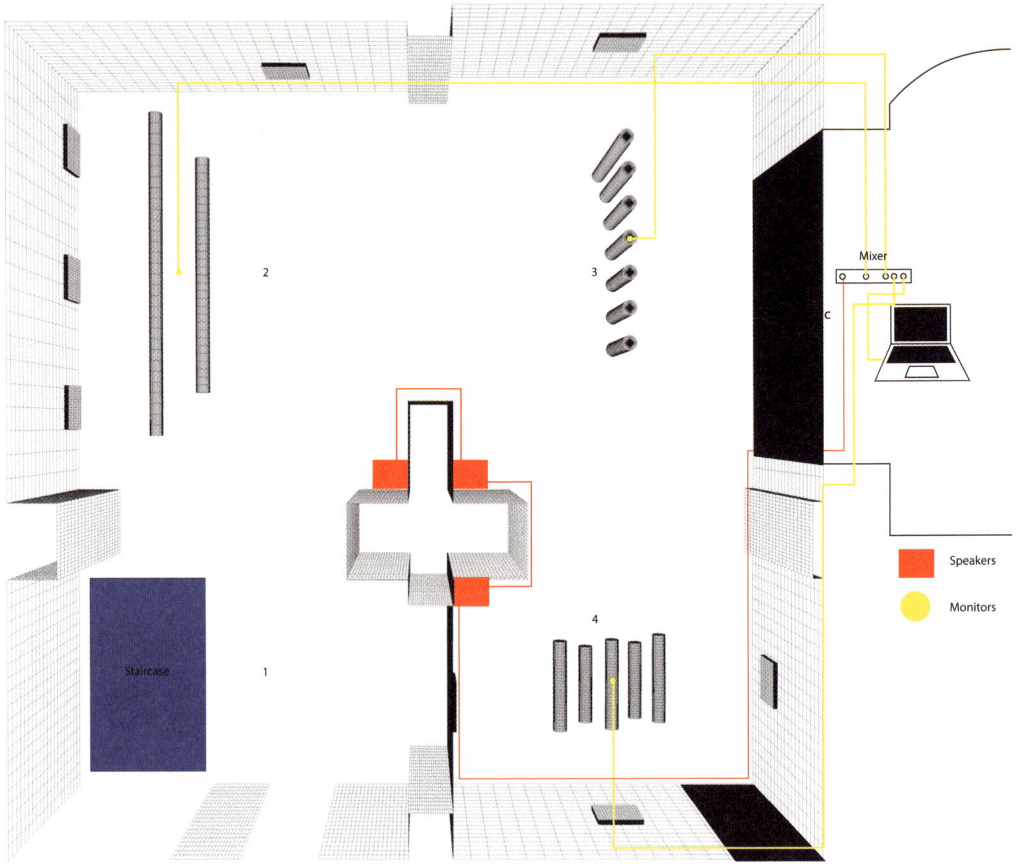

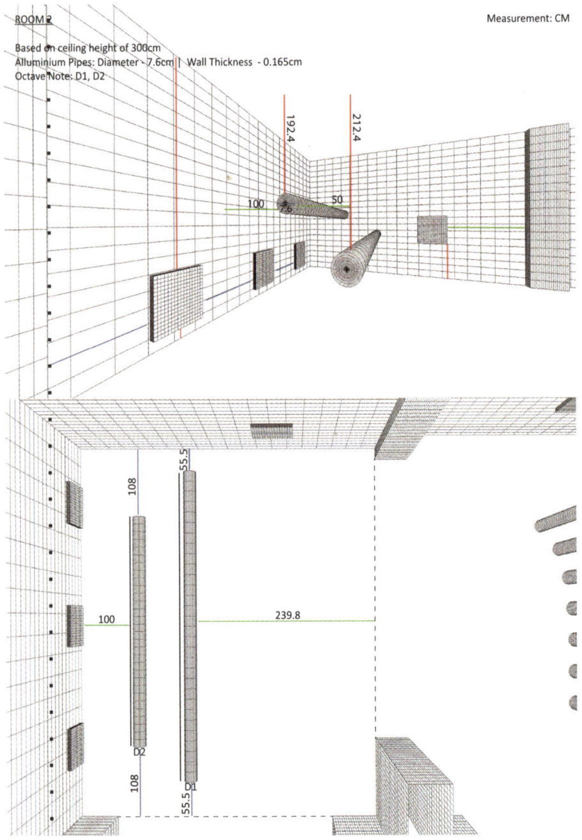

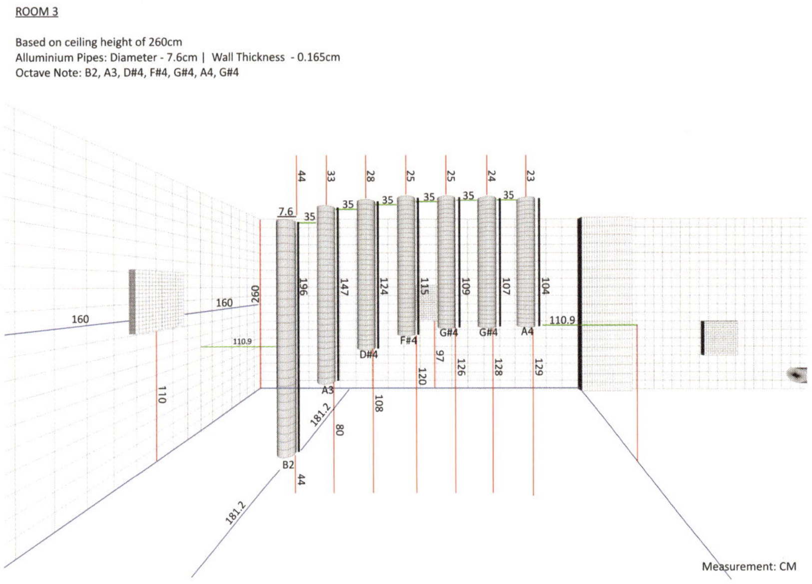

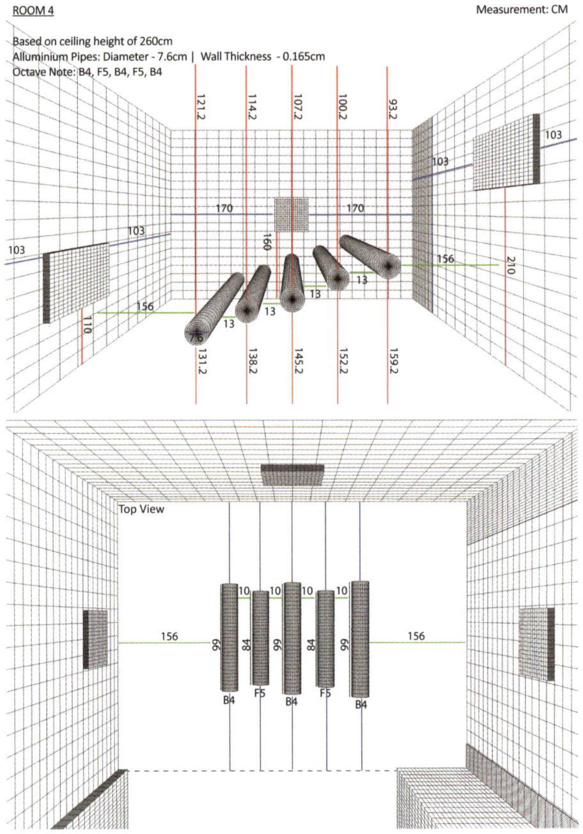

String wave calculation has shown that wave tensions exist between the center and the surface of the Earth, which also refers to the living and nonliving entities existing on the surface. The deep connection also creates tension which is also known as gravity.

In 1952, Schumann's resonance was measured at 7.83 and in 2017 at 36.70; however, the higher reading could have been the higher-order harmonics, although this was not scientifically proven.

I was intrigued by this data and the relation in how humans feel and transfer energy.
I experimented with the higher-order harmonics using 7.83 and 36.70 as fundamentals to direct the arrangement of the sounding pipes. Closely spaced frequencies will interact to produce a third frequency which would create richer overtones when played together.

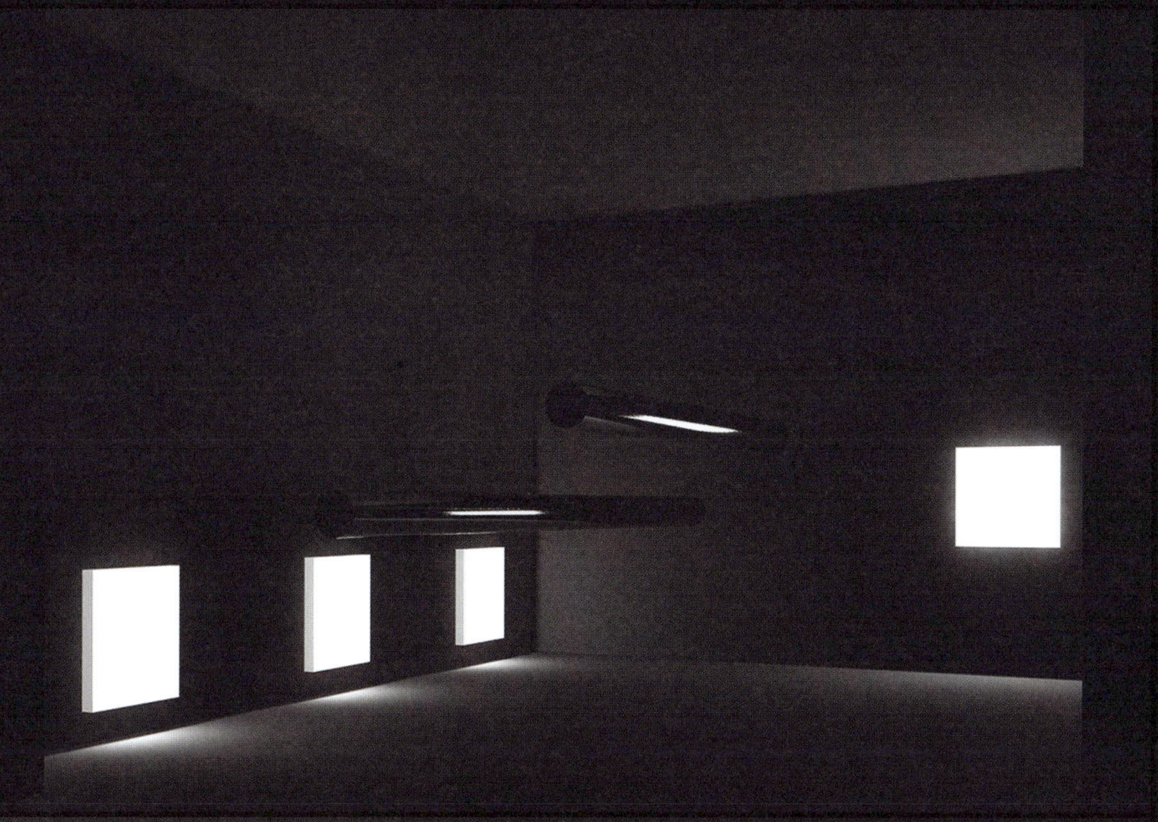

Combining the measurements is a way of listening to how Earth may have sounded if we were present in 1952 and 2017, and how bodies would interact with these vibrations, merging an alternate sense of time and space. Higher frequency (Venus and Red/Orange) sounds attenuate quickly in the atmosphere compared to lower frequencies. At a distance, the human ear does not hear the same sound when in close proximity; some of the high-frequency sounds can be significantly attenuated or missing, dissipating into the air faster than the lower harmonics.

Once the pipes were positioned, I recorded each one taking away the sound of the strike and feeding it back into the space through speakers. This process would encourage the participants to interact with the pipes, setting a tone when playing.

Light formed as a Dot, Vertical and Horizontal line was triggered by the sound of the hitting pipes, bending and pulsating, enhancing temporality with the human and the sounding object. It is crucial to have a physical element to give a sense of active participation in the installation.

When a person has a certain amount of control over what they are hearing, it can also encourage playfulness.

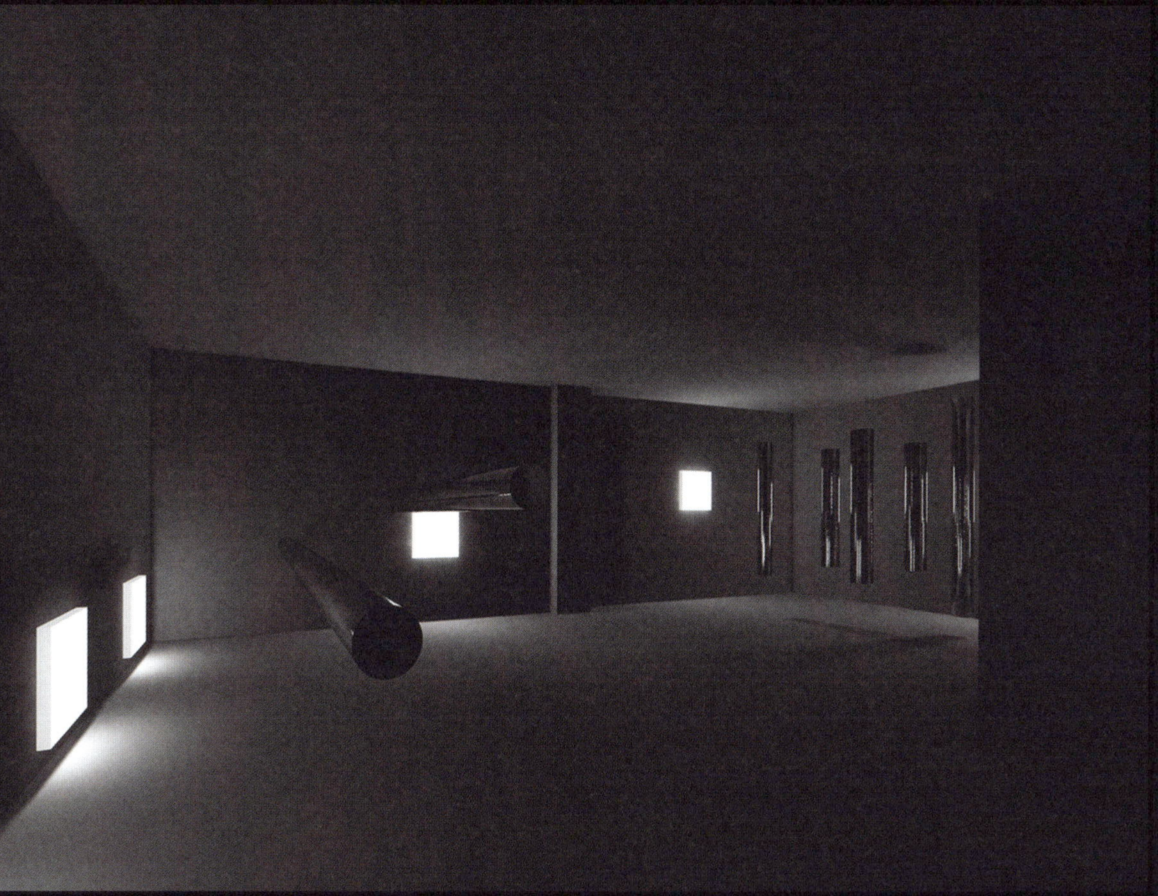

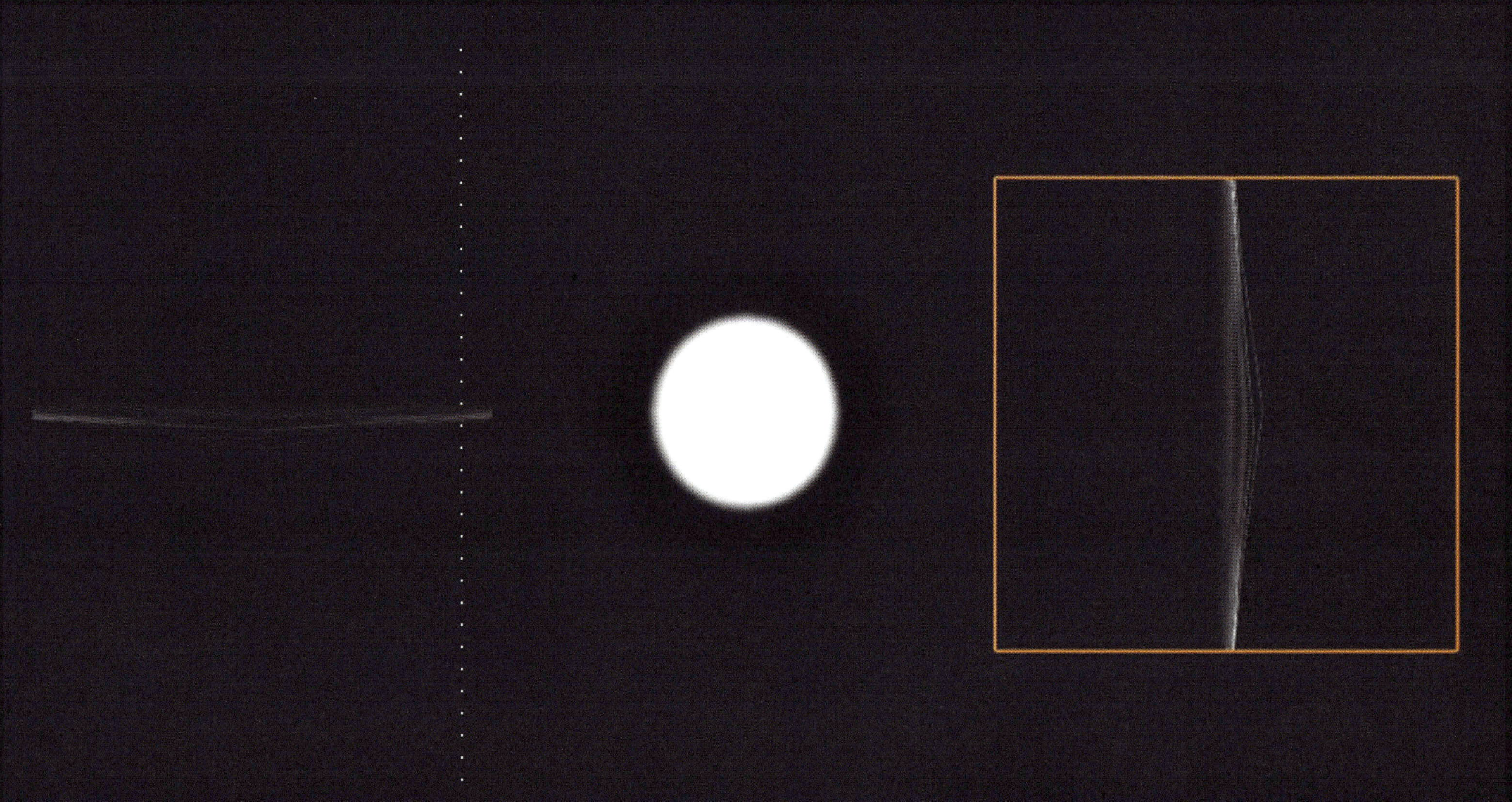

The installation set-up includes a node-based visual program, Touchdesigner, the microphones go into the mixer then through the computer.

Audio is analyzed using filters to dampen and increase the strength of the response. After the audio is analyzed, the sound velocity is used as a reference to trigger the light parameter.

The light geometry is mapped in sequential order to each LED panel.

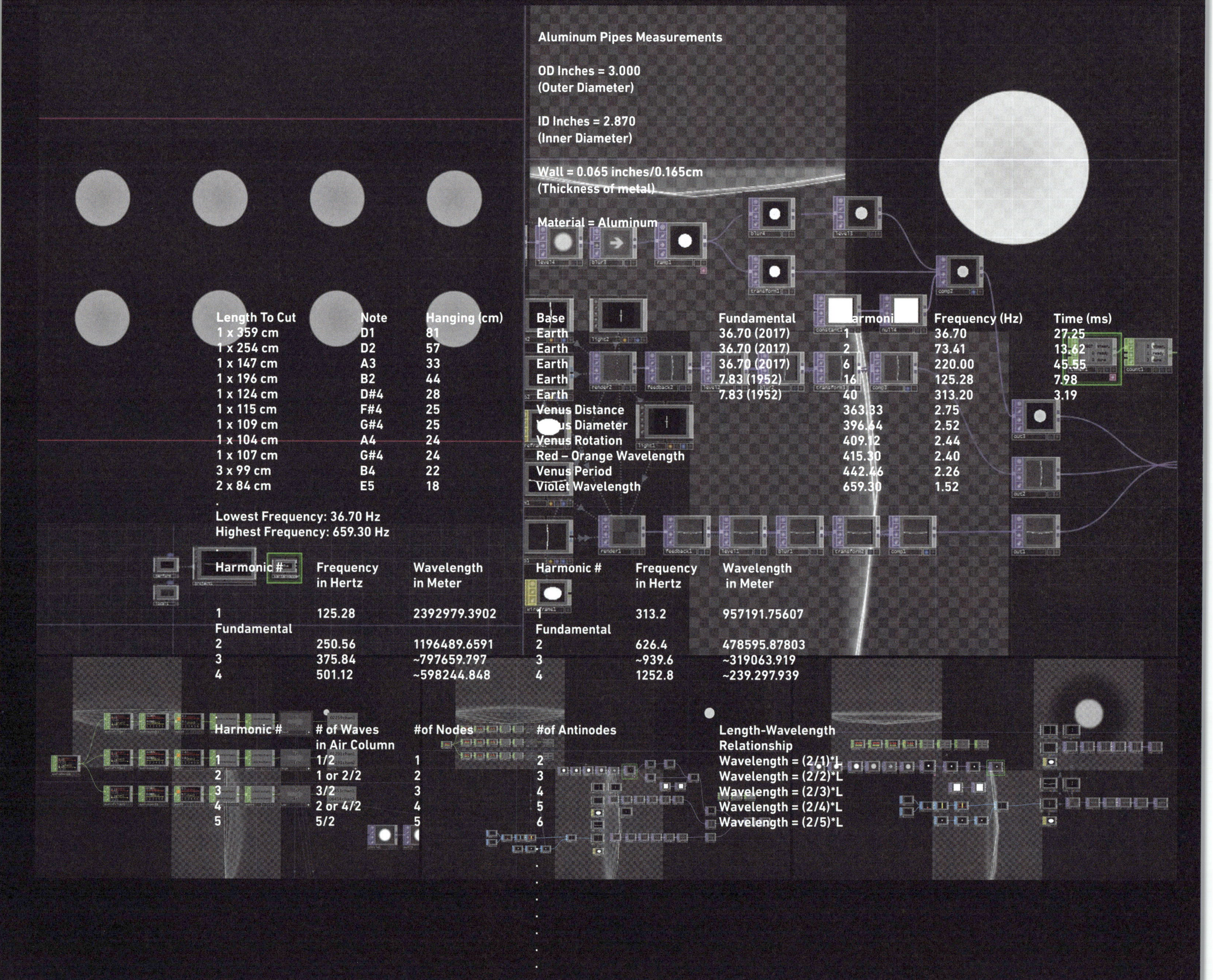

Aluminum Pipes Measurements
OD Inches = 3.000
(Outer Diameter)
ID Inches = 2.870
(Inner Diameter)
Wall = 0.065 inches/0.165cm
(Thickness of metal)
Material = Aluminum
Length To Cut
Note
Hanging (cm)
1 x 359 cm D1 81
1 x 254 cm D2 57
1 x 147 cm A3 33
1 x 196 cm B2 44
1 x 124 cm D#4 28
1 x 115 cm F#4 25
1 x 109 cm G#4 25
1 x 104 cm A4 24
1 x 107 cm G#4 24
3 x 99 cm B4 22
2 x 84 cm E5 18
Lowest Frequency: 36.70 Hz
Highest Frequency: 659.30 Hz
Base
Fundamental
Harmoni
Frequency (Hz)
Time (ms)
Earth 36.70 (2017) 1 36.70 27.25
Earth 36.70 (2017) 2 73.41 13.62
Earth 36.70 (2017) 6 220.00 45.55
Earth 7.83 (1952) 16 125.28 7.98
Earth 7.83 (1952) 40 313.20 3.19
Venus Distance 363.33 2.75
us Diameter 396.64 2.52
Venus Rotation 409.12 2.44
Red – Orange Wavelength 415.30 2.40
Venus Period 442.46 2.26
Violet Wavelength 659.30 1.52
Harmonic # Frequency in Hertz Wavelength in Meter
1 125.28 2392979.3902
Fundamental
2 250.56 1196489.6591
3 375.84 ~797659.797
4 501.12 ~598244.848
Harmonic # Frequency in Hertz Wavelength in Meter
1 313.2 957191.75607
Fundamental
2 626.4 478595.87803
3 ~939.6 ~319063.919
4 1252.8 ~239.297.939
Harmonic #
# of Waves in Air Column
#of Nodes
#of Antinodes
1 1/2 1 2
2 1 or 2/2 2 3
3 3/2 3 4
4 2 or 4/2 4 5
5 5/2 5 6
Length-Wavelength Relationship
Wavelength = (2/1)*L
Wavelength = (2/2)*L
Wavelength = (2/3)*L
Wavelength = (2/4)*L
Wavelength = (2/5)*L

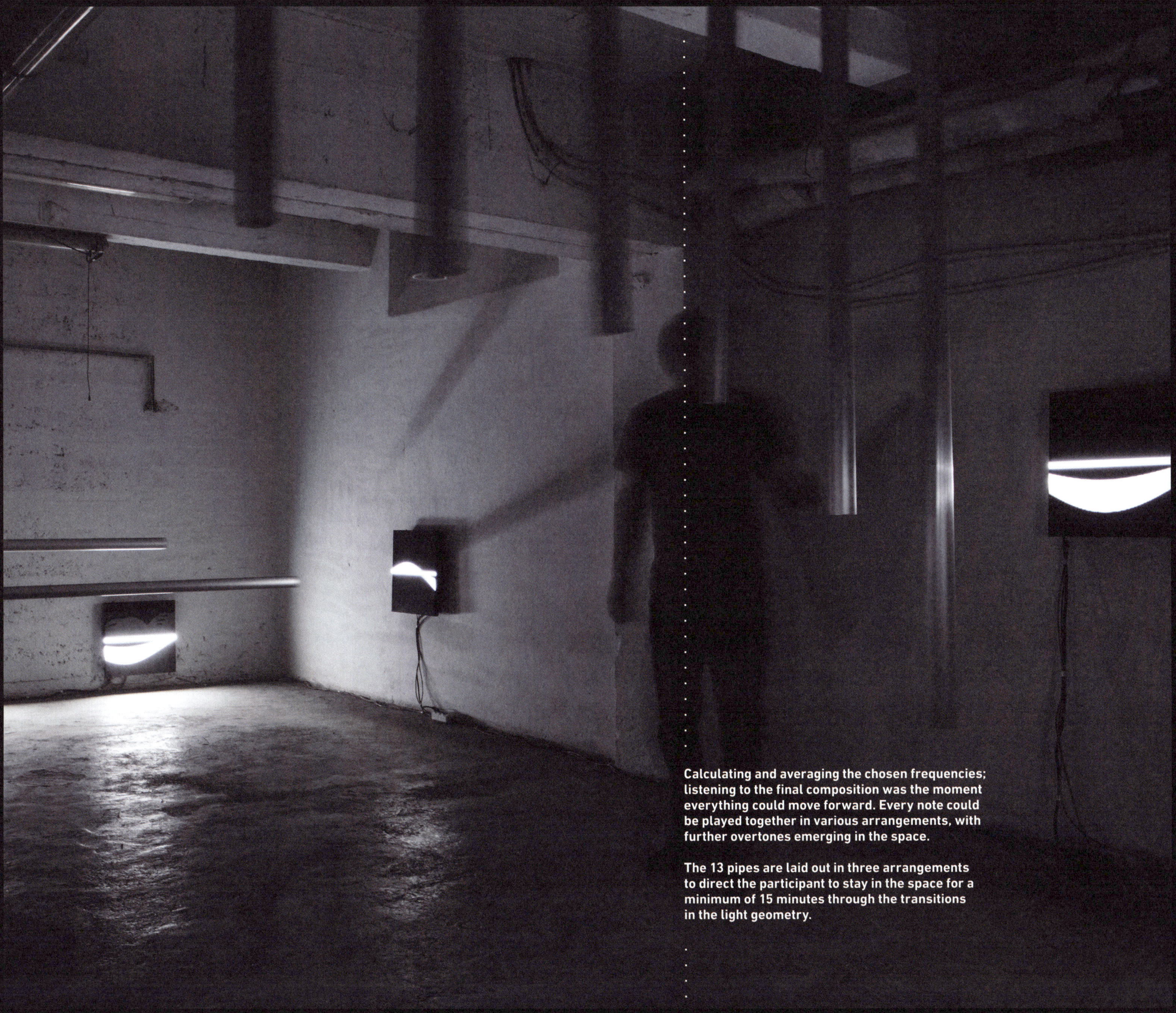

Calculating and averaging the chosen frequencies; listening to the final composition was the moment everything could move forward. Every note could be played together in various arrangements, with further overtones emerging in the space.

The 13 pipes are laid out in three arrangements to direct the participant to stay in the space for a minimum of 15 minutes through the transitions in the light geometry.

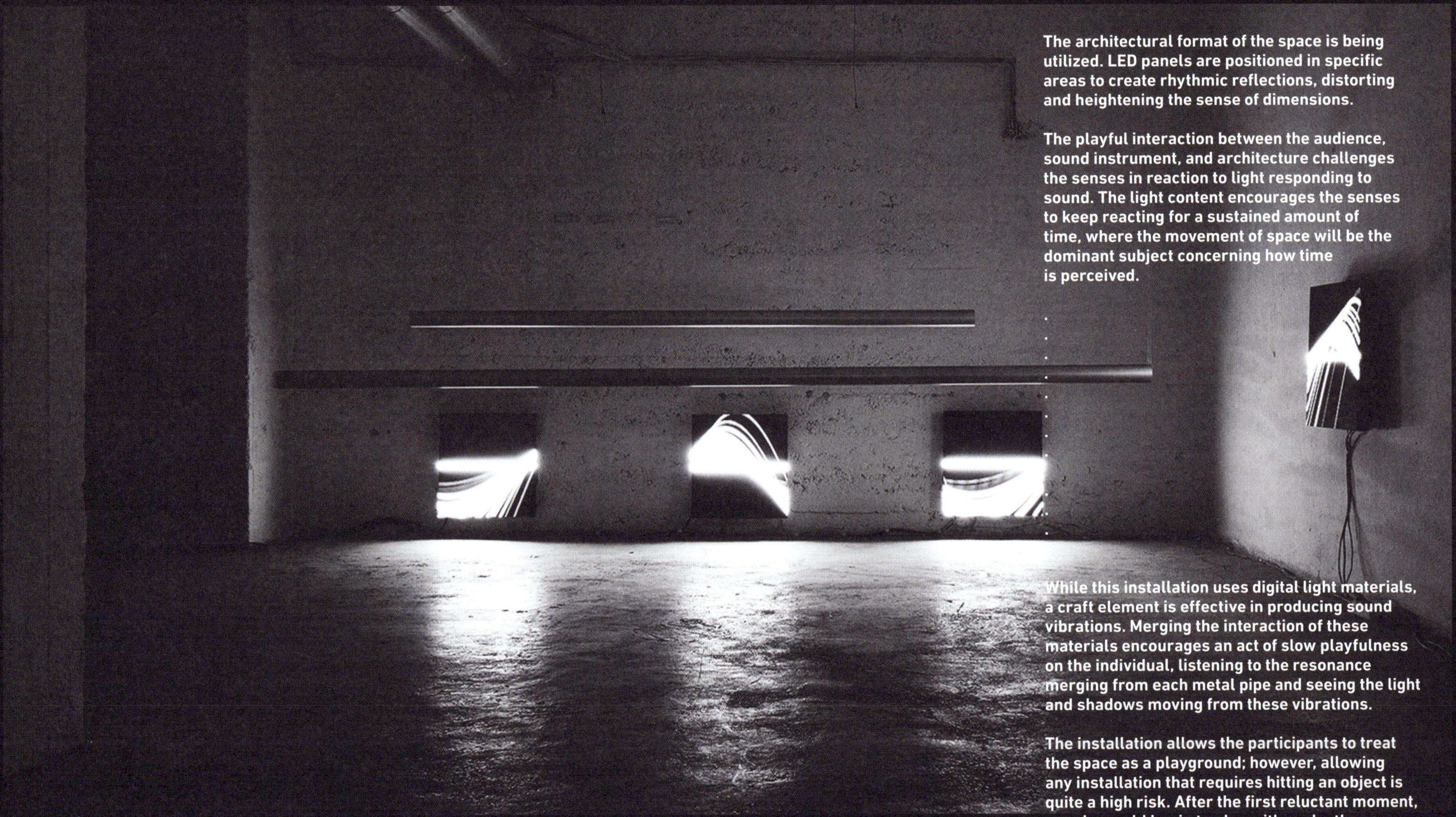

The architectural format of the space is being utilized. LED panels are positioned in specific areas to create rhythmic reflections, distorting and heightening the sense of dimensions.

The playful interaction between the audience, sound instrument, and architecture challenges the senses in reaction to light responding to sound. The light content encourages the senses to keep reacting for a sustained amount of time, where the movement of space will be the dominant subject concerning how time is perceived.

While this installation uses digital light materials, a craft element is effective in producing sound vibrations. Merging the interaction of these materials encourages an act of slow playfulness on the individual, listening to the resonance merging from each metal pipe and seeing the light and shadows moving from these vibrations.

The installation allows the participants to treat the space as a playground; however, allowing any installation that requires hitting an object is quite a high risk. After the first reluctant moment, people would begin to play with each other, also feeling calm and aware of their behavior with the environment.

It took a few tries for the user to understand their temporality with the object, especially those not experienced with physical instruments. Nonetheless, humans can relate to their more profound levels of sound consciousness and corporal perception in harmonic structures, allowing us to hear a wide range of timbre.

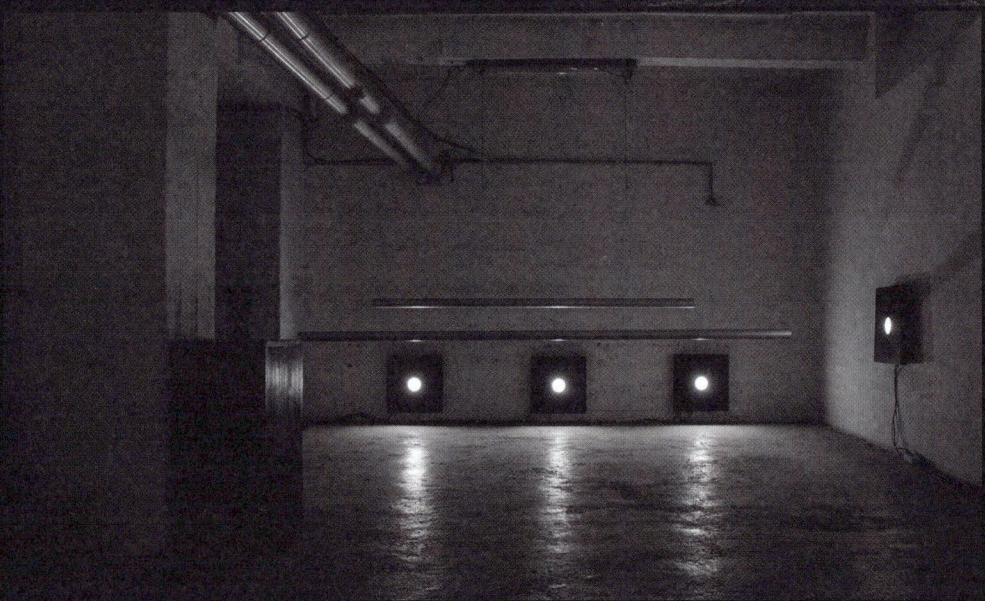

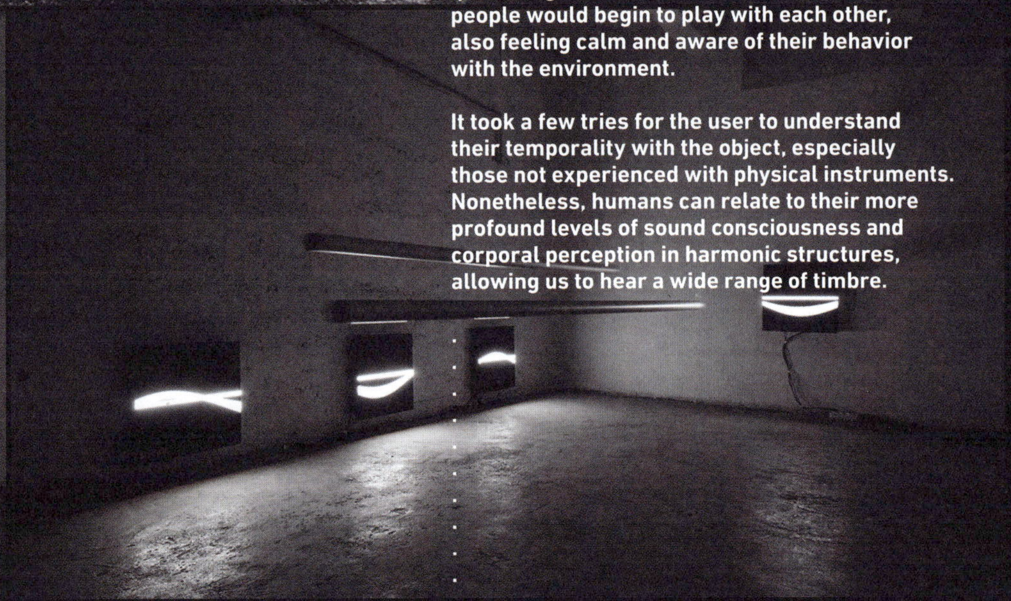

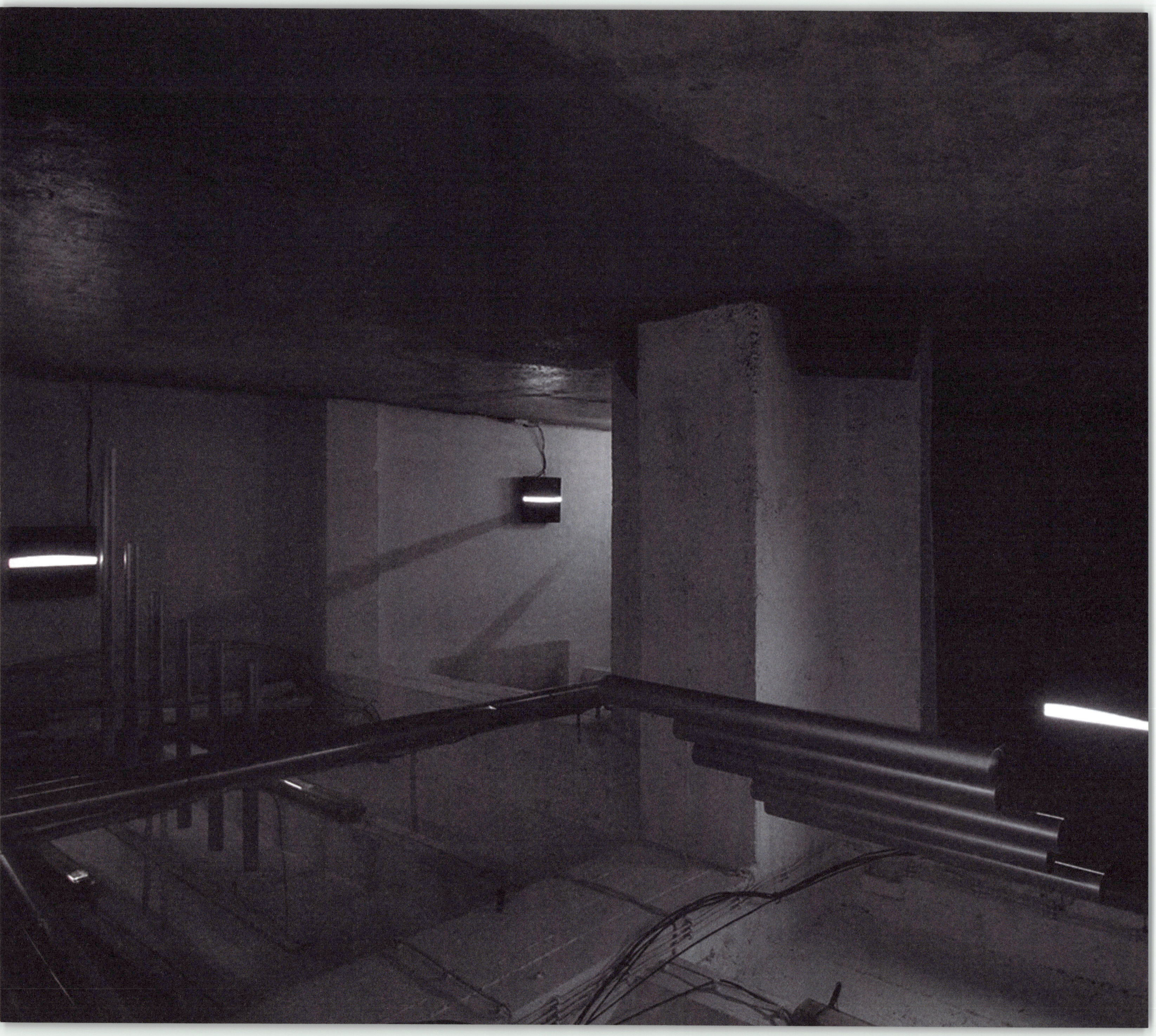

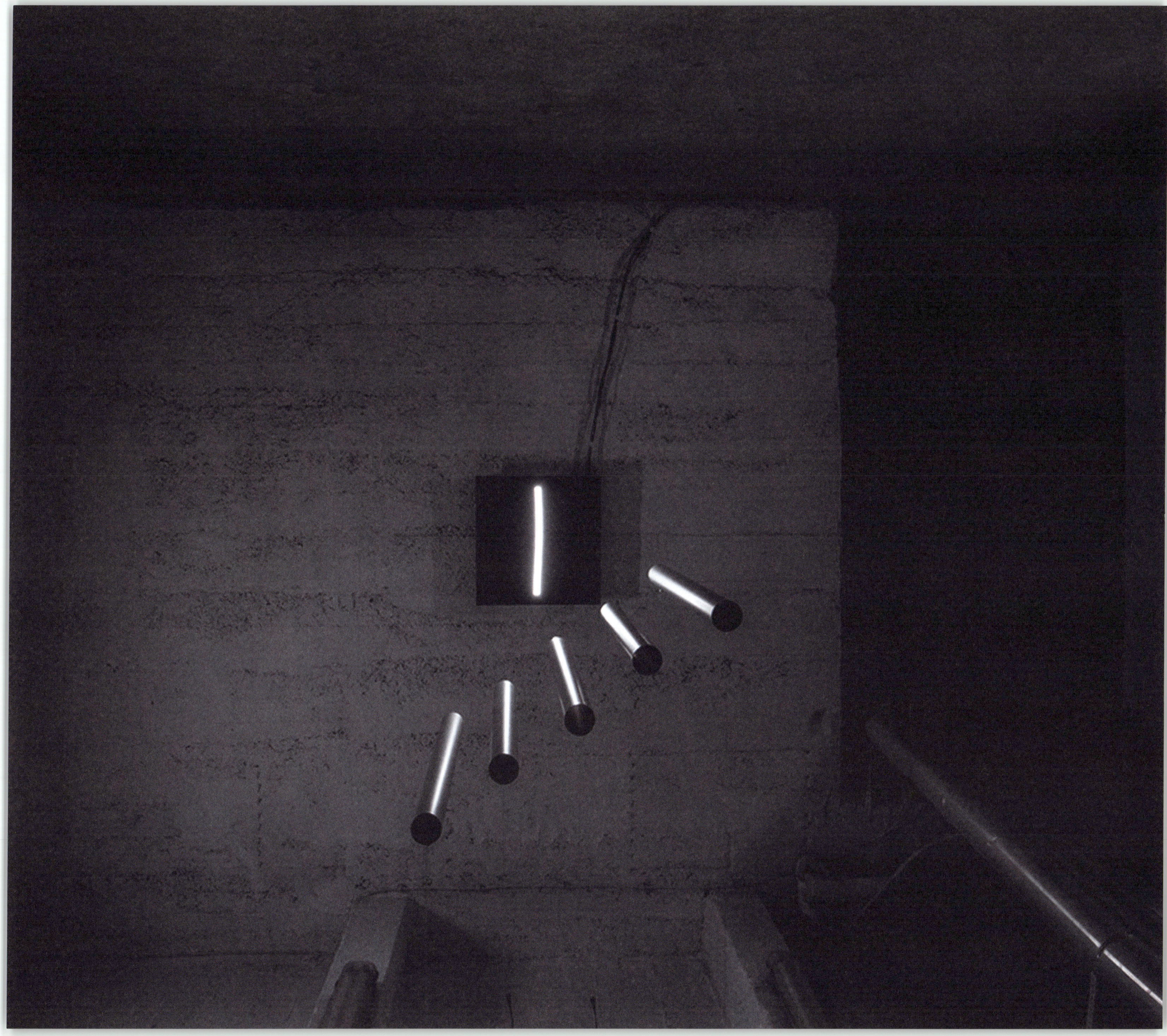

Name:

Tina Touli

Info:

Tina Touli is a London-based creative director, graphic communication designer, maker, speaker, and educator at Central Saint Martins, University of the Arts, London.

She works in various design fields, both digital and print design, including branding, typography, web design, animation.

Her work is mainly known for blending the physical and the digital world, working across different platforms and mediums.

Projects:

A CHANGE FOR A CHANCE
p. 375
Z BY HP
p. 376
30 YEARS OF ADOBE ILLUSTRATOR
p. 380
&PIZZA CHRISTMAS 2019
p. 382
36 DAYS OF TYPE
p. 383
FOLLOW YOUR BLISS
p. 384
WHAT ABOUT WATER?
p. 386

URL:

tinatouli.com

Mail:

tt@tinatouli.com

Instagram:

@tinatouli

Tina Touli

Conversation with Tina Touli

At the dawn of a new era.

You have to pursue your curiosity to create something outstanding. Studio Tina Touli in South East London is a hot shop to have on your radar. At the intersection of physical design and digital finishing, breathtaking moments are created.

We stand at the beginning of a new age. All tools, from the painting brush to graphic applications, are understood. We look at what is yet to come.

Tina Touli lets us participate in her process.

Typography plays a central role in your work. Where does this enthusiasm for "giving the created form a semantic level" originate?

When I was a child, my German mother taught me how to read and write in German and bought me a book to learn calligraphy. I never really bothered to ask her why I was learning calligraphy at that point, just because I enjoyed it so much. It was the most exciting part of my homework, and I always looked forward to it. I was much more interested in learning how each letter could be drawn in many different and beautiful ways than actually learning the language.

After so many years, I realized how significant the impact was, how these little exercises built and enhanced my passion for typography. This medium is so much more than just beautiful characters. It plays a vital role in communication, and it is so closely connected with emotions.

Good typography establishes a graphic balance, clearly delivering what is supposed to be communicated.

When looking at your works, one also senses the presence of particular curiosity in the process. Besides the concept, how big is the part of "playing" and "letting things happen" in your way of working?

Sometimes, the most powerful designs come from a simple concept.

By trying things out, interacting with "objects" from the digital and the physical world lets them influence the outcome, even if things work out differently from the initial thoughts. Once you interact and understand your "objects'" strengths and weaknesses, they can become your tools or prototypes or even the results of your design.

It is a process lead journey in which the analog and digital world can blend to create new strategies, approaches, and techniques.

Different design processes and inspirations can lead to unique outcomes.

You are the link between analog and digital. How do you weigh your tools? How do you define striving for perfection?

Is there a preferred working routine, or is it adjusted accordingly?

The digital world can offer us all these exciting tools and potentials for designing. But sometimes, it feels that this digital entity lacks tactile materiality.

On the other hand, the physical world can do all these fantastic things, but it is the digital one that makes everything possible.

The digital impact can effectively distort the physical world. Digital layers can be placed over the analog to enrich the outcomes and create new unique designs, approaches, and techniques.

For me, it is all about merging the two worlds in different ways and balance the needs of each project accordingly.

We are in a time of continuous change. Your assumption or outlook on how the work of designers will evolve? What would be your wish?

More and more creatives are inclined to follow the same process, starting and finishing their projects on their computer, ignoring all the inspiration from our immediate surroundings. This process can impact our creative outcomes, working in front of a screen and simply reflecting without absorbing the content rather than creating something new, finding their voice.

The question is, do you want to be a creator or be the follower of somebody else's creative voice?

As a designer, you work on free projects to try out new techniques. Where do you get your inspiration from, also considering that you work a lot with analog processes?

I like the potential of design; I am open-minded about mediums, processes, interactions, and techniques. I enjoy working on different projects that require diverse skills and techniques.

What motivates me and keeps me going is the excitement of something new.

Learning and creating something different from the last time, something unexpected, excites me the most. We usually try to find inspiration from other professionals. That is probably the most convenient source, but most likely, it will lead us to an infinite loop.

Looking at the work of other professionals from totally different fields could be a better approach that can perhaps lead us to more unique outcomes.

How about exploring our immediate surroundings? Anything around me that can stimulate any of my senses can be inspirational and an "object" for investigation.

A hole on paper, a glass of water, the ribbon used to wrap presents, even the sketchbook as an object itself.

There is endless inspiration in the physical world that we tend to ignore and fail to implement in our work. I am inclined to believe that the more unexpected the recourse of inspiration will be, the most likely it is to create original work and shape your voice.

Being a lecturer, you are frequently in touch with students either at the university or in the form of workshops.

Can you draw something positive, enriching your work from this kind of profession by passing on knowledge?

I am always interested in sharing my processes and learnings to open conversations, inspire and motivate others. Help students develop unique solutions and find their ways of being productive and helpful for the community.

For me, teaching is a two-way process, you are sharing, but at the same time, you are receiving so much more back. That feeling of satisfaction from helping others. That feeling of pride when you and your students achieve while experimenting in a workshop.

I always see teaching as an excellent opportunity to exchange knowledge and learn, to help each other push the boundaries of our creativity.

Please use an example to explain your process from sketch to finished work. A project I would appreciate deeper insight on is Z BY HP.

Please guide us through the steps.

One of the most common questions that I am asked is where do I seek inspiration?

Creating a campaign showcasing new techniques and ideas that will hopefully be a reference and inspiration for other creatives was the aim of this ad. As designers, we do not want to think of any technical issues and limitations while creating.

We want to have an uninterrupted creative experience and freedom to Create Anything, Anywhere, and Anytime.

The Z BY HP collection provides limitless possibilities, breaking any boundaries between creativity and technology.

It extends devices to become a continuation of us and our creativity.

The key messages of Create Anything, Anywhere, and Anytime are designed using various techniques, from physical experimentations to 3D visuals and sketchy graphics, reflecting the concept of a device created by a group of creatives for all types of creatives.

Tina Touli and Christoph Grünberger
November 2020

CREATE ANYTHING

An abstract composition of shapes is created to represent the concept of ANYTHING.

The look and feel of the composition remind me of space and planets, pushing the idea of ANYTHING even further. The "behind the scenes" of the design creation is revealed in the ad when zooming out of the graphics and dragging the glass tray with the abstract composition on the side.

The ZBook 2 by HP, a device that allows you to create ANYTHING reveals.

CREATE ANYWHERE

Living in this contemporary era where we are so busy that we sometimes end up having a quick lunch at the tube or finishing up our presentation on the bus on our way to work, being able to work from anywhere is crucial.

Having a device with no place restrictions, super light, easy to carry around, and quickly use from anywhere, is like a dream come true!

In this scene, custom typography has been combined with clouds, representing the concept of a "dream" and, at the same time, the idea of literally ANYWHERE.

CREATE ANYTIME

Especially if you are a night owl like me, and you often work till late, having a device like the ZBook 2 that allows you to efficiently lie down on the sofa and carry on creating with your pen is the ideal setup.

You can easily create ANYTIME.

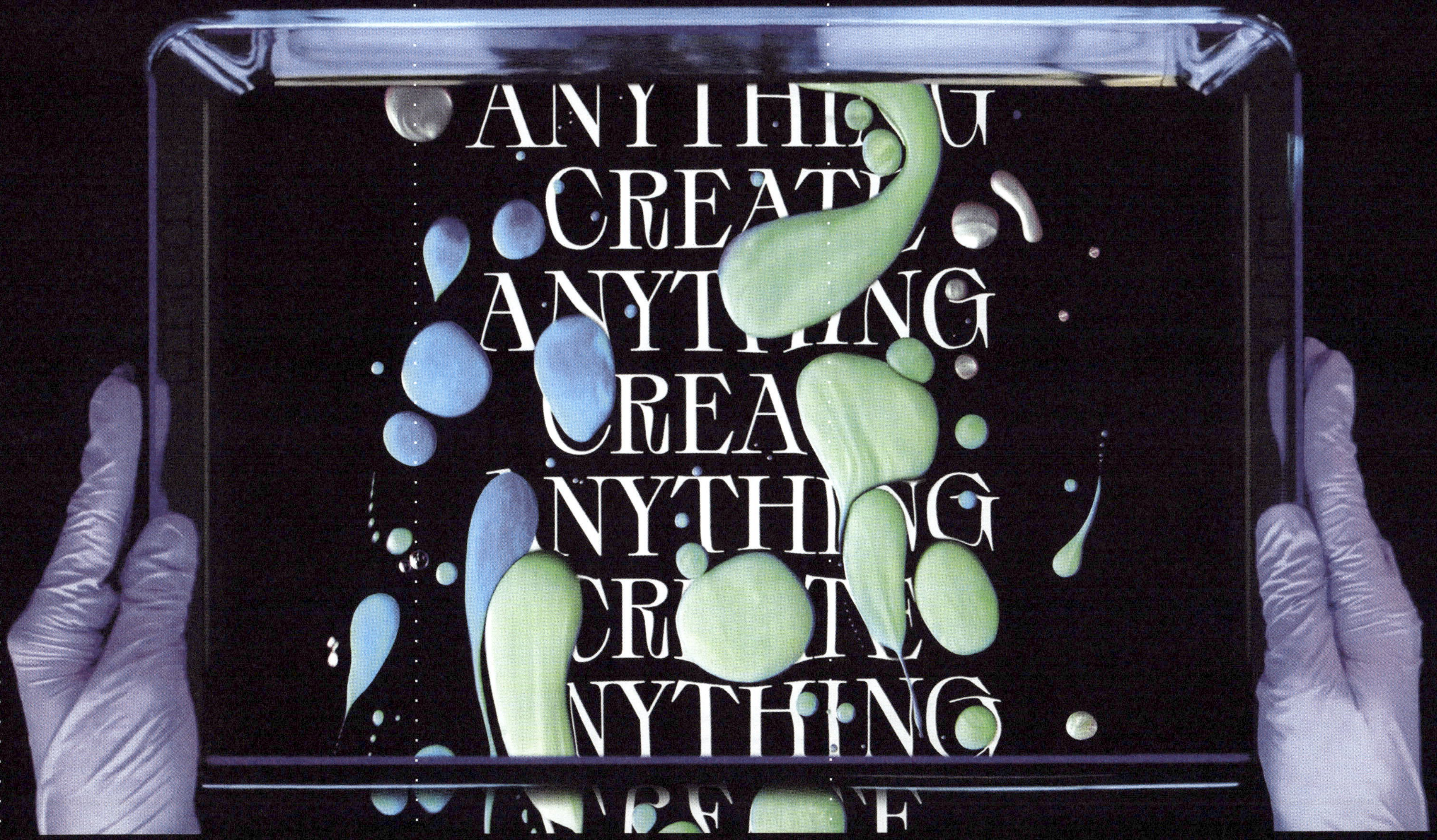

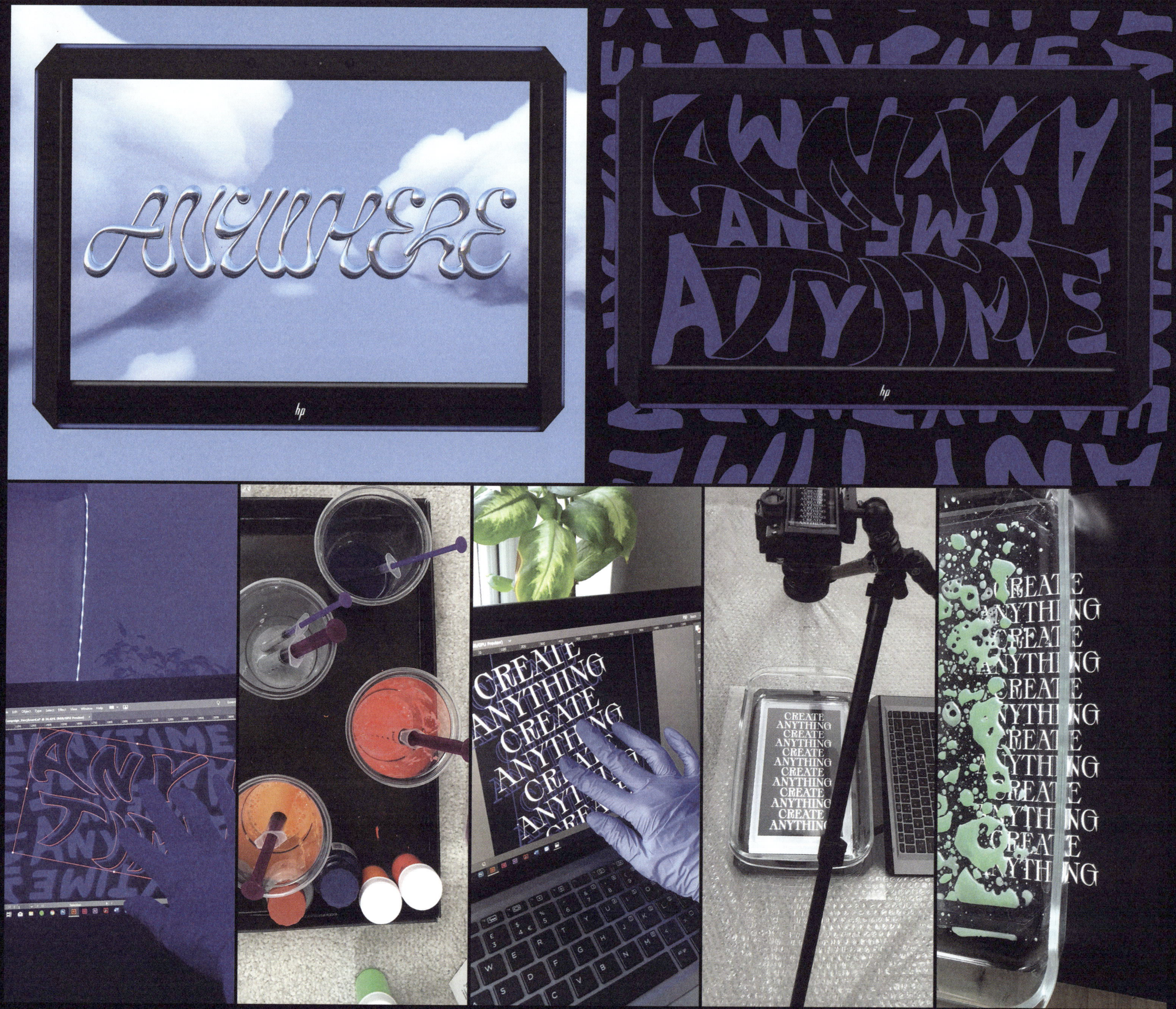
ANYWHERE
ANYTIME
CREATE
ANYTHING

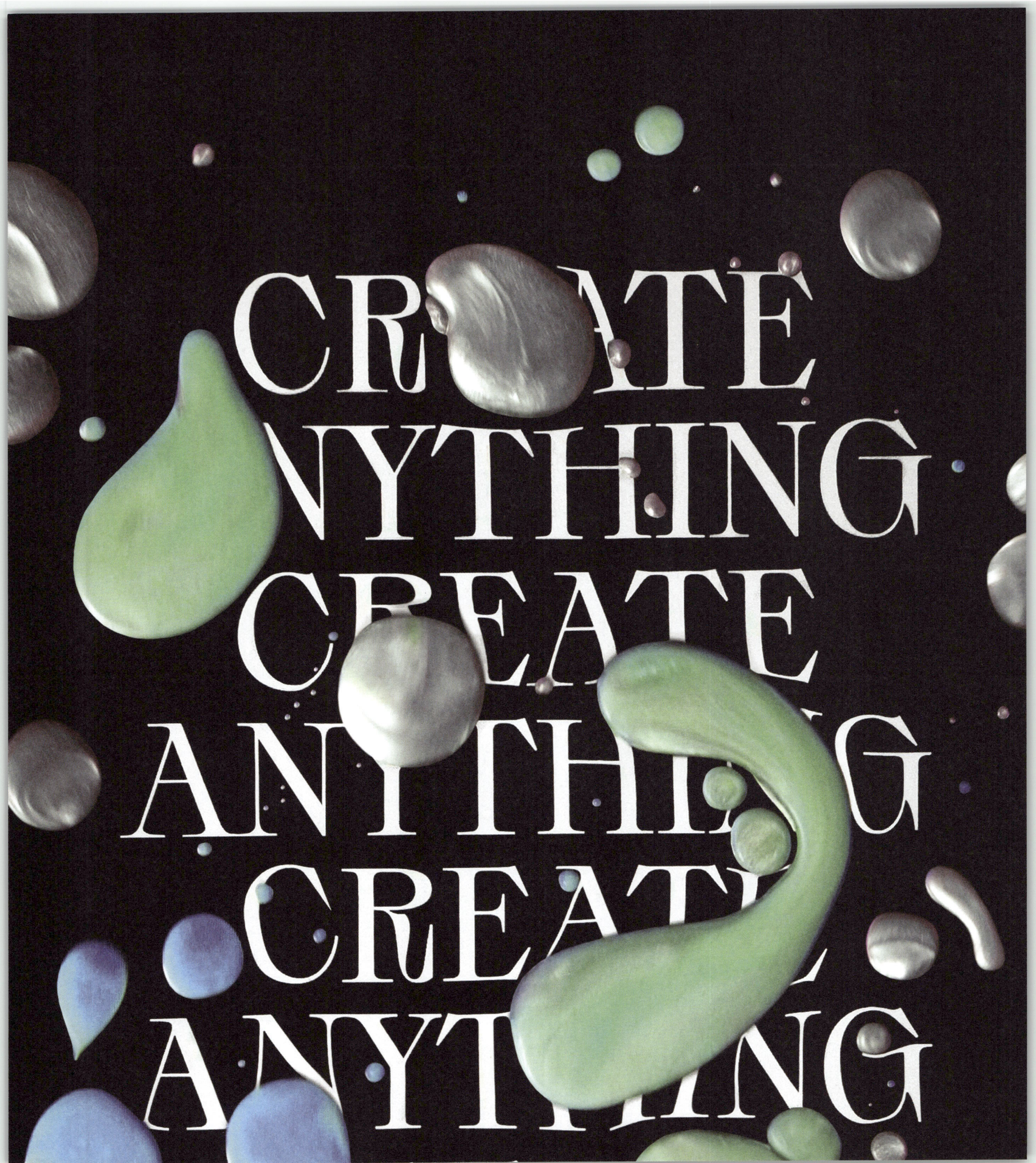
CREATE
NYTHING
CREATE
ANYTHING
CREATE
ANYTHING

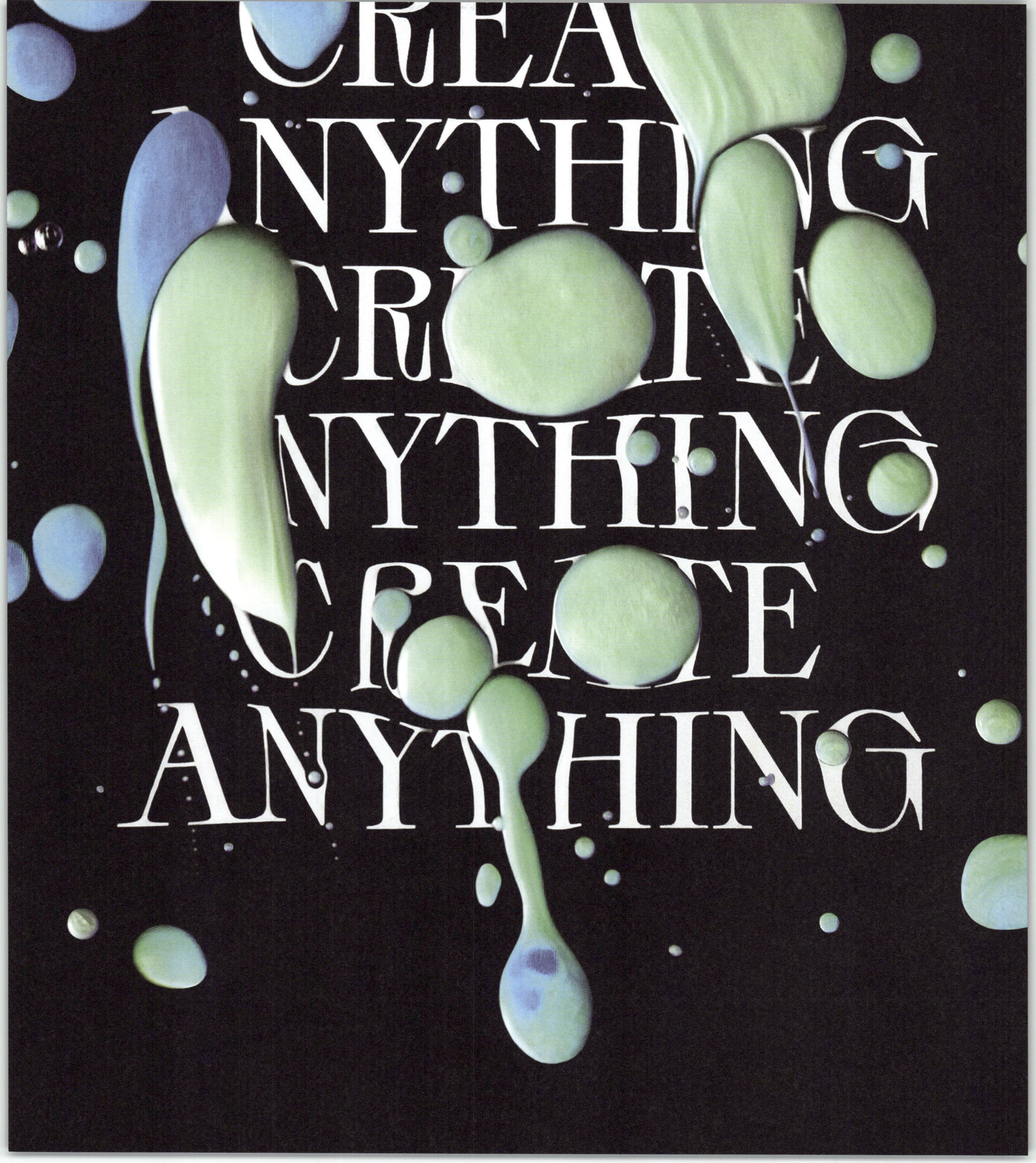
CREA
NYTHING
ANYTHING

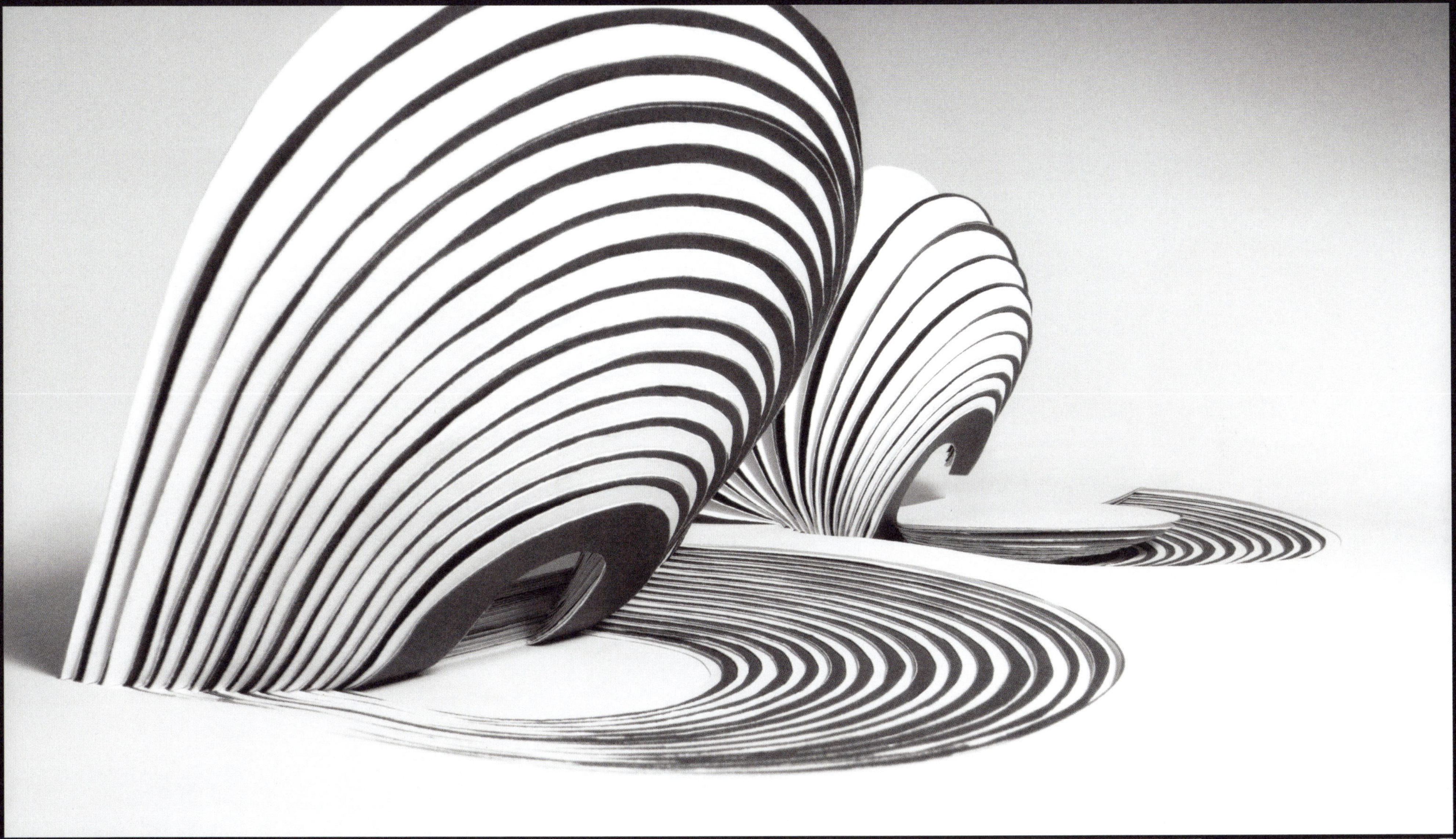

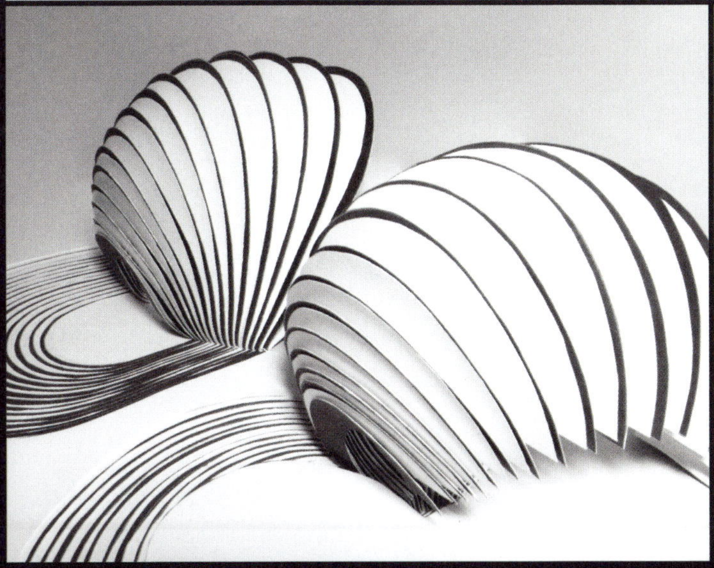

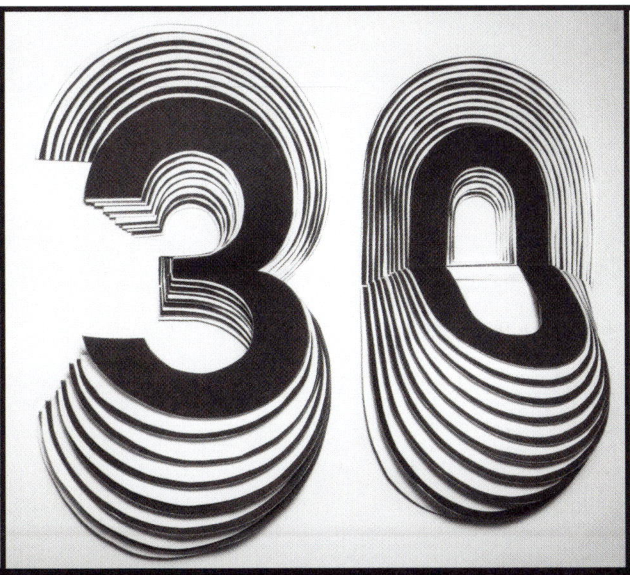

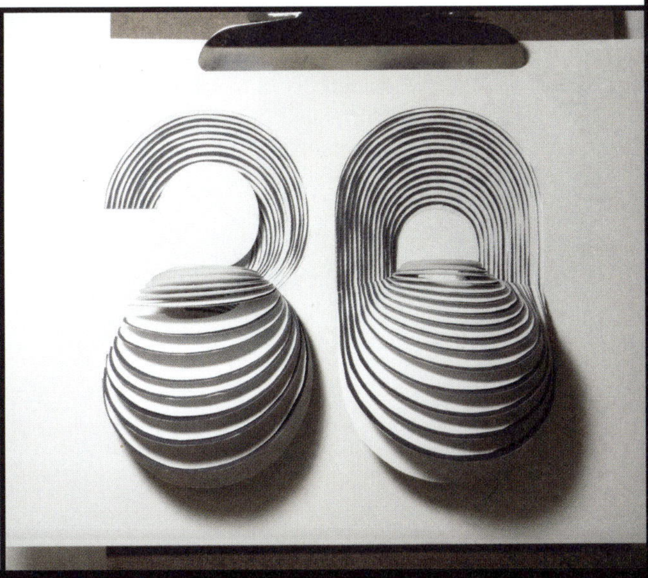

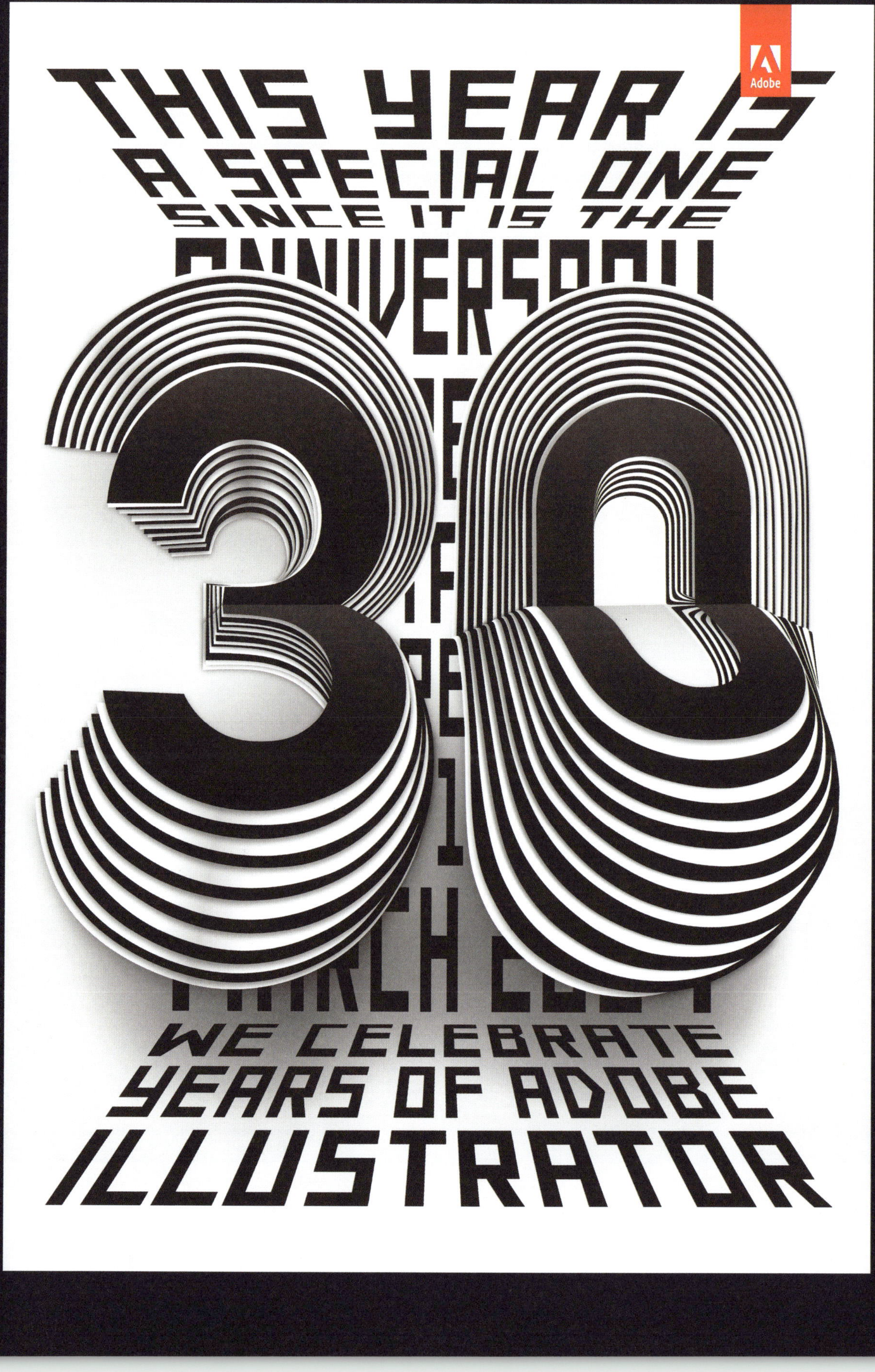

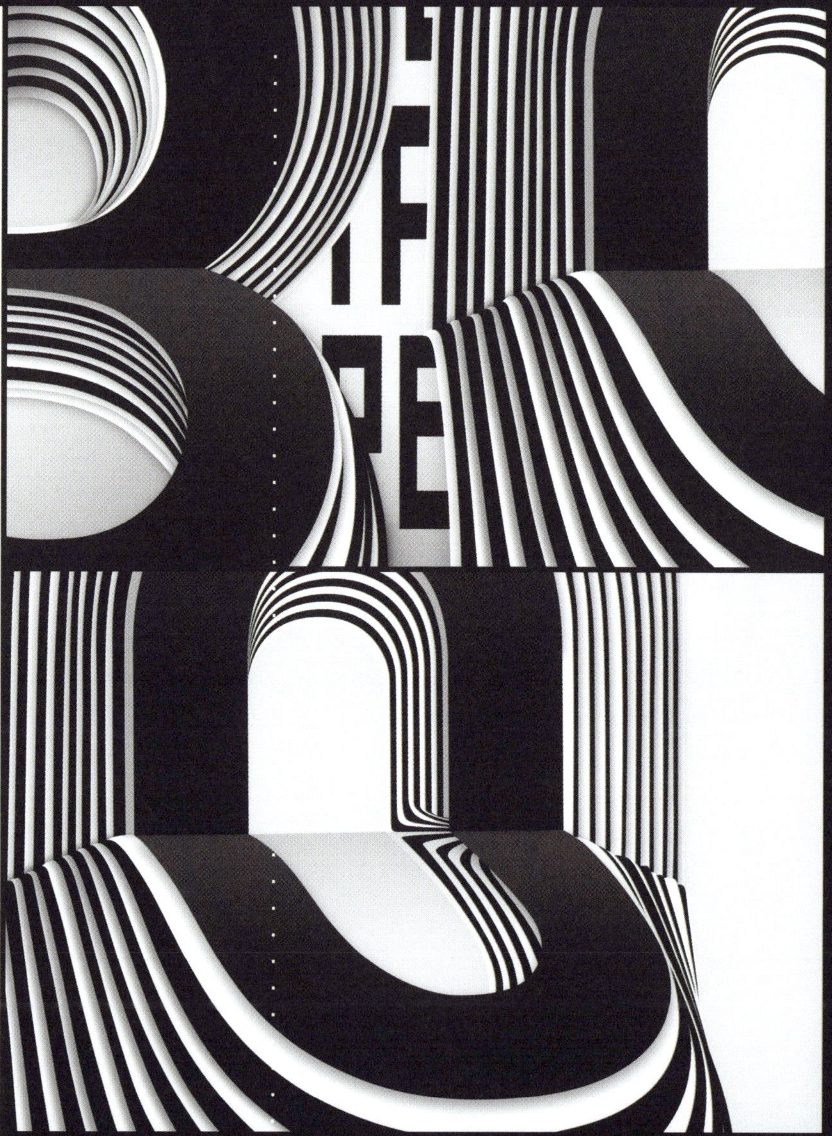

30 YEARS OF ADOBE ILLUSTRATOR
Client: Adobe Live Stream

2017 was an exceptional year celebrating 30 YEARS OF ADOBE ILLUSTRATOR.

A poster for this special anniversary has been designed during the Graphic Design Adobe Live Stream. Inspired by how we flip the pages of a book, representing the past, present, and future, a three-dimensional paper sculpture is created and used to guide the design.

It depicts the number "30," a horizontally symmetrical number, standing for the 30 YEARS OF ADOBE ILLUSTRATOR.

&PIZZA CHRISTMAS 2019
Client: &pizza
Art Direction: Shehan Abrahams
Design: Tina Touli

&pizza is a US pizza restaurant chain.

A brand that takes personal pride in being their best. That looks for an opportunity, creates and shares new ideas, and embraces unconventional thinking.

A paper sculpture of two ampersands connected has been created, photographed, and edited digitally to shape the packaging of &pizza for the Christmas 2019 period.

The packaging has been inspired by the ribbons used on the Christmas presents and the concept of connection and communication that represents the brand.

Stand together and lift each other.

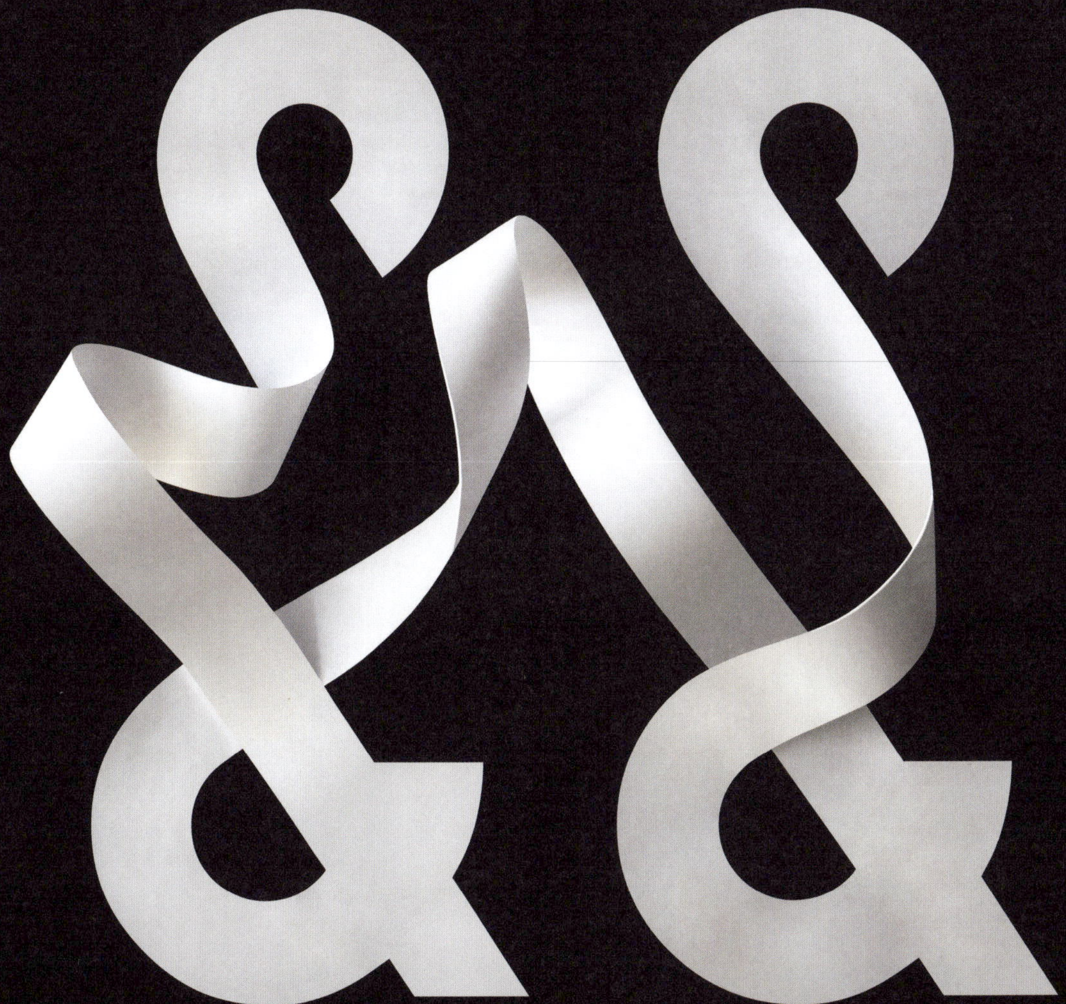

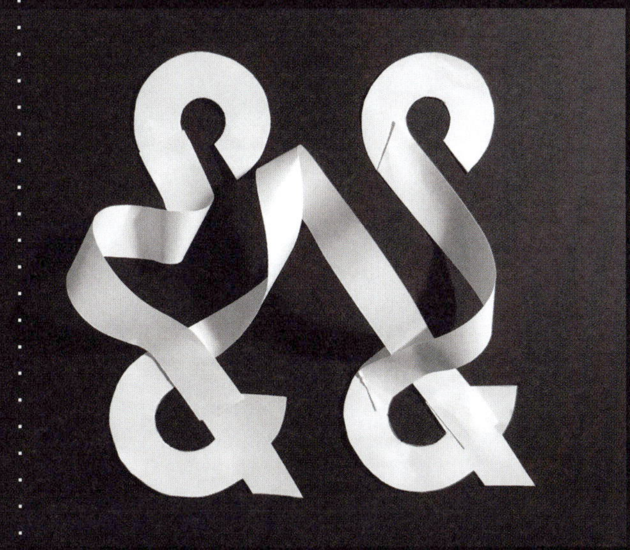

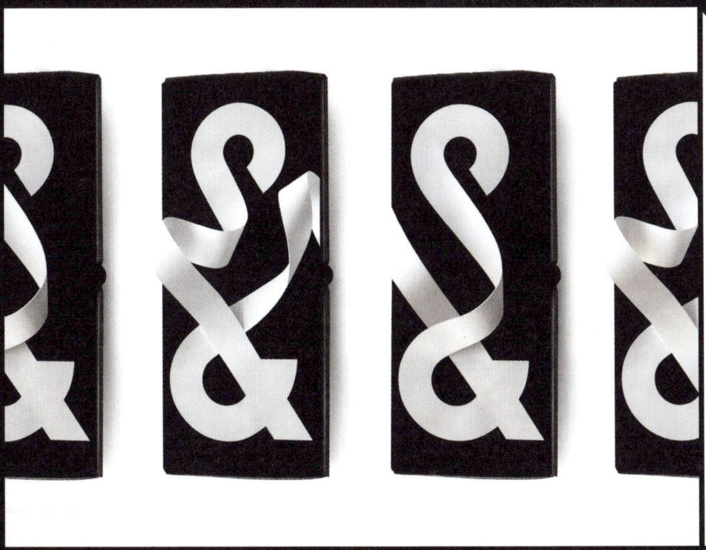

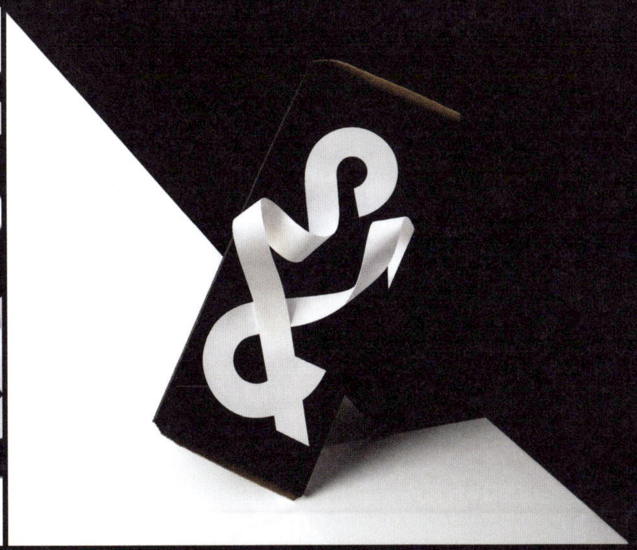

36 DAYS OF TYPE
Client: 36 Days of Type

36 DAYS OF TYPE is a project that invites designers, illustrators, and graphic artists to express their particular interpretation of the letters and numbers of the Latin alphabet.

A yearly open call explored the creative boundaries of letterforms. Participants are challenged to design a letter or number each day for 36 consecutive days, as a global and simultaneous act showing the outcome of the ability to represent the same symbols from thousands of different perspectives.

A project that aims to be a space for creation around typography and its endless graphic possibilities.

It has been a great honor to be the guest designer for the "T" letter for the 36 DAYS OF TYPE 2020 edition.

My work; mainly known for blending the physical and the digital world. Anything around us can be inspirational, even a gift ribbon itself, just like my contribution for the 36 DAYS OF TYPE letter "T."

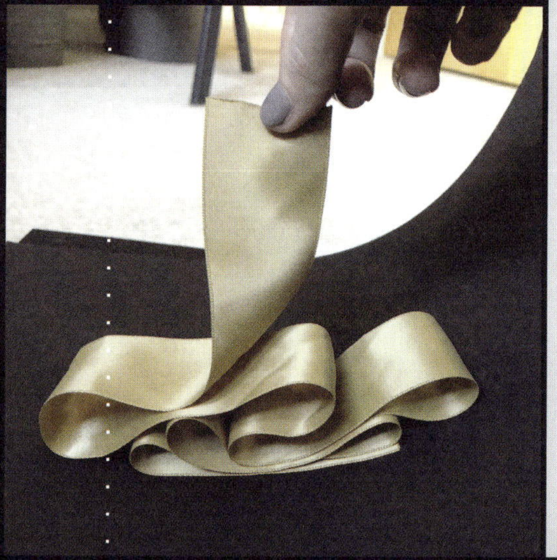

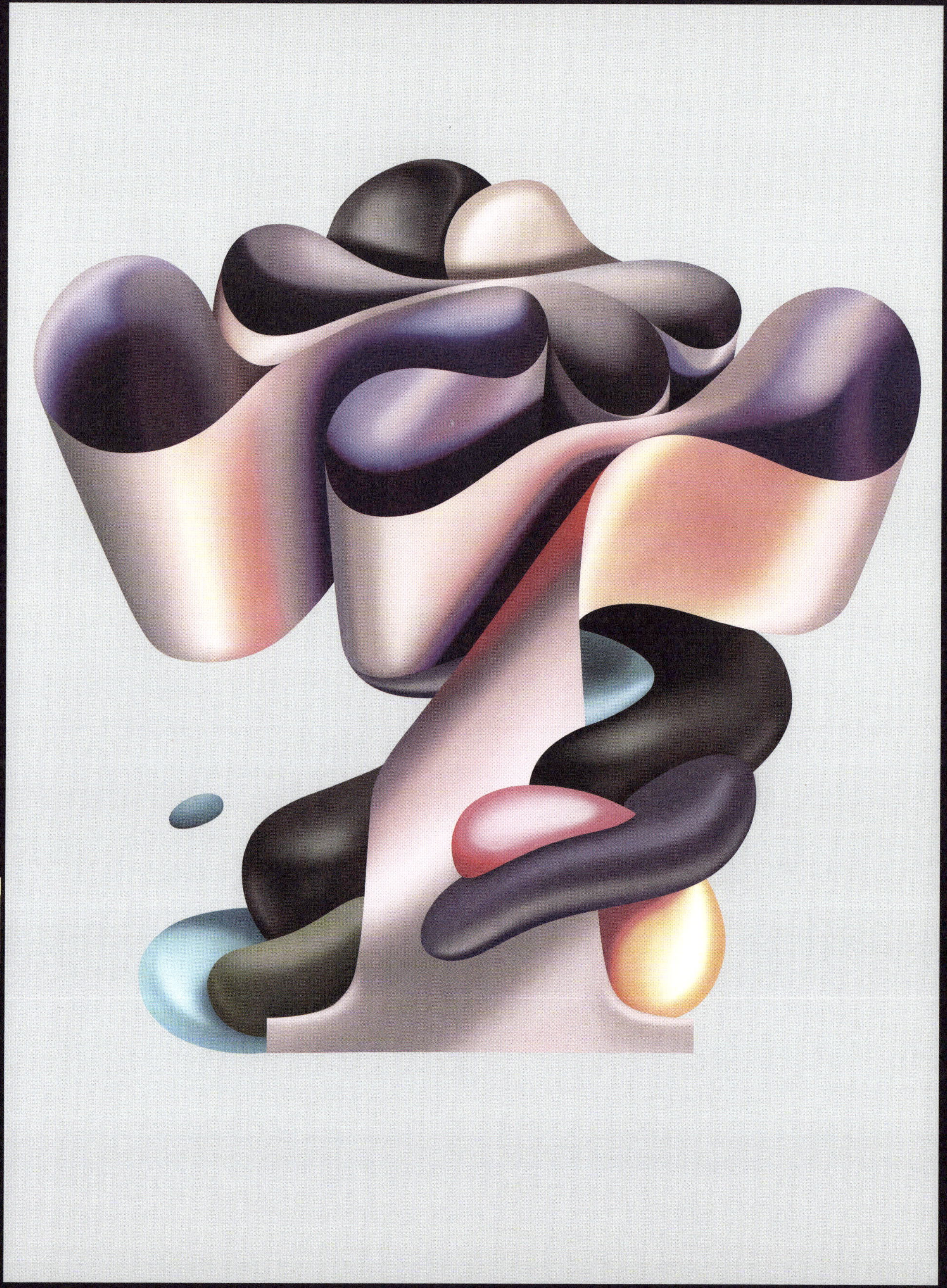

FOLLOW YOUR BLISS
Client: Skullcandy

Let's feel Blissful!

We could all use a little extra happiness; we're hoping to inspire you to look forward to more Blissful times and remember the people and experiences that give you those warm and fuzzy feels. Join Skullcandy on the journey and celebrate a different feel-good mood every month through music performances, interviews, and exclusive product drops. Because nothing changes the way, we feel like music.

During the pandemic, things feel a bit tough, and everyone could use some positivity in whatever small way we can. We want to help inspire some good vibes. That's why the Mood Boost; a campaign with a mission to boost mental health, one uplifting mood at a time, has been launched.

This month, we're feeling Blissful.

For April 2020, Skullcandy collaborates with Tina to help bring the Blissful mood to life.

They provided a specific mood (blissful) and a color palette (green earth tones with red secondary colors), and the freedom to define her interpretation of the theme while creating a digital toolkit for the campaign. A print of the hero artwork was bundled with limited-edition earbuds. Re-interpreted Skullcandy "skulls" have been designed using the Blissful mood and its color palette as a theme. Environment design graphics have been created for short-form music video performances and interview content, where artists shared stories and thoughts on the mood of the month.

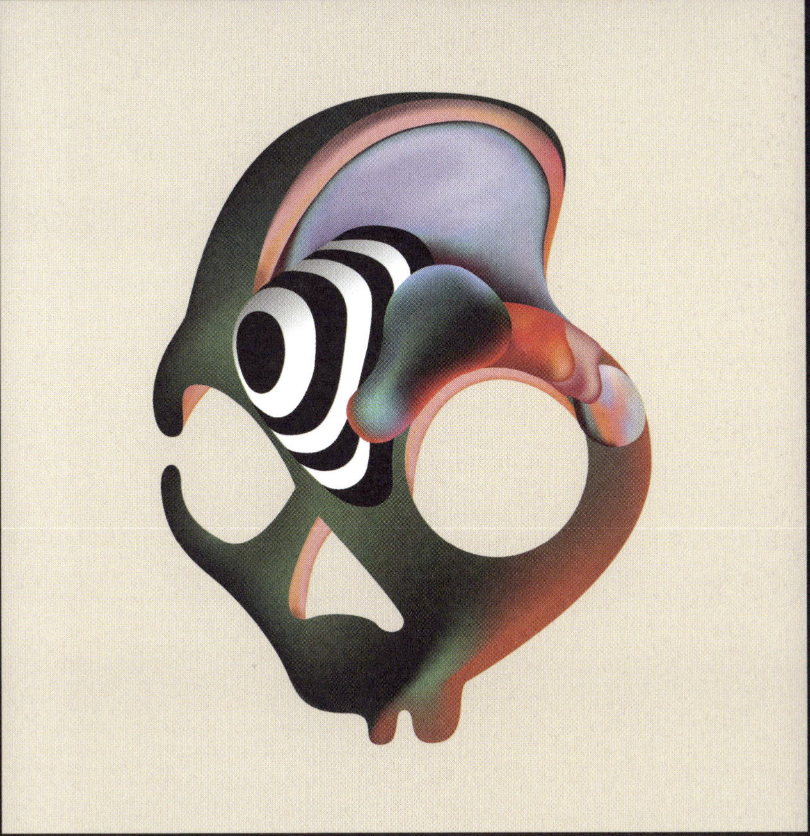

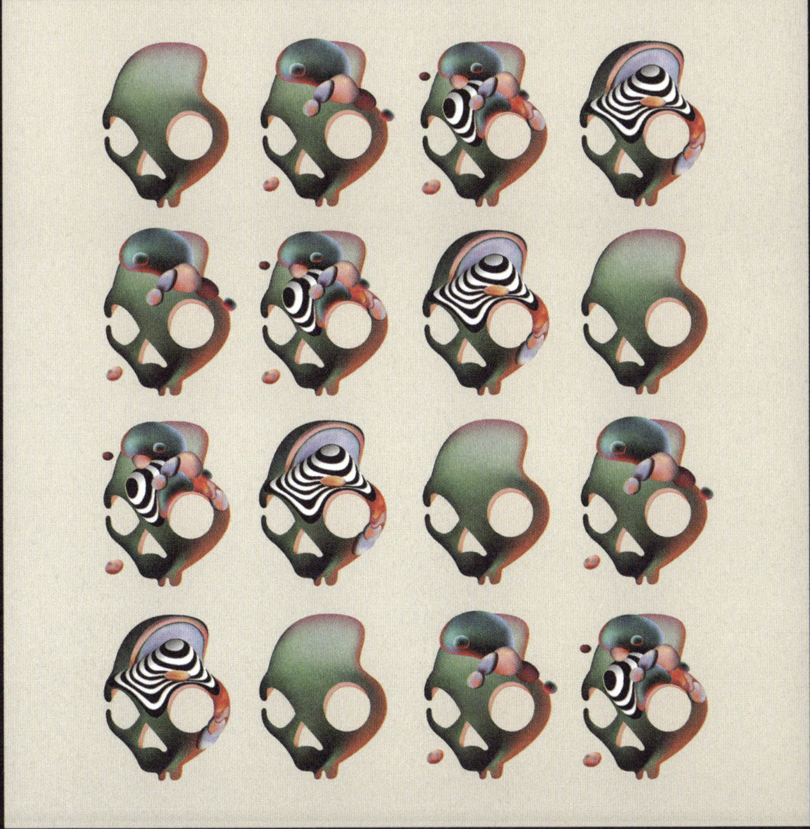

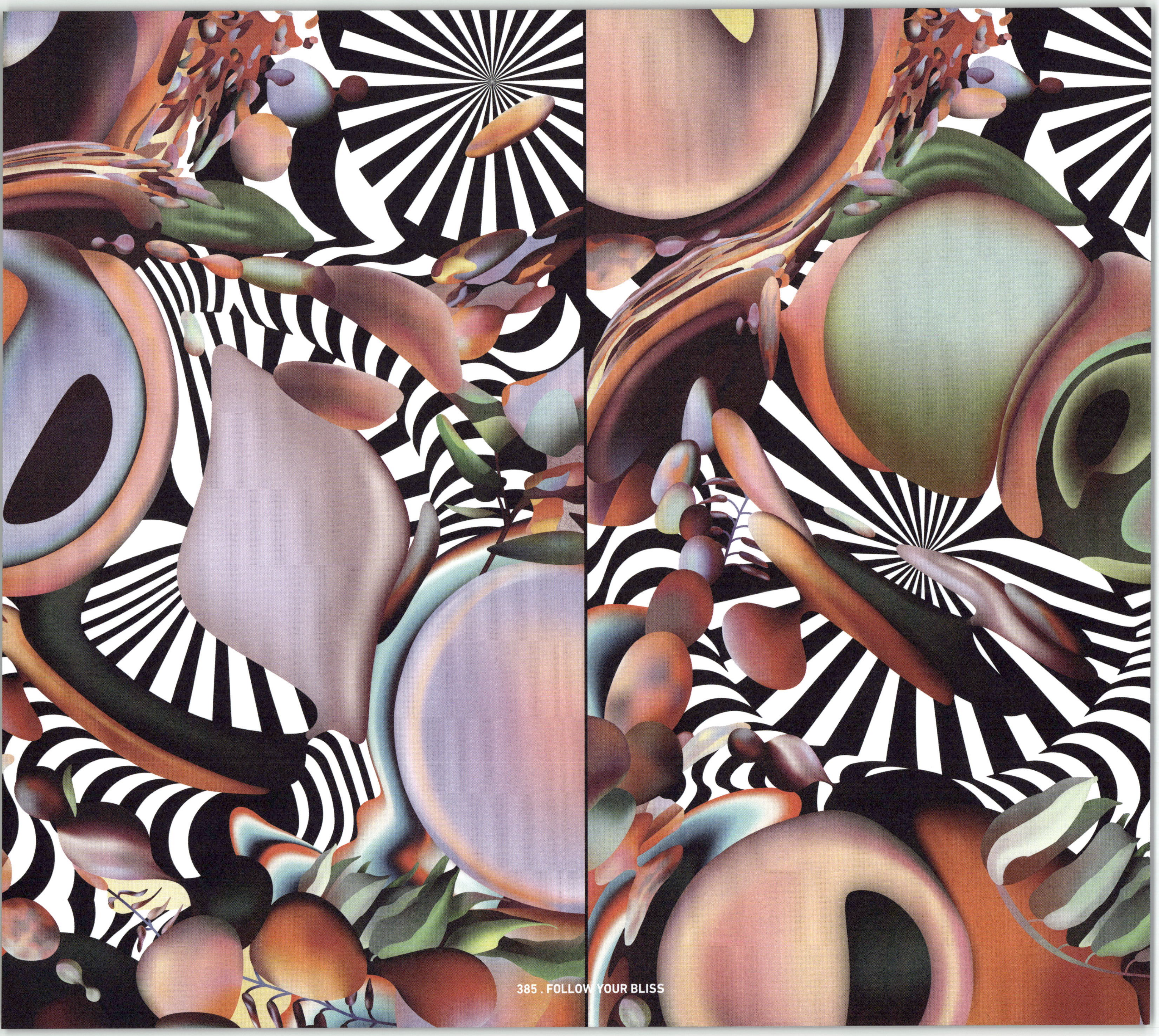

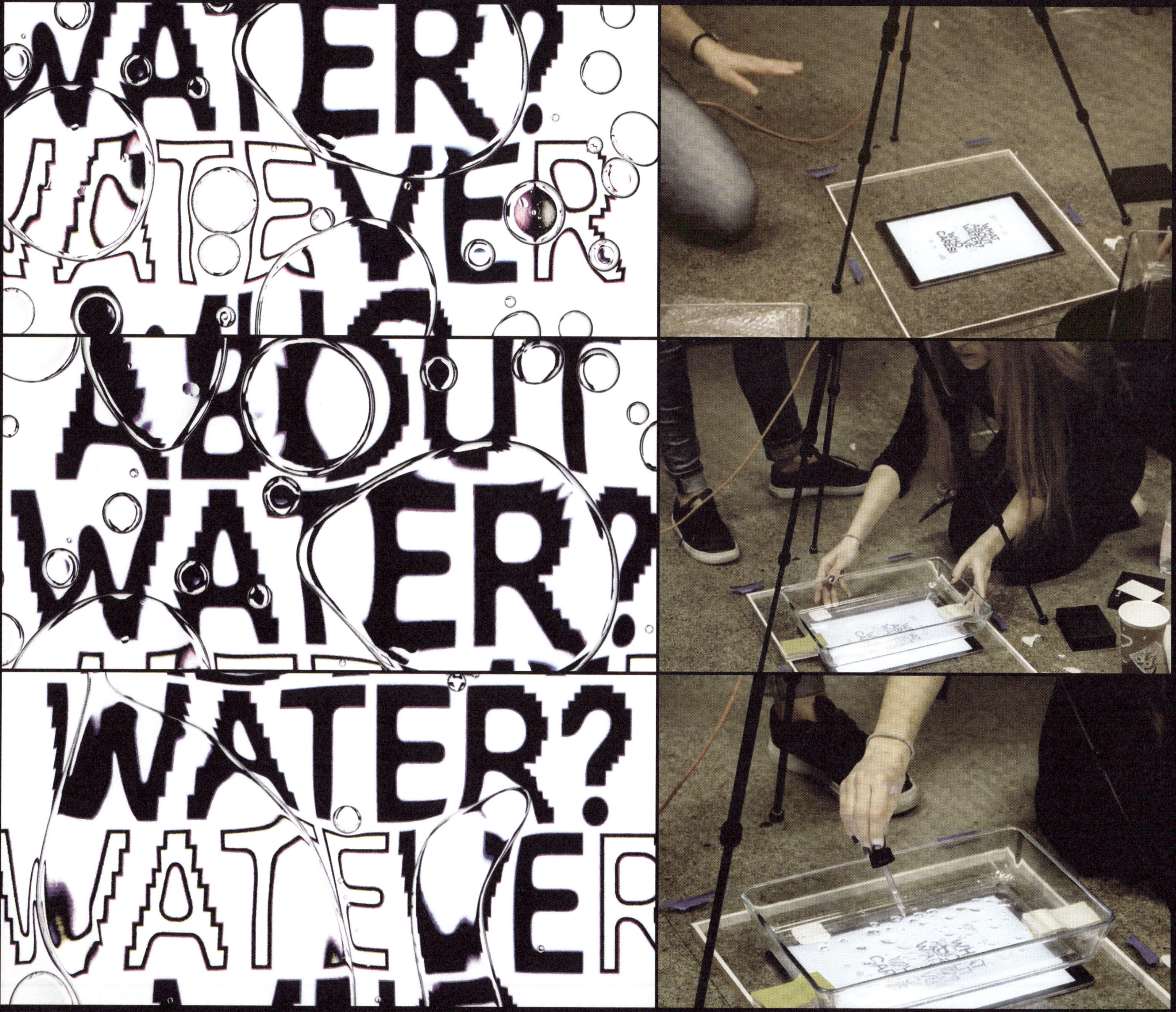
WATER?
ABOUT
WATER?
WATER?

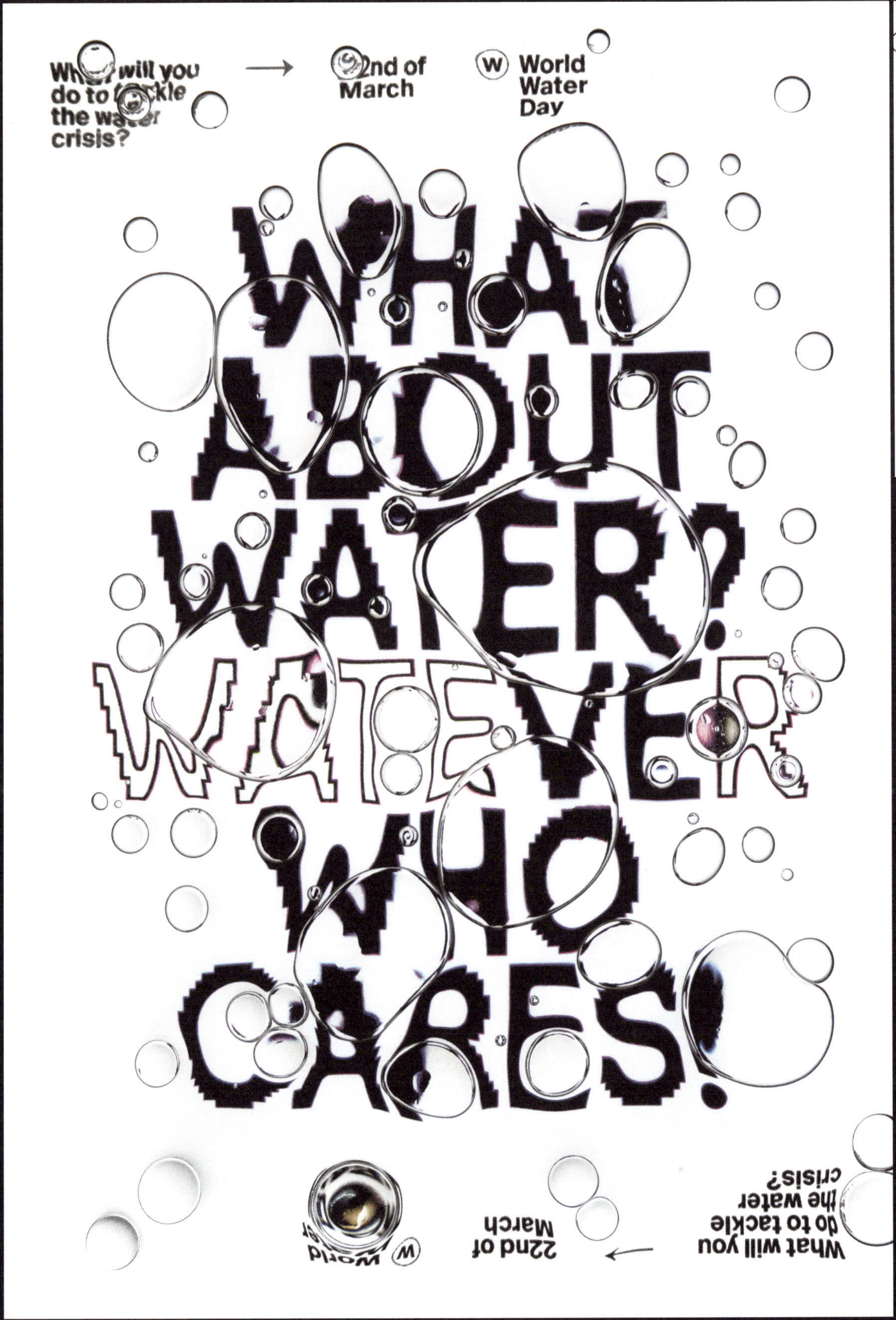

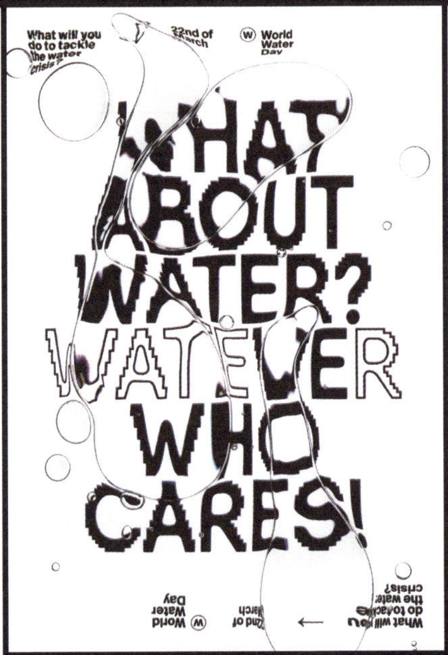

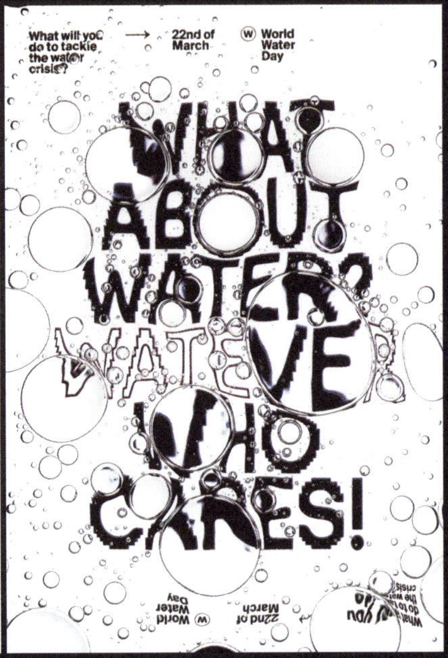

WHAT ABOUT WATER?
Client: Adobe Live Stream

Every year on the 22nd of March, we celebrate "World Water Day." A collection of five posters and a video for this special day have been designed during the Graphic Design Adobe Live Stream in San Francisco.

Water awareness campaigns usually "ask" the viewer to change his/her behavior, highlighting the importance of freshwater. In contrast, the phrase "What about water? Whatever, who cares!" has been used for this poster collection, calling the viewer to question his/her way of thinking towards the importance of water.

In earlier experimentations, during a self-initiated project in collaboration with Jakob Ritt and Yunxin Stella Wang, we developed a technique where oil-based and water-based liquids were "mixed" to create interesting shapes and distortions used for design outcomes. Inspired by these experimentations, this technique has been used to bring the water element to the project more uniquely and excitingly.

Ryan Uhrich

Name:

Ryan Uhrich

Info:

Hi, I am a Vancouver-based motion designer/3D artist working in film, tv, games, and advertising.

I specialize in 3D design & look development as well as fictional technology concepts and simulations.

I love problem-solving and exploring beautiful aesthetics.

Project:

ENTROPY

URL:

ryanuhrich.ca

Mail:

ryan.uhrich@gmail.com

Instagram:

@a.mor.phous

References:

- Star Trek Beyond
- Batman vs Superman
- Altered Carbon
- Enders Game
- Marvel Studio's Loki - Outro

Q&As

Please explain the main idea and what gave the impulse?

I think of ENTROPY as a visual exploration of energy, fluidity, and movement. There's beauty in the chaos; when order leads to disorder.

ENTROPY was born out of experimentation with particles and simulations using various techniques for manipulating forces with algorithms.

What challenges did you face for this project? And what surprises?

The main challenge was to make the movement look and feel more organic because out of the box; it looked very uniform.

I experimented with drag coefficients and was able to map those values volumetrically, resulting in an organic type of flow. Discovering this got me excited to keep going.

Please describe the technical environment.

The medium is my playground and it needs to be fun.

I like to use software that is quick for me to jump in and start iterating.

I use Cinema 4D, X-Particles, Octane Render, or Red Shift for a lot of my work, including the ENTROPY series.

Real-time feedback is critical; it keeps me excited to push harder and see where I can take it.

Tell us about your aesthetical approach.

This process started as black and white particle explorations, and at some point, I decided it was worth adding texture and began to play with color, lighting, and environment.

I love contrast and vibrant colors.

What's next? Your vision?

I hope to find time to explore more physical phenomena within a 3D environment.

I am always excited when technology mimics nature.

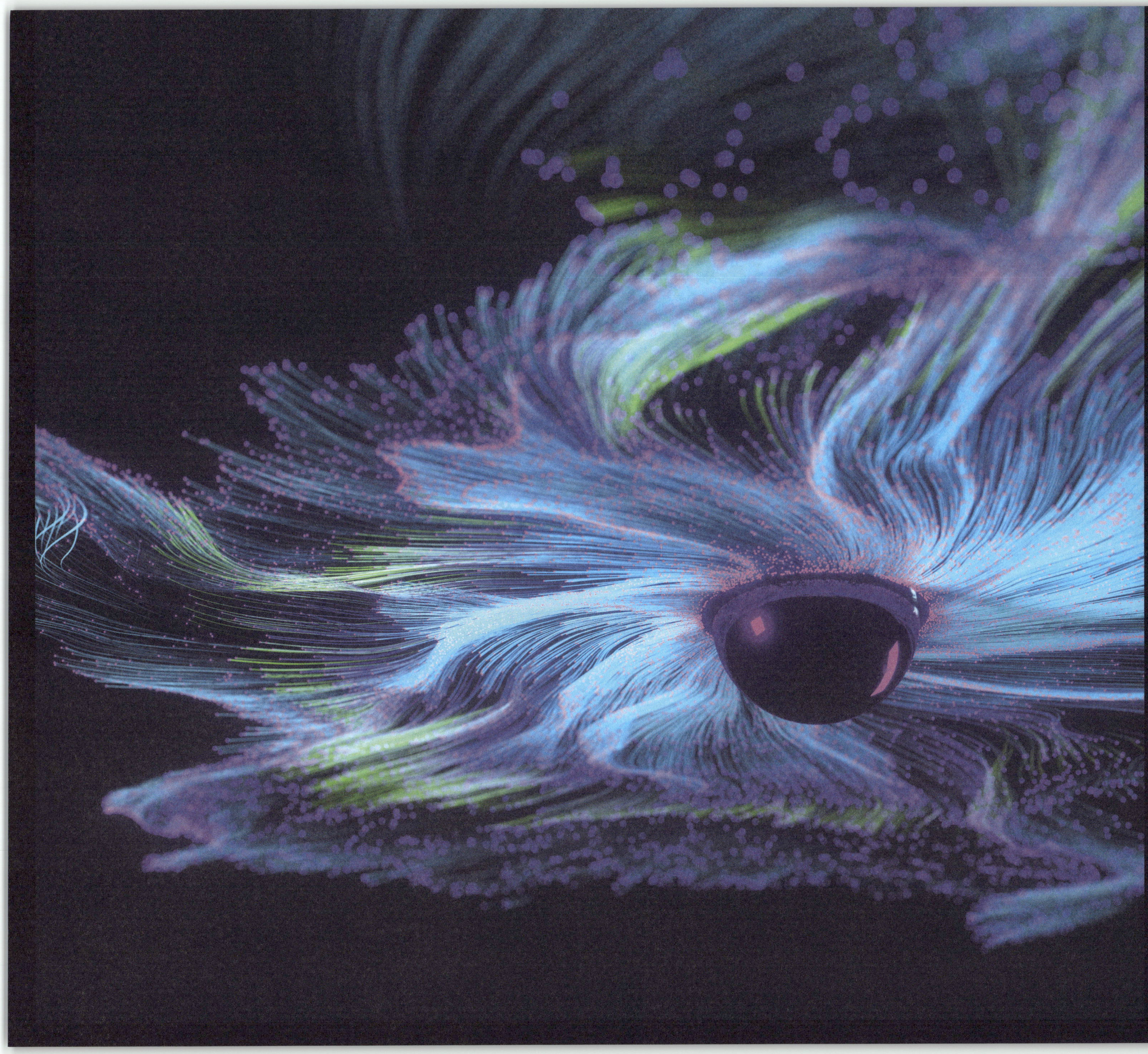

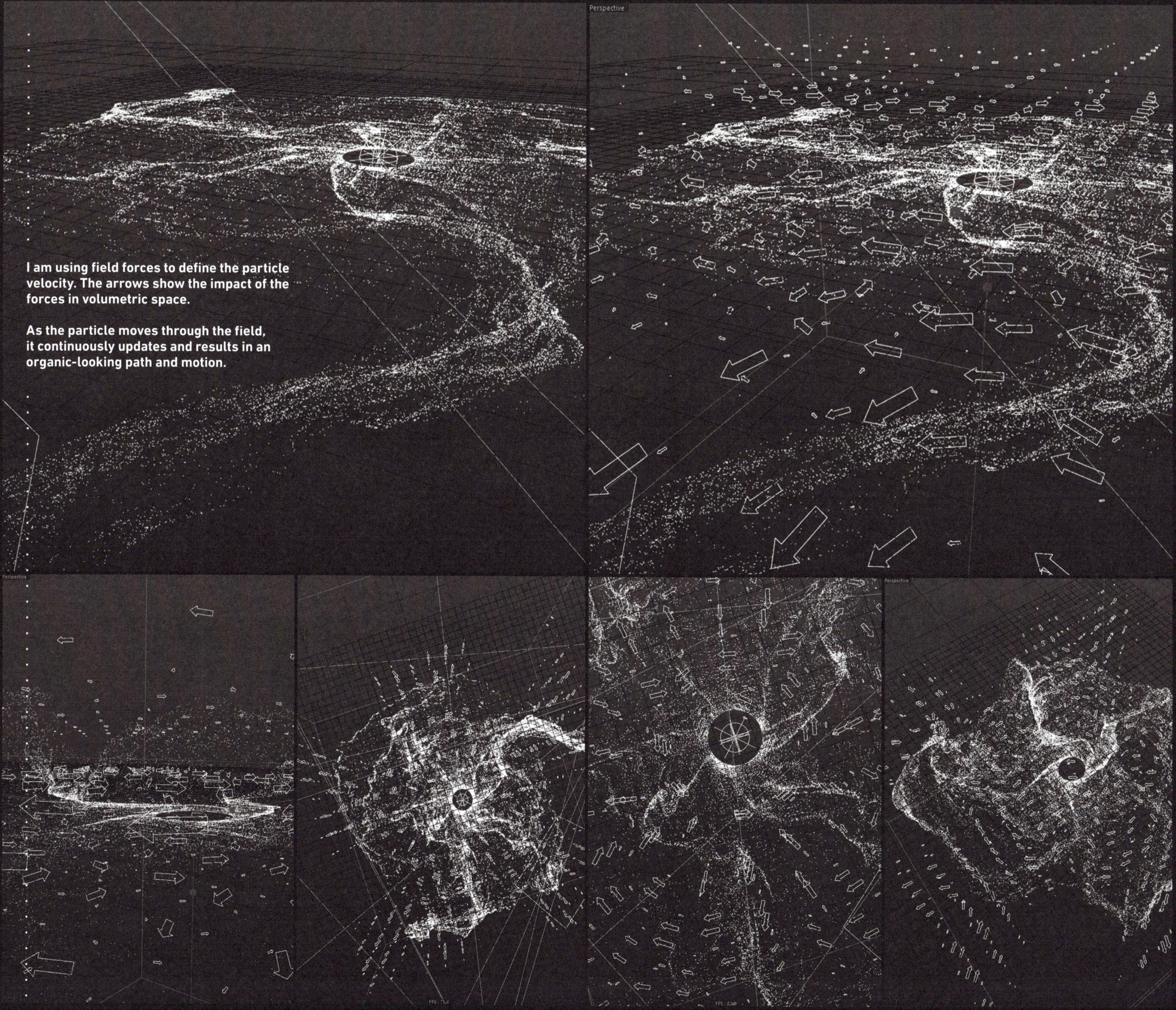

I am using field forces to define the particle velocity. The arrows show the impact of the forces in volumetric space.

As the particle moves through the field, it continuously updates and results in an organic-looking path and motion.

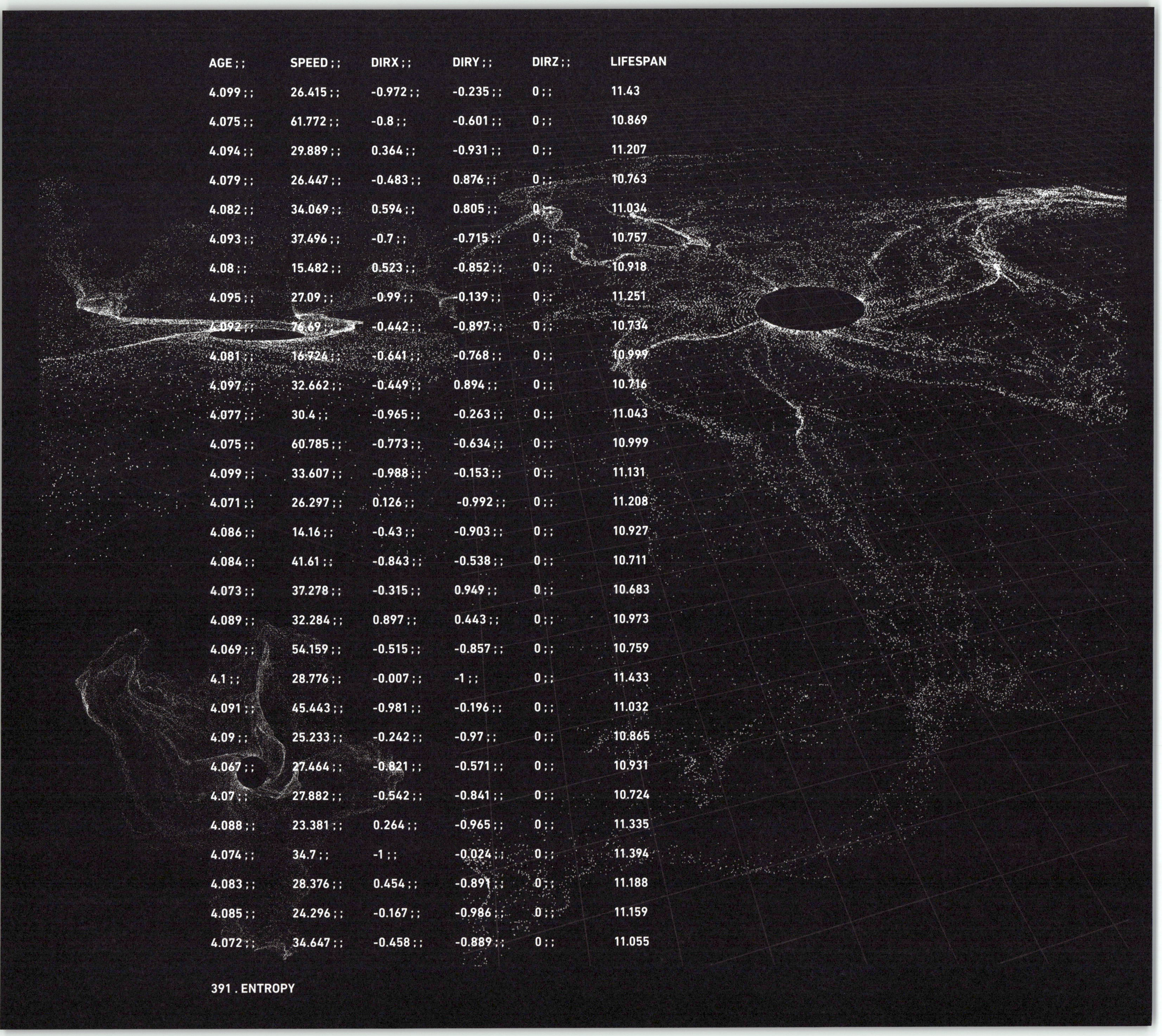

AGE ; ;	SPEED ; ;	DIRX ; ;	DIRY ; ;	DIRZ ; ;	LIFESPAN
4.099 ; ;	26.415 ; ;	-0.972 ; ;	-0.235 ; ;	0 ; ;	11.43
4.075 ; ;	61.772 ; ;	-0.8 ; ;	-0.601 ; ;	0 ; ;	10.869
4.094 ; ;	29.889 ; ;	0.364 ; ;	-0.931 ; ;	0 ; ;	11.207
4.079 ; ;	26.447 ; ;	-0.483 ; ;	0.876 ; ;	0 ; ;	10.763
4.082 ; ;	34.069 ; ;	0.594 ; ;	0.805 ; ;	0 ; ;	11.034
4.093 ; ;	37.496 ; ;	-0.7 ; ;	-0.715 ; ;	0 ; ;	10.757
4.08 ; ;	15.482 ; ;	0.523 ; ;	-0.852 ; ;	0 ; ;	10.918
4.095 ; ;	27.09 ; ;	-0.99 ; ;	-0.139 ; ;	0 ; ;	11.251
4.092 ; ;	76.69 ; ;	-0.442 ; ;	-0.897 ; ;	0 ; ;	10.734
4.081 ; ;	16.724 ; ;	-0.641 ; ;	-0.768 ; ;	0 ; ;	10.999
4.097 ; ;	32.662 ; ;	-0.449 ; ;	0.894 ; ;	0 ; ;	10.716
4.077 ; ;	30.4 ; ;	-0.965 ; ;	-0.263 ; ;	0 ; ;	11.043
4.075 ; ;	60.785 ; ;	-0.773 ; ;	-0.634 ; ;	0 ; ;	10.999
4.099 ; ;	33.607 ; ;	-0.988 ; ;	-0.153 ; ;	0 ; ;	11.131
4.071 ; ;	26.297 ; ;	0.126 ; ;	-0.992 ; ;	0 ; ;	11.208
4.086 ; ;	14.16 ; ;	-0.43 ; ;	-0.903 ; ;	0 ; ;	10.927
4.084 ; ;	41.61 ; ;	-0.843 ; ;	-0.538 ; ;	0 ; ;	10.711
4.073 ; ;	37.278 ; ;	-0.315 ; ;	0.949 ; ;	0 ; ;	10.683
4.089 ; ;	32.284 ; ;	0.897 ; ;	0.443 ; ;	0 ; ;	10.973
4.069 ; ;	54.159 ; ;	-0.515 ; ;	-0.857 ; ;	0 ; ;	10.759
4.1 ; ;	28.776 ; ;	-0.007 ; ;	-1 ; ;	0 ; ;	11.433
4.091 ; ;	45.443 ; ;	-0.981 ; ;	-0.196 ; ;	0 ; ;	11.032
4.09 ; ;	25.233 ; ;	-0.242 ; ;	-0.97 ; ;	0 ; ;	10.865
4.067 ; ;	27.464 ; ;	-0.821 ; ;	-0.571 ; ;	0 ; ;	10.931
4.07 ; ;	27.882 ; ;	-0.542 ; ;	-0.841 ; ;	0 ; ;	10.724
4.088 ; ;	23.381 ; ;	0.264 ; ;	-0.965 ; ;	0 ; ;	11.335
4.074 ; ;	34.7 ; ;	-1 ; ;	-0.024 ; ;	0 ; ;	11.394
4.083 ; ;	28.376 ; ;	0.454 ; ;	-0.891 ; ;	0 ; ;	11.188
4.085 ; ;	24.296 ; ;	-0.167 ; ;	-0.986 ; ;	0 ; ;	11.159
4.072 ; ;	34.647 ; ;	-0.458 ; ;	-0.889 ; ;	0 ; ;	11.055

391 . ENTROPY

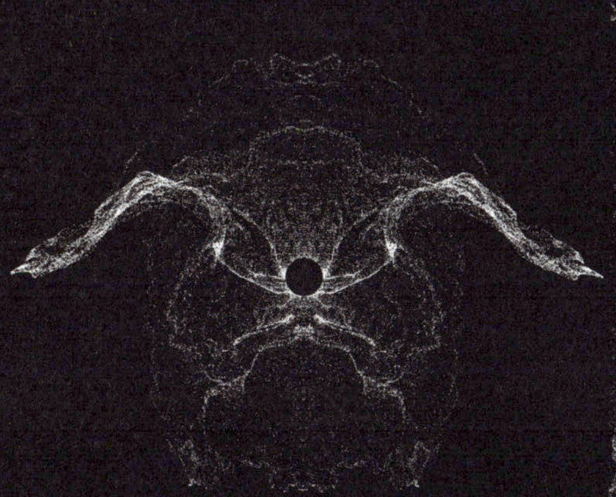

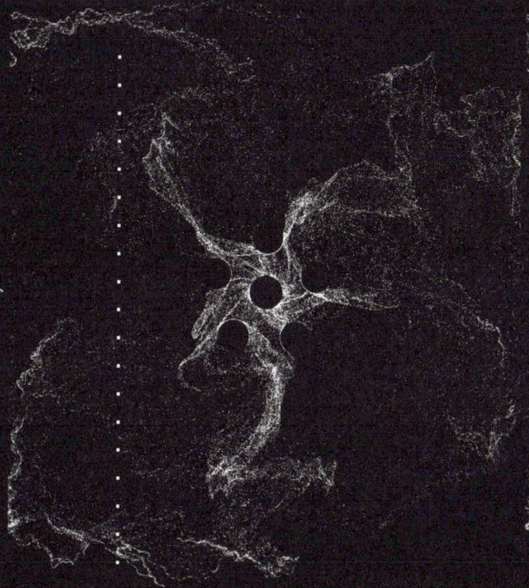

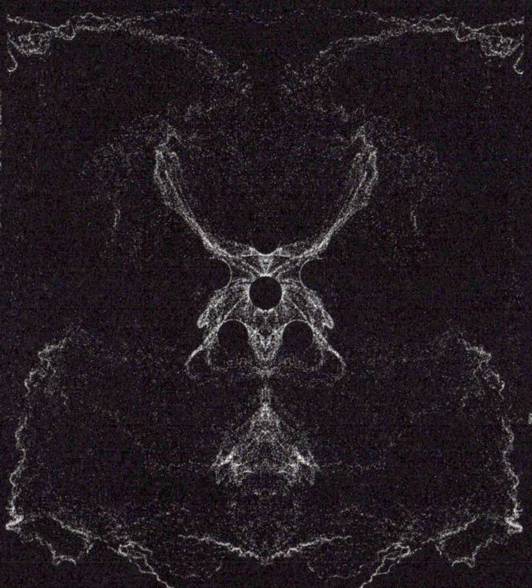

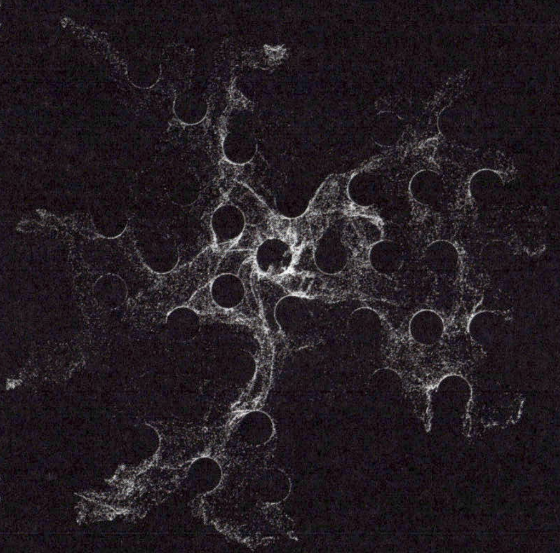

At this stage, the particles are also subjected to various structures to make the result more interesting.

By colliding and avoiding certain areas, particles start to reveal, and "voids" begin to form.

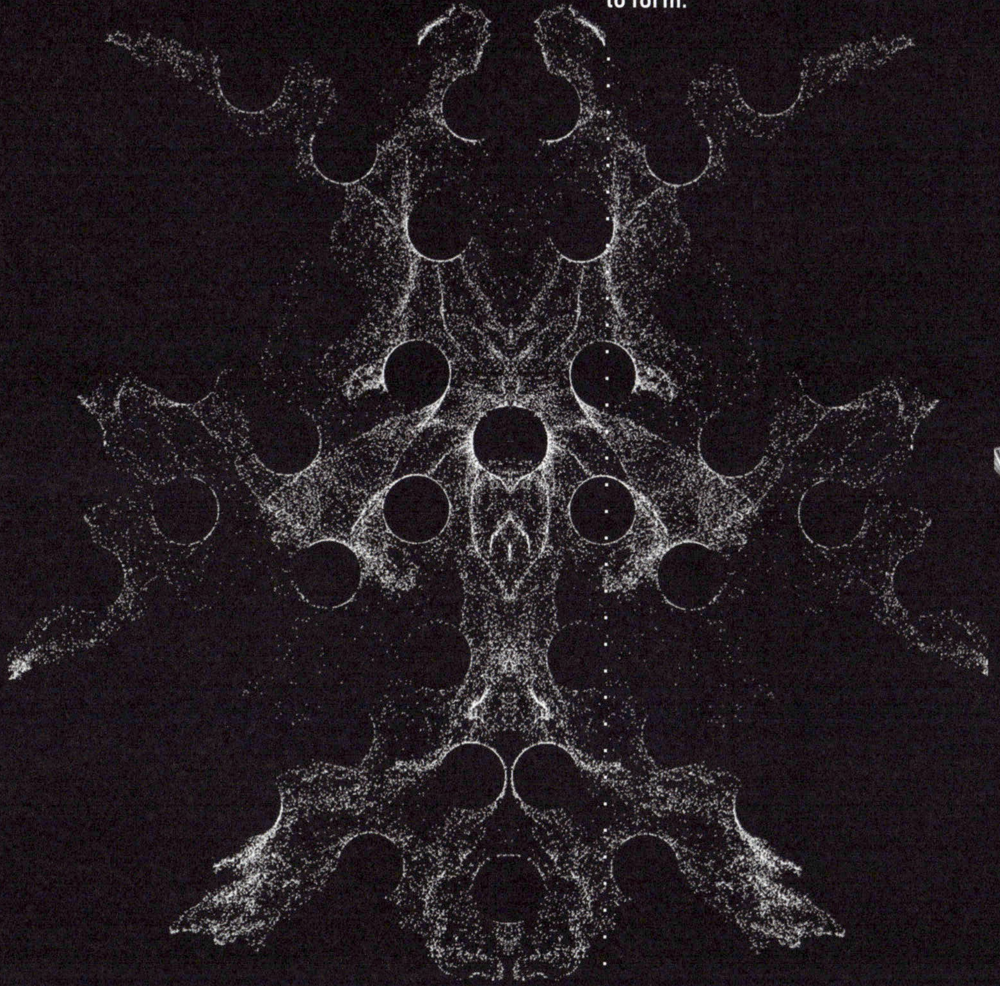

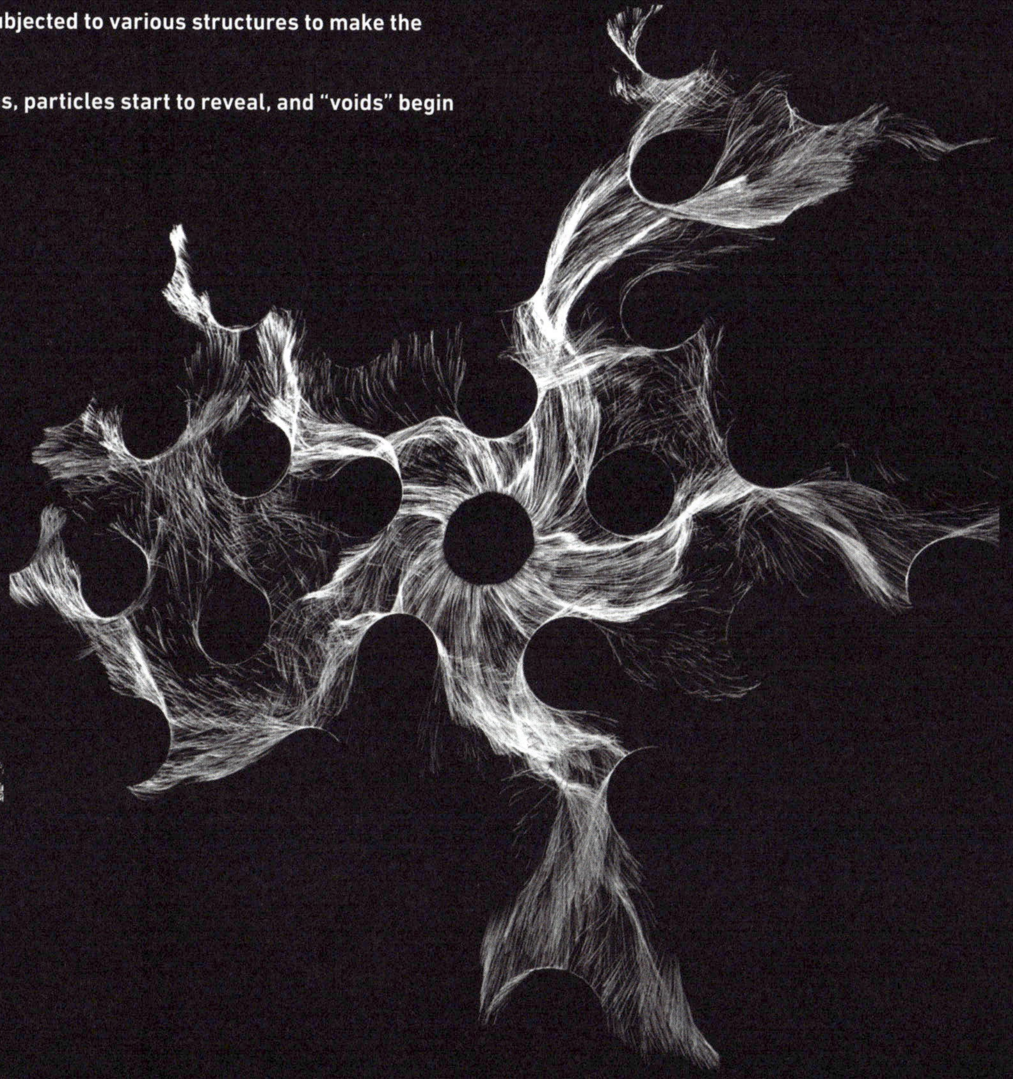

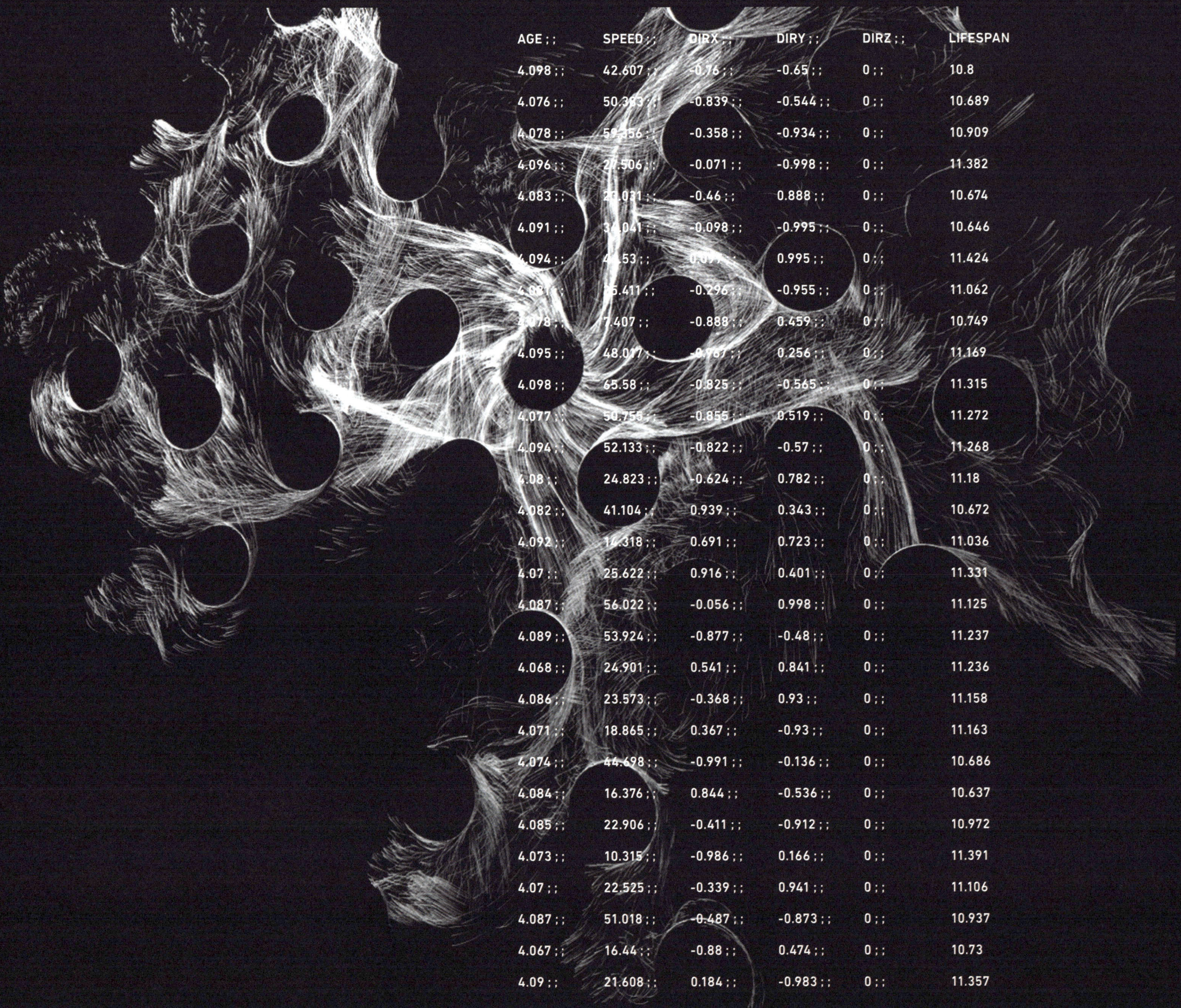

AGE ; ;	SPEED ; ;	DIRX ; ;	DIRY ; ;	DIRZ ; ;	LIFESPAN
4.098 ; ;	42.607 ; ;	-0.76 ; ;	-0.65 ; ;	0 ; ;	10.8
4.076 ; ;	50.383 ; ;	-0.839 ; ;	-0.544 ; ;	0 ; ;	10.689
4.078 ; ;	59.356 ; ;	-0.358 ; ;	-0.934 ; ;	0 ; ;	10.909
4.096 ; ;	27.506 ; ;	-0.071 ; ;	-0.998 ; ;	0 ; ;	11.382
4.083 ; ;	20.031 ; ;	-0.46 ; ;	0.888 ; ;	0 ; ;	10.674
4.091 ; ;	34.041 ; ;	-0.098 ; ;	-0.995 ; ;	0 ; ;	10.646
4.094 ; ;	44.53 ; ;	0.0[illegible] ; ;	0.995 ; ;	0 ; ;	11.424
4.081 ; ;	[illegible]5.411 ; ;	-0.296 ; ;	-0.955 ; ;	0 ; ;	11.062
4.078 ; ;	7.407 ; ;	-0.888 ; ;	0.459 ; ;	0 ; ;	10.749
4.095 ; ;	48.017 ; ;	-0.967 ; ;	0.256 ; ;	0 ; ;	11.169
4.098 ; ;	65.58 ; ;	-0.825 ; ;	-0.565 ; ;	0 ; ;	11.315
4.077 ; ;	50.755 ; ;	-0.855 ; ;	0.519 ; ;	0 ; ;	11.272
4.094 ; ;	52.133 ; ;	-0.822 ; ;	-0.57 ; ;	0 ; ;	11.268
4.08 ; ;	24.823 ; ;	-0.624 ; ;	0.782 ; ;	0 ; ;	11.18
4.082 ; ;	41.104 ; ;	0.939 ; ;	0.343 ; ;	0 ; ;	10.672
4.092 ; ;	14.318 ; ;	0.691 ; ;	0.723 ; ;	0 ; ;	11.036
4.07 ; ;	25.622 ; ;	0.916 ; ;	0.401 ; ;	0 ; ;	11.331
4.087 ; ;	56.022 ; ;	-0.056 ; ;	0.998 ; ;	0 ; ;	11.125
4.089 ; ;	53.924 ; ;	-0.877 ; ;	-0.48 ; ;	0 ; ;	11.237
4.068 ; ;	24.901 ; ;	0.541 ; ;	0.841 ; ;	0 ; ;	11.236
4.086 ; ;	23.573 ; ;	-0.368 ; ;	0.93 ; ;	0 ; ;	11.158
4.071 ; ;	18.865 ; ;	0.367 ; ;	-0.93 ; ;	0 ; ;	11.163
4.074 ; ;	44.698 ; ;	-0.991 ; ;	-0.136 ; ;	0 ; ;	10.686
4.084 ; ;	16.376 ; ;	0.844 ; ;	-0.536 ; ;	0 ; ;	10.637
4.085 ; ;	22.906 ; ;	-0.411 ; ;	-0.912 ; ;	0 ; ;	10.972
4.073 ; ;	10.315 ; ;	-0.986 ; ;	0.166 ; ;	0 ; ;	11.391
4.07 ; ;	22.525 ; ;	-0.339 ; ;	0.941 ; ;	0 ; ;	11.106
4.087 ; ;	51.018 ; ;	-0.487 ; ;	-0.873 ; ;	0 ; ;	10.937
4.067 ; ;	16.44 ; ;	-0.88 ; ;	0.474 ; ;	0 ; ;	10.73
4.09 ; ;	21.608 ; ;	0.184 ; ;	-0.983 ; ;	0 ; ;	11.357

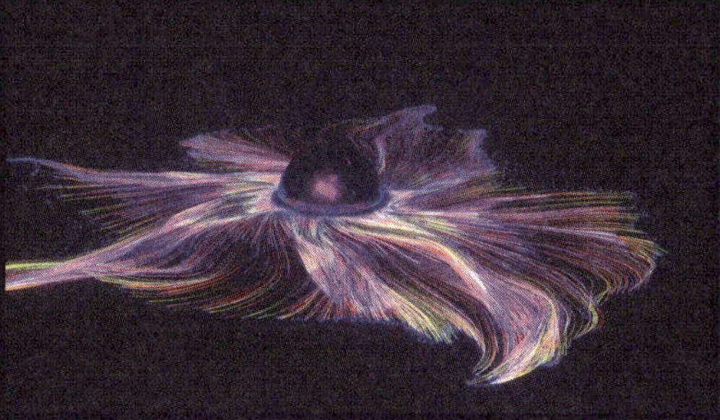
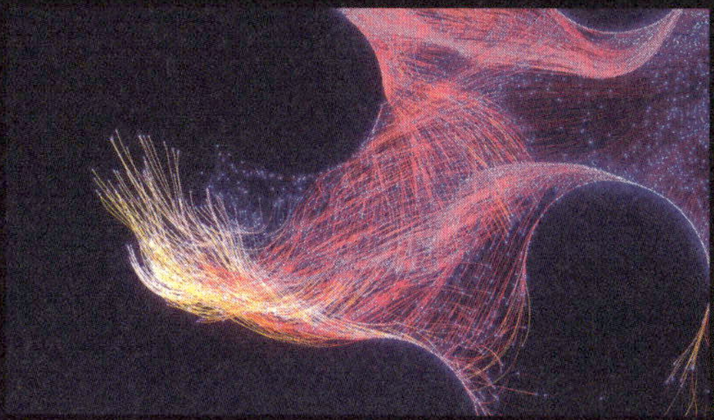
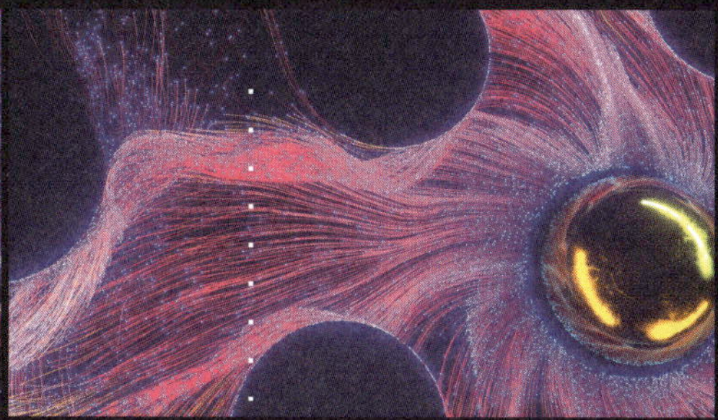
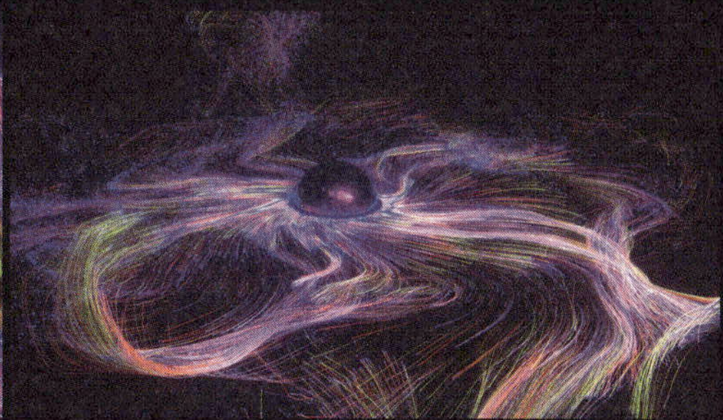
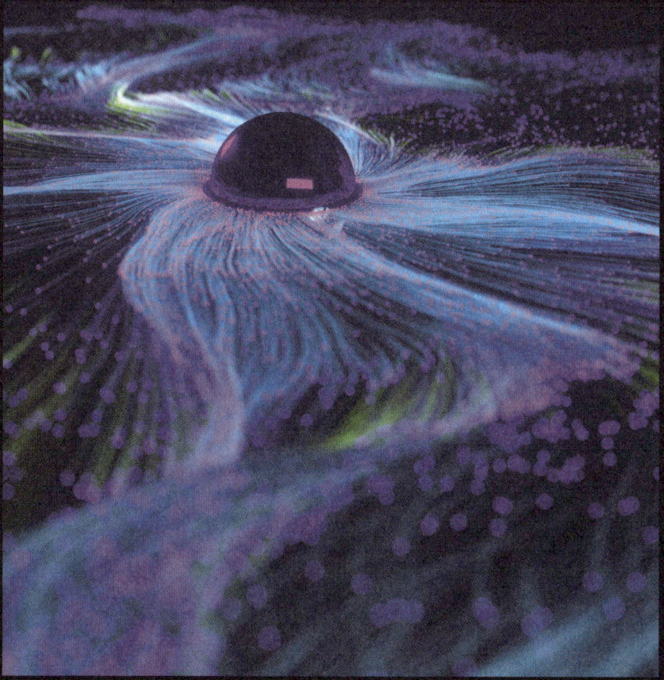
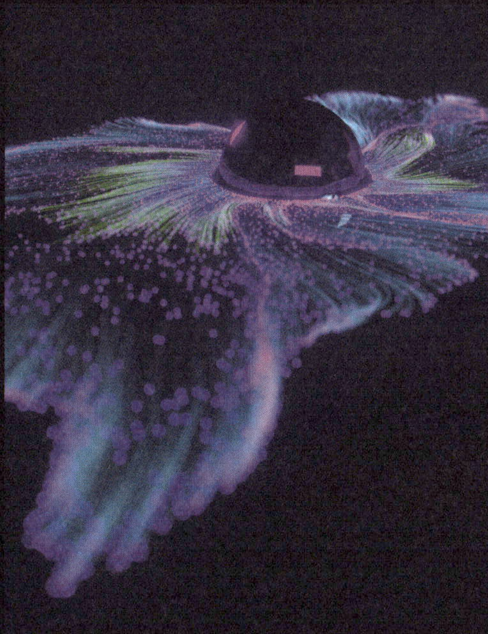
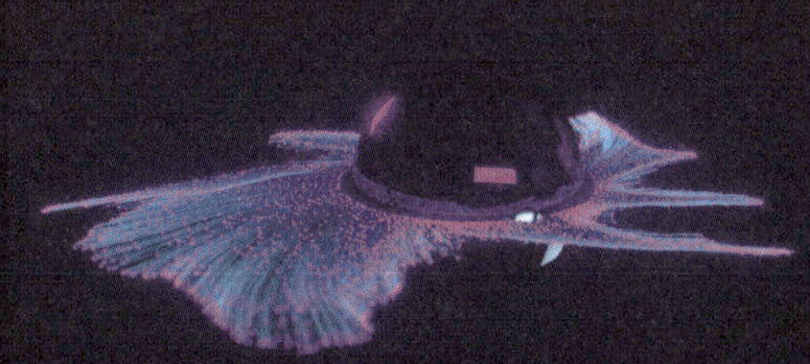

Color, materials, and environment are injected into the system.

Here I am adding path trails, a gradient spectrum, and a reflective element for the focal point.

The result is organic and tactile but also digital.

Reminiscent of flowers, weather patterns, or paths of energy dispersing into the environment.

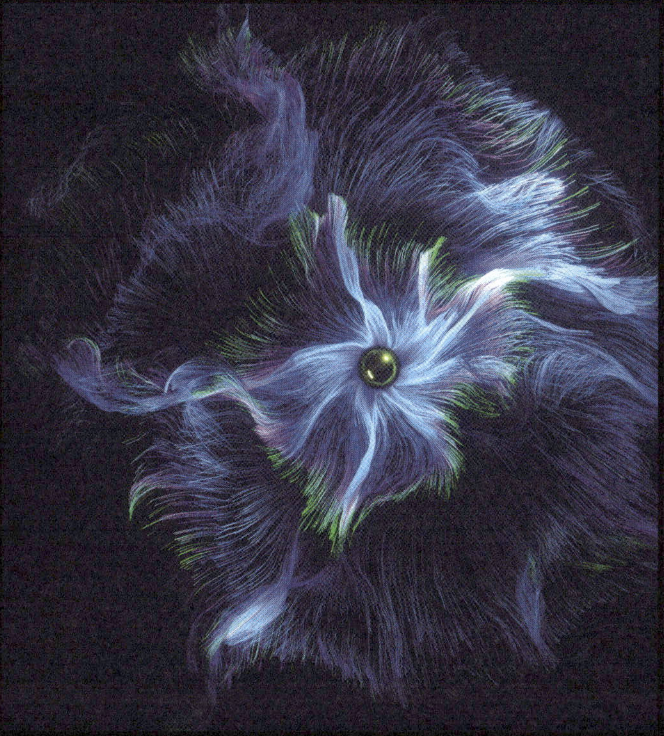
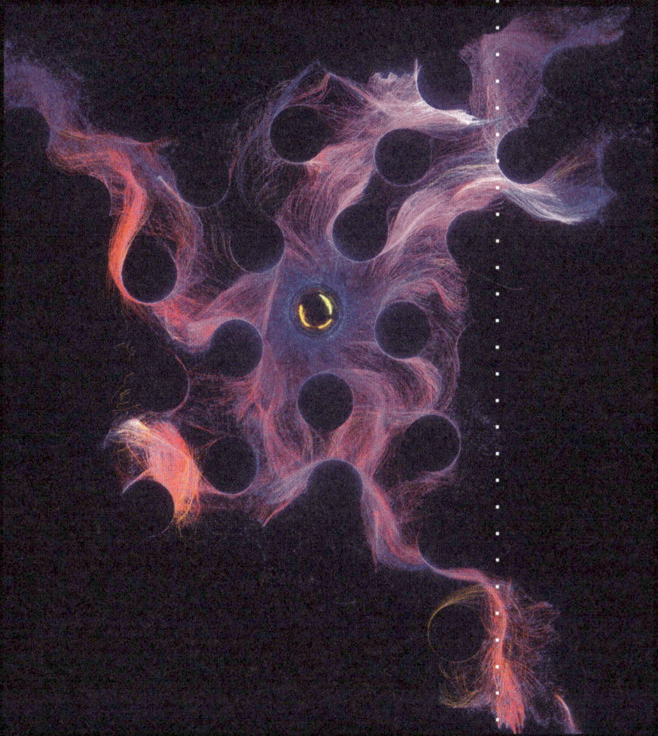
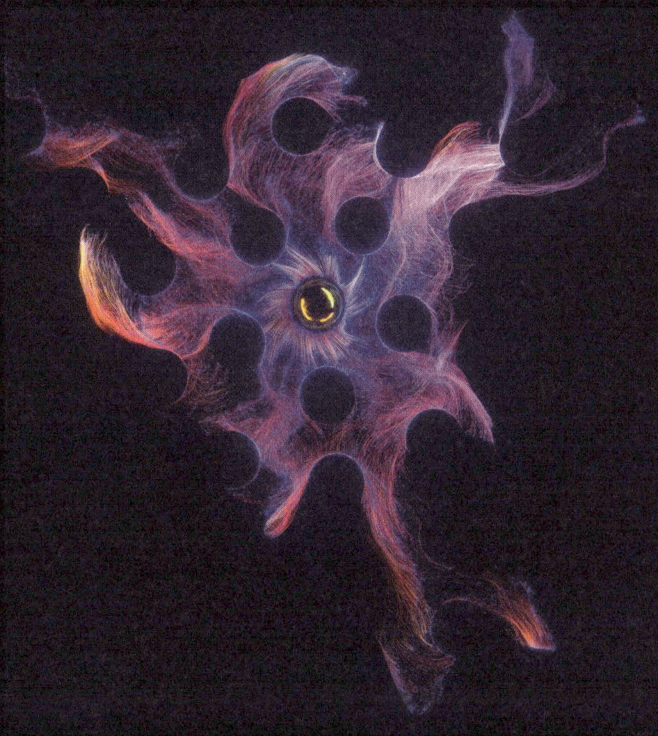

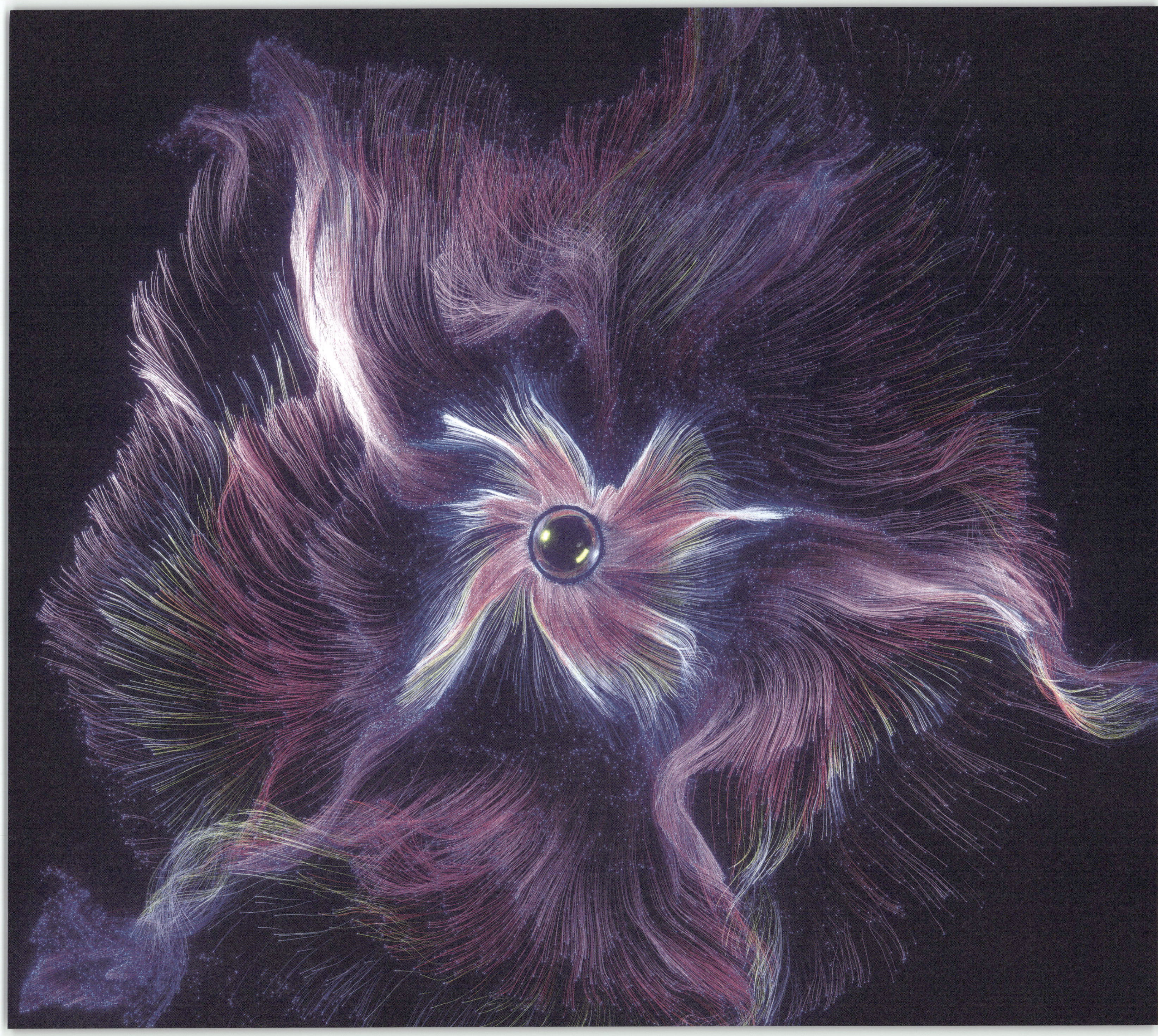

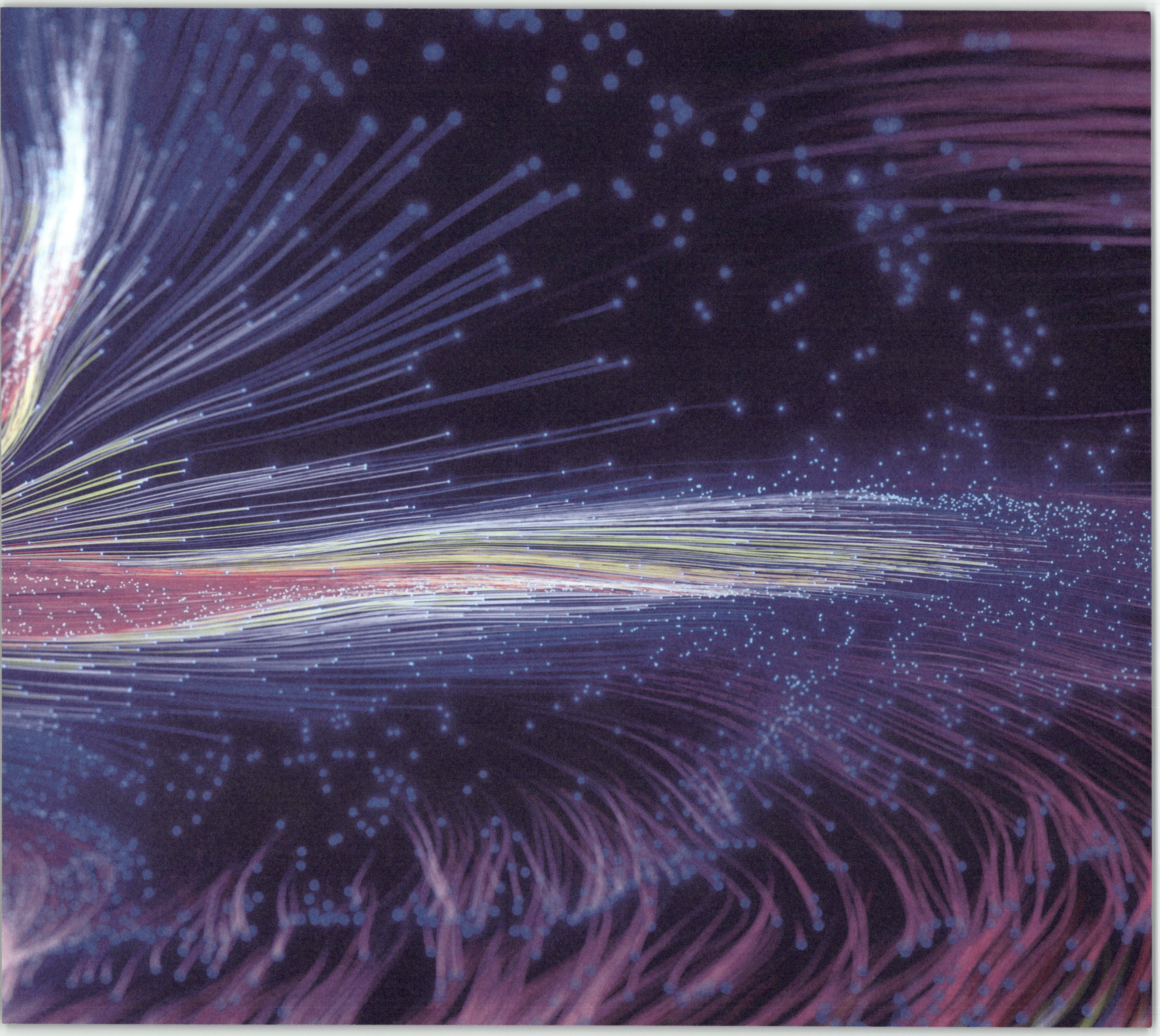

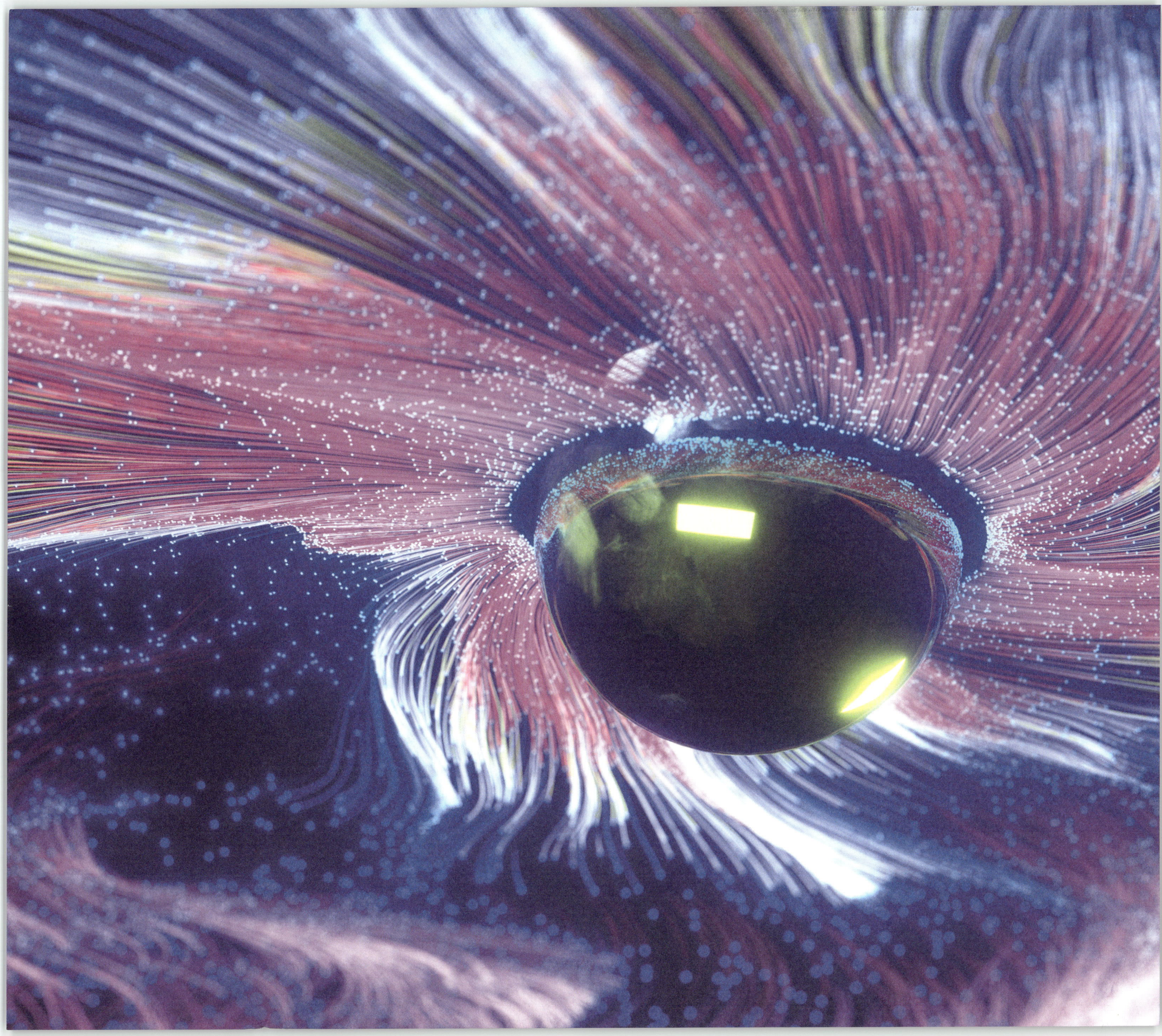

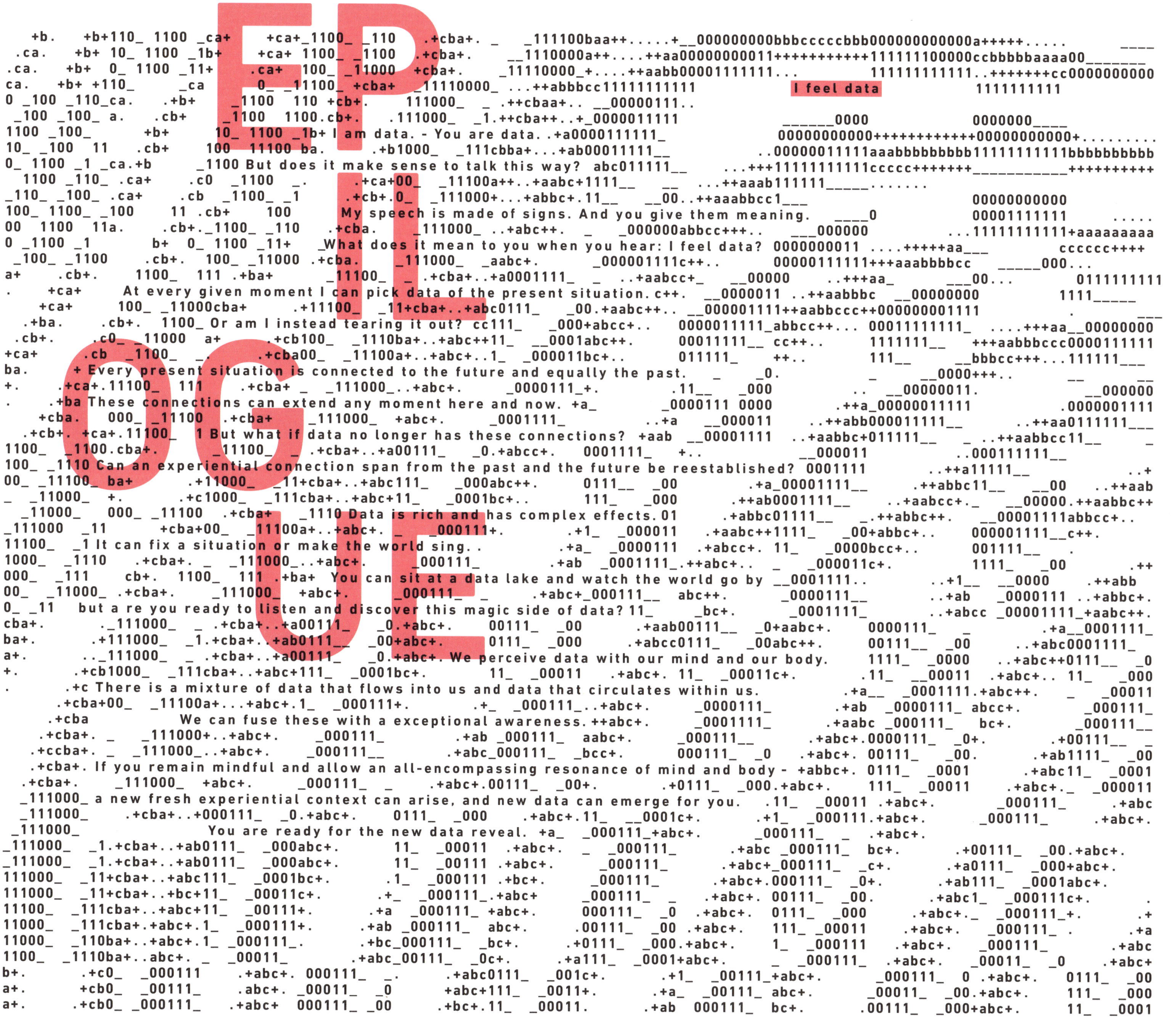
EPILOGUE
I feel data
I am data. - You are data.
But does it make sense to talk this way?
My speech is made of signs. And you give them meaning.
What does it mean to you when you hear: I feel data?
At every given moment I can pick data of the present situation.
Or am I instead tearing it out?
Every present situation is connected to the future and equally the past.
These connections can extend any moment here and now.
But what if data no longer has these connections?
Can an experiential connection span from the past and the future be reestablished?
Data is rich and has complex effects.
It can fix a situation or make the world sing.
You can sit at a data lake and watch the world go by
but a re you ready to listen and discover this magic side of data?
We perceive data with our mind and our body.
There is a mixture of data that flows into us and data that circulates within us.
We can fuse these with a exceptional awareness.
If you remain mindful and allow an all-encompassing resonance of mind and body -
a new fresh experiential context can arise, and new data can emerge for you.
You are ready for the new data reveal.

```
_1100_ 110_.   +b. .b. 10_0_10 10 +a  c+  c+  10__10_ 11  .+cbaa+++111111__  _    .+bc.    0011_ _00+bc+.      000000_  _1+    +a.
_1100_ _100    .c+  c+  0 10 10_1_1c. .b  .b. _10 110 _11  +cba++...00111111_  .    .+bc. 1  0011_ _0.+abc+..    0000__  _11.   .ca.
11100 _100 1  +a  .b  .__0_10 10 1a  c+  c+  10__10_ 110 .cba+..   000001111_ +.    .+bc.11  0011_ _  .+abc++.. ___    _111    .ca
1100  110 _1 +b.  c+  c 10 10_0_10. .b. .b.  10 110 _100.+ba+.    0000000111_c+.    .+bc011  0011_    .+abbcc++      __1110    +b+
100_ 110_ 10.c+  +a  +a10 10 10 10  ++  c+  +0__10_ 110_+ba+.    __000000111ab+.    .+b0011  00111     .+aabbc____1111100    .+b+
00_ _100 110+a  .b.  .b.10_1__0_10  .b.  .b.  c0 110 _100 ca+.        ___00001+ab+.    .+_0011  _001.      .++aa11111111000    .ca.
0_ _100 _10 b.  c+  c+ 0 10 10 10_ ++  ++  +b__10_ 110_ b+.          _0000.+abc.    . _0011_ _00c+       ...1111100000_  .+ba.
_ _110__10 Perhaps you're motivated because data comes in capsules of experience. bc.   _ _0011_ _0ac+.      000000000_   .cb+
_110_ 100 1  .b.  c.   10 10 10_1++  ++  .b._10_ 100_ 1+       ...111___  _0   +abc.   1_ _0011_ +abc+.      000000__    .+ca+   .
110_ 110 100 110+a  .b.  .b.10_1__0_1 They can shine in the context of wisdom and form new connections.       _       _.+cb+.   .
.ca.  .b+  10__10 10   .a  +a  +_10 10 10__ +b.   +ba.00_  _11111bbbbccc+..  _00011_  0    +ac+.  _ _0001111__        ..11000  110
.ca.  .c+ Will you grant data to grow where where it currently doesn't?  bbcc+.  _00011_      +ab+. 1_  _0001111...    ...++1000_ _110
.cb+   ca   10 10__1__1 +a  ++  c+10_10 10__1+b.   +b+. 0  _1111000++++aaabbc+__  _00111 +.    .abc.111_  _00001c+++++++ccb000_  1100
+b+   +b.  +0__10 10 10.b. .b  .b 0 10__10 10c+   .ca.  _ _11100000....+++aabc11_  _00111c+.    .+bc0011_   _000bbbbccbbbba00_  _1100
b+   .b+  But some forces disrupt this process of special connection and growth.        .+a_00111_   __++aaaaaaa++__  _1100_
a.  .c+   c+ 10__10 10 a  .a  +a   10__10 100+   +b+.   _1110000___       ..+01111_ _000.abc.     . _000111__   ....++....   _11100_
.   ca   +0__10 10 10   These forces can obscure vast amounts of data that is meant for you.     .    _  _0001111_          __11100_
+a.  +a. 10 10__0__1  +a  +a  +10 _10 10_    +b+    .11000_          _000111_  _  .+ac+.   11_  _000111          11111000_
+b.  .b.+b.  +0__10 10 10.b.  .b   .b 0 10__10 10c+   These forces are awaiting your arrival..+abc.  011_   _0000          1110000_
.b+  .c+  .0 10 10 10_ c+  c+  +a0 100 10_ 1  +b+    +c000_   _111         _000111_     .abc+.00111_   _00+..        1 00000_
.c+   ca  You merely have to find the right distance and stay with them...    __  _000111.     .+ab+_000111_   _bcc+++.....0000__  _1
100 100 10    .a  .b.  0 10__10 10 .b.  +b.  _ 110_ _110.       ...00000001111      .+ab11  _00011_c+.       ..+  ___000000ccbbaa+.
110 _10 10   These forces will become gentle and gradually uncover more data for you.   .+a111_  _0011abc+.       __       ___aaa++..
10 _10 110 1 c+  +a  .b 10 10__10 +b.   +a.  . 110_ 11000      ..+ccc00000000000+..      .0011_  _000.+abc+.      111___     ++...
0__10__10                But the question you must ask yourself is: how aware do you want these forces to be?     111
_ 10_ 10 _10b.  c+  +a 10 10 100 1a   +a.  .b100  1100_    .+ccbaaa       __bbcc+.      _000111  _   .+abbc+. 00000111111
100 10__10 +  +a  .b. 0 10_ 10 10+  .b+   ca10_ 1100_ _   .+cbba+++        aabbc++.     _000111_       .+aabc+ _000000000       ..
110 100 10 To find an excellent way to deal with this power, you need preciseness of experience. 000111.      .++ab     __00000       ..+c
10 110 10__1 .b.  c+  + 10__10 10_  +b.  .ca.0_ 1100  _1.+cba++.    1111111111_ ..++abbc+.111_  _0001c+.       .+11__    __....+++ccb
0 _10 10_+a  .b.  0 10_ 10 10 But too much data too quickly can confuse the accuracy of experience and thought. 11111__   cccccbbaa
__10 _10 10_+a  .b.  c+10 10__10 _ +a.  .b+   _110_ _110cba+.      11110011111       .++ab000111_  _0+abcc+.     00011111111aaaaaaa++.
_10__10 10 Are you ready to decelerate and decompress the flow of data?  000000      .++_0000111_   .+abbc+.    _0000001111+++++...
+a   c+  .b0 _10 10 10 +a   c+  .0 110 _100 .ca.    .cb_  _1111000   .....   000111111_ ++abc+.       _0000111__            0000000000
+a.  +a   c+__10 10__10.b.  +a   + _10_ 100 _cb+    .+ba  _11110000...++++++..00000011111 .++abc+.  1_  _0000111+..          00000000__
b.  +a.  c  10 10__10.b.  +a   + _10_ 100 _cb+     .+ba  _1111     Data only responds to you...+abc+.111_  __0000bcc++..
.  +b.  +a  10__10 10__a  .c+   ca110 _100 _1a.    +cb+._1110000___cccbbbbbbbb   __000000      .++abc01111_   _00+aabbcc++..___    ___
.b.  +a. 10 10__10.b. ... when you are there,   .cba. 1110000__  bbaaaaaaaaaa_     __000        ..+a00001111_    ..++aabbcc1111111111
.b+  .b.  +0 10__10 10  +b.   .b+ 00 110_ 110.   .+ba+  11000__    aa+++++++++1___     __.        .. _00001111__     ..++aa0111111111
.c+  .b.  10 10__10.b.  +a   + _10_ 100 _cb+    .+b ... when you ask, ........11111___   ++..       _  __0000111          ..0000000000
c+  .c+  .b.110 10__10  ca   +a.  _ 100 _110_   +ca+.   000_   __11..         11111111__ bcc+..     11_   _00000.          _________
+  .c+  .b   10 10__10.b.  +a   + _10_ 100 _cb+    .+ba  _111      ... if you listen and    1aabbc++.    1111__   _00c++..       _
c+  .c+  0 _10 100 1b.  .c+   +_100 _100 _ .+ba.    0_  __11111          00000000111.++aabcc+..0001111__   abbcc++..  1111111___
ca   c+ _10 10__10.b.  +a   + _10_ 1... don't know any better. 100        __000000000  ..++abbcc_000001111__..+aabbccc+0111111111
ca   ca   c_10__10 _10   +b.  .ca10_ 110_ _1+ca+     .+  _11110000         ____0000      ..++ab  __00000111    ..++aaab0000000000
110 100 10_    ca   +a._10_ 100 _1   +ba.   .00  11100_ ba+.        __          .....       00000011111+abbc++..   111111__   ++aaaabbbb
10 110 100 This data is ok. 110 _10   .ca.   .+0_ _1100_  a+.          ______++++++....   ___0000011..++abbcc+..0000111111_   .....+++
0 110 100 10 +b.   .b+  10 _10_ 110 .+b+    +b_ _1100_  _+.        .  ___111111ccccccc++++     __0000    ..++aabcc__000000111
110 110 1 0 10__10.b.  +a   + _10_ 100 _cb+     .+b ..              You are ok. I am ok. bcc1___     __0       ..+aa    __00000
110 110 110 b+   .ca    +_ 100 _10_ .ca.    .cb+ 11000   _11         ..+c11111111100++++++aaaab11111___            ..11__      __+...
10 110 110 1+    ca.   .b 110 _100 _ca.    .+b+.11100_ _111       .++cb11110000000........+++011111111__...         0111111___ bcccc+++++
0 110 110 _1    +a.   .c+110_ 100 _1b+     +ba. 1100_ _1110     ..+ccba10000000000           .00000011111cc++..      000001111111++aaaabbbb
110 _10 _0 +b.   .b+  10 _10_ 110 .+b Yes, I feel Data,0    ..+cbba+0000000____           _0000000001aabbcc+++..  __00000000     ....+++
110 _10 _10_ +b.   ca. 0_ 110_ 110.   .cb+   00_  _11000  .++cbaa+.0000___               ____0000.+++aabbbcc+_     ___00
10 110 _10     0b.  c+  +a 10 10 100 1a   +a.  .b100       .++1100000000           .0000001111 ... and it's a bliss to be alive!111__
0 110 _10_ 1b+   +b.    _100 _100_ .+ba.    0  _11000_ .+cbba+..  _    ____1           111_____          ...+0011111111_++....
b.  .ca   +b0 110_ 100 b+   .+b+   _100_ _1100+ba+.     ._11110000_          ..11111111111.....      __         ___0   ...+++aaa1111111___
.   .c+   +b+ 110_ 110__+    +b+    100_ _1100_ca+.     .+1110000__         ...++11000000000ccc++++++..11111___            ...0000111111
.c+   +b+ _10_ 110_ 1.    +b+.    100 _1100_ a+.     .+c110000_  _     ...++ccc00000000000bbbbbbbcccc011111111111          __00000000
.b+   +b+  10_ 110_ 11    +ca.    .00  1100_  +.     .+cb10000_   _1 ..++cccbbb0000000____++++aaaaaaa000000001111...           __
+b+    +b+   0_ 110_ 110   .ca.    .+0  11000  1.     .+cba000__  __11.++ccbbbaaa____         .........++____00000000cccc+++....11111_____
b+    +b+    +_ 110_ 110_ .ca.     +b_ _1100    _1      .+cba+00_   _1111+ccbbaa+++.          +++++......            ____aaaabbbbccc0011111111
.    +b+    +b 110_ 1100 .ca+     +ba _1100_ _11     .+cba+.0_   _11110cbbaa++....   _____0000aaaaaaaaaaa0_______     .....+++++a0000000000
```


ASCII routine by Andreas Gysin . https://play.ertdfgcvb.xyz/

I would like to thank all the artists participating, for their contribution, their time and permission to show their outstanding work, which makes this book what it is.

I am also very thankful to many others, whose names are not listed here, who have supported me along the way through word and deed.

Without all of them, I would not have been able to create this work.

URL:

theageofdata.net

Instagram:

@theageofdata

DATA IS US

Support & Thanks:

David Gilbert/davidgilbert.de
Florian Hausberger/florianhausberger.com
Mario Jilka/theforeignoffice.co
Kero/Detroit Underground™/detroitunderground.net
Andreas Lutz/andreaslutz.com
NXSCN . new future press
Ulrich Rothe
Richard Seabrooke/thetenthman.com
Gordon Spurs/gordonspurs.com
Tati & Sandro/ARTECHOUSE/artechouse.com
Christoph Tratberger
Julien Van Havere/Search System/searchsystem.co
Franek Zbieszczyk
and
everyone at TOCA ME/toca-me.com

Realized with the help of a kickstarter campaign

kickstarter.com/projects/niggliverlag/the-age-of-data-embracing-algorithms-in-art-and-design

Campaign Management:

Sandra Ellegiers

Thanks to all the backers for making this book happen!

Welcome to the Age of Data!

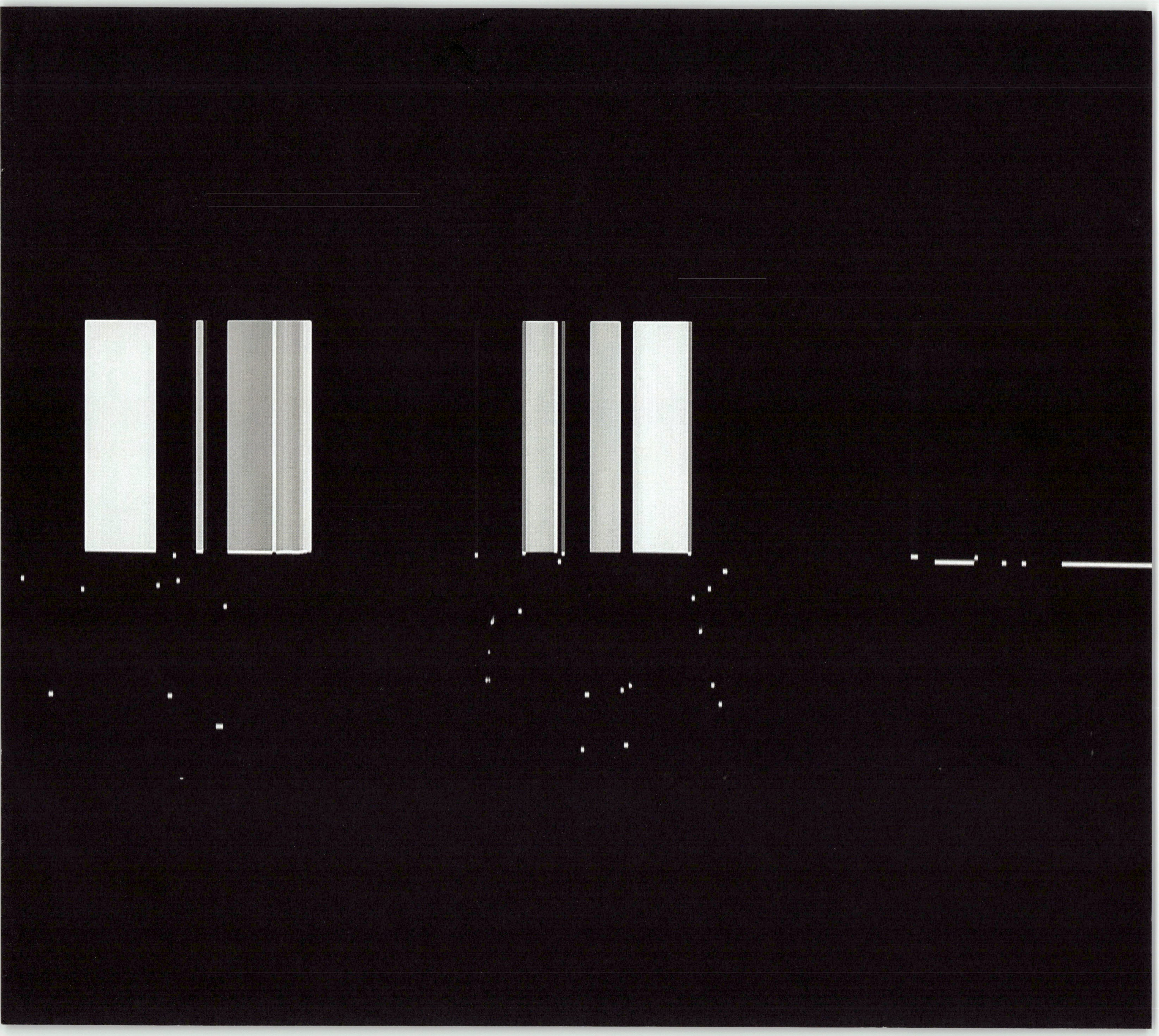